W9-CCX-979

THE OXFORD DICTIONARY OF THE
MIDDLE AGES

THE OXFORD DICTIONARY OF THE MIDDLE AGES

Edited by Robert E. Bjork

VOLUME I

A–C

UNIVERSITY PRESS

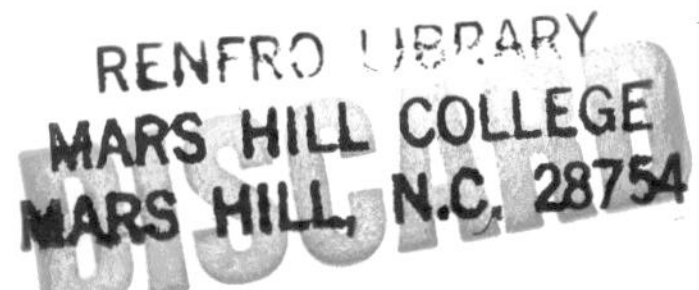

OXFORD
UNIVERSITY PRESS

Great Clarendon Street, Oxford OX2 6DP

Oxford University Press is a department of the University of Oxford.
It furthers the University's objective of excellence in research, scholarship,
and education by publishing worldwide in

Oxford New York

Auckland Cape Town Dar es Salaam Hong Kong Karachi
Kuala Lumpur Madrid Melbourne Mexico City Nairobi
New Delhi Shanghai Taipei Toronto

With offices in

Argentina Austria Brazil Chile Czech Republic France Greece
Guatemala Hungary Italy Japan Poland Portugal Singapore
South Korea Switzerland Thailand Turkey Ukraine Vietnam

Oxford is a registered trade mark of Oxford University Press
in the UK and in certain other countries

Published in the United States
by Oxford University Press Inc., New York

First published 2010

British Library Cataloguing in Publication Data
Data available

Library of Congress Cataloging in Publication Data
Data available

Library of Congress Control Number: 2010923327

Typeset by Graphicraft Limited, Hong Kong
Printed in China
by C&C Offset Printing Co., Ltd.

ISBN 978-0-19-866262-4

1 3 5 7 9 10 8 6 4 2

ADVISORY AND EDITORIAL BOARD

CONTENTS

INTRODUCTION

THE *Oxford Dictionary of the Middle Ages* (*ODMA*) is designed to be a resource of first resort for specialists and non-specialists alike for all key aspects of European history, society, religion, and culture, *c.*500 to *c.*1500. Since neighbouring areas of Asia and North Africa helped shape the civilization of the West, we have likewise included relevant aspects of the Byzantine empire, the Islamic dynasties, and Asiatic peoples such as the Avars and Mongols. The *ODMA* is also designed to give readers direct access to material they will have difficulty finding elsewhere. In particular, you will find in the *ODMA* extraordinary coverage of central and eastern Europe, archaeology, medicine, and music, as well as separate and substantial entries on women and children for all the geographical areas. Over 800 scholars explore these and all other topics through scores of entries ranging in size from 60 to 10,000 words and ranging in focus from such things as individual artifacts, people, and towns to general histories and large concepts, such as feudalism. All entries are supported by up-to-date bibliographies, and all are made extremely easy to use by the navigational tools developed for this reference work. Besides abundant cross-references within each entry to other entries and signpost entries showing readers where to find information on topics that do not have entries themselves (for example, **calligraphy** *See* WRITING AND WRITING MATERIALS), the *ODMA* begins and ends with two different kinds of index: a thematic index in which all entries are grouped by topic and a general index in which all subjects are listed alphabetically. Over 500 illustrations and 50 maps give the *ODMA* further substance and utility, enhancing, not merely complementing, the scholarly work resident in these pages. Despite its four volumes and close to 1,300,000 words, the *ODMA* cannot claim to be an exhaustive treatment of so sprawling a subject as the Middle Ages. Because of its history, however, and the nature of its construction, it can claim to be unusually balanced.

First, the Editorial Board consists of two groups of scholars, one responsible for nine geographical and the other for seventeen topical areas (see the list of Editors and Contributors, below). The interaction between these two groups ensures that major topics are not slighted or ignored. With his or her own special focus in mind, each editor scrutinized the headword list for the *ODMA* as the list developed and made certain that it gave adequate attention to his or her area of concern. Second, the list began with what amounts to a survey of the existing knowledge about and coverage of the field: the compilation of the list of headwords from several English dictionaries or encyclopedias of the Middle Ages.

During the summer of 1998, all the possible headwords were collated into a master list, which became the provisional headword list for *ODMA*. This list consisted of some 9,000 items. Each headword was assigned to one or more of eighteen geo-cultural and/or 23 thematic categories. Those categories now constitute the basis of the Thematic Listing of Entries of the *ODMA*. The entire list was then sorted by those categories to determine the percentage of the list devoted to each area.

Two points about the headword list thus produced are worth emphasizing here. The first is the unbalanced geographical coverage: France got 13.9% of the entries; Italy 13.5%; England 9.6%; Germany and Austria 7.9%; central and eastern Europe 5.9%; Spain and Portugal 5.4%; Scotland, Ireland, and Wales 2.6%; Scandinavia 2.4%; and the Low Countries 1.5%. The second is a curious under-representation of what should have been major topics. Ecclesiastical history comprised 22.9% of the list, but philosophy and theology only 3%, medieval Latin only 0.3%, and the Bible and exegesis only 0.2%. The various vernacular languages and literatures were similarly neglected (from 0.1% for Slavic to 1.5% for Romance) as was archaeology (0.1%) and art and architecture (4.1%).

From a purely statistical and superficial point of view, the *ODMA* has been able to rectify this situation easily by devoting a specific number of words to each geographical area and a balanced and reasonable percentage of total coverage to each topical category as well. But by so doing, it has also addressed some slightly more serious and hidden problems. One might assume, for example, that although the original list was imbalanced as a whole, it could have been balanced within individual areas. This was not necessarily true. Even the list for the Low Countries, to take the least represented geographical region, contained three problems that the *ODMA* would correct: it was weighted heavily toward religious figures, it omitted many important women (including religious mystics), and it reflected some knowledge about Flanders but little about Brabant, Holland, and the rest of the Low Countries. The early headword list for the Romance languages and literatures, on the other hand, was heavily Franco-centric and was also biased toward canonical writers. The *ODMA*, on the other hand, includes Occitan, Italian, and Spanish material as well as a large body of Iberian writing in non-Romance languages. While thus correcting the geographical and topical imbalances and misrepresentations of the early list, the *ODMA* also serves as a corrective to the marginalization of certain topical categories such as archaeology. By devoting an analytical overview of up to 10,000 words with ample cross-referencing and indexing to this and other major topics, the *ODMA* gives those neglected areas their due and thereby promotes a true inter-disciplinarity.

The complete, collated list of headwords together with a sub-list specific for each editorial area and culled from the master list was then sent to each member of the Editorial Board along with guidelines for developing the headword list for the *ODMA*. The members were advised that they should not feel constrained by the collated lists despite their relatively authoritative appearance. The lists were intended to serve as a beginning, a mere impetus for thought.

Finally, the nine geographical editors were advised to keep space limitations in mind as they developed their lists and were given the following estimate of how many words would be allotted to each area:

Geographical Allotments	
England:	130,000 words
central and eastern Europe:	100,000
France:	200,000
Germany and Austria:	170,000
Italy and Sicily:	100,000
Low Countries:	100,000
Scandinavia:	100,000
Scotland, Ireland, Wales:	70,000
Spain and Portugal:	130,000
Sub-total	1,100,000

The seventeen topical editors were likewise asked to arrange for the writing of major and minor articles in their areas totaling about 12,000 words and to coordinate their efforts with those of the geographical editors.

Topical Allotments	
Sub-total	200,000
Total *ODMA* word count	1,300,000

The various parameters of the project thus having been set, the final headword list for the *ODMA*—totaling over 5,000 entries—emerged at last, and invitations were issued worldwide to 840 scholars to write the required articles while the Editorial and Advisory Boards and I worked on other essential details of the project such as putting together lists of illustrations and maps to accompany the text. The result of this painstaking, meticulous, and laborious collaboration you now have in hand: a cornucopia of facts, new insights, figures, illustrations, maps, and thorough treatments of topics given short shrift elsewhere. The *ODMA*'s breadth is one of its most distinctive aspects, and we hope that it and many other compelling features will bring you back to this research tool time and time again.

REB

December 2009

ACKNOWLEDGEMENTS

ONLY with the support of several institutions and scores of individuals can a reference work of this magnitude come to fruition, and I would like to express my deep and abiding gratitude for that support here. At Arizona State University, the College of Liberal Arts and Sciences had the foresight to establish and generously fund the Arizona Center for Medieval and Renaissance Studies (ACMRS) over the years and gave me the latitude in my position as Director to make ACMRS the home of the *ODMA* from its inception in 1998. The Office of the Vice Provost for Research also supplied additional funds for me to hire two research assistants at the beginning of the project. At Oxford University Press, the late Michael Cox, who originally commissioned me to undertake this project, and his successors, Pamela Coote and Joanna Harris as well as their highly skilled assistant, Jo Spillane, have all been alacritous with their help and enthusiasm and sound guidance at all stages of work. Helen Nash, Carrie Hickman, and Jamie Crowther at the Press also provided invaluable aid at crucial moments as we moved into the final stages of production, and hundreds of infelicities, errors, and inconsistencies were caught and corrected by Ruth Ogden and Bernadette Mohan in page proofs under the expert direction of Clare Jenkins. At ACMRS, three staff members in particular—Jennifer Michaud, William F. Gentrup, and Leslie MacCoull—devoted hundreds of intense hours to the project, and the *ODMA* is much the better for their investing their considerable expertise in it. In the formative years of the *ODMA*, Lynn Sims also contributed a great deal at the right time as did several research assistants: Geoffrey Gust, Neil Waldrop, Darin Merrill, Stephanie Volf, Anthony Cantelmo, Stephanie Valencia, Anthony Richardson, Julie Stone, Jamie Robinson, Kyle Anderson, Kasandra Castle, and William Bolton. I am also grateful for two years of research leave, one at the Institute for Advanced Study (2004–5), Princeton, and the other at home in Scottsdale and sponsored by the National Endowment for the Humanities (2006–7), during which I was able to complete a great deal of work on this project while labouring on two others.

The Advisory and Editorial Boards for and the Contributors to the *ODMA* have given the work its shape and substance, and I thank them profoundly for that and for their commitment to the whole enterprise. They are all listed separately, below, as a small token of my and the Press's appreciation. In addition, a large number of scholars went far beyond what I originally requested of them as contributors or advisers and deserve special mention: M. Teresa Tavormina, Thomas Head, Florin Curta, Thomas J. Mathiesen, Caroline Walker Bynum, David Pelteret, Henry Ansgar Kelly, Walter Goffart, Dimitri Gutras, Paul M. Cobb, Albrecht Classen, John Marenbon, Richard Sharpe, Cynthia Neville, Joel

Rosenthal, Thomas Glick, Donald Kagay, Andrew S. Rabin, Helen Conrad-O'Briain, Katja Ritari, Sarah Gordon, Alan Stahl, Marc Boone, Andrea Dickens, Thomas J. A. Heffernan, Michael Lapidge, Elisabeth Hollender, Judith Baskin, Edwin Seroussi, Susan Boynton, Thomas Izbicki, Yom Tov Assis, Benjamin Hudson, James A. Brundage, Helene Scheck, Angel Saenz-Badillos, Jérôme Hayez, Walter Prevenier, Toby Burrows, Shmuel Shepkaru, Sam Riches, Paul Shore, Richard Utz, Scott Gwara, Michael Grünbart, A. S. McGrade, Michael Hicks, Asa Mittman, Irina Kolbutova, Michael Frassetto, Walter P. Simons, Kelly DeVries, Raymond Cormier, Katharine Simms, Kirsten Wolf, Seán Duffy, Jeffrey Spier, David Townsend, William Tronzo, Rita Copeland, Georgi Papulov, Diane Reilly, Alex Woolf, Bill Dohar, Nora Berend, Bianca Kuehnel, Susan Kramer, Jelena Bogdanovic, Raeleen Chai Elsholz, Irven Resnick, Roger Wieck, Constance Bouchard, Anne Scott, and Cynthia Kosso. Victoria Agee and Francine Cronshaw stepped in at the last moment to compile a magnificent general index.

Finally, I am most grateful for and to my wife, Mary, and daughter, Francesca, who support me daily in innumerable ways and who have lovingly put up with me under the burden of this massive project for such a long time.

REB

December 2009

EDITORS AND CONTRIBUTORS

EDITORS

GENERAL EDITOR

Robert E. Bjork, FEA, is Foundation Professor of English and Director of the Arizona Center for Medieval and Renaissance Studies (ACMRS), Arizona State University. His research interests lie primarily in Old English literature and Scandinavian studies. (REB)

ADVISORY BOARD

Giles Constable, FBA, FMAA, is Professor Emeritus in the School of Historical Studies at the Institute for Advanced Study, Princeton.

Helen Cooper, FBA, is Professor of Medieval and Renaissance English at the University of Cambridge (Magdalene College). Her research interests include Chaucer, romance, and the links between medieval and early modern literature. (HC)

† **R. R. Davies**, FBA, was the Chichele Chair of Medieval History, University of Oxford (All Souls College). Past President of the Royal Historical Society, Davies specialized in medieval British history, particularly the history of Wales. (RRD)

Roberta Frank, FMAA, is Marie Borroff Professor of English at Yale University, and writes about and teaches Old English and Old Norse literature. (RFr)

Edward James is Professor of History at University College, Dublin.

EDITORIAL BOARD

Theodore M. Andersson (SCANDINAVIA), now retired, taught for over forty years at Harvard, Stanford, and Indiana Universities, and is Professor Emeritus of Germanic Studies at the last institution. He specializes in medieval Icelandic literature, especially the sagas, and, secondarily, early German literature. (TMA)

János M. Bak (CENTRAL AND EASTERN EUROPE) is Professor Emeritus of the University of British Columbia, Vancouver, BC, and the Central European University, Budapest. His main interest has been the history of rulership. (JMB)

Elizabeth A. R. Brown, FMAA, (FRANCE) is Professor Emerita of History, Graduate School and Brooklyn College, City University of New York. (EARB)

Gene A. Brucker, FBA, FMAA, (ITALY, SICILY, AND LATIN GREECE), Shepard Professor Emeritus of History, Department of History, University of California, Berkeley, specializes in Italian Renaissance history. His latest book is *Living on the Edge in Leonardo's Florence* (2005). (GAB)

† **R. R. Davies** (SCOTLAND, IRELAND, AND WALES). Advisory Board. See above. (RRD)

† **S. R. Epstein** (SOCIAL AND ECONOMIC HISTORY) was Professor of Economic History, London School of Economics and Political Science.

Margot E. Fassler (MUSIC AND THE LITURGY) is the Robert Tangeman Professor of Music History at Yale University. (MEF)

Michael S. Flier (SLAVIC LANGUAGES AND LITERATURES) is Oleksandr Potebnja Professor of Ukrainian Philology at Harvard University. His fields of specialization include Slavic linguistics and the semiotics of Slavic medieval culture. (MSF)

Paul H. Freedman, FMAA, (SPAIN AND PORTUGAL) teaches history at Yale University and has written on Spain, the peasantry, and church history. Recently he has published work on spices and the history of cuisine. (PHF)

Simon Gaunt (ROMANCE LANGUAGES AND LITERATURES) is Professor of French at King's College, London. He specializes in Old French and medieval Occitan literature. (SG)

John B. Gillingham, FBA, (ENGLAND) is Emeritus Professor of History at the London School of Economics and Political Science. His interests include English political and military culture, and views of neighbouring peoples, especially Celtic. (JBG)

Richard Helmholz, FMAA, (LAW) is Professor of Law, University of Chicago. He does research on canon and Roman law in English legal history, principally in the ecclesiastical courts, 13th to 17th centuries. (RH)

John Hines (ARCHAEOLOGY) is Professor in the School of History and Archaeology, Cardiff University. He works with the archaeology, philology, literature, and history of medieval northern Europe, and on interdisciplinary methods. (JHi)

C. Stephen Jaeger, FMAA, (GERMANIC LANGUAGES AND LITERATURES) is Gutgsell Professor (Emeritus), University of Illinois, Urbana-Champaign. His interests are medieval literature, vernacular and Latin, history of education, and history of social forms. He is the author of *Origins of Courtliness* (1985), *The Envy of Angels: Cathedral Schools and European Social Ideals* (1994), and *Ennobling Love* (1999). (CSJ)

Herbert L. Kessler, FMAA, FAAAS, (ART AND ARCHITECTURE) is Professor of the History of Art at Johns Hopkins University. He has been a visiting professor at Harvard, Emory, and Williams and the Bibliotheca Hertziana in Rome. He is the author of eleven books and some 135 articles and reviews.

Felice Lifshitz (GERMANY AND AUSTRIA) is Professor of History at Florida International University. She is author of *The Norman Conquest of Pious Neustria: Historiographic Discourse and Saintly Relics, 684–1090* (1995) and *The Name of the Saint: The*

Martyrology of Jerome and Access to the Sacred in Francia, 627–823 (2006). (FL)

David C. Lindberg, FMAA, (SCIENCE) is Hilldale Professor Emeritus of the History of Science at the University of Wisconsin, and has authored or edited fourteen books, including *The Beginnings of Western Science* (1992). (DCL)

Pamela O. Long (TECHNOLOGY) is an independent historian and has published extensively in the history of science and technology. Her books include *Openness, Secrecy, Authorship: Technical Arts and the Culture of Knowledge from Antiquity to the Renaissance* (2001). (POL)

David Luscombe, FBA, (PHILOSOPHY) is Emeritus Research Professor of Medieval History, University of Sheffield. He has written about medieval conceptions of hierarchy and about Peter Abelard, editing some of Abelard's works. (DLu)

† **Joseph H. Lynch**, FMAA, (ECCLESIASTICAL HISTORY) was Distinguished University Professor and Joe R. Engle Designated Professor of the History of Christianity at the Ohio State University, and published on ancient and medieval church history. (JHLy)

Ivan G. Marcus (JUDAICA) is Frederick P. Rose Professor of Jewish History and of Religious Studies, Yale University.

Steven P. Marrone (INTELLECTUAL HISTORY) is Professor of History at Tufts University. His most recent book is *The Light of thy Countenance: Science and Knowledge of God in the Thirteenth Century* (2001). (SPM)

Ian Netton (ISLAM) is Sharjah Professor of Islamic Studies, University of Exeter.

David Nicholas (LOW COUNTRIES) is Kathryn and Calhoun Lemon Professor Emeritus of History at Clemson University. His books include *Medieval Flanders* (1992), *The Later Medieval City* (1997), *Urban Europe, 1100–1700* (2003), and *The Northern Lands: Germanic Europe, c.1270–c.1500* (2009). (DN)

Huw Pryce (SCOTLAND, IRELAND, WALES) is Professor of History, University of Wales (Bangor). His publications include *Native Law and the Church in Medieval Wales* (1993), *The Acts of Welsh Rulers, 1120–1282* (2005) and, as co-editor, *Power and Identity in the Middle Ages* (2007). (HP)

† **Timothy Reuter** (GERMANY AND AUSTRIA) was Professor of Medieval History at the University of Southampton.

Linda Ehrsam Voigts, FMAA, (MEDICINE) is Curators' Professor Emerita of English, University of Missouri-Kansas City, and is responsible, with Patricia Deery Kurtz, for e-versions of catalogues of medieval scientific and medical writings in Latin (e-Thorndike-Kibre) and in Old and Middle English (e-Voigts-Kurtz). (LEV)

Jan Ziolkowski, FMAA, (MEDIEVAL LATIN) is Arthur Kingsley Porter Professor of Medieval Latin, Harvard University.

CONTRIBUTORS

Phillip I. Ackerman-Lieberman is Assistant Professor of Jewish Studies at Vanderbilt University, working on the economic and social history of the Jewish community under medieval Islam. (PIAL)

Melitta Weiss Adamson is Professor of German, Comparative Literature, and History of Medicine at the University of Western Ontario, Canada. She has published widely on food and preventive medicine in the Middle Ages. (MWA)

Jan A. Aertsen is Emeritus Director of the Thomas Institute at the University of Cologne (Germany). His main area of research is medieval philosophy, in particular metaphysics and the thought of Thomas Aquinas. (JAA)

Maria Teresa Agozzino is Assistant Professor in Folk Studies at Western Kentucky University. Her research interests include folk belief, calendric customs, Wales and the Welsh Diaspora, Arthuriana, and folkloristics. (MTA)

F. R. P. Akehurst is Professor of French at the University of Minnesota. He has published on the troubadours and translated Old French Customary law texts. (FRPA)

Kevin Alban, O. Carm., is the Bursar General of the Order of Carmelites and a lecturer at Pontifical Beda College, Rome, and Heythrop College, London. His research interests include medieval Carmelite history and Mariology. (KJA)

Francesca Yardenit Albertini is Professor of Jewish History of Religion at the University of Potsdam, Germany. Her research focuses on the hermeneutics of holy texts, on Jewish philosophy of religion in the ancient world and in the Middle Ages as well as on Jewish bioethics. (FYA)

N. W. Alcock, FSA, is Emeritus Reader, University of Warwick, and past president of the Vernacular Architecture Group. His principal research relates to vernacular architecture, especially cruck construction and the correlation of documentary evidence and standing buildings. (NWA)

Ahmed H. al-Rahim is Assistant Professor of Islamic Studies at the University of Virginia. He is the co-editor of *Before and After Avicenna* (2003) and the author of *The Creation of Philosophical Tradition: Biography and the Reception of Avicenna's Philosophy from the 11th to the 14th Centuries AD* (forthcoming). (AHR)

Lourdes María Alvarez is Director of the Center for Medieval and Byzantine Studies at the Catholic University of America. Her research currently focuses on mysticism and poetry in Islamic Spain. (LMA)

Björn Ambrosiani is Professor and Project Director for The Birka Project at Riksantikvarieämbetet, Swedish National Heritage Board, Stockholm, and works on settlement history and early towns in northern Europe. (BA)

Mark Amsler is with the Departments of English and of Applied Language Studies and Linguistics, University of Auckland, researching the history of linguistics, medieval literatures and culture, and literacy and pragmatics. (MA)

Benjamin William Anderson is a PhD candidate, History of Art, at Bryn Mawr College. His research interests include late antique and early medieval art and architecture. (BWA)

Theodore M. Andersson Editorial Board. See above. (TMA)

Eyðun Andreassen is Professor of Oral Literature, University of the Faroe Islands, Tórshavn, researching folk legends and medieval oral ballads, and other aspects of oral literature. (EA)

Justine M. Andrews is an Assistant Professor at the University of New Mexico. Her research interests include crusader art, medieval Cyprus, the late Byzantine Empire, illuminated manuscripts, and icons and Gothic architectural sculpture. (JMA)

† **Jane Andrews Aiken** was a Professor of Art History at Virginia Polytechnic Institute and State University. She published widely on the history of artist's perspective and its ties with the theory

and practice of mathematics and technology during the ancient and medieval periods. (JAAi)

Stanko Andrić is Senior Research Fellow at the Croatian Institute of History in Slavonski Brod, and works on the medieval history of Slavonia (northern Croatia). (SA)

Gabriele Annas is Senior Research Fellow of the Historical Commission, Bavarian Academy of Sciences and Humanities, Munich, studying the history of the Holy Roman Empire in the later Middle Ages. (GA)

Haki Antonsson is a Lecturer in Scandinavian Studies at University College London. Research interests include Scandinavia and its relation with Europe *c.*1000–*c.*1250. (HA)

Adrian Armstrong is Professor of Early French Culture at the University of Manchester. He specializes in late medieval French poetry, particularly Rhétoriqueur poetry, and in the materiality of medieval literature. (AA)

Lawrin Armstrong is an Associate Professor of Medieval Studies at the University of Toronto. He studies law and economic thought in medieval Italy, and teaches history, Latin, and diplomatics. (LDA)

Jonathan J. Arnold is an Assistant Professor at the University of Tulsa, where he teaches ancient and medieval history. His research focuses on barbarian Europe, especially Gaul and Italy. (JJA)

Jon Arrizabalaga is Senior Researcher in the History of Science at the Spanish National Research Council (CSIC), Barcelona. His research interest has been mostly focused on medicine, health and disease. He has published (with John Henderson and Roger French) *The Great Pox* (1997). (JA)

Paul Arthur, FSA, is Professor of Medieval Archaeology at the University of Salento, Italy, conducting research on Byzantine and medieval economy, settlement patterns, and the landscape around the Mediterranean. (PRA)

William B. Ashworth, Jr is Associate Professor of History at the University of Missouri-Kansas City, with a special research interest in Renaissance astronomy, natural history, and scientific illustration. (WBA)

Yom Tov Assis is Professor of Medieval Jewish History at the Hebrew University of Jerusalem. He specializes in the history of the Jews in the Iberian Peninsula and Provence-Languedoc and the Sephardi Diaspora following the Expulsion. (YTA)

Lorraine C. Attreed is a Professor of History at Holy Cross College in Worcester, Massachusetts. She has published on English urban history, the reign of Richard III, medieval Anglo-Iberian diplomacy, and historical film. (LCA)

Elizabeth Aubrey is Professor of Music at the University of Iowa. She is a scholar of the songs of the trouvères of medieval France and the troubadours of Occitania. (EAu)

David Stewart Bachrach is Associate Professor of Medieval History at the University of New Hampshire. His research focuses on military history of medieval Germany and England. (DSB)

Vera Bácskai is Professor Emeritus at Eötvös Loránd University, Budapest. Her main fields of research are medieval, early modern and modern urban history, and early modern and modern social history. (VB)

Lola Badia is Professor of Catalan Literature at the University of Barcelona and Director of the Centre de Documentació Ramon Llull, and works on the editing and study of medieval romance texts. (LB)

Sverre Bagge is Professor of Medieval History, University of Bergen and Director of the Centre for Medieval Studies. Research interests include medieval historiography, state formation, and political thought and culture. (SHB)

Michael D. Bailey is Associate Professor of History at Iowa State University, and works primarily on the history of magic and superstition in the late medieval period. (MDB)

Michael G. L. Baillie is a dendrochronologist and palaeoecologist, with strong research interests in refined chronologies and the causes of abrupt environmental changes observed in tree-ring and historical records, leading to interest in terrestrial and extraterrestrial causes of atmospheric loading. (MGLB)

János M. Bak Editorial Board. See above. (JMB)

Géza Balázs is a linguist, folklorist, and head of department at Eötvös Loránd University, Budapest, Hungary. Fields of study include anthropological linguistics, text linguistics, and actual Hungarian language. (GBa)

Spurgeon Baldwin is Professor of Romance Languages and Literatures at the Universities of Illinois (Emeritus 1990) and Alabama (Emeritus 2000). He specializes in medieval vernacular translations of the Vulgate and encyclopedic works. (SWB)

Anthony Bale is Senior Lecturer in Medieval Studies at Birkbeck College, University of London. He has written on medieval Anglo-Jewry and literary antisemitism, including a monograph *The Jew in the Medieval Book: English Antisemitisms, 1350–1500* (2006). (APB)

C. Matthew Balensuela, Professor of Music at DePauw University, specializes in the history of music theory. His publications include *Music Theory from Boethius to Zarlino* (2008), an edition of the *Ars cantus mensurabilis mensurata per modos iuris*, and articles in the *New Grove Dictionary*. (CMB)

Bridget Kennedy Balint is Assistant Professor of Classical Studies at Indiana University, Bloomington. Her primary field of study is the Latin literature of the high Middle Ages. (BKB)

Rebecca A. Baltzer is Professor Emerita of Musicology, University of Texas, Austin, and has worked on the Notre-Dame School and Ars antique, 13th-century manuscript codicology, and medieval Parisian liturgy. (RAB)

Stanislaw Baranczak is Alfred Jurzykowski Professor of Polish Language and Literature, Harvard, and specializes in modern Polish literature, Polish poetry of the 19th and 20th centuries, and literary translation. (SBa)

Attila Pál Bárány is a Lecturer for the Department of History, Debrecen University, Hungary, and for the Department of History, Miskolc University, Hungary. His research speciality is medieval Anglo-Hungarian/German relations. (APBá)

John W. Barker is Professor Emeritus of History at the University of Wisconsin. He specializes in Byzantine, Crusading, and Venetian History. His teaching and writing interests include the study of music in relation to history and art. (JWB)

Geraldine Barnes is McCaughey Professor of English Language and Early English Literature in the Department of English at the University of Sydney. Her main areas of research are Old Icelandic and Middle English romance. (GB)

Michael P. Barnes is Professor Emeritus of Scandinavian Studies at University College London. His interests include Migration- and Viking-Age Scandinavian, runes and runic inscriptions, history of Norse in the British Isles, and Faroese. (MPB)

Terry Barry is Associate Professor in the Department of History, School of Histories and Humanities, Trinity College Dublin. His publications include *The Archaeology of Mediaeval Ireland* (latest edition 2004). (TB)

Milena Bartlová is Professor of Medieval Art History at Masaryk University in Brno, Czech Republic. Her specialities include the art of central Europe in the 14th and 15th centuries. (MB)

Simon Barton is Professor of Spanish History, University of Exeter. His research and teaching interests are medieval Iberian history, particularly aristocratic society, Crusade and cross-border relations. (SFB)

Thomas W. Barton is Assistant Professor of History at the University of San Diego. He works on the social history of conquest and settlement within the Crown of Aragon. (TWB)

László Bartosiewicz, PhD, DSc, teaches archaeozoology at the Loránd Eötvös University, Budapest, and is Reader at the University of Edinburgh. He studies animal–human relationships as reflected by excavated animal remains. (LBa)

Rozmeri Basic is Associate Dean of the Weitzenhoffer Family College of Fine Arts and Associate Professor of Art History at the University of Oklahoma. Teaching and research interests include Aegean, Etruscan, Byzantine, and post-Byzantine art and architecture. (RB)

Judith R. Baskin is Knight Professor of Humanities and Associate Dean of Humanities at the University of Oregon. She writes about women in rabbinic and medieval Jewish cultures. (JRB)

Elisheva Baumgarten is a professor at Bar Ilan University. She specializes in the history of Jewish women and family and in Jewish-Christian relations in medieval Germany and Northern France. (EMB)

Henry Bayerle is Assistant Professor of Latin at Oxford College of Emory University. His main research interests are Latin epic and the medieval reception of the classics. (HB)

Martha Bayless is Associate Professor of English at the University of Oregon. She specializes in the intersection between medieval literature and culture. (MJB)

Cordelia Beattie is Senior Lecturer in Medieval History at the University of Edinburgh. She is the author of *Medieval Single Women: The Politics of Social Classification in Late Medieval England* (2007). (CBe)

Matthias Becher is Professor of Medieval History at the University of Bonn, Germany. His main areas of research are the Frankish kingdoms and the history of the Welf family. (MBe)

Brigitte Miriam Bedos-Rezak is Professor of History at New York University specializing in the semiotic anthropology of the central Middle Ages, and considers the agency of signs of identity and media of communication in terms of social relations, legal practices, and conceptions of personhood and authority. (BMBR)

Elena Bellomo teaches at the Università degli Studi di Genova, Italy. She has published extensively on the Military Orders in Italy and the Italian participation in the Crusades. (EB)

Nora Berend is Senior Lecturer at the University of Cambridge and Fellow of St Catharine's College. She works on the social and religious history of the central medieval period. (NB)

David Berger is Ruth and I. Lewis Gordon Professor of Jewish History at Yeshiva University. He specializes in medieval Jewry, Jewish-Christian relations, and the intellectual history of the Jews. (DB)

John W. Bernhardt is Professor of History, San Jose University, USA. His fields of specialization include history of the medieval church and history of medieval Germany, 800–1350. (JWBe)

Alan E. Bernstein is Emeritus Professor of Medieval History, University of Arizona. Author of *The Formation of Hell* (1993), he also has research interests that include elite and popular culture, the comparative history of religion, and the history of belief in hell. (AB)

Walter Berschin is Professor of Medieval Latin (Heidelberg) and fellow of the academies of Barcelona, London, and Vienna. He publishes on medieval biography and monastic culture, and Greek in the Middle Ages. (WB)

Luigi Andrea Berto is Assistant Professor of History at Western Michigan University. He is interested in early medieval Italy and medieval Venice. (LAB)

Edel Bhreathnach is Academic Project Manager of the Míchéal Ó Cléirigh Institute, University College Dublin. Her areas of interest are early medieval Irish history, archaeology, and literature, as well as religious orders, especially Franciscans in the late medieval and early modern period. (EBh)

Joseph Biancalana is Joseph P. Kinneary Professor of Law at the University of Cincinnati College of Law. He has written on various topics in English medieval legal history. (JBi)

Jessalynn Lea Bird, DPhil (Oxon.), is an independent scholar. Her research includes the Crusades, sermons and pastoral literature, medieval theologians (especially Peter the Chanter's circle), and intellectuals' impact on social, religious, and economic trends. (JLB)

Marianna D. Birnbaum is Professor Emerita of Hungarian Studies at the University of California, Los Angeles, and has worked on central European humanism, Jews in early modern Europe, and literature theory. (MDBi)

Anna Bitner-Wróblewska, PhD, works at the State Archaeological Museum in Warsaw. Her principal field of research is archaeology of the Balts in Roman and Migration periods. She is involved in a project to reconstruct the Balts' heritage damaged or dispersed during WW II. (ABW)

Robert E. Bjork General Editor. See above. (REB)

Michael Shane Bjornlie is an assistant professor at Claremont McKenna College. His academic interests include the literary culture, social and economic history, and archaeology of late antiquity and the early Middle Ages. (MSB)

Grzegorz Błaszczyk is professor in the Department of History of East Europe, Institute of History, Adam Mickiewicz University, Poznań. He researches Polish-Lithuanian relations and the history of Lithuania and Belarus. (GBł)

R. Howard Bloch, Sterling Professor of French, Chair of the Humanities Program, Yale University, has published abundantly on the relationship between medieval literature and social institutions and on 19th-century medievalism. (RHB)

Nils Blomkvist is Professor of Medieval History at Gotland University, Visby. His main research topic is the medieval process of Europeanization on the Baltic Rim. (NBl)

Jill Elizabeth Blondin is Associate Professor of Art History at the University of Texas at Tyler, and researches the patronage of Pope Sixtus IV ('Power Made Visible', *Catholic Historical Review*, 2005). (JEB)

Uta-Renate Blumenthal is an Ordinary Professor of History at The Catholic University of America. Main interests include institutional and legal history of the central Middle Ages. (URB)

Adrian J. Boas of the University of Haifa specializes in archaeology of the Crusader period. He is the author of *Crusader Archaeology* (1999), *Jerusalem in the Time of the Crusades* (2001), *Archaeology of the Military Orders* (2005), and *Domestic Settings* (forthcoming), and he is currently directing a major research project at Montfort Castle. (AJB)

Jelena Bogdanović specializes in the architectural history of Byzantine, Slavic, western European, and Islamic medieval cultures, and teaches at East Carolina University. (JBo)

Flavio Boggi is Senior Lecturer in the History of Art at University College Cork. His research interests are focused upon the art of late medieval and Renaissance Tuscany. (FB)

Marc Boone is Professor of Medieval History at the University of Ghent. His research interests include urban history, late medieval social and political history of the Low Countries, and 'Burgundy'. (MGRB)

Urszula Borkowska is Emeritus Professor of History at The John Paul II Catholic University of Lublin, Poland. (UB)

Claudia Bornholdt is Assistant Professor for medieval German and Scandinavian literature and language in the Department of Germanic Languages and Literatures at the University of Illinois, Urbana-Champaign. (CB)

Joyce Boro is Associate Professor of English at Université de Montréal. She is the editor of *Berners's Castell of Love* (2007) and author of several articles on romance and book history. (JB)

Jostein Børtnes is Professor Emeritus at the University of Bergen, where he held the chair of Russian literature (1984–2007). His most recent book is *The Poetry of Prose* (2007). (JBør)

Jurjen M. Bos was educated at the University of Amsterdam, and has since 1988 been teaching and researching medieval and post-medieval archaeology at the State University of Groningen, The Netherlands. (JMBo)

Anne-Marie Bouché is Associate Professor of Art History, Florida Gulf Coast University. Her research specialties are Romanesque manuscript illumination, iconography, and Mosan art. She has published on the Floreffe Bible, the tympanum of Conques, and the Morgan Old Testament (M638). (AMB)

Constance B. Bouchard is Distinguished Professor of Medieval History at the University of Akron. Her many books include *Sword, Miter, and Cloister* (1987) and *Every Valley Shall Be Exalted* (2003). (CBB)

Marie Bouhaïk-Gironès is a Researcher at Universiteit van Amsterdam, and works on theatrical practices. Her publications include *Les Clercs de la Basoche et le théâtre comique (Paris, 1420–1550)* (2007) and *Le Théâtre polémique français (1450–1550)* (2008). (MBG)

Emmanuel Constantine Bourbouhakis, PhD, is Lecturer in Classics and Byzantine Literature at Harvard University. (ECB)

Charles R. Bowlus is Professor Emeritus, University of Arkansas at Little Rock, where he taught for thirty years. He continues to publish books and articles on medieval German history. (CRB)

Jeffrey A. Bowman is Associate Professor of History at Kenyon College. He has published articles on law, society, and sanctity in Spain and Mediterranean France. He is the author of *Shifting Landmarks*, which received the American Historical Association's Premio del Ray. (JAB)

Matthieu Boyd studies medieval Celtic, Francophone, and other literatures at the Department of Celtic Languages and Literatures, Harvard University, as well as literature in modern Breton and the other modern Celtic languages. (MBo)

Susan Boynton is Associate Professor of Historical Musicology at Columbia University, and works on medieval Western monastic liturgy and chant (particularly in France, Italy, and Spain), music drama, prayer, and troubadour song. (SB)

Úlfar Bragason is Research Professor, The Árni Magnússon Institute for Icelandic Studies. He has published extensively on Sturlunga saga. His research focuses on medieval Icelandic literature and the Icelandic emigration to America. (ÚBr)

Benjamin Brand is Assistant Professor of Music History at the University of North Texas. His areas of interest include plainsong, ritual, and music pedagogy in medieval and Renaissance Italy. (BB)

Paul Brand is Senior Research Fellow at All Souls College, University of Oxford. He researches and publishes on English and Irish medieval legal history, primarily of the 12th to the 14th centuries. (PAB)

Stefan Brink is Professor and Director of the Centre for Scandinavian Studies, University of Aberdeen. His research interests include the society, culture, language, law, and landscape history of early Scandinavia. (SBr)

Elizabeth A. R. Brown Editorial Board. See above. (EARB)

George Hardin Brown, FMAA, is Professor Emeritus of English and Classics, Stanford University. He specializes in Anglo-Saxon and Anglo-Latin literature, history, and culture, particularly the works of the Venerable Bede. (GHB)

Michael Brown is Reader in Scottish History at the University of St Andrews and author of *James I* (1994), *The Black Douglases* (1998), and *The Wars of Scotland, 1214–1371* (2004). (MBr)

Warren C. Brown is in the Division of Humanities and Social Sciences, California Institute of Technology. His current areas of interest include early medieval social and political history, especially the history of power and of documentary practices. Publications include *Unjust Seizure* (2001) and *Conflict in Medieval Europe* (with Piotr Górecki, 2003). (WCB)

Alexander M. Bruce is Professor of English, University of Montevallo, and has written *Scyld and Scef: Expanding the Analogues* (2002) and essays on Old and Middle English language and literature, folklore, and pedagogy. (AMBr)

Gene A. Brucker Editorial Board. See above. (GAB)

James A. Brundage, FMAA, is Professor Emeritus at the University of Kansas, and specializes in the history of medieval canon law. His most recent book is *Medieval Origins of the Legal Profession* (2008). (JABr)

Caroline Bruzelius is Professor of Art and Art History, Duke University, and works on medieval architecture, especially mendicant and monastic architecture, the buildings of women religious, and urban burials and their impact. (CAB)

Charles Burnett, PhD (Cantab.), is Professor of the History of Islamic Influences in Europe at the Warburg Institute, University of London, and has published widely on the transmission of Arabic learning. (CBu)

Joëlle Burnouf is Professor of Medieval Archaeology at Université de Paris I Panthéon-Sorbonne, and Team Director of environmental archaeology. Her main areas of research and teaching are medieval archaeology and environmental archaeology. (JBu)

Toby Burrows is Principal Librarian of the Scholars' Centre in the University of Western Australia Library. His research interests include the medieval encyclopedic tradition and medieval Biblical exegesis. (TNB)

Keith Busby is Professor of French at the University of Wisconsin. His major area of interest is the production of vernacular manuscripts in medieval Francophonia. His publications include *Gauvain in Old French Literature* (1980), *Chrétien de Troyes's Perceval* (1993), and *Codex and Context* (2002). (KB)

Paul Bushkovitch, PhD (Columbia), is Professor of History at Yale, and is the author of *Religion and Society in Russia* (1992) and *Peter the Great* (2001). He is currently investigating the image of monarchs in Russia 850–1740. (PB)

Giulio Busi is Full Professor of Jewish Studies at the Freie Universität Berlin. He is the editor of the series *The Kabbalistic Library of Giovanni Pico della Mirandola*. (GBu)

Colleen Dorelle Butler is a PhD student at the University of Toronto's Centre for Medieval Studies. Her thesis focuses upon the construction of identity in medieval Insular literature, Latin and vernacular. (CDB)

Sara M. Butler is an Assistant Professor at Loyola University, New Orleans. Her main area of research is marriage and the law in later medieval England. (SMB)

Börje Bydén is Assistant Professor of Greek at Stockholm University. His research interests lie mainly in the field of ancient philosophy and its legacy, especially in the Byzantine period. (BBy)

Stanisław Bylina is Professor at the Institute of History of the Polish Academy of Sciences, Warsaw, and works on medieval Christianity in east-central Europe, including Christianization and popular and elite religious culture. (SBy)

Caroline Walker Bynum, FMAA, FAAAS, is Professor of Medieval History at the Institute for Advanced Study, Princeton. Recent books include *Metamorphosis and Identity* (2001) and *Wonderful Blood* (2007), which won the Gründler Prize. (CWB)

Miriam Cabré is Lecturer in Medieval Romance Literature at the University of Girona. She has worked mainly on the poetry of the troubadour Cerverí de Girona and on medieval Catalan lyrics. (MC)

Montserrat Cabré is Associate Professor of the History of Science, Universidad de Cantabria, Spain, where she teaches history of medicine and women's studies. She works on self-care and household medicine. (MCab)

James Cain is Associate Professor of Literature, Massachusetts Institute of Technology. His main areas of research include the politics of Anglo-Norman courtly literature of the 12th century and genres of narrative from epic and romance to history and hagiography. (JCa)

Martin Camargo is Professor of English and Medieval Studies at the University of Illinois. His many publications focus on medieval Latin rhetoric and on Middle English literature. (MJC)

Fergus Cannan is a historian who specializes in the sculpture and art of medieval England, and the military and social history of Scotland and Ireland. (FC)

Joseph Canning is an Affiliated Lecturer of the History Faculty, Cambridge University, and researches in medieval political thought. His publications include *The Political Thought of Baldus* (1987) and *A History of Medieval Political Thought* (1996 and 2005). (JC)

María José Carrillo-Linares is Associate Professor of English at the University of Huelva (Spain), with research interests in the history of English, medieval medical texts, and Middle English word geography. (MJCL)

Martin Carver is Professor Emeritus at the Department of Archaeology, University of York, UK. He has worked on numerous early medieval sites in England, Scotland, France, Italy, and Algeria, including the princely burial ground at Sutton Hoo and the Pictish monastery at Portmahomack. He is currently editor of *Antiquity*. (MCa)

Brian A. Catlos, Department of History, University of California, Santa Cruz, works on inter-communal political, social, and economic relations across medieval Europe and the Islamic world, and on the medieval Mediterranean. (BAC)

Raeleen Chai-Elsholz, PhD, is an independent scholar and a graduate of Bryn Mawr College and the Sorbonne (Paris IV). (RCE)

Jane Chance is Andrew W. Mellon Distinguished Chair in English, Rice University, and has published twenty-two books, including two volumes of *Medieval Mythography* (1994 & 2000), *The Mythographic Chaucer* (1994), and *The Genius Figure in Antiquity and the Middle Ages* (1975). (JCha)

T. M. Charles-Edwards, FBA, is Jesus Professor of Celtic, University of Oxford, and works mainly on medieval Irish and Welsh history and literature. (TMCE)

Martin Chase is Associate Professor of English and Medieval Studies at Fordham University. Relevant publications include *Einarr Skúlason's Geisli* (2005) and *Lilja* (2007). (MLC)

Robert Chazan, FMAA, is S. H. and Helen R. Scheuer Professor of Jewish History in the Skirball Department of Hebrew and Judaic Studies at New York University. (RC)

Fredric L. Cheyette, FMAA, is Professor Emeritus of History, Amherst College, and has focused on the social and legal history of France and England, environmental history, Chrétien de Troyes' romances, and troubadour poetry. (FLC)

Claudia Chierichini is Assistant Professor of Italian at Mount Holyoke College, and teaches medieval and Renaissance Italian literature. Her research considers the influence of Classical literature on Italian medieval and Renaissance literature. (CC)

Mark Chinca is Senior Lecturer of German, University of Cambridge. He is a Fellow at Trinity College, Cambridge, and specializes in German medieval literature. (MGC)

Tom Christensen is Magister in Nordic and European Archaeology at the University of Copenhagen and Curator at Roskilde Museum. (TChr)

Tina Chronopoulos is RCUK Academic Fellow in Latin at King's College London. Her research interests include hagiography and medieval Latin literature, including reception of and commentaries on Classical authors. (TC)

Sima M. Ćirković is Emeritus Professor at the University of Belgrade, and does research in the archives of Dubrovnik, Venice, Budapest, and Mount Athos, publishing on the society and economy of the Balkan states. (SMĆ)

Robert L. A. Clark has published broadly on medieval theatre, devotion, gender issues, and text-image relationships in illuminated manuscripts. With Kathleen Ashley, he is the editor of *Medieval Conduct* (2001). He teaches French at Kansas State University. (RCl)

Albrecht Classen is University Distinguished Professor of German Studies at the University of Arizona, focusing on medieval and early modern cultural history and mentality. His most recent book is a study of 16th-century German jest narratives (2009). (AC)

M. A. Claussen is Professor of History at the University of San Francisco. He has written on Late Antiquity and Carolingian history and religion. (MAC)

Paul M. Cobb is Associate Professor of Islamic history at the University of Pennsylvania. (PMC)

Adam S. Cohen of the University of Toronto specializes in early medieval art, manuscript illumination, visual exegesis, and Jewish art. He is author of *The Uta Codex: Art, Philosophy, and Reform in Eleventh-Century Germany* (2000). (ASC)

Samuel Cohn is Professor of Medieval History at Glasgow University. His areas of interest are disease and popular revolt. He has authored eleven books, most recently *Cultures of Plague: Medical Thought at the End of the Renaissance* (2009). (SKC)

Georges Comet is Emeritus Professor of Medieval History, University of Aix-en-Provence, France. He is a specialist in the history of medieval agriculture and its techniques, and in the use of images as historical documents. (GC)

Ellen Condict is a doctoral student in English literature at Baylor University. Areas of research interest include medieval literature and philosophy, Chaucer, dream visions, and Victorian poetry. (EMC)

William J. Connell is Professor of History and holder of the Joseph M. and Geraldine C. La Motta Chair in Italian Studies at Seton Hall University. (WJC)

Helen Conrad-O'Briain is an Adjunct Lecturer and Research Associate at the School of English and Centre for Medieval and Renaissance Studies, Trinity College Dublin. She has published on Vergil's *Fortleben*, *anima naturaliter Christiana*, and the origins of science fiction. (HCOB)

John J. Contreni, FMAA, is Professor of History, Purdue University. His research centres on the liberal arts, the Bible, schools, schoolbooks, and teacher-student relations, especially during the Carolingian age. (JJC)

Robert Cook taught English medieval literature at Tulane University from 1962 to 1989. He then moved to the University of Iceland, where he is now Professor Emeritus. (RGC)

Glen M. Cooper is Professor of History at Brigham Young University. His interests include the history of Græco-Islamic science and medicine, Galen and Galenism in Islam and Byzantium, and the transmission of science, Greek to Arabic to Latin. (GMC)

Helen Cooper Advisory Board. See above. (HC)

Rita Copeland, of the University of Pennsylvania, has most recently published (with co-author Ineke Sluiter) *Medieval Grammar and Rhetoric: Language Arts and Literary Theory, AD 300–1475* (2009). (RCo)

Ricardo Córdoba de la Llave has been a Professor of Medieval History at the University of Córdoba since 1990. Among his research interests are technology and material culture in the Middle Ages. (RCór)

Margaret Cormack is Professor of Religious Studies at the College of Charleston. She has published *The Saints in Iceland* (1994) and edited *Sacrificing the Self* (2002) and *Saints and Their Cults Around the Atlantic* (2007). (MJCo)

Raymond J. Cormier specializes in medieval comparative literature (French, Latin, and Celtic), and he has published extensively in those areas. His latest monograph is entitled *High Medieval Adaptations of Virgil's Aeneid* (2010). (RJC)

Sally J. Cornelison is Associate Professor of Art History at the University of Kansas. Her research focuses on saints' cults and relics in late medieval and Renaissance Florence. (SJC)

Lynn T. Courtenay, MA, PhD, FSA, Emerita University of Wisconsin-Whitewater, is an Honorary Research Fellow in Art History at University of Wisconsin-Madison. She researches medieval architecture and is currently working on the Maison Dieu at Tonnerre. (LTC)

William J. Courtenay, FMAA, is C. H. Haskins and Hilldale Professor of History, University of Wisconsin, and specializes in medieval intellectual, university, and religious history, especially for the late Middle Ages. (WJCo)

S. Peter Cowe is Narekatsi Professor of Armenian Studies in the Department of Near Eastern Languages and Cultures, University of California, Los Angeles. His research interests include medieval intellectual history, lyric, and nationalism. (SPC)

Mark Crane teaches History and Latin at Nipissing University in North Bay, Ontario. His main research interest is the Latin print culture of Paris between 1500 and 1540. (MLCr)

Peter Crooks is a specialist on English Ireland in the later Middle Ages. He is editor of *Government, War, and Society in Medieval Ireland* (2009) and Deputy Director of the Irish Chancery Project, Trinity College Dublin. (PJAC)

Richard Cross is John A. O'Brien Professor of Philosophy at the University of Notre Dame. He is the author of *The Metaphysics of the Incarnation* (2002) and *Duns Scotus on God* (2005). (RCr)

William C. Crossgrove is Professor Emeritus of German Studies and Comparative Literature at Brown University. He works on medieval German technical literature, especially herbals and other texts dealing with agriculture and medicine. (WCC)

Katy Cubitt is Senior Lecturer in Early Medieval History at the University of York. She is currently completing a book on penance entitled *Sin and Society in Tenth- and Eleventh-Century England* and has published widely on the Anglo-Saxon Church. (KC)

Linda Page Cummins is Area Coordinator of Musicology at the University of Alabama. Her main research interests are medieval music theory and early 20th-century music. (LPC)

Florin Curta is Professor of Medieval History and Archaeology, University of Florida. She has published on medieval Eastern Europe, including *The Making of the Slavs* (2001) and *Southeastern Europe in the Middle Ages, ca. 500–1250* (2006). (FCu)

Zbignew Dalewski is Professor of Medieval History at the University of Bialystok and at the Institute of History of the Polish Academy of Sciences in Warsaw, and specializes in medieval political culture. His publications include *Ritual and Politics: Writing the History of a Dynastic Conflict in Medieval Poland* (2008). (ZD)

Christopher J. Daniell was an Honorary Visiting Fellow at the Centre for Medieval Studies, University of York. His research interests include death and burial in medieval England and the medieval history of York. (CJD)

Maria Amalia D'Aronco, Professor of Germanic Philology at the University of Udine, has published extensively on Anglo-Saxon and Middle English language and literature, herbals, and early medieval medicine. (MAD)

John Reuben Davies is Research Fellow in Scottish History, School of History and Classics, University of Edinburgh. He specializes in the ecclesiastical history of medieval Scotland and Wales. (JRD)

† **R. R. Davies** Advisory Board. See above. (RRD)

Craig R. Davis is Professor of English Language and Literature at Smith College in Northampton, Massachusetts, where he teaches Old and Middle English, Old Norse, and Medieval Welsh. (CRD)

Joseph Maurice Davis teaches medieval Judaism at Gratz College in Philadelphia. His work focuses on the Jews of central and eastern Europe in the 16th and 17th centuries. (JMD)

RáGena C. DeAragon is Associate Professor of History at Gonzaga University. Research and publications interests include 12th-century English social history. (RCD)

Sible de Blaauw is Professor of Early Christian Art and Architecture at the Radboud Universiteit Nijmegen, The Netherlands. His scholarship focuses upon the interchange between architecture and liturgy and the reception history of early Christian monuments. (SdB)

Scott DeGregorio is Associate Professor of English Language and Literature at the University of Michigan at Dearborn. He works on Anglo-Saxon literature and culture, especially Bede, and patristic and medieval exegetical traditions. (SDD)

Alan Deighton is Lecturer in German at the University of Hull. He is also the author of articles on various aspects of medieval German literature and iconography. (ARD)

George E. Demacopoulos is Associate Professor of Historical Theology and Co-Founding Director of the Orthodox Christian Studies Program at Fordham University. He specializes in the contact and discord between the Christian East and West from late Antiquity to the early Modern era. (GED)

Luke Demaitre is Visiting Professor at the Center for Biomedical Ethics and Humanities, University of Virginia. Recent publications include *Leprosy in Premodern Medicine* (2007), and 'AIDS and medieval leprosy' (2008). (LED)

James D'Emilio is Associate Professor of Humanities, University of South Florida (Tampa), and studies medieval Galicia, the Church in medieval Iberia, and art and architecture in Iberia (800–1300). (JPD)

Walter B. Denny is Professor of Art History at the University of Massachusetts, Amherst, and Senior Consultant in the Department of Islamic Art, Metropolitan Museum of Art, New York. His work concentrates on Ottoman Turkey, Islamic carpets and textiles, and East-West issues. (WBD)

Nancy van Deusen, FMAA, is Professor of Musicology, Claremont Graduate University, and has published extensively on music within the medieval city of Rome, medieval cathedrals, the medieval sequence within its Latin codicological and palaeographical contexts, and music as medieval science. (NvD)

Eva de Visscher is British Academy Post-doctoral Research Fellow at Oriel College, Oxford. Her research interests include Jewish-Christian relations, biblical exegesis, and the use of magic in the Middle Ages. (EdV)

Kelly DeVries is Professor of History at Loyola University Maryland. He is the author or co-author of 14 books and more than 60 articles on medieval military history and technology. He is also an Honorary Historical Consultant for the Royal Armouries, UK. (KDV)

Andrea Janelle Dickens is Assistant Professor of Church History at the United Theological Seminary, Dayton. Her research interests include medieval Cistercian mysticism, the reception of Augustine, and medieval women's theological writings. (AJD)

William J. Diebold is Jane Neuberger Goodsell Professor of Art History and Humanities at Reed College, Portland, Oregon, and specializes in early medieval art and its modern reception. (WJDi)

Peter Dinzelbacher is an interdisciplinary medievalist, and has published over forty books on the Middle Ages and edited *Mediaevistik*. His main fields are the history of mentalities and religious history, especially mysticism. (PD)

Muhammad Ashraf Ebrahim Dockrat is Lecturer in the Department of Semitic Languages, University of Johannesburg, teaching classical Arabic and Islamic studies. His research interests are in Qur'anic interpretation. (MD)

Ben Dodds is Lecturer in History at Durham University. His research includes the late-medieval peasant economy in England, with additional interests in the history of the continental European peasantry, especially that of Spain. (BD)

William J. Dohar is Adjunct Associate Professor in the Religious Studies Department at Santa Clara University in California. His areas of interest include medieval pastoral care, ecclesiastical organization, and late medieval England. (WJD)

L. S. Domonkos is Professor Emeritus of Medieval and Renaissance History at Youngstown State University. His areas of research include the Renaissance in Hungary and the history of universities. He is the author of numerous articles and co-editor of three volumes, including *The Laws of the Medieval Kingdom of Hungary*, Vol. 3 (1996). (LSD)

John E. Dotson is Professor Emeritus, Department of History, Southern Illinois University at Carbondale. His field is medieval maritime and business history, particularly of Genoa and Venice. (JED)

Simon Doubleday is Associate Professor of History at Hofstra University. His current research projects address the

ethical-political dimensions of medieval studies, and the figure of María Pérez, La Balteira. (SRD)

Ute Drews is the Curator of the Wikinger Museum Haithabu with overall responsibility for exhibitions. The museum is part of the State Museum for Archaeology at Gottorf Palace in Schleswig-Holstein, Germany. (UD)

Anne M. Dropick teaches at Yale University. Her professional interests include medieval and Renaissance literature and civilization, philology, visual arts, and the history of the book. (AMD)

Thérèse-Anne Druart is Ordinary Professor of Philosophy at The Catholic University of America, Washington, DC. She specializes in medieval Arabic philosophy. (TAD)

Donald F. Duclow is Professor Emeritus of Philosophy at Gwynedd-Mercy College. He writes on the medieval Christian Neoplatonic tradition, and published *Masters of Learned Ignorance: Eriugena, Eckhart, and Cusanus* (2006). (DFD)

Seán Duffy is Senior Lecturer in Medieval History at Trinity College Dublin. His areas of specialty are Anglo-Irish relations, the medieval 'Celtic Fringe', and the history and archaeology of Dublin. (SD)

Jan Dumolyn is Lecturer in the Department of Medieval History of Ghent University. His research interests include the social and political history of the late medieval Netherlands. (JDu)

Joan Dusa received a doctorate in History from the University of California, Los Angeles, and writes on the history of East-Central Europe and the Balkan peninsula in the Middle Ages. (JDus)

Francis A. Dutra is Professor of History at the University of California, Santa Barbara. He is a specialist in the histories of Portugal and Brazil. (FAD)

Joseph Dyer taught music history at the University of Massachusetts, Boston. His research interests include the medieval liturgy of Rome, psalmody, the music of monasticism, music theory, and performance practice. (JDy)

Lesley-Anne Dyer is a doctoral candidate, University of Notre Dame, and studies the influences of philosophical realism upon medieval theology. She completed her MPhil thesis at the University of Cambridge on John Wyclif. (LAD)

P. S. Eardley is Associate Professor of Philosophy at the University of Guelph. He specializes in medieval philosophy. (PSE)

Theresa Earenfight is Associate Professor of History (Seattle University), and author of *The King's Other Body: Maria of Castile and the Crown of Aragon* (forthcoming). She studies gender and royal authority in medieval Spain. (TME)

Bruce Stansfield Eastwood is Professor of History, Emeritus, at the University of Kentucky. He now studies medieval astronomy and cosmology in western Europe, 600–1200, with a current project on 'Charlemagne and the Christian Revival of Science'. (BSE)

Martin Elbel is a Lecturer in Early Modern History at the University of Olomouc. (ME)

Ivana Elbl is Associate Professor in the Department of History of Trent University and the Director of its graduate programme. Her work focuses on late medieval Portugal and its overseas expansion. She is currently completing a new biography of Henry the Navigator. (IE)

Martin Malcolm Elbl of Trent University researches late medieval economic history, with emphasis on technology, cross-cultural exchange, business decision-making, and marginal economies or social groups. (MME)

L. M. Eldredge, now retired, was Professor of English at the University of Ottawa. His research has focused primarily on medieval ophthalmology. (LME)

Oliver B. Ellsworth is Professor Emeritus of Musicology at the University of Colorado at Boulder. His main area of research is late medieval music theory. (OBE)

Jutta Eming teaches medieval German literature at the Freie Universität Berlin. Recently she has worked on theories of emotions, the history of medieval theatre, and in the broader field of performance studies. (JE)

Richard K. Emmerson is Dean of the School of Arts at Manhattan College, and studies representations of apocalypticism in medieval illustrated manuscripts, art, drama, and visionary poetry. (RKE)

James B. Tschen Emmons is a professor with Northern Virginia Community College's Extended Learning Institute. His research focuses upon early medieval Irish history and literary culture, especially hagiography. (JBTE)

Libby Karlinger Escobedo is an Assistant Professor of Art History at Aurora University and a former Reader for the Index of Christian Art, Princeton University. Her PhD is from Bryn Mawr College. (LKE)

Nicholas John Evans is Hunter-Marshall Research Fellow at the Centre for Scottish and Celtic Studies, University of Glasgow, and works on medieval Ireland and Scotland, especially identity, perceptions of the past, and socio-political developments. (NJE)

Thor Ewing is an independent medievalist with a special interest in pre-Christian northern Europe, and the author of *Viking Clothing* (2006) and *Gods and Worshippers* (2008). (TE)

Richard C. Famiglietti specializes in the history of France in the 14th–15th centuries. His published monographs include *Royal Intrigue* (1986), *Tales of the Marriage Bed* (1992), *The Lit de Justice* (with Elizabeth A. R. Brown, 1994), and *Lordship in Medieval France* (forthcoming). (RCF)

Margot E. Fassler Editorial Board. See above. (MEF)

Anthony Faulkes is Emeritus Professor of Old Icelandic at the University of Birmingham (UK). (ARF)

Kirsten Anne Fenton is a Teaching Fellow at the University of St Andrews. Her research interests include gender, national identity, and historical writing (especially William of Malmesbury) within the Anglo-Norman world. (KAF)

Manuel Pedro Ferreira is Associate Professor at the Universidade Nova de Lisboa, Portugal, and has been working on French and Iberian medieval music since the mid 1980s. In 1995 he founded the early music ensemble Vozes Alfonsinas, which he also directs. (MPF)

George Ferzoco is Research Fellow of Medieval Religious Studies at the University of Bristol. His research deals mainly with textual and visual aspects of medieval education and propaganda. (GPF)

Alison Finlay is Reader in Medieval English and Icelandic at Birkbeck, University of London. Her research interests are in Icelandic Kings' sagas, Sagas of Icelanders, and skaldic poetry. (AF)

R. C. Finucane is Distinguished Professor of History at Oakland University in Rochester, MI. His publications include two books on medieval miracles, *Miracles and Pilgrims* (1977, 1995) and *The Rescue of the Innocents* (1997, 2000). (RCFi)

Klaus-Dietrich Fischer is Professor of Medical History, Mainz University and a member of the Institute for Advanced Study, Princeton (2008–9). He studies the transmission and content of Latin medical works, including those on veterinary medicine, from antiquity and the early Middle Ages. (KDF)

Marie Therese Flanagan is Professor of Medieval History, The Queen's University, Belfast. Her research area is 12th-century Ireland, both before and after Anglo-Norman intervention. (MTF)

Joe Flatman is the County Archaeologist of Surrey and a Lecturer at the Institute of Archaeology, London. He researches and teaches aspects of medieval archaeology, history, and art history. (JCF)

Michael S. Flier Editorial Board. See above. (MSF)

Christoph Flüeler is Professor of Palaeography, Codicology, and Medieval Latin at the University of Fribourg, working on medieval political philosophy, the reception of Aristotle, and virtual manuscript libraries. (CF)

Sarah Foot is Regius Professor of Ecclesiastical History at Oxford. She works on Anglo-Saxon history (particularly the Church and English identity) and is currently writing a life of King Æthelstan. (SRIF)

Jerold C. Frakes is Professor of Comparative Literature and German at the University of Southern California. His research interests include medieval German, Norse, Latin, and Yiddish, medieval epic, and Europe and Islam. (JCFr)

Roberta Frank Advisory Board. See above. (RFr)

Arnold E. Franklin is Assistant Professor of Jewish History at Queens College, City University of New York. His research focuses on Jewish culture in the Islamic world. (AEF)

Mary Franklin-Brown is Assistant Professor at the University of Minnesota. Her recent publications include 'The Obscure Figures of the Encyclopedia' and *Discourses of Encyclopedism in the Scholastic Age*, both forthcoming. (MFB)

Adam Joseph Franklin-Lyons is Professor of History at Marlboro College, and studies agricultural and economic history in the Mediterranean. He focuses on famines and subsistence crises in the Crown of Aragon. (AJFL)

Michael Frassetto teaches history at the University of Delaware and is author of *Heretic Lives: Medieval Heresy from Bogomil and the Cathars to Wyclif and Hus* (2007), and editor of *Christian Attitudes toward the Jews in the Middle Ages* (2006). (MCF)

Paul H. Freedman Editorial Board. See above. (PHF)

Richard Freedman is Professor of Music at Haverford College. His research explores the roles of patronage, printing, and piety in the musical life of the 16th century. (RF)

Gad Freudenthal is Senior Research Fellow, Centre National de la Recherche Scientifique, and works on the history of ancient and medieval science in Jewish cultures. He is the author of numerous publications and the editor of *Aleph*. (GF)

Carole Collier Frick is Professor of History at Southern Illinois University, Edwardsville, and is the author of *Dressing Renaissance Florence: Families, Fortunes, and Fine Clothing* (2002). (CCF)

Jan Frolík of the Institute of Archaeology, Academy of Sciences of the Czech Republic, works on the archaeology of medieval towns and hillforts and on the history of Prague Castle. (JFr)

Thomas A. Fudge is Director of the Hewitt Research Foundation in Washington. His research interests include heresy and popular religion, especially Hussites, and ecclesiastical history. (TAF)

Signe Horn Fuglesang is a Professor of Art History at the University of Oslo. Her research interests include north European medieval art, specializing in the Viking period. (SHF)

Beatrix Fülöpp-Romhányi is an assistant professor at the Institute for History of the Gáspár Károli Calvinist University (Budapest, Hungary). Her area of interest is medieval church history. (BFR)

Erika Gál is an archaeozoologist and Postdoctoral Research Fellow at the Archaeological Institute of the Hungarian Academy of Sciences. Her research interests include the archaeology of birds and mammals, and bone manufacturing. (EG)

Brenda Gardenour received her PhD in Medieval History from Boston University. Her research examines the interrelationship of medical and hagiographical texts in 13th- and 14th-century Europe. (BG)

Mark Gardiner is Senior Lecturer at the Queen's University Belfast. His research interests include the archaeology of late medieval England, particularly rural landscape and domestic architecture. (MFG)

Cristian Gaşpar is a PhD candidate at Central European University, Budapest. His research interests include Byzantine and Early Christian studies, hagiography, Indo-European linguistics, Romanian linguistics, and philology. (CG)

Simon Gaunt Editorial Board. See above. (SG)

Ottó Sándor Gecser is Assistant Professor, Department of Sociology, Eötvös Loránd University, Budapest. He is also a postdoctoral researcher, OTKA (Hungarian Scientific Research Foundation), Department of Medieval Studies, Central European University, Budapest. (OSG)

William Gentrup is Assistant Director of the Arizona Center for Medieval and Renaissance Studies. His research and teaching fields are Renaissance literature and the Bible. (WFG)

Francis G. Gentry is Emeritus Professor of German at the University of Wisconsin-Madison and The Pennsylvania State University. His area of teaching and research is Medieval German literature. (FGG)

Ioannis Georganas is a Researcher (Antiquity) at the Foundation of the Hellenic World. His main area of research is the archaeology of Late Bronze and Early Iron Age Greece. (IG)

Sharon E. J. Gerstel is Professor of Byzantine Art at the University of California, Los Angeles. Her research focuses on late Byzantine religious art and the archaeology of the Byzantine village. (SEJG)

Frederick W. Gibbs of the University of Wisconsin at Madison studies the intersection of medieval medicine and natural philosophy, with attention to how the body interacts with the world around it. (FWG)

Pedro Gil-Sotres is Professor of History of Medicine at the University of Navarra, Spain. Present on the Executive

Committee of the Arnaldi de Villanova Opera Medica Omnia, his research has focused on the medieval period. (PGS)

Jan Gilbert is a freelance journalist. She has published various articles on Spanish ballads, has a PhD on ethno-religious identities in Spanish frontier ballads, and has held a research fellowship in medieval Iberian literature at Trinity Hall, Cambridge. (JG)

Jane Gilbert is Senior Lecturer in French at University College London, and a comparativist working in English, French, and modern theory. (JGi)

Jennifer D. Gilchrist holds a Master's degree from the Centre for Medieval Studies, University of Toronto. She focuses on the devotional literature and culture of late-medieval England. (JDG)

Andrew Gillett is Research Fellow and Associate Professor in Late Antiquity at Macquarie University. His research interests include late Roman and early medieval communication and historiography. (AKG)

John B. Gillingham Editorial Board. See above. (JBG)

Cédric Giraud is Assistant Professor of Medieval History at the University of Nancy (2). His research interests include 12th-century theology and Anselm of Laon. (CGi)

Florence Eliza Glaze is Associate Professor of History, Coastal Carolina University, and Fellow of the American Academy in Rome, and specializes in the study of medicine from antiquity to the year 1200. (FEG)

Thomas F. Glick is Professor of History and Geography at Boston University. He has written extensively on medieval irrigation systems. (TFG)

Hans-Werner Goetz is Professor of Medieval History, University of Hamburg. He works on medieval mentality and historiography, and on the political, social, constitutional, and gender history of the early Middle Ages. (HWG)

Eric J. Goldberg is Associate Professor of History at Williams College. He specializes in the politics and culture of early medieval Europe. (EJG)

Randall Goldberg is pursuing a PhD at Indiana University. His research interests include early modern European music and music literature, 18th-century music, and Jewish identity in American music. He teaches music history at Youngstown State University. (REG)

Harvey Goldblatt is Professor of Medieval Slavic Literature at Yale University and the author of numerous publications on the literary civilization of Slavia orthodoxa. His current interests include the Igor Tale and the Cyrillo-Methodian literary tradition. (HG)

Judith K. Golden is a research scholar for the Index of Christian Art at Princeton University. Her research interests include Gothic manuscript illumination, especially of saints, women as patrons, and 13th- and 14th-century France and England. (JKG)

Peter B. Golden is Professor Emeritus (History) and Academic Director of the Middle Eastern Studies Program at Rutgers University. He studies the interaction of the Turkic nomads of medieval Eurasia with the surrounding Slavic, Iranian, Byzantine, Islamic, and Caucasian peoples. (PBG)

David M. Goldfrank is Professor of History, Georgetown University, and has written *The Monastic Rule of Iosif Volotsky* (1983, 2000), *The Origins of the Crimean War* (1994), and *Nil Sorsky: The Authentic Writings* (2008), and co-authored *A History of Russia: Peoples, Legends, Events, Forces* (2004). (DMG)

Bernard R. Goldstein is University Professor Emeritus at the University of Pittsburgh, and has written extensively on the history of astronomy, particularly in antiquity and the Middle Ages. (BRG)

Camilo Gómez-Rivas is Assistant Professor in the Department of Arab and Islamic Civilizations at the American University in Cairo. He writes on law and society in the Islamic Maghrib. (CGR)

Sarah Gordon is Associate Professor of French, Utah State University, and is author of *Culinary Comedy in Medieval French Literature* (2006) and publications on food, sexuality, and disability in Old French literature. (SGo)

Piotr Górecki is Professor of History at the University of California, Riverside. He specializes in the history of society, communities, and the law in medieval Poland. (PSG)

Timothy Graham is Director of the Institute for Medieval Studies and Professor of History, University of New Mexico, and is a specialist in palaeography and codicology, as well as co-author of *Introduction to Manuscript Studies* (2007). (TG)

Edward Grant is the author of 12 books and over 90 articles on medieval science and natural philosophy, and is Distinguished Professor Emeritus of History and Philosophy of Science at Indiana University, Bloomington. (EGr)

Gundula Grebner is Researcher at the Department of History, Goethe-Universität, Frankfurt am Main. She is working on Italian notarial culture and law schools, on the court of Frederick II, and on Jewish history. (GG)

Monica H. Green is Professor of History at Arizona State University. Her research interests include the history of medicine in medieval Western Europe. (MHG)

Borislav Grgin works at the Department of History, University of Zagreb. His areas of interest are late medieval Croatian and central European history, and his publications include *Europe and the Mediterranean in the Middle Ages* (2006) and *The Romanian Lands in the Middle Ages and in the Early Modern Age* (2006). (BGr)

Frank Griffel is Professor of Islamic Studies in the Department of Religious Studies, Yale University. He specializes in Islamic intellectual history, particularly the introduction of Aristotelian philosophy into Islamic theology. (FG)

Ralph A. Griffiths is Emeritus Professor of Medieval History at Swansea University. His research interests include the society and politics of the British Isles during the later Middle Ages. (RAG)

Kaaren Grimstad is Associate Professor in the Department of German, Scandinavian and Dutch at the University of Minnesota. Her teaching and research include Old Norse language, literature, and culture. (KG)

Stefanie Gropper is Professor for Scandinavian Studies at Tübingen University. Her special field of research is translation studies in medieval Scandinavian literature. (SGr)

Michael A. Grünbart is Assistant Professor at the University of Münster. His research interests include Byzantine literature, the history of Byzantine aristocracy, material culture, and daily life. (MAG)

Ryszard Grzesik is Docent at the Institute for Slavistics of the Polish Academy of Sciences, and works on medieval central European history, especially relations between Poland and Hungary, and on the narrative sources. (RG)

Aðalheiður Guðmundsdóttir is a part-time teacher in folklore in the Faculty of Social and Human Sciences at the University of Iceland. Main areas of research are Old Norse literature and folktale studies. (AGu)

Darius von Güttner-Sporzyński is Research Fellow at School of Historical Studies, the University of Melbourne. He is the author of the forthcoming *Poland and the Crusades in the Twelfth Century*. (DvG)

Alison Gulley, Assistant Professor of English at Lees-McRae College, teaches classes in medieval and Renaissance literature as well as modern British literature. She has published articles in *Medievalia*, the *Chaucer Encyclopedia*, and several other literary journals. (AG)

Terry Gunnell teaches folkloristics at the University of Iceland. He is author of *The Origins of Drama in Scandinavia* (1995), and editor of *Masks and Mumming in the Nordic Area* (2007). (TAG)

Dimitri Gutas is Professor of Arabic, Yale University, and works on the medieval Graeco-Arabic translation movement and its lexicography, the transmission of Greek philosophical texts into Arabic (especially Theophrastus), and Arabic philosophy (especially Avicenna). (DG)

Scott Gwara received his PhD in Medieval Studies from the University of Toronto in 1993. He teaches English literature at the University of South Carolina. (SGw)

Margaret E. Hadley, PhD (Yale University), is an independent scholar, and does research on medieval and Renaissance manuscript illumination in northern Europe. Her dissertation on French-language missals appeared in 2007. (MEH)

Mark Hagger is Lecturer in Medieval History, Bangor University, and works on the political, institutional, and social history of Normandy and Anglo-Norman England, 950–1200, and Anglo-Norman charters and chronicles. (MH)

John Haines is Associate Professor at the University of Toronto and researches the history of music in the Middle Ages. (JDH)

Tracy Chapman Hamilton is Associate Professor of Art History at Sweet Briar College. Her research interests include medieval women, patronage, topography, and pilgrimage. *Poetry and Politics: The Artistic Patronage of Marie de Brabant* is forthcoming. (TCH)

Lars Ivar Hansen is Professor in Medieval and Early Modern history at the University of Tromsø, Norway. His main research interests concern economic and social conditions, inter-ethnic relations, and networks of social interaction. He is co-author of a textbook in Sámi history before 1750. (LIH)

Syed Nomanul Haq is Senior Faculty at the Lahore University of Management Sciences (LUMS) in Pakistan where he leads the history program. Trained in medieval Islamic intellectual history, his research and teaching lie in the history of philosophy and of science, literature, and culture. (SNH)

Antonina Harbus is Associate Professor of English at Macquarie University, Sydney. Her research interests include Anglo-Saxon understandings of dreams, the mind, and the self. (AJH)

Franklin T. Harkins received his PhD in medieval theology from the University of Notre Dame and is currently at Fordham University where he teaches historical theology. (FTH)

Anthea Harris is Lecturer in Archaeology at the University of Birmingham. She works on the archaeology and history of long-distance contacts in the early medieval world, particularly the 5th to 8th centuries, with a special focus on Byzantine external relations. (ALH)

Joseph Harris is Professor of English and Folklore at Harvard University. His scholarly publications centre on Old English, Old Norse, comparative mythology, runology, and the study of orality and literacy. (JHa)

Wolfgang Haubrichs of the Department of German Studies, University of Saarland, is a member of the Akademie der Wissenschaften Mainz and Österreichische Akademie der Wissenschaften. His areas of research include German medieval studies, history of German language, onomastics, and Romance-Germanic language contacts. (WH)

David J. Hay is an Associate Professor of History at the University of Lethbridge. He specializes in high medieval military and gender history, especially the career of Matilda of Tuscany. (DJH)

Jérôme Hayez is a Researcher at the Centre National de la Recherche Scientifique, Institut d'Histoire Moderne et Contemporaine, Paris. His main fields of research include practical letter-writing, 1250–1600, and Italian merchants' careers and social networks, 14th to 15th centuries. (JHay)

Thomas Head is Professor of History, Hunter College and the Graduate Center of the City University of New York, and has written widely on the cult of saints and early Capetian France. (TFH)

Patrick Stephen Healy is a Research Fellow at Trinity College Dublin. His research interests include the Investiture Controversy of the late 11th century and the medieval transmission of canon law collections. (PSH)

Luba Hédlová is a PhD student at the Department of Art History, Masaryk University Brno, Czech Republic. Her research is in medieval sculpture and early print in the central European region, historiography, and methodology of art history. (LH)

Thomas J. Heffernan holds the Kenneth Curry Chair in the Humanities at the University of Tennessee. He studies the period of the historical martyrdoms with particular attention to the Christian church in Roman North Africa. (TJH)

Joseph Held is Professor Emeritus of Rutgers University, former Dean of the Faculty at the Camden, NJ campus, elected member of the Hungarian Academy of Sciences, and author of ten books and many articles. (JHe)

Knut Helle is Professor Emeritus of Medieval History at the University of Bergen. Research interests include medieval political institutions, urbanization, and legal history. (KH)

Richard Helmholz Editorial Board. See above. (RH)

John C. Hendrickson is an independent scholar and writer, and has graduate degrees in religion, history, literature, and political science. Specialisms include comparative Christian theology, political and ethical theories, and Victorian literature. (JCH)

Michelle M. Herder is Assistant Professor of History at Cornell College. Her research centres on religious women in Catalonia in the late Middle Ages. (MMH)

Jan Herlinger is Derryl and Helen Haymon Professor of Music at Louisiana State University, and has edited and translated treatises of Marchetto da Padova and Prosdocimus de Beldemandis. (JH)

Lars Hermanson is a scholar and Associate Professor for the Department of History, Uppsala University. His main area of research is the élite's political culture in 13th- to 14th- century Scandinavia. (LOH)

Michael W. Herren is Distinguished Research Professor Emeritus, York University, Toronto, and has written extensively on early medieval Latin culture, including the Hisperica Famina, Virgilius Grammaticus, Aldhelm, Eriugena, and Insular church history. (MWH)

Alfred Hiatt is a Reader in the School of English and Drama, Queen Mary, University of London. His research interests include forgery and document culture, medieval maps, and spatial representation. (AH)

Michael A. Hicks is Professor of Medieval History, University of Winchester, and works on late medieval political and aristocratic England, especially Bastard Feudalism, the Wars of the Roses, and the Yorkist kings. (MAH)

David Hiley is Professor at the Institut für Musikwissenschaft, University of Regensburg, and is a specialist in medieval liturgical chant, especially its regional and local traditions. (DDH)

John-Paul Himka is Professor of East European and Ukrainian history in the Department of History and Classics at the University of Alberta. (JPH)

S. Adam Hindin of Harvard University is a historian of medieval European art and architecture. His current research explores the social interpretations of visual material in Gothic Bohemia. (SAH)

John Hines Editorial Board. See above. (JHi)

Amanda Jane Hingst is an independent scholar in Madison, WI. Her research interests include 11th- and 12th-century northern European history, especially the Anglo-Norman world. (AJHi)

Ivan Hlavácek is Professor Emeritus of Historical Auxiliary Sciences, Faculty of Arts, Charles University of Prague. His main fields of interest are the diplomatics of the High Middle Ages, administrative history, codicology, and library history. (IH)

Hana Jana Hlaváčková is a Researcher at the Academy of Sciences of the Czech Republic, and teaches art history at Charles University, Prague, specializing in Bohemian and Byzantine art, illuminated manuscripts, and iconography. (HJH)

Jean-Claude Hocquet is 'Directeur de Recherche' Emeritus, Centre National de la Recherche Scientifique, and has taught at Paris, Venice, and Lille. His work is on Venice, the Mediterranean, salt, maritime trade, weights and measures, and public finance. (JCHo)

Richard C. Hoffmann is Professor Emeritus and Senior Scholar in Medieval and Early Modern History at York University, Toronto. His research interests include the environmental, economic, and social history of medieval Europe. (RCH)

Kelly M. Holbert is the Exhibition Coordinator at the Smith College Museum of Art. Her area of specialty is metalwork, enamel, and ivories of the 12th to 14th centuries. (KMH)

Elisabeth Hollender is Professor of Religious Studies, Ruhruniversity Bochum. Her research includes medieval Hebrew literature from Ashkenaz, medieval Hebrew poetry, and medieval commentaries on Hebrew liturgical poetry. (EHo)

Alizah Holstein received her doctorate from Cornell University in 2006. She specializes in the cultural and social history of medieval Rome. (AHo)

Andrew Holt is a doctoral student at the University of Florida, working on the Crusading era, and is co-author, with James Muldoon, of *Fighting Words: Competing Voices from the Crusades* (2008). (APH)

Richard Holt is Professor of Medieval History at the University of Tromsø, Norway. His chief areas of research are in medieval urban history and the history of technology. (RAH)

Wendy Marie Hoofnagle is Assistant Professor of English, University of Northern Iowa. She specializes in Anglo-Norman literature and cultural history, particularly the impact of Carolingian customs on Anglo-Norman society. (WMH)

Peregrine Horden is Professor of Medieval History, Royal Holloway, University of London, and has written extensively on the history of medicine, charity, disease, and the environment in the Middle Ages. (PH)

Kateřina Horníčková, a PhD candidate, is completing a dissertation on ecclesiastical treasures in medieval Bohemia. Her interests cover relics, minor arts, and artworks in their confessional context. (KHo)

Elliott Horowitz is Associate Professor of Jewish History at Bar-Ilan University, Israel, and co-editor of the *Jewish Quarterly Review*. (EHor)

Maryanne Cline Horowitz is a Professor of History at Occidental College and an Associate, University of California, Los Angeles. Her research interests include intellectual history, and France and Italian city-states, 12th through 17th centuries. (MCH)

John D. Hosler is Assistant Professor of History at Morgan State University in Baltimore, Maryland. He researches the military, political and religious history of 11th- and 12th-century England and France. (JDHo)

Jason M. Houston is Assistant Professor of Italian, University of Oklahoma. Professor Houston specializes in literature of the Italian Trecento and Italian Humanism. (JMH)

John McDonald Howe is Professor of History, and teaches medieval and religious history at Texas Tech University. He studies Greek and Latin ecclesiastical history of the 10th, 11th, and 12th centuries. (JMHo)

Jonathan H. Hsy is Assistant Professor of English at the George Washington University. His research and teaching interests include Middle English poetry, merchant culture, sociolinguistics, and medieval romance. (JHH)

Benjamin Hudson is Professor of History and Medieval Studies, Pennsylvania State University, and has published *Irish Sea Studies, 900–1200* (2006), *Viking Pirates and Christian Princes* (2005), and *Kings of Celtic Scotland* (1994). (BH)

Joseph P. Huffman is former Academic Dean and Professor of European History, Messiah College. His fields are medieval England and Germany (especially Cologne) and their social history, including immigration and assimilation. (JPHu)

Erwin Huizenga, PhD, researches medieval medicine and surgery, astrology and alchemy. He specializes in the interaction between

theory and practice in medicine, and the vernacular transmission of utilitarian, scientific knowledge. (EHu)

Hans Hummer is Associate Professor at Wayne State University, and is a specialist in the political and social history of the Frankish realms in early medieval Europe. (HH)

R. Stephen Humphreys is the King Abdul Aziz Al Saud Professor of Islamic Studies at the University of California, Santa Barbara. His research and teaching deal with the history of Islamic societies in both medieval and modern times. (RSH)

Zsolt Hunyadi is Adjunct Professor, Department of Medieval and Early Modern Hungarian History, University of Szeged, and works on the military-religious orders in east-central Europe, as well as the Crusades and Hungary. (ZsH)

Alexander Y. Hwang is Assistant Professor of Historical Theology at Louisville Presbyterian Theological Seminary. His interests include Augustine, Augustinianism, monasticism, and Latin palaeography. (AYH)

Moshe Idel is the Max Cooper Professor of Jewish Thought at Hebrew University in Jerusalem and has also served as a visiting professor and research scholar at several universities and institutions in the United States and Europe. His numerous publications include *Kabbalah: New Perspectives* and *Studies in Ecstatic Kabbalah*. (MI)

Gabriela Ilnitchi Currie is Assistant Professor in the School of Music at the University of Minnesota. Her research examines the intersection of medieval musical, scientific, and philosophical thought. (GIC)

Patricia Clare Ingham is Associate Professor of English and Medieval Studies at Indiana University, Bloomington. She is Editor of *Exemplaria: A Journal of Theory in Medieval and Renaissance Studies*, and has authored *Sovereign Fantasies: Arthurian Romance and the Making of Britain* (2001) and *Postcolonial Moves: Medieval through Modern* (2003). (PCI)

Vyacheslav V. Ivanov is Distinguished Professor, Department of Slavic Languages and Literatures, University of California, Los Angeles. (VVI)

Thomas M. Izbicki holds a doctorate in medieval history from Cornell University. His research mostly focuses on conciliarists and papalists in the 15th and 16th centuries. (TMI)

Martin Jacobs is Associate Professor of Rabbinic Studies and of Jewish, Islamic, and Near Eastern Studies, Washington University in St Louis. He works on medieval Jewish historiography and travel literature and Jewish-Muslim polemics. (MJ)

C. Stephen Jaeger Editorial Board. See above. (CSJ)

Ármann Jakobsson is Senior Lecturer in Old Icelandic literature, University of Iceland, and author of *Tolkien og Hringurinn* (2003). His interests include royal biographies, childhood and old age, and giants and monsters. (ÁJ)

Sverrir Jakobsson is a Doctor of Philosophy from Háskóli Íslands, University of Iceland. He has written *Við og veröldin: Heimsmynd Íslendinga, 1100–1400* (2005), and numerous articles. (SJ)

Zrinka Nikolic Jakus is Assistant Professor, Department of History, at the University of Zagreb, Croatia. Her areas of interest are urban nobility, gender, family, and hagiography. Her publications include *Kith and Kin: Dalmatian Urban Nobility in the Early Middle Ages* (2003) and *Introduction to the Study of History: Historiographical Practica* (2009). (ZNJ)

Sarah James is Lecturer in Medieval Literature at the University of Kent. Her research centres on late medieval vernacular theological writing, and its historical and cultural contexts. (SJa)

Emilia Jamroziak is a Senior Lecturer at the University of Leeds. Her research focuses on religious and cultural history of the central Middle Ages, especially Cistercian monasticism in northern and central Europe. (EMJ)

Zdenka Janeković Römer is Senior Researcher, Institute for Historical Sciences, Croatian Academy of Sciences and Arts, Dubrovnik, and works on political and social practices, culture, and religion in late medieval-early modern Croatia. (ZJR)

Henrik Janson is Associate Professor in History at the University of Göteborg. He specializes in European and Scandinavian early and high Middle Ages. (HJ)

Sven-Bertil Jansson, PhD, now retired, was Senior Archivist at the Centre for Swedish Folk Music and Jazz Research (Svenskt visarkiv), Stockholm. (SBJ)

Gerhard Jaritz is Professor of Medieval Studies at Central European University and a senior research fellow at the Austrian Academy of Sciences. Research interests include history of daily life and material culture. (GJ)

Peter Jeffery is Michael P. Grace Professor of Medieval Studies at Notre Dame, and Scheide Professor of Music History Emeritus at Princeton University. (PJ)

Judith Jesch is Professor of Viking Studies at the University of Nottingham. She has published extensively on Old Norse language, literature, and culture. (JJ)

Phyllis G. Jestice is Professor and Chair of the History Department at the University of Southern Mississippi. Her research area is Germany in the central Middle Ages. (PGJ)

Jenny Jochens is Professor Emerita of History, Towson University, and has written two monographs on Old Norse women and numerous articles on social and family life in the Old Norse world. She spends her retirement years between Baltimore and Paris. (JJo)

Klaus-Frédéric Johannes studied at Heidelberg. His research interests are in late medieval political history and theory, diplomatics, constitutional and legal history, conciliarism, philosophical history, and imperial relations with the papacy. (KFJ)

Eric F. Johnson is Assistant Professor of Medieval and Early Modern History at Kutztown University of Pennsylvania. His research interests include the history of Provence and popular religious culture. (EFJ)

Peter Murray Jones is Fellow and Librarian at King's College, Cambridge. He has published *Medieval Medicine in Illuminated Manuscripts* (1998) and other studies on medicine and science. (PMJ)

Tomasz Jurek is Professor at the Institute of History, Polish Academy of Sciences, Poznań. He specializes in medieval history of Poland, especially Silesia. His main publications are *The Successor of the Kingdom of Poland: Henry the Duke of Glogów* (1993), and *Foreign Knights in Silesia until the Middle of the 14th Century* (1996). (TJ)

Abdul Nasser Kaadan, MD, PhD, is Chairman of the History of Medicine Department at Aleppo University, Professor of History of Medicine, and the President of the International Society for History of Islamic Medicine. (ANK)

Bernice M. Kaczynski is Professor of History at McMaster University and the Centre for Medieval Studies, University of Toronto. Her research interests include intellectual history, manuscripts, and medieval Greek and Latin. (BMK)

Donald Kagay is Professor of History, Albany State University, Georgia, and specializes in medieval legal and military history. He has published *War, Government, and Society in the Medieval Crown of Aragon* (2007). (DJK)

David Kalhous is a Researcher at the Centre for Studies in Central European History, Masaryk University, Brno, working on early medieval hagiography and power structures in early medieval Europe. (DK)

Marianne Kalinke is Trowbridge Chair of Literary Studies and Emerita Professor of Germanic Languages, and is an authority on cultural and literary relations between medieval and early modern Scandinavia and the continent. (MEK)

Antonín Kalous teaches at the Palacký University, Olomouc, Czech Republic. His main interest lies in the late-medieval political, cultural, and church history of central Europe, especially humanism, papal legates, and Matthias Corvinus. (AK)

Ephraim Kanarfogel is Professor of Medieval Jewish History, Graduate School of Jewish Studies, Yeshiva University. He works on medieval Jewish intellectual and social history, and rabbinic literature and culture. (EK)

Damir Karbic is a Researcher at the Croatian Academy of Sciences, Institute of Historical and Social Research, Zagreb, and a Lecturer in the Department of History, University of Zagreb. (DKa)

Sarah Kay is Professor of French at Princeton University. She is a specialist in medieval French and medieval Occitan literature and modern French thought. (SK)

Michel Kazanski is Directeur de Recherche at Centre National de la Recherche Scientifique. His areas of research include the archaeology of barbarian culture during the Migration Age, and Proto-Byzantine material culture (4th to 7th centuries). He is the co-author of *Tsibilium, vol. 2: La nécropole apsile de Tsibilium* (2007), and *Morskoj Čulek* (2007). (MK)

Catherine Keen is Senior Lecturer in Italian at University College London. Her research focuses on Dante and the medieval Italian lyric tradition, especially on themes of politics and exile. (CMK)

Derek Keene is Leverhulme Professor of Comparative Metropolitan History at the Institute of Historical Research, University of London. His research concerns cities in Britain and Europe between 600 and 1700. (DKe)

Menachem Kellner is Professor of Jewish Religious Thought at the University of Haifa. Research interests include medieval Jewish philosophy and studies on dogma, Maimonides, Gersonides, and Abravanel. (MKe)

Dorothy Kelly is a Lecturer at the University College Dublin. Her research interests include early medieval art of Ireland and Britain, specializing in sculpture, particularly the high crosses of Ireland and western Scotland. (DKel)

F. Douglas Kelly is Professor Emeritus of French and Medieval Studies at the University of Wisconsin-Madison. His research interests include medieval French literature, Occitan literature, and medieval Latin and medieval French poetics. (FDK)

Henry Ansgar Kelly, FMAA, is Professor Emeritus of English and Medieval-Renaissance Studies, University of California, Los Angeles. He has worked on canon law and common law (procedure), religious history (demonology, liturgy), and literature (tragedy, Chaucer). (HAK)

David J. Kennedy is Vice-Dean and Precentor of Durham Cathedral, part-time Lecturer in Liturgy in the University of Durham, and member of the Church of England Liturgical Commission. (DJKe)

Beverly Mayne Kienzle is John B. Morrison Professor of the Practice in Latin and Romance Languages, Harvard Divinity School, and works on Hildegard of Bingen, sermons and preaching, Catharism, and hagiography. (BMKi)

Margaret L. King is Professor of History at Brooklyn College and the Graduate Center, City University of New York. She specializes in the history of the Italian Renaissance, especially Venice, humanism, women, and the history of childhood. (MLK)

Ian Kirby was the first Professor of English at Háskóla Islands, and is Professor Emeritus of Lausanne University. His principal publications relate to Bible translation and quotation in western Scandinavia. (IJK)

Andrea Kiss is a Lecturer at the University of Szeged, Hungary. Her research interests include environmental historical geography, landscape history, and climate history. (AKi)

Mikhail B. Kizilov is Kreitman Fellow at Ben Gurion University of the Negev, Beer Sheva, Israel. His research interests include late medieval to early modern Crimea, Khazars, and Jewish communities of the Crimea. (MBK)

Gábor Klaniczay is Permanent Fellow of Collegium Budapest at the Institute for Advanced Study, and Professor at the Central European University. His research interests are in comparative history, and the historical anthropology of sainthood, miracles, visions, shamanism, and witchcraft. (GK)

John Klassen is Professor Emeritus, Department of History, Trinity Western University. His areas of interest are friendship, domestic morality, and women in the economy. His publications include *The Letters of the Rožmberk Sisters: Gender and Family in Fifteenth-Century Bohemia* (2001) and 'The Public and Domestic Faces of Ulrich of Rožmberk' (2000). (JMK)

Holger A. Klein is Associate Professor of Art History and Archaeology, Columbia University, specializing in late antique, early medieval, and Byzantine art history and archaeology. (HAKl)

Uta Kleine is Lecturer in Medieval History at Fernuniversität Hagen. Among her research interests are the social history of medieval religion, the history of literacy and mediality, the conceptions and uses of images, and the forms of social organization and domination in rural communities. (UK)

Christian Kleinert is Research Associate at the Historisches Seminar, Goethe-Universität, Frankfurt am Main. He concentrates on late medieval French and church history, and on the history of the gypsies. (CK)

H. K. Klemettilä is a Postdoctoral Researcher of the Academy of Finland. Her interests include the cultural history of the late Middle Ages, representations of executioners, and abuse of animals. (HKK)

Karen M. Kletter is Assistant Professor of History, Methodist University. Her fields include medieval England, intellectual history, historiography, Jewish-Christian relations,

and reception of Classical and Jewish works in medieval Europe. (KMK)

Michael Knapton is an associate professor at Udine University, Italy. His research interests concern state and society in Venice and northeast Italy, 12th–18th centuries. (MWSK)

James E. Knirk is Professor at the Museum of Cultural History, University of Oslo, and head of Norway's Runic Archives. He studies runic inscriptions, kings' sagas, and Old Norse manuscripts. (JEK)

Paul W. Knoll is Professor of History, Emeritus, University of Southern California. His primary interests are the history of late medieval Poland, the University of Cracow, and the conciliar movement. (PWK)

Zbigniew Kobyliński is Professor at the Institute of Archaeology and Ethnology, Polish Academy of Sciences, and at the Cardinal Stefan Wyszyński University, Warsaw, and works on central European archaeology and heritage management. (ZK)

Mira B. Kofkin is a doctoral student in history at Binghamton University. Her dissertation topic is the role of saints' cults in the English primacy dispute. (MBKo)

Irina Dmitrievna Kolbutova is a translator and copy-editor at the University Press of St Andrew's Biblical Theological Institute, Moscow. Her areas of research are medieval philosophy, theology, and Christian iconography. (IDK)

Gabriela Kompatscher Gufler is Associate Professor of Latin Philology, Institute for Languages and Literatures, University of Innsbruck, and specializes primarily in medieval Latin language and literature. (GKG)

Petr Kopal of the Institute for the Study of Totalitarian Regimes in Prague works in both central European history and film studies. She has written two dissertations, 'Cosmas of Prague' and 'The Medieval Film'. (PK)

† **Zoltan Kordé** was Associate Professor at the University of Szeged, Hungary. He was the author of several studies and books dealing with the institutions of the Szeklers in the Middle Ages, in particular in the 1400s. (ZKo)

Genevra Kornbluth specializes in early medieval art history, particularly Carolingian and Merovingian. She is the author of *Amulets, Power, and Identity in Early Medieval Europe* (forthcoming). (GAK)

Cynthia K. Kosso is Professor of History, Northern Arizona University, and works on late antique Mediterranean environment and economy, particularly Rome and Greece, emphasizing the intersection between history and archaeology. (CKK)

† **Zoltan J. Kosztolnyik** was Emeritus Professor of History at Texas A&M University, specializing in Hungarian medieval history and canon law. (ZJK)

Anna Kovács received her PhD in medieval studies from the Central European University, Budapest. She specializes in material culture and self-representation in the late Middle Ages. (AMK)

Jacek Kowzan studied at the universities of Wroclaw and Glasgow, and now lectures at the Podlaska Academy, Poland. His research interests include the late medieval and early modern eschatology. (JK)

Olga Kozubska-Andrusiv, PhD (Budapest), teaches in the Department of Classical, Byzantine, and Medieval Studies at the Ukrainian Catholic University, Lviv. Her fields of research include the history of Gothic architecture, urban development, and medieval town law. (OKA)

Matt Kozusko is Associate Professor of English at Ursinus College. He also serves as review editor for *Borrowers and Lenders*. His research interests include theatre history and Shakespeare. (MBKoz)

Joel L. Kraemer is John Henry Barrows Professor Emeritus, Divinity School, University of Chicago. He is the author of *Moses Maimonides: The Life and World of One of Civilization's Greatest Minds* (2008), *Humanism in the Renaissance of Islam* (1992) and *Philosophy in the Renaissance of Islam* (1986). (JLK)

Claus Krag is Professor Emeritus of History at Telemark University College in the Faculty of Arts and Sciences, and works on Norwegian history during the Viking Age and high Middle Ages. (CKr)

Susanne Kramarz-Bein is Head of the Scandinavian Department, University of Münster, teaching Scandinavian studies, and medieval and modern Scandinavian literature and culture. She specializes in Norwegian courtly literature (13th century) and culture. (SKB)

Susan R. Kramer has a PhD from Columbia University. She has taught at Columbia and at Sarah Lawrence College. She specializes in the cultural and intellectual history of the high Middle Ages. (SRK)

Jill Kraye is Professor of the History of Renaissance Philosophy and Librarian at the Warburg Institute, and studies the influence of ancient philosophy from the late Middle Ages to early modern times. (JAK)

Juhan Kreem obtained his PhD in 2002 at Tartu University. He is a research fellow in the Tallinn City Archives. His research fields include history of the Teutonic Order and urban history. (JKr)

Jerome Kroll is Professor of Psychiatry Emeritus at the University of Minnesota Medical School, and has published on mental illness in the Middle Ages and, with Bernard Bachrach, *The Mystic Mind* (2005). (JKro)

Bianca Kühnel is Jack Cotton Professor of Architecture and Fine Arts at the Hebrew University of Jerusalem. Her main areas of research are medieval art and architecture, and the Holy Land in Western art. (BK)

Péter Kulcsár, Emeritus of University Miskolc, Hungary, has research interests in cultural history, historiography of the Middle Ages, and humanism. He is author of *Petrus Ransanus: Epithoma rerum Hungararum* (1977) and *Mythographi Vaticani I et II.* (Turnhout 1987). (PKu)

Michael Kulikowski, PhD, is Professor and Head of History at the Pennsylvania State University, and the author of *Late Roman Spain and Its Cities* (2004) and *Rome's Gothic Wars* (2007). (MKu)

Andrew P. Kurt is Visiting Assistant Professor of History at Western Carolina University in North Carolina. His specializations are early medieval Spain and Muslim-Christian relations in al-Andalus and in the Red Sea region. (APK)

Janusz Kurtyka is Associate Professor, Institute of History of Polish Academy of Sciences and President of the Institute of National Remembrance in Poland. Research interests are social history, elites, and structures of power in medieval and early modern Poland. (JKu)

Stanislava Kuzmová is completing a dissertation in the Medieval Studies Department of the Central European University, Budapest, on sermons on St Stanislaus of Cracow and their role in his cult. (SKu)

Anna Kuznetsova is Senior Researcher in the Institute of Slavonic Studies of the Russian Academy of Sciences, Moscow. She studies Christian missions in central and eastern Europe. (AMKu)

W. R. Laird is Associate Professor of History and Humanities at Carleton University, Ottawa, Canada. His research interests include motion and mechanics in the Middle Ages and Renaissance. (WRL)

Lisa Lampert-Weissig is Associate Professor of English Literature and Comparative Medieval Studies at the University of California, San Diego. Her research interests include Middle English literature, Middle High German literature and the history of anti-Semitism. (LLW)

Kate Lang is Associate Professor of History and Chair of the Department of History at the University of Wisconsin-Eau Claire. Her research interests include medieval Islamic cultural history. (KHL)

John Langdon is a professor at the University of Alberta. His research interests include medieval technology, agriculture, economics. and child labour. Recent publications include *Mills in the Medieval Economy* (2004), and 'Commercial Activity and Population Growth in Medieval England', *Past and Present* (2006) (with James Masschaele). (JL)

Lidia Lanza is a postdoctoral student in the University of Fribourg, Switzerland. She studies the medieval reception of Aristotle's *Politics*. (LL)

Michael Lapidge, FBA, is Emeritus Fellow of Clare College, Cambridge. His many publications on Anglo-Saxon literature include *The Cult of St Swithun* (2003) and *The Anglo-Saxon Library* (2006). (ML)

Carolyne Larrington is Supernumerary Fellow and Tutor in Medieval English at St John's College, Oxford. Her research interests are in Old Norse, psychology and medieval literature, and Arthurian texts. (CAL)

Hynek Látal is a Fellow at the Faculty of Philosophy, University of South Bohemia, Czech Republic, with main areas of research in central European late Gothic architecture. (HLá)

James M. Lattis is Director of UW Space Place and Faculty Associate in the Department of Astronomy of the University of Wisconsin-Madison. He specializes in the history of astronomy. (JML)

Whitney A. M. Leeson of Roanoke College is an Associate Professor with a PhD in Anthropology. Research interests include repentant prostitutes, Mary Magdalene, history of witchcraft, gift exchange, and medieval France. (WAML)

Peter M. Lefferts is Professor of Music History, University of Nebraska-Lincoln. He specializes in medieval English music and notation, music theory in Latin and English, and the tonal behaviour of polyphony. (PML)

Rainer Leng is Private Lecturer of History at the University of Würzburg, Germany. His research includes medieval history, history of science and technology, social history, and illustrated technical manuscripts. (RL)

Gail Lenhoff is Professor of Slavic Languages and Literatures, University of California, Los Angeles, and has authored articles and books on Russian hagiography, history, and cultural patronage in the pre-Petrine period. (GL)

James Francis LePree is an Adjunct Assistant Professor in the History Department at the City College of New York. He specializes in early Carolingian religious and political literature. (JFL)

Dorota Lesniewska works at the Slavic Institute of the Polish Academy of Sciences, Poznań, and is interested in Bohemian medieval history, and Polish and Bohemian historiography. (DL)

Andrew W. Lewis is Professor of History at Missouri State University. His research centres on the history of northern and central France from the 11th to 13th centuries. (AWL)

Henrietta Leyser is Senior Research Fellow of St Peter's College, Oxford. Her publications include *Christina of Markyate* (2004) and *Medieval Women: A Social History of Women in England, 450–1500* (1995). (HL)

Felice Lifshitz Editorial Board. See above. (FL)

Evelyn Lincoln is Associate Professor of the History of Art and Architecture and Italian Studies at Brown University. Her research interests include the history of printing and printmaking in Italy. (EL)

David C. Lindberg Editorial Board. See above. (DCL)

Thomas Lindkvist is Professor of Medieval History, University of Gothenburg, and does research on agrarian and social history, the social conditions and emergence of a kingdom in Sweden, and Sweden's Christianization. (TL)

John Lindow is Professor of Scandinavian at the University of California, Berkeley. His research and teaching focus on Old Norse language and literature and on northern European folklore. (JLi)

Joyce Tally Lionarons is Professor of English at Ursinus College. Her research centres on Old English and Old Norse literature. (JTL)

Janet Senderowitz Loengard is Professor of History Emerita at Moravian College. Her research interests include late medieval and early modern English legal history. (JSL)

Pamela O. Long Editorial Board. See above. (POL)

Philip Longworth was Professor of History at McGill University. His research interests include the eastern European frontier-lands and the Russian Academy of Sciences great expedition to the Caucasus in the 1770s. (PL)

Dubravko Lovrenović is Associate Professor of History, University of Sarajevo, and specializes in south-eastern Europe during the late medieval period. His dissertation, 'Hungary and Bosnia, 1387–1463', was published in Sarajevo (2006). (DLo)

John Lowden is a professor at Courtauld Institute of Art, and has published six books, including *The Making of the Bibles Moralisées* (2000), *Medieval Ivories and Works of Art* (with John Cherry, 2008), and *The Jaharis Gospel Lectionary* (2009), and more than eighty articles. (JHL)

Christian Lübke is Professor of East-European History, Historisches Institut, Ernst Moritz Arndt University of

Greifswald. He specializes in Poland and the Baltic countries. (CL)

Pavel Vladimirovich Lukin, PhD, is a Senior Research Fellow at the Institute of Russian History, Russian Academy of Sciences. He was awarded the 2003 medal and prize for young scientists by the Russian Academy of Sciences. (PVL)

Niels Lund is Professor of History, University of Copenhagen, and does research in Viking history, in particular the Scandinavian settlement in England, and in Scandinavian military organization in the Middle Ages. (NL)

Ingunn Lunde is Professor of Russian at the University of Bergen. Her research interests include medieval Slavic culture, 19th–21st century Russian literature, and contemporary Russian language culture. (IL)

F. Thomas Luongo is Associate Professor of History, Tulane University. His research interests include Catherine of Siena, medieval urban religious culture, and representations of sanctity and authorship in medieval manuscripts. (FTL)

Maria Lupescu Mako is in the Faculty of History and Philosophy, Babes-Bolyai University, and is a Fellow and Alumna of the Central European University, Budapest, and the Hungarian Academy of Sciences. She is co-editor of *Dicționarul mănăstirilor din Transilvania, Banat, Crișana și Maramureș* [The Dictionary of the Monasteries from Transylvania, Banat, Crișana, Maramureș]. (MLM)

David Luscombe Editorial Board. See above. (DLu)

† **Joseph H. Lynch** Editorial Board. See above. (JHLy)

Anne McClanan is Professor of Medieval Art at Portland State University. Her research concerns medieval Italy, Byzantium, and the depiction of the natural world in medieval art. (ALM)

Winder McConnell is Professor of German and Director of the Teaching Resources Center at the University of California, Davis. His research interests include medieval German heroic epic and courtly romance. (WM)

Leslie S. B. MacCoull is an Academic Associate at the Arizona Center for Medieval and Renaissance Studies, and is a papyrologist specializing in Coptic documents. She has served the Society for Coptic Archaeology for thirty-one years. (LSBM)

John M. McCulloh is Professor of History, Kansas State University, and specializes in ecclesiastical history and hagiography. He has published primarily on martyrologies, relics, and St William of Norwich. (JMM)

William C. McDonald is Professor of German at the University of Virginia, and has published widely on Arthurian literature (primarily Hartmann von Aue), Michel Beheim, and the Tristan legend. (WCM)

Christopher J. McDonough is Professor Emeritus, Classics, University of Toronto, and recently completed a bilingual edition of the poetry of Hugh Primas and Peter of Blois as part of the Dumbarton Oaks Medieval Library. (CJMc)

Timothy J. McGee is a music historian whose area of research is music performance practices before 1700. His latest book, *The Ceremonial Musicians of Late Medieval Florence*, was published in 2009. Currently he is Honorary Professor at Trent University in Peterborough, Ontario. (TM)

A. S. McGrade is Professor Emeritus of Philosophy, University of Connecticut, and is the author of *The Political Thought of William of Ockham* and editor of *The Cambridge Companion to Medieval Philosophy*. (ASMc)

Michael McGrade studies music of the European Middle Ages. He taught music history at Brandeis University and Williams College and is currently Director of Graduate Admissions at Worcester Polytechnic Institute. (MRM)

Brian Patrick McGuire is of Roskilde University, Denmark. His area of research is the western Church and society 1000–1500. He is the author of *The Cistercians in Denmark* (1982), *Friendship and Community* (1988), *The Difficult Saint* (1991), *Brother and Lover* (1994), *Jean Gerson and the Last Medieval Reformation* (2005), plus several books in Danish. (BPM)

Megan McLaughlin is Associate Professor of History at the University of Illinois. She is currently completing a book on the relationship of sex, gender, and authority during the Investiture Controversy. (MM)

Michael McVaugh is Wells Professor of History Emeritus, University of North Carolina. He has published *Medicine Before the Plague* (1993) and *The Rational Surgery of the Middle Ages* (2006). His current research centres on medieval Arabic-Latin translation. (MRMc)

Thomas F. Madden is Professor of Medieval History at Saint Louis University. His books include *The New Concise History of the Crusades* (2005) and *Enrico Dandolo and the Rise of Venice* (2003). (TFM)

Eliana Magnani is a Researcher at the Centre National de la Recherche Scientifique. Her research interests include the early and central Middle Ages and gift exchange and social bonds in medieval Latin society. (EMSC)

Ömer Mahir Alper is an associate professor at Istanbul University. His research interests include Islamic philosophy, Ottoman intellectual thought, and metaphilosophy. (ÖMA)

Demeter Malat'ák is a researcher and editor at the Masaryk University, Brno, Czech Republic. His research focus is mainly directed to royal representation in the medieval Czech lands. (DM)

Anu Mänd is a Senior Researcher at the Institute of History at Tallinn University. Research interests include social and cultural history of the Middle Ages. (AM)

C. Griffith Mann is Chief Curator at the Cleveland Museum of Art, and is a specialist in Italian medieval art, focusing on civic patronage, pictorial narrative, and relic cults. (CGM)

Jill Mann, FBA, is Emerita Notre Dame Professor at the University of Notre Dame and is a Life Fellow of Girton College, Cambridge. Her research interests include Middle English and medieval Latin. She is the author of *From Aesop to Reynard: Beast Literature in Medieval Britain* (2009). (JM)

Vivian B. Mann is the Director of the Master's Program in Jewish Art at the Graduate School of the Jewish Theological Seminary, and Curator Emerita of The Jewish Museum in New York. (VBM)

Christina Maranci is the Dadian Oztemel Chair of Armenian art at Tufts University. Her research focuses on the early medieval art of the Transcaucasus, the subject of her book, *Medieval Armenian Architecture: Constructions of Race and Nation* (2001). (CM)

John Marenbon, FBA, is a Senior Research Fellow at Trinity College, Cambridge. He works on medieval philosophy and has recently published *Medieval Philosophy: An Historical and Philosophical Introduction* (2007). (JMar)

Vasileios Marinis is Assistant Professor of Christian Art and Architecture at Yale University. His research focuses on the interaction of architecture and ritual in Byzantine Constantinople. (VM)

Robert Mark is Professor of Architecture and Civil Engineering, Emeritus, Princeton University, and pioneered application of modern engineering modelling to study historic buildings. Publications include *Experiments in Gothic Structure* (1982), *Light, Wind, and Structure* (1990), and *Architectural Technology up to the Scientific Revolution* (1993). (RM)

Sophie Marnette is Lecturer in Medieval French at the University of Oxford and Fellow of Balliol College. She studies the evolution of literary genres, narrator, and point of view. (SM)

Erno Marosi is Professor of Art History, Eötvös Loránd University, Budapest, and a Senior Fellow, Research Institute for Art History, Hungarian Academy of Sciences, Budapest. Among his numerous publications are *Steinskulpturen der Arpadenzeit* (1978), *König Ludwig I. von Anjou* (1982), and *König Sigismund von Luxemburg* (1987). (EM)

Steven P. Marrone Editorial Board. See above. (SPM)

Kimberly Marshall is the Goldman Professor of Organ and Director of the School of Music at Arizona State University. She is an authority on the late medieval organ and its music. (KAM)

Richard Marsina is Ordinary Professor at Trnava University, Faculty of Arts, Department of History, Slovak Republic, specializing in medieval diplomacy and Slovak historiography. He is the editor of *Codex diplomaticus et epistolaris Slovaciae (805–1260)*, 2 vols. (RMa)

Christopher J. Martin is Associate Professor of Philosophy at the University of Auckland. He works in the history of formal and philosophical logic. (CJMa)

Lister M. Matheson is Professor of English at Michigan State University and an International Fellow of Queen's University, Belfast. His research interests include medieval chronicles, codicology, and Middle English language and dialects. (LMM)

Thomas J. Mathiesen, FAAAS, is Distinguished Professor and David H. Jacobs Chair in Music at Indiana University. (TJM)

Mirjana Matijević-Sokol is Professor of History, University of Zagreb. She teaches auxiliary sciences of history and medieval Latin. She is the co-editor of *Historia Salonitana* (2006). (MMSo)

E. Ann Matter, FMAA, is William R. Kenan, Jr Professor of Religious Studies and Associate Dean for Arts and Letters at the University of Pennsylvania. Her forthcoming book, with Carla P. Weinberg, is an English translation of the *Ogdoas*, by Alberto Alfieri. (EAM)

Robert A. Maxwell of the University of Pennsylvania specializes in Romanesque art. He has published *The Art of Medieval Urbanism: Parthenay in Romanesque Aquitaine* (2007) and edited *Representing History, 1000–1300: Art, Music, History* (2010). (RAM)

Maureen Fennell Mazzaoui is Professor of History at the University of Wisconsin-Madison. Her research interests include the economic and social history of medieval Europe, textile history, and medieval and Renaissance Italy. (MFM)

Massimo Mazzotti teaches history of science at the University of California, Berkeley. His research explores the social dimension of early modern science, with a focus on the development of technology and mathematics in southern Europe. (MMa)

Rob Meens is a historian at the University of Utrecht. His research interests include the religious and cultural history of the early Middle Ages. (RMe)

John Megaard, a Slavicist, teaches in Oslo and has published articles on saga writing before Snorri Sturluson and on the extent of Snorri's authorship. (JMe)

Leidulf Melve is Professor of Medieval Studies, Centre for Medieval Studies, Bergen. He specializes in intellectual history, political history, historiography, theory/method. (LM)

David C. Mengel of Xavier University has published on medieval central Europe in *Speculum*, *Past & Present*, *Bohemian Reformation and Religious Practice*, and elsewhere. His current book project focuses on 14th-century Prague. (DCM)

Constant Mews is Director of the Centre for Studies in Religion and Theology, Monash University, and author of *The Lost Love Letters of Heloise and Abelard* (2008) and *Abelard and Heloise* (2005). (CJM)

Giedrė Mickūnaitė is Associate Professor at Vilnius Academy of Fine Arts in Lithuania. Research interests include medieval Lithuanian culture and reception of the Middle Ages in later epoques. (GM)

Pawel Migdalski is a doctoral candidate at the University of Szczecin. Research interests include central European historiography and medieval studies. (PM)

Nadejda Vladimirova Miladinova, MPhil, researches Byzantine philosophy, orthodoxy, and heresy in Byzantium, as well as Orthodox theology during the Ottoman period. (NVM)

Kathleen Miller is completing her PhD in English literature at Baylor University. (KMi)

Donka Minkova is Professor of English at the University of California, Los Angeles (since 1983), and author and editor of numerous books and articles, working mainly on the history of the English language, phonology, and metrics. (DMi)

Milena Minkova is Associate Professor of Classics at the University of Kentucky. Her recent work concerns the 12th-century Renaissance, Latin prose composition, and Latin pedagogy. (MYM)

Colin Paul Mitchell is Assistant Professor of History at Dalhousie University. He researches and teaches the medieval history of the eastern Islamic world, specializing on the Safavid dynasty of Iran. (CPM)

Piers D. Mitchell of the University of Cambridge is a paleopathologist, medical historian, and medical practitioner. His research interests focus on health and disease in the Crusades and the medieval world. (PDM)

Asa Simon Mittman of California State University, Chico, is the author of *Maps and Monsters in Medieval England* (2006), and *Inconceivable Beasts* (with Susan Kim, forthcoming), and is co-director of Digital Mappaemundi (with Martin Foys). (ASM)

Karol Modzelewski is Vice-President of the Polish Academy of Science, Warsaw, and Professor of Medieval History at Warsaw University. He is author of *Barbarzynska Europa* (2004). (KM)

Luca Mola is Associate Professor, Department of History, and Director of the Centre for the History of Innovation and Creativity, University of Warwick. Among his many publications is *The Silk Industry of Renaissance Venice* (2000). (LMo)

Ken Mondschein is currently a Visiting Fellow at Harvard University and expects to receive his PhD from Fordham University. His interests are in medieval intellectual history. He also teaches fencing at the Higgins Armory Museum. (KMo)

Catherine M. Mooney is Associate Professor at Boston College's School of Theology and Ministry, Chestnut Hill, Massachusetts. Her research focuses on Christian church history, spirituality, and saints. (CMM)

R. Scott Moore is Assistant Professor of History at Indiana University of Pennsylvania. His research interests include trade and exchange in the Mediterranean, late antiquity, and Cyprus. (RSM)

Alexander Medico More is a doctoral candidate in the department of History at Harvard University. His research and publications focus on the economic and legal history of government in the Middle Ages. (AMM)

Karl Morrison, FMAA, is Lessing Professor of History and Poetics at Rutgers University. His books include *Tradition and Authority in the Western Church: c.300–1140* (1969) and *'I am You': The Hermeneutics of Empathy in Western Literature, Theology, and Art* (1988). (KFM)

Robert G. Morrison is Associate Professor of Religion at Bowdoin College. He is interested in Islamic astronomy and is the author of *Islam and Science: The Intellectual Career of Nizam al-Din al-Nisaburi* (2007). (RGM)

Victoria M. Morse is Assistant Professor of History at Carleton College. Her research interests include Italian urban and religious history and the history of cartography. (VMM)

Richard E. Morton, a graduate of Oxford University, is Professor Emeritus in the Department of English, McMaster University, Canada. His most recent publications have examined Early Modern translations of Greek and Latin classics. (REM)

Thomas C. Moser, Jr is Associate Professor of English at the University of Maryland, College Park. His research interests include medieval Latin lyric, Neoplatonism, Chaucer, and Middle English literature. (TCM)

Joan L. Mueller teaches systematic theology and spirituality at Creighton University, Omaha, NE, and specializes in the early Franciscan movement. She has written extensively on Clare of Assisi, Agnes of Prague, and the early Franciscans. (JLM)

James Muldoon is Professor of History (Emeritus) at Rutgers University and currently an Invited Research Scholar at The John Carter Brown Library. He is a specialist in the history of medieval canon law and has written extensively on the role of canon law in the early development of international law. (JMu)

Heribert Müller is Chair in Medieval History, Goethe-Universität, Frankfurt am Main, and works on the history of Cologne and the Rhineland and of France and Burgundy, and on church history. (HM)

Bret Mulligan is Assistant Professor of Classics at Haverford College. His interests include Latin poetry (especially of late antiquity), epigrams, epistolary literature, and the classical tradition. (BEM)

Else Mundal is Professor of Old Norse Philology at the Centre for Medieval Studies, University of Bergen. She has published widely on Old Norse literature and culture. (EMu)

J. M. Murray is Professor of History and Medieval Studies, Medieval Institute, Western Michigan University. Trained at Northwestern and the University of Ghent, he studies the economic and urban history of late-medieval northern Europe. His latest book is *Bruges: Cradle of Capitalism, 1280–1390* (2005). (JMMu)

Sarah Jane Murray is Assistant Professor of Medieval Literature and French in the Honors College, Baylor University. (SJM)

Grzegorz Mysliwski is Assistant Professor of History, University of Warsaw. His areas of interest are economy and culture in the Middle Ages, and his publications include *Wrocław in the Economic Space of Europe* (2009) and 'Boundaries and Men in Poland' in *Medieval Frontiers: Concepts and Practices* (2002). (GMy)

Balázs Nagy is Associate Professor of Medieval European History at Eötvös Loránd University and at the Department of Medieval Studies, Central European University, Budapest. His main field of interest is medieval economic and social history. (BN)

Joseph Falaky Nagy is Professor of English at the University of California, Los Angeles. He teaches and writes on medieval Celtic literatures, especially Irish. (JFN)

Teodora P. Navid is an independent scholar and teaches art history classes at Diablo Valley College (Emeritus Center), Walnut Creek, CA. Current research interests include medieval Bulgarian architecture and pilgrimage. (TPN)

Leonard F. Nedashkovsky is Senior Assistant in the Department of Archaeology and Ethnography, Kazan State University. He has written on the Golden Horde in *Ukek: The Golden Horde City and its Periphery* (2004) and *The Golden Horde Cities of the Low Volga Region and their Periphery* (2009). (LFN)

Cary J. Nederman is Professor of Political Science at Texas A&M University. He is author, most recently, of *Lineages of European Political Thought* (2009) and *Machiavelli* (2009). (CN)

Carol Neel is Professor of History at Colorado College. Her research interests include medieval affinities, families of origin, and religious communities. She has written on the Carolingian noblewoman Dhuoda and the 12th-century Premonstratensians. (CLN)

William Nelles is Professor of English at the University of Massachusetts, Dartmouth, where he teaches courses in medieval literature and narrative theory. Publications include *Frameworks: Narrative Levels and Embedded Narrative* (1997). (WN)

Janet L. Nelson, DBE, FMAA, FBA, is Emeritus Professor of Medieval History, King's College, London. Her main areas of research include earlier medieval politics, culture, political ideas, and gender. (JLN)

Elod Nemerkenyi is a specialist in medieval Latin and the classical tradition in the Middle Ages. He currently teaches Classical and Medieval Latin at the University of Budapest. (EN)

Beverley S. Nenk is Curator of Medieval Collections, Department of Prehistory and Europe, the British Museum, and does research on medieval ceramics and the archaeology of medieval Jewry. (BSN)

Cynthia J. Neville is the George Munro Professor of History at Dalhousie University, Halifax, Canada. She has published extensively on the social and cultural encounter between Gaels and Europeans in Scotland in the period between 1100 and 1400. (CJN)

Richard Newhauser of Arizona State University has written works including *Sin: Essays on the Moral Tradition in the Western Middle Ages* (2007), *The Early History of Greed* (2000), and, as co-editor, *Pleasure and Danger in Perception* (2010). (RNe)

William R. Newman of Indiana University is a historian of alchemy, chemistry, and natural philosophy. His most recent book is *Atoms and Alchemy* (2006). (WRN)

David Nicholas Editorial Board. See above. (DN)

Bronagh Ní Chonaill is Lecturer in the Departments of Celtic and History, University of Glasgow. Her research interests include Irish and Welsh laws in the Middle Ages and childhood through the ages. (BNíC)

Alexandar N. Nikolov is Assistant Professor in Medieval History of Europe, at the University of Sofia, Bulgaria. His research interests include migrations, frontier societies, and 'proto-orientalism'. (ANN)

Bertil Nilsson is Professor of the History of Christianity at the University of Gothenburg, Sweden, and has done research in medieval canon law and the process of Christianization in the Nordic countries. (BNi)

Thomas F. X. Noble, FMAA, is Professor of History at the University of Notre Dame. His research interests are medieval Rome and the papacy, the Carolingians and controversial literature pertaining to sacred art. (TFXN)

Brian Noell is an instructor in the History Department at Yale University. His research focuses on Cistercian culture and the interactions between monks and scholars in the central Middle Ages. (BRN)

Sæbjørg Walaker Nordeide is Postdoctoral Research Fellow at the Centre for Medieval Studies at the University of Bergen, Norway. Research interests include medieval archaeology, Christianization, urbanism, and bishops' palaces. (SWN)

† **John D. North**, formerly at Oxford, was Emeritus Professor of the University of Groningen. He wrote on the history and philosophy of cosmology, from prehistory to the present day. (JDN)

Richard North read Old English at Oxford and teaches it in University College London. His publications include *Heathen Gods in Old English Literature* (1997) and *The Origins of* Beowulf (2006). (RN)

Robert Novotný, at the Centre for Medieval Studies, Prague, does research on the social history of the late Middle Ages, especially history of the nobility, and Hussitism. (RNo)

Vivian Nutton, FBA, is Emeritus Professor of the History of Medicine at University College London. His books include *Ancient Medicine* (2004) and *Pestilential Complexities: Understanding Medieval Plague* (2008). (VN)

Robin S. Oggins, PhD, FRHistS, is retired from Binghamton University. His recent publications include *The Kings and Their Hawks* (2004) and 'Game in the Medieval English Diet' (2008). His current research encompasses medieval English hunting. (RSO)

Katherine O'Brien O'Keeffe is Professor of English, University of California, Berkeley, and specializes in the literary culture of Anglo-Saxon England. Her research focuses on cultural transmission, manuscript culture, and early medieval subjectivity. (KOO)

Lea T. Olsan is Professor Emerita of English at the University of Louisiana at Monroe, and has written articles on incantations, amulets, charms, prayers, and magical experiments in late antique, Anglo-Saxon, and late medieval manuscripts. (LTO)

Bjørnar Olsen is Professor of Archaeology at the University of Tromsø, Norway, and works on material culture, theory, and northern and Sámi archaeology, on all of which he has published numerous works. (BO)

Vibeke Olson is an assistant professor at the University of North Carolina, Wilmington. Her research interests include 12th-century French architecture and sculpture and the economics of labour and production. (VCO)

Åslaug Ommundsen is Doctoral Fellow at the Centre for Medieval Studies at the University of Bergen, Norway. Her research centres on medieval manuscripts and book fragments, particularly liturgical. (ÅO)

Ynez Violé O'Neill received her PhD at the University of California, Los Angeles under Lynn White, Jr. She is interested in the development of pre-Vesalian anatomy and physiology, and is Professor Emerita of Medical History at UCLA. (YVO)

Nicholas Orme, FMAA, is Emeritus Professor of History at Exeter University and an honorary canon of Truro Cathedral. His books include *Medieval Children* (2001) and *Medieval Schools* (2006). (NO)

Jan K. Ostrowski is Professor of the History of Art, Jagiellonian University, Cracow, and Director of Cracow's Wawel Castle. He directs the programme to catalogue historical monuments in Poland's former eastern territory. (JKO)

John S. Ott is Associate Professor of History at Portland State University. He is co-editor of *The Bishop Reformed: Studies of Episcopal Power and Culture in the Central Middle Ages* (2007). (JSO)

Patrick Ottaway is Manager of Archaeological Consultancy, PJO Archaeology, and specializes in ironwork of the Anglo-Saxon and medieval periods. (PJO)

Päivi Pahta is Professor of English Philology at the University of Tampere. Her research interests include manuscript studies, corpus linguistics, the history of scientific and medical writing, and language contact. (PP)

Mária Pakucs is a Researcher at the Nicolae Iorga Institute of History. Her research interests include the history of trade in central and south-eastern Europe and the social history of Reformation in Transylvania. (MP)

Josie Panzuto is a doctoral candidate in the English Department at the University of Montreal, and is currently writing her dissertation, a critical edition and study of Robert Copland's *History of Helyas, Knight of the Swan*. (JP)

Stratis Papaioannou is Dumbarton Oaks Assistant Professor of Byzantine Studies at Brown University. His research interests include late antique and medieval Greek literature and culture. (SP)

Michael Papio is Associate Professor of Medieval Italian at the University of Massachusetts, Amherst. He specializes in Dante, Boccaccio, Masuccio Salernitano, Pico della Mirandola, and the novella tradition. (EMP)

Georgi R. Parpulov is temporary Departmental Lecturer in Byzantine Art and Archaeology at the University of Oxford. (GRP)

Joseph F. Patrouch is Associate Professor of History at Florida International University. His research and teaching interests include late medieval and early modern central Europe, with an emphasis on the Habsburg Dynasty. (JFP)

James R. Payton, Jr is Professor of History at Redeemer University College. His main areas of teaching and research are eastern European history, church history, and eastern Orthodoxy. (JRP)

Kathy L. Pearson is University Professor of History at Old Dominion University. She teaches ancient and medieval history, and her current research examines medieval environmental history and foodways. (KLP)

Frederik Pedersen, Senior Lecturer in History, is Lecturer in Scandinavian Studies, University of Aberdeen, and has published *Marriage Disputes in Medieval England* (2000) and is co-author, with A. Forte and R. Oram, of *Viking Empires* (2005). (FGP)

David A. E. Pelteret's publications include *Slavery in Early Mediaeval England* (1995). He was a major contributor to the Prosopography of Anglo-Saxon England database (www.pase.ac.uk). He is currently writing a book on Anglo-Saxon travellers in England and abroad. (DAEP)

Stephen Penn is Lecturer in Medieval Literature at the University of Stirling. He has published articles on scholastic literary theory, John Wyclif, and medieval European Latin literature. His translations of selected Latin texts by Wyclif will be published in 2010. (SWP)

Kenneth Pennington, FMAA, is Kelly-Quinn Professor of Ecclesiastical and Legal History at the Catholic University of America. His publications include *The Prince and the Law* (1993) and *The History of Medieval Canon Law in the Classical Period* (2008). (KP)

Ralph Penny is Emeritus Professor of Romance Philology and Research Professor at Queen Mary, University of London. His main research interests are the history of Spanish, variation in Spanish, and historical sociolinguistics. (RJP)

Patrick Périn is Director of the National Archaeological Museum at St-Germain-en-Laye and Associate Professor at Université Paris 1, Panthéon-Sorbonne, and works on medieval art and archaeology (ethnicity, population, habitats, funerary practices, artefacts, trade, and beliefs). (PPé)

Barbara Perlich is an architectural historian in Berlin and was Visiting Professor at the Bauhaus-University, Weimar. She now works at the Berlin Institute of Technology, primarily on medieval architecture and conservation of existing structures. (BCP)

Alexandra Pesch is a medievalist and archaeologist. She specializes in the early Middle Ages including images and art (especially gold bracteates), central places, and communication structures in medieval times. (AP)

Greg Peters is Assistant Professor of Medieval and Spiritual Theology at Biola University. He specializes in the areas of 11th- and 12th-century monastic reform movements as well as Protestant theologies of monasticism. (GP)

Peter Petkoff is a Law Lecturer in the Brunel Law School of Brunel University, West London. He specializes in canon law. (PPet)

Kiril Petkov is Associate Professor of Mediterranean History at the University of Wisconsin-River Falls, and does research on cross-cultural and interfaith interaction and the role of religion in the premodern eastern Mediterranean. (KPe)

Richard W. Pfaff, FMAA, is Professor Emeritus of History, University of North Carolina, Chapel Hill. His research areas include the medieval church, especially liturgy, hagiography, and monasticism, as well as medieval English history, manuscripts, and history of scholarship. (RWP)

Carl Phelpstead is a Senior Lecturer in Old Norse-Icelandic and Medieval English Literature at Cardiff University. His research interests are in the Icelandic sagas, hagiography, medieval masculinities, and medievalism. (CLP)

William D. Phillips, Jr, is Professor of History at the University of Minnesota. He specializes in medieval and early modern Europe, the European expansion, and the history of Spain. (WDP)

Montserrat Piera is Associate Professor of Spanish at Temple University. Her field is medieval and early modern Spanish and Catalan literature, with emphasis on chivalric novels and women writers. She is author of *'Curial e Guelfa' y las novelas de caballerias espanolas* (1998). (MPi)

Marc Pierce is Assistant Professor in the Department of Germanic Studies at the University of Texas at Austin. He works on historical linguistics, especially Germanic linguistics, and medieval Germanic studies. (MPie)

Laura Marie Piotrowicz, a priest of the Anglican Church of Canada, is adjunct faculty in Religious Studies at Niagara University, while pursuing studies at University of St Michael's College, Toronto. (LMP)

Jan M. Piskorski is Professor of Comparative European History at the University of Szczecin, specializing in the history of colonization and migration, historiography, and east-central Europe. (JMP)

Miloslav Polivka is a Researcher in the Institute of History, Academy of Sciences of the Czech Republic. He specializes in the history of the Czech lands and central Europe in the late Middle Ages, with particular focus on the Hussites and Czech-German relations in their political, economic, and military context. (MPo)

Sara M. Pons-Sanz is Lecturer in Medieval English at the University of Nottingham. Her research interests include the linguistic contact between speakers of Old English and Old Norse. (SMPS)

Kevin R. Poole is Assistant Professor of Spanish in the Department of Spanish and Portuguese at Yale University. He specializes in medieval literature and is particularly interested in apocalypse belief and its relation to Christian-Muslim relations in medieval Spain. (KRP)

Sara S. Poor is Associate Professor of German Literature at Princeton University. Her research interests include women mystics, women and medieval epic, manuscript studies, and gender studies. (SSP)

Cosmin Popa-Gorjanu is Lecturer in Medieval History in the Department of History at the 1 December 1918 University, Alba

Iulia, Romania. His areas of interest are medieval Romanian principalities, central Europe, and medieval nobility. (CPG)

James F. Powers is Professor Emeritus in History at Holy Cross College. He is the author of two books on medieval Spanish towns and has interests in military, urban, and art history. (JFPo)

Walter Prevenier, FMAA, is Professor Emeritus, University of Ghent, and works on late medieval social history, including marriage and the family, crime, and social and political networks, as well as palaeography and textual editing. (WP)

Frances Pritchard is the Curator (Textiles) at the Whitworth Art Gallery, University of Manchester, and has worked in museums since 1977. She has written extensively on medieval textiles, particularly from urban excavations. (FAP)

Huw Pryce Editorial Board. See above. (HP)

F. Regina Psaki is the Giustina Family Professor of Italian Language and Literature at the University of Oregon. Her research specialization is medieval Italian and French literature. (FRP)

Joseph Pucci is Associate Professor of Classics, of Medieval Studies, and of Comparative Literature, Brown University. He studies and teaches late and medieval Latin literary culture, focusing on poetry. (JPu)

Andrew Shepard Rabin is Assistant Professor of English at the University of Louisville. His research examines the relationship between law and literature in Anglo-Saxon England. (ASR)

Gianluca Raccagni is a British Academy Postdoctoral Fellow at Cambridge University. His research interests include Italian medieval history, specifically the Italian regional leagues (12th–15th centuries). (GR)

Pierre Racine, Professor Emeritus, Université Strasbourg, specializes in medieval Italy, and has published *Les villes italiennes du milieu du XIIe siècle au milieu du XIVe siècle* (2004) and *Frédéric Barberousse, 1152–1190* (2009). (PR)

Oliver Rackham, FBA, is a Fellow of Corpus Christi College, Cambridge, and Professor of Historical Ecology, Cambridge University. (OR)

Manu Radhakrishnan, a PhD candidate in Princeton's History Department, studies vernacular hagiography in late medieval and Renaissance Italy and the social history of the broader Byzantine and Islamic Mediterranean world. (MR)

Raluca L. Radulescu is Senior Lecturer in Medieval Literature at Bangor University, Wales. She has published articles and books on late medieval gentry culture, Arthurian literature, late medieval genealogy, and popular romance. (RLR)

Martyn Rady is Professor of Central European History at the School of Slavonic and East European Studies, University College London. He writes mainly on Hungarian medieval and legal history. (MRa)

Richard Raiswell is Assistant Professor of History at the University of Prince Edward Island. His research centres upon European knowledge of Asia before 1600, and premodern demonology. (RAR)

M. R. Rambaran-Olm is a PhD candidate at the University of Glasgow. Research interests include Old English prose and poetry, medieval military history, scriptural exegesis and the Pearl poet, and humanities computing. (MRRO)

Lynn Ransom is Project Manager of the Schoenberg Database of Manuscripts at the University of Pennsylvania. Her research interests include Gothic illumination, Franciscan devotional practices, and medieval book culture. (LRa)

Ann Marie Rasmussen is Associate Professor, Department of Germanic Languages and Literature, Duke University, and works on the intersections of gender, sexuality, and poetics in medieval German literature and culture. (AMR)

Irmengard Rauch is Professor of Germanic Linguistics at the University of California, Berkeley, and the author of *The Old Saxon Language* (1992), *Semiotic Insights* (1999), *The Gothic Language* (2003), and *The Phonology/Paraphonology Interface and the Sounds of German Across Time* (2008). (IR)

Jonathan S. Ray is Samuel Eig Assistant Professor of Jewish Studies at Georgetown University. His research focuses on medieval and early modern Jewish history. (JSR)

Marian Rębkowski is a Professor at the University of Szczecin. His research interests include medieval archaeology. (MRę)

A. Compton Reeves, FRHistS, is Professor Emeritus of History at Ohio University. His primary research interests are late medieval England and Wales. He is author of *Pleasures and Pastimes in Medieval England* (1995). (ACR)

Charles J. Reid, Jr is Professor of Law, University of St Thomas, Minnesota, and has published *Power Over the Body, Equality in the Family: Rights and Domestic Relations in Medieval Canon Law* (2004). (CJR)

Diane J. Reilly is Associate Professor of History of Art at Indiana University. Her research focuses on religious manuscripts and monastic reform, particularly in 11th- and 12th-century France. (DJR)

Irven M. Resnick is Professor of Philosophy and Religion at the University of Tennessee at Chattanooga. He writes on medieval philosophical theology, and has translated several works by Albertus Magnus. (IMR)

Orsolya Réthelyi is University Lecturer at the Department of Dutch Studies, Eötvös Loránd University, Budapest. She is author of various publications on Mary of Hungary, regent of the Low Countries, and her research interests include medieval and early modern Netherlandic literature. (ORé)

Andrew Reynolds is Reader in Medieval Archaeology at University College London. He specializes in early medieval archaeology in the British Isles and the study of buildings and landscapes using archaeological methods and techniques. (AJR)

Roger E. Reynolds is Senior Fellow and Professor of Liturgy and Law, Pontifical Institute of Medieval Studies and Centre for Medieval Studies, University of Toronto. His areas of research include medieval liturgy, canon law, and palaeography. (RER)

Gary Richardson is an associate professor at the University of California in Irvine and a Faculty Research Fellow at the National Bureau of Economic Research. He researches topics in economic history. (GRi)

Samantha Riches is Co-ordinator of the Centre for North-West Regional Studies at Lancaster University. Her research interests include pseudo-historical saints, monstrosity, gender, and the interplay between these areas. (SJER)

Michael Richter is Professor Emeritus of Medieval History at the Universität Konstanz, Germany. His research interests are Celtic countries and oral culture, and his publications include *Medieval Ireland: The Enduring Tradition* (2005) and *Bobbio in the Early Middle Ages* (2008). (MRi)

John M. Riddle is Alumni Distinguished Professor, North Carolina State University, Raleigh, and author of seven books including *The Middle Ages* (in press). (JMR)

Steve Rigby is Professor of Medieval Social and Economic History at the University of Manchester. His areas of interest and research are medieval social and economic history, medieval literature, and social theory and history. His publications include *Marxism and History* (1998) and *English Society in the Later Middle Ages* (1998). (SHR)

Thomas Riis is Professor of Regional History (Schleswig-Holstein) in the University of Kiel, and works on medieval social and economic history, especially the history of towns. (TR)

Magnus Rindal is Professor of Old Norse Philology at the University of Oslo, Norway. (MRin)

Katja Ritari is a Postdoctoral Researcher at the Department of World Cultures, Study of Religions, at the University of Helsinki, Finland. Research interests include early medieval Irish hagiography and theology. (KR)

Ágnes Ritoók is Curator of the Archaeological Department of the Hungarian National Museum. Her field of research is archaeology and history of the 11th–13th centuries (especially Zalavár). (ÁRi)

Hedwig Röckelein of the Seminar in Medieval and Modern History, University of Göttingen, works on medieval relic cults, pilgrimage, Mariology, hagiography, gender studies, biography, and Christian-Jewish relations. (HR)

Emily Rodgers is a Graduate Fellow at Baylor University. (EMR)

Else Roesdahl, FSA, FRHS, is Professor of Medieval Archaeology at the University of Aarhus, with research interests in the Viking Age, conversion archaeology, and medieval material culture. (ER)

Edward H. Roesner is Professor of Music at New York University. His research interests include the polyphonic music of the 12th, 13th, and early 14th centuries. (EHR)

Serena Romano is Professor of History of Art of the Middle Ages and Chair of the Department of History of Art at the University of Lausanne, Switzerland. Her research interests include painting, sculpture, and iconography in Rome, Tuscany, and central Italy from the 12th to 15th centuries, with a focus on Giotto. (SR)

Andrew Vincent Rosato is with the Medieval Institute, University of Notre Dame. His area of research is medieval theology and philosophy. (AVR)

Roy S. Rosenstein is Professor of Comparative Literature and English at the American University of Paris. He served as advisor to Kibler and Zinn, eds, *Medieval France: An Encyclopedia* (1995). (RSR)

Joel T. Rosenthal, FMAA, is Distinguished Professor Emeritus at the State University of New York at Stony Brook, and has published on medieval English social history: widows, old age, family structure, and lay religion. (JTR)

Barbara H. Rosenwein is Professor of History at Loyola University of Chicago. Her research interests include Cluny and medieval immunities and the history of emotions. (BHR)

Jay Rubenstein is an associate professor at the University of Tennessee. His research focuses on the intellectual history of the Middle Ages, the First Crusade, and medieval historiography. (JCR)

Adeline Rucquoi is Directeur de Recherches, Centre National de la Recherche Scientifique, and also works at the EHESS (École des Hautes Études en Sciences Sociales) on medieval Iberian history, especially political and cultural history. (AR)

Conrad Rudolph is Professor of Art History at the University of California, Riverside. He has interests in medieval social theories of art, monasticism and art, and art and social change. (CR)

Teofilo F. Ruiz teaches medieval and early modern history at the University of California, Los Angeles. His *Crisis and Continuity* (1994) received the American Historical Association's Premio del Rey prize. His most recent book is *Spain: Centuries of Crisis* (2007). (TFR)

Timothy Runyan is Manager of the Maritime Heritage Program, US National Oceanic and Atmospheric Administration, and Professor at East Carolina University. (TJR)

Marina Rustow is Associate Professor of History, Emory University, and author of *Heresy and the Politics of Community: The Jews of the Fatimid Caliphate* (2008). (MAAR)

Leah Rutchick, Visiting Scholar at the University of North Carolina, Chapel Hill, studies the ritual, liturgical, and cultural context of architecture and sculpture in southern Europe and northern Spain. (LR)

Angel Saenz-Badillos is Professor of Hebrew Language and Literature, Universidad Complutense, Madrid, Spain. His main teaching and research interests are in Sephardic culture, medieval Hebrew poetry and philology in Spain, and the history of the Hebrew language. (ASB)

Marianne Sághy is Associate Professor of Medieval Studies, Central European University, Budapest, working on the political, religious, and cultural history of late antiquity and the Middle Ages. (MSág)

György Ságvári is Senior Curator, head of the Department of Uniforms of Military History Museum, Budapest. His main field of research is the history of armies, particularly the history of hussars and Hungarian uniforms. His books are available in Hungarian, English, and German. (GyS)

Zahia Smail Salhi is head of the Department of Arabic and Middle Eastern Studies, University of Leeds, and the Executive Director of the British Society for Middle Eastern Studies (BRISMES). She works on Arabic and Francophone literature, gender, and the status of women in Islam. (ZSS)

Esa-Jussi Salminen is a Finno-Ugrist, and researches the Udmurt language and has lectured in Finnish language at the Mari State University (2003–5) and the Udmurt State University (2005–7). (EJS)

Fernando Salmón is Professor of the History of Medicine at the University of Cantabria (Santander, Spain). His main area of research is medicine and the medieval universities. (FS)

Henryk Samsonowicz is a professor in the Institute of History at Warsaw University. His publications include *The Long Tenth Century* (2008). (HS)

Norbert M. Samuelson is Grossman Chair of Jewish Studies, Department of Religious Studies, Arizona State University, and publishes in the fields of medieval and modern Jewish philosophy and science. (NMS)

Jonathan Sands Wise received his PhD in philosophy from Baylor University in 2009, specializing in ethics and ancient and medieval philosophy. (JDSW)

Marc Saperstein relocated to London in June 2006 to become Principal of the Leo Baeck College. He is widely recognized as a leading authority on the history of Jewish preaching. (MSa)

Michelle M. Sauer, PhD, is Associate Professor of English and Women Studies, University of North Dakota, and publishes on anchoritism, mysticism, hagiography, and queer theory. (MMS)

Birgit Sawyer is Professor of Medieval History at the University of Trondheim. Research interests include medieval Scandinavian historiography, and, previously, the Christianization of Scandinavia, runic inscriptions, and women's history. (BIS)

Peter Sawyer, FMAA, is Emeritus Professor of Medieval History at the University of Leeds. His current research interests include medieval Scandinavian history; previously, he focused on early English history, especially Anglo-Saxon charters and the Domesday Book. (PHS)

Larry Scanlon is Associate Professor of English and Director of Medieval Studies at Rutgers, the State University of New Jersey. He specializes in medieval literature, gender and sexuality, multiculturalism, cultural theory, and pedagogy and composition theory. (LFS)

Walt Schalick is a historian and practising physician at the University of Wisconsin working on medieval medical pharmacology and on disability history in both the medieval and modern periods. (WS)

Helene Scheck is Associate Professor of English at the State University of New York, Albany. Her current research interests centre on women's intellectual culture in early medieval Europe, from 750–1050. (HSc)

Raymond P. Scheindlin is Professor of Medieval Hebrew Literature at the Jewish Theological Seminary of America. His most recent book is *Song of a Distant Dove: Judah Halevi's Pilgrimage* (2007). (RPS)

Felicitas Schmieder is Professor of Medieval History at the Fernuniversität, Hagen, Germany. Her fields are German urban history, history of perception of foreigners, prophecy and politics, and cross-cultural exchanges. (FSchm)

Elizabeth Schoales is Adjunct Professor in Celtic Studies at St Francis Xavier University. Her research interests include Welsh prophetic poetry and the Anglo-Norman Arthurian chronicle tradition. (ELS)

Kerstin Schulmeyer teaches at the Johann Wolfgang Goethe-Universität in Frankfurt am Main. (KS)

James A. Schultz is Professor of German at the University of California, Los Angeles. He has written on narrative theory, the history of childhood, and, most recently, courtly love and the history of sexuality. (JAS)

Marc Carel Schurr is a professor at the University of Fribourg. His research interests include the history of art and architecture. (MCS)

Frederick Schwink is Associate Professor of Germanic Languages, Linguistics, Medieval Studies, and the Classics, University of Illinois at Urbana-Champaign. His areas of interest include Germanic and Indo-European historical linguistics, language typology, and history of linguistics. He is the author of *The Third Gender: Studies in the Origin and History of Germanic Grammatical Gender* (2004). (FSch)

Volker Scior is Assistant Professor for Medieval History at the University of Osnabrueck, Germany. His research and teaching is in medieval communication and mobility, perception of strangers in the Middle Ages, history of historiography, and modern views on the Middle Ages. (VS)

Anne Scott, Professor of English and Executive Secretary of the Western Regional Honors Council, has co-edited two interdisciplinary collections of essays on the topics of fear and water from late antiquity through the early modern period. (AMS)

Terence Scully is Professor Emeritus of French at Wilfrid Laurier University. He studies the theory and practice of cookery across Europe during the late Middle Ages. (TPS)

Neslihan Şenocak is Professor of European History at Eastern Mediterranean University in North Cyprus. She has published on the intellectual activities of the Franciscan order, and is currently working on crime in medieval Perugia. (NŞ)

Edwin Seroussi is the Emanuel Alexandre Professor of Musicology and Director of the Jewish Music Research Centre at the Hebrew University of Jerusalem. He has published on Sephardic music, Jewish liturgy, and Israeli popular music. (ES)

Michael H. Shank is Professor of the History of Science, University of Wisconsin-Madison. He studies the natural philosophy and astronomy of the 14th and 15th centuries, especially at the University of Vienna. (MHS)

Richard Sharpe, FBA, is Professor of Diplomatic in the University of Oxford and a Fellow of Wadham College. His publications include *English Benedictine Libraries* (1996) and *Titulus: Identifying Medieval Texts* (2003). (RS)

Joseph Shatzmiller is Smart Family Professor of Judaic Studies, Duke University, and is the author of *Shylock Reconsidered: Jews, Moneylending, and Medieval Society* (1990) and *Jews, Medicine, and Medieval Society* (1994). (JS)

Deborah J. Shepherd is a Postdoctoral Associate at the Center for Medieval Studies, University of Minnesota-Twin Cities. She is an archaeologist specializing in early medieval Britain and Scandinavia. (DJS)

Shmuel Shepkaru is Associate Professor of Jewish Studies and History at the University of Oklahoma. He is the author of *Jewish Martyrs in the Pagan and Christian Worlds* (2005). (SS)

Karl B. Shoemaker is Associate Professor of History and Law, University of Wisconsin-Madison. His research interests include medieval legal and social history, and medieval canon law. His recent publications include *Sanctuary and Crime in the Middle Ages* (2010). (KBS)

Paul Shore is Visiting Fellow at the Jesuit Institute at Boston College. His publications include *The Eagle and the Cross* (2002) and *Jesuits and the Politics of Religious Pluralism* (2007). (PJS)

Ian Short is Emeritus Professor of French at Birkbeck College, University of London. A specialist in Anglo-Norman, he has recently published an edition and translation of Gaimar's *Estoire des Engleis* (2009). (IS)

Claudius Sieber-Lehmann is Associate Professor at the Historisches Seminar der Universität Basel, Switzerland. His areas of research are the history of the Swiss Confederation, ecclesiastical history, cultural history, and medieval Latin. (CSL)

A. Edward Siecienski is Assistant Professor of Religion and Byzantine Studies at Richard Stockton College of New Jersey. His research interests include patristic and Byzantine studies with a particular emphasis on ecclesial relations between East and West. (AES)

Gabriela Signori is Professor of Medieval History and Chair, Department of History and Sociology, University of Konstanz, Germany. Her main area of research is the social history of late medieval towns: law, gender, culture, and religion. (GSi)

Gísli Sigurðsson is a Research Professor at Árnastofnun at the University of Iceland and Professor II at the University of Stavanger. His work focuses on oral tradition and medieval texts. (GS)

Jón Viðar Sigurðsson is Professor at the Department of Archaeology Conservation and History, University of Oslo. His research fields are Icelandic and Norwegian history *c.*900–1300. His main publications include *Chieftains and Power* (1999), *Frå høvdingmakt til konge- og kyrkjemakt* (1999), *Kristninga i Norden* (2003), and *Det norrøne samfunnet* (2008). (JVS)

Rudolf F. Simek is Professor of Medieval German and Scandinavian Literature at the University of Bonn. His research interests include Germanic mythology and religion, Viking Age culture, Old Norse literature, and medieval science. (RFS)

Katharine Simms lectures in medieval history at Trinity College Dublin, specializing in medieval Gaelic Ireland. Her publications include *From Kings to Warlords* (1987), and *Medieval Gaelic Sources* (2009). (MKS)

Robert Šimůnek of the Institute of History, Academy of Sciences of the Czech Republic, Prague, specializes in the medieval history of the Czech lands, especially the nobility and historical topography. (RŠi)

Zaza Skhirtladze is a professor at the Institute of Art History and Theory, Tbilisi State University. His current research interests are east Christian and Georgian art, and recent publications include *The Original Cladding of the Portaitissa Icon* (2005), *Tomb of St David Garejeli* (2006), and *Early Medieval Georgian Wall Painting* (2008). (ZSk)

Izabela Skierska is of the Polish Academy of Sciences, Poznan. Her areas of interest are ecclesiastical history of medieval Poland and medieval settlement. Her publications include *The Obligation to Attend Mass in Medieval Poland* (2003) and *Sabbatha Sanctifices: A Feast Day in Medieval Poland* (2008). (ISk)

Peter Slemon is Associate Director at the Center for the History of Music Theory and Literature at Indiana University. His research speciality is Renaissance music history. (PJSl)

František Šmahel, DSc, FBA, is a professor at the Centre for Medieval Studies in Prague. His research interests include the history of Charles University, Hussite Revolution, early humanism, and the Reformation. (FŠm)

A. Mark Smith is Curator's Professor of History at the University of Missouri, Columbia, and teaches both medieval history and history of science, his scholarly focus being on the latter. (AMSm)

Damian J. Smith is Associate Professor of History, Saint Louis University. He is the author of *The Book of Deeds of James I* (2003) co-translated with Helena Buffery, *Innocent III and the Crown of Aragon* (2004), *Pope Celestine III* (2008) co-edited with John Doran, and *Crusade, Heresy, and Inquisition in Aragon-Catalonia* (2009). (DJSm)

D. Vance Smith is Professor of English at Princeton University. His research interests include intellectual history, scholasticism (especially medieval physics and logic), continental philosophy, William Langland, and Chaucer. (DVS)

William H. Smith is an instructor in the Department of English at Weatherford College. His research focuses on Old English literature and medieval science. (WHS)

Clare Marie Snow is a doctoral candidate at the Centre for Medieval Studies, University of Toronto. Her dissertation examines Marian imagery and modes of mediation in late medieval England. (CMS)

Peter G. Sobol has taught history of science at Indiana University, Oklahoma University, and the University of Wisconsin, and is a frequent lecturer on topics in the history of astronomy. (PGSo)

Tim Soens is Lecturer in Medieval and Environmental History at the University of Antwerp, Belgium. He has published on the history of water management and local politics in medieval Flanders. (TSo)

Paolo Squatriti is Associate Professor of History and Romance Languages and Literatures at the University of Michigan, and works on various aspects of the natural environment in early medieval Europe. (PS)

Peter Stabel is Professor of Medieval History at the University of Antwerp. His current research interests are urban history and the social and economic history of the late medieval and early modern Low Countries. (PSt)

Robin Chapman Stacey is Professor of History at the University of Washington, Seattle. Her areas of interest are medieval history, Celtic studies, and legal history. Her publications include *Dark Speech: The Performance of Law in Early Ireland* (2007) and *Learning to Plead in Medieval Welsh Law*, Studia Celtica 38 (2004), 107–24. (RCS)

Alan M. Stahl is Curator of Numismatics at Princeton University. His areas of research include the Merovingian era and the late medieval Mediterranean and Venice. (AMSt)

Anne Stalsberg is Magister Artium, Associate Professor of Archaeology at the Norwegian University of Science and Technology, and Curator at the Museum of Natural History and Archaeology specializing in Scandinavian Viking Age finds in Old Rus'. (ASt)

Ralf M. W. Stammberger is an associated member of the Hugo von Sankt Viktor-Institut, Frankfurt am Main, Germany, and an assistant at the curia of the diocese of Limburg, Germany. (RMWS)

Kay Staniland was the Curator of Costume and Textiles, Museum of London, 1971–98. She is an independent researcher in prehistoric and medieval dress, and the clothing and textiles provided for the medieval English royal household. (KSt)

Anne Rudloff Stanton is Associate Professor of Art History and Archaeology at the University of Missouri, Columbia. Her research interests include English Gothic illuminated manuscripts and royal art patronage. (ARS)

D. N. Starostine is Assistant Professor at St Petersburg University, Russia, and has been a Mellon Fellow of the Pontifical Institute of Medieval Studies, Toronto. (DNS)

Adrian Stevens, Senior Research Fellow in German and Honorary Senior Lecturer in Comparative Literature, University College London, is author of numerous articles on Gottfried von Strassburg's 'Tristan' and on medieval German courtly literature generally. (AKS)

Devin J. Stewart is Associate Professor at Emory University, and is a specialist in Arabic and Islamic studies. His research focuses on Shiite Islam, Islamic law, the Qur'an, and Arabic dialects. (DJSt)

Marilyn Stokstad is Judith Harris Murphy Distinguished Professor, History of Art Emerita, University of Kansas. She is the author of *Art History* (2007), *Medieval Art* (2004), *Medieval Castles* (2005), and *Santiago de Compostela in the Age of Great Pilgrimages* (1979). (MStok)

Jacquelyn Tuerk Stonberg is Assistant Professor of Art History at Kean University in New Jersey. She focuses her research on Byzantine art and the history of magic. (JTS)

Marilyn Stone works in foreign languages, translation, and interpreting at New York University. (MSt)

M. W. F. Stone was formerly Professor of Renaissance and Early Modern Philosophy at the Katholieke Universiteit, Leuven, Belgium. He has published widely in the field of late medieval moral philosophy, and is the author of *Malum proprium mentientis: La theorie scolastique du Mensonge* (2009). (MWFS)

Jenna Louise Stook is a PhD candidate at the University of Calgary. Her dissertation research focuses on medieval Christian representations of Muslims in Middle English romances. (JLS)

Eleonora Stoppino is Assistant Professor of Italian Studies, University of Illinois at Urbana-Champaign. Her research and teaching interests include the epic and chivalric poem, popular cantari in 15th and 16th century Italy, conduct texts, historiography and genealogy, gender studies, and narratology. (ESt)

Mel Storm is Professor of English at Emporia State University, Emporia, Kansas. His research interests include Old and Middle English, and publications have appeared in *Chaucer Review*, *Studies in Philology*, *Philological Quarterly*, and *Publications of the Modern Language Association of America*. (MS)

Peter Stotz is Professor Emeritus, Medieval Latin Language and Literature, University of Zurich. He has published *Ardua spes mundi* (1972), *Sonderformen der sapphischen Dichtung* (1982), *Handbuch zur lateinischen Sprache des Mittelalters* (1996–2004), and *Lateinische Sprache und Literatur des Mittelalters*, for which he was series editor. (PSto)

J. A. Stover is a graduate student in medieval Latin at Harvard University, and Preceptor of Christian Latin at Harvard Divinity School. His interests are in 12th-century Latin commentaries. (JASt)

Jerzy Strzelczyk is a professor at the Institute of History, Adam-Mickiewicz University in Poznan, Poland. Special interests are medieval history of Europe, Slavic-German relations in the Middle Ages, women's history, and literature by women. (JStr)

Robert S. Sturges is Professor of English at Arizona State University. His books include *Medieval Interpretation* (1991) and *Chaucer's Pardoner and Gender Theory: Bodies of Discourse* (2000). His research interests include devotional literature and drama. (RSS)

Frederick C. Suppe is Associate Professor of History at Ball State University. His research focuses on the relationship between medieval England and Wales, including military institutions, cross-cultural marriages, and interpreters. (FCS)

Edith Sylla is Professor of History at North Carolina State University. She works on the application of mathematics within Aristotelian natural philosophy and the early history of mathematical probability. (EDS)

Vasileios Syros is a Junior Research Fellow of the Academy of Finland. His teaching and research interests cluster around the history of medieval and early modern political thought. (VSy)

Péter Szabó of the Institute of Botany, Academy of Sciences of the Czech Republic, specializes in central European woodland and landscape history. He has published *Woodland and Forests in Medieval Hungary* (2005). (PSz)

Béla Zsolt Szakács of Pázmány Péter Catholic University and Central European University is an art historian dealing with medieval architecture and Christian iconography. He is the author of a monograph on *Hungarian Angevin Legendary* (2006) and editor of the *Guide to Visual Resources of Medieval East-Central Europe* (2001). (BZS)

Paul E. Szarmach, FMAA, is Executive Director of The Medieval Academy of America and Editor of *Speculum* (from 2006). His scholarly interest is Old English prose with special reference to Latin backgrounds and the House of Wessex. (PES)

Blanka Szeghyová is a Junior Research Fellow at the Institute of History in Bratislava, Slovakia. Her research interests include crime and punishment, the history of mentalities, and early modern urban history. (BSz)

Katalin Szende is Associate Professor at the Department of Medieval Studies, Central European University, Budapest. Her main interest is the history of towns in the Carpathian Basin, especially their society, economy, topography, and literacy. (KSz)

László Szende is a historian, archaeologist, and archivist, and works as a department leader at the Hungarian National Museum. His area of research is Hungarian history in the Anjou era (13–14th centuries). (LSz)

Irma Taavitsainen is Professor of English Philology and Director of the Department of English at the University of Helsinki. Her research focuses on historical pragmatics and corpus linguistics. (IAJT)

Cheryl Tallan is an independent scholar, and is co-author of *The JPS Guide to Jewish Women, 600 BCE–1900 CE* (2003). Her bibliography on medieval Jewish women is on the Hadassah-Brandeis website. (CT)

Adena V. Tanenbaum, Associate Professor, Department of Near Eastern Languages and Cultures, Ohio State University, works on medieval Hebrew literature from Islamic lands. She is the author of *The Contemplative Soul* (2002). (AVT)

Paola Ymayo Tartakoff is a doctoral student at Columbia University. Her dissertation examines Jewish conversion to

Christianity and the Papal Inquisition in the 14th-century Crown of Aragon. (PYT)

M. Teresa Tavormina is Professor of English at Michigan State University. Her research interests include Middle English medical writing, Langland, Chaucer, and medieval devotional literature. (MTT)

Craig Taylor is Senior Lecturer in Medieval History at the University of York. His research interests focus on chivalric and political cultures in late medieval France and England. (CDT)

Elizabeth C. Teviotdale of Western Michigan University has written *The Stammheim Missal* (2001). Her research focuses on early medieval liturgical manuscripts and their illumination. (ECT)

Daniel E. Thiery is Assistant Professor of History at Iona College. His research interests include late medieval/ Reformation English history and the history of violence in western civilization. (DET)

Erik Thoen is Senior Full Professor (Gewoon Hoogleraar) at Ghent University, Belgium. He specializes in social, economic, and environmental history, as well as historical geography of the Middle Ages and the Old Regime. He is coordinator of the CORN project on comparative rural history. (ET)

Alfred Thomas is Professor of English, Germanic, and Slavic Studies, University of Illinois at Chicago. He is the author of *Anne's Bohemia* (1998), *A Blessed Shore* (2007), *The Bohemian Body* (2007), and *Prague Palimpsest* (2010). (AT)

Erik Thunø, of the Department of Art History at Rutgers University, specializes in early medieval art. His current research is on early medieval apse mosaics and the viewer. (ETh)

Hava Tirosh-Samuelson is Professor of History, Director of Jewish Studies, and Irving and Miriam Lowe Professor of Modern Judaism at Arizona State University, and studies Jewish intellectual history, emphasizing philosophy and mysticism. (HTS)

Lara Tohme is the Knafel Assistant Professor in the Humanities at Wellesley College. Her research focuses on medieval Mediterranean architecture in Syria, Southern Italy, Sicily, and North Africa. (LT)

Maria-Claudia Tomany, PhD, works as an Assistant Professor and Director of Scandinavian Studies at Minnesota State University, Mankato. Her research focuses on Old Norse literature. (MCT)

Shawkat M. Toorawa teaches Arabic literature and Islamic studies at Cornell University. His areas of research include the literary structure of the Qur'an, and the writerly culture of 9th-century Baghdad. (SMT)

Marco Toste is a PhD student in the University of Fribourg, Switzerland. He studies the medieval reception of Aristotle's *Politics*. (MTo)

Szilard Toth is a Finno-Ugrist and researcher of the Old Estonian literary language, and has lectured on different Finno-Ugric languages at the Universities of Szeged and Tartu, the Udmurt State University, and the University of Latvia. (ST)

Diane Touliatos-Miles is Distinguished Professor of Musicology at the University of Missouri-St Louis, and has an international reputation for her research in ancient Greek music, eastern medieval music, and the earliest women composers. (DTM)

Alain Touwaide is a Historian of Sciences at the Smithsonian Institution, specializing in medicine of Byzantium and the eastern Mediterranean, particularly Greek medical manuscripts and texts, and medicinal plants. (ATo)

David Townsend is Professor of Medieval Studies and English in the Centre for Medieval Studies, University of Toronto. His research focuses on the editing, interpretation, and translation of medieval Latin texts. (DT)

William Tronzo of the Department of Visual Arts, University of California, San Diego, has published on medieval and early modern art and is preparing a study of the medieval-early Renaissance designed landscape. (WT)

Torfi H. Tulinius is Professor of Medieval Icelandic Studies at the University of Iceland. He has written *The Matter of the North* (2002) and *Skáldið í skriftinni* (2004). (THT)

Terence Tunberg is Professor of Classics at the University of Kentucky, and is a specialist in the history of Latin prose style. (TT)

Jo Rune Ugulen, PhD, is Senior Archivist at the National Archives of Norway, Oslo. His areas of interest include medieval social and political history, and nobility. (JRU)

Richard W. Unger, FMAA, is a member of the Department of History at the University of British Columbia. He has written on shipbuilding and brewing in the Middle Ages and the Renaissance. (RWU)

Sabetai Unguru is Professor Emeritus in The Cohn Institute for History and Philosophy of Science and Ideas of Tel-Aviv University. His research interests are the history of ancient mathematics and medieval optics. (SU)

William Urban is the Lee L. Morgan Professor of History and International Studies at Monmouth College in Monmouth, Illinois. He is the author of several books on the Baltic crusades. (WU)

Daniel Ursprung is an assistant at the Department of Eastern European History, University of Zurich. His research is on south-east European and Romanian history, and he has published *Herrschaftslegitimation zwischen Tradition und Innovation* (2007). (DU)

Richard Utz is Professor and Chair in the English Department at Western Michigan University. His scholarship focuses on late medieval English culture, the postmedieval reception of medieval culture, and the history of English studies. (RJU)

Anne Van Arsdall is affiliated with the Institute for Medieval Studies, University of New Mexico, and her main research interests are early medieval Western medicine, herbals, transmission of knowledge outside texts, and the 14th-century Old French *Chronicle of the Morea*. (AVA)

Glen Van Brummelen is Professor of Mathematics at Quest University, Squamish, Canada, and specializes in the mathematics and astronomy of ancient Greece and medieval Islam. He recently published *The Mathematics of the Heavens and the Earth: The Early History of Trigonometry* (2009). (GVB)

Theresa M. Vann is the Josef S. Micallef Curator of the Malta Study Center, Hill Museum and Manuscript Library, St John's University, Collegeville, MN. She has researched and published extensively on the Crusades and the military religious orders. (TMV)

Trpimir Vedriš is an assistant at the university of Zagreb, Croatia, where he teaches early medieval Croatian history and the history of Christianity. His main research interests are in hagiography and the early medieval history of central and southern Europe. (TV)

Katja Vehlow is an assistant professor at the University of South Carolina, Columbia. Research interests include medieval history, historiography, and inter-religious polemics. (KV)

László Veszprémy is Head of the Institute of Military History at the Institute and Museum of Military History, Budapest. His main fields of interest include Latin historiography and military history. (LV)

Gabor Viragos is Director General at the Field Service for Cultural Heritage. His areas of interest are the Roman Age and medieval archaeology and history. His publications include *The Social Archaeology of Residential Sites* (2006). (GV)

András Vizkelety is an Ordinary Member of the Hungarian Academy of Sciences. His main research interests include medieval manuscripts, and multilingual literacy in the Middle Ages. At present he is editing a 15th-century Latin translation of a Middle High German chronicle. (AV)

Linda Ehrsam Voigts Editorial Board. See above. (LEV)

Annette Volfing is Reader in Medieval German Studies, Oriel College, Oxford, and has written on Heinrich von Mügeln, on John the Evangelist in Middle High German literature, and on Albrecht's 'Jüngerer Titurel'. (AMV)

Kathryn R. Vulic is Associate Professor of Medieval Literatures at Western Washington University, specializing in Middle English devotional literature. (KRV)

Mary F. Wack is Vice Provost for Undergraduate Education and Professor of English, Washington State University, and the author of *Lovesickness in the Middle Ages: The Viaticum and its Commentaries* (1990). (MFW)

Stephen Wagner holds a PhD in Art History from the University of Delaware. He has been teaching at the Savannah College of Art and Design since 2004. He recently published an article on manuscripts from Echternach in the online journal *Peregrinations*. (SMW)

Faith Wallis, of the Department of History and Department of Social Studies of Medicine, McGill University, specializes in medieval science, particularly the works of Bede, and in textual traditions of medical learning. (FW)

Steven A. Walton is Assistant Professor in the Science, Technology, and Society Program at Penn State University. He works on premodern technologies and their users, especially military technologies. (SAW)

Fiona Watson is a writer and broadcaster. She is the author of *Under the Hammer: Edward I and Scotland* (2006) and *Scotland: A History* (2002). She is currently working on a book on the historical Macbeth. (FJW)

Laura Weber is a PhD candidate in musicology at Yale University. She specializes in the music of the Middle Ages, with a particular interest in theory and notational practices. (LW)

Laura Weigert is Associate Professor of Art History at Rutgers University. Her research and publications focus on late medieval and early modern northern European art, architecture, and visual culture. (LJW)

Olga Weijers is of the Huygens Instituut, Royal Academy of Arts and Sciences, the Hague, and IRHT (CNRS), Paris. Her last publication is *Queritur utrum: Recherches sur la 'disputatio' dans les universités médievales* (2009). (OW)

Julian Weiss is Professor of Medieval and Early Modern Spanish at King's College London. He has published widely on medieval and Renaissance poetics, courtly lyric, and clerical narrative verse. (JW)

Stig Welinder is Professor in Archaeology at Mid Sweden University, Hämösand. His research interests are archaeological theory and historical archaeology. His current book is an overview of the prehistory of Sweden: *Sveriges historia 1. 13 000 f.Kr.–600 e.Kr.* (2009). (SW)

Jonas Wellendorf is Postdoctoral Research Fellow at the Centre for Medieval Studies, University of Bergen, and works on Old Norse literature, mainly learned and religious, and on medieval translation practices. (JWe)

Amanda Weppler is a doctoral student at the University of Notre Dame. Her research interests include Dante, Italian, and philosophy and theology. (AMW)

Haijo Jan Westra is a professor in the Department of Greek and Roman Studies, University of Calgary, and has written on Latin literature in late antiquity and the Middle Ages and is now working on Neo-Latin descriptions of Canada and indigenous peoples from the 17th century. (HJW)

Diana Whaley is Professor of Early Medieval Studies, Newcastle University, and researches Old Icelandic literature and English place names. She is also an editor with the project Skaldic Poetry of the Scandinavian Middle Ages. (DCW)

Elspeth Whitney is an Associate Professor of History at the University of Nevada, Las Vegas. She has published in the fields of medieval technology and the European witch hunts. (EW)

Nancy L. Wicker is Professor of Art History at The University of Mississippi. Her research interests include Scandinavian Migration Period jewellery, animal-style art, gender archaeology, and Viking-Age female infanticide. (NLW)

Roger S. Wieck is Curator of Medieval and Renaissance Manuscripts at the Pierpont Morgan Library, New York. (RSW)

Annemarieke Willemsen is an archaeologist and art historian, and Curator of the Medieval Department of the National Museum of Antiquities at Leiden, and works mainly on children and toys of the past. (AW)

Laura L. Williams is a Latin palaeographer who earned her PhD in Medieval Studies from Yale University. She studies medieval literature and history and has taught English, history, and humanities. (LLWi)

Daniel Williman is Professor Emeritus of Latin and History, Binghamton University. His latest book is *Calendar of the Letter of Pierre de Cros, Chamberlain to Pope Gregory XI (1371–1378)* (2010). (DHW)

Elizabeth Moore Willingham is Associate Professor of Spanish at Baylor University. Her interests include Old French and Spanish language and literature, miracle narratives, text study, manuscript art, and religious history. (EMW)

Blake Wilson is Professor of Music and Director of the Dickinson Collegium at Dickinson College. He has published extensively on the musical culture of late medieval and Renaissance Italy. (BMW)

Hanneke Wilson is the author of *Wine and Words in Classical Antiquity and the Middle Ages* (2003) and trains the Oxford University wine-tasting team. (HMW)

Jean Wirth is Professeur Ordinaire of Medieval Art History at the University of Geneva. (JWi)

Benjamin C. Withers, who specializes in Anglo-Saxon manuscripts, is Professor of Art History at the University of Kentucky and chair of the Department of Art. (BCW)

Ronald Wixman is Professor Emeritus, Department of Geography, University of Oregon. His research focuses on geographies of ethnicity, culture and religion, particularly on eastern and central Europe, the former Soviet Union and its successor states, and the Middle East. (RW)

Kenneth Baxter Wolf is John Sutton Miner Professor of Medieval History at Pomona College, and has published broadly on Christian views of Islam and the idea of sanctity as it relates to poverty. (KBW)

Kirsten Wolf is the Torger Thompson Chair and Professor of Old Norse and Scandinavian Linguistics at the University of Wisconsin-Madison. Her primary areas of research are Old Norse-Icelandic philology and hagiography. (KW)

Ian Wood is Professor of Early Medieval History at the University of Leeds. His main areas of research are on the Burgundian and Merovingian kingdoms, Bede, and the history of mission. (IW)

Alex Woolf is Lecturer in the School of History at the University of St Andrews and has published on a range of topics in early Insular history. His publications include his monograph *From Pictland to Alba* (2007). (AWo)

John Wreglesworth is an independent scholar. He holds an honours History degree from Manchester University and a doctorate from Leeds University. Research interests are in early medieval Europe, especially Spain. (JWr)

Stephen Wright is Ordinary Professor of English at the Catholic University of America (Washington, DC). His research focuses on medieval English, German, Latin, French, Dutch, and Swedish drama, art, and music. (SKW)

Jonathan Yaeger is a PhD candidate in Musicology at Indiana University. His dissertation is on the experiences of Leipzig's Gewandhaus Orchestra in the GDR era. (JLY)

M. K. K. Yearl is an independent scholar who specializes in medieval religion and medicine. Her current research is on the use of medical theory in medieval pastoral care. (MKKY)

Grzegorz Zabinski is a medievalist from Upper Silesia in Poland, specializing in medieval and early Renaissance military history. He is the author of *Codex Wallerstein: A Medieval Fighting Book from the Fifteenth Century* (2002). (GZ)

Hannah Zdansky is a PhD student in the literature program at the University of Notre Dame, specializing in the intersection of Celtic and classical traditions in medieval texts. (HZ)

Nada Zecevic, PhD, graduated from Central European University, Budapest. She focuses on the medieval Balkans, families, and migrations. She is currently preparing her monograph on the Tocco family in Greece, and works with the Institute of International Education, Budapest. (NZ)

Julia Zernack is Professor of Old Norse and Scandinavian Studies, Goethe-Universität, Frankfurt-am-Main. She has authored publications on Old Norse literature in medieval and post-medieval times, and on the history of Scandinavian and German studies. (JZ)

Alfons Zettler is Professor of Medieval History, Technische Universität, Dortmund. His publications include *Die frühen Klosterbauten der Reichenau* (1988), *Offerenteninschriften auf den frühchristlichen Mosaikfußböden Venetiens* (2000), and *Geschichte des Herzogtums Schwaben* (2003). (AZ)

Victor Zhivov is a Professor in the Department of Slavic Languages and Literatures at the University of California, Berkeley, and he is Deputy Director for the Institute of Russian Language at the Russian Academy of Sciences. His research interests are in the history of Slavic cultures, orthodoxy, and philology. (VZ)

Harold C. Zimmerman teaches in the Honors College at East Tennessee State University. His primary areas of interest are Anglo-Saxon literature, history, and language. (HCZ)

Grover A. Zinn, FMAA, is the William H. Danforth Professor of Religion, Emeritus, Oberlin College. His research interests include Hugh and Richard of St-Victor, medieval mysticism, monasticism, religious thought, Biblical interpretation, iconography, and manuscript studies. (GAZ)

Lilian H. Zirpolo is co-editor/co-publisher of *Aurora, The Journal of the History of Art* and author of *Ave Papa/Ave Papabile* (2005) and the *Historical Dictionary of Renaissance Art* (2008). (LHZ)

Jack Zupko teaches in the Philosophy Department at Emory University. A specialist in later medieval philosophy, he has published numerous research articles and three books, including *John Buridan: Portrait of a Fourteenth-Century Arts Master* (2003). (JAZ)

Ronald Zupko is Professor of Medieval History Emeritus, Marquette University. He specializes in the science, technology, and economic history of the Middle Ages and is a broadly published authority on metrology, the study of weights and measures. (REZ)

KEY TO EDITORS AND CONTRIBUTORS

Key to Contributor Initials

AA	Adrian Armstrong
AB	Alan E. Bernstein
ABW	Anna Bitner-Wróblewska
AC	Albrecht Classen
ACR	A. Compton Reeves
AEF	Arnold E. Franklin
AES	A. Edward Siecienski
AF	Alison Finlay
AG	Alison Gulley
AGu	Aðalheiður Guðmundsdóttir
AH	Alfred Hiatt
AHo	Alizah Holstein
AHR	Ahmed H. al-Rahim
ÁJ	Ármann Jakobsson
AJB	Adrian J. Boas
AJD	Andrea Janelle Dickens
AJFL	Adam Joseph Franklin-Lyons
AJH	Antonina Harbus
AJHi	Amanda Jane Hingst
AJR	Andrew Reynolds
AK	Antonín Kalous
AKG	Andrew Gillett
AKi	Andrea Kiss
AKS	Adrian Stevens
ALH	Anthea Harris
ALM	Anne McClanan
AM	Anu Mänd
AMB	Anne-Marie Bouché
AMBr	Alexander M. Bruce
AMD	Anne M. Dropick
AMK	Anna Kovács
AMKu	Anna Kuznetsova
AMM	Alexander Medico More
AMR	Ann Marie Rasmussen
AMS	Anne Scott
AMSm	A. Mark Smith
AMSt	Alan M. Stahl
AMV	Annette Volfing
AMW	Amanda Weppler
ANK	Abdul Nasser Kaadan
ANN	Alexandar N. Nikolov
ÅO	Åslaug Ommundsen
AP	Alexandra Pesch
APB	Anthony Bale
APBá	Attila Pál Bárány
APH	Andrew Holt
APK	Andrew P. Kurt
AR	Adeline Rucquoi
ARD	Alan Deighton
ARF	Anthony Faulkes
ÁRi	Ágnes Ritoók
ARS	Anne Rudloff Stanton
ASB	Angel Saenz-Badillos
ASC	Adam S. Cohen
ASM	Asa Simon Mittman
ASMc	A. S. McGrade
ASR	Andrew Shepard Rabin
ASt	Anne Stalsberg
AT	Alfred Thomas
ATo	Alain Touwaide
AV	András Vizkelety
AVA	Anne Van Arsdall
AVR	Andrew Vincent Rosato
AVT	Adena V. Tanenbaum
AW	Annemarieke Willemsen
AWL	Andrew W. Lewis
AWo	Alex Woolf
AYH	Alexander Y. Hwang
AZ	Alfons Zettler
BA	Björn Ambrosiani
BAC	Brian A. Catlos
BB	Benjamin Brand
BBy	Börje Bydén
BCP	Barbara Perlich
BCW	Benjamin C. Withers
BD	Ben Dodds
BEM	Bret Mulligan
BFR	Beatrix Fülöpp-Romhányi
BG	Brenda Gardenour
BGr	Borislav Grgin
BH	Benjamin Hudson
BHR	Barbara H. Rosenwein
BIS	Birgit Sawyer
BK	Bianca Kühnel
BKB	Bridget Kennedy Balint
BMBR	Brigitte Miriam Bedos-Rezak
BMK	Bernice M. Kaczynski
BMKi	Beverly Mayne Kienzle
BMW	Blake Wilson
BN	Balázs Nagy
BNi	Bertil Nilsson
BNíC	Bronagh Ní Chonaill
BO	Bjørnar Olsen
BPM	Brian Patrick McGuire
BRG	Bernard R. Goldstein
BRN	Brian Noell
BSE	Bruce Stansfield Eastwood
BSN	Beverley S. Nenk
BSz	Blanka Szeghyová
BWA	Benjamin William Anderson
BZS	Béla Zsolt Szakács
CAB	Caroline Bruzelius
CAL	Carolyne Larrington
CB	Claudia Bornholdt
CBB	Constance B. Bouchard
CBe	Cordelia Beattie
CBu	Charles Burnett
CC	Claudia Chierichini
CCF	Carole Collier Frick
CDB	Colleen Dorelle Butler
CDT	Craig Taylor
CF	Christoph Flüeler
CG	Cristian Gaşpar
CGi	Cédric Giraud
CGM	C. Griffith Mann
CGR	Camilo Gómez-Rivas
CJD	Christopher J. Daniell
CJM	Constant Mews
CJMa	Christopher J. Martin
CJMc	Christopher J. McDonough
CJN	Cynthia J. Neville
CJR	Charles J. Reid, Jr
CK	Christian Kleinert
CKK	Cynthia K. Kosso
CKr	Claus Krag
CL	Christian Lübke
CLN	Carol Neel
CLP	Carl Phelpstead
CM	Christina Maranci
CMB	C. Matthew Balensuela
CMK	Catherine Keen
CMM	Catherine M. Mooney
CMS	Clare Marie Snow
CN	Cary J. Nederman
CPG	Cosmin Popa-Gorjanu
CPM	Colin Paul Mitchell
CR	Conrad Rudolph
CRB	Charles R. Bowlus
CRD	Craig R. Davis
CSJ	C. Stephen Jaeger
CSL	Claudius Sieber-Lehmann
CT	Cheryl Tallan
CWB	Caroline Walker Bynum
DAEP	David A. E. Pelteret
DB	David Berger
DCL	David C. Lindberg
DCM	David C. Mengel
DCW	Diana Whaley

DDH	David Hiley	EMW	Elizabeth Moore Willingham	GV	Gabor Viragos
DET	Daniel E. Thiery	EN	Elod Nemerkenyi	GVB	Glen Van Brummelen
DFD	Donald F. Duclow	ER	Else Roesdahl	GyS	György Ságvári
DG	Dimitri Gutas	ES	Edwin Seroussi	GZ	Grzegorz Zabinski
DHW	Daniel Williman	ESt	Eleonora Stoppino	HA	Haki Antonsson
DJH	David J. Hay	ET	Erik Thoen	HAK	Henry Ansgar Kelly
DJK	Donald Kagay	ETh	Erik Thunø	HAKl	Holger A. Klein
DJKe	David J. Kennedy	EW	Elspeth Whitney	HB	Henry Bayerle
DJR	Diane J. Reilly	FAD	Francis A. Dutra	HC	Helen Cooper
DJS	Deborah J. Shepherd	FAP	Frances Pritchard	HCOB	Helen Conrad-O'Briain
DJSm	Damian J. Smith	FB	Flavio Boggi	HCZ	Harold C. Zimmerman
DJSt	Devin J. Stewart	FC	Fergus Cannan	HG	Harvey Goldblatt
DK	David Kalhous	FCS	Frederick C. Suppe	HH	Hans Hummer
DKa	Damir Karbic	FCu	Florin Curta	HJ	Henrik Janson
DKe	Derek Keene	FDK	F. Douglas Kelly	HJH	Hana Jana Hlaváčková
DKel	Dorothy Kelly	FEG	Florence Eliza Glaze	HJW	Haijo Jan Westra
DL	Dorota Lesniewska	FG	Frank Griffel	HKK	H. K. Klemettilä
DLo	Dubravko Lovrenović	FGG	Francis G. Gentry	HL	Henrietta Leyser
DLu	David Luscombe	FGP	Frederik Pedersen	HLá	Hynek Látal
DM	Demeter Malat'ák	FJW	Fiona Watson	HM	Heribert Müller
DMG	David M. Goldfrank	FL	Felice Lifshitz	HMW	Hanneke Wilson
DMi	Donka Minkova	FLC	Fredric L. Cheyette	HP	Huw Pryce
DN	David Nicholas	FRP	F. Regina Psaki	HR	Hedwig Röckelein
DNS	D. N. Starostine	FRPA	F. R. P. Akehurst	HS	Henryk Samsonowicz
DSB	David Stewart Bachrach	FS	Fernando Salmón	HSc	Helene Scheck
DT	David Townsend	FSch	Frederick Schwink	HTS	Hava Tirosh-Samuelson
DTM	Diane Touliatos-Miles	FSchm	Felicitas Schmieder	HWG	Hans-Werner Goetz
DU	Daniel Ursprung	FŠm	František Šmahel	HZ	Hannah Zdansky
DvG	Darius von Güttner-Sporzyński	FTH	Franklin T. Harkins	IAJT	Irma Taavitsainen
DVS	D. Vance Smith	FTL	F. Thomas Luongo	IDK	Irina Dmitrievna Kolbutova
EA	Eyðun Andreassen	FW	Faith Wallis	IE	Ivana Elbl
EAM	E. Ann Matter	FWG	Frederick W. Gibbs	IG	Ioannis Georganas
EARB	Elizabeth A. R. Brown	FYA	Francesca Yardenit Albertini	IH	Ivan Hlavácek
EAu	Elizabeth Aubrey	GA	Gabriele Annas	IJK	Ian Kirby
EB	Elena Bellomo	GAB	Gene A. Brucker	IL	Ingunn Lunde
EBh	Edel Bhreathnach	GAK	Genevra Kornbluth	IMR	Irven M. Resnick
ECB	Emmanuel Constantine Bourbouhakis	GAZ	Grover A. Zinn	IR	Irmengard Rauch
		GB	Geraldine Barnes	IS	Ian Short
ECT	Elizabeth C. Teviotdale	GBa	Géza Balázs	ISk	Izabela Skierska
EDS	Edith Sylla	GBł	Grzegorz Błaszczyk	IW	Ian Wood
EdV	Eva de Visscher	GBu	Giulio Busi	JA	Jon Arrizabalaga
EFJ	Eric F. Johnson	GC	Georges Comet	JAA	Jan A. Aertsen
EG	Erika Gál	GED	George E. Demacopoulos	JAAi	Jane Andrews Aiken
EGr	Edward Grant	GF	Gad Freudenthal	JAB	Jeffrey A. Bowman
EHo	Elisabeth Hollender	GG	Gundula Grebner	JABr	James A. Brundage
EHor	Elliott Horowitz	GHB	George Hardin Brown	JAK	Jill Kraye
EHR	Edward H. Roesner	GIC	Gabriela Ilnitchi Currie	JAS	James A. Schultz
EHu	Erwin Huizenga	GJ	Gerhard Jaritz	JASt	J. A. Stover
EJG	Eric J. Goldberg	GK	Gábor Klaniczay	JAZ	Jack Zupko
EJS	Esa-Jussi Salminen	GKG	Gabriela Kompatscher Gufler	JB	Joyce Boro
EK	Ephraim Kanarfogel	GL	Gail Lenhoff	JBG	John B. Gillingham
EL	Evelyn Lincoln	GM	Giedrė Mickūnaitė	JBi	Joseph Biancalana
ELS	Elizabeth Schoales	GMC	Glen M. Cooper	JBo	Jelena Bogdanović
EM	Erno Marosi	GMy	Grzegorz Mysliwski	JBør	Jostein Børtnes
EMB	Elisheva Baumgarten	GP	Greg Peters	JBTE	James B. Tschen Emmons
EMC	Ellen Condict	GPF	George Ferzoco	JBu	Joëlle Burnouf
EMJ	Emilia Jamroziak	GR	Gianluca Raccagni	JC	Joseph Canning
EMP	Michael Papio	GRi	Gary Richardson	JCa	James Cain
EMR	Emily Rodgers	GRP	Georgi R. Parpulov	JCF	Joe Flatman
EMSC	Eliana Magnani	GS	Gísli Sigurðsson	JCFr	Jerold C. Frakes
EMu	Else Mundal	GSi	Gabriela Signori	JCH	John C. Hendrickson

JCha Jane Chance
JCHo Jean-Claude Hocquet
JCR Jay Rubenstein
JDG Jennifer D. Gilchrist
JDH John Haines
JDHo John D. Hosler
JDN John D. North
JDSW Jonathan Sands Wise
JDu Jan Dumolyn
JDus Joan Dusa
JDy Joseph Dyer
JE Jutta Eming
JEB Jill Elizabeth Blondin
JED John E. Dotson
JEK James E. Knirk
JFL James Francis LePree
JFN Joseph Falaky Nagy
JFP Joseph F. Patrouch
JFPo James F. Powers
JFr Jan Frolík
JG Jan Gilbert
JGi Jane Gilbert
JH Jan Herlinger
JHa Joseph Harris
JHay Jérôme Hayez
JHe Joseph Held
JHH Jonathan H. Hsy
JHi John Hines
JHL John Lowden
JHLy Joseph H. Lynch
JJ Judith Jesch
JJA Jonathan J. Arnold
JJC John J. Contreni
JJo Jenny Jochens
JK Jacek Kowzan
JKG Judith K. Golden
JKO Jan K. Ostrowski
JKr Juhan Kreem
JKro Jerome Kroll
JKu Janusz Kurtyka
JL John Langdon
JLB Jessalynn Lea Bird
JLi John Lindow
JLK Joel L. Kraemer
JLM Joan L. Mueller
JLN Janet L. Nelson
JLS Jenna Louise Stook
JLY Jonathan Yaeger
JM Jill Mann
JMA Justine M. Andrews
JMar John Marenbon
JMB János M. Bak
JMBo Jurjen M. Bos
JMD Joseph Maurice Davis
JMe John Megaard
JMH Jason M. Houston
JMHo John McDonald Howe
JMK John Klassen
JML James M. Lattis
JMM John M. McCulloh
JMMu J. M. Murray
JMP Jan M. Piskorski
JMR John M. Riddle
JMu James Muldoon
JP Josie Panzuto
JPu Joseph Pucci
JPD James D'Emilio
JPH John-Paul Himka
JPHu Joseph P. Huffman
JRB Judith R. Baskin
JRD John Reuben Davies
JRP James R. Payton, Jr
JRU Jo Rune Ugulen
JS Joseph Shatzmiller
JSL Janet Senderowitz Loengard
JSO John S. Ott
JSR Jonathan S. Ray
JStr Jerzy Strzelczyk
JTL Joyce Tally Lionarons
JTR Joel T. Rosenthal
JTS Jacquelyn Tuerk Stonberg
JVS Jón Viðar Sigurðsson
JW Julian Weiss
JWB John W. Barker
JWBe John W. Bernhardt
JWe Jonas Wellendorf
JWi Jean Wirth
JWr John Wreglesworth
JZ Julia Zernack
KAF Kirsten Anne Fenton
KAM Kimberly Marshall
KB Keith Busby
KBS Karl B. Shoemaker
KBW Kenneth Baxter Wolf
KC Katy Cubitt
KDF Klaus-Dietrich Fischer
KDV Kelly DeVries
KFJ Klaus-Frédéric Johannes
KFM Karl Morrison
KG Kaaren Grimstad
KH Knut Helle
KHL Kate Lang
KHo Kateřina Horníčková
KJA Kevin Alban
KLP Kathy L. Pearson
KM Karol Modzelewski
KMH Kelly M. Holbert
KMi Kathleen Miller
KMK Karen M. Kletter
KMo Ken Mondschein
KOO Katherine O'Brien O'Keeffe
KP Kenneth Pennington
KPe Kiril Petkov
KR Katja Ritari
KRP Kevin R. Poole
KRV Kathryn R. Vulic
KS Kerstin Schulmeyer
KSt Kay Staniland
KSz Katalin Szende
KV Katja Vehlow
KW Kirsten Wolf
LAB Luigi Andrea Berto
LAD Lesley-Anne Dyer
LB Lola Badia
LBa László Bartosiewicz
LCA Lorraine C. Attreed
LDA Lawrin Armstrong
LED Luke Demaitre
LEV Linda Ehrsam Voigts
LFN Leonard F. Nedashkovsky
LFS Larry Scanlon
LH Luba Hédlová
LHZ Lilian H. Zirpolo
LIH Lars Ivar Hansen
LJW Laura Weigert
LKE Libby Karlinger Escobedo
LL Lidia Lanza
LLW Lisa Lampert-Weissig
LLWi Laura L. Williams
LM Leidulf Melve
LMA Lourdes María Alvarez
LME L. M. Eldredge
LMM Lister M. Matheson
LMo Luca Mola
LMP Laura Marie Piotrowicz
LOH Lars Hermanson
LPC Linda Page Cummins
LR Leah Rutchick
LRa Lynn Ransom
LSBM Leslie S. B. MacCoull
LSD L. S. Domonkos
LSz László Szende
LT Lara Tohme
LTC Lynn T. Courtenay
LTO Lea T. Olsan
LV László Veszprémy
LW Laura Weber
MA Mark Amsler
MAAR Marina Rustow
MAC M. A. Claussen
MAD Maria Amalia D'Aronco
MAG Michael A. Grünbart
MAH Michael A. Hicks
MB Milena Bartlová
MBe Matthias Becher
MBG Marie Bouhaïk-Gironès
MBK Mikhail B. Kizilov
MBKo Mira B. Kofkin
MBKoz Matt Kozusko
MBo Matthieu Boyd
MBr Michael Brown
MC Miriam Cabré
MCa Martin Carver
MCab Montserrat Cabré
MCF Michael Frassetto
MCH Maryanne Cline Horowitz
MCS Marc Carel Schurr
MCT Maria-Claudia Tomany
MD Muhammad Ashraf Ebrahim Dockrat
MDB Michael D. Bailey
MDBi Marianna D. Birnbaum
ME Martin Elbel

MEF Margot E. Fassler
MEH Margaret E. Hadley
MEK Marianne Kalinke
MFB Mary Franklin-Brown
MFG Mark Gardiner
MFM Maureen Fennell Mazzaoui
MFW Mary F. Wack
MGC Mark Chinca
MGLB Michael G. L. Baillie
MGRB Marc Boone
MH Mark Hagger
MHG Monica H. Green
MHS Michael H. Shank
MI Moshe Idel
MJ Martin Jacobs
MJB Martha Bayless
MJC Martin Camargo
MJCL María José Carrillo-Linares
MJCo Margaret Cormack
MK Michel Kazanski
MKe Menachem Kellner
MKKY M. K. K. Yearl
MKS Katharine Simms
MKu Michael Kulikowski
ML Michael Lapidge
MLC Martin Chase
MLCr Mark Crane
MLK Margaret L. King
MLM Maria Lupescu Mako
MM Megan McLaughlin
MMa Massimo Mazzotti
MME Martin Malcolm Elbl
MMH Michelle M. Herder
MMS Michelle M. Sauer
MMSo Mirjana Matijević-Sokol
MP Mária Pakucs
MPB Michael P. Barnes
MPF Manuel Pedro Ferreira
MPi Montserrat Piera
MPie Marc Pierce
MPo Miloslav Polivka
MR Manu Radhakrishnan
MRa Martyn Rady
MRę Marian Rębkowski
MRi Michael Richter
MRin Magnus Rindal
MRM Michael McGrade
MRMc Michael McVaugh
MRRO M. R. Rambaran-Olm
MS Mel Storm
MSa Marc Saperstein
MSág Marianne Sághy
MSB Michael Shane Bjornlie
MSF Michael S. Flier
MSt Marilyn Stone
MStok Marilyn Stokstad
MTA Maria Teresa Agozzino
MTF Marie Therese Flanagan
MTo Marco Toste
MTT M. Teresa Tavormina
MWA Melitta Weiss Adamson
MWFS M. W. F. Stone
MWH Michael W. Herren
MWSK Michael Knapton
MYM Milena Minkova
NB Nora Berend
NBl Nils Blomkvist
NJE Nicholas John Evans
NL Niels Lund
NLW Nancy L. Wicker
NMS Norbert M. Samuelson
NO Nicholas Orme
NŞ Neslihan Şenocak
NvD Nancy van Deusen
NVM Nadejda Vladimirova Miladinova
NWA N. W. Alcock
NZ Nada Zecevic
OBE Oliver B. Ellsworth
OKA Olga Kozubska-Andrusiv
ÖMA Ömer Mahir Alper
OR Oliver Rackham
ORé Orsolya Réthelyi
OSG Ottó Sándor Gecser
OW Olga Weijers
PAB Paul Brand
PB Paul Bushkovitch
PBG Peter B. Golden
PCI Patricia Clare Ingham
PD Peter Dinzelbacher
PDM Piers D. Mitchell
PES Paul E. Szarmach
PGJ Phyllis G. Jestice
PGS Pedro Gil-Sotres
PGSo Peter G. Sobol
PH Peregrine Horden
PHF Paul H. Freedman
PHS Peter Sawyer
PIAL Phillip I. Ackerman-Lieberman
PJ Peter Jeffery
PJAC Peter Crooks
PJO Patrick Ottaway
PJS Paul Shore
PJSl Peter Slemon
PK Petr Kopal
PKu Péter Kulcsár
PL Philip Longworth
PM Pawel Migdalski
PMC Paul M. Cobb
PMJ Peter Murray Jones
PML Peter M. Lefferts
POL Pamela O. Long
PP Päivi Pahta
PPé Patrick Périn
PPet Peter Petkoff
PR Pierre Racine
PRA Paul Arthur
PS Paolo Squatriti
PSE P. S. Eardley
PSG Piotr Górecki
PSH Patrick Stephen Healy
PSt Peter Stabel
PSto Peter Stotz
PSz Péter Szabó
PVL Pavel Vladimirovich Lukin
PWK Paul W. Knoll
PYT Paola Ymayo Tartakoff
RAB Rebecca A. Baltzer
RAG Ralph A. Griffiths
RAH Richard Holt
RAM Robert A. Maxwell
RAR Richard Raiswell
RB Rozmeri Basic
RC Robert Chazan
RCD RáGena C. DeAragon
RCE Raeleen Chai-Elsholz
RCF Richard C. Famiglietti
RCFi R. C. Finucane
RCH Richard C. Hoffmann
RCl Robert L. A. Clark
RCo Rita Copeland
RCór Ricardo Córdoba de la Llave
RCr Richard Cross
RCS Robin Chapman Stacey
REB Robert E. Bjork
REG Randall Goldberg
REM Richard E. Morton
RER Roger E. Reynolds
REZ Ronald Zupko
RF Richard Freedman
RFr Roberta Frank
RFS Rudolf F. Simek
RG Ryszard Grzesik
RGC Robert Cook
RGM Robert G. Morrison
RH Richard Helmholz
RHB R. Howard Bloch
RJC Raymond J. Cormier
RJP Ralph Penny
RJU Richard Utz
RKE Richard K. Emmerson
RL Rainer Leng
RLR Raluca L. Radulescu
RM Robert Mark
RMa Richard Marsina
RMe Rob Meens
RMWS Ralf M. W. Stammberger
RN Richard North
RNe Richard Newhauser
RNo Robert Novotný
RPS Raymond P. Scheindlin
RRD R. R. Davies
RS Richard Sharpe
RSH R. Stephen Humphreys
RŠi Robert Šimůnek
RSM R. Scott Moore
RSO Robin S. Oggins
RSR Roy S. Rosenstein
RSS Robert S. Sturges
RSW Roger S. Wieck
RW Ronald Wixman
RWP Richard W. Pfaff

RWU Richard W. Unger
SA Stanko Andrić
SAH S. Adam Hindin
SAW Steven A. Walton
SB Susan Boynton
SBa Stanislaw Baranczak
SBJ Sven-Bertil Jansson
SBr Stefan Brink
SBy Stanisław Bylina
SD Seán Duffy
SdB Sible de Blaauw
SDD Scott DeGregorio
SEJG Sharon E. J. Gerstel
SFB Simon Barton
SG Simon Gaunt
SGo Sarah Gordon
SGr Stefanie Gropper
SGw Scott Gwara
SHB Sverre Bagge
SHF Signe Horn Fuglesang
SHR Steve Rigby
SJ Sverrir Jakobsson
SJa Sarah James
SJC Sally J. Cornelison
SJER Samantha Riches
SJM Sarah Jane Murray
SK Sarah Kay
SKB Susanne Kramarz-Bein
SKC Samuel Cohn
SKu Stanislava Kuzmová
SKW Stephen Wright
SM Sophie Marnette
SMB Sara M. Butler
SMĆ Sima M. Ćirković
SMPS Sara M. Pons-Sanz
SMT Shawkat M. Toorawa
SMW Stephen Wagner
SNH Syed Nomanul Haq
SP Stratis Papaioannou
SPC S. Peter Cowe
SPM Steven P. Marrone
SR Serena Romano
SRD Simon Doubleday
SRIF Sarah Foot
SRK Susan R. Kramer
SS Shmuel Shepkaru
SSP Sara S. Poor
ST Szilard Toth
SU Sabetai Unguru
SW Stig Welinder
SWB Spurgeon Baldwin
SWN Sæbjørg Walaker Nordeide
SWP Stephen Penn
TAD Thérèse-Anne Druart
TAF Thomas A. Fudge
TAG Terry Gunnell
TB Terry Barry
TC Tina Chronopoulos
TCH Tracy Chapman Hamilton
TChr Tom Christensen
TCM Thomas C. Moser, Jr
TE Thor Ewing
TFG Thomas F. Glick
TFH Thomas Head
TFM Thomas F. Madden
TFR Teofilo F. Ruiz
TFXN Thomas F. X. Noble
TG Timothy Graham
THT Torfi H. Tulinius
TJ Tomasz Jurek
TJH Thomas J. Heffernan
TJM Thomas J. Mathiesen
TJR Timothy Runyan
TL Thomas Lindkvist
TM Timothy J. McGee
TMA Theodore M. Andersson
TMCE T. M. Charles-Edwards
TME Theresa Earenfight
TMI Thomas M. Izbicki
TMV Theresa M. Vann
TNB Toby Burrows
TPN Teodora P. Navid
TPS Terence Scully
TR Thomas Riis
TSo Tim Soens
TT Terence Tunberg
TV Trpimir Vedriš
TWB Thomas W. Barton
UB Urszula Borkowska
ÚBr Úlfar Bragason
UD Ute Drews
UK Uta Kleine
URB Uta-Renate Blumenthal
VB Vera Bácskai
VBM Vivian B. Mann
VCO Vibeke Olson
VM Vasileios Marinis
VMM Victoria M. Morse
VN Vivian Nutton
VS Volker Scior
VSy Vasileios Syros
VVI Vyacheslav V. Ivanov
VZ Viktor Zhivov
WAML Whitney A. M. Leeson
WB Walter Berschin
WBA William B. Ashworth, Jr
WBD Walter B. Denny
WCB Warren C. Brown
WCC William C. Crossgrove
WCM William C. McDonald
WDP William D. Phillips, Jr
WFG William Gentrup
WH Wolfgang Haubrichs
WHS William H. Smith
WJC William J. Connell
WJCo William J. Courtenay
WJD William J. Dohar
WJDi William J. Diebold
WM Winder McConnell
WMH Wendy Marie Hoofnagle
WN William Nelles
WP Walter Prevenier
WRL W. R. Laird
WRN William R. Newman
WS Walt Schalick
WT William Tronzo
WU William Urban
YTA Yom Tov Assis
YVO Ynez Violé O'Neill
ZD Zbignew Dalewski
ZJK Zoltan J. Kosztolnyik
ZJR Zdenka Janeković-Römer
ZK Zbigniew Kobyliński
ZKo Zoltan Kordé
ZNJ Zrinka Nikolic Jakus
ZsH Zsolt Hunyadi
ZSk Zaza Skhirtladze
ZSS Zahia Smail Salhi

THEMATIC LISTING OF ENTRIES

Below is a listing of the entries in *ODMA* ordered by topic. To locate a subject which does not have its own entry, please consult the General Index (pp. 1791–841). The listing is outlined as follows; within each category it is also divided by geographical region, people group, or a 'generic' section.

1. COUNTRY AND PLACE NAMES

Central and eastern Europe

Albania
Balaton, Lake
Baltic Sea
banates
Banská Bystrica
Belgrade
Black Sea
Bohemia (Moravia)
Bosnia
Brașov
Bratislava
Brno
Buda
Bulgaria
Carpathian mountains
Cheb
Cherson
Cluj-Napoca
Cracow
Crimea
Croatia
Dalmatia
Esztergom
Finns, Estonians, and Livs
Galich
Gdańsk
Gniezno
Golden Horde
'Great Moravia'
Hradec Králové
Hungary-Croatia
Kassa
Kaunas
Kiev
Kołobrzeg
Krušné (Erz mountains)
Kutná Hora
Levoča (Leutschau, Lőcse)
Lithuania (pre-union)
Livonia
Lublin
Lviv
Mazovia
Moldavia
Mosapurg-Zalavár
Moscow
Nitra
Novgorod (republic of)
Old Balts (Baltic peoples)
Olomouc
Oradea
Pécs
Plzeň
Poland (and Lithuania after 1385)
Pomerania
Poznań
Prague
Pripet marshes
Pskov
Reval
Riga
river Danube
river Dnieper
river Dniester
river Don
river Elbe
river Oder
river Vistula
river Volga
Rostov Velikii
Rus' (Kievan, Lithuanian, Muscovite)
Sandomierz
Serbia
Silesia
Smolensk
Sopron
Split
Suzdalia
Szczecin
Székesfehérvár
Szepes Spiš
Tmutarakan'
Toruń
Trakai
Transylvania
Trogir
Tver'
Ural mountains
Velebit mountains
Vilnius
Vladimir (Volodymyr, Volyn')
Vladimir (Suzdalia)
Wallachia
Warsaw
Wrocław
Yaroslavl
Zadar
Zagreb

Crusader states

Acre
Antioch

Damietta
Edessa
Jaffa
Nicosia
Palestine
Ramallah (Ramlah, Ramleh)
Sidon
Tiberias
Tripoli

England
Bernicia
Channel Islands
Deira
Dumnonia
East Anglia (kingdom and earldom)
Elmet
England, Anglo-Saxon
England, post-Conquest
Essex (East Saxons)
Hwicce
Kent (kingdom)
Lindsey kingdom
London
Mercia (kingdom and earldom)
Northumbria (kingdom and earldom)
Salisbury
Sarum
Sussex (kingdom)
Tintagel
Wessex (kingdom and earldom)

France
Abbeville
Aigues-Mortes
Aix-en-Provence
Amboise
Amiens
Angers
Angoulême
Anjou
Aquitaine
Arles
Armorica
Arras
Artois
Autun
Auvergne
Auxerre
Avignon
Avranches
Bar, duchy of
Bayeux
Béarn
Beaucaire
Besançon
Béziers
Blois
Bordeaux
Bourbon, duchy of
Bourges
Brittany
Burgundy (county)
Burgundy (duchy)
Burgundy (kingdom)
Caen
Cahors
Calais
Cambrai
Carcassonne
Champagne
Chantilly
Charolais
Cherbourg
Chinon
Clairvaux
Clermont
Compiègne
Coucy
Dauphiné
Dijon
Dreux
Évreux
Foix (county)
Fontainebleau
France
Grenoble
Guienne
Île-de-France
Langres
Languedoc
Laon
Le Puy
Limoges
Lyons
Mâcon
Marseilles
Meaux
Moissac
Monaco
Mont Cenis Pass
Montpellier
Montségur
Nancy
Nantes
Narbonne
Nice
Orange
Orléans
Paris
Périgord
Perpignan
Picardy
Poissy
Poitiers and Poitou
provins
Quierzy (palace)
Rennes
Rethel
Rheims
Rouen
Roussillon
St-Germain-des-Prés
St-Malo
St-Quentin
Savoy
Senlis
Sens
Septimania
Soissons
Toulouse
Touraine
Tours
Troyes
Uzès
Val d'Aran
Valenciennes
Valois
Vannes
Vendôme
Vermandois
Vexin
Vienne
Villa Franca (Ville Franche)
Vincennes

Germany/Austria
Alsace
Anhalt
Augsburg
Austrasia
Baden
Bamberg
Basel
Bautzen
Bavaria
Berlin
Black Forest
Brandenburg (town, bishopric)
Brandenburg, margravate of
Brunswick
Burgundy (kingdom)
Chur
Cleves
Cologne
Constance
Dorestad
Dortmund
Dresden
Eichstätt
Erfurt
Forchheim (palace)
Franconia
Frankfurt
Freiberg
Freising
Fritzlar
Geneva
Germany (kingdom)
Goslar
Greifswald
Halberstadt
Halle

Anastasis
apse
arch
architects, architecture
Arma Christi
art
art, Dominican
art, Franciscan
art and architecture: Benedictine
art and architecture: Cistercian
art and architecture: Cluniac
art and architecture: early Christian
art and architecture: Gothic
art and architecture: Romanesque
artist
atelier
atrium
aureole
baldachin
baptistery
basilica
bay system
bell tower
bema
Bible, illustration of the
Biblia Pauperum
canon table
cathedral
ceramics
chancel
chancel screen
chapel
chapter house
chevet
church types
clipeus
cloister
colour
copies
corbel
crucifix
Deesis
devotional image
diaconicon
diptych
dome
dossal
drawings and model books
drollery
Ecce homo
ekphrasis
enamel
encaustic
Evangelist symbols
exonarthex
feast cycle in art
fibula
finial
flabellum
flèche
fleuron
flushwork
fresco
galilee
gallery
gargoyle
gems and jewellery
Gothic design and construction techniques
grisaille
grotesque
halo
hammer beam
holy water font
hours, books of
iconography: iconoclasm
iconography: iconostasis
iconography: icons and manufacture of
iconography: icons, types of Christ, Mary, others
initials, decorated
interlace
International Style 1400
lancet window
lierne
lustreware
Mandylion
manuals, artistic
manuscript illumination
Master of the St George Codex
metalwork
misericord
missorium
mosaics, techniques of
mullion
naos
narthex
nave
nymphaeum
opus mixtum
opus reticulatum
opus sectile
oratory
oriel
orphrey
painting
painting, techniques of
panel painting
parekklesion
pastophories
paten
patronage, art
pendentive
perspective, artist's
pietà
pilaster
pilaster strip
pluvial
polyptych
portrait
predella
prie-dieu
pulpit
pyx, pyxis
quatrefoil
refectory
reliquary
reredos
rib
rose window
sacristy
sculpture
sculpture, techniques of
solea
soufflet
spandrel
spolia
squinch
stained glass, techniques of making
stringcourse
Synthronon
tapestry
tempera painting
terra sigillata
tetraconch
tierceron
tracery
traditio legis
Transenna
transept
trefoil
tribune
triclinium
triforium
triptych
triumphal arch
Trumeau
tympanum
vault
voussoir
westwork
wheel window

Germany / Austria

art and architecture: Merovingian
art and architecture: Ottonian
Bernward of Hildesheim, St
Erwin of Steinbach
Konrad of Soest
Master of the *Registrum Gregorii*
Meister Bertram
Muldenfaltenstil
Odo of Metz
Parler family and their works

Islamic world

Alamut
alcázar
art, Mudéjar
art, Umayyad

art and architecture: Abbasid
art and architecture: Almoravid
art and architecture: Arabic
art and architecture: Ayyubid
art and architecture: Ghaznavid
art and architecture: Islamic
art and architecture: Mamluk
art and architecture: Sasanian
art and architecture: Seljuk
mihrab
minaret
minbar
mosque
muqarnas
naqsh
qubba
Umar, mosque of

Italy/Sicily
Altichiero da Zevio
Antelami, Benedetto
Arditi, Andrea
Arnolfo di Cambio
art and architecture: Angevin
Avanzo, Jacopo
Barna da Siena
Bartolo di Fredi
Bonanno Pisano
Cavallini, Pietro
Cimabue, Giovanni
Coppo da Marcovaldo
Cosmati and Cosmatesque work
Daddi, Bernardo
Duccio di Buoninsegna
Gaddi family
Giotto di Bondone
Giovanni da Milano
Giovanni di Bartolo
Giovannino de' Grassi
Giusto de' Menabuoi
Guido da Siena
Isaac Master
Jacopo di Cione
Lanfranc of Modena
Lorenzetti, Ambrogio and Pietro
Luca di Tommè
Maitani, Lorenzo
maniera greca
Martini, Simone
Maso di Banco
Nanni di Banco
Nardo di Cione
Orcagna (Andrea di Cione)
Paolo di Giovanni Fei
Pisano, Andrea
Pisano, Giunta
Pisano, Nicola and Giovanni
Rusuti, Filippo
Segna di Bonaventura
Spinello Aretino
Torriti, Jacopo
Traini, Francesco
Vanni, Andrea
Vanni, Lippo
Vassallettus
Wiligelmo da Modena
Wolvinus

Judaica
Ark of the Covenant
art and architecture: synagogue

Low Countries
art and architecture: Merovingian
art and architecture: Mosan
Boendale, Jan van
Bosch, Hieronymus
Campin, Robert (Master of Flémalle)
Geertgen van Haarlem
Godefroid de Huy
Goes, Hugo van der
Hocsem, Jan van
Justus of Ghent
Limbourg brothers
Marmion, Simon
Master of the St Lucy Legend
Master of the St Ursula Legend
Memling, Hans
Rainer of Huy
Sluter, Claus
Van Eyck, Hubert and Jan
Werve, Claus de
Weyden, Rogier van der

Scandinavia
art and architecture: Scandinavian
interlace
stavkirke

Scotland/Ireland/Wales
art, Celtic
art, Pictish
art and architecture: Insular
Cormac's chapel
high crosses, Irish
Insular script
Trim castle

Spain/Portugal
art and architecture: Mozarabic
Beatus manuscripts
Juan de Burgos
Plateresque style
Roberto d'Oderiso

2.2. Intellectual history

Byzantium
Apostolis, Michael
Argyros, Isaac
Bryennius, Nicephorus
Cedrenus, George
Chalcondyles, Demetrius
Chalcondyles, Laonicus
Constantine III Leichudes
Cosmas Indicopleustes
George of Trebizond
Gregoras Nicephorus
Gregory Palamas, St
Jacob of Edessa
Lascaris, Constantine
Origen
Zonaras, Johannes

Central and eastern Europe
Academia Istropolitana
Charles University
Jagiełłonian University

England
Cambridge, University of
John of Salisbury
Langton, Stephen
Oxford, University of
Renaissance, Northumbrian
William of Ockham

France
Abbo, St
Alan of Lille
Badius, Jodocus
Buridan, John
Chartres, school of
Eudes of Deuil
Gautier of St-Victor
Ivo, St
Jacques de Vitry
John of Jandun
Odo Rigaud
Olivi, Peter John
Peter Lombard
Peter the Chanter
Petit, Jean
Renaissance, Carolingian
Robert of Sorbonne

Generic
Arts, Faculty of the
baccalarius
education, schools of law
epigraphy
intellectual history
literary nominalism
literature of *Correctoria*
manuscript studies
Martianus Capella
Master of Arts
quodlibet
rector
schoolmen
studium generale
summa
universities

Germany/Austria
Anselm of Havelberg
Bernold of Constance
Dietrich of Niem
Ebstorf world map
Henry of Langenstein
Henry Suso
Ludolf of Saxony
Lupold von Bebenburg
Marsilius of Inghen
Otto of Freising
Reuchlin, Johannes
Wolfger of Prüfening

Islamic world
Azhar, al-
Hafiz
Ibn Battuta, Muhammad ibn Abdallah
Idrisi, Abu Abdallah Muhammad ibn Muhammad al-Sharif
Muslim ibn al-Hajjaj al-Qushayri al-Naysaburi

Italy/Sicily
Cyriacus of Ancona
Hostiensis

Judaica
Abravanel, Isaac
Asher ben Yehiel
Berakhia ben Natronai Ha-Naqdan
Duran, Simon ben Zemah
education, Jewish elementary schools
Eldad ha-Dani
Eviatar ben Elija ha-Kohen
Fasi, Isaac ben Jacob al-
Isaac ben Moses Levi
Jacob Anatoli
Jacob ben Asher
Kimhi, David
Kimhi, Joseph
Kimhi family
literacy, Jewish
Meir ben Barukh of Rothenburg
Menahem ben Suruk
Meshullam ben Qalonimos of Lucca
polemics, Jewish (with Christians)
polemics, Jewish (with Muslims)
Rashi
women, learned Jewish
Yehiel ben Joseph of Paris

Low Countries
Bate, Henry
Cantimpré, Thomas of
Hegius, Alexander
Odo of Tournai
Wazo of Liège

Scotland/Ireland/Wales
John Scottus Eriugena
Sedulius Scot(t)us

Spain/Portugal
Abulafia, Meir
Benjamin of Tudela
Ibn Ezra, Abraham ben Meir
Ibn Ezra, Moses ben Jacob
Isidore, St
Jimenez de Rada, Rodrigo
Judah Halevi
Julian of Toledo
Leander of Seville
Moses ben Nahman
Peñafort, Ramón de
Petrus Alfonsi

2.2.1. Bible and exegesis

Byzantium
Gennadius I
Origen
Theophylact of Ochrida

Christian, Latin
Ambrose, St
Andrew of St-Victor
Augustine, St
Bede, St
Bible, illustration of the
Bible, Latin
Bible, translations of the
bible epic
Bible moralisée
Biblia pauperum
Cassian, John
Easter
encyclopedias
etymology
exegesis
exegesis, Latin Christian biblical
gloss and commentary
Glossa ordinaria
Haimo of Auxerre
Honorius Augustodunensis
Hrabanus Maurus
Hugh of St-Victor
Jerome, St
literatures: allegorical
Nicholas of Lyre
Pope Gregory I
Rupert of Deutz
St-Victor (abbey) and Victorines
sermon
translations, Bible (Scandinavian)

Judaica
Ahimaaz, Scroll of
Eleazar ben Judah of Worms
Emanuel ben Solomon the Roman
exegesis, Jewish biblical
exegesis, Jewish liturgical
gematria
halakhah
Hasidei Ashkenaz
homiletics, Jewish
Ibn Ezra, Abraham ben Meir
Isaac ben Abraham
Isaac ben Samuel of Dampierre, Rabbi
Jacob ben Meir
Kabbalah
Karaites
Karo, Joseph
Kimhi, David
Masoretes
midrash, medieval
Mishnah
Moses ben Nahman (Nahmanides)
Rashi
Samuel ben Meir
Talmud
Tosafists

2.2.2. Philosophy and theology

Byzantium
Aeneas of Gaza
Anastasius
Arethas of Caesarea
Bessarion, Cardinal John
Cabasilas, Nicolas
Eustratios of Nicaea
Euthymius Zigabenus
Fulgentius of Ruspe
Gennadius II
Glycas, Michael
Iamblichus
John Italos
John of Damascus
John Philoponus
Leontius of Byzantium
Maximus the Confessor, St
Metochites, Theodore
Michael of Ephesus
Nemesius
Nicetas Stethatos
Nikephoros Blemmydes
Nikephoros Choumnos
philosophy, Byzantine
Photius
Pletho, Georgius Gemistus
Plotinus
Proclus
Prodromus, Theodore
Psellos, Michael
Pseudo-Dionysius the Areopagite
Severus of Antioch
Stephen of Alexandria
Theodore of Smyrna
theology, Byzantine
Three Chapters, The

Xiphilinos, John VIII
Zacharias Rhetor

England
Alexander of Hales
Anselm, St
Bradwardine, Thomas
Burley, Walter
Chobham, Thomas
Crispin, Gilbert
Daniel of Morley
Duns Scotus, John
Easton, Adam
FitzRalph, Richard
Gilbert of Hoyland
Grosseteste, Robert
Haymo of Faversham
John Dumbleton
John of Salisbury
Kenningham, John
Marsh, Adam
Netter of Walden, Thomas
William de la Mare
William of Ockham
Wyclif, John, and Wycliffites

France
Abelard, Peter
Alberic of Paris
Almain, Jacques
Amalric of Bène
Bernard of Auvergne
Capréolus, John
Claudianus Mamertus
David of Dinant
Eustace of Arras
Faustus of Riez
Fredegisus of Tours
Garland of Besançon
Garlandus Computista
Gerard of Abbeville
Gilbert de la Porrée
Godfrey of Fontaines
Guillaume of St-Thierry
Hadoard
Isaac of Stella
James of Douai
John of La Rochelle
John of Mirecourt
John of Paris
Lambert of Auxerre
Lanfranc
Lefèvre d'Étaples, Jacques
Lupus
Nicholas of Autrecourt
Odo of Ourscamp
Pecock, Reginald
Peter of Auvergne
Peter of la Palud
Philip the Chancellor
Radulphus Brito
Ratramnus of Corbie
Robert of Courçon
Siger of Brabant
Simon of Tournai
Thierry of Chartres
Vital du Four
William de Congenis

Generic
analogy
apocatastasis
Aristotelianism
Atomism
Augustinianism
beatific vision
Categories
City of God
Confessions of St Augustine
Defensor Pacis
demonology and demons
dialectic
Donatists
ethics
florilegia
free will
Hermetic writings
Hexameron
hylomorphism
logic
Mariology
metaphysics
miracles
mysticism, Christian
Neoplatonism
nominalism
ontological argument, the
Pelagianism
philosophy, western
predestination
Purgatory
realism
scholasticism
Scotism
Secretum secretorum
Sentences, Four Books of
Stoicism
theology, Western
Thomism
transcendentals
universals

Germany / Austria
Albertists
Albertus Magnus, St
Biel, Gabriel
Ebendorfer, Thomas
Eckhart, Meister
Elizabeth of Schönau, St
Hermann of Carinthia
Manegold of Lautenbach
Thomas à Kempis
Thomas of Erfurt
Versor, Johannes

Islamic world
Ahl al-Kitab
Ashari, Abu l-Hasan Ali ibn Ismail al-
Averroës
Avicenna
Ghazali, Abu Hamid Muhammad ibn Muhammad al-
Hunayn ibn Ishaq (Johannitius)
Ibn Tufail, Abu Bakr Muhammad ibn Abd al-Malik
Ibn Tumart, Muhammad ibn Abdallah
Isaac ben Abraham ibn Latif
Maimonides, Moses
Mutakallimun
philosophy in the Islamic world
theology, Islamic

Italy / Sicily
Acciaiuoli, Donato
Adelnulf of Anagni
Barbaro, Ermolao
Barlaam of Calabria (Seminara)
Bartholomew of Pisa
Bombolognus of Bologna
Bruno, Giordano
Cajetan, Thomas
Guido Terrena
Hannibaldus de Hannibaldis
James of Viterbo
John of Ripa
Matthew of Aquasparta
Nifo, Agostino
Paul of Venice
Peter of Trabes
Pomponazzi, Pietro
Prepositinus of Cremona
Ptolemy of Lucca
Remigio de' Girolami
Salutati, Coluccio
Thomas Aquinas, St

Judaica
Abraham ben David, Ibn Daud
Abraham ben David of Posquieres
Abraham ben Moses
Abraham ben Shmuel Abulafia (Saragossa)
Anan ben David
Ashkenaz
blood libel accusation
Eleazar ben Judah of Worms
Elijah ben Moses Abba Delmedigo
Falaquera, Shem Tov ben Joseph
Gershom ben Judah of Mainz
Gershom ben Solomon of Arles
Hasidei Ashkenaz
Isaac Albalag
Isaac ben Moses Levi

Isaac ben Moses of Vienna
Jews, medieval
Judah ben Samuel ('the Hasid')
Kaddish, mourners'
Kaspi, Joseph
Maimonides, Moses
messianism and apocalypticism, Jewish
Moses ben Joshua of Narbonne
mysticism, Jewish
philosophy, Jewish
ritual murder accusation
Saadia ben Joseph Gaon
Samuel Ibn Tibbon
Sefarad
Solomon ben Judah ibn Gabirol
Solomon ibn Adret (Rashba, Shelomo ben Abraham)
Sophonias
Talmud commentaries
theology, Jewish
Yetzirah, Book of

Low Countries
Dionysius the Carthusian
Everard of Ypres
Giles of Lessines
Henry of Ghent
Odo of Tournai
Sibert of Beka
Walter of Bruges

Scandinavia
Boethius of Dacia
Elucidarius
homily books (Scandinavian)
Martin of Dacia

Scotland/Ireland/Wales
Clement of Llanthony
John of Wales
Peter of Ireland

Spain/Portugal
Averroës
Braulio of Saragossa
Dominic Gundisalvi
John of Segovia
Martin of Bracara
Torquemada, Juan de

2.3. Languages and literatures

2.3.1. German languages and literatures

England
alliterative verse
Beowulf
Cædmon
Caxton, William
Chaucer, Geoffrey
Clanvowe, Sir John
Clanvowe, Sir Thomas
Cynewulf
Everyman
Gower, John
Hoccleve, Thomas
Langland, William
languages: Germanic—Old and Middle English
Lawman (Laȝamon, Layamon)
literatures: Arthurian legend
literatures: English—ME prose and poetry
literatures: English literature—OE prose and poetry
Lydgate, John
Malory, Sir Thomas
Mandeville's Travels
Metham, John
Morte Arthur
Scogan, Henry
Skelton, John
Trevisa, John
Usk, Thomas
Worcester, William

Germany/Austria
Alberic
Albrecht (von Scharfenberg)
Albrecht von Eyb
Albrecht von Halberstadt
Albrecht von Johannsdorf
Alexander legend
Alexanderlied
alliterative verse
Altswert, Master
Ambraser Heldenbuch
Anfortas
Apollonius von Tyrland
Arzneibücher
Ava, Frau
Balmung
Beheim, Michael
Berthold von Holle
Bligger von Steinach
Boner, Ulrich
Boppe
bridal quest epic
Bruder Wernher
Brunhild
Burggraf von Regensburg
Burkhart von Hohenfels
Dietmar von Aist
Dietrichepik
Dietrich von Bern
Dreikonigsspiele
Dukus Horant
Ebner, Christine
Ebner, Margaret
Eckenlied
Eckhart, Meister
Eilhart von Oberge
Elisabeth von Nassau-Saarbrücken
Eulenspiegel, Till
Ezzo
Ezzolied
Fleck, Konrad
folklore and mythology: Germanic
Folz, Hans
Frauendienst (Minnedienst)
Freidank
Friedrich von Hausen
Fuetrer, Ulrich
Georgslied
Gottfried von Neifen
Gottfried von Strassburg
Göttweiger Trojanerkerieg
Graf Rudolf
Hadamar von Laber
Hadlaub, Johannes
Hagen of Tronje
Hartlieb, Johannes
Hartmann von Aue
Heiligen Leben
Heinrich der Teichner
Heinrich von dem Türlin
Heinrich von Freiberg
Heinrich von Hesler
Heinrich von Meißen
Heinrich von Melk
Heinrich von Morungen
Heinrich von Mügeln
Heinrich von Neustadt
Heinrich von Veldeke
Heinrich von Wittenwiler
Heldenbuch
Heliand
Herbort von Fritzlar
Hermann von Sachsenheim
Herrand von Wildonie
Herzog Ernst
Hildebrandslied
Hiltbolt von Schwangau
Hrotsvitha of Gandersheim
Hugo von Langenstein
Hugo von Trimberg
Hürnen Seyfried, Das Lied vom
Jansen Enikel
Johann von Würzburg
Kaiser Heinrich VI
Karlmeinet
Klage, Diu
Klingsor (Clinschor)
König Rother
Konrad von Ammenhausen
Konrad von Fussesbrunnen
Konrad von Heimesfurt
Konrad von Megenberg
Konrad von Stoffeln
Konrad von Würzburg
Kriemhild
Kudrun
languages: Germanic

languages: Germanic—Old High German, Middle High German
Liederbuch der Clara Hätzlerin
literatures: Arthurian legend
literatures: Germanic
Lohengrin
Lucidarius
Ludwigslied
Lutwin
Malleus Maleficarum
Manesse, Manuscript of
Marienlyrik
Marner, Der
Mechthild von Magdeburg
Meinloh von Sevelingen
Meistergesang, Meistersinger
Merseburger Zaubersprüche
Minnesinger
Muspilli
Neithart von Reuental
Nibelungenlied
Notker Teutonicus
Orendel
Oswald von Wolkenstein
Otfrid von Weissenburg
Ottokar von Steiermark
Otto von Botenlouben
Passional
Petruslied
Pfaffe Lamprecht
Pleier, Der
Prose Lancelot
Rabenschlacht
Reinbot von Durne
Reinfried von Braunschweig
Reinmar 'the Elder'
Reinmar von Hagenau
Reinmar von Zweter
ritterliches Tugendsystem
Rolandslied
Rothe, Johannes
Rudolf von Ems
Rudolf von Fenis
Salman und Morolf
Seifried Helblinc
Siegfried
Spervogel and Herger
Spielmannsepik
Spruchdichtung
Steinmar
Stricker, Der
Suchenwirt, Peter
Süßkind von Trimberg
Tannhäuser
Tauler, Johannes
Thomasin von Zirclaria
Thüring von Ringoltingen
Ulrich von Etzenbach
Ulrich von Liechtenstein
Ulrich von Türheim
Ulrich von Winterstetten
Ulrich von Zatzikhoven
Väterbuch
Walther von der Vogelweide
Wartburgkrieg
Wernher der Gartenære
Wernher von Elmendorf
Wessobrunner Gebet
Wiener Genesis
Wigamur
wilde Alexander, Der
Winileod
Winsbecke, Der
Wirnt von Gravenberg
Wisse–Colin
Wolfdietrich
Wolfram von Eschenbach
Zaubersprüche

Low Countries
Hadewijch
Maerlant, Jacob van
Ysengrimus

Scandinavia
Ari Þorgilsson
Baldr
Barlaam and Josaphat's saga
bishops' sagas
blood brother
Breta sögur
bridal quest epic
Christian poetry in Iceland
eddic poetry
Eufemiavisorna
Færeyinga saga
Fáfnir
Fenrir
Flateyjarbók
folklore and mythology: Scandinavian
Fornsvenska legendariet
Freyja
fylgja
gnomic verse, Scandinavian
Gunnlaugr Leifsson
Hjaðningavíg
Icelandic sagas
Jómsvíkinga saga
Karlamagnús saga ok kappa hans
kings' sagas
Konungs skuggsjá
languages: Germanic—Scandinavian
legendary sagas
Loki
Maríu saga
Midgard serpent
Nordic ballads
Norse heroic legends
Oddr Snorrason
Odin
Orkneyinga saga
Postola sögur
Ragnarok
rímur
Rómverja saga
Scandinavian love poetry
Scandinavian paleography
Scandinavian romances
Sigurd
skaldic poetry
Skjöldunga saga
Snorra Edda
Snorri Sturluson
Strengleikar
Sturla Þórðarson (Thorardson)
Sturlunga saga
Þættir
Theodoricus monachus
Þiðreks saga af Bern
Thómas saga erkibyskups
Thor
Trójumanna saga
Valkyries
Völsunga saga
Yggdrasill
Ynglinga saga

2.3.2. Medieval Latin

Byzantium
Corippus, Flavius Cresconius
Pseudo-Methodius

Central and eastern Europe
Callimachus Experiens
Charles IV Autobiography (*Vita Caroli*)
Janus Pannonius
John Vitéz of Zredna
Pelbartus of Temesvár
Renaissance, Croatian-Dalmatian
Trojan origins

Crusader states
William of Tyre

England
Aelred, St
Aldhelm, St
Alexander Neckam
Alfred of Sareshel
Asser
Bartholomew the Englishman
Byrhtferth of Ramsey
Cambridge Songs
Eadmer of Canterbury
Ecloga Theodoli
Eddius (Aeddius Stephanus, Stephen of Ripon)
Florence of Worcester
Fridegodus
Geoffrey of Vinsauf
Gervase of Canterbury
Gervase of Tilbury

Herbert of Bosham
John of Garland
John of Howden
John Peckham
Joseph of Exeter
Lawrence of Durham
literatures: Anglo-Latin
Nicholas Trevet
Nigel Longchamp
(Nigel Wireker, Nigel of Canterbury)
Orderic Vitalis
Orm (Ormin, *The Ormulum*)
Osbern of Gloucester
Peter Helias
Reginald of Canterbury
Roger of Howden
Simeon of Durham
Wulfstan of Winchester

France

Abbo of St-Germain-des-Prés
Adalbero of Laon
Adam of Petit-Pont
Adam of St-Victor
Adhemar of Chabannes
Adso of Montier-en-Der
Agobard of Lyons
Aimoin of Fleury
Alberic of Aix-la-Chapelle
Alcuin
Alexander of Villa Dei
Andreas Capellanus
(André Le Chapelain)
Angilbert of St-Riquier
Anselm of Laon
Arnulf of Lisieux
Arnulf of Orléans
Baudri of Bourgeuil
Benedict of Aniane, St
Berengar of Tours
Bernard Gui
Bernard of Chartres
Bernard Silvestris
Charles IV
Clarembald of Arras
Dhuoda
Ermoldus Nigellus
Flodoard of Rheims
Fulbert of Chartres
Geoffrey of Auxerre
Gerson, John
Gervase of Melkley
Gilbert of Tournai
Godescalc (Gottschalk) of Orbais
Godfrey of St-Victor
Gregory of Tours
Guibert of Nogent
Gui of Amiens
Haimo of Auxerre
Heiric of Auxerre
Heloise
Hilary of Orléans
Hilary of Poitiers
Hildebert of Lavardin
Hrabanus Maurus
Hucbald of St-Amand
Hugeburc
Hugh of Fleury
Hugh of Fouilloy
Hugh of Orléans
Jacob of Voragine
John of Alta Silva (Haute Seille)
John of Hauville
Jonas of Orléans
Letald of Micy
Loire Valley poets
Marbod of Rennes
Matthew of Vendôme
Nithard
Odo, St
Odo of Meung
Paschasius Radbertus
Peter Comestor
Peter of Blois
Peter of Celle
Peter of Poitiers
Peter Riga
Pseudo-Turpin
Ralph of Torte
Remigius of Auxerre
Roscelin of Compiègne
Sidonius Apollinaris
Smaragdus
Stephen of Rouen
Suger
Theodulf of Orléans
Usuard
Vitalis of Blois
Walahfrid Strabo
Walter of Châtillon
Waltharius
Warner of Rouen
William of Auvergne
William of Auxerre
William of Blois
William of Champeaux
William of Jumièges

Generic

ancients and moderns
anonymity
anthology
Archpoet
ars dictaminis and ars dictandi
ars praedicandi
artes poeticae
beast fable and epic
Bible, Latin
Bible, translations of the
bible epic
bilingualism
biography, Latin
cento
codex aureus
colophon
comedy, Latin
commentary
commonplace
courtesy books
courtly love
court poetry
Dares Phrygius
debates
dialogue
dictionary
Dictys Cretensis
didactic poetry
drama
Ecbasis captivi
eclogue
epic, medieval Latin
epigram
epithalamium
etymology
exegesis, Latin Christian biblical
exemplum
forgeries, literary
genre
gloss and commentary
glossary
Goliards
Golias
grammar, Latin
hagiography
hermeneumata
hermeneutic Latin
Historia Apollonii
imitatio
Joca (Ioca) monachorum
Jordanes
lament
languages: Latin, medieval
Laudes urbium
letters
Liber de causis
Liber pontificalis
libraries, medieval
linguistics, medieval
literary criticism
literatures: allegorical
literatures: apocalyptic
locus amoenus
Ludus de Antichristo
lyric, medieval Latin
macaronic
Menippean satire
metaphor and simile
metre, Latin
Mirabilia urbis Romae
mythography
novel, Latin
opus geminum
orality

2.3.4. Romance languages and literatures

France

Adam de la Halle
Aimoin of St-Germain-des-Prés
alexandrine
Alexis, Vie de St
Amadis de Gaula
Amis et Amiles
Arnaut Daniel
Aucassin et Nicolette
ballade
Benoît de St-More
Bernart de Ventadorn
Bertran de Born
Blondel de Nesle
Bodel, Jean
Cent Nouvelles Nouvelles
Chanson de Roland
chansons de geste
Charles, duke of Orléans
Charny, Geoffroi de
Chartier, Alain
Châtelain de Coucy
Chrétien de Troyes
Christine de Pizan
Commynes, Philippe de
Conon de Béthune
Deschamps, Eustache
Dia, Comtessa de
Doon de Mayence
Eulalia, Séquence de Ste
Fierabras
fin'amor
Flamenca
Floire et Blancheflor
Folquet de Marselha
Froissart, Jehan
Gace Brulé
Gautier of Arras
Gerson, John
Girart de Roussillon
Girart de Vienne
Giraut de Borneil
Graal, La Queste del Saint
Guilhem IX
Guillaume de Lorris
Guillaume d'Orange cycle
Guillaume Le Maréchal, Histoire de
Guiot de Provins
Guiraut Riquier
Hélinand de Froidmont
Hue de Rotelande
Huon de Bordeaux
Jean de Meun
Jeu d'Adam (Ordo representacionis Ade)
jongleur (joglar)
la Marche, Olivier de
Lancelot cycle
languages: French
languages: Occitan
la Sale, Antoine de
literatures: Arthurian legend
literatures: French
literatures: Occitan
Machaut, Guillaume de
Marcabru
Marguerite, Vie de Sainte
Marie de France
Marie l'Égyptienne, Vie de Sainte
matière de Bretagne
Mélusine
Mézières, Philippe de
mort le roi Artu, La
Ogier le Danois
pastourelle
Pathelin, Farce de Maistre Pierre
Peire Cardenal
Peire d'Alvernhe
Peire Vidal
Perceval (Parzival)
Quatre Fils Aymon, Les
Quinze Joies de Mariage
Raimbaut d'Aurenga
Raoul de Cambrai
Renart, Jean
Renaud de Montauban
Rhétoriqueurs
Robert de Blois
Robert de Boron
Robert de Clari
romance, French
Roman de la rose
Roman d'Eneas
Roman de Renart
Roman de Silence
Roncesvalles
Rudel, Jaufre
Rutebeuf
sirventes
Strasbourg Oaths
Thaon, Philippe de
Thibaut de Champagne
Tristan and Yseult
troubadour
trouvère
Uc de Saint Circ
Villehardouin, Geoffroi de
Villon, François
Wace, Robert
Yvain

Generic

Alexander romances
canso, canzone, chanson
Crusade Cycle
fabliaux
Ganelon (Gano)
Gawain romances
Guinevere
literatures: Arthurian legend
Mirror for Princes
philology, Romance
sextina
trobairitz

Italy/Sicily

Boccaccio, Giovanni
Dante Alighieri
Decameron
De vulgari eloquentia
dolce stil nuovo
Guido Cavalcanti
Guido Guinzelli
Guittone d'Arezzo
Jacopo da Lentini
Jacopone da Todi
languages: Italian
Latini, Brunetto
literatures: Italian
Petrarch, Francesco
Pinar Florencia
Rustichello da Pisa
Sicilian School
Sordello

Low Countries

Lemaire de Belges, Jean
Molinet, Jean

Spain/Portugal

Alexandre, Libro de
Alfonso X ('el Sabio', 'the Learned', 'the Wise')
Baena, Juan Alfonso de
Berceo, Gonzalo de
caballería, libros de
Calila e Dimna
Cartagena, Alonso de
Cartagena, Teresa de
Celestina
Cerverí de Girona
Cid, Cantar de Mio
Eiximenis, Francesc
Encina, Juan del
Fernán González, Poema de
Flores, Juan de
Guillem de Berguedà
Imperial, Francisco
Juan Manuel
languages: Castilian/Spanish
languages: Catalan
languages: Portuguese
literatures: aljamiado
literatures: Aragonese
literatures: Castilian
literatures: Catalan
literatures: Galician-Portuguese
Llull, Ramon
Lopes, Fernão
López de Ayala, Pero
Madrigal, Alfonso Fernández de

2.3.5. Slavic languages and literatures

Central and eastern Europe

2.4. Medicine

Central and eastern Europe

England

France

Generic

Germany / Austria

Islamic world
Arabic medicine in the Latin West
Avicenna (Ibn Sina)
Razi, Abu Bakr Muhammad ibn Zakariyya al-

Italy/Sicily
Antonio Guaineri
Burgundio of Pisa
Constantinus Africanus
Del Garbo, Dino and Tommaso
Frugardi, Roger
Gariopontus
Gentile da Foligno
Lanfranc of Milan
Luzzi, Mondino da
Michele Savonarola
Peter of Abano
Petrus de Crescentiis
Roland of Parma
Salerno, School of
Taddeo Alderotti
Theodoric Borgognoni
William of Saliceto

Low Countries
Scellinck, Thomas
Yperman, Jan

Judaica
Isaac Israeli
Maimonides, Moses
physicians, Jewish

Spain/Portugal
Arnau de Vilanova
Peter of Spain

2.5. Music and liturgy

Byzantium
Akathistos hymn
Byzantine chant
Byzantine dance
Byzantine instruments
Byzantine rite
Byzantine secular music
church of the East (Assyrian church of the East)
Coptic church, liturgical practices of
Cosmas Melodus, St
Heirmos
hymnody, Byzantine
kanon
Kassia
kontakion
liturgical books, Greek
Liturgy of Jerusalem
Liturgy of St James
Liturgy of St Mark
menologion
Noeane
Oktoechos
Pachymeres, Georgios
Psellos, Michael
trisagion
Typikon, liturgical

England
Alanus, Johannes
contenance angloise
Dunstable, John
Hanboys, Johannes
Hothby, John
John of Garland
Odington, Walter
Power, Leonel
Robert of Flamborough
Robert of Handlo
Theinred of Dover
Winchester Tropers

France
Aegidius of Murino
Andrieu Contredit d'Arras
Aurelian of Réôme
Baude Cordîer
Beleth, Jean
Binchois, Gilles
Busnoys, Antoine
Chevalier, Ulysee
Cluny, music and liturgy of
Colin Muset
Compère, Loyset
Coussemaker, (Charles) Edmond (Henri de)
Després, Josquin
Du Fay, Guillaume
Florus of Lyons
Gallican chants
Gallican Psalter
Gallican rites
Gautier of Coincy
Giraut de Borneil
Grocheio, Johannes de
Guilhem IX
Guy of Orchelles
homme armé
Hue de la Ferté
Humbertus de Romans
Jaufre Rudel
Jehannot de l'Escurel
jeu-parti
Johannes de Muris
lai-descort
Lambertus
La Rue, Pierre de
Leoninus
Magnus of Sens
Michel, Jean
missals, French
Missale Gallicanum Vetus
Missale Gothicum
Musical instruction in Paris schools 1200–1300
Notre-Dame School
Odorannus of Sens
ouvert and *clos*
Perotinus
Petrus de Cruce
Philippe de Vitry
Raimbaut de Vaqueiras
Roman de Fauvel
Salomo, Elias
Senleches, Jaquemin de
song sources: secular and monophonic—northern French
song sources: secular and monophonic—southern French

Generic
absolutions of the dead
adventus regis
alba (aube)
Alia musica
alta capella
anointing of the dead
Anonymous IV
antiphon, antiphonal
antiphons, Marian
ars antiqua
ars nova
ars subtilior
asperges
Augustine, Rule of
Ave maris stella
Ave verum corpus
Bangor, Antiphoner of
basse danse
bells
Benedicamus Domino
Benedicite
Benedictus
calendar, ecclesiastical
Canon of the Mass
cantio
cantor
cantus coronatus
cantus firmus (cantus prius factus)
Caput Masses
carol (to 1400)
carol (1400–1500)
cauda
cheironomy
chekker
Cistercian chant
Cisterican liturgy
clausula
collect
colours, liturgical
communion in both kinds
composers, minor (15th century)
conductus (monophonic)

conductus (polyphonic)
confirmation
Confiteor
consolamentum
consubstantial
copula
coronation / consecration of kings and queens
cosmos
counterpoint
Credo
customaries and ordinals, music and liturgy in
custos
dances and dance music
dedication of the church, rite of
descant
Dies irae
discant
Divine Office
Dominican liturgy and chant
Dominican rite
drama
education, music in
envoy
Eucharistic veneration and vessels
euchologion
expositio missae
Exposition of the Blessed Sacrament
Exultet
Exultet roll
faburden (*fauxbourdon*)
farced epistle (*epître farcie*)
feria, ferial
font
Fools, Feast of
formes fixes
fraction
gestures, Christain liturgical
Gloria in Excelsis Deo
Gloria, laus, et honor
Gloria Patri
Golden Rose
Good Friday
Gospel
Gradual
Great Responsory
Guidonian hand
Harrowing of Hell
hexachord
hocket, hoketus
Holy Saturday
holy water
hymnody, Latin
iconography of music
improvisation
incipit
instrumental music, forms of
Introit
invitatory
Ite missa est
Jesu, redemptor omnium
jubilus
Landini cadence
Latin (as pronounced by singers and liturgists)
lauda
Laudes crucis
lectionary
Lent
Liber tramitis
Liber usualis
Libri memoriales
litany
liturgical books, Latin
liturgical furnishings
liturgical vestments
liturgical year
liturgy
madrigal
Magnus liber organi
Mandatum
marriage rites
Martianus Capella, commentaries on
martyrology
Mass
Mass, cyclic
Matins
Maundy Thursday
melisma
mensural notation, mensuration
Metrologus
minor orders
minstrels
Miserere
modal rhythm
modes, melodic
modes, rhythmic
monochord
monophony (15th century)
Morrow Mass
motet (to 1300)
motet (1300–1400)
motet and Mass (1400–1500)
music, oral tradition in
Musica and *Scolica enchiriadis*
musica ficta
musical instruments
musical notation
musica mensurabilis
music theory
Notker Balbulus of St Gall
Nunc Dimittis
O Antiphons
Offertory
Office for the Dead
Old Roman chant
Orate Fratres
Ordinals of Christ
ordination
Ordines Romani
Oremus
organ
organum, organum purum
O Salutaris Hostia
ostensorium (monstrance)
paliotto
Pange lingua gloriosi
Panis angelicus
paschal candle
paschal vigil
pax, liturgical
performance practice
pitch, concept of
plainchant, sources of
plainsong
polyphonic chanson (1400–1500)
polyphonic music, sources: to 1300
polyphonic music, sources: 1300–1400
polyphonic music, sources: 1400–1500
polyphony: to 1300
polyphony: 1300–1400
prayers and devotional material
Presanctified, Mass of the
prima signatio
processions
prone
prosula (verba)
psalmody
psalters
Quadragesima
Quinquagesima
Requiem
rhymed offices
rondeau in monophonic song
sacrament, reservation of
sacramentals
sacrament house
Sanctus
Sanctus bell
Sanctus candle
scapular
Schola cantorum
Septuagesima
sequence
Sexagesima
sign of the cross
Solesmes
solfège (solmization)
songs, polyphonic (14th century)
substitute clausula
Sursum Corda
synaxis
Te Deum (Laudamus)
tenor, motetus, triplum, quadruplum
tropes, ordinary
tropes, proper
tuning
veneration of the cross
Vere dignum
versicle
versus
vigil

rugs and carpets
salt and salt production
sanitation
scarlet
seals and sigillography
ships, seafaring, and navigation
shoes and shoemakers
siege machines
signatures
silk
soap
sorcery
spear
spectacles
spinning
stained glass, techniques of making
steel
stirrup
stockings and hose
stone
surveying
swords and daggers
technical writing (*Fachliteratur*)
technology
textiles and cloth-making
timber
tin, pewter, and lead
tools
tools, agricultural
transport, land
trebuchet
vehicles
vernacular buildings: construction and form
Viking ship
warfare
wattle-and-daub
weaving, techniques of
weights and measures
wheelbarrow
wood and woodworking
woodcut
wool
writing and writing materials

Germany/Austria
Feuerwerkbuch
Gruter, Conrad
gunners' manuals
Housebook, Medieval
Kyeser, Konrad
Roriczer, Mathes
Schmuttermayer, Hanns
Schwarz, Berthold
Theophilus Presbyter

Islamic World
Geoponica
Jazari, Ibn al-Razzaz al-
kilim
noria
qali
qanat
saqiya
shaduf

Italy/Sicily
Alberti, Leon Battista
Brunelleschi, Filippo
carroccio
Cennini, Cennino
Dondi dall'Orologio, Giovanni
Filarete (Antonio Averlino)
Fontana, Giovanni
Francesco di Giorgio Martini
Gattaponi, Matteo
Guido da Vigevano
Opicino de Canistris (Opicinus)
Piero della Francesca
Taccola, Mariano di Jacopo
Valturio, Roberto

Low Countries
Coster, Laurens Janszoon

3. HISTORICAL CONTEXT AND INQUIRY

3.1. Archaeology

Byzantium
archaeology: Constantinople and Byzantium
archaeology: the Levant

Central and eastern Europe
archaeology: the Balkans
archaeology: the Baltic culture group
archaeology: east/central Europe (Slavonic)
archaeology: Russia, Belarus, and the Ukraine
Mikulčice and related sites

England; Scotland/Ireland/Wales
archaeology: Britain
archaeology: Ireland

France
archaeology: France

Generic
animal finds in the East and West
archaeology
historiography
prosopography

Germany/Austria
archaeology: Germany and Austria

Italy/Sicily
archaeology: Italy

Low Countries
archaeology: Low Countries and the Frisian islands/coastlands

Spain/Portugal
archaeology: Iberia

3.2. Classical tradition/late antiquity

Generic
aetas Virgiliana, *Horatiana*, and *Ovidiana*
ancients and moderns
anthology
Aristotelianism
artes poeticae
Augustine, St
bestiary
bible epic
biography, Latin
comedy, Latin
Dares Phrygius
Dictys Cretensis
Dioscorides in the MA
Ecloga Theoduli
eclogue
epigram
epigraphy
Galen and Galenism in the MA
gloss and commentary
grammar, Latin
hermeneumata
Hippocrates in the MA
Historia Apollonii
imitatio
Jerome, St
Kiranides (Cyranides) in the MA
Laudes urbium
letters
literatures: allegorical
locus amoenus
Maximian
Medicina Plinii
Menippean satire
metre, Latin
mythography
Neoplatonism
novel, Latin
opus geminum
Oribasius in the MA
Palladius in the MA
panegyric
Patrologia Latina
Priscian
progymnasmata
pronunciation, Latin
prose style, Latin
prosimetrum
Pseudo-Dionysius the Areopagite
Renaissance and antiquarianism
rhetoric
rhythmic poetry

Soranus of Ephesus
Stoicism
Theophrastus
topos
translation
Trojan origins
verse style, Latin
Virgil's Wheel

France
Merovech
Sulpicius Severus

Italy and Sicily
Amarcius
Boethius, Amicius Manlius Severinus
Cassiodorus, Flavius Magnus Aurelius
Donatus, Aelius
Ficino, Marsilio
Fulgentius
Pamphilus
Pico della Mirandola, Giovanni
Poliziano, Angelo
Salutati, Coluccio
Servius
Sidonius, Apollinaris
Valla, Lorenzo

Spain and Portugal
Orosius

3.3. Historical writings

Central and eastern Europe
annals and chronicles: central / eastern Europe—Annals of Hungary
annals and chronicles: central / eastern Europe—Chronica Poloniae Maioris
annals and chronicles: central / eastern Europe—Chronicle of Dzierzwa
annals and chronicles: central / eastern Europe—Chronicon Aulae Regiae
annals and chronicles: central / eastern Europe—Livonian Rhymed Chronicle
annals and chronicles: central / eastern Europe—Polish-Hungarian Chronicle
annals and chronicles: central / eastern Europe—Slavic chronicles, chronographs, and histories
Anonymus (P. dictus magister)
Bonfini, Antonio
Cosmas of Prague
Gesta principum Polonorum
Henry of Livonia
Jan Długosz
Janko of Czarnków
John of Thurocz
Magister Wincenty Kadłubek
Micha Madii
Nestor the Chronicler
Obsidio Jadrensis
Peter of Zittau
Simon of Kéza
Thomas, archdeacon of Split

England
Æthelweard
annals and chronicles: England (1)—Anglo-Saxon Chronicle
annals and chronicles: England (2)—Abingdon
annals and chronicles: England (3)—Anonimalle
annals and chronicles: England (4)—Crowland
annals and chronicles: England (5)—Peterborough Chronicle
Bede, St
Coggeshall, Ralph of
curia regis rolls
Devizes, Richard of
Elmham, Thomas
Exeter Book
Fantosme, Jordan
FitzThedmar, Arnold
Gaimar, Geoffrey
Hardyng, John
Hexham, Richard and John of
Higden, Ranulf
Hugh the Chanter
Huntingdon, Henry of
Jocelin of Brakelond
letters patent
Maitland, Frederic William
Mannyng of Brynne, Robert
manorial court rolls
Roger of Wendover
Rous, John
Stubbs, William
Usk, Adam
Vita Edwardi Regis
Wavrin, Jean de
Whethamsted, John
William of Malmesbury
William of Newburgh

France
annals and chronicles: France—Grandes Chroniques de France
Aubri of Trois-Fontaines
Basin, Thomas
Dudo of St-Quentin
Fredegar
Gilles le Muisit
Glaber, Ralph
Guillaume le Breton
Guillaume of Nangis
Guy of Bazoches
Joinville, Jean (Jehan) Sire de
Normandy and Norman history
Peter of Vaux-de-Cernay
Vincent of Beauvais

Germany / Austria
Alpert of Metz
annals and chronicles: Germany / Austria—Kaiserchronik
Arnold of Lübeck
Behaim, Albert
Berthold of Zwiefalten
Burchard of Ursperg
Ebendorfer, Thomas
Ekkehard of Aura
Frutolf of Michelsberg
Gesta Treverorum
Godfrey of Viterbo
Heinrich Taube of Selbach
Helmold of Bosau
Henry of Livonia
Hermann of Reichenau
Historia Welforum
Johann von Viktring
Johannes von Winterthur
Lampert of Hersfeld
Landesgeschichte
Levold von Northof
Matthias von Neunburg
Monumenta Germaniae Historica
Otto of St Blasien
Regesta Imperii
Reichstagsakten, Deutsche
Ruotger of Cologne
Staatssymbolik
Verfassungsgeschichte
Vita Heinrici IV

Islamic world
Ibn Khallikan
Masudi, Abu al-Hasan Ali ibn al-Husayn

Italy / Sicily
Polo, Marco
Salimbene de Adam

Judaica
annals and chronicles: chronicles (Hebrew) of First Crusade in 1096

Low Countries
Galbert of Bruges

Scandinavia
Ágrip af Nóregskonungasögum
Fagrskinna
Grammatical Treatises
Hauksbók
Heimskringla
Historia Norwegiae
Landnámabók
Morkinskinna
Oratio contra clerum Norvegiae
Sæmundr Sigfússon
Saxo Grammaticus

antipope
apostolic life (*vita apostolica*)
archdiocese
archpriest
Arianism
Art of Dying (*Ars moriendi*)
asceticism
Ash Wednesday
asylum (sanctuary), right of
Augustinian order
Babylonian captivity
beghards and beguines
bishop's accoutrements
bull, papal
camera, apostolic
canoness
canonization
Canon of Scripture
canons, regular and secular
cardinal
cardinal virtues
carnival
Cashel, Synod of
catacomb
cathedral chapter
celibacy of the clergy
chaplain
chapter (capitulum)
chapter house
chapter of faults
chrism
Christmas
church, collegiate
church history
Cistercian order
clergy
Clericis Laicos
coenobitism
collections, canonical
conclave, papal
concordat
consistory
corrody
councils, ecclesiastical
cowl
creeds: Apostles', Athanasian, Nicene
cross
crown of thorns
crusades
cure of souls
devotio moderna
Dictatus papae
dimissorial letters
diocese
docetism
Docta Ignorantia
doctor of the church
Donation of Constantine
double monastery
Easter
Ecclesia militans
Ecclesia triumphans
ember days
episcopi vagantes
Eucharist
excommunication
Execrabilis
exorcism
extra ecclesiam nulla salus
extravagantes
fasting
filioque, dispute over
flagellants
Fools, Feast of
fraternities
Free Spirit, doctrine of the
Frequens
friars
Friends of God
Gelasian doctrine
general chapter
great seal
Gregorian Reform
hagiography
heaven
hell
heresy, western Europe
hermits
Holy Lance
Holy See
Holy Week
Humiliati
imitation of Christ
Immaculate Conception of the Virgin Mary
immunity
indulgences
inquisition
interdict
Investiture Controversy
Joseph (father of Jesus)
Jubilee Year
Keys, Power of the
Knights Hospitaller
Knights Templar
laity
law, canon
lay abbot
lay brother
legate, papal
Libelli de lite
Liber censuum
Liber extra
Liber sextus
Libri memoriales
limbo
locus sanctus
Mary Magdalene, cult of
Mary, Mother of Christ
millenarianism
missions, medieval
monastery
monasticism
Nicolaitism
nomen sacrum (*nomina sacra*)
oblate
Palm Sunday
papacy
papal court (*papal curia*)
papal register
pastoral care
Pater Noster
patriarch
Patrimony of St Peter
patron of a benefice
pectoral crosses
penance
penitentials
penitentiary
Per Venerabilem
Petrine doctrine
pilgrimage
pilgrim's guides
poverty, religious
preaching
prebend
procurations
proprietary churches
Provisors, Statutes of
Purgatory
recluse
relics
religious orders
Rogation, Feast of
rood
rosary
sacraments
Saladin tithe
Satan
Savigny, Order of
Schism, Great Western
Schism of 1054
sermon
Servus servorum Dei
seven deadly sins
seven gifts of the Holy Spirit
simony
stigmata
stylites
Sunday
tithe and tithing
tonsure
transubstantiation
Trinitarians, Order of
Trinity
Two Swords, Doctrine of the
typology
Veronica, St
Vicar of Christ
visitation, canonical
visitations, episcopal
vows
White Monks

women, churching of
women, religious

Germany/Austria
Abraham of Freising
Adalbert, St
Adalbert of Bremen
Adelheid, St
Admont (monastery)
Adolf I of Altena
Albero of Trier
Albert II of Magdeburg
Altmann of Passau, St
Amadeus of Lausanne, St
Angilram of Metz
Anno of Cologne, St
Aribo of Mainz
Arnulf, St
Baldwin of Luxemburg
Bardo of Mainz
Basel (bishopric)
Basel, Council of
Benediktbeuern (abbey)
Benno of Osnabrück
Bernward of Hildesheim, St
Berthold of Henneberg
Bremen (suffragan)
Brixen, Synod of
Bruno of Cologne, St
Bruno the Carthusian, St
Busch, Jan
Canossa, Meeting of
Christian I von Buch
Christian of Prussia
Chrodegang, St
Conrad of Gelnausen
Conrad of Hochstaden
Conrad of Lichtenau
Conrad of Mainz
Conrad of Marburg
Corvey (monastery)
David of Augsburg
Dietrich I
Dietrich von Moers of Cologne
Eberhard of Berg, St
Eberhard of Rohrdorf
Eberhard of Salzburg
Echternach (monastery)
Egbert
Emmeram of Regensburg, St
Forchheim, meeting of
Frederick of Mainz
Fulda (monastery)
Gandersheim
Gertrude, St ('the Great')
Gutenberg, Johannes
Haimerad (Heimrad)
Helfta, convent of
Henry Suso
Hermann of Metz
Hersfeld (monastery)
Hildegard of Bingen
Hirsau
Johannes Trithemius
Johannes von Neumarkt
Jordan of Saxony
Lorsch (monastery)
Lull, St
Mechthild of Hackeborn
Melk (monastery)
Michelsberg
Mondsee (monastery)
Niklashausen, Drummer of
Otto, St
Philip of Heinsberg
Prüm (monastery)
Quedlinburg
Radegunda, St
Rainald of Dassel
Reichenau (monastery)
Rupert of Salzburg, St
St Blasien (monastery)
St Gall (monastery)
Salzburg
Severin, St
Siegfried of Mainz
Tegernsee (monastery)
Teutonic Knights, Order of
Three Magi of Köln
Ulrich, St
Virgilius of Salzburg, St
Weissenburg (monastery)
Wibald
Wiching
Willehad, St
William of Hirsau, St
Willigis of Mainz, St
Wolfgang, St
Worms, Synod of

Italy/Sicily
Albergati, Niccolò
Anagni, Outrage (Humiliation) of
Angelo Clareno
Anthony of Padua, St
Antoninus, St
Arialdo, St
Aureoli, Petrus
Autpert, Ambrose
Benedict of Nursia, St
Benedictine order
Bernardino of Siena, St
Bonizo of Sutri
Cadalus (antipope)
Canossa
Catherine of Genoa, St
Catherine of Siena, St
Clara of Assisi, St
Clement VII (antipope)
Colombini, Giovanni
councils, Lateran
Decretum Gratiani
Dionysius Exiguus
Dolcino, Fra
Felix V (antipope)
Florence, Council of
Frances of Rome, St
Francis of Assisi, St
Franciscan order
fraticelli
Giovanni Gualberto, St
Humbert of Silva Candida
Jerome, St
Joachim of Fiore
Joannes Andreae
John XXIII (antipope)
John Capistran
Lateran palace
Margaret of Cortona, St
Monte Cassino (abbey)
Peter Damian
Pian dei Carpini, Giovanni
Pisa, Council of
Pope Agatho
Pope Alexander II
Pope Alexander III
Pope Alexander IV
Pope Alexander VI
Pope Benedict XII
Pope Boniface VIII
Pope Calixtus II
Pope Celestine V
Pope Clement VI
Pope Eugenius III
Pope Eugenius IV
Pope Gelasius I
Pope Gregory I
Pope Gregory VII
Pope Gregory IX
Pope Hadrian I
Pope Hadrian IV
Pope Honorius III
Pope Innocent III
Pope Innocent IV
Pope Joan (antipope)
Pope John XXII
Pope Leo I ('the Great')
Pope Leo IV
Pope Leo IX
Pope Martin V
Pope Nicholas I
Pope Pius II
Pope Urban VI
Romuald, St
Sacchoni, Rainerio
Segarelli, Gerard
Shroud of Turin
Spiritual Franciscans
Tancred
Ubertino of Casale
Vatican
Vatican library
Waldensians

Zabarella, Francesco
Zita of Lucca, St

Low Countries
Alexian brothers and nuns
Amandus, St
Arkel, Jan van
devotio moderna
Dymphna, St
Gertrude, St
Groote, Geert
Lobbes (abbey)
Notker
Ruysbroeck, Jan van
St Bertin (abbey)
Stavelot (abbey)
Tanchelm
Utrecht Psalter
Wessel, Johann
William of Ruysbroeck
Windesheim (abbey)

Scandinavia
Absalon of Lund
Ansgar, St
Birgitta of Sweden, St
Catherine of Sweden, St
conversion of Scandinavia
Eskil, St
Guðmundr Arason
homily books (Scandinavian)
Scandinavian church
sermon literature (Scandinavian)
translations, Bible (Scandinavian)

Scotland/Ireland/Wales
Arbroath (abbey)
Armagh
Brendan, St
Bridget of Ireland, St
Celtic church
clas churches
Clonmacnoise
Columba, St
Columban, St
Comyn, John
Culdees
David, St
Dunfermline (abbey)
Finan, St
Holyrood (abbey)
Iona (abbey)
Irish church, early organization of
Kells, Synod of
Kentigern, St
Kilian, St
Laudabiliter (papal privilege)
Llandaff, Book of
Malachy, St
Mellifont (abbey)
Melrose (abbey)
Palladius, St
Patrick, St
Purgatory, St Patrick's
Sulien (bishop)

Spain/Portugal
Albornoz, Cardinal Gil Álvarez Carillo de
auto da fé
conversos
Córdoba martyrs
Dominic, St
Dominican order
Elias of Cortona
Elipandus
Felix (bishop of Urgell)
Fructuosus, St
Gelmírez, Diego
Hosius (bishop of Córdoba)
Ildefonso, St
Jimenez de Cisneros, Francisco
Monte Corvino, John of
Montserrat (monastery)
Paulus Albarus
Ripoll, Santa Maria de
Santiago de Compostela
Santo Domingo de Silos (monastery)
Toledo, councils of
Torquemada, Tomás de
Vincent Ferrer, St

4.2. Legal history

Byzantium
Basilica, The
logothete
Rhodian Sea Law
Theodosian Code
Tribonian

Central and eastern Europe
Assizes of Romania
aviticitas
Buda Stadtercht
castellan
corona regni (Hungary, Bohemia, Poland)
county (Hungary)
Golden Bull (of Andrew II of Hungary)
Jus regale montanorum
law code, Poljica
law code, Vrana
Lithuanian Metrica
Lithuanian statutes
Loca credibilia
Nihil novi and its predecessors
noble diet (Hungary, Bohemia)
Pacta conventa
palatine (Hungary, Poland-Lithuania)
Rožmberk family
Russkaya Pravda
Statuta Łaskiego
Statute of Dubrovnik
Statutes of Casimir
tavernical court
Tripartitum of Werbőczy
ustavy of the Rus' principalities
veche
Vinodol, law code of
voivode

England
abjuration of the realm
Arches, Court of
Arundel's Constitutions
assize
Bracton, Henry de
burgage tenure
chancery
Chancery, Court of
Circumspecte Agatis
Clarendon, Assize of
Clarendon, Constitutions of
common burdens
Common Pleas, Court of
coroner
distraint
distraint of knighthood
entail
escheat
Fleta
forest law
forms of action, English
Fortescue, Sir John
frankpledge
'Glanvill'
Glanvill, Ranulf de
Grand Assize
Inns of Court
juries
justices itinerant
King's Bench, Court of
Labourers, Statute of
law, English common
Lyndwood, William
Magna Carta
Merton, Statute of
nisi prius
Northampton, Assize of
Oswaldslow
primogeniture
privy seal
quo warranto
sake and soke
scutage
serjeants at law
sheriff
shire
soke
sokeman
Statute of York

4.3. Military history

Central and eastern Europe
'Black Army' of Matthias Corvinus
Cossacks
Dózsa uprising
druzhina
Grunwald (Tannenberg), battle of
Hunyadi, John
hussars
Hussite wars and leaders
Indagines
Kosovo Polje, battle of
Kulikovo Pole, battle of
Lake Chud (Peipus), battle of
Liutizi uprising
Mohács, battle of
Muhi, battle of
Nicopolis, Crusade of
noble levy
Order of St George
Peace of Toruń
portalis, militia
Scanderbeg
strel'tsy
Swordbrothers
Varna, Crusade of
vojniki

Crusader states
Hattin, battle of
Militia Christi
Montreal (castle)
Tiberias, battle of

England
Ashingdon, battle of
Badon, Mount
Barnet, battle of
Barons' War
benevolence
Blore Heath, battle of
Bosworth Field, battle of
Bramham Moor
Brunanburh, battle of
Buckingham's rebellion
Burghal Hidage
Buttington, battle of
Dyrham, battle of
Ellendun, battle of
Fulford Gate, battle of
fyrd
Great Army
Harrying (Harrowing) of the North
Hastings, battle of
Hingston Down, battle of
Homildon Hill
housecarl
Hundred Years War
Lincoln, battles of
Lincolnshire Rebellion
Maldon, battle of
Masefield, battle of
Mortimer's Cross
Neville's Cross, battle of
Norman Conquest
Northampton, battle of
Norwich Crusade
Otterburn
Roses, Wars of the
St Albans, battles of
Saxon shore
Shrewsbury, battle of
Stamford Bridge, battle of
Standard, battle of the
Stoke, Battle of
Tewkesbury, battle of
Tower of London
Towton, battle of
Wakefield, battle of
Wat's Dyke
Winwaed

France
Agincourt
Boucicaut, Jean II le Meingre, called
Bouvines, battle of
Buch, Jean III de Grailly, captal de
Clisson, Olivier IV de
Crécy, battle of
Du Guesclin, Bertrand
échorcheurs
Fontenay, battle of
francs-archers
Fréteval, battle of
Hundred Years War
Jacquerie
Montfort, Simon de
Montjoie St-Denis!
Norman Conquest
Praguerie (revolt of 1440)
Rais, Gilles de
Richemont, Arthur, Comte de
routiers
Val-ès-Dunes

Generic
arsenals and navies
chevauchée
maritime history
militias, urban and rural

Germany/Austria
Andernach, battle of
Fossa Carolina
Lechfeld, battle of
Morgarten, battle of
Mühldorf, battle of
Reichsheerfahrt
Riade (Merseberg), battle of
Stellinga uprising
Unstrut (Langensalza), battle of
Welfesholz, battle of
Worringen, battle of

Islamic world
armies, Islamic
Baybars, al-Bunduqdari
Cotrone, battle of
emir (amir)
Mongol invasion of Europe
Nur al-Din Mahmud ibn Zengi
Ridda (Riddah), War of al-
Saladin
Tamerlane
Tarik ibn Ziyad

Italy/Sicily
Cotrone, battle of
Legnano, battle of

Low Countries
Cassel, battle of
Courtrai (Kortrijk), battle of
Ghent War
maritime Flanders, revolt of
Rosebeke, battle of
Sluis, battle of

Scandinavia
Berserk
Danevirke
Garðar (Garðaríki)
horse fights
Scandinavian military history
Stiklastaðir, battle of
Svolðr, battle of
Varangians

Scotland/Ireland/Wales
Anglo-Scottish wars
Bannockburn, battle of
Caernarfon (castle)
Clontarf, battle of
Flodden, battle of
Largs, battle of
Stirling, battle of
warfare in Ireland and Wales

Spain/Portugal
Alarcos, battle of
Alcántara, Order of
Aljubarrota, battle of
Barbastro Crusade
caballeros villanos
Calatrava, Order of
Catalan Grand Company
Covadonga, battle of
Guadalete, battle of
Muret, battle of
Nájera, battle of
Navas de Tolosa, battle of
Roncesvalles
Salado, battle of

4.4. Political history: rulers and dynasties

Central and eastern Europe
Angevins in central Europe
Árpád dynasty
confederation of Poland–Lithuania
Frankapani
free royal cities
Garai
Gediminids
George of Poděbrady
Habsburgs (Hapsburgs) in central Europe
Jagiełłonian dynasty
Kurozwencki of Kurozwęki
Matthias Corvinus
Mindaugas
Musachi
Order of the Dragon
Otakar Přemysl II
Piast dynasty
Přemysl dynasty
Rurikid dynasty
senate, royal council
Šubići
Tenczinski
Trpimirid dynasty
Újlaki, Nicholas
zhupan (comes, ispán)

Crusader states
Bohemond I of Taranto
Constantinople, Latin empire of
Cyprus, kings of
Godfrey de Bouillon
Guy of Lusignan
Jerusalem, kings of
Melisande, queen of Jerusalem
Raymond of Poitiers
Tripoli, counts of
Yolande of Brienna

England
Adela of Louvain
Ælfthryth
Ælle of the South Saxons
Æthelbald
Æthelbert
Æthelflaed
Æthelred II
Æthelstan
Alfred the Great
Arthur of Brittany
Arundel, earls of
baronial reform movement
Beaufort family
Bigod family
Bretwalda
Burgh, Hubert de
Byrhtnoth
Cambridge (earldom)
Catherine of Valois
Ceawlin
Cerdic
Clare family
Clarence, dukes of
Cnut
Cobham, Eleanor
Cornwall (earldom, dukedom, bishopric)
Cromwell, Ralph Lord
Danelaw
de la Pole family
Derby / Ferrers, earls of
Devon, earls of
Eadred
Eadwig
Ecgberht
Edgar ('the Aethling')
Edgar I
Edith
Edmund I
Edmund II
Edward ('the Confessor')
Edward ('the Martyr')
Edward I
Edward II
Edward III
Edward IV
Edward V
Edward of Lancaster
Edward of Woodstock
Edward the Elder
Edward the Exile
Edwin
Eleanor of Aquitaine
Eleanor of Castile
Emma of Normandy
Essex (earldom)
Exeter (earldom, dukedom)
Falaise, Treaty of
Fastolf, Sir John
Fauconberg, Thomas
FitzNigel, Richard
FitzPeter, Geoffrey
Flambard, Ranulf
Gaveston, Piers
Gloucester (earldom)
Godiva
Godwine
Good Parliament, the
Guthrum
Halfdan I
Harold I Harefoot
Harold II Godwinson
Harthacnut
Hastings, William, Lord
Henry (earl of Lancaster)
Henry, Young King
Henry I
Henry II
Henry III
Henry IV
Henry V
Henry VI
Henry VII
Henry of Blois
heptarchy
Hereward 'the Wake'
Howard family
Humphrey
Isabella of Angoulême
Isabella of France
Joan ('Fair Maid of Kent')
John ('Lackland')
John of Gaunt
John of Lancaster
Lancaster (earldom, dukedom)
Lancastrian dynasty
Leofric (earl)
Longchamp, William
Magonsætan
Mandeville, Geoffrey de
Margaret of Anjou
Marshal, William
Matilda (empress)
Matilda II
Matilda of Boulogne
Matilda of Flanders
Merciless Parliament
Modus tenendi parliamentum
Montfort, Simon de (earl of Leicester)
Mortimer family
Mowbray family
Neville, Richard
Neville family
Norman dynasty
Northampton (earldom)
Northumberland (earldom, dukedom)
Odo of Bayeux
Offa
Oldcastle, Sir John
Ordainers
Oswald, St (king of Northumbria)
Oswy
Oxford, earldom of
parliament
Pembroke (earldom)
Penda
Percy family
Perrers, Alice
Philippa of Hainaut
Plantagenet, George
Plantagenet / Angevin dynasty
Privy Council
Provisions of Oxford
Rædwald
Rheged
Richard (earl of Cornwall)
Richard I
Richard II
Richard III
Richard of York
Robert (earl of Gloucester)
Robert of Bellême

Roches, Peter des
Roger of Salisbury
St Brice's Day massacre
Salisbury (earldom, dukedom)
Scrope, Richard le
Sicilian Adventure
signet
Simnel, Lambert
Siward
Somerset
Southampton Plot
Stafford, earls of, and dukes of Buckingham
Stafford family
staller
Stanley family
Star Chamber
Stephen (king of England)
Stigand of Canterbury
Straw, Jack
Suffolk (earldom, dukedom)
Swein Forkbeard
Thomas of Lancaster
Thorkell the Tall
Tiptoft, John
Tostig
Tudor dynasty
Vere family
Vortigern
Wales, prince of
Walter, Hubert
Waltheof
Walworth, William
Warbeck, Perkin
Wedmore, Peace of
White Ship
William I
William II
William of Wykeham
Winchester (earldom)
Windsor, Treaty of
Woodville, Anthony
Woodville, Elizabeth
Woodville family
York (kingdom, dukedom, earldom)
York dynasty
Yorkist

France
Anne of Brittany
Anne of France
Armagnac, house of
Armagnacs and Burgundians
Beaujeu, house of
Berry, duchy of
Blois, house of
Bourbon, house of
Buch, captals of
Capetians
Carolingian dynasty
Charlemagne
Charles II ('the Bad')
Charles II ('the Bald')
Charles III ('the Fat')
Charles III ('the Simple')
Charles IV
Charles V
Charles VI
Charles VII
Charles VIII
Christian King, Most
Dagobert I
Dauphin
Garlande, Stephen of
Hugh Capet
Jeanne (queen of Navarre and France)
Lorraine, dukes of
Louis IX, St
Lusignan, house of
Montmorency family
Navarre, kings and queens of
Odo of Bayeux
Philip II Augustus
Philip IV
Philip VI
Provence, counts of
René of Anjou
Robertian dynasty
rois fainéants
Sorel, Agnès
Thierry II
Thierry III
Trencavels

Generic
assembly, royal
charter, private
city-state
communes and community
duke, duchy
earl
kingship, queenship, and monarchy
peerage
Secretum secretorum

Germany/Austria
Adela of Elten
Adolf (VIII) of Schleswig-Holstein
Andechs dynasty
Aribonid dynasty
Arnulf of Carinthia
Bautzen, Treaty of
Berg dynasty
Billung dynasty
Forchheim, meeting of
Frederick III
Freiburg School
Henry II (emperor)
Henry Raspe
Henry the Lion
Hermann of Thuringia
Hohenzollern family
Holy Roman Empire
interregnum
Jacqueline of Bavaria
Louis II
Louis the German
Louis the Pious
Luitpoldings
Luxembourg dynasty
Meißen, margraves of
Roman Empire
Romans, king of the
Rudolf of Rheinfelden
Wettin family
Wittelsbach family
Zähringer (dynasty)

Islamic world
Abu Bakr
Aghlabid dynasty
Ahmad ibn Tulun
Ali (Ali ibn Abi Talib)
Almohads
Almoravids
Assassins, sect of
Ayyubid dynasty
Buyids
caliphate
caliphate, Abbasid
caliphate, Fatimid
caliphate, Umayyad
Ghana
Ghassanids
Ghaznavid dynasty
Hamdanid dynasty
Idrisid dynasty
imam
Islamic Empire
khan
Mamun, al-
Mangu Khan (or Mongke)
Mansur, al-
Marinid dynasty
Nasrid dynasty
Saffarid dynasty
Saladin (Salah al-Din)
Secretum secretorum
Seljuk Turks
Umar I (Ibn al-Khattab)
Uthman ibn Affan
Zirid dynasty

Italy/Sicily
Arnold of Brescia
Baldus of Perugia
Canossa (castle)
Carrara family
Charles I of Anjou
Cola di Rienzo
Colonna family
consuls

Lucrum camerae
Magyars
non-privilege towns
pre-urban settlements and emporia in central / eastern Europe
Romanians (Vlachs)
servientes regis
shamanism, remnants of
Slavs
Székely (Siculi, Szeklers)
Szlachta (knights)
Tatars
thirtieth (customs)
travel and exploration: travellers to and from central and eastern Europe
women in central and eastern Europe

England
alderman
allod and freehold
Anglo-Saxons
baron, baroness
Brembre, Nicholas
bridge-building brotherhoods
Bukerel family
Cade's Rebellion
carucate
children in England
Cinque Ports
commendation
copyhold, copyholder
croft
Danegeld
deserted villages
Dialogus de scaccario
Domesday Book
duke, duchy
ealdorman
earl
Exchequer
forest charter
Garter, Order of the
gesith
groat
Henley, Walter of
hue-and-cry
hundred
Hundred Rolls
journeymen
Jutes
knights of the shire
Laxton
livery companies
Northampton, John of
Offa's Dyke
Paston family and letters
Peasants' Rebellion of 1381
pipe rolls
poll tax
Robin Hood
ship burial
Stamford cloth
staple
Staple, Company of the
Steelyard, Merchants of the
stews
thrymsas
Tribal Hidage
Tyler, Wat
Whittington, Dick
women in England
yeoman

France
bastides
Bourgeois de Paris
Cabochiens
Cahorsin
Capitulare de villis vel curtis imperialis
Chambre des Comptes
children in France
'courts of love'
droit du seigneur
fairs: fairs of Champagne
League of Public Weal
Marcel, Étienne
Marigny, Enguerran de
marmousets
mayor of the palace
Pastoreaux, crusades of the
sénéchal
women in France

Generic
accounting and bookkeeping
administration, royal
administration, urban
adultery and concubinage
adventus regis
Alps and Alpine passes
animal pets
animals, domestic, draft, and wild
aseity
bandits and outlawry
banking, finance, and taxation
barbarians
bastard feudalism
bill of exchange
Black Death, social and economic impact
bourgeois (borghese, burgher)
bracteate
bullion and bullion famine
burial customs and medieval cemetaries
Camposanto
chace
charnel house
charters of franchise and liberties
chivalry and knighthood
Cistercian entrepreneurs
city-state
climate and climatic change
clothing and costume
colonialism
comitatus
commercial handbooks
commercial revolution
communes and community
confraternities
cooking and cookery books
coral
coronation, rites of
cottar
courtliness and courtesy
crime and criminality
crusades, economic and social features of
crypt
Dance of Death
'Dark Ages'
death
demography and population
despotism and tyranny
dowry and trousseau
duelling
echevin (alderman, *scabinus*, *Schöffen*)
economic and social history
economic thought
education
education, curriculum
enclosure
environment
estate management and organization
ethnography, medieval
exploration and colonization
fairs
falconry
famine
Fechtbücher ('fencing books')
festivals
feudalism
feudal revolution
fief and money fief
field systems
folklore and popular culture
folly and madness
food, drink, and diet
foods, prepared
food supply and food trades
forests and woodlands
friendship
frontiers and frontier societies
gardens
genealogy
gentry
gift and tribute
gleaning
grain crops
guilds
heraldry
homage
homosexuality
honour and shame
hotels, inns, and taverns
housing and building trades

hunting and fowling
incest
instruments
insurance
itinerary, royal
just price
kinship, family, marriage, divorce
knight
knitting
labour legislation
land tenure
libraries, medieval
literacy and writing
loculus
lordship and town
luxury, consumption, and sumptuary laws
markets
Memento mori
mercenary companies
migration
migration of peoples
money and coinage
moneylending, credit, and usury
mons pietatis (*monte di pietà*)
mountains and mountain societies
nation and nationhood
nobility
oaths and oath-taking
old age
olives and olive oil
out-burghership (*bourgeoisie foraine*)
paganism
parish
pastoralism and transhumance
patronage, literary
peasant resistance and revolts
peasants
pilgrimage
piracy
poverty and poor relief
prisons and punishment
proverbs, riddles, exempla
prostitution
public order
race and minorities
rape
reclamation
royal entry
royal household
salt, tax on
sarcophagus and tomb
scriptorium
serfdom
servanthood
ship burial
slavery and slave trade
spices and the spice trade
sports, games, and pastimes
stock breeding and selection
suburb
sugar
taxation
theoretical approaches: social and economic history of the MA
three estates
town and country (*pagus, contado*)
trade and commerce: Mediterranean European
trade and commerce: northwest Europe
trade, collapse and revival
travel and mobility
underwear
urbanism
urban revolts
Uzzano
vassalage
wardrobe
waterworks
widowhood
wine production and trade
women, economic and social roles of
year 1000

Germany/Austria

Brenner Pass
children in Germany and Austria
Drang nach Osten
free cities
Fugger dynasty
Hanse and Hanseatic League
Pied Piper of Hamelin
Reichstag
Rhenish League
St Gotthard pass
Urbar
William Tell legend
women in Germany and Austria

Islamic world

Aisha
Alids
Allah
Bedouin
Berbers
children in Islam
emir (amir)
Fatima
Five Pillars of Islam
hadith
Hasan, al-
Hilal (Banu Hilal)
Husayn, al-
Ibn Tumart, Muhammad ibn Abdallah
imam
Islamic civilization
Ismaili Sect
Kharijites
madrasah
mosque
muezzin (muadhdhin)
Muhammad
Mumin, Abd al-
Prester John
Ramadan
Shia (Shiah, Shiites)
sunna
women in Islam

Italy/Sicily

Bartholomew of Pisa
Bianchi e Neri ('Whites and Blacks')
Calimala
Camposanto
capitano del popolo
Ciompi, Revolt of the
colonate
compagnie di ventura
condottieri
consulate (Italian towns)
contado
Cotrugli, Benedetto
Datini, Francesco di Marco
florin
funduk
incastellamento
Lombard League
magnati e popolani
Medici
Patarines
Pegolotti, Francesco Balducci
Pian dei Carpini, Giovanni
podestà
popolo
tower societies
women in Italy

Judaica

Amram ben Sheshna
anti-Semitism
Ashkenaz
badge, Jewish
Bartinoro, Ovadia
betrothal rings, Jewish
children in Jewish society
courtiers, Jewish
David ben Zakkai
Dulcea of Worms
excommunication (Christian/Jewish)
exilarch
festival cycle customs
Geniza, Cairo
gestures, Jewish liturgical
ghetto
godparents, Jewish
Hai ben Sherira
Ibrahim ibn Jaqub
Jewish clothing and distinctive dress
Jewish philosophical translations
Jewish quarters
Jews, medieval
Joseph ibn Megash
Judah ben Meir of Mainz

—— *The Abbreviation of the Introduction to Astrology* (1994).
D. Pingree, *The Thousands of Abū Ma'shar* (1968).
—— *Albumasaris De revolutionibus nativitatum* (1968).

Abu Nuwas (Hassan, al-Hasan ibn Hani) (*c.*750–*c.*815) Born in Ahwaz; regarded as one of the greatest poets of Abbasid times. Although he mastered various themes, he is mainly known for his *Khamriyat* (wine songs) and *Ghulamiyat* (poems of boy-love). He is remembered for revolutionary innovations in both the themes and the structure of the Arabic poem. ZSS

P. F. Kennedy, *Abu Nuwas: A Genius of Poetry* (2005).

Abyssinia (Ethiopia) Christian-ruled empire in the Horn of Africa and Upper Nile, whose orthodox church depended upon the patriarchate of Alexandria. Muslim expansion during the 7th and 8th centuries disrupted the Ethiopian state's trade routes and helped isolate its church. By the 12th century a new Christian dynasty established power and built notable monuments. Their successors further strengthened church power while relying on a mobile capital. Zara Yakob (d. 1468) imposed Christianity in his entire dominion; meanwhile, Islamization in the coastal plains was connected to the Muslim *slave trade. The war of attrition between Christian Abyssinia and the Muslim sultanates lasted until the reign of Claudius (r. 1540–59), when with Portuguese help he defeated the Muslims in battle (1543). AHR

R. Grierson and S. Munro-Hay, *Red Sea, Blue Nile: The Civilisation of Ancient and Medieval Ethiopia* (2002).
S. Munro-Hay, *Aksum* (1991).
T. Tamrat, *Church and State in Ethiopia, 1270–1527* (1972).

Academia Istropolitana The third medieval university foundation in *Hungary. In 1465 *Matthias Corvinus petitioned Pope Paul II to authorize the establishment of a *studium generale in his kingdom, since the universities of *Pécs (1367) and Óbiuda (1395) were no longer in existence. The foundation *bull was issued on 19 May 1465. The university was to have four faculties and enjoy the same scholarly privileges as *Bologna. The king chose Pozsony (*Bratislava) as the site of the new institution and named the archbishop of *Esztergom, *John Vitéz, as the first chancellor. The king provided some buildings for the *studium* and later added a *bursa*. Vitéz was in charge of recruiting the professors and, with some advice and support from Vienna, met with considerable success. Teachers and students assembled for the start of the academic year in the fall of 1467, and the institution initially flourished. While the faculties of arts and theology did function, there is no reference to the teaching of law or *medicine. Following the fall of Vitéz from royal favour and his death in 1472, the university soon fell into decay, its building reverting to other uses. It is unclear why Matthias, a patron of scholars, did not take steps to preserve this institution. LSD

R. Marsina, *LMA* 1 (1977), 70.

accessus ad auctores *See* LITERARY CRITICISM.

Acciaiuoli, Donato (1429–78) Florentine humanist and member of the Platonic Academy, he was a statesman and ambassador to *Medici's *Florence. A student of Johannes Argyropulus, he commented on Aristotle and translated Plutarch's lives of Hannibal and Scipio. *See also* FICINO, MARSILIO. LL

L. Bianchi, 'Un commento umanistico ad Aristotele: l'*Expositio super libros Ethicorum* di Donato Acciaiuoli', *Medioevo e Rinascimento*, 30 (1990), 29–55.
E. Garin, *Medioevo e Rinascimento: Studi e ricerche* (1954), 211–87.

accounting and bookkeeping After the Roman tax- and estate-accounting practices discernible from papyri, more sophisticated systems arose in the MA. 'Double-entry' bookkeeping means bilateral accounts in two parallel columns where each transaction is entered twice, once as a credit and once as a debit, making it possible for a merchant to know at any particular time whether he has a profit or a loss. Whether the practice reached *Italy from the Arab world is debated, but it was ostensibly introduced along with Arab commercial arithmetic in the early 13th century. There are 12th-century bilateral accounts in the Cairo *Geniza, but with debits listed first and then credits, not yet side by side. The Geniza documents suggest that merchants used sheets of paper folded lengthwise, making a portable four-page notebook. The oldest surviving Italian account book dates from 1211, but double-entry ledgers do not appear until the 14th century, probably in *Venice. According to Luca Pacioli's *Summa de arithmetica* (1494), a merchant should keep three separate account books: the memorandum book (continuing details of the transaction); the journal, a dated record of the transactions recorded in the memorandum book, recording income and expenditures converted into a single currency; and the ledger, in which figures from the journal would be entered twice, assets on one side (including receivables and inventories), liabilities on the other. TFG

F.-J. Arlinghaus, 'Bookkeeping', *Medieval Italy: An Encyclopedia*, ed. C. Kleinhenz (2004), 147–50.
M. Chatfield and R. Vangermeersch, eds, *The History of Accounting: An International Encyclopedia* (1996).

Accursius, Franciscus (d. 1263) Compiler of the standard commentary (*Glossa ordinaria*) on Justinian's *Corpus iuris civilis* taught in medieval *universities and law schools. Accursius was a pupil of *Azo. JABr

absolutions of the dead Prayers for escape from judgement, remission of sins, and reception into paradise, after the conclusion of the *Requiem Mass and before the recessional and the *burial rites in medieval western funeral *liturgy. DJKe

G. Rowell, *The Liturgy of Christian Burial* (1977).

R. Rutherford, *The Death of a Christian: The Rite of Funerals* (1980).

Abu al-Hasan al-Shushtari (1212–69) Muslim mystical poet of Hispano-Arabic song forms (*muwashshah* and *zajal*), often in the Andaluso-Arabic vernacular, and combining calls to ecstatic spirituality with *tropes of drinking and love. He also composed odes in classical Arabic. LMA

L. Alvarez, 'The Mystical Language of Daily Life: Vernacular Sufi Poetry and the Songs of Abū al-Hasan al Shushtarī', *Exemplaria*, 17 (2005), 1–32.

Shushtarī, *Poesia estrófica: céjeles y/o muwaššahāt*, tr. F. Corriente (Arabic ed., 1960) (1988).

Abu Bakr (*c*.572–634; r. 632–634) First caliph; early Muslim convert and confidant of *Muhammad. Shortly after the Muslim community's emigration (*Hijra*) to *Medina in 622, Muhammad married Abu Bakr's daughter Aisha. Upon Muhammad's death Abu Bakr was selected as his successor. His *caliphate was characterized principally by armed struggle with apostate tribes. He is buried in Medina beside Muhammad. SMT

H. Kennedy, *The Prophet and the Age of the Caliphates* (2004).

W. Madelung, *The Succession to Muhammad: A Study of the Early Caliphate* (1997).

A. I. Tayob, 'Political Theory in al-Tabari and his Contemporaries: Deliberations on the First Caliph in Islam', *Journal for Islamic Studies*, 18–19 (1998–99), 24–50.

Abu Hanifa (al-Numan ibn Thabit) (d. 767) Iraqi Sunni Muslim jurist, founder of the Hanafi school of **sharia*; a pupil of the jurist Hammad. Abu Hanifa collaborated with his students in evaluating contemporary doctrines, discussing issues to create new formulations so as to shape a law system capable of dealing with new problems as society changed. His jurisprudence was probably the most flexible and adaptable of the four Sunni law schools. He probably never composed any writings; his teachings were collected by his disciples. Being opposed to the contemporary regime, he also never accepted a judgeship, for which he died in prison. ANK

C. Melchert, *The Formation of the Sunni Schools of Law* (1997).

Abulafia, Meir (Ramah) (*c*.1165–1244) Born in *Burgos into an aristocratic Jewish family, he married the daughter of Joseph ibn Shoshan, the treasurer of Alfonso VIII of *Castile. Settling in *Toledo in 1194, he became a scholar and communal leader, composing influential commentaries on *Talmudic tractates. Conversant in Arabic, he was the first known translator of Hispano-Arabic poetry into Hebrew. Becoming concerned that *Maimonides' rationalism challenged traditional Jewish understanding of the afterlife, in 1202 he responded to the correspondence between Maimonides and the Jewish scholars of Lunel by writing to Jonathan ha-Kohen of Lunel. Ramah's letter generated controversy and provoked rebuttals. The debate ended in 1204 after Maimonides' *Treatise on Resurrection* became available in the Hebrew translation by *Samuel ibn Tibbon, making it clear that both sides had misinterpreted Maimonides. However, the deeper issues concerning the place of rationalism in Jewish society continued to simmer and erupted in the 1230s in a more acrimonious controversy. At that stage, Ramah became marginally involved by writing to *Moses ben Nahman, but his cause was taken up and radicalized by Jewish scholars in *France. HTS

B. Septimus, *Hispano-Jewish Culture in Transition: The Career and Controversies of Ramah* (1982).

H. Tirosh-Samuelson, *Happiness in Premodern Judaism: Virtue, Knowledge and Well-Being* (2003).

Abul-Barakat al-Baghdadi (*c*.1080–*c*.1165) Jewish *physician and philosopher, who converted to Islam. Born in northern Iraq, he was educated in *Baghdad, where he was a court physician. His criticism of *Avicenna was influential in the Muslim east. He wrote on a variety of philosophical and scientific topics, including the intellect and soul (between which he made no distinction), God, space (infinite and empty), time, and *motion. *See also* COSMOLOGY. FG, DCL

H. A. Davidson, *Alfarabi, Avicenna, and Averroes on Intellect: Their Cosmologies, Theories of the Active Intellect, and Theories of Human Intellect* (1992).

W. Madelung, 'Abū'l-Barakāt al-Bagdādī', *Encyclopaedia Iranica*, vol. 1, 266–8.

S. Pines, 'Abu'l-Barakāt al-Baghdādī', *DSB*, vol. 1, 26–9.

—— *Studies in Abū'l-Barakāt al-Baghdādī* (1979).

Abu Mashar al-Balkhi (787–886) Islamic astrologer, who justified *astrology by appealing to both Aristotle and pre-Islamic Iranian thought, asserting astrology's divine origin by positing a Hermes-like universal teacher. The celestial orbs helped reunite human souls with the divine. His two major astrological works were his *Great Introduction* and *Grand Conjunctions*. In *astronomy, his *Zij al-Hazarat* (*Ephemeris of the Thousands*) combined Indian parameters with Ptolemaic planetary theory. RGM

Abu Mashar al-Balkhi, *Kitāb al-Madkhal al-kabīr ilā 'ilm al-nujūm: Liber introductorii maioris ad scientiam judiciorum astrorum*, ed. and tr. R. Lemay (1995–6).

C. Burnett *et al.*, eds and trs, *On Historical Astrology* (2000).

miscarriage after the foetal formation called 'quickening', that is, discernible foetal movement, but convictions were rare. According to English *assize records, juries did not return convictions for abortions or miscarriages, even those caused by assault. If a woman contrived an assault leading to a miscarriage, court records do not identify a crime because it could not be proved that the foetus would have been viable. Civil courts consistently maintained that before *baptism, there could be no homicide, and—despite some patristic assertions to the contrary—the church did not actively dispute the convention. JMR

A. McLaren, *A History of Contraception* (1990).
J. Noonan, *Contraception* (1986).
J. Riddle, *Eve's Herbs* (1997).

Abraham, bosom of The place to which the poor man Lazarus is carried after death in the parable of Lazarus and Dives (Luke 16:22–23). It came to be thought of as *heaven or the abode of the righteous dead. In medieval representations of the Last Judgement, Abraham is often shown bearing souls of the blessed in a cloth. ECT

K. Kohler, 'Abraham's Bosom', *Jewish Encyclopedia* (2002).

Abraham ben David, Ibn Daud (*c.*1110–80) Scholar, philosopher, and astronomer from *Córdoba; settled in *Toledo after 1148; first in Spain to adopt *Aristotelianism in interpreting Judaism. In *Sefer ha-Qabbalah* he gives an account of rabbinic history, refuting *Karaism and emphasizing Sefardi culture. He explains how Jewish centres of learning independent of Babylon emerged. His book *The Exalted Faith* is the first Aristotelian Jewish philosophy work before *Maimonides. YTA

T. A. M. Fontaine, *In Defence of Judaism: Abraham ibn Daud* (1990).

Abraham ben David (Rabad) **of Posquieres** (d. 1198) Known for his glosses to *Maimonides' *Mishneh Torah*; also authored *Talmudic commentaries (surviving in fragments) and halakhic monographs; both a philosopher and apparently also a mystic. EK

J. Cohen, 'Rationales for Conjugal Sex in Rabad's "Ba'alei ha-Nefesh"', *Frank Talmage Memorial Volume*, ed. B. Walfish (1992–3), 71–84.
I. Ta-Shma, *Ha-Sifrut ha-Parshanit la-Talmud*, vol. 1 (2000).
I. Twersky, *Rabad of Posquieres* (1980).

Abraham ben Moses (Abraham Maimuni) (1186–1237) Nagid (head) of the Jewish community of *Egypt; jurist and pietist, influenced by Sufi doctrine. Many of his **responsa* survive. PIAL

M. Friedman, 'Responsa of R. Abraham Maimonides from the Cairo Geniza', *Proceedings of the American Academy for Jewish Research*, 56 (1990), 29–49.
S. Goitein, 'Abraham Maimonides and his Pietist Circle', *Jewish Medieval and Renaissance Studies*, ed. A. Altmann (1967), 145–64.

Abraham ben Shmuel Abulafia (Saragossa, 1240–*c.*1291) The founder of the prophetic school of *Kabbalah. He combined *Maimonides' philosophical esotericism with the linguistic techniques of the Rhenan Jewish pietists, known as *Hasidei Ashkenaz, and claimed to be both a prophet and the Messiah. He was active in Spain, *Italy, and the Byzantine Empire. MI

M. Idel, *The Mystical Experience in Abraham Abulafia* (1988).
E. Wolfson, *Abraham Abulafia: Kabbalist and Prophet* (2000).

Abraham of Freising (r. 957–93/94) (bishop) After the Hungarian incursions, Abraham restored *Freising to a position of prominence. An early tutor of the future Henry II, Abraham was rewarded for his services to the crown territories. A MS probably written for him contains the oldest extant Slovenian texts; *manuscript book production and illumination also increased in Freising under Abraham. ASC

J. Mass, *Geschichte des Erzbistums München und Freising* (1986), vol. 1, 113–19.

Abravanel, Isaac (1437–1508) Sefardi statesman, financier, and scholar. Born in Portugal and broadly educated, Abravanel served the king as financial advisor until he had to flee to *Castile in 1483. There he began to write commentaries on the Prophets and eschatological works (*Migdal Yeshuot*) but soon entered the service of the *Catholic Monarchs, Ferdinand and Isabel. He supported the war against *Granada. In 1492 he left for *Naples and again entered royal service, dying in *Venice. YTA

J.-C. Attias, *Isaac Abravanel, La mémoire et l'espérance* (1992).

Abrogans *See* LITERATURES: GERMANIC.

Absalon of Lund (1128–1201) Educated in *Paris, he became bishop of *Roskilde (1158), then archbishop of *Lund, Denmark (1178). He participated in the conquest and conversion of pagans (especially of Rügen), had great political influence at the royal court, introduced canon *law and monastic reforms, and was a patron of historical writing. *See also* CONVERSION OF SCANDINAVIA. NB

F. Birkebæk *et al.*, eds, *Absalon, fædrelandets fader* (1996).
K. Friis-Jensen and I. Skovgaard-Petersen, eds, *Archbishop Absalon of Lund and his World* (2000).

absolution Administered after *penance, absolution is the authoritative declaration of forgiveness by a priest, following confession. The Fourth Lateran *Council of 1215 made individual confession to a priest obligatory at least once a year, and especially in preparation for receiving the *Eucharist at *Easter. *See also* CLERGY; SACRAMENTS. DJKe

M. Dudley and G. Rowell, eds, *Confession and Absolution* (1990).
J. T. McNeill and H. M. Gamer, *Medieval Handbooks of Penance* (1990).

well. *See also* DIALECTIC; ETHICS; PHILOSOPHY, WESTERN; POLEMICS, JEWISH (WITH CHRISTIANS); STOICISM.

JMar, MEF

J. Brower and K. Guilfoy, eds, *The Cambridge Companion to Abelard* (1997).
The Letters of Abelard and Heloise, tr. B. Radice, rev. M. T. Clanchy (2003).
M. T. Clanchy, *Abelard: A Medieval Life* (1997).
J. Marenbon, *The Philosophy of Peter Abelard* (1997).
C. Mews, 'Heloise and Liturgical Experience at the Paraclete', *Plainsong and Medieval Music*, 11 (2002), 1–25.
—— *Abelard and Heloise* (2005).
M. Stewart and D. Wulstan, *The Poetic and Musical Legacy of Heloise and Abelard: An Anthology of Essays by Various Authors* (2003).
C. Waddell, '"Ephithalamica": An Easter Sequence by Peter Abelard', *MQ* 72 (1986), 239–71.
—— ed., *Hymn Collections from the Paraclete*, 2 vols (1989).
—— ed., *The Old French Paraclete Ordinary, Paris, BN fr 14410 and the Paraclete Breviary, Chaumont, BM, Ms 31*, 3 vols in 5 (1983–5).
—— ed., *The Paraclete Statutes 'Institutiones Nostrae': Troyes, Bibliothèque Municipale, MS 802, ff. 89r–90v* (1987).
L. Weinrich, 'Peter Abelard as a Musician', *The Musical Quarterly*, 55 (1969), 295–312, 464–86.

Abiell, Guilermo (Guillem) (*fl.* 1380–1416) Catalan master builder, whose major work is the Hospital of the Holy Cross (Santa Creu), *Barcelona. The *hospital, begun in 1401, is conspicuous for its courtyard plan and large, single-span halls with open timber roofs and diaphragm masonry *arches. He also worked on various churches in Barcelona including S. Maria del Pi. LTC

A. Conejo da Pena, 'Assistència i hospitalitat a l'edat mitjana. L'arquitectura dels hospitals catalans: del gòtic al primer renaixement', Ph.D. thesis (Barcelona, 2002).
F. De P. Verrié, *El Hospital de la Santa Cruz*, vol. 4 (1953).

abjuration A formal disavowal or renunciation that heretics were required to perform upon reconciliation with the church; often accompanied by *penance and imposition of hands or unction. Rituals for abjuration vary in the sources but came to be schematized in the age of *inquisitions.

KBS

E. Martène, *De Antiquis ecclesiae ritibus libri* (1736–38).

abjuration of the realm (12th–16th centuries) English legal process whereby felons forswore their goods and the realm of England and were granted passage beyond the kingdom. Abjurers were required to select a port of departure and to behave as penitent exiles. KBS

A. Réville, 'L'*abjuratio regni*: Histoire d'une institution anglaise', *Revue historique du droit français et étranger*, 50 (1892), 1–42.

abortion, contraception, and infanticide Medieval attitudes and practices about birth control derived from customary practices of various ethnic groups and were reinforced and justified by scriptural passages and by Greek philosophy. Pre-Christian customs held that the husband decided whether a pregnancy should be completed and, upon birth, whether the child was accepted. If unaccepted, the father had the right to expose or to sell the newborn.

In antiquity and into the MA a woman was considered pregnant when she declared herself so or her condition was obvious, because of the belief that an unspecified period lapsed between the time of insemination and the acceptance of the seed by the woman's body. During this period, if a woman wished, she had access to a number of *herbs that stimulated the production of human hormones to restore menstrual regularity. Using these was not regarded as abortion. Greek concepts that influenced Christian theological opinions varied. Aristotle raised the question about when a foetus was capable of independent life in a foetal state and answered that it was when the foetus was 'formed', or in modern terms, was a person. St *Augustine adopted this position in accord with Roman practices. Stoics asserted that independent life, that is, the soul (*psychē*, Latin: *anima*), began when the child took its first breath.

Early medieval ecclesiastical sources identify contraception and abortion as sins deserving of punishment, especially for those who administered the procedures—usually drugs—but with lesser punishments for the women who received them. The underlying ecclesiastical principle was that there should be no interference as to who was to be born, a principle that applied as much to fertility enhancers as it did to contraceptives and abortifacients.

From the 10th century onward, a number of church positions can be identified. Birth control could be considered a sin, based on conduct or 'right reason', according to *Thomas Aquinas, not on the assertion that the foetus (*conceptus*) was alive and independent. Other church authorities reflected a theme introduced by *Regino of Prüm (*c.*830) that both infanticide and contraception were homicide. *Gratian's *Decretum* condemned contraception and abortion on the grounds that they countered rightful sexual intercourse for procreation. Some church records also condemn contraception because the theologians mistakenly thought Onan's sin ('spilling seed upon the ground', Genesis 38:8–10) was an explicit scriptural prohibition of contraception. By the late MA recorded infanticide was rare.

Aquinas extended the Augustinian/Stoic/Aristotelian principle when he said that the foetus was formed at approximately the period of ensoulment. God alone conferred the soul. Exodus 21:22–3 was interpreted to mean that a person striking a pregnant woman and causing a miscarriage was fined if the foetus was not fully formed and received a stronger penalty if it was fully formed.

By the later MA, civil courts, rather than ecclesiastical courts, dealt with abortion cases. Late medieval cases in secular law confirm felony only if an assault caused until its cession to *Burgundy (1435); annexed by *France (1477), returned to Crown rule (1696). Site of 1514 wedding of Louis XII and Mary *Tudor. LMP

B. Chevalier, *Les bonnes villes de France du XIVᵉ au XVIᵉ siècle* (1982).

abbey *See* MONASTERY.

Abbo, St, abbot of Fleury (*c.*945–1004; r. 988–1004) A student of *Pope Silvester II, Abbo was a distinguished scholar, writing on canon *law, *hagiography, *grammar, and the *calendar. As abbot, he was an influential monastic reformer and partisan of the *Capetians. Murdered by rebellious monks in Gascony, he was celebrated as a saint. TFH

R.-H. Bautier *et al.*, eds, *L'Abbaye de Fleury en l'an mil* (2004).
T. Head, *Hagiography and the Cult of Saints: The Diocese of Orléans, 800–1200* (1990).
M. Mostert, *The Political Theology of Abbo of Fleury* (1987).
A. Notter, ed., *Lumières de l'an mil en Orléanais* (2004).

Abbo of St-Germain-des-Prés (d. after 921) Composed the *Bella Parisiacae urbis*, an epic describing the *Viking siege of *Paris (885–6), glossing the poem himself; he also wrote sermons. CJMc

A. Adams and A. G. Rigg, 'A Verse Translation of Abbo of St Germain's *Bella Parisiacae urbis*', *Journal of Medieval Latin*, 14 (2004), 1–68.
F. Brunhölzl, *Geschichte der lateinischen Literatur des Mittelalters* (1975–92), vol. 2, 118–21, 574–75.

Abd al-Rahman I *See* CÓRDOBA, EMIRATE AND CALIPHATE OF.

Abd al-Rahman II *See* CÓRDOBA, EMIRATE AND CALIPHATE OF.

Abd al-Rahman III *See* CÓRDOBA, EMIRATE AND CALIPHATE OF.

Abelard, Peter (1079–1142) A great logician, a powerful moral philosopher, a daring theologian, and a composer and liturgist. Abelard was prodigiously gifted at *logic, which he studied first with *Roscelin and then, at *Paris (*c.*1100), with *William of Champeaux. He quickly set up his own school and became famous as a teacher; the *Dialectica*, a long, profoundly original textbook of logic, probably illustrates his teaching in the period (*c.*1105–15).

Around 1115 Abelard began an affair with *Heloise, an intellectually gifted woman he was teaching privately. They married secretly and had a son, but Heloise's uncle, apparently thinking that Abelard intended to abandon his niece, arranged for thugs to break into his room and castrate him. Abelard decided, as a result, to become a monk, at *St-Denis, and he insisted that Heloise should become a nun.

Abelard went on teaching logic but also developed an interest in theology. He left his *monastery, began his own monastico-scholastic community, then became abbot of a remote Breton monastery, before going to teach again in Paris (*c.*1131–9). The first version of his *Theologia Summi Boni* was already condemned at the Council of *Soissons (1121). In 1140, at St *Bernard of Clairvaux's instigation, the Council of *Sens condemned a set of propositions supposedly taken from Abelard's work. Abelard sought refuge with *Peter the Venerable, abbot of *Cluny, and he died at Chalon-sur-Saône, a dependency of Cluny, in 1142.

The most important works from his later years were two further versions of his *Theologia* (*Theologia Christiana*, *c.*1125; *Theologia Scholarium*, *c.*1134), a *dialogue between a philosopher, a Christian, and a Jew (*c.*1130), and *Scito teipsum* ('Know yourself') or the *Ethics* (*c.*1138).

Much of Abelard's fame, from the time of *Petrarch to the present day, comes from a series of *letters exchanged between himself and Heloise nearly fifteen years after they separated, which tell the story of their romance and of Heloise's constant adoration for Abelard, despite her outwardly religious life. The authenticity of the correspondence has been questioned, but most scholars now accept it as genuine. Heloise also claimed that his love songs circulated widely, but none has been identified. His most ambitious liturgical work, a complete hymn collection created for Heloise's convent the Paraclete, survives without music (with the exception of a melody for the hymn 'O Quanta Qualia'). A handful of noted sequences and of laments (*planctus) are attributed to Abelard (or perhaps to Heloise) based on autobiographical resonances, the state of the sources, and the considerable liturgical information present in books from the Paraclete.

Abelard rediscovered propositional logic, known to the Stoics in antiquity, and reinvented again at the turn of the 20th century. He located ethical value, just as Kant would do, entirely in the goodness or badness of the will: he spoke about this in terms of consenting to acts that express love or contempt for God, because they follow or contradict what the agent believes to be God's law. An optimistic view of the universal knowledge of *natural law saved this view from extreme subjectivism.

As a theologian, Abelard tried to make sense of Christian teaching about the *Trinity in terms of God's power, knowledge, and love and of Christ's life and crucifixion, which he saw as presenting an example of overwhelming love and self-sacrifice that humans need to imitate in order to act

Aachen (Aix-la-Chapelle) (town, palace) West central German town, known for its hot springs. Aachen's significance is linked to *Charlemagne, who created a *Carolingian palace complex there, where he was buried. Successive Carolingian and German rulers gained legitimacy from possessing Aachen. Otto I began the tradition of German rulers being crowned in Aachen, Otto III was buried there, and Frederick I 'Barbarossa' orchestrated the *canonization of Charlemagne (1165). Important *relics, including Charlemagne's, established Aachen as a late medieval *pilgrimage site. JWBe

A. Hausmann, *Aachen im Mittelalter: königlicher Stuhl und kaiserliche Stadt* (1997).
M. Kramp, ed., *Krönungen: Könige in Aachen—Geschichte und Mythos* (2000).

Aachen cathedral.

Aaron ben Elijah of Nicomedia (Aaron the Younger) (1328–69) *Karaite jurist, biblical commentator, and philosopher. His philosophical work *Etz Hayyim* ('Tree of Life') is modelled after *Maimonides' *Guide of the Perplexed*, though his philosophical positions are often at odds with the latter in favour of Mutazilite opinions. Aaron frequently quotes Rabbanite literature. PIAL

J. Fürst, *Geschichte des Karäerthums* (1869).
I. Husik, *A History of Mediaeval Jewish Philosophy* (²1959).
L. Nemoy, *Karaite Anthology* (1952).

abacus *See* MATHEMATICS.

Abbas, al- (*c*.567–*c*.653) *Muhammad's uncle; a merchant who accepted Islam and joined in the conquest of *Mecca (630). The Abbasid *caliphal dynasty, which took its name from him, claimed descent from his son Abd Allah, so Abbasid sources celebrate him. KL

W. Madelung, *The Succession to Muhammad* (1997).

Abbeville Lowest point on the Somme, the city was near the English crossing point for the battle of *Crécy (1346). Ownership alternated between the English and French

PBA	*Proceedings of the British Academy*
PG	*Patrologiae cursus completus. Series Graeca*
PL	*Patrologiae cursus completus. Series Latina*
PRMA	*Proceedings of the Royal Musical Association*
QFIAB	*Quellen und Forschungen aus italienischen Archiven und Bibliotheken*
QSt	*Quaderni storici*
RArte	*Rivista d'arte*
RB	*Revue bénédictine*
RBK	*Reallexikon zur byzantinischen Kunst*
RbM	*Revue belge de Musicologie*
RBPH	*Revue belge de philologie et d'histoire*
REA	*Revue des études augustiniennes*
REJ	*Revue des études juives*
RH	*Revue historique*
RHE	*Revue d'histoire ecclésiastique*
RHM	*Römische historische Mitteilungen*
RIS	*Rerum Italicarum scriptores*
R-L	*Reallexikon der germanischen Altertumskunde*, 2nd edn.
RlangR	*Revue des langues romanes*
RMab	*Revue Mabillon: Archives de la France monastique*
RMM	*Revue de métaphysique et de morale*
RPh	*Romance Philology*
RQCAK	*Römische Quartalschrift für christliche Altertumskunde und Kirchengeschichte*
RSBN	*Rivista di studi bizantini e neoellenici*
RSJB	*Recueils de la société Jean Bodin pour l'histoire comparative des institutions*
SAGM	*Sudhoffs Archiv für Geschichte des Medizin und der Naturwissenschaften*
SCH(L)	*Studies in Church History* (London)
SCH(L).S	*SCH(L). Subsidia*
SGSG	*Studi gregoriani per la storia di Gregorio VII e della riforma gregoriana*
SHG	*Subsidia hagiographica*
SMed	*Studi medievali*
SMGB	*Studien mi Mitteilungen zur Geschichte des Benediktinerordens und seiner Zweige*
SMGH	*Schriften der Monumenta Germaniae historica*
SOPMA	T. Kaeppeli, *Scriptores ordinis praedicatorum medii aevi*
SS	*Scandinavian Studies*
SSASH	*Studia Slavica Academiae Scientiarum Hungaricae*
TAPS	*Transactions of the American Philosophical Society*
TRHS	*Transactions of the Royal Historical Society*
TSMAO	*Typologie des sources du Moyen Age occidental*
TSz	*Történelmi Szemle*
Verfasserlexikon	*Die deutsche Literatur des Mittelalters. Verfasserlexikon* ([2]1978–)
ZBLG	*Zeitschrift für bayerische Landesgeschichte*
ZDA	*Zeitschrift für deutsches Altertum und deutsche Literatur*
ZDP	*Zeitschrift für deutsche Philologie*
ZGO	*Zeitschrift für die Geschichte des Oberrheins*
ZKG	*Zeitschrift für Kunstgeschichte*
ZRG.G	*Zeitschrift der Savigny-Stiftung für Rechtsgeschichte. Germanistische Abteilung*
ZRG.K	*Zeitschrift der Savigny-Stifung für Rechtsgeschichte. Kanonistische Abteilung*
ZRG.R	*Zeitschrift der Savigny-Stifung für Rechtsgeschichte. Romanistische Abteilung*

OTHER ABBREVIATIONS

AM	Arnamagnæan Manuscript Collection
AN	Anglo-Norman
AS	Anglo-Saxon
b.	born
bk	book
BL	British Library
BN	Bibliothèque nationale de France
c.	*circa* (around)
cf.	confer (compare)
ch., chs	chapter, chapters
CL	Classical Latin
comm.	commentary (by)
comp.	compiler, compiled by
Cz.	Czech
d.	died
DBE	Dame of the British Empire
diss.	dissertation
ed., eds	editor (edited by), editors
edn.	edition
EMHG	Early Modern High German
et al.	*et alii* (and others)
FAAAS	Fellow of the American Academy of Arts and Sciences
facs.	facsimile
FBA	Fellow of the British Academy
f.d.	feast day
FEA	Fellow of the English Association
fem.	feminine
fig.	figure
fl.	*floruit* (flourished)
FMAA	Fellow of the Medieval Academy of America
fol., fols	folio, folios
FRHistS	Fellow of the Royal Historical Society
FSA	Fellow of the Society of Antiquaries
ft	foot, feet (unit of measure)
gen.	general, genitive
g	gram(s)

Goth.	Gothic
ha	hectare(s)
Hung.	Hungarian
idem, eadem	the same (author) (m. and f.)
imper.	imperative
inf.	infinitive
intro.	introduction (by)
km	kilometre
Lat.	Latin
lit.	literally
Lith.	Lithuanian
loc.	locative
m	metre
MA	Middle Ages
masc.	masculine
ME	Middle English
MHG	Middle High German
ML	Medieval Latin
MS, MSS	manuscript, manuscripts
n. c.	not catalogued
n.d.	no date
neut.	neuter
NHG	New High German
no., nos.	number, numbers
nom.	nominative
n.s.	new series
NWRuss.	northwestern Russian
OE	Old English
OFr.	Old French
OHG	Old High German
OIcel.	Old Icelandic
ON	Old Norse
OP	Ordo Praedicatorum
OS	Old Saxon
PDE	Present-Day English
pl.	plural (2pl. = second person plural)
Pol.	Polish
pres.	present
pt	part
repr.	reprint(ed)
rev.	revised (by)
Russ.	Russian
s.	saeculo / seculo (century)
S., SS.	San or Sancta, Sanctae
sec., secs	section, sections
ser.	series
sg.	singular (1sg. = first person singular)
St, Sts	Saint, Saints
Suppl.	Supplement
s.v.	sub voce (under the heading)
tr., trs	translated by (translation), translator(s)
Ukr.	Ukrainian
vol., vols	volume, volumes
vs.	versus

Superscript number preceding date of publication indicates the edition cited.

NOTE TO THE READER

Alphabetical arrangement Entries are arranged in letter-by-letter alphabetical order up to the first punctuation in the headword, with spaces and hyphens ignored.

Cross-references Cross-references occurring within the text of an entry are marked with an *asterisk. Those not in the entry text are indicated at the end of the entry in SMALL CAPITALS after '*See*' or '*See also*'.

Subheadings Short subheadings divide up many entries of 1,000 words or more. Entries with subheadings start with the headword and a sentence or two of broad definition, followed by a numbered list of the subheadings as a brief table of contents. The subheadings are repeated in the correct places in the entry.

Contributor's initials These appear in small capitals at the end of the main text, ranged right, and before the bibliography. A key to these is printed on pp. XLV–XLIX, and brief biographies of the editors and contributors on pp. XV–XLIV.

Bibliographies These consist of the most important works available on the topic.

Formatting

1. BIOGRAPHICAL ENTRIES. These begin with the person's name as the headword, followed by dates in parentheses (both birth and death year when known). For entries on rulers, known regnal dates are also given in parentheses within the opening sentence fragment.

2. NAMES. People are listed under their most commonly used name, following the standard spelling (see below). Where English names of foreign subjects are in common usage, the English form is used in preference to the foreign (for example, Frederick II, *not* Friedrich II).

Epithets and sobriquets Epithets are used as part of the headword *only* where there is no more conventional name. Normally, well-known epithets and sobriquets are indicated within single quotes, for example:

Hereward 'the Wake' (*fl.* 1070–71)
William I ('the Lion'), king of Scotland (1143–1214)

Alternative spellings/alternative names and forms, and foreign originals Where other spellings of the name are commonly found, up to two **alternative spellings** are supplied in Roman type and in parentheses following the standard spelling. Similarly, commonly used **alternative names and forms** are given in parentheses after the standard form, for example:

Averroës (Abu al-Walid Muhammad ibn Rushd) (1126–98)
Adam Scottus (Adam of Dryburgh)
William of Newburgh (Willelmus Parvus)

3. TITLES. Titled people are referred to by both title and family name (where known), the better known form appearing first, for example:

Plantagenet, George, duke of Clarence (1449–78)
or
John of Gaunt, duke of Lancaster (1340–99)

4. PLACE NAMES. **Headwords** If there is an established English form, that form is used, followed in brackets by the form current in 2010 in the language of the country in which the place is located; if there is not, the form current in 2010 in the language of the country in which the place is located is used. If there are other alternative names (for example, for Aachen: Aix-la-Chappelle; for Bratislava: Pressburg, Posonium; for Regensburg: Ratisbonne), they are included in the brackets as well.

Running text The headword, but *not* the local, English, or alternative forms in brackets, is used throughout the text. English spellings are used in preference to foreign ones wherever possible, (for example, Lyons, *not* Lyon; Marseilles, *not* Marseille; Hanover, *not* Hannover; Florence *not* Firenze).

NOTE: These rules apply also to geographical features and to names of peoples, *mutatis mutandis*.

5. STANDARD SPELLINGS. The headwords reflect standard spellings where these exist.

6. DATES. In biographies, if only one date is known, it is qualified by b. (born) or d. (died) together with before or

after. Uncertain dates are indicated as such with *c.* for *circa* and *fl.* for *floruit*. **Alternative dates** are indicated by an oblique slash (solidus), for example, 1294/8 [= 1294 or 1298]. A **sequence of dates** is indicated by a hyphen, thus: 1153–7; 1353–1402. A **range of dates** is signified by a multiplication sign, thus: b. 1430×39 [= born between 1430 and 1439]. In combinations using a range of birth dates followed by a single death date, the final year is inserted in full to avoid ambiguity, for example, (1342×7–1390) [= born between 1342 and 1347, and died in 1390].

7. MEASUREMENTS. Measurements are given in metric, rounded to the nearest whole number (for example, 35 km). Medieval units of measurement are followed by their modern equivalent or an approximation thereof in parentheses.

8. ARABIC. No diacritical marks have been used in transliterated Arabic words.

The **Thematic Listing of Entries** on pp. LI–LXXXIII provides a topical method of approaching entries.

EJ	*Encyclopaedia Judaica*
ELH	*English Literary History*
EME	*Early Medieval Europe*
EMH	*Early Music History*
ESM	*Early Science and Medicine*
EThL	*Ephemerides theologicae Lovanienses, Bruges, Louvain, etc.*
FMAS	*Frühmittelalterliche Studien*
FOEG	*Forschungen zur osteuropäischen Geschichte*
FranS	*Franciscan Studies*
FrSt	*Franziskanische Studien*
GDU	*Grand dictionnaire universel du XIXe siècle français historique, géographique, mythologique, bibliographique, littèraire, artistique, scientifique, etc.*, P. Larousse, 17 vols (1982)
GGB	*Geschichtliche Grundbegriffe. Historisches Lexikon zur politisch-sozialen Sprache in Deutschland*
GRLMA	*Grundriss der romanischen Literaturen des Mittelalters*
Hist(L)	*History. The Journal of the Historical Association*
HR	*Historical Research: the Bulletin of the Institute of Historical Research*
HSJ	*Haskins Society Journal*
HThR	*Harvard Theological Review*
HZ	*Historische Zeitschrift*
IMU	*Italia medioevale e umanistica*
JAMS	*Journal of the American Musicological Society*
JBAA	*Journal of the British Archaeological Association*
JEconH	*Journal of Economic History*
JEEH	*Journal of European Economic History*
JEH	*Journal of Ecclesiastical History*
JEGP	*Journal of English and Germanic Philology*
JGO	*Jahrbücher für Geschichte Osteuropas*
JHI	*Journal of the History of Ideas*
JHMAS	*Journal of the History of Medicine and Allied Sciences*
JMH	*Journal of Medieval History*
JÖB	*Jahrbuch der österreichischen Byzantinistik*
JQR	*Jewish Quarterly Review*
JRS	*Journal of Roman Studies*
JTS	*Journal of Theological Studies*
JWCI	*Journal of the Warburg and Courtauld Institutes*
KLNM	*Kulturhistorisk leksikon for nordisk middelalder*
LMA	*Lexikon des Mittelalters*
MA	*Le Moyen Age. Revue d'histoire et de philologie*
MÆ	*Medium Ævum*
M&H	*Medievalia et humanistica*
MD	*Musica Disciplina*
MedIb	*Medieval Iberia: An Encyclopedia*, ed. E. M. Gerli (2003)
MedIsl	*Medieval Islamic Civilization: An Encyclopedia*, ed. J. W. Meri and J. L. Bacharach, 2 vols (2006)
MedScan	*Medieval Scandinavia: An Encyclopedia*
MEFRM	*Mélanges de l'école française de Rome: moyen age, temps modernes*
MGH	*Monumenta Germaniae historica*
MGH.AA	*MGH [Scriptores]. Auctores antiquissimi*
MGH.Const	*MGH [Leges]. Constitutiones et acta publica imperatorum et regum*
MGH.DR	*MGH [Diplomata]. Diplomata regum et imperatorum Germaniae (Die Urkunden der deutschen Könige und Kaiser)*
MGH.ES	*MGH. Epistolae selectae*
MGH.LL	*MGH [Scriptores]. Libelli de lite imperatorum et pontificum saeculis XI. et XII. conscripti*
MGH.PL	*MGH [Antiquitates]. Poetae latini Medii Aevi*
MGH.QG	*MGH. Quellen zur Geistesgeschichte des Mittelalters*
MGH.SRG	*MGH [Scriptores]. Scriptores rerum Germanicarum in usum scholarum*
MGH.SRG.NS	*MGH [Scriptores]. Scriptores rerum Germanicarum in usum scholarum. Nova series.*
MGH.SRM	*MGH [Scriptores]. Scriptores rerum Merovingicarum*
MGH.SS	*MGH [Scriptores]. Scriptores (in folio)*
MIC.S	*Monumenta iuris canonici. Subsidia*
MIÖG	*Mitteilungen des Instituts für Österreichische Geschichtsforschung*
MKHIF	*Mitteilungen des Kunsthistorischen Instituts in Florenz*
MLQ	*Modern Language Quarterly*
MQ	*Musical Quarterly*
MRSFM	*Medioevo: Rivista di Storia della filosofia medievale*
MRTS	Medieval and Renaissance Texts and Studies
MS	*Mediaeval Studies*
MSHP	*Mémoires de la Société de l'histoire de Paris et de l'Ile-de-France*
NBL	*Norsk biografisk leksikon*
NCE	*New Catholic Encyclopedia*
NCMH	*New Cambridge Medieval History*
NDB	*Neue deutsche Biographie*
NGD2	*New Grove Dictionary of Music*, 2nd edn.
NM	*Neuphilologische Mitteilungen*
OCA	*Orientalia christiana analecta*
ODB	*Oxford Dictionary of Byzantium*
ODNB	*Oxford Dictionary of National Biography*
OED	*Oxford English Dictionary*
PaP	*Past and Present, A Journal of Scientific History*

BIBLIOGRAPHICAL ABBREVIATIONS

AASS	*Acta sanctorum*, 3rd edn.
ABR	*American Benedictine Review*
AcM	*Acta musicologica*
ADipl	*Archiv für Diplomatik Schriftgeschichte, Siegel- und Wappenkunde*
AFP	*Archivum fratrum praedicatorum*
AGN	*Algemene Geschiedenis der Nederlanden*
AHAH	*Acta historiae artium Academiae scientiarum Hungaricae*
AHC	*Annuarium historiae conciliorum*
AHDLMA	*Archives d'histoire doctrinale et littéraire du Moyen Age*
AHMA	*Analecta hymnica medii aevi*
AHR	*The American Historical Review*
AKG	*Archiv für Kulturgeschichte*
ALMA	*Archivum latinitatis medii aevi*
AnBol	*Analecta bollandiana*
ANF	*Arkiv för nordisk filologi*
ANOH	*Annaler for nordisk oldkyndighed og historie*
AntJ	*Antiquaries Journal*
APH	*Acta Poloniae historica*
AQDGMA	*Ausgewählte Quellen zur deutschen Geschichte des Mittelalters*
Archiv	*Archiv für das Studium der neueren Sprachen und Literaturen*
ArtB	*Art Bulletin*
ASE	*Anglo-Saxon England*
ASNSP	*Annali della reale Scuola normale superiore di Pisa*
ATS	*Antikvarisk Tidskrift för Sverige*
Aug(L)	*Augustiniana. Tijdschrift voor de studie van Sint Augustinus en de Augustijnenorde*
AUMLA	*Journal of the Australasian Universities Language and Literature Association*
AUU	*Acta universitatis Upsaliensis*
BAACT	*British Archaeological Association Conference Transactions*
BAR	British Archaeological Reports
BAr	*Bulletin archéologique du Comité des travaux historiques et scientifiques*
BECh	*Bibliothèque de l'Ecole des chartes*
BEHE	*Bibliothèque de l'Ecole des hautes études*
BGPTM	*Beiträge zur Geschichte der Philosophie und Theologie des Mittelalters*
BHL	*Bibliotheca hagiographica latina antiquae et mediae aetatis*
BHM	*Bulletin of the History of Medicine*
BIHR	*Bulletin of the Institute of Historical Research* (to 1986, then *HR*)
BISI	*Bollettino dell'Istituto storico italiano per il Medio Evo (e archivio muratoriano)*
BM	*Bulletin monumental*
BMCL	*Bulletin of Medieval Canon Law*
BMGS	*Byzantine and Modern Greek Studies*
BRUO	A. B. Emden, *A Biographical Register of the University of Oxford to* AD *1500*
BZ	*Byzantinische Zeitschrift*
CALMA	*Compendium auctorum latinorum medii aevi*, ed. C. Leonardi and M. Lapidge (2000–).
CAr	*Cahiers archéologiques*
CCCM	*Corpus Christianorum: Continuatio mediaevalis*
CCM	*Cahiers de civilisation médiévale X^e–XIIe siècle*
CCSL	*Corpus Christianorum: Series latina*
CH	*Church History*
ChauR	*Chaucer Review*
CHR	*Catholic Historical Review*
CLLA	*Codices liturgici latini antiquiores*
CM	*Current Musicology*
CPG	*Clavis patrum Graecorum*
DAEM	*Deutsches Archiv für Erforschung des Mittelalters*
DB	*Deutsche Bibliographie*
DBI	*Dizionario biografico degli italiani*
DDC	*Dictionnaire de droit canonique*
DHGE	*Dictionnaire d'histoire et de géographie ecclésiastiques*
DMA	*Dictionary of the Middle Ages*
DoA	*Dictionary of Art*
DOP	*Dumbarton Oaks Papers*
DRMH	*Decreta Regni Mediaevalis Hungariae*
DSB	*Dictionary of Scientific Biography*
EcHR	*Economic History Review*
EHR	*English Historical Review*
EI	*Encyclopedia of Islam*

M. Bellomo, *The Common Legal Past of Europe* (1995).
J. A. Clarence Smith, *Medieval Law Teachers and Writers, Civilian and Canonist* (1975).
H. Lange, *Römisches Recht im Mittelalter* (1997).

accusatorial procedure *See* PROCEDURE, LEGAL.

acheiropoieta [Greek, 'objects not made by [human] hands'] Primarily used of direct impressions of Christ's face (the Kamoulianai Christ, the *Mandylion of *Edessa, the *Veronica of Rome, and the *Shroud of Turin), a category first attested in the 6th century. BWA

H. Belting, *Likeness and Presence*, tr. E. Jephcott (German original, 1990) (1993).
H. L. Kessler and G. Wolf, eds, *The Holy Face and the Paradox of Representation* (1998).

Acht und Bann A link between *Acht* (*outlawry) and *Bann* (*excommunication) was created when *Frederick II barred excommunicates from royal courts (1220) and forbade inhabitants of royal towns (1231/32), then of the entire kingdom (1235), to deal with excommunicates. Excommunicates who did not seek forgiveness within six weeks of sentencing could be formally outlawed by royal courts. FL

E. Klingelhöfer, *Die Reichsgesetze von 1220, 1231/1232 und 1235* (1955).

Ackermann von Böhmen, Der ('The Ploughman from Bohemia'). Written after 1400 in Saaz (Žatec) by *Johannes von Tepl, later an imperial notary in *Prague, this allegorical debate between a widowed ploughman and Death shows influences of the Platonic, Aristotelian, and Roman philosophical traditions, as well as of scholastic and humanistic rhetoric. A product of early modern German humanism in Prague, it is one of the first works of modern German literature, enjoying great popularity in the 15th–16th centuries (sixteen extant MSS, seventeen early prints). JCFr

K. Bertau, ed. and tr., *Johannes von Saaz*, 2 vols (1994).

acolyte *See* MINOR ORDERS.

Acre (Akko) Ancient port on the eastern Mediterranean shore. It was lost by *Byzantium to Chosroes II in 614, briefly regained, and lost to the Arabs in 638. Conquered in 1104 during the First *Crusade, it throve as St Jean d'Acre. Captured by *Saladin in 1187, it was besieged in 1189 by the deposed king of *Jerusalem, *Guy of Lusignan, whose forces were then surrounded by the *Ayyubids. The drawn-out battle became a *cause célèbre* in the Latin West, the object of *Richard I and *Philip II Augustus's Third Crusade. After the garrison capitulated in 1191, Richard massacred several thousand prisoners. The town declined in Latin hands until falling to the Mamluk al-Ashraf in 1219; it came under Ottoman rule in 1516. BAC

D. Jacoby, 'Crusader Acre in the Thirteenth Century: Urban Layout and topography', *Studi Medievali*, 20 (1979), 1–45.
The Travels of Ibn Jubayr, trans. W. Wright (1907).

Acta Sanctorum A major resource for the culture of the European MA and begun by the Societé des *Bollandistes (Jesuit) in *Antwerp and *Brussels in the 17th century, this encyclopedia of the saints is organized according to the feast day of each saint and comprises 68 volumes. The first two volumes for January were published in 1643 and the last for December in 1940. *See also* HAGIOGRAPHY; LITURGY. REB

R. Lechat, 'Les "Acta sanctorum" des Bollandistes,' *CHR* 6 (1920–21), 334–342.
L. Sheppard, 'The Bollandists and their *Acta Sanctorum*,' *ABR* 8 (1957), 219–34.

Adalard, abbot of Corbie (*c.*751–826) The grandson of Charles Martel, he served in the court of Pepin the Short. Around 814 Pepin's advisors suspected Adalard of impropriety with Bernard, Pepin's son, who aspired to the crown. Adalard was banished for seven years. Upon his return, he helped establish the monastery of *Corvey in Westphalia. GP

M. Sot, 'Adalard of Corbie', *Encyclopedia of the Middle Ages*, ed. A. Vauchez *et al.* (2000), vol. 1, 13.

Adalberon of Rheims (*c.*920–89) Becoming archbishop in 969, he soon engaged *Pope Silvester II as personal secretary and school master. His support of *Hugh Capet was crucial to Hugh's election as king in 987. TFH

M. Bur, 'Adalbéron, archevêque de Reims, reconsidéré', *Le Roi de France et son royaume autour de l'an mil*, ed. M. Parisse *et al.* (1992), 55–63.
H. Lattin, tr., *The Letters of Gerbert* (1961).

Adalbero of Laon (*c.*947–1030) Politically active bishop of *Laon (r. 977–1030). Adalbero is notorious for betraying Charles of Lorraine, the last *Carolingian claimant to the throne, whom he turned over to *Hugh Capet, the first *Capetian. He plotted with Otto III against the Capetians in 995 and outlined the theory of the 'three orders' or *'three estates' in his *Carmen ad Rotbertum*. MCF

G. Duby, *The Three Orders: Feudal Society Imagined* (1980).

Adalbert, St, archbishop of Magdeburg (r. 968–81) Bishop, missionary, annalist. Adalbert was the first bishop of Otto I's new foundation of *Magdeburg, which served as a centre for converting the Slavs. Adalbert founded numerous dioceses, including Naumberg, Meißen, and *Merseburg, and wrote a continuation of the *Chronica* of *Regino of Prüm. ASC

D. Claude, *Geschichte des Erzbistums Magdeburg bis in das 12. Jahrhundert* (1972).

Adalbert of Bremen (d. 1072) (archbishop) Adalbert greatly enriched the archbishopric after his appointment in 1043; friendships with Pope Clement II and *Pope Leo IX and influence over young Henry IV marked his high ecclesiastical and political status. ASC

Adam of Bremen. *History of the Archbishops of Hamburg-Bremen*, tr. F. Tschan, new intro. T. Reuter (2002).

Adalbert of Prague (Vojtěch)**, St** (*c.*957–97) After St *Wenceslas, the major patron saint of *Bohemia and the first patron saint of *Poland. In 982 he was elected the second bishop of *Prague; he attempted to reform the Bohemian church but was opposed by the prince and some *clergy. In 988 he left Bohemia for *Italy but returned in 992 at the request of Boleslav II, with whom he co-founded the monastery at *Břevnov near Prague. In 996 he went to Poland and was martyred on an expedition to Prussia. AT

M. Teich, ed., *Bohemia in History* (1998), 39–58.

Adalboldus, bishop of Utrecht (*c.*970–1026; r. 1010–26) A treatise on the three *Boethian types of *musica*, featuring scholastic, *music-theoretical, and *astronomical notions, and two short texts on the division of the *monochord, all previously attributed to him, are now considered *anonymous. GIC

Adalboldi episcopi Ultraiectensis Epistola cum tractatu de musica instrumentali humanaque ac mundana, ed. J. Smits van Waesberghe (1981).

Adam de la Halle (le Bossu) (1240×50–*c.*1288) French poet and dramatist. Adam spent most of his career in *Arras, before joining the Neapolitan court of *Charles I of Anjou, king of *Naples, in the early 1280s. His best-known works are two plays, of which Jean *Bodel's *Jeu de saint Nicolas* is a crucial intertext. The *Jeu de la Feuillée* (*c.*1276) is a satirical revue unique in medieval French theatre. In the pastoral *Jeu de Robin et Marion* (*c.*1281) plots from the poetic genres of *pastourelle* and *bergerie* are acted out. Adam also composed a wide variety of poems and songs. AA

Adam de la Halle, *Œuvres complètes*, ed. P.-Y. Badel (1995).

J. Maillard, *Adam de la Halle: perspective musicale* (1982).

G. D. McGregor and J. H. Logan, *The Broken Pot Restored: Le Jeu de la Feuillée of Adam de la Halle* (1991).

Adam of Bremen Summoned to *Bremen in 1066/7 by Archbishop *Adalbert soon after he and his see had suffered setbacks, Adam was made *scholasticus* and given the task of writing the *Gesta Hammaburgensis ecclesiae pontificum*, a history of the bishoprics of *Hamburg and Bremen, united in 848, up to Adalbert's death (1072), proclaiming their achievements, in particular their successes in the mission to the heathen, which he described as 'the first duty of the church of Hamburg' from its establishment under St *Ansgar. The third and longest book is a remarkable biography of Adalbert describing his rise to power and his fall; the last is a survey of *Scandinavia and beyond, the main area of Adalbert's missionary ambitions. The work was ready by 1075 and dedicated to Adalbert's successor, Liemar, but no copy of that version is known. The many surviving MSS incorporate alterations and additional notes made by Adam until his death soon after 1081, and later by others. Adam's *Gesta* figures prominently in discussions of early Scandinavian history but is a misleading guide because he exaggerated the success of Hamburg-Bremen's missionaries and mistakenly accepted the Danish king Sven Estridsen as a trustworthy source. PHS

Gesta Hammaburgensis ecclesiae pontificum, ed. B. Schmeidler, *MGH.SRG* (1917).

A. K. G. Kristensen, *Studien zur Adam von Bremen Überlieferung* (1975).

N. Lund, *Harald Blåtands død* (1998).

B. Sawyer and P. Sawyer, *Die Welt der Wikinger* (2002), 351–6.

Adam of Fulda (*c.*1445–1505) German composer and theorist. His *De musica* offers important perspectives on 15th-century music, praising *Du Fay and *Binchois while complaining about uneducated *minstrels. His German songs and Latin sacred works were printed in the 16th century. RF

Adam of Fulda, *De musica, Scriptores ecclesiastici de musica sacra potissimum*, ed. M. Gerbert, 3 vols (1784; repr.1963), vol. 3, 139ff.

J. Heidrich, *Die Deutschen Chorbücher aus der Hofkapelle Friedrichs des Weisen* (1993).

Adam of Marsh *See* MARSH, ADAM.

Adam of Orleton, bishop of Hereford, Worcester, and Winchester (*c.*1275–1345) Orleton was a canon lawyer and diplomat favoured and promoted by *Pope John XXII. Although involved in political upheavals, he was a second-rank figure disparaged by a particular chronicler. MAH

R. M. Haines, *The Church and Politics in the Fourteenth Century: The Career of Adam Orleton c.1275–1345* (1978).

Adam of Perseigne (d. 1221) *Cistercian abbot of Perseigne (1188–1221), near Alençon. Adam is best known as a spiritual writer of over 200 *sermons and 35 *letters. He helped preach the Fourth *Crusade and conferred with the mystic *Joachim of Fiore. AJD

J. Bouvet, 'Correspondance d'Adam, Abbé de Perseigne, 1188–1221', *Archives Historiques du Maine*, 13 (1953), 101–60.
L. T. Merton, 'La Formation monastique selon Adam de Perseigne', *Collectanea ordinis Cisterciensium Reformatorum*, 19 (1957), 1–17.

Adam of Petit-Pont (Balsamiensis, Parvipontanus) (1105–*c.*1170), born near *Cambridge, studied in *Paris where *c.*1147 he became a *canon of *Notre-Dame, before returning to England. He authored the *De utensilibus*, a wordbook listing everyday objects, and the *Ars disserendi*, a logic treatise. CJMc

T. Hunt, *Teaching and Learning Latin in 13th-Century England* (1991), vol. 1, 165–76.
C. H. Lohr, 'Medieval Latin Aristotle Commentaries: Authors A-F', *Traditio*, 23 (1967), 323–4.

Adam of St-Victor (d. *c.*1146) The most illusive of well-known Victorines from the 12th century, the *sequence poet Adam was apparently the *cantor of the cathedral of *Notre-Dame in *Paris from 1106, leaving the cathedral for the Abbey St-Victor in 1133, where he died. MEF

M. Fassler, 'Who was Adam of St Victor? The Evidence of the Sequence Manuscripts', *JAMS* 37 (1984), 233–69.
——*Gothic Song: Victorine Sequences and Augustinian Reform in Twelfth-Century Paris* (1993).
J. Grosfillier, *Les Séquences d'Adam de Saint-Victor. Étude littéraire (poétique et rhétorique)* (2008).

Adam Scottus (Adam of Dryburgh) (*c.*1140–1212) Abbot, theologian. He moved from the *Premonstratensian house of Dryburgh to the *Carthusian house in Witham. He wrote sermons and theological texts including *De tripartito tabernaculo* and the *Liber de quadripartito exercitio cellae*. HB

J. Bullock, *Adam of Dryburgh* (1958).
C. Holdsworth, 'Dryburgh, Adam of', *ODNB*, vol. 16, 1016–17.

Addai and Mari, liturgy of *See* MASS.

Adela of Elten (*c.*955–*c.*1021) Her death resulted in a struggle over foundational assets between Adela and her sister, the abbess Luitgard. Trying to secure land for her husband Balderich, she took to violent measures, causing upheaval in the *Lower Lorraine after 1010. HM

T. Fischer, 'Probleme um Adela und Balderich: Zur Geschichte eines niederrheinischen Grafenpaares um 1000', *Mittelalter an Rhein und Maas*, ed. U. Ludwig and T. Schilp (2004), 87–106.

Adela (Adeliza) **of Louvain** (*c.*1103–51) Second wife of *Henry I of England and queen consort from 1121–35. Literary *patron of such works as Philippe de *Thaon's *Bestiaire*. Married William d'Aubigny after Henry's death. WMH

A. Strickland, *Lives of the Queens of England*, 6 vols (1893–99).
L. Wertheimer, 'Adeliza of Louvain and Anglo-Norman Queenship', *HSJ* 7 (1995), 101–15.

Adelard of Bath (*c.*1080–*c.*1150) A pioneer in introducing Arabic *science into the Latin curriculum of the *seven liberal arts. After studying in *France, he spent many years in *Antioch and Sicily before settling in his native city of *Bath. He wrote an exhortation to the study of *philosophy, which he called *De eodem et diverso* ('On the Same and the Different'), and an entertaining dialogue on *Questions concerning Natural History* in which he advocated the use of reason (which he alleges that he had learnt from the Arabs) rather than the reliance on authorities. He made the first complete translation (from Arabic) of Euclid's *Elements*, which became the basis of all the versions of Euclid in the MA. His other translations covered the fields of *astronomy, *astrology, and *magic. His last work was probably an original text on *cosmology and the use of the 'little model of the universe', the astrolabe, which he dedicated to the future *Henry II of England in 1150. CBu

C. Burnett, ed., *Adelard of Bath: An English Scientist and Arabist of the Early Twelfth Century* (1987).
——ed. and tr., *Adelard of Bath: Conversations with his Nephew: On the Same and the Different, Question on Natural Science, and On Birds* (1998).

Adelheid (Adelaide)**, St** (*c.*931–99) Wife of Otto I and empress 951–73. She exercised influence in the German (or [Holy] Roman) empire as wife, mother, and grandmother of consecutive emperors. *See also* ROMAN EMPIRE. TFH

P. Corbet et al., eds, *Adélaïde de Bourgogne: Genèse et representations d'une sainteté impériale* (2002).
S. Gilsdorf, tr., *Queenship and Sanctity: The Lives of Mathilda and the Epitaph of Adelheid* (2004).

Adenulf of Anagni (d. 1289/90) *Canon of *Paris, nephew of *Pope Gregory IX. He wrote *commentaries on Aristotle's *Topics* and on the *Psalms* (edited among the works of *Albertus Magnus), **Quodlibeta*, and **Sermons*. He is the author of one of the most successful treatises on canonical procedure. *See also* LAW, CANON. LL

M. Grabmann, *Mittelalterliches Geistesleben* (1956), vol. 3, 306–22.
L. Ott, 'Die Wissenschaftslehre des Adenulf von Anagni', *Mélanges offerts à Etienne Gilson* (1959), 465–90.

Adhemar of Chabannes (989–1034) Monk, chronicler, composer of liturgical music, and forger. More of his autograph MSS survive than for any other author from the early MA. He is best known for his history of *Aquitaine from the 9th to the early 11th century. This chronicle was begun at St-Cybard in *Angoulême, but after a failed effort to become abbot there Adhemar moved to the monastery of St-Martial of *Limoges. There he undertook to demonstrate that St Martial, the monastery's patron, had been one of the original apostles. Although he did not persuade his contemporaries, and had to leave Limoges in disgrace, the 12th-century monks of the house believed him. Adhemar, who had a classical liberal-arts education and was respected as a *scribe and copyist, also wrote on apocalyptic themes, gave accounts of contemporary *heresies and *Peace of God councils, made drawings with religious themes, and composed a number of musical works, notably a liturgy for St Martial. He died on *pilgrimage to *Jerusalem. CBB

Adhemar of Chabannes, *Chronicon*, ed. P. Bourgain, *CCCM* 129 (1999).

J. Gillingham, 'Ademar of Chabannes and the History of Aquitaine in the Reign of Charles the Bald', *Charles the Bald: Court and Kingdom*, ed. M. Gibson and J. Nelson (1981), 3–14.

R. Landes, *Relics, Apocalypse, and the Deceits of History: Ademar of Chabannes, 989–1034* (1993).

adiastematic *See* MUSICAL NOTATION.

***ad limina* visit** (*visitatio ad limina apostolorum*) A custom as early as 743 that bishops consecrated at *Rome should return for a visit 'to the thresholds of the apostles' every two years, making a donation to the pope. By the 13th century all bishops appointed by papal letter were included, and the offerings were mandatory. DHW

W. E. Lunt, *Papal Revenues in the Middle Ages*, 2 vols (1934), vol. 1, 61–3.

administration, royal A neutral notion of 'state', independent from the person of the ruler, is unknown in the MA. Administrative as well as legislative and judicial power emanated from the right of a ruler (emperor, king, duke, count; pope, bishop) over a certain area, which did not have to be a coherent territory. Within this area, the ruler and his dynasty developed administrative powers to control and exert power, essentially in a twofold way: a *chancery using the growing power of written control over a number of subjects; a demesnial administration aiming at managing the prince's resources and the dues of the subjects. Because of economic growth from the 12th century on, medieval kings were able to enhance the number of local representatives of their power (*bailiffs and receivers) and to replace feudal and hereditary authorities by remunerated office holders, who were replaceable and revocable. A clear correlation between early economic growth and early administrative development has been demonstrated in the cases of, for instance, the duchy of *Normandy and the county of *Flanders (with the former influencing developments in England from 1066 on). The more wealth a ruler possessed, the more efficient was his administration over a socially more and more complex society. In the late MA, the ruler no longer depended exclusively upon his demesnial income but had more or less regular tax incomes (*aides*) at his disposal. A complex system of internal control developed, in which the local and regional layers of administration were controlled by the action of centralized institutions directly responsible to the king or theoretically presided over by him (Parlement of Paris). At a regional level, the dukes and counts imitated royal administrative structures within their own territories, though they submitted ultimately to royal control. On the ideological level, administration was imbued with Roman and canon *law as taught at the *universities and developed the notion of *bien publique*, which justified its action and its development. A post in the royal (or ducal, or whichever) administration often offered a sure way to realize social promotion, since intellectual and social capacities (and not exclusively birth) were required. In the course of the MA, typical, urban-centred *corps d'état* developed with their own rules and behaviour. As a specific professional group and as representatives of the highest authority, they enjoyed judicial and fiscal privileges, investing largely in artistic and intellectual goods and ultimately aiming at achieving noble rank through the prince whose dynasty they served. *See also* CHAMBRE DES COMPTES; ESTATE MANAGEMENT AND ORGANIZATION.

MGRB

P. Contamine, O. Guyotjeannin, and R. Le Jan, *Le Moyen Age. Le roi, l'Église, les grands, le peuple, 481–1514* (2002).

G. Leyte, *Domaine et domanialité publique dans la France médiévale (XIIe–XVe siècles)* (1996).

A. Marchandisse, J.-L. Kupper, eds, *A l'ombre du pouvoir. Les entourages princiers au Moyen Age* (2003).

W. Paravicini, K. F. Werner, eds, *Histoire comparée de l'administration (IVe–XVIIIe siècles)* (1980).

administration, urban The organization of an urban settlement with its complex social relations and its orientation towards secondary and tertiary economic activities necessitated an early administrative development aiming at controlling and securing transactions and agreements between burghers (and between burghers and temporary residents, such as foreign merchants). In Southern Europe and in the kingdom of *Germany, part of these functions were dealt with by *notaries public; in northwestern Europe and *France local office holders and judges, *échevins often linked or coinciding with the local *patriciate, were responsible for offering secure testimony and keeping the records, thus establishing the first nucleus of what were to become the municipal archives. In many respects, this development of using written testimonies to a large extent becomes common after the cultural 12th-century *renaissance. The growth of the early *universities and the even wider spread network of schools where essential techniques of writing, the elaboration of diplomatic documents, and bookkeeping were offered, made possible the training of specialized urban administrators, capable of dealing in the name of the town with the prince's administration (often urban specialists were drained away to princely institutions) and with the church, which in former centuries held the monopoly on the written word. Parallel with this development, cities all over Europe (though in a multitude of scales, directly linked with the number of inhabitants and the participation in a broader urban network) developed a proper financial administration. This responded to a need not only to defend the city, finance the building of walls and gates, but also to invest in infrastructure (port installations, *bridges, town halls, marketplaces, tools to control water) and in the exercise of power, both political (with particular interest in the city's participation in representative institutions and exchange of information within an urban network, such as the German *Hanse) and judicial (the *aldermen, who were also judges, were responsible for maintaining peace within the city and thus needed to organize the living memory of repressive and controlling measures they imposed). A specific sector of the cities' administration embraced the need to secure instruments of social protection, often under direct urban control or mixed control, involving ecclesiastical institutions: *hospitals and social networks aimed at defending specific groups, such as the orphans, whose administration gave way in many cities to specific urban institutions. All these tasks led to a general system of urban taxation and hence the development of administrations charged with collecting taxes (in many cases farmed out to private investors). In Mediterranean Europe, administrations emphasized direct taxation (from the type *catasto*; see Florence in 1427, or *estime*), in north-western Europe, indirect taxes (or excises). As in the field of legislation, fiscal techniques that were developed in cities inspired to a large extent what happened afterwards on the level of the 'State'. *See also* BANKING, FINANCE, AND TAXATION; URBANISM.

MGRB

T. Dutour, *La ville médiévale. Origines et triomphe de l'Europe urbaine* (2003).
D. Nicholas, *The Later Medieval City 1300–1500* (1997).
W. Prevenier, T. De Hemptinne, eds, *La diplomatique urbaine en Europe au Moyen Age* (2000).

Admont (monastery) Oldest surviving *monastery in *Styria, Austria; founded 1074 by Archbishop Gebhard of *Salzburg with an endowment left by Countess Hemma of Friesach and Zeltschach; famed for its *scriptorium. A *convent was established for the education of noble girls.

HSc

A. Beach, 'Admont', monasticmatrix.usc.edu/monasticon/index.php?function=detail&id=2777.
L. Rudolf, *Stift Admont, 1074–1974* (1974).

Adolf I of Altena, archbishop of Cologne (d. 1205) Supporter of the *Guelph faction, especially in the coronation of Otto IV (1198). In order to secure his rights as an imperial prince as well as money, he changed allegiances in 1204 and was excommunicated and deposed by *Pope Innocent III.

HM

W. Janssen, *Das Erzbistum Köln im späten Mittelalter I* (1995).

Adolf of Nassau *See* ROMAN EMPIRE.

Adolf (VIII) **of Schleswig-Holstein** (1401–59) Last Schauenburg ruler of *Schleswig and Holstein; opponent of the kings of Denmark. This duke's death without male heirs ended almost 350 years of rule by the Schauenburgs in Holstein and later Schleswig.

JFP

W. Meyer, ed., *Schauenburger: 350-jährige Herrschaft in Schleswig-Holstein* (1985).

Adolf of Vienna (2nd half of 13th century–after 1315) Poet and scholar; pupil of Ulrich of Vienna, to whom he dedicated his satirical poem 'Doligamus' in 1315. He recommends labour as the only antidote to women's powers of seduction.

MAG

P. Casali, ed., *Doligamus: Gli inganni delle donne* (1997).
E. Habel, 'Der "Doligamus" des Adolfus von Wien', *Studi Medievali*, n.s. 11 (1938), 103–47.

Adolphe de la Marck, bishop of Liège (1313–44) Appointed by the pope rather than being elected by the cathedral chapter, Adolphe opposed the towns of the prince-bishopric and the crafts of Liège in favour of the patricians and promoted his family interests, arousing strong resistance.

DN

J. Lejeune, *Liège et son pays: Naissance d'une patrie (XIIIe–IVe siècles)* (1948).

Adomnán (Adamnan)**, St** (*c.*624–704) Ninth abbot of *Iona. He urged his followers to adopt the Roman dating of *Easter, and promulgated the *Cáin Adomnáin* ('Adomnán's Law'), protecting women, children, and *clergy during warfare. His most famous work is the *Life of St Columba*.

SJM, HZ

Adomnán, *Life of St Columba*, tr. R. Sharpe (1995).
T. O'Louglin, ed., *Adomnán at Birr, AD 697* (2001).

Ado of Vienne (*c.*800–875) Monk at Ferrières, *Prüm, and *Lyons; archbishop of *Vienne by 860. At Lyons he compiled a *martyrology, which he expanded at Vienne. He also wrote a chronicle and several saints' lives. His works reveal limited regard for historical accuracy. JMM

Ado, *Chronicon*, *PL* 123, 23–138.

J. Dubois and G. Renaud, *Le martyrologe d'Adon* (1984).

W. Kremers, *Ado von Vienne, sein Leben und seine Schriften* (1911).

Adoptionism The theological position that Jesus, born human, earned divinity through sinless devotion to God's will and was 'adopted' by the Father at his *baptism reappeared in Spain in the late 8th century under *Elipandus, bishop of *Toledo, and *Felix, bishop of Urgell. Their voices survive only in the polemics of *Alcuin of York. Adoptionism was condemned by *Charlemagne, *Pope Hadrian I, and by several Frankish councils in the 790s. Felix, whose diocese was within Carolingian rule, died under house arrest in *Lyons; but Elipandus, deep in the *caliphate of Córdoba, never recanted. Scholars disagree about whether Adoptionism was a popular movement, and whether it was a response to *Islam. *See also* HERESY: CENTRAL EUROPE; HERESY: WESTERN EUROPE. EAM

A. Cabaniss, 'The Heresiarch Felix', *CHR* 39 (1953), 130–31.

J. C. Cavadini, 'Elipandus and his Critics at the Council of Frankfort', *Das Frankfurter Konzil von 794: Kristillisationspunkt karolingischer Kultur*, ed. R. Berndt (1977), vol. 1, 788–807.

—— *The Last Christology of the West: Adoptionism in Spain and Gaul, 785–820* (1992).

J. B. Russell, *Dissent and Reform in the Early Middle Ages* (1968), 11–14.

Adornes family Merchants in *Genoa since the 12th century; in the 14th–15th, seven members became doge; lost political influence in 1528. Branches became successful in Spain and *Flanders. **Anselm Adorno-Adornes** was prominent in the duke of *Burgundy's circle in *Bruges, writing an account of travel to the Holy Land (1470–71). MGRB

G. Petti Balbi, 'Adorno', *LMA*, vol. 1, 164–5.

Adso of Montier-en-Der (d. 992) *Benedictine abbot and author of *Libellus de Antichristo* (*c*.950), which organizes patristic *exegesis and legendary beliefs concerning the end of the world into a future 'life' of *Antichrist from birth to death. *See also* LITERATURES: APOCALYPTIC. RKE

Adso Dervensis, *De Ortu et Tempore Antichristi*, ed. D. Verhelst, *CCCM* 45 (1976).

Adso of Montier-en-Der, 'Letter on the Origin and Time of Antichrist,' tr. B. McGinn, *Apocalyptic Spirituality* (1979).

adultery and concubinage Concubinage as an exclusive, long-term sexual relationship between two unmarried persons was generally tolerated by the medieval church. Typically, the concubine enjoyed some rights and legal protection as a de facto wife as did her 'natural' children who held greater rights than 'bastards' born of adulterous liaisons. Canonists forbade laymen to keep simultaneously more than one concubine, a wife and a concubine (that is, adultery), or two or more wives (bigamy). WAML

J. A. Brundage, 'Concubinage and Marriage in Medieval Canon Law', *JMH*, 1 (1975), 1–17.

—— *Law, Sex, and Christian Society in Medieval Europe* (1987).

Advent *See* LITURGICAL YEAR.

adventus regis Ceremonial royal arrival in a city or monastery. Having Hellenistic, Roman, and Christian prototypes, the medieval *adventus regis* emphasized the king's Christian liturgical reception. Various *ordines ad regem suscipiendum* describe these ceremonies. JWBe

E. H. Kantorowicz, 'The "King's Advent" and the Enigmatic Panels in the Doors of Santa Sabina', *Art Bulletin*, 26 (1944), 207–31.

M. McCormick, *Eternal Victory* (1986).

advocates *See* LEGAL PROFESSION.

advowson Right of nomination to a benefice. Advowsons are 'presentative' when the *patron of a benefice presents a candidate to the bishop for induction and 'collative' when the bishop institutes a cleric directly in his own right. *See also* CLERGY. WJD

G. Le Bras, *Institutions ecclésiastiques de la Chrétienté medievale* (1964).

E. Mason, 'The Role of the English Parishioner, 1100–1500', *JEH* 26 (1976), 17–29.

Aeddius Stephanus *See* EDDIUS.

Aegidius de Zamora, Johannes (Juan Gil) (*c*.1240–*c*.1316) Spanish *Franciscan. His *Ars musica* (*c*.1270) primarily concerns *plainchant and draws on earlier authorities (*Boethius, *Guido Aretinus, *Bartholomew the Englishman). He also comments on contemporary *musical instrumental practice, particularly the use of the *organ in church. *See also* MUSIC THEORY. CMB

M. Robert-Tissot, ed., *Johannes Aegidius de Zamora 'Ars musica'* (1974).

Aegidius of Murino (*fl.* mid 14th century) Music theorist of the **ars nova* style. His *De motettis componendis* teaches basic principles for composing isorhythmic *motets. No compositions are attributed to Aegidius, but he is praised in two motets. REG

D. Leech-Wilkinson, *Compositional Techniques in the Four-Part Isorhythmic Motets of Philippe de Vitry and his Contemporaries*, 2 vols (1989).

Ælfheah, St, archbishop of Canterbury (954–1012) Bishop of *Winchester (984–1005) and archbishop of *Canterbury (1005–12). Ælfheah was murdered in April 1012 after many months' detention by an invading pagan *Viking army. HCZ

N. Brooks, *The Early History of the Church of Canterbury* (1984).
H. Warton, 'Vita S. Elphegi', *Anglia Sacra*, 2 vols (1691), vol. 2, 122–47.

Ælfric, abbot of Eynsham (Grammaticus) (*c*.955–*c*.1010) Student of *Æthelwold of *Winchester, monk, and mass-priest, Ælfric was the most prominent writer of his time, developing both an expository and a narrative style. He was a second-generation reformer of the *Benedictine revival whose responses to the religious and political issues of his day and his connections to powerful magnates such as *Æthelweard and Æthelmær mark him as a participating intellectual. Though Ælfric had a strong concern for right doctrine and practice, not all his views were shared by his contemporaries. Ælfric chose not to *preach on Holy Thursday, Good Friday, and Holy Saturday, while others did, and he was clearly uncomfortable about doctrines surrounding the Blessed Virgin *Mary despite her popularity. Ælfric's corrections of his own work (as in BL MS Royal C. xii), his worrying over *scribes and their errors, and his tendency to keep revising his own work suggest that he saw himself as a self-conscious author. *See also* WULFSTAN, ST (ARCHBISHOP OF YORK). PES

P. Clemoes, ed., *Aelfric's Catholic Homilies: The First Series* (1997).
M. M. Gatch, *Preaching and Theology in Anglo-Saxon England: Aelfric and Wulfstan* (1977).
H. Gneuss, *Aelfric von Eynsham und seine Zeit* (2003).
M. Godden, ed., *Aelfric's Catholic Homilies: The Second Series* (1979).
—— ed., *Aelfric's Catholic Homilies* (1998).
J. C. Pope, ed., *Homilies of Aelfric: A Supplementary Collection* (1967–68).

Ælfthryth (d. 999/1001) Second wife of King *Edgar I, stepmother to King *Edward 'the Martyr', and mother of *Æthelred II 'the Unready' (r. 978–1013, 1014–16). Because of her ambitions for her son, some suspected her in Edward's murder although modern scholars tend to accept her innocence. She remained influential until her death. *See also* ENGLAND, ANGLO-SAXON. AG

E. B. Fryde, D. E. Greenway, S. Porter, and I. Roy, eds, *Handbook of British Chronology* (1986), 27.

Ælle of the South Saxons King (*c*.477–514) and arguable founder of the dynasty, according to the late 9th-century *Anglo-Saxon Chronicle*. It records a tradition that Ælle and his three sons landed in *Sussex in 477 and engaged in battles at 'Cymenesora' (477), 'Mearcreadesburne' (485), and 'Andredesceaster' (491). *Bede's *Historia ecclesiastica* documents that Ælle was titled *Bretwalda (overlord) of the Saxon kingdoms south of the Humber. *See also* ROMAN EMPIRE. SGw

B. Colgrave and R. A. B. Mynors, eds, *Bede's Ecclesiastical History of the English People* (1969).
J. Earle and C. Plummer, eds, *Two of the Saxon Chronicles Parallel* (1927).

Aelred (Ailred)**, St**, abbot of Rievaulx (1109–67) A priest's son from Hexham, probably educated at the Scottish court. Here he felt guilty about a love affair, the content of which he never makes clear but which may have involved another man. After a visit to the fledgling *Cistercian community of Rievaulx, he was called to the monastic life (1134). Aelred became a central figure at Rievaulx and was elected abbot (1147), remaining thus until his death. He was apparently loved by almost everyone who knew him and in his writings celebrated friendship in the Christian life. BPM

D. Bell, 'Ailred (Ælred, Æthelred) of Rievaulx (1110–1167)', *ODNB* vol. 1, 491–3.
C. Waddell, 'The Hidden Years of Ælred of Rievaulx: the Formation of a Spiritual Master', *Cistercian Studies Q*, 41 (2006), 51–63.

Aeneas of Gaza (5th/6th century) Teacher of *rhetoric. The Christian sophist Aeneas, pupil of the Neoplatonist Hierokles of Alexandria, taught *philosophy and rhetoric at Gaza and left 25 letters addressed to pupils and friends. In his *dialogue *Theophrastus*, the well-known peripatetic philosopher, is convinced by Christian arguments. *See also* NEOPLATONISM. MAG

L. M. Positano, *Epistole* (^{2}1962).
M. Wacht, *Aeneas von Gaza als Apologet: Seine Kosmologie im Verhältnis zum Platonismus* (1969).

aesthetics A branch of *philosophy that appeared during the 18th century in Germany. Aesthetics in the MA refers to contemporary discussions of the nature and perception of beauty.

1. Defining aesthetics
2. Natural beauty
3. Imitation

1. *Defining aesthetics*

This term only partially applies to the theory of particular arts (for example, *rhetoric, *painting), which are largely defined by their utilitarian ends, and still less to the problem of the history of taste, in the sense of implicit qualities of beauty that could be inferred from works of art. (Aesthetics includes the sense of taste but is not the practice of it.) Hence, two preliminary comments offer themselves. On the one hand, no medieval works devoted specifically to aesthetics exist because philosophy was inseparable from theology. Serious reflections on the beautiful are found in relation to Creation, the properties of the Son in the *Trinity, and, in the most varied contexts, in regard to the nature of light or the virtue of temperance. On the other hand, contrary to modern aesthetics born out of German idealism, the medieval conception of beauty places much more emphasis on the beauty of nature (as a divine work) than on the creation of beauty through art. In particular, consideration of the beautiful in representational art is almost non-existent.

2. *Natural beauty*

The principal characteristics of medieval aesthetics have been fairly consistent since St *Augustine and *Boethius. Beauty is defined as that which pleases by its appearance. It is difficult to distinguish from 'the good' because the appearance of good things also gives us pleasure. This is as true for the most profane delights as for God's love, which is neither beautiful nor good, but which is in itself beauty and goodness. Throughout the MA, aesthetic judgements combine or contrast, more or less, supersensitive beauty and the beauty of earthly things, of which the latter can be viewed as a foretaste of heavenly bliss/beatitude or, conversely, as a dangerous temptation that leads to the ruin of the soul. Augustine, Boethius, and later St *Bernard value the immaterial forms of beauty and associate them with interiority. On the other hand, the work of *Pseudo-Dionysius the Areopagite, evidenced in the commentaries of *John Scottus Eriugena and *Hugh of St-Victor, views the beauty of material things as an emanation of the divine. As opposed to a rigourism frequent in the Romanesque period, the great scholars of the 13th century, in particular St *Thomas Aquinas and St *Bonaventure, display a remarkable indulgence toward the pleasures of the senses. Thus, Aquinas justifies the 'companionable delights' of the sexual act, which the beauty and adornment of the woman enhances and renders more delightful.

The two characteristics of beauty that most interested the MA are the symmetry of the parts of an object and the light that emanates from it. Following Cicero, the human body is frequently cited as an example of harmonious arrangement and well-proportioned limbs. Thus, Boethius says, 'the beauty of limbs seems to be a commensurable characteristic'. But well-proportioned parts are also a characteristic of the human soul, made in the Trinitarian image of God. When observing perfect arrangements and proportions in things, the soul experiences a correspondence with its own nature, which stimulates aesthetic pleasure according to the principle that 'like agrees with like'. Cicero adjoins the sweetness of *colour to the proportion of limbs to define the beauty of the body. But, in the Neoplatonic tradition of Dionysius the Areopagite, it is radiance or luminosity more than colour that characterizes beauty. It creates an aesthetic hierarchy of objects, ranging from gold to smoke, and determines the quality of their appearance. According to medieval *optics, the full perception of an object results from, in effect, the internal light or energy of one's soul, the luminosity of the medium (that is to say, of the air), and, finally, the radiance of the object itself. Like the best symmetry, brightness produces a correspondence between the soul and the object.

Proportionality and the diffusion of light are some manifestations of the one in the many. The quantitative study of these phenomena constitutes **musica*, a theoretical discipline in which musical composition and, even more so, vocal and instrumental performance are subordinate. If arithmetic is concerned with the properties of numbers, music concerns the numerical relations between the most sonorous objects as well as their sensory effects. *Musica* starts from the statement, attributed to Pythagoras, that the sounds produced by hammers in which the weights are in the proportions 1/2 (octave), 2/3 (quint or fifth), and 3/4 (quarter or fourth) are consonant, sweet-sounding. This concord is, according to the definition of Boethius, 'the harmony of dissimilar voices brought to unity'. The musical harmony that emerges from a series of consonances can be thought of in objective terms, as an intrinsic aesthetic quality of the sounded object, as well as in subjective terms, such as its effect on the listener. The human soul enjoys the conformity of music to its own internal harmony, but the body is not to be outdone in its taste, for music reflects the balance of *humours, and the listener will prefer music that corresponds best to his temperament.

If beauty is generally thought of in terms of the one within the many, it may be viewed as a tension between polar opposites. The vocabulary of aesthetics gives value as much to *simplicitas* (for example, geometric regularity) as to *varietas*, diversity. Beauty can only be understood in a structured whole. One part or one quality of this mixture is not beautiful in itself, but by its harmonization with the whole. To take some examples found in *scholastic philosophy, red is without doubt more beautiful than black, but it is ugly in an eye, whereas black can be a harmonious ingredient in a painting. It is through this kind of observation that the problem of ugliness is treated. Whatever the optimism during the MA about the beauties of the Creation, it was necessary to admit that certain beings are ugly. The solution to this problem is borrowed from St Augustine: that which we consider evil or ugly has its place in the beauty of the universal order, in order to bring out good or beauty by contrast (*Enchiridion* 10–11).

3. *Imitation*

Creation being a divine work and thus perfect, the arts are supposed to imitate it. This is of course the case of painting and literature, but also of music which imitates cosmic harmony. Imitation is not just the representation of objects by images or words; even the methods of manufacture should draw their inspiration from nature, which teaches them in some fashion. This concept of *imitatio*, however, leads to a frequent devaluation of art, even by St Augustine when he claims that statues are less beautiful than animals (*De diversis quaestionibus*, 78). Above all, this notion eliminates the question of what is *artistic* beauty. The beauty of a work of art comes from the nature it imitates: 'It is necessary to prefer nature to art and art to the absence of art, because art imitates nature. Also, what beauty it [art] has comes from nature, from which it looks to imitate beauty' (Boethius, *In topica Ciceronis*, 6). Sometimes a passage from St Bonaventure with a contrary view has been cited, affirming that an image is said to be beautiful because it is well drawn, but also because it represents its model well, in a way that 'the image of the devil is said to be fair when it represents well the ugliness of the devil and it is therefore also ugly' (*Sentences*, I, d. 31, p. 2, a. 1, q. 3). In fact, this paradox very clearly recalls the issue of the place of ugliness in a harmonious whole.

But the theme of the imitation of nature also allows for the enhanced value of art by comparing the Creator with the *artist and sometimes the artist with the Creator. Bonaventure compares the creation of man to the fabrication of a statue (*De reductione artium ad theologiam*, 12), and the frontispiece of a **Bible moralisée* (Vienna, Österreichische Nationalbibliothek, ms. 2554) shows God creating the world with the aid of a compass. If theologians do not go so far as to compare reciprocally the artist to God, medieval sculptors occasionally suggest this relationship. The sculptor Nicolas put his signature on the creation of Adam on the doors of San Zeno in *Verona. Even better, the sculptor Noël praised himself on the portal of the church of Autry-Issard in the Bourbonnais region for having 'made' in turn the God who created the world and restored it by the Incarnation. 'I, God, made everything. Having been made man, I remade everything. Noël made me' (*Cuncta Deus feci. Homo factus cuncta refeci. Natalis me fecit*). JWi

R. Assunto, *Die Theorie des Schönen im Mittelalter* (1964).
E. De Bruyne, *Etudes d'esthétique médiévale* (1946; 1998).
U. Eco, *Arte e bellezza nell'estetica medievale* (1987).
H. L. Kessler, *Spiritual Seeing: Picturing God's Invisibility in Medieval Art* (2000).
C. Rudolf, *Artistic Change at St Denis* (1990).

aetas Vergiliana, Horatiana,* and *Ovidiana Traube described the 8th and 9th centuries as *aetas Vergiliana*, the 10th and 11th as *aetas Horatiana*, and the 12th and 13th as *aetas Ovidiana*. While useful, the labels underrate the influence of Terence, Silver Latin poets like Lucan and Statius, and Christian poets like Sedulius and Prudentius. Vergil's influence is obvious in the **Waltharius* (possibly before 900) or **Karolus Magnus et Leo Papa*; he inspires *Aldhelm and *Bede with emulation; but 'the poet' is also *Dante's guide. Horace's influence and MSS re-emerge in the later 9th century. His *Epistles* and *Satires* suited the reforming spirit of the 11th century; the lyrics do not yet find favour, although the author of the **Ecbasis captivi* knew them. Ovid's vogue originates in 12th-century scholarship in the Loire valley. Nevertheless, the *Metamorphoses* already influenced Aldhelm, and Ovid's presence remains strong in Latin and vernacular verse long after the epoch Traube stressed. HCOB

C. Baswell, *Virgil in Medieval England* (1995).
J. Dimmick, 'Ovid in the Middle Ages: Authority and Poetry', *Cambridge Companion to Ovid*, ed. P. Hardie (2002), 264–87.
R. Hexter, 'Ovid in the Middle Ages: Exile, Mythographer, and Lover', *Brill's Companion to Ovid*, ed. B. W. Boyd (2002), 413–42.
Lectures médiévales de Virgile (1985).
A. Orchard, *Aldhelm's Poetic Art* (1984).
E. A. Schmidt, *Zeitgenosse Horaz: Der Dichter und seine Leser seit zwei Jahrtausend* (1996).
L. Traube, *Vorlesungen und Abhandlungen: Einleitung in die lateinische Paläographie des Mittelalters*, ed. V. P. Lehmann (1911; repr. 1965), vol. 2, 113.

Æthelbald, king of Mercia (r. 716–57) According to *Bede and other sources, Æthelbald ruled over all the southern English kingdoms by the 730s. Ecclesiastical reaction to Æthelbald was mixed: he did encourage church reform, and the 8th-century *Life of Guthlac* praises him, saying God gave him the throne. But St *Boniface denounced Æthelbald for his treatment of churches and monasteries, including violence against *clergy, and one anonymous visionary places him in *hell. Æthelbald's reign (longest among AS kings) ended with his murder by his bodyguard. *See also* ANGLO-SAXON CHURCH; ANGLO-SAXONS; ENGLAND, ANGLO-SAXON. AMBr

J. Campbell, ed., *The Anglo-Saxons* (1982).
D. P. Kirby, *The Earliest English Kings* (2000).

Æthelbert, king of Kent (r. *c*.560–616) Identified by *Bede as one of the seven overlords (or *Bretwaldas) who ruled the unified AS kingdoms. Converted by St *Augustine of Canterbury after 597, Æthelbert was also the first Christian AS; his law code, written between 597–616 and the oldest piece of writing in OE, reflects his new faith as it outlines penalties for crimes against the church. Though his immediate successors reverted to *paganism, Æthelbert gave Christianity legitimacy in AS *England. AMBr

P. H. Blair, *An Introduction to Anglo-Saxon England* ([2]1995).
J. Campbell, ed., *The Anglo-Saxons* (1982).
D. P. Kirby, *The Earliest English Kings* (2000).

Æthelflæd ('Lady of the Mercians') (d. 918) Daughter of *Alfred the Great and wife of Æthelred of *Mercia, Æthelflæd exercised exceptional power in the first two decades of the 10th century. The *Anglo-Saxon Chronicle*, in its B, C, and D versions, recount her strategic plans to build and rebuild Tamworth and Stafford, her struggle at Derby, and her successes in Wales. Called 'lady of the Mercians', and never queen, Æthelflæd could not pass her power on to her daughter Ælfwynn. PES

P. E. Szarmach, 'Æthelflaed of Mercia *mise en page*', *Words and Works: Studies in Medieval Language and Literature in honour of Fred C. Robinson*, ed. P. S. Baker and N. Howe (1998), 105–26.

Æthelfryth *See* NORTHUMBRIA.

Æthelred *See* ÆTHELFLAED.

Æthelred II ('the Unready') (r. 978–1016) King of the English, called *unræd* ('redeless or without counsel'). Yet he maintained control of the throne for 38 years in a disastrous period marked by internal strife and Scandinavian incursions, including the English defeat under *Byrhtnoth at the battle of *Maldon (991) and the subsequent institutionalization of *danegeld. Within this generalized insecurity there were nevertheless some positive indicators of administrative stability and efficiency. Concurrently, the *Benedictine revival led to a golden age of AS prose. *See also* LITERATURES: ENGLISH—OE PROSE. RSR

C. R. Hart, *Chronicles of the Reign of Ethelred the Unready: An Edition and Translation* (2006).

S. Keynes, *The Diplomas of King Aethelred the Unready, 978–1016* (1980; repr. 2005).

A. Williams, *Aethelred the Unready: The Ill-Counseled King* (2003).

Æthelstan (893/4–939) King of the Anglo-Saxons (924/5–27), king of the English (927–939), son of *Edward 'the Elder', and grandson of *Alfred the Great. Most famously commemorated in the OE poem 'The Battle of *Brunanburh' in which his army defeats the combined forces of the Scots, Picts, and Norse, Æthelstan is regarded now and was regarded in his own time as the king of all England as reflected in charters and coins, the latter of which declare him 'king of the whole of Britain'. He achieved great success in international diplomatic affairs, at least four of his half-sisters marrying into noble families on the continent, and he was an important book and relic collector. The major source of information for his life and reign is *William of Malmesbury's *Gesta regum Anglorum*. REB

D. Dumville, *Wessex and England from Alfred to Edgar* (1992), 141–71.

S. Foot, 'Æthelstan (Athelstan) (893/4–939)' *ODNB* vol. 1, 420–28.

Tomb of Æthelstan, king of the English, at the monastery at Malmesbury.

Æthelweard (*fl.* later 10th century) AS author, probably *ealdorman of the western provinces. He composed a Latin chronicle up to 975, based mainly on a lost version of the *Anglo-Saxon Chronicle* but with independent information, especially for the period 893 to 946. DAEP

A. Campbell, ed., *The Chronicle of Æthelweard* (1962).

W. Jezierski, 'Æthelweardus Redivivus', *EME* 13 (2005), 159–78.

Æthelwold, St, bishop of Winchester (904×9–84) A key figure in the Benedictine reform movement in 10th-century England, Æthelwold was one of the most prominent scholars of his day. Among his most important scholarly works are his **Regularis Concordia* and his English translation of the Rule of St *Benedict. REB

M. Gretsch, *The Intellectual Foundations of the English Benedictine Reform* (1998).

B. Yorke, 'Æthelwold (St Æthelwold, Ethelwold) (904×9–984)' *ODNB* vol. 1, 434–8.

Aethicus Ister (7th/8th century?) Pseudonymous author of a cosmography-cum-travelogue entitled *Cosmographia*, allegedly edited by *Jerome. The work describes 'Aethicus'' *periplous* through the barbarian world, recording his observations and 'Jerome's' censures. The latinity is continental, but traces of Insular literary culture are marked. MWH

M. Herren, 'The "Cosmography" of Aethicus Ister: Speculations about its Date, Provenance, and Audience', *Nova de veteribus: mittel- und neulateinische Studien für Paul Gerhard Schmidt*, ed. A. Bihrer *et al.* (2004), 79–102.

O. Prinz, ed., *Die Kosmographie des Aethicus* (1993).

Afonso I Henriques, king of Portugal (*c.*1109–8 December 1185) First acknowledged king of Portugal. Son of Teresa (daughter of *Alfonso VI, king of *Castile-León) and Count

Henri (cousin of Raymond of *Burgundy), he became count of Portugal upon Teresa's death in 1128. He proclaimed himself king of Portugal in 1140. Like his mother, Afonso Henriques resisted the claims of the kingdom of Castile-León to Portuguese sovereignty. He refused to recognize the imperial coronation of his first cousin, *Alfonso VII, as emperor of all Spain in 1135, and he sought the independence of the Portuguese church from the Castilian ecclesiastical hierarchy. Alfonso VII denied his cousin's claim to a Portuguese throne until the Treaty of Zamora in 1143. Finally, in 1179, *Pope Alexander III formally recognized Afonso Henriques as monarch. Afonso Henriques fought many campaigns against the Muslims, conquering *Lisbon in 1147 (with the aid of crusaders en route for the Second Crusade) and defending Santarém in 1184. TMV

Alexander Herculano de Carvalho e Araujo, *História de Portugal: Desde o começo da monarchia até o fim do reinado de Afonso III*, 4 vols (1980–1983).

B. W. Diffie, *Prelude to Empire: Portugal Overseas before Henry the Navigator* (1960).

F. A. Dutre, 'Portugal: to 1279' *DMA*, vol. 10, 39–42.

Afonso II, king of Portugal (r. 1211–1223) Leprous, overweight, militarily undistinguished, Afonso II had a short reign beset by his brothers' pretensions to the throne, invasion by *León, the complicated struggle with his sisters concerning their father Sancho I's testament, and jurisdictional disputes with Archbishop Estêvão of *Braga, because of which Afonso died *excommunicate. But bolstered by Roman and canon *law, supported by a small group of faithful nobles and exceptional jurist clerics (Julião Pais, Gonçalo Mendes, Julião of Coimbra, Paio of Oporto, Vicente of *Lisbon, Silvestre Godinho, Lanfranco), his rule saw the creation of perhaps the most centralized royal government in Europe. Afonso's court of 1211 affirmed the universality of the judicial and legislative power of monarchy. The year 1212 saw the first initiatives to establish a notariate to give legal form to contracts and guarantee their authenticity. The diplomas issued by the royal chancery were systematically registered from 1217. The *inquiriçoes* (investigations) of 1220 saw royal rights and revenues registered through much of Afonso's land. *See also* CHANCERY; KINGSHIP, QUEENSHIP, AND MONARCHY. DJSm

J. Mattoso, *Identificação de um país. Ensaio sobre as origens de Portugal 1096–1325* (1995).

A. D. de Sousa Costa, *Mestre Silvestre e mestre Vicente, juristas da contenda entre Afonso II e suas irmãs* (1957).

Afonso III, king of Portugal (1210–79; r. 1248–79) Second son of *Afonso II and *Urraca, daughter of Alfonso VIII of *Castile. The prince spent his youth in *France at the court of his aunt, Queen Blanche, and married *Matilda, widow of Count Philip of Boulogne. In 1245, *Pope Innocent IV, heeding the *clergy's complaints, ordered Sancho II's subjects to obey his brother, Afonso. Afonso returned to Portugal and was crowned in 1248, after the defeat and death of Sancho II. In 1249, he drove the Muslims from the *Algarve. The Treaty of Badajoz (1267) settled disputes with Castile over the conquered territories, after Afonso's marriage (1253) to Beatriz, illegitimate daughter of *Alfonso X of Castile, and the birth (1261) of *Dinis. Townspeople first participated in parliament (**cortes*) at Leiria (1254), and they supported the king when his later inquests into aristocratic and clerical estates and privileges sparked conflicts. These led to the king's *excommunication and the imposition of a papal *interdict by 1277. JPD

L. Krus, 'Escrita e poder: as Inquirições de Afonso III', *Estudios Medievais* 1 (1981), 59–79.

A. H. R. de Oliveira Marques and J. J. Alves Dias, 'Itinerários de D. Alfonso III (1245–1279)', *Arquivos do Centro Cultural Português* 15 (1980), 453–519.

Afonso IV, king of Portugal (1291–1357; r. 1325–57) Only son of *Dinis I and Isabel, daughter of Pedro III of *Aragon. In 1309, he married Beatriz, daughter of Sancho IV of *Castile. He rebelled against his father because of Dinis's favours toward his illegitimate sons. After he became king, Queen Isabel settled his conflict with his half-brother, Afonso Sanches (d. 1329). The mistreatment of Afonso's daughter, Maria, by her husband, Alfonso XI of Castile, provoked

Afonso IV of Portugal, probably early 19th-century.

dynastic conflict, exacerbated by the marriage of Afonso's son, Pedro, to Constanza, daughter of Infante *Juan Manuel, cousin and rival of Alfonso XI. Faced with the invasion of the Moroccan *Marinids, the kings made peace and defeated the Muslims at *Salado in 1340. With social and economic legislation, Afonso grappled with the effects of the *Black Death. In 1355, the king's reputed involvement in the murder of Prince Pedro's lover, Inés de Castro, a Galician noblewoman, led to the prince's rebellion. They reconciled before the king's death in 1357. JPD

A. H. R. de Oliveira Marques, *Chancelarias portuguesas: D. Afonso IV*, 3 vols (1990–92).

——M. T. Campos Rodrigues, and N. J. Pizarro Pinto Dias, eds, *Cortes Portuguesas: Reinado de D. Afonso IV (1325–1357)* (1982).

Agde, Council of (506) Sponsored by Alaric II, who hoped to gain the support of his Catholic Gallo-Roman subjects, Agde was intended to be the first 'national' Visigothic council. *Caesarius of Arles was the presiding metropolitan bishop. JJA

K. Schäferdiek, *Die Kirche in den Reichen der Westgoten und Suewen bis zur Errichtung der westgotischen katholischen Staatskirche* (1967).

age-related medical care In his *Aphorisms* (1.2), a major source of medical learning, *Hippocrates urged the practitioner to take into account the patient's age as a crucial variable. Different ages were susceptible to different ailments, from the aphthae of babies to the hearing loss of old men (3.24–31). Moreover, life proceeded by distinct seasons, in analogy with the meteorological year (3.18). A fourfold periodicity suited the schemes of the *humours and primary qualities. Thus, like spring, childhood was a moist stage between cold/phlegmatic and warm/sanguine; youth, like summer, was hot and between moist/sanguine and dry/choleric; and so on.

A second foundation of age-related medicine was the teaching, primarily of *Galen, that life proceeded as a finite interaction between heat and moisture. Maintaining this process was the objective of dietetics and *hygiene, particularly in *regimens of health. Proper care of the non-*naturals, such as nutrition and *exercise, promoted progress from the potential 'drowning' of infancy. Excess, on the contrary, such as gluttony (*see* SEVEN DEADLY SINS) or sexual passion, prematurely caused the drying-out of old age. The patient's age was decisive in individualized guidelines, or **consilia*. General *regimina* and *therapeutic compendia addressed the middle-aged male, for example, as revealed by the emphasis on wine and preoccupation with gout and stone; health concerns of women between menarche and menopause were left to *gynaecology.

The most sustained discussions of specific ages foreshadowed the development, respectively, of paediatric and geriatric medicine. The first and last years of life also proved increasingly relevant to *public health, in the establishment of certain institutions. Special municipal and voluntary *hospitals gave shelter—and, when needed, medical assistance—to children and the old. Shelters for infants took in destitute foundlings and orphans, whereas homes for the elderly might be almshouses for the poor or residences for prosperous pensioners. LED

J. Agrimi and Ch. Crisciani, *Les 'Consilia' médicaux* (1994).

A. R. Colón and P. A. Colón, *Nurturing Children: A History of Pediatrics* (1999), ch. 4.

L. Demaitre, 'The Care and Extension of Old Age in Medieval Medicine', *Aging and the Aged in Medieval Europe*, ed. M. M. Sheehan (1990), 3–22.

Aghlabid dynasty (800–909) In 800, the Abbasid caliph Harun al-Rashid granted **Ibrahim ibn al-Aghlab**, governor of Zab, a gift: he could rule *Ifriqiyah* (Tunisia and eastern Algeria) autonomously on condition of annual tribute. The Aghlabid realm with *Kairouan as its capital, was, however, beset with revolutions and civil strife, including from the theologians, from the beginning to its end in 909, but it also managed to capture Byzantine Sicily.

The Aghlabids were famous for their waterworks, which improved agriculture in their domains. They were also enthusiastic builders. Under **Abu Iqal al-Aghlab** (837–40) a mosque was built at Susa; later on **Abu al-Abbas Muhammad** endowed a mosque that still exists. According to *Ibn Khaldun, **Abu Ibrahim** himself built 'ten thousand forts, constructed of stone and mortar and furnished with iron gates'.

Under the Aghlabids, Kairouan became a meeting point of east and west. Whilst they did not evolve a local interpretation of Islamic law, the scholars followed one of the eastern schools of thought, but eclectically, Kairouan became the leading centre of the Malikite school. The foremost Maliki scholars of the age, such as Asad ibn Furat (d. 828), Sahnun (d. 854), Abu Zakariyyah Yahya ibn Umar al-Kinani (d. 901), Isa ibn Miskin (d. 907), and Abu Uthman al-Haddad (d. 914) flourished in this time. Kairouan was also a hotbed of philosophical argument among Sunnis, Murjiia, and the Jabriyyah, which sometimes even turned violent. The scholars followed the orthodoxy of the east, but under the Mutazili Ahmed ibn Aghlab, they also had to undergo a type of *mihna* (inquisition). Although orthodoxy settled in quickly thereafter, Mutazili influence was not quick to be eradicated, and towards the end of the dynasty a Mutazili scholar was appointed as a judge.

The dynasty ended when the Fatimids converted the Kutama *Berbers to Shiism, getting them to accept al-Mahdi Ubaidullah as the promised messiah. The last, **Abu Mudar**

Image of the battle of Agincourt.

Ziyadat Allah, fled Kairouan for *Cairo in 909, dying in *Jerusalem. *See also* CALIPHATE, ABBASID; CALIPHATE, FATIMID. MD

J. D. Wyrtzen, 'Aghlabids', *MedIsl* vol. 1, 19–20.

Agilbert, St (*c*.625–90) Frankish priest, later bishop of *Dorchester in *Wessex. The ranking church official at the Synod of *Whitby, he invited St *Wilfrid to speak for him. Afterwards, Agilbert returned to Gaul where he was installed as bishop of *Paris, a see he retained until death. MMS

M. Deanesly, *The Pre-Conquest Church in England* (1963).
I. Macdonald, *Saints of Northumbria* (1997).

Agincourt (Azincourt) A small village in the Pas-de-Calais which on 25 October 1415 was the site of the greatest English victory of the *Hundred Years War. The French army cornered an exhausted raiding force led by King Henry V, but was provoked into taking the offensive, thereby sacrificing the advantages of superior numbers and terrain. Perhaps 5,000 Frenchmen were killed and many leading nobles were captured. The victory paved the way for a full-scale English invasion two years later. CDT

A. Curry, ed., *Battle of Agincourt: Sources and Interpretations* (2000).
—— ed., *Agincourt, 1415* (2000).

Agius of Corvey (d. after 876) Monk; composed didactic *Versus computistici* for ecclesiastical and royal patrons. His *Vita Hathumodae* and *Epicedium Hathumodae*, memorializing *Gandersheim's first abbess, are especially noteworthy. JJC

F. Brunhölzl, *Histoire de la littérature latine du Moyen Age*, vol. 1/2 (1991), 140–43, 198.
J. J. Contreni, 'Counting, Calendars, and Cosmology', *Word, Image, Number: Communication in the Middle Ages*, ed. idem and S. Casciani (2002), 75.

Agnellus of Ravenna Iatrosophist and author, according to MS Milan, Ambr. G. 108 inf., of lectures on three introductory Galenic treatises (*De sectis*, *Ars medica*, *De pulsibus ad tirones*). Because of the colophon in the MS, he is supposed to have taught in *Ravenna at an epoch situated between 550 (the rise of the possible medical school of Ravenna) and AD 751 (the end of the Byzantine exarchate). The circulation of the texts might prove wider than generally assumed. ATo

Agnellus of Ravenna, 'Lectures on Galen's *De sectis*' (1981).
E. Glaze, 'Master-Student Medical Dialogues: the Evidence of London, British Library, Sloane 2839', *Form and Content of Instruction in Anglo-Saxon England in the Light of Contemporary Manuscript Evidence*, ed. P. Lendinara et al. (2007), 467–94.
N. Palmieri, *Agnellus de Ravenne. Lectures galéniques: le De pulsibus ad tirones* (2005).

Agnes of Prague (1211–82) Early *Franciscan woman who joined Clare of Assisi in following Francis' ideal of poverty. The youngest daughter of King Přemysl Otakar I of *Bohemia and Queen Constance of *Hungary, Agnes possessed the political clout to bargain with the *papacy, paving the way for the approval of a Franciscan Rule for women, that is, the *Rule of St Clare*.

Rejecting a series of marriage offers, including one from Emperor Frederick II, Agnes followed the example of her cousin Elizabeth of Hungary and founded a monastery for sisters and a hospital for the poor and sick in *Prague. Using her royal dowry for these projects, she left the monastery without a landed endowment according to Franciscan practice, but heavily endowed the hospital.

Nervous about the precariousness of Agnes's monastery, *Pope Gregory IX forcibly endowed it with the resources bequeathed to the hospital. Agnes resisted appealing to Clare of Assisi for instruction and, with the help of her brother, King Wenceslas I, persuaded Gregory to reverse his decision. Faithful to her *Privilege of Poverty* until the end, Agnes, exhausted by *famine, died on 2 March 1282. Pope John Paul II canonized her on 12 November 1989, just days before the Velvet Revolution. JLM

A. Marini, *Agnese di Boemia* (1991).
J. Mueller, *Clare's Letters to Agnes: Texts and Sources* (2000).
—— 'Agnes of Prague and the Juridical Implications of the Privilege of Poverty', *FranS* 58 (2000), 261–87.
J. Polc, *Agnes von Böhmen 1211–1282: Königstochter—Äbtissin—Heilige* (1989).

Agnus Dei *See* MASS.

Agobard of Lyons (769–840; r. 816–40) (archbishop) Born in Spain, Agobard, a politically and intellectually active prelate, spent 835–8 in exile in *Italy. His writings treat theology, *liturgy, pastoral concerns, heresy, superstitions, church politics, and his perception of growing Jewish influence in Christian society. JJC

E. Boshof, *Erzbischof Agobard von Lyon: Leben und Werk* (1969).
F. Brunhölzl, *Histoire de la littérature latine du Moyen Age*, vol. 1/2 (1991), 166–77.

Agricola, Alexander (1445/6–1506) Netherlandish composer. His *chansons* are in ornate melodic style. His *masses rework borrowed contemporary melodic material, while his *motets, Magnificats, and Lamentations are based on *plainsong. RF

A. Agricola, *Opera Omnia*, ed. E. R. Lerner, 5 vols (1961–70).
A. W. Atlas, *Alexander Agricola at the Aragonese Court of Naples* (1985).
R. C. Wegman, 'Agricola, Bordon and Obrecht at Ghent', *RbM* 51 (1997), 23–62.

agricultural technology Broadly defined, agricultural technology involves the production, processing, and marketing of a constellation of edible and non-edible commodities produced on farms. These commodities ranged from the most basic foodstuffs, such as *grain and meat products, to those, such as *wool and *flax, that formed the basis for substantial *textiles and *clothing industries. Over the past 100 years of scholarship, however, views concerning the development of medieval agricultural technology and its nature have ranged from seeing such technology move at a glacially slow pace to one where the word 'revolution' has seemed much more appropriate.

1. Food production
2. Tools and land use
3. Crops
4. Food processing, food variety, and elite consumerism
5. Markets and transport

1. Food production

Curiously, in the current state of knowledge, one of these striking technological clusters does *not* seem to have involved improving *food production in a straightforward calorific sense, long thought to provide a basic ceiling for population growth in medieval societies. The most recent and comprehensive studies of medieval agriculture, particularly that of Bruce Campbell for England, has shown that medieval agriculture had much more flexibility in meeting demands for its products, and that the reason why medieval agricultural production sometimes seems anaemic to modern-day observers was *not* because of a deficient technology for the needs of the time but because of insufficient demand; David Stone's work on decision-making by manorial officials and its strong market orientation related to prevailing grain and livestock prices points in the same direction. Medieval agricultural technology was always robust enough in normal circumstances to satisfy its fundamental role of keeping humans alive and healthy. Only in times of exceptionally unfortunate circumstances, such as in the dreadful weather from 1315–17, would the technological and productive foundation of agriculture break down to the point that real suffering would occur on a widespread scale.

2. Tools and land use

This is not to say that significant technological adjustments improving agricultural production in this straightforward calorific sense did not occur during the period. Woodland clearance (*see* FORESTS AND WOODLANDS) and the draining of marshes markedly increased the extent of cropland, certainly up to about 1300, some of this dependent upon technological improvements to *tools, such as more effective axes, adzes, and bill-hooks. The slow development of the *plough from a simple scratch (ard) type to one capable of turning a more substantial furrow—the mouldboard plough—was evident in the period from about 900–1200 and was accompanied more generally by the increased use of *iron in tools, from ploughshares through to hand-tools like hoes, mattocks, scythes, and sickles. This may have been intimately connected with the development of various *field systems, particularly the large, open field divided into long strips shared out amongst the various families in the community, a pattern particularly evident for many areas across northern Europe. How effective this was in raising agricultural productivity is debatable, however, since strip farming in particular seems to have been a strategy to spread risk evenly throughout the community rather than to improve production. In a similar fashion, oft-mentioned changes to the motive power of ploughs, especially in relation to the introduction of horses to cultivation from no later than the 12th century, may well have been done from the point of view of reducing costs rather than increasing overall crop production on a per-acre or per-worker basis. Certainly, the introduction of horses to ploughing was scarcely all-encompassing, varying considerably from region to region and indeed from class to class (*peasants seem to have used horses more for ploughing than did lords, for example).

3. Crops

If there were a key development in the production of food in a basic calorific sense, it was probably in the development and stabilization of hardier and more versatile crop regimes. Out of earlier strains of *grains like spelt and millet, a quadripartite cereal regime of wheat, rye, barley, and oats developed over much of northwest Europe by AD 1000 to cater for *bread, drink, and animal fodder. The most important addition to these four were legumes—peas, beans, and vetches—which were known from before the millennium, but only reached significant proportions from the 13th century onwards, mainly as a fodder crop for *animals but also for their fertilizing properties. After the *Black Death, which saw a shift from arable to pastoral regimes in many regions, legume-growing grew even more popular, in effect providing that first surge towards fodder crops that would feature so prominently in the later Agricultural Revolution (as recently surveyed in magisterial fashion by Ambrosoli). In the Islamic world, hard wheat was probably introduced from *Abyssinia by at least the 11th century as an important addition to basic foodstuffs, which most famously would eventually form the basis for the pasta so well-known around the Mediterranean, probably from around the 13th century. Of equal importance for the North African and Middle Eastern world over the medieval period was the introduction of sorghum (for dishes such as couscous) from sub-Saharan Africa and rice from *India and China. Both crops were in a sense complementary, sorghum being suited to semi-arid areas from the Middle East through North Africa to Spain, while rice became a significant crop addition to the river systems of the Middle East and the Nile.

The combined effect of these improvements, often very incremental and regionally oriented, may have seen crop yields peaking sometime during the 13th century, as argued by Georges Duby in particular. Certainly, after that, yields per unit of land, as calculated, for instance, by Campbell and Overton in a very careful study for eastern England, seem to have remained steady until the 18th century. As a result, the scholarly enthusiasm for a medieval agricultural 'revolution', promoted so vigorously by Duby, White, and Gimpel, has been considerably muted of late, to the extent that, in a technological sense, the issue of food production on the farm (that is, supplying the basic calories for society) may have been secondary to other technologically driven factors that impinged upon agriculture from other directions.

4. Food processing, food variety, and elite consumerism

So what were these other directions? One area was in the processing of foods. The impressive application of water power to grain grinding over the early MA has long been known, and was followed by the even more spectacular (in terms of the speed of dissemination) exploitation of wind power, where tens of thousands of *windmills were built across Europe in the space of little more than a hundred years from the late 12th to the late 13th century. The importance of demand is paradoxically revealed in this dissemination of water and wind power by what it did not do, or was very slow in doing—that is, in turning such new power sources to other activities. Thus, despite the great emphasis often placed by the scholarly literature upon the application of water power for industrial uses during the MA, such as for *fulling cloth, crushing oak bark for tannin (for the *leather trades), sawing *wood, forging, or smelting *iron, and so forth, this activity was decidedly anaemic in contrast to the capital and labour devoted to *mills for grinding grain. The almost obsessive focus of water and wind power for processing grains shows the strength of the demand for this particular aspect of food production, suggesting that—until at least 1300, when milling capacity for grains at last reached surfeit—it was a particular bottleneck for the provision of usable nutrients for human bodies.

Another area very responsive to technological change—or the geographical spread of new food products—was in increasing the variety of foodstuffs to titillate human palates (rather than simply satisfying calorific shortfalls), a phenomenon having some connection to the importation of *spices from the east. This was particularly evident in the Islamic world, where the dissemination of many different *fruit and vegetable types from the east, recorded in detail by Watson, transformed the culinary world of the Mediterranean in particular. Thus, from the 10th century, various citrus fruits, including oranges, lemons, and limes, made their way through the Islamic world to the European west, as did watermelons. Eggplant (aubergine) and spinach—as vegetable alternatives—made their way along the same route to Spain in the 10th and 11th centuries. Perhaps most crucially for future dietary patterns across the world was the transmission of *sugar cane, also gradually making its way east to west from India until it reached Spain by at least the 12th century. There was less of this variety in foodstuffs further north, where growing conditions were not suitable for some of the exotic plant species grown in Islamic territories, but one of the more famous developments in northern climes was the development of hopped *beers, which first reached significant levels of production in *Germany during the 13th century and expanded first through the *Low Countries and into England over the 14th and 15th centuries, before becoming established as a mature industry in the 16th century, in the process affecting the drinking patterns over a great swathe of northern Europe from Russia to the British Isles.

This concern for variety stretched to non-edible agricultural products. For example, the desire for higher quality cloth drove the search for better fibres, as in the case of wool reached by the development of the merino breed of sheep in Spain, so fundamentally important for the development of the Flemish 'new draperies' in the 15th century (*see* STOCK BREEDING AND SELECTION). The pinnacle in terms of clothing was found in the development of *silk production, a very specialized form of 'agriculture', known in *Italy and the Byzantine world from the 12th century. As Hunt and Murray have argued, it was these consumer preference issues, often established by elites (especially for such things as spices and silks), that principally drove the technologies for business practice, from double-entry bookkeeping (*see* ACCOUNTING AND BOOKKEEPING) to up-to-date shipping technology.

5. Markets and transport

But the most critical area attracting arguably the most diverse and potent cluster of technological developments affecting agriculture in the MA was in the area of marketing and transport. *Markets and *fairs sprang up across much of the medieval world in the 12th and 13th centuries, and in many ways developed a technology to match. This was felt both on land and on water. Land *transport for much of Europe and northern Africa was transformed over the period 1000–1300, especially by the overwhelming emergence of horse-drawn transport, a feature replicated by the development of camel transport in North Africa and the Middle East. Except for areas where terrain, particularly hilly areas with heavy soils, still required the slow, but more tenacious, oxen, horse-hauled carts—and sometimes perhaps wagons—tended to dominate across most of western Europe in particular, a trend reinforced by the use of horses (and sometimes mules or donkeys) as pack-animals. These changes required concomitant adjustments to the transport infrastructure as a whole. This was felt not so much in the matter of *roads, which, except for occasional stretches of paving in and around cities, still tended to be earthen, but the system as a whole was considerably improved and extended in the number of *bridges and causeways that arose around this much more horse-oriented transport.

Of equal importance were developments in water transport, both for maritime and inland water transport. Often extremely subtle adjustments, very technical in nature, were made to accommodate various commercial and economic interests impinging on water routes. Thus, on the Thames river in England, at least upstream to the inland port of Henley upon Thames, a barge called a 'shout', seemingly of Dutch design originally, was introduced sometime around the 13th century. To accommodate these and other shallow-drafted types of boats, mill-weirs on this stretch of the Thames were seemingly each equipped with a 'flash' and a winch. The flash consisted of removable pieces of board, which allowed a temporary flow of water over the top of the weir, which a boat such as the shout could 'shoot' if going downstream, or, if going upstream, could be hauled over the flow of water going through the open flash by means of a winch and cable. In such a fashion, seemingly conflicting demands upon water systems represented by mills and water transporters could be reconciled. Similarly, on the high seas, a host of important technological adjustments, involving new ship designs and navigational techniques, including the *compass, in effect transformed the ability to move agricultural products economically over distances as extensive as from the North or *Baltic seas to the *Levant.

In short, examining the technological base of agriculture from the perspective of the farm alone can give an incomplete picture of agriculture and its important technological elements in the MA. Rather it is better situated within the larger medieval *'commercial revolution', as Spufford labelled the marked economic expansion in Europe during the 13th century in particular. Technologies affecting agriculture were most strongly felt in allowing farmers to participate in this commercial revolution, that is, by having their produce processed and transported efficiently to markets, local and beyond. It was this commercial revolution, largely involving agriculture, that would bring the western 'Old World' back into a sort of equality with China and would provide the springboard for future European expansion in the post-medieval period. *See also* DEMOGRAPHY AND POPULATION; FURNACES AND FORGES; METEOROLOGY; PASTORALISM AND TRANSHUMANCE; WATERWORKS. JL

M. Ambrosoli, *The Wild and the Sown: Botany and Agriculture in Western Europe, 1350–1850*, tr. M. McCann Salvatorelli (Italian original, 1992) (1997).

G. Astill and J. Langdon, eds, *Medieval Farming and Technology: The Impact of Agricultural Change in Northwest Europe* (1997).

B. M. S. Campbell, *English Seigniorial Agriculture, 1250–1450* (2000).

—— and M. Overton, 'A New Perspective on Medieval and Early Modern Agriculture: Six Centuries of Norfolk Farming, *c*.1250–*c*.1850', *PaP* 141 (1993), 38–105.

G. Duby, *Rural Economy and Country Life in the Medieval West* (1968).
P. Fowler, *Farming in the First Millennium AD: British Agriculture between Julius Caesar and William the Conqueror* (2002).
J. Gimpel, *The Medieval Machine* (1977).
D. Harrison, *The Bridges of Medieval England: Transport and Society, 400–1800* (2004).
E. S. Hunt and J. M. Murray, *A History of Business in Medieval Europe 1200–1550* (1999).
J. Langdon, *Horses, Oxen, and Technological Innovation: The Use of Draught Animals in English Farming from 1066 to 1500* (1986).
J. Munro, 'Spanish *Merino* Wools and the *Nouvelles Draperies*: An Industrial Transformation in the Late Medieval Low Countries', *EcHR* 58 (2005), 431–84.
R. B. Peberdy, 'Navigation on the River Thames between London and Oxford in the Late Middle Ages: A Reconsideration', *Oxoniensia*, 61 (1996), 311–40.
M. M. Postan, ed., *The Cambridge Economic History of Europe*, vol. 1, *The Agrarian Life of the Middle Ages* ([2]1966).
N. J. G. Pounds, *An Economic History of Medieval Europe* ([2]1994).
P. Spufford, *Money and its Use in Medieval Europe* (1988).
D. Stone, *Decision-Making in Medieval Agriculture* (2005).
R. Unger, *Beer in the Middle Ages and the Renaissance* (2004).
A. M. Watson, *Agricultural Innovation in the Early Islamic World* (1983).
L. White, Jr, *Medieval Technology and Social Change* (1962).

agricultural treatises Medieval Europe inherited ancient Latin agricultural writings, most importantly by Cato the Elder, Varro, Columella, and Palladius. Medieval writers sometimes used ancient writings but also wrote from their own experience.

The earliest Arabic work on agriculture, the *Filaha al Nabatiyya* (*Nabataean Agriculture*) by Ibn Wahshiyya, was either written in Arabic or translated from Nabataean around the end of the 8th century. Medieval treatises included many by Egyptian authors, treating kinds of land, manure, irrigation and water supply, *tools, tasks of cultivation, *fruit trees, vegetables, *grains, legumes, and other crops. Further west, on the Iberian Peninsula, a rich tradition of Arabic agricultural writing included a treatise on agronomy by Ibn Wafid (d. 1075) and another by Muhammad b. Ibrahim Ibn Bassal (d. 1105), both of which were translated into Castilian.

Treatises in England from the 13th century were tied to 'high farming', the direct management of demesne agriculture by lords. Robert *Grosseteste, bishop of Lincoln, compiled the *Rules* for the countess of *Lincoln between 1240 and 1242. The anonymous *Seneschaucy* treated the duties of the various officers of an *estate. Walter of *Henley, who may have had experience as a *bailiff, wrote the *Husbandry* *c.*1276–90. These and other tracts emphasized close supervision, hands-on control, and careful *accounting practices to maximize profits on the demesne.

In *Italy, a jurist, Pietro de' Crescenzi, wrote an important agronomical treatise, *Opus ruralium commodorum* (*c.*1304–09). A learned compendium in twelve books, it focused on the management of the villa. Crescenzi was concerned to adopt farming practices to specific local conditions and frequently compared the teachings of authorities with actual experience. *See also* GEOPONICA; WATERWORKS. POL

M. Ambrosoli, *The Wild and the Sown: Botany and Agriculture in Western Europe, 1350–1850*, tr. M. McCann Salvatorelli (Italian original, 1992) (1997).
L. Bolens, *Agronomes andalous du Moyen-Âge* (1981).
G. E. Fussell, *The Classical Tradition in Western European Farming* (1972).
D. Oschinsky, *Walter of Henley and Other Treatises on Estate Management and Accounting* (1971).
M. al-Shihabi *et al.*, '*Filāha*, agriculture,' *EI* ([2]1965), 899–910.
P. Toubert, 'Crescenzi, Pietro de' (Pier, Petrus de Crescentiis),' *DBI*, 30: 649–57.
F. Toufic, 'L'agriculture nabatéenne et les Geoponica', *De Kêmi à Birit Nari*, 1 (2003), 77–94.

Ágrip af Nóregskonungasǫgum Anonymous synoptic history of the kings of Norway from the death of Hálfdan the Black *c.*880 to the accession of Ingi the Hunchback *c.*1136 and originally perhaps to the accession of Sverrir Sigurðarson in 1177. This *kings' saga was probably written in Norway in the 1190s, but the MS is Icelandic and dates from the first half of the 13th century. REB

T. M. Andersson, 'Kings' Sagas (*Konungasögur*)', *Old Norse-Icelandic Literature: A Critical Guide*, ed. C. J. Clover and J. Lindow (2005), 197–238.
M. Driscoll, ed., *Ágrip af Nóregskonungasögum* (1995).

Ahimaaz, Scroll of (*Megillat Yuhasin*) A Hebrew family chronicle in rhymed prose written by Ahimaaz ben Paltiel (1017–*c.*60) in southern *Italy. The narrative text covers the 9th and 10th centuries when the author's forebears were leaders of their communities and well-known poets. EHo

B. Klar, *Megillat Ahimaaz: Hu megillat yuhasin le-Rabbi Ahimaaz birabbi Paltiel* (1944).
M. Salzman, *The Chronicle of Ahimaaz* (1924).

Ahl al-Kitab [Arabic, 'People of the Book'] *Quranic term for Jews and Christians recognizing them as fellow believers and stressing that God had given them the Bible. Islamic law required a *poll tax and prohibited bearing arms, riding horses, and building places of worship, in exchange for protection, freedom of worship, and the right to govern intra-communal affairs. DJSt

J. D. MacAuliffe, *Qur'anic Christians: An Analysis of Classical and Modern Exegesis* (1991).

Ahmad ibn Tulun (835–84) Civil servant, assigned as lieutenant to the governor of *Egypt, he took over the fiscal administration, built a private slave army, and occupied Syria (882), being thereafter Egypt's de facto ruler, though

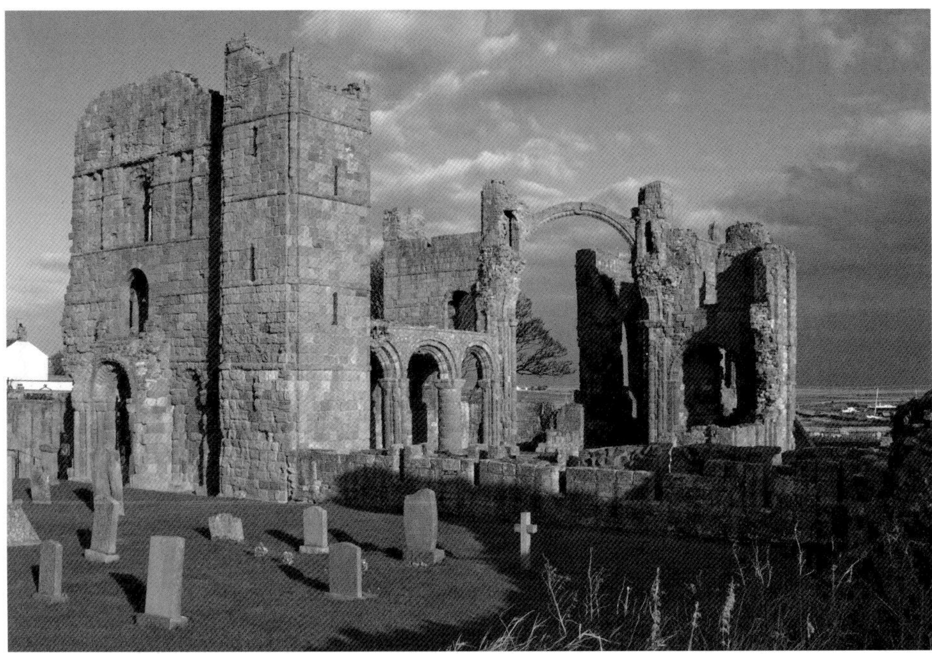

Lindisfarne, founded by Aidan.

perhaps continuing formally to acknowledge the caliph. He was succeeded by two sons before Abbasid rule was re-established in 905. The mosque he founded in *Cairo still stands. BAC

T. Bianquis, 'Autonomous Egypt from Ibn Tūlūn to Kāfūr, 868–969', *Cambridge History of Egypt*, ed. C. Petry, vol. 1 (1998), 86–119.
S. Sears, 'Ibn Tulun', *MedIsl*, vol. 1, 373–4.

Aidan of Lindisfarne, St (d. 651) Irish missionary and monk-bishop from *Iona to the *Northumbrians. *Bede wrote admiringly of his life and humility while disapproving of his Irish tradition for the dating of *Easter. Brought to England by King *Oswald, his interpreter to the people, Aidan gave to a beggar the royal steed received from Oswald's successor, Oswine. GHB

Bede, *Ecclesiastical History of the English People*, ed. B. Colgrave and R. A. B. Mynors (1969), vol. 3/3, 5, 14–17, 26.

Aigues-Mortes *Louis IX of *France chose this fishing village in the marshes of the Rhône delta in 1240 to be the port of departure for his *crusades, since the southern French coastline to the east and west was under the rule of the king of *Aragon and the German emperor respectively. Aigues-Mortes lost its importance as a port city when the French crown expanded its southern holdings, but its fort continued to be used as a prison throughout the MA. EFJ

Histoire d'Aigues-mortes (1894).
W. Jordan, *Louis IX and the Challenge of the Crusade: A Study in Rulership* (1979).

Ailly, Pierre d' (Petrus de Alliaco) (d. 1420) Doctor of theology, cardinal, church reformer. As chancellor of the University of *Paris and chaplain of King *Charles VI, he went to *Avignon to heal the Great *Schism, denying bishops jurisdiction from God and asserting the supremacy of the general council, itself not infallible but which alone receives its power directly from Christ. His rejection of papal infallibility, promoted in works like his *Tractatus super reformatione ecclesiae*, was influential in the Reformation. His less original *De imagine mundi* stated that the Indies were reachable by sailing west: a copy was annotated by Columbus before he set sail. *See also* PISA, COUNCIL OF. RSR

B. Guénée, *Between Church and State: The Lives of Four French Prelates in the Late Middle Ages*, tr. A. Goldhammer (French original, 1987) (1991), 102–258.
L. B. Pascoe, *Church and Reform: Bishops, Theologians, and Canon Lawyers in the Thought of Pierre d'Ailly (1351–1420)* (2005).
L. A. Smoller, *History, Prophecy, and the Stars: The Christian Astrology of Pierre d'Ailly (1350–1420)* (1994).

Ailred *See* AELRED.

Aimo *See* HAIMO OF AUXERRE.

Aimoin of Fleury (*c*.965–d. after 1008) Historian, hagiographer; monk at *Fleury (980/85), pupil of *Abbo. His writings include the *Historia Francorum* and the historically detailed *Vita Abbonis*. TC

Aimoin of Fleury, *Vita Abbonis, L'Abbaye de Fleury en l'an mil*, vol. 1, ed. R.-H. Bautier and G. Labory (2004).

Aerial view of Aigues-Mortes.

——*Historia Francorum, Recueil des historiens des Gaules et de la France*, ed. M. Bouquet (1869–1904; repr. 1967–8), vol. 3, 21–143.
R. Love, 'Aimoin of Fleury', *CALMA*, vol. 1, 90–91.

Aimoin of St-Germain-des-Prés (d. 889) Monk and hagiographer. Aimoin entered the *Benedictine monastery of *St-Germain-des-Prés before 845; from 872 he was responsible for the house's archive and *scriptorium. His writings deal with *relic translations and attendant miracles. JWr

Historia translationis S. Vincenti, PL, vol. 126, 1011–28.
A. Christys, 'St-Germain-des-Prés, St Vincent and the Martyrs of Cordoba', *EME* 7 (1998), 199–216.

Aisha (Aishah) (614–78) *Muhammad's favourite wife; daughter of *Abu Bakr, opponent of *Ali at the Battle of the Camel (656). Sources portray Aisha as loving, pious, eloquent, and knowledgeable. KL

N. Abbott, *Aishah the Beloved of Muhammad* (1942).
D. A. Spellberg, *Politics, Gender and the Islamic Past* (1994).

Aix-en-Provence This Roman resort town became a regional capital of Gaul in the late empire. Originally under the ecclesiastical control of *Arles, it became an archbishopric in the 8th century, and in the 9th became the capital of the county of Provence. The patronage of the local counts made it a renowned centre of arts and learning. Its *university, known for its law school, was founded in 1409. With the death of René the Good in 1480, Aix passed to *France, and became the seat of the Parlement of Provence. EFJ

M. Bernos, N. Coulet, C. Dolan-Leclerc, and P. A. Février, *Histoire d'Aix-en-Provence* (1977).

Akathistos hymn (*c.*6th century) Anonymous **kontakion*, originally for the *Annunciation; still sung on Sundays and a Saturday in Great Lent. Its form consists of two prooimia and twenty-four oikoi (stanzas). The earliest notated music dates from the 13th century. DTM

L. M. Peltomaa, *The Image of the Virgin Mary in the Akathistos Hymn* (2001).
E. Wellesz, ed., *The Akathistos Hymn* (1957).

Akhtal, al- (Ghiyath ibn Harith) (d. 710) Christian Arab poet, known as al-Akhtal. He impressed the Umayyad Abd al-Malik and became his court poet, using panegyrics to laud the Umayyad princes and defend them in political intrigues. His competitor, al-Jarir, was a Muslim, and the two would lampoon each other, as Jarir tried to uphold Islamic tradition whilst al-Akhtal favoured 'pagan' *Bedouin themes. MD

S. Stetkevych, *The Poetics of Islamic Legitimacy: Myth, Gender, and Ceremony in the Classical Arabic Ode* (2002).

Akolouthia *See* LITURGICAL BOOKS, GREEK.

Alamut Mountain stronghold of the Nizari Ismaili sect ('Assassins') in the Elburz Mountains in *Iran. Built in the 9th century, Alamut was conquered by the Nizaris in 1090; they remained there until the *Mongol invasions in the 1250s. At *c.*2000 metres high, Alamut was a formidable centre of resistance against the orthodox *Seljuk state in the 12th century. CPM

M. Hodgson, *The Secret Order of the Assassins* (repr. 2005).

al-Andalus Arabic name given to the geographical area of the Iberian Peninsula that came under Muslim control in the MA, from 711 to 1492. This period is often referred to as a cultural golden age of Islam. Traces of the encounter between Muslims and Christians can still be found today in Spain, especially in the architecture of the southern region of *Andalusia.

Scholars have long debated the extent of the Arab influence on modern Spanish culture. Americo Castro affirmed that Spanish culture is greatly indebted to the Muslim and Jewish traditions of al-Andalus, while Claudio Sánchez-Albornoz denied it. Following their leads, many scholars today interpret the legacy of al-Andalus in widely diverging terms. What is undeniable, however, is that the peculiar socio-religious situation of the Iberian Peninsula during the MA is unique in western European history.

Before the Muslims arrived, the Iberian Peninsula was governed by the *Visigoths, whose rulers were constantly engaged in internal disputes and warfare. In 711 a faction of disgruntled Visigoths enlisted the help of the Muslims to overthrow their rival, King Rodrigo. Thus Arab and *Berber armies, under the leadership of *Tarik, crossed the Strait of Gibraltar, defeated Rodrigo, and proceeded to conquer the rest of the Visigothic lands. Although their advance towards the north was brought to a halt by the Frankish ruler Charles Martel in 732, the Muslims still managed to subdue the entire Iberian Peninsula in three years.

Initially, al-Andalus functioned as a Muslim colonial settlement ruled by a governor who was chosen by the Umayyad caliph in *Damascus. Around 750, however, the Umayyad dynasty was deposed by the rival family, the Abbasids, and the last Umayyad prince, Abd al-Rahman, fled from Damascus to Spain, where he united all factions and managed to carve out an independent and sovereign state, the emirate of *Córdoba. He ruled from 756 to 788. One of his descendants, Abd al-Rahman III, elevated the emirate to the category of *caliphate by proclaiming himself caliph in 929.

At the height of Umayyad rule, the Islamic realm in Spain achieved an unprecedented level of prosperity and refinement. Under Abd al-Rahman III, *Córdoba, capital of al-Andalus, was the most brilliant city in Europe. The arts and sciences flourished, particularly philosophy. Eminent scholars such as *Averroës and *Maimonides produced their influential works during this period. New literary genres such as the *muwashshah* were created and cultivated by Muslims as well as Jews. Great advances in agricultural exploitation were accomplished also in this period. Jews and Christians, although reduced to the status of *dhimmi* (non-Muslims 'protected' under Muslim law), seem to have benefited as well from the prosperity and the general climate of tolerance which prevailed in al-Andalus.

After a long period of internal strife (*fitnah*) between 1009 and 1031 and a succession of puppet caliphs, the caliphate collapsed and al-Andalus became fragmented into a number of weak smaller kingdoms (**taifa*), ruled by various 'party kings'. In addition, the Christian armies were beginning to be more effective in combating their Muslim enemies and were increasingly threatening the *taifa* kingdoms' fragile borders. Thus the 'party kings' sought help from their North African allies, the *Almoravids, and later, in 1171–73, the more fanatical *Almohads. The consequence of these interventions was the end of the independence of al-Andalus.

By the time of the Almohads' invasion the three major Christian powers in the Peninsula—*Castile, *Aragon, and Portugal—had become very strong, and they forged an alliance that succeeded in eventually destroying the Almohads at the battle of Las *Navas de Tolosa in 1212. During the next forty years the Christian rulers recovered nearly all of the territory of al-Andalus: Córdoba was won in 1236, *Valencia in 1238, and *Seville in 1248. Consequently, by the 13th century al-Andalus consisted only of the city of *Granada, ruled by the Nasrid dynasty. But in 1492 this city fell and surrendered to the *Catholic Monarchs, Queen Isabella of Castile and King Ferdinand of Aragon. Eventually, all Muslims who did not convert were expelled from Spain and al-Andalus ceased to exist, except in the imagination of nostalgic Arab poets and contemporary scholars who wishfully like to think of al-Andalus as a place and time where Muslims, Christians, and Jews coexisted in peace. MPi

A. Castro, *España en su historia* (1948).

P. Chevedden, D. Kagay, P. Padilla, and L. Simon, eds, *Medieval Spain and the Western Mediterranean: Essays in Honor of Robert I. Burns, S.J.* (1995–6).

R. Collins, *The Arab Conquest of Spain, 710–797* (1989).

T. Glick, *Islamic and Christian Spain in the Early Middle Ages* (1979).
L. P. Harvey, *Islamic Spain, 1250 to 1500* (1990).
S. K. Jayyusi, ed., *The Legacy of Muslim Spain* (1992).
M. Marín, J. Samso, and M. I. Fierro, eds, *The Formation of Al-Andalus: History and Society* (1998).
M. R. Menocal, *The Ornament of the World: How Muslims, Jews and Christians Created a Culture of Tolerance in Medieval Spain* (2002).
M. D. Meyerson and E. D. English, eds, *Christians, Muslims and Jews in Medieval and Early Modern Spain* (2000).
C. Sánchez-Albornoz, *España, un enigma histórico* (1956).

Alan of Lille (1128–1203) Poet and theologian who came to be known as the *Doctor universalis* because of the range of his learning. There is little reliable information about his life, but he was probably born in *Lille, may have studied in *Paris, lived in southwestern *France, and entered the *Cistercian order late in life. He wrote important works against the *Cathars and a number of theological works. His collection of verse maxims, *Parabolae*, was a popular educational work, and his *commentary on human *vice, *De planctu Naturae*, and the *epic poem and allegory on creation, the *Anticlaudianus*, enjoyed a wide readership throughout the MA. MCF

Alan of Lille, Anticlaudianus, or the Good and Perfect Man, tr. J. J. Sheridan (1973).
——*Plaint of Nature*, tr. J. J. Sheridan (1980).
G. Evans, *Alan of Lille: The Frontiers of Theology in the Later Twelfth Century* (1983).

Alanus, Johannes (d. 1373) English composer of the *motet *Sub arturo plebs*, and possibly of four songs attributed to 'Magister Alanus', and two sacred works attributed to 'Aleyn'. PML

R. Bowers, 'Fixed Points in the Chronology of English Fourteenth Century Polyphony', *Music and Letters*, 71 (1990), 313–35.
D. Fallows, 'Alanus, Johannes', *NGD2* 1/276.

Alarcos, battle of (19 July 1195) The last great victory of the Muslims in Spain. By the Christian fortress of Alarcos on the Guadiana, the *Almohad forces of al-*Mansur crushingly defeated the army of Alfonso VIII of *Castile. *See also* RECONQUISTA. DJSm

Actas de Alarcos 1195. Congreso Internacional Conmemorativo de VII centenario de la batalla de Alarcos, ed. R. Izquierdo (1996).
A. Huici, *Las grandes batallas de la Reconquista* (1956).

alb *See* LITURGICAL VESTMENTS.

alba (aube) Song in which the coming dawn (Old Occitan *alba*) causes the separation of two lovers. From such early specimens as *Giraut de Borneil's 'Reis glorios', the genre lived on as the OF *aube* and the German *Tagelied*. JDH

P. Bec, *La lyrique française au moyen âge (XIIe–XIIIe siècles)* (1977–8).
M. de Riquer, ed., *Las albas provenzales* (1944).

Albania Medieval name for the territory of the modern republic of Albania. Inhabited by a presumed autochthonous Albanian population, this region was nominally subjected to the Byzantine Empire until the 12th century, when Norman attacks and internal crises in *Byzantium permitted the rise of local chieftains. At the end of the 13th century, the area was occupied by the *Angevins of *Naples who named it the 'Kingdom of Albania'. The interest struggle between the Byzantines and the Angevins in the 14th century prompted the rise of powerful local kindreds such as the Arianiti, *Thopia, *Musachi, and Spata. From 1392, coastal urban centres were subjected to Venetian authority, while the hinterland eventually fell under the power of the Castrioti kindred, gradually giving way to the Ottomans (sançak-i Arvanid). Following the resistance led by *Skanderbeg, the fall of Shkodër in 1479 marked the completion of the Ottoman conquest of the region. NZ

A. Ducellier, *La façade maritime de l'Albanie au moyen âge: Durazzo et Valona du XIe au XVe siècle* (1981).
——*L'Albanie entre Byzance et Venise, X^e–XVe siècles* (1987).
C. Gaspares, *The Mediaeval Albanians* (1998).
A. Gegaj, *L'Albanie et l'invasion turque au XVe siècle* (1937).
O. J. Schmitt, *Das Venezianische Albanien (1392–1479)* (2001).
G. Stadtmüller, *Forschungen zur Albanischen Frühgeschichte* (²1966).
L. Thallóczy, *Illyrisch-albanische Forschungen*, 2 vols (1916).

Albarus, Paulus *See* PAULUS ALBARUS.

Albergati, Niccolò (1357–1443) *Cardinal and bishop of *Bologna who attended the councils of *Basel and *Ferrara. *Pope Martin V and *Pope Eugenius IV employed him on important diplomatic missions to *France and northern *Italy. A learned man, he wrote theological and other treatises. FB

G. Cantagalli, *Il beato Nicolo Albergati* (1928).
P. De Toth, *Il beato cardinale Nicolo Albergati e i suoi tempi, 1375–1444* (1934).

Alberic (Elberich) Dwarf of Germanic mythology and literary heroic tradition. In the *Nibelungenlied* he is the guardian of the Nibelungs' hoard. In the *Dietrichepen* he fashioned Dietrich of Bern's sword. In the *Ortnit* and **Wolfdietrich* the dwarf-king Elberich is Ortnit's father, who assists Ortnit on his *bridal quest and bequeaths to him (and later Wolfdietrich) the sword Rose. CB

R. Simek, *Lexikon der germanischen Mythologie* (³2006).

Alberic of Aix-la-Chapelle (Albert of Aachen) (*fl.* 1100–1150) Canon, author of the *Historia Ierosolimitana*, an important source for the history of the popular *crusade. In twelve books it recounts the First Crusade and the history of the kingdom of *Jerusalem (1099–1119). Alberic relied on eyewitnesses and written sources rather than his own experience. TC

S. B. Edgington, *Albert of Aachen: Historia Ierosolimitana, History of the Journey to Jerusalem* (2007).

Alberic of Monte Cassino (*c.*1030–after 1105), monk and deacon; composed a dictaminal manual, *hagiography, a grammatical treatise, *homilies, and (probably) a polemic against *Berengar of Tours. CJMc

C. H. Lohr, 'Medieval Latin Aristotle Commentaries: Authors A-F', *Traditio*, 23 (1967), 338.
C. M. Radding and F. Newton, *Theology, Rhetoric, and Politics in the Eucharistic Controversy, 1078–1079* (2003).
L. Rockinger, ed., *Briefsteller und Formelbücher des elften bis vierzehnten Jahrhunderts* (1863), 3–46.

Alberic of Paris (*fl.* mid 12th century) One of the leading teachers of *logic in *Paris in the 1130s and 1140s. Later, he visited *Bologna and returned with different views. He was a relentless critic of many of *Abelard's theories, and he produced a particularly powerful argument against his system of propositional logic. No surviving texts can be reliably attributed to him, but his ideas are quoted very frequently in logical *commentaries of the 1140s and 1150s. JMar

C. J. Martin, 'Embarrassing Arguments and Surprising Conclusions in the Development of Theories of the Conditional in the Twelfth Century', *Gilbert de Poitiers et ses contemporains*, ed. J. Jolivet and A. De Libera (1987), 377–400.
L. M. de Rijk, 'Some New Evidence on Twelfth-Century Logic', *Vivarium*, 4 (1966), 1–57.

Albero of Trier (d. 1152) Appointed archbishop of *Trier in 1131 and papal *legate to *Germany in 1137, Albero ardently supported papal reform and the new reform orders. Politically, he engineered Conrad III's election as king in 1138 and strengthened his archbishopric's territorial power against secular princes. JWBe

Georg Waitz, ed., *Gesta Alberonis archiepiscopi auctore Balderico*, *MGH.SS*, 8 (1848), 243–60.

Albert II of Magdeburg (1170–1232) (archbishop) Educated at *Magdeburg, Albert then studied in *Paris and *Bologna before returning to the city as prior, being elected archbishop in 1205. Albert was active in Hohenstaufen politics and served as papal *legate in *Germany from 1212. He also founded the new Gothic cathedral in Magdeburg. ASC

H. Silberborth, *Erzbishof Albrecht II. von Magdeburg von seiner Erwählung bis zum Tode Ottos IV* (1910).

Albert III Achilles *See* BRANDENBURG, MARGRAVATE OF.

Albertano of Brescia (*c.*1200–*c.*1270) Judge, notary, scholar. Countering Italian cities' factionalism, Albertano sought solutions in personal moral development and civic cooperation. He was among the first to look to ancient Rome for ethical and institutional guidance. AHo

J. Powell, *The Pursuit of Happiness in the Early Thirteenth Century* (1992).
R. Witt, 'Medieval *Ars Dictaminis* and the Beginnings of Humanism: A New Construction of the Problem', *Renaissance Quarterly*, 35 (1982), 1–35.

Alberti, Leon Battista (1404–72) Major *humanist and scholar of the 15th century from an exiled Florentine family. Alberti wrote important treatises on *painting, *sculpture, and *architecture, and on mathematical and literary topics. He was the first to explain in writing the new Florentine artist's *perspective and was also an architect who designed buildings, such as *Sant'Andrea* in *Mantua. POL

L. B. Alberti, *L'architettura (De re aedificatoria)*, ed. and tr. G. Orlandi; intro. and notes P. Portoghesi, 2 vols (1966).
—— *Opere volgari*, ed. C. Grayson (1973).
—— *'On Painting' and 'On Sculpture': The Latin Texts of 'De pictura' and 'De statua'*, ed. and tr. C. Grayson (1972).
J. Gadol, *Leon Battista Alberti: Universal Man of the Early Renaissance* (1969).
A. Grafton, *Leon Battista Alberti: Master Builder of the Italian Renaissance* (2000).
R. Tavernor, *On Alberti and the Art of Building* (1998).

Albertists Followers of *Albertus Magnus, mentor of *Thomas Aquinas. Albert had been particularly receptive to *Aristotelianism, though he was also influenced by *Neoplatonism. He insisted on the importance of *philosophy to theology, and believed human reason can distinguish between natural truth and divine revelation.

The term originated with a group of *schoolmen at the University of *Cologne during the 15th and 16th centuries, participants in *debates between the philosophies of *realism and *nominalism. The former group was divided into two camps—the Thomists and the Albertists. By 1425, the two factions began being defined in opposition to each other.

The movement began in *Paris under the auspices of Jean de Maisonneuve but quickly spread to other *universities at *Leuven, *Heidelberg, *Basel, *Prague, *Padua, Copenhagen, *Tübingen, *Cracow, *Uppsala, and Ingolstadt among others. The most prominent Albertist was Flemish-born Heymeric van de Velde (or Heinrich von Kampen, d. 1460).

Albertists were moderate realists, well grounded in natural philosophy and *rhetoric, and preferred deductive reasoning over inductive, as *logic is speculative, not practical. Adherents further believed in 'cosmic sympathy', the idea that God's life permeates the whole universe, and a hierarchal approach to salvation, wherein individuals achieved states according to levels of perfection.

Though the Albertists never gained the dominance enjoyed by the Thomists, their numbers were strong among the German Dominican-influenced mystics, including Meister *Eckhart, *Henry Suso, Jan van *Ruysbroeck, and Johannes *Tauler. Other influential Albertists include *Nicholas of Cusa and Wessel Gansfort (d. 1489). *See also* THOMISM. MMS

J. A. Weisheipl, ed., *Albertus Magnus and the Sciences: Commemorative Essays* (1980).
H. Wilms, *Albert the Great, Saint and Doctor of the Church* (1933).

Albert of Aachen *See* ALBERIC OF AIX-LA-CHAPELLE.

Albert of Bavaria (1336–1404) Duke of Bayern-Straubing, regent for his brother Count William V (1358–89) and count (1389–1404) of *Holland, *Hainaut, and *Zeeland. Albert reversed his dynasty's preference for Hainaut, establishing his residence in The *Hague, where his court became a cultural centre. After 1392 discords re-erupted between the Hook and Cod factions. Albert campaigned against *Guelders and invaded *Frisia. His son William of Ostrevant dominated the Dutch government during Albert's last years. DN

H. P. H. Jansen, *Middeleeuwse Geschiedenis der Nederlanden* (1971).
M. Vandermaesen, 'Het graafschap Henegouwen 1280–1384', *AGN* 2: 441–51.
F. P. van Oostrom, *Court and Culture: Dutch Literature, 1350–1450* (1992).

Albert of Habsburg *See* ROMAN EMPIRE.

Albert of Jerusalem (*c*.1150–1214) *Canon Regular of Mortara, bishop of Bobbio (1184), of Vercelli (1185–1205), and *Patriarch of *Jerusalem (1205–14). He legislated for the canons of Biella and in 1201 for the *Humiliati. As patriarch, he gave a *formula vitae* to the Carmelite *hermits. KJA

L. Mingetti, 'Alberto vescovo di Vercelli (1185–1205): contributo per una biografia', *Aevum*, 59 (1985), 267–304.
V. Mosca, *Alberto patriarca di Gerusalemme, tempo–vita–opera* (1996).

Albert of Metz (**Alpertus Mettensis**) (d. after 1021/4) Monk in *Metz and later in the bishopric of *Utrecht. He wrote a biography of Theoderic of Metz, a chronicle of the lower *Rhine region known as *De diversitate temporum*, and possibly the *Miracula Waldburgae*. RMe

H. van Rij, tr., *Alpertus van Metz: Gebeurtenissen van deze tijd; Een fragment over bisschop Diederik I van Metz. De mirakelen van de heilige Walburg in Tiel* (1999).

Albert of Saxony (Albertutius) (1360–90) Secular *Master of Arts at *Paris, first rector of the University of Vienna, and later bishop of *Halberstadt. His works included sets of questions on Aristotle's *Physics* and *De caelo*, which closely followed John *Buridan's teaching, and a *Tractatus proportionum*, based largely on Thomas *Bradwardine's *De proportionibus*. In his treatment of problems such as projectile motion and acceleration in free fall, he combined the Oxford mathematical analysis of *motion, including Bradwardine's rule, with Buridan's *impetus theory. Albert's works were printed both in *Italy and in *France around 1500 and so became important sources for late-medieval natural *philosophy in the 16th century. WRL

C. H. Lohr, 'Medieval Latin Aristotle Commentaries', *Traditio*, 23 (1967), 348–52.
E. A. Moody, 'Albert of Saxony', *DSB* vol. 1, 93–5.
J. Sarnowsky, *Die aristotelische-scholastische Theorie der Bewegung: Studien zum Kommentar Alberts von Sachsen zur Physik des Aristoteles*, *BGPTM* 32 (1989).

Albert of Stade (d. after 1265) Abbot of St Mary's in Stade from 1232, entered the *Franciscan cloister there in 1240. He composed the *Annales*, a history of the world up to 1256, and the *Troilus*, a monumental epic on the Trojan War, indebted to *Dares Phrygius. CJMc

Albert of Stade, *Annales Stadenses auctore Alberto*, ed. J. M. Lappenberg, *MGH.SS* 16 (1959), 271–379.
T. Gärtner, *Klassische Vorbilder mittelalterlicher Trojaepen* (1999).

Albertus Magnus, St (b. 1193×1206–1280) A German Dominican distinguished as a natural scientist, philosopher, and theologian, Albertus of Lauingen was known as 'the Great' in his own lifetime. Much uncertainty exists concerning the date of his birth as well as of his entry to the Order of Preachers. After entering the *Dominican order, however, he arrived in *Cologne about 1229–30 to study theology, later becoming a *lector* at *Hildesheim in 1233. From Hildesheim, Albertus went to teach at Freiburg, *Regensburg, and *Strasbourg. Between 1240 and 1243, Albertus arrived in *Paris at the Dominican priory of St James. There, he became a teacher to St *Thomas Aquinas and regent master at the University of Paris. In Paris too he digested the new translations of Aristotle, along with the works of Jewish and Arab commentators. By 1250, having again returned to Cologne to open a Dominican *studium generale, Albertus had conceived the notion of making Aristotle intelligible to the Latins, becoming one of the few *Scholastics to write commentaries on *all* of the medieval Aristotle, including not only Aristotle's logic, metaphysics, and ethics but his natural science as well, to include both Aristotle's *De animalibus* and the (pseudo-Aristotelian) *De plantis*. But because Albertus insisted that one cannot truly be a philosopher without knowing both Aristotle and Plato, he also composed important commentaries on the writings of the Neoplatonist *Pseudo-Dionysius. From 1254–57, Albertus was prior provincial of the German Dominicans. From 1260–62 Albertus held the bishopric of Regensburg; in 1263 Pope Urban IV appointed him to preach the *crusade in German lands. From 1264 until 1267 Albertus was likely in residence among the Dominicans in *Würzburg, and after 1269–70 he was again in Cologne as *lector emeritus* at the Dominican cloister of the Holy Cross (*Heiliges Kreuz*), where he would remain until his death on 15 November 1280. Albertus was canonized and recognized as a doctor of the church in 1931, while in 1941 Pope Pius XII named Albertus Magnus patron saint of natural scientists.

Albertus' literary output was staggering, and includes some seventy philosophical, scientific, and theological treatises comprising more than twenty thousand pages in MS, making him perhaps the most prolific Latin author of the whole of the MA. In addition, he composed *sermons, liturgical works, and scriptural commentaries upon each of the four gospels, as well as upon many of the prophetic books of the Old Testament.

Two incomplete printed editions of the collected works have been published: one edited by Peter Jammy, OP (Lyons: 1651) and one by Abbé Auguste Borgnet (Paris: 1890–99). A critical edition projected for forty-one volumes, the Cologne edition (1951–), is now in progress at the Albertus-Magnus-Institut in Bonn; nearly 50 per cent of the titles have been published. *See also* GEOLOGY AND MINERALOGY. IMR

I. M. Resnick and K. F. Kitchell Jr, *Albert the Great: A Selectively Annotated Bibliography (1900–2000)* (2004).
B. Tremblay, 'Modern Scholarship (1900–2000) on Albertus Magnus: A Complement', *Bochumer Philosophisches Jahrbuch für Antike und Mittelalter*, 11 (2006), 159–94.

Albigensian Crusade, Albigensians *See* CATHARS AND CATHARISM.

Albornoz, Cardinal Gil Álvarez de (*c.*1295–1367) Cardinal, statesman, and general. Born at Cuenca; raised in Saragossa; studied in *Toulouse, where he graduated in canon *law around 1325. Between 1325 and 1350, he was King Alfonso XI of Castile's chaplain and counsellor, ambassador, and chancellor of *Castile. In 1338, he succeeded his uncle Jimeno as archbishop of *Toledo, where he tried to improve his clergy's morality. Albornoz left Castile after the king's death, went to *Avignon, and was made a cardinal by *Pope Clement VI. Appointed as a papal *legate and vicar by Pope Innocent VI and Pope Urban V, Albornoz led several military expeditions in *Italy between 1353 and 1363 to pacify and organize the *Papal States; he restored the pope's authority and promulgated the *Constitutiones Aegidianae* in 1357. In 1364, he founded a college in *Bologna for 24 Spanish students. AR

J. Beneyto, *El Cardenal Albornoz: hombre de Iglesia y de Estado en Castilla y en Italia* (1986).
E. Chauvin, *La politique militaire du Cardinal Gil Albornoz, légat du pape en Italie (1353–1357)* (1992).
El Cardenal Albornoz y el Colegio de España en Bolonia, ed. E. Verdera y Tuells (1972–79), 6 vols.
I. M. Sánchez, 'El Cardenal Albornoz y su obra', *Revista de Estudios Políticos*, 183–4 (1972), 400–404.

Albrecht (**von Scharfenberg**) Author of *Der Jüngere Titurel*, a late-13th-century MHG Grail romance, based on works by *Wolfram von Eschenbach, but expanding Wolfram's treatment to give events a moral and soteriological meaning. Whether this 'Albrecht' is the Albrecht von Scharfenberg mentioned by Ulrich *Fuetrer is uncertain. MGC

Albrecht, *Der Jüngere Titurel*, ed. W. Wolf and K. Nyholm, 3 vols (1955–92).
W. Schröder, ed., *Wolfram-Studien*, 8 (1984).

Albrecht 'the Bear' *See* BRANDENBURG, MARGRAVATE OF.

Albrecht von Eyb (1420–75) German humanist, Eichstätt canon; translated from Italian and Latin (especially Plautus) into German. Composed marriage treatise, *Ehebüchlein*, and several Latin treatises. AC

E. Bernstein, 'Albrecht von Eyb', *Deutsche Dichter der frühen Neuzeit (1450–1600)*, ed. S. Füssel (1993), 96–110.
J. A. Hiller, *Albrecht von Eyb, Medieval Moralist* (1939).
F. J. Worstbrock, *Deutsche Antikerezeption 1450–1550* (1976).

Albrecht von Halberstadt Author of a German adaptation of Ovid's *Metamorphoses* (1190 / 1210). The adaptation, unique in its time for being based directly on a classical literary text, stays relatively close to its source. In the prologue Albrecht names Hermann of Thuringia, possibly his patron, who is known to have fostered German versions of classical material by Heinrich von Veldeke and Herbort von Fritzlar. The original work, of which only fragments survive, is known in its entirety only in the adaptation by Jörg Wickram (printed 1545). JAS

G. Wickram, *Werke*, vol. 7–8, ed. J. Bolte (1905–6).

Albrecht von Johansdorf (1185–1209) MHG poet; composed thirteen courtly love songs and introduced the *Wechsel* (lover-lady dialogue poem). Also composed *crusade songs minus the traditional conflict between religion and love. AC

H. Bekker, *The Poetry of Albrecht von Johansdorf* (1978).
S. Ranawake, 'Albrecht von Johansdorf', *Wolfger von Erla*, ed. E. Boshof and F. P. Knapp (1994), 249–80.
D. P. Sudermann, *The Minnelieder of Albrecht von Johansdorf* (1976).

Albucasis (d. 1013) Arabic surgeon, working in southern Spain near *Córdoba. He wrote on all medical subjects in his work *Kitab al-Tasrif*. Treatise thirty of this massive compilation, the *Cirurgia*, became especially influential during the MA. Extensive parts on *bloodletting and *cauterization from it were copied extensively by surgeons and *barber surgeons, both in Latin and in vernacular languages. *See also* SURGEONS AND SURGERY; ARABIC MEDICINE IN THE LATIN WEST. EHu

T. Makhluf, *L'oeuvre chirurgicale d'Abul-cassim Khalaf ibn Abbas Ez-Zahrawi dit Abulcasis* (1930).

M. S. Spink and G. L. Lewis, eds, *Albucasis on Surgery and Instruments: A Definitive Edition of the Arabic Text with English Translation and Commentary* (1973).

Alcántara, Order of Founded in San Julián del Pereiro before 1176, when approved by *Pope Alexander III. Affiliated to the Order of *Calatrava by 1187, it adopted the *Cistercian rule. Its headquarters were transferred to Alcántara on the Tagus river in 1218. The order, which held many possessions, particularly in Extremadura along the Portuguese frontier, played a notable role in the defence of the Christian frontier and in the campaigns of *Ferdinand III, but from the 14th century, it was drawn increasingly into the domestic politics of the Castilian rulers, and the administration of the order was ultimately annexed by the *Catholic Monarchs (1494). *See also* RECONQUISTA; RELIGIOUS ORDERS. DJSm

Colección diplomática medieval de la Orden de Alcántara (1157–1494), ed. B. Palacios Martín (2000).

C. A. Martínez, *Las Ordenes Militares Hispanicas en la Edad Media* (2003).

J. O'Callaghan, 'The Foundation of the Order of Alcántara, 1176–1218', *CHR* 47 (1962), 471–86.

alcázar A Spanish word derived from the Arabic *al-qasr* that refers to a fortified palace or *castle. During the Islamic occupation of Spain, 'alcázar' was used to identify the residences of the *emirs and caliphs. *See also* CALIPHATE; ISLAMIC EMPIRE. LT

A. Weissmüller, *Castles from the Heart of Spain* (1967).

alchemy Alchemy intersected the medieval cultures of *scholasticism and the artisanal world of metallurgy, *pigment-making, and the manufacture of simulated natural products more generally. This unusual mixture of traditions found its origin in late antique Graeco-Roman *Egypt and reached a level of considerable sophistication in the medieval Islamic world. After its entry in the Latin West in the 12th century, alchemy acquired a new face, thanks to its intensive study at the hands of influential university-trained scholastics such as Roger *Bacon and *Albertus Magnus. Traditional alchemical *topoi* were often combined with the increased emphasis on Aristotelian natural *philosophy that was characteristic of the schools. Both of these figures wrote extensively on alchemy—Roger in his three famous *Opera* to *Pope Clement IV, and Albert in his *Libri mineralium* (or *De mineralibus*). In addition, they had major pseudonymous alchemical corpora foisted upon them posthumously.

As the 13th century came to a close, this scholastic tendency in Latin alchemy reached its apogee in the *Summa perfectionis* by *Geber, a pseudonymous author who adopted the name of the famous Arabic alchemist and sage Jabir ibn Hayyan for his masterpiece. Geber's work was written in the clear and comprehensible style of a scholastic *summa, avoiding the extended allegories and enigmas that had often been associated with alchemy since its antique origins. In part, Geber owed his clear expression to the Persian alchemical writer Muhammad ibn Zakariyya al-*Razi, who had also reacted against the excessively veiled writing of some alchemists. But Geber also introduced new elements to alchemy, such as a comprehensive corpuscular theory of *matter based largely on the tradition of Aristotle's *Meteorology*, Book 4, a new emphasis on imitating the underground processes that nature herself uses in generating *metals, and a theory that the alchemist should focus his chrysopoetic efforts on mercury alone, rather than looking for the 'philosophers' stone' in hair, blood, oils, and other materials derived from living beings.

The Latin world soon added a new twist to the scholastic alchemy of authors like Geber. Various schools of alchemy associated with the more radical groups within the *Franciscan order sprang up during the 14th century, and these groups transformed the discipline by leading it into the territory of Christian eschatology, chiliasm, and revelation. The *Testamentum* of pseudo-Ramon *Llull, whose author appropriated the name of the famous Franciscan tertiary, saw alchemy as a means of separating matter from the dark impurity acquired by the Fall of Adam. The pseudonymous corpus ascribed to the equally famous Catalan physician and prophet *Arnau de Villanova used the passions of Jesus as a model for the alchemical work, thus incorporating Christianity into the very technology of alchemy. John of Rupescissa, a Franciscan exponent of radical *poverty, wrote a hugely popular *Liber de quinta essentia omnium rerum* that used alchemy as the basis for a reformed *medicine where *distillation acquired central importance. At the same time, John was a prophetical writer who incorporated the popular themes of the coming of *Antichrist and the tribulation of the elect into his other alchemical writings.

The alchemical fusion of scholastic philosophy and theology with genuine experimental knowledge led to real and influential developments in science and *technology. Greek-speaking alchemists had invented distillation apparatus in the late antique period, and the technology was diffused in the MA into the area of perfume-making and, by the 12th century, into the realm of distilling alcohol from *wine. Rupescissa and others linked this product to pharmacology, thus laying the basis for the vast distilling industry that would flourish in early modern Europe, reaching its medical apogee in the Paracelsian movement. By the first third of the 14th century, many alchemical writers were also explaining how to make the mineral acids—hydrochloric, nitric, and sulfuric—and these remarkable corrosives

The chapiter folowing convenient for to de
Shewith the councels of the subtile werk

Compone lapidem alisque repugnancia

Separatis elementis sub igne subtile sigillo

Mane prope vas nota colores

opened the path to entirely new metallurgical industries. The laborious, dry assaying processes of cupellation and cementation could now be supplemented by much faster analytical techniques employing the mineral acids. The technological prowess of alchemists was also recognized by painters and others in the fine arts. At the beginning of the 15th century, the famous painter and technical writer Cennino *Cennini advised those in need of 'artificial' pigments such as orpiment and vermilion to buy these products from alchemists. While alchemy also had numerous detractors who rejected the goal of chrysopoeia and portrayed the would-be gold-makers as frauds, even they, typically, had to admit that the technological fruits of the aurific art had provided a remarkable contribution to European culture. *See also* ARTISANS AND CRAFTWORK; COSMETICS, PERFUME, AND BEAUTY AIDS; GOLD AND SILVER; PHARMACY; PSEUDONYMOUS LITERATURE; UNIVERSITIES. WRN

R. Halleux, *Les textes alchimiques* (1979).
W. R. Newman, *The Summa Perfectionis of Pseudo-Geber* (1991).
—— *Promethean Ambitions: Alchemy and the Quest to Perfect Nature* (2004).
B. Obrist, *Les débuts de l'imagerie alchimique (XIVe–XVe siècles)* (1982).
J. Perarnau, ed., *Actes de la 'II trobada internacional d'estudis sobre Arnau de Vilanova'* (2005).
M. Pereira, *The Alchemical Corpus Attributed to Ramon Lull* (1989).
—— and B. Spaggieri, *Il 'Testamentum' alchemico attribuito a Raimondo Lullo* (1999).

Alcuin (Albinus, Alcuinus, Flaccus) (*c*.740–804). Abbot of St Martin's at *Tours 796–804, adviser to *Charlemagne, renowned teacher and theologian, and a major figure in the Carolingian *Renaissance whom Charlemagne's biographer, *Einhard, considered exceptionally learned in all fields. He was born in Northumberland and educated at the cathedral school of *York, where he later taught and eventually became *deacon. In the 770s, he was sent on a mission to Charlemagne, then met him again on a journey to *Parma in 780–1, when the king invited him to join his court, which he seems to have done as late as 786 for an initial three and a half years. During that time he rediscovered some late antique works by *Boethius and other neglected works such as the pseudo-Augustinian *De categoriis decem* (On the Ten Categories), which has great import in the history of logic, and *De imagine Dei* (On the Image of God), a work on the nature of man sometimes attributed to Alcuin himself; he also wrote his first (extant) exegetical work, *Interrogationes et Responsiones in Genesin* (Questions and Responses on Genesis). He returned to Northumbria for three years, continued his prodigious scholarly and poetic output, and was back in Charlemagne's court in 793 when the *Vikings sacked *Lindisfarne. At court, he produced yet more letters and scholarship on topics as diverse as *grammar, *rhetoric, *dialectic, and possibly arithmetic and music, and from 796 to his death in 804, he was abbot of St Martin's. It was during that period that he composed most of his major works.

Alcuin's intellectual influence is immense. Besides contributing to the fields noted above, among other things, he devoted much time to writing against *adoptionism (for example, *Libri septem contra Felicem* [Seven books against Felix]), wrote statements on *baptism and a *commentary on the Gospel of St John, contributed to the development of the liturgy, introduced *votive masses to the Continent, produced for Charlemagne an emended text of the Vulgate Bible, introduced the Carolingian minuscule script to the *scriptorium along with new standards of accuracy and clarity for text production, and raised the standard for the correct pronunciation of Latin as he helped Charlemagne try to realize his goal of revitalizing the greatness of ancient Rome in Charlemagne's modern state. Alcuin's voluminous corpus includes 270 extant letters and numerous poems showing great variety of form and technique. *See also* RENAISSANCE, CAROLINGIAN. REB

Alcuinus, *PL* 100–101.
—— 'Carmina', *Poetae Latini aevi Carolini*, ed. E. Dümmler, *MGH.PL*, 1, 160–351, 631–3.
—— *The Bishops, Kings, and Saints of York*, ed. and tr. P. Godman (1982).
D. A. Bullough, *Carolingian Renewal: Sources and Heritage* (1991).
—— 'Alcuin [Albinus, Flaccus] (*c*.740–804)', *ODNB*, vol. 6, 602–8.
—— *Alcuin: Achievement and Reputation* (2004).
M. Lapidge, 'Alcuin of York', *The Blackwell Encyclopaedia of Anglo-Saxon England*, ed. idem *et al.* (1999), 24–5.
J. Marenbon, *From the Circle of Alcuin to the School of Auxerre: Logic, Theology, and Philosophy in the Early Middle Ages* (1981), 30–66.
L. Wallach, *Alcuin and Charlemagne* (1959).

alderman By *c*.1100 the term identified at least two categories of office-holders in English *towns. One was the head of a *guild. Aldermen (occasionally *senatores*) were also responsible for neighbourhood administration: in some towns they had only police responsibilities, but elsewhere they enjoyed judicial powers and a political role, notably in *London. DKe

S. Reynolds, *An Introduction to the History of English Medieval Towns* (1977).

Aldfrith *See* NORTHUMBRIA.

Aldhelm, St, abbot of Malmesbury, first bishop of Sherborne (*c*.640–709/10) The first AS Latin author, whose stylistic influence on the medieval Latin tradition endured until the 10th century. He studied in *Canterbury where the Greek and Mediterranean cultures of Archbishop *Theodore and Abbot *Hadrian profoundly affected AS intellectual life and Aldhelm in particular. Aldhelm's distinctive style combined Greek-like words, alliteration, complicated sentences, and archaic and unusual vocabulary

Alchemy master preparing ingredients, from *The Ordinals of Alchemy* by Thomas Norton, *c*.1477.

culled from *glossaries. His collection of puzzles or *riddles (*aenigmata*) was popular and widely imitated. Inspired by Symphosius, Aldhelm moved the puzzle genre in a distinctly pedagogical direction. In addition to their bookish and serious subject matter (nature, education, church life), the riddles introduced readers to Latin versification. His *De metris* (*On Metre*) and *De pedum regulis* (*On Rules for the Metrical Feet*) served as fundamental schoolbooks for centuries. Along with the riddles and a treatise on the mystical significance of the biblical *number seven, they appeared originally in the *Epistola ad Acircium* dedicated to King *Aldfrith of Northumbria (686–705). Aldhelm also composed a prose and poetical *De virginitate* (*On Virginity*). These works praised and justified virginity with powerful examples of biblical and post-biblical male and female virgins. JJC

F. Brunhölzl, *Histoire de la littérature latine du Moyen Age*, pt 1, vol. 1 (1990), 196–201.
M. Lapidge, 'Aldhelm', *The Blackwell Encyclopaedia of Anglo-Saxon England*, ed. idem *et al.* (2001), 25–7.
—— and M. Herren, *Aldhelm: The Prose Works* (1979).
—— and J. L. Rosier, *Aldhelm: The Poetic Works* (1985).

ale- and beer-making The brewing of ale and beer and the making of *bread were intimately related: both began with cereal *grains or if necessary the seed of wild grasses, and both relied upon a yeast to convert some of the starch or *sugar into soluble carbohydrates in the grain to alcohol. In the plan of the 9th-century *Benedictine monastery of *St Gall, the brewery shares the same building, probably the same grains, and effectively the same yeast, with the bakery.

Because grains grew more abundantly than grape vines in northern climates and soils, ale and beer were favoured as beverages over wine in Scandinavia, northern and central Germany, the Lowlands, and Britain.

Ale-making followed a basic recipe known for at least a millennium. The grain, preferably barley, occasionally with a proportion of oats, was allowed to germinate into malt which was then dried in a warm area or kiln, sieved, and milled; that grain was let stand in hot water (though not boiling) in a copper kettle along with optional *herbs or *spices for flavour. The liquid or 'wort' containing sugars and proteins was drawn off and cooled, and yeasts, either ambient or reserved from previous batches, began the fermentation process. In preparing beer, brewers boiled crushed hop catkins, valued as a preservative and for their somewhat bitter flavour, with the wort. All such additives were either filtered from the wort or contained in fabric bags or wicker baskets.

British ale was normally drunk within several days while still fresh, perhaps still fermenting and cloudy. The use of hops was long established on the continent but hesitantly accepted in Britain only by the 15th century; hops were later outlawed (1530–52) by Henry VIII, who proclaimed the historic and dominant virtue of ale.

Until the 15th century, brewing was fundamentally a domestic activity managed by women. Even when it became a remunerative urban industry, a high proportion of *guild members remained brewsters. Over time various ordinances, both local and national, regulated the ingredients of ale and beer, the proportion of them to water, the frequency of brewing, and the quality and sale of the product. *See also* FOOD, DRINK, AND DIET; FOOD SUPPLY AND FOOD TRADES. TPS

J. Bennett, *Ale, Beer, and Brewsters in England: Women's Work in a Changing World (1300–1600)* (1996).
I. S. Hornsey, *A History of Beer and Brewing* (2003).
O. Nordland, *Brewing and Beer Traditions in Norway* (1969).
R. W. Unger, *A History of Brewing in Holland, 900–1900* (2001).
—— *Beer in the Middle Ages and Renaissance* (2004).

Aleksii (*c*.1293–1378) From 1354 metropolitan of *Kiev (residing in *Moscow). Aleksii strove with intermittent success to unite East Slavic dioceses under Moscow, to suppress the rival Lithuanian hierarchy, and to further Muscovite interests, both secular and ecclesiastical. He was largely responsible for the 14th-century monastic revival in Muscovy and the proliferation of *coenobitic communities that strengthened his power. He was canonized in 1448 and venerated as the founder of Muscovite Orthodoxy. VZ

E. Golubinskii, *Istoriia russkoi tserkvi*, vol. 2/1 (1900).
J. Meyendorff, *Byzantium and the Rise of Russia* (1989).

Aleppo (Halab) City in northern Syria. The 10th- and 11th-century city flourished under the *Hamdanids, while under the *Seljuks it resisted a crusader siege in 1124–5, becoming a key Syrian city for Zengi, *Nur al-Din, and *Saladin. BAC

J. Nielsen, 'Between Arab and Turk: Aleppo from the 11th till the 13th centuries', *ByF* 16 (1991), 323–40.

Alexander II, king of Scotland (1198–1249) Succeeded *William I in 1214. Alexander's reign witnessed the first successful efforts of the MacMalcolm dynasty to impose royal authority over the entire extent of modern-day Scotland, but these efforts were much bedevilled. The king's early years saw challenges to the throne from the families of MacWilliam and MacHeth, descendants of the dispossessed son of Malcolm III and his first wife. Later, there were revolts in *Moray, Inverness-shire, Caithness, and *Galloway, as well as armed disaffection from the Gaelic rulers of Argyll and the Isles, who looked to Norway for support. Alexander successfully countered all these risings, though he failed ultimately to win the allegiance of Argyll and died at Kerrara fighting an invasion by its ruler, Ewen.

By contrast, the years of Alexander II's rule marked an important and generally peaceful phase in Anglo-Scottish history. These good relations in turn generated conditions favourable to the rapid maturation within the kingdom of the institutions of central government. Especially notable

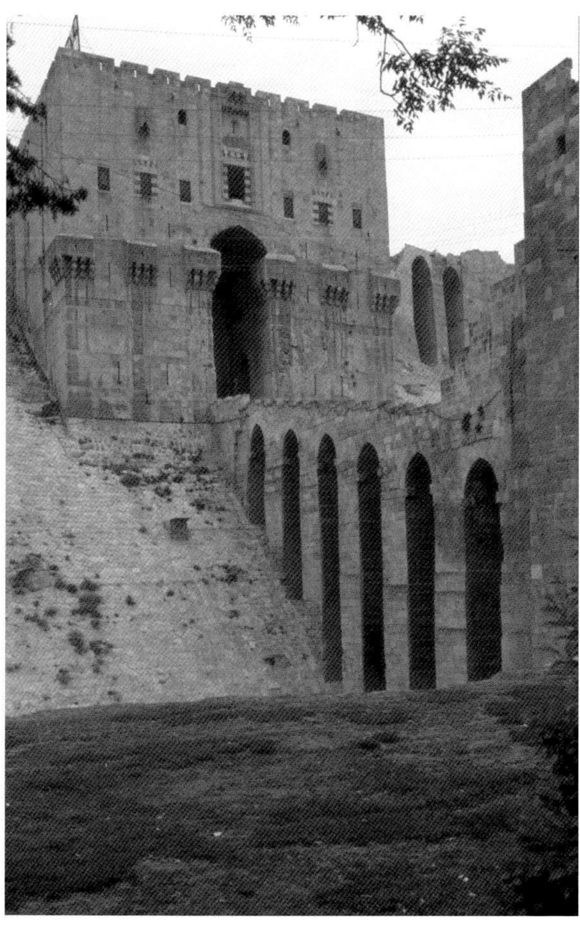

Aleppo. Entrance to the citadel.

were the elaboration of a body of distinctly Scottish common law, which drew on both native Gaelic practices and more recent English jurisprudence, and the earliest efforts to codify the customs of the Anglo-Scottish border lands. *See also* LAW IN THE BRITISH ISLES, ENGLISH; LAW, SCOTTISH; SCOTLAND, IRELAND, WALES: SCOTLAND AND WALES 1064–1536. CJN

A. D. M. Barrell, *Medieval Scotland* (2000).
A. A. M. Duncan, *Scotland: The Making of the Kingdom* (1975).
H. L. MacQueen, *Common Law and Feudal Society in Medieval Scotland* (1993).
R. A. McDonald, *Outlaws of Medieval Scotland: Challenges to the Canmore Kings, 1058–1266* (2003).

Alexander III, king of Scotland (1241–86) Reigned 1249–86. Although later medieval historians often looked back on Alexander III's rule as a golden age of prosperity and tranquillity before the violent conflicts of the wars of independence, in fact his early years were troubled by bitter fighting among rival Scottish noblemen and his father-in-law, *Henry III of England, for control over the young king's person. Soon after he assumed governance of the realm in 1260, however, Alexander proved himself a fiercely competent ruler. His defeat of King *Hákon Hákonarson IV of Norway at the battle of *Largs (1263) signalled the eclipse of Norse influence in Caithness and Ross. Relations with England remained cordial despite Alexander's refusal to swear *homage for Scotland before an ambitious *Edward I. The king's military achievements and a strong economy in the later 13th century offered ideal conditions for the rapid growth of many of the royal boroughs and the development of a series of long-lasting *trade links with the continent. The years 1249–86 also saw the elaboration of key institutions of central government. The reign ended suddenly in 1296, when Alexander III died unexpectedly, leaving no direct heir to succeed him; it was followed by the commencement of a long war against England. *See also* ANGLO-SCOTTISH WARS; SCOTLAND, IRELAND, WALES: SCOTLAND AND WALES 1064–1536. CJN

A. A. M. Duncan, *Scotland: The Making of the Kingdom* (1975).
N. Reid, ed., *Scotland in the Reign of Alexander III* (1990).

Alexander legend Medieval fascination with the figure of Alexander goes back to the 3rd-century Greek romance of Pseudo-Callisthenes, which became known to the west in large part, though not exclusively, through the 10th-century Latin translation by Leo of *Naples. A common factor of the *Alexander romances is the depiction of the marvelous and fantastic, the wonders of the mysterious East. Alexander is the model of the king of kings, the ruler of the world. The further the distance to antiquity, however, the more religiously tinged the image became, and Alexander came to epitomize the transitory nature of earthly existence. In the German tales, Alexander is also enmeshed in the process of universal history, which, in the German texts, leads inexorably to the continuation of the *Roman Empire under German rulers. The first appearance of Alexander in a German text occurs in the **Annolied* (*c.*1080) and is presented within the parameters of the *translatio imperii* according to the Book of Daniel and *Jerome's commentary. Alexander tales are found in all European vernaculars as well as in Hebrew, eastern Christian, and Islamic literatures. FGG

W. J. Aerts *et al.*, *Alexander the Great in the Middle Ages: Ten Studies on the Last Days of Alexander in Literary and Historical Writing* (1978).
J. Brummack, *Die Darstellung des Orients in den deutschen Alexandergeschichten des Mittelalters* (1966).
G. Cary, *The Medieval Alexander* (1956).
J. Cölln *et al.*, *Alexanderdichtungen im Mittelalter: Kulturelle Selbstbestimmung im Kontext literarischer Beziehungen* (2000).
R. Stoneman, *Legends of Alexander the Great* (1994).

Alexanderlied MHG epic about Alexander the Great, composed *c.*1140–50 by *Pfaffe Lamprecht, who was confronted

Alexander Romances: a hare with a crossbow hunts a man. A *monde renverse* scene from a lower margin in *The Romance of Alexander.*

with the problem of writing about a non-Christian hero. This was resolved by contextualizing Alexander within Christianity and depicting him as part of God's plan for mankind. MPie

S. M. Johnson, 'Pre-Courtly Epics', *A Companion to Middle High German Literature to the 14th Century*, ed. F. G. Gentry (2002), 397–429.

Alexander Neckam (Nequam) (1157–1217) Born and educated in St Albans, England, he studied and became a regent master in *Paris before returning to lecture in theology at *Oxford *c*.1190. After 1197 he joined the *canons regular in the Augustinian abbey of St Mary's in Cirencester, where he was elected abbot in 1213. He died on 31 March 1217 at Kempsey in Worcester. His scholarship produced works on *Martianus Capella, *grammar, lexicography, biblical *exegesis, including a Marian interpretation of the Song of Songs, and *natural history, notably in the *De naturis rerum*, the *Laus sapientie diuine*, and the *Suppletio defectuum*. *See also* GLOSS AND COMMENTARY. CJMc

R. W. Hunt, *The Schools and the Cloister: The Life and Writings of Alexander Nequam (1157–1217)*, ed. and rev. M. Gibson (1984).

Alexander Neckam, *Suppletio defectuum, Book 1: Alexander Neckam on Plants, Birds and Animals*, ed. C. J. McDonough (1999).

Alexander of Hales (d. 1245) English *Franciscan theologian. He was a Master at *Paris by 1210, and he replaced lecturing on the Bible with lecturing on *Peter Lombard's **Sentences*. His works include his youthful *Exoticon*, about difficult words, the *Glossa in 4 libros sententiarum*, and his last work, the *Summa fratris Alexandri*, of which the fourth part was written after his death. Although he knew Aristotle, and quoted his works, Aristotelian thought did not seriously inform his theology. *See also* EXEGESIS; GLOSS AND COMMENTARY; SCHOLASTICISM. AJD

'Alexander of Hales', *The History of Franciscan Theology*, ed. K. Osborne (1994), 1–38.

I. Herscher, 'A Bibliography of Alexander of Hales', *FranS* 5 (1945), 434–54.

Alexander of Roes (13th century) Canon, probably identical to Andreas of Leysberg OFM, in service to Cardinal Jacob Colonna; criticised conditions at the Roman curia. In his major work *Memoriale de Prerogativa Romani Imperii* he demarcated the division of powers among royalty, *clergy, and intellectuals. Despite being repeated in *De Pavo*, his ideas had no political influence. KFJ

H. Grundmann and H. Heimpel, eds, *Alexander von Roes: Schriften* (1958).

Alexander of Villa Dei (Villedieu) (d. *c*.1250) Grammarian and mathematician, author of the *Doctrinale puerorum*, on Latin grammar, morphology, and syntax. Also ascribed to him are a *Summarium biblicum*, *De sphaera*, and the *Ecclesiale*. CJMc

Alexander of Villa Dei, *Carmen de Algorismo*, ed. J. O. Halliwell (1839).

——*Doctrinale*, ed. D. Reichling (1893).

——*Ecclesiale*, ed. L. R. Lind (1958).

——*Massa compoti*, ed. R. Steele, *Opera hactenus inedita Rogeri Baconi* 6 (1926).

Alexander romances Generic term for the large group of enormously popular narrative poems, mainly in French and with a rich iconographic tradition, devoted to the life of Alexander the Great. Deriving initially from classical sources, particularly the 2nd-century Greek pseudo-Callisthenes and its Latin adaptations, Alexander romances were the major vernacular source, before *Marco Polo and *Mandeville, for European knowledge of Asia, particularly *India and the so-called marvels of the east. As the tradition advances, Alexander increasingly becomes a model of *chivalry, kingship, and learning, with his prodigious abilities variously stressed depending on the version. Though often referred to as romances, these texts have more in common with the **chanson de geste*, using the characteristic *laisse* form and concentrating on conquest, war, and feudal politics. Versions of the *Romance of Alexander* were already in circulation before 1150, but after *c.*1160 new poems proliferated, notably those by Lambert le Tort (*c.*1170), Thomas of Kent (*c.*1175–5, *Le Roman de toute chevalerie*, in AN French), and Alexandre de Paris (*c.*1180–85). This last had the widest circulation, becoming something of a vulgate and leading, in the 13th century to frequent recasting and continuations as well as prose versions. The dodecasyllabic-line, apparently pioneered in French by Lambert le Tort, became so closely associated with narratives of Alexander's life that the form came to be known as the Alexandrine. *See also* ALEXANDER LEGEND; ALEXANDERLIED; ROMAN D'ALEXANDRE, LE. SG

M. Gosman, *La Légende d'Alexandre le Grand dans la littérature française du XIIe siècle* (1994).

D. Maddox and S. Sturm-Maddox (eds), *The Medieval French Alexander* (2002).

Alexandre, Libro de Castilian *Alexander romance (*c.*1210) and the founding text of the *mester de clerecía*, the literary movement associated with the new University of Palencia. Its mono-rhymed *alexandrine quatrains (*cuaderna vía*) are largely based on *Walter of Châtillon's *Alexandreis* and treat the themes of imperial glory, earthly greed, and divine retribution with originality, subtlety, and dramatic power. *See also* LITERATURES: CATALAN. JW

A. Arizaleta, *La Translation d'Alexandre: recherches sur les structures et les significations du 'Libro de Alexandre'* (1999).

J. Cañas, ed., *Libro de Alexandre* (1988).

J. Weiss, *The 'Mester de Clerecía': Intellectuals and Ideologies in Thirteenth-Century Castile* (2006).

alexandrine Late medieval French metre named after a 12th-century example, the **Roman d'Alexandre*. Rhymed in couplets, the lines have twelve syllables (thirteen when the rhyme is feminine), and there is a caesura (pause) after the sixth syllable. Alexandrines were revived by Racine and Molière in the 17th century. DHW

K. Voretsch, *Introduction to the Study of Old French Literature* (1931).

Alexian Brothers and Nuns A religious community specifically devoted to caring for the sick, with special attention to the dying. The order traces its origins to the *Beghard communities of the *Low Countries, particularly *Brabant, though many of their activities were centred in *Cologne and *Aachen. During the *Black Death they were particularly active, caring for the ill and burying the dead. During this time they were commonly referred to as Cellites, derived from *cella*, meaning small church, monastic room, or grave—all of which embody the spirit of these men. Others called them 'Passage Brothers' (referring to their assistance to the dying), 'Poor Brothers', 'Bread Brothers', and 'Soul Brothers'. After the plague diminished, the group took over funerary practices and vigils, earning them the additional name 'Brothers of Chant'.

In 1427, this group of men built a *chapel dedicated to St Alexus, patron of the poor, in Aachen. They became known as the Brothers at the chapel of St Alexus, later shortened to Alexian Brothers. In 1472, they adopted the Rule of *Augustine and were officially recognized by Pope Sixtus IV as the Order of Cellites. A group of women who had assisted the brothers in their ministries became Cellitine sisters, also dedicated to works of corporal mercy. Their motherhouse is at Cologne. *See also* APOSTOLIC LIFE; PASTORAL CARE; POVERTY AND POOR RELIEF; RELIGIOUS ORDERS. MMS

M. Frisbie, *The Story of the Alexian Brothers* (1984).

C. J. Kauffman, *Tamers of Death: The History of the Alexian Brothers from 1300 to 1789* (1976).

W. J. Marx, *The Development of Charity in Medieval Louvain* (1936).

Alexis, Vie de St (late 11th-century?) The oldest and most celebrated French life of Alexis is preserved in the Hildersheim MS prepared for *Christina of Markyate and is hailed as one of the 'monuments' of French literature, though there are many other French versions of his life. The only child of patrician parents, Alexis dashes their expectations by becoming a nameless beggar and shelters unrecognized under the stairs outside their house, his sanctity being acclaimed and his identity revealed only after his death. *See also* BIOGRAPHY, LATIN; LITERATURES: FRENCH. SK

C. Storey, ed., *'La Vie de Saint Alexis': Texte du manuscit de Hildesheim (L)* (1968).

alfalfa *See* LUCERNE.

Alfanus of Salerno (Alphanus) (1020?–85) Poet, medical author, friend of Desiderius and *Pope Gregory VII; archbishop of Salerno (1058); wrote poetry in classicizing metres, hymns, and saints' lives, and translated Greek medical treatises into Latin. TC

Alfanus, *I carmi di Alfano*, ed. A. Lentini and F. Avagliano (1974).

——*Nemesii episcopi Premnon physicon ... a ... Alfano in latinum translatus*, ed. C. Burkhard (1917).

L. Ghilli, 'Alfanus of Salerno', *CALMA*, vol. 1, 179–80.

Alfonsine tables *See* ASTRONOMY.

Alfonso I el Batallador (*c.*1073–1134) Alfonso became king of *Aragon and *Navarre in 1104. His reputation as a warrior secured him the nickname *Batallador* during a career of expanding the frontiers of Aragon. In 1109 he married *Urraca, the widowed daughter of the king of *Castile-León, potentially unifying two peninsular monarchies. However, the couple proved incompatible, and Pope Paschal II soon annulled the marriage on the grounds of *consanguinity. Eventually surrendering the territories he claimed in Castile, Alfonso turned instead to the siege of Saragossa, capturing the Muslim stronghold in 1119. His conquest of the upper Ebro Valley nearly tripled the size of his kingdom. Alfonso was badly defeated and severely wounded at the battle of Fraga (17 July 1234) against the Muslims, and he died some days later. Navarre separated itself from Aragon at his death. JFPo

R. del Arco y Garay, 'Notas biográficas del rey Alfonso I el Batallador', *Boletín de la Real Academia de la Historia*, 133 (1953), 111–209.
J. M. Lacarra, *Vida de Alfonso el Batallador* (1971).
B. F. Reilly, *The Kingdom of León-Castilla under King Alfonso VII 1126–1157* (1998).
—— *The Kingdom of León-Castilla under Queen Urraca 1109–1126* (1982).

Alfonso V of Aragon (IV of Catalonia, 'the Magnanimous') (1396–1458) Eldest son of Fernando de Antequera (Fernando I, 1414–16) and Leonor of Albuquerque, Alfonso was a Castilian prince of the *Trastámara family who acceded to the Crown of *Aragon at his father's death in 1416. Alfonso shrewdly balanced his Aragonese, Castilian, and Italian interests. He was often at war with and against his family in *Castile and against the Angevins and the Genoese in *Italy. After conquering *Naples in 1442, he ruled it directly after entrusting his Spanish realms to his brother, *Joan II, and his wife, *María de Castile. The conquest of Naples strengthened economic ties between Italy and Spain, and under Alfonso's patronage, the court at Naples became a centre of Renaissance humanism. He had no children with María, but he had three illegitimate children, María, Leonor, and Ferran, who succeeded him in Naples. In the Crown of Aragon, Alfonso was succeeded by his brother, Joan. TME

A. Ryder, *Alfonso the Magnanimous: King of Aragon, Naples, and Sicily, 1396–1458* (1990).
—— *The Kingdom of Naples under Alfonso the Magnanimous* (1976).

From the prayer book of Alfonso V of Aragon.

Alfonso VI of Castile-León (*c.*1040–1109) Son of Ferdinand I of Castile, king of *León 1065–1109 and king of *Castile 1072–1109. Though his father divided his realms among his three sons, Alfonso reunited them after one brother was killed and the other imprisoned. Alfonso campaigned vigorously against the Muslim princes of Iberia, forcing them to pay tribute. He also captured the ancient capital city of *Toledo in 1085. This victory prompted Muslims to seek assistance from the North African *Almoravids, who reversed some of Alfonso's gains. He restored the archbishoprics of Toledo and *Salamanca, granted several Castilian monasteries to *Cluny, and introduced Roman *liturgy into Castile. He also maintained ties across the Pyrenees, introducing French *clergy into Castile and marrying two of his daughters to Burgundian noblemen. Though married several times, Alfonso had only one son, whose death in 1108 led Alfonso to designate his daughter *Urraca his successor. MMH

A. L. Conde, *Alfonso VI, el rey hispano y europeo de los tres religiones: 1065–1109* (1994).
B. F. Reilly, *The Kingdom of León-Castilla under Alfonso VI, 1065–1109* (1988).

Alfonso VII of Castile-León (*c.*1104–1157) Son of Queen *Urraca and Raymond of Burgundy, king of *Castile-León 1126–1157. Emulating his grandfather *Alfonso VI, Alfonso VII used the title 'emperor of all Spain', putting him at odds with *Alfonso I of *Aragon until the latter's death. Taking advantage of that death, Alfonso VII reclaimed Castilian territories lost to Aragon during Urraca's reign. He had less success attempting to reclaim control of Portugal from Alfonso I. An indefatigable campaigner, Alfonso VII also regularly led armies against the Muslim rulers of eastern *Andalusia and Almeria. Though his final siege of Almeria was unsuccessful, and the *Almohad invasion of Spain reversed many of his territorial gains, Alfonso's pursuit of the *Reconquista was significant. A traditional monarch, Alfonso VII generously patronized the church, including *Cluny, the *Cistercians, and the *Knights Hospitaller. At his death, his kingdoms were divided between his two sons Sancho III of Castile and Fernando II of León. MMH

L. S. Belda, ed., *Chronica Adefonsi Imperatoris* (1950).

B. Reilly, *The Kingdom of León-Castilla under King Alfonso VII, 1126–1157* (1998).

Alfonso X ('el Sabio', 'the Learned', 'the Wise') (1221–84) King of *Castile-León (1252–84), son of *Ferdinand III, and uncle of Juan *Manuel. Even in a century that boasted rulers such as *Frederick II and *Louis IX, and in spite of his unsuccessful quest to become (Holy) *Roman emperor, Alfonso X still is remarkable in his achievements, particularly his contribution to the cultural life of his kingdom.

Alfonso and his teams of scholars and translators were responsible for a variety of historical, legal, scientific, and literary works, which, along with official documents, were composed in the vernacular at the king's insistence. Many of these works were vast in their range. For example, in their composition of the national and universal histories the *Estoria de España* and *General estoria*, Alfonso's collaborators drew on an array of sources including Latin and Arabic histories, the Bible, *hagiography, and vernacular epics. Similarly broad in their scope were Alfonso's legal works: the **Fuero real*, *Espéculo*, and *Siete partidas*. Only the first of these codes was promulgated during the monarch's lifetime, the most important and influential of them, the encyclopedic *Siete partidas*, having to wait until 1348 for its promulgation.

Other works produced under the aegis of Alfonso include translations from Arabic of astronomical and astrological treatises such as the *Tablas alfonsíes*, which detailed the movements of the planets; the **Cantigas de Santa Maria*, a collection of Marian miracles which, unlike those of Gonzalo de *Berceo, were composed in Galician Portuguese; and the *Libro de ajedrez, dados e tablas*, a recreational work translated and revised from the original Arabic. *See also* ANNALS AND CHRONICLES: SPAIN/PORTUGAL; LITERATURES: GALICIAN-PORTUGUESE; SCIENCE, TRANSMISSION OF; STUDIUM GENERALE. JG

R. I. Burns, ed., *The Worlds of Alfonso the Learned and James the Conqueror: Intellect and Force in the Middle Ages* (1985).

——ed., *Emperor of Culture: Alfonso X the Learned of Castile and his Thirteenth-Century Renaissance* (1990).

J. F. O'Callaghan, *The Learned King: The Reign of Alfonso X of Castile* (1993).

E. S. Procter, *Alfonso X of Castile: Patron of Literature and Learning* (1951).

C. J. Socarras, *Alfonso X of Castile: A Study on Imperialistic Frustration* (1976).

Alfred of Sareshel (Alfred Anglicus) *Canon of Lichfield, belonged to the circle of *Gerard of Cremona at the school for translators in *Toledo. Around 1210 he translated from the Arabic the *De vegetabilibus* of Nicolaus Damascenus and wrote a *commentary on Aristotle's *Meteorologica*. He dedicated his major work, *De motu cordis*, to *Alexander Neckam. CJMc

C. H. Lohr, 'Medieval Latin Aristotle Commentaries: Authors A-F', *Traditio*, 23 (1967), 355–6.

Alfred the Great (849–99) Born at Wantage as the youngest son of King Æthelwulf of *Wessex, Alfred survived three briefly reigning older brothers to become king of Wessex in 871. In spite of several serious setbacks, including a retreat into the Somerset marshes at Athelney, Alfred rallied to defeat a 'great heathen army' of Danish Vikings under *Guthrum at Edington in 878. After this decisive victory, Alfred worked to establish a system of garrisoned *burhs* (boroughs; fortified towns) and other defences throughout his kingdom, including a navy with newly designed ships that could reach any point of attack on the coasts within hours. In 886 he took over *London and received the formal submission of the Anglian king of western *Mercia, *Æthelred, who married Alfred's daughter *Æthelflæd. Alfred thereafter styled himself 'King of the *Anglo-Saxons' as ruler of a new national polity of all English-speaking peoples not under control of the Danes.

Alfred looked to an Old Testament model to reform the law codes of his kingdom and invited to his court at *Winchester scholars from other lands, including several Mercians, Grimbald a Frank, John the Old Saxon, and Bishop *Asser from St David's in Wales. The king founded monastic houses at Shaftesbury and Athelney and began a programme of education with the systematic translation of those Latin works he deemed 'most necessary for men to know' into OE, 'the language that we can all understand'. These texts include the **Pastoral Care* of *Pope Gregory I the Great (in a Preface to which Alfred describes his project), the *Consolation of Philosophy* by *Boethius, St *Augustine's *Soliloquies*, the first fifty Psalms, Gregory's *Dialogues*,

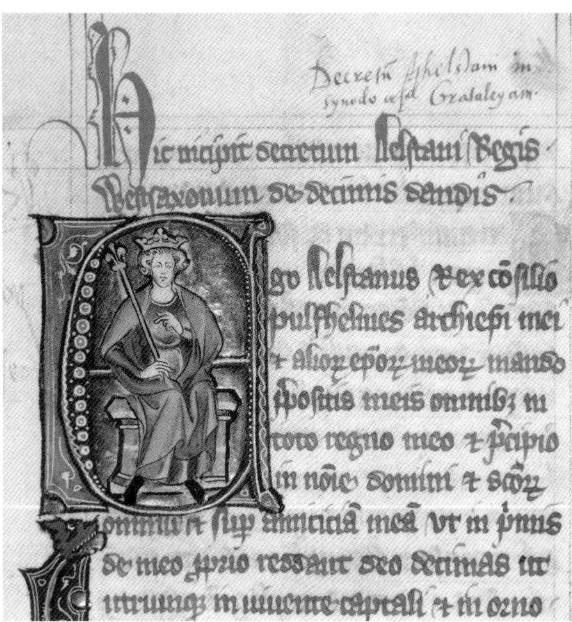

Illuminated initial depicting Alfred the Great.

*Orosius' *Histories against the Pagans*, and probably *Bede's *Ecclesiastical History of the English People*. The king also commissioned the compilation in OE of the *Anglo-Saxon Chronicle*, which includes a genealogy of the West Saxon royal family going back to the legendary Scylding kings of ancient Denmark, the antediluvian patriarchs from the Book of Genesis, and finally Adam and Christ 'the son of God'. On his mother Osburh's side, Alfred claimed to be of Gothic ancestry through the Jutish kings of Wight. An interest in traditional poetry in his native tongue may have been acquired from his mother, and some scholars associate Alfred's court with the preservation of heroic poems like **Beowulf*.

Alfred encouraged trade and economic development in the *burhs* under the oversight of royal agents who established new *mints, reformed the coinage to a much higher standard, and rationalized the system of taxation, improving existing administrative structures to get more service from nobles and work from peasants. The king reorganized London by moving the trading centre inside the city walls and laying out streets, markets, and landing-places for a new commercial emporium. Alfred also increased royal wealth through the annexation of ecclesiastical property, for which Pope John VII criticized him. In his will Alfred took steps to exclude from the succession his nephew Æthelwold, a legitimate pretender of the royal family, in favour of his son *Edward 'the Elder'. King Alfred was buried at Winchester in 899.

Alfred emulated the successful nation-building of the Frankish kings and is seen as a key figure in the creation of the English nation as a distinctive political and cultural entity. However, whereas the *Carolingians demonstrated their power with elevated thrones, elaborate coronations, and gorgeous treasures designed to exalt the king, Alfred chose a much more familiar style of rule, one in which he shared his hopes and expectations with his people as a firm but wise pastor of his flock. In letters prefacing the newly translated books or in gifts of rich handles for book-pointers like the Alfred Jewel, the king sought personally to inspire his subjects to a common project of national learning and collective responsibility.

Asser composed a biography of the king in 893 that suggests Alfred suffered some psychological stress and sexual anxiety from his competing roles as Germanic warrior and Christian scholar, as well as a chronic intestinal ailment recently diagnosed as Crohn's disease. This less-than-flattering portrayal of the king's character has led a few scholars to see Asser's *Life* as a late-10th-/early-11th-century fabrication. The 13th-century chronicler Matthew *Paris was the first author to designate King Alfred 'the Great'. CRD

R. Abels, *Alfred the Great: War, Kingship, and Culture in Anglo-Saxon England* (1998).

Alfred the Great: Asser's 'Life of King Alfred' and Other Contemporary Sources, tr. S. Keynes and M. Lapidge (1983).

T. Reuter, ed., *Alfred the Great* (2003).

A. P. Smyth, *King Alfred the Great* (1995).

Algarve Southernmost region of present-day Portugal, stretching from the mouth of the Guadiana river in the east to Cape St Vincent in the west. Its history reaches back to antiquity. Its principal towns started as Phoenician and Carthaginian settlements, later taken over by Rome and eventually Islam. The westernmost region of *al-Andalus, the Algarve was not at the centre of events but nonetheless developed a rich economy and Islamic cultural tradition, the architectural legacy of which still survives. After the breakup of the Umayyad state in Spain, al-Andalus became a patchwork of petty Muslim states (**taifas*), despite the Almohad attempt at restoring its unity. The discord and political instability in Muslim Spain and Morocco paved the road for the massive military campaigns prosecuted in the four decades after the battle of Las *Navas de Tolosa by the three main Christian kingdoms of the peninsula: *Castile, *Aragon, and Portugal. The decisive development in the reconquest of the Algarve was the push by Sancho II of Portugal along the Guadiana river in the 1230s. In 1238 and 1239 he captured key locations near Guadiana's estuary, including Mértola, Tavira, and Cacela, cutting off the remaining Muslim communities from the rest of al-Andalus. Sancho's brother, *Afonso III, completed the conquest of

Algarve in 1349–1250. The fall of Faro and of Silves, the former capital of a prosperous *taifa*, marks the end of the Portuguese reconquest. However, the kingdom of Algarve did not formally and conclusively become part of Portugal until 1267 when *Alfonso X finally surrendered his claim to suzerainty if not the title 'king of the Algarve', also employed by the Portuguese kings.

Under Portuguese rule, the Algarve became a maritime frontier, subject to Muslim raids and a staging area for Portuguese corsair activity and piracy. Its vulnerability to Muslim attacks explains the support of its municipalities for the 15th-century expansion in North Africa, in the hope of forging a new frontier zone. Thinly populated, Algarve had most of its inhabitants concentrated in coastal towns. Of these, Tavira, Faro, Lagos, and Silves were the most important. Despite population problems, exacerbated first by the shock of conquest and after 1348 by recurring epidemics, the Algarve occupied an important place in the Portuguese economy, particularly exports. Its *fruit and almonds travelled as far as *Flanders, *England, and the Baltic. *Fisheries constituted another ubiquitous industry.

In the 15th century, the Algarve came to play a significant role in the Portuguese overseas expansion. It was the last staging area before the conquest of Ceuta in 1415. Although it is not true that Prince *Henry the Navigator spent much of his adult life on the Sagres promontory, the Algarve was very important to him. In the last three decades of his life he expended considerable effort to acquire lands and other real estate there. He eventually prevailed on the Crown to grant him Lagos, Sagres, and other places in the western Algarve and near the Guadiana estuary, but the agriculturally rich Silves eluded him, remaining a royal town. Of his new holdings, Lagos was the most essential. A staging area for the early expeditions along the Atlantic coast of northwestern Africa, Lagos was the location of the first *slave auction in 1445 and, together with Lisbon, an administrative centre for the African enterprise. Its role, however, declined after Prince Henry's death and the subsequent centralization of customs and administrative activities associated with the African commerce in Lisbon. Algarve, however, continued to play a substantial role in Portuguese overseas activities, in particular in the Atlantic islands and Morocco, as well as strategic defence of the kingdom into the 16th century. IE

S. Boissellier, *Naissance d'une identité portugaise: la vie rurale entre Tage et Guadiana de l'Islam à la reconquête (X^e–XIVe siècles)* (1999).

M. da Fátima Botão, *Silva, a capital de um reino medievo* (1992).

A. Iria, 'O Algarve e a ilha da Madeira no sèculo XV (documentos inéditos)', *Studia*, 38 (1974), 131–515.

—— *Da importância geo-política do Algarve, na defesa marítima de Portugal, nos séculos XV a XVIII* (1976).

—— *A liderança de Silves na região do Algarve nos sèculos XIV e XV* (1995).

A. Iria, ed., *O Algarve e os descobrimentos*, vol. 2 of *Descobrimentos portugueses, documentos para a sua história*, ed. J. Martins da Silva Marques (1988).

N. Magalhães, *O legado arquiectónico Islámico no Algarve* (2002).

M. da Graça Maia Marques, ed., *O Algarve da antiguidade aos nossos dias: elementos para a sua história* (1999).

C. Picard, *Le Portugal musulman, VIIIe–XIIIe siècle: l'Occident d'al-Andalus sous domination islamique* (2000).

algebra *See* MATHEMATICS.

Alhacen (Abu Ali al-Hasan ibn al-Hasan ibn al-Haytham) (d. after 1039) Physicist whose contributions to *optics and the scientific method are outstanding.

1. Early life and travels
2. Optics
3. Other scientific contributions
4. Influence

1. *Early life and travels*

Known in the west as Alhazen, ibn al-Haytham was born in 965 in *Basra to a family of *engineers and was educated in Basra and *Baghdad. Thereafter he went to *Egypt, where he discovered a way of controlling the Nile flood, reasoning that constructing a dam would enable water to be stored for irrigation in the dry season, and flooding could be prevented at other times. He pitched his idea to the ruler of Egypt, *Fatimid caliph al-Hakim, who provided the financial backing and workmen to complete the task, but the money fell short. He also travelled to Spain and, during this period, had ample time for his scientific pursuits, which included *optics, *mathematics, physics, *medicine, and developing the scientific method, on each of which he has left several books.

2. *Optics*

He examined the passage of light through various media and discovered the laws of refraction. He also carried out the first experiments on the dispersion of light into its constituent *colours. His book *Kitab al-Manazir* was translated into Latin in the MA, as was his work on the colours of sunset. He dealt at length with the theory of various physical phenomena like shadows, *eclipses, and the *rainbow, and he speculated on the physical nature of light. He was the first to describe accurately the various parts of the eye and give a scientific explanation of the process of vision. He also attempted to explain binocular vision and gave a correct explanation of the apparent increase in size of the sun and moon when near the horizon. He is known for the earliest use of the camera obscura. He contradicted Ptolemy's and Euclid's theory of vision according to which objects are seen by means of light rays emanating from the eyes; according to him the rays originate in the object of vision, not in the eye. Through these researches on optics, he has been considered the father of modern optics.

The Latin translation of his main work, *Kitab al-Manadhir*, greatly influenced western scientists, for example Roger *Bacon and Kepler, and brought about great progress in experimental methods. His research in catoptrics centred on spherical and parabolic mirrors and spherical aberration. He made the important observation that the ratio between the angle of incidence and refraction does not remain constant, and investigated the magnifying power of *lenses. His catoptrics contain the important problem known as Alhazen's problem. It comprises drawing lines from two points in the plane of a circle meeting at a point on the circumference and making equal angles with the normal at that point. This leads to an equation of the fourth degree.

3. *Other scientific contributions*

In his book *Mizan al-Hikmah*, Ibn al-Haytham discussed the density of the atmosphere and related it to its height. He also studied atmospheric refraction. He discovered that twilight ceases or begins only when the sun is nineteen degrees below the horizon, and he attempted to measure the height of the atmosphere on that basis. He also discussed theories of attraction between masses, and it seems he was aware of the magnitude of acceleration due to gravity.

His contribution to mathematics and physics was extensive. In mathematics, he developed analytical geometry by establishing linkages between algebra and geometry. He studied the mechanics of *motion of a body and was the first to maintain that a body moves perpetually unless an external force stops it or changes its direction of motion, seemingly anticipating Newton's first law of motion.

4. *Influence*

Few of his two hundred works have survived; even his optics treatise survived only through its Latin translation. During the MA his books on *cosmology were translated into Latin, Hebrew, and other languages. He also wrote on evolution. In his writing, one can see a clear development of the scientific method as developed and applied by the Muslims, comprising the systematic observation of physical phenomena and their linking together into a scientific theory. This was a major breakthrough in scientific methodology and placed scientific pursuits on a sound foundation comprising a systematic relationship amongst observation, hypothesis-making, and verification. His influence on the physical sciences in general, and optics in particular, ushered in a new era in optical research, in theory and practice. His optics treatise was translated into Latin by *Witelo (1270), making the west aware of his theories on refraction and vision and of the importance of empirical experimentation. *See also* EXPERIMENT AND EXPERIMENTAL SCIENCE; METEOROLOGY; PHILOSOPHY, NATURAL. MD

A. M. Smith, *Alhacen's Theory of Visual Perception* (2001).
B. Steffens, *Ibn al-Haytham: First Scientist* (2005).

Ali (**Ali ibn Abi Talib**) (*c.*599–661) Cousin and son-in-law of *Muhammad; fourth caliph (656–61); first Shiite *imam; an early *Quran scribe. *Hasan and *Husayn, his sons with Muhammad's daughter Fatima, are the second and third Shiite Imams. Ali's *caliphate was characterized by accusations of failure to prosecute his predecessor *Uthman's assassins, civil war, and the secession of hardline *Shia partisans, one of whom assassinated him for his capitulations to the Umayyad Muawiya, his eventual successor. Ali's wisdom and oratory are collected in the 11th-century *Peak of Eloquence*. SMT

Ali ibn Abi Talib, *Nahjul Balagha: Peak of Eloquence*, tr. S. A. Reza, 3 vols (1973; 1984).
H. Kennedy, *The Prophet and the Age of the Caliphates* (2004).
W. Madelung, *The Succession to Muhammad: A Study of the Early Caliphate* (1997).
E. L. Petersen, *'Ali and Mu'awiya in Early Arabic Tradition*, tr. P. L. Christensen (1964).
al-Tabari, *The First Civil War*, tr. G. R. Hawting (1996).

Alia musica (early 10th century) Compendium of theoretical treatments applying Greek concepts of octave species and modes (from *Boethius) to *Carolingian church music, albeit with misinterpretations that would profoundly affect later music theory. REG

D. E. Cohen, 'Notes, Scales, and Modes in the Earlier Middle Ages', *Cambridge History of Western Music Theory*, ed. T. Christensen (2002), 331–38.

Alids Descendants of *Ali ibn Abi Talib, son-in-law and second cousin of *Muhammad. Alids and their supporters (*shia*) have always claimed that the Sunni Umayyad (661–750) and Abbasid (750–1258) dynasties had usurped the legitimate rule of Ali and his scions. Competing genealogical claims have resulted in a number of Alid groups (Imami, Zaidi, Ismaili) from North Africa to Afghanistan, with some (for example, Fatimids in *Egypt) successfully establishing themselves as Shiite dynasties during the MA. CPM

S. H. Jafri, *The Origins and Early Development of Shi'a Islam* (2002).
W. Madelung, *The Succession to Muhammad: A Study of the Early Caliphate* (1997).

Alimpii *See* DORMITION, CATHEDRAL OF THE.

Aliscans *See* GUILLAUME D'ORANGE CYCLE.

aljama Derived from the Arabic *al-jamaa*, meaning 'the gathering' or 'the assembly', the term *aljama* denotes a self-governing Jewish or Muslim community in the medieval Iberian Peninsula (*al-Andalus). It has also been used to refer to the physical area inhabited by this community. Use of the term became common in Iberia in the 13th century and spread to Sicily and southern *Italy. PYT

Y. Baer, *A History of the Jews in Christian Spain*, 2 vols (1966; repr. 1992).
J. Ray, *The Sephardic Frontier: The Reconquista and the Jewish Community in Medieval Iberia* (2006).

Aljubarrota, battle of (14 August 1385) Struggle between *Castile and Portugal to decide the possession of Portugal. Castilian king Juan I moved his nearly 14,000 troops through Biera into Estremadura down the road to *Lisbon. Portuguese king João I positioned his nearly 80,000 men on a rise in the road. Juan moved wide to the west of the Portuguese position and came up behind Portuguese forces on the same road late in the day, cutting João off from Lisbon and re-supply. Juan wanted to place his forces on a rise and fight the following day, but his knights refused and launched an attack uphill against João's repositioned army. Portugal's pikemen and archers devastated the Castilian cavalry and broke their assault. Juan retreated, ending the greatest medieval threat of Castilian occupation. JFPo

P. L. de Ayala, *Crónica del rey don Juan, primero de Castilla e de León, Biblioteca de Autores Españoles*, 68 (1953).
F. Lopes, *Crónica del Rey Dom Joham I da boa memória, Primeira Parte e Segunda Parte*, ed. A. B. Freire and W. H. Entwistle, 2 vols (1977).
P. E. Russell, *The English Intervention in Spain and Portugal in the Time of Edward III and Richard II* (1955).

Allah Biblical God in the *Quran and Islamic tradition, also termed *al-Rahman* 'the Merciful One' in some Quranic passages. Allah had been a supreme deity in the pre-Islamic Arabian pantheon, associated with three daughter goddesses, al-Lat ('the Goddess'), al-Manat ('Fate'), and al-Uzza ('the Powerful One'). God's 'beauteous names' (*al-asma al-husna*) are divine epithets, for example, *al-Karim* 'the Generous', *al-Muti* 'the Giver', used in theophoric personal names (for example, Abd al-Karim) and in prayers and supplications. Islamic tradition upholds strict monotheism and divine transcendence, condemning the attribution of any of God's power to other entities. DJSt

G. S. Reynolds, ed., *The Qur'an in its Historical Context* (2008).

Alleluia *See* MASS.

alliterative verse (*Stabreim*) Although a common poetic device in general, only in the older North and West Germanic languages (OE, ON, OS, OHG, OLG) was alliteration a basic stylistic principle. By supporting the work's meaning structurally through varying but regular types of metrical patterns, alliteration was an essential component of Germanic poetry and not a mere stylistic conceit. While OE and ON provide the most numerous illustrations of alliterative verse, there are also some examples in OHG (**Hildebrandslied*) and OS (**Heliand*). The basis of the alliterative verse is the Germanic long line consisting of two hemistichs separated by a caesura. The most important stress is the first stress of the second half-line. It determines the alliterative pattern. The first half-line may contain one or two alliterative stresses: *H*iltibrant enti *H*aðubrant untar ‖ *h*eriun tuem (Hildebrand and Hadubrand between two armies). Identical consonants—above *h*—alliterate; certain consonant clusters—*sp*-, *st*-, *sk*- (*sc*-)—alliterate only with each other; all vowels alliterate indiscriminately with each other. Only accented syllables alliterate; unaccented syllables, even those beginning with the alliterating letter, are unimportant. FGG

K. E. Gade, *A Bibliography of Germanic Alliterative Meters: Comparative Germanic, Old Norse, Old English, Middle English, Old Saxon, Old High German* (2000).
A. Heusler, *Deutsche Versgeschichte mit Einschluß des altenglischen und altnordischen Stabreimverses* ([2]1956).
W. Hoffmann, *Altdeutsche Metrik* (1967).
W. P. Lehmann, *The Development of Germanic Verse Form* (1956).
K. von See, *Germanische Verskunst* (1967).
E. Sievers, *Altgermanische Metrik* (1893).
T. Turville-Petre, *The Alliterative Revival* (1977).

allod and freehold Allodial land was heritable property owned absolutely, that is, with full rights and no obligations to an overlord, subject to claims of relatives and tenants. In some regions of *France, such property could be held of another person, although services were generally less onerous than those associated with *fiefs. EARB

S. Reynolds, *Fiefs and Vassals: The Medieval Evidence Reinterpreted* (1994).
E. Z. Tabuteau, *Transfers of Property in Eleventh-Century Norman Law* (1988).

All Saints, Feast of *See* LITURGICAL YEAR; LITURGY.

Almagest *See* ASTRONOMY.

Almain, Jacques (*c.*1480–1515) French philosopher and theologian. He studied and taught *arts and theology at the University of *Paris, and wrote treatises on moral, political, and natural *philosophy as well as *logic. He maintained that both individuals and communities had God-given inalienable rights, and he defended conciliar authority in the church against unrestricted papal power. *See also* CONCILIAR MOVEMENT; PAPACY. JAK

J. H. Burns, ed., *The Cambridge History of Political Thought, 1450–1700* (1991), 147–51, 657–8.

Almansor *See* RAZI, AL-.

Alma Redemptoris Mater *See* ANTIPHONS, MARIAN.

Almohads Founded by *Ibn Tumart, a *Berber of the Masmuda who having returned from the east, influenced by the teaching of al-Gazali (d. 1111), affirmed the absolute unity of God. Hence his followers were called unitarians, that is al-Muwahhidun, hence Almohads. Critical of the laxity of the *Almoravids, Ibn Tumart insisted on rigorous maintenance of the teachings of Islam through the *Quran and the Sunna, declaring himself mahdi. Below him was an inner council plus the Council of Ten and the Council of Fifty, which contained representatives of the Masmuda tribes. Under Ibn Tumart's successor, the caliph Abd al-*Mumin, expansionist wars were waged. First success came slowly, but in 1147 *Marrakesh was taken from the Almoravids, and the central Maghreb was then conquered (1152–9). In *al-Andalus, Cadiz and Jérez recognized the caliph (1146), and *Seville was captured (1147). While establishing their power in the southern Iberian Peninsula, they met resistance in the eastern peninsula from the independent Ibn Mardanish (1147–72) and in the west from *Afonso I Henriques. This deflected the Almohads from waging war against *Castile during the minority of Alfonso VIII, and while Abu Yaqub Yusuf (1163–84) turned Seville into an impressive capital of architectural splendour, advances in the north were negligible. The situation changed under Abu Yusuf Yaqub (1184–99), a brilliant general who consolidated Almohad power in North Africa, recaptured Alcacer do Sol and Silves from Portugal (1191), and inflicted a massive defeat on Castile at the battle of *Alarcos (1195). He took the name al-*Mansur. Now the Almohads reached to the height of their power, their armies dominant, their fleet powerful in the Mediterranean, their finances efficiently administered, their lands home to the writer-physician Ibn Tufayl and the great philosopher Ibn Rushd (*Averroës). Under al-Nasir (1199–1213), they conquered the Balearics (1203) and subdued the region of Ifriqiya (Tunisia and eastern Algeria) (1206–7). In 1211, al-Nasir crossed to the Peninsula, capturing the fortress of Salvatierra from Castile, and declaring war on all Christians. But on 16 July 1212, through both the caliph's miscalculations and divisions between his Andalusian and African troops, his army was crushingly defeated by the Christians at the battle of Las *Navas de Tolosa. The Almohads never recovered. After the reign of Yusuf II (1213–24), Christian political crises having delayed the end, a power struggle ensued with Abd al-Wahid proclaimed caliph in Morocco and al-Adil recognized in much of al-Andalus. The disintegration of authority allowed the Christians to take *Córdoba (1236), *Valencia (1238), and Seville (1248). In the Maghreb, Almohad doctrines were challenged and revolt spread. In 1229, the governor of Ifriqiya had declared himself independent, followed by those of Tlemcen and central Maghreb. *Marrakesh remained, a remnant of empire, until 1269, when it fell to the *Marinids. *See also* RECONQUISTA. DJSm

H. Kennedy, *Muslim Spain and Portugal* (1998).
R. Le Tourneau, *The Almohad Movement* (1969).
A. H. Miranda, *Historia política del Imperio Almohade* (1956–7).
M.-J. V. Molíns, *El retroceso territorial de al-Andalus* (1997).

almoner Monastic officer responsible for collecting and distributing food, clothes, and alms to the poor; he also had general care of any who recommended themselves to the charity of the *monastery. On occasion, the almoner would travel into towns to visit the ill in need of food or medication. *See also* CIVIC MEDICINE; POVERTY AND POOR RELIEF. GP

B. Harvey, *Living and Dying in England, 1100–1540: The Monastic Experience* (1993).

Almoravids *Berber followers of a religiously inspired movement that established an empire in northwest Africa and Spain during the 11th and 12th centuries. By the 10th century Islam had reached the nomadic Berbers in the Sahara south of Morocco's Atlas Mountains. After Abd Allah ben Yasin (d. 1059), a religious scholar, failed to impose a puritanical form of Islam among the Guddala, he found a more receptive audience among the Lamtuna, a rival tribe. He formed a close association with Yanya ben Umar (d. 1056) and his brother *Abu Bakr of the Banu Targut. Together they created a cross-tribal confederation.

Ibn Yasin called his followers *al-Murabitun* (Almoravids). By choosing this title from a word (with *Quranic precedent) that meant to band together for fighting, he emphasized a religious, rather than tribal, identity. They recognized the Abbasid *caliphs and followed the conservative Malikite school of Quranic interpretation. Their ascetic zeal, with the aspiration to abolish non-Quranic taxes, was acceptable to pious Muslims. The Almoravid expansion was by the force of persuasion as well as by the weight of arms.

In 1054 Ibn Yasin and Yahya ben Umar advanced along the trans-Saharan trade routes. After their deaths, Abu Bakr, as sole leader. established a new capital at *Marrakesh (*c.*1070), linking the former Saharan heartlands with anticipated conquests in northern Morocco. On leaving to suppress rebellion among the Saharan Berbers, Abu Bakr entrusted Marrakesh to a cousin, Yusuf b. Tashfin (d. 1106), who barred his return. Until his death Abu Bakr campaigned in the south Sahara. From Marrakesh, Ibn Tashfin spread Almoravid rule from the Atlantic to western Algeria, governing an empire of city-dwellers, nomads, and peasants.

Responding to appeals from the **taifa* kingdoms after the fall of *Toledo (1085) to Christian forces, Ibn Tashfin crossed to Spain, inflicted a defeat on Alfonso VI of León at Sagrajas, but failed to exploit the success and went back to Morocco. He returned to Spain on three occasions (1088, 1090, 1097). Ibn Tashfin reunited *al-Andalus after 1090 by annexing all of the *taifa* states except for Saragossa. Despite the gulf between rough Berber tribesmen and the sophisticated Andalusian elite, the Almoravids were welcomed for their piety, readiness to abolish non-canonical taxes, and military prowess. Ibn Tashfin and his successor stemmed the

Christian advance without recovering Toledo and the middle Tagus valley.

Under Ali b. Yusuf b. Tashfin (d.1143), who made four visits (1107, 1109, 1117, 1121), Almoravid armies largely dominated Spain until 1118. The loss of Saragossa (1118) to *Aragon and a revolt in *Córdoba (1121) indicated a deteriorating position. The real threat lay in Morocco from another fundamentalist Berber movement, the *Almohads (*al-Muwahhidun*), after 1120. In 1147 the Almoravid dynasty fell with the Almohad capture of Marrakesh. Diminishing resources, the need to raise extra taxes, and military defeat undermined the Almoravids in Spain. The last Almoravid governor to resist the Almohads died at *Granada in 1149.

JWr

M. Fierro, 'Almoravids', *MedIsl* vol. 1, 39–40.
H. Kennedy, *Muslim Spain and Portugal* (1996).
V. Lagardère, *Les Almoravides* (1989).

Alp Arslan I *See* SELJUK TURKS.

Alpert of Metz (*fl.* 1005–25) Monastic author of two historical works: the *Diversitate temporum* (*c*.1005) and *Fragmentum de Deoderico primo episcopo Mettensi* (*c*.1024) provide information about the *Low Countries and imperial affairs.

ASC

Alpertus van Metz, *Gebeurtenissen van deze tijd & Een fragment over bisschop Diederik van Metz*, ed. and trans. (Dutch), H. van Rij and A. S. Abulafia (1980).

Alphonse de Poitiers *See* POITIERS AND POITOU.

Alps and Alpine passes The Alps Mountains cover over 80,000 square miles from the south of *France to Slovenia. The source of many of Europe's important rivers, the mountains created a barrier to easy travel between the Italian peninsula and the rest of the continent. A number of important passes, including Great St Bernard, *St Gotthard, *Brenner, Felber Tauern, and those in the east around Tarvis, channelled communications. Control of these important, if difficult, crossings helped buttress religious, political, and economic control in the region. Northern European armies were led into the Italian peninsula repeatedly using these routes.

Many of the routes mentioned had been known in pre-historic times and had been improved by the Romans. Medieval Europeans often re-utilized existing paths, such as the Brenner or Tauern passes. Most of these did not allow for wagons, so a combination of pack animals, human labour, and water travel was used. The merchandise carried was correspondingly compact and lightweight, except in cases where logs or other heavy goods were shipped downstream via rafts.

Travel continued for much of the year, adverse weather notwithstanding. A complex network of *hospices and *monasteries was built to assist the travellers, those under way for commercial purposes or travelling southward on Christian *pilgrimage. The most famous of such hospices were those founded in the mid-10th century by St Bernard de Menthon, the Archdean of Aosta Diocese, near the two passes that now bear his name. The establishment of Christian religious houses in the Alpine region of Europe around 1000 played important roles in the region's religious, economic, and political development. These houses included ones at Einsiedeln and *St Gall.

The pastoral economy of the Alpine valleys encouraged heterogeneity and particularism. Until competition from sea trade, among other factors, developed in the 14th century, the Alps were home to a flourishing and complex set of societies using a variety of spoken languages (including French, Italian, German, Slovenian) and a rich imaginative culture still reflected in the hundreds of legends, sagas, and tales about the various mountains, valleys, rocks, and rivers of the area. Culture tended to be local and tied to particular valleys. Later, *mining activities were introduced, particularly in those areas under the control of the *Habsburg dynasty such as the County of *Tyrol or the Styrian March. The pastures high in the mountains, between the tree and snowlines, were home to seasonal societies tied to livestock and woodworking.

Seigneurial authority did not develop strongly in many parts of the region. This is partly reflected in the variety of Christian practice that is recorded, particularly in the western reaches. Known now as *'Waldensians', the followers of non-orthodox Christian religious practice were first noted in the region beginning in the mid 14th century, particularly on the borders of the French kingdom and the Duchy of *Savoy. *See also* INNSBRUCK; STYRIA.

JFP

J.-F. Bergier, *Pour une histoire des Alpes, Moyen Âge et Temps modernes* (1997).
J. E. Tyler, *The Alpine Passes: The Middle Ages (962–1250)* (1930).

Alsace The territory between the Vosges Mountains, *Rhine river, and Jura Mountains, known by the 7th century as 'Alsace'. Roman military settlement in the area included a base at what would become the most important Alsatian city, *Strasbourg (Latin: *Argentoratum*). This city reportedly became the seat of a bishop in the 3rd or 4th century.

The region was incorporated into the Frankish realm around 500. The following centuries saw extensive Christian *missionizing and the establishment of *monastic houses such as Murbach and Wissembourg. St Odilia (d. *c*.720) is credited with founding the important cloister at Mont Ste-Odile. This was the only period in Alsatian history when it was governed as a single political unit: a *duchy which existed for about a century. In the mid 9th century the famous *'Strasbourg Oaths' taken by two of *Charlemagne's grandsons began the division of the Frankish empire. This resulted in the inclusion of Alsace in the empire, where it would remain.

Alsace was home to many important cities, including Colmar and Haguenau. It benefited from *trade routes along the Rhine. The bridge built at Strasbourg in the later 14th century was for a long time the last one across the river before its mouth. The accession of Werner I as bishop of Strasbourg in 1001 marked the beginning of another important development in the history of Alsace: the increasing role of the *Habsburg dynasty there.

By the 14th century, the Habsburgs' interests had moved farther east. The development of independent *Swiss cantons, the accession of *Basel to the cantons' federation in 1501, and the growth of *Burgundy in the 15th century left Alsace isolated and divided. JFP

A. Acker, ed., *Encyclopédie de l'Alsace* (1982–6).

alta capella Term used to refer to the shawm band in the 15th century, known also in England as Waits and in *Italy as *pifferi*. It consisted of two to four shawm players and a slide trumpet (after *c.*1490, replaced by a trombone). As distinct from the other loud (*alta*) instruments such as trumpets and percussion, this ensemble performed for dances and also was capable of performing more sophisticated, composed polyphonic repertory. TM

H. M. Brown and S. Sadie, eds, *Performance Practice: Music Before 1600* (1989).

R. W. Duffin, ed., *A Performer's Guide to Medieval Music* (2000).

altar, altar decoration, and utensils A table-high structure in a church, at which the *Mass, culminating in the consecration of bread and wine (*Eucharist), is celebrated. The Christian altar is the result of two ritual traditions from antiquity: the sacrifice and the meal. Both received a Christian significance through Christ's Last Supper (Mark 14:22–31). This double association has also determined the formal evolution of the Christian altar.

The altars in the pre-Constantinian house churches may still have been transportable, table-like pieces of furniture. From the 4th century onwards, when altars were placed in monumental church buildings, they tended to become fixed, solid structures, usually executed in *stone. This was certainly not a direct reversion to pagan antecedents of sacrificial altar blocks but was a consequence of a more complicated association of the sacrifice of Christ with that of the martyrs, and, hence, of the altar with martyrs' tombs. Accordingly, altars adopted the additional significance of a tomb, of which *relics became the concretization. In the medieval west all altars were equipped with relics. Conversely, table-like structures without the function of relic containers remained the rule in the eastern churches.

In their shape, western medieval altars may vary from massive blocks and chests with solid sides to more transparent table forms. Unlike most Greek and Roman antecedents they have a separate upper slab (*mensa*), obviously reminiscent of the table. Early Christian churches sheltered only one altar. Due to the multiplication of private masses, secondary altars were common from *Carolingian times onward. The high altar was originally free-standing in front of the *apse. Later, it was moved towards the end of the *chancel whereas secondary altars could be built directly against walls or pillars.

The support (*stipes*) and the *mensa* are the essential elements of the altar and are solemnly consecrated by the bishop. All the other components are secondary in nature

Set of nested beakers, Prague (1310–35), partially in gilt silver. Found in a house in Kutná Hora, Bohemia.

and are normally only blessed for sacred use. The block itself could be covered by a frontal or 'antependium', usually decorated. Older examples with *metal reliefs have been preserved, but frontals of fabric were most common. The altarpiece of *wood, metal, or stone was mounted above or behind the altar. This screen-like structure contained an iconographical programme directly focused on the liturgical function of the Mass or a devotional meaning (for example, patron saints). Although a relatively late addition (11th–13th centuries), the altarpiece became visually the most dominant element of the late medieval altar.

Until the 9th century, nothing was placed on the altar *mensa* except those *liturgical furnishings and books and Eucharistic vessels to be used during the Mass. Candlesticks usually stood on the floor in front of the altar during the service. Gradually, the candlesticks and a *cross became indispensable attributes of the altar, permanently placed on the *mensa* or a special shelf attached to it. *See also* MARTYROLOGY; SARCOPHAGUS AND TOMB. SdB

'The Altar from the 4th to the 15th Century', *Hortus Artium Medievalium*, 11 (2005).
J. Braun, *Der christliche Altar in seiner geschichtlichen Entwicklung* (1924).
J.-P. Caillet, 'L'arredo dell'altare', *L'arte medievale nel contesto (300–1300)*, ed. P. Piva (2006), 181–204.
V. Fuchß, *Das Altarensemble: Eine Analyse des Kompositcharakters früh- und hochmittelalterlicher Altarausstattung* (1999).

Altdeutsche Genesis (before 1075) EMHG *epic commentary on Genesis in end-rhyme; the poet (a Carinthian cleric) possessed mediocre talents, but his aim was a comprehensible exposition of the divine plan, not learnedness. There are two 12th-century MS transmissions: 1) Vienna and 2) Klagenfurt/Millstatt. FGG

F. G. Gentry, *Bibliographie zur frühmittelhochdeutschen geistlichen Dichtung* (1992), 112–23.

Altichiero da Zevio (*c.*1335–93) Veronese painter responsible for designing and executing the *fresco cycles in the oratory of San Giorgio and chapel of San Giacomo in *Padua and the Cavalli chapel in Sant'Anastasia in *Verona, among others. *See also* CHAPEL; ORATORY. DJR

G. L. Mellini, *Altichiero et Jacopo Avanzi* (1965).
P. Pettenella, *Altichiero e la pittura veronese del trecento* (1961).
J. Richards, *Altichiero: An Artist and his Patrons in the Italian Trecento* (2000).

Altmann of Passau, St (d. 1091) (bishop) Altmann reformed and founded several *monasteries, including Gottweig, where he was venerated as a saint (without official *canonization). A staunch supporter of *Pope Gregory VII, Altmann was named papal *legate in *Germany and driven from his see by Henry IV. ASC

E. Boshof, *Die Regeste der Bischöfe von Passau 731–1206* (1992).

Altswert, Master (late 14th century) Composed four love narratives ('Reden') in which he criticized his own time and raised social and moral issues concerning love. He was also the first to develop the idea of the 'Venusberg' which the poet enters and learns the true values of love. AC

W. L. Holland and A. von Keller, eds, *Meister Altswert* (1850).
E. A. McCormick, 'Meister Altswert's *Kittel*', *Germanic Review*, 35 (1960), 1–15.

alum and astringents Of substances used medically to shrink tissues and lessen the discharge of blood or mucus, the best-known was alum (aluminum potassium sulfate), a salt used in compresses to heal wounds. However, alum was better known as a detergent used in everything from the *fulling of *wool to dentifrices, and as a mordant to fix dyes. Many common *herbs, including Herb Robert (a species of cranesbill), sage, and thyme, had astringent properties and were applied topically for skin irritations and as antiseptics or used in poultices to cure wounds. *Avicenna recommended astringent wine as an antiseptic. TFG

Alvarus Cordubensis *See* PAULUS ALBARUS.

Amadeus of Lausanne, St (1110–59) Imperial counsellor, papal legate, bishop, and abbot. Amadeus is best known for his eight *sermons on the Blessed Virgin *Mary, two works addressed to monks, and an epistle to his persecuted spiritual sons of the *Lausanne church. AJD

Collectanea ordinis Cisterciensum Reformatorum (1959), 1–65.
A. Dimier, *Amédeé de Lausanne, disciple de saint Bernard* (1949).

Amadís de Gaula Most famous of the Spanish **libros de caballería*. References to this neo-Arthurian work can be traced from the mid 14th century onwards, although the first extant edition appeared much later in 1508. Despite its 16th-century date, this four-volume edition was probably reworked *c.*1492 by Garci Rodríguez de Montalvo. *See also* LITERATURES: ARTHURIAN LEGEND. JG

J. M. C. Blecua, *Amadís: heroísmo mítico cortesano* (1979).
S. Gil-Albarellos, *'Amadís de Gaula' y el género caballeresco en España* (1999).

Amalar of Metz (*c.*775–*c.*850) Archbishop of *Trier (809), administrator of the Lyons diocese (835); travelled to the Constantinopolitan court on *Charlemagne's behalf. His influential, controversial *Liber officialis* introduced exegesis to the *liturgy and championed symbolic and allegorical interpretations of Christian ritual. JJC

F. Brunhölzl, *Histoire de la littérature latine du Moyen Âge*, vol. 1/2 (1991), 186–8, 304–5.
C. A. Jones, *A Lost Work by Amalarius of Metz* (2001).

Amalric of Bène (Amalric of Chartres) (d. *c.*1206) Master in *Paris, whose teaching, usually termed pantheistic, was condemned by the synod in Paris (1210) in the form propagated by his followers called the Amalricians. IDK

G. Dickson, 'The Burning of the Amalricians', *JEH*, 40 (1989), 347–69.
P. Lucentini, 'L'eresia di Amalrico', *Eriugena redivivus: Zur Wirkungsgeschichte seines Denkens im Mittelalter und im Übergang zur Neuzeit*, ed. W. Beierwaltes (1987), 174–91.

Amandus, St (d. *c*.675) Missionary bishop influenced by Columbanian *monasticism. Worked mainly in the region of modern Belgium and was briefly bishop of Maastricht. Founder of the *monastery in Elnone that later would bear his name: St Amand. RMe

I. Wood, *The Missionary Life: Saints and the Evangelization of Europe, 400–1050* (2001).

Amarcius (Sextus Amarcius Gallus Piosistratus) (*c*.1100) Pseudonym for the author (probably a German cleric) of a four-book, Horatian-style hexameter didactic work titled *Sermones*. The author packs his text with references to authors of pagan and Christian antiquity, satirizes moral decline, and calls for a life of virtue. GKG

Amarcius, *Sermones*, ed. K. Manitius, *MGH.QG* 6 (1969).
C. White, '*Quid facit cum psalterio Horatius*? The "Sermones" of Sextus Amarcius—Horatian or Christian?', *Mittellateinisches Jahrbuch*, 26 (1991), 103–16.

Amatus of Montecassino (d. before 1098–9?) Perhaps Bishop Amatus of Paestum (1047–58?); monk at *Monte Cassino by 1061. Author of both the (poorly transmitted) earliest account of the Norman conquest of southern *Italy and of an epic on the deeds of St Peter. JMHo

Amatus of Montecassino, *History of the Normans*, tr. P. Dunbar with G. Loud (2004).
A. Lentini, *Il Poema di Amato su S. Pietro Apostolo* (1958).

Amaury de Chartres *See* AMALRIC OF BÈNE.

ambo A raised platform from which liturgical readings were spoken or sung. It usually stood in the *nave, attached to a *chancel enclosure, sometimes in a pair. In the high MA, the ambo was superseded by a lectern for the readings and by the *pulpit for other functions. SdB

J.-P. Sodini, 'L'ambon dans l'église primitive', *La Maison-Dieu*, 193 (1993), 39–51.
G. Vrins, 'De Ambon, oorsprong en verspreiding tot 600', *Feestbundel F. van der Meer*, ed. E. van der Grinten (1964), 11–55.

Amboise On the Loire, east of *Tours; fortified site, lordship seat from 840; enclave of counts of *Anjou in struggles with counts of *Blois. Rebuilt in the early 12th century, then confiscated and added to the royal demesne in the 1430s. Louis XI, often in residence, began expansions, founding the Order of St Michael (1469). Birthplace of *Charles VIII who built a Gothic chapel and began transforming the castle into a Renaissance château with an Italianate garden. JFP

Château Amboise, built 15th–16th centuries.

J.-P. Babelon and J.-B. Leroux, *Le Château d'Amboise* (2004).
E. Thomas, 'Les logis royaux d'Amboise', *Revue de l'art*, 100 (1993), 44–57.

Ambraser Heldenbuch Compiled between 1503 and 1516 by the customs official Hans Ried (Bozen) for Maximilian I, the *Ambraser Heldenbuch* is a collection of twenty-five medieval German texts of diverse genres, including the only extant copy of the heroic epic **Kudrun*. WM

H.-J. Koppitz, *Studien zur Tradierung der weltlichen mittelhochdeutschen Epik im 15. und beginnenden 16. Jahrhundert* (1980).
F. Unterkircher, ed., *Ambraser Heldenbuch: Vollständige Faksimile-Ausgabe im Originalformat. Kommentar* (1973).

Ambrose, St (*c*.339–97) Lawyer, prefect, drafted as bishop of *Milan (373/4); one of the Latin church's *Four Doctors. He influenced *Augustine's conversion, wrote many homiletic and exegetical works, and was an early composer of influential Latin *hymnody. Ambrose had forceful and effective dealings with contemporary emperors, particularly Theodosius, whom for ordering a massacre he threatened with excommunication until he had gone through several months of penance. Ambrose was influential in Theodosius' making Christianity the official state religion of Rome (as against polytheism) and backing Nicene orthodoxy (versus *Arianism). Ambrose was considered unusual in his day for reading silently to himself rather than out loud. JCH

N. B. McLynn, *Ambrose of Milan* (1994).
J. Moorhead, *Ambrose: Church and Society in the Late Roman World* (1999).
G. Nauroy, ed., *Lire et éditer aujourd'hui Ambroise de Milan* (2007).
D. H. Williams, *Ambrose of Milan and the End of the Arian-Nicene Conflicts* (1995).

Ambrosian chant Liturgical song of the *Ambrosian rite of *Milan. Strophic 'Ambrosian' hymns (some by *Ambrose) were widely influential. Some prose chants are related to eastern Greek troparia. PJ

T. Bailey, *The Transitoria of the Ambrosian Mass* (2003).
CLLA 060, 550–57.
R. Weakland, 'The Office Antiphons of the Ambrosian Chant', Ph.D. thesis (Columbia, 2000).

Ambrosian rite Liturgical tradition of the *Milan diocese, ascribed to *Ambrose, but surely later. Most MSS date from the 12th century or later; the rite was reformed in the *Carolingian era. The morning office exhibits structural similarities to the Greek rite of *Jerusalem. PJ

B. G. Baroffio, 'Iter Liturgicum Ambrosianum', *Aevum*, 74 (2000), 583–603.
CLLA 501–95.
M. Navoni, *Dizionario di liturgia ambrosiana* (1996).

ambry (aumbry) A recess in a church wall for keeping sacred *Eucharistic vessels and *liturgical books. It later developed into a tabernacle for the hosts used in Holy *Communion. *See also* LITURGICAL FURNISHINGS. SdB

J. H. Walker and S. J. P. van Dijk, *The Myth of the Aumbry: Notes on Medieval Reservation Practice and Eucharistic Devotion* (1957).

ambulatory A walkway surrounding the *apse or *chancel end of a church, usually a continuation of the aisles, serving to facilitate circulation behind the sanctuary. Ambulatories existed already in the early Christian period (for example, S. Sebastiano, *Rome). From the Romanesque period onwards they could be extended by means of radiating *chapels (for example, Cluny III, late 11th century). *See also* ART AND ARCHITECTURE: ROMANESQUE. SdB

J. Herschman, 'The Norman Ambulatory of Le Mans Cathedral and the *chevet* of the Cathedral of Coutances', *Gesta*, 20 (1981), 323–32.
S. Heywood, s.v. 'Ambulatory', *The Dictionary of Art* (1996), vol. 1, 767–8.

melioratio terrae Medieval term for land reclamation. An initial colonizing phase of settlement extension covered *Carolingian Europe in the 8th and 9th centuries. The second wave swept almost all of Europe from the 11th to the 14th centuries, mainly in fringe areas: the British Isles, the Iberian Peninsula, and the lands east of the *river Elbe. Colonization reached *Bohemia, *Poland, and *Hungary in the 12th century through guest institutions, which received privileges to cultivate the new lands. From the 13th century mostly German settlers gradually made their way eastwards. They were granted 'German law' (**jus theutonicum*), defined on the conquered Slav territories between the Elbe and Oder rivers in the later 12th century. This was first granted only to foreign arrivals, but was soon applied also to the native population. Medieval *colonization is usually associated with adoption of grain-growing, growth in number of towns, and increased liberties for peasants and burghers. The debate on the meaning of medieval colonization, particularly for east-central Europe, continues, but it shaped the cultural landscape of Europe until the industrial age. It should not however be equated with 'Germanization', since these were largely independent processes. *See also* ESTATE MANAGEMENT AND ORGANIZATION. JMP

R. Bartlett, *The Making of Europe: Conquest, Colonization and Cultural Change* (1993).
A. Körmendy, *Melioratio terrae: Vergleichende Untersuchungen über die Siedlungsbewegung im östlichen Mitteleuropa im 13.–14. Jahrhundert* (1995).
J. M. Piskorski, ed., *Historiographical Approaches to Medieval Colonization of East Central Europe* (2002).
—— 'The Medieval Colonization of Central Europe as a Problem of World History and Historiography', *German History*, 22 (2004), 323–43.

Amerus English music theorist active in *Italy. His *Practica artis musice* (1271) covers basic chant theory (intervals, musical hand, mutations, characteristics of the eight modes) and includes two tonaries (for French and English churches; for the Roman curia). The penultimate chapter is an introduction to *mensural notation. JDy

C. Ruini, ed., *Ameri Practica artis musice (1271)* (1977).

amice *See* LITURGICAL VESTMENTS.

Amiens Episcopal town in *Picardy, *c.*125 km north of *Paris. A Gallic settlement and later a Roman city, it was an episcopal see since at least the early 6th century. The counts of Amiens ruled the town and its surroundings from the 9th century until 1190, when *Philip II Augustus joined it to the *Capetian domain. By the 13th century Amiens was an important economic centre with around 3,000 inhabitants. It is practically synonymous with its High Gothic *cathedral, one of the most architecturally significant in Europe. When the previous church was destroyed by fire in 1218, Bishop Evrard de Fouilloy commissioned the architect Robert de Luzarches to replace it. Luzarches completed the lower portion of the west façade, the three-aisle *nave (at 43 m the tallest of its era), and the western *transept aisles. His successor, Thomas de Cormont, completed the eastern transept aisles, choir aisles, and seven radiating choir chapels. Major construction ended under his son Regnault, who concluded and vaulted the transept and choir. Important artistic elements

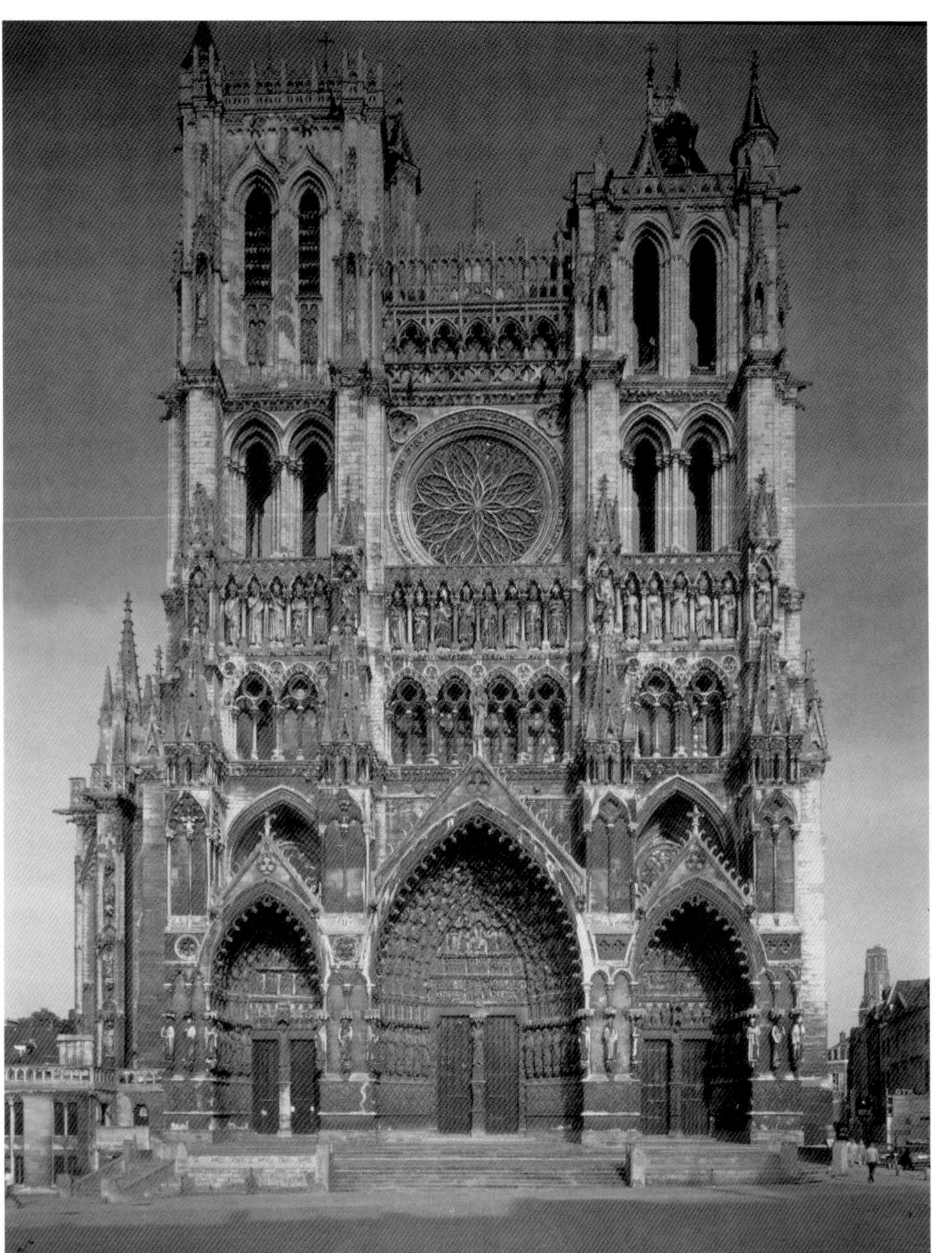

Cathedral at Amiens.

included an octagonal pavement labyrinth with figures of the architects and patron (1288, destroyed early 19th century; reconstructed) and particularly the west façade portal sculpture, which was once richly painted and whose programme derives partly from Chartres and *Notre-Dame in Paris. SAH

S. Murray, *Notre Dame, Cathedral of Amiens* (1996).
—— *A Gothic Sermon* (2004).
D. Verret and D. Steyaert, eds, *La couleur et la pierre* (2002).

Amis et Amiles OFr. **chanson de geste*, *c.*1200, concerning physically identical friends. When Amiles is accused of having slept with *Charlemagne's daughter Belissant, Amis secretly and successfully takes his place in the ensuing judicial trial by *battle. An *angel promises him *leprosy when, maintaining his disguise, he offers to wed Belissant. Amiles, on God's instructions, slaughters his infant sons and bathes the leprous Amis in their blood, curing him. The elevation of male *friendship both idealizes and problematizes a central *epic theme. Versions are found throughout Europe. *See also* LITERATURES: FRENCH. JGi

S. N. Rosenberg and S. Danon, trs, *Ami and Amile: A Medieval Tale of Friendship* (1996).

amor hereos *See* LOVESICKNESS.

ampulla A small rounded flask with a narrow mouth and two handles, usually made of metal or earthenware. Ampullae often contained *holy water or oil from *pilgrimage sites and regularly display relief images, such as a saint or Chi-Rho monogram. An example of a pilgrim's pewter ampulla depicting Christ's Resurrection (Palestine, 6th–7th century) is in the collection of Dumbarton Oaks, Washington, DC. JTS

A. Grabar, *Ampoules de Terre Sainte* (1958).

Amram ben Sheshna (d. *c.*875) (Gaon) Jurist and rabbinic leader best known for composing the earliest known Jewish prayer book, in the form of a responsum sent to Spain. Amram may have been at the head of a faction that broke away from the Babylonian academy of Sura. PIAL

R. Brody, *The Geonim of Babylonia and the Shaping of Medieval Jewish Culture* (1997).
G. Cohen, *The Book of Tradition* (1967).

Amsterdam City in the county of *Holland. A small *town that only developed into a real city during the 13th and 14th centuries from a *Frisian peat settlement. Gradually, a port developed and it was dammed *c.*1270. Along the dyke of the river Amstel an urban nucleus of *artisans, merchants, and shipmasters would develop into what would become a metropole in the 17th century. In 1306 Amsterdam was granted *urban privileges. During the later MA the role of Amsterdam shipmasters in the North Sea and the *Baltic *trade steadily grew. JDu

W. Frijhoff, ed., *Geschiedenis van Amsterdam* (2004), vol. 1.

amulets *See* CHARMS, INCANTATIONS, AND AMULETS.

Anacletus II, Pope (1130–38) (antipope) In the papal *election of 1130 a small group of *cardinals elected Cardinal-Deacon Gregory, the favourite of the powerful Frangipani faction. He took the name Honorius II. Hours later a larger group elected Piero Pierleoni, the favourite of the faction headed by his family. He took the name Anacletus II. As both elections were irregular, *schism ensued. *Rome, much of *Italy, and Scotland supported Anacletus, while England, *France, Germany, and St *Bernard of Clairvaux supported Honorius. Emperor Lothar III effected Honorius' return to Rome in 1132, but he could not secure control. Nevertheless, support for Anacletus dwindled, and on his death in 1138 no one was elected to succeed him.

Anacletus, a *Cluniac monk, had been cardinal-priest of Santa Maria in Trastevere, and a *legate in England and France. He represented the Cluniac-*Gregorian strand of reform. Pierleoni's family had converted from Judaism in the mid 11th century. TFXN

H. K. Mann, *The Lives of the Popes in the Early Middle Ages* (1925), vol. 9, 4–56.
R. Manselli, 'Anacleto II, antipapa', *Enciclopedia dei Papi* (2000), vol. 2, 268–70.
F. J. Schmale, *Studien zum Schisma des Jahres 1130* (1961).
M. Stroll, *The Jewish Pope* (1987).

anaesthetics and soporifics Medieval recipes do not always meet definitions used in modern anaesthesia, but the intended result was the same—to make a person 'slepe so þat he schal fele no kuttyng' (*Arderne). Such recipes occur in hundreds of *therapeutic compendia and *surgery treatises in Latin and vernacular languages and take three forms: inhalants (soporific sponge); drinks; and ointments for application to the skin or under the tongue. They call for one or more active agents such as opiates, hemlock, henbane, and alcohol, and they often include such laxatives as briony, apparently for speedy evacuation of dangerous drugs from the body. Rendering a person unconscious was not difficult, but the difference between a state desired for surgery or *cautery on one hand and death from respiratory depression on the other is small. Surgery texts sometimes urge great caution in the use of anaesthetics or warn against it. Geographical differences are reflected in these recipes. The soporific sponge, utilizing mandragora, is found frequently on the continent but is less common in England, while the drink called 'dwale' is rare on the continent, but occurs in scores of English MSS. LEV

M. Baur, 'Recherches sur l'histoire de l'anesthésie avant 1846', *Janus*, 31 (1927), 24–270.
E. S. Ellis, *Ancient Anodynes* (1946).
J. Poulin, *L'Anesthésie avant l'emploi du chloroforme et de l'éther* (1931).
L. E. Voigts and R. P. Hudson, '"A drynke þat men callen dwale to make a man to slepe whyle men kerven hem": A Surgical Anesthetic from Late Medieval England', *Health, Disease and Healing in Medieval Culture*, ed. S. Campbell *et al.* (1992), 34–56.

Anagni, Outrage (Humiliation) **of** (1303) When *Pope Boniface VIII asserted his supremacy over *Philip IV of *France with the bull *Unam sanctam*, the king's councillor Guillaume de *Nogaret, in concert with Boniface's enemies, the *Colonna, captured and abused the pope in his family palace at Anagni. Rescued by the people, Boniface died three weeks later (11 October 1303). DHW

'William of Hundlehy's Account of the Anagni Outrage', tr. H. G. J. Beck, *CHR* 32 (1947), 200–201.

analogy The doctrine of analogy was discussed in medieval *logic, *metaphysics, and theology. Medieval theories of analogy ultimately stem from Aristotle's comments on a special type of equivocation. Normally, an equivocal term has completely different definitions in each of its uses. In *Metaphysics* 4.2, Aristotle describes how the multiple use of a term can have different senses that are related to each other through one central meaning. Many theologians invoke analogy when explaining how we can talk meaningfully about God with terms drawn from creatures. In *Summa theologiae* I.13, *Thomas Aquinas explains how terms designating certain kinds of perfections are predicated of God. Perfections such as goodness or knowledge are found in creatures in a limited form but of themselves do not imply limitation. One can literally predicate these perfections of God, after removing the limiting qualifications connoted in their application to creatures. God is good in a way that is neither completely different from nor completely identical to the way that created beings, who participate in his goodness, are themselves good. *Henry of Ghent argued that Aquinas's theory of analogy was reducible to pure equivocity. Henry's elaborate explanation for how analogical concepts can be known (*Summa quaestionum ordinariarum*, aa. 21, 24) prompted *Duns Scotus to develop his doctrine of the univocity of being in response. *See also* ARISTOTELIANISM. AVR

E. J. Ashworth, 'Signification and Modes of Signifying in Thirteenth-Century Logic: A Preface to Aquinas on Analogy', *Medieval Theology and Philosophy*, 1 (1991), 39–67.
A. de Libera, 'Les sources gréco-arabes de la théorie médiévale de l'analogie de l'être', *Les études philosophiques*, 3–4 (1989), 319–45.
R. McInerny, *Aquinas and Analogy* (1996).

Anan ben David (8th century) Sectarian leader learned in rabbinic lore and descended from a Davidic line, passed over for the Rabbanite exilarchate in favour of his brother. Rejecting Talmudic legal exegesis, Anan's *Sefer ha-Mitzvot* ('Book of Precepts') became a cornerstone of *Karaite literature as this sect eventually looked to Anan as their founder. PIAL

G. Cohen, *The Book of Tradition* (1967).
L. Nemoy, *Karaite Anthology* (1952).

Anastasis The image representing the descent of Christ into *hell from where he released the Old Testament righteous. This image denotes his Resurrection and became the feast icon of *Easter Sunday in the Orthodox church. *See also* HARROWING OF HELL; ICONOGRAPHY: ICONS, TYPES OF CHRIST, MARY, OTHERS; LITURGY. IDK

A. Kartsonis, *Anastasis: The Making of an Image* (1986).
I. Shalina, 'Pskovskie ikony "Soshestvie vo ad": o liturgicheskoj interpretatsii ikonographicheskih osobennostej', *Vostochnohristianskij hram: litugija i iskusstvo*, ed. A. M. Lidov (1994), 230–64.

Anastasius, patriarch of Antioch (d. 598) An opponent of some of Justinian's doctrinal positions, he was deposed from Antioch's Chalcedonian headship by Justin II and sent to *Constantinople where he met *Pope Gregory I, the future 'Great' pope. He composed treatises on the *Trinity and the Incarnation (also surviving in Latin and Syriac) that were used in the Iconoclast controversy. *See also* ICONOGRAPHY: ICONOCLASM. LSBM

CPG 6944–6969.
A. Papadakis, 'Anastasios I', *ODB*, vol. 1, 87.

Anastasius Bibliothecarius (d. *c.*878) Successively Roman priest, antipope, papal secretary, and papal librarian. His career included *excommunication, deposition, and restoration. He counted popes and kings among his patrons and adversaries. A scholar, he translated Greek works into Latin and revised *John Scottus Eriugena's translation of *Pseudo-Dionysius. JJC

M. McCormick, 'Anastasius Bibliothecarius', *ODB*, vol. 1, 88–9.
B. Neil, *Seventh-Century Popes and Martyrs: The Political Hagiography of Anastasius the Librarian* (2007).

anathema *See* EXCOMMUNICATION.

anatomy and physiology Pre-modern thinkers—indeed most writers until William Harvey (d. 1657)—did not distinguish between anatomy and physiology. Form and design (anatomy) were assumed to reflect the function (physiology) intended by an all-wise Creator or Prime Mover. The study of body structure began in the early MA with the simple concepts and limited vocabulary found in the Roman writers Celsus and Pliny. Awareness of more detailed Greek and Hellenistic investigations came through a complex process of transmission through first Christian and then Islamic cultures of the Middle East. Study through actual observation began surprisingly early in the MA, but developed slowly.

1. Beginnings in Pliny, Celsus, and Isidore of Seville
2. Recovery of Hippocratic, Galenic, and other ancient texts
3. Development of empirical investigation and the use of images

1. Beginnings in Pliny, Celsus, and Isidore of Seville

Greek was the medical language of the Roman Empire. Heirs to the Latin tradition in the west, where knowledge of the Greek language was virtually unknown after about the 6th century, therefore, were deprived of even the basic terms to designate parts of the body. In the *Historia naturalis* of the Roman encyclopedist Pliny, there are scattered remarks on the practices of practical *medicine but very little on human structure or function. Terms and concepts in the 8th book of Celsus' *De medicina*, purportedly a treatise on the bones, are often confused, and the same word is used to designate several different anatomical structures. *Isidore of Seville (570–636) tried to repair this lacuna in the Latin vocabulary by devoting a chapter in each of his works, *Etymologiae* and *Differentia*, to defining and explaining the terms for parts of human structure.

Glimmerings of classical anatomical knowledge were also obtained by the Latin West through translations of Greek Christian theological writings. The works of the Cappadocian Fathers, which were early translated from

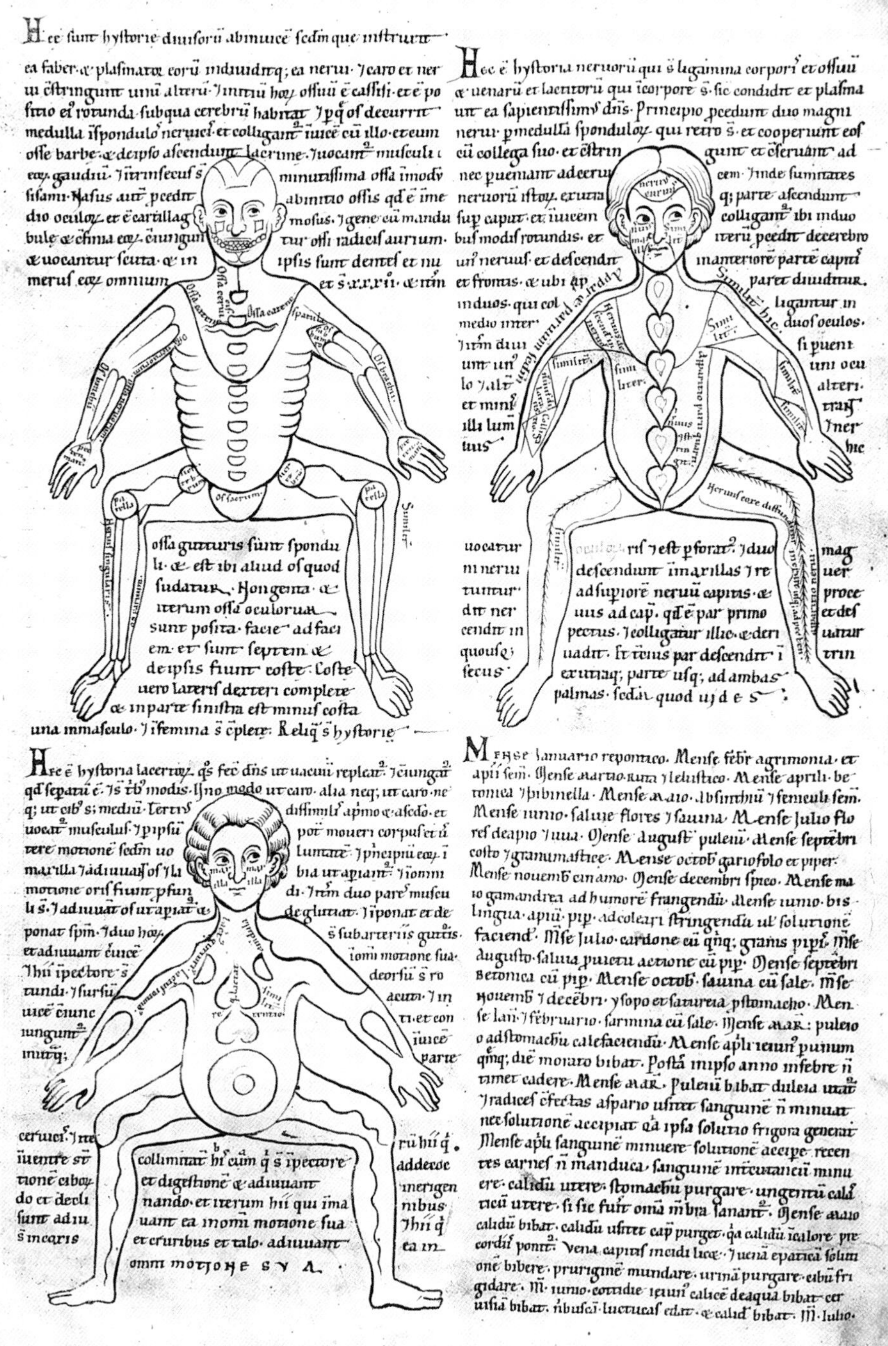

Fünfbilderserie or the Five-Figure series of anatomical images, Munich.

Greek to Latin, exemplify this stream of knowledge. Most significant in this transfer of anatomical ideas and terms is the writing of Gregory of Nyssa, whose systematic anthropological treatise, *On the Making of Man*, played an important role in transmitting Greek nomenclature and concepts to Latin scholars in the early MA.

2. *Recovery of Hippocratic, Galenic, and other ancient texts*

Another Christian apologist of this era, Nemesius of Emesa, in his *On the Nature of Man* uses concepts and terminology from classical medicine to argue for human primacy over the created world. These arguments fascinated

*Alfanus, bishop of Salerno who, in the 11th century, rendered Nemesius' treatise into Latin. His appetite whetted by this sampling of Hellenistic anatomy and physiology, and knowing that many Greek medical works had been rendered into Arabic during the great Islamic translation efforts of the 8th to 9th centuries, Alfanus was ready to encourage a learned and reputedly well-travelled monk, *Constantinus Africanus, to undertake a massive project of translation from Arabic to Latin.

Modern anatomical nomenclature contains survivals of Constantinus' efforts to create a new Latin anatomical vocabulary. These include such terms as *pia mater* and *dura mater* for membranes surrounding the brain.

3. Development of empirical investigation and the use of images

Constantinus' versions of practical Islamic anatomical compendia inspired new western investigations into animal and human anatomy as recorded in the *Anatomia porci*, the *Anatomia Mauri*, and the so-called *Second Salernitan Anatomical Demonstration*. A mysterious set of anatomical images (often called, not quite accurately, the Fünfbilderserie) seems to have appeared about this time. Their origins remain controversial, but they are undeniably an attempt to depict graphically the structure and function of the human body.

In later generations, disputes between practical battlefield surgeons such as Ugo of Lucca and academic practitioners seem to have prompted more detailed examination of human structure, especially as it related to wound management. Such inquiries were advanced by Ugo's son, *Theodoric Borgognoni, and the physician-surgeons *William of Saliceto and *Lanfranc of Milan. This effort culminated in *Henri of Mondeville's vigorous but ultimately unsuccessful struggle to centre the discipline of anatomy and the study of *surgery around the use of images. Traditional barriers and technological limits were too great.

As knowledge of human form and function increased, its usefulness to other areas of knowledge also widened. Anatomists were asked to establish cause of *death, and pressures from legal authorities pushed physicians to undertake forensic *dissections. The earliest medico-judicial dissection seems to be the case of a certain Azzolino, whose death in February 1302 aroused a suspicion of murder. After an autopsy examination by two physicians and three surgeons, the conclusion, 'after the anatomization of the parts', was reached that no foul play had been involved.

Shortly thereafter in 1316, Mondino da *Luzzi, a professor in *Bologna, finished his *Anathomia*, which has been termed the first 'modern' book on anatomy, since it is wholly devoted to the subject and is based at least in part on empirical evidence its author obtained from dissections. Mondino's successors in Bologna carried on the practice of human dissection, and by 1410, the practice was so common that in that year even the pope's body was given a post-mortem examination.

Academic dissection spread from Bologna to other university cities of *Italy and *France throughout the 15th century, but with the recovery of texts translated directly from the Greek in that century, dissection became more of a demonstration of the correctness of the classical texts than an experience-based investigation. Affairs remained in this static condition until Berengario da Carpi (1560–1530) began to raise questions, especially about a brain structure called the *rete mirabile*, which he could not find (*Galen had incorrectly generalized to humans a structure he found very obvious in goats), and began a new effort to integrate illustration and text. While these may appear small advances from our point of view, they did prepare the way for the earthshaking achievements of Andreas Vesalius, who as a student found the *Paris academic climate stifling, and came south to the still-vital centres of Bologna and *Padua to lay the groundwork for his *De humani corporis fabrica* (1543). YVO

G. Corner, *Anatomical Texts of the Earlier Middle Ages* (1927).
T. Hunt, *The Medieval Surgery* (1994).
Y. O'Neill, 'Diagrams of the Medieval Brain,' *Iconography at the Crossroads*, ed. B. Cassidy (1993), 91–105.
—— 'Meningeal Localization: A New Key to Medieval Texts, Diagrams and Surgical Practice,' *Mediaevistik*, 6 (1993), 211–38.
N. Siraisi, *Medieval and Early Renaissance Medicine* (1991).
C. Talbot, *Medicine in Medieval England* (1967).
O. Temkin, *Galenism* (1973).

anchoress, anchorite A Christian who desired to live a contemplative existence in isolation. Medieval anchorites were enclosed in small, sparsely furnished cells often attached to churches. Windows provided access to necessities, such as *Mass, the *Eucharist, food, and conversation.

Anchorites came from all classes and professions. Their only *vows were chastity, obedience, and 'stability of abode'. *Literacy, especially in the vernacular, seemed to be the norm, and women outnumbered men almost two-to-one.

An anchorite's primary duty was to pray for humanity, but some took on other tasks, such as sewing vestments or dispensing advice; others, like Billfrith of *Lindisfarne, illuminated MSS, or became authors, like *Julian of Norwich. MMS

M. Sauer, *The Wooing Group and A Discussion of the Love of God* (2006).
A. Warren, *Anchorites and their Patrons in Medieval England* (1985).

ancients and moderns Medieval readers and writers were strongly aware of their relationship to the past. They viewed classical learning as their inheritance and assumed the responsibility of safeguarding and transmitting it for the sake of posterity. Thus many writings embody the essential ancient-modern connection, or *translatio studii* (the transfer of knowledge from one place and time to the next), theme of the Atlantis myth in Plato's *Timaeus* (known to the western MA in Calcidius' Latin version). *Marie de France explains in her *Lais* that the ancients wrote obscurely so that future readers would 'gloss the letter'—that is, bring to light the meaning with which the books were invested. And in the preface to *Cligès* (*c*.1175), *Chrétien de Troyes explains that learning first had its seat in Greece, then it came to Rome, and now it has come to *France. The concept is best summarized by *John of Salisbury in *Metalogicon* 1. 24. According to John, *Bernard of Chartres explained to his students that the moderns were just dwarves compared to the giants of antiquity. And yet, perched on the giants' shoulders, the dwarves possess a unique advantage: they see farther than the ancients ever could. Active engagement with ancient textual traditions led to numerous translations and adaptations of pagan texts, including Plato, Ovid, Cicero, Horace, Statius, and Livy. EMR

R. Brusegan and S. Sticca, *The Polyphonic Voice in Marie de France's 'Translatio Studii'* (2005).
M. Colish, *Medieval Foundations of the Western Intellectual Tradition* (1999).
E. Jeauneau, *Translatio Studii* (1995).

Ancilla Dei [Latin, 'Servant of God'] Expression designating Christian women in Late Antiquity in *epigraphic inscriptions, and after the 7th century, women converted to a religious life. EMSC

M. E. Goodich, '*Ancilla Dei*: The Servant as Saint in the Later Middle Ages', *Lives and Miracles of the Saints: Studies in Medieval Hagiography* (2004), 119–36.
H. Leclercq, 'Ancilla Dei', *Dictionnaire d'archéologie chrétienne et de liturgie* (1924), vol. 1, 1973–93.

Andalusia Southernmost province of modern Spain whose name derives from the Arabic term for the Iberian Peninsula, much of which was under Arab-Islamic rule between 711 and 1492. This rule extended over much of the peninsula in its first three centuries but diminished beginning in the late 11th century as a result of the expansion of the Christian states to the north. *Al-Andalus evolved from being part of the Umayyad administrative province of Ifriqiya (Tunisia and eastern Algeria; governed from *Qainouan) (711–756) into a largely autonomous province ruled from *Córdoba (756–929), which later became the seat of a *caliphate (929–1031). The latter broke up into a collection of petty kingdoms (1031–1091), which were then conquered by two successive *Berber dynasties ruled from *Marrakesh (1091–1232). These were succeeded by the small principality of *Granada, which survived for over two centuries (1232–1492). On a major frontier between Dar al-Islam and the Latin West, al-Andalus contributed significantly to the cultural and economic life of medieval Europe through the transmission of knowledge and technology. The changing frontier affected the lives of sizable Muslim, Jewish, and Christian communities whose by turns harmonious and acrimonious interaction created characteristic cultural forms as well as significant legal and political models of peace and conflict among the Abrahamic faiths.

1. Beginnings to 912
2. The pinnacle of Umayyad and Islamic rule to 976
3. Seeds of civil war
4. Fragmentation
5. The Nasrid dynasty and Granada

1. *Beginnings to 912*

The quick success of *Tariq ben Ziyad points to the weakness of the *Visigothic kingdom. In 711 Tariq landed in Gibraltar and with 12,000 men routed the regular troops of King Rodrigo at Wadi Lago, taking the capital, *Toledo, within a year *Mawali* (tribal clients or freedmen) of *Berber origin formed the predominant demographic of the invading Muslim army. An Arab military aristocracy answering to the caliphate in *Damascus formed the leadership. This leadership raided northward as far as *Poitiers, where Abd al-Rahman al-Ghafiqi clashed with Charles Martel in 732 and vied internally for control until a surviving Marwanid pretender to the defeated Umayyad caliphate, *Abd al-Rahman I, managed to claim the governorship of al-Andalus in 756 and pass it onto his son Hisham I, establishing a dynasty that would last until 1031.

Abd al-Rahman I (who began construction on the Great Mosque of Córdoba, an architectural wonder attesting to the power of the Spanish Umayyads) and his first successors oversaw the political unification of their emirate (or principality), quelling a series of rebellions of the native population that by the middle of the 10th century had converted to Islam in its majority, but as *muwallads* (second-generation converts) was not always integrated. The emirate's northern border stabilized around the valley of the Ebro river. In the northeast it fell beyond Huesca, Lerida, and Tarragona, but fell short of Pamplona and *Barcelona (lost in 801). Al-Andalus under the Marwanid governors built a powerful state and developed urban centres more significant and numerous than those in the contemporary Latin West and western North Africa.

2. *The pinnacle of Umayyad and Islamic rule to 976*

The reign of Abd al-Rahman III, together with that of his son al-Hakam II (961–976), forms the pinnacle of both Umayyad and Islamic rule in the peninsula. After putting down another *muwallad* rebellion, that of the Banu Hafsun, Abd al-Rahman III assumed the title of caliph in 929 on account of the power of the Umayyad state and in response to the threat of the Shiite *Fatimids, with whom the Umayyads fought a proxy war in North Africa. The great library at Córdoba (said to contain 400,000 volumes) and the

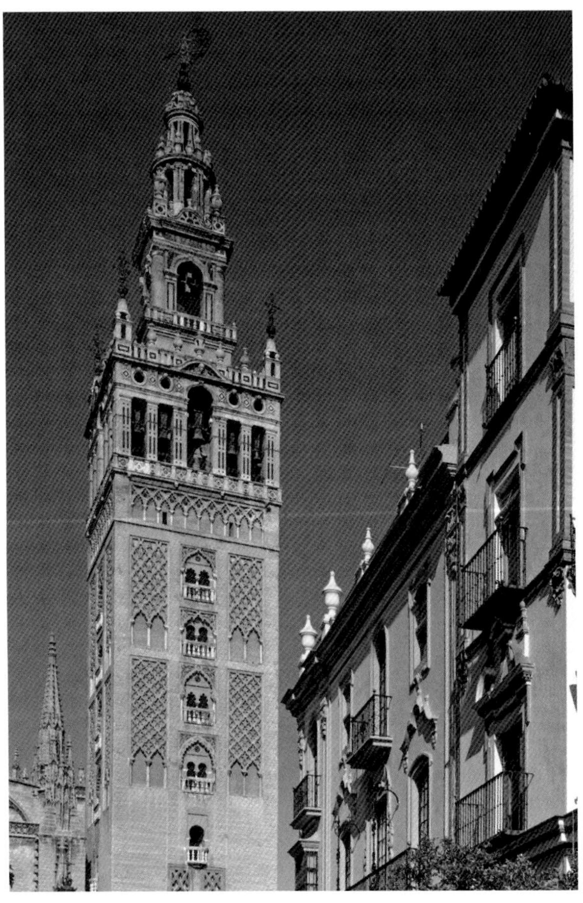

Church tower in Andalusia (La Giralda tower, Seville, Spain).

palatine city of Madinat al-Zahra attest to the power of the caliphate. The sacking of the latter by Berber troops in 1010 provided a poignant symbol of its demise.

3. Seeds of civil war

These troops had been introduced by Ibn Abi Amir (who later assumed the title of al-*Mansur bi-Llah). The *hajib* (majordomo) of the third caliph, Hisham II (976–1009), al-Mansur established himself as the absolute military power in the peninsula, taking tribute from *Castile, sacking and burning *Barcelona, razing the church of *Santiago de Compostela (the bells of which were hung in the great mosque of Córdoba), and expanding further into western North Africa. His wholesale usurpation of power, however, sowed the seeds for a civil war between Umayyad loyalists and Amirids when al-Mansur's second successor, Abd al-Rahman (Sanjul), claimed the caliphate for himself.

4. Fragmentation

Córdoba never recovered, and al-Andalus fragmented into petty kingdoms whose courts vied for power and prestige but lacked the Umayyad state's ability to undertake large projects and raise a powerful army. They were thus forced to pay protection money to the emboldened Christian states. Al-Andalus's most famous man of letters, Ibn Hazm, wrote for one of these courts.

Effective Muslim military power appeared in Mauritania and southern Morocco, where a Berber dynasty founded *Marrakesh (1070) and unified the region. Invited by the leaders of the petty kingdoms to intervene in the peninsula after the fall of Toledo in 1085 to *Alfonso VI, the *Almoravids, under Yusuf b. Tashfin, defeated the Christian army at the battle of Zallaqa in 1086 and conquered most of the Muslim kingdoms of the peninsula in 1091.

The Almoravid dynasty was defeated by a different tribal confederation of the High Atlas region (the *Almohads, inspired by the Mahdi Ibn Tumart) who then took control of the once again fragmented Muslim kingdoms of Iberia. The Almohad defeat at Las *Navas de Tolosa in 1212 initiated their collapse, followed by a great southward sweep of the Christian states, who took Córdoba (1236), *Valencia (1238), and Seville (1248), among others. With some important differences, both Almoravids and Almohads, as the first large non-Arab Islamic states of the region, legitimated their rule through their status as defenders of Islam and reformers of religious practices. Two of al-Andalus's most famous philosophers, *Ibn Tufail and *Averroës, were active in the Almohad court. The famous Murcian mystic (the culmination of a movement that had begun in the 11th century), Muhyi al-Din b. al-Arabi, was also active in the Almohad period. And the Córdoban Jewish philosopher Moses *Maimonides was forced to emigrate to *Egypt due to the Almohads' hostility to minorities.

5. The Nasrid dynasty and Granada

Ibn al-Ahmar (Muhammad I), through his alliance with *Ferdinand III, managed to secure a region comprising *Granada (the capital), Málaga, and Almeria, where he founded the *Nasrid dynasty, which played off allegiances to Castile and the Marinids until its capitulation to the *Catholic Monarchs, 2 January, 1492. Unlike previous Andalusian states, Granada's population was almost entirely Muslim. The palace begun by Ibn al-Ahmar, the Alhambra, marks the final splendor of Muslim rule in the peninsula.

A series of expulsions took place after Granada's capitulation including that of the Jews in 1492, as well as of the *Moriscos in 1609. The Andalusian heritage is evident through, among others, the thousands of Arabic loanwords in the Spanish language, as well as in the artistic style of Mudéjar, which was further developed in the New World.

See also ART, MUDÉJAR. CGR

L. P. Harvey, *Islamic Spain, 1250 to 1500* (1990).

É. Lévi-Provençal, *L'Espagne musulmane au xème siècle* (1932).

M. R. Menocal, R. P. Scheindlin, and M. A. Sells, eds, *The Literature of Al-Andalus* (2000).

B. F. Reilly, *The Medieval Spains* (1993).
J. B. Vilá, *Los Almorávides* (1998).
D. Wasserstein, *The Rise and Fall of the Party-Kings: Politics and Society in Islamic Spain 1002–1086* (1985).

Andechs dynasty A noble dynasty with properties in western *Bavaria (*castle Andechs on the Ammersee), *Tyrol (control of the *Brenner Pass), and around *Bamberg. Visible on the scene from the end of the 10th century, the family rose, with **Berthold IV** and his children, to European-wide significance around 1200 as allies of the Staufer. His father was elevated to margrave of Istria and duke of Merania; his daughters **Agnes** and **Gertrude** married the kings of *France (*Philip II) and *Hungary (Andrew II), respectively; his daughter **Hedwig** and granddaughter **Elizabeth** became saints; the County Palatine of *Burgundy, the Patriarchate of *Aquileia, and the bishopric of Bamberg were in their possession.

The family patronized *courtly love poetry (*Minnesang*), architecture (construction of the Bamberg *cathedral), and the foundation of (among others) the towns of *Innsbruck and Bayreuth. They were harmed by the murder of King Philip of *Swabia at Bamberg (1208) and, in subsequent competition with the *Wittelsbacher, never recovered. The dynasty died out around the middle of the 13th century. *See also* ROMAN EMPIRE. GG

A. Frenken, 'Hausmachtpolitik und Bischofsstuhl: Die Andechs-Meranier als oberfränkische Territorialherren und Bischöfe von Bamberg', *ZBLG* 63 (2000), 711–86.
J. Kirmeier and E. Brockhoff, eds, *Herzöge und Heilige: Das Geschlecht der Andechs-Meranier im europäischen Hochmittelalter* (1993).

Andernach, battle of (876) When his half-brother *Louis the German died, *Charlemagne's remaining grandson, *Charles II 'the Bald', sought to increase his kingdom but was opposed by his nephew Louis the Younger. The issue was decided at Andernach when Charles's cavalry became bogged down in the mud. Unable to manoeuvre, Charles's army was routed and he barely escaped. KDV

B. S. Bachrach, '*Caballus et Caballarius* in Medieval Warfare', *The Study of Chivalry*, ed. H. Chickering and T. H. Seiler (1988), 173–211.

Anders Sunesen (Andreas Sunonis), archbishop of Lund (1160×70–1228) Having studied theology and law in *Paris, *Bologna, and *Oxford, he translated the Scanian Law into Latin and wrote a didactic poem, *Hexaëmeron*, consisting of 8,040 verses of Latin hexameter. HB

S. Ebbesen, ed., *Anders Sunesen: stormand, teolog, administrator, digter: femten studier* (1985).

Andreas Capellanus (André Le Chapelain) Author of *De amore* (1174×1238), a work dealing with the nature and effects of love, the 'Rules of Love', and the evils of women and love. It purportedly demonstrates how a man could win love, but actually depicts women rejecting their suitors; at the end the author even repudiates love. The work was translated into numerous European vernaculars. Little is known of Andreas outside his treatise. *See also* COURTLY LOVE. CBB, CJMc

K. Andersen-Wyman, *Andreas Capellanus on Love?* (2005).
Andreas Capellanus, *De Amore*, ed. E. Trojel and F. P. Knapp (2006).
A. Karnein, *De Amore in volkssprachlicher Literatur* (1985).
D. A. Monson, *Andreas Capellanus, Scholasticism and the Courtly Tradition* (2005).

Andrew of St-Victor (d. 1175) Exegete, canon regular, abbot. A student of *Hugh, Andrew followed him in the literal interpretation of scripture, using contemporary Jewish sources and commentary. He was twice abbot of an English Victorine house. He commented on the literal sense of the Octateuch, historical books, the Major and Minor Prophets, Proverbs, and Ecclesiastes. GAZ

Andrew of St-Victor, *Opera*, ed. C. Lohr *et al.*, CCCM 53-53F (1986).
R. Berndt, *André de Saint-Victor (†1175), exégète et théologien* (1991).

Andrieu Contredit d'Arras (*c.*1220–48) French *knight, crusader, and **trouvère*, author of eighteen *chansons*, a *pastourelle*, a *jeu-parti*, and a lai, most of which survive with melodies. EAu

M.-G. Grossel, 'Le chevalier-ménestrel Andrieu Contredit d'Arras', *Arras au moyen âge*, ed. M.-M. Castellani and J.-P. Martin (1994), 81–96.
D. H. Nelson and H. van der Werf, eds, *The Songs Attributed to Andrieu Contredit d'Arras* (1992).

Anegenge *See* LITERATURES: GERMANIC.

Aneirin ap Dwywei Poet *c.*600. One of five poets active at this time in *Historia Brittonum* §62. A 13th-century codex, *Llyfr Aneirin*, contains two recensions of *The Gododdin* and the later of these, 'A', is preceded by a rubric stating 'This the Gododdin: Aneirin sang it'. Within the text of both a stanza survives giving the poet's matronym and bewailing his death, throwing doubt on his authorship. In the Triads Aneirin's slaying was counted as one of the Three Unfortunate Hatchet-blows of the Island of Britain. Dwywei is said elsewhere to have been the daughter of Lleenog and the wife of Dunod, both members of the Coeling dynasty. AWo

R. Bromwich, ed. and tr., *Trioedd Ynys Prydein: The Triads of the Island of Britain* (2006).
D. Huws, ed., *Llyfr Aneirin: facsimile* (1989).
J. T. Koch, ed. and tr., *The Gododdin of Aneirin: text and context from Dark-Age North Britain* (1997).

Anfortas In *Wolfram von Eschenbach's *Parzival*, son of the late Grail King, Frimutel, and Parzival's maternal uncle. Dealt a sexual wound by a heathen adversary while jousting in the service of *amor*, he is kept alive by the Grail, but eventually freed from his suffering and succeeded by Parzival when the latter finally asks: 'Uncle, what is troubling you?' WM

J. Reichert, '"Slaying the Dragon": Der letzte Heilversuch an Anfortas im "Parzival" Wolframs von Eschenbach' (483, 6–18), *Mediaevistik*, 14 (2001), 149–78.

Angelo Clareno (1247/55–1337) Leading exponent of the *Spiritual Franciscans. Angelo vigorously opposed the Conventual wing of the order and was, consequently, persecuted for his strict observance of St Francis' rule. *See also* FRANCISCAN ORDER. FB

Angelo Clareno, *A Chronicle or History of the Seven Tribulations of the Order of Brothers Minor*, tr. D. Burr and E. R. Daniel (2005).
G. L. Potestà, *Angelo Clareno: Dai poveri eremiti ai fraticelli* (1990).

angels [Greek, *angelos* 'messenger'; cf. Hebrew, *mal'ak*] Belief in angels was a robust, dynamic aspect of medieval Latin and Greek Christianity, Islam, and Judaism. Its fundamentals were derived from Scripture and, in the west, from patristic authors such as *Augustine and *Pope Gregory I the Great, but topics in angelology were discussed productively throughout the MA. Scholastic theology in the 13th century, notably that of *Thomas Aquinas and *Bonaventure, represents the climax of this discussion. Angels were richly polysemic entities, but their basic function and mode of existence was as intermediaries between God and humans. They served as theophanies (visions, manifestations) of God and carried prayers to him. Consequently they attracted widespread popular devotion. The Archangel Michael, patron of several important *pilgrimage sites, is an outstanding example. There was also firm belief in personal guardian angels. The idea that there were nine distinct orders of angels was received from the late-5th-century *Celestial Hierarchy* of *Pseudo-Dionysius the Areopagite, which was glossed repeatedly by medieval authors. (There was a corresponding hierarchy of fallen angels, called the *exordo* by *Alan of Lille.) For Bonaventure and others, the hierarchy of angels (or the six wings of the seraphim, and so forth) corresponded to stages of the soul's progress towards God, with the cherubim and seraphim, the angels nearest to God, representing the ideal of wisdom and of love respectively. *See also* ADAM OF ST-VICTOR; BERNARD, ST; DEMONOLOGY AND DEMONS; DUNS SCOTUS, JOHN; FRANCIS OF ASSISI, ST; FRANCISCAN ORDER; HUGH OF ST-VICTOR; JOHN SCOTTUS ERIUGENA; SCHOLASTICISM. MBo

S. Chase, ed. and tr., *Angelic Spirituality: Medieval Perspectives on the Ways of Angels* (2002).

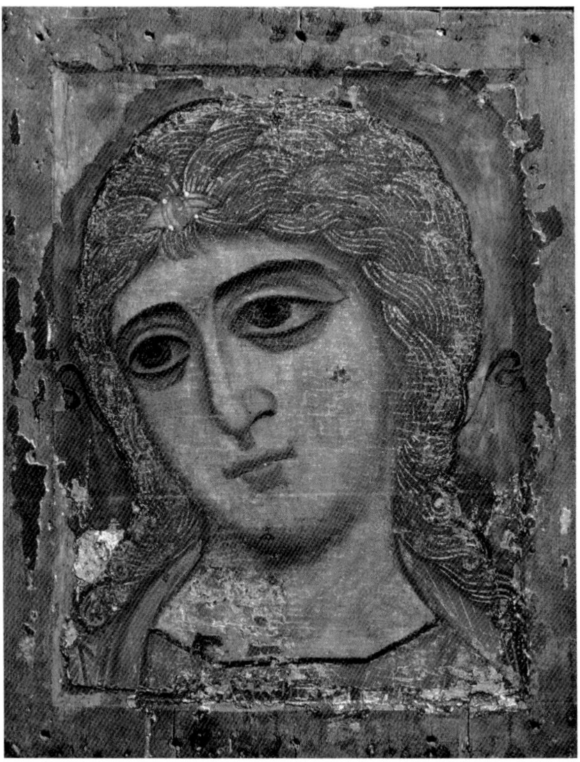

Icon of (Arch)angel with the Golden Hair. Novgorod School, 1130–90. Russian Museum, St Petersburg.

I. Iribarren and M. Lenz, eds, *Angels in Medieval Philosophical Inquiry* (2008).
D. Keck, *Angels and Angelology in the Middle Ages* (1998).

Angers City on the Maine river, 310 km southwest of *Paris. By the mid 4th century it was a Christian bishopric. From the late 10th century it was the seat of the counts of *Anjou. The city contained fortifications constructed by *Louis IX, a Romanesque *cathedral, several important *monasteries, and a *university founded in 1244 and officially recognized in 1337. TFH

S. Fanning, *A Bishop and his World before the Gregorian Reform: Hubert of Angers, 1006–1047* (1988).
F. Lebrun *et al.*, *Histoire d'Angers* (1975).
L. Pietri and J. Biarne, *Topographie chrétienne des cités de la Gaule, V: Province ecclésiastique de Tours* (1987).

Angevins *See* ANJOU.

Angevins in central Europe Descendants of *Charles of Anjou and a branch of the *Árpád dynasty, Charles I (1301/08/10–42) and Louis I (the Great) (1326–82, r.1342–82), through marriage, conquest, and diplomacy expanded Hungarian territory to encompass *Poland, *Wallachia,

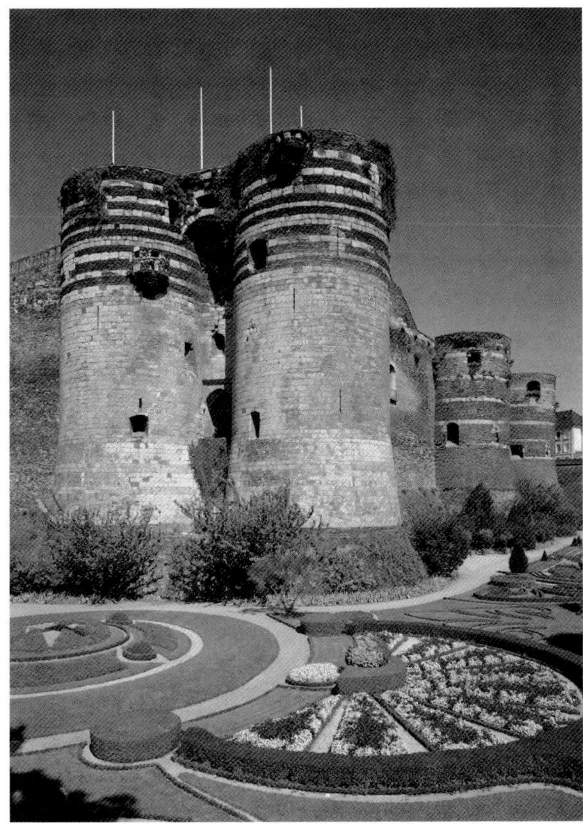

The Château of Angers, completed 1238.

*Dalmatia, *Croatia, *Bosnia, and *Bulgaria, centralized royal power, and stimulated the growth of towns, trade, and mining to create prosperity for central Europe in the MA.

Charles Robert, great-grandson of Charles of Anjou, assumed the throne as Charles I in 1310. He reorganized the county system of governance, centred around a castle ruled by an ispan, increasing the legal power (*ius gladii*), privileges, land, and military obligations to a stratum of nobles who collected taxes (**lucrum camerae*) and provided military support (**banderia*) for the king. He founded a uniform currency (*florin) and encouraged foreign commerce with Poland, Bohemia, and Bavaria, stimulating the growth of towns and crafts.

Louis I, who succeeded his father in 1342, strengthened and expanded the Hungarian empire. By defeating *Venice he gained control of the eastern Adriatic. He made contracts with patricians to whom he guaranteed protection in return for taxes and military support. But his grants of land privileges (*avicitias*) and tax farms (*nona*) to nobles held back regional development. Steeped in western European culture, Louis founded the University of *Pécs in 1367 and introduced humanist ideas, art, and architecture into Hungary. As a *miles Christi* he fought the Lithuanians, the Serbs, and the Turks. But under Sigismund of Luxembourg, his successor, the empire shrank and towns deteriorated throughout the 15th century. JDus

E. Fügedi, *Castle and Society in Medieval Hungary (1000–1437)*, tr. J. M. Bak (Hungarian original, 1977) (1986).

L. Makkai, 'The Independent Hungarian Feudal Monarchy to the Battle of Mohács (1000–1526)', *A History of Hungary*, ed. E. Pamlényi (1975), 62–92.

Angilbert of St-Riquier (750–814) Raised in *Charlemagne's court, Angilbert led royal diplomatic missions to Rome. Installed as abbot of St-Riquier, he undertook an imaginative building programme for the richly endowed community. An accomplished composer of *panegyric poetry, he also wrote statutes for his monks. JJC

P. Godman, *Poets and Emperors: Frankish Politics and Carolingian Poetry* (1987).

S. Rabe, *Faith, Art, and Politics at Saint-Riquier: The Symbolic Vision of Angilbert* (1995).

Angilram of Metz (d. 791) *Austrasian nobleman, bishop of *Metz (768–91), and advisor to *Charlemagne. Angilram served as Charlemagne's royal chaplain from 784 until his death on 26 October 791. He died while accompanying Charlemagne on campaign against the Avars. EJG

J. Fleckenstein, *Die Hofkapelle der deutschen Könige*, vol. 1 (1959).

R. McKitterick, *The Frankish Kingdoms under the Carolingians, 751–987* (1983).

Anglo-Saxon Chronicle *See* ANNALS AND CHRONICLES: ENGLAND (1)—ANGLO-SAXON CHRONICLE.

Anglo-Saxon church The origins of the English church lie in the mission dispatched from Rome by *Pope Gregory I the Great in 597, 40 of his monks, led by St *Augustine, the future archbishop of Canterbury. St Augustine was successful in converting the Kentish king, *Æthelbert, who then held overlordship over the other AS rulers. Through his authority, the mission was able to spread to *Essex, *East Anglia, and *Northumbria. However, its dependence upon royal authority meant that success fluctuated according to political circumstances. In Northumbria, a marriage alliance between King *Edwin and Æthelbert's daughter resulted in the establishment of Paulinus, another Gregorian missionary, as bishop of *York. But upon Edwin's death in 633, Paulinus was forced to flee. Christian mission was resumed in Northumbria under King *Oswald whose exile in Ireland led him to introduce missionaries from *Iona under St *Aidan. The coexistence of Irish and Roman traditions in the early English church resulted in a clash of cultures and beliefs which came to a head at the Synod of *Whitby in 664 when King Oswiu adopted Roman customs and the leaders of the pro-Irish faction departed for Ireland. The appointment of *Theodore of Tarsus (602–90), a great scholar from the Byzantine empire domiciled in *Rome, by Pope Vitalian as archbishop of *Canterbury in 669 was a major influence on the development of the church, particularly on diocesan structure. Episcopal provision was stabilised with roughly twelve sees in the kingdoms south of the Humber and five in the north. Bishops were not only important pastoral leaders but also played a major part in royal council. Within the *diocese, pastoral care was administered from mother-churches (known as minsters), religious communities responsible for large territories. These communities were not necessarily strictly monastic. A great variety of religious houses existed in England; some like *Bede's monasteries at *Wearmouth and Jarrow adopted a rule close to that of St *Benedict, while others were communities of clerks. Bede denounced some foundations as totally secularised, existing only to allow their founders' kin to take advantage of the tax-free status of ecclesiastical land. But it is thought that most AS *monasteries were mixed communities, all bearing pastoral responsibility. These sprang up rapidly from the late seventh century under the patronage of kings, bishops, and nobles. In some areas—notably *Wessex—minster churches were founded at nodal points, royal estates, to provide pastoral care and were closely allied with royal power. By the late 8th century, the English church was wealthy, learned, and perhaps increasingly secularised. Communities such as Wearmouth and Jarrow and York were international centres for learning. The efflorescence of the church also produced major saints such as *Cuthbert, bishop of *Lindisfarne, and Bishop *Wilfrid of York and resulted in an important *missionary impulse with monks from Northumbria and Wessex, notably St *Boniface, travelling to the continent, to the Frankish kingdoms and to Germany to evangelize the pagan Saxons there, whom they saw as their kindred.

But the development of the church was abruptly halted by the *Viking raids, first recorded in 794 when the church of Lindisfarne was raided. These culminated in the conquest of northern and eastern England and in the Scandinavian settlement of the *Danelaw. Although the settlers seem quickly to have been converted to Christianity and become active patrons of the local church, the areas they settled witnessed the decline of the monastic life and the cessation of a number of dioceses. The number of sees shrank, in Northumbria to two, and East Anglia was ultimately served by one bishop. The Midlands received ministry from one huge see based at *Dorchester. Many religious communities either disappeared or became small houses of hereditary *clergy. However, the causes of these changes may have been various: there is evidence for a decline in scholarship and Latin learning before the raids intensified and the West Saxon rulers, who brought the Danelaw under their control, preferred to have it served by a small number of bishops, often with bases like Dorchester closer to the West Saxon heartlands, rather than revive ancient sees.

King *Alfred lamented that loss of scholarship and the ravaging of monasteries and launched an educational programme to provide key texts in OE. He recruited scholars from the Frankish realms to assist in these endeavours and founded two monasteries himself, but his example in this respect was not followed by his nobility. It was not until the second half of the 10th century, that strict *monasticism in accordance with the *Benedictine Rule was revived. King *Edgar supported the reform of the monastic life by three outstanding bishops, Archbishop *Dunstan of Canterbury (d. 988), Bishop *Æthelwold of Winchester, and Archbishop *Oswald of Worcester and York. Influenced by continental monastic reforms, particularly those of *Fleury, and impelled by a vision of the early AS church as strictly monastic, these three fostered the foundation or reform of numerous monasteries in the south and east of England, chief amongst them New Minster, *Winchester, Abingdon, *Ely, and *Ramsey. Edgar himself imposed in a single monastic customary to be used by all monasteries, the **Regularis Concordia*. Benedictine reform houses became influential as foyers of learning and MS production. The late 10th and early 11th centuries also saw a strong impulse to strengthen pastoral care, particularly with the provision of vernacular homilies. At the same time, the local churches began to be founded by secular lords on their estates, the beginning of the parish system. These small estate churches were initially subordinated to the old mother churches and not all had rights of *burial or *baptism. By the end of the 11th century, the parish network of churches as we know it was largely in place. On the eve of the *Norman Conquest, the English church was governed by able prelates such as Archbishop Ealdred of York (d. 1069) and was already open to continental and Norman influence, partly through long-established connections with northern *France and partly through the promotion by *Edward 'the Confessor' of Norman and continental clerics such as Giso of Wells (d. 1088). The low reputation of the archbishop of Canterbury, the pluralist Stigand, should not obscure the vitality and strength of the AS church. KC

J. Blair, *The Church in Anglo-Saxon Society* (2005).
H. Mayr-Harting, *The Coming of Christianity to Anglo-Saxon England* ([3]1991).

Anglo-Saxons The Germanic-speaking peoples of post-Roman Britain identified by their two largest ethnic groups, Angles from southern Denmark and Saxons from north-western Germany. Angles occupied the Midlands and north of England; Saxons settled the Thames Valley and territories to the south and west. The West Saxon king *Alfred adopted the title 'King of the Anglo-Saxons' in 886 with the submission of the Anglian king *Æthelred of western *Mercia. CRD

S. Foot, 'The Making of *Angelcynn*: English Identity Before the Norman Conquest', *TRHS*, 6th series, 6 (1996), 25–49.

S. Reynolds, 'What Do We Mean by "Anglo-Saxon" and "Anglo-Saxons"?' *Journal of British Studies*, 24 (1985), 395–414.

Anglo-Scottish wars (1296–1513) The process of nation-building and territorial consolidation that took place in later medieval Europe provoked hostilities and often fed a growing awareness of defined national identities that might transcend older racial groupings. The wars between the neighbouring kingdoms of *Scotland and England, which broke out in 1296, formed part of that process, leading to centuries of bloodshed and informing relations between the two nations that still resonate today.

On the death of his brother-in-law *Alexander III of Scotland in 1286, *Edward I of England pressed for the marriage of the Scottish heiress, Margaret of Norway, with his son and heir. When Margaret died, Edward offered to judge who should be the next king but also pushed long-standing English claims of overlordship on the leaderless Scots. His choice—John *Balliol—found his sovereignty severely restricted, and the Scots allied themselves with England's enemy, *France. Edward duly invaded in 1296, Balliol's army was defeated, and the king and most of the nobility imprisoned. Scotland was taken under direct English rule.

Within a year, spontaneous revolts ignited throughout the country, the most famous of which was led by the unknown William *Wallace. After defeating Edward's army at *Stirling Bridge, Wallace became Guardian of Scotland for King John Balliol. After his own defeat by Edward in July 1298, the guardianship then passed into more traditional noble hands. With French and papal support, the Scots expected their king's return in 1302, but European politics turned against them. They sued for peace with Edward in 1304, though Wallace fought on until his capture and execution in 1305.

However, in February 1306, Robert *Bruce, grandson of a claimant to the throne, made himself king after murdering a rival and former Guardian, John *Comyn. Despite initial failure, the death of Edward I in 1307 and his own military prowess brought King *Robert I increasing control of his kingdom. The battle of *Bannockburn in 1314 reinforced his position within Scotland, forcing his enemies to support him or lose their Scottish lands. But *Edward II would not give up English claims of overlordship, despite Scottish invasions of England and Ireland. However, the English king's deposition in 1326 brought Bruce a peace treaty in 1328 from Edward III's regency government.

*Edward III soon renewed hostilities, promoting the claim of King John Balliol's son, Edward, against Bruce's son, later *David II. The *Hundred Years War between England and France, however, brought an end to sustained campaigning in Scotland. Although hostilities flared up from time to time, including the disastrous battle of *Flodden in 1513, Scotland had effectively regained its independence. The issue was finally resolved when the Scottish king, James VI, became king of England in 1603. *See also* NATION AND NATIONHOOD. FJW

G. W. S. Barrow, *Robert Bruce and the Community of the Realm of Scotland* (1988).

R. Frame, *The Political Development of the British Isles, 1100–1400* (1995).

M. Penman, *David II, 1329–71* (2004).

F. Watson, *Under the Hammer: Edward I and Scotland* (2005).

Angoulême City on the Charente river. The see was founded in the 4th century, but the first known bishop was St Cybard (d. 581), who gave his name to the city's *monastery. Seized by *Clovis in 507, Angoulême was the capital of an independent county in the 9th century. In the 11th century it became part of the duchy of *Aquitaine and in the 12th part of the Angevin empire. During the late MA, England and *France fought over Angoulême. Its greatest monument is the *cathedral of St Peter, begun *c.*1110. MCF

J. Boussard, *Historia pontificum et comitum Engolismensium* (1957).

Anhalt Situated on the upper *river Elbe, the *castle of Anhalt was built *c.*1123 near Ballenstedt abbey. Bernhard, the first count, died in 1212. His son Henry was created prince in 1218 and Anhalt became a principality. Upon Henry's death, Anhalt was subdivided into three regions. When the Aschersleben line died out in 1315, that region passed to the bishop of *Halberstadt. The Anhalt-Bernburg line ended in 1468, and the lands were reabsorbed into the remaining Anhalt-Zerbst line, which split into two lines, Anhalt-Köthen and Anhalt-Dessau, in the early 16th century. HSc

G. Schlenker *et al.*, *Geschichte in Daten: Anhalt* (1994).

Aniane (abbey) Founded by Benedict of Aniane in 782 in the diocese of *Montpellier, and endowed by *Charlemagne, Aniane was one of the two 'exemplary cloisters' of the *Carolingian monastic reform. Embroiled in controversy with its neighbouring monastery of Gellone through much of the MA, the house was sacked by Calvinists in 1562. The *monastery was secularized in 1790 by the revolutionary government. MAC

L. Cassan and E. Meynial, eds, *Cartulaires des abbayes d'Aniane et de Gellone publiés d'après les manuscrits originaux* (1900).

A. Rastoul, 'Aniane (Abbaye d')', *DHGE* 2 (1924), 277–79.

animal finds in the east and west Archaeozoology reveals both sacred and secular human-animal relationships, adding scientific evidence to written and pictorial sources. Most finds represent opportunistic exploitation of cattle, sheep, and pigs at rural settlements. Urban deposits often reflect centralized redistribution, especially of beef. Game remains occur mainly at high-status sites, as *hunting became the domain of *nobility; they may also indicate poaching by commoners.

Beaver bones are associated with *Lenten practices, as aquatic mammals were considered 'fish'. Jewish and Islamic dietary restrictions are manifested in the absence of pig and shellfish species from excavated samples.

While Christian graves contain no animals, dogs were sometimes buried alongside people outside consecrated ground. Cat and dog skeletons covered by pots are thought to represent pagan rituals, given the roles of these animals in witchcraft. Some dog bones from high-status settlements are of sophisticated breeds, reconfirming iconographic evidence.

Milk/*wool production may be inferred from the remains of cows and sheep. Draught animals, except cattle, tend to be absent from food remains, although, in defiance of an 8th-century papal prohibition, horses were eaten in peripheral regions. Bones of camel, widely documented in countries under Islamic influence, and water-buffalo are rarely found. Mules, popular in iconographic sources, can be archaeologically identified only by their teeth. Other exotic animals are represented by imported artefacts (for example, elephant, hippopotamus, or walrus ivory).

By the MA, archaeological remains of poultry become more frequent, even sometimes exceeding those of domestic mammals. Among domestic fowl, chickens were the main source for meat and eggs. Geese and ducks were exploited for down, while pigeons were also kept for manure and even message delivery. Turkeys reached Europe only after *Columbus, and were found in high-status settlements, as were tame and wild birds.

Like *hunting and fowling, *falconry and the consumption of small birds were privileges of the *nobility. Partridges, quail, and small songbirds were eaten in *castles and *estates. Cranes and peacocks were kept in courts for pleasure, their feathers adorning *knights. The plumage and wings of herons, egrets, and eagles were also used in decoration.

Bird bones were also carved. Wind *instruments made from hollow wing bones are especially common: fine flutes were made from large raptors, while modest versions were made from domestic geese. Pathological symptoms in bird bone offer evidence of the occurrence and spread of disease. *See also* ANIMALS, DOMESTIC, DRAUGHT, AND WILD; ARCHAEOLOGY; FOOD, DRINK, AND DIET. LBa, EG

L. Bartosiewicz, *Animals in the Urban Landscape in the Wake of the Middle Ages* (1995).

S. Bökönyi, *History of Domestic Mammals in Central and Eastern Europe* (1974).

—— *Fowling* (1985).

S. J. O'Day *et al.* eds, *Behaviour Behind Bones* (2003).

D. Serjeantson, *A Dainty Dish: Consumption of Small Birds in Late Medieval England* (2001).

D. Sweeney, ed., *Agriculture in the Middle Ages* (1995).

animal husbandry Concerned not only with 'domestic animals,' but also *bees and silkworms. Throughout the MA, animals for the most part were allowed to wander free; thus horses, for example, were often raised in the *forest. *Animals mainly were of interest for their aid in work, such as pulling and *transportation. The goods they provided—horns, intestines (as sausage casings), hides, *parchment, meat, *wool, and manure—followed secondarily.

In the past 25 years, *archaeology and *zoology have considerably increased our knowledge of medieval animals and animal husbandry. The amount of meat in the human diet was small, but it increased in the 13th century and mostly came from pigs and sheep. Animal size decreased from antiquity to the 13th century, whereas in the 15th century size began to increase. Sheep were the most common domestic animals, making up approximately one to two thirds of all livestock. The horse represented only four to seven per cent of the total, because horses were expensive to maintain with regard to food, horseshoes, and general care. In certain regions, such as England, *Lombardy, *Catalonia, and *Burgundy, the horse was hardly used at all.

Animal breeding modified the medieval landscape. It brought about the reduction of fallow fields (*saltus*) and an increase in *enclosures and in crop rotation. It encouraged the sowing of oats (for horses) and led to an increase in grass meadows. Modifications of the environment continued even when animal breeding experienced a crisis at the beginning of the 14th century. With the demographic recovery, the cultivation of fields took precedence over animal husbandry, while in the 15th century animal husbandry became a focus of economic interest. *See also* FOOD, DRINK, AND DIET; GRAIN CROPS; SILK; STOCK BREEDING AND SELECTION. GC

F. Audoin-Rouzeau, *Hommes et animaux en Europe de l'époque antique aux Temps modernes* (1993).

R. Delort and F. Audoin-Rouzeau, 'L'élevage médiéval', *Ethnozootechnie*, 59 (1997), 1–86.

J. Langdon, *Horses, Oxen and Technological Innovation: The Use of Draught Animals in English Farming from 1066 to 1500* (1986; repr. 2002).

animal pets Medieval pets included dogs, cats, birds, and monkeys. Dogs were primarily kept for *hunting, herding, and vermin-catching but were often valued for companionship as well. Ladies were known for doting on lapdogs, but the individualized effigies of dogs on owners' tombs show that both sexes could cherish their pets. Such sculptures sometimes even record the names of the dogs, such as 'Jakke' and 'Terri'.

Cats were kept primarily as vermin-catchers and also supplied skins for clothing. Solitary people such as *anchoresses often were quickest to regard cats as companions as well as mousers; the 9th-century Irish monk's poem about his cat Pangur Ban is a famous instance. Occasionally cats were also depicted on tombs, as in one instance where the owner's feet rest on his cat, whose feet rest on a mouse.

Birds were also popular, especially talking birds such as parrots ('popinjays'), magpies, and jackdaws. Monkeys were imported from at least the 13th century. Other animals might be given names, particularly horses, cows, and bears used in bear-baiting. Even bees were thought to respond to human speech, but relations with such animals were usually utilitarian at heart. MJB

N. Orme, *Medieval Children* (2001).
K. Thomas, *Man and the Natural World* (1983).

animals, domestic, draught, and wild Medieval people formed complex relationships with other living beings, which can be categorized as (a) those animals they found useful, either for food, work, raw materials (like wool), sport, or even companionship, (b) those animals they were neutral towards (perhaps small birds or small mammals like squirrels or even cats), and (c) animals to which they were actively hostile, like foxes, wolves, and snakes (animals particularly associated with the devil), which they did their best to eradicate from their natural world.

Medieval people gathered a constellation of the first category of animals about themselves, many as repositories for *food. This was most obvious in the case of cattle, which provided meat and milk products for virtually all of medieval Europe, while in other cultures, particularly the Middle East and northern Africa, sheep and goats provided a regime similar to what cattle did for Europe. Some of these meat animals were viewed very differently across the medieval world, none more so than the pig, an essential foodstuff for Europe, but reviled in the Islamic and Jewish worlds, because of very sharply drawn religious prescriptions. Most of these animals provided valuable by-products, hides in the case of cattle and goats, *wool in the case of sheep. Some of these were raised to an impressive industrial status, as in the case of sheep, the great flocks of which dotted (in particular) the English and Spanish landscapes to serve *clothing and *textile entrepôts such as *Flanders.

The area of greatest change in terms of animal use over the medieval period occurred in the employment of animals for work. One could argue that the great surge in economic activity and population that occurred virtually across the Eurasian continent over the so-called 'long 13th century' —roughly speaking 1185–1315—was placed almost literally on the backs of new work animals. The camel certainly promoted this in the drier areas, where the animal, among other things, made the Sahara accessible for long-range trade routes over the MA. The horse, long used as a riding beast and pack-animal, came into its own during the 12th and 13th centuries as an animal for hauling and to a lesser extent for ploughing. This was particularly the case in northwest Europe, where oxen were largely replaced by horses as beasts of *transport, a change facilitated by new *harnessing combinations, of which the padded horse-collar was a very notable element.

Also important was the use of animals for leisure and *sport. Here the horse was a pre-eminent beast, especially for jousting. This was much encouraged as essential training for the 'heavy' cavalry much employed in *warfare by medieval Europeans. Less obvious is that great pool of animals, especially deer and wild boar, that were in effect displaced from their natural place in the 'wild' and confined to very managed (if often extensive) areas of *forest and woodland for the sport of the aristocracy. In these pursuits, many animals virtually became companion beings to humans. Horses, particularly those for the elite pursuits of war and *hunting, must have become something akin to pets, and the same must also have applied to dogs, important in hunting and appearing in all sorts of breeds in the MA. *Chaucer's nun, who loved her little dogs, is unlikely to have been a solitary figure then, and the lack of emotional connection often assumed between medieval people and their animals, similar to that allegedly felt for their children, is probably a myth.

Finally, medieval people's fascination and, in the main, easygoing companionship with animals is most obviously reflected in the illuminated *bestiaries that were produced in such large numbers in the medieval period. These listings of animals, real or fanciful, represented a fundamental accounting of the natural world as medieval Christianity understood it. The interaction of animals and humans, from adversarial to companionable, formed a central theme of the bestiaries, and animal behaviour was generally seen as an allegory for (mostly) the foibles of human conduct, as reflected in the medieval fascination with Aesop's fables. Here, as nowhere else, the medieval animal and human worlds met in seamless symbiosis. *See also* AGRICULTURAL TECHNOLOGY; BEAST FABLE AND EPIC; HARNESS; LEATHER AND LEATHERWORKING; PLOUGHS AND PLOUGHING; STOCK BREEDING AND SELECTION. JL

R. Baxter, *Bestiaries and their Users in the Middle Ages* (1998).
R. W. Bulliet, *The Camel and the Wheel* (1975).
R. H. C. Davis, *The Medieval Warhorse: Origin, Development, and Redevelopment* (1989).
J. Langdon, *Horses, Oxen, and Technological Innovation: The Use of Draught Animals in English Farming from 1066 to 1500* (1986).
A. C. Leighton, *Transport and Communication in Early Medieval Europe, AD 500–1100* (1972).
R. Trow-Smith, *A History of British Livestock Husbandry to 1700* (1975).

Anjou Territory in the lower Loire valley based on *Angers, the Roman *Civitas Andegavensis*, a walled city surrounded by suburbs it eventually absorbed. In the early 10th century, Viscount Fulk the Red usurped a comital title that his descendants would hold for three centuries. Through early mastery of castle-building and diplomacy, they gained *Tours and other centres. The marriage of Count Geoffrey *Plantagenet (1129–51) with an heiress to the English throne ultimately resulted in an Angevin empire that dominated western Europe and *Outremer until Angers was captured by *Philip II Augustus in 1202. JMHo

B. Bachrach, *Fulk Nerra, the Neo-Roman Consul, 987–1040* (1993).
J. Boussard, 'La vie en Anjou aux XIe et XIIe siècles', *MA* 56 (1950), 29–68.
W. Jessee, *Robert the Burgundian and the Counts of Anjou, ca. 1025–1098* (2000).
J. McNeill and D. Prigent, eds, *Anjou: Medieval Art, Architecture and Archaeology* (2003).

annals and chronicles Forms of history writing, organized by year or by other narrative principles.

1. Overview
2. Late antiquity and the early MA
3. Carolingian chronicles
4. Chronicles in the German MA
5. Iberian chronicles
6. Medieval English chronicles
7. Medieval Italian chronicles
8. Medieval French chronicles
9. Slavic chronicles
10. End of the MA

1. Overview

After classical antiquity, writers of different backgrounds composed accounts of past events with various emphases, sponsorships, and goals, embodying different degrees of accuracy and using both learned and vernacular languages. These accounts could be structured as ongoing narratives or as year-by-year summaries. While chronicles were often commissioned by nobles and ecclesiastics, annals were originally composed anonymously to record developments within religious houses. At first prompted by the AS missionaries in *Germany, annals such as the *Annales regni francorum* (741–829), the *Annales Corbeienses* (9th century), the *Annales Quedlinburgenses*, and the *Annales Hildesheimenses* (10th century) also proved useful for early Germanic rulers. Secular annals were first commissioned by *Charlemagne. Irish and Welsh authorities in the 7th and 8th centuries also commissioned annals, such as the *Annales Cambriae*, the *Annals of Tigernach*, the *Annals of Inisfallen*, and the *Annals of Ulster*. By contrast, chronicles deal with longer time periods and/or larger geographical areas and tend to provide interpretations. Many chronicles are highly composite texts, including a range of different genres. Chronicles can be divided into world chronicles, national chronicles, monastic chronicles, *crusade and other war chronicles, city chronicles, and family chronicles.

Another genre is that of *gesta* (*res gestae*) describing the life and actions of individuals and peoples, often relying on anecdotes and moralizations, and utilizing a literary style like that of the **chansons de geste*, often with *panegyric intent. Examples are *Paul the Deacon's *Gesta Episcoporum* (*Deeds of Bishops*, 783–91); *Hrotsvitha of Gandersheim's *Gesta Oddonis* (*c.*965–68; *Deeds of Emperor Otto I*); *Wipo's *Gesta Chuonradi II Imperatoris* (11th century; *Deeds of Emperor Conrad II*); *Saxo Grammaticus' *Gesta Danorum* (*Deeds of the Danes*); and the popular *Gesta Romanorum* (oldest MS from 1342) collected by an anonymous English or German poet (or poets), an anthology including historical narratives, legends, and fairy tales.

Most major medieval chronicles are world chronicles beginning with Creation and going on to the author's own time. These world chronicles often divide history, following *Augustine, into six major time periods (*aetates*) marked by Christ's birth and the traditional four empires, and then taking up a specific subject. World chronicles can be divided into linear chronicles, determined by the sequence of events (*series temporum*); narrative chronicles, emphasizing the multiplicity of accounts (*mare historiarum*); and encyclopedic chronicles, offering a holistic world view (*imago mundi*). Many chronicles deal with local or regional history, such as, from central Europe, Ottokar of Styria's *Österreichische Reimchronik* (early 14th century), the *Braunschweiger Fürsten-Chronik* (after 1274), the *Livländische Reimchronik* (late 13th century; largely based on Martin of Troppau's chronicle), Nikolaus of Jeroschin's *Krônike von Pruzinlant* (1331ff), Priester Eberhard's *Gandersheimer Reim-Chronik* (*c.*1216), Gotfrid Hagen's *Boich van der stede Colne* (1270), the *Magdeburger Schöppen-Chronik* (end of the 14th century), the *Zimmerische Chronik* (1566), and Ulrich of Richenthal's *Chronik des Konstanzer Konzils* (1414–18).

2. Late antiquity and the early MA

Eusebius of Caesarea (*c.*260–*c.*339) laid the foundation for postclassical chronological writing in Greek, with his *Church History* and his two-part *Chronicle*, the first part of which (*Chronographies*) relates world history from ancient Mesopotamian and biblical kings to the Egyptians, Greeks, and Romans down to 225, while the second part (*Canons*) consists of chronological tables from Abraham, accompanied by regnal years of successive rulers from various kingdoms. *Orosius' *Historiarum adversus paganos libri septem* (*c.*417) was influenced by Augustine's *City of God* and covered the time from the foundation of Rome until 417, with particularly detailed information for the years 387–417. His work included secular as well as religious history. While Byzantine historical writers were mostly laymen, westerners were predominantly clerics or monks, such as *Fulgentius (*De aetatibus mundi*), *Gregory of Tours (*Historia Francorum*, begun in 576), and *Bede, famous for his *Historia ecclesiastica Gentis Anglorum* (731; *Ecclesiastical History of the English People*) in which he attempted to separate facts from hearsay. Bede's account is a reliable source of information for early English history since the author used English and continental documents. Both Gothic and Roman history were of interest to Magnus Aurelius *Cassiodorus, who composed works on both peoples. *Julian of Toledo outlined the history of the Visigoths in Spain in his *Historia de Wambae regis Gothorum Toletani expeditione* (673). Early Irish history is recorded in the *Book of *Armagh*, containing the *Life of St Patrick* and the *Life of St Martin*, both in Latin, copied in Armagh in 807.

3. *Carolingian chronicles*

Eusebius's chronicles had been translated into Latin and expanded by *Jerome up to 378, followed by *Isidore of Seville's *Chronica maiora*, covering from Creation to 615, *Regino of Prüm's world chronicle, the annals of the monastery of *Fulda (*Annales Fuldenses antiqui* for 680–901), the *Annales Mosellani*, the *Annales Alamannici*, the *Annales Guelferbytani*, the *Annales Juvavenses* (Salzburg), and *Frutolf of Michelsberg's chronicle (*c.*1100), among many others. Especially comprehensive and detailed are the *Annales Laurissenses* (741–829), also called the *Royal Annals* because they reflect political and military events in the *Carolingian empire. The first part (741–88) was written after the fall of Tassilo of *Bavaria. The second part, extending from 788 to 801, was written by two scribes, one of whom might have been *Angilbert of St Riquier. The fourth part (801–29) was written by four scribes, the role of *Charlemagne's biographer *Einhard being disputed. *Paul the Deacon, a *Lombard monk of *Monte Cassino, wrote a *Historia gentis Langobardorum*, a *Historia Romana*, and a history of the bishops of *Metz. Under *Louis the Pious and his sons another major chronicle was written by the layman *Nithard, Charlemagne's grandson, whose *Historiarum libri quatuor* deal with the last years of Charlemagne up to 843 when the Frankish Empire was divided among Louis's sons. He included the famous account of the *Strasbourg Oaths in 843. In a time of political and military turmoil, chroniclers were highly active: witness the *Annals of St Bertin* (until 882) and Prudentius of Troyes's *Annals of St Vaast* (until 900), continued by Archbishop *Hincmar of Rheims using primary material. Regino of Prüm's *Chronicon* outlines history from the birth of Christ until 906. Other types of texts, such as saints' lives, *biographies of bishops and popes, and even *epics, could be kinds of history writing.

4. *Chronicles in the German MA*

Medieval Germany witnessed the production of numerous chronicles and annals, such as the episcopal annals of *Hildesheim (to 1040), the annals of *Halberstadt (lost), the annals of *Salzburg, and the annals of *Cologne (to 1028). *Widukind of *Corvey outlined the history of *Saxony in his *Rerum gestarum libri tres* (begun in 967), closely paralleled by *Thietmar of Merseburg's *Chronicon*. Whereas the former heavily relied on literary sources and attacked the Franks, the latter emphasized the history of the later Saxon kings and added fictionally derived material. During the 10th century many bishops' lives were written, both influenced by classical models and reporting recent events, such as the *Life of Udalric*, bishop of *Augsburg, the *Life of Meinwerk of Paderborn*, the *Life of Burchard of Worms*, and the *Life of Bernward of Hildesheim*. Monastic annals also gained in significance, such as the *Annals of Reichenau*, the *Annals of Altaich*, *Lampert's *Annals of Hersfeld* (containing Emperor Henry IV's *Canossa meeting in 1077), and the *Chronicle of Bernold of St Blasien*. Growing tensions in 11th- and 12th-century Germany prompted increased chronicle writing. By the later 11th century we perceive a shift from accumulation of facts to more interpretation, as exemplified by *Hermannus Contractus of Reichenau's (1013–54) world chronicle (*Chronicon*). Hermannus' wide-ranging work was continued after 1055 by his student Berthold, then by the universal chronicle of Ekkehard of Aura (1050–1125), who rewrote the work five times with corrections and updates. The years 1099 to 1125 are most detailed and also reflect personal opinions on the *Investiture Controversy and the *crusades.

Although the three *Lives* of St *Otto of Bamberg focus primarily on his personal accomplishments, they are also important historical accounts, the first written by a monk of Priefling, the second by Ebo, a monk of *Michelsberg in *Bamberg, and the third by Herbord, also from Michelsberg. Other important *Lives* were those of *Albero of Trier by Balderich, of *Norbert of Xanten, and of *Wibald, abbot of *Corvey.

One of the most erudite and philosophically founded chronicles, titled *Chronica*, was written by *Otto of Freising, grandson of Emperor Henry IV, who was educated in *Paris, entered the *Cistercians, and became bishop of Freising in 1137. His chronicle was closely modelled after Augustine's *City of God*, describing the duality between this world and heaven. Otto supported the crusades, yet was deeply pessimistic. In 1147 Otto completed the *Chronica* and immediately began his *Gesta Friderici I imperatoris* (*Deeds of Emperor Frederick I*) but died in 1158 before completing it. His student Rahewin continued his master's work and added his own letters and other documents, offering first-hand insights into the early years of Frederick's reign. Otto's masterpiece was complemented by three contemporary chronicles: the *Annals of Marbach*, *Burchard of Ursberg's *Chronicle*, and the *Annales colonienses maximi* (*Great Annals of Cologne*) that offered an overview of world history from Creation to 1144, and then covered until 1238, guaranteeing it wide popularity. The same model was realized by *Albert of Stade (*Annals of Stade*). Another significant chronicle from northern Germany, the **Gesta Hammaburgensis ecclesiae pontificum* (*Deeds of the Bishops of the See of Hamburg*, 788–1072) by *Adam of Bremen, also included much geographical information about *Scandinavia including its outlying territories, reflecting the Christian mission in those areas from 788 to 1072. A major world chronicle was written by Martin von Troppau (or Opava), also known as Martinus Polonus (d. 1278; *Chronicon pontificum et imperatorum*, *Chronicle of Popes and Emperors*), which was often copied and contains the famous legend of *Pope Joan.

Vernacular German chronicles emerged in the middle of the 12th century, first with the anonymous rhymed **Kaiserchronik* (*c.*1126–46), which became extremely popular. Eike von Repgow produced a Middle Low German *Sächsische Weltchronik* (middle of the 13th century, mostly in prose; soon translated into MHG and Latin). Conrad IV commissioned the poet *Rudolf von Ems to write a world chronicle in the 1240s in MHG verse. Margrave Henry III of Meißen (1247–88) asked an anonymous author to compose the *Christherre-Chronik*. One of the most popular German world chronicles was *Jansen Enikel's *Weltchronik* (latter half of the 13th century), which contains many literary narratives only vaguely related to the matter at hand. At about the same time appeared the *Magdeburg Weichbildchronik*, which combines world history with local history up to the time of King William of Holland (d. 1256). Other contemporary German chronicles were the *Braunschweigische Reimchronik*, the **Livonian Rhymed Chronicle* (up to 1290), and *Ottokar von Steiermark's *Österreichische Reimchronik* (from the death of Emperor *Frederick II in 1250 until the uprising by the Austrian nobility in 1309). One of the most comprehensive world chronicles was composed by Heinrich von München sometime in the first half of the 14th century. Other noteworthy chronicles were the *Oberrheinische Chronik* (1337, anonymous); Dietrich Engelhus's (*c.*1362–1434) world chronicle, first in Latin, later translated into German in 1424; and, with a narrower focus, Gottfried Hagen's *Buch von der Stadt Köln* (*Book of the City of Cologne*, *c.*1270). Two Nuremberg *scribes, Johannes Plattenberger and Theodorich Truchsess, composed a German world chronicle in 1459 (*Excerpta chronicarum*), which in turn became one of the sources for Hartmann Schedel's (1440–1514) monumental *Liber Chronicarum*, first printed in 1493 and illustrated with woodcuts, offering a pictorial history from Creation to the time of Emperor Maximilian I.

Jakob Twinger von Königshofen wrote a universal world chronicle in 1386 (*Deutsche Chronik*). Another urban author, Konrad Justinger, wrote a *Chronik der Stadt Bern* (*Chronicle of the City of Bern*) in 1421. The famous Council of *Constance (1414–18) is dealt with in Ulrich von Richental's *Chronik* (1420–30; first printed in 1483).

5. Iberian chronicles

Early Spanish history is covered by Idatius' *Chronicon* (379–469), the chronicle by John of Biclara (567–90), and Isidore of Seville's *Historia Gothorum, Vandalorum et Suevorum*. Besides Julian of Toledo (above), Victor Vitensis, bishop of Byzacena, had outlined the history of the Vandals in North Africa in his *History of the Persecution of the Province of Africa by Gaiseric and Huneric* (429–84). The *Crónica de 754*, composed under Muslim rule, includes Byzantine, Visigothic, and Arabic as well as local history; the *Chronicon Albeldense* was completed in 883 at the court of King Alfonso III of *Asturias. The *Historia Silense*, completed in 1110 by a monk in the convent of Seminis, deals with the early Christian Iberian Peninsula. The *Gesta Comitum Barcinonensium* was written by several monks between 1162 and 1272. In the *Llibre dels Feits* King *James I of Aragon provides an autobiographical account, from 1207 to 1276, when he died; the continuation was probably written by monks under the king's supervision. Bernat *Desclot composed a second royal chronicle in 1286 (*Libre del rei En Pere*). Another famous chronicle was the strongly autobiographical one by Ramón *Muntaner. King *Pere IV of Aragon commissioned the *Crónica dels reys d'Aragó e comtes de Barcelona* and an account of his own reign, *Crónica del Rey Don Pedro IV*. Other contemporary chronicles were authored by Lopez de Ayala (1332–1407) and Gutierro Diaz de Gomez (1379–1449). Extremely successful proved to be Diego de Valera's *Crónica abreviada de Espana* (1411/12–*c.*1488). One of the last major medieval Spanish chronicles was written by Pere Tomic in 1438, the *Histories e conquestes del reyalme d'Aragó é principat de Catalunya*.

6. Medieval English chronicles

The earliest chronicle written in England was the *Anglo-Saxon Chronicle*, compiled in *Winchester or *Canterbury between 855 and 892. A short Latin chronicle to 975, which melds Bede and the *Anglo-Saxon Chronicle*, was written by Æthelweard (d. *c.*998). After the *Norman Conquest, historical writing in AS practically disappeared. The only noteworthy exceptions were the continuations of the *Anglo-Saxon Chronicle* in two versions until 1070 (Parker), then to 1080 (Worcester), and finally to 1154 (*Peterborough Chronicle*), written by a number of different scribes from different times. Most English chronicles employ prose, not verse, perhaps owing to a decline of learning after the Danish invasions. The only subsequent major chronicle, seemingly inspired by anti-Norman sentiment, was written by *Robert of Gloucester *c.*1300 (the *Metrical Chronicle*). Shortly after 1327 Thomas Bek of Castleford composed an English chronicle in verse, and Robert *Mannyng completed his chronicle, also in English, in 1338, both deploring the Norman invasion. Latin chronicles produced in England were very numerous, such as Richard of Devizes's *Winchester Annals*

(1277), Thomas Wykes's *Chronicle* (1289), the anonymous *Annals of Waverley* (1291), John of Oxnead's *Chronicle* (1293?), the anonymous *Peterborough Chronicle* (1295), Richard de Morins's (d. 1242) *Annals of Dunstable* (continued until 1297), Bartholomew Cotton's *English History* (*Historia Anglicana*) (1298, covering 449 to 1298), William Rishanger's *Chronicle* (a continuation [1259–1306] of Matthew *Paris's *Chronica maiora* [*c*.1241–51]) and his *Life of Edward I* (after 1307), and the *Chronicle of the Barons' War* (*c*.1312), and Walter of Hemingburth's *Chronicon*, covering 1066 to 1346. One of the most comprehensive chronicles was written by Ranulf *Higden, his *Polychronicon*, a compilation of many different sources, treating a wide range of topics, among them world history from Creation to 1352. This work was copied and excerpted many times and translated into English by John *Trevisa in 1387. Another major compilation work was Sir Thomas Gray's *Scalacronica*, in French, begun in a Scottish prison in 1355 and continued after his release in 1358. A *Malmesbury monk wrote the *Eulogium Historiarum*, basically the same work as Higden's but extending it to 1366. Other world chronicles were Richard of Cirencester's (d. *c*.1401) *Speculum historiale*, Thomas Otterbourne's *Chronica regum Angliae* (from the legendary Brutus to 1420), and Thomas *Walsingham's *Chronica maiora*; but the interest in this genre then declined, except for a number of chronicles of King *Richard II and subsequent kings, and of individual convents, such as the *Evesham Chronicle* (714–1418) and the *Bermondsey Annals* (until 1432). The *Chronicle of the Brute* was printed by *Caxton in 1480 and extends Walsingham's chronicle to the year 1461. Up to 1333 it is a translation of the French *Brut d'Engleterre*, but then offers independent information. One of the most famous late medieval English chronicles was John Capgrave's *Abbreuiacion of Cronicles* (*c*.1462/63), which ended with the year 1417.

7. *Medieval Italian chronicles*

After the 8th-century work of Paul the Deacon (above), the years 774–888 were covered by the chronicle of Erchempert, and the period 574–974 by the *Chronicon Salernitanum*, which focused principally on the duchy of *Benevento, shedding important light on the relations between Greeks and Arabs in southern *Italy. The history of Robert Guiscard and his followers, who founded the Norman kingdom of Sicily, was described in the chronicles by *Amatus of Monte Cassino (for the years 1016–78), Goffredo Malaterra, and William of Apulia (both 11th century). In the 11th century the monk Leone Marsicano began the chronicle of Monte Cassino (*Chronica Monasterii Casinensis*), which was continued by *Peter the Deacon. The archbishop of Salerno, Romualdo Guarna (Romualdo Salernitano), wrote a universal chronicle, covering from Creation to 1178. Drawing from personal experience in politics, his work excelled through its eyewitness accounts, though his chronicle was also influenced by the Bible, the Fathers, and Isidore of Seville. Hugo Falcandus, a contemporary of Romualdo, wrote a chronicle account of the kingdom of Sicily (*Liber de regno Siciliae*) between 1154 and 1169.

Royal or ducal rulers, city councils, bishops, and other powerful entities commissioned chronicles, especially because the chronicle effectively served for the patron's self-aggrandizement. The Norman conquest of southern Italy led to the production of a number of important chronicles reflecting this event, such as Amatus' *Historia Normannorum* (*c*.1075–to *c*.1101), which has survived only in a French translation (*Ystoire de li Normant*, after 1268). Robert Guiscard is the centre of attention in Malaterra's *Historia Sicula*, which begins with the first conquest of Sicily and goes to 1099. The early part was written in poetic form, but a later continuator (to 1265) resorted to the traditional annalistic prose style. Highly hostile to the Normans, Falco of Beneventum wrote his *Chronicon de rebus aetate sua gestis* (completed in 1154 or later), in which he depicts *Roger II as a tyrant. The opposite position can be found in the chronicle written by Alexander of San Salvatore, *De rebus gestis Rogerii Siciliae* (ended in 1136, probably with the author's death). The subsequent years, particularly 1154 to 1169, are covered by Falcandus.

In the late 11th century, the Milanese priest Landulph Senior wrote a history of his city in four books, followed by the unrelated Landulph Junior's account for the years 1095–1137. The history of *Milan was recorded by Arnulf of Milan in his *History of his Own Time* (*Rerum sui temporis* [five books, 925–1077]), subsequently continued by Landulph Senior, who dealt with the years until 1085, and then by his son Landulph de S. Paulo, up to 1137, in his *Mediolanensis Historia*. The history of *Genoa from 1099 to 1163 was dealt with by Caffaro, whereas the history of *Pisa was reflected by Bernardo Marangone, who began with Creation and concluded with the years 1136–82, for this period drawing from personal experience. Although the Franciscan *Salimbene de Adam of *Parma focused on his own city, he intended to write a chronicle of Italy and Europe, and also of his monastic order. Salimbene freely incorporated hearsay accounts and reflected on his personal impressions, often transgressing the traditional boundaries of a traditional chronicle. By contrast, his contemporary, the Dominican *Jacob of Voragine, limited himself to the more or less verifiable events that had occurred in his own city. The history of *Padua was written by Rolandino in his *Chronica in factis et circa facta Marchie Trivixane*, covering the years 1200–1262, that is, the rise and fall of the tyrant Ezzelino da Romano, followed by Albertino *Mussato, who emphasized the events surrounding Emperor Henry VII. The history of Milan was recorded by Galvano Fiamma (1283–1344) who favoured the dynasty of the *Visconti. Other major *Lombard chroniclers were Pietro Azario of Novara (*fl.* 1250–1362), Bonincontro Morigia of Monza (*fl.* until 1349), Ferreto dei Ferreti, and the 15th-century authors Galeazzo and Bartolomeo Gattari.

Already during the 12th century numerous annals came into existence, such as the *Annals of Cremona* (from 1096), the *Annals of Piacenza* (from 1130 to 1235), the *Annals of* **Florence* (from 1110), Bernard Marangonis's *Chronicon Pisanum* (1136–75), and the *Annals of Genoa* (*Annales Januenses*) by Caffaro (concluded in 1163).

No chronicle can be simply taken at face value, since they all reflect their authors' political, religious, and ethical orientations, which find dramatic expression in Dino Compagni's (*c*.1246–1324) retrospective history of the factional strife in early-14th-century Florence. Though a White *Guelph, Compagni was spared the fate of being expelled from the city by the Black Guelphs, as were many of his compatriots including *Dante Alighieri, but he lost his official post and lived the life of an exile within Florence. His *Cronica delle cose occorrenti ne' tempi suoi* focuses on the years 1280–1312 and was begun in 1310, when the expedition of Henry VII had raised hopes for the return of the Guelph party, and finished in 1313. Instead of listing events in chronological order, Compagni successfully analysed causes, developments, and motives from his personal perspective, offering a highly complex, synthesizing view of history. Like Compagni, the Florentine Giovanni Villani (*c*.1280–1348) offered a historical overview in his *Nuova cronica*, incorporating material from his own experiences in the city administration and as an international merchant. Not surprisingly, however, like many other chroniclers, Villani begins his account with the destruction of the biblical tower of Babel and takes us to the year 1348 when he died. His brother Matteo continued the chronicle thereafter. The traumatic experiences of the *plague injected a gloomy perspective into this chronicle, which ultimately transformed the entire genre of medieval chronicles from a straightforward assembly of historical facts to a narrative account of past events seen through a personal lens, offering evaluation, criticism, and reflection. Villani's chronicle enjoyed an enormous success far into the 15th century and received several printings.

Other late medieval vernacular city chronicles testify to the great interest in local history on the part of the merchant authors, such as the anonymous *Storie Pistoresi*, Raniero Sardo's *Cronaca di Pisa*, and Giovanni Sercambi's (1348–1424) chronicles of *Lucca. The fascination with chronicle writing even turned toward domestic life, as documented by the accounts written by Donato Velluti and Giovanni Morelli. These late medieval chronicles were mostly composed in Italian, such as the Genoese annals for the years 1298 to 1435 by the notaries Giorgio and Giovanni Stella, whereas *humanists increasingly turned toward Latin.

8. *Medieval French chronicles*

In *France also, chronicles and annals constituted favourite genres of intellectual writing. The Rheims monk *Flodoard begins his *Annals* in 922 and continues them until 966, the year of his own death, focusing on the history of the late *Carolingians. The following thirty-plus years are discussed in Richer's *Historiarum libri quatuor* (966–99). *Aimoin of Fleury undertook a grand chronicle of the *History of the Franks*, but only up to 654; this was continued later until 1164. Whereas *Paris produced fairly few and rather poor chronicles, both *Champagne and *Burgundy were centres of major chronicle literature. The *Acts of the Bishops of Auxerre* and the *Chronicle of St Bénigne* at *Dijon, written by the monk John, cover from the 5th to the 12th centuries. *Adhemar of Chabannes, a monk in the abbey of St Martial in *Limoges, wrote a brief history of the abbots of his monastery, the *Annales Lemovicenses* (687–1030), a *Chronicon Aquitanicum* (830–1028), and a *Chronicon* offering a more global historical perspective: Book I treats Merovingian history; Book II outlines the history of the Frankish mayors and of *Charlemagne; and Book III discusses the history of France from 841 to 1028. The earliest Norman chronicler was Dudo, a canon of St Quentin who lived at the Norman court in Rouen and wrote, on behalf of Duke Richard I, the first history of Normandy, *De moribus et actis primorum Normanniae ducum*, completed in 1015. *William the Conqueror's history (*Gesta Guillelmi ducis*) was recorded by William of Poitiers, archdeacon of Lisieux.

One of the most famous French chroniclers was *Guibert of Nogent, who wrote not only an autobiography in Latin (*De vita sua sive monodiarum suarum libri tres*) and a treatise on the veneration of *relics (*De pignoribus sanctorum*) but also a popular history of the First Crusade (*Gesta Dei per Francos*) in which he voiced considerable criticism of the participants and the moral depravity resulting from the Christians' victory. This did not, however, prevent him from expressing his pride in France's being the leader in this crusade. Most unusual proved to be Galbert's *De multro, traditione et occisione gloriosi Karoli comitis Flandiarum*, in which the notary and official Count *Charles 'the Good' of Flanders details the events surrounding the murder of his patron on 2 March 1127. Another noteworthy development concerns the more or less official appointment of the monks of *St-Denis as the recognized court historians of the French monarchy, best represented by Abbot *Suger, who composed *Gesta Ludovici regis grossi* (*Life of Louis the Fat* [*Louis VI]) and the famous, reflective account of the architectural history of France, his *Liber de rebus in sua administratione*. The reign of *Philip II Augustus is described in Rigord's *De gestis Philippi Augusti Francorum regis* (first part between 1187 and 1196, the second before 1207) and in William the Breton's *De gestis Philippi Augusti* (*c*.1214–20), both having served under the king.

A more global perspective of church history is pursued by *Orderic Vitalis (d. 1142) in his *Historia ecclesiastica*, which is characterized by philosophizing and personal reflections. *Gislebert of Mons, chancellor of *Baldwin V, count of Hainaut, wrote the *Chronicon Hanoniense* sometime after 1200. Most famous was *Vincent of Beauvais's universal history, the *Speculum historiale* (1244–60), which exerted long-term influence on late medieval *scholasticism and *historiography. The chronicle genre continued to proliferate.

The oldest extant historical account in OF was written by *Geoffrey Gaimar (*Estoire des Engleis*, 1136–37), who composed it on behalf of Constance FitzGilbert, wife of a nobleman in Lincolnshire. The first part (lost today) is based on *Geoffrey of Monmouth's rather fanciful *Historia Regum Britanniae* (*c.*1135; includes the story of King Arthur) and deals with the history of the Britons. The second part, to a large extent simply a translation of the *Anglo-Saxon Chronicle* and relying on a variety of other sources, both written and oral, relates the history of the Anglo-Saxons. From then on many other OF chronicles were written throughout the MA, such as those by Georges *Chastellain and Olivier de *La Marche. Jean *Wavrin translated the Latin *Annales Hannoniae* as *Chroniques de Hainaut*, which was richly illustrated. Perhaps most famous was the luxuriously embellished *Chroniques* by *Froissart, written between 1470 and 1475 on behalf of the lord of *Bruges, with a focus on the *Hundred Years War. Most French chronicles written before 1300 were in verse, but then prose gradually became acceptable and finally the norm for historiography.

9. *Slavic chronicles*

The Slavic world comes into focus in Helmbold's (d. 1177) *Chronicon Slavorum*. Almost as a continuation, *Arnold of Lübeck also dealt with Slavic history from 1171 to 1209. The history of *Bohemia was recorded by *Cosmas of Prague in his *Chronicae Bohemorum* (Chronicles of the Bohemians), which was continued to 1167 by Vincent, a prebendary of *Prague, and to 1198 by Gerlach, abbot of Mühlhausen. One of the oldest extant Russian chronicles is the *Povest' vremennych let'* by the monk *Nestor of the monastery of Petschora in *Kiev, written in 1113. We also know of the (now lost) *Oldest Kiev Chronicle* (*c.*1030–40), the *Nikonov Chronicle* by the monk Nikon (1073), and the *Original Chronicle* from 1095 (the first *Novgorod Chronicle*). Nestor's chronicle was followed by a second version (1116), then by the third version of the *Povest' vremennych let'* in 1118, to mention just a few of the many subsequent chronicles. The most important Polish chronicle was written by *Jan Długosz, whose *Annales seu cronicae inclyti regni Polonorum* (1458–61, continued until 1480) became the standard textbook for early modern Polish historiography.

10. *End of the MA*

At the end of the MA, both the number and the volume of chronicles produced all over Europe increased. One of the most important French chronicles, the **Grandes Chroniques de France* (written 1274–1493), which starts in legendary Troy and goes to 1461, propagandistically advocated the glory of the French nation. Late medieval historiography also included more images and relied on graphic designs, as in the hugely popular *Fasciculus Temporum Omnes Antiquorum Chronicas Complectens* by the German Carthusian Werner Rolevinck (1425–1502). Finally, humanistic perspectives transformed the medieval chronicle. AC

R. J. Bartlett, ed., *History and Historians: Selected Papers of R. W. Southern* (2004).

A.-D. von den Brincken, *Studien zur lateinischen Weltchronistik bis in das Zeitalter Ottos von Freising* (1957).

P. Damian-Grint, *The New Historians of the Twelfth-Century Renaissance* (1999).

D. M. Deliyannis, ed., *Historiography in the Middle Ages* (2003).

J.-P. Genet, ed., *L'Historiographie médiévale en Europe* (1991).

D. Hay, *Annalists and Historians: Western Historiography from the Eighth to the Eighteenth Century* (1977).

E. Kooper, ed., *The Medieval Chronicle*, 2 vols (1999–2002).

B. Smalley, *Historians in the Middle Ages* (1974).

G. M. Spiegel, *Romancing the Past: The Rise of Vernacular Prose Historiography in Thirteenth-Century France* (1993).

R. Sprandel, *Chronisten als Zeitzeugen: Forschungen zur spätmittelalterlichen Geschichtsschreibung* (1994).

annals and chronicles: central / eastern Europe—Annals of Hungary Though the genre surely existed in medieval *Hungary, only the *Bratislava (Pozsony) Annals survive, in a sacramentary from *c.*1200. The first part (997–1115) originated at the royal court, was continued in NE Hungary to 1187 and finished in a *Benedictine monastery in 1203, and later stored in the chapter library of Bratislava (hence its name). For mid-11th-century Hungarian history the Altaich Annals are of central importance, based on local Hungarian information, later incorporated into the Hungarian Chronicle. Other annalistic collections, like the 15th-century Somogyvár annals and king-lists, may go back to lost annals, but provide no new information. LV

N. Kersken, *Geschichtsschreibung im Europa der 'nationes': Nationalgeschichtliche Gesamtdarstellungen im Mittelalter* (1995).

Scriptores rerum Hungaricarum, ed. I. Szentpétery (1937).

Repertorium fontium historiae medii aevi (1967).

annals and chronicles: central / eastern Europe—*Chronica Poloniae Maioris* Chronicle composed in the late 13th century (or possibly the 14th), by either Godisław Basco, *custos* of Poznań, or Bishop Bochuwał of Poznań. The work's importance lies in its view of Polish history emphasizing the importance of the region of Great Poland. The chronicle's views on the origins of the

Poles and on 13th-century developments are especially interesting. PWK

Chronica Poloniae Maioris, ed. B. Kürbis (1970).
J. Dąbrowski, *Dawne dziejopisarstwo polskie do roku 1480* (1964).
B. Kürbis, *Dziejopisarstwo wielkopolskie XIII i XIV wieku* (1959).
—— *Studia nad Kronika Wielkopolska* (1952).

annals and chronicles: central/eastern Europe—Chronicle of Dzierzwa Polish chronicle from the beginning of the 14th century. Its author was a *Cracow *Franciscan or canon connected with the court of Władysław Łokietek. He based himself on Vincent Kadłubek's Latin work; this work's relation to the *Chronicon Poloniae Maius* is controversial. RG

J. Banaszkiewicz, *Kronika Dzierzwy: XIV-wieczne Kompendium Historii ojczystej* (1979).
W. Drelicharz, *Annalistyka małopolska XIII–XV wieku* (2003).

annals and chronicles: central/eastern Europe—*Chronicon Aulae Regiae* (*Königsaaler Geschichtsquellen*) Chronicle written by the abbots Ota (d. 1314) and Peter of Zittau (d. after 1338) of the *Cistercian *monastery in Zbraslav near *Prague. It covers the period of the last *Přemyslid kings and the accession of the Luxembourgs to the Bohemian throne (1278–1338) and is a unique source not only for Czech history of the age but also of the neighbouring countries. Peter belonged to the king's entourage as his diplomat and recorded events he witnessed himself. The chronicle is written in prose with almost 4,000 lines of hexameters inserted. It is preserved in only a few MSS, of which the oldest, in the *Vatican Library, is likely to be Peter's autograph. The fullest version is contained in a Jihlava MS from the end of the 14th century with miniatures representing Bohemian rulers. It was first printed in 1602. JFr

Chronicon aulae regiae, ed. J. Emler (2004).
Die Königssaaler Geschichts-Quellen, ed. J. Loserth (1875; repr. 1970); tr. F. Heřmanský, *Kronika Zbraslavská* (1952).
J. Loserth, 'Die Königsaaler Geschichtsquellen. Kritische Untersuchung über die Entstehung des Chronicon Aulae Regiae', *Archiv für österreichische Geschichte*, 51 (1873), 449–99.
A. Seibt, *Studien zu den Königsaaler Geschichtsquellen* (1898).

annals and chronicles: central/eastern Europe—Livonian Rhymed Chronicle Source for the 13th-century Baltic *crusade. Its anonymous author was probably from the *Teutonic order in Livonia. Written in MHG, it consists of 12,017 lines and covers *c.*1180 to 1290. Organized by masters of the order, it focuses on military deeds. The chronicle is sometimes designated the Older Rhymed Chronicle, to distinguish it from the Younger Rhymed Chronicle by Bartholomäus Hoenecke (14th century). JKr

Livländische Reimchronik, ed. L. Meyer (1876).
A. V. Murray, 'The Structure, Genre and Intended Audience of the Livonian Rhymed Chronicle', *Crusade and Conversion on the Baltic Frontier 1150–1500*, ed. idem (2001), 235–51.

annals and chronicles: central/eastern Europe—Polish-Hungarian Chronicle Chronicle preserved in two versions in Polish MSS, written *c.*1227 in *Croatia; narrating the primary history of the *Hungarians, based on written and oral tradition as well as on the *Legenda sancti Stephani*. It is the source of Hungarian information in later medieval Polish narratives. *See also* POLAND. RG

R. Grzesik, *Kronika węgiersko-polska* (1999).

annals and chronicles: central/eastern Europe—Slavic chronicles, chronographs, and histories With their entry into Christendom, the Slavs created writing traditions based on established literary models and conceptions of history. From the Cyrillo-Methodian mission to *Great Moravia in the mid 9th century to the Great *Schism of the church (1054), a united religious and cultural community of 'Christian Slavdom' (*Slavia Christiana*) stretched from the Czech lands to the East Slavs, coexisting with the dominant Greek and Latin traditions. By the early 12th century, however, two Slavic cultural communities emerged, based on confessional distinctiveness and ethno-linguistic affinity. 'Orthodox Slavdom' (*Slavia Orthodoxa*), extending from the eastern Balkans to East Slavic territory, shared a common confession (Orthodoxy), a common language (Church Slavonic), and recognition of the spiritual jurisdiction of the 'eastern' Orthodox church. 'Roman Slavdom' (*Slavia Romana*), stretching from the West Slavs to the western Balkans, owed its allegiance to the 'western' Roman church. In both communities writing activity embraced schemes and norms generated by the relationship between religious power and secular authority.

The Orthodox Slavs first turned to Byzantine historiographic writings as models, especially to the 'Christian' chroniclers, such as John Malalas and George Hamartolos—both of whom they translated from Greek into Church Slavonic—writers who conceived 'local' historical events within a universal framework governed by providence. Early Bulgarian literature provided the paradigmatic foundation for the common literary conventions of *Slavia Orthodoxa*, but the most significant preserved examples of 'original' (non-translated) Orthodox Slavic chronicle writing were produced elsewhere, notably in *Rus'.

Rus' 'chronicles' (*letopisi*) differed from western European annals, particularly in their compilatory nature and their role as text carriers. The inclusion of heterogeneous materials often meant that other compositional patterns prevailed over the annalistic format. Beyond serving as a collection of factual sources, this type of East Slavic 'compilation' (*svod*) or 'miscellany' (*sbornik*) yielded an anthology of narrative compositions of literary as well as historical value.

The earliest preserved East Slavic chronicle is the *Tale of Bygone Years* (*Povest' vremennyx let*), assembled by a compiler-reviser in the early 12th century. The *Tale* features a heterogeneity of textual components and literary styles as well as motifs underscoring the unity of Rus' and its unique place in the Christian oikoumene. The textual history of the *Tale* illustrates a process that applied for centuries to the compilation of similar literary monuments in many local centres of *Slavia Orientalis*. Such compilations became repositories of all kinds of writings, often inserted with little or no contextual adaptation.

The *Tale* became part of later annalistic compilations, for which it provided a common introductory section. In the 12th century, the rise of many religious and political centres in the East Slavic lands fostered chronicle writing that supported the aspirations of local rulers and monasteries. In the 13th century increasing fragmentation under *Tatar rule further underscored the local tendencies of East Slavic chronicles. With the growth of *Moscow from the 15th to the 17th century, new compilations reflected the pan-Russian ambitions of the Muscovite rulers, whereas writings from other centres, such as the *Pskov Chronicles, often revealed anti-Muscovite sentiments.

It is noteworthy that the 16th-century *Book of Degrees of the Imperial Genealogy* (*Kniga stepennaia tsarskogo rodosloviia*), which exalted Moscow's claim to leadership of all Orthodox Christendom, is likely modelled after both earlier Rus' chronicle writing and historical legends and a Serbian miscellany known as the *Lives of the Serbian Kings and Archbishops*. In Rus' and *Serbia the conception of history was indissolubly linked with the sacred nature of kingship and the notion of the righteous dynasty. Among the noteworthy Serbian chronicles are the *Peć Chronicle* (*c*.1391), the *Koporin Chronicle* (1456), and the *Karlovci Chronicle* (1503).

With the expulsion of Slavic monks from the Sázava monastery at the end of the 11th century, the westernization and Latinization of Czech Christianity entered its definitive phase. All Slavs subject to the Roman church adopted Latin as a sacred language and as a secular administrative language, making them participants in the *latinitas europea* and the cultural 'rules of the game' for Roman Catholic civilization.

In the first quarter of the 12th century, *Cosmas of Prague compiled his Latin chronicle of Czech history (*Chronica Bohemorum*), among the first major 'Roman Slavic' historiographic writings to describe the events of a Slavic state (*Bohemia) and dynasty (*Přemysl) against a 'western' and 'Catholic' background. Additionally, it provides us with a model for future chronicle writing among the Roman Slavs, by including both local writings (for example, the *Privilegium Moravensis ecclesiae*) and non-local sources (for example, the chronicle by *Regino of Prüm), and by offering a paradigm for writing in Slavic vernaculars.

Among the most important Polish chronicles written in Latin were the early-12th-century *Chronicae* by Gallus Anonymus (d. 1116), the earliest Polish historiographic source relying on non-extant documents; the *Chronica* by Wincenty Kadłubek (d. 1223); and the *Annals* of *Jan Długosz.

The *Croatian lands were marked by competing and often conflicting cultural traditions. In the later 12th century the Latin compilation known as the chronicle of the priest of Duklja (*Ljetopis Popa Dukljanina*) was written to demonstrate the superiority of the diocese of Bar over that of *Split, and it reveals a complex history of expansion and subsequent translation from Church Slavonic. Some five decades later, *Thomas, archdeacon of Split, wrote the *History of the Bishops of Salona and Split*, promoting Split as heir to the metropolitan rights of Salona and reporting on the Fourth and Fifth crusades as well as the *Mongol invasion of 1241–2.

The Czechs were the first in *Slavia Romana* to extend the use of the vernacular. The rhymed *Chronicle of Dalimil* (*Dalimilova kronika*), compiled early in the 14th century, was the first written in the Czech language, but based primarily on earlier Czech historiographic sources written in Latin. By the Renaissance, all components of *Slavia Romana* would begin to write in the vernacular, either producing new chronicles or translating from Latin and thereby offering new histories of Slavic peoples, their relations with other states, and their place in world history. HG

J. Allan, ed., *The Annals of Jan Długosz: Annales seu cronicae incliti regni Poloniae* (1997).

S. Bărlieva, 'Xroniki', *Kirilo-Metodievska Enciklopedija*, vol. 4 (2003), 453–8.

B. Bretholz, *Die Chronik der Böhmen des Cosmas von Prag* (1923).

S. H. Cross and O. P. Sherbowitz-Wetzor, eds, *The Russian Primary Chronicle: Laurentian Text* (1973).

J. Daňhelka *et al.*, eds, *Staročeská kronika tak řečeného Dalimila* (1988).

G. M. Danijel and D. Petrović, eds, *Životi kraljeva i arhiepiskopa srpskih* (1988).

J. Dąbrowski, ed., *Ioannis Dlugossii Annales; seu, Cronicae incliti Regni Poloniae* (1964).

Gallus Anonymus, *Gesta principum Polonorum: The Deeds of the Princes of the Poles* (2003).

D. Karbić *et al.*, eds, *Historia Salonitanorum atque Spalatinorum pontificum: History of the Bishops of Salona and Split* (2006).

A. Koševev, ed., *Polnoe sobranie russkix letopisej* (1997–2002).

K. Maleczyński, ed., *Gallus Anonymus, Cronica et gesta ducum sive principum Polonorum* (1952).

S. Nikolova, 'Istoričeski săčinenija', *Kirilo-Metodievska Enciklopedija*, vol. 2 (1995), 129–38.

A. Przezdziecki, ed., *Wincenty Kadłubek, Chronica Polonorum: sive originale regum et principum Poloniae* (1862).

F. Šišić, ed., *Letopis popa Dukljanina* (1928).

L. Stojanović, ed., *Stari srpski rodoslovi i letopisi* (1927).

M. Weingart, *Byzantské kroniky v literatuře církevněslovanské*, 2 vols (1922–23).

annals and chronicles: chronicles (Hebrew) **of First Crusade in 1096** Hebrew narratives of the crusaders' massacres of German (*Ashkenazic) Jews in the spring and summer of 1096; known as Solomon bar Simson's Chronicle, Eliezer bar Nathan's Chronicle, and the Mainz Anonymous. Eliezer bar Nathan's account was widely circulated; the other two survived in a single MS each. The accounts attributed to Solomon and Eliezer may date to the 12th century; the Mainz Anonymous is difficult to date.

These chronicles describe the attacks and the Jewish reactions in cities along the *Rhine and on the Moselle, depicting the crusaders' demands. The chronicles concentrate on those who chose death over *baptism. All forms of resistance were defined as martyrdom (*qiddush ha-Shem*, 'sanctifying the Name'); all individuals were viewed as God's sacrifices (*qorbanot*). Utilizing biblical and rabbinic symbols, the chronicles present martyrdom as religious ritual, embellishing their accounts through imagination and ideology. This style of reporting has given the chronicles a formative effect on the Ashkenazic collective memory and Jewish *historiography. SS

R. Chazan, *God, Humanity, and History: The Hebrew First Crusade Narratives* (2000).
J. Cohen, *Sanctifying the Name of God: Jewish Martyrs and Jewish Memories of the First Crusade* (2004).
E. Haverkamp, *Hebräische Berichte über die Judenverfolgungen während des ersten Kreuzzugs* (2005).
I. G. Marcus, 'From Politics to Martyrdom: Shifting Paradigms in the Hebrew Narratives of the 1096 Crusader Riots', *Prooftexts*, 2 (1982), 40–52.
L. Roos, *'God Wants It!': The Ideology of Martyrdom in the Hebrew Crusade Chronicles and its Jewish and Christian Background* (2006).

annals and chronicles: England (1)—*Anglo-Saxon Chronicle*

A chronicle in variant versions extending from Julius Caesar's arrival in Britain until 1154.

The Chronicle survives in eight MSS, assigned by scholars the *sigla* A to H. Its core, the so-called 'common stock' (best represented by MS A), was assembled in *c*.892, probably under the aegis of King *Alfred. It was added to in stages at various ecclesiastical centres, some versions incorporating other putative sources such as the 'Mercian Annals', primary evidence for events in *Mercia in 902–24. Extant MSS sometimes influenced other versions. MS E, the so-called *'Peterborough Chronicle', continued to receive vernacular entries up to 1154, important both for information about English post-Conquest events and for exemplifying the linguistic transition from OE to ME. Other texts also contain versions of the Chronicle, including *Asser's *Life of Alfred*, *Æthelweard's *Chronicle*, the *Annals of St Neots*, the *Waverley Annals*, Geoffrey *Gaimar's *L'Estoire des Engleis*, and works by *William of Malmesbury, *Florence of Worcester, Henry of *Huntingdon, and *Simeon of Durham. The complex relationships of the texts lying behind these latter versions have still to be explored fully. DAEP

J. Bately, *The Anglo-Saxon Chronicle: Texts and Relationships* (1991).
—— ed., *The Anglo-Saxon Chronicle: A Collaborative Edition, The A-Text*, vol. 3 (1986).
S. Irvine, ed., *The Anglo-Saxon Chronicle: A Collaborative Edition, The E-Text*, vol. 7 (2004).
C. Plummer, ed., *Two of the Saxon Chronicles Parallel*, 2 vols (1892–9; reissued 1952).
M. J. Swanton, tr., *The Anglo-Saxon Chronicle* ([2]2000).

annals and chronicles: England (2)—Abingdon

Two 11th-century chronicles, MSS 'B' and 'C' of the *Anglo-Saxon Chronicle*, compiled at Abingdon in northern *Wessex, based on copies of the lost original under King *Alfred's rule to 891 and subsequently continued independently. 'B' runs from AD 1 to 977; 'C' from 60 BC to 1066. REM

D. Dumville and S. Keynes, eds, *The Anglo-Saxon Chronicle*, vols 4 and 5 (1983).
G. N. Garmonsway, ed. and tr., *The Anglo-Saxon Chronicle* (1953).
H. A. Rositzke, ed., *The C-Text of the Old English Chronicles* (1940).

annals and chronicles: England (3)—Anonimalle

So named (obsolete for 'anonymous') by 16th-century historians. A 14th-century AN chronicle from St Mary's abbey, *York, with well-informed accounts of the *'Good Parliament' (1376) and the *Peasants' Rebellion of 1381. REM

W. Childs and J. Taylor, eds, *The Anonimalle Chronicle, 1307–1334* (1991).
V. H. Galbraith, ed., *The Anonimalle Chronicle, 1333–1381* (1927).
C. Given-Wilson, *Chronicles: The Writing of History in Medieval England* (2004).

annals and chronicles: England (4)—Crowland

A Latin chronicle compiled at Crowland abbey in Lincolnshire, supposedly under abbot Ingulph in the early 12th century, but probably forged in the 15th century to support monastic land-claims. The early sections were much damaged in the Cottonian Library fire (1731), but the later contemporary narrative provides detailed comment on the Wars of the *Roses, condemning *Richard III and lauding the triumph of *Henry VII. REM

N. Pronay and J. Cox, eds, *The Crowland Chronicle Continuations: 1459–1486* (1986).

annals and chronicles: England (5)—Peterborough Chronicle

The title given to the final of four distinct versions of the *Anglo-Saxon Chronicle*, describing the post-*Norman Conquest history of England from 1070–1154. The latter part of this text (1122–54) was composed by the monks of Peterborough abbey, who provided a non-courtly perspective on historical events and continued to use and slowly adapt their traditional AS language, although AN had become the country's official language after 1066. *See also* LANGUAGES: ANGLO-NORMAN. RJU

C. Clark, ed., *The Peterborough Chronicle, 1070–1154* (1970).
D. L. Shores, '*The Peterborough Chronicle*: Continuity and Change in the English Language', *South Atlantic Bulletin*, 35/4 (1970), 19–29.

annals and chronicles: France—*Grandes Chroniques de France* (*de St-Denis*) The official history of *France, principally compiled in both Latin and French at the abbey of *St-Denis until the end of the 15th century. CDT

B. Guenée, 'Les *Grandes chroniques de France*: le roman aux rois (1274–1518)', *Les lieux de mémoire*, ed. P. Nora, 3 vols (1986), vol. 1/2, 189–214.
G. M. Spiegel, *The Chronicle Tradition of Saint-Denis: A Survey* (1978).

annals and chronicles: Germany/Austria—*Kaiserchronik* (between 1126 and 1147/52) First vernacular verse chronicle in the German-language area. Composed in *Regensburg, the chronicle covers the history of the *Roman Empire from its beginnings to the German emperor Conrad III. It incorporates a variety of stories from *hagiography, legends, folk-tales, and chronicles, most famously those of Sylvester, Faustinianus, Lucretia, and Crescentia. CB

H. F. Massmann, *Der keiser und der kunige buoch oder die sogenannte Kaiserchronik* (1854).
F. Ohly, *Sage und Legende in der Kaiserchronik* (1940; repr. 1968).
E. Schröder, ed., *Die Kaiserchronik eines Regensburger Geistlichen* (1895; repr. 1964).

annals and chronicles: Ireland—Irish annals Although the earliest surviving MSS of most Irish annals date from the later medieval and early modern periods, the Irish annalistic tradition may be traced back to 8th-century Iona and was subsequently developed in a number of *monastic centres in Ireland itself. Written in both Irish and Latin, compilations such as the 'Annals of Ulster', the 'Annals of Tigernach', and the 'Annals of Innisfallen' provide a wealth of *prosopographical and narrative detail about Ireland and the wider *Gaelic world. *See also* ANNALS AND CHRONICLES; LITERATURES: HIBERNO-LATIN. HP

G. MacNiocaill, *The Medieval Irish Annals* (1975).

annals and chronicles: Spain/Portugal—*Crónica de 754* Traditionally known as the *Mozarabic Chronicle*, the anonymous Latin *Chronicle of 754* is the most important single source of information in any language about the Muslim conquest of Spain and its aftermath. Apparently written by a Spanish-Christian ecclesiastic with ties to the new regime, it fits within the universal chronography tradition of Eusebius, providing an outline of events occurring simultaneously in the Arab, Byzantine, and Spanish worlds. Beginning with the accession of Heraclius (610), the author recounts the emperor's unexpected success over the Persians only to use his failure to credit God with the victory to explain the subsequent rise of *Muhammad and the Arabs. After describing the Muslim conquests in the east, the author backtracks to cover Iberian history from the accession of the *Visigothic king Sisebut (612) to the middle of Yusuf's term as governor (754). Although he depicts the Muslim conquests in the east as a scourge, the author resists the temptation to treat the invasion of Spain similarly, explaining that the Visigothic king Roderic simply did not enjoy the undivided support of his nobility. The author also shows remarkable even-handedness when describing the Muslim governors of *Córdoba, who replaced the Christian kings of *Toledo. References to the religious identity of the new regime are surprisingly few and muted. KBW

R. Collins, *The Arab Conquest of Spain, 710–797* (1989).
E. L. Pereira, ed., *Crónica mozárabe de 754: edición crítica y traducción* (1980).
K. Wolf, *Conquerors and Chroniclers of Early Medieval Spain* (1999).

annals and chronicles: Wales—Chronicle of the Welsh Princes Three chronicles, written in Middle Welsh, generically known as *Brut y Tywysogyon* ('The Chronicle of the Princes'), each of which appears to derive from a lost Latin chronicle composed shortly after *Edward I's conquest of Wales. Conceived as a continuation of the Welsh translations of *Geoffrey of Monmouth's *Historia Regum Britanniae*, 'The Chronicle of the Princes' covers the period from 682 to 1282 (with additional coverage beyond that in two of the versions), and is the single most important narrative source for medieval Welsh history. *See also* LANGUAGES: WELSH; SCOTLAND, IRELAND, WALES: EARLY WALES TO 1064; WARFARE IN IRELAND AND WALES. HP

T. Jones, tr., *Brut y Tywysogyon, or, The Chronicle of the Princes, Peniarth MS. 20 Version* (1952).

Anne, St Mother of the Virgin *Mary. In apocryphal works, Anne and Joachim, a barren couple, conceive Mary miraculously and give her to the temple in *Jerusalem to be raised. This legend, based on the story of Hannah in 1 Samuel 1–2, is found in much medieval church art. Anne is often represented with Mary, holding a book, or holding Mary, who holds Jesus. *See also* IMMACULATE CONCEPTION OF THE VIRGIN MARY. EAM

K. Ashley and P. Sheingorn, eds, *Interpreting Cultural Symbols: Saint Anne in Late Medieval Society* (1990).
V. Nixon, *Mary's Mother: Saint Anne in Late Medieval Europe* (2004).

Anne Neville *See* RICHARD III.

Anne of Brittany, queen of France (1477–1514) Duchess of *Brittany in 1488, married by proxy to Maximilian of Austria in 1490, Anne wed *Charles VIII in 1491 and had six children, none of whom survived their father, dead in 1498. Married to Louis XII in 1498 after his divorce from *Jeanne of France, Anne bore him four children of whom two daughters survived, one (Claude) bringing *Brittany to *France through her marriage to Francis I. EARB

A. Le Roux de Lincy, *Vie de la reine Anne de Bretagne, femme des rois de France Charles VIII et Louis XII*, 4 vols (1860–61).

Musées du Château de Nantes, *Anne de Bretagne: une histoire, un mythe* (2007).

Anne of France, lady of Beaujeu and duchess of Bourbon (1461–1522) Eldest child to survive of Louis XI and Charlotte of *Savoy; wife in 1473/74 of Pierre de Beaujeu (1438–1503), duke of Bourbon in 1488; until 1488 regent with Pierre for her brother *Charles VIII (1470–98); she and Pierre quieted opposition and achieved the marriage of Charles and *Anne of Brittany. EARB

P. Pélicier, *Essai sur le gouvernement de la dame de Beaujeu, 1483–1491* (1882).

P. Pradel, *Anne de France 1461–1522* (1986).

Annolied *See* ANNO OF COLOGNE.

Anno of Cologne, St, archbishop (d. 1075) Building campaigns, monastic reform, and political intrigue were among Anno's methods for increasing *Cologne's prestige. A problematic figure, he was praised in the *Annolied* (*c.*1077) and venerated in a luxurious reliquary of *c.*1183. ASC

J. Rotondo-McCord, 'Body Snatching and Episcopal Power: Archbishop Anno II of Cologne, Burials in St Mary's *ad gradus*, and the Minority of Henry IV', *JMH* 22 (1996), 297–312.

Annunciation, Feast of *See* LITURGY.

anointing of the dead There is sporadic evidence for the anointing of the body in the early medieval west, imitating Christ's burial and recalling baptismal anointing. In developed medieval rites, anointing was administered before death. DJKe

M. Dudley and G. Rowell, eds, *The Oil of Gladness: Anointing in the Christian Tradition* (1993).

G. Rowell, *The Liturgy of Christian Burial* (1977).

anonymity The vast number of anonymous and pseudonymous texts that circulated in the MA was a product of the medieval attitude to *authorship and 'authority' (*auctoritas*). This attitude considered that only the classical poets of antiquity or the Church Fathers of late antiquity were 'authors'; their medieval successors were considered to be mere 'writers' or 'compilers' who lacked the weight of *auctoritas*. *Bernard of Chartres expressed this medieval inferiority complex perfectly in the 12th century when he asserted that contemporaries were to the ancients as 'dwarves on the shoulders of giants'. Medieval writers, therefore, often sought either to remain anonymous or to cloak their compositions under the aegis of more venerable authors. PSH

B. Smalley, *Historians in the Middle Ages* (1974).

M. Swan, 'Authorship and Anonymity', *A Companion to Anglo-Saxon Literature*, ed. P. Pulsiano and E. Treharne (2001), 71–83.

Anonymous IV Music theorist who wrote his only surviving treatise *c.*1280. Its originality lies in his reference to *Leoninus and *Perotinus, as well as his discussion of irregular modes and of the music writing trade. *See also* MUSIC THEORY. JDH

F. Reckow, *Der Musiktraktat des Anonymus 4* (1967).

J. Yudkin, *The Music Treatise of Anonymous IV: A New Translation* (1985).

Anonymous of Melk (*c.*1135) Putative compiler of the *De scriptoribus ecclesiasticis*, which ends with *Rupert of Deutz. Interspersed are literary-historical notices on little-known medieval authors, including *Ekkehard IV as the *'Waltharius' poet. *See also* WOLFGER OF PRÜFENING. FGG

F. J. Worstbrock, *Verfasserlexikon*, vol. 10, 1352–60.

Anonymous of the Hussite Wars Illustrated MS (Munich, clm 197, 1^r^–48^v^), discovered 1524–57 by Johann Albrecht Widmanstetter, bound together with Mariano *Taccola's *De Ingeneis*, and sold to the Bavarian duke Albrecht V (1558). It consists of two fascicles from different authors: *A* (1^r^–28^r^) was designed *c.*1472–76 with marginal notes in the east Franconian dialect; *B* (29^r^–48^v^) *c.*1486–92 without any text. *A* refers to older sources possibly written by a military leader entrusted with repelling the Hussites. Some notes refer to specific incidents of the *Hussite Wars such as a drawing of an armoured piece of artillery that was used in the siege of Saaz (1421) according to notes by Erkinger of Seinsheim. The coloured pen-and-ink images are crudely drawn, without perspective, and difficult to decipher, but are most relevant for the history of engineering. The main subjects are military devices (firearms, protective shields, battle-wagons), weight-raising systems, underwater breathing apparatus (influenced by Konrad *Kyeser), grinding machines, and building equipment. The author was especially interested in driving and gearing technologies such as the waterwheel, flywheel drive, brake mechanisms, and crankshaft. RL

B. S. Hall, ed., *The Technological Illustrations of the So-called 'Anonymous of the Hussite Wars'* (1979).

R. Leng, *Ars belli* (2002), vol. 1, 231–3, vol. 2, 196–7.

Verfasserlexikon vol. 4, 329–32.

Anonymus (P. dictus magister) Hungarian historian *fl. c.*1200, called also *praedictus*, a *notary of a certain King

Béla, mostly identified as Béla III (d. 1196). His *Gesta Hungarorum* survives in a single 13th-century MS (Budapest, OSzK Clm. 304, 1st ed. 1746), as the earliest extant *Hungarian chronicle, describing Hungarian prehistory from Scythia to the occupation of the *Carpathian basin (895/6), and arguing for a mythical contractual power-sharing between nobles and princes. It is the first written source naming *Attila the Hun as the ancestor of the *Árpád dynasty. Used both oral traditions and written sources (Regino, Histories of Troy and of Alexander the Great), to epic effect. Gives a detailed description of the country, connecting place names with heroes of the past, for the 9th–10th centuries without any historical authenticity, still disputed by modern historians. LV

Anonymus, *A magyarok cselekedetei*, tr. L. Veszprémy (1999).
Die 'Gesta Hungarorum' des anonymen Notars, ed. G. Silagi (1991).
K. Szovák, 'Wer war der anonyme Notar? Zur Bestimmung des Verfassers der Gesta Ungarorum', *Ungarn-Jahrbuch*, 19 (1991), 1–16.
I. Kapitánffy, 'Der ungarische Anonymus und Byzanz', *Byzance et ses voisins: Mélanges à la mémoire de Gy. Moravcsik*, ed. T. Olajos (1994), 69–76.

Anselm, St, archbishop of Canterbury (*c.*1033–1109) A philosopher, theologian, and archbishop whose major contributions to early scholastic theology include the distinctive method of *fides quaerens intellectum*, the *'ontological argument' for the existence of God, and the satisfaction theory of the atonement.

Born in 1033 in Aosta, in his mid-twenties Anselm entered the *Benedictine school at *Bec in *Normandy where he came under the tutelage of *Lanfranc. In 1063 Anselm succeeded Lanfranc as prior and was consecrated abbot in 1078. Toward the end of his priorate Anselm produced the *Monologion* (1075–6) and the *Proslogion* (1077–8), both contemplative works offering philosophical or rational proofs for the existence of God. The *Monologion* propounds what has become known as the 'ontological argument', namely, that if God is (as Anselm maintained) 'that than which nothing greater can be thought' (*id quo nihil maius cogitari possit*) then this entity necessarily exists, not merely in human understanding but also in reality.

Anselm produced philosophical works such as *De Veritate*, *De Libertate Arbitrii*, and *De Casu Diaboli* while the abbot at Bec (1078–93). As archbishop of *Canterbury (1093–1109), he composed several theological treatises including *De conceptu virginali et de peccato originali* (1099), *De Processione Sancti Spiritus* (1102), and his magnum opus, *Cur Deus Homo* (1095–8). In this latter work Anselm presents 'necessary reasons' for the Incarnation. He argues that God had to become human in order for humankind to be saved because humans alone are obliged to make satisfaction for their sin, yet God alone is actually able to do so. Anselm's treatise, which rejected the widely-held ransom theory, represents the most significant contribution to atonement theology in the MA.

During *Lent in 1109, Anselm became seriously ill and died on Wednesday of Holy Week (April 21, his feast day). His cult became firmly established in the following centuries, and in 1720 he was declared a *'doctor of the church'. *See also* PHILOSOPHY. FTH

R. W. Southern, *Saint Anselm: A Portrait in a Landscape* (1990).
—— *Saint Anselm and his Biographer: A Study of Monastic Life and Thought, 1059–c.1130* (1963).

Anselm of Besate (Anselmus Peripateticus) (11th century) Educated in *Padua and Reggio; served in the chapel of Henry III. His *Rhetorimachia* (*c.*1046/48), in epistolary form, combines rhetorical precepts with lively denunciations of clerical vice. CJMc

Anselm of Besate, *Rhetorimachia*, ed. K. Manitius, *MGH.QG* 11/2 (1958), 95–183.
B. Pabst, *Prosimetrum: Tradition und Wandel einer Literaturform zwischen Spätantike und Spätmittelalter* (1994), vol. 1, 379–87.

Anselm of Havelberg (*c.*1100–1158) Frontier bishop. Born near *Liège, educated at *Laon, entered *Premonstratensian order. While bishop of Havelberg (1129–55), he led a *crusade in the East Baltic region as papal *legate. He served his emperors, especially Frederick I 'Barbarossa', in many capacities. Dealings with *Byzantium as imperial ambassador and as archbishop of *Ravenna (1155–8) led to his great book on differences between the Greek and Latin churches. *See also* ROMAN EMPIRE. KFM

W. Bomm, 'Neue Lebensmodelle in einer funktionalen Gesellschaft', *Macht und Ordnungsvorstellungen*, ed. S. Weinfurter and F. M. Siefarth (1998), 169–91.
J. T. Lees, *Anselm of Havelberg: Deeds into Words in the Twelfth Century* (1998).

Anselm of Laon (*c.*1050–1117) French theologian, educated by Anselm of Bec; taught at *Paris (*c.*1076). With *William of Champeaux, he championed the *realist side of the scholastic debate. He later established a theological school at *Laon, which Peter *Abelard attended (*c.*1114). Some of the **Glossa ordinaria* is attributed to him. AMW

G. Mazzanti, 'Anselmo di Laon, Gilberto l'Universale, e la *Glossa Ordinaria* alla Bibbia', *Bullettino dell'Istituto italiano per il Medio Evo*, 102 (2001), 1–19.

Ansgar (Anskar)**, St** (*c.*801–65) After missions to the Danes and, more successfully, to *Birka, he became archbishop of *Hamburg with responsibility for mission among Danes, Svear, and Slavs. From 848 he held it jointly with Bremen. The *Vita Anskarii*, by his successor Rimbert, reports that he built churches in Ribe and *Schleswig and in 852 revived the Birka mission after a pagan revolt. PHS

I. Wood, *The Missionary Life* (2001), 123–41.

Antelami, Benedetto (late 12th century) Emilian sculptor whose work, informed by both antique Roman and contemporary French *sculpture, includes the free-standing prophets in façade niches of Fidenza cathedral and the extensive exterior and interior narrative programmes of the *baptistery and *cathedral of *Parma. DJR

C. Frugoni, ed., *Benedetto Antelami e il Battistero di Parma* (1995).
M. Woelk, *Benedetto Antelami: Die Werke in Parma und Fidenza* (1995).

anthology The medieval anthology is a creation of late antiquity. Manuscripts preserving these collections usually include shorter works of, and excerpts from, well-established poets (and at times prose writers) who would have their own MS transmission. They would also contain, more importantly, the smaller oeuvres of minor poets, and individual poems, many being pseudepigrapha. Anthologies have attracted interest both as collections and as the witnesses to individual works and *authors.

The collection printed as the *Anthologia Latina* represents material drawn from many sources. At its heart is a probably North African collection preserved in the uncial Codex Salmasianus (Paris BN Lat.10318; *Codices Latini Antiquiores*, vol. 5, 593; s.viii[ex]), its best witness, probably copied in north *Italy or southern *France. It is not clear if its contents represent a single late antique anthology. Such a collection might have been only a nucleus to which material was added at various times and places between the latest date for its original assemblage (in the third or fourth decade of the 6th century) and the MS. It contains the elusive Symphosius, 6th-century Africans like Dracontius and Luxorius, and texts composed neither in the 6th century nor in North Africa, like the *Pervigilium Veneris*.

While the Salmasianus is the sole witness for some of its texts, several other 9th- or 10th-century MS anthologies overlap it to varying degrees. The most important of these is the 9th-century Codex Thuaneus (Paris BN Lat. 8071), the descendant of a fragmentary late-8th-century MS now in Vienna (Österreichische Nationalbibliothek MS.277; *Codices Latini Antiquiores*, vol. 10, 1474).

The anthology was not, however, limited to ancient poets. The **Cambridge Songs*, based on a German collection but preserved in an English MS, were 'modern' when the MS was written in the later 11th century. Poets like *Baudri of Bourgueil, *Hildebert of Le Mans, *Marbod of Rennes, Hugh Primas, and *Peter Riga were anthologized and largely maintained their popularity in and through MS collections into the 15th century. Such collections were fluid, and the MS reality reflects prevailing fashion, availability, and practical interests, often pedagogical or pastoral.

Among the MS anthologies that have attracted continuing scholarly attention are that of Oxford Bodleian MS. Rawlinson G. 109, the so-called **Carmina Burana*, and the largely ME Harley Lyrics. HCOB

D. R. S. Bailey, ed., *Towards a Text of 'Anthologia Latina'* (1979).
—— *Anthologia Latina* (1982).
B. Bischoff, ed., *Carmina Burana*, 2 vols (1967–71).
A. Boutemy, 'A propos d'anthologies poétiques au XIIe siècle', *RBPH* 19 (1940), 229–33.
P. Dronke, *Medieval Latin and the Rise of the European Love-Lyric* ([2]1968).
S. Fein, ed., *Studies in the Harley Manuscript: The Scribes and Contexts of the British Library MS Harley 2253* (2000).
G. Glauche, *Schullektüre im Mittelalter* (1970).
L. D. Reynolds, ed., *Texts and Transmission* (1986).
A. G. Rigg, 'Medieval Latin Poetic Anthologies (I)', *MS* 39 (1977), 281–330.
—— 'Medieval Latin Poetic Anthologies (II)', *MS* 40 (1978), 387–407.
—— 'Anthologies and Florilegia', *Medieval Latin*, ed. F. A. C. Mantello *et al.* (1996), 708–12.

Anthony, duke of Brabant (1406–15) Second son of Philip the Bold, duke of *Burgundy; succeeded Joan, last native duchess of *Brabant, in 1406. As a pawn of his dynasty, he immediately reorganized Brabant's institutions along Flemish-Burgundian lines. Later on he restored, in a more independent fashion, most of the Brabantine traditions. In this perspective he married Elisabeth of Görlitz, the German emperor's niece. Nevertheless he died, a loyal vassal of the French king, in the battle of *Agincourt (1415). WP

W. Blockmans and W. Prevenier, *The Promised Lands: The Low Countries Under Burgundian Rule, 1369–1530* (1999), 38–9, 54–8.

Anthony (Antony) **of Padua, St** (1188/95–1231) Born in *Lisbon, he was a canon regular and then became a *Friar Minor. Struck by the martyrdom of some Franciscans in Morocco, he decided to go to Africa to preach. There he became ill and had to return. On the way back, Anthony landed in Italy. He participated in the Franciscan general chapter of 1221 in *Assisi and then went to Romagna. There, for the first time, Anthony gave a public exhortation, revealing brilliant oratorical skills and extensive scholarship. Later, he engaged in preaching against heresy and taught *theology in *Bologna. After some apostolic ministry and teaching in France between 1224 and 1227, Anthony was elected the minister provincial of Lombardy. In this position, he continued his preaching, collected in his *Sermones*, and also went to *Padua for the first time. In 1230 he left the provincial appointment and took part in the delegation to *Pope Gregory IX that discussed the Franciscan Rule. Returning to Padua, he dedicated himself to preaching against *usury

A picture from the 1450s of St Anthony of Padua with the Bible in his hand. Panel in the church of S. Maria d'Aracoeli, Rome.

and on behalf of insolvent debtors. There he died in 1231. *See also* CANONS, REGULAR AND SECULAR; FRANCISCAN ORDER. EB

Le fonti e la teologia dei sermones antoniani: Atti del Congresso internazionale di studio sui 'Sermones' di s. Antonio da Padova, Padova, 5–10 ottobre 1981 (1982).

A. Rigon, *Dal Libro alla folla, Antonio da Padova e il francescanesimo medievale* (2002).

'Vite' e vita di Antonio da Padova: Atti del Convegno internazionale sull'agiografia antoniana, Padova, 29 maggio-1 giugno 1995 (1997).

Antichrist *Apocalyptic leader of evil expected to appear before Doomsday, persecute the faithful, and deceive Christians and Jews by claiming to be Christ. RKE

R. K. Emmerson, *Antichrist in the Middle Ages: A Study of Medieval Apocalypticism, Art, and Literature* (1981).

R. Rusconi, 'Antichrist and Antichrists', *The Encyclopedia of Apocalypticism*, ed. B. McGinn (1998), vol. 2, 287–325.

Antidotarium Nicolai (12th century?) A collection of recipes for compound medicines based on plants and minerals, originally in Latin, and arranged in alphabetical order starting with *Aurea Alexandrina*. It was a compulsory text in a number of European *universities.

The authorship and date of composition are uncertain, but the earliest extant Latin MSS are 12th century. In some early copies, the name Nicolas appears associated with the collection. An authorial prologue precedes the recipes in one branch of the work. The earliest MSS in this branch date from the 13th century. Several vernacular translations appeared in the 14th and 15th centuries. *See also* MEDICAL TRAINING; THERAPEUTIC COMPENDIA. MJCL

D. Goltz, *Mittelalterliche Pharmazie und Medizin: Dargestellt an Geschichte und Inhalt des Antidotarium Nicolai, mit einem Nachdruck der Druckfassung von 1471* (1976).

antinomianism (Greek, *anti* 'against' + *nomos* 'law') The belief that God's grace liberates Christians from an obligation to moral law. The teaching of antinomianism was primarily an early church phenomenon. From 500–1500 it occurred occasionally, usually in combination with *mysticism or Gnosticism. Some groups, condemned as heretical, practised sexual licence—at times even including *prostitution—as an expression of Christian freedom. Antinomianism was rare within Judaism or Islam. *See also* FREE SPIRIT, DOCTRINE OF THE; HERESY. JCH

M. D. Lambert, *Medieval Heresy* ([3]2002).

G. Leff, *Heresy in the Later Middle Ages* (1967).

Antioch Commercial, cultural, and military hub; Seleucid, then Roman capital of Syria; seat of the *magister militum* for Oriens and of the patriarch of the east. Thereafter Antioch entered an unstable period, suffering earthquakes (528) and Persian attacks and occupation (609–28), then falling under Arab rule (636–7) and shrinking. Regained by *Byzantium in 969, it became an Armenian fiefdom in 1078, before falling to the *Seljuks in 1084 and to the crusaders in 1098, becoming the centre of a principality established by *Bohemond I, which endured until 1268 despite repeated Byzantine attempts at reconquest, dynastic entanglements with Armenian Cilicia, and the threat from Muslim-controlled Syria. An ally of the *Mongols under Bohemond VI, it was finally surrendered to *Baybars and remained in Mamluk control until seized by the Ottomans in 1517. SPC

C. Kondoleon, ed., *Antioch: The Lost Ancient City* (2000).

antiphon, antiphonal From Greek and Latin *antiphona*, 'sounding over against'. In Latin medieval liturgical chant, an antiphon is a short chant sung before a psalm or canticle and repeated after it. The adjective 'antiphonal' is sometimes used to describe *psalmody performed with framing antiphons in this way. However, 'antiphonal' could also be defined (for example, by *Isidore of Seville) as performance by two choirs in alternation. *See also* PSALMODY. DDH

M. Huglo and J. Halmo, 'Antiphon', *NGD2*, vol. 1, 735–48.

Antiphoner *See* LITURGICAL BOOKS.

antiphons, Marian Chants performed after the office of compline beginning in the 13th century. The four principal Marian antiphons were 'Alma Redemptoris Mater', 'Ave Regina Caelorum', 'Salve Regina', and 'Regina Caeli'. Many other antiphons honouring Mary were sung during the *Divine Office and in *votive services, sometimes polyphonically. SB

S. Boynton, 'Marian Antiphons', *Medieval France: An Encyclopedia*, ed. W. Kibler *et al.* (1995), 589.

Antipodes *See* GEOGRAPHY.

antipope One who assumes papal office without regard to the rules of election under canon *law. This occurred most frequently in the early church, over doctrinal differences, and in the high MA, as church and empire fought to control the office. *See also* GREGORIAN REFORM; INVESTITURE CONTROVERSY; PAPACY. AHo

G. Barraclough, *The Medieval Papacy* (1968).

A. Mercati, 'The New List of the Popes', *MS* 9 (1947), 71–80.

antiquarianism and antique revival *See* RENAISSANCE AND ANTIQUARIANISM.

anti-Semitism Though the 19th-century term 'anti-Semitism' was unknown in the MA, many themes of anti-Jewish sentiment have their genesis in medieval western Christendom. While the medieval perceptions originate in classical Christian doctrine and teachings concerning the Jews, for example their enmity to Christ and their responsibility for his death, the special circumstances of western Christendom and its Jewish minority led to the elaboration of a series of anti-Jewish allegations that have become part of western folklore ever since.

Key elements among these anti-Jewish perceptions were Jewish involvement in *banking and *moneylending, leading to undue power and harm; worldwide Jewish connections that brought Jews from around the globe together in an anti-Christian alliance; regularized acts of physical violence against Christians and regularized acts of blasphemy against Christian holy things and places. The common element in all these allegations is the notion of Jewish enmity toward Christianity and Christians. Inherited from the New Testament and the Church Fathers, this core notion was expanded during the MA to form a legacy to modern anti-Semitic thinking and action.

The most dramatic element in this web of perceptions is the notion of a hatred so deep as to move Jews, whenever possible, to physical violence. Jewish anti-Christian violence was alleged to involve more than the antipathies normally evoked by inter-communal tensions and rivalries. Jews were purportedly moved to kill their Christian neighbours in a variety of ways, sometimes individually and sometimes more massively through contamination of the water supply—the *well-poisoning accusation; alternatively, they were perceived to murder out of a compulsion to re-enact their historic crime of crucifying Jesus—the *ritual murder accusation; sometimes it was claimed that their acts of murder were to fulfill dictates of Jewish law—the *blood libel accusation. All these allegations became part of the stock of medieval European folklore and modern anti-Semitic propaganda, despite regular investigation and repudiation by the authorities of both church and state. RC

M. Frassetto, *Christian Attitudes towards the Jews in the Middle Ages* (2006).

S. F. Kruger, *The Spectral Jew* (2006).

Antonians, Order of *See* RELIGIOUS ORDERS.

Antonii, St (d. 1073) Layman from the city of Liubech who founded the *Kievan Caves monastery. Tonsured on Mount Athos, he received the monastic name of Antonii. On his return to *Rus' he settled in a cave at Berestovo, the princely residence just south of *Kiev. Other anchorites (*see* ANCHORESS, ANCHORITE) joined him and proceeded to excavate a larger cave, a church, and cells. Sometime after Prince Iziaslav Iaroslavich succeeded his father (1054), Antonii fled to *Chernigov and founded another monastery under the patronage of Sviatoslav Iaroslavich. JBør

S. Franklin and J. Shepard, *The Emergence of Rus' 750–1200* (1996).

Antoninus, St, archbishop of Florence (1389–1459) Dominican moral theologian. An observant *Dominican, he reformed several Italian houses before founding San Marco, *Florence, in 1436. Appointed archbishop in 1446, he was distinguished as an ecclesiastical judge, preacher, and moralist. *See also* MEDICI; PREACHING. LDA

D. Peterson, 'Archbishop Antoninus: Florence and the Church in the Earlier Fifteenth Century', Ph.D. thesis (Cornell, 1984).

Antonio Guaineri (1380s? d. after 1455) Pavian citizen, court physician, and university professor whose writings emphasize practice over theory and bear witness to contemporary social conditions. He studied at *Padua and *Pavia and began teaching at Pavia soon after completing his doctorate in 1412. He was subsequently employed by the commune of Chieri in Piedmont and eventually became physician at the court of *Savoy. He travelled in the entourage of prelates and princes to whom some of his works were dedicated. His numerous writings covering various topics including *plague, poisons, fevers, arthritis, *baths, and a *gynaecological treatise were printed both separately and collectively in the 16th century. Some were translated into Italian and Hebrew—a testament to his reputation as a successful practitioner. His explanations of illness were mostly naturalistic, but he supplemented these with recourse to *astrology, *magic, and *alchemy when *humoral theories proved insufficient. He also used folk remedies reputed to be efficacious. Influenced by *Peter of Abano's psychological writings in the *Conciliator*, he consciously included magical rituals aimed at stirring the imagination of the patient to increase the healing effects of his treatments by benign frauds. MR

D. M. Carrara, 'Guaineri, Antonio', *DBI* 60 (2003), 111–15.

D. Jacquart, 'Theory, Everyday Practice, and Three Fifteenth-century Physicians', *Osiris*, 2nd series, 6 (1990), 140–60.

—— 'De la science à la magie: Le cas d'Antonio Guaineri, médecin italien du XVe siècle', *Littérature, Médécine, Société*, 9 (1988), 137–56.

L. Thorndike, *A History of Magic and Experimental Science* (1934), vol. 4, 215–31.

Antwerp (Anvers) Before the medieval settlement that grew into the city, the site had known Roman and late antique inhabitants. The early *castrum/civitas* was destroyed by *Vikings in 836, and its successor community was constructed a bit north along the Scheldt. Owing to its favourable location along a navigable waterway leading to the North Sea, the mouths of the *Rhine and Meuse downstream, and prosperous *Brabant and *Flanders upstream, the town grew considerably in the 12th and 13th centuries. But the true age of expansion commenced with the founding of the Antwerp *fairs in 1317 and the improvement of the town's access to the sea caused by storm surges late in the 14th century. The fairs developed into meeting places of regional and international merchants, meshing with the growing economy of southern *Germany, a role that increased in importance even after the annexation to Flanders in 1356. As a commercial satellite of *Bruges, the town counted about 7,000 inhabitants in 1374, a number that swelled during the two periods of the fair when even foreign merchants resident at Bruges journeyed there to make purchases. This period of interdependence was broken by the boom in English cloth exports, which were welcome in Antwerp but banned in Flanders; the growth of south and central European *mining and metal export; and the policies of Maximilian of Austria, who ordered the colonies of foreign merchants in Bruges to migrate to Antwerp. Thereafter the town grew rapidly to number some 30,000 inhabitants in 1500. JMMu

E. Sabbe, *Anvers, métropole de l'Occident (1492–1566)* (1951).

H. van der Wee, *The Growth of the Antwerp Market and the European Economy, Fourteenth–Sixteenth Centuries* (1963).

Antwerp town hall.

apanage [OF, *apaner*; ML, *appanere* 'to provide with sustenance' [lit. 'bread']] The apanage was a grant from French sovereigns to younger princes who had little possibility of advancing to the throne. These grants consisted of regions over which the royal offspring exercised full property rights with the exception that they could not sell or alienate the apanage. The grants were heritable and remained under the full control of the prince's line unless he produced no male heirs. In that case, the apanage reverted to royal control.

Despite the reluctance of the *Capetians to divide the royal patrimony, the practice of granting apanages increased greatly during the 13th century when the counties of Alençon, *Anjou, *Artois, *Auvergne, Maine, *Poitou, Perche, and *Orléans were all ruled by the younger princes. With the accession of the *Valois dynasty in 1328 and the outbreak of the *Hundred Years War in 1337, decades of intermittent conflict brought great swaths of French territory under English domination and gave rise to a long era of weak French kings and 'over-mighty subjects' drawn from the ranks of apanage holders and led by the houses of *Burgundy and *Armagnac. Even with the emergence of absolutism in the 17th century, monarchs continued granting apanages. DJK

C. T. Wood, *The French Apanages and the Capetian Monarchy* (1966).

apiculture *See* BEEKEEPING.

apocatastasis Greek word meaning 'restoration' of everything or the 'reconciliation' of good and evil. Some Greek Fathers, *Origen notably, developed it into the doctrine of 'universalism' or universal redemption in God. Although condemned at *Constantinople (553), traces are found in *Maximus the Confessor and *John Scottus Eriugena. *See also* COUNCILS, ECCLESIASTICAL. AYH

H. von Balthasar, *Dare We Hope 'That All Men be Saved'?*, tr. D. Kipp and L. Krauth (German original, 1986–87) (1988).

apocrisiarius [Greek, *apókrisis* 'an answer'] Term used in the 6th and 7th centuries for representatives of bishops (especially of *Rome) to the eastern Roman imperial court in *Constantinople. A number of *apocrisiarii* subsequently became popes themselves, including *Pope Gregory I. *See also* ENVOY. AKG

A. S. Gillett, *Envoys and Political Communication in the Late Antique West* (2003), 266–7.

Apocrypha *See* BIBLE, LATIN.

Apollonius of Tyre Belonging to the popular genre of the love-and-adventure novel, this is the most important and influential incest story of late antiquity and the MA. While early MSS (5th/6th centuries) were anonymously written in Latin, the story was translated into all European languages during the MA through the early modern period. It features a case of consummated father-daughter incest contrasted with the appropriate relationship between a good father (Apollonius) and his daughter, and it contains a succession of exotic adventures. German versions were written by *Heinrich von Neustadt (early 14th century) and Heinrich Steinhöwel (1473). It also influenced Shakespeare. *See also* APOLLONIUS VON TYRLAND. JE

E. Archibald, *Apollonius of Tyre: Medieval and Renaissance Themes and Variations* (1991).

J. Eming, 'Inzestneigung und Inzestvollzug im mittelalterlichen Liebes- und Abenteuerroman ("Mai und Beaflor" und "Apollonius von Tyrus")', *Historische Inzestdiskurse: Interdisziplinäre Zugänge*, ed. eadem, C. Jarzewbowski, and C. Ulbrich (2003), 21–45.

Apollonius von Tyrland (*c*.1300) MHG verse romance by Heinrich von Neustadt based on **Apollonius of Tyre*, embellished with fanciful, exotic adventures. Court surroundings are downplayed in favour of more middle-class values. *See also* APOLLONIUS OF TYRE. AC

A. Classen, 'Die Freude am Exotischen als literarisches Phänomen des Spätmittelalters: Heinrichs von Neustadt', '*Apollonius von Tyrland*', *Wirkendes Wort*, 54 (2004), 23–46.

'*Apollonius von Tyrland*', ed. S. Singer (1906; repr. 1967).

Apostles' Creed *See* CREEDS: APOSTLES', ATHANASIAN, NICENE.

apostolic life (*vita apostolica*) Religious life based on the model of the Apostles. Associated with monks, who claimed the Apostles were the first monks, it was adopted by heretics around the year 1000. In the 12th century, monastic reformers and the new orders of *canons followed it. It was adopted by the *Waldensians and the *mendicant orders and later assumed a violent character under Fra *Dolcino. *See also* HERESY; MONASTICISM. MCF

C. H. Lawrence, *Medieval Monasticism* ([3]2000).

apostolic see *See* PAPACY.

Apostolis, Michael (*c*.1420–1474×86) Copyist of MSS, teacher, and writer. He studied with John Argyropoulos and taught at the Petra monastery in *Constantinople. After Turkish imprisonment in 1453, he lived in Crete, visited *Italy, and copied about 115 MSS for Cardinal *Bessarion. He left a collection of proverbs and many *letters. *See also* MANUSCRIPT BOOK PRODUCTION; MANUSCRIPT STUDIES. MAG

D. Geanakoplos, *Greek Scholars in Venice* (1962), 73–110.

E. Legrand, *Bibliographie hellénique* (1885), vol. 2.

H. Noiret, *Lettres inédites de Michel Apostolis* (1889).

Apostolos *See* LITURGICAL BOOKS, GREEK.

apothecaries *See* MEDICINE.

apprenticeship An arrangement usually governed by a contract or formal agreement whereby a young person learned a skilled *craft or trade from a master. The duration of apprenticeships depended on the age of the apprentice at the time of the agreement and the level of difficulty of the trade. Extant European apprenticeship contracts are associated with *guilds, although they could also exist independently, as in *Flanders. Early guild statutes always address the issue of apprenticeship, and it has been argued (Epstein, 1998) that medieval craft guilds emerged in order to provide transferable skills through apprenticeship. Extant apprenticeship contracts require that the master teach the pupil the trade and that the pupil learn it. Often the master provided food, clothing, and (sometimes) *tools, while the pupil began with simple tasks and gradually learned the more challenging aspects of the craft.

The earliest apprenticeship contracts (after paramonê papyri) are notarial documents that date from the 12th and 13th centuries. Boys and girls between the ages of ten and fourteen entered apprenticeships created by contracts made between a parent or guardian and the master. They often experienced long years of training, usually five to ten years, beginning as helpers or servants. Older apprentices between the ages of fourteen and 21 also could spend many years, but were more likely to receive a small *wage. Contracts often specified that the apprentice could not leave to work with another master without the express permission of the original master. Children trained in a craft by their own parent acquired their skills without formal apprenticeship contracts and without a specific termination date. Apprentices were sometimes required to produce a masterpiece, demonstrating skill in the craft. *See also* ARTISANS AND CRAFTWORK; JOURNEYMEN. POL

S. A. Epstein, *Wage Labor and Guilds in Medieval Europe* (1991).

—— 'Craft Guilds, Apprenticeship, and Technological Change in Pre-industrial Europe', *JEconH* 58 (1998), 684–713.

apse [Latin, *apsis* 'arch'] A semicircular or polygonal termination of a building, as a rule *vaulted. In early Christian *basilicas, the main apse projected from the church as an articulated unit. It served to house the seats of the *clergy and as a backdrop to the *altar, frequently exhibiting the prominent decoration of the interior. Later, the apse was an integral part of the **chevet*. SdB

S. de Blaauw, 'L'abside nella terminologia architettonica del Liber Pontificalis', *Mededelingen van het Nederlands Instituut te Rome*, 60–61 (2002), 105–14.

Apuleius *See* HERBARIUM APULEI.

***aqua ardens, aqua vitae*, and quintessence** *See* DISTILLATION.

aquaculture Distinctive techniques for rearing certain freshwater fish under human management in fully regulated natural or artificial water bodies were developed by medieval Europeans, perhaps by *estate managers in central *France about 1100, and adopted on lay and clerical properties across interior Europe. Not merely a system of storing wild catches, aquaculture entailed controlling the water in dammed ponds, which were then filled, stocked with selected young fish, and some years later drained to harvest the adults. Procedures for breeding selected stock and then protecting and feeding the larvae were followed. Methods likely pioneered with native bream (*Abramis brama* L.) were adapted around 1250 to the faster-growing common carp (*Cyprinus carpio* L.), a recent arrival from the Balkans. Rotating production in several large artificial water bodies gave continual annual yields. Fresh pond fish were a luxury for inland consumers ill-served by traditional wild and distant marine fisheries. *See also* FISHING AND FISHERIES. RCH

M. Aston, ed., *Medieval Fish, Fisheries and Fishponds in England*, 2 vols (1988).
P. Benoit, 'Le carpe dans l'Occident médiéval', *Dans l'eau, sous l'eau: Le monde aquatique au Moyen Âge*, ed. D. James-Raoul and C. Thomasset (2002), 227–36.
R. C. Hoffmann, 'Carp, Cods, Connections: New Fisheries in the Medieval European Economy and Environment', *Animals in Human Histories: The Mirror of Nature and Culture*, ed. M. Henninger-Voss (2002), 3–55.

aqueducts and fountains *See* WATERWORKS.

Aquileia (patriarchate) This town is located in the Veneto, very near the Adriatic coast and 90 km from *Venice. Late antique Aquileia had its own *mint from 313 and sometimes served as an imperial residence in the 3rd to 5th centuries. The church of Aquileia vaunted apostolic origins, though no documentary or archaeological evidence supports Mark's visit, likely a *Carolingian invention. In 381 an ecumenical council in Aquileia denounced *Arianism. Aquileia's bishop attained the rank of *patriarch in the 4th century, only to have the patriarchate transferred to Grado in the 6th century following the depredations of *Attila the Hun in 452 and the *Lombards in 568.

The very early *cathedral of Aquileia, located on pre-Constantinian foundations, was built by Bishop Theodore (ruled 313–9). This building may have originated as a three-part early Christian meeting house. Its well-preserved floor *mosaics depict abundant marine life, the seasons, individuals (perhaps donors), and the story of Jonah.

Aquileia's later cathedral was founded by the early-11th-century archbishop Poppo and was decorated with *frescoes in the *crypt and above in the cathedral narrating the early history of the Aquileian church. ALM

T. E. A. Dale, *Relics, Prayer and Politics in Medieval Venetia* (1997).
G. Marini, ed., *I mosaici della Basilica di Aquileia* (2003).
G. C. Menis, *Il complesso episcopale Teodoriano di Aquileia e il suo battistero* (1986).
S. Ristow, 'Zur Problematik der spätrömischen Reste auf dem Gelände der Domkirche zu Aquileia', *Jährbuch für Antike und Christentum*, 37 (1994), 97–109.

Aquitaine One of the largest and most important duchies in medieval *France, Aquitaine was an independent principality, a part of the great Angevin empire, and a major French province. The region lacked linguistic, cultural, and even geographic unity and included the counties of Agenais, Angoumois, Aunis, *Auvergne, *Berry, Bordelais, La Marche, *Limousin, *Périgord, *Poitou, Uzerches, Quercy, Rouergue, and Saintonge. Aquitaine contained the archdiocese of *Bordeaux and *Bourges and had episcopal sees at Agen, *Angoulême, Périgueux, *Poitiers, Saintes, and *Limoges, which boasted the duchy's greatest *monastery, St Martial of Limoges.

The duchy's origins can be found in its organization by the Romans. It had connections with *Visigothic Spain and was loosely incorporated into the Frankish kingdom by *Clovis. *Charlemagne attached Aquitaine firmly to the Frankish empire and created the sub-kingdom of Aquitaine. In the 9th and 10th centuries, Carolingian decline and *Viking invasion led to the sub-kingdom's collapse and the emergence of the duchy under the counts of Poitou, who claimed the title of duke. From William III (d. 963) to William XI (d. 1137), son of the *troubadour and father of *Eleanor, Aquitaine was ruled by a line of Williams, most notably William V, the Great (993–1030), under whom Aquitaine achieved its greatest prominence and the *Peace of God flourished. The region welcomed *Cluniac and *Gregorian reform, sent knights on crusade, and expanded commercially, especially in the *wine trade. In the 12th century, Eleanor's marriages joined Aquitaine to France and then to the Angevin empire and England. Aquitaine caused

Aquitaine: illumination of Louis the Pious driving away Pippin I.

repeated struggles between England and France and contributed to the outbreak of the *Hundred Years War. The French won the war and took control of Aquitaine in 1453, but the duchy suffered from the war as well as from *famine and *plague in the 14th century. MCF

L. Auzias, *L'Aquitaine carolingienne, 778–987* (1937).

J. Dhondt, *Études sur la naissance des principautés territoriales en France, IXe–Xe siècles* (1948).

M. W. Labarge, *Gascony, England's First Colony, 1204–1453* (1980).

J. Martindale, 'The Kingdom of Aquitaine and the Dissolution of the Carolingian Fisc', *Francia*, 11 (1985), 131–91.

Aquitanian polyphony *See* POLYPHONY: TO 1300.

Arabia Area comprising the peninsula (*jazirat al arab*, 'island of the Arabs') and islands located south of present-day Jordan and Iraq. With no major rivers, the area depends on the water table and monsoon rains in the south and southwest for cultivation. Its desert interior was the home of nomadic herding peoples (*Bedouin), while agriculture was practised in oases and in the fertile south, along with *fishing in coastal areas. *Mining and pearl harvesting were important industries from ancient times.

In the pre-Islamic era (termed *jahiliyya*, 'ignorance') Arabia was home to independent tribes of diverse social and religious customs. Classical-era Arabia was drawn into Mediterranean, East African, and Persian spheres by trade, notably of frankincense; this encouraged emigration, particularly to Syria and *Mesopotamia. Contact with these areas intensified as the 6th-century Perso-Byzantine war pushed Indian-Mediterranean trade southwards and Arabs were recruited as military clients. Acculturation and urbanization encouraged monotheism, including Christianity and Judaism, and indigenous forms.

In the 600s *Mecca became a leading trade centre, and here *Muhammad received the revelations (from *c.*610) that signalled him as the final prophet of the Abrahamic tradition of *Islam* ('surrender to God'). Threatened by the Meccan elite, Muhammad moved to *Medina on 22 September 622 in the *Hijra* ('flight') that initiated the Islamic era. In 630 Mecca submitted, and by Muhammad's death in 632 Arabia had been brought under Muslim control. Polytheism was proscribed, while there was an uneven accommodation of Jews and Christians.

The restyling of the pre-Islamic *hajj* (pilgrimage) ensured the central role of Mecca, and, despite tensions and struggles within the Islamic community after his death, four individuals were named in turn as Muhammad's successor (*khalifa*, *caliph). Under their leadership, particularly of *'Umar I, Islam erupted from the peninsula, and *Palestine, Syria, Mesopotamia, *Egypt, and Libya were conquered. After the death of *'Uthman, *Ali's succession was resisted by the Meccan merchant clan, the Umayyads. These gained the upper hand in the ensuing civil war, and with Ali's assassination (661) took the caliphal title.

Under the Umayyads (661–750) the political centre of Islam shifted north to *Damascus. Arabia throve under their patronage, but became increasingly independent under the Abbasids—a refuge for rebellious movements, including *Kharijites and Qarmatians, the latter abducting the Black Stone of the Kaaba in 930.

In succeeding centuries, Arabia remained important as the location of the Muslim holy sites but became a political, economic, and cultural backwater. In the 1170s *Saladin endeavored to reimpose *Sunni orthodoxy and political unity, and in 1180 Renaud de Châtillon launched an ineffectual naval attack. From the 12th century Yemen, Mecca, and the Gulf area were ruled by local dynasties, sometimes under the control of Egypt or *Persia. In 1514 the Portuguese seized several ports, and in 1517 the Ottomans were recognized in Mecca and *Medina. BAC

P. Crone, *Meccan Trade and the Rise of Islam* (1987).
W. Daum, ed., *Yemen: 3000 Years of Art and Civilisation in Arabia Felix* (1988).
H. M. al-Naboodah, 'Arabia', *MedIsl*, vol. 1, 53–6.
R. Sanger, *The Arabian Peninsula* (1954).

Arabic medicine in the Latin West Medical texts had been written in Arabic in the Islamic world by Christian, Jewish, and Muslim doctors from the late 8th century onwards. The earliest translations of these medical works from Arabic into Latin were made in southern *Italy in the late 11th century, when *Constantine the African arrived in Salerno, the most flourishing Latin medical school at the time. Being disappointed at the level of theoretical *medicine there, he returned to North Africa to fetch relevant Arabic texts and proceeded to translate them, first at Salerno and later in the *Benedictine mother house of *Monte Cassino, where he died before the end of the century. At *Qairouan Constantine would have benefited from the succession of three Arabic doctors there, Ishaq al-Imrani, *Isaac Israeli, and Ibn al-Jazzar. He introduced the genre of psychological medicine by translating Ishaq al-Imrani's *Book on Melancholy*, and he translated the books on fevers, diets, and urines by Isaac Israeli. Most important was his translation of Ali ibn Abbas al-Majusi's *Complete Book of the Medical Art*, of which the whole of the first part (on theory) was translated, but only certain books of the practice, which were consequently supplemented from other translations, especially of works by Ibn al-Jazzar and Isaac. The resultant volume was called *Pantegni* and was diffused widely throughout Europe, thanks partly through the network of Benedictine monasteries of which Monte Cassino was the head.

In his own preface to *Pantegni*, Constantine listed the sixteen books by *Galen that formed the basis of ancient training in medicine at Alexandria, but it largely fell to his successors to recover these Greek works via the Arabic. A popular small collection of medical works (**Articella*) by Greek authorities was put together around his time, consisting of *Hippocrates' *Prognostics* and *Aphorisms*, Theophilus on urines, Philaretus on pulses, and Galen's *Megatechni* (on therapeutics). The *Articella* was introduced by an *Isagoge* of 'Johannitius', who is the 9th-century Baghdadi translator and doctor *Hunayn ibn Ishaq, and whose versions of Hippocrates seem to be sources for the *Aphorisms* and *Prognostics* in the *Articella*.

It was, however, later in the 12th century that the bulk of Arabic medical texts were translated as a result of the work of *Gerard of Cemona. He went to *Toledo, according to the students who sketched his biography, out of love for Ptolemy's *Almagest*, but translated there 21 works of medicine from Arabic into Latin—by far the largest category of his translations. He included nine of Galen's sixteen texts from the Alexandrian curriculum and added to these major works of the Islamic tradition, both of the east—Isaac Israeli's *On the Elements* and *On the Description of Things and their Definitions*, a comprehensive book of medicine by Abu Bakr Muhammad ibn Zakariyya al-*Razi (Rhazes) (*The Book for Almansor*), and *Avicenna's *Canon*—and of *al-Andalus: Abu-l-Qasim az-Zahrawi's *Surgery*, and the *Book of Simple Medicines and Foods* of Ibn al-Wafid, who had practised medicine in Toledo in the previous century.

Additions to this Arabic-Latin corpus were made in the 13th century, including the largest text by al-Razi—the *Continens (Hawi)*, which is a corpus of case notes on patients, and *Averroës' principal medical work, the *Colliget*. The translation, in the second half of the 13th century, of Ibn Butlan's *Taqwim al-sihha (Taquinum sanitatis)*, in which attributes of medicines were set out in tabular form, generated a series of lavishly illustrated MSS.

Beside books, Muslim or Jewish doctors were also influential in the west. Muslim doctors attended crusaders; a turbanned 'Achim medicus' was at the bedside of King William II of Sicily, and a convert from Judaism, *Petrus Alfonsi, became doctor to the English king *Henry I.

Arabic medicine filled a vacuum in the early medieval Latin tradition. Latin texts extant before Constantine's translations were for the most part brief and lacked any physiological theory. Arabic medicine, on the other hand, was closely linked with the natural sciences (the term 'physica' could refer to both subjects) and, through its rigorous system of quaterneries—the four qualities, the four elements, the four *humours, the four seasons, the four directions, and so forth—to *cosmology and *astrology. The intellectual rigour of Arabic medicine also appealed to philosophical speculation. For example, the detailed anatomy of the eye and the descriptions of the operation of the visual spirit was used by philosophers, from *William of Conches (mid 12th century) onwards, in their accounts of visual perception. The subtle 'animal spirit', located in the head, which controlled all the sensations and conveyed them to the reasoning and memorizing ventricles of the brain, had to be carefully distinguished from the incorporeal soul.

Within the field of medicine itself, the Arabic texts contributed massively to Latin medical terminology, in which Arabic terms were sometimes retained (for example, *nucha*, the spinal marrow, *zirbum*, the omentum; *tiriacum*—'treacle'—for a cure-all made of many ingredients). At other times a Latin calque was invented (for example, the *dura mater* and *pia mater* for the two meninges covering the brain). *Herbals often provided names in several different languages, for ease of identification. Stephen of Antioch in the 1120s appended a trilingual index (Greek, Arabic, and Latin) to his translation of al-Majusi's *Complete Book of the Medical Art* (a more literal translation than that of Constantine), which was vastly expanded in the *Clavis sanationis* ('the key to good health') of Simon of Genoa at the very end of the 13th century.

Among the medical techniques introduced in these Arabic works was the couching of a cataract, the use of catgut to sew up wounds, and of a drill to crush urethral stones. The first description of measles in the west occurs in the *Canon* of Avicenna. Therapy was as important as cure, and *regimens of health (including dietetics, bathing, exercise, and a healthy state of mind) figure prominently.

As the MA progressed and more works of Galen were translated directly from Greek (especially by Nicholas of Reggio in the 14th century), Arabic medicine started to lose its dominant position. With the rise of Renaissance humanism, those who relied on the works of Avicenna, Rasis, Isaac, and the others began to be sharply criticised for not using the Greek sources directly. The Latin translations were regarded as being written in a barbaric language, full of incomprehensible words and errors. Nevertheless, Avicenna's *Canon of Medicine* remained the main teaching tool in medical faculties until the late 17th century. *See also* ALBUCASIS. CBu

D. Jacquart and F. Micheau, *La Médecine arabe et l'occident médiéval* (1990).

Arabic numerals Originating from Hindu sources, Arabic numerals developed two variants, eastern and western (*gobar*), the latter marking the roots of our own Hindu-Arabic numerals, structured into a decimal place-value system. Through Latin translations of al-*Khwarizmi's *Algebra and Arithmetic*, the west became acquainted with the new numbers. Instrumental in the dissemination of the new arithmetical knowledge were *Pope Silvester II and other abacists, as well as algorists (adepts of the new arithmetic) and, significantly, *Leonardo Fibonacci of Pisa. *See also* MATHEMATICS. SU

G. Flegg, *Numbers: Their History and Meaning* (1983).
K. Menninger, *Zahlwort und Ziffer* (1958), tr. as *Number Words and Number Symbols* (1969).

Arabic sources of Scandinavian history During the *Viking Age, the Scandinavians travelled to places as far apart as the *river Volga, the Caspian and *Black Sea area, *Baghdad, and the Mediterranean. They therefore encountered plenty of opportunities for direct contact with Arabic-speaking peoples. First-hand and indirectly acquired information on the Scandinavians and their homeland can be found in the works of Arabic-writing travellers, geographers, and historians.

The best-known account of the activities of the Scandinavians in the east may be that by the ambassador *Ibn Fadlan, who provides us with an eyewitness description of the traditions of the Rus' merchants in the Volga in the 920s. However, Ibn Khurradadhbih (d. *c.*911) may be our earliest source for the activities of the Rus'. Our knowledge of the latter is supplemented by Ibn Rusta's (*fl.* 10th century) and al-Balkhi's (d. 934) geographical treatises.

Arabic writers in the west refer to the Scandinavians as Majus. The historian al-Yaqubi (d. *c.*905) is the first to identify them explicitly with the Rus'; he is also the first to refer to the activities of the Scandinavians in Spain. Ibn Dihya (d. 1235) describes an exchange of embassies between the Majus and Abd al-Rahman II (r. 822–52), who is said to have chosen al-*Ghazali as the main ambassador. The Majus, however, seem to have been present in the Mediterranean before attacking Spain: the great historian *Ibn Khaldun suggests that they were in today's Morocco as early as *c.*760.

The Scandinavians' homeland is depicted by al-*Idrisi, whose Ptolemaic world map features *Iceland, the Faroes, and the rest of Scandinavia, including various towns. *Schleswig receives particular attention in the work of al-Qazwini (d. 1283). SMPS

J. E. Montgomery, 'Ibn Fadlan and the Rusiyyah', *Journal of Arabic and Islamic Studies*, 3 (2000), 1–25.
Richard Perkis, 'Arabic Sources for Scandinavia(ns)', *MedScan*, 17–18.
S. M. Pons-Sanz, 'Whom did al-Ghazāl Meet? An Exchange of Embassies between the Arabs from *al-Andalus* and the Vikings', *Saga-Book*, 28 (2004), 5–28.

Aragon Originally a county, Aragon became a kingdom, roughly corresponding to the modern autonomous community of Aragon, under the rule of Ramiro I in 1035. It formed part of the Crown of *Aragon.

1. 8th through 11th centuries
2. 12th century
3. 13th century
4. 14th through 15th centuries

1. 8th through 11th centuries

A product of the Muslim invasions of Spain in the 8th century, the lands of the valleys above the river Aragon were home to Christian refugees who sought protection from the Franks, before Aznar Galíndez (*c.*809–39) established a measure of control over the small county. The *Benedictine monastery of San Pedro de Siresa and then that of San Juan de la Peña served as its religious and intellectual centres. After Frankish withdrawal, the county was under the domination of the kingdom of Pamplona until the death of *Sancho III (1035), when a realm some six times the extent of the original county passed to Sancho's natural son Ramiro, who had governed Aragon since 1015. Ramiro also gained control of the counties of Sobrarbe and Ribagorza, governing 'as if king'. Ramiro's son, Sancho Ramírez (1062–94) was the first king of the dynasty and also succeeded in *Navarre (1076). He took the bold step of submitting his kingdom to papal protection, introduced the Roman rite, and encouraged artists and settlers from southern *France, particularly to Jaca, which became an important city en route to Compostela. With increased French and Catalan support, Sancho took advantage of Muslim divisions and the Moors of Huesca, Saragossa, and Tudela were forced to pay tribute. The rewards for Sancho's consolidating genius bore fruit under his sons. Peter I (1094–1104) captured Huesca (1096) and Barbastro (1100), and took control of the major fortresses up to Saragossa and Tudela.

2. 12th century

*Alfonso I added Saragossa (1118), then Tarazona and Tudela (1119), then Calatayud and Daroca (1120). Imbued with a crusading spirit, Alfonso left his considerable domains to the orders of the Sepulchre, the Hospital, and the Temple, a move unacceptable to the majority of the Aragonese nobles, who feared the lands would fall to *Castile. They placed Alfonso's younger brother Ramiro (monk and bishop-elect of Roda) on the throne. Navarre broke from Aragon at this time. Ramiro (1134–57) returned to the monastic life in 1137, having provided a daughter, Petronila, who was betrothed to Count *Ramon Berenguer IV of *Barcelona (1131–62). The fates of the Aragonese and the Catalans, peoples of different customs and temperaments, were to be tied together for the next six centuries. The history of the one cannot be understood without the history of the other. The early rulers (1137–1213) of the Crown of Aragon were adept

Alfonso II confirming the Sales Privileges to the merchants of the city of Barcelona, from the customs and recollections of Pere Albert, 13th–14th century (vellum).

at balancing the interests of the different parties of the union. The key military successes of Ramon Berenguer IV were the capture of Tortosa (1148), Fraga, and Lleida (1149), the latter acting as a bridge between his lands. The restoration of the ecclesiastical province of Tarragona (1154) united the episcopal sees of Aragon and *Catalonia. With the founding of Teruel (1171), Aragon moved close to its ultimate extent, while the interests of both Aragonese and Catalans were pursued north of the Pyrenees by Alfonso II (1162–96) and Peter II (1196–1213).

3. 13th century

Victory at Las *Navas and defeat at *Muret altered the Aragonese future. Expansion north ceased while the paths south and east were opened to a ruler, *James I (1213–76), of Catalan sympathies who never forgave the Aragonese nobles for his troubled minority. Though the Aragonese contributed to the conquest of *Majorca and more so to that of *Valencia, their rewards were not commensurate with their efforts, and the king's use of Roman *law to challenge their ancient customs led the nobles into revolt on a number of occasions. From 1244, Lleida was defined as within the boundaries of Catalonia, and the balance within the union was lost. The situation worsened under *Peter III with the Aragonese protesting that they had not been consulted on the Sicilian conquest and were being taxed unlawfully. Thus, the Aragonese Unión was born (1283), while Peter faced off French invasion with little

Aragonese support. Alfonso III (1285–91) capitulated to the Unión in 1287, accepting that the Justiciar and the *cortes had to consent to any process of the king against a member of the Unión.

4. 14th and 15th centuries

The conciliatory James II (1291–1327) was able to revive Aragonese enthusiasm for his campaigns against Castile and in the Mediterranean, though the Aragonese suffered badly through the failed Almeria campaign. While the Crown of Aragon was the leading power in the western Mediterranean world, Catalonia was the dominant force within the Crown. Under Peter IV (1336–87), the Unión revived and the Aragonese nobles and towns humiliated the king at the *cortes* of Saragossa (1347) but, as the *Black Death spread, Peter reaffirmed his authority, though swearing to uphold the *fueros and privileges of Aragon. War with Castile proved exhausting for Aragon, invaded in 1362 by *Pedro I of Castile and only spared greater damage through Pedro's capacity for making enemies. Resentment at the extravagance of the court and demands for administrative reforms dominated Aragonese relations with the crown, particularly under the pro-Catalan John I (1387–96). After many divisions, it was the Castilian Ferdinand I (1412–16), a candidate more favoured by the Aragonese, who succeeded at the *Compromise of Caspe. But the foreign enterprises and Castilian wars of *Alfonso V again threw the Aragonese into conflict with the crown over money and appointments. These troubles developed under John II (1458–79) with the revolt against the imprisonment of *Carlos, prince of Viana (1460). At the close of the medieval period, Aragon was a land conservative in its institutions, proud of its rights, narrow in its ambitions. *See also* LITERATURES: ARAGONESE; RECONQUISTA. DJSm

J. L. Abadía, *Los fueros de Aragón* (1976).
L. G. Antón, *Las Uniones aragonesas y las cortes del reino (1283–1301)*, 2 vols (1975).
A. U. Arteta, *Historia de Aragón. La formación territorial* (1981).
T. Bisson, *The Medieval Crown of Aragon* (1986).
J. M. Lacarra, *Aragón en el pasado* (1972).
A. C. López, ed., *Aragón en su historia* (1980).

Aragon, Crown of An appellation used to refer to the federation of realms that came to include *Catalonia, *Aragon, *Valencia, and an array of Mediterranean possessions. The crisis following *Alfonso I of Aragon's death without a successor was resolved through the marriage of his daughter to Count *Ramon Berenguer IV of *Barcelona in 1137, an alliance that united Barcelona-dominated Catalonia with the kingdom of *Aragon under a single count-king. Initially Catalonian and Aragonese shared interests in the merger, which promised to foster collaboration in the capture of Muslim lands. Gradually, however, a climate of division, competition, and conflict emerged between the Catalans and Aragonese, sparking occasional revolts that threatened royal authority and the federation itself. Sources of tension included ambiguity over the primacy of these two dominant peoples within the federation, their respective uneven influence over the royal dynasts, and differing rights to exploit the conquered lands in Valencia and the Mediterranean. The growth of independent territorial governments, separate parliamentary sessions (the *cortes), and distinct traditions of law also fostered division. The *Compromise of Caspe replaced the defunct ancient Barcelona line of count-kings with the Castilian *Trastámara dynasty in 1412, a step towards absorption by *Castile that would not materialize until the marriage of the *Catholic Monarchs (1479). The Crown of Aragon nevertheless enjoyed relative autonomy, retaining independent administration, laws, and privileges, until the 18th century. TWB

T. Bisson, *The Medieval Crown of Aragon* (1986).
S. Cawsey, *Kingship and Propaganda: Royal Eloquence and the Crown of Aragon c.1200–1450* (2002).

Arator *See* BIBLE EPIC.

aratrum An ard, sometimes called a 'scratch plough' without a mouldboard and with or without wheels. In normal use it separated the earth by pushing it equally to each side, opening a shallow trench without returning the soil to it. It has been used from antiquity to the present day with local improvements, corresponding to particular agricultural needs. *See also* AGRICULTURAL TECHNOLOGY; PLOUGHS AND PLOUGHING. GC

B. Gille, 'Recherches sur les instruments du labour au Moyen Âge', *BECh* 120 (1962), 5–38.
A. Haudricourt and M. J.-B. Delamarre, *L'homme et la charrue à travers le monde* (1955).

Arba'ah Turim Composed in *Toledo *c.*1330 by *Jacob ben Asher, comprising four units: *Hoshen Mishpat* (civil law); *Even ha-Ezer* (marital law); *Yoreh De'ah* (dietary and purity laws); and *Orah Hayyim* (religious observances). Jacob was influenced by the Pietists, *Nahmanides, *Maimonides, and Provençal sources. *Arba'ah Turim* was popular in Spain, North Africa, *Germany, and *Italy; its quadripartite structure was retained by Joseph *Karo. EK

Y. D. Galinsky, 'Arba'ah Turim ve ha-Sifrut ha-Hilkhatit shel Sefarad be-Me'ah ha-14', Ph.D. thesis (Bar-Ilan University, 1999).
E. E. Urbach, 'Mi-Darkei ha-Qodifaqazyah: 'Al Sefer ha-Turim le-R. Ya'aqov b. Asher', *Jubilee Volume of the American Academy for Jewish Research* (1980), 1–14.

Arbeo of Freising (*c.*723–83) Bishop from 764/5, Arbeo built up his diocese's resources and supported the *Carolingians. He composed lives of Corbinian, considered the first Latin work by a German, and of *Emmeram. JJC

F. Brunhölzl, *Histoire de la littérature latine du Moyen Âge*, vol. 1/1 (1990), 228–30.

Ploughing with an aratrum. From the Utrecht Psalter.

F. Glaser, F. Brunhölzl, and S. Benker, *Vita Corbiniani, Bischof Arbeo von Freising und die Lebensgeschichte des hl. Korbinian* (1983).

Arbroath (abbey) *Monastery in Angus, Scotland, founded by *William I, 'the Lion', in 1178 for *Benedictine monks, dedicated to St Thomas *Becket, and site of the Declaration of Arbroath in 1320. The richly endowed abbey declined after 1500, falling into ruin after the Reformation. *See also* ROBERT I (BRUCE). MTA

G. W. S. Barrow, *Robert Bruce and the Community of the Realm of Scotland* (1996).

Arbroath, Declaration of *See* ARBROATH; SCOTLAND, IRELAND, WALES: SCOTLAND AND WALES 1064–1536.

arch A load-bearing rather than decorative member, an arch spans an opening or a frame or supports a *bridge, *roof, or wall. The arch derives its stability from the weight it supports. Medieval arches were of various forms, curved or pointed, composed of *voussoirs. *See also* SPANDREL. JBo

C. E. Armi, *Design and Construction in Romanesque Architecture* (2004).
K. A. C. Creswell, *Early Muslim Architecture*, 2 vols (1940–69).
R. Ousterhout, *Master Builders of Byzantium* (1999).

archabbot *See* CLERGY.

archaeology (and the study of the MA)

1. Scope, methods, and objectives
2. Sites, objects, and materials
3. An appraisal

1. Scope, methods, and objectives

What is particular to archaeology as a source of knowledge and understanding of the past is that it is the science of material life. Much of its basic evidence is man-made—artefacts, structures, landscapes, and even selectively bred crop-plants and domesticated animals. However, archaeology is equally concerned with the concrete realities of biological, climatological, and geographical history: the form and conditions of human life revealed by osteology and the chemical analysis of elements in human bone tissue; both general trends and exceptional events in the global environment; and the way, often in correlation with climatic developments, the land, seas, and coasts have changed.

In the modern history of professionalized scholarship, archaeology and its near neighbour history initially established *modus operandi* that avoided awkward clashes rather than trying to work together. Archaeology either concentrated on topics beyond contemporary documentation, such as prehistory, or found an uncontroversial role for itself in the recognition and appreciation of monumental works of art and engineering. There are still major centres of university archaeology in Europe whose structure and ethos assume that prehistory is the core of their discipline, and where post-Roman archaeology is marginalized if not excluded. Another consequence of this historical situation is that the 20th-century development of medieval archaeology was characterized by a predilection for applying methods and objectives derived from the archaeology of other periods and contexts. That could take the form of either a marked concentration on the ruins of monumental structures such as *monasteries and *castles, or the careful preservation and display of, say, pre-Reformation altarpieces; or of a determination to identify lacunae in the historical record—which are indeed many and wide—and to insert the attitudes and techniques of prehistoric archaeology into those.

In relation to much of Europe, North Africa, and the Near and Middle East, medieval archaeology consequently remains quite undeveloped. In some areas it is a subject in its infancy; in others, one still struggling for recognition. In certain ways, though, it has never had to be discovered or invented: from the period of the Renaissance itself there has been some recognition of and appreciation for the difference and intrinsic interest of the physical remains of the preceding MA—in the collections of antiquaries, for instance, or the cult of ruins of the picturesque movement and its successors. In Roman Catholic lands medieval structures and *relics could retain particular values. Indeed, societal cognition of medieval archaeology is profoundly complicated by

The Declaration of Arbroath, 6 April 1320 (ink on vellum).

the fact that the idea of 'the medieval'—always, in a real sense, a *recent* past—varies significantly according to the local, usually national, experiences of the last two millennia. If the 'Middle' Ages are so named as the intermediary period between the ancient world of the Roman Empire and the Renaissance of classicism and humanism that started in earnest in the 15th century, one definitive parameter is absent from areas never ruled by Rome. In much of northern and eastern Europe, and Ireland and Scotland, we rather have Iron-age material cultural history continuing for most of the first millennium—in the eastern Baltic lands, well beyond then. Over much of the south and southeast, Arab conquest and the spread of Islam in the 7th century eventually brought about a radically different cultural orientation and a trajectory of periods and watersheds unlike those in Christian Europe. Even beyond those horizons, trading links between Europe and other parts of Asia render it meaningful to talk of a MA in relation to, say, *India, China, and Japan.

Despite the great range of contexts thus incorporated within the concept of the MA, a special and general challenge faced in medieval archaeology—indeed increasingly one of the most significant contributions of this branch of scholarship to general theory and method in the humanities—is the necessity of exploring constructive relationships between material and textual evidence as the means of reconstructing and understanding the past. In some medieval contexts the quantity and range of our evidence is in both respects very small indeed; in others, apparently very copious—although, if so, usually only in respect of certain facets of the past. Of course, straightforward comparison of the stories immediately told by history and archaeology respectively will always be valuable: for that, it is crucial that the scholar is genuinely multidisciplinary to the extent of understanding the strengths and weaknesses of analysis and reasoning in both areas—able to distinguish secure facts from well-founded probabilities or more speculative hypotheses in turn. An equally valid and constructive approach, however, is not to separate and contrast the two disciplines but to unite them and their distinctive forms of evidence as undifferentiated examples of an overarching category of 'cultural production'. Texts can be treated as a special class of artefact, albeit a class that may also, in records or descriptions, reflect aspects of its ambient material culture in a unique way. Given that the MA saw practically every society of the Old World (as delimited above) become functionally literate by its close, no comprehensive concept of medieval archaeology can exclude the impact of generalized literacy within material life.

An absolute requirement for the archaeology of any given period is to be able to identify the relevant evidence—to establish which features, deposits, and artefacts can be dated within its particular time-frame. Archaeology has several reliable dating methods, including laboratory-based techniques that have been discovered and refined over the past sixty years, the applicability of which has leapt ahead with the availability of powerful digital computing capacity. An essential method in archaeological excavation is the observation of stratigraphy: the intrinsic relative chronology (using quasi-logical operators 'earlier than', 'later than', and their negatives, in binary relationships) of superimposed layers. In any such sequence of layers and features we can also hope to find regularly changing artefact assemblages that reflect serial change amongst the objects available at successive times. The artefacts themselves are analytically grouped into types, which may be very broad—such as *'pottery', 'weaponry'—or as precise as, say, a brooch-type of which only two or three extant specimens are known. Typology itself can be used as a dating method, with reliable general principles concerning how artefact-types and styles of decoration are likely to change over time in respect of the stylization and redundancy of features. A few special artefacts, especially *coins, may bear their own historically specific dating, having been struck, perhaps, under the authority of a particular king. The powerful new dating techniques applying natural science and mathematics are not in fact essentially different in character from these earlier-developed methods. Radiocarbon, thermoluminescence, and archaeomagnetic dating find physical traces in objects or features that can be sampled and dated in terms of a calendrical age before the present within a certain range of probability. Statistical techniques such as Principal Components Analysis and Correspondence Analysis, most recently supplemented by Bayesian mathematics, provide ways of searching for structure in collections of data analogous to the pattern of changing artefactual assemblages in sequences of layers.

All of these techniques have proved their value in medieval archaeology. Short of an inscription that might fix the production of a given item to a specific day, however, potentially the most precise dating method is that based on the sequences of varying growth-rings of trees: dendrochronology. With a very favourable sample—with the bark still in situ, and a certain stage in the regular annual life cycle of microfauna such as insects captured inside it—this can locate the formation of a structure or deposit even thousands of years ago to within a few weeks. Frustratingly, the survival of large enough samples of preserved wood from the medieval world is highly variable. Widespread surveys using dendrochronology have proved very illuminating in identifying, inter alia, major phases of *timber construction, such as watermills in early medieval Ireland and house-building in the late MA; precise and very useful dates for the Norwegian Viking ships from Gokstad, *Oseberg, and Tune have also been produced by this method. Dendrochronology has also made exceptional contributions to palaeoenvironmental and climatic study. In the areas of formerly Roman Europe, for instance, it has been possible to trace widespread deforestation towards the end of the Roman period and the gradual re-establishment of woodland in the second half of the first millennium. Great interest has been attracted recently by the evidence for seriously adverse climatic conditions, probably the result of a near-global dust-veil created by a massive volcanic eruption or even a comet or meteor strike, in the late 530s—also coinciding with the Justinian *plague in Constantinople, graphically recorded by Procopius and reflected in annals in several other parts of the world. It is indeed of the greatest contemporary relevance, in light of the current anxieties and controversy over global warming, that we can observe considerable climatic fluctuation in the period *c.*400–1600 through this and other evidence, alongside huge variation in the human population level.

The material life of the MA is represented by a wide variety of types of site, deposit, and artefact, which in turn reflect many different facets of human experience and human behaviour within this long period and the enormous area concerned. While it will be appropriate to separate and categorize these in an overview of this kind, before that it must be stressed that a key question facing the interpretative archaeologist is how far superficially diverse aspects of material life—for instance the technology of farming on the one hand, and customs in the *burial of the dead on the other—may nonetheless be understood as consistent and even congruent reflexes of an intrinsic cultural whole. It is, for instance, easy to understand that a marked diversity and apparent hierarchy in the elaboration and opulence of funerary deposits may coincide with sharp qualitative and quantitative contrasts in the form of housing—even if, in fact, no directly associated settlements and cemeteries have ever been found. That the appearance of churches, *mosques, or synagogues, of new styles of burial practice, of new patterns and elements of economic production and distribution, and of changes in landscape exploitation in an area, may all be connected is equally self-evident. As has been a feature of the humanities in general, though, a strong trend in recent archaeological thought has been away from collectivist and deterministic characterizations of human behaviour towards a more individualistic attitude, typified above all by an interest in the concept of 'agency'. This has also been associated with attempts to analyse past consciousness: to find the cognitive correlates of intrinsically inert and silent material structures and objects, and the 'symbolic' rather than the purely utilitarian value those things may have been endowed with by some persons in particular circumstances.

2. Sites, objects, and materials

The practical range and diversity of medieval archaeology within the parameters explained above is huge, and to attempt any sort of practical overview in anything short of a dedicated 'Dictionary of the *Archaeology* of the MA' risks fundamental omissions, damaging simplifications, and (worst of all) over-generalization. Nevertheless, a summary conspectus that is more than a mere catalogue will serve a useful purpose if it can provide a real framework for the critical comparison of what is undertaken in the name of medieval archaeology in different places. This also allows a number of significant trends in the history of the subject itself to be highlighted, illustrating its dynamism and significance, or identifying issues for further work.

We may start with the circumstances in which medieval populations lived, and within which they had to make their livings. Quite a recent development in medieval archaeology has been the reconstruction of past landscapes: looking at the overall interrelationship of settlements and intensively exploited, usually cultivated, lands alongside other resources such as waterways and wetlands, rough pasture, heath and woodland, seacoasts and communication routes. A concept that has proved heuristically effective is that denoted by the French term *pays*: not implying a homogeneous topographical context so much as a zone that appears consistent and to have its complementary niches exploited—or indeed left—in an integrated way. We can properly think of the *pays* as a natural territory, and the correlation between such geographical entities and the social networks and political territories that archaeology and history can reveal may follow from this.

The study of human settlements must of course be closely correlated with effective landscape archaeology. Throughout the MA settlement was predominantly agrarian and rural. A key theme here for diachronic and regional comparison is the varying fortunes of the grouped households of several peasant farmers: those directly responsible for agricultural production. A primary distinction amongst settlement patterns is that between 'nucleated villages' of such character and the dispersal of individual households through the countryside. Those contrasts are often analysed as characteristics of the *pays*, although there are cases where historical and administrative differences seem more determinative factors than environmental adaptation. In the earliest centuries of the MA there is a striking contrast between North Africa and the *Levant, where villages survive as particularly strong and stable units under both Byzantine and subsequently Arab rule, while rural settlement continuity from the Roman period is much more elusive in western Europe. We also find widespread dislocation in the course of rural settlement history in the first millennium beyond the Roman *limes*, although what has become the famous type-site of Vorbasse in Jutland gives us a good view of how a settlement could periodically relocate within the existing landscape and modulate in its internal structure.

As the MA progressed, however, a consolidation in the pattern of villages was widespread in Europe, while the southern and eastern Mediterranean lands eventually saw their own relocation of rural settlement. Social developments closely associable with this phenomenon in Europe were the growth of a parochial system of local churches, frequently under secular patronage, and the concomitant emergence of what—with a huge pinch of salt—can be called the 'manorial system' (*see* ESTATE MANAGEMENT AND ORGANIZATION): in fact both the nature of *manses*, 'manors', and their origins varied radically. It may actually be claimed as a crucial contribution of the archaeological evidence to demonstrate how inchoate and unstable the cumulative progress of manorialization actually was. This understanding is congruent with the inconsistency of the relevant historical evidence, although the latter tends not to record how often dominant houses prove to have been demolished or superseded elsewhere. The longer-term history that can be written from archaeology is likewise confirming and illustrating how communities of free *peasants with no local manorial lordship might collaboratively develop practices and structures such as common- and open-field agriculture as a voluntary, protective strategy. Those developments cannot always be attributed to imposition from above.

The history of urban settlement is even more one of deep and inconsistent change across the MA. Towns are of course large things, and thus very amenable to archaeologists to find and work on: archaeology has made serious and substantial contributions to our knowledge of *urbanism between the ancient world and the modern, especially in the long 'proto-historic' period from the 5th century to the 11th. There has, however, been an intense debate amongst archaeologists over how 'the town' should be defined. It is impossible to rehearse that here; it may be proposed, nonetheless, that a crucial characteristic of the town is that it is a forum for specialized exchange. That exchange may involve the distribution of material goods, but can equally be the determination of essentially immaterial, social arrangements such as jurisdiction, marriage contracts, or religious ceremonies. At a true town, the level and importance of such activities supports a resident population markedly greater than that of any typical contemporary rural settlement within the same cultural and social system.

The value of putting this conceptualization of urbanism first is that it emphasizes that systems of specialized exchange can function perfectly well without towns—indeed the adaptation of the geographers Kristaller and Losch's central-place theories to first-millennium sites found in northern Europe represents that in a particularly significant way in current archaeological research. This in turn enables us to focus on the distinctive characteristics of true urbanism through a series of comparative, in some cases evolutionary, perspectives including genuinely proto-urban contexts. In this respect, as indeed throughout settlement archaeology, essential evidence of the role and interrelationship of the sites is their material artefactual assemblages: the evidence for production, exchange, and consumption there. Out of countless examples that might be considered, we could note the archaeological evidence in the form of both loom-fragments and textile remains for the gradual spread of loom-types, in particular the horizontal treadle-loom, from the Mediterranean lands to towns in northern and western Europe. In its own way this embodied a small social and economic revolution there, as weaving changed from a domestic craft entirely within the female domain to an urban industry, with the weaver becoming the epitome of the male working-class artisan.

It is equally clear, however, that the material economy alone was just one of several equally valent factors of urbanism. The concept of the seat of government lying in a town, or rather city, survived from the Roman period at sites such as *Paris, *Toledo, Carthage, Alexandria, and of course *Constantinople, although the Roman senate itself removed to *Ravenna, where outstanding buildings and *mosaics survive from the periods of Ostrogothic and then Byzantine overlordship. The conflation of secular authority and town-life was a slow process over much of Europe, where the military aristocracy was economically supported by control of agricultural land and remained deeply rural, residing, inter alia, in impressive halls and ring-forts. An institution of social and ideological power that exercised earlier and thus apparently more significant influence on urbanization was the church: there is a close connection between ecclesiastical centres and effective market sites, to the extent, indeed, that in Ireland the 'monastic town' has proved to be a fruitful if not unchallenged concept.

In the Islamic world, the governors and troops of the caliphs took over ancient towns as going concerns, but their fiscally based policy of maintaining paid armies in central barracks reinforced the urban core of this cultural system. In Europe, before the creation of permanent armies but as communal conscription became more substantial, the military utility of towns as refuges and muster-points was a further important factor in the progress of urbanization. It is true that the widespread provision of defensive walls largely from the 12th century onwards can be attributed to motives of symbolic display and the commercial/fiscal control of movement in and out of the town, but towns certainly could be subject to assault and siege.

More personal and intimate knowledge of the people of the MA, rather than of the structures and circumstances of their lives, can be gained through funerary archaeology, even though that is the archaeology of the dead. Cemeteries and monuments are often respected places that can survive well, not infrequently via adaptation and reuse, and thus offer substantial repositories of information. The MA came to be dominated in the areas of our concern by Christianity and Islam, both religions with a fundamental concern for how the dead were treated. Almost throughout the period, however, pre-Christian burials in 'barbarian' Europe tend to be characterized by the inclusion of artefacts as grave-goods, which may be elaborate and copious, excellent for dating, and symbolically expressive of identity and ideology. The dominant Abrahamic rites are nonetheless equally amenable to study and interpretation.

Irrespective of the external customs, physical anthropology, the osteological study of the body, can yield unparalleled insights into the conditions of life. Although the figures themselves are approximate, statistics on life-expectancy are produced by estimates of age at death: these support comparisons not just between different periods and places but most importantly intra-societally, for instance between the sexes. Analysis of skeletal pathology has proved valuable, for one in yielding graphic impressions of general health and physical stress levels in populations, and also in adding to our understanding of the history of diseases such as *leprosy. The most controversial aspect of the study of human remains is the irrepressible interest in genetic relationship and descent. Peculiarities that are likely to be inherited by children from parents can be identified and in some cases do form convincing patterns of closeness of lineage within particular burying communities. Efforts have been made to retrieve DNA samples from medieval human remains, but this is far from easy and there is much dispute over how reliable the results are. The major recent discussions of medieval demography in terms of DNA distributions in fact sample modern populations and seek to extrapolate from these to purported population movements and connections in the past. Nearly all such exercises have been shockingly naive in terms of the historical models adopted, although more critical statistical modelling and historical complexity is now being applied, and these data may eventually produce significant insights. Another area of new laboratory-based analysis of the dead is the attempt to identify a person's area of origin by comparing chemical isotopes derived from groundwater. This too needs to undergo much refinement of calibration before it is genuinely reliable and informative, but such an outcome can be anticipated.

The treatment of the dead in terms of funerary ritual and the form of interment proves to be a highly expressive reflection of the social and ideological context, and thus is an indispensable complement to settlement archaeology. Even while the church seemed to enforce a material egalitarianism on the dead, seeking to lay all in the grave to await resurrection and judgement naked but for a shroud or a baptismal shirt, and unadorned, social distinction proved ineradicable. The holy and the powerful came to be buried within churches, or, as with *Charlemagne's burial in a doorway, to participate posthumously in dynamic and dramatic manipulations of sacred space; exhumation and translation became honorific rituals; monuments and inscriptions around the grave superseded conspicuous consumption within it, although in fact ecclesiastics could still be interred with artefacts associated with their vocation; the culmination in the late MA came in the construction of chantry *chapels, again spaces for memorial performance, around the tomb within a public church. The potential of medieval Christian burial archaeology is only newly being appreciated, but it is evidently great.

Meanwhile, it is solely material evidence that reveals the persistence, in areas of Europe, of ritual activity that sits very curiously with Christian orthodoxy. The deliberate deposition of symbolically charged objects—usually artefacts, although it may be food—has a very long history indeed, right back to the Stone Age. In Roman-period and early post-Roman, non-Christian Europe, we refer to 'votive hoarding' or simply 'sacrifice' in respect of weaponry, jewellery—mostly gold—or *amulets deliberately deposited in lakes or rivers or on dry land with apparently no intention of retrieval. That these can represent a gift-exchange approach to gods and powers is an entirely reasonable interpretation. Yet the custom survived conversion to Christianity, so that even from high-medieval England we have far more swords recovered from river-beds than can possibly be explained by accidental loss as is so often asserted. It is often, in fact, difficult to pin down the motivation for hoarding, between pragmatic hiding for safekeeping and ritual riddance. The question itself has not been recognised and addressed widely enough, and it should be a priority for medieval archaeology to redress this.

The official religions, meanwhile, also established themselves materially in buildings and possessions to an exceptional degree in the MA. We can usually recognize churches, monasteries, mosques, and synagogues from regularities and peculiarities of design, and, on occasion, the provision of special ritual or liturgical structures such as the Jewish *mikvah* (ritual bath) or Christian font. The extension of Christianity through Europe, replacing pre-Christian traditional religions of the Germanic, Slavonic, Baltic, and Finno-Ugric peoples of the north, was a continuous process throughout the MA, and the often problematic archaeology of that only partially knowable range of genuinely prehistoric European religion has emerged as an important element of medieval archaeology. Recent years have seen remarkable successes both in identifying and understanding major pre-Christian sites—often through a combination of archaeological and toponymic analysis—and in elucidating spiritual practice, for instance in respect of *Sámi *shamanism. The monumentality of the medieval church meant that its archaeology—particularly in terms of art and architectural history—was prominent in the formative years of medieval archaeology. It has correspondingly been recently somewhat sidelined. However, new developments such as more careful attention to the archaeology of the Early Modern period, especially to the impact of the Reformation, which was itself intensely concerned with the materiality of the church, have brought church archaeology into the sights of modern symbolic archaeology. We can look forward to mature interpretative studies of the archaeology of medieval religion in future years.

Besides the huge *cathedrals and thousands of churches that still so conspicuously represent medieval material life in modern landscapes and towns, the MA left another imposing masonry legacy that for many is at the core of their idea of 'the medieval'—the *castle. Superseding the earlier construction and use of intermittently occupied hill-forts and domestic strongholds, the moated and walled castles, of timber early on but later of stone, of course represent a material development in the logistics of *warfare. The crucial factors leading to the development of these massive bases and refuges, however, were more social and political than technological. The major formal changes in warfare between the early and high MA, when the castles emerged —the adaptation of effective riding *harness, derived ultimately from migrant Asiatic steppe peoples in the earlier MA, and the skilful design and manufacture of body armour (*see* ARMS AND ARMOUR)—supported a wide-ranging cult of *chivalry that rooted itself in the castle and its grounds: gardens and deer-parks. Various *crusades carried these structures to the eastern Mediterranean and the eastern Baltic lands.

There is yet another vast field of archaeological study, namely the identification and exploration of the many different categories of artefact produced, traded, and used in this period. As noted in the context of interpretation of settlement sites, this evidence illustrates the complexity of exchange relationships, from near subsistence-level self-sufficiency at one extreme to the dominance of commercially modulated professional specialization at the other: a distinction that can stand as a valid if summary characterization of the contrast between the material culture of the beginning of the MA and that of the transition to the modern world. Understanding this range of material fully requires a technical expertise akin to the increasing specialization that is seen in the MA: out of the range of accessible raw materials, care was taken not to waste any usable commodity—*metal, *wood, *ceramic, *stone, *textile, *leather, bone, and more. An intriguing but well-attested fact is that increasing occupational specialization and levels of production and trade did not always go hand in hand with technical advances in production. Ceramic history is a good case in point, where the fluctuation between the adoption and abandonment of fast and slow wheels was remarkable over several centuries, although from the 12th century onwards the more consistent introduction of *glazing and later development of stonewares show the start of a more consistently progressive sequence that was to continue to the 18th century. In that light, perhaps one of the most telling, though little considered, developments in the artefactual archaeology of the late MA is the regular appearance of intricate mechanical apparatus—in instruments such as the astrolabe, *clocks, even table furniture. Literary references as in Chaucer's *Squire's Tale* imply that these were generally regarded as little more than curiosities at the time. Yet they represent the start of a sequence of invention that would culminate in the Industrial Revolution.

3. An appraisal

This overview and summary of medieval archaeology has attempted to show in what ways the field can be appreciated as something rather more than just descriptive expertise in the material culture of the 5th to 16th centuries, distinguished from the archaeology of other periods merely by particular facts of material technology and production as they happened then to be, not by any intrinsic qualities of perspective. It is possible to propose a theory of material life that made the MA, and thus medieval archaeology, special. At the core of that theory lies the empirically verifiable fact that the material world was, in medieval cognition, massively imbued with meaning, and so was used—and argued both over and through—as a medium of expression and communication. The strength of material semiotics, as objects were variously used, for instance, in gift-exchange (*see* GIFT AND TRIBUTE), ritually, to express or reflect identity and allegiance, or ideologically in cosmological or theological similes, is something that an informed and sensitive reading of the extensive textual sources from the period in full conjunction with the archaeology impresses on us most insistently. Even within the MA this led to outbursts of iconoclasm, Islamic and Orthodox Christian (*see* ICONOGRAPHY: ICONOCLASM); at the end of the period it provoked the Protestant reformers. Medieval material culture and art were truly languages used for discourses specific to this age.

Importance has also been attached here to aspects of continuity and change at either end of the period, simultaneously defining and querying the chronological concept of the MA as a period between the ancient and the modern. The 19th-century French scholar Ernest Renan is usually cited as the first modern intellectual to identify the roots of contemporary European nationalism with the early medieval processes we now call ethnogenesis, and several regional reviews below reflect this issue. The contemporary prominence of historical genetics represents further (subconscious?) recognition that major political issues of our own times are not just reflected but genuinely rooted in that period. The MA were fundamental in the transformation and production of social structures, identity, and ideology alike. A comprehensive knowledge of the period is indispensable to an informed understanding of those issues, and the proper study of medieval archaeology is essential to any meaningful programme of medieval studies. JHi

Archéologie médiévale, 35 vols+ (1971–).

P. J. Crabtree, ed., *Medieval Archaeology: An Encyclopedia* (2001).

G. P. Fehring, *Die Archäologie des Mittelalters: Eine Einführung* (³2000).

C. M. Gerrard, *Medieval Archaeology: Understanding Traditions and Contemporary Approaches* (2003).

James Graham-Campbell and Magdalena Valor (eds), *The Archaeology of Medieval Europe*, vol. 1: *Eighth to Twelfth Centuries* AD (2007).

Medieval Archaeology, 51 vols+ (1957–).

archaeology: the Balkans Aside from work at Pliska (1899), medieval archaeology in the Balkans began in earnest only after 1945. Although many of its components, especially cemetery archaeology, have a much longer history of study, the main catalyst for this growth was the post-war shift in emphasis from political and constitutional to social and economic history. This coincided in time with, and was ultimately caused by, the imposition of Communist regimes under Soviet control. As a consequence, archaeology was organized along the lines of Soviet multidisciplinary studies of 'material culture history', and received a considerable degree of institutional attention. Massive long-term investments, with no parallel in contemporary western Europe, have made possible large-scale explorations of several key sites, some of which resulted in total excavation, following the principles first championed by Soviet archaeologists. By directing the attention to how ordinary people lived, the Marxist paradigm encouraged the development of settlement archaeology, as opposed to cemeteries, the primary focus of pre-war research. During the last decade, more attention was paid to questions of ethnicity, power, and gender. Together with a shift in emphasis to the late MA, coupled with drastic cuts in state funding, the field is now largely defined by rescue archaeology, especially in connection with the building of motorways and pipelines.

1. Settlement sites
2. High-status sites, churches, and monasteries
3. Cemeteries

1. *Settlement sites*
Zhivka Văzharova's excavations at Popina (1955–61) and Garvan (1964–80) mark the beginnings of the 'material culture' approach. In addition to the first monographs on medieval villages, Văzharova attempted to write economic and social history on the basis of *ceramic assemblages or *metal finds. Economic and social issues are also central to more recent studies of later medieval settlements in *Bulgaria, such as Kladenci (10th century), Kovachevo, Diadovo (11th and 12th centuries), and Khisar (11th and 13th centuries). By contrast, most settlement sites in former Yugoslavia were excavated during the 1970s and 1980s as part of micro-regional studies, the purpose of which was to generate a long-range diachronic view of settlement history, from prehistory to the Early Modern age. This is especially the case of László Szekeres' and Nebojša Stanojev's work in Bačka and Vojvodina, respectively. In addition to settlement patterns, such micro-regional studies focused on details of medieval rural life and economy, especially on buildings, heating facilities, rural technology, and ceramic production. Despite great regional variety, which has so far discouraged comprehensive surveys, such studies reveal a great deal of specific detail. No manor comparable to those known from western Europe has so far been identified, while, despite some evidence for mobility, excavations show a long-term continuity of settlement at a micro-regional scale. More research into settlement history of the Balkans, particularly between the 11th and 15th centuries, is needed before deciding whether the medieval village in the Balkans is a result of displacement and economic rearrangements following the Byzantine conquest, or owes more to earlier patterns than previously thought. During the 1980s, a number of settlement sites have been excavated in northeastern Bulgaria (Khuma, Durankulak, and Skala), which were fortified during the 10th century before the Byzantine conquest, although the degree to which the fortification served any military purpose is still debated.

2. *High-status sites, churches, and monasteries*
Documentary history has a leading role in the Balkans in establishing national priorities for archaeological work, and that has provided the stimulus for the excavation agendas on such high-status sites as Pliska and Preslav. Pliska was discovered in 1899 by Karel Škorpil on the basis of a thorough study and comparison of Byzantine sources. Similarly, the identification with Iustiniana Prima (Emperor Justinian's foundation) of the 6th-century city excavated since 1912 in Caričin Grad (*Serbia) has been based exclusively on written sources, for no inscription was found that contains the name of that city. Historical questions about power in 8th- to 10th-century as well as 13th-century Bulgaria, in connection with questions of early urban development in the medieval Balkans, have prompted systematic excavations of the palace compounds in Pliska and Preslav and of the urban site at Veliko Tărnovo, respectively. Similar questions motivated the work of Marko Popović at Ras, an 11th- and 12th-century Byzantine border fortress that became one of the earliest capitals of Nemanjid Serbia. General questions about settlement and economic and social history have also generated long-term research projects in coastal areas. Examples include excavations of Byzantine forts or cities, such as Nufăru (Romania), Nesebăr (Bulgaria), or Butrint (*Albania). Churches, long a subject of interest in architectural and art history, became the target of archaeological research during the 1960s and 1970s. Most significant in that respect is the pioneering work of Totiu Totev at Tuzlalăka, a 10th-century monastery near Preslav. His work was the inspiration for the remarkable development of the Bulgarian archaeology of monastic sites. Ninth- and 10th-century churches in *Croatia, some of abbeys, have recently been the object of intensive research. A most recent example is the French-Croatian excavation, since 1995, of a *Carolingian abbey at Velika Gospa, in Istria.

3. *Cemeteries*
The growth in the 1960s and 1970s of cemetery archaeology, especially in Yugoslavia, led to a quick increase in the volume of data, to such an extent that entire chronological gaps in the knowledge of the early MA have been virtually eliminated by 1990. Without extensive archives, research in what is now *Croatia had to lean heavily on archaeological evidence, especially for the 8th and 9th centuries. This is not to be viewed as a weakness, because archaeology gives information of a character different from that provided by written sources. Many of the changes to our perception of 8th- and 9th-century society in Croatia and Bulgaria have resulted from archaeological fieldwork. Cemeteries were initially used to answer far-reaching questions about social history, but the connection to written sources was also recognized. This in turn generated an abundant literature, both in the Balkan countries and abroad, tackling such controversial issues as ethnicity and the conversion to Christianity.

Despite its relatively recent history, archaeology has quickly become a key discipline for the study of the medieval Balkans. Besides the remarkable amount of data generated to fill gaps in knowledge, the discipline has provided invaluable information for times and places for which no documentary record exists. *See also* ART AND

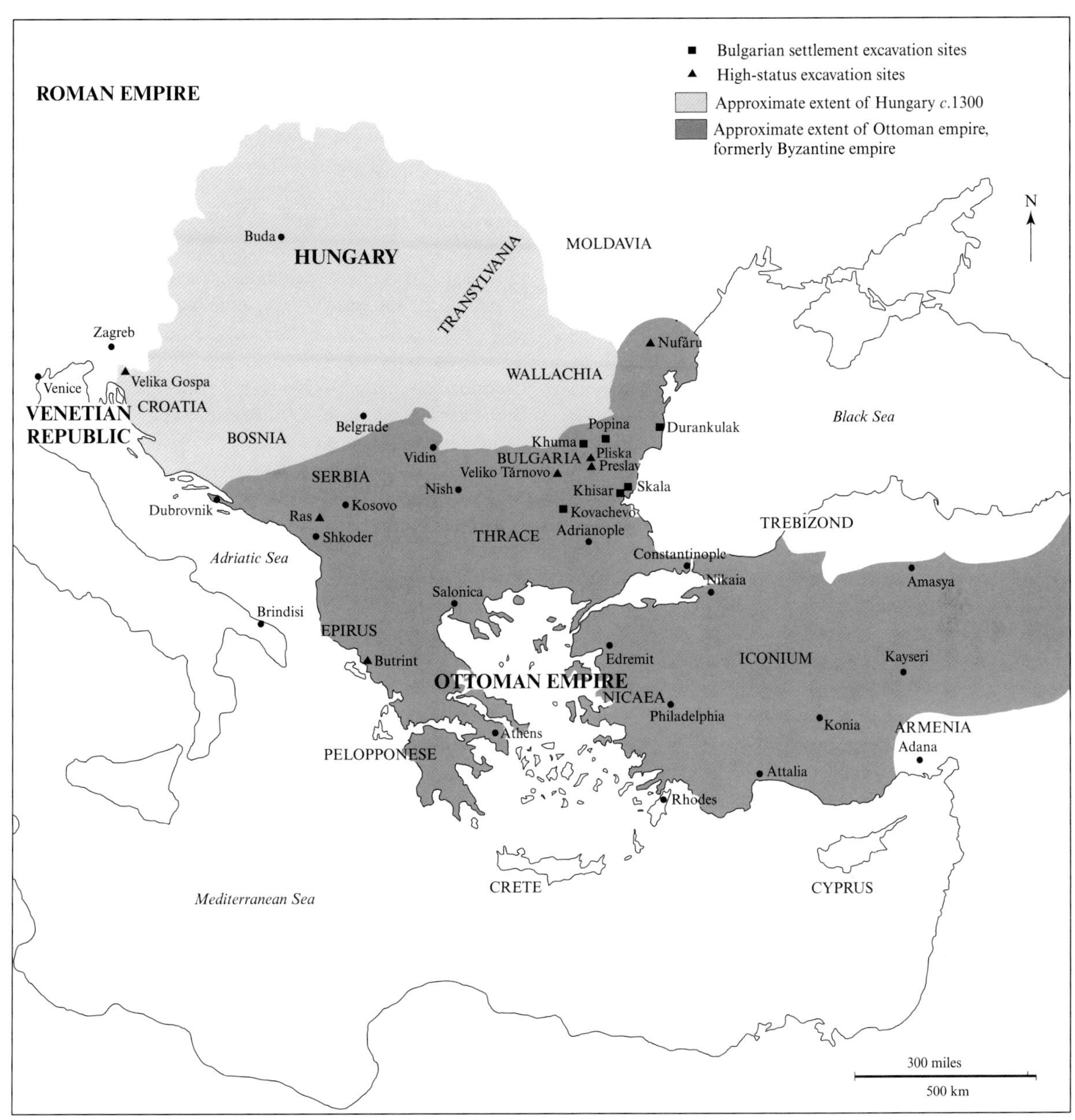

Medieval archaeological sites in the Balkans.

ARCHITECTURE: BULGARIAN / BYZANTINE / SERBIAN; BOSNIA; BYZANTIUM; CHURCH TYPES; DESERTED VILLAGES; ECONOMIC AND SOCIAL HISTORY; LOCATORES; MONASTICISM; PEASANTS. FCu

B. Borisov, *Djadovo I. Mediaeval Settlement and Necropolis (11th–12th Century)* (1989).

Carevgrad Tărnov, 5 vols (1973–80).

H. Evans, *Early Medieval Archaeology of Croatia AD 600–900* (1989).

U. Fiedler, *Studien zu Gräberfeldern des 6. bis 9. Jahrhunderts an der unteren Donau* (1992).

T. Ivanov, ed., *Nessèbre*, 2 vols (1969, 1980).

R. Kostova, 'Bulgarian monasteries, ninth to tenth centuries: interpreting the archaeological evidence', *Pliska-Preslav*, 8 (2000), 190–202.

G. Mănucu-Adameșteanu, 'Nufăru (jud. Tulcea)—oraș bizantin fortificat la Dunărea de Jos (sec. X–XIII)', *Arheologia medievală*, 2 (1998), 79–86.

M. Popović, *Tvrđava Ras* (1999).

R. Rashev and I. Dimitrov, *Pliska: 100 godini arkheologicheski raskopki* (1999).

T. Šekelj-Ivančan, *Catalogue of Medieval Sites in Continental Croatia* (1995).
N. Stanojev, *Srednjovekovna seoska naselja od V do XV veka u Vojvodini* (1996).
L. Szekeres, *Középkori települések Északkelet-Bácskában* (1983).
H. Todorova, ed., *Durankulak* (1989).
T. Totev, *Great Preslav* (2001).
Z. Văzharova, *Slaviano-bălgarskoto selishte krai selo Popina, Silistrensko* (1954).
—— *Srednovekovnoto selishte s. Garvăn, Silistrenski okrăg (VI–XI v.)* (1986).

archaeology: the Baltic culture group (That is, members of the Baltic linguistic family of Indo-European.) From the 5th century BC Balts settled on the southwestern shores of the Baltic Sea; they were named after it in the 19th century. From their homeland on the upper reaches of the Dvina, *Dnieper, and Oka rivers, Balts migrated to the seacoast and settled the lands between the lower *river Vistula and middle reaches of the Dvina. The Balts are represented today by Lithuanians and Latvians; many other groups, including the western Baltic Couronians, Old Prussians, and Yotvingians, became extinct or assimilated.

1. Tribal divisions
2. Internal diversity
3. Pagan religion and conversion to Christianity
4. Conquest by Teutonic Knights and Order of the Knights of the Sword
5. The Polish-Lithuanian union

1. Tribal divisions

Balts in Tacitus' *Germania* were termed *Aestii*, referring to inhabitants of the amber-rich shore of the Baltic Sea; the name is also found in *Cassiodorus and *Jordanes (6th century), and in *Wulfstan (9th century). The appellation 'Kúrland' (land of the Couronians) appeared in Scandinavian sagas before 800. In his *Chronicon terrae Prussiae* (after 1326) Peter of Duisburg, chronicler of the *Teutonic order, named several western Balt tribes settled in what today is northeastern *Poland, the Kaliningrad region, and the area of *Lithuania at the mouth of the Neman. Further names of Letto-Lithuanian tribes were recorded in the 9th century by Rimbert in his *Vita Ansgarii* and by later chroniclers.

2. Internal diversity

The archaeological record reflects the cultural diversity of ancient Balt tribes. Based on differences in funerary practices, archaeologists have distinguished two zones: a zone of flat cemeteries in the coastal region, and one of barrow cemeteries farther inland. At first in both these zones cremation and inhumation were equally common, but gradually cremation displaced inhumation. After the 7th century, in the southwest, cemeteries are harder to interpret. Stone structures are present in some areas, absent in others. A feature common to the entire Balt environment is horse burial. First recorded in the 1st–2nd centuries in the west, by the 5th–6th centuries (*'Migration of Peoples') it had spread across the entire region and persisted among Latvians and Lithuanians until the 14th century.

The diversity of Balt cultures is also manifested in distinctive ornament forms and dress fittings; jewellery shows remarkable continuity of tradition with largely the same repertoire of forms across hundreds of years (for example, crossbow brooches, pins with cruciform heads). Imported models (for example, Scandinavian zoomorphic style) were modified to suit local fashion (Couronian zoomorphic style).

Settlement patterns show similar continuity. Cemeteries continue to be used by the same community over many centuries, occasionally even for more than a millennium. Settlements focused around hill-forts which were accompanied by open-plan holdings. The territory held by each tribe was divided into hierarchically ranged territorial units. Apart from the Lithuanians, who established their principality during the 13th century, the Balts failed to form a lasting political organization transcending tribal divisions.

3. Pagan religion and conversion to Christianity

Pagan religion persisted long (*see* PAGANISM), with cremation being practised, and burnt remains being buried with grave-goods. Balts venerated the sun, moon, and stars. Rather than building temples, they worshipped at sacred sites, paying homage to groves, trees, stones, springs, lakes, rivers, bogs, and hills. Some of these sites (for example, Romove) were sacred to all tribes. Some pagan practices, for example animal sacrifice, persisted for a time even after the advent of Christianity.

The first recorded attempt at converting Balts to Christianity was made in 997 by *Adalbert of Prague, who missionized among the Old Prussians. His mission was backed by Bolesław I the Brave of Poland, who wished to extend his influence to the Prussian territory bordering Poland. After Adalbert's martyrdom by the Prussians a mission was undertaken among the Yotvingians in 1009 by *Bruno of Querfurt. Following an initial success, Bruno was murdered by pagan members of the same tribe. The early 13th century brought further efforts by the *Cistercians and, from 1230, by the Teutonic order. The *Teutonic Knights imposed Christianity by force and rapidly overran Prussian and Yotvingian lands. From 1202 Christianization began to be brought to the eastern Balts in Latvia by the Order of the Knights of the Sword. Lithuania ultimately embraced Christianity in 1386 after its grand duke Jogaila (Jagiełło) was crowned king of Poland, and Lithuania joined Poland in a dynastic union. Although some earlier Lithuanian dukes had also converted to Christianity (for example *Mindaugas in 1251), their success at converting their subjects was short-lived.

4. Conquest by Teutonic Knights and Order of the Knights of the Sword

A lasting imprint on Balt history was made by German military monastic orders which in the course of the 13th century subjugated numerous Balt tribes except for those in much of the territory of present-day Lithuania. Invited in 1226 by a duke of the Polish province of Mazovia whose lands were being harassed by raiding Prussians, the Teutonic Knights installed themselves in the border country between Polish and Prussian lands. By 1283 they had conquered all Old Prussian and Yotvingian tribes and established their own state with its capital at Marienburg (Malbork). The native Balt population was either exterminated or resettled; the survivors became Germanized. The strong and aggressive Teutonic State started to pose a threat to the neighbouring Lithuanian and Polish principalities. The threat to Lithuania increased further when the Teutonic Knights united themselves with the German Order of the Knights of the Sword (also known as Livonian Knights).

By the late 12th century German missionaries from the *Hamburg archbishopric had started penetrating the Dvina estuary region. In 1201 they founded the city of *Riga which became the seat of the local bishop. Together with the Order of the Knights of the Sword, the bishop of Riga conquered the Letgallian, Selonian, Semigallian, and Couronian tribes and started to threaten Lithuania.

5. The Polish-Lithuanian union

In the face of a common threat from the Teutonic order, Lithuania and Poland entered into a dynastic union at Krevo in 1385. The Lithuanian grand duke Jogaila married Queen Jadwiga of Poland, and Poland and Lithuania were united for four centuries in a 'Commonwealth of Two Nations' until this state was dismantled in the late 18th century. ABW

A. Bitner-Wróblewska, *From Samland to Rogaland: East-West Connections in the Baltic Basin during the Early Migration Period* (2001).
Die Balten: Die nördlichen Nachbarn der Slawen (1987).
E. Mugurēvičs, 'Die Balten im frühen Mittelalter nach schriftlichen Quellen', *Archaeologia Baltica*, 4 (2000), 71–80.
J. Okulicz, 'Einige Aspekte der Ethnogenese der Balten und Slawen im Lichte archäologischer und sprachwissenschaftlicher Forschungen', *Quaestiones Medii Aevi*, 3 (1986), 7–35.
S. C. Rowell, *Lithuania Ascending: A Pagan Empire within East-central Europe, 1295–1345* (1994).
Sēļi un Sēlija/Selonians and Selonia (2005).
V. Vaitkevičius, *Studies on the Balts' Sacred Places* (2004).
Žiemgaliai/The Semigallians: Baltų archeologijos paroda: Katalogas/Baltic Archaeological Exhibition: Catalogue (2005).

archaeology: Britain The medieval archaeology of Britain presents a rich and diverse resource that includes both upstanding and below-ground remains and a substantial but variable material culture across the MA. The period covers the centuries following the departure of the Roman army from Britain in the early 5th century to the mid 16th century and the dissolution of the *monasteries; it is broadly divided by the 11th century into the early and late MA.

1. Principal types of evidence
2. Topics and themes
3. Curation and management
4. Sources of new information
5. A select list of sites and finds

1. Principal types of evidence

In southern, central, and eastern England, material culture of a distinctive Germanic character is found in inhumation and cremation cemeteries. The earliest of these cemeteries contain early-5th-century graves, while most appear to have been in use during the 6th and 7th centuries. Graves of this period, particularly the 6th century, often contain weapons in male graves, and sets of brooches and other dress fittings, but graves of both sexes often included a wide array of other object types. During the late 6th and 7th centuries high-status barrow burials are found at *Sutton Hoo (Suffolk) and Taplow (Buckinghamshire) among others, and these reflect the emergence of dominant families and ruling elites during this time. Field monuments of the early period survive as earthworks, such as the barrows at Sutton Hoo, while linear earthworks, including *Offa's Dyke (English/Welsh borders) and Wansdyke (south-central England), represent a high degree of social organization from at least the 8th century.

*Viking activity during the 9th century and then again in the late 10th and 11th centuries has left little in the archaeological record. Approximately 30 burials are known from England, for example from Repton (Derbyshire) and Aspatria (Cumbria). The only known barrow cemetery of Scandinavian type is that at Ingleby (Derbyshire). Settlement archaeology, including *burials, is better attested in the western and northern Isles, particularly Orkney and the Outer Hebrides. The Vikings are scarce in Wales, although the only known crannóg (artificial island) was a 10th-century insular royal residence, occupied during a period of English military activity in 916. Crannógs are found largely in the Western Isles of Scotland, although none has revealed Pictish occupation. The earliest crannógs are occupied from the 8th century as at Loch Glashan, Argyllshire. They continue to be occupied into the later medieval period up to recent times. Crannógs are also found in Ireland.

In southwestern Britain, Wales, northern Britain, and Scotland, a distinctly different social and material culture developed during the 5th to 7th centuries. In northern and western England, evidence for populations expressing a Germanic social identity is not found, if at all, until the 7th century. In these regions a culture similar to that in western Britain as a whole developed. The kings of *Northumbria resided at the reused hillfort of Bamburgh, while the Picts re-occupied the promontory hillfort at Burghead, on the Moray Firth, Morayshire. Radiocarbon dates from Burghead indicate 4th- and 6th-century activity, while the discovery of two silver horn mounts decorated in the English Trewhiddle Style attest to activity into the 9th century. In eastern Scotland the Picts have left an accomplished record in their sculpture. Settlements of the Pictish period are rare. Evidence for activity during the 5th to 9th or even 10th centuries in the Inner and Outer Hebrides is scarce.

It is evident from excavations at sites like Dinas Powys (Glamorgan), South Cadbury (Somerset), and Dunadd (Argyllshire) that elite power bases were established within hillforts of Iron-age origin throughout western Britain. These sites are characterized by refurbished fortifications, including gateways, feature large timber halls, and contain finds of imported Mediterranean pottery of 5th- to 7th-century date. In other regions, former Roman towns were evidently central places from at least the 6th century, for example *Bath, Cirencester, and *Gloucester. From the later 6th century in England, a series of un-enclosed and apparently fortified elite residences is known from either excavations or aerial photographs (sometimes both). Timber buildings aligned end-to-end, with substantial enclosures, characterize the best known of the 6th- and 7th-century high-status sites at *Yeavering and Millfield in Northumbria. Middle AS (*c.*650–*c.*850) royal buildings are suggested at *Northampton, but the successive timber and stone structures there are probably associated with the adjacent minster church. In the late AS period (*c.*850–*c.*1050) royal accommodation has been excavated at Cheddar (Somerset) and, probably, Kingsholm (Gloucester). There are numerous fine examples of royal accommodation of the later MA, ranging from the White Tower of later 11th-century origin (with later additions) at the Tower of London, to Hampton Court (Middlesex) built in the mid 16th century. Clarendon Palace (Wiltshire), excavated in the 1920s, was a rural residence occupied throughout the later MA and survives as a substantial field monument. *Castles of wide variety survive in the British landscape: most notable are those built under *Edward I in North Wales as at Beaumaris and *Caernarfon, although many fine smaller castles survive throughout Britain, notably in the Welsh Marches.

Stone-built housing of the lordly and merchant classes survives from the 12th century, at Boothby Pagnell (Lincolnshire) and at the Jew's House in *Lincoln. Timber-framed buildings of the late MA are plentiful in lowland England, with counties such as Shropshire and *Kent exhibiting many fine examples of housing and agricultural buildings from across the social spectrum.

Evidence for rural settlement survives in both upland and lowland regions of Britain. Field remains dating to the early medieval period are scarce, and most sites are known via excavation. In upland regions, deserted later medieval settlements survive as surface remains of stone footings and boundary walls of farmsteads, as on Dartmoor at Hound Tor (Devon). In lowland regions, the medieval settlement pattern often partly survives in the topography and morphology of many existing villages, while *deserted settlements are widespread, commonly surviving as earthworks. Attendant *field systems also survive in lowland areas in the form of ridge and furrow, predominantly in central and southern England, but also in other regions. Open fields did not develop in certain upland regions, nor in Kent and much of Devon and *Cornwall. Field boundaries in these latter regions may in part be much older than the medieval period. The deserted village at Wharram Percy (North Yorkshire) was excavated over a period of 40 years and is a key site presented to the public and surviving as earthworks with a ruined parish church.

The earliest urban centres lay in England where excavations at Southampton (Hamwic), Ipswich (Gippeswic), *London (Lundenwic), and *York (Eoforwic) have revealed substantial settlements closely tied into a European network of trade and communication, developing from the 7th century but with earlier origins. Finds of coins and *pottery attest to foreign trading links, while many insular coins attest to a developed monetary economy from the early 8th century.

The larger medieval towns developed suburbs, a process that began before the *Norman Conquest. There were major periods of urban growth in the 9th–10th and 12th–13th centuries when the number of towns increased rapidly, in many cases as planned ventures. The form of many medieval towns may be traced in their modern layouts, as at *Salisbury (Wiltshire), *Oxford, and York.

Medieval *cathedrals are numerous, with fine examples in *Canterbury, London, and York, among others. Parish churches survive throughout the British Isles with a significant number of AS origin. The remains of later medieval monastic houses provide a substantial legacy of the wealth and impact of *monasticism on landscapes throughout the British Isles. Despite the devastating impact of the mid-16th-century dissolution, much survives above ground, sometimes on a spectacular scale, for example at Fountains and Rivaulx abbeys in Yorkshire or at Tintern abbey, Monmouthshire. Many monasteries have been extensively excavated, such as Hulton abbey (Staffordshire), and Jedburgh abbey and the monastic hospital at Soutra, both in southern Scotland.

2. *Topics and themes*

The scholarly study of medieval archaeology in Britain has a long history of division between those who study the early and the later MA. Study of the early period has until recently focused on the material culture of early AS cemeteries (5th–7th centuries), although the study of AS architecture has a long history from the perspective of art and architectural history. The study of towns using material remains did not develop in earnest until the 1950s, as a response to post-war redevelopment, but accelerated during the 1970s and 1980s when many historic urban centres were redeveloped. There is a rich archaeological data set, particularly for the later medieval period, for the study of urban development from many British towns. Urban archaeology remains a vibrant field, largely in England and Scotland, examining the origins and development of towns through the MA. The study of rural settlement has been somewhat polarized, with much emphasis on the early AS period and the extensive excavation of only a few sites, notably Mucking and West Heslerton. The over-arching paradigm for research into the early AS period was, and is, that provided by written accounts of the arrival of Germanic migrants into England. The distinction on archaeological grounds between secular and monastic settlements of the 7th–9th centuries is a recent research theme, while the potential of burial archaeology of the 9th–16th centuries is only now being fully realized. Church archaeology developed in earnest from the 1970s and the archaeological study of cathedrals is now well established alongside traditional art- and architectural-historical approaches to the built environment. Recent work on ecclesiastical buildings has emphasized their social functions, often via their symbolism, and this has led to a more holistic view of later medieval society that examines castles, monasteries, and other structures in a comparable and comparative way.

The origin of the medieval village in England has been a major research theme since the 1950s. Research has now broadened to include a wider range of settlements, including dispersed farms and hamlets and specialized communities, such as those on coasts or near forests. New methodologies, such as large-scale test-pitting as developed at Whittlewood in central England, reflect a move towards an attempt to understand the broader development of settlements and their landscapes first, rather than older approaches that concentrated on individual buildings, often in pursuit of high-status occupation.

The study of *ceramics played an important part in the early development of medieval archaeology and continues to do so largely from an economic perspective. Recent studies have widened the focus of artefact-based studies to consider gender roles and the place of children in society.

Overall, the role of archaeology has long been seen as augmenting historical narratives, although archaeology is now taken seriously by many in the field at large as capable of constructing an independent narrative of medieval life.

3. *Curation and management*

The archaeological resource in Britain is managed on a daily basis by many organizations. National bodies (English Heritage, CADW, and Historic Scotland) provide academic and management guidance to government, local authorities, and others concerned with the care of sites or directly engaged with research projects. Local authorities monitor the process of ensuring an archaeological response to development plans, and many new medieval sites have come to light since strict procedures (PPG 16) were implemented in England in 1990. County museums, many of which were founded by benefaction during the 19th century, are mainly charged with housing material from excavations, and many such museums are home to their respective county archaeological societies. Archaeology departments can be found in many universities, both older and newer, throughout Britain. Local amateur societies flourished during the post-war period, and continue to do so in many areas; they tend now to concentrate on bringing excavations to publication and conducting survey work rather than excavation. Many museums and universities now run outreach programmes in order to diversify access to archaeology, though comparatively little archaeology is taught in schools. Evening courses continue to be popular.

4. *Sources of new information*

Current developments in the field are manifold. New techniques are allowing a reassessment of old problems. Isotope analysis of human remains is facilitating a fresh approach to long-running debates, such as the issue of migration in the early AS period. The increasing use of Optically Stimulated Luminescence (OSL) is allowing dates to be ascribed to sites where finds are rare or absent, and this latter aspect frequently characterizes archaeological sites in the north and west of Britain. Carbon 14 dating is an increasingly refined technique and important work has been done, particularly on human remains of middle and late AS date. Dendrochronology is now a widespread and commonly used technique, and many medieval *timber buildings and other wooden structures and fittings are dated in that way. Many of the rescue excavations in English towns in the 1970s and 1980s have been published or are expected soon. During the 1990s exploratory regional schemes were initiated to engage users of metal-detectors in a more inclusive study of the past. The Portable Antiquities Scheme now has officers across England who liaise with detector-users and attempt to record discoveries for both academic study and public interest. Much new material is now available for study. (Metal-detecting is illegal in Scotland and Ireland.)

The building of roads and housing provides much new information. Planning authorities in Britain now require archaeological assessment in advance of construction projects, and this has generated a substantial body of so-called 'grey literature' or unpublished client reports detailing new discoveries.

5. A select list of sites and finds

Beaumaris (Anglesey, Wales): castle; Canterbury (Kent, England): cathedral and other remains; Cressing (Essex, England): timber-framed tithe barn; Edinburgh (Scotland): castle and National Museum of Scotland; Fountains abbey (Ripon, West Yorkshire, England): Cistercian monastery; *Iona (Western Isles, Scotland): site of Columban monastery with early sculpture; *Jarrow (County Durham, England): monastery of the Venerable *Bede with reconstruction; London (England): collections in British Museum and Museum of London; Offa's Dyke (English/Welsh border): substantial 8th-century frontier earthwork; Salisbury (Wiltshire, England): cathedral and townscape; Singleton (West Sussex, England): museum of timber-framed buildings; Sutton Hoo (Suffolk, England): site of late-6th-century high-status barrow burials and visitor centre; Tarbat (Easter Ross, Scotland): site of Pictish monastery with museum containing sculpture; York (England): major city, built heritage and museums; Wharram Percy (North Yorkshire, England): excavated church and village presented to public. AJR

G. Astill and A. Grant, eds, *The Countryside of Medieval England* (1988).
C. Batey and J. Graham-Campbell, *Vikings in Scotland* (1998).
J. Blair, *The Church in Anglo-Saxon Society* (2005).
K. Dark, *Britain and the End of the Roman Empire* (2000).
C. Dyer, *Making a Living in the Middle Ages* (2002).
S. Foster, *Picts, Gaels and Scots* (1996).
C. Gerrard, *Medieval Archaeology: Understanding Traditions and Contemporary Approaches* (2003).
J. Grenville, *Medieval Housing* (1997).
G. Henderson and I. Henderson, *The Art of the Picts* (2004).
D. Hinton, *Gold and Gilt, Pots and Pins* (2005).
B. Hope-Taylor, *Yeavering: An Anglo-British Centre of Early Northumbria* (1977).
J. Hunter and I. Ralston, eds, *Archaeological Resource Management in the UK* (2002).
A. Reynolds, *Later Anglo-Saxon England: Life and Landscape* (1999).
J. Schofield and A. Vince, *Medieval Towns: the Archaeology of British Towns and their European Setting* (2003).
J. Steane, *The Archaeology of Medieval England and Wales* (1985).
M. Welch, *The English Heritage Book of Anglo-Saxon England* (1992).
P. Yeoman, *Medieval Scotland: An Archaeological Perspective* (1995).

archaeology: Constantinople and Byzantium

1. Constantinople
2. Byzantium
3. Byzantine archaeology as a discipline

1. Constantinople

Constantinople has been the subject of comparatively little archaeological research. From the 15th century, foreign visitors made descriptions and visual representations of the city's topography, including its remaining Byzantine features. By the 19th century, the standing archaeology was attracting attention, particularly the ecclesiastical monuments and city walls. The Fossati brothers' restoration of Hagia Sophia brought that building more fully to western attention, and Van Millingen's study of the city walls set new standards. During the 20th century study of Constantinople gained ground. Talbot Rice and others excavated within the Great Palace area, Ogan excavated on the acropolis, and Mamboury focused on the area between Topkapi Sarayi and the sea walls.

Photographic evidence of Istanbul's old city was compiled in the early 20th century. More recently, Constantinople's archaeology and topography attracted serious study from for example Eyice, Fıratlı, Guilland, Janin, Mango, and Müller-Wiener, who set high standards of recording, interpretation, and presentation. Attempts were made to correlate textual evidence with physical remains.

Since the 1960s, large-scale excavations have yielded evidence for settlement patterns, material culture, and monumental architecture. Harrison's excavation at Saraçhane revealed the remains of the enormous 6th-century church of St Polyeuktos. Striker's excavations at Kalenderhane centred round a church, with a bath house and other structures. Hagia Sophia continued and continues to be the subject of research. Its associated structures include a baptistery and a treasury, and the remains of the Patriarchate can possibly be identified. The Great Palace area has continued to attract attention, and is now being studied by three-dimensional digital imaging. The walls, evidence for Byzantine defence, are a repository of *spolia and newly found inscriptions; near them are a hypogeum plus tombs.

Since the 1990s, museum campaigns have included a harbour site and the Great Palace area. A recent street-by-street survey has recorded hundreds of previously unknown Byzantine features and artefacts, including spolia, cisterns, walls, structures, inscriptions, and *pottery. Another survey, in the city's hinterland, has examined the water supply. Scholars are increasingly addressing topics other than the traditional monumental buildings. Analyses of commercial areas, street plans, private housing, and shops have been published since 1990.

Archaeologists tend to use historians' periodizations: Early Byzantine (4th–7th centuries), Middle Byzantine (8th–13th centuries), and Late Byzantine (14th–15th centuries). Some spolia from the earlier town of Byzantion were reused in Constantinople, for example the pagan goddess heads in the 6th-century Basilica cistern (Yerebatan Sarayi). The centre of the Early Byzantine city was on the promontory jutting into the Sea of Marmara. Both the main city and Galata on the adjacent side were bounded by defensive walls: the Constantinian land-walls were superseded in the 5th century by the Theodosian walls further to the west. The so-called sea walls survive in several places.

Constantinople was laid out along classicizing lines, mirroring Rome. It had wide porticoed streets giving on to large fora with showpiece statuary, including marble columns topped by imperial statues. The southeast part of the city centre was marked by the Great Palace, a huge complex which was extended and elaborated throughout the Early and Middle Byzantine periods, before largely going out of use in the Late Byzantine period when the imperial family moved to the Blachernae Palace in the northwest of the city.

Texts and archaeology together permit a reconstruction of the Great Palace as a congeries of administrative buildings, churches (including the Nea), and private dwellings, plus open spaces and walkways. An impressive find has been the covered peristyle walkway (probably 6th century) with substantial mosaics. On its western side the palace overlooked the Hippodrome, with a balcony or box for imperial appearances. The Hippodrome itself showcased statuary, including ancient obelisks and the bronze serpent-column from Delphi; a marble seat has even been excavated. The palace's northern entrance—the 'Chalke' gate—led to an open area known as the Augusteion; this was flanked on its northern side by the church of Hagia Sophia (founded in the 5th century). The current church, dating to the mid 6th century, represents the culmination of Early Byzantine architectural and ecclesiastical programmes.

Hagia Sophia lies near the foot of a hill beneath which were vaulted brick-built cisterns. In the 6th century the church of Hagia Eirene was built at the southern foot of the hill, while the Mangana *monastery complex occupied the area towards the base of its eastern slopes. At the summit were the remains of pagan temples, replaced in the 5th century by the Forum of Leo. In the early 12th century under imperial *patronage a new complex was built on the heights to serve as a charitable institution for orphans and the needy. The changing use of this area reflects the ways in which urban infrastructure changed between the Early and Late Byzantine periods.

The main approach to the city centre was via the Mese, a wide colonnaded or porticoed street whose western end lay at the Golden Gate in the west of the city and whose eastern end was near the northwestern edge of the Hippodrome. Although laid out in the 4th century, this remained in use at least until the 13th century. The Milion or central distance marker denoted the eastern end of the Mese. Various imperial fora were incorporated into the Mese, including the Fora of Constantine and Theodosius. Sculpture associated with the Forum of Theodosius can still be seen in this area. The site of the Forum of Constantine is marked by a single porphyry column (the 'burnt column').

Away from the immediate city centre and the main colonnaded streets, the suburbs held thousands of private dwellings and, presumably, shops and workshops to service the population. These are largely unknown archaeologically, although attempts have been made to identify aspects of the street layout in various parts of the city. It is still not clear how densely Constantinople was settled throughout its history, but there were several open spaces outside the city centre, including large open-air cisterns (two of which can still be seen) and market gardens or urban farms. Late Byzantine Constantinople was far less densely populated than in earlier centuries.

Churches and monasteries were dotted all over both the city centre and the suburbs. The important Early Byzantine monastic complex of St John Stoudios (Imrahor Camii) and the church of the Holy Apostles (Fatih Camii) were both located in the west of the city. By the Late Byzantine period, there were over a hundred more churches and monasteries. Several of these survive, converted to mosques or still in use as churches. St Saviour in Chora (Kariye Camii) contains impressive Late Byzantine wall paintings, as does the church of the Pammakaristos monastery (Fethiye Camii); the three conjoined churches forming part of the Pantocrator monastic complex (Zeyrek Camii) have been subject to extensive recording and restoration; and the Myrelaion church (Bodrum Camii) incorporates a rotunda building which had been part of an Early Byzantine townhouse.

2. *Byzantium*

This last example serves to illustrate an urban transformation which took place not only in Constantinople but throughout the Byzantine empire. Whereas in the Early Byzantine period private wealth had been displayed by the construction of large townhouses in prime locations, by the Middle Byzantine period, and often earlier, the aristocracy was patronizing the building of churches and founding monasteries to display its wealth.

Prior to that development, typically late antique cities on the Constantinopolitan model had been laid out empire-wide—in Greece (Thessaloniki, Corinth, Athens), Asia Minor (Ephesus, Sardis, Sagalassos, Anemourion, Pergamon), Syria (Beirut), the Holy Land (*Jerusalem, Jerash), and North Africa (Carthage). These cities' pattern of development conformed closely to that of Constantinople: wide colonnaded streets, monumental arches and statuary, open fora, large churches, and townhouses. In the mid 6th century, a Byzantine 'new town', Justiniana Prima (Caričin Grad), was planned in the Balkans according to these principles.

This classicizing of urban space took place in the context of another development, beginning in the 5th century and continuing into the Middle Byzantine period and beyond: a rapid proliferation of churches and associated structures. New churches were built both in the city and the countryside; even smaller villages sometimes had several churches by the Middle Byzantine period. These were often very elaborate, clearly the key repository of available disposable wealth. Temple-to-church conversions also took place. In the Holy Land, almost every place associated with the life of Christ or other important biblical events was marked by a church or shrine.

As *monasticism spread, first within *Egypt and *Palestine-Syria and then more widely, many monasteries and hermitages were constructed, some at key religious sites. Within a few years these were attracting large numbers of pilgrims who required accommodation and refreshment. The desire to express Christian faith not only in material terms but also through travel had a significant impact on the Byzantine landscape. Although focused on the Near Eastern provinces in the Early Byzantine period, after the loss of these territories to the Arabs in the 7th century it was Constantinople's shrines and churches which remained the focus for pilgrimage and patronage, thus providing further impetus for investment in religious institutions.

Rural life is not yet fully understood. Before the 7th century, villages throughout the empire appear to have been quite prosperous: this is evident in the artefacts (*pottery, coins, and glass) and in the quality and quantity of buildings. Agricultural life seems to have flourished. After the 7th century, the evidence is less clear. Some archaeologists argue for a period of economic contraction in both towns and villages, but it is difficult to generalize, and most recent evidence seems to indicate that, if some settlements declined, others continued to expand into the 8th and 9th centuries. During the Middle Byzantine period, some towns (for example Pergamon) experienced a geographical shift, with hilltop administrative centres being developed, often fortified. Secular buildings were typically located there whilst ecclesiastical or monastic buildings were to be found at lower altitudes, often surrounded by stone dwellings or farms.

3. Byzantine archaeology as a discipline

Much of the ambiguity over the fate of settlements after the 7th century derives from the fact that Byzantine settlement archaeology (including burial archaeology) is still a young field. While several important sites have been published in recent years (for example Amorium, Beirut, Sagalassos, Ephesus, Sardis), synthetic work from a wholly archaeological perspective has lagged behind. Analyses have also been hindered by the lack of archaeological indicators—such as pottery, glass, coins, *seals—from stratified contexts in Constantinople itself. Nevertheless, settlement archaeology is expected to make a vital contribution to our understanding of the relationship between urban and rural centres, as well as the economic transitions delineating the Early, Middle, and Late Byzantine periods.

As a discipline, Byzantine archaeology has often taken its cue (though not often its theory) from Roman archaeology. This probably explains why, for most sites, the Early Byzantine period is far better understood than the Middle or Late periods. There has long been a desire to understand where Byzantium fits the central concerns of Roman archaeology, in particular with questions of 'decline' and 'continuity' or, in more recent years, 'transition' and 'transformation'. Whilst its 'Roman' heritage remained vital throughout its history, Byzantium's material culture was also characterized by a highly visible ecclesiastical and monastic presence, a distinctive repertoire of artefactual evidence, and a settlement pattern heavily influenced by networks of exchange, pilgrimage, immigration, and economic change. The potential for much of this archaeological evidence is yet to be fully explored. ALH

'Constantinople: The Fabric of the City: Symposium', *DOP* 54 (2000), 157–264.
K. Dark, 'Archaeology', *Palgrave Advances in Byzantine History*, ed. J. Harris (2005), 166–84.
Y. Hirschfeld, *The Judean Desert Monasteries in the Byzantine Period* (1992).
A. Laiou, ed., *The Economic History of Byzantium*, 3 vols (2002).
C. Lightfoot and M. Lightfoot, *Amorium* (2007).
C. Mango, *Studies on Constantinople* (1993).
—— and G. Dagron, eds, *Constantinople and its Hinterland* (1995).
T. Mathews, *The Byzantine Churches of Istanbul* (1976).
N. Necipoğlu, ed., *Byzantine Constantinople* (2001).
M. Rautman, *Daily Life in the Byzantine Empire* (2006).

archaeology: east/central Europe (Slavonic)

1. Ethnogenesis of the Slavs
2. Formation of the earliest Slavic states

1. Ethnogenesis of the Slavs

The name Slavs (*Sclaveni*) first appears in the mid 6th century in *Jordanes and Procopius of Caesarea, where it designates the peoples inhabiting large areas of east central Europe from the upper *river Vistula basin in the north, along the eastern *Carpathian Mountains to the lower *river Danube basin in the south and to the *river Dnieper in the east. The lack of ancient written sources for the Slavs' ethnogenesis resulted in lively discussions among linguists, historians, and archaeologists for over two centuries. In these discussions archaeology plays a special role, since it provides abundant source material and possesses a chronology. What archaeology can do is define typical material correlates of Slavic culture in the mid 6th century and search for their earlier prototypes.

In the early epoch settlements were small, located on riverine terraces, with dwellings in the form of sunken square huts having an oven in one corner. Material items included handmade, undecorated clay pots, bone and antler tools, and clay spindle whorls. Typical is the lack of distinct crafts and of evidence for trade, as well as the paucity of weapons and of metal items. This pattern first appears in the late 4th to early 5th centuries in river basins in present-day western Ukraine and Moldova, within settlements of the Cherniakhov culture.

In eastern Europe such a pattern is found in the middle and upper Dnieper basin, where assemblages are called the *Kiev culture. This culture has different dwellings, with postholes but no ovens. Archaeologists conclude that after the Huns' attacks people relocated from the Dnieper to the Carpathian zone, in contact with the Gothic polity. This contact prompted them to develop their own dwelling forms and survival strategies. They were subsequently joined by groups from elsewhere, resulting in demographic growth.

By the 5th–6th centuries at least four ceramic cultures are identified: Praha-Korchak, Penkovka, Kolochin, and Tushemla-Bantserovshchina. Migrations led the Slavs toward Byzantine territory: we find them in Romania (the Ipotesti-Cindesti culture, distinguished by imported Byzantine ceramics and metalwork). Wheel-made pottery and trans-frontier trade began, attested also by finds of Byzantine coins. Slavs served in the Byzantine army, and we find their ceramics in Byzantine fortresses. This coexistence, leading to acculturation of the Slavs, ended in the early 6th century: Procopius relates numerous Slavic raids after 518. Accordingly Justinian built a defence system, which worked both to protect *Byzantium and to isolate the Slavs. This strengthened Slavic ethnic identity on the lower Danube. Here the assemblage called the Suchava-Sipot culture emerged, a culture without Byzantine ties or influences. Instead we find typically Slavic ornamented bow fibulae.

However, Slavs also tried to settle within the empire's borders. In 550 the first *sclavinia* (enclave of Slavic settlement) came into existence, on the Adriatic coast of present-day Bosnia. In 581 there was a *sclavinia* around Thessalonica, and in 586 Slavs settled in the Peloponnese, displacing many inhabitants. The new population may have been not unwelcome in an empire that had suffered from demographic catastrophe in the *plague of 541/42 and its consequent fall in tax revenue. After *c.*557, when the nomadic Avars subjugated the Slavic tribes on the Romanian plain and organized their own state, Slavic migration into Byzantine territory took place mostly within the framework of Avar raids, proceeding southwards along the Adriatic coast. Heraclius invited the Croats to free Dalmatia from the Avars *c.*620–26, which resulted in a permanent settlement of this Slavic people on the Dalmatian coast and in the valley of the Sava.

While in Dalmatia the Slavs maintained their ethnicity, the Slavic peoples who settled Macedonia and the Peloponnese quickly acculturated and have left almost no archaeological traces. Only the area of the former Roman province of Moesia (*Bulgaria) shows affiliations with the Ipotesti-Cindesti culture, in the assemblages named the Popina culture. Despite the arrival of the Bulgars in the later 7th century and the formation of their state by 679, the Slavic culture did not disappear in this region; rather, the nomads underwent Slavicization in the 8th and 9th centuries.

Archaeological find of hoard of gold from Nagyszentmiklós, dating 8th–9th centuries. Kunsthistorisches Museum, Vienna.

The second direction of Slavic migrations led northwest along the Carpathians to the territory of present-day western and central *Poland and later to the *river Elbe basin in eastern Germany. While written sources seem to suggest that before the Slavs arrived this territory was largely unpopulated, the incomers probably encountered pre-Slavic inhabitants (remnant Goths, Vandals, and Burgundians [*see* ARMAGNACS AND BURGUNDIANS]). The typical Slavic square sunken huts with corner ovens rarely appear in this region. Oval pits, probably the sunken parts of above-ground shelters, are also found. This implies that in western Poland in the late 6th to early 7th century there was another Slavic culture centre, emerging through contact between the migrating Slavic-tradition-bearing groups and non-migrating peoples. Archaeological evidence of contact and/or of population continuity comes from Březno, from *Pomerania, and from *Saxony. The earliest Slavic archaeological culture in western Poland and eastern Germany is called the Sukow-Dziedzice culture.

2. *Formation of the earliest Slavic states*

After the migration stage came stabilization. This stage, which in the Balkans ended in the 8th century but north of the Carpathians continued until the early 10th, is archaeologically visible in the construction of fortresses, usually on the tribal territories' margins. Slavic culture still remained relatively uniform: from the Balkans to the Baltic wheel-made pottery with linear decoration is widespread.

The so-called 'state of Samo' is considered the earliest Slavic state, in the sense of a political entity comprising more than one tribe. This state was formed probably in the territory of Moravia (*see* BOHEMIA), probably *c.*623 by a Frankish merchant who organized the Slavs to rebel against the Avars: it was a short-lived creation, which did not survive the death of its ruler in 658×61; it has left no archaeological remains.

One of the earliest examples of Slavic statehood formation is *'Great Moravia', created *c.*833 after the Moravian prince Mojmir took Slovakia. As a result of conquests, especially under Svjatopluk (871–94), this state encompassed lands of the present-day Czech Republic, southern Poland, southeastern Germany, and part of *Hungary. It survived until being conquered by the Hungarians at the turn of the 9th–10th centuries. The Christian mission of *Cyril and Methodius, who devised a written version of the Old Slavic language and propagated Christianity via the Slavic liturgy, spurred the rapid progress of Christianization. The first towns outside the Mediterranean sphere of influence emerged here from gradual enlargement of the small strongholds that served as fortresses and seats of rulers (Stare Mesto and Mikulčice). An aristocratic elite gathered around a prince, controlling long-distance trade. In the towns we find numerous churches surrounded by cemeteries containing richly furnished graves. Specialized districts for craftsmen and marketplaces also emerged in these early towns. The same archaeological correlates of early state formation and of an emerging 'feudal' social structure can be observed in other early Slavic polities, such as Carantania, as well as in *Croatia and *Serbia in the 8th and early 9th centuries.

The mechanism of the later formation of the Polish state was similar. A tribe called the Polanie began to expand in the early 10th century, destroying tribal strongholds in western Poland and building new ones in newly acquired territories. In the process of conquest an important role was played by mercenaries, partly of Scandinavian origin, as attested by finds of Scandinavian weapons and graves manifesting Scandinavian *burial customs. One of the capitals of this new state became *Gniezno, probably once the site of a pagan temple. Conversion to Christianity in 966 brought change: in the strongholds stone architecture emerged, both of sacred (churches) and of lay character (princely seats patterned after *Carolingian palaces). Around them grew up specialized neighbourhoods for craftsmen's workshops and marketplaces. This process of the emergence of towns in the central European Slavic zone was broken only at the beginning of the 13th century, by the practice of founding completely new towns, with regular layouts and new inhabitants, mostly invited from western Europe.

The original uniformity of Slavic culture was disrupted by the arrival of the Hungarians (*c.*896) in the Hungarian plain, blocking contacts between the southern and the northern Slavs, and further by the east-west ecclesiastical divide of 1054, which drew a line between the Slavic peoples who accepted Christianity from *Byzantium and used the Cyrillic alphabet (Ruthenia, Bulgaria, Serbia) and those of the Roman sphere who used the Latin alphabet (Croatia, Bohemia, Poland). ZK

F. Curta, *The Making of the Slavs* (2001).
M. Gojda, *Ancient Slavs: Settlement and Society* (1991).
Z. Kobyliński, 'The Slavs', *NCMH,* vol. 1: *c.500–c.700*, ed. P. Fouracre (2005), 524–44.
M. Parczewski, *Die Anfänge der frühslawischen Kultur in Polen* (1993).

archaeology: France

1. History of the discipline
2. Migration of peoples (5th century)
3. Urban archaeology
4. Monumental archaeology
5. Rural archaeology
6. Funerary archaeology
7. Craft production and trade
8. Environmental archaeology

1. *History of the discipline*

From its rise in the mid 19th century to when it took shape (and was taught) in the 1970s, the medieval archaeology of France has encompassed three main areas: elite dwellings, places of worship (especially for the high MA), and Merovingian funerary remains. Long supported by amateur archaeologists, and then with excavations run by scientific teams from regional services, universities, and the CNRS, it is today linked with 'preventive' archaeology (with its own national institute).

2. *Migration of peoples (5th century)*

The older view was one of various 'barbarian' peoples becoming established in Roman Gaul, each with its corresponding material culture. Re-study of museum material and recent excavations are revising this view. The 5th-century Vandals, Suevi, Alans, and Huns left no archaeological traces; but late-4th- and early-5th-century objects found in northern Gaul can be attributed to eastern Germanic people and steppe nomads (Huns, Alano-Sarmatians) who served in the Roman army and were integrated into the population, as their graves are mixed in with those of Roman provincials. The settlement and kingdoms of the *Visigoths in *Aquitaine (419–507) and of the Burgundians (*see* ARMAGNACS AND BURGUNDIANS) in eastern Gaul (443–534), well-attested in literary sources, are little represented: this may have been because these dominant Germanic minorities, benefiting from their status as *foederati*, integrated more rapidly without leaving a distinct material culture. The Franks, many of whom were already integrated into the Roman defensive system from the Loire to the *Rhine since late antiquity (we recognize them, as well as the Saxons and *Frisians, by their tombs of men with weapons, especially axes, and of women with fibulae like those found on the North Sea coast), present an archaeological identity, at least for the period when the Merovingian dynasty conquered Gaul (late 5th–early 6th century). The Frankish minority, who shared cemeteries with the Gallo-Roman natives, are marked by their practice of clothed inhumation together with grave-goods: witness a few male burials (those of 'chiefs') with typical weaponry (hooked spears, franciscae) and female burials following western Germanic fashions (2 pairs of fibulae, one on the breast or neck, the other by the waist or on the shoulders). But after the second half of the 6th century, the Merovingian horizon no longer manifests a Frankish identity, except for a few elite tombs whose furnishings (especially with particular zoomorphic ornaments) witness to a desire to affirm a Germanic origin.

3. *Urban archaeology*

At the end of the 1960s, along with rebuilding of ancient city centres to accommodate motorcars, city archaeology came dramatically into its own in a whole north European context emphasizing notions of the 'erosion of the past', with British work at *York and *Winchester being models. Topographically, Merovingian cities continue late antique ones, being also marked by their walls (whose revised chronology attests their more recent, non-defensive character), their refuse dumps, public and Christian monuments, and cemeteries. The urban and suburban built environment is nevertheless substantially changed, especially by the building of new Christian churches. Except for *Toulouse (the Hôpital Larrey), where the remains of an urban palace—that of the Visigothic kings?—were uncovered in 1988, civil architecture is absent. Structures inherited from late antiquity were largely reused. Inside city walls zones called 'terres noires' have been found; long thought to be evidence of non-occupation, these sediments could also correspond to dwelling or peripheral zones. From the mid 1980s urban rescue archaeology has followed public works like the Paris 'Grand Louvre' or the *Lyons Métro. This has also encouraged the study of ordinary city buildings.

To date, urban archaeology has helped establish specific chronologies for each place, but has also disclosed the common rhythms and processes, inherited from earlier epochs, of at least the more important medieval cities: open Iron-age settlements, ancient *civitates* and *vici*, late antique and high medieval Christian cities. What is new has been to show: 1) that the high MA is the time when cities were created, with new ones born between the 6th and the 9th centuries; 2) that the 12th century consolidated this phenomenon and changed the city's material form; and 3) that a 'new wave' of city creations took place during the 13th century, and within extant ones great public works were achieved, affirming civic power: the word *ville* itself appears in the 13th century.

4. *Monumental archaeology*

Many excavations under standing churches or on the site of vanished ones have revealed the dynamism of Merovingian architecture, embodied in France by not many standing examples. This research has revealed both enlargements of late antique churches and new constructions. In towns, cathedral groupings (*Lyons, *Rouen, Digne, *Aix-en-Provence, *Autun, St-Jean-de-Maurienne) and funerary *basilicas (for example St-Laurent and St-Just in Lyons, St-Pierre in *Vienne, St-Laurent in Grenoble, St-Pierre-l'Estrier in *Autun, St-Martin in *Angers, St-Clément in Mâcon) have been excavated. Striking results have come from work on baptisteries, such as at Lyons, Grenoble, *Rheims, Meysse, Broude, and Rouanne. Other excavations have revealed churches totally unknown to the written sources, such as at Maguelone (Hérault), *Marseilles (rue Malaval), Rézé near *Nantes, and Notre-Dame-de-Bondeville (Seine-Maritime), with its liturgical arrangements still in place and its interesting tombs. Monastic archaeology has progressed correspondingly less on sites where high-medieval sites have been built over by later constructions. Other than *Cluny, we should note the remarkable dig at Hamages (Nord) where the evolution of a 7th-century monastery can be followed until its destruction in the 9th century, as well as those at St-Germain d'Auxerre, St-Cybard in the Périgueux, Ganagobie, Fontevrault, St-Claude, and Landevennec. Updating of archaeological techniques for buildings has let us know the ordinary civil building, propose new chronologies, and redate structures hitherto dated only by stylistic analysis.

5. *Rural archaeology*

The last 30 years have seen an extraordinary development of this field, notably in northern France. Hundreds of digs following large-scale projects have permitted the excavation of habitation sites where 'agricultural units', often scattered within an enclosure, consisted of a wooden dwelling house, domestic 'cabanes' with dug-out floors and roofs resting on two, four, or six posts, granaries on posts or silos dug in the earth, a well, and other more modest adjunct structures for agricultural or craft uses. Most of these settlements were built no earlier than the 7th to 8th centuries (as is confirmed by corresponding burials), but then abandoned during the 9th to 11th centuries. This phenomenon seems to have resulted from specially favourable climatic conditions that gave rise to an economic expansion and population growth in the 7th century, necessitating the building of more dwellings. Their abandonment (leaving the church and cemetery to perhaps survive longer) seems to have been due to a land reorganization by the seigneurial rulership. On the other hand, the location of old Merovingian cemeteries (late 5th–6th centuries), almost always next to actual villages and hamlets, shows that the latter are mostly the direct descendants of Merovingian settlements (of ancient origin or not) that endured. Numerous recent excavations, notably in the Moselle valley, have confirmed this. So, around AD 1000, the rural population was much denser than it was to be later on, as the organization and dividing up of the landscape still depended on a structure going back to the end of the second Iron Age and to the Roman Empire.

'Preventive' archaeology has also let us know more about the dispersed settlement of the MA: monastic granges (the farm at la Cense), hamlets (Trainecourt in the Calvados; Vitry-sur-Orne, on the Moselle), and farms. It has also revealed how resources were exploited: *pottery centres, *glassworking centres, metalworking centres, such as in Lorraine and in the Sarthe and the Berry.

6. *Funerary archaeology*

Only in recent decades have Merovingian cemeteries benefited from truly scientific excavation, particularly on the level of funerary structures and of anthropology. We have several reference sites that lend themselves to innovative study. At least in northern France where clothed inhumation was practised, typological-chronological classifications of grave-goods have been made, which, in their seven main phases, coincide with those established for the *Rhine basin and southwest *Germany. In southern France, where clothed inhumation was rare or absent, the accent is on funerary practices, especially on modes of burial, with a solid chronology established. Anthropological work has borne much fruit, for example on taphonomy (placing the tombs in a filled-in space or not), palaeodemography, and palaeopathology, though it is still difficult to construct a synthesis with so many local variables. But the overall impression is that people suffered more from bad nutrition than from lack of food. A new theme in funerary archaeology today is to combine archaeological and anthropological results, so as to make promising social reconstructions.

For the following medieval period, funerary archaeology work is complicated by the long time cemeteries remained in use in a small space and the disappearance of grave-goods. Still, several parish or monastic cemeteries have been partially excavated and their study bodes well for the future.

7. *Craft production and trade*

Long limited to the laboratory study of objects or by the bias of experimental archaeology, Merovingian craftsmanship is starting to be understood through the uncovering of actual production structures, such as potters' or bronzesmiths' hearths, furnaces, sites for glass bead manufacture (sometimes out of imported glass) or for bone- and antler-working (combs, awls, and so forth). Mapping types of objects, sometimes made in the same moulds or decorated by the same templates, bears witness to local (*ceramic), inter-regional (metal jewellery or accessories), and long-distance (Mediterranean bronze vessels) trade. For example, laboratory study of garnets shows that they were first imported from *India or Ceylon, then (from the end of the 6th century) from central Europe, when the Byzantines no longer controlled the Red Sea.

For the MA proper, study of techniques has progressed especially since the 1980s in the area of *mining, with excavations at Brandes (Isère) and Pampailly (Rhône), and in areas along the south border of the Massif Central (Cévennes), the Alpes du Sud, the Limousin, the Vosges, and the eastern Pyrenees. Large-scale works have allowed the uncovering of metalworking sites (ironworking) in Lorraine, the Berry, and the Sarthe. Study of water technology has shown the importance and the high level of what was achieved, especially by monasteries (in the Île-de-France, Burgundy, and the Franche-Comté). From the mid 1990s there have been many studies on medieval ceramics, with concentration on artefacts coming from production and consumption sites, notably in Normandy, *Brittany, the *Auvergne, *Alsace, and *Touraine.

8. *Environmental archaeology*

The innovation of the last 20 years has been further use of the results coming from archaeological strata, so as to understand medieval relationships between societies and their surroundings. These works have engaged specialists in environmental and archaeoscientific studies: the study of eco-facts (archaeozoology, archaeobotany), of geological sediments, and of materials (geoarchaeology). These studies have brought out, among other findings, that not only were the early MA not a period of reforestation, but rather (with regional differences of course) a period when landscapes remained open and were cleared. One can also observe the diversity of areas utilized, between grassland and arable, and the extension of territory: lands used in antiquity whose flora were used by humans. Studies of valleys show how human societies affected the land: rivers and watered regions, and even human-directed water-courses during the first millennium: changing riverbeds, building dykes, *mills, fishponds, and navigation works. These results lead us to reconsider why sites were located where they were and why they were moved and to revise some interpretations in the urban and rural spheres. At the beginning of the 21st century archaeological work in France is allowing us to present a different MA. JBu, PPé

M. de Boüard, *Manuel d'archéologie médiévale: de la fouille à l'histoire* (1975).
J.-P. Bravard and M. Magny, eds, *Les fleuves ont une histoire* (2002).
J. Burnouf *et al.*, eds, *La dynamique des paysages protohistoriques, antiques, médiévaux et modernes* (1997).
J.-P. Demoule, ed., *La France archéologique* (2004).
B. Effros, *Merovingian Mortuary Archaeology and the Making of the Early Middle Ages* (2003).
P. Périn, *La datation des tombes mérovingiennes* (1980).
E. Peytremann, *Archéologie de l'habitat rural dans le nord de la France du IVe au XIIe siècle*, 2 vols (2003).
J. Plumier and M. Regnard, eds, *Voies d'eau, commerce et artisanat en Gaule mérovingienne* (2005).
Les premiers monuments chrétiens de la France, 3 vols (1995–8).

archaeology: Germany and Austria

1. Introduction
2. The early MA and the Carolingian period
3. The high MA

1. *Introduction*

In Germany and Austria, medieval archaeology is a relatively young branch of scholarship. However, its importance for regional history and its relevance to the identity of locally dominant populations are high—and indeed increasing with every high-profile excavation. The creation of local town archaeologies helps to meet these concerns. Other focal issues are the study of churches, monasteries, and cemeteries, of castles and fortifications, of deserted villages, and also of craft and technology, industry and transport. Medieval displays in museums are growing in range.

Although medieval archaeology succeeds pre- and protohistoric archaeology, in Germany and Austria these subjects are normally institutionally separated, both in universities and in public heritage management. The remit of pre- and protohistory usually ends in the 9th century. The *Carolingian period is a transitional phase, sometimes classified one way, sometimes the other. 'Mittelalterarchäologie' proper is concerned with the period from the 10th century to the 15th and joins up closely with early modern archaeology.

Medieval archaeology has long since developed distinctive methods and techniques. *Pottery is the backbone of all interpretations and datings. Over the last thirty years the typology, production, and dating of various forms of medieval ceramics and vessel-forms has steadily been refined; likewise with several other classes of artefact (for example buckles, horse-*harness, brooches). The cataloguing of finds has been of greater significance than in pre- and protohistoric archaeology and has been undertaken systematically in several regions. At the same time, the assessment of archives has been vital: documents, *saints' lives or annals, and above all old maps and other pictorial sources provide copious information. To make use of such sources, medieval archaeology has to adopt an interdisciplinary approach. Also common is collaboration with those responsible for historic buildings, as many such are still standing in the heart of medieval structures such as *castles, *monasteries, and churches. However, medieval archaeology adds a great deal to what the historical sources alone can offer. Excavations produce information on the material culture and thus on the physical life of the people at particular sites.

2. *The early MA and the Carolingian period*

From the 5th century to the 8th, central Europe can be viewed as two distinctive parts. This division was founded upon the *limes* of the Roman Empire along the Rhine–Main frontier. After the collapse of the western empire, the Frankish/Merovingian realm arose west of the *Rhine, subsequently expanding, as the *Carolingian empire, to the east and north. This was followed by the high-medieval state of the Ottonians and Salians, under whom the borders were pushed further east and north. This division persists, archaeologically, in certain types of artefact and find-complexes.

Franks, Burgundians (*see* ARMAGNACS AND BURGUNDIANS), Alamans, and Goths settled in the south and west: groups who saw themselves as autonomous nations superseding Roman provincial governments. They usually established centres in former Roman towns. In contrast to their northern neighbours they were already Christian in a way: they had at least partially abandoned their traditional *Odin-cult and for various reasons loosened their ties with the other Germanic peoples. This is apparent in artefact finds similar to late-antique models, and particularly in the decoration of precious items with the polychrome style using colourful gemstones. From the 6th century onwards, more conspicuous Christian symbolism appears. Typical of these regions as a whole is the occurrence of row-grave cemeteries from the mid 5th century onwards. There are also some special burials (for example the boys' and women's graves within *Cologne cathedral), furnished with wheel-thrown pottery, drinking glasses, and zoomorphic brooches.

The other area is defined archaeologically in the 5th and 6th centuries by certain types of bow brooch, gold *bracteates, and decorated weapons, some with animal motifs. This is the pagan Germanic area. Its culture is expressed in the common use of a symbolic language and the employment of *runic script. The heartlands were southern *Scandinavia, northern *Germany, and eastern *England. The dead were mostly cremated and interred in huge cemeteries, although barrows containing both cremation and inhumation graves are also known. The organization of the social elites rested upon a series of multifunctional central places;

in Germany, however, research into these is in an early stage. These stand above the ordinary rural settlements in their diverse and rich finds. In the 7th and 8th centuries their function was taken over by major trade centres such as the well-studied *Hedeby, whose dense timber buildings can be examined not only by excavation but also by geophysical survey. There were also settlements of the character of central places further south, some of which show long-term continuity.

The first Christian churches were built as early as the 4th century, but there is little archaeological evidence of these. It has been possible to excavate a few churches of the 5th and 6th centuries. Churches and monasteries multiplied in the Merovingian period, even in the formerly pagan territories. These were often small timber structures, although important and sometimes long-lived complexes appeared too (for example *Reichenau, *Lorsch, *Regensburg). In the south and west many of these structures were placed in Roman buildings, which affected their appearance, while in the north new types of building had to be created. East of the Rhine and in the north new sees emerged, some in existing settlements, others on 'greenfield sites'. These soon developed into the first large towns of those territories (for example *Münster, *Hamburg). The large stone-built monasteries of the 8th and 9th centuries that appeared in the converted lands as emblems of the new faith, culture, and way of life were, like the new communication routes, key products of a world in flux on the threshold of the high MA. The new, ordered, and uniform spirit of this age was manifested in the *St Gall monastery plan: a model design created *c*.800, whose idealized structure of four wings around a *cloister came to be adopted as basic.

Other evidence of missionary activity and of conversion comes from small finds of the 7th century onwards. Religious pendants, brooches, and *amulets can probably be associated with the work of individual missionaries; certainly it is possible to use these to trace the Carolingian-period missions, promoted from Rome, *France, and England, and later also the Frankish mission to other parts of northern and central Germany. These objects include above all the enamelled disc and cross brooches of the 8th to 10th centuries, alongside individual finds with pictorial art in what is known as the Tassilo Chalice Style. Objects such as book-mounts, book-clasps, and styli imply the diffusion of literacy. These are found primarily in the vicinity of monasteries. A profusion of monasteries and parish churches sprang up after the Saxon wars of *Charlemagne, even in those areas that had previously had pagan populations, which they structured in a new and enduring manner. The progressive adoption of unfurnished burial points to the changes in religious outlook; above all, the practice of burial either beside or in a church. These churches and their cemeteries are rarely found because they were usually built over in the following centuries. A few, however, can be studied archaeologically, if only in part.

3. The high MA

Starting in the *Carolingian period, palace-sites as fortified places could be developed as spectacular residences (for example *Aachen); several have been excavated. New palaces gained status in the 10th century especially (for example *Goslar), and without delay in the steadily expanding eastern territories of the state. The physical origins of several castles lie in the 10th and 11th centuries. The 'high *castles' (for example the Rhine castles) that appeared on clifftops or plateaux stand in contrast to the 'lowland castles' surrounded by moats on the plains. *Chivalry, feudal lordship, and nobility were displayed in these fortified sites. Many castles began as 'mottes': *timber or stone buildings defended by palisades and sometimes with walls and moats. In terms of artefact finds, these are not very different from agrarian settlements. However, the nobility's and knights' need for defence and display grew steadily, and in the 12th and 13th centuries large stone castles were built over many small sites. These comprised various buildings and functional zones that the archaeological finds help to identify and enable us to reconstruct. Now we also find items associated with aristocratic culture (harness-mounts, spurs, dress accessories, candlesticks, *hunting and hawking equipment, *musical instruments, gaming pieces and boards, and so forth) as well as objects that reflect the military aspect of the castles (for example weaponry, training weaponry, pieces of armour, crossbow bolts, sling- and cannon-shot). Although life in the castles had been very simple and harsh to start with, in the 13th century signs of an elevated and refined lifestyle and greater comfort can be found (for example hand-basins, aquamaniles, ceramic serving- and tableware, drinking glasses, stove-tiles). Many castles were destroyed in the course of the innumerable noble quarrels or as the outcome of various wars; some, however, were subsequently rebuilt as great castles, barracks, or new fortifications and remained in use into modern times.

In several cases, castles and the settlements that grew up around them developed into genuine towns. Towns also emerged near monasteries and *cathedrals and at other important locations. Archaeology helps us to identify the *crafts, often zoned, and their particular tools and techniques (for example tanners, bakers, potters, weavers, smiths, and shoemakers). Drains and ditches yield well-preserved organic finds. Food-waste in particular (animal bone, shellfish, eggshells, fruit-pips) illustrates the real life of the population. This, indeed, is where urban archaeology redresses the balance for the 'history of the common man'; without it, information that was never documented would be lost. As a matter of fact, the early fortifications and the initial phases of growth of the towns, and the positions of the churches, monasteries, aristocratic courts, or administrative buildings, cannot be traced in those records either, but can be found through archaeology.

Amongst the aspects of medieval life still visible in many places are churches. The small timber buildings of the Merovingian period were succeeded as early as the Carolingian period by large stone *basilica structures. From these derived the two high-medieval architectural styles, the Romanesque (11th to mid 12th centuries) and the Gothic (12th/13th–15th centuries) (*see* ART AND ARCHITECTURE: GOTHIC/ROMANESQUE). Excavations in churches frequently reveal earlier buildings of which little was previously known. Church excavations also produce other typical items of these periods, such as candelabras, coins, bone beads, crucifixes, toy figures, buckles, book-mounts, leather spectacles, and inkhorns.

In complementing the written sources, archaeology is able both to test and to substantiate long-standing historical ideas. Archaeology provides an essential counterbalance and check upon documentary evidence. With its complex methodology and the multifaceted results that it yields, it has become an indispensable historical science concerned with the physical reality of medieval life. AP

Beiträge zur Mittelalterarchäologie in Österreich, 1– (1985–).
Die Franken: Wegbereiter Europas (1996).
G. P. Fehring, *Die Archäologie des Mittelalters* ([3]2000).
—— and W. Sage, eds, *Mittelalterarchäologie in Zentraleuropa: Zum Wandel der Aufgaben und Zielsetzungen* (1995).
F. Felgenhauer, 'Zum Stand mittelalterarchäologischer Forschung in Österreich', *Mitteilungen der österreichischen Arbeitsgemeinschaft für Ur- und Frühgeschichte*, 25 (1974/5), 245–53.
K. Fuchs *et al.*, eds, *Die Alamannen* (1997).
Fundort Kloster: Archäologie im Klösterreich (2000).
Landesdenkmalamt Baden-Württemberg und die Stadt Zürich, *Stadtluft, Hirsebrei und Bettelmönch: Die Stadt um 1300* (1992).
M. Wemhoff and C. Stiegemann, eds, *799: Kunst und Kultur der Karolingerzeit* (1999).
A. Wieczorek and H.-M. Hinz, eds, *Europas Mitte um 1000* (2000).
J. Zeune, ed., *Alltag auf Burgen im Mittelalter* (2006).

archaeology: Iberia Medieval archaeology in Spain and Portugal emerged as a distinct field in the 1980s; previous sporadic work was usually ideologically targeted. Influenced by German nationalism, archaeologists sought to place the *Visigoths within 'pan-Germanism'; hence it was argued that Visigothic settlement was centred in *Castile, the allegedly 'German' culture of which was opposed to the Guadalquivir valley's 'Romanism'. This doctrine was fabricated to promote the Visigothic kingdom as the progenitor of the Crown of Castile. Early study of Mozarabic churches led to the overvaluation of Visigothic influence on later Spanish culture. The archaeology of Islamic Spain (*al-Andalus) in the 1930s–1950s was better developed thanks to the conservation and restoration of the Alhambra.

1. Extensive archaeology
2. Hydraulic archaeology
3. Religious archaeology
4. Archaeology of the Christian kingdoms

1. Extensive archaeology

The transfer of control over archaeology to the autonomous regions in the 1980s stimulated a boom in medieval archaeology and local history. Extensive archaeology is about settlement patterns and sequential occupancy, drawing on the traditions and techniques of landscape archaeology and historical geography, focussing on rural social organization. The long occupancy of the southern half of the peninsula by a Muslim society made Spain an opportune place to introduce this approach. The original reference of **incastellamento* was Latin Europe, where *castles came to be points of control over peasant villages they ruled. In Spain and Portugal, however, the pioneering work in extensive archaeology was focused on Islamic society wherein castles did not control peasants but rather served for protection. Thus many castles built in al-Andalus before the 12th century were 'castle-refuges', possessing walls and walled enclosures to protect peasants and their animals in insecure times. In this arrangement, a castle (*hisn*, pl. *husun*) formed a single unit that included several villages (*qura*, sg. *qarya*), which might be termed a '*hisn-qarya* complex'. Such complexes had a number of associated features: they were almost always irrigated (*see* WATERWORKS), and the villages were settled by tribal subgroups, Arab or *Berber. Villages were farmed collectively, having no measured bounds.

Irrigation was organized tribally. Because agriculture tended to be based on irrigation, immigrating tribal groups' site selection was based on a calculation of the optimal population size and the amount of water available. Hence settlements were typically in small valleys, fed by spring water tapped by **qanats* (galleries) and distributed by gravity flow in surface canals. Optimization, however, was a function not of economic efficiency but rather of tribal perceptions of the size of a settlement (numbers of families) comprising an ideal segment.

The early focus on castles imposed limits on how rural society could be analysed. A link between castle and village was assumed, but it has proved difficult to be precise about the nature, intensity, and continuity of such links. Since *husun* did not control surrounding settlements, they yielded less archaeological information than feudal castles. If *husun* were primarily defensive, against whom were they defending? Until the 12th and 13th centuries, when defence against Christian incursions became an issue, these castles were not located on the Muslim-Christian frontier.

Early settlement (in the 8th century) was, to a degree, concentrated on the Mediterranean littoral, where food could be easily gathered or hunted in tidal marshlands—the future habitat of rice, an Indian crop diffused by the Arabs

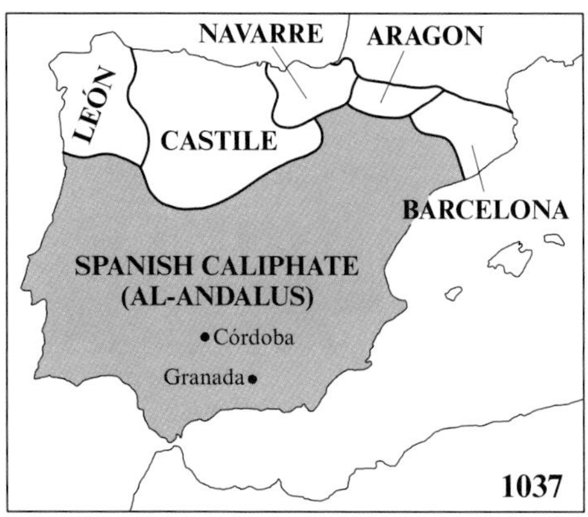

Early Iberia, 8th–12th centuries.

Muslim territory

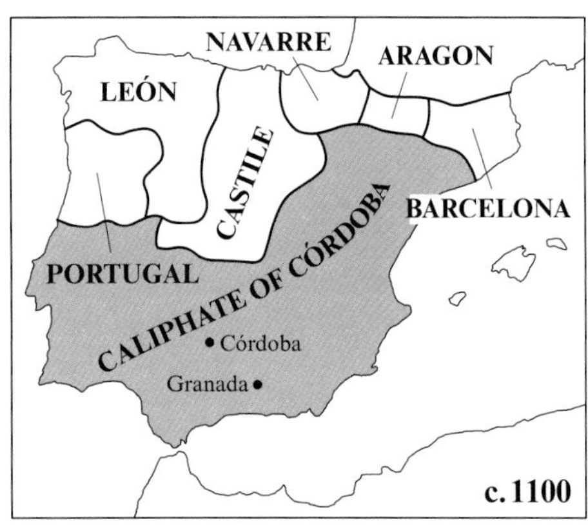

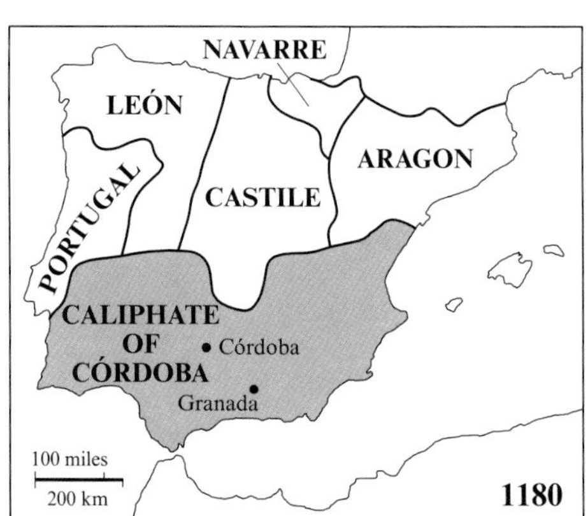

which seems not to have arrived in the peninsula until the late 9th century.

Extensive archaeology, based on field surveys and aerial photographs, is less given to utilizing stratigraphic excavation. The retrenchment of western Mediterranean maritime trade in *terra sigillata* (Roman incised wares) goes along with the ruralization of Roman settlement from the 4th century and the change in ceramic production from industrial shops with men using kick-wheels and glaze to rural household production by women producing wares on turntables. These wares were unglazed, and the repertory of forms narrowed to a few standard staples of cookware, stew-pots (*ollas*) and the like. These forms display continuity with late Roman forms: however, their presence alone is no indication of the ethnicity of its producers, because such simple cookwares were standard in all Mediterranean societies. Thus the oldest *pottery finds in the mountain districts of the eastern littoral (the kingdom of Denia) are unglazed common wares, dating to the late 10th century; their Roman form does not prove any continuity of settlement from Roman times. These high-altitude settlements were abandoned by Romans and resettled later by Arabs and Berbers. In the same region, castles yield sherds of glazed pottery imported from *Toledo until its fall in 1085, and subsequently from *Valencia and Murcia.

A purely archaeological approach to ethnicity is problematic. The physical remains of sites are, with one exception, opaque with respect to ethnicity, the exception being a specifically Berber house style. Therefore complementary material must be used to identify the dispersion of ethnic groups. One approach is to identify ethnicity via place names (either current or medieval). Tribal subgroups are reflected in a great number of place names in 'Beni-', literally 'sons of'. It has been possible to map villages settled as a result of segmentation (for example, the Berber Beni Ajjans in *Valencia, Mallorca, and so forth). The pattern is frequently revealing, for example Beni Gudala and Beni Massufa, neighbouring Moroccan tribes settling near each other in the huerta of Valencia. Sometimes Arabic and Berber tribes are paired in both the Maghrib and *al-Andalus. These toponymic patterns can then be matched with historical literature attesting to the presence of tribal segments—Arab or Berber—in specific places. Irrigation appurtenances are similar in all cultures, and popular

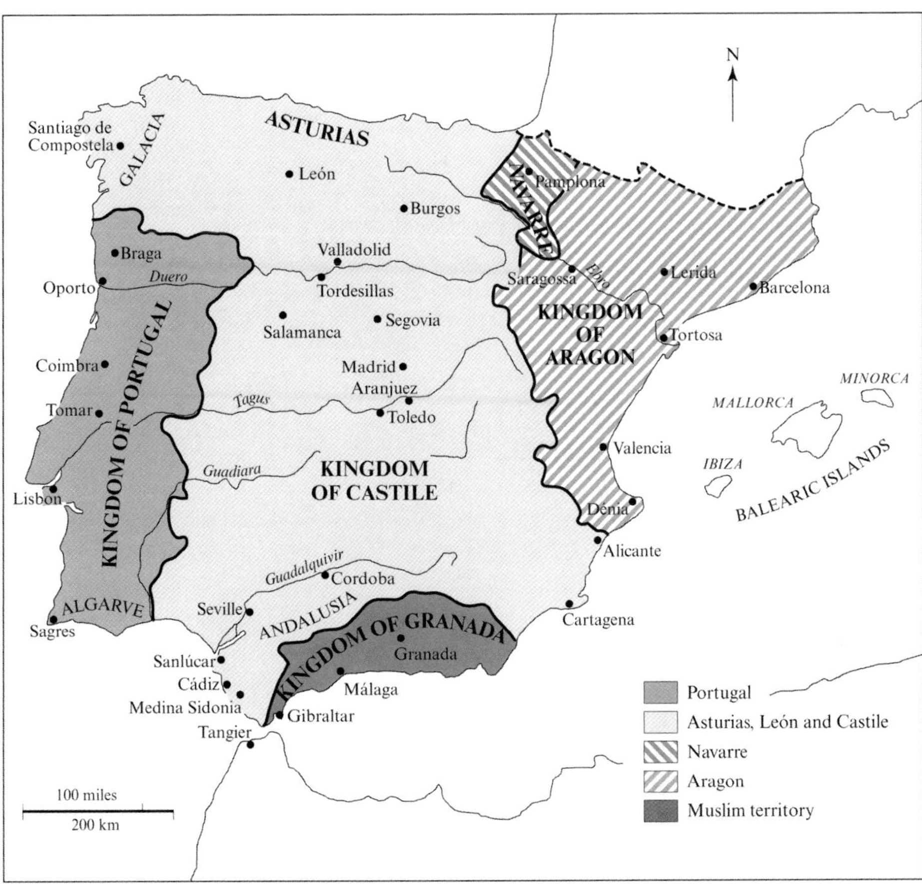

Later Iberia, 13th–15th centuries.

diffusionist traditions attributing a local landscape element to 'the time of the Moors' are almost always wrong.

2. *Hydraulic archaeology*

An interesting offshoot of extensive archaeology is a subspeciality known as hydraulic archaeology. A group founded by Miquel Barceló is centred at the Autonomous University of Barcelona. It has developed a distinctive methodology based on a painstaking field protocol that involves walking and measuring irrigation channels from source to end, and on that basis deducing the original design of the system in Islamic times. This is important because peasant life scarcely shows up in the archaeological register, and irrigation layouts, articulating what Barceló describes as the point of water catchment, the direction and slope of the supply canals, the location of the regulation reservoirs, and the sites of mills, entail a specific kind of social organization required for the system's operation. The fact that there is a close connection between the institutional requirements of irrigation and tribal social structure has made it possible to form a coherent explanation of tribal settlement. Segmentary social organization is marked by villages with names compounded with Beni-, 'sons of', as seen above. So in eastern Spain there occur dozens of villages with names like Benimamet (sons of Muhammad), Beniquinena (Kinana, an Arab clan), or Benissomada (Sumata, a Berber clan). Replication of particular names, via segmentation, and their association with irrigation generates further inferences. This makes for a determinist archaeology, one of the axioms of which is that a culture creates an artefact or an institution to adjust itself better to a particular environment.

Even if *castles can be dated by ceramic fragments, the chronology of the surrounding villages cannot. So peasant settlement 'has no archaeological identity other than its own spatial form. Its historical content is its form' (Barceló, *Design*, 20). A 'palaeoandalusian' period (8th century) has been identified on the basis of bilingual coinage and the sharing of cemeteries, both of which reveal the ethnic dynamics of early Muslim occupation. Selected place names have been used to identify places in northern Spain where Arab and Berber occupancy was too fleeting to leave substantial material remains: thus place names in *quinta* ('one-fifth') reflect the reservation for the state of one-fifth of a conquered territory; *aguilar* ('eagle's nest') describes a high-altitude fortification; others reflect *moro* and *sarracín*, generic words for 'Muslim'; and so forth. The clustering of such place names in the *Duero valley and points north are taken as indices of Muslim settlement.

3. Religious archaeology

It has been noted that the access roads of remote *Mozarab (Christian) settlements in al-Andalus preserve imprints of cart wheels, which is a physical sign of Christian settlement because wheeled vehicles had disappeared from the Arabic-speaking world. Martínez Enamorado discovered a second church at Bobastro, the mountain citadel of the rebel Ibn Hafsun, probably demonstrating the deep social repercussions of his conversion from Islam to Christianity.

4. Archaeology of the Christian kingdoms

Caves in northern Spain were inhabited throughout the MA: many have been studied along with the ceramic deposits found in them. The repertory of wares found was very narrow (only five forms in early medieval Cantabria) compared to that of al-Andalus. The sequence of occupancy in rural habitats has been studied in *Catalonia and various sites in the central meseta, typically using the methods of extensive archaeology in deserted (*despoblados*) villages. Frontier sites are particularly interesting given the constant warfare across them. Here, beginning in the 12th century, it was not uncommon to find double-walled villages, with a castle and church within. Here, walls made of stone or brick contrast with the rammed-earth construction of Andalusian walls. The high value placed on wheat in Christian Spain, where feudal dues were commonly collected in kind, particularly wheat, accounts for the attraction of silos as an object of archaeological study. Indeed, silos tend to cluster chronologically between the 11th and 13th centuries, the feudal epoch par excellence. Sometimes ovens are found in the vicinity of silos. Castles and watchtowers have received extensive study, as have churches and monasteries.

Two ceramic phases have been detected in the west of the peninsula: an early phase (8th through 10th centuries), characterized by the predominance of unglazed stew-pots (*ollas*) over all other forms; and then a later period (11th through 13th centuries) characterized by the diversification of forms and the increasing incidence of painted decorations in the form of wavy or parallel lines and other simple geometric motifs. Still later, in the early 14th century, 'loza dorada' copied from Muslim motifs appear, most notably in the pottery town of Manises near *Valencia. When Christian armies conquered, then settled, the former heartland of Islamic Spain, the adoption of standard Muslim wares had the effect of expanding the typically reduced repertoire of forms that characterized early medieval Christian pottery. Northern Catalan grey-wares (*cerámica gris*) were likewise restricted to a few forms, in particular the *olla* (stew-pot), at the same time (11th century) that the downdraft Roman kiln disappears and is replaced by a Persian- or Arab-style vaulted updraft kiln.

Though irrigation systems have received comparatively scant archaeological treatment, watermills have been extensively studied. Archaeologists have noted the salience of vertical seigneurial *mills in Catalonia, not only for milling wheat but also for fulling cloth or finishing leather (as early as 1126). TFG

R. Azuar, *Denia islámica: Arqueología y poblamiento* (1989).

M. Barceló, ed., *Arqueología medieval: En las afueras del 'medievalismo'* (1988).

—— *The Design of Irrigation Systems in al-Andalus* (1998).

A. Bazzana, *Maisons d'al-Andalus: Habitat médiéval et structures du peuplement dans l'Espagne orientale*, 2 vols (1992).

—— P. Cressier, and P. Guichard, *Les chateaux ruraux d'al-Andalus* (1988).

T. F. Glick, *From Muslim Fortress to Christian Castle: Social and Cultural Change in Medieval Spain* (1995); rev. Spanish ed. *Paisajes de conquista: Cambio cultural y geográfico en la España medieval* (2006).

—— and L. P. Martinez, 'Mills and Millers in Medieval Valencia', *Wind and Water in the Middle Ages*, ed. S. A. Walton (2006), 189–211.

S. Gutiérrez, *Cerámica común paleoandalusí del sur de Alicante (siglos VII–X)* (1988).

H. Kirchner, *La construcció de l'espai pages a Mayûrqa; les valls de Bunyola, Orient, Coanegra i Alaró* (1997).

—— *La ceràmica de Yâbisa: Catàleg i estudi dels fons del Museu Arqueològic d'Eivissa i Formentera* (2002).

—— and C. Navarro, 'Objetivos, métodos y práctica de la arqueología hidráulica', *Archeologia Medievale*, 20 (1993), 121–50.

V. Martínez Enamorado, 'Sobre las "Ciudades Iglesias" de Ibn Hafsun: Estudio de la basilica hallada en la ciudad de Bobastro (Ardales, Málaga)', *Madrider Mitteilungen*, 45 (2004), 507–31.

archaeology: Ireland

1. Introduction
2. Pre-Norman period
3. Urban archaeology
4. Rural settlement
5. Future directions

1. Introduction

Many archaeological investigations have been carried out in Ireland over the last decade or so, especially as a result of redevelopment in historic urban centres, the expansion of peripheral housing estates, and the programme of infrastructure improvements, especially roads. The National Roads Authority has a branch of professional archaeologists who oversee the mitigation programmes necessary for each new project, and they subcontract excavations and monitoring to commercial archaeological companies. Therefore most recent excavations on medieval sites have been developer-driven rather than research-driven. One advantage of these large-scale investigations is the location of many sites of all periods that, because they had left no surface trace, would have remained unknown.

Although the volume of archaeological work has grown, the volume of public information has fallen because often contract archaeologists do not have either the time or the resources to produce finished reports. This is somewhat mitigated by the requirement that a stratigraphical report for every site be submitted to the regulatory bodies: the Heritage Service of the Department of the Environment, Heritage and Local Government, and the National Museum of Ireland. These, however, are not generally available, and there is no means of ensuring that they meet basic standards.

A positive recent trend in medieval settlement archaeology has been the concentration on the interaction of the sites both with other settlement sites and with the natural landscape, rather than solely on the monuments. This approach has been encouraged by the Heritage Council. The state also channels funds to the Discovery Programme. Indeed, one current undertaking of the Discovery Programme focuses on medieval rural settlement; the other, on Lake Settlement, also has a medieval component.

2. *Pre-Norman period*

This phase of human settlement, from the spread of literacy and learning associated with the 5th-century coming of Christianity to Ireland up to the 12th century, is now more generally known as the early medieval period. Two major excavations of ringforts, the defended farmsteads of the first millennium at Lisleagh, County Cork, and Deer Park Farms, County Antrim, have provided much useful evidence of both house structures and the agricultural bases of these communities. Evidence of the broader economic infrastructure of this period has also been forthcoming. Especially valuable was the discovery of the tidal *mill near the monastic complex of Nendrum, Mahee Island, in Strangford Lough in County Down. There has also been much useful research and archaeological excavation carried out at the important monastery of *Clonmacnoise, County Offaly, on the river Shannon that has provided us with a broader idea of the economic foundations of such an ecclesiastical settlement.

Archaeological evidence has also recently been forthcoming of the *Viking phase of Cork City, while in *Dublin archaeological excavations in the Temple Bar area of the city have confirmed that there was Hiberno-Norse activity in the city as early as the 9th century. Excavations have also indicated that there was settlement activity in the same area in the 8th century, which seems to have possibly been influenced by urban developments in nearby Anglo-Saxon England.

The discovery of an important early Hiberno-Scandinavian site on the banks of the River Suir at Woodstown, County Waterford, has also caused scholars to re-evaluate their understanding of Viking activity in the area. Sometime in the mid to late 9th century some type of Viking settlement seems to have occurred here at a pre-existing Irish site. Apart from some enclosures and other linear features, the evidence consisted of many Viking-type artefacts such as silver ingots and parts of weapons, all found in the topsoil, as well as some well-stratified lead weights, and a Viking warrior *burial. Although the excavations to date have been limited, more extensive investigations are hoped for in future.

3. *Urban archaeology*

Much of Ireland's medieval archaeology has of necessity been carried out in urban areas. For two towns, Galway and Waterford, the archaeological record has been virtually fully published. Dublin has been covered by fascicles published by the Royal Irish Academy on various artefact types recovered by National Museum excavations, the latest on the medieval *pottery assemblages. More research also needs to be carried out on the hinterlands of these important urban centres. The Discovery Programme's Dublin project has attempted to reconstruct a picture of rural settlement, landownership, landuse, and farming practices within a 30 km radius of the city centre (forthcoming).

We also know more about the growth and development of the layouts of many smaller urban settlements in the MA. For example, excavations have taken place over the last decade in smaller towns such as Kilmallock, County Limerick, and Drogheda, County Louth.

4. *Rural settlement*

Numerous new medieval settlement sites have been excavated in advance of road construction. Excavation of a moated site at Camross, County Wexford, has shown that future work must extend beyond the perimeter of the moat itself, since a medieval pottery kiln was found just outside the moat. At another moated site at Coolamurry in the same county, excavation uncovered significant portions of a large wooden gatehouse and drawbridge, as well as many artefacts, including a perfect specimen of copper-alloy dividers, a unique find so far in Ireland. The excavator speculated that the carpenters and craftsmen might have used these dividers when they were constructing the major wooden structures of the site.

The Discovery Programme has also instituted a remote-sensing survey of the moated site in County Roscommon probably constructed by the O'Conors in the 13th century as a power base, the construction of which was described in contemporary bardic poetry. Increasingly it is now thought that the Gaelic-Irish nobility constructed moated sites in imitation of their Anglo-Norman neighbours. At another site at Tulsk in the same county, Discovery Programme excavations on what appeared to be a significant raised earthwork have located a major stone defensive construction of the 17th century overlying earlier settlement occupation stratigraphy. In 2006, some of the same research team utilizing new site-prospecting techniques, including orthorectified aerial photographs, have also excavated parts of an interesting field pattern and associated medieval settlement sites in the area of Carns, also in North Roscommon close to the important Rathcroghan prehistoric landscape complex.

Within these Gaelic-Irish areas it has also been found that the crannógs, artificial or natural islands in lakes that were occupied, and which are usually dated to the early medieval period, were often occupied from the 13th to the 15th centuries as well. Also, at the site of one of the palaces of the bishop of Elphin at Knockvicar, County Roscommon, recent excavations have produced evidence of a possible *Black Death period mass burial.

5. Future directions

Future research will obviously further embrace the concept of medieval landscape studies. Another Heritage Council priority is dealing with the backlog of unpublished excavation reports by offering grants to excavators.

Doubtless there will be further refinements in the accuracy of dating medieval *pottery types, still the major artefact type by which a chronology can be established for many sites. When scientific dating methods come into play, it is dendrochronology more than any other method that has revolutionized the accuracy with which we can date medieval buildings constructed of oak. For instance, dendrochronological dating by the palaeoenvironmental laboratory (Queen's University, Belfast) of pieces of the oak scaffold poles recovered from the putlog holes in the stone *keep of Trim castle, County Meath, revealed that much of it was constructed in the 1180s, rather than at the start of the following century, as had been thought. This dating technique has also shown how widely used good Irish oak timbers were in the rest of Europe, with examples being found in the Danish Skudelev IV Viking warship of the early 12th century, and as major structural timbers in the roof of *Salisbury cathedral in England in the 13th century. Much more accurate dating of small samples from many sites has also been achieved by utilizing the AMS (Accelerator Mass Spectrometry) radiocarbon dating method, again by the Belfast palaeoenvironmental laboratory.

There is now a growing consensus among scholars that the medieval period in Ireland did not end until the middle of the 17th century with the Cromwellian wars, as it is not till then that the medieval rural settlement pattern and the artefactual assemblies associated with them dramatically changed. Thus, as a result, the post-medieval period in Irish archaeology would commence at a much later date than in much of the rest of Europe. TB

N. Brady, 'Mills in Medieval Ireland', in *Wind and Water*, ed. S. A. Walton (2006), 39–68.

W. Davies, 'The Celtic Kingdoms', and C. Stancliffe, 'Religion and Society in Ireland', in *NCMH*, vol. 1: *c.500–c.700*, ed. P. Fouracre (2005), 240–46, 397–425.

L. R. Laing, *The Archaeology of Celtic Britain and Ireland, c.400–1200* (2005).

A. O'Sullivan, *Crannógs in Early Medieval Ireland* (2005).

P. F. Wallace, *The Viking Age Buildings of Dublin* (1992).

archaeology: Italy Italy is still strongly dominated by its classical past, which is why medieval archaeology began comparatively late. The peninsula was a melting pot of cultures, from Roman to Gothic and *Lombard, and from Byzantine to Saracen, Norman, and Angevin. Whilst medieval art and architecture, from ecclesiastical items to majolica ceramics, has attracted interest since the 19th century, little thought was given to archaeological contexts. Nonetheless, some early archaeological interest in the *Migration period followed the discovery of the Lombard cemeteries of Castel Trosino, Nocera Umbra, and Cividale del Friuli, with their wealth of grave goods, at the end of the century. Stratigraphic excavations began around the same time, when Boni dug beneath the bell-tower of St Mark's in *Venice (1885). Contemporaneously, Orsi was to promote the archaeology of Byzantine Sicily. However, almost 50 years had to pass, witnessing the substantial destruction of post-classical remains in *Rome, Ostia, and elsewhere under Mussolini, before any general interest began to be shown in post-classical archaeology. After the war it was, above all, foreign attention to the MA in the 1950s and 60s that sowed the seeds of modern medieval archaeology in Italy.

In 1961, the Polish Institute of Material Culture of Warsaw began excavation at Torcello in the Venetian lagoon, attempting to explain the birth of *Venice. Other major collaborative excavations (Castelseprio, Capaccio Vecchia) soon followed.

Under John Ward-Perkins, director of the British School at Rome, British archaeologists began taking interest in the medieval remains revealed by the South Etruria Project during the 1950s and 60s. Daniels excavated the papal farm of S. Cornelia, north of Rome, whilst Whitehouse began putting medieval *pottery chronology on a sure footing and also developed medieval archaeology in the centre and south of the peninsula, excavating at various sites such as the monastery of Farfa, the *Swabian castle of Lucera, and the village of S. Maria d'Anglona. Blake and Bryan Ward-Perkins collaborated with the Italians in the north.

The French School began its own major excavation project at the later medieval hilltop site of Brucato, Sicily, under the direction of Pesez, followed by a host of other excavations in central and southern Italy, particularly by Noyé. The Germans, with archaeologists such as Bierbrauer, concentrated on the *Lombards, with the excavation of the Alpine *castrum* of Ibligo-Invillino, mentioned by *Paul the Deacon in the 8th century.

On the Italian side, the principal instigators of a systematic medieval archaeology were Mannoni in Liguria and Francovich in Tuscany, both of whom, from the 1970s, posed concrete research objectives, excavating sites, establishing local chronologies, and creating schools. Major excavations, in particular at hilltop sites such as Montarrenti, Rocca San Silvestro, and Sant'Antonino di Perti, helped show the way.

Since the destruction in pre- and post-war times, urban archaeology has developed apace, revealing much of the MA. *Pavia was the first town to be examined systematically within the limits of a modern urban environment, followed by *Brescia and *Verona. An important urban project has been that by Manacorda of the Crypta Balbi in the centre of *Rome, with excavation and publication of a site that was transformed from a Roman theatre to an early medieval and later monastic complex. In *Milan, opportunity for excavation was provided by the construction of a new metro line in the 1980s. In *Naples it was the earthquake of 1981 that stimulated urban archaeology, with further opportunities now provided by a new metro line. In Otranto, urban archaeology is a result of building works linked to the growth in tourism. Nonetheless, the north continues to be best served. Whilst major excavations at Bari and Reggio Calabria remain substantially unpublished, the municipal council of Cesena has backed scholars in evaluating archaeological deposits in the town. All this has led to rethinking the transition between antiquity and the MA in Italy, and in characterizing medieval towns.

Conservation in towns with emphasis on major buildings has stimulated the stratigraphical analysis of stone architecture, with great prominence now given to changes in building techniques and materials. Lesser work has been done on early medieval architecture as on all forms of wooden and earth-built structures. The discovery of sunken-feature buildings or *Grubenhäuser* of north and central European type, and the large-scale excavations at Poggibonsi, near *Siena, with its numerous post-built houses, are helping to change the scene. Monastic archaeology has also blossomed, with such fruitful excavations as S. Salvatore a Brescia and S. Vincenzo al Volturno, both begun in the 1980s, by Brogiolo and Hodges respectively.

Though the first university course in medieval archaeology was given in Milan in 1966, it was not until 1984 that Italian universities first offered posts in the discipline. The landmark year 1974 saw the appearance of the annual *Archeologia Medievale* which has become the principal vehicle for all aspects of the discipline and not just in Italy. It is largely because of this journal that research is often well published, with a goodly number of final excavation reports. By setting an example, it has helped to promote standards. Increasing interest in the field is also now shown by the foundation of the Italian society of medieval archaeologists (SAMI) in 1996, and by annual conferences.

The first handbook of Italian medieval archaeology in Italy was published in 1997. What are the directions for future research? Much work needs to be done on the countryside. Though Italy has witnessed a host of field surveys, many are still inclined towards understanding the classical landscape. So little is known about villages, their genesis and individual characteristics, and how they related to the differing environments found throughout the country, that historians and archaeologists still debate as to when they became the dominant form of rural land management. Recent studies tend to suggest that villages already began to populate the landscape by the 8th century. Early sites made great use of wood and other decomposable materials, and often it was not until the turn of the millennium that churches and other buildings were regularly built of stone. Earthworks, field systems, and other rural infrastructures are equally in need of study, as are those pertaining to manufacture, such as *mills, olive presses, or salt pans.

The extraction and working of *iron is a major research topic in Tuscany, whilst in Alpine areas archaeologists have researched the large medieval soapstone industry. More generally, a number of *pottery kiln sites have been excavated, with medieval ceramics becoming better known in Italy than in any other Mediterranean country. It is now possible to chart the decline of late Roman ceramics and the rise of painted wares through the 5th and 6th centuries. A class of thick lead-glazed pottery (*vetrina pesante*) appeared by the 8th century, through links with the Byzantine East. However, much Italian pottery remained regionalized, with distinct north and south cultural facies. By the 12th century, through contact with the Maghreb and Norman Sicily, painted lead-glazed table wares became ubiquitous. These were soon followed by more up-market tin-glazed pottery (*protomaiolica* or *maiolica arcaica*), which reached an apex by the Renaissance.

The study of many other objects lags far behind that of ceramics, with more interest being given for example to Lombard decorative metalwork than to later medieval metalwork and technology. Numerous lead pilgrim badges and **ampullae*, for instance, are still lacking any regional study, and far too little is known about organic artefacts. Similarly, many issues covered by environmental archaeology, from physical anthropology to archaeozoology and palaeobotany, are still in want of sufficient specialists and general support from archaeologists.

From a methodological point of view, more reliance, particularly for the dating of early medieval contexts, needs to be made on radiocarbon dating. That said, information technology, led by the University of Siena, is permitting ever more detailed recording and informed overviews. With more information now available, we can also note some lacunae in the development of the discipline. There is still little theoretical work, as most archaeologists are content with simply excavating. This hampers free-thinking visions of the past, as opposed to reconstructions with archaeology simply illustrating models drawn from historical sources. This is partly a responsibility of the Ministry of Cultural Heritage, which still views prehistoric and classical remains as objects of study by archaeologists, and post-classical remains as principally the field of architects and art historians, paying little attention to the historical landscape. There is also limited outreach to the general public, without whose support medieval archaeology will remain largely the domain of a restricted group of specialists. The possibility of a rosy future now depends upon changing the positions of central, regional, and local government and on bringing the discipline to ever-greater public view. This is a race against time, as progress daily witnesses the destruction of our buried heritage. PRA

G. P. Brogiolo and S. Gelichi, *La città nell'alto medioevo italiano: Archeologia e storia* (1998).

R. Francovich and G. Noyé, eds, *La storia dell'alto medioevo italiano (VI–X secolo) alla luce dell'archeologia* (1994).

S. Gelichi, *Introduzione all'Archeologia Medievale* (1997).

R. Hodges and R. Francovich, *Villa to Village* (2003).

T. Mannoni and E. Giannichedda, *Archeologia della Produzione* (1996).

archaeology: the Levant In this region the MA can be defined as the period from the Islamic conquests of Byzantine territory beginning in the 7th century until the Ottoman conquests of *Egypt and Syria in the 16th century. Archaeological research has concentrated on central aspects of Islamic and Christian material culture including urban and rural settlements, religious and commercial buildings, bath houses, domestic buildings, fortifications, industrial installations, *burials, and fine and minor arts. In recent years research has expanded into previously neglected areas like the study of human skeletal remains and botanical and faunal analyses.

1. Umayyads (661–750)
2. Abbasids (750–c.950)
3. Tulunids (868/869–906) and Fatimids (969–1171)
4. Franks (1099–1291)
5. Ayyubids (1171–1250)
6. Mamluks (1250–1517) and early Ottoman rule (16th century)

1. *Umayyads (661–750)*

Umayyad rule contributed to the establishment of an individual Islamic architectural style. Though influenced by Sassanid and Byzantine models and employing existing construction techniques, materials, and decoration, it was already distinctive and innovative, as evidenced by the earliest major religious monument, the Dome of the Rock (mosque of *Umar) built by Abd al-Malik in 691, and the two great mosques built by al-Walid, the al-Aqsa mosque in *Jerusalem (699) and the Great Mosque of *Damascus (705).

The Umayyads built large courtyard palaces south of the Temple Mount in Jerusalem and a number of other palaces including Qasr al-Hayr al-Sharqi, Qasr al-Hayr al-Gharbi, Mshatta, and Khirbat al-Mafjar. In these they employed the *quadriburgium* design, a rectangular fortification with projecting corner towers familiar from Roman/Byzantine military camps and Byzantine fortresses. Some Islamic urban settlements (among others *Fustat, al-*Basra, Ayla at Aqaba, Anjar in Lebanon) also adopted this design. Construction under the Umayyads was of high quality, employing *ashlar masonry and sun-baked brick.

In the minor arts the Umayyads continued earlier traditions. The stucco at Khirbat al-Mafjar shows Sassanid influence, and the mosaics in the Dome of the Rock, the *mosques of al-Walid I, and the bath house at Khirbat al-Mafjar reflect a combination of Sassanid and Byzantine artistic traditions. The carved wooden panels from the al-Aqsa mosque may be examples of Coptic work. The same continuation of classical and Sassanid traditions can be seen in other minor arts such as textiles and metalwork. Umayyad ceramics closely follow Byzantine forms and decoration, with minor variations. Umayyad *glass also represents technologically and stylistically a continuation of the Byzantine industry. It is largely free-blown with open and closed vessel forms and continues the light blue to blue-green colouring of Byzantine glass, with some additional shades (amber and dark green) introduced in the 8th century. In the early period of Umayyad rule some of the coinage followed Byzantine prototypes, imitating the coins of Heraclius and Constans II. The figure of the *caliph replaced that of the emperor, and Islamic inscriptions replaced Greek ones until the reform of Abd al-Malik (696–7), when epigraphic coins were introduced. The principal denominations minted were gold dinars, silver dirhams, and copper fulus.

2. *Abbasids (750–c.950)*

Under the Abbasids (from 750), Islamic architecture and arts began to evolve with greater individuality and distinction. The Abbasids built major mosques and palaces in Iraq and founded the city of Samarra, but there is little evidence for important building in Syria and Palestine except for substantial rebuilding of the al-Aqsa mosque. Secular architecture included the cisterns at Ramla and the Nilometer at *Fustat (861).

An important contribution to the potter's art was made in this period throughout the Levant: the first large-scale use of glazes for tableware (mostly jugs and bowls) and cooking vessels. Lead and tin-opacified glazes were employed in decorative techniques influenced by Chinese wares, which were now reaching Near Eastern markets. The use of clay tripods to separate bowls in the kiln enabled the potters to fire large numbers of vessels at one time without danger of them adhering to one another. The Abbasids also achieved a high standard in the art of woodcarving.

3. *Tulunids (868/869–906) and Fatimids (969–1171)*

Under the Tulunid dynasty in Egypt the mosque of Ahmad ibn Tulun north of Fustat, with its spiral minaret (rebuilt in the 14th century), was completed in 879. It was influenced by the mosque of Samarra rather than by Egyptian prototypes.

The Fatimids, *Shiites who came to power in Egypt in 969, made major contributions to urban architecture: the walls of *Cairo, several mausolea, the two large congregational mosques of al-Azhar (970) and al-Hakim (990–1013) in Cairo, and several smaller mosques. In Jerusalem the al-Aqsa Mosque was largely reconstructed after the earthquake of 1033. Excavations at Fustat have thrown light on urban domestic building in the Fatimid and Tulunid periods.

*Glass manufacture included the introduction of enamel decoration, which developed further under both the Franks and the Mamluks. It also employed the techniques of trailing, marvering, cameo, mould-blowing, and lustre and produced stamped glass coin weights. The lustre technique was effectively employed in ceramics, and the Fatimids introduced decorative incised filters in the necks of unglazed water jugs. They manufactured high-quality metalware, wood and ivory carvings, and objects carved in rock crystal. Hoards of bronze vessels have been recovered from Caesarea and *Tiberias (close to 1,000 items). Hoards of silver and gold jewellery, the former decorated with repoussé or niello, the latter with filigree and granulation, were found at Caesarea, *Jerusalem, and Tiberias.

4. *Franks (1099–1291)*

The First *Crusade occupied Jerusalem on 15 July 1099 and Frankish rule subsequently expanded over western Syria, Lebanon, and the Holy Land. Almost every aspect of the material culture of the Franks in the east was influenced, in varying degrees, by the west, *Byzantium, and the Muslim east.

The small size of the Frankish settlement and the standing army forced the Franks to rely on massively constructed fortresses. The military orders became particularly adept at constructing technologically innovative and powerful structures which could withstand sieges and enable them to retain and administer their lands. Numerous surveys of *castles have been undertaken, and excavations have uncovered the remains of the castles of Arsuf, Atlit, Belmont, Belvoir, *Krac des Chevaliers, Karak, Montfort, and Safed. In many of these castles defensive techniques, such as the use of machicolation, were adopted from Byzantine and Muslim fortifications. Ongoing excavations are uncovering a castle building site, the Templar castle of Vadum Jacob north of the Sea of Galilee, which was destroyed in 1179 while still under construction.

An important architectural achievement was the construction of several hundred churches, the foremost being the new church of the *Holy Sepulchre, which adopted, with certain changes, the Romanesque pilgrimage-church plan used in the churches on the route to and at *Santiago de Compostela. With some other exceptions, such as the octagonal church of the Ascension in Jerusalem and the twelve-sided castle church at Atlit, most Frankish churches were tri-apsidal basilicas in the Romanesque and, after the mid 12th century, the Gothic styles. In other urban architecture (markets, bath houses, and private dwellings) the eastern influence is prominent in design and decoration, alongside typically western Romanesque and Gothic elements.

Frankish rural settlement, now known to have been on a larger scale than was once believed, was nonetheless limited in both the number of settlers and the period in which it was possible for the Franks to occupy unfortified sites. Surveys and excavations have revealed that in both their administration of the largely Muslim countryside and in their own settlements the Franks employed western-type buildings and village plans. For administration they built local versions of the European manor house and *maison forte*. For their settlements they adopted the western street-village.

The Franks imported ceramics and purchased local wares but were apparently not involved in ceramic manufacture. The kingdom of Jerusalem imported ceramics from Cyprus, Port St Symeon (the port of Antioch), Syria, Egypt, Byzantium, southern Italy and Sicily, and Spain. Ceramics were often decorated with Christian designs like mounted knights, women in western dress, crosses, and heraldic shields. Muslim influence is prominent in the technology of much of this production.

The Franks minted gold, silver, and bronze coins, the basic currency unit being the gold bezant, an imitation of the Fatimid dinar of al-Amir (until 1251). The silver *deniers and bronze obols displayed legends in Latin and various representations including the Tower of David and the Holy Sepulchre. The Franks also minted *seals and lead tokens.

Glass was manufactured in the coastal region north of *Acre. This was also one of the regions where sugar cane was grown and where sugar refineries were built. Excavations have uncovered a glass factory (Somalariyya) and a sugar refinery (Khirbat Manot). One of the lasting contributions of the crusader period was the production of cane *sugar as a full-scale industry.

In other areas research has been conducted on textiles, burial techniques, human bones (to study the effects of disease and battle injuries), and soil from latrines (to provide information on contemporary intestinal disorders).

5. Ayyubids (1171–1250)

The Ayyubids came to power with the overthrow of the Fatimids, reinstating *Sunni Islam in Egypt and Syria. *Nur al-Din sent a Kurdish general, Shirkuh, and his nephew *Saladin to Egypt, aiming to unite Syrian and Egyptian resources in the holy war (*jihad*) against the Frankish states. Within two years Saladin had become independent sultan of Egypt, and after Nur al-Din's death he united Egypt and Syria and began to attack the Frankish states in earnest. Consequently, much of the architecture of this dynasty was of a military nature (Ajlun, Qalat Nimrud, the citadels at Aleppo and Damascus, and defensive works in Jerusalem). The desire to spread Sunni Islam can be seen in the establishment of theological colleges (**madrasahs*) such as the converted church of St Anna in Jerusalem and in the transformation of al-Azhar in Cairo and many buildings in the main Syrian centres into Sunni institutions. Though the Ayyubids were a comparatively short-lived dynasty, they constructed some important buildings like the citadel in Cairo and built a series of road-stations (*funduqs/khans*) on the routes connecting Syria and Egypt.

6. Mamluks (1250–1517) and early Ottoman rule (16th century)

The Mamluks, freed slaves of Turkish or *Mongol origin who had converted to Islam, came to power by overthrowing the Ayyubids. Under Sultan *Baybars, they defeated the Mongols at Ayn Jalut (1260) and began a systematic occupation and destruction of Frankish towns and castles, culminating in the fall of Acre in 1291. The Mamluks contributed to the material culture of the region in architecture and in fine and minor arts. In Jerusalem they built *madrasahs*, caravanserais (*khans*), markets (*suqs*), and bath houses, in a distinctive architectural style that included extensive use of carved panels, striped masonry (*ablaq*), stalactite-like decoration (*muqarnas*), and joggled inlays.

In 1517 the Ottomans ousted the Mamluks in the Near East. A major building project carried out by Sulayman the Magnificent between 1538 and 1541 was the reconstruction of the defences of Jerusalem. The exterior of the Dome of the Rock was decorated with Iznik tiles. In Cairo the mosque of Sulayman Pasha was built in 1528, and in Damascus Sulayman's architect Sinan built the Tekiyya complex (mosque, kitchens, and pilgrims' camping grounds) in 1555. AJB

D. Behrens-Abouseif, *Islamic Architecture in Cairo: An Introduction*, supplements to *Muqarnas* vol. 3 (1989).

A. J. Boas, *Crusader Archaeology: The Material Culture of the Latin East* (1999).

——*Jerusalem in the Time of the Crusades* (2001).

N. Brosh, *Jewellery and Goldsmithing in the Islamic World* (1987).

M. Burgoyne, *The Architecture of Islamic Jerusalem* (1976).

—— and D. Richards, *Mamluk Jerusalem: An Architectural Study* (1987).

K. A. C. Cresswell, *Early Muslim Architecture* (1969).

E. Ettinghausen and O. Grabar, *The Art and Architecture of Islam, 650–1250* (1997).

J. Folda, *Crusader Art in the Twelfth Century* (1995).

R. W. Hamilton, *The Structural History of the Aqsa Mosque: A Record of Architectural Gleanings from the Repairs of 1938–42* (1949).

——*Khirbat al-Mafjar: An Arabian Mansion in the Jordan Valley* (1959).

D. Hill, *Islamic Architecture and its Decoration AD 800–1500* (1967).

R. Hillenbrand, *Islamic Architecture: Form, Function and Meaning* (1994).

H. Kennedy, *Crusader Castles* (1995).

M. Meinecke, *Die mamlukische Architektur in Ägypten und Syrien (648/1250 bis 923/1517)*, 2 vols (1992).

A. Petersen, *A Gazetteer of Buildings in Muslim Palestine* (2001).

D. Pringle, 'Church Building in Palestine before the Crusades', *Crusader Art in the Twelfth Century*, ed. J. Folda (1982), 5–46.

——'Crusader Castles: The First Generation', *Fortress*, 1 (1989), 14–25.

——'Crusader Jerusalem', *BAIAS* 10 (1991), 105–13.

——*The Churches of the Crusader Kingdom of Jerusalem*, vol. 1 (1993).

——*Secular Buildings in the Crusader Kingdom of Jerusalem: An Archaeological Gazetteer* (1997).

——*Fortification and Settlement in Crusader Palestine* (2000).

J. Sauvaget and M. Ecochard, *Les Monuments Ayyubides de Damas* (1938–50).

archaeology: Low Countries and Frisian islands/coastlands The MA in the Low Countries began with the collapse of Roman Imperial rule here, accompanied, mainly in the 3rd to the 5th century AD, by *migrations. Subsequently, the Franks (formerly partly Frisians?) achieved a high level of tribal organization in the south, leading to early state formation, while the new Frisians (partly Danes) began to follow suit over much of what are now the Netherlands north of the former *limes*, especially the *terpen* zone. The Saxons proper, in archaeological terms at least, are known mostly from their building traditions on the sandy soils in the east. The ethnic term 'German' is archaeologically not really relevant to the Early Middle Ages. The 9th-/10th-century *Vikings are discussed below.

1. Migration
2. Hoards and coins
3. The Vikings
4. Water

1. Migration

A problem of the Migration Period has been confusion over the continuity of settlement locations without, necessarily, continuity of occupation or exploitation. The *Dark Ages remain obscure; in the north, especially, the 4th and 5th centuries are in deep shadow. The *terpen* zone, a few centuries later one of the most densely populated areas of Europe, may well have been deserted between AD 350 and 425.

Frankish splendour is best known from the grave goods in and around the tomb of King Childeric at Tournai; in the north we lack these graves, but do have the equally rich royal brooch of Wijnaldum, of which several more fragments were recently found, and the jewellery workshop there. *Dorestad, the main port of northwestern Europe in its time, was contested between Franks and Frisians in the 7th and early 8th centuries, lying between these marked spheres of influence in the Dutch central river area. Much of the more recent Dorestad excavation results (palisades, gold hoards, and so forth) have yet to be published. The early medieval cemeteries in the south of the Low Countries, below the *limes*, are mostly of the Frankish tradition; in the north they seem to be, until the full Conversion, a medley of habits and rituals. Fortunately, more has become known through recent excavations such as Oosterbeintum (*Frisia), though Frisian practices remain quite unclear.

2. *Hoards and coins*

A Frisian gold horizon of the 7th century is evident mostly in hoards, not grave goods. The controlled Wijnaldum excavations have provided new insights into socio-economic circumstances in early medieval Frisia. They confirm the importance of gold in the 6th and 7th centuries; at the same time the role of coins has had to be thoroughly reconsidered. The span of time between production and deposition appears to be far greater than formerly believed. Roman silver and bronze coins were circulating up to Carolingian times. Coins could be halved or quartered; scales were abundant. In the Dutch (Frisian) *terpen* zone this system must have been introduced by immigrant Danes. The Franks have left us many written records, but what exactly was going on north of the Dutch river area was largely beyond their horizon, and what they do report is heavily biased. For early Frisian history we depend mainly on archaeology, which indicates that Tacitus' Frisians had a different ethnic background from those we later see fighting and trading with the Franks, and intermarrying, even royally. The Franks finally overwhelmed the Frisians in the course of the 8th century, but it did not take long for the political landscape of this part of northwestern Europe to change again.

3. *The Vikings*

An interlude often referred to is the periodic presence of Vikings, mainly in the 9th century. They are reported to have looted and burned both in the north and in the south, but archaeology is unable to confirm this. Thanks to metal-detector finds, the Viking presence in the Netherlands is now better known from hoards and stray finds, although still on a modest scale. Apart from sword deposits in rivers, these finds all seem to have a non-military character. Hoards such as those found on the former island of Wieringen seem to point to Vikings settling peacefully in local communities. They either left or quite quickly assimilated. This 'old boys' network' of Franks, Frisians, and Danes/Vikings, with their common roots, ought to include the Anglo-Saxons too: especially the Jutes who crossed the North Sea to settle within what would become England.

4. *Water*

These contacts around the North Sea draw our attention to another common factor: water. The orientation of the Holocene parts of the Low Countries was not primarily to land, but to the sea. The archaeology of the maritime cultural landscape is a prominent topic of recent research. Intertribal and international traffic usually went by water, which remained important in the ensuing period as well.

In the 9th, 10th, and 11th centuries, different areas were confronted with very diverse aspects of water. After the early expansion of the Frankish empire, a period of fragmentation set in. Battle and conquest continued, but expansion was now mostly directed internally. In the Low Countries, this proved as successful as the former outward expansion. This period is known as that of the great reclamations. On the sandy soils two key processes intensified. Deforestation created more arable land. The use of heather turf mixed with (sheep) manure and urine to fertilize fields became common practice. Rapid demographic growth (and thus more income) resulted; unfortunately, it also led to the extension of blow sands. Climatically, the 10th-century dry period did not help. The groundwater level fell; in the coastal area the Younger Dunes, as they are known geologically, were forming; and in many areas people had to abandon their fields in search of water. Nevertheless, the use of turf and dung persisted in many areas, resulting in relatively isolated regions that were self-sufficient to a greater extent than before, but generally quite poor. Slowly, specialization became essential, but no market system was available. Only in the south (for example *Flanders) could fledgling urbanization appear. Others, who can largely still be called Frisians, sought to expand into the waterlogged (former) raised bog areas behind the coastline. These raised bog areas, metres above sea level, had their own groundwater level, but were oligotrophic. By digging ditches (to lower the groundwater), building dykes (to keep out the water from unreclaimed areas), and manuring, these could be turned into arable land. This process took place first on a private, entrepreneurial basis, later under the supervision of various lords and bishops. Lowering the water table caused rapid subsidence of the surface through oxidation and shrinkage. The by now densely populated areas could no longer grow their own crops, and there were insufficient markets for their dairy products (13th/14th centuries). The 'non-governmental communities' did not all abandon their homesteads, but took up the old Frisian practice of trade, and went to the Baltic to get their corn. In the aptly named region of Waterland in Holland, for instance, farming became at best of secondary importance. The coastal areas now needed trade, but they had had to dam their main rivers. Thus the 13th-century dam towns, such as *Amsterdam, *Rotterdam, and many others, came into existence, where ships were towed or goods transferred. Only after the arrival of large numbers of religious refugees from the south in the 16th and 17th centuries could the countryside return to dairy farming. With southern (formerly Frankish) money this produced the familiar landscape of cattle and windmills. Whereas religion had helped the Franks conquer the Frisians in the Early MA, now the 'Franks' contributed to bring the Golden Age of the 'Frisians' (17th century). All these processes led to the relocation of settlements, in different circumstances, creating an extensive soil archive, which is unfortunately inadequately protected for future research by the law.

It is hard to define an end of the MA in the Low Countries; archaeological interest in many aspects of society continues well into the Age of Industry. JMBo

J. C. Besteman, J. M. Bos, D. A. Gerrets, H. A. Heidinga, and J. de Koning, eds, *The Excavations at Wijnaldum: Reports on Frisia in Roman and Medieval Times*, vol. 1 (1999).

J. C. Besteman, J. M. Bos, and H. A. Heidinga, eds, *Medieval Archaeology in the Netherlands: Studies Presented to H. H. van Regteren Altena* (1990).

J. M. Bos, *Landinrichting en archeologie: het bodemarchief van Waterland* (1988).

H. A. Heidinga, *Medieval Settlement and Economy North of the Lower Rhine: Archaeology and History of Kootwijk and the Veluwe (the Netherlands)* (1987).

Reiss Museum, Mannheim, *Die Franken: Wegbereiter Europas vor 1500 Jahren: König Chlodwig und seine Erben* (1996).

archaeology: Russia, Belarus, and the Ukraine

At the beginning of the MA, the eastern landmass of Europe was divided between two ethno-cultural blocs. The northern part, forest and steppe, was occupied by sedentary peoples: Slavs, Balts, and Finns. The steppes north of the Black Sea were under the control of nomads, Huns, and Bulgars, primarily Turkic-speaking although with an Ugric minority.

1. Slavs, Balts, and Finns
2. Scandinavians
3. 10th through 13th centuries
4. 14th through 17th centuries
5. The steppe peoples

1. *Slavs, Balts, and Finns*

In the steppe and the forest zone, the 5th- to 7th-century Slavs are represented by three archaeological culture groups. The *Prague culture (Prague-Korčak), identified with the 6th-century Sclavenes, is found in the area between the *river Dnieper and the middle *river Danube. The Pen'kovka culture, associated with the Slavic-speaking Antes, is located in the steppe strip between the Donetz and the lower Danube. The third, the Koločin culture, is found in the Dnieper basin, north of present-day *Kiev.

A number of Slavonic culture groups emerged in the 8th century. In the west, between the Dnieper and the *Carpathians, appeared the Luka-Rajkoveckaja culture, a descendant of the Prague culture. There are some similar sites in both southern Belarus and in present-day Moldova. These represent the Slavonic peoples known as the Poljane, Drevljane, Dregoviči, Uliči, and Volynjane in the Russian chronicles and external historical records. A further influx of Slavs penetrated east of the Dnieper in the late 7th and first half of the 8th century, where they left sites of the Volyncevo type, the Romny-Borševo culture, which formed during the 8th century. This took in the area east of the Dnieper and the basins of the upper Don and upper Oka, with the cultures of the Severjane, Radimiči, and Vjatiči groups. Further north, in the basin of the upper Dnieper and western Dvina, the so-called Long Barrow (*kurgan*) culture, with a major Balt component, corresponds to the Slavonic Kriviči group. Further north still, in the Ilmen' and Lake Ladoga area, a culture of large barrows called *sopka* is associated with the Slovenes of *Novgorod.

The lands of central and northern Russia were occupied during the early MA by Finnish groups. Most of them were assimilated by the Slavs, and constitute one ancestral component of the medieval Russian people. Others, notably the Mordves of the Volga and the Karelians of northern Russia, have preserved their linguistic and cultural differences.

2. *Scandinavians*

According to the tradition recounted in the medieval Russian chronicles, groups of Scandinavian origin known as *Varangians or *Rus' and led by Rurik entered eastern Europe during the 9th century and took possession of Kiev, the future capital of 10th- to 13th-century Russia. Archaeology clearly reveals a Scandinavian presence from the middle of the 8th century onwards at Ladoga. From the late 9th/early 10th century cultural elements of Scandinavian origin are evident in the material of the *pre-urban settlements and in the burials of elite warriors, at Novgorod (Rjurikovo Gorodisče), Kiev, *Chernigov, Gnezdovo (near *Smolensk), Šestovicy (near Chernigov), Timirevo (near Jaroslavl'), amongst others. The archaeological evidence traces the integration of the Scandinavians into the Slavonic milieu during the 10th century.

3. *10th through 13th centuries*

The archaeological culture of 10th- to 13th-century Russia, known as Kievan Rus', represented by excavations in towns and a large number of rural settlement sites and burials, is essentially Slavonic in character. Alongside the cemetery excavations, however, rural settlement archaeology also bears witness to the presence and assimilation of non-Slavonic groups. In the north these were Finnish groups, whose cultural affinity remains visible in their burial practices and female costume into the 13th century. In western Belarus, in the Niemen basin, archaeology reveals the gradual integration of Baltic groups. In Ukraine, in the middle Dnieper basin, the footprints of the Turkic steppe peoples, confederates of the princes of Kiev, are their numerous barrows.

Large-scale urban excavations have been carried out both in major centres, such as Kiev, Novgorod, Chernigov, Polotsk, *Pskov, *Rostov, *Suzdal', *Vladimir, Vitebsk, and Grodno, and in numerous small towns (Izyaslavl', Peresopnica, Volkovyisk). The remains of the earliest pre-urban settlements, linked to international trade, have been found from the 9th century at Ladoga, Rjurikovo Gorodišče (later Novgorod), Gnezdovo (later Smolensk), and Sarskoe (near Rostov Velikij). During the 10th and the earlier 11th centuries these centres either transformed into medieval towns or were superseded by alternative centres, adapted to the promotion of the power of the Kievan princes and subsequently, in the 12th and 13th centuries, under the control of local princes, descendants of the *Rurikid dynasty. Research has revealed the high level of urban culture in Kievan Rus'. Building in the Russian towns was primarily in timber, which is well preserved in waterlogged conditions in Novgorod, Ladoga, and Kiev. At Novgorod, excavation has notably revealed the presence of wooden roadways. These towns were the major centres of production and trade, as well as the centres of political power. The discovery in Novgorod of nearly a thousand birchbark documents of the 11th to 15th centuries is evidence of a high level of education amongst the urban population. These texts constitute an important source for the reconstruction of urban life in medieval Russia.

4. 14th through 17th centuries

The conversion of Kievan Rus' by the Byzantines imparted an eastern Christian character to this culture. This is the foundation upon which the medieval Russian, Ukrainian, and Belarusian culture of the 14th to 17th centuries was formed. The study of architectural monuments other than churches is advanced, especially in towns such as Kiev, Novgorod, Smolensk, and Vladimir. Strong influence from Byzantine architecture has been revealed, albeit alongside the emergence of local schools during the 12th century.

5. The steppe peoples

The medieval archaeology of the steppe peoples of Russia and Ukraine is well developed. In their periods of migration, the nomads left distinctive burials across the steppe. This applies to the Huns, the Bulgars, the Hungarians, the Pechenegs, and the Polovtsy. However, the birth of the great steppe empires, such as the kingdom of the Khazars or the Tatar *Golden Horde, was accompanied by a relatively higher level of settlement, resulting in the appearance of highly developed urban cultures. In the basin of the Don and Donetz, the 8th century saw the formation of the Saltov-Majackoe culture, representing the Alan and Bulgar population of the Khazar kingdom. This culture features large fortified settlements and cemeteries. The Saltov culture disappeared in the 10th century under the assaults of nomads from the east (Magyars and Pechenegs) on the one hand and of the Rus' under the Kievan prince Svjatoslav on the other.

From the 11th century to the early 13th, the Turkic-speaking peoples of the steppe—Pechenegs and Polovtsy—are known through their many *kurgans*. At the same time the Turkic Bulgars of the Volga became sedentary. Their advanced medieval culture is known principally through excavations of their towns, such as Bulgar (the capital), Bilyar, and Suvar.

In 1223–40 the Tatars seized the steppe. They delivered a lethal blow to the culture of the Volga Bulgars and conquered Russia. In the 13th and 14th centuries the Tatar Golden Horde was the superpower of eastern Europe. Tatar barrows are profusely scattered across the steppe of Russia and Ukraine. But the archaeology of the Tatars is known above all from the excavations of the towns of the Volga such as Saraï-Berke. These towns reveal the extensive sedentarization of a large number of the steppe nomads as well as the strong influence of the Islamic culture of central Asia.

The Tatar invasion of 1237–40 was the end of Kievan Rus'. Russia suffered an insurmountable shock: Kiev was razed to the ground, as were many other centres, and the lands were depopulated. However, archaeology shows that northern Russia, particularly Novgorod, preserved its high level of economic and cultural life. The lands of Belarus and Ukraine, the latter devastated by the Tatars, were invaded from *Lithuania and integrated in the 13th–15th centuries into that Grand Duchy. In central and northern Russia the principalities (such as *Moscow, Tver', and Riazan) and urban republics (Novgorod and Pskov) preserved their autonomy and their Russian dynasties, albeit under Tatar protection. Towards 1480 the great princes of Moscow succeeded in reuniting the Russian territories under their rule, and freed them from the guardianship of the Golden Horde. The archaeological evidence bears witness to the gradual establishment of medieval Russian ('Muscovite Russian'), Ukrainian, and Belarusian cultures, and of significant demographic and economic growth from the 15th century onwards. MK

Arheologija Ukrainskoj SSR, vol. 3 (1986).

V. D. Baran, ed., *Etnokul'turnaja karta Ukrainskoj SSR v I tys. n.e.* (1985).

Drevnaja Rus': Byt i kul'tura (1997).

Drevnaja Rus': Gorod, zamok, selo (1985).

Finno-ugry i balty v epohu srednevekov'ja (1987).

M. Kazanski, A. Nercissian, and C. Zuckerman, eds, *Les centres proto-urbains russes entre Scandinavie, Byzance et Orient* (2000).
S. A. Pletneva, *Kočevniki južnorusskih stepej v epohu srednevekov'ja* (2003).
V. V. Sedov, *Vostočnye slavjane v VI–XIII vv.* (1982).
—— *Drevnerusskaja narodnost'* (1999).
Stepi Evrazii v epohu srednevekov'ja (1981).

archaeology: Scandinavia (including Finland and Estonia) **and Iceland** The broad geographical expanse from *Iceland to Estonia and from Denmark to the North Cape encompasses vastly different topographies, climates, vegetation, and ways of life, from mixed agriculture in the south to reindeer herding by *Sámi in northern Fenno-Scandinavia, with fishing, fur-trading, and iron production often supplementing farming and herding. Diverse types of archaeological evidence across this region are difficult to summarize.

1. History of the discipline
2. Chronologies
3. Burials
4. Votive offerings and hoards
5. Fortifications
6. Settlements, towns, and trade
7. Christianization and urbanization

1. *History of the discipline*

Scandinavian archaeology began with antiquarian interest in stray finds and standing monuments, including *rune stones. Beginning in the 19th century, prehistorians concentrated on excavating cemeteries, and the periodization of the Three-Age system (Stone, Bronze, and Iron Ages) was initiated by the Dane Christian Jürgensen Thomsen and refined by the Swede Oscar Montelius. Settlement archaeology was a later concern except for a few notable sites. In Estonia, socialist agendas emphasized connections with Russia rather than Scandinavia. Later medieval historical archaeology was born in the 1960s, largely as a result of rescue excavations in urban areas. Indeed, much recent research is indebted to the construction of highways, pipelines, and public structures. Norwegian and Swedish archaeology tends toward the theoretical, while Danish and Finnish research traditions are more descriptive.

2. *Chronologies*

What is called the early MA in Continental Europe is part of the prehistoric or proto-historic Iron Age in Scandinavia; 'medieval' indicates the Christian period following the Viking Age, *c.*1050, or as late as the 12th and 13th centuries in Finland and Estonia. Scandinavia is such a diverse area that chronological terminologies vary considerably. In Denmark, the period AD 1–400 is called the Roman Iron Age (after imports of Roman prestige goods), 400–800 is the Germanic Iron Age, and 800–1050 is the *Viking Age. Norway's periodization is similar, except that 400–600 is called the Migration period (reflecting migrations in the rest of Europe, not Scandinavia) and 600–800 is the Merovingian period (due to limited Frankish contacts), and the Viking Age is considered the last phase of the Iron Age. The Migration period (400–550) in Sweden is followed by the Vendel period (550–800), after an eponymous site in Uppland. In Finland, the Viking Age is succeeded by the crusade period (1050–1150) in western Finland, to as late as 1300 in Karelia. In Estonia, the years 450–800 are called the Middle Iron Age, and the Late Iron Age includes both the Viking Age (800–1050) and the Latest Iron Age (1050–1225), succeeded by the *crusades of the medieval period. Finally, Scandinavian archaeology in Iceland commences with the traditional Viking Age settlement date of *c.*874.

3. *Burials*

Iron-age *burials differ from medieval, with cremation and inclusion of grave goods common before conversion, while inhumations become more frequent under Christian influence. The largest Roman Iron-age cemetery in Denmark at Møllegårdsmarken on Fyn has over 2,000 cremation graves. Although many graves—especially cremations—are invisible on the surface, some are marked by stone settings or earthen mounds, as at Viking Age *Birka in Sweden where *c.*3,000 graves reflect diverse burial practices including cremations and interments (in wooden coffins or chamber graves) rich with remains of textiles, dress accessories, weapons, tools, and household goods. *Ship burials at Tune, *Oseberg, Gokstad, and Borre in Norway also contain abundant grave goods. Mound burials reflect several generations of Iron-age elites at Gamla Uppsala and also at Vendel and Valsgärde in Sweden, where some were inhumed in boats while others were cremated. Other exceptional mounds extend from Migration period Högom in northern Sweden to Viking Age Denmark at Mammen, Søllested, and Jelling. Burial in birchbark wrappings was typical of Sámi burials as at Vivallen in Jämtland. Cremation marked by stone settings was the most common Finnish and Estonian burial rite except in western Finland as at Luistari where a large inhumation cemetery was used from the Merovingian through the crusader period. Weapons and spears are commonly found in Finnish burials, but precious metals are mostly lacking. Recent excavations are beginning to illuminate burial traditions of the Middle Iron Age in Estonia, while Late Iron-age Estonia is characterized by sand barrows and stone-marked inhumation and cremation graves.

4. *Votive offerings and hoards*

Besides metalwork found in graves, large numbers of weapons and coins were intentionally deposited in the ground or in watery contexts. Roman Iron-age and early Germanic Iron-age–Migration-period weapons and military equipment (and sometimes preserved wood) have been discovered in bogs at Vimose, Illerup, Kragehul in Denmark;

Thorsbjerg and Nydam in Schleswig; Sjörup and Sösdala in Skåne; and Skedemose on Öland. These finds may reflect ritual sacrifice and offerings to gods following battle successes. Viking Age metal hoards including Arabic dirhams as well as AS and German coins were hidden in the ground apparently in times of unrest, especially on the Baltic islands of Bornholm, Öland, *Gotland, and Åland. Other hoard finds include Sámi metal depositions such as in Jämtland and Härjedalen in Sweden and Hedmark in Norway.

5. Fortifications

Defensive structures include hillforts, ringforts, and military enclosures. Thousands of walled fortified strongholds were constructed in hilly terrain beginning in the Migration period in Norway and in eastern Sweden, and extending into the latest Iron Age as at Linnavuori (which means 'hillfort'), Finland, and Varbota, Estonia. Such hillforts controlled transportation routes and served as refuges in turbulent times. Stone and earthen ringforts were built at Eketorp, Ismanstorp, Gråborg on flatter ground on the Baltic island of Öland, and a 2 km-long stone wall was constructed at Torsburen on Gotland. Banked enclosures surrounded geometrically arranged longhouses at Aggersborg (Jutland), Fyrkat (Jutland), Nonnebakken (Fyn), Trelleborg (Zealand), and Trelleborg (Skåne). These Danish structures are dated around 980 dendrochronologically and may have housed military garrisons. Tree-ring dating also elucidates construction stages of the *Danevirke, a 30 km-long defensive earthwork built across the Jutlandic peninsula to defend Denmark from the Franks.

6. Settlements, towns, and trade

Solitary farmsteads in the west and north contrasted with villages in the south and east. Examples of excavated farms with longhouses, feasting hall, and boathouses include chiefly estates such as Åker and Borg in Norway, which were inhabited for centuries. At Vorbasse in Jutland, the location of longhouses shifted only slightly over a thousand years. Other Danish settlements include Lejre in Zealand, Sejlflod in Jutland, and Sorte Muld on Bornholm. Stone enclosures and foundations of twenty-four Migration-period buildings at Vallhagar on Gotland comprise one of the largest Iron-age settlements, and longhouses characteristic of southern Scandinavia have been excavated at Gene in northern Sweden. Well-preserved Iron-age farms are also found in Rogaland and on Andøya in Norway. A structure at Hofstaðir on Lake Mývatn in Iceland's interior is interpreted as a feasting hall or pagan temple. Few Iron-age settlements have been discovered in Finland beyond Åland, as hunting and fishing remained important and swidden agriculture required frequent shifting of settlements. Hut platforms indicate seasonal dwellings for northern Sámi hunters and fisher folk.

Some farms with craftworking centres matured into seasonal market sites with long-distance trade connections. *Metalworking and other crafts were carried out at Helgö in Sweden, where exotic goods including a Buddha statuette were discovered. An early craft production centre and harbour at Lundeborg was paired with an elite centre at Gudme in Fünen. Early market and harbours were located at Åhus and Löddeköpinge in Scania, and Paviken and Fröjel on the coast of Gotland. Trade was indebted to developments in ship construction documented from early ship burials at Haithabu (*Hedeby), Nydam, and Kvalsund; later Viking Age burials at Tune, Oseberg, Godstad, and Borre; and trading vessels scuttled at Skuldelev, Denmark. The wooden causeway at Ravning Enge, dendrochronologically dated to 979, provides unusual evidence of land transport. Trading sites with permanent craftworkers developed into proto-towns or ports-of-trade, such as Ribe where Rhenish glass was discovered among 8th-century jewellery and bead-making workshops. Hedeby in Schleswig, Kaupang (Skiringssal) in Norway, and Birka and Sigtuna in Sweden were significant Viking Age market centres. The Finnish settlement at Varikkoniemi was town-like, and Pirkkala (named after Birka) was a fur-trading centre. Finns traded fish across the Gulf of Finland to obtain grain from Estonia, and Tallinn emerged as a seasonal trading place. Fishing was important along coastal Arctic Norway, and metalwork finds attest to Sámi contacts across the north to Karelia.

7. Christianization and urbanization

During conversion to Christianity, there was economic continuity. Viking Age chieftains' farms were incorporated into medieval systems as fishing in Iceland and in the Norwegian Lofoten and Vesterålen Islands became more intensive, providing stockfish for Europe. Throughout Scandinavia, early towns such as *Uppsala, *Lund, Hamar, *Trondheim, and Viborg became centres of craft specialization, ecclesiastical power, and economic power, as evidenced by coin minting. Additional towns developed as commercial centres, including Odense, *Roskilde, and Århus in Denmark; Lödöse, Visby, Skara, and eventually Stockholm and Kalmar in Sweden; *Bergen, *Oslo, and Stavanger in Norway; Turku (Åbo) and Viipuri (Viborg) in Finland; and Tartu and Tallinn in Estonia.

Medieval archaeology is often considered urban archaeology, yet stone churches began to replace rural wooden ones, too. Besides cathedrals and churches, other masonry structures include *castles, which partly replaced the functions of Iron-age hillforts that fell into disuse, and *monasteries built with church revenues. Monasteries betray close connections with their founders, both west and east, as demonstrated by Orthodox monasteries at Valamo and Konevitsa in Karelia. Contacts between Scandinavia and the eastern Baltic continued, especially from Gotland to Estonia's island Saaremaa, and fur-trading interactions between Sámi and Scandinavians continued. Cemeteries shifted from chieftains' manors to churchyards, except in Estonia where village cemeteries were used into early modern times. Analysis of human remains from cemeteries, for example, Löddeköpinge (Skåne), Västerhus (Jämtland), and Helgeandsholmen (in Stockholm), provides information about the demography of medieval populations.

While research traditionally has focused on artefact studies and chronologies, publication of excavations—Iron Age and medieval—is vital. The application of scientific methods should be increasingly applied to general discussions of power and gender relations, ethnicity and identity, and the lives of individuals in the past. A broad theoretically informed archaeology of Scandinavia has yet to be written. *See also* CHILDREN IN SCANDINAVIA; CONVERSION OF SCANDINAVIA; SCANDINAVIA; SCANDINAVIAN CHURCH. NLW

E. Baudou, *Norrlands Forntid—ett historisk perspektiv* (1992).
G. Bigelow, *The Norse of the North Atlantic* (1991).
G. Burenhult, *Arkeologi i Sverige, vol. 3. Samhällsbyggare och handelsmän* (1984).
——*Arkeologi i Norden* (1999).
H. Clarke and B. Ambrosiani, *Towns in the Viking Age* ([2]1995).
W. W. Fitzhugh and E. I. Ward, eds, *Vikings: The North Atlantic Saga* (2000).
J. Graham-Campbell, ed., *Cultural Atlas of the Viking World* (1994).
L. Hedeager, *Iron-Age Societies* (1992).
K. Helle, ed., *The Cambridge History of Scandinavia*, vol. 1 (2003).
J. Jensen, *Danmarks Oldtid: Yngre Jernalder og Vikingetid 400–1050 e. Kr.* (2004).
V. Lang, ed., *Archaeological Research in Estonia, 1865–2005* (2006).
N.-K. Liebgott, *Dansk Middelalder Arkæologi* (1989).
B. Myhre, 'Chieftains' Graves and Chiefdom Territories', *Studien zur Sachsenforschung*, 6 (1987), 169–87.
U. Näsman, 'The Germanic Iron Age and Viking Age in Danish Archaeology', *Journal of Danish Archaeology*, 8 (1989), 159–87.
B. Nilsson, ed., *Kristnandet i Sverige* (1996).
P. Purhonen, *Kristinuskon saapumisesta Suomeen* (1998).
K. Randsborg, *The Viking Age in Denmark* (1980).
E. Roesdahl, *Viking Age Denmark* (1982).
B. Sawyer and P. Sawyer, *Medieval Scandinavia: From Conversion to Reformation circa 800–1500* (1993).
D. J. Shepherd, *Funerary Ritual and Symbolism: An Interdisciplinary Interpretation of Burial Practices in Late Iron Age Finland* (1999).
T. Sjøvold, *The Iron Age Settlement of Arctic Norway*, 2 vols (1967–1974).
B. Solberg, *Jernalderen i Norge* (2000).
J.-P. Taavitsainen, *Ancient Hillforts of Finland* (1990).
T. L. Thurston, *Landscapes of Power, Landscapes of Conflict: State Formation in the South Scandinavian Iron Age* (2001).
P. Urbanczyk, *Medieval Arctic Norway* (1992).
I. Zachrisson, 'A Review of Archaeological Research on Saami Prehistory in Sweden', *Current Swedish Archaeology* 1 (1993), 171–82.

archangel *See* ANGELS.

archbishop *See* CLERGY.

archdeacon *See* CLERGY.

archdiocese Ecclesiastical province under the jurisdiction of an *archbishop and consisting of several *dioceses. Their borders were usually based on imperial Roman administrative units. Aside from their priestly functions, archbishops' primary duties included visitation of dioceses, convening provincial synods, and supervision of vacant sees. MBKo

R. W. Southern, *Western Society and the Church in the Middle Ages* (1990).

archers Every medieval army utilized missile troops, almost always archers. Both mounted archers, especially prominent among forces that originated in the steppes, and infantry archers appeared frequently on medieval battlefields. Most came from the lower or urban classes, although they were not always irregular troops; some were also hired as mercenaries. KDV

J. Bradbury, *The Medieval Archer* (1985).

Arches, Court of The spiritual court for the province of *Canterbury situated in the parish church of St Mary-le-Bow (*de Arcubus*), a *London peculiar within the archbishop's jurisdiction. As a court of original jurisdiction, Arches could initiate causes, but was far busier as an appellate court for the province's *dioceses. Court officials heard various cases including complaints between *clergy, disputes over ecclesiastical property rights, moral lapses of clergy and laity alike, and the disposition of legacies. WJD

D. Logan, *The Medieval Court of Arches* (2005).
O. Reichel, *The Canon Law of Church Institutions*, vol. 1 (1922).

architects, architecture A diversity of styles emerged in both secular and religious architecture between *c.*500–*c.*1500 in Europe, Asia, and Northern Africa. This development was a result of combining the needs of local populations with the cultural and economic values of the regions. In addition to the Byzantine Empire with its influential early architectural forms, the Islamic monuments emerged as the important stylistic contribution to the overall building activities. In western Europe, the *Carolingian dynasty based its designs on the earlier Merovingian structures, and without its successive Ottonian dynasty, the Romanesque and Gothic periods would not have been exceptionally innovative in shaping the variety of their regional styles.

1. Byzantine
2. Islamic
3. Merovingian
4. Carolingian
5. Ottonian
6. Romanesque
7. Gothic

1. Byzantine

The emperor Justinian (527–65) through his *patronage of architecture established the unique features of Byzantine

monuments. There are two basic categories of Byzantine constructions. *Ashlar masonry was typical for Syria, Palestine, Asia Major, and in parts of Armenia and Georgia. The second category of building was brick and rubble, used predominantly in Constantinople (Istanbul), the western coast of Asia Minor, the Balkans, and *Italy. The superb example of the church of St Sophia (Hagia Sophia) in Istanbul was constructed in 532–7 by Anthemius of Tralles, geometrician and theorist, and *Isidorus of Miletus, geometrician, both recorded as *mechanikoi*. The other category of Byzantine masters consisted of *architectones* or master builders. After the 6th century there are no preserved records of any Byzantine architect.

2. *Islamic*

In the century after the death of the prophet *Muhammad (*c*.632), the Muslims derived their unique style synthesizing the arts of the Byzantines, the Copts, the Romans, and the Persians. Islamic architecture developed in parts of *Egypt and North Africa, Spain and Persia in predominately religious structures that were based on early Byzantine models like the *mosque of *Umar (Dome of the Rock, Qubbat-al-Sakhra) in *Jerusalem, constructed in 691–2 under the patronage of the Umayyad *caliphate (661–750). In the middle of the 8th century, the last of the Umayyads arrived in Spain, and the Great mosque of *Córdoba was begun in 785. The culture of Islamic Spain reached its climax in Moorish style. No records of known architects of the early monuments have been preserved.

3. *Merovingian*

The first Germanic-Frankish dynasty (*c*.500–751) favoured large *basilicas with *timber roofs and *bell towers. A typical example is the 7th-century *baptistery of St John in *Poitiers, made of stone and brick with classical capitals. Remains of other Merovingian monuments have been found in *Auxerre, Jouarre, and *Lyons.

4. *Carolingian*

The Frankish king *Charlemagne became a new (Holy) *Roman emperor *c*.800, uniting the vast territory stretching from Spain to *Germany and *Italy. As a patron of the arts, he commissioned *Odo of Metz to build him a *chapel in *Aachen, dedicated *c*.805, with prominent use of luxurious materials, rich ornamentations, and heavy structures loosely based on early Byzantine models. The development of monastic orders required complex structures such as those seen in the design for the ideal monastery of *St Gall (*c*.820) in Switzerland.

England was never part of the Carolingian empire. Under the patronage of King *Alfred the Great the fortified strongholds known as *burhs* (boroughs) were erected as defence structures against the *Viking raids. Later, King *Edward 'the Elder' built the system of massive fortresses all over the territory of *Wessex.

5. *Ottonian*

Charlemagne's successors established the Ottonian kingdom, which lasted from 936 to 1002. Influenced by Carolingian forms, Ottonian architecture consisted of massive and symmetrical basilicas of which the church of St Michael in *Hildesheim (1001–36) is a very good example. It was built by *Bernward, who was elected bishop of Hildesheim in 993 and was canonized in 1193.

6. *Romanesque*

The architecture of western Europe from about AD 1000 to about the late 1100s was called Romanesque, meaning 'in the Roman style'. It was the invention of masonry vaulting that gave a birth to a new design of building known as the monumental *cathedral. To support these heavy stone *vaults, architects used massive walls and piers, creating a typical plan that treated the entire structure as a complex composed of smaller units, called *bays. The *nave in Romanesque churches was higher and narrower than in earlier structures and included clerestory windows. Doors and *windows were usually covered by round or pointed *arches. These openings were small and decorated with mouldings, carvings, and *sculptures.

In Italy, there is a great diversity of Romanesque architectural styles, and the architects continued to use decorative elements such as classical capitals, multicoloured marble, open arcades, colonnades, *galleries, and carved façades.

In *France, Romanesque architecture is characterized by various vaulted styles. Provençal churches have pointed *domes and façades decorated with tiers of wall arcades filled with sculpture. In central France, architects built structures containing a long choir with side aisles and an *ambulatory with radiating chapels. In Burgundy the barrel-vaulted and multi-aisled basilica became a favourite design. Norman architects developed an original style that was based on monuments with complex groined vaulting systems, and façades with flanking towers.

In Germany, Romanesque structures were often planned on a monumental scale. Many of them are extremely tall and have an *apse on both ends. Numerous round or octagonal towers were especially popular.

In England, after the *Norman Conquest in 1066, and from about 1120 to 1200, builders erected monuments with heavy walls and compound piers, rectangular apses, double *transepts, and deeply recessed portals.

7. *Gothic*

It was the design of the abbot *Suger, who remodelled the abbey church of *St-Denis in Paris, thus making this monument the symbol of the beginning of Gothic architecture, which flourished in the Catholic countries of Europe until the end of the 15th century, with the highest achievements in France and England. It is characterized by the elongated silhouettes of tall pillars and spires, emphasis on height in

interior spaces, pointed arches, rib vaulting, and the flying buttress. It developed a great complexity of forms noticeable in all types of secular and religious structures.

Gothic architecture in France may be divided into four periods: Early Gothic (1130–90), Lancet Gothic (1190–1240), Rayonnant Gothic (1240–1350), and Late or Flamboyant Gothic (1350–1520).

Gothic architecture in England is divided into three styles: Early English (1200–1275), Decorated (1300–1375), and Perpendicular (1400–1575).

The complexity of structures in Romanesque and Gothic architecture required precise division in craftsmanship. The *masons were trained as stone and brick masons, while other specialists included carpenters, *glass specialists, and master carvers who were working in materials such as *wood and *metals. The masons were the highest ranked of all labourers regarding their skills, although no record about the actual training of masters and their working methods exists before the 16th century. It was in the 13th century in France that the profession of architect was defined more precisely as the prominent role of someone who acted as a supervisor and did not participate in actual physical work. The most prominent architectural theoreticians of the times were St *Thomas Aquinas and *Villard de Honnecourt. *See also* ART AND ARCHITECTURE: BYZANTINE / CAROLINGIAN / GOTHIC / ISLAMIC / MEROVINGIAN / OTTONIAN / ROMANESQUE; CASTLES, FORTIFICATIONS, AND FORTRESSES. RB

F. B. Andres, *The Medieval Builder and his Methods* (1993).
E. Brownie, *Romanesque Architecture* (2005).
F. Bucher, 'Medieval Architectural Design Methods, 800–1560', *Gesta*, 11 (1972), 37–51.
K. Conant, *Carolingian and Romanesque Architecture, 800–1200* (1992).
P. Crossley, 'Medieval Architecture and Meaning: The Limits of Iconography', *The Burlington Magazine*, 130 (1988), 116–21.
J. D. Dodds, B. F. Reilly, and J. W. Williams, *The Art of Medieval Spain AD 500–1200* (1993).
T. Frisch, *Gothic Art, 1140–c.1450: Sources and Documents* (1987).
J. Harvey, *The Master Builders: Architecture in the Middle Ages* (1971).
N. Hiscock, *The Wise Master Builder: Platonic Geometry in Plans of Medieval Abbeys and Cathedrals* (2000).
J. Hoag, *Islamic Architecture* (2004).
D. Knoop and G. P. Jones, *The Medieval Mason* (1967).
S. Kostof, *A History of Architecture: Settings and Rituals* (1995).
U. Laule, *Architecture of the Middle Ages*, ed. R. Toman (2004).
C. Mango, *Byzantine Architecture* (1985).
R. Marks, *Gothic: Art for England 1400–1547*, ed. R. Marks and P. Williamson (2003).
C. McClendon, *The Origin of Medieval Architecture: Building in Europe, AD 600–900* (2005).
R. Ousterhout, *Master Builders of Byzantium* (1999).
N. Pevsner, 'The Term "Architect" in the Middle Ages', *Speculum*, 17 (1942), 549–62.
C. Radding, *Medieval Architecture, Medieval Learning: Builders and Masters in the Age of Romanesque and Gothic* (1992).
L. R. Shelby, 'The Role of the Master Mason in Medieval English Building', *Speculum*, 39 (1964), 307–403.
R. Stalley, *Early Medieval Architecture* (1999).
H. M. Taylor and J. Taylor, *Anglo-Saxon Architecture*, 3 vols (1965–78).
C. Wilson, *The Gothic Cathedral: The Architecture of the Great Church, 1130–1530* (2005).

architecture: Anglo-Saxon The building traditions in England following the Germanic resettlements in the mid 5th century and extending to the era following the *Norman conquest in the late 11th and early 12th centuries, with the Danish invasions of the 9th century providing a key point of separation.

The Germanic tribes settled a landscape that still housed substantial Roman stone construction. However, archaeological excavations reveal that Anglo-Saxons relied on two basic, well-formed traditions of *timber construction. One consists of an excavated sunken floor, a structure that resembles traditional Grubenhäuser found on the continent, though it remains unclear whether the excavated area was used for habitation or storage. Remains of rectangular, post-built halls have also been found, which appear to have been built simply or with complex suspended floors and carpentry depending on social context. Large and complex secular buildings were built for royal use, as evidenced by the finds at *Yeavering, in *Yorkshire. Early churches were also constructed in wood, with *Lindisfarne and Yeavering providing notable archaeological evidence.

Construction in stone was closely associated with the Roman church. *Bede records that *Benedict Biscop sent for *masons from Gaul to build churches at the *monasteries of *Wearmouth and Jarrow; crypts at *Hexham and Ripon attest to other ambitious structures built by *Wilfrid, archbishop of York. The early missionaries in *Kent looked back to continental traditions as well, witnessed by traces of early churches at *Canterbury and the surviving nave of St Peters, Bradwell (7th century). By the mid 8th century, perhaps influenced by *Carolingian developments, Anglo-Saxons undertake more ambitious designs based on the aisled *basilica, evidenced by the surviving church at *Brixworth and the excavations at Cirencester.

The Danish invasions of the late 9th century redirected interest toward defences and town planning (*burhs* or boroughs), though surviving churches at Deerhurst and *Repton and reports of King *Alfred's project at Athelney demonstrate a continued vitality in ecclesiastical building.

The political stability established by Alfred's successors and the advent of the monastic reform movement brought greater wealth and ambition to the architectural design. Prosperity enabled the construction of churches such as St Mary's, Breamore, and at Greensted (a unique survival of a wooden church). Reformers, having spent time in

continental houses, introduced Carolingian features such as westwork and multiple chapels at the east end. The extension of the Old Minster at *Winchester, housing the important cult of St *Swithun, is an important example of this trend. The political unrest of the early 11th century, caused by renewed *Viking invasions that ended with the capture of the English throne by the Danish king *Cnut, corresponded with a slowdown in building. AS architecture is seen to lag behind developments on the continent until the construction of *Westminster Abbey, heavily influenced by contemporary Norman models, by *Edward 'the Confessor' in the mid 11th century. BCW

E. Fernie, *The Architecture of the Anglo-Saxons* (1983).
R. Morris, *The Church in British Archaeology* (1983).
H. M. Taylor, and J. Taylor, *Anglo-Saxon Architecture*, 3 vols (1965–78).

Archpoet (*c.*1130–*c.*1167) Anonymous German poet known for his 'Confessions of *Golias', included in the **Carmina Burana*, and nine other surviving poems celebrating worldly pleasures. Little is known of his life beyond what is revealed in his poems. He notes that he was from the knightly order, and he most likely acquired a classical education and clearly knew the Roman poets and the Bible. He reveals that he was a member of the entourage of *Rainald of Dassel, archbishop of *Cologne and archchancellor of Frederick I 'Barbarossa', and travelled throughout *Germany and *Italy with Rainald. Although a servant of the archbishop, he refused Rainald's request to write an epic poem on Frederick's Italian campaigns. He did, however, write a hymn praising the emperor that used Christological language. His poems are characterized by parody of *sermons and confessions and often include requests for money, food, or clothing. One poem contains a moving description of Christ's death, but concludes by declaring that if the reader has compassion for Christ then he should also take pity on the Archpoet. His most famous verse proclaims his desire to die in a tavern so that wine may be near his mouth at that moment while angels sing 'May God have mercy on this drinker'. MCF

F. Adcock, ed. and tr., *Hugh Primas and the Archpoet* (1994).
P. Dronke, 'The Archpoet and the Classics', *Latin Poetry and the Classical Tradition*, ed. P. Godman and O. Murray (1990), 57–72.

archpriest A priest who occupies a position of pre-eminence among other priests. From the early 5th century this senior priest of a city or rural area performed many of the bishop's liturgical and governmental functions in his absence or during a vacancy. The Council of Trent (1545–63) replaced the archpriest title with the office of '*vicar forane*' ('dean' in English), but it continues in Eastern Orthodoxy and Eastern-Rite Catholicism. *See also* BYZANTINE RITE; CLERGY. JCH

A. Amanieu, 'Archiprêtre', *Dictionnaire de Droit Canonique* (1935), vol. 1, 1004–26.
M. C. Miller, *The Formation of a Medieval Church: Ecclesiastical Change in Verona, 950–1150* (1993).

Arculf Little-known, late-7th-century Gallic bishop, who visited *Palestine, *Egypt, and *Constantinople (*c.*679–82). A storm-battered return took him to *Iona where Abbot *Adomnán (679–704) used Arculf's experiences as the basis of 'De Locis Sanctis', a description of the holy places in the early years of the Umayyad *caliphate. *See also* JEWISH LITURGICAL POETRY; LOCUS SANCTUS. JWr

Adamnan, *De Locis Sanctis*, ed. D. Meehan (1958).

ard *See* ARATRUM.

Ardennes, counts of This four-generation line, descending from **Wigericus** (d. 916/19) and **Kunigunde** and ending with **Gozelo** *c.*1028, held a countship based on the old *Carolingian pagus of Ardennes and the advocacy of *Stavelot. The line was part of an interrelated cluster of families known as the house of Ardennes, which included the counts of Verdun, Bar, and *Luxembourg. The house, which monopolized affairs in Lorraine between the 10th and 12th centuries and played important roles elsewhere, produced prominent abbesses, many bishops of Laon, *Metz, *Rheims, and Verdun, and the dukes of Lorraine and *Bavaria. HH

Arderne, John (1307/8–*c.*1380) A craft-trained surgeon, who states in his *Practica* of fistula-in-ano that he practised in Newark in Nottinghamshire, England, from 1349, moving to *London in 1370. He claims to be the only *surgeon who can perform the operation for fistula-in-ano and lists his patients. His writings are notably attentive to the practicalities of treatment and make considerable use of case histories and visual illustrations. PMJ

J. Arderne, *Treatises of fistula in ano haemorrhoids and clysters*, ed. D'A. Power (1910).
P. Jones, 'Arderne, John (*b.* 1307/8, *d.* in or after 1377)', *ODNB*, vol. 2, 368–9.

Arditi, Andrea (di Ardito) (*fl.* 1324–38) Tuscan goldsmith from Antella. His sole surviving work is the enamelled and gilded silver *reliquary bust of St Zenobius from 1331 (*Florence cathedral), which was commissioned during Francesco da Cingoli's tenure as bishop. Arditi pioneered the *basse-taille* or translucent *enamel technique in northern Tuscany. *See also* GOLD AND SILVER. FB

C. Strocchi, 'Lo smalto traslucido a Firenze: prime osservazioni sulla bottega di Andrea Arditi', *ASNSP* 3/18 (1988), 137–50.

arenga Diplomatic term for the introductory formula setting a *charter within a religious, moral, or legal framework, often drawing upon scriptural, patristic, or liturgical

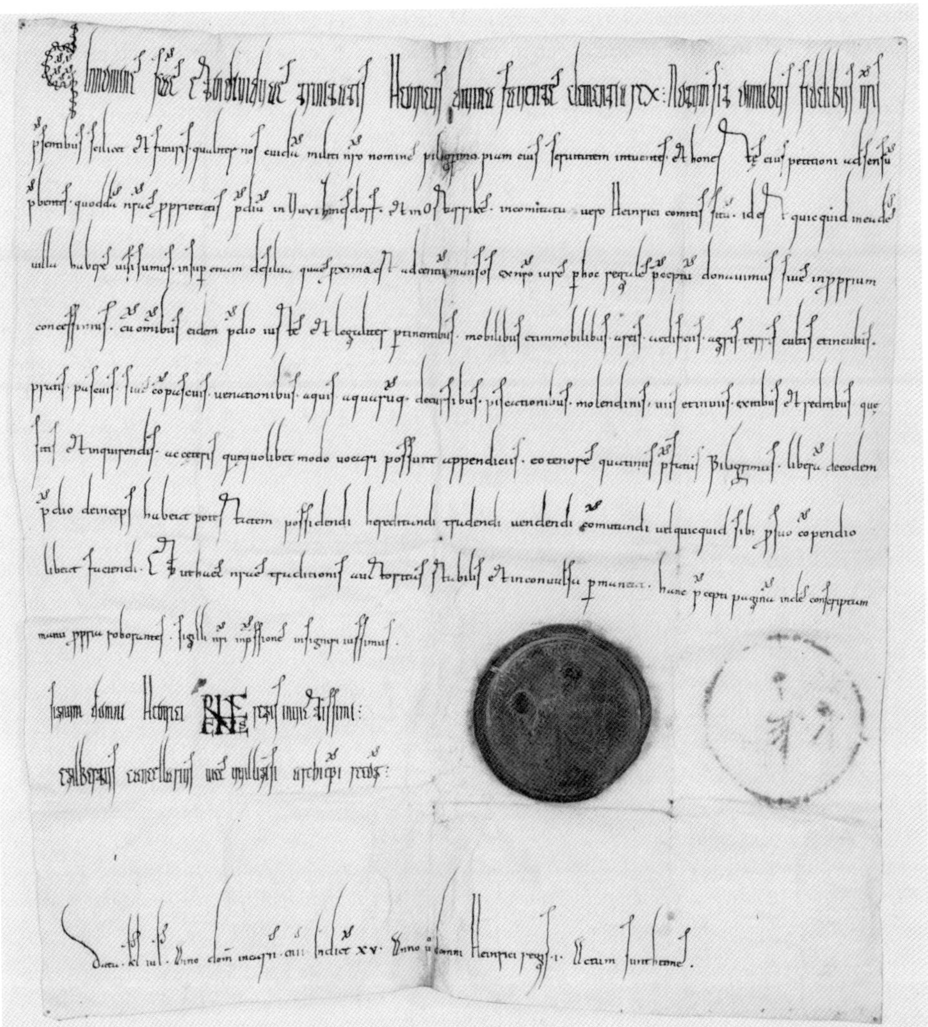

Detail from the text of an arenga or narratio.

material. In the charters of ecclesiastical and lay authorities, the 'harangue' usually proclaims an entitled lord's legitimacy and divine mandate; in monastic charters, it expresses a patron's desire for mercy, forgiveness of sins, and salvation. HH

Arethas of Caesarea (d. 932/944) Archbishop, book collector and scholar. Arethas played a part in Byzantine politics by opposing Leo VI's plans on a fourth marriage (the Tetragamy). But his fame rests mainly on the remnants of his library: eight volumes are preserved, all of them with scholia in Arethas' own hand. BBy

Arethas, *Scripta minora*, ed. L. G. Westerink, 2 vols (1968–72).
N. G. Wilson, *Scholars of Byzantium* ([2]1996).

Arezzo A Tuscan city located in the upper valley of the Arno river, Arezzo flourished in the 13th century as a Ghibelline *commune rival to *Siena and *Florence. An important Etruscan centre, then a Roman colony, Arezzo became rapidly Christian and one of the first *dioceses in Tuscany: the second bishop of Arezzo was San Donato, the 4th-century evangelist who later became the diocese's patron. Dominated by the Ostrogoths between 480 and 530, likely occupied by the *Lombards by 599, Arezzo remained nonetheless under the influence of Roman culture until the early 8th century, since its bishops were of Latin descent, and there existed a cathedral school. During the 10th and 11th centuries the area was under bishops loyal to the emperors, and civic and cultural achievements are documented. Communal consuls were elected in 1098. Ghibelline feudal families provided bishops and wielded power. In the early 13th century the *university was founded, and important poetic and scientific works were written in the Tuscan vernacular. Internal rivalries and Arezzo's defeat in the battle of Campaldino won by Florentine *Guelphs in 1289 contributed to a decline, briefly interrupted under the rule

of Bishop Guido Tarlati (1312–27). Sold to Florence in 1337, Arezzo rebelled unsuccessfully from 1408 to 1530. *See also* ITALY AND SICILY. CC

R. Black, *Studio e scuola in Arezzo durante il Medioevo e il Rinascimento* (1996).
M. Falciai, *Storia di Arezzo* (1928).
V. F. Pardo, *Arezzo* (1986).
U. Pasqui, ed., *Documenti per la storia della città di Arezzo nel medio evo*, 4 vols (1899–1937).

Argenteuil (monastery) A 7th-century women's abbey near Versailles, developed under *Carolingian patronage. Few records survive, none for the century before *Heloise was a lay student there *c.*1115. After *Abelard's castration she took vows at Argenteuil and eventually became the last abbess there. In 1129 Abbot *Suger of *St-Denis fought the bishop of Paris for control of Argenteuil and won, replacing the nuns with monks under a prior. The priory then steadily declined until in the 16th century it was a mere ruin with no monks, only a commendatory to collect its remaining revenues. DHW

DHGE, vol. 4, 22–32.

Argyros, Isaac (1300–*c.*1375) Byzantine monk, astronomer, mathematician, and student of Nicephorus *Gregoras. Argyros compiled numerous astronomical texts, most of them based on Persian works. He also wrote an introduction to the production of an astrolabe and *commentaries on ancient astronomers such as Ptolemy as well as three treatises against the theologian *Gregory Palamas. *See also* THEOLOGY, BYZANTINE. IG

I. Ševčenko, *Society and Intellectual Life in Late Byzantium* (1981).
A. Tihon, *Études d'astronomie byzantine* (1994).

Arialdo, St (d. 1066) A Milanese church reformer who helped lead the Pataria movement against *simony and clerical unchastity. Ariald was murdered in 1066 by his opponents; the pope declared him a martyr in 1067. PGJ

H. E. J. Cowdrey, 'The Papacy, the Patarenes and the Church of Milan', *TRHS* 18 (1968), 25–48.
O. Zumhagen, *Religiöse Konflikte und kommunale Entwicklung* (2002).

Arianism An understanding of Arianism may be pieced together from surviving documents, though many were written by its opponents, notably *Athanasius and *Hilary of Poitiers. Arius (*c.*260–336) and his followers believed the Son or Incarnate Logos was a created being and therefore not coeternal with the Father. Controversy arose over this and other complex trinitarian issues. Still, Arians shared with orthodox Christians practices like baptizing in the name of all three Persons of the *Trinity.

Arian beliefs were rejected by Constantine I, who convened the Council of Nicaea (325) where the term *homoousios* defined the oneness of substance or essence between the Father and the Son. Constantius II and Valens, however, tolerated Arianism before it was officially suppressed under Theodosius I at the Council of Constantinople (381).

Meanwhile, Ulfila (Wulfila) had begun converting the Visigoths to Arian Christianity in 341. Other barbarian peoples, such as the Vandals, Alamanni, and *Burgundians, likewise received this form of Christianity. Persecutions occurred between Arian and orthodox Christians under their rule, particularly by the Vandals in Africa. The *barbarians came to orthodox Christianity over the centuries; the *Lombards as late as the end of the 7th century. *See also* CREEDS: APOSTLES', ATHANASIAN, NICENE; FILIOQUE, DISPUTE OVER. RCE

H. Chadwick, *The Early Church, The Pelican History of the Church*, vol. 1 (1967; rev. ed. 1993).
A. C. Gregg and D. Groh, *Early Arianism: A View of Salvation* (1981).
M. Simonetti, *La crisi ariana nel IV secolo* (1975).
B. Williams, *Arius: Heresy and Tradition* (2002).

Aribo (*fl.* *c.*1068–78) German author of a treatise *De musica* introducing two Christological diagrams, the *caprea* and the *figura circularis*, framing his treatment of the tetrachords, *modes, modal pitches, and division of the *monochord, and placing these in the context of a *Neoplatonic music-theoretical *ordo naturalis*. *See also* MUSIC THEORY. GIC

Aribo, *De musica*, ed. J. Smits van Waesberghe (1951).

Aribonid dynasty Succession of *Bavarian nobles first appearing in documents in the late *Carolingian period. Members of the family were known to have made donations to the monasteries of Göß and Seeon. The most famous of the line was *Aribo, archbishop of *Mainz, who witnessed the transition from Ottonian to Salian imperial rule, favouring the former. Because of his refusing to crown Queen Gisela, Aribo's relationship with Conrad II, the first Salian ruler, became strained. SMW

T. Reuter, *Germany in the Early Middle Ages c.800–1056* (1991).
L. Sträter, *Aribo Erzbischof von Mainz 1021–1031* (1953).

Aribo of Mainz (d. 1031; r. 1021–31) (archbishop) A primary supporter of Conrad II, he crowned him in 1024 and served as his chancellor in *Germany and *Italy. Aribo brought *Ekkehard IV of St Gall to head the *Mainz cathedral school. ASC

J. Fleckenstein, *Die Hofkapelle der deutschen Könige* (1966).

Aristotelianism The modern term 'Aristotelianism', and its application to very different periods of intellectual history, suggests the idea that the central tenets of Aristotle's thought can be codified in a set of finite propositions which then establish and define a distinctive philosophical and scientific system. On this basis, one might assume that there is a recognizable phenomenon known as 'medieval Aristotelianism' and that it is appropriate for historians to classify the long and complex engagement of medieval thinkers with the ideas of Aristotle under that heading. One problem with adopting this approach is that it does not always assist us to make sense of what medieval readers were doing when they encountered Aristotle's works. For these individuals there was no such thing as the 'Aristotelianism' of the type envisaged by modern authors, but rather a body of texts such as the *Analytics*, *Categories*, *Topics*, *Physics*, *Metaphysics*, *De anima*, *Nicomachean Ethics*, *Politics*, and *Poetics*, which conditioned the scope and point of their philosophical and scientific enquiries. Seen from a pre-modern or medieval perspective, the highly suggestive term 'Aristotelianism' can refer to nothing more than the actual reading of Aristotlian texts, and engaging with Aristotle's ideas and teaching rather than to something like an abstraction or codification of 'Aristotelian' principles.

The texts and methods of Aristotle permeated and defined several aspects of medieval learning for many hundreds of years. Since a plethora of Aristotelian ideas, concepts, and arguments became part of a common philosophical and scientific vocabulary and heritage, they cannot be considered the property of a general 'school'. Even explicit theoretical engagements with Aristotle range from deployments of single phrases or sentences through to more sustained criticism of a particular range of arguments, and a single writer may reveal all these relations to Aristotle over works in different fields of learning or even in the same work. Thus we find Aristotelian ideas being used and disputed in very different intellectual contexts, ranging from the writings of masters in the Arts Faculty of *Paris such as *Siger of Brabant, *Boethius of Dacia, and much later John *Buridan, to the varied and contested appropriation of Aristotelian principles in the work of theologians such as *Albertus Magnus, *Bonaventure, *Thomas Aquinas, and *Duns Scotus.

Mention of the theologians brings us to the very complex interaction of Aristotelian thought with the Jewish, Islamic, and Christian faiths. The difficulties faced by Christian writers of the so-called 'high scholastic' period are perhaps best known to us, even though they may be said to be similar to those problems addressed by Islamic and Jewish writers in earlier times. Almost all of the putative 'Christian Aristotelians' in the Latin West were members of the *clergy. Most spent what we would now term their professional lives in teaching and writing, not just the *seven liberal arts and *philosophy, but *sacra doctrina* or theology. Controversy remains as to whether or not and as to how much and in what form 'Aristotelian philosophy' may be found. When we try to isolate what we now demarcate as 'philosophy' from other fields of learning, we face similar problems. Medieval students of Aristotle studied a vast range of topics that he broached in his encyclopedic corpus, from logic to poetics, from the physics of moving bodies through the species of plants and animals to the movement of the heavens above. For medieval writers this vast expanse of learning was all 'Aristotelian', and all equally 'philosophy', and even though it was thought to inform further theological enquiry, it was deemed to be inferior to that knowledge gained from the study of God's revelation.

Nowhere is this tendency more apparent than in the writings of an individual who has been deemed by posterity to be a great 'medieval Aristotelian', Thomas Aquinas. Despite a tendency on the part of his modern interpreters to claim that Thomas 'baptized' Aristotle by forcing the latter's ideas into the Procrustean bed of Christian theology, Thomas used Aristotle's ideas as a means to an end. Concerned to win his way through to the discovery of the truth about a particular issue, Thomas was prepared to trump Aristotle's teaching, whether it be on *hylomorphism or else on human happiness, whenever he deemed it was inadequate to meet the requirements of *sacra doctrina* or the needs of the pressing theological questions of his time. His attitude to Aristotle, though deferential, is never slavish, and he maintains a cautious and highly critical sense of the ways in which Aristotle can and cannot be appropriated to theological discourse. In this respect his writings represent an approach to the texts of Aristotle that remained a conspicuous feature of medieval intellectual life. MWFS

B. Dod, 'Aristoteles Latinus', *The Cambridge History of Later Medieval Philosophy*, ed. N. Kretzmann, A. Kenny, and J. Pinborg (1982), 45–79.

C. Lohr, 'The Medieval Intepretation of Aristotle', *The Cambridge History of Later Medieval Philosophy*, 80–98.

F. E. Peters, *Aristoteles Arabus* (1968).

F. van Steenberghen, *Aristotle in the West: The Origins of Latin Aristotelianism*, tr. L. Johnson (French original, 1946) (1955).

M. W. F. Stone, 'The Debate on the Soul in the Second Half of the Thirteenth Century: A Reply to William Charlton', *Whose Aristotle? Whose Aristotelianism?*, ed. R. W. Sharples (2001), 78–104.

arithmetic *See* MATHEMATICS.

Ari Þorgilsson (d. 1148) The first author of narrative prose in Icelandic. Born 1067/8 at Helgafell and spent his youth at Haukadalr, where he was educated. Virtually nothing is known about his later life, except that he was ordained priest. The only surviving work that can with certainty be ascribed to Ari is a short history of Iceland, the *Libellus Islandorum*, often called *Íslendingabók* ('Book of Icelanders'), written between 1122 and 1133. KW

J. Benediktsson, ed., *Íslendingabók—Landnámabók* (1968).

S. Grønlie, tr., *Íslendingabók—Kristni saga* (2006).

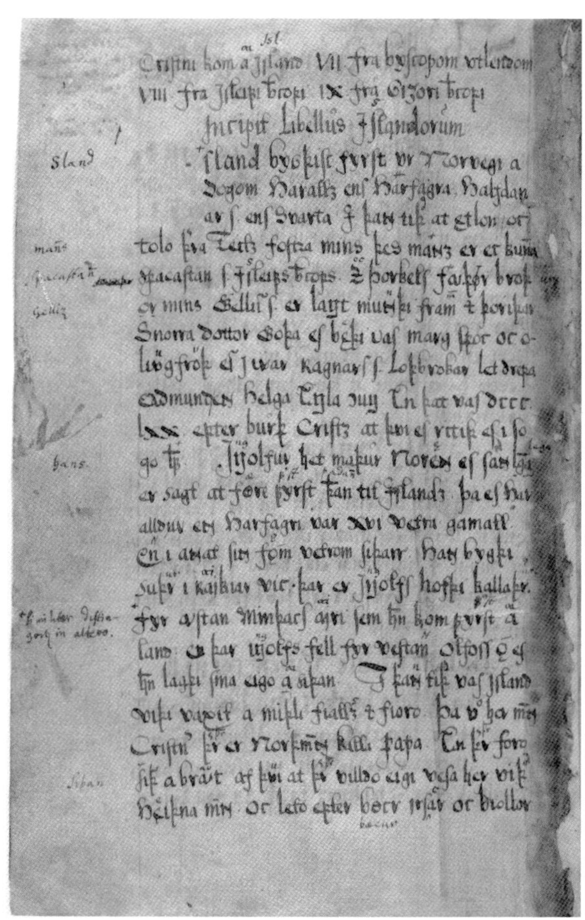

Page from Ari Þorgilsson's *Íslendingabók*.

Arkel, Jan van, bishop of Utrecht (1342–64) Appointed to *Utrecht by the pope as the Dutch candidate, by 1355 he had largely recovered the resources that Utrecht had lost. In 1364 he was transferred to Liège, where in 1373 he accepted the 'Peace of the Twenty-two'. DN

H. P. H. Jansen, 'Holland, Zeeland en het Sticht 1100–1433', *Archief voor de geschiedenis van de Katholieke Kerk in Nederland*, 2 (1982).

Ark of the Covenant Gold-sheathed wooden box containing the tablets inscribed with the Law, guarded by cherubim. The Ark was related to cosmological and Old Testament themes, the church, Christ, and the Virgin. JBo

L. Brubaker, 'The Elephant and the Ark', *DOP* 58 (2004), 175–95.
K. Weitzmann and H. Kessler, *The Frescoes of the Dura Synagogue and Christian Art* (1990).

Arles (city, kingdom) Situated at the mouth of the Rhône delta in southern *France, Arles was an important administrative centre in the late Roman Empire. After a period of decline under the Franks, it became the capital of an independent kingdom after the break-up of the *Carolingian empire. It was integrated into the (Holy) *Roman Empire in 1033, and the remnants of the kingdom were ceded to France in 1378. From the 14th century onwards, Arles's importance in the region was eclipsed by nearby *Avignon. EFJ

A. Hofmeister, *Deutschland und Burgund im früheren Mittelalter: eine Studie über die Entstehung des Arelatischen Reiches und seine politische Bedeutung* (1963).

Arma Christi The Latin term meaning 'weapons of Christ' and referring to the symbolic representations of the instruments of Christ's Passion (for example, nails, *crown of thorns). The *Arma Christi* were the weapons with which Christ gained victory over *death. They functioned as mnemonic signs for meditation and *devotional images on the whole Passion narrative. *See also* CHURCH HISTORY; CROSS; CRUCIFIX. LRa

R. Suckale, 'Arma Christi', *Städel-Jahrbuch*, 4 (1977), 177–208.

Armagh Archiepiscopal see in northern Ireland. Armagh's abbots claimed special authority as St Patrick's heirs because the see was founded by St *Patrick near an ancient ritual site. With 12th-century reforms, the abbot of Armagh became archbishop and primate of the Irish church; the primacy was lost to *Dublin in the 14th century. PGJ

N. B. Aitchison, *Armagh and the Royal Centres in Early Medieval Ireland* (1994).
D. N. Dumville, *St Patrick, AD 493–1993* (1993).

Armagh, Book of Irish MS of the early 9th century. Once believed to be the work of St *Patrick, the Book of *Armagh contains some of the earliest examples of OIr, including several documents related to the life and works of the saint. WHS

L. Bieler and F. Kelly, eds, *The Patrician Texts in the Book of Armagh* (1979).
J. Gwynn, ed., *Liber Ardmachanus: The Book of Armagh* (1913).

Armagnac, house of The county of Armagnac gained prominence during the *Hundred Years War. The name Armagnac was attached to one of two political parties in the early 15th century. Bernard VII of Armagnac's followers supported *Charles VII, but his heirs sporadically opposed the French kings. EARB

C. Samaran, *La maison d'Armagnac au XVe siècle* (1907).

Armagnacs and Burgundians Nicknames of the opposing political factions that waged intermittent civil war during the reigns of *Charles VI and *Charles VII. After the onset of Charles VI's schizophrenia (1392), Charles's brother Louis, duke of Orléans, developed a rivalry, first with his uncle Philip the Bold, duke of *Burgundy (d. 1404), and then with Philip's son John the Fearless, who had Louis murdered

Aerial view of the amphitheatre and surrounding city of Arles.

on 23 November 1407. The ensuing conflict was resolved by the Peace of Chartres (9 March 1409), whereby the king pardoned John and declared that the murder had been committed for the good of the kingdom. By royal command, Louis's sons, Charles, duke of *Orléans, and Philip, count of Vertus, swore not to pursue vengeance, but on 15 April 1410 an alliance (the 'League of Gien') was formed against Burgundy by the dukes of Berry, Orléans, and *Brittany, and the counts of Armagnac, Alençon, and Clermont. In addition, a marriage was arranged between Charles of Orléans and Bonne, daughter of Bernard, count of Armagnac. Open war was prevented by the Peace of Bicêtre (2 November 1410), the result of the king's threat to confiscate all property of members of the League. Charles of Orléans opened new hostilities on 30 January 1411 with the kidnapping of the lord of Croy, a Burgundian ambassador. The king ordered Croy's release, but Charles refused. On 14 July, Charles and his brothers sent the king a list of complaints (the Manifesto of Jargeau), in which they declared that John's pardon in 1409 had been against divine law, and thus the oaths given at Chartres were invalid. Not waiting for the king's reply, Charles summoned his vassals for war and on 31 July sent Burgundy a defiant letter announcing that henceforth he would seek to harm him however he could. During the hostilities of summer 1411, the Parisians coined the nickname Armagnacs for the pro-Orléans faction. On 3 October the government declared Orléans and his allies rebels. Undismayed, the Armagnacs took the bridge of St-Cloud (13 October) and the town of St-Denis. On 14 October, having intercepted letters incriminating the duke of Berry as a partisan of Orléans, the royal council, presided over by the king's eldest son, Louis, duke of Guyenne, ordered the summoning of the *arrière-ban* to fight the rebels, who now officially included the duke of Berry. In November–December, Guyenne led the royal army that took Berry's castles of Etampes and Dourdan. The king led an expedition against Berry (May–July 1412) culminating in the siege of Bourges. Guyenne negotiated a treaty, Berry surrendered the keys to *Bourges on 15 July, and the peace was formalized at *Auxerre (22 August 1412). Burgundy upset the balance when, attempting to check the duke of Guyenne's anti-Burgundian policy, he incited the riot of the *Cabochiens in *Paris in April 1413. The Cabochiens fell in August 1413, and Burgundy fled Paris, which allowed the Armagnacs to increase their influence. The king, accompanied by the duke of Guyenne, led a military campaign against John the Fearless that ended with the Peace of *Arras (September 1414, finalized 22 February 1415). Guyenne sought to maintain a royalist party, independent of the Armagnacs, but his death in 1415 worked in their favour. Bernard of Armagnac, named constable of France after *Agincourt (1415), became leader of the Armagnacs after the duke of *Anjou left Paris in 1417, since Berry had died (1416) and Orléans and Bourbon, captured at Agincourt, were prisoners in England. The queen (Isabeau of *Bavaria) worked against Bernard, and in retaliation he engineered her exile. With the

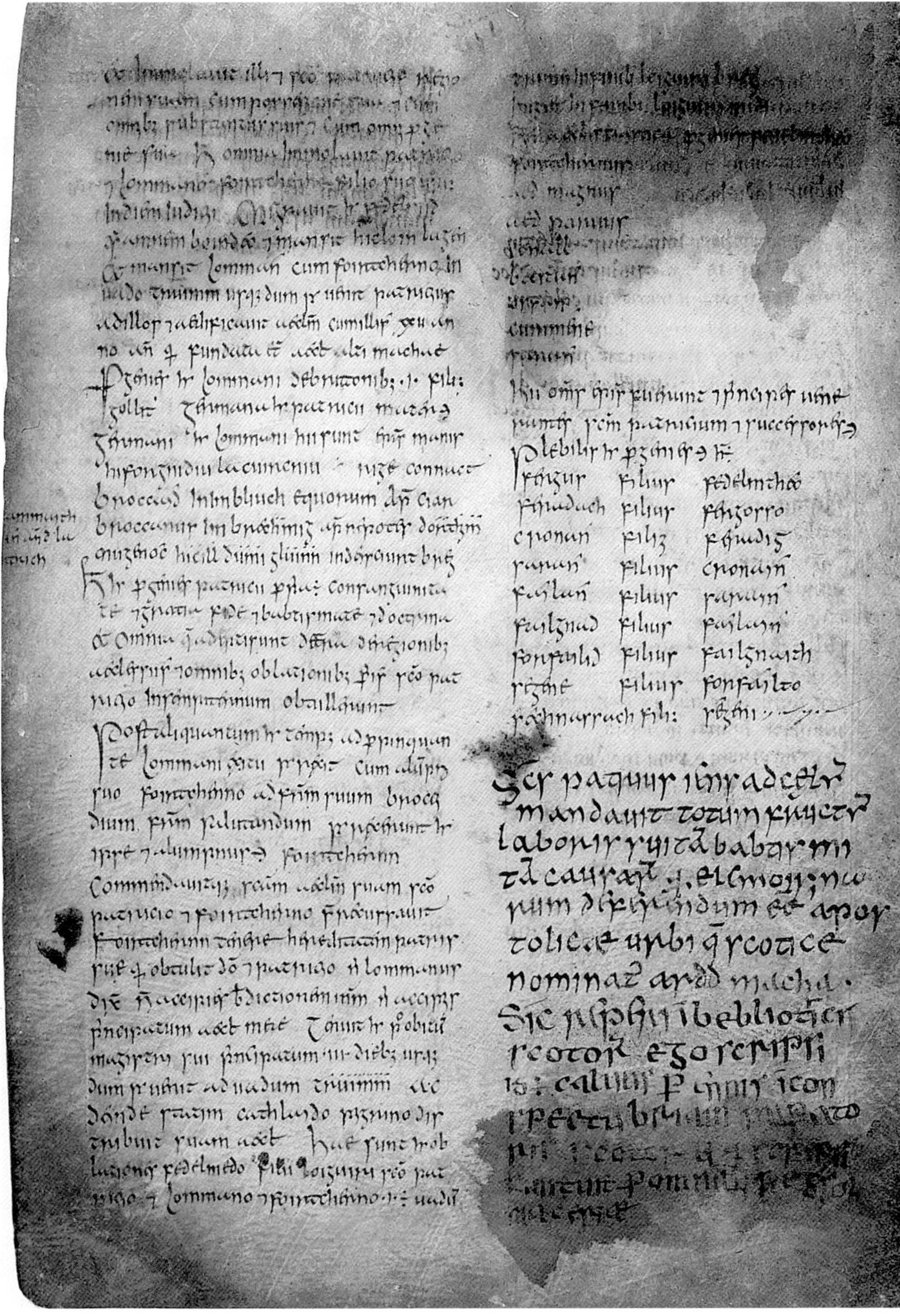

A page from the Book of Armagh.

help of Burgundy, she escaped and, claiming that the king was a prisoner of the Armagnacs, set up a rival government in *Troyes. In May 1418 the Burgundians stormed Paris, and Bernard was put to death in July, before Isabeau entered the city with Burgundy. The king's present heir (Charles VII), spirited out of Paris by an Armagnac during the May invasion, became head of the anti-Burgundian faction, which nevertheless continued to be called the Armagnacs. RCF

R. C. Famiglietti, *Royal Intrigue: Crisis at the Court of Charles VI 1392–1420* (1986).

F. Lehoux, *Jean de France, duc de Berri, sa vie, son action politique (1340–1416)*, 4 vols (1966–8).

Arme Heinrich, Der *See* HARTMANN VON AUE.

armies, Islamic Pre-Islamic Arabia, with the exception of Yemen, had no known standing armies. The first Islamic army was prepared and led by *Muhammad under the new religious obligation of *jihad*. However, it was with the early Islamic conquests that a distinction was drawn between Muslim combatants and non-combatants and that Islamic standing armies as such came into being. These armies were not settled with the conquered populations, but installed in newly established garrison cities like *Basra and Kufa in Iraq and *Fustat in *Egypt. The earliest armies were often grouped by Arab tribal affiliation, while they were paid from war spoils distributed through the *caliph's treasury. Under the Umayyads, Arab military chiefs began relying on non-Arab clients (*mawali*) and non-Muslim auxiliaries, who were exempted from paying the *poll tax. The Abbasid dynasty began using slave soldiers (*mamluk*, pl. *mamalik*), many of whom were Turks from central Asia, whose outsider, often non-Muslim, status in Islamic society ensured their allegiance to the caliph alone. However, with the passage of time, these slave soldiers became a distinct and powerful military caste, and on more than one occasion seized political power for themselves, ultimately establishing the Mamluk dynasty in Egypt (1250–1517). Slave soldiers and armies were a distinctly Muslim phenomenon and a pervasive feature of medieval Islamic military history. AHR

P. Crone, *Slaves on Horses: The Evolution of the Islamic Polity* (1980).
H. Kennedy, *The Armies of the Caliphs: Military and Society in the Early Islamic State* (2001).

armillary sphere *See* ASTRONOMY.

Armorica Roman name for the northwest peninsula of *France. Part of Celtic Gaul, Armorica was conquered by Julius Caesar in 56 BC and incorporated into the Roman province of Lugdunensis. Following the fall of the empire in the 5th century, Briton migrants from *Cornwall and *Devon settled in Armorica, from whom the area's later name *Brittany derives. ELS

L. Fleuriot, *Les origines de la Bretagne: l'émigration* ([2]1982).

arms and armour It is difficult to separate medieval soldiers from the arms they carried and the armour they wore: the *knight in shining armour with his *lance; the *Viking protected by helmet and shield, wielding a battleaxe; the English longbowman; the Genoese crossbowman. Although arms and armour could not on their own determine victory in a medieval conflict—victory and defeat was always as result of the skills and resolve of the individual warriors—they often determined strategy and tactics.

From the fall of Rome to the end of the MA, when *gunpowder weapons and plate armour appeared and proliferated, medieval soldiers used similar arms and were clad in similar armour. The *spear (of various lengths), *sword, axe, club / mace, and *bow were used as weapons, and mail armour (sometimes redundantly called chain mail), wooden shields, and metal helmets as armour.

The two oldest weapons in history are the club and the spear. Originating as only wooden, or wood and stone, weapons, by the early MA they had acquired metal heads. A club, which when metal-tipped would be called a mace, was used to crash down on opponents most often resulting in broken bones and heavily bruised muscles. Spears, with sharp-edged heads, were most often thrust at opponents, causing stabbing or slashing wounds. The ancient Greeks had lengthened the spear to as much as 21 feet during the time of Alexander the Great, but by the early MA, it was no more than eight to ten feet, a standard used throughout the MA. Smaller, lighter spears, sometimes called javelins, could also be thrown, while longer, heavier spears, lances, were used by cavalry, either in a thrusting or crouched position.

It is only in the Bronze Age that the sword was invented, and by the 6th to 8th centuries, swords were made of the highest quality *iron by the best smiths. Some swords from the period were also pattern-welded, a process of construction whereby bars of steel would be twisted together, over and over, before being flattened and their edges and tips sharpened. The result was a sword of extraordinary strength and durability. So impressive was the work of these smiths, and so proud of it were they, that frequently they inscribed their names down the face of the blades. Swords of the greatest early medieval heroes were also named: Excalibur (Arthur) and Durendal (Roland). From the high to the late MA, the sword had become the standard weapon for all soldiers but especially for the more wealthy knights.

Long, often narrow and very sharp daggers were also carried by all medieval soldiers. These were most effective when an armoured opponent was disabled, and vulnerable spots in the armour—the neck, armpit, and groin—could be penetrated.

Axes were also used as weapons in the early and high MA, shifting their use as agricultural and domestic tools to the battlefield. Frankish soldiers were particularly known for their short throwing axes, *fransiscae*, while Vikings were characterized by their broad-headed and long-handled battle axes. Axes like these largely disappeared from use around 1000, to be replaced throughout the rest of the MA by axe-like staff weapons such as halberds, partisans, ahlspeisses, vouges, goededags, holy-water sprinklers, and so forth.

Ancient armies used *archers only as auxiliary troops, mainly for skirmishing and harassing rather than directly facing an opponent. The Huns changed this as a tactic. With mounted archers as their main military units, the Huns rode throughout the Roman Empire defeating any army they encountered. Their skill as bowmen firing from horseback was unsurpassed and showed that archers could be effective regular army units. Later in the MA, their like were English longbowmen and Genoese crossbowmen. The former used a longbow made of particularly flexible yew wood with strong iron-headed arrows that when shot by well-trained archers were deadly accurate and penetrative. The latter used a more sophisticated mechanical bow that increased the force by which a projectile could be shot, sometimes up to 400 lbs. of pull.

Almost all early medieval warriors wore armour and carried shields. The most protective armour was mail. Coats of mail, which until the 12th century covered the torso, thighs, and upper arms and afterwards covered the entire body, were made of thousands of interlocking iron rings (70,000–90,000 for a normal-sized Carolingian byrnie or Norman armour). When worn with a protective garment underneath, a jerkin of padded felt or leather, mail was virtually impregnable to slashing or thrusting weapons, as can be seen by the sparsity of torso wounds found in medieval military burials.

Medieval shields were made of wood. Many shields also had metal rims and bosses, with early medieval shields decorated with metal animal images but otherwise unadorned; later medieval shields were painted with the *heraldry of the unit's noble leader or general. Infantry using round and kite-shaped shields of the early and high MA could overlap them to form a protective defensive formation, the shield wall. By the end of the MA, cavalry shields disappeared, or in jousts became small *targes*, or targets, attached to the plate armour, while infantry shields had both become small and round, *bucklers*, or large and oblong or square, *pavises*.

As the head was the most vulnerable part of the body, special care was taken in providing protection for it in the form of a helmet. In tournaments, where regulations meant that peripheral vision was not important, helmets tended to be made of thick metal and were closed tightly around the skull with just a small slit open through which the eyes could look only forward. For military purposes, however, the need for a greater range of vision, more air, and the ability to communicate required the helmet to be more open. The variety of helmet styles throughout the MA can probably be attributed to fashion and preference rather than utility. All helmets were made of a single piece of metal hammered into shape or of several metal pieces welded or riveted together, with padding, an undercap, or a mail coif worn between helmet and head; some also had mail attached to them to protect the neck.

In the 14th and 15th centuries, several technological changes and innovations in arms and armour were introduced. Longbow archery became more prevalent, and crossbows, now made in metal, more powerful. Both fired projectiles that could be outfitted with strong steeled heads. Metal plates also began to be used more often to cover parts of the body, until by the middle of the 15th century when plate armour began to replace mail as the preferred armour for more wealthy soldiers. Finally, gunpowder weapons were introduced and became more numerous and prominent; by the beginning of the 15th century, some were hand-held, and by the end of the 16th century they had replaced almost all medieval weapons, except sword and dagger, and had made armour of any kind obsolete. KDV

C. Blair, *European Armour: circa 1066 to circa 1700* (1958).
K. DeVries, *Medieval Military Technology* (1992).
—— and R. D. Smith, *Medieval Weapons: An Illustrated History of their Impact* (2007).
D. C. Nicolle, *Arms and Armour of the Crusading Era, 1050–1350*, 2 vols (1988).
E. Oakeshott, *The Sword in the Age of Chivalry* (1964; repr. 1994).
M. Strickland and R. Hardy, *The Great Warbow: From Hastings to the Mary Rose* (2005).
J. Waldman, *Hafted Weapons in Medieval and Renaissance Europe: The Evolution of European Staff Weapons between 1200 and 1650* (2005).

Arnau de Villanova (*c.*1240–1311) Medieval physician, university teacher, and spiritual reformer. His early biography is poorly known, but he was certainly born in the Crown of *Aragon. He earned his medical degree at *Montpellier in the 1260s. In 1281, Arnau moved to *Barcelona to serve the Aragonese royal family and later was also physician to several 14th-century popes. This role at the royal and papal courts was not an impediment to his development as an author of medical works at the medical school of Montpellier, where he taught from 1289 to 1301. From the early 1280s to the date of his death, Arnau touched upon almost all medical genres and subjects in his writings, developing an original epistemological position that bridged the gap between belief in *medicine as science and an anti-intellectual medical empiricism. Tradition has attached Arnau's name to some *alchemical works, but there is no historical evidence to support his authorship. In Montpellier, the flourishing of Arnau's medical production paralleled his growing interest in spiritual matters, following the reformist views of certain *Franciscan groups. His spiritual writings of an eschatological and prophetic nature brought him serious problems with the church. Travelling by sea, Arnau died off the coast of *Genoa in 1311. FS

Arnau de Vilanova, *Arnaldi de Villanova Opera Medica Omnia*, ed. L. García Ballester, M. McVaugh, J. A. Paniagua, P. Gil Sotres, F. Salmón, and J. Arrizabalaga (1975–).
——*Arnaldi de Villanova Opera Theologica Omnia*, ed. J. Perarnau (2004–).

Arnaut Daniel (*fl. c.*1180–95) *Troubadour from the *Périgord whose eighteen (possibly twenty) surviving lyrics evince a predilection for extreme formal complexity, semantic ambivalence, unusual vocabulary, and difficult rhymes. His *vida* confirms his work was regarded as difficult by his contemporaries, but he was much admired by *Dante, who describes him as *miglior fabbro del parlar materno* (the best craftsman in the vernacular) in *Purgatorio*, 26/117, and by modern poets such as Ezra Pound and T. S. Eliot. Two of his melodies survive. *See also* TROUBADOURS; VIDAS AND RAZOS. SG

M. Eusebi, ed., *Arnaut Daniel: Il sirventese e le canzoni* (1984; repr. 1995).

Arnold of Brescia (*c.*1100–1155) Heretic who joined the communal revolt at *Rome in the mid 12th century. Born in *Brescia, Arnold studied in *Paris, possibly with Peter *Abelard, whom he later defended. Returning to Brescia, he criticized the clergy's corruption and the bishop's failure to implement reform quickly enough. He was condemned at the Council of *Sens and sent to Rome as a penitent in 1140. In Rome, he witnessed the corruption of the *papal court (curia) and developed a more radical agenda that merged with the revolutionary programme of the Roman *commune. He taught that *clergy who had possessions could not be saved, opposed papal claims to temporal power, and helped lead the revolt of the commune. Cooperation between the pope and emperor led to Arnold's capture and execution; he was burned, and his ashes were cast on the Tiber. *See also* HERESY. MCF

R. I. Moore, *The Origins of European Dissent* (1985).

Arnold of Lübeck (d. *c.*1212) *Benedictine abbot; North-German chronicler with regional perspective yet treating the Holy Land (*crusades, *Henry the Lion's *peregrinatio*). Translator of *Hartmann von Aue's *Gesta Gregorii*. VS

Arnold of Lübeck, *Chronica Slavorum*, ed. G. H. Pertz, *MGH.SRG* 14 (1868); ed. J. M. Lappenberg, *MGH.SS* 21 (1869), 100–250.
—— *Gesta Gregorii peccatoris*, ed. J. Schilling (1986).
V. Scior, *Das Eigene und das Fremde* (2001).

Arnolfo di Cambio (*c.*1245–1302) Pupil of Nicola *Pisano, he collaborated on the *pulpit of the *cathedral of *Siena and on the arch of St *Dominic (*Bologna). His remaining sculptures (the bust of *Charles I of Anjou and part of the tombs of the cardinals Annibaldi, de Braye, and *Pope Boniface VIII) demonstrate a harmonious style, influenced by the classic tradition and the works of the *Cosmati. He also designed the tabernacles of San Paolo fuori le Mura, Santa Cecilia in Trastevere, and the initial project of the Duomo of *Florence. EB

A. M. Romanini, *Arnolfo di Cambio e lo 'Stil novo' del gotico italiano* (1980).

Arno of Reichersberg (*c.*1100–1175) Provost, reformer; brother of *Gerhoch. In the *Apologeticus contra Folmarum* and the *Scutum canonicorum* Arno discussed contemporary issues of dogma. HB

E. M. Buytaert, 'The Apologeticus of Arno of Reichersberg', *FranS* 11 (1951), 1–47.
P. Classen, *Gerhoch von Reichersberg* (1960).
I. Peri, 'Die Konzeption des Heilsgeschehens und die Frage nach dem Ursprung des Bösen im Hexaemeron Arnos von Reichersberg', *Miscellanea mediaevalia*, 11 (1977), 104–12.

Arnpeck, Veit (1435/40–1495/1505) Bavarian historian. He wrote the *Chronica Baioariorum*, which he also translated into German, a *Chronicon Austriacum* down to 1488, and the *Liber de gestis episcoporum Frisingensium*. HB

G. Leidinger, ed., *Veit Arnpeck, Sämtliche Chroniken* (1915).
D. Rödel, 'Veit Arnpeck: Publikumsbezogene Zweisprachigkeit bei *Chronica Baioariorum* und *Bayerischer Chronik*', *Wissensliteratur im Mittelalter*, 14 (1993), 227–70.

Arnulf, counts of Flanders (918–1071) **Arnulf I 'the Great'** (r. 918–65) initially controlled only the area around *Bruges, but after 933 concentrated on east *Flanders. He introduced the *Benedictine rule, making his relatives lay abbots, and ordained that all feudal bonds passed through the count. He expanded into *Vermandois and *Artois, leading to disputes with *Normandy, which necessitated surrendering territory to Lothair IV. While Arnulf I styled himself 'marquis', Lothair designated him *princeps*. **Arnulf II** (r. 965–88) became count at age four. Rebellions of nobles eroded his power, and his early death precipitated another minority regime. **Arnulf III** (1070–71) ruled only briefly and was killed in battle in a coup engineered by his uncle Robert 'the Frisian'. DN

J. Dunbabin and A. C. F. Koch, 'Het graafschap Vlaanderen van de 9de eeuw tot 1070', *AGN* 1: 54–83.
France in the Making, 843–1180 (1985).
D. Nicholas, *Medieval Flanders* (1992).

Arnulf, St, bishop of Metz (*c.*580–*c.*640) Ancestor of the *Carolingians. Late in life Arnulf took vows at Remiremont, where he was buried and revered as a saint. EJG

J. Jarnut, *Agilolfingerstudien: Untersuchungen zur Geschichte einer adeligen Familie im 6. und 7. Jahrhundert* (1986).
P. Riché, *The Carolingians: A Family Who Forged Europe*, trans. M. I. Allen (French original, 1983) (1993).

Arnulf of Carinthia (887–99) (emperor) Bastard son of Carloman; chosen king by the East Franks (887). After victories (891–2) he staged shows of power in *Italy (894) and *Germany (895), and was crowned emperor at Rome (896). His reign ended in scandal (899), but his son Louis succeeded him. JLN

T. Reuter, *Germany in the Early Middle Ages 800–1056* (1991), 119–26.
—— 'Sex, Lies and Oath-helpers: The Trial of Queen Uota', *Medieval Polities and Modern Mentalities*, ed. J. L. Nelson (2006), 217–30.

Arnulf of Lisieux (d. 1184) (bishop) An ecclesiastical leader of the Second *Crusade. A preacher and author, he attempted to reconcile the ambitions of the kings of *France and England. His correspondence, which he compiled, documents how extensively he was in contact with many leading contemporaries. His numerous sermons and poems, both religious and circumstantial, are characterized by epigrammatic conciseness. RSR

C. P. Schriber, *The Dilemma of Arnulf of Lisieux: New Ideas versus Old Ideals* (1990).

—— tr., *The Letter Collections of Arnulf of Lisieux* (1997).

Arnulf of Orléans (late 12th century) Grammarian from the school of *Orléans who wrote encyclopedic commentaries on Ovid and Lucan. There are two so-called elegiac comedies attributed to him, *Lidia* and *Miles Gloriosus*, the latter with less certainty. MYM

Arnulfi Aurelianensis Glosule Ovidii Fastorum, ed. J. R. Rieker (2005).

Arnulfi Aurelianensis Glosule super Lucanum, ed. B. M. Marti (1958).

F. Bertini, ed., *Commedie latine del XII e XIII secolo*, vol. 4 (1983), vol. 6 (1998).

F. Ghisalberti, 'Arnolfo d'Orléans, un cultore di Ovidio nel secolo XII', *Memorie del Reale Istituto Lombardo di Scienze e Lettere*, 24 (1932), 157–234.

Árpád dynasty Hungarian rulers from the mid 890s to 1301. **Árpád**, son of Álmos, elected chief of the *Magyar tribal alliance, led his peoples into the *Carpathian Basin in the mid 890s. While his immediate successors had difficulty maintaining control over the tribal chiefs who led marauding ventures into the Latin West and the Byzantine southeast, his great-grandson **Géza** (d. 997) established his reign after the defeat of the raiders at Augsburg (Lechfeld) in 955. He turned toward the Latin West so that his son **Vajk**, baptized **Stephen** (d. 1038; canonized in 1083), could be crowned king on the first day of 1001 with the consent of Rome and of Emperor Otto III. Problems of inheritance—primogeniture challenged by *seniorat*, that is, inheritance by the oldest male member of the kin—caused internal strife in the royal family for over a century. Stephen died heirless and the crown passed to the descendants of his uncle **Vazul**. Among them, **Ladislas I** (d. 1095; canonized 1192) and **Coloman the Learned** (d. 1116) were able to rebuild a firm political-economical, spiritual-social foundation. The last change in the dynastic line followed when Coloman's son died without a male heir. During the 12th century younger brothers frequently challenged the ruling kings, mostly with Byzantine backing. Finally, **Béla III** (d. 1196), who grew up in *Byzantium, guided the political destiny of the realm with a firm hand. Under **Andrew II** (d. 1235) domestic conflicts threatened the throne until he issued the *Golden Bull of 1222 in order to involve the nobility along with the church hierarchy in governing the affairs of the realm. Under **Béla IV** (d. 1270), political discontent grew so strong that the king had difficulty summoning a force against the invading Mongols, who after the defeat of the Hungarian army at *Muhi in 1241, devastated the country. After their withdrawal, the king could proceed with reconstruction as a 'second founder of the realm'. Fierce domestic struggles between powerful baronial cliques weakened the monarchy under **Ladislas IV 'the Cuman'** (d. 1290, whose mother was a *Cuman). The right to the throne of the last Árpád scion, **Andrew III** (d. 1301), was already challenged by claimants from the female line of the dynasty (*Anjou). During the three centuries of Árpád reigns, marriages of kings and princesses connected the dynasty to the rulers of the neighbouring countries as well as to those of western and Mediterranean Europe. Ever since the canonization of Stephen, together with his son Emeric (Imre, Henry, d. 1031) and even more after that of Ladislas, the dynasty was referred to as that 'of the holy kings'. This dynastic holiness was enhanced by the widespread reputation of saintly princesses in the royal family, St Elisabeth of Hungary/Thuringia and the Dominican nun Margaret. ZJK

T. von Bogay, ed., *Die heiligen Könige* (1976).

G. Klaniczay, *Holy Rulers and Blessed Princesses: Dynastic Cults in Medieval Central Europe*, tr. E. Pálmai (Hungarian original, 2000) (2002).

Z. J. Kosztolnyik, *Hungary Under the Early Árpáds* (2002).

—— *Hungary in the Thirteenth Century* (1996).

G. Kristó, *Die Arpaden-Dynastie* (1993).

F. Makk, *The Árpáds and the Comneni* (1989).

Arras Religious and mercantile centre in the French *Artois region and the medieval county of *Flanders. Home of the powerful *Benedictine abbey of St Vaast, where the *Burgundian-French Peace of Arras was negotiated (1435). DJR

J. G. Dickenson, *The Congress of Arras, 1435: A Study in Medieval Diplomacy* (1955).

A. Jacques *et al.*, *Histoire d'Arras* (1988).

Arrouaise, Order of *See* RELIGIOUS ORDERS.

ars antiqua Style of musical composition in the later 13th century, as viewed from the 14th-century perspective of the **ars nova*. *Jacques of Liège in *Speculum musicae* (1320s) disparaged contemporary music, praising the style of his predecessors and the theorists *Franco of Cologne and Magister *Lambertus. Later 13th-century polyphony is marked by a concentration on the *motet, especially three-voice double motets, but contemporaneous MSS still contain examples of *organum, *clausula, *conductus, and *hocket, which had largely disappeared by the 1320s. The musical *ars antiqua* has come to be understood as the time between the *Notre-Dame School (to *c.*1250) and the *ars nova* (1310s–20s), but some scholars use the term to encompass music of the Notre-Dame School as well, thus going from *c*.1160 to the early 14th century. This broader period encompasses the development of *modal rhythm and its transformation into fully mensuralized music (**musica mensurabilis*) based on 'perfections', beats with only triplet subdivision. Also evident are the beginnings of monophonic vernacular song collections (from the 1230s), notated instrumental music, and the *polyphonic *chanson*. All these developments show an increasing emphasis on written musical documents. Secular works and their MS sources also reflect the rising *patronage of aristocratic courts, as opposed to a largely ecclesiastical musical culture. *See also* POLYPHONY: TO 1300. RAB

G. A. Anderson and E. H. Roesner, 'Ars Antiqua', *NGD2*, vol. 2, 79–80.

C. Page, *The Owl and the Nightingale: Musical Life and Ideas in France, 1100–1300* (1989).

ars dictaminis* and *ars dictandi These terms designated both the subfield of medieval *rhetoric concerned with *letter writing and a textbook devoted to that subject. A fusion of long-standing epistolographic practices and Ciceronian rhetorical theory, the *ars dictaminis* began to take shape in the late 11th century, in the pedagogical writings of the monk *Alberic of *Monte Cassino, and emerged as a distinctive discipline in a series of textbooks written at *Bologna during the first few decades of the 12th century. By the end of that century, similar textbooks were in use throughout western and central Europe. They continued to be produced in great numbers through the end of the 15th century, when different models of epistolary style and structure came to dominate the schools and chanceries.

Every treatise on the *ars dictaminis* concerned itself with the parts of a letter and the elements of epistolary style. Although some teachers disagreed on the number and nomenclature of the various parts, a five-part schema based on Cicero's analysis of a forensic speech proved especially influential. The *salutatio* (greeting) identified the sender and recipient, clearly indicating their hierarchical relationship to one another. This was followed by an *exordium* (introduction) or *captatio benevolentiae* (securing of good will) that was designed to dispose the recipient favourably towards the letter's specific message by relating it to some general truth. Next came the *narratio* (statement of the facts in the present case), the *petitio* (request), and *conclusio* (formal closing). Conditions for omitting one or more of these standard parts were also specified. The only stylistic feature unique to letters was the *cursus*, a system of rhythmical clause endings that became a regular element of the *ars dictaminis* by the last quarter of the 12th century. Among the other topics of style frequently treated in letter-writing manuals, as in other medieval composition textbooks, were the techniques for varying the same expression, the rhetorical figures, and the vices to be avoided. Some treatises also distinguished among various types of letters, especially letters intended to be sent and letters meant to function as official records. The latter often were treated separately in textbooks on the *ars notaria* (notary's art).

Although a few textbooks consisted mainly of precepts and theory—notably Bene of *Florence's *Candelabrum*—more typically they devoted most of their space to models and illustrative examples. Some of the most influential textbooks, such as those by Bernard of Meung, Guido Faba, and Boncompagno of Signa, contain hundreds of model letters, along with model phrases for use in the *salutatio*, proverbs for use as *exordia*, and the like; and the letter collections of *Peter of Blois, Peter of Vinea, and Richard of Pofi were pressed into service as letter-writing textbooks. The preponderance of models for imitation or copying enabled even those with limited facility in Latin to move quickly from the classroom to the production of the myriad documents that late medieval social, political, and economic relations required. Similarly user-friendly were the letter-writing manuals in the vernacular that began to appear in Italy as early as the 13th century. Although manuals in French were produced in England during the last half of the 14th century, the first English-language textbooks date from the 16th century and were shaped more by the newer epistolary models of the Renaissance than by the medieval *ars dictaminis*. MJC

M. Camargo, *Ars Dictaminis, Ars Dictandi*, *TSMAO* 60 (1991).

J. J. Murphy, '*Ars dictaminis*: The Art of Letter-Writing', in *Rhetoric in the Middle Ages* (1974; repr. 2001), 194–268.

W. D. Patt, 'The Early *Ars dictaminis* as Response to a Changing Society', *Viator*, 9 (1978), 133–55.

Transmundus, *Introductiones dictandi*, ed. and tr. A. Dalzell (1995).

R. Witt, 'Medieval "Ars dictaminis" and the Beginnings of Humanism: A New Construction of the Problem', *Renaissance Quarterly*, 35 (1982), 1–35.

F. J. Worstbrock, M. Klaes, and J. Lütten, *Repertorium der Artes dictandi des Mittelalters, Teil 1: Von den Anfängen bis um 1200* (1992).

arsenals and navies An arsenal consisted of a yard for shipbuilding, a repair shop, a magazine for storing detached pieces and disarmed hulls, and a workshop for making armaments, as well as sails and oars, rigging, anchors, crossbows and bolts, and, at the end of the MA, artillery. Two more numerous professional groups worked there: carpenters and caulkers, who used pitch and oakum. Every port of moderate importance possessed an arsenal (from Arabic *dar al-sina'a*, dockyard). Between the 13th and 14th centuries, western Muslims maintained arsenals at the ports of Tunis, Mahdia, Oran, Hunayn, Almeria, and Malaga. *Venice possessed the greatest fortified arsenal, which had continued to expand in response to the needs of the naval wars against pirates and rival towns, and against the Turks, who seized the arsenal of *Constantinople in 1453. The Arsenale at

Venice built *ships for the Commune—warships, whether galleys or *cocche* or *kogge*—while individuals employed private shipyards to build commercial vessels. The Commune was careful to guarantee supplies of wood for shipbuilding to the Arsenale, and implemented forestry policies to ensure the permanent availability of construction wood. The Arsenale was a 'war machine' whose specialized magazines were organized into batteries: all that belonged to the armament of a given galley was stored beneath a roman numeral corresponding to that on the ship's prow. In the event of a threat, these items could all be installed very quickly. The Arsenale was capable of arming a hundred light and twelve heavy *galleys within a few weeks; the vessel would move from one magazine to the other, receiving its own equipment at each stop. This organization of space provided efficient control over the quantities of materials used and the time taken to do the work. The Arsenale at Venice supplied and oversaw two other arsenals at Crete and Corfu.

The types of ship were many and varied. Long, narrow, low-draught boats contrasted with those that were large and high on the water. In the first category are the galleys and all oared vessels (*lenys*); in the second are the bigger ships (*nao*, *nave*) and all the sail-vessels (*tarides*, **coche*, *carracks). The galley could also move by sail whenever a little wind blew (its *lateen sails making an excellent sailboat); the rowers, who were free and salaried, were used for manoeuvres into and out of ports, in times of windless weather, and during combat. The MA made continual progress in naval technology, such as the substitution of a sternpost rudder for the side-mounted tillers, the segmentation of sails across multiple masts (three on larger ships), and the simultaneous adoption of lateen and squared sails to make better use of the compass rose. Some ships remained faithful to a single type of sail—whether a squared sail on yards or a lateen on antennae—the latter type being adopted by the Spanish caravel. Tonnage was not a distinguishing criterion; the sailboats, like the *kogge*, could transport 400–700 tons (*botti*), while bigger vessels, like the *navi* (*naos*), carried to 2000 tons until the end of the 15th century. The merchant galleys had a smaller gauge, roughly between 150 and 250 'tons' (*miera*, quite a thousand pounds). Commercial vessels supplied with forecastles and tops could be armed for war and receive soldiers for their defence, or for hunting corsairs. The galleys could also be used for commercial purposes, but the size of their crew (180 rowers on a trireme—a galley with three levels of oars that reappeared at the beginning of the 14th century) and lack of space limited their capacity and increased costs; they were therefore employed as transport for light and costly goods, such as spices, while round sail-vessels were used to transport heavy goods, such as salt, wine, grains, and oil, or voluminous materials such as *wool and *cotton. JCHo

G. Bellavitis, *L'arsenale da Venezia: Storia di una grande struttura urbana* (1983).
E. Concina, 'La casa dell'arsenale', *Storia di Venezia: Il mare*, ed. A. Tenenti and U. Tucci (1992).
J.-C. Hocquet, *Il sale e la fortuna di Venezia* (1990).
—— *Venise et la Mer, XIIe–XVIIIe siècles* (2006).
F. C. Lane, *Navires et constructeurs à Venise pendant la Renaissance* (1965).
C. Picard, 'Les arsenaux musulmans de la Méditerranée et de l'océan Atlantique (VIIe–XVe siècles)', *Chemins d'outre-mer: Études sur la Méditerranée médiévale offertes à Michel Balard*, 2 vols (2004), vol. 2, 691–710.

Ars medicinae *See* ARTICELLA.

ars nova Term used by 20th-century music historians. It has been used variously to identify all the music of the 14th century, French music of the 14th century, and French music of approximately the first half of the 14th century. It may be set in opposition to an **ars antiqua* (all music of the 13th century, or all music between the *Notre-Dame School and *c.*1300) and to an **ars subtilior* of the later 14th century. It derives from discussions of new rhythmic and notational possibilities for mensural (metrical) music in English and French music treatises, beginning in the 1310s and 1320s; these use the language of an *ars moderna*, *ars modernorum*, or *ars nova* that is contrasted to an earlier *ars vetus* or *ars antiqua*. Used as a title, the expression occurs in the unique explicit ('Explicit ars nove musice') of a text by *Johannes de Muris otherwise known as the *Notitia artis musice* or *Summa musice* (1319–21), and in the unique explicit ('Explicit ars nova') of one text from a body of material of about the same date associated with the teachings of Philippe de *Vitry. PML

D. Fallows, 'Ars Nova', *NGD2*, vol. 2, 80–81.
S. Fuller, 'A Phantom Treatise of the Fourteenth Century? The Ars Nova', *Journal of Musicology*, 4 (1985), 23–50.
P. M. Lefferts, 'An Anonymous Treatise of the Theory of Frater Robertus de Brunham', *Quellen und Studien zur Musiktheorie des Mittelalters*, ed. M. Bernhard, vol. 3 (2001), 217–51.

ars praedicandi While the singular term refers generally to the theory of preaching, the specific phrase *artes praedicandi* designates the rhetorical manuals written from 1200 onward, the date of *Alan of Lille's *Summa de arte praedicatoria*. The *artes*, of which more than 300 MSS are extant, advise preachers on the formal composition of *sermons, the modes of *preaching, the moral behaviour of the preacher, and the delivery of sermons.

The *artes* have their sources in scripture and Jewish tradition, classical oratory, and patristic authors, especially *Augustine and *Pope Gregory I the Great. The *artes* define and illustrate the four senses of scripture (historical, allegorical, tropological, anagogical) and discuss the *circumstantiae* (*quis, quibus, ubi, quando, quomodo, quid*). They also specify structural plans and methods of composition rooted in classical oratory. The exemplary scholastic or university sermon opens with a prologue, then states a theme, normally a brief passage of scripture, separates the theme into divisions and subdivisions, and supports its conclusion for each with authorities, normally from scripture or patristic writings but also taken from **florilegia*, and other illustrative devices such as *similitudines, distinctiones*, and exempla (*see* PROVERBS, RIDDLES, AND EXEMPLA), learned or popular. As the scholastic sermon developed in the *university, so the complexity of the *artes* increased to include methods of expanding the theme (*amplificatio*). BMKi

M. G. Briscoe, *Artes praedicandi*, and B. H. Jaye, *Artes orandi*, *TSMAO* 61 (1992).
P. B. Roberts, 'The *Ars Praedicandi* and the Medieval Sermon', *Preacher, Sermon and Audience in the Middle Ages*, ed. C. A. Muessig (2001), 41–62.

ars subtilior Modern historians' term for a *polyphonic music tendency (*c*.1370–1420), describing works of subtlety and artifice, in which composers exploited stylistic aspects and potential implications of contemporary systems for notating rhythm and tonal behaviour to create visually audacious, musically complex works. Found from *England to Cyprus, and in *Mass, *motet, and *chanson*, the 'more subtle art' is associated with the *grandes ballades* of the Chantilly codex (1390s). PML

N. S. Josephson, 'Ars Subtilior', *NGD2*, vol. 2, 81–2.
P. M. Lefferts, '*Subtilitas* in the Tonal Language of *Fumeux fume*', *Early Music*, 16 (1988), 176–83.
Y. Plumley and A. Stone, eds, *Chantilly Codex/Codex Chantilly*, 2 vols (2007).

art Apart from formulaic phrases (for example, 'black arts', *'Master of Arts') or ones no longer used, the word 'art' today designates what not long ago were called the 'Fine Arts'—*painting, *sculpture, *architecture, and the performing arts (*drama, *dance, *music, and so forth). Since the 19th century, moreover, the word has more often designated a stock of material objects: a work on medieval art is more concerned with the artefacts of the period than the knowledge and activity of medieval artists. Like the Greek *technè*, the Latin *ars* denotes the creative faculty—an applied knowledge and technical ability. *Ars* is contrasted with *scientia*, a theoretical understanding, not subordinate to the action or creation. Paradoxically, our own scientific practice, oriented largely around practical applications and depending upon the manipulation of objects, corresponds better to the medieval conception of *ars* than to that of *scientia*.

1. Categorizing art
2. Art as production
3. Categorizing artists
4. Status and professionalization

1. *Categorizing art*

Throughout the MA, the arts were divided into the *seven liberal arts (*grammar, *rhetoric, *logic, *arithmetic, *geometry, music, *astronomy) and the *mechanical arts, such as painting and *metallurgy. The fine arts did not occupy a predominant place in the category of mechanical arts, which varied greatly. *Hugh of St-Victor, for instance, in his *Didascalion* (*PL* 176, 760), divides this category into the art of *wool making, *military art, navigation, *agriculture, *hunting, *medicine, and theatre. Painting and sculpture are listed briefly as subdivisions of architecture, itself part of military art. *Richard of St-Victor's enumeration of the fine arts, under the generic heading of 'artificial work, that is, the work of industry', is almost comical to our eyes: 'carving, painting, *writing, agriculture, and innumerable other things' (*PL* 196, 83). It is remarkable that a discipline like law, despite its full development in the 12th century, could not find a place among either the liberal or the mechanical arts.

2. *Art as production*

No medieval word simultaneously covered several arts, such as painting, sculpture, and architecture, like the modern phrase 'fine arts' or 'visual arts'. The vocabulary of the arts in the MA systematically emphasizes the specific technique, never indicating what the arts have in common; it relies not on *aesthetic categories—not on the perspective of the *viewer*—but rather on modes of production, from the point of view of the professional. Moreover, the label 'mechanical arts' stands in contradiction to the idea, endlessly repeated from *Anselm to *Thomas Aquinas, that the architect or artisan conceives in his mind the intended form, and then works the material in accordance with his preliminary design. The intellectual component of the artist's work is thus recognized, but it is not clearly distinguished from that of other mechanical arts. In the absence of standardized industrial production, the difference between a painter and a cobbler is, from this perspective, a matter of degree, comparable to the difference between a great painter and an average one. Furthermore, the price of durable art supplies, especially *parchment, and ignorance of scale drawing before the mid 13th century led to a scarcity of preliminary drawings. Until the advent of one-to-one scale-drawings, the genesis of a building was essentially held in the architect's mind, by a mental feat of undoubted value. In the case of the figurative arts, iconographic creation and the intellectual work of composition were also mental, right up until the moment of drawing the work on its support—a fact of which many art historians are ignorant, preferring to imagine large numbers of lost 'model books'. Once again, however, the difference between this work and that of more modest artisans is only a matter of degree.

3. *Categorizing artists*

Professionals were categorized in much the same way as the disciplines. The word *artista* referred to a member of the school of arts—the liberal arts—and was never used in an artistic context. The words closest in actual usage to our term 'artist', *artifex* and *opifex*, might just as easily have denoted the cobbler as the painter. One should not, however, regard this fact as an indication that the arts were held in low esteem: the most frequent occurrences of *artifex* in the *Patrologia Latina* concern God in the role of Creator, and *architectus* is there employed only for him. Just as with the occupations themselves, the most common designations for artists rely on modes of production: *pictor, sculptor, aurifaber*, and so forth. Architects, likewise, are generally lumped in with stonecutters (*lapicida, lathomus, magister lapidus*), and so are sculptors. The more precise terms that appear in the 13th century, such as *imagiers tailleurs* and *imagiers peintres* from Etienne *Boileau's *Livre des métiers*, do not indicate any form of emancipation. These terms designate the makers of small objects, such as *crucifixes and ivory mirror-valves, which require a relatively serial production in the context of increasing specialization. It was this context, no less evident in miniature-painting—a task that fell to laymen who were often illiterate—that produced the relative devaluation of the figurative arts against which Renaissance painters reacted, assigning their activity rather to the liberal arts.

4. *Status and professionalization*

Even if the vocabulary were stable, we would be unable to describe as a whole the status of art and the artist during the MA. Until the 12th century, and sometimes later still, it is very difficult to put into perspective the roles of sponsor and labourer in the conception of a work. It is probable that for less physical work, such as *manuscript illumination and *metalsmithing, designer and worker are united in the cleric (sometimes an important personage, as with *Einhard at the court of *Charlemagne), who often acted as sponsor at the same time. In such cases, artistic activity did not define the condition of its author, but rather augmented his prestige. The status of Romanesque sculptors is less certain, although we notice that they frequently signed their works. Our information about the cost of artistic work is so scanty that it must have often involved non-monetary exchanges, or even donations.

The professionalization of these vocations is evident in the 13th century, and thus we begin to find information about the cost of artistic work. During the construction of *Exeter cathedral, the sculptors distinguished themselves from the stonecutters by their salaries, which were four times greater. Their recognition is evident, but it is hardly comparable to the growing estimation of artists during the modern era. Only *relics and other *mirabilia* could fetch the price that paintings would later achieve. We know, for instance, that Christ's *crown of thorns cost St *Louis IX 135,000 pounds, and that the *Ste-Chapelle of Paris, designed to house it, cost him a further 40,000. While the price of artworks remained low around 1400, and very inferior to what was offered for exotic curiosities, some great artists now began to enjoy an enviable status at courts on account of their art. A self-*portrait can be found among the busts of court nobles sculpted by Peter *Parler for the *triforium of *Prague cathedral. The *Limbourg Brothers enjoyed not only the protection of Jean Duc de *Berry, but also his friendship, without making a great fortune. It was due, in the end, to the resale of artworks, and to the production of works adapted for resale, such as independent paintings on conventional subjects, that artistic talent began to be measured by a monetary standard from the 16th century onwards. *See also* DRAWINGS AND MODEL BOOKS. JWi

E. Boileau, *Le Livre des métiers*, ed. R. de Lespinasse and F. Bonnardot (1879).
E. de Bruyne, *Etudes d'esthétique médiévale* (1946; repr. 1998).
J. A. Givens, 'The Fabric Account of Exeter Cathedral as a Record of Medieval Sculptural Praxis', *Gesta*, 30 (1991), 112–18.
H. L. Kessler, *Seeing Medieval Art* (2004).
P. O. Kristeller, 'The Modern System of the Arts', *Renaissance Thought, II* (1965), 163–227.

art, Anglo-Saxon The art of *England from the early MA through the mid 11th century, though in the field of *manuscript illumination, it is generally restricted to the late 9th through the mid 11th centuries. The period of AS art theoretically ends at the *Norman Conquest of 1066, but many have observed a strong artistic continuity across this political divide. The Anglo-Saxons were particularly notable for MS production, with main centres in *Canterbury and *Winchester. Much of this production stemmed from the *literacy campaigns of *Alfred the Great and from the *Benedictine reform initiated by Sts *Dunstan, *Oswald, and *Æthelwold. In addition to MS illumination, significant stone *sculpture survives. It has been argued that the Anglo-Saxons themselves held *textiles in highest regard, though very few examples remain.

The book arts were held in high esteem in AS *England, as attested by the number of abbots and bishops mentioned in *colophons as *scribes, illuminators, and *bookbinders. Two scripts are generally used, English Caroline Minuscule for Latin texts and AS Pointed Minuscule for OE texts, often appearing together in bilingual MSS.

There are two main illumination styles recognized. The 'Winchester Style,' influenced by *Carolingian Court School models, used lavish colours, elaborate foliate frames, and heavy gilding. The Benedictional of St *Æthelwold typifies the style. The 'Utrecht Style' is named for its primary influence, the Carolingian *Utrecht Psalter, characterized by dynamic, energetic line work, in either monochrome or coloured inks, unpainted but sometimes tinted with ink washes. Three English copies of the Utrecht Psalter survive, the earliest of which is the Harley Psalter, from Christ Church, Canterbury.

The Illustrated Hexateuch is most noteworthy, with over 400 images displaying an OE paraphrase of the first six biblical books. It is not only the earliest surviving work with a substantial portion of the Bible in a vernacular language, but is also the source of well-known *tropes, including the jawbone used by Cain to kill Abel, and the 'horned' Moses.

Much stone carving survives from the period, the most important extant example being the *Ruthwell Cross, a 17-foot-tall pillar from the late 7th or early 8th century, with vine-scroll *interlace along two sides, surrounded by *runic inscriptions containing portions of 'The Dream of the *Rood', and biblical scenes on two faces, surrounded by biblical inscriptions in Roman capitals. *See also* ARCHITECTURE: ANGLO-SAXON; ART, CELTIC; ART, INSULAR; ART AND ARCHITECTURE: CAROLINGIAN; LITERATURES: ENGLISH—OE PROSE; PSALTERS. ASM

M. Brown, *Anglo-Saxon Manuscripts* (1991).
——*A Guide to Western Historical Scripts, from Antiquity to 1600* ([2]1999).
M. Budny, *Insular, Anglo-Saxon, and Early Anglo-Norman Manuscript Art at Corpus Christi College, Cambridge: An Illustrated Catalogue* (1997).
R. G. Calkins, *Illuminated Books of the Middle Ages* (1983).
C. R. Dodwell, *Anglo-Saxon Art: A New Perspective* (1982).
C. de Hamel, *A History of Illuminated Manuscripts* (1986; repr. 1994).
T. Ohlgren, *Inventory of Insular and Anglo-Saxon Illuminated Manuscripts* (1991).
——*Insular and Anglo-Saxon Illuminated Manuscripts: An Iconographic Catalogue, c.AD 625 to 1100* (1986).

art, Bohemian Subsequent to the political and economic rise of the kingdom of *Bohemia, artistic production there constantly increased and reached an impressive level of quality in the late MA. Even during the Romanesque period, the *patronage of the king and important *barons yielded outstanding buildings (the *cathedral and St George's *monastery on the Hračany in *Prague; the abbeys of Třebíč, Milevsko, and Teplá), wall paintings (Znojmo round church), and illuminated *manuscripts (Codex Vyšehradensis [*c.*1086], National Library, Prague). Gothic art reflects the further advancement of the Bohemian kings (*Agnes monastery in Prague; bridge and *castle in Písek; monastery of Porta Coeli, Tišnov). Under the reign of *Charles IV, who was crowned emperor of the (Holy) *Roman Empire in 1355, Prague became the leading centre of artistic production in central Europe. Peter *Parler of Schwäbisch Gmünd built a new Gothic cathedral on the Hračany in a highly original style that had a formative influence on architects of later generations, and artists like Master Theodoric, Tomaso da Modena, Nikolaus Wurmser, and the Master of Višší Brod contributed paintings of exceptional quality (pictorial decoration of Karlstein castle [1348–67]; altarpiece from Višší Brod, National Gallery, Prague). Towards 1400, the works of Bohemian sculptors (*Beautiful Madonna* from Česky Krumlov, Kunsthistorisches Museum, Vienna; *Beautiful Madonna* from Thorún, lost since 1945) and painters (*St Vitus Madonna*, National Gallery, Prague) were developed in the 'Beautiful Style', a brilliant, lavishly decorated variant of the *'International Style'. *See also* ART AND ARCHITECTURE: GOTHIC/ROMANESQUE. MCS

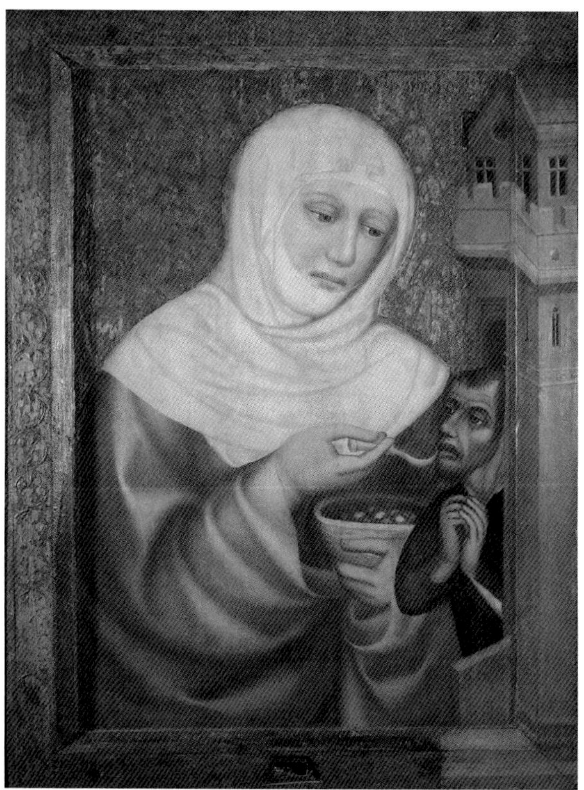

This example of Bohemian art is one of Master Theodoric's portraits of 'St Elizabeth' before 1365. National Museum, Prague.

T. Petrasová and H. Lorenzová, eds, *Dějiny českého výtvarného umění*, vols 1/1, 1/2 (1984, 1989).

art, Celtic Style of art produced in Europe in the period from the Iron Age through to *c.*AD 600, characterized by stylized motifs and curvilinear *interlacing, with little use of naturalism or narrative. Composite creatures and mythological monsters such as *dragons and griffins are commonly depicted, and an interest in the natural world is apparent in imagery of birds, fish, animals, and vegetation.

Many motifs appear as trios; the triskele—a symbol of three interlocked spirals, bent human legs, or other protrusions subject to rotational symmetry—persists into the modern era, for example in the flag of the Isle of Man.

The Celts were not a homogenous group, racially or linguistically. They flourished *c.*450–*c.*50 BC in temperate continental Europe, but extended to *c.*AD 600 in Britain and Ireland. Attempts to define an area as 'Celtic' are largely dependent on the discovery of Celtic artefacts: at their greatest, 'Celtic' lands were virtually as extensive as the Roman Empire, although they were never subject to central control. Celtic art can be found at locations from Ireland to Asia Minor, and also in North Africa, although there is no evidence that Celts settled there.

The most significant origin of, and influence on, Celtic art is identified as the La Tène culture, named after a site in Switzerland. La Tène art first appeared around the mid 5th century AD, and seems to be influenced by art from Scythia, Thrace, and Dacia, and particularly the decoration used on Greek pottery and Etruscan metalwork. The depiction of plant motifs and mask-like human heads can be traced to imported artefacts. The main objects that exhibit this 'Early' or 'Strict' style of decoration are weapons, jewellery (*see* GEMS AND JEWELLERY), drinking vessels, equipment for horses, and chariot fittings. In this Early period red coral imported from the Mediterranean and enamels were incorporated into metalwork to provide further adornment.

In the first half of the 4th century BC, there is evidence of Celtic expansion into *Italy and the *Carpathian basin; Rome was occupied by Celts between 387 and 385 BC. The art of the period *c.*350–*c.*250 BC has been termed the 'Waldalgesheim' style, after the last known Rhenish burial that contained imported Mediterranean goods. However, the Rhineland was peripheral to the distribution area of the new style of art and is not thought to be the origin of its development. The objects of this period are generally less rich than those of the Early style, and they are characterized by abstract treatments of both plant motifs and human heads.

From *c.*300–*c.*125 BC the Celts continued to expand their sphere of influence, moving south into Greece, north into Serbia, and east into Turkey. Much of the art of this period is associated with iron scabbards, so the term applied is 'Sword style'. The motif of a pair of dragons' heads is commonly found just below the mouth of scabbards; it is thought that the dragon may have been invoked as a sign of status or as an apotropaic charm. The 'Plastic style' also appeared at this time, characterized by high-relief S shapes and triskeles on gold and bronze objects rather than iron artefacts.

The period from *c.*125–*c.*50 BC is known as 'the *Oppida*', as Celtic territory contracted under threats from Rome, northern and eastern Europe; fortified towns appeared from Britain to Slovakia. These towns had a trading aspect, for goods imported from south of the *Alps reappear at this time, whilst the indigenous Celtic art is characterized by a relatively uniform style, suggesting close connections between the various Celtic peoples. Greater realism is found in decoration, suggesting Roman influence, and many more portrayals of human bodies, especially in wood, survive from this period than the earlier eras.

Beyond the *Oppida* period, Celtic art seems to survive only in Britain and Ireland, although much of what has been discovered is difficult to date with certainty. Artefacts tend to have insular *iconography: there are few La Tène imports from mainland Europe, and influences are hard to decipher. British and Irish *metalwork finds often combine engraving with repoussé work. The Roman occupation of Britain seems to have affected artistic production, with Roman-style artefacts found in areas of strong Romanization, but Celtic-style art arising anew in northern England, and for the first time in Scotland, as refugees were displaced. With the departure of the Romans, Celtic art formed the basis of the 'Insular art' style of Britain and Ireland. SJER

J. V. S. Megaw and M. R. Megaw, *Celtic Art from its Beginnings to the Book of Kells* (1989).

art, Dominican The Order of Preachers' commitment to scholarship and teaching had far-reaching repercussions for 13th- and 14th-century art. *Dominican *patronage of the age can be associated with intellectually demanding altarpieces, mural *paintings, and *stone monuments that are frequently inventive in design and didactic in function.

The cult of St *Dominic was promoted through purposeful depictions of the saint and his *miracles. Ambitious early examples include Nicola *Pisano's sarcophagus for Dominic's shrine (*c.*1264–7; Bologna, S. Domenico), which also refers to the order's expansion, and Francesco *Traini's *St Dominic* altarpiece (1345; Pisa, Museo Nazionale), which links Dominican teaching with apostolic authority. The order's crucial role in society was reinforced in Andrea Bonaiuti's sophisticated allegorical *frescoes in the *chapter-house of S. Maria Novella (Florence; 1366–8) that also honour the intellect of *Thomas Aquinas, a Dominican saint. Earlier celebrations of Aquinas as a divinely inspired writer appear in Simone *Martini's Santa Caterina *polyptych (*c.*1319–20; Pisa, Museo Nazionale), the *Triumph of Aquinas* altarpiece (of disputed attribution; *c.*1340–45; Pisa, S. Caterina), and Andrea *Orcagna's Strozzi altarpiece (1357; Florence, S. Maria Novella). To judge by the Dominican Constitution and Fra Angelico's frescoes in the dormitory of S. Marco in Florence (1440–45), the order recognized the potential of art as an aid in devotional meditations. *See also* ALTAR, ALTAR DECORATION, AND UTENSILS. FB

J. Cannon, 'Dominican Patronage of the Arts in Central Italy: The Provincia Romana, *c.*1220–*c.*1320', Ph.D. thesis (London, 1980).

——'Simone Martini, the Dominicans and the Early Sienese Polyptych', *JWCI* 45 (1982), 69–93.
W. Hood, *Fra Angelico at San Marco* (1993).
A. F. Moskowitz, *Nicola Pisano's Arca di San Domenico and its Legacy* (1994).

art, Franciscan Even before the death of the order's founder, *Francis of Assisi (1226), the *Franciscan order had expanded first around the Mediterranean and subsequently throughout Europe. It rapidly recognized and systematically exploited the visual and *decorative arts as a means of expressive communication and missionary propaganda. The constantly growing number of *friars urgently required churches and convents: local bishops often assigned the new order disused or ruinous churches, often in the *suburbs, which the Franciscans adapted for their use. New churches were also built, often simple in plan and austere in decoration following the norms established by the order's *General Chapter at *Narbonne (1260): these prohibited stone *vaulting outside the sanctuary, elaborate decoration, and free-standing *bell-towers. There were, however, numerous exceptions prompted by the growing numbers of friars, and, in the larger convents, their desire to study. The primary exception was the church of San Francesco, *Assisi, built as the founder's burial place and already under construction in 1228, two years after the saint's death. San Francesco was a large, single-naved church designed on two levels, the Lower church still retaining Romanesque architectural features, the Upper church markedly more Gothic with strong links to contemporary northern French architecture.

In *Italy particularly, there was an intense, rapidly increasing demand for *panel paintings with the image of Francis. Influenced by eastern Mediterranean models, these panels displayed a standing Francis flanked by scenes from his life and *miracles. They were produced for churches and convents of the order, particularly in Tuscany, in part by specialized workshops. They evince clear links with the written sources, notably the official biographies of Francis by Thomas of Celano and *Bonaventure. The panels show a restricted range of episodes, concentrating on emblematic scenes such as the Sermon to the Birds and the Stigmatization, and a few post-mortem miracles, which had the advantage of emphasizing the founder's resemblance to Christ. They may also have memorialized places visited by Francis himself, in Umbria and the east. Some of these panels, like that now in the Bardi chapel in Santa Croce (Florence), datable to *c.*1235–40, utilized a wider repertory of biographical scenes, often with programmatic intent. San Francesco at Assisi was, however, the crucible for Franciscan *painting. A first cycle of Francis' life was painted *c.*1260 in the Lower Church, paralleling the two 'lives' of Christ and Francis; it was followed shortly thereafter by a sequence of *stained glass windows in the Upper Church. Towards the end of the century a major cycle of 28 scenes of the Life of St Francis was painted in the *nave of the Upper Church, attributed to a workshop guided by *Giotto.

An impressive series of books containing *manuscript illuminations commissioned for or by the Franciscans is to be found in Italy and elsewhere in Europe and beyond. There were many Franciscan houses around the Mediterranean with painted cycles: fragments have been found in the Kalenderhane Camii at Istanbul. The contact with Palaeologan (Byzantine) art may have influenced not only the palette but also the affective emotional expressiveness of Franciscan painting. This is one of the specific Franciscan contributions to medieval European spirituality, characteristic not only of works commissioned by the order itself but also of works commissioned for Franciscan destinations. The popularity and authority of the order and its saints during the Trecento remained important. Francis and *Anthony of Padua appeared in *fresco cycles and in altarpieces and *polyptychs often in non-Franciscan contexts. Cycles derived from Assisi decorated many churches and family *chapels. This phenomenon formed part of a lively artistic competition in the 14th century between the various *religious orders, most notably the other mendicant orders, the *Dominicans, *Augustinians, and Carmelites, each striving for a prominent role in medieval society. *See also* ART AND ARCHITECTURE: BYZANTINE / GOTHIC / ROMANESQUE; HAGIOGRAPHY; LITURGY; STIGMATA. SR

H. Belting, *Die Oberkirche von San Francesco in Assisi* (1977).
D. Blume, *Wandmalerei als Ordenspropaganda* (1983).
F. Bologna, 'Povertà e umiltà: il "San Ludovico" di Simone Martini', *Studi storici*, 10 (1969), 231–59.
L. Bourdua, *The Franciscan and Art Patronage in Late Medieval Italy* (2004).
W. Cook, *Images of St Francis of Assisi* (1999).
A. Derbes, *Picturing the Passion in Late Medieval Italy: Narrative Painting, Franciscan Ideology, and the Levant* (1996).
C. Frugoni, *Francesco e l'invenzione delle stimmate* (1993).
K. Krüger, *Die frühe Bildkult der Franziskus in Italien* (1992).
L. Little, *Religious Poverty and the Profit Economy in Medieval Europe* (1978).
F. Martin, *Die Apsisverglasung der Oberkirche von S. Francesco in Assisi* (1993).
S. Romano, *La basilica di San Francesco ad Assisi: Pittori, botteghe, strategie narrative* (2001).
C. L. Striker and Y. D. Kuban, *Kalenderhane in Istanbul: The Buildings, their History, Architecture, and Decoration* (1997).

art, Mudéjar Traditionally refers to Iberian works produced by Muslims under Christian rule, from the conquest of *Toledo in 1085 to the 16th century. The role of Muslim craftsmen is debated, but the term describes richly textured brick architecture, tile and stucco adornment, and intricately coffered wooden ceilings. Examples include churches of Toledo, Sahagún, and Teruel; synagogues in Toledo and

*Andalusia; 14th-century palaces at Tordesillas and Astudillo; and the *Alcázar of *Pedro I in *Seville. *See also* ART AND ARCHITECTURE: ALMORAVID / MOZARABIC. JPD

P. Araguas, *Brique et architecture dans l'Espagne médiévale (XIIe–XVe siècle)* (2003).
M. J. Feliciano, L. Rouhi, *et al.*, 'Interrogating Iberian Frontiers', *Medieval Encounters* 12 (2006), 317–532.
R. J. L. Guzmán, *Arquitectura mudéjar: del sincretismo medieval a las alternativas hispanoamericanas* (2000).

art, Pictish Art created by the inhabitants of northern Scotland in the MA. It consists of incised stones, cross slabs, monuments, and *metalwork and is characterized by its use of zoomorphic and geometric patterns. The arrival of Christianity in the region resulted in Christian symbols, such as the *cross, being incorporated into the more traditional patterns. For many years art historians considered Pictish art rudimentary, but recent work has helped foster a better understanding of both its historical importance and aesthetic qualities. *See also* ART AND ARCHITECTURE: INSULAR / SCANDINAVIAN; SCOTLAND, IRELAND, WALES: EARLY 'SCOTLAND' TO 1124. RSM

G. Henderson and I. Henderson, *The Art of the Picts: Sculpture and Metalwork in Early Medieval Scotland* (2004).

art, Umayyad Art produced during the Umayyad *caliphate developed diverse late antique tendencies: Byzantine, Sasanian, Jewish, Palmyrene, central Asian. Major surviving monuments include the public-religious (the Dome of the Rock or *Umar *mosque, the al-Aqsa mosque, the mosque of *Damascus), the private-secular (Qusayr Amra, Mshatta, Qasr al-Hayr east and west, Khirbat al-Mafjar), and luxury objects ('post-Sasanian' silver, the Humeima ivories, the al-Faddayn brazier). While the public monuments are not iconic, the private are richly figural. *See also* ART AND ARCHITECTURE: BYZANTINE / SASANIAN / SYNAGOGUE; ICONOGRAPHY: ICONOCLASM. BWA

F. B. Flood, *The Great Mosque of Damascus* (2001).
G. Fowden, *Qusayr 'Amra* (2004).
O. Grabar, *The Formation of Islamic Art* (²1987).

art and architecture: Abbasid The Abbasid caliphate (750–1258) is the second Islamic dynasty. The Abbasids succeeded the Damascus-based Umayyad dynasty (661–750) and moved the focal point of the Islamic political and cultural world eastward from Syria to Iraq. In 762, the Abbasid caliph al-*Mansur founded a new capital, the round City of Peace (*madinat al-salam*) in *Baghdad. The Abbasids later founded Samarra, north of Baghdad, which served as the capital of the caliphate for a brief period between 836 and 883. During the period between the 9th and 11th centuries, Baghdad and Samarra became the most affluent and admired cities in the Islamic world. This period also marks the cultural pinnacle of the Abbasid caliphate. However, by the mid 11th century, Abbasid political unity along with caliphal control over the empire deteriorated due to the rise of independent and semi-autonomous local dynasties in *Egypt, *Iran, and other parts of the empire. The Abbasid caliphate eventually collapsed with the invasion of Baghdad by the *Mongols in 1258.

The Abbasid period is artistically important because it witnessed the development of new artistic and architectural styles that greatly influenced the art and architecture produced throughout the rest of the Islamic world. A new way of carving surfaces, the so-called bevelled style, as well as a repetition of abstract geometric or abstracted vegetal forms were widely used as wall decoration and became popular in other media such as *wood, *metalwork, *textiles, and *pottery. At this time, the technique of lustre painting over a white *glaze was also probably introduced in Samarra. The popularity of this glazing technique, which gives pottery a metallic sheen, became widely popular throughout the Islamic and western worlds.

Abbasid architecture is marked by its borrowings from Persian and central Asian models and by its monumental scale. Most Abbasid buildings were constructed out of brick and employed carved and moulded stucco for ornament. Among the extant architecture from this period, the palace of Jawsaq al-Khaqani (*c.*836) and the mosques of al-Mutawakkil (848–52) and Abu Dulaf (859–61) in Samarra are the most emblematic of the Abbasid style. Other surviving Abbasid mosques are the late-9th-century mosque of Ibn Tulun in *Cairo, the Tarik Khane of Damghan in Iran (750–89), as well as the 9th-century Masjid-i-Tarikh in Balkh, Afghanistan. LT

F. Déroche, *The Abbasid Tradition Qur'ans of the 8th to the 10th Centuries AD* (1992).
R. Ettinghausen and O. Grabar, *The Art and Architecture of Islam 650–1250* (1987), 75–125.
J. Hoag, *Islamic Architecture* (1987), 23–31.
J. Lassner, *The Topography of Baghdad in the Early Middle Ages* (1970).
A. Northedge, *The Historical Topography of Samarra* (2005).
H. Philon, *Early Islamic Ceramics: Ninth to Late Twelfth Centuries* (1980).

art and architecture: Almoravid The Almoravids (*al-Murabitun* in Arabic) ruled Morocco and *al-Andalus (Muslim Spain) between *c.*1062 and 1150. Due to the Almoravids' adherence to the conservative Malikite school of Islamic law, their art and architecture is best characterized as austere. The Almoravid disdain for the luxury arts (*textiles, *metalwork, ivory carving, and so forth) is evident in that there are very few extant objects from this period. What remains dates mostly to the reign of the last Almoravid sultan, Ali ibn Yusuf (r. 1106–46). One of the best surviving examples of Almoravid craftsmanship is the beautifully carved wood and inlay *minbar (pulpit) now in the al-Kutubiyya mosque in *Marrakesh, the capital of the Almoravids. An inscription on this minbar's left side states that it was built in *Córdoba on the first day of Muharram 532 AH (19 September, 1137) for the congregational mosque in Marrakesh. In North Africa the mosques of Algiers (*c.*1097), Tlemcen (1136), and Qarawiyin in *Fès (1135) are among the most important architectural examples from this period.

LT

J. Bloom, 'The Masterpiece Minbar', *Saudi Aramco World* (May/June 1998), 2–11.
J. Dodds, ed., *Al-Andalus: The Art of Islamic Spain* (1992).
G. Marçais, *L'architecture musulmane d'Occident* (1954).

art and architecture: Angevin (in Italy) The ruling family of Sicily and southern *Italy, 1266–1414, known as Angevins after their place of origin, *Anjou (France). Angevin rule on the whole, however, did not represent a simple case of French artistic values imported to southern Italy, but rather an ongoing process of artistic integration with strong indigenous traditions.

1. Charles I
2. Charles II
3. Robert I
4. Aristocratic and merchant patronage

1. *Charles I*

In 1266, *Charles of Anjou, youngest son of Louis VIII of France, conquered the kingdom of Sicily from the last heir of the Hohenstaufen dynasty, Manfred. The new regime, although characterized by political and economic instability, produced a flourishing of art and architecture, especially in *Naples. Surviving evidence of French artisanship can be found in *metalwork and *enamels, such as the *reliquary head of San Gennaro, commissioned by Charles II (1288–1309) for the *cathedral of Naples, and other reliquaries donated to San Nicola in Bari.

There are several distinct phases of architecture produced under Angevin rule. Charles I repaired the *castles at Lagopesole, Melfi, Bari, and Mola di Bari with elements in tune with contemporary trends in French fortification design. At Lucera he constructed a fortified enclosure for a community of French settlers brought in to counterweigh the adjacent Muslim population; these new walls were similar in style to those of *Aigues Mortes (France), constructed in the 1240s by *Louis IX.

Charles of Anjou's most conspicuous architectural project was the Castel Nuovo of Naples, a new royal residence built on the southwest side of the city. Construction was initiated in 1279, but work continued during the reigns of Charles II and Robert (1309–43). Charles II constructed the royal *chapel at the castle in its present form, and in *c.*1330 King Robert employed *Giotto to decorate it and the choir of the church of St Chiara in Naples. Only minute fragments survive of Giotto's decoration at these sites; the castle itself was largely rebuilt in the 15th century by Alphonse II.

In ecclesiastical architecture, evidence of French influence is especially evident in the first decades. The most conspicuous example is Sant'Eligio al Mercato, a hospital founded by a *confraternity of French merchants, to which Charles I gave two parcels of land in 1270 and 1279 at the new market (the Campo Moricino, or Piazza del Mercato). The church resembles the king's other foundation of St-Jean-de Malte in *Aix-en-Provence, which housed the tomb of his first wife, Beatrice. At Sant'Eligio the south portal is in a distinctly French Rayonnant style. Evidence of French workmanship is also visible in the monument to Isabelle of Aragon in the cathedral of Cosenza (Calabria).

Other monuments, however, suggest a fusion of French and Italian influences. The most striking of these is the Franciscan church of San Lorenzo in Naples of the 1270s. Because the choir is rib-vaulted, and the plan has an *ambulatory and radiating chapels, the structure recalls French models. The handling of the structure, however, is archaic by French standards, and suggests instead that the church was designed within a Franciscan building tradition of the second half of the 13th century. In the late 1290s Charles II gave funds for the completion of the church, which was enlarged several decades later with the vast single *nave flanked by lateral chapels that can be seen today.

2. *Charles II*

The most important phase of Angevin patronage was that of Charles II. With his financial support many churches were founded, built, restored, or repaired in the kingdom of Sicily. He was an especially ardent patron of the *Dominicans and also subsidized the construction of several *cathedrals and *Franciscan houses. Among his many projects were the foundation or reconstruction of the churches of San Domenico and San Pietro Martire in Naples. The king also subsidized the reconstruction of the cathedral of Naples, a centrally important monument in southern Italy. Here one can see a distinct preference for local architectural idioms and techniques: the piers integrate the columns of the previous (early Christian) *basilica, and the high *transept suggests affiliation with the building traditions of Constantinian Rome. The *apse of the cathedral contained the tombs of several members of the ruling family, including Charles I's.

Beginning in *c.*1307, Queen Mary of Hungary, wife of Charles II, supported the reconstruction of the Clarissan church of Sta. Maria Donnaregina, one of the most striking *Gothic monuments of Naples. The upper choir for the nuns' community was decorated by Pietro *Cavallini and his school, although it was badly damaged by a fire in the late 14th century. Queen Mary (d. 1325) was buried in the church in a tomb executed by Tino di Camaino, who had been brought to Naples in *c.*1323 to carve the tomb of Catherine of Austria, still in San Lorenzo. Tino's work initiated a new style of sculpture in Naples.

Charles II was also responsible for significant public works in Naples and other cities such as L'Aquila, Brindisi, and Barletta. He repaired city walls, constructed new roads, established a new port, and occupied himself with the water supply and drainage of Naples.

3. Robert I

Although King Robert is mostly known as a patron of poetry and literature, his wife, Sancia of Mallorca, was devoted to the *Franciscan order and especially active in the foundation of convents for women in Naples and Provence. The most conspicuous example is the vast convent of Sta. Chiara in Naples. This magnificent complex, founded to serve communities of Clarissan nuns and Franciscan friars, was initiated in 1310 and completed *c.*1340. The church consists of a vast single *nave flanked by lateral chapels with galleries placed above the chapels; the nuns' choir at the far end of the nave was directly behind the main altar. As noted above, Giotto was employed to decorate this choir; he was one of many Tuscan artists employed in the service of the court.

In about 1325 Sta. Chiara became the necropolis of the Angevin royal dynasty with the burial of the heir to the throne and his family in 1328. The tombs were carved by Tino da Camaino and his workshop. At his death in 1343 King Robert was buried at Sta. Chiara in a monumental tomb carved by Pacio and Giovanni Bertini, placed behind the main altar. The bombardments of 1943 seriously damaged these tombs, and Robert's in particular is a fragment of the original composition.

At her death in 1345 Queen Sancia was buried at her foundation of Sta. Croce, founded slightly to the west of the Castel Nuovo. Her tomb, now destroyed, is recorded in drawings by Seroux d'Agincourt in the *Vatican Library.

4. Aristocratic and merchant patronage

Although standard narratives on this period emphasize the role of the king and court in the cultural life of the kingdom, recent research indicates that there was also a strong tradition of religious *patronage by the mercantile and urban aristocracy, evident in commercial areas such as Naples, Amalfi, and Ravello on the west coast and Barletta and Brindisi on the east. At Ravello the Rufolo family was an important patron of the cathedral, and other families participated in the construction or decoration of the other churches in the city. At Barletta in the 1290s a consortium of eminent citizens undertook a Gothic extension to Sta. Maria Maggiore that more than doubled the length of the church.

Under Queen Joanna the role of Naples as a cultural and artistic centre declined. In 1348 she moved the royal court to *Avignon, and the vicissitudes of her reign were serious impediments to a continued flourishing of the visual arts. One notable exception is the church of the Incoronata, founded between the old city and the Castel Nuovo. This charitable foundation consists of two parallel naves, a type of architecture frequently found in hospitals, and decorated in the 1350s with a cycle of the Seven Sacraments by Robert d'Odorisio.

Noble patrons in other cities in the kingdom continued to produce remarkable works of art: for example, the church of Sta. Maria della Consolazione in Altomonte (Calabria), the churches founded by the *Orsini family in Nola, or the tombs in Teggiano (Campania) and Gerace (Calabria) were demonstrations of continued noble and courtly art patronage in the provinces. It was not until the early 15th century and the court of Ladislao and Joanna II that a strong and identifiable court culture re-emerged gloriously—if ephemerally—in the kingdom of Naples. CAB

F. Aceto, 'Tino di Camaino a Napoli: una proposta per il sepolcro di Caterina d'Austria e altri fatti angioini', *Prospettiva*, 67 (1992), 53–65.
F. Bologna, *I pittori alla corte angioina di Napoli 1266–1414* (1969).
C. Bruzelius, *The Stones of Naples: Church Building in the Angevin Kingdom, 1266–1343* (2004).
P. L. de Castris, *Arte di corte nella Napoli angioina* (1986).
L. Enderlein, *Die Grablegen des Hauses Anjou in Unteritalien: Totenkult und Monumente* (1997).
G. Galasso, *Il Regno di Napoli: il Mezzogiorno angioino e aragonese (1266–1494)* (1992).
E. Leonard, *Les Angevins de Naples* (1954).
T. Michalsky, *Memoria und Repräsentation: die Grabmaler des Königshauses Anjou in Italien* (2000).
G. Vitolo, *Tra Napoli e Salerno: la costruzione dell'identità cittadina nel mezzogiorno Medievale* (2001).

art and architecture: Anglo-Norman When the Normans conquered England in 1066, there was an extraordinary and thriving artistic tradition already in place, particularly in regard to *manuscript illumination. While the political and ecclesiastical hierarchies underwent tremendous upheaval following the military conquest, many scholars of the period have noted that the majority of illuminators continued to work within a largely AS artistic vocabulary for several decades.

The situation was rather different in regards to architecture. Very few structures remain from the AS period. Much of this had been constructed of perishable materials, but even buildings constructed in stone were often replaced with AN buildings, shortly after the *Norman Conquest. The Anglo-Saxons had, until this point, worked largely in their traditional mode, rather than joining in the Romanesque movement that was spreading through the Continent, with *Westminster Abbey, begun in 1054, as the one noteworthy exception. In post-Conquest

*England, more monumental structures were being built than anywhere else in the world. The AN churches, in particular, stand among the greatest works of the Romanesque period, including, among many others, *Canterbury, *Norwich, *Ely, *Winchester, *Rochester, and, perhaps most dominant, *Durham.

The tremendous *building programme undertaken by the Normans was as political in motivation as it was devout. In *Normandy, *William I had bolstered his power through church reform, and carried this out swiftly in England as well. He rapidly replaced the church hierarchy, and his new bishops and abbots bore *feudal responsibilities as well as ecclesiastical ones. The major building programme begun at this point functioned as visible evidence of the power and ability, as well as the piety, of the new rulers. These new structures were especially designed to impress the Anglo-Saxons, and thereby to convince them of the legitimacy (and incontestability) of the Normans.

The Normans were great builders of two building types, *castles and churches, and they seem to have seen little difference between them in their basic approach. Both tend toward mighty walls, capped with fortifications, and bold simplicity in design. The churches stand out among the whole of medieval architecture for their tremendous *naves, not soaring in height as French *Gothic works would later be, but rather extremely long and low, creating impressive processional spaces and clear, dramatic sightlines from the west portals, through to the flat glass windows in their unusual, square *apses.

Again, in MS art, the Normans can be credited with bringing the Romanesque more solidly to England, which had previously worked in its own, independent idiom. The AN works are more solid in character, with bolder and brighter contrasts of colour and less use of the loose, sketchy inks and washes and gentle colours favoured by many AS houses. The Normans also brought new, more angular scripts, which replaced the rounder AS hands. The resulting works are something of a hybrid, bearing the characteristics of both conqueror and conquered.

Many works of the period contain elaborate, decorated *initials, particularly of the man-and-beasts variety, in which human figures, animals, and monsters all struggle against one another, within writhing, highly energetic foliage. While the period is not known for one great masterpiece, there are a few very noteworthy survivals, including the *Eadwine Psalter (the second copy of the *Utrecht Psalter), the Shaftesbury Psalter, and the Dover, Lambeth, and Winchester Bibles.

As with building, the AN were very productive in the *scriptorium. Christ Church, Canterbury, for example, was more productive between 1070 and 1150 than at any other time, according to extant evidence. The *monasteries were the main production houses in the period, reorganized under Archbishop *Lanfranc, originally of *Bec (sometimes with strong resistance, as at St Augustine's, Canterbury, where the AS monks walked out in protest of the appointment of a Norman abbot to their house). The most significant of these houses were Christ Church, *Bury St Edmunds, St Augustine's, *Canterbury, and St *Swithun's. *See also* ART AND ARCHITECTURE: INSULAR / NORMAN / ROMANESQUE; CHURCH TYPES; PALAEOGRAPHY. ASM

BAACT, vol. 3: *Medieval Art and Architecture at Durham Cathedral* (1980).
W. Braunfels, *Monasteries of Western Europe* (1972).
C. R. Dodwell, *The Canterbury School of Illumination, 1066–1200* (1954).
E. Fernie, *The Architecture of Norman England* (2000).
P. Johnson, *Cathedrals of England, Scotland and Wales* (1990).
C. M. Kauffmann, *Romanesque Manuscripts, 1066–1190* (1975).
S. N. Vaughn, *The Abbey of Bec and the Anglo-Norman State, 1034–1136* (1981).
F. Wormald, *The Survival of Anglo-Saxon Illumination after the Norman Conquest* (1944).

art and architecture: Arabic With the spread of Islam from the Arabian Peninsula westward across North Africa and into Spain in the century following the death of the prophet *Muhammad in 630, new forms of artistic expression exhibiting a combination of Persian and Byzantine influences began to flourish in the areas of Islamic domination. Carpet-making, ceramic *pottery, decorative tile, and *metalwork, which had long been in existence in Persia and the Far East before the formation of Islam, together with new architectural styles particularly linked to the new faith, covered the artistic landscape as the religion spread geographically.

1. General artistic characteristics
2. Damascus and Jerusalem
3. Hispano-Arab art and architecture

1. *General artistic characteristics*

Of the various forms of artistic expression linked to Arabian culture, *architecture, especially *mosques, is by far the most widely developed and recognized. Like Christian churches, Islamic mosques seek to serve the faithful by providing a space of adequate size for large gatherings while also offering an aesthetically pleasing place in which one may pray with tranquillity. Unlike many Christian churches that find their aesthetic value in the statuary, *stained glass, or paintings found within their walls, mosques contain no such characteristics due to the Islamic prohibition of graven images. Instead, the walls of mosques often contain ornately designed *engravings or paintings of phrases taken from the *Quran and written in Arabic *calligraphy. Due to the sacredness of the Quranic writings and the desire for aesthetic beauty predominant in Arab art, architects and calligraphers hold the highest respect among artists of Arab visual expression. Structurally, the main hall of most mosques takes the form of a square in which the faithful face the *mihrab*, a decorative niche in the centre of the *qibla* wall that indicates the direction of the Kaaba in *Mecca. Also particular to mosques is the *minaret, a tower from which traditionally the **muezzin* calls the faithful to prayer five times each day. Also common to Arabian architecture is the use of horseshoe *arches as frames for *windows and doors.

Outside of architecture, carpet-making and the production of *ceramic tiles and *pottery became widespread throughout the Arab world as early as the 9th century. In the main, these products exhibited the same aesthetic desires for beauty through parallelism and geometric motifs as seen in architectural design, and often floral or animal scenes were chosen as the themes for *rugs or tile paintings. Despite the prohibition of graven images, some artists did choose to portray the human form in some scenes of the early years of this form of Arab art.

2. *Damascus and Jerusalem*

As Islam moved north and west, gaining more territory geographically, the cities of *Damascus and *Jerusalem gained importance as both religious and cultural centres. As a result, much of the Arabian architecture found throughout North Africa and Spain in the MA took these two cities as their models. The mosque of *Umar, a shrine in Jerusalem built by Byzantine craftsmen under the orders of the caliph Abd al-Malik between 687–91, is located on the spot where Muslims believe *Muhammad to have ascended into Heaven for a consultation with Moses and where Jews believe Abraham to have laid Isaac for the sacrifice demanded of him by God. This octagonal building is considered not only one of Islam's most holy places but also one of the most popular examples of Middle Byzantine art. During the *crusades, the Dome of the Rock fell into the hands of the *Augustinians, but was later returned to the Muslims when *Saladin took control of the city in 1187.

The Great Mosque of Damascus, also known as the Umayyad Mosque, built on the site of a demolished *cathedral dedicated to St John the Baptist, has since the early 8th century been considered one of the most impressive mosques in the world. Built between 706–14 by the Umayyad caliph al-Walid I (668–715), it became the model upon which the Great Mosque of *Córdoba in Spain was later designed. As with the Dome of the Rock, Byzantine builders were sent from *Constantinople to build the mosque at Damascus, covering its walls with colourful mosaics depicting the wonders of paradise. At the time of its construction, the Great Mosque of Damascus was the largest mosque in the world, with dimensions measuring 153 m by 99 m, though the mosque at Córdoba later grew to even larger proportions.

3. *Hispano-Arab art and architecture*

In Europe the influence of Arabian art and architecture is nowhere more prominent than in Spain. The Arabian invasion of 711 meant for Spain nearly eight hundred years of cultural exchange between Iberian Christians and Hispano-Arabs in which new forms of art and architecture came into being. Though Islam spread to over two-thirds of Iberia, Arabian cultural norms took deepest roots in *al-Andalus, the southern portion of the peninsula. There mosques and Arabian palaces were built in grandiose style in imitation of those found in the Middle East, and from there Christian artists and architects went north with new ideas and designs.

During the *caliphate of *Córdoba (912–1031), Abderramán III (912–61) brought the Andalusian city to the height of its grandeur by having over 700 mosques and 300 public baths built. Schools of ceramics and metallurgy were established, and *envoys from Constantinople, Germany, Italy, France, and England were sent to gather news of the riches and artistic beauty of Córdoba, as it had become the most glamorous capital city in all of Europe. Central to the city's renown was the *Mezquita*, or the Great Mosque of Córdoba, begun in 785 during the emirate of Abderramán I (756–88) and expanded a total of three times. The original building consisted of a square enclosure of 74 m from side to side, to which was added a hexagonal-domed *mihrab* in 965 by caliph Hakim II (d. 976). Decorated with calligraphic writings from the Quran and intricate stucco and stonework, the *mihrab* was entered through a brilliant horseshoe arch and came to be known as the most beautiful *mihrab* in the Arab world. From 987–8, caliph al-*Mansur (938–1002) ordered the mosque enlarged to the dimensions of 180 m north to south and 130 m east to west, with over 1000 columns made of jasper, onyx, marble, and granite supporting horseshoe arches of alternating red and white stripes. In 1236 Córdoba fell into Christian hands and the great mosque was re-consecrated as the cathedral of the Assumption of the Virgin.

The second of the great Arabian architectural projects in Spain was the Alhambra, a palace fortress of 142,000 m^2 built above the town of Granada between 1248–1354 for the Nazri kings of the kingdom of *Granada. The palace is most known for the intricate calligraphy and stucco formations that adorn the interior walls, details that exhibit the demand for elegance placed on the artists and architects of the Nazri period. Fountains and neatly arranged gardens provided a paradisiacal setting in which the royal family passed their time in tranquil luxury. To accompany the Alhambra fortress, the Generalife palace was built during the reign of Muhammad III (1302–9) as a summer house for the Nazri sultans. As with the Alhambra, the Generalife consists of ornately decorated rooms overlooking fountains, pools, and patio gardens, and it is believed that this small palace conserves even today the best example of Andalusian garden architecture ever to have existed.

The presence of Arabian style in Christian art and architecture may be found in Mozarabic and Mudéjar churches and MSS in the northern regions of the Iberian Peninsula. Such buildings as the *monastery of *Santo Domingo de Silos and San Miguel de Escalada clearly exhibit the influence of Arabian arches and motifs in the colonnades of the *cloisters. The early *Beatus *Commentaries on the Apocalypse* are the best examples of Arabian influence on the use of colour and decorative motifs in *manuscript illuminations. *See also* ART AND ARCHITECTURE: BYZANTINE/MOZARABIC; ART, MUDÉJAR; CALIPHATE, UMAYYAD; ISLAMIC EMPIRE; WATERWORKS. KRP

J. F. Arenas, *Mozarabic Architecture* (1972).
H. Atasoy, A. Bahnassi, and M. Rogers, *The Art of Islam* (1990).
G. Beaugé and J. F. Clément, *L'image dans le monde arabe* (1995).
D. Behrens-Abouseif, *Schönheit in der arabischen Kultur* (1998).
S. Bianca, *Urban Form in the Arab World: Past and Present* (2000).
S. S. Blair and J. M. Bloom, *The Art and Architecture of Islam, 1250–1800* (1994).
J. G. Davies, *Temples, Churches, and Mosques: A Guide to the Appreciation of Religious Architecture* (1982).
M. Gómez-Moreno, *Iglesias Mózarabes: Arte Español de los Siglos IX a XI* (1919).
E. J. Grube, *The World of Islam* (1967).
——*Architecture of the Islamic World: Its History and Social Meaning* (1995).
R. Hillenbrand, *Islamic Architecture: Form, Function, and Meaning* (1994).
R. J. López-Gúzman, *Arquitectura Mudéjar: del Sincretismo Medieval a las alternativas hispanoamericanas* (2000).
B. Pavón-Maldonado, *Arte Toledano: Islámico y Mudéjar* (1973).
J. Pereira, *Islamic Sacred Architecture: Stylistic History* (1994).
U. Vogt-Göknil, *Mosquées: Grands Courants de l'Architecture Islamique* (1975).
R. Yeomans, *The Story of Islamic Architecture* (2000).

art and architecture: Armenian Medieval Armenia's visual culture bears strikingly distinctive features as well as evidence of close contact with neighbouring traditions. Art in the region is generally categorized into three periods. The first, from the 4th to the 8th centuries, saw the emergence of ecclesiastical architecture. The earliest surviving churches are basilical in form, constructed with rubble masonry, and feature stone *vaults carried on piers. In the 7th century, the *basilica was superseded by a centralized, domed form unique to the Transcaucasus. At the church of Hripʿsimē (618), a cubic shell, enlivened by triangular niches, is topped by four gabled cross arms which meet at a square base supporting a faceted drum and conical roof. The variety and number of churches produced during this era is remarkable; moreover, many are dated by inscriptions. Relief sculpture appears on church exteriors, consisting of profiled door and window mouldings, capitals derived from classical orders, and figural sculpture including biblical images, aristocratic scenes, and donor portraits. The first known examples of Armenian MS art, a set of four folios, are generally dated to this period. Bound within the Ejmiacin Gospels (Erevan, Matenadaran, MS. 2374GF), they feature scenes from the infancy of Christ. The large-eyed, curly-haired figures, executed in deep mineral pigments, find correspondences in Syriac MSS and Sasanian traditions. Departures from Byzantine iconographic formulae may reflect the circulation of apocryphal texts such as the Armenian Infancy Gospel.

The second period comprises the 9th to 11th centuries, when Armenia was controlled by two royal dynasties. A key monument of this era is the palace chapel of Ałtʿamar, begun *c.*915. In plan it recalls 7th-century *quatrefoils. The form was sheathed in an elaborate programme of figural reliefs, including biblical images, *hunting and feasting scenes, and donor portraits. Another important building of the era is the cathedral of Ani (989–1001). A domed basilica, the structure is enlivened by profiled piers, pointed arches, and exterior blind arcades. The same period witnessed an increase in MS painting, as indicated by the large number of surviving gospel books. A series of painting styles emerged, including an abstract, schematized tradition associated with clerical production, and a Byzantinizing, naturalistic mode used in deluxe royal commissions. Sculpted steles, known as 'cross-stones' (*xačʿkʿars*), also survive from this era, bearing relief decoration of crosses and vegetal ornament.

The third period, from the 12th to the 15th centuries, witnessed architectural experimentation in monastic building. Church forehalls (*gawits*) are often vaulted with intersecting ribs placed laterally or diagonally across space. **Muqarnas* forms, appropriated from Seljuk *art and architecture, also appear. A rich array of relief sculpture, including sculpted tympana and vegetal decoration, decorates wall surfaces. *Xačʿkʿars* become more exuberant, often including figural scenes. Wall painting from this period is particularly well preserved in the *fresco cycles of the church of Tigran Honencʿ at Ani (1218). From the 12th to the 14th centuries, the Armenian kingdom of Cilicia (southwest Anatolia) produced a corpus of MSS impressive in both number and visual sophistication. The painter Tʿoros Roslin, commissioned by the royal Hetʿumids to illustrate a series of gospel books, created works celebrated for their inventive marginalia, subtle psychology, and luxurious gold surfaces. Cilician MSS are infused with a swirl of artistic influences, including Byzantine, *crusader, *Franciscan, and Mongol art.

In Greater Armenia, under successive periods of Georgian, Turkish, and Mongol rule, questions of identity played a crucial role in visual culture. The Glajor Gospels (Los Angeles, UCLA Spec. Coll., Armenian MS. 1 [1300–1307]), produced in the region of Siwnik in southwestern Armenia, offers a striking assertion of Armenian exegetical thought and liturgical practice. In the Lake Van region, the influence of Mongol visual traditions fostered a painting style characterized by bold abstraction and bright, colourful patterns. In the 16th and 17th centuries, Armenian art continued to flourish in diaspora communities. The Armenians of *Constantinople, for example, produced a rich corpus of MSS informed by both traditional pictorial formulae and the arrival of European print culture. CM

S. Der-Nersessian, *Armenian Art* (1978).
—— *Miniature Painting in the Armenian Kingdom of Cilicia* (1993).
J. Durand, I. Rapti, and D. Giovannoni, *Armenia Sacra: Mémoire chrétienne des Arméniens (IVe–XVIIIe siècles)* (2007).
C. Maranci, *Medieval Armenian Architecture* (2001).
T. F. Mathews, 'The Early Armenian Iconographic Program of the Ejmiacin Gospel', *East of Byzantium: Syria and Armenia in the Formative Period*, ed. N. G. Garsoïan, idem, and R. W. Thomson (1982), 199–215.
—— and R. S. Wieck, eds, *Treasures in Heaven: Armenian Illuminated Manuscripts* (1994).
J.-M. Thierry and P. Donabédian, *Armenian Art* (1987).

art and architecture: Ayyubid The Ayyubid dynasty ruled in *Egypt between 1171–1250, in Syria and southeast Anatolia between 1180–1260, and in the Yemen between 1174–1229. The dynasty was established in 1169 by the Kurdish Zengid general Salah al-Din (known in the west as *Saladin). During his reign (1169–93), Salah al-Din ended the *Shia Fatimid *caliphate of Egypt in 1171 and brought Aleppo and *Damascus under his control in 1183 and 1186, respectively. *Cairo eventually became the main capital of the sultanate, and Damascus its second major city. The struggle between the Muslims and the crusaders dominates the history of the Ayyubids, and this period is perhaps best known for the Muslim reconquest of *Jerusalem, first in 1187 and later in 1244. Even though the sultanate depended on slave soldiers (mamluks) for its military organization, the dynasty's eventual demise beginning in 1250 was largely caused by the mamluks themselves, who overthrew the last Ayyubid sultan in Egypt and founded the Mamluk sultanate (1250–1517).

The Ayyubids were great patrons of architecture, and many buildings survive from this period in such cities as Cairo, Damascus, and Aleppo. Notable among the secular architecture are the fortified citadels of Cairo (1187) and Aleppo (early 13th century). The dynasty's adherence to *Sunna doctrine is reflected architecturally by the building of many *madrasahs (religious colleges), such as the Zahiriya in Aleppo (1219) and Salih Najm al-Din Ayyub in Cairo (1243). The triumph of Sunnism is also manifested in commemorative buildings, such as in the mausoleum of one of the main Sunni theologians, *Imam al-Shafii (1211). In addition, this period is characterized by the rise in the role of women as patrons of architecture, as is evidenced in the Madrasa al-Sahiba in Damascus (1233), which was commissioned by Salah al-Din's sister Rabia Khatun, as well as the Mausoleum of Salih Najm al-Din Ayyub (1250), built by his wife Shajarat al-Durr.

In the arts, the Ayyubids are known particularly for their works in inlaid *metalwork, *enamelled *glass, carved *wood, and *ceramics, particularly lustre- and underglaze-painted wares. Signatures of artists on some of the metalwork indicate that the majority of the craftsmen were from Mosul in Iraq. Techniques established and developed during this time formed the foundation of the arts in the later periods. *See also* WOMEN IN ISLAM. LT

E. Baer, *Ayyubid Metalwork with Christian Images* (1989).
D. Behrens-Abouseif, *Islamic Architecture in Cairo: An Introduction* (1989), 78–93.
R. S. Humphreys, 'Women as Patrons of Religious Architecture in Ayyubid Damascus', *Muqarnas*, 11 (1994), 35–54.
N. D. MacKenzie, *Ayyubid Cairo: A Topographical Study* (1992).
J. Raby, ed., *The Art of Syria and the Jazira 1100–1250* (1985).
J. Sauvaget, *Les Monuments ayyoubides de Damas*, 4 vols (1938–50).
Y. Tabbaa, *Constructions of Power and Piety in Medieval Aleppo* (1997).

art and architecture: Benedictine The Benedictine houses of monks and nuns founded throughout Europe from the middle of the 6th century onwards, although connected by little or no supra-regional hierarchy, shared several characteristic architectural features. The Benedictine Rule dictated that the bulk of the monks' daily activities take place inside a protective enclosure, and that the buildings intended to accommodate the monastic round of work, study, and prayer be interconnected in some way, typically with a *cloister. Benedictine monks and nuns were to eat, sleep, and pray the *Divine Office communally, necessitating a *refectory, dormitory, and *oratory. Later foundations also incorporated a *chapter house, used both for the daily reading of a chapter of the Benedictine Rule and for organizational and disciplinary gatherings. Benedictine architectural complexes thus can usually be identified by their component parts.

The order, as such, never mandated a distinctive architectural layout or decorative style. The early-9th-century *St Gall plan, possibly drafted in response to the monastic reforms of the *Carolingian king *Louis the Pious, was apparently never adopted as a binding model for monasteries within the Carolingian realm. Therefore, the appearance of most Benedictine monasteries was guided by regional tastes and traditions. In a few cases, the ground plan or elevation of a particularly noted Benedictine abbey church could be influential. The ground plan of the 11th-century church at *Monte Cassino may have been copied because of the abbey's reputation as *Benedict's own *monastery. More organized branches of the Benedictine order such as the *Cluniacs and *Cistercians, however, could be identified with a style of architecture, inspired either by the home region of the order or by the architectural philosophy of the order's spiritual leaders. Cluniac daughter-houses may have imitated the mother-house's pointed *arches and *apses in echelon scheme, or later its *pilgrimage *chevet. Conversely, these churches may have copied similar local models. The Cistercians, alone among the Benedictines, instituted a system of oversight intended to impose architectural uniformity among its daughter-houses. Until the late MA, Cistercian churches usually exhibited a lowered vertical profile, square east end, and no *bell tower. In addition, Cistercian houses internationally copied the pointed arches characteristic of the Burgundian mother-house. Some Cistercian innovations, such as the practice of placing the dormitory perpendicular to the cloister, were intended to accommodate the reformed lifestyle of the monks. Similarly, adjustments to the *crypt level of Benedictine churches in Lorraine incorporated, through architectural layout or *altar designation, symbolism particular to the *Gorze reform.

Art can be associated with the Benedictine order most easily through its *patronage rather than its content or appearance. Some objects that commonly incorporated artwork in the MA were necessary to the practices mandated by the Benedictine Rule. Thus, each Benedictine monastery commissioned, bought, or created the accoutrements of Benedictine life, including decorated Bibles, *missals, *graduals, *breviaries and *antiphonals, liturgical plate, and *liturgical vestments. Art in Benedictine contexts, however, did not employ a consistent style, *iconography, or medium, and thus none of these objects would have been identifiably Benedictine. Again, the exception to this may be artistic innovations that were the products of Benedictine monastic reform. For example, *crucifixion images in AS England may have served a specifically Benedictine liturgical devotion. Likewise, MS images of St Benedict wearing a diadem expressed reformers' commitment to monastic leadership, and Romanesque cloister *sculpture in *France and Spain may have reflected a renewed emphasis on the *apostolic life. DJR

W. Braunfels, *Monasteries of Western Europe: The Architecture of the Orders* (1972), 7–110.

K. J. Conant, *Benedictine Contributions to Church Architecture* (1949).

R. Deshman, '*Benedictus Monarcha et Monachus*: Early Medieval Ruler Theology and the Anglo-Saxon Reform', *FMAS* 22 (1988), 204–40.

P. Fergusson, *Architecture of Solitude: Cistercian Abbeys in 12th-century England* (1984).

I. H. Forsyth, 'The *Vita Apostolica* and Romanesque Sculpture: Some Preliminary Observations', *Gesta*, 25 (1986), 75–82.

R. Gameson, *The Role of Art in the Late Anglo-Saxon Church* (1995).

W. Horn, 'On the Origins of the Medieval Cloister', *Gesta*, 12 (1973), 13–52.

T. W. Lyman, 'The Politics of Selective Eclecticism: Monastic Architecture, Pilgrimage Churches and "Resistance to Cluny"', *Gesta*, 27 (1988), 83–92.

L. Pressouyre, 'St Bernard to Saint Francis: Monastic Ideals and Iconographic Programs in the Cloister', *Gesta*, 12 (1973), 71–92.

B. Raw, *Anglo-Saxon Crucifixion Iconography and the Art of the Monastic Revival* (1990).

W. Sanderson, *The Monastic Reform in Lorraine and the Architecture of the Outer Crypt, 950–1100* (1971).

art and architecture: Bulgarian Over most of its history, the medieval Bulgarian state covered the territory of the modern republics of *Bulgaria and Macedonia. While outstanding monuments of Byzantine art are found there in Sofia, Ohrid, Nerezi, Bachkovo, Mělník, and Nesebăr, this entry discusses only works commissioned by Bulgarian patrons.

Tastes that the Bulgar *nobility brought from its steppe homeland inform the first major monuments of Bulgarian art: a large rock-cut relief of a hunting horseman at Madara and a treasure of gold vessels from Nagy-Szent-Miklós (Vienna, Kunsthistorisches Museum). Their style has connections with Sasanian Iran; their imagery is related to a semi-nomadic way of life. Nomadic customs delayed the emergence of masonry architecture, the earliest remains of which, excavated at the first Bulgarian capital Pliska, date to *c.*800. Khan Omurtag (ruled 814–31) undertook a major building campaign, documented by stone inscriptions in Greek.

The adoption of Christianity in 864 occasioned the construction of numerous churches: the remains of a large three-isle *basilica survive at Pliska and those of a *trefoil monastery church associated with Bishop *Kliment were found in Ohrid. The Byzantine cross-in-square plan became widespread once smaller *parish churches started to be built, for example most of those excavated in Preslav, the capital after 893. A novel feature of Preslav buildings is their rich decoration of carved marble and of glazed *ceramic tiles. Among the latter are found the earliest known works of Bulgarian icon-painting. A large jewellery hoard from Preslav, including pieces with cloisonné *enamel, was buried when the city fell to the Byzantines in 971. The last significant monuments of the First Bulgarian Empire (681–1018) lie on the shores of Lake Prespa, where Tsar Samuel (ruled 971–1014) built a basilica to house the *relics of St Achilles of Larissa (*c.*983) and a cross-in-square funerary church for his parents (993).

In Tărnovo, the capital of the Second Bulgarian Empire (1185–1396), the churches of Sts Peter and Paul and of the Forty Martyrs of Sebaste preserve fragmentary wall *paintings from *c.*1220–40. Together with an icon of the Holy Face in *Laon and with the murals of the church of Sts Nicholas and Panteleimon (1259) at Boyana outside Sofia, they represent local painting styles developed on the basis of late-12th-century Byzantine models. A hundred years later, the *frescoes of a rock-cut church near Ivanovo (1360s) show complete assimilation of a new, late-Byzantine style coming from *Constantinople. Its gradual adoption in Tărnovo can be traced through a series of *illuminated MSS made there in the course of the 14th century: the Chilandari *Gospels of Tsar George II Terter (1322), the Sofia *Psalter (1337), the Vatican Manasses (c.1349) and London Gospels (1356) copied for Tsar John Alexander (ruled 1331–71), and the Moscow 'Tomić Psalter' (1360s).

The key surviving monument of 14th-century architecture, the church of Sts Peter and Paul in Nikopol (Nikopolis), displays façade articulation and decorative brickwork similar to those of late-Byzantine buildings. Secular *metalwork, as exemplified by a hoard found also at Nikopol (Pleven, Museum), shows the influence of Gothic art. Works commissioned by regional nobles in the west of the country were less open to outside influences, as shown by the 14th-century wall paintings of the churches in Donja Kamenica, Staničenje (1332), Berende, Kalotina, and Zemen. Local artistic schools became dominant after the Ottoman conquest of the Balkans destroyed royal courts and wiped away most state borders. The murals of the Dragalevtsi monastery outside Sofia (1476) were painted by Ohrid masters, those of the nearby monasteries of Kremikovtsi (1493) and Poganovo (1500) are by a workshop probably based in Kastoria, and the Tărnovo church of Sts Peter and Paul was repainted in the 1520s by artists from *Wallachia. Medieval traditions determined the character of Bulgarian art until the 18th century. *See also* ART AND ARCHITECTURE: BYZANTINE / GOTHIC / SASANIAN; MASONS.

GRP

A. Ančev, ed., *La Bulgarie médiévale: Art et civilisation* (1980).
E. Bakalova, 'Sur la peinture bulgare de la seconde moitié du XIVe siècle', *L'école de la Morava et son temps*, ed. V. Djurić (1972), 61–75.
Corsi di cultura sull'arte ravennate e bizantina, 15 (1968), 7–30, 113–30, 241–93.
B. Filov, *Geschichte der altbulgarischen Kunst* (1932).
A. Grabar, *La peinture religieuse en Bulgarie* (1928).
K. Mijatev, *Die mittelalterliche Baukunst in Bulgarien* (1974).
O. Minaeva, *From Paganism to Christianity: Formation of Medieval Bulgarian Art* (1996).
V. Pace, ed., *Treasures of Christian Art in Bulgaria* (2001).
D. Piguet-Panayotova, *Recherches sur la peinture en Bulgarie du bas moyen âge* (1987).
L. Praškov, ed., *Trésors d'art médiéval bulgare* (1988).
A. Tschilingirov, *Die Kunst des christlichen Mittelalters in Bulgarien* (1978).

art and architecture: Byzantine

1. *Early Byzantine*

Early Byzantine art is stylistically varied, continuing earlier developments. Classicizing elements combine with a late Roman tendency towards hieratic and frontal arrangement of figures, abstraction, linearity, and golden backgrounds.

Iconographic themes in church wall decoration are also diverse. Wall *mosaics in sanctuaries feature eucharistic scenes, donor portraits, and symbolic representations of paradise or theophanies. *Nave walls usually bear figures of standing martyrs and prophets, as well as New Testament narrative scenes. Church domes are treated as representations of heaven, for example the Rotunda in Thessalonike (c.500).

Floor mosaic production flourishes in the 4th through 6th centuries, with a preference for geometric decoration and secular themes (hunts, nature, pastoral scenes) even in church buildings. The floor mosaic in a court of the Great Palace at *Constantinople depicts animals, circus episodes, and bucolic scenes.

The monastery of St Catherine at Sinai preserves the most comprehensive collection of Byzantine panel icons. The earliest (6th–7th century) continue late antique traditions in technique, media, and style. The *iconography includes portraits of Christ (for example the 6th-century Pantocrator), of the Theotokos, saints, and scenes of divine revelation such as the Transfiguration.

There are few extant *illuminated MSS from before iconoclasm. The Rossano Gospels (c.550–600) is the oldest surviving illustrated Greek gospel book. The late antique painterly style is evident in it and other MSS (the Rabbula Gospels, 586; and the Vienna Genesis, 6th century).

Archaeology and textual sources attest to large-scale production of ivory objects, especially 4th to 6th century. Examples include *reliquaries, consular *diptychs, boxes, and combs. The iconography occasionally combines Christian and classical themes. The Barberini Ivory, probably depicting Justinian, demonstrates the high quality of carving.

Few monuments survive from the Iconoclastic period (726–843). Their decoration consists mostly of *crosses and vegetal or animal motifs. Aniconic decoration is preserved in some churches in Constantinople, on Naxos, and in Cappadocia.

The *basilica is the predominant church type before iconoclasm. There are numerous variations in spatial arrangement (for example number of aisles) and construction techniques (building material, roofing). From the 6th century on, elements such as a central tower or a central dome are combined with a basilican plan. Hagia Sophia, the great church of Constantinople rebuilt by Justinian (532–37), is itself a domed basilica of unprecedented size, its dome measuring c.31 m across.

2. *Middle Byzantine*

From the late 10th century most Byzantine churches follow a hierarchic system of decoration intended to reflect the cosmos. The themes include Christ Pantocrator in the dome, surrounded by the heavenly court; the Theotokos, often holding the Christ child, in the *altar *apse; depictions of the Great Feasts in the middle zone, below the dome; and saints, usually located in the lowest level closest to the congregation. To this period belong three exceptional monuments in Greece: the *monastery of Hosios Loukas in Boeotia (*c.*1000–1050); the katholikon of the Nea Moni on Chios (1042–55), probably executed by a Constantinopolitan workshop; and the church at Daphni (*c.*1080) near Athens.

Cappadocia preserves hundreds of rock-cut churches and structures, many decorated in fresco. Some of the finest ensembles, dating primarily to the 10th century, are found in the Göreme Valley. Byzantine Southern *Italy contains additional rock-cut and built churches with close iconographic and stylistic connections to metropolitan works.

Several illuminated MSS survive from the Middle Byzantine period. To the 9th century date the Khludov Psalter, with anti-Iconoclastic iconography, and the Paris Homilies of Gregory of Nazianzos. Some 10th-century examples, such as the Paris Psalter, the Joshua Roll, and the Bible of Leo Sakellarios, embody a return to a classicizing style. The 11th-century Menologion of Basil II is probably a creation of the imperial scriptorium.

Middle Byzantine icon painting becomes more firmly connected to the Byzantine liturgy. Certain themes, like the *Akra Tapeinosis* (Man of Sorrows), are influenced by hymnography. The liturgical calendar inspires the development of icons depicting the major church feasts (the 'Twelve Feasts'), as well as calendar icons. Painted panels acquired a permanent place within the church building on the iconostasis, on portable stands, or hung on the walls or columns.

This period saw the flourishing of enamels, the predominant technique being cloisonné. Enamel decoration was used in crowns, reliquaries, liturgical vessels, book covers, and icon revetments. A large group of 11th- and 12th-century Byzantine enamels is assembled on the Pala d'Oro in St Mark's, *Venice.

After a break in the 8th century, ivory production resumes in *Byzantium probably in the late 900s. The iconography is largely imperial representations (for example, Christ crowning Constantine VII) and religious themes (for example, the Harbaville Triptych). Scenes inspired by classical mythology are also executed (for example, the Veroli Casket).

Programmes in monumental wall decoration complement the form of Middle Byzantine churches, which are predominantly centralized domed buildings. Cross-in-square structures, for example the church of the Theotokos *tou Libos* in Constantinople (907), are the most common, although other types exist: the domed octagon (Nea Moni, Chios), the triconch (the late-10th-century katholikon of the Great Lavra, Mount Athos), and others. During the Latin occupation of Constantinople (1204–61) several local architectural styles appeared in the new centres of the fragmented empire: Arta, Nicaea, and Trebizond.

3. *Late Byzantine*

Despite adverse political, social, and economic circumstances, civil wars, and a shrinking empire, some of the finest examples of Byzantine art were produced during this period. It is difficult to treat the art of the empire's last centuries as a whole; nevertheless, inspiration from classical models permeates all of late Byzantine art. Extended narrative cycles, such as the Ministry and Passion of Christ, the Life of the Theotokos, and episodes from the lives of saints, appear frequently. At the same time new monumental compositions emerge, for example scenes illustrating the *Akathistos Hymn. Liturgical themes, especially in the sanctuary, also abound.

Painted compositions from the late 1200s are characterized by multiplication of figures and heavy modelling of the human body (for example Karyes, Mount Athos; the Kilise Camii, Constantinople; and the churches painted by Michael Astrapas and Eutychios). In the early 14th century, figures become more elegant and elongated. The *fresco and mosaic cycles of the Chora monastery in *Constantinople (*c.*1315–20) epitomize this style. Several outstanding fresco and mosaic ensembles in Thessalonike also belong to this period. The churches of Mistra, in southern Greece, span the whole of the late Byzantine period and represent the variety of styles in use.

Icon production proliferated in the late Byzantine centuries. As in monumental painting, panel paintings display a great range of subjects. The stylistic conventions of panel painting come to influence monumental painting and *manuscript illumination. To this period belong a group of sumptuous micro-mosaic icons, usually representing saints or the major feasts of the church.

MS illumination also testifies to the great artistic flourishing of late Byzantium. In the late 13th and early 14th centuries there is a conscious return to a classicizing style, and earlier MSS are replicated. Many illustrated gospel books were produced, some containing extensive narrative cycles.

Late Byzantine architecture is characteristically eclectic in both spatial articulation and exterior wall decoration. Such subsidiary spaces as *chapels, *exonarthexes, *ambulatories, and porticoes become standard features. Special attention is given to the exterior articulation of spaces: niches and *pilasters enliven the exterior surfaces. Ceramoplastic decoration on the church exterior is prominent, especially on the east façade.

Intense building activity followed the reconquest of Constantinople and lasted until *c.*1330; most new projects in the capital are either renovations or additions to existing buildings. Theodore Metochites restored the monastery of Chora, to which he added a funerary chapel (parekklesion), two *narthexes, a belfry, and a northern annex.

In Thessalonike, several churches show close ties to Constantinopolitan buildings, although the Greek churches tend to be more regular and symmetrical. Many important late Byzantine buildings are found in Mistra. These reveal inspiration from the architecture of both Greece and Constantinople, along with Gothic elements from western Europe. VM

R. Cormack, *Byzantine Art* (2000).
A. Cutler and J. W. Nesbitt, *L'arte bizantina e il suo pubblico* (1986).
—— and J.-M. Spieser, *Byzance Médiévale* (1996).
O. Demus, *Byzantine Mosaic Decoration* (1976).
H. C. Evans, ed., *Byzantium: Faith and Power (1261–1557)* (2004).
—— and W. D. Wixom, eds, *The Glory of Byzantium: Art and Culture of the Middle Byzantine Era AD 843–1261* (1997).
A. Goldschmidt and K. Weitzmann, *Die byzantinischen Elfenbeinskulpturen des X.–XIII Jahrhunderts*, 2 vols ([2]1979).
E. Kitzinger, *Byzantine Art in the Making* (1980).
R. Krautheimer, *Early Christian and Byzantine Architecture* ([4]1986).
J. Lowden, *Early Christian and Byzantine Art* (1997).
H. Maguire, *Earth and Ocean: The Terrestrial World in Early Byzantine Art* (1987).
—— *Art and Eloquence in Byzantium* (1981).
C. Mango, *Byzantine Architecture* (1976).
—— *The Art of the Byzantine Empire 312–1415: Sources and Documents* (1986).
T. Mathews, *Byzantium: From Antiquity to Renaissance* (1998).
R. Ousterhout, *Master Builders of Byzantium* (1999).
L. Safran, ed., *Heaven on Earth: Art and the Church in Byzantium* (1998).
M. Spiro, *Critical Corpus of the Mosaic Pavements on the Greek Mainland, Fourth/Sixth Centuries, with Architectural Surveys* (1978).
W. F. Volbach, *Elfenbeinarbeiten der Spätantike und des frühen Mittelalters* ([3]1976).
C. Walter, *Art and Ritual of the Byzantine Church* (1982).
K. Weitzmann, *Studies in Classical and Byzantine Manuscript Illumination* (1971).
—— ed., *Age of Spirituality: Late Antique and Early Christian Art, Third to Seventh Centuries* (1979).
—— *et al.*, *The Icon* (1982).
K. Wessel, *Byzantine Enamels* (1967).

art and architecture: Carolingian Literally, art and architecture produced in areas ruled by a monarch of the *Carolingian dynasty. Geographically, while borders were somewhat fluid, this usually included western *Germany, the *Low Countries, most of *France, and parts of *Italy. Chronologically, Carolingian rule in some of these areas began in 751 with Pepin III and extended into the 10th century, although most of what is usually considered Carolingian art was made between the last years of the 8th century and the end of the 9th.

1. Centres and patrons
2. Art and artists
3. Architecture

1. *Centres and Patrons*

This historico-political definition of the period is not completely arbitrary from the art-historical perspective, for the leading centres of Carolingian art production were royal courts and the religious establishments closely associated with them. Thus, a significant portion of art and architecture during the Carolingian era was made in the ambient of the ruling dynasty.

The most important Carolingian court was *Charlemagne's at *Aachen; however, the Carolingian pattern of royal succession, with all of a ruler's sons dividing his lands, meant that the boundaries of kingdoms and the locations of courts shifted throughout the period. Other important courts responsible for significant artistic commissions (although not necessarily themselves centres of production) were those of Charlemagne's grandsons *Charles 'the Bald' and *Louis the German. *Monasteries and episcopal seats, while neither itinerant nor transient, were somewhat less susceptible to shifting political currents, but their role in art production shifted often, since it depended greatly on the predilections of individual bishops and abbots. Important ecclesiastical centres included the bishoprics of *Metz (especially under Drogo) and *Rheims and such monasteries as *Fulda, *Lorsch, *St-Denis, *St Gall, *St Riquier, and *Tours.

2. *Art and artists*

Major media were painting (both in MSS and on the walls of churches and secular structures; independent panel painting was essentially unknown), *metalwork in *gold, silver, bronze and less precious metals, *embroidery, and the carving of ivory and crystal. Larger-scale sculpture in stone and wood was also practised, although it was not the important medium it later became. Most Carolingian art (especially textile) has been lost, although MSS and, to a lesser degree, ivories, survive in relatively large numbers. Because *illuminated MSS, thanks to the evidence of their texts, are more easily dated and localized than most other forms of artistic production, they provide the basis of what is known of the chronological sequence and local peculiarities of Carolingian art.

Carolingian art is generally characterized by great material richness, technical excellence, and extremely rich intellectual content, with some iconographic programmes of a complexity and sophistication not previously encountered in Christian art. Under what material and intellectual conditions were these remarkable objects produced? Exploring the role of *patrons in providing the material, social, and intellectual preconditions for Carolingian artistic production has been a central concern of modern art history, although the importance of patrons vis-a-vis artists is still disputed. As with all medieval artists, the status of the Carolingian art maker was very different from that of the modern. It is a misconception that Carolingian artists were anonymous monks: a number have left their names in the historical record (most often book illuminators, but also *goldsmiths such as *Wolvinus) and only a few of these were clerics. Attempts to recover further Carolingian artistic personalities through the traditional art-historical method of connoisseurship have met with limited success, precisely because that tool was developed to identify individuals prized for their individuality, with a signature style, something that does not appear to have been a desideratum in the era. But the makers of Carolingian art were not simply interchangeable pawns; the technical skill required to make art and its material richness meant that artists were regarded with respect, but none had the social or intellectual prestige of the aristocratic or clerical elites who were likely responsible for conceiving the iconographic programs of most Carolingian art.

Like all medieval Christians, the Carolingians had to confront the question of whether images were justified. They tended to answer with a qualified yes, agreeing with *Pope Gregory I the Great's dictum that pictures were neither to be adored nor destroyed. This issue was particularly fraught for the Carolingians because *Byzantium, their rival and model, changed its position from *iconoclasm to iconodulism and back twice during the period. One Carolingian confrontation with the image question culiminated in *Theodulf of Orléans' **Libri Carolini*, the longest medieval treatise on images.

Formally, Carolingian art manifests various syntheses between the more abstracting art of the Carolingians' 'barbarian' predecessors and the illusionistic representational styles characteristic of late antique Rome and Byzantium. Whether (and to what degree) this synthetic character represents continuity with past visual cultures, either Mediterranean or northern European, or a conscious, artificial attempt to emulate and invoke these cultures, has been a point of dispute in almost all scholarship on Carolingian art since 1900 (thus forming the particular art-historical contribution to the more general debate about the nature of the Carolingian renaissance).

Carolingian art was influential throughout much of the MA because of the success of this formal synthesis and the immense prestige of the Carolingians, typically looked upon as the first kings of *France and *Germany. In Germany, the Ottonians and Salians drew upon Carolingian models with special frequency. More generally, Carolingian forms and buildings lie behind many of the artistic developments of the Romanesque.

3. Architecture

Although modern art-historical writing traditionally distinguishes between architecture and the other visual arts, it is not clear this distinction would have meant much to the Carolingians. Carolingian architecture, especially churches, originally housed most Carolingian art, much of which was used in the *liturgy, while architecture served as the support for a major artistic medium, wall painting. Carolingian architecture is difficult to characterize with certainty because the extant evidence is so scant; only a handful of buildings remain and they are not representative of the full range of construction.

As with so much of Carolingian culture, the period's architecture was not entirely innovative, but involved the standardization and reworking of previously established types. Nonetheless, the architecture of the era was of great importance in the MA thanks to the historically high status of the Carolingians and the sheer extent of their building programmes: it has been estimated that over 400 *monasteries were built or rebuilt in the century after Pepin the Short became king.

Carolingian churches can be divided into two main groups: *basilicas and centrally planned structures. Carolingian church basilicas include Seligenstadt and Michelstadt-Steinbach, the prestigious lost monastic churches at Fulda and St-Denis, and the church laid out in the so-called *St Gall plan, a never-built 9th-century design for a complete monastic complex. In the Carolingian period, when stone vaulting was very rarely used, such buildings were covered with timber roofs. The basilica's popularity as a building type for the Carolingians is easy to understand; simple to construct and highly adaptable in size and scale, it was well suited to the Christian liturgy and evoked the prestigious form of the most important churches in Christendom, the early Roman basilicas.

Some Carolingian churches were centrally planned, dominated not by an axis, but by a single central point or area. Like the basilica, this building type had a long history, going back to classical and late antiquity. The most famous centrally planned structure of the MA is Carolingian, Charlemagne's palace *chapel at Aachen, part of a large complex established around 790.

A non-church structure from the period is the so-called gateway to the monastery at Lorsch, a small free-standing building pierced by three arches at ground level and with a room on the upper floor decorated with wall paintings. Its function is debated, but its combination of highly classicizing elements (notably the Corinthian capitals of the engaged columns and the very form of the building, with a triple opening reminiscent of the arch erected in Rome for Constantine) with more typically medieval features (the brightly coloured stone work; the upper storey, with its stone reminders of timber

construction) made the Lorsch building distinctively Carolingian. WJDi

D. Ganz., '"Pando quod Ignoro": In Search of Carolingian Artistic Experience', *Intellectual Life in the Middle Ages: Essays Presented to Margaret Gibson*, ed. L. Smith and B. Ward (1992), 25–32.

A. Goldschmidt, *Die Elfenbeinskulpturen aus der Zeit der karolingischen und sächsischen Kaiser*, 2 vols (1914).

C. Heitz, *L'architecture religieuse carolingienne: les formes et leurs fonctions* (1980).

W. Horn and E. Born, *The Plan of St Gall*, 3 vols (1979).

J. Hubert, J. Porcher, and W. Volbach, *The Carolingian Renaissance*, tr. J. Emmons, S. Gilbert, and R. Allen (French original, 1968) (1970).

W. Koehler, *Die karolingischen Miniaturen*, 6 vols (1930ff.).

P. Lasko, *Ars Sacra, 800–1200* ([2]1994).

C. McClendon, *The Origins of Medieval Architecture: Building in Europe*, AD *600–900* (2005).

J. van Schlosser, *Schriftquellen zur Geschichte der karolingischen Kunst* (1892; repr. 1988).

art and architecture: Cistercian The *Cistercian order was founded in 1098 at *Cîteaux, in Burgundy, by a group of monks who had left a reformed but traditional *Benedictine *monastery in hope of living a more authentic expression of the Benedictine Rule. Artistically, the Cistercians are distinguished for three things: some of the most original *manuscript illumination of the MA, the most significant policy restricting the use of art in the west prior to the Reformation, and a superb architecture that had an unusually strong impact throughout the western sphere of influence. These subjects are successively related, broadly speaking, to the general attitude toward art of the first three generations of Cistercians.

1. The first generation
2. The second generation
3. The third generation

1. *The first generation*

Although the order was founded on the basis of very strict consuetudinary reform, the evidence suggests the first generation's attitude toward art was little different from that of traditional *monasticism. The simplicity of the first stone church of Cîteaux seems to have been determined by financial necessity, not monastic principle, and the sources indicate there was a wide variety of precious liturgical artworks and lavish vestments. Furthermore, for a monastery of such apparently limited means, early Cîteaux devoted exceptional resources to book painting, creating some of the most stunning MS illumination of the time. Among a large number of surviving works, the Bible of Stephen Harding (*c.*1109; Dijon, Bib. mun. 12–15) is exceptional for its originality, sense of design, and fine execution. But even this is surpassed by the famous Cîteaux *Moralia in Job* (*c.*1111; Dijon, Bib. mun. 168–170, 173), a MS whose creativity and imagination in the depiction of images of violence and daily life were only rarely matched and never surpassed. These images evocatively express the first generation's conception of monastic spirituality through the use of monstrous forms, knightly imagery, and scenes of monastic labour.

2. *The second generation*

When St *Bernard of Clairvaux (1090–1153) approached Cîteaux in 1113 to ask for admittance, there was little to distinguish it from other foundations of the new ascetic orders that were beginning to spring up everywhere. This was the defining moment for the order both institutionally and artistically, and would lead to one of the greatest expansions in the history of western monasticism. Artistically, Bernard would radically transform the Cistercian attitude toward art through both internal legislation and external polemic, creating the culture of artistic *asceticism that was to become such a distinctive part of Cistercian identity.

Within the order, it seems that Bernard and his party were the force behind the early legislation on art of *c.*1115–19. Statute 10 severely restricts the use of precious materials such as *gold, *silver, *gems and jewellery, and *silk in the *liturgy, and prohibits more than a single colour for the chasuble. Statute 20 calls for the almost total elimination of sculpture and painting from the monastery, allowing only a painted crucifix. Together, the two statutes struck at the *aesthetics of excess associated with the twin economic foundations of early-12th-century monasticism: the Cult of the Dead expressed in liturgical services (*Absolutions of the Dead and *Office for the Dead) and the Cult of Relics (*pilgrimage), the two being seen as increasing social entanglements and decreasing the loss of monastic seclusion.

Bernard took the issue of the sensory saturation of the holy place outside of the order in 1125 with his famous polemic, the *Apologia*, the most penetrating critique of art within its social and spiritual contexts of the MA. In this, he follows a sequence from the investment in art to attract donations to the use of liturgical art to carry this out, to the equation between excessive art and holiness, to art as opposed to the care of the poor, and finally to art as a spiritual distraction to the monk. The resultant controversy over the place of art within monastic culture would act as a spur to certain aspects of the art programme of Abbot *Suger (*c.*1081–1151) at *St-Denis, near *Paris—which marks the inception of *Gothic architecture and sculpture—particularly the opposing claim that complex art could function in a manner similar to scriptural study, most notably in the medium of the *stained glass window.

3. *The third generation*

The foundations of the first and second generations were made with relatively small communities and without anticipation of the even greater growth that was to follow. With the phenomenal influx of postulants into the order with

what might be called the third generation, the Cistercians were compelled to address the question of a monumental architecture. This situation was greatly affected by the strong Cistercian policy of uniformity in all matters pertaining to monastic life. Nowhere is the Cistercian conception of monastic architecture as the consciously constructed space of the regular life better expressed than at Fontenay, in Burgundy, most of whose structures date from *c*.1139–47. An important contemporary traditional Benedictine monastery might have a sculpted façade, a *nave vaulted with heavy semicircular barrel *vaults pierced with clerestories, an interior with rich architectural ornamentation and capital sculpture, and rubble walls covered with paintings—the most important churches sometimes having the main sanctuary surrounded with an *ambulatory bearing an elaborate series of *chapels (the pilgrimage plan). In contrast, Fontenay has an essentially unadorned façade, a nave vaulted with a pointed, ribbed barrel vault resting on finely articulated but purposefully simple compound piers, no clerestory (although there are aisle windows), and unpainted walls. The main sanctuary is flat-ended with one aisle running along the east side of the *transept to provide additional chapel space. There is an absolute minimum of architectural ornamentation, aesthetic effect being realized through superb proportions, a uniformly high level of stonework (often *ashlar), and the restriction of most of the light to the east and west ends. The cloistral and work buildings are of the highest quality, with excellent groin vaults and stonework being employed throughout. The traditional ideas that Cistercian architecture was subject to rigid centralized control and that it prepared the way for Gothic are now more flexibly understood. However, the Cistercians were the first actual monastic order in the modern sense and a conscious, if adaptable, uniformity of architecture certainly did contribute to the internationalization of architecture and to the spread of new building methods from *Scandinavia to Spain, and from Ireland to the *crusader states.

Illuminated MSS continued to be made in the second and third generations, although now with generally more restrained imagery. It was not MS illumination, however, that was becoming an issue. The pre-eminent artistic legislation of the third generation is Statute 80. According to a literal interpretation, it prohibits both the use of more than one colour and the depiction of imagery in the creation of illuminated *initials; more importantly, it also restricts the colour of windows to 'white' and forbids any imagery in these whatsoever. Unlike earlier Cistercian legislation on art, which attempted to initiate new monastic ideals, Statute 80 was directed against the apparently constant erosion of the earlier principles of artistic asceticism. If the controversy over art raised by the Cistercians had had its effect on Suger in his development of the stained glass window, then Suger also had his effect on the Cistercians in that they were now forced to deal with the embrace of this very medium, apparently throughout the order.

Gradually, Cistercian resistance to art began to weaken further; first in the size, structure, and uniformity of churches, and then in the use of ornamentation and imagery, with some Cistercian churches eventually being little different from the great secular churches. The Cistercian ideal of artistic asceticism, however, lived on, being taken up by the new *mendicant orders such as the *Franciscans and *Dominicans until they, too, succumbed to the 'perpetual law' (*William of Malmesbury, *Gesta Reg.* 4:337) of inevitable relapse. CR

M. Aubert, *L'architecture cistercienne en France* (1943–47).
C. Bruzelius, *L'apogée de l'art gothique: L'église abbatiale de Longpont* (1990).
A. Dimier, *Recueil de plans d'églises cisterciennes* (1949; supplement 1967).
—— *L'art cistercien hors de France* (1971).
—— *L'art cistercien: France* (1982).
H. Eydoux, *L'architecture des églises cisterciennes d'Allemagne* (1952).
P. Fergusson, *Architecture of Solitude: Cistercian Abbeys in Twelfth-Century England* (1984).
H. Hahn, *Die frühe Kirchenbaukunst der Zisterzienser* (1957).
A. Laabs, *Malerei und Plastik im Zisterzienserorden* (2000).
D. Negri, *Abbazie cistercensi in Italia* (1981).
C. Norton, '*Varietates Pavimentorum*', *CAr* 31 (1983), 69–114.
C. Oursel, *La miniature du XIIe siècle à l'abbaye de Cîteaux* (1926).
L. Pressouyre, ed., *Saint Bernard et le monde cistercien* (1990).
C. Rudolph, *The 'Things of Greater Importance': Bernard of Clairvaux's Apologia and the Medieval Attitude Toward Art* (1990).
—— *Violence and Daily Life: Reading, Art, and Polemics in the Cîteaux* Moralia in Job (1997).
R. Stalley, *The Cistercian Monasteries of Ireland* (1987).
I. B. Torviso, ed., *Monjes y Monasterios: El Cister en el medioevo de Castilla y León* (1998).
M. Untermann, *Forma Ordinis: Die mittelalterliche Baukunst der Zisterzienser* (2001).
A. Wyrwa, ed., *Monasticon Cisterciense Poloniae* (1999).
H. Zakin, *French Cistercian Grisaille Glass* (1979).
Y. Załuska, *L'enluminure et le scriptorium de Cîteaux au XIIe siècle* (1989).

art and architecture: Cluniac For three hundred years after its foundation in 909/910, the Burgundian abbey of *Cluny was perhaps the most important monastic house in western Christendom, with, at its height, over 1,400 *priories. Cluny was also a major centre of art production, and its own 12th-century church (Cluny III) surpassed in size all others of its day.

1. Architecture and furnishings
2. Sculpture
3. Manuscripts and wall painting
4. A Cluniac art?

1. Architecture and furnishings

Of the constructions that followed the abbey's foundation (Cluny I, consecrated in 927), we know little apart from the

church's petite dimensions and general *basilica form. Excavations yield a clearer picture of the second church consecrated in 981. Cluny II consisted of a cross-shaped church, seven bays long in the *nave and terminating in a western *narthex three bays deep. Its long aisled choir featured a large central, rounded *apse flanked by two smaller ones; one additional apse projected from each *transept arm, creating a staggered effect of eastern apses. A small number of other Cluniac establishments built their churches in similar fashion (for example, Romainmôtier), an emulation perhaps aided by the so-called *Farfa Customary* (1043) that recorded the mother abbey's general dimensions. At Cluny Abbot *Odilo (994–1049) began also new auxiliary constructions and was said by his biographer to have 'found the cloister in wood, and made it into marble'.

Under abbots Hugh of Semur (or *Hugh of Cluny) and *Peter the Venerable (1122–56), the abbey grew dramatically, its monastic population swelling to over 450 by the mid 12th century. Work on a church commensurate in stature began under Hugh before 1088 (date of an official *fundatio*) and continued after the church's dedication in 1130. Cluny III was unprecedented in scale (187 m long) and monumental extravagance. The nave rose three stories and stretched eleven bays long. In the eastern end, five *chapels radiated from a *vaulted *ambulatory encircling the choir. This hemicycle opened at its western end onto a small transept outfitted with two apses and onto yet a second, even larger transept with another four apses. At the west end a triple portal provided access into the church, and a triple-aisled narthex of five *bays extended the church further westward. Enlargement to the *cloister and the construction of additional auxiliary buildings occupied the abbacies of Pons (1109–22) and Peter the Venerable.

Some 20th-century scholars have related the complex yet harmonious church plan to the application of Pythagorean proportional geometry in relation to the musical ratios of chant, an interest stemming from Cluny's enthusiasm for liturgical celebration. In the early 12th century, however, the plan was attributed to a miracle: the monk Gunzo received a dream vision in which Sts Peter and Paul instructed him in the layout of the new church. Cluny III came to an ignominious end in 1809 when it was dynamited; its gradual dismantlement followed, leaving only the southwest transept standing. This one transept—whose vaults tower at over 30 meters—represents a small fraction of Cluny III's total size, yet it is sufficient to evoke still the church's former splendour.

Construction of Cluny III benefited from the generosity of Europe's wealthiest patrons, such as the Castilian king *Alfonso VI and England's *Henry I. Contemporary accounts mention also royal gifts of *liturgical furnishings in gold, silver, and bronze. *Matilda of England, for example, gave funds for casting *bells and fashioning a large seven-branched candlestick, while *Henry of Blois furnished the great cross that stood on the high altar. Other aspects of the decoration are more difficult to reconstruct, although old sources indicate that the apse was decorated with a *fresco depicting Christ in Majesty. Decorated fragments of a low limestone arcade also offer an idea of the *chancel screen used to enclose the choir from the spaces occupied by the laity. Sections of decorative pavement, including areas of stone-incrusted designs, as well as painted tiles, also survive. The opulence of Cluny III famously inspired fierce condemnations from the ascetically minded Cistercian, St *Bernard of Clairvaux (*Apologia*, 1125), and thus the abbey became for a time a conspicuous lightning rod in a debate on the appropriateness of ostentatious art in monastic settings.

2. *Sculpture*

The few sculptural survivals of Cluny II (for example, *interlace fragments, several capitals) scarcely permit an appreciation of early production, but the more numerous capitals, reliefs, and hundreds of small fragments left behind from Cluny III, including the decorative work in the surviving south transept, show the abbey to have been at the forefront of sculptural arts.

The west portal (according to early drawings and descriptions) featured on its central *tympanum a representation of Christ in Majesty. Christ, seated within a mandorla, was buffered on both sides by two angels and the four symbols of the *Evangelists. Approximately two dozen figures occupied the lintel, representing probably the Ascension, the Resurrection, and Three Marys at the Tomb. A *spandrel figure of St Peter (now in Providence, Rhode Island), the best preserved element, with locks of hair falling away in rhythmic curls, keenly chiselled cheeks, and layered drapery cascading in plate-like folds, all showcase Cluny's taste for refinement.

The most famous works are the eight capitals that survive from the choir hemicycle. Apart from one entirely foliate work (closely imitating a Corinthian style), the other capitals include figures, most of which are difficult to identify. One capital, for example, includes female figures on each face that may represent the three Theological Virtues and a *cardinal virtue. Another features personifications of Spring and Summer on two faces while on the third face an inscription identifies Prudence. Inscriptions identify the four musicians of one capital as the First Four Tones of *Plain-Chant, while another capital likely completes the set with the Last Four Tones. Just as these identifications are vexed, so is their combined meaning for the choir decoration. Even their date (*c.*1088 or *c.*1115) has been widely debated. (Questions of date have dogged Cluny studies, as the abbey's sculpture has been viewed as pivotal to an understanding of Romanesque sculpture.) Nonetheless, even

taken individually the hemicycle capitals demonstrate well Cluny's interest in allying notions of allegory, spiritual theology, and *liturgy to their sumptuous arts, yielding a rarefied quality of artistic cultivation.

3. Manuscripts and wall painting

Cluny's importance to the *painting arts must have been great, but its actual impact is difficult to ascertain. Owing to the loss of Cluny III, examples of monumental painting must be gleaned from dependencies, such as fragments from La Charité-sur-Loire and especially the apse decoration at nearby Berzé-la-Ville. According to some scholars, such surviving works reflect Roman traditions, as much in the colour palette and compositional organization into registers as in the use of antique motifs. (Similar Roman associations have been claimed for the church's monumental sculpture, owing to the striking presence of fluted *pilasters, egg-and-dart decoration, and antique-styled acanthus patterns on capitals.) At Berzé-la-Ville, the apse's subject matter itself harkens to Rome: the *traditio* (Christ conferring authority to Peter and Paul as leaders of the Roman church) was indeed pregnant with meaning at Cluny, for the church was dedicated to those two apostles. Scholars have also noted that this Roman style is allied to a Byzantine tendency, marked by heavy ornamentation and white, streaky highlights on faces and drapery.

A similar Italo-Byzantine style is found in the few surviving *illuminated MSS from the abbey. The best known include the so-called Parma Ildefonsus (a 10th-century treatise on the Virgin composed by the Toledan archbishop St *Ildefonso) and a lectionary, both produced around 1100. In addition to the style, the iconography of Pentecost in the latter MS shares parallels with some eastern traditions. Close study of the Parma Ildefonsus by Meyer Schapiro also underscored the presence of an indigenous Burgundian style (ultimately derived from Ottonian traditions) marked by a more sober palette, thick, decorative borders, and spiralling foliage.

4. A Cluniac art?

An abbey of such importance and wealth may well have coordinated, even directed, building projects and decorative programmes at its priories, and there is some textual evidence of this. Cluny's abbots did actively acquire other establishments to draw them into the mother abbey's orbit, and some of the most notable monasteries of the period were Cluniac (for example, *Moissac, Vézelay, Souvigny, St-Gilles-du-Gard, La Charité-sur-Loire, Polirone, Lewes, Thetford, Fontanella, Payerne). Determining just how closely the scattered possessions conform, however, is difficult, and although several studies have attempted to demonstrate singularity of purpose (namely, Evans), the resulting picture is still quite eclectic. Cluny's customs and statutes, even if they recorded the mother abbey's dispositions, did not, as was the case among the *Cistercians, legislate architectural projects. Even the organization of the claustral buildings reveals nothing distinctive but instead follows patterns honed by *Benedictines centuries earlier.

With so many monasteries under its sway, Cluny may have had more diffuse influence than directed. Cluny III's elaborate arrangement of radiating and transept chapels, all easily accessed in succession via the wide aisles, for example, could have contributed to the popularity of this plan already well adapted to pilgrim traffic. In the realm of sculpture, the treatment of certain iconographic subjects appears on capitals at neighbouring Burgundian churches, and the style of large ensembles such as that found at Vézelay, *Autun, and Paray-le-Monial has its origins in Cluny work. The *tympanum arrangement of Christ in Majesty, soon one of the most frequently selected subjects for portal sculpture, probably owes something of its popularity to Cluny as well. Most of all, however, Cluny's own artistic accomplishment offered a model of monastic production. It distinguished itself by the unprecedented construction of its own church and its refined monumental decoration. *See also* ART AND ARCHITECTURE: BYZANTINE / OTTONIAN / ROMANESQUE. RAM

C. E. Armi, *Masons and Sculptors in Romanesque Burgundy: The New Aesthetic of Cluny III* (1983).

W. Cahn, I. H. Forsyth, W. W. Clark, eds, *Current Studies on Cluny*, special issue of *Gesta*, 27 (1988).

K. J. Conant, *Cluny: Les églises et la maison du chef d'ordre* (1968).

J. Evans, *Cluniac Art of the Romanesque Period* (1950).

—— *The Romanesque Architecture of the Order of Cluny* (²1972).

P. Garrigou-Grandchamp, M. Jones, *et al.*, *La ville de Cluny et ses maisons: XIe–XVe siècles* (1997).

Le gouvernement d'Hugues de Semur à Cluny: actes du colloque, Cluny, septembre 1988 (1990).

D. Russo, 'Espace peint, espace symbolique, construction ecclésiologique: Les peintures de Berzé-la-Ville', *Revue Mabillon*, 11 (2000), 57–87.

F. Salet, *Cluny et Vézelay: l'œuvre des sculpteurs* (1995).

M. Schapiro, *The Parma Ildefonsus: A Romanesque Illuminated Manuscript from Cluny and Related Works* (1964).

art and architecture: Coptic The term 'Coptic' is an Arabicized derivation of the Greek word for Egyptian, *Aiguptios*, and as such was employed by the Arabs to describe those Egyptians who remained Christian after the conquest of the country in 640–2. In art and architecture, the name 'Coptic' is specifically applied to objects and buildings produced by the Christian population of *Egypt from the 4th to the 13th centuries. Coptic art reached its highest point between the 5th and early 7th centuries, when local and external aesthetic trends were united under the banner of Christianity.

1. Architecture
2. Sculpture, painting, and textiles

1. *Architecture*

The preferred form of church architecture during the early Christian period in Egypt was the *basilica. The earliest monumental, securely dated examples are the *cathedral at Hermopolis Magna (al-Ashmunayn), *c*.430–40; the church of Dayr Anba Shinudah near Sohag (Sawhaj), *c*.440; and the large church of the Pachomian *monastery at Pbow (Faw Qibli), founded in 459. The *pilgrimage site of Abu Mina, where the tomb of the miracle-working St Menas was venerated, witnessed the construction of several large basilicas, most notably the Great Basilica (5th century) and the North Basilica (1st half of the 6th century). These are three-aisled buildings (except the one at Pbow, which has five aisles) with a semicircular main *apse preceded either by a *transept (as at Hermopolis Magna and Abu Mina) or by a square sanctuary with lateral apses, an arrangement that resulted in a tri-lobed east end (as at Sohag and the 6th-century basilica at Dendera). The transept is less frequent, and its appearance is attributed to the influence of Aegean models, while the tri-lobed *chancel has more in common with Syrian and North African architecture. Distinctly local features are the grouping of sanctuary rooms behind a straight eastern wall, the so-called 'return aisle' across the west end of the nave, and the additional triumphal *arch in the east end of the *nave, in front of the sanctuary opening, which later gave rise to the *khurus* (choir) of the medieval Egyptian church. Churches with a centralized plan are generally rare and reproduced imported models (for example, the east church at Abu Mina, mid 6th century).

After the Arab conquest, the basilica began to adopt more sophisticated vaulting designs under the influence of Islamic religious architecture. Cupolas over the nave became the preferred roofing method in Upper Egypt, while barrel *vaults were popular in Lower Egypt. Smaller domed churches constructed over four inner pillars or columns (similar to the Byzantine cross-in-square type) were introduced in the Fatimid period (969–1171). During this time the Coptic church structure adopts the *khurus*, a tripartite transverse room in front of the sanctuary, as a required feature. Its front wall functioned in a manner similar to that of the Byzantine *templon* (*chancel screen), namely a barrier restricting lay access to the east end. In the late MA, the axially oriented basilica plan gave way to a more compact grid system of vaulted square *bays (as exemplified by the monastic church of St Theodore at Madinat Habu).

2. *Sculpture, painting, and textiles*

*Sculpture and carving encompasses works for private and public use in a variety of media: *stone, *wood, ivory, and bone. Architectural members (capitals, friezes, pediments, and niche-heads) comprise the largest category of preserved examples. These were executed in either imported (marble) or local (limestone, sandstone) material. Although numerous skilled workshops existed in the early Christian period, urban and monastic churches in Egypt utilized a considerable amount of **spolia* from earlier (usually pagan) buildings. Oxyrhynchos, Ahnas, Bawit, Saqqara, and the monasteries near Sohag are among the important sites for architectural sculpture carved contemporaneously with the building it decorates. On the whole, the findings do not support the notion of a uniform Coptic style although the Late Antique tendency toward growing stylization and simplification is evident. Certain 6th-century capitals from Bawit and Saqqara testify to the fact that Constantinopolitan capital types were known and imitated locally.

The funerary stele is another popular category of Coptic sculpture. Generally fashioned out of limestone, its surface decoration ranges from a simple pattern to multiple figures in an elaborate pseudo-architectural setting. Stuccoed and painted polychrome details are frequently part of its ornamental scheme. Few stelae were found in their original context, and fewer yet contain inscriptions allowing for their exact dating. One of the only sites where Coptic stelae have been found *in situ* is at the monastery of Apa Jeremiah, Saqqara.

By the end of the 8th century, production of carved stone sculpture in Egypt seems to have come to an end. However, woodwork gained greater prominence in the decoration of churches and became the dominant sculptural genre during the medieval period. Of particular interest are the sanctuary screens, door panels, and lintels from the churches in Old *Cairo (for example, the screen from the church of St Barbara, now in the Coptic Museum of Cairo, or the door from the church of al-Muallaqa, now in the British Museum), many of which testify to the assimilation of contemporary Islamic ornamental motifs.

The iconographical repertoire of Coptic funerary murals shows a remarkable similarity with early Christian *sepulchral art from other parts of the empire. Salvation symbols and themes, including orants, the *miracles of Christ, and Old Testament allegories, are depicted frequently both in the east and the west. However, the majority of extant Coptic murals are found in a monastic context and therefore carry a broader Christian message. The archaeological sites of Isna, Kellia, Saqqara, and Bawit contain now-abandoned monastic cells that preserve *frescoes from several centuries of occupation. Their walls are covered with images of venerated monks, local saints, and monastery founders, as well as 'iconic' representations of Christ, the Virgin, and other biblical figures. A mural composition from the *oratory known as Cell A at the monastery of Apa Jeremiah in Saqqara (7th century, now in the Coptic Museum of Cairo) is instructive as it depicts a scene of personal devotion: a monk (probably the cell's owner) prostrated at the feet of St Apollo.

The painted decoration of churches often consists of several superimposed layers due to a practice of periodic renewal. Consequently, few are earlier than the 10th century. The main apse and *dome often contain the image of Christ in Majesty, as is the case at Dayr Anba Shinudah near Sohag (apse painted in 1124) and the monastery of St Antony in the eastern desert (dome painted 1232–3). Scenes from the Old Testament and the lives of Christ and the Virgin are reserved for the walls, while pillars and columns are adorned with saints. Several fresco layers (from the 9th to the 13th centuries) with festival scenes and rows of holy figures have been uncovered in the monastery church of the Syrians in the Wadi Natrun.

Small-scale *painting in *encaustic or tempera entered the repertoire of Coptic art early on. The precursors of these icons of holy persons were locally produced mummy portraits and painted *panels of pagan gods. Early Coptic icons, such as the 6th-century one of St Menas and Christ (Louvre, Paris), have much in common with monastic oratory frescoes of standing figures (for example, Bawit and Saqqara).

Decorated *textiles are certainly the most characteristic product of Coptic art. These include garments, tunic ornaments, curtains and hangings, covers, and parts of shrouds. Themes from the Hellenistic tradition such as mythological characters, scenes on the Nile, dancing girls, and personifications remain constant although their *iconography becomes more stylized with time. Christian symbols and subjects are less common, but large figural compositions such as the enthroned Virgin with Child in the Cleveland Museum of Art (6th or 7th century) seem to have been popular as hangings in churches and homes of the pious. *See also* ARCHAEOLOGY: CONSTANTINOPLE AND BYZANTIUM; ART AND ARCHITECTURE: BYZANTINE / ISLAMIC; COPTIC CHURCH, LITURGICAL PRACTICES OF; ISLAMIC EMPIRE. TPN

A. S. Atiya, ed., *The Coptic Encyclopedia*, 8 vols (1991).
A. Badawy, *Coptic Art and Archaeology: The Art of Christian Egyptians from the Late Antique to the Middle Ages* (1978).
J. Beckwith, *Coptic Sculpture, 300–1300* (1963).
M. Capuani, *Christian Egypt: Coptic Art and Monuments Through Two Millennia* (2002).
P. M. Du Bourguet, *The Art of the Copts* (1971).
F. D. Friedman, ed., *Beyond the Pharaohs: Egypt and the Copts in the 2nd to 7th Centuries AD* (1989).
G. Gabra, *Coptic Monasteries: Egypt's Monastic Art and Architecture* (2002).
P. Grossmann, *Christliche Architektur in Ägypten* (2002).
H. Hondelink, ed., *Coptic Art and Culture* (1990).
C. Ihm, *Die Programme der christichen Apsismalerei vom vierten Jahrhundert bis zur Mitte des achten Jahrhunderts* (1960).
J. Lafontaine-Dosogne, *Textiles coptes* (1988).
J. Leroy, *La peinture murale chez les coptes*, 2 vols (1975–82).
M.-H. Rutschowscaya, *Coptic Fabrics* (1990).
A. I. Sadek, 'L'icône copte', *Monde Copte* 18 (1990), 11–18.
H.-G. Severin, 'Frühchristliche Skulptur und Malerei in Ägypten', *Spätantike und frühes Christentum*, ed. B. Brenk (1977), 243–53.
T. K. Thomas, *Late Antique Egyptian Funerary Sculpture* (2000).
L. Török, *Transfigurations of Hellenism: Aspects of Late Antique Art in Egypt, AD 250–700* (2005).
H. Torp, 'Leda Christiana: The Problem of the Interpretation of Coptic Sculpture with Mythological Motifs', *Acta ad Archaeologiam et Artium Historiam Pertinentia*, 4 (1969), 101–12.
C. C. Walters, *Monastic Archaeology in Egypt* (1974).

art and architecture: crusader (12th century) Crusader art and architecture are defined by location, content, and a typical blend of local and imported styles. Historical and geographical conditions in the Latin kingdom of *Jerusalem (1099–1187) determined the formation and appearance of this synthesis. The holy places, restored to Christianity by the Latin crusaders, provided focal points for artistic production: the most significant expressions of crusader architecture, sculpture, and painting, both monumental and miniature, were inspired by and executed at central *loca sancta*. The holy places were the meeting ground of the Latin conquerors, the eastern environment, and the local traditions.

1. Church of the Holy Sepulchre
2. Church of the Ascension
3. The Nativity church
4. The St Jeremiah church
5. The Scriptorium in the Holy Sepulchre

1. Church of the Holy Sepulchre

The crusader church of the *Holy Sepulchre (1149) brought under one roof the three liturgical foci of the site, Anastasis, Golgotha, the Finding of the Cross (commemorated in the 11th century by the underground chapel of St Helena), in an oriented *basilica with transept and Romanesque *chevet. The chevet with three radial *chapels balances the opposite already extant Anastasis rotonda, achieving a spatial unity lacking in the two predecessor structures (4th and 11th centuries). The Holy Sepulchre is the only crusader church to display an ambulatorium and a chevet, thus most accurately reflecting the architectural style current in the west. It was the first to commemorate the place of the Crucifixion by a high chapel over the site known as Adam's tomb to the right of the south, main double entrance to the church, reached by flights of stairs within and without the building.

The Holy Sepulchre church is also remarkable in the relatively rich quantity of figural sculpture preserved in situ: two lintels, one decorated with scenes from Christ's public life up to the Entry into Jerusalem, the other with inhabited scrolls (kept at the Rockefeller Museum in Jerusalem since 1948). The interior was adorned with *mosaics, of which a single fragment, a figure of Christ from an Ascension, is preserved.

2. Church of the Ascension

Most crusader churches in the Holy Land retain the early Christian basilical plan with no transept, which was usual in the region. Even where a transept is recognizable from the exterior, there is little correspondence within, as in the case of St Anne in Jerusalem, where the only indication of one is a dome. The early Christian basilical plan is usually accompanied by an interior space of Romanesque flavour, produced by narrow aisles and densely planted columns (St George, Ramlah; Annunciation, Nazareth), pointed *arches, barrel and cross *vaults (St Anne). Pointed arches and domes in crusader architecture may perhaps indicate a local continuity in which the Muslim buildings on the Temple Mount played a role.

The church of the Ascension on the Mount of Olives offers confirmation that Muslim architecture influenced the crusaders. Its octagonal shape, ground plan, and dimensions clearly refer to the *Dome of the Rock. The particular crusader blend of styles is further exemplified by the Romanesque sculptural decoration.

3. The Nativity church

The Nativity church in *Bethlehem possesses the most important extant series of crusader wall mosaics, witness to a historical episode of trilateral cooperation between the crusader king Amalric, the Byzantine emperor Manuel Comnenos, and Bishop Raoul of Bethlehem. The mosaics placed on the walls of the early Christian basilica represent ecumenical and regional church councils, flanked by angels moving eastwards from the window intervals, and by busts of Christ's ancestors. The transept walls were covered by scenes from Christ's public life, with a figure of Mary in the main *apse. A series of saints venerated in the western and eastern churches is painted on the columns of the nave. The decoration programme reflects cooperation between Byzantine artists, western patrons, and local interests of a theological (the Nativity *locus*) and a political nature.

4. The St Jeremiah church

The St Jeremiah church in Abu-Ghosh was also built and decorated during the time of Manuel Comnenos' involvement in the *crusader state. The basilical church plan is almost quadratic; the style and technique of the wall paintings are evidence of the presence of Byzantine artists, but the interior with its narrow openings, square columns, and pointed arches indicates Romanesque influence. Even the paintings, notwithstanding their Byzantine style and composition, are unusual in their location within the church space, probably intended to enhance the content of the *locus sanctus*.

5. Scriptorium in the Holy Sepulchre

A *scriptorium active at the Holy Sepulchre produced a distinct group of *illuminated MSS of which the Psalter of Queen Melisende now in the British Museum is the most elaborate. Its illuminations and ivory book covers are western in content and style, although they demonstrate awareness of Byzantine (the illuminations) and Islamic (the book covers) traditions associated with the respective media.

BK

H. Buchthal, *Miniature Painting in the Latin Kingdom of Jerusalem* (1957).

H. Buschhausen, *Die süditalienische Bauplastik im Königreich Jerusalem von König Wilhelm II. bis Kaiser Friedrich II.* (1978).

J. Folda, ed., *Crusader Art in the Twelfth Century* (1982).

—— *The Nazareth Capitals and the Crusader Shrine of the Annunciation* (1986).

—— *The Art of the Crusaders in the Holy Land 1098–1187* (1995).

V. Goss and C. V. Bornstein, eds, *The Meeting of Two Worlds: Cultural Exchange between East and West during the Period of the Crusades* (1986).

H. W. Hazard, ed., *The Art and Architecture of the Crusader States*, vol. 4 of *A History of the Crusades*, ed. K. M. Setton (1977).

L.-A. Hunt, 'Art and Colonialism: The Mosaics of the Church of the Nativity, Bethlehem (1169), and the Problem of "Crusader Art"', *DOP* 45 (1991), 69–85.

Z. Jacoby, 'Le Portail de l'Église de l'Annonciation des Nazareth au XIIe siecle', *Monuments Piot* 64 (1981), 141–94.

—— 'The Workshop of the Temple Area in Jerusalem in the Twelfth Century: Its Origin, Evolution and Impact', *ZKG* 45 (1982), 325–94.

B. Kühnel, *Crusader Art of the Twelfth Century: A Geographical, an Historical, or an Art-Historical Notion?* (1994).

G. Kühnel, 'Das Ausschmückungsprogramm der Geburtsbasilika in Bethlehem, Byzanz und Abendland im Königreich Jerusalem', *Boreas*, 10 (1987), 133–49.

—— 'Die Konzilsdarstellungen in der Geburtskirche in Bethlehem', *BZ* 86/87 (1993/94), 86–107.

—— 'Kreuzfahrerideologie und Herrscherikonographie: Das Kaiserpaar Helena und Heraklius in der Grabeskirche', *BZ* 90 (1997), 396–404.

—— 'Das restaurierte Christusmosaik der Calvarienberg-Kapelle und das Bildprogramm der Kreuzfahrer', *RQ* 92 (1997), 45–71.

—— *Wall Painting in the Latin Kingdom of Jerusalem* (1988).

D. Pringle, *The Churches of the Crusader Kingdom of Jerusalem: A Corpus*, vols 1–3 (1993–2007).

M.-L. B. Thiele, 'Die Mosaiken der "Auferstehungskirche" in Jerusalem und die Bauten der "Franken" im 12. Jahrhundert', *FMAS* 18 (1973), 442–71.

D. H. Weiss, *Art and Crusade in the Age of St Louis* (1998).

art and architecture: early Christian In its most common definition, the art and architecture of the Roman Empire from the 4th through the 6th century. Chronological boundaries tend to vary depending on preferences of periodization, stretching from as early as 200 to as late as 750.

1. Definition
2. Images
3. Structures
4. Wall painting, sarcophagi, sculpture, and other art forms

1. *Definition*

The use of the term early Christian as a period designation is problematic because Christian art and architecture developed within the cultural context of a multi-ethnic and multi-religious empire during the 3rd century and started to dominate the cultural landscape of the Mediterranean basin not before the 5th century. Having emerged from Jewish roots, Christianity did not immediately develop a culture of religious image-making or distinct architectural forms for places of worship. Evidence for a Christian material culture is absent during the 1st and much of the 2nd century.

2. *Images*

By the beginning of the 3rd century, common images and symbols such as the dove, fish, ship, or anchor were considered appropriate decoration for seal rings used by Christians. Other images with a long pedigree in the ancient world such as the sheep-bearer were likewise adopted by Christians during this period. Together with Old Testament scenes depicting the stories of Jonah, Daniel, Moses, Noah, and others, allegorical representations of Christ as the Good Shepherd are among the earliest surviving works of art produced for Christian patrons in the Roman *catacombs, where they served to decorate *burial chambers. Towards the end of the 3rd century, wealthy Christians started to commission marble sarcophagi decorated with biblical imagery as well as small-scale independent sculptures of biblical themes and figures. The earliest clearly identifiable Christian sarcophagus is preserved at S. Maria Antiqua in Rome (*c*.270). *Artists and workshops responsible for the execution of such sarcophagi were not necessarily Christian, but served Christian and non-Christian clients alike.

3. *Structures*

While early Christian communities are known to have gathered in private homes from apostolic times until the end of the Great Persecution (303–11), only one such structure has survived. A courtyard house excavated at Dura Europos in Syria was adapted for Christian use between 232 and 256. It contained a meeting room and a *baptistery decorated with *frescoes depicting Christ as the Good Shepherd, Adam and Eve, and other biblical scenes (now Yale University Art Gallery). The victory of Emperor Constantine over Maxentius in 312 marked a turning point in the history of early Christian art and architecture as it elevated Christianity's status to a religion favoured by the emperor. Beginning with the *Basilica Constantiniana* (now S. Giovanni in Laterano, begun *c*.313), the first large-scale Christian church and *cathedral of Rome, Constantine commissioned and endowed numerous churches in *Italy and beyond. Many of these structures were longitudinal in plan featuring a tall colonnaded *nave flanked by a pair of one or two lower side aisles and terminating in a semicircular *apse. This building type derived from secular Roman market *basilicas and was first adapted for Christian use in Constantine's cathedral for Rome. Other churches constructed during this period were modelled on different building types featuring u-shaped, cruciform, circular, hexagonal, or octagonal plans, sometimes combining them with standard basilican structures as in Constantine's churches of the Holy Sepulchre in *Jerusalem (*c*.328–35) and the Nativity in Bethlehem (*c*.333). Baptisteries were often conceived as independent structures with a centralized plan. Richly decorated early examples include the Lateran baptistery in *Rome (*c*.313; remodelled 423–40), S. Giovanni in Fonte in *Naples (*c*.400), and the Orthodox baptistery in *Ravenna (*c*.400–450). Marble panelling, *mosaics, and frescoes are most commonly used to decorate church interiors. The cathedral of *Aquileia (313–19), the mausoleum of Constantine's daughter Constantia (now S. Costanza, *c*.350), and the church of S. Maria Maggiore (432–40), both in Rome, preserve much of their original mosaic decoration, variously employed to adorn floors, walls, and *vaults. The earliest large-scale apse mosaic in a church setting survives at S. Pudenziana in Rome (*c*.400), depicting Christ among his apostles.

4. *Wall painting, sarcophagi, sculpture, and other art forms*

Evidence of monumental wall painting survives largely in the Roman catacombs, which remained in use throughout the 4th century. The city's production of Christian sarcophagi likewise continued until about 400, the sarcophagus of Junius Bassus (*c*.359) in the *Vatican being one of the finest examples. Architectural sculpture and fragments of liturgical furnishings are known from across the empire, attesting to the lavish decoration of parish churches, *monasteries, and Christian *martyria*. Wooden decorative sculpture has survived only rarely, a prominent example being the doors of S. Sabina in Rome (*c*.430). By the 5th century, the Late Roman Empire was thoroughly Christianized and *Constantinople had gained profile as one of its most important artistic centres. Imperial, aristocratic, and ecclesiastical *patrons competed with each other in the foundation and endowment of churches. Secular and ecclesiastical *metalwork objects, MSS, and carved ivories attest to the continuation of Classical styles and Roman artistic traditions during this period. Early evidence for the production of illustrated biblical books survives in a few fragments known as the *Quedlinburg Itala* in *Berlin (Staatsbibliothek, early 5th century). An early ivory casket with portrait busts and scenes from the Old and New Testaments survives in *Brescia (Museo Civico, *c*.400), likely made to contain saintly *relics. The rise of the Christian cult of saints is reflected in an increasing number of surviving *reliquaries and an emergence of major cult centres in Asia Minor, Syria-Palestine, and North Africa. While the boundaries between early Christian and *Byzantine art and architecture are fluid, the 6th century can be considered a period of transition, in which new artistic trends emerge that can no longer be described in terms of earlier forms and developments. HAKl

B. Brenk, *Spätantike und frühes Christentum* (1977).
A. Effenberger, *Frühchristliche Kunst und Kultur: Von den Anfängen bis zum 7. Jahrhundert* (1986).
P. C. Finney, *The Invisible God* (1994).
W. E. Kleinbauer, *Early Christian and Byzantine Architecture: An Annotated Bibliography and Historiography* (1992).
G. Koch, *Early Christian Art and Architecture: An Introduction* (1996).
R. Krautheimer, *Early Christian and Byzantine Architecture* ([4]1986).
Liebieghaus, Museum Alter Plastik, *Spätantike und frühes Christentum* (1984).
J. Lowden, *Early Christian and Byzantine Art* (1997).
T. F. Matthews, *The Early Churches of Constantinople: Architecture and Liturgy* (1971).
R. Milburn, *Early Christian Art and Architecture* (1988).
J. Spier, ed., *Picturing the Bible: The Earliest Christian Art* (2007).
K. Weitzmannn, ed., *Age of Spirituality: Late Antique and Early Christian Art. Third to Seventh Century* (1979).

art and architecture: Georgian The roots of ecclesiastical building activity in art and architecture in Georgia may be traced to the declaration of Christianity as the official religion in the 320s during the reign of King Mirian. From then through the 4th to 7th centuries, churches, from large *cathedrals to small *chapels, and other Christian monuments including wooden and stone *crosses and stelae, were erected in various parts of the country.

1. Development of basilicas and domed churches
2. Mural painting, mosaics, and frescoes
3. The monastic impetus
4. Middle Georgian art and architecture (*c*.975–1080)
5. High Georgian art and architecture (*c*.1080–1220)
6. Late Georgian art and architecture (*c*.1220–1450)

1. *Development of basilicas and domed churches*

Georgian historical sources preserve information on many of these, namely the churches of Svetitskhoveli, Samtavro, Erusheti, Manglisi, Tsilkani, Nekresi, Nikozi, Ujarma, Bichvinta, and Tsikhegoji churches and the episcopal sees of Mere and Akhiza.

Two main types of ecclesiastical structures, the *basilica and the domed church, have been constructed in Georgia since early Christian times. Both forms exhibit wide variation throughout the different regions of the country and over the course of centuries. Due to their architectural rendering the churches of Nekresi (4th–5th centuries), Bolnisi (478–93), Urbnisi (5th–6th centuries), and Vazisubani (6th century) are distinguished among early Christian basilicas. Gradual refinement of one of the variations of the cruciform-domed church—a *tetraconch—had resulted in the erection of the late-6th-century church of the Holy Cross (Jvari) in Mtskheta. In this period the tetraconch became widespread not only in various regions of Georgia (Ateni Sion in Kartli, Martvili in Egrisi, Shuamta in Kakheti, Dranda in Apkhazeti, Chamkhusi in Tao), but in neighbouring Armenia. Subsequently, a more complex compositional and constructional variation of the domed church based on its plan, the tetraconch with a circular *ambulatory, was worked out (Bana, 7th century). Additional variations of the domed church, such as the croix-libre or semi-croix-libre (Erelaant Saqdari, Idleti and Shiomgvime—all of the 6th century; Samtsevrisi—first half of the 7th century), the croix-inscrite (Tsromi, 626–34), the tetraconch inscribed in the octagon (Manglisi, 5th century and Davitiani, 5th–6th centuries) were also established in Georgian ecclesiastical architecture from an earlier period.

2. *Mural painting, mosaics, and frescoes*

The oldest examples of Christian mural *painting, *mosaics, and *frescoes are known from the 6th–7th centuries (Ateni Sion and Tsromi). Only certain parts of the interior were covered with the painted decoration—mainly the *chancel and the *dome. Murals of this epoch share the principles of the monumental art of the Holy Land in the selection and depiction of holy images.

3. *The monastic impetus*

The mid-6th-century arrival of the so-called 'Syrian Fathers' in Georgia marks a certain stage in the further strengthening development of *monasticism in Georgia as well as the evaluation of monastic art. Monasteries of Zedazeni, Shiomgvime, Gareja, Martq'opi, Iq'alto, Nekresi, and Khirsa had in the course of the centuries developed into the most significant centres of artistic creative activity, preserving specific examples of architecture, mural painting, and stone carving. For centuries these sites had not lost their initial purpose—monastic life—and strong building activity had actually never ceased in all the monasteries founded by the 'Syrian Fathers'.

The development of Christian art in Georgia did not cease during the Arab domination beginning in the mid 7th century. As far as ecclesiastical building activity in this period is concerned, Tao-Klarjeti is distinguished among other regions of the country. Here numerous monasteries were founded through the efforts of St Grigol Khantzteli (759–861) and his disciples. This was a new stage in monastic building activity in Georgia, considerably differing by its character and scale from the earlier monasticism based on Syro-Palestinian ascetic traditions. Numerous churches were erected by the reverend father himself and his disciples, including Khandzta, Nuka Saqdari, Nedzvi, and Vachedzori (all 9th century), Opiza (9th to 10th centuries), and Khandzta (10th century).

Georgia avoided the *iconoclastic controversy affecting the larger part of eastern Christendom. Hence, an uninterrupted course of development of the Christian figurative tradition was retained. The oldest iconographical themes and images were preserved unaltered up to the MA. Murals were still executed; interior facades of the churches, stelae, and chancel barriers were decorated with reliefs; and painted and metal icons and cloisonné *enamels were produced.

Beginning from this period, which witnessed the gradual liberation of the country from invaders and the establishment of a united kingdom, certain changes are discernible in ecclesiastical architecture (Samshvilde Sion, 759–77; Kabeni and Gurjaani, both of the 8th century; Tsirkoli, Vachnadziani, and Iqalto, all of the beginning of the early 9th century; Taoskari, turn of the 9th to the 10th century), mural painting (Telovani, 8th century; Armazi, 864; Akura, 850s; Sabereebi, four paintings of the 9th and 10th centuries), *metalwork (icon of Transfiguration from Zarzma, 886), and sculptural decoration of the church facades (Opiza, 9th century), chancel barriers, stelae (Opiza, Gveldesi, Usaneti), and *manuscript illumination (Adishi Gospel, 897). They are distinguished by a striving towards new modes of expression, close to a deeper Christian spirituality.

4. Middle Georgian art and architecture (c.975–1080)

The heyday of medieval Georgian art coincides with the late 10th to early 11th centuries. In the cruciform-domed churches of this period, the interiors of the churches are completely covered with frescoes. Great attention was also paid to the sculptural decoration of the facades. Along with decorative *arches, ornamental framings and terminations of the doors and *windows, separate motifs, images of the saints and Christian symbols, are scattered all over the facades.

The massive cathedrals erected in the late 10th and early 11th centuries, namely Kutaisi, Svetitskhoveli, Alaverdi, and Ishkhani, are distinguished by their large scale, the originality of the constructional and artistic solution, and the richness and diversity of ornamental decoration. Of the same period are frescoes and stone reliefs distinguished by supreme refinement and exquisiteness—the murals of Otxta Eklesia, Oshki, Khakhuli, Ishkhani; the chancel barriers of Shiomgvime, Sapara, and Khovle; metal and painted icons; numerous enamels; and richly illuminated MSS. Among them are processional crosses of Ishkhani and Breti, Sagolasheni and Shemokmedi panels, a pre-altar cross from Mestia, the chalice from Bedia church, an enamelled *cross from Shemokmedi, the Martvili *quatrefoil, icons of the Virgin (from Zarzma, Martvili, Labechina, Tsageri), the first Jruchi Gospel, and the Synaxarion of Zacharia, archbishop of Bana. Local schools of painting with specific artistic traits were formed in different regions of the country, namely the Gareja desert and Svaneti, whose work survives in murals of the main church and refectory of Udabno monastery in Gareja and the Nezguni, Cvabiani, and Svipi churches in Svaneti.

An intensification of activity is discernible in the Georgian monasteries in *Jerusalem, Mount Athos, Sinai, *Antioch, *Cyprus, and so forth, also increased artistic production around this time. Monuments of architecture (for example, churches on the Black Mountain and the monastery of the Holy Cross in *Jerusalem built by the abbot Prochore), wall painting (the frescoes of the painter John Iveropulos for the ossuary chapel of the monastery of Petritson, 1070s), icon painting (late-11th-century icons by the painter John Tokhabi in Sinai monastery of St Catherine), and the MS illumination (Alaverdi Gospel copied and illuminated in the Kalipos monastery near Antioch in 1054) testify to the influence of Byzantine culture.

5. High Georgian art and architecture (c.1080–1222)

The century and a half from the reign of Davit Agmashenebeli (1089–1125) up to the invasion of Khwarazmians and Mongols in the 1220s, a period that also witnessed the strengthening of the Georgian state, was an epoch of incomparable efflorescence of national and spiritual culture. Ecclesiastical art—especially the fine arts—was an inseparable part of the homogeneous cultural-historical development of that period. This was the apex of the evolution and refinement of the artistic traditions that were consistently established in the course of the previous centuries. The monuments of this period are extraordinary, namely, the murals of Ateni Sion (1080s) and the chancel mosaics and *narthex frescoes of the main church of the Gelati monastery (1120s); the wall paintings executed by the royal painters Tevdore and Michael Maglakeli in Upper Svaneti in the course of the first half of the 12th century; the murals in Vardzia (1184–6), Natlismcemeli (1190s), Kincvisi (*c.*1205), Betania (beginning of the 13th century), Bertubani (*c.*1210), and Akhtala (1220s); the miniatures of the Second Jruchi, Gelati, and Vani Gospels (12th and early 13th centuries); and numerous painted and chased icons (among them the Khakhuli *triptych of the second quarter of the 12th century and works of the goldsmiths Beka and Beshken Opizari). The variations of the cruciform-domed church, which had been established earlier, were still predominant in the ecclesiastical architecture of the 12th–13th centuries. This type of structure was the basis of the artistic character of the main church of the Gelati monastery and the churches of Tigva, Betania, Ikorta, and Kvatakhevi.

6. Late Georgian art and architecture (c.1223–1450)

Despite continuous devastating invasions, beginning in the second half of the 13th century, artistic production continued unabated in the country, now divided into separate princedoms. The activity of local ruler-donors greatly contributed to these developments. This tendency is especially conspicuous in the princely domain of Samtskhe-Saatabago, the rulers of which—the Jaq'eli house—had commissioned the erection and painting of numerous churches, including Sapara (1290s), Zarzma (early 14th century), and Ch'ule (1381). Vast fresco ensembles were produced in western Georgia, namely in Ubisi, Khobi, Sori, and Martvili. In the late 14th century, Cyr Manuil Eugenikos, a Constantinopolitan painter specially invited to Georgia by the order of Vameq Dadiani, ruler of Odishi, executed the Tsalenjikha murals. All these decorations more or less distinctly and consistently reflected the Byzantine Palaeologan style. Examples of this artistic trend are also evident in the Ubisi triptych (second half of the 14th century) and in the miniatures of the Mokvi Gospel (1300).

The difficulties caused by devastating invasions and the disintegration of the country beginning in the 15th century left an imprint on the character of Georgian creative activity and accordingly on art. In the course of the late MA, the age-old tradition of Christian art was mainly continued in the monasteries. With the aid of the royal court and nobles, they preserved contacts with the most significant spiritual centres of eastern Christendom threatened by that time—the Holy Land, Mount Athos, and Sinai. *See also* ART AND ARCHITECTURE: BYZANTINE; CHURCH OF THE EAST. ZSk

G. Abramishvili and A. Javakhishvili, *Jewellery and Metalwork in the Museums of Georgia* (1986).

N. Aladashvili, *Monumental'naja skulptura gruzii* (1977).

——G. Alibegashvili, and A. Volskaia, *Zhivopisnaja shkola Svaneti* (1983).

G. Alibegashvili and A. Volskaia, 'Georgian Icons', *Icons*, ed. K. Weitzmann *et al.* (1982).

A. Alpago-Novello *et al.*, *Art and Architecture in Medieval Georgia* (1980).

S. Amiranashvili, *Istorija Gruzinskoi monumental'noi zhivopisi* (1957).

——*Les émaux de Géorgie* (1962).

V. Beridze, *Architecture de Tao-Klarjeti* (1981).

——G. Alibegashvili, A. Volskaia, L. Khuskivadze, *et al.*, *The Treasures of Georgia* (1984).

—— and E. Neubauer, *Die Baukunst des Mittelalters in Georgien vom 4. bis zum 18. Jahrhundert* (1981).

G. Chubinashvili, *Pamjatniki tipa Djvari* (1948).

——*Peshchernye Monastyry David Garedji* (1948).

——*Arkhitektura Kakheti* (1958).

——*Gruzinskoe chekannoe iskusstvo* (1959).

W. Djobadze, *Early Medieval Georgian Monasteries in Historic Tao, Klarjeti and Savseti* (1992).

A. Eastmond, *Royal Imagery in Medieval Georgia* (1998).

L. Khuskivadze, *Gruzinskie émail* (1981).

R. Mepisaschili and W. Tsintsadze, *Die Kunst des alten Georgien* (1977).

T. Sheviakova, *Monumentalnaia zhivopis rannego srednevekov'ya Gruzii* (1983).

R. Shmerling, *Malye formy v arkhitekture srednevekovoj Gruzii* (1962).

——*Khudozhestvennoe oformlenie gruzinskoi rukopisnoi knigi IX–XI stoletii*, vols 1 and 2 (1968, 1979).

N. Thierry, 'La peinture Médiévale géorgienne', *Corsi di cultura sull'arte ravennate e bizantina* (1973).

T. Velmans and A. Alpago-Novello, *Miroire de l'invisible. Peintures murales et architecture de la Géorgie (VIe–XVe siècles)* (1996).

T. Virsaladze, *Osnovnye etapy razvitija gruzinskoi srednevekovoi monumental'noi zhivopisi* (1977).

art and architecture: Ghaznavid The first Islamicized Turkish dynasty in the eastern Islamic world, the Ghaznavids (977–1186), ruled over an empire comprising eastern Iran, Afghanistan, Pakistan, and northern *India. In terms of cultural orientation, the Ghaznavids were responsible for promoting the Persian literary and artistic renaissance begun by their predecessors, the Samanids (819–1005) of the Farghana valley, after three centuries of domination by Arab culture. Thanks to a vigorous literary tradition, a number of contemporary court chronicles—*Tarikh-i Masud* by Baihaqi and the *Tabaqat-i Nasiri* by Juzjani—exist to inform us regarding the Ghaznavid construction of numerous palaces, *mosques, and public works in main centres such as the capital Ghazna, Balkh, Bost, Termez, Herat, and Nishapur. These sources also attest to the court production, through workshops (*kar-khanas*), of textiles, carpets, robes, and handcrafted luxury goods.

Centuries of *warfare, earthquakes, floods, and erosion have erased much of the physical evidence and material culture left behind by the Ghaznavids. Probably the largest and most impressive archaeological site is Lashkar-i Bazar on the banks of the Helmand, near Bost, in southwest Afghanistan. This was first examined systematically by the French between 1949 and 1951, revealing a comprehensive palace complex measuring *c.*7 km × 2 km. Art historians have examined the physical structure and layout of the Lashkar-i Bazar to suggest that the Ghaznavid architectural programme was a continuation of not only pre-Islamic Iranian building practices and styles (walled rectangular precincts, court pools with reservoirs, garden complexes) but also Achaemenian and Sasanian concepts of imperial space in the form of audience halls, *porticoes, and throne rooms.

Turks such as the Ghaznavids were first introduced to the Islamic world in the 9th century as slave troops serving the Abbasid caliphate in and around the Tigris-Euphrates river complex. Transferred east to Afghanistan as military governors where they later became self-proclaimed dynasts, the Ghaznavids likely brought architectural and aesthetic standards from this region, which had been dominated by Persian traditions for close to 1500 years. Undoubtedly the greatest contribution of the Ghaznavid dynasty was their patronage of the Persian poet Firdausi (d. 1020) and his lifelong project of recording the epic poem, the *Shah nama* ('Book of Kings'). Some scholars have suggested that the Persian verses inscribed on tiled slabs in the Southern Palace in the Lashkar-i Bazar are in fact quotations from Firdausi's poem. In any case, the figural representation of animals, horsed figures, and fantastic creatures on tiled surfaces, along with an extensive fresco of Turkish palace guardsmen in the throne room, depict a court that actively sponsored and promoted long-standing Iranian aesthetic traditions. Other monumental architecture includes a Ghaznavid palace built in Termez on the Oxus that was later restored and expanded by Bahramshah in 1129–30. Here we sense the prevalence of a 'Ghaznavid style' as many of the features in the main palace at Lashkar-i Bazar are discovered at its counterpart in the Termez site, including extensive inscriptions of floral designs, birds, animals, and human figures. The inclusion of distinctive figural representations have led some to suggest that the Ghaznavids probably brought back examples of fine Hindu artwork and sculptures from their plundering raids into the Indo-Gangetic plain. The legacy of these raids in terms of aesthetic influence has probably been overstated, seen in the 1880 decision by the invading British army to 'liberate' from Kabul a pair of massive sandalwood gates that allegedly had been looted by Mahmud from a Hindu temple in Somnath and transported to Afghanistan. Likewise, for many years it was believed that the minarets of Ghazna had been erected as 'victory towers' by Mahmud or his son Mas'ud when, in fact, they have now been attributed to a much later phase of Ghaznavid history. The most significant legacy of the Ghaznavids with respect to art and architecture was their ability to transmit certain classical Persian traditions to the succeeding dynasty of the *Seljuks, who are widely considered responsible for the flourishing of medieval Persian art, architecture, literature, and poetry. CPM

C. E. Bosworth, *The Ghaznavids* (1963).

—— 'The Development of the Persian Culture under the Early Ghaznavids', *Iran*, 6 (1968), 33–44.

R. Hillenbrand, *Islamic Architecture* (1994).

G. Schlumberger, 'Le palais Ghaznevide de Lashkar-i Bazar', *Syria*, 29 (1952), 251–70.

J. Sourdel-Thomine, 'Ghaznawids: Art and Monuments', *EI*, vol. 2, 1053–5.

art and architecture: Gothic With the advent of the Gothic style, architecture became a leading form of artistic expression during the late MA. Despite regional peculiarities it shared a common language of forms and artistic principles throughout Europe. The most typical features of Gothic architecture are the use of *rib *vaults, *buttresses on the exterior, and huge *windows filled with *tracery and *stained glass. Its beginnings can be traced back to *England and northwest *France in the first half of the 12th century. During the 13th century the new style spread all over Europe, resulting in the first 'international style' around 1300. In the 14th century central Europe and England developed further innovations in architectural design, generating the second international style around 1400 as well as later Gothic styles such as the 'flamboyant' and the 'perpendicular'.

1. Early to High Gothic and Early English (*c*.1130–*c*.1240)
2. Rayonnant Gothic and Decorated Style (*c*.1240–*c*.1350)
3. Late Gothic: flamboyant and perpendicular (*c*.1350–*c*.1500)

1. *Early to High Gothic and Early English*

The first strides toward a Gothic-style architecture were achieved almost simultaneously in England and France via a development of Norman Romanesque architecture. In France, it was on the occasion of rebuilding the abbey church of *St-Denis, royal necropolis in the vicinity of *Paris (1134–44), and of *Sens cathedral (1143–63) that the ingredients of the new style were put together for the first time: a systematic combination of rib vaults and buttresses together with a penchant for pointed *arches. The architect of St-Denis also introduced the choir with *ambulatory and radiating *chapels as a feature that would become a mainstay in French Gothic architecture. This is also true for the western façade with its characteristic two towers and three openings that correspond to the three *naves. Sens cathedral added to this the monumental appearance of a huge, vertically shaped interior and a simple, but effective, tripartite elevation consisting of arcades, *triforium instead of a *gallery, and clerestory. In the next decades, flying buttresses allowed for higher and thinner walls that were pierced by large windows.

The buildings of the High Gothic period, namely the cathedrals of Chartres (begun in 1194; all subsequent years for churches are building *start* dates unless otherwise noted), *Rheims (1210), and *Amiens (1220), further standardized the style by dividing the inner space into a row of identical, oblong *bays (*travées*) of quadripartite rib vaults. The windows now covered the whole surface of the clerestory and were filled first with plate tracery (Chartres), later with free-standing tracery made up of round shafts (Rheims). Another important element is the steady enhancement of height, starting with the already impressive 36 meters at Chartres to the breathtaking 48 meters of Beauvais cathedral (1225). Its collapse in 1248 seems to have stopped the competition, since from then on no more attempts were made to surpass the height of the Beauvais cathedral's interior.

In England, rib vaults had already been introduced as early as 1093 when the construction of *Durham cathedral was begun. However, the Gothic style was not completely embraced until the construction in 1175 of a new choir for *Canterbury cathedral by William of Sens, a master from France who must have been aware of the new artistic and technological innovations. After his death in 1178 he was followed by William the Englishman. The change of architects resulted in a rather original style that initiated Early English Gothic. It is characterized by the use of pointed arches, rib vaults, and buttresses, but, distinctive from the French cathedrals, the galleries persisted, choirs with rectangular terminations were preferred, and the horizontal elements of the elevation were more accented. Also, some elements that came out of the Romanesque tradition, such as 'Lady' chapels, crossing towers, and the use of two *transepts, were maintained. Compared to continental buildings of the same period, the English churches impress by the richness of sculpted details as well as by their overall size. The patrons and architects in England tended to replace the continental verticalism by a horizontal expansion of their structures. That same horizontalism also characterizes the English façades, which often conceal the structure of the building behind and are placed like a roodscreen in front of the naves. Other splendid examples of Early English Gothic, besides Canterbury cathedral, include the cathedrals of *Worcester (1175), Wells (*c.*1180), *Lincoln (1192), and *Salisbury (1220). Another important innovation occurred around 1200 when Lincoln cathedral was vaulted. Its architect introduced *tiercerons, which allowed him to the supply the vaults with a decorative pattern of ribs. From then on, decorative rib vaults developed into a characteristic of Gothic architecture in England.

In central Europe, the strong Romanesque architectural tradition that had created quite original designs inhibited the direct assumption of French models for a long time. It took the transformation of a Romanesque model into the High Gothic style of *Rheims cathedral, as was done by the master of Toul cathedral (*c.*1220), to allow a broader reception of the new Gothic style. After Toul, great churches in this style were built all over the (Holy) Roman Empire, first in *Trier (Liebfrauenkirche, 1228), followed by Marburg (Elisabethkirche, 1235) and *Metz (*c.*1235). As many examples show, the 'lodges' (working groups of *masons, sculptors, and *architects) in Lorraine and northern Burgundy proved to be constant sources of artistic inspiration for German architects, and Toul cathedral's one-storeyed, polygonal *apse with *tracery windows was to become the standard form for central European Gothic choirs.

2. Rayonnant Gothic and Decorated Style

The term 'Rayonnant' refers to the completely glazed (that is, *stained glass) walls of churches such as in the nave of the abbey church of *St-Denis (1231) and those of *Ste-Chapelle at the royal palace on the Île-de-la-cité in Paris (*c.*1241–8). The refinement of flying *buttresses and the use of ironwork to strengthen the structure helped to create an eye-catching architecture of deceptive transparency, studded with richly decorated tracery. Whereas the thin wall structure filled with stained glass became a specialty of the French lodges, the English concentrated on the ornamental effect of the traceries. They developed a wealth of new tracery designs, ranging from geometrical to reticulated and, finally, curvilinear forms (*Westminster Abbey, 1245; *Lichfield cathedral, after 1257; *Exeter cathedral, *c.*1275; abbey church of Bristol, 1298; Wells cathedral, retro choir, *c.*1320).

In central Europe only the clerestory of Metz cathedral (*c.*1245), Cologne cathedral (1248), and the nave of *Strasbourg cathedral (*c.*1250) could be called pure examples of Rayonnant architecture modelled after French examples of the 1240s. Things did change fundamentally with the construction of the western façade of Strasbourg cathedral (1276), which echoes the second generation of French Rayonnant buildings, such as the cathedral of Clermont-Ferrand (1248) and the papal collegiate *church of St-Urbain in *Troyes (1262). This second Rayonnant style retained the thin-wall structure, but completed the stained glass windows with membrane-like mural surfaces covered by the elegant, sharp-edged mouldings of the more and more autonomous tracery. In Strasbourg, this style was adopted and further developed in a way that was to leave its mark on the architecture all over central Europe. Thus, towards the year 1300, the second Rayonnant style became truly international, generating such exceptional buildings as the cathedrals of *Limoges (1273), *Regensburg (Ratisbonne) (*c.*1275), and *York (nave, 1292).

3. Late Gothic: flamboyant and perpendicular

In England, innovative designs such as the decorative rib-vaults and curvilinear tracery already had a long tradition when Peter *Parler built a new cathedral for Emperor *Charles IV in *Prague (1344). The result was a highly original architecture that became the definitive model for central European Late Gothic. Its main characteristics are richly varied patterns of flamboyant tracery and decorative rib-vaults that combine into reticulated or star-shaped figures. With the appearance of Peter Parler, central Europe took a leading role in the artistic development of Gothic, which resulted in another international phenomenon. The use of the new style was not limited to *cathedrals or collegiate churches, as the cities now began to build their *parish churches in the forms and dimensions of cathedrals. Splendid examples include *Ulm's minster (1377), and the great hall-churches of Schwäbisch Gmünd (*c.*1320), *Kutná Hora (Kuttenberg, 1389), and Landshut (St Martin, *c.*1385; Heiliggeist, 1407). The English variant of Late Gothic became the Perpendicular style, whose main features are completely glazed walls that are divided by the perpendicular lines of the tracery and crowned by fan vaults. *See also* ART AND ARCHITECTURE: ROMANESQUE. MCS

P. Frankl, *Gothic Architecture*, ed. and rev. P. Crossley (2000).

D. Kimpel and R. Suckale, *Die gotische Architektur in Frankreich, 1130–1270* (1985).

N. Nußbaum, *German Gothic Church Architecture* (2000).

M. C. Schurr, *Gotische Architektur im mittleren Europa, 1220–1340* (2007).

C. Wilson, *The Gothic Cathedral: The Architecture of the Great Church, 1130–1530* (1990).

art and architecture: Insular The term 'Insular' refers to the cultures of the British Isles from the mid 6th through the late 9th centuries, sometimes called 'Northumbro-Irish' to suggest the two main zones of production. These cultures were so intertwined that it is often impossible to determine if a work was made in Ireland or *England, or in England by Irish craftsmen, and so on. Insular art was influenced by Celtic and Roman works and in turn impacted not only the later arts of the British Isles, but also Continental art, through missions and strong ties between monastic centres. The Insular period was particularly rich in artistic production, especially in *manuscript illumination, producing the Book of *Kells, the *Lindisfarne Gospels, and other well-known masterpieces.

Insular MSS are characterized by elaborate decoration, integration of decorative elements, images, and scripts, and extensive use of *interlace. Insular scribes used slightly different methods in preparing their materials, using thicker *vellum, with little differentiation between hair and flesh, and distinct scripts, including an *Insular Half-Uncial and Minuscule, which include a handful of *runic derivatives (æ, ð, þ, known as 'ash', 'eth', and 'thorn').

The dominant book type was the *Gospel, which was usually (and lavishly) decorated with prefatory pages preceding each Gospel. *Carpet pages, elaborate decorative pages bearing some formal similarity to eastern textiles, serve as protective covers for each Gospel account and sometimes for St *Jerome's 'Novum Opus', perhaps taking the place of the actual covers used when the books were bound separately. These tend to be geometric, often containing one or more crosses within their overall structure. Designs are commonly filled with interlace composed of lines and elongated beasts. Carpet pages typically face *incipit pages containing the opening of each Gospel, written in elaborate display scripts, such that these pages can frequently contain only the first few words of the text. These are often followed by author portraits of the Evangelists, inspired by late antique works, generally showing the figure seated, within an architectural frame, in the act of writing. In some cases, the *Evangelist symbols accompany the figure, as if providing dictation.

A particular innovation of the period is the *Chi-Rho* page, containing a monogram consisting of the first two letters of 'Christ' as spelled in Greek and used as an abbreviation. These appear at Matthew 1:18, which relates the birth of Jesus. Early *Chi-Rho* examples contain only slight elaboration of the letters, but in certain examples, such as the Book of Kells, the letters are allowed to swell, taking over the entire page. They may be filled with interlace and, as in the Kells example, may contain a wealth of animal and monstrous figures within and around the letters.

Little Insular architecture survives, as much was constructed in perishable materials or replaced by the *Normans. A few early works do survive, some expressing clearly the ideals of Insular *monasticism. The beehive huts of Skellig Michael (island off the west coast of Ireland), rebuilt in the mid 9th century following *Viking raids, are simple, even harsh structures, composed of field stones, stacked and *corbelled without *mortar into a series of small individual cells. The church on the site is somewhat larger, but of the same simple format. Except for a cross of lighter-coloured stones over the door to the church, they are without decoration, and they are as a rule windowless. Such brutal structures bear out the devotion of Insular monks to the precepts of their rules.

Significant portions of the *double monastery at *Wearmouth and Jarrow, where *Bede spent almost his entire life, survive. These suggest relatively simple stone structures, with peaked *roofs, limited use of round *arches, and, perhaps surprisingly, stained glass windows. *See also* ARCHITECTURE: ANGLO-SAXON; ART, CELTIC; CANON TABLE; NORTHUMBRIA. ASM

J. J. G. Alexander, *A Survey of Manuscripts Illuminated in the British Isles: Insular Manuscripts, Sixth to the Ninth Century* (1978).
M. Brown, *Anglo-Saxon Manuscripts* (1991).
——*A Guide to Western Historical Scripts, from Antiquity to 1600* (²1999).
M. Budny, *Insular, Anglo-Saxon, and Early Anglo-Norman Manuscript Art at Corpus Christi College, Cambridge: An Illustrated Catalogue* (1997).
R. G. Calkins, *Illuminated Books of the Middle Ages* (1983).
——*Medieval Architecture in Western Europe* (1998).
C. de Hamel, *A History of Illuminated Manuscripts* (²1994).
G. Henderson, *From Durrow To Kells: The Insular Gospel-Books, 650–800* (1987).
T. Ohlgren, *Inventory of Insular and Anglo-Saxon Illuminated Manuscripts* (1991).
——*Insular and Anglo-Saxon Illuminated Manuscripts: An Iconographic Catalogue, c.AD 625 to 1100* (1986).

art and architecture: Islamic The term Islamic as it is often applied to art and architecture describes the art and architecture created for the service of Islam as well as secular art and architecture produced in lands under Islamic rule or influence, regardless of the artist's, architect's, or patron's religious affiliation. Medieval Islamic art and architecture include objects and buildings from a vast geographic region, spanning from the Iberian Peninsula in the west to the Indian Peninsula in the east. The medieval Islamic world was composed of various ruling dynasties. The historical, cultural, and regional varieties of these individual dynasties are reflected in the art and architecture. However, there are some features that are common to all of Islamic art and architecture. *Calligraphy and inscriptions are perhaps the two most prevalent features in Islamic artistic production. Arabic script is considered the noblest form of expression because of its association with the Muslim holy book, the *Quran, which is written in Arabic. Another characteristic of Islamic art is total surface decoration with geometric or vegetal patterns and motifs. In addition, figural imagery is an important aspect of Islamic art. Such images occur primarily in secular arts and appear in a wide variety of media, such as MSS and *textiles. Among medieval Islamic cultures the so-called minor arts were the primary means of artistic expression. Illuminated MSS, textiles and carpets, inlaid *metalwork, blown glass, glazed *ceramics, and carved wood, ivory, and stone all became highly developed art forms. In architecture, the most prevalent Islamic building-type is the *mosque. In the medieval period, the three most common mosque types were the hypostyle mosque, the four-iwan mosque, and the centrally planned mosque. Despite the variety in their forms, all mosques share specific liturgical features such as the *minaret, the **minbar* (pulpit), the *qibla* (directional wall towards Mecca), and the **mihrab* (a niche in the *qibla* wall that indicates the position of the prayer-leader). Lavish palaces, gardens, and mausoleums were also common throughout the medieval Islamic world. LT

S. Blair and J. Bloom, *The Art and Architecture of Islam 1250–1800* (1994).
R. Ettinghausen *et al.*, *Islamic Art and Architecture 650–1250* (2001).
O. Grabar, *The Formation of Islamic Art* (1987).

art and architecture: Mamluk (1250–1517) Military slaves of Turkish descent who ruled *Egypt, Syria, and *Palestine. They are considered among the greatest *patrons of the arts in the history of Islam, and the cities of *Cairo and *Damascus were leading intellectual and cultural centres. Their preserved secular and religious monuments display monumental *domes, slender *minarets, and ornamented façades with pointed arched *windows. In addition, the Mamluks were famous for producing *manuscripts, *metalwork, *textile, *glass, and *pottery. RB

O. Grabar, *Islamic Visual Culture, 1100–1800* (2006).
H. Stierlin and A. Stierlin, *Splendour of an Islamic World: The Art and Architecture of the Mamluks* (1997).

art and architecture: Merovingian The cultural productions of the Frankish tribes settling in parts of what are now modern France, Belgium, and western Germany between the 5th and 8th centuries. Surviving examples of elaborate jewellery, MSS, and ecclesiastical architecture reflect a continuation of Roman traditions combined with an abstract, Germanic, ornamental vocabulary.

Merovingian nobles manifested their aristocratic status visually through functional and decorative personal adornment. Polychrome jewellery, particularly garnet cloisonné, was especially prized by both men and women. The burial of King Childeric (d. 482) preserved a particularly impressive collection of items of male adornment, focusing on military items such as weapon mounts, belts as well as ornamental bees/cicadas likely worn on the king's cloak to signify royalty or fertility. Circular brooches set with garnet were an important component of the attire of noble women.

The conversion of Childeric's son *Clovis to Christianity created a demand for basic Christian texts and documents of church practice. The polychrome effect of jewellery, along with Insular influences brought by *missionaries such as St *Columban as well as artefacts such as Coptic *textiles, informed the inventive art of Merovingian MSS. The *Gelasian Sacramentary (Vatican MS. Reg.lat 316) displays a basic repertoire of birds and fish shaped to form the display letters of a text, each filled with patterns of red, green, and yellow in tight compartments of colour. Merovingian artists limited their figural treatments, though novel use of the crucifixion in the Gellone Sacramentary (BN MS.lat. 12048, 143v) is an early use of word illustration.

Contemporary written sources and archaeological remains indicate that building activity was significant. Only a fraction survives relatively intact, perhaps a result of a deliberate attempt to discredit the dynasty by the revisionists of the *Carolingian dynasty that replaced them. Free-standing *baptisteries, which were not in favour in later centuries and thus were spared rebuilding, survive in *Aix-en-Provence, Riez, and Fréjus. These octagonal structures, with a central font covered with a cupola on pillars, recall early Christian and Byzantine prototypes. Bishop *Gregory of Tours in his *History of the Franks* records that King Clovis ordered buildings constructed in *Paris, and Queen Cholthilda erected a *basilica over the tomb of St *Germanus at Auxerre. Gregory also commends the construction of the basilica of St *Martin at Tours (*c.*472; not extant), which contained 120 columns, 8 doors, and 52 *windows. A surviving basilica at St Pierre, *Vienne, relies on masonry side-walls to support a *timber *roof; the interior elevation is composed of two superimposed orders adorned with re-used Roman marble columns. Reused columns found in the *crypt at Jouarre, once part of a large basilica, are topped with late-Roman, Corinthian-style capitals imported from Spain.

Two of the most impressive survivals of Merovingian architecture are preserved in *Poitiers. The baptistery of St Jean (7th century) presents a centralized cruciform plan, flanked by three (originally) square *apses and a rectangular entrance porch. The exterior, composed of Roman-style *brick, terracotta, and coloured *stone adornments, is ornamented with surface features such as triangular pediments, embedded *pilasters and arcades, and carved capitals to create a polychrome effect. The so-called Hypogeum des Dunes (*c.*700), a barrel-*vaulted, free-standing *memoria or funerary *chapel, was reached by descending twelve steps protected by apotropaic carvings of Mediterranean-inspired vine-scrolls and griffins combined with Germanic geometric or animal patterns.

Merovingian *sculpture was largely ornamental and architectural in nature. Exceptions are the elaborately sculpted *sarcophagi of St Theodichilde and St *Agilbert, the first abbots and abbesses of the *double monastery at Jouarre.

Merovingian *craftsmen gained respect in other Germanic kingdoms, evidenced most notably by the importation of *masons from Gaul into *Northumbria by *Benedict Biscop. Merovingian work in garnet, stone, and MS *painting preserved and passed along Roman and Germanic traditions of craftsmanship, combining both into an inventive and influential aesthetic. *See also* ART AND ARCHITECTURE: COPTIC/INSULAR; CLOTHING AND COSTUME; GEMS AND JEWELLERY; LITURGICAL BOOKS, LATIN. BCW

B. Arrhenius, *Merovingian Garnet Jewelry: Emergence and Social Implications* (1985).
G. Bandmann, *Early Medieval Architecture as Bearer of Meaning*, tr. K. Wallis (German original, 1951) (2005).
B. Effros, *Merovingian Mortuary Archaeology and the Making of the Early Middle Ages* (2003).
Gregory of Tours, *The History of the Franks*, tr. L. Thorpe (1974).
J. Hubert, J. Porcher, and W. F. Volbach, *Europe in the Dark Ages* (1969).
C. B. McClendon, *The Origins of Medieval Architecture: Building in Europe, AD 600–900* (2005).
I. N. Wood, 'Art and Architecture of Western Europe', *Cambridge Medieval History*, vol. 1, *c.500–c.700*, ed. P. Fouracre (2005), 760–75.

art and architecture: Mosan A regional 'school' of medieval art centred in the diocese of *Liège on the Meuse river in eastern Belgium. Between the 11th and 13th centuries this French-speaking part of the *German Empire became a crucible for stylistic and iconographic innovation. Mosan *artists made important contributions to the development of *sculpture, *stained glass, and *manuscript illumination, and were particularly renowned for *metalwork and *enamel.

Among the most important early works of Mosan Romanesque art is the *Stavelot Bible (1094–7). Its full-page gospel frontispiece of Christ in Majesty derives its clarity and flatness and opaque body colours and gold from Ottonian illumination, but other features—the subdivision of the figure into cell-like units, dark outlines, abstract facial features with Byzantinizing shadows and white highlights, nested v-folds, and rhythmic patterning of surfaces—are characteristically Romanesque. Genesis begins with a huge initial 'I' ('In principio') containing an ambitious exegetical programme. Three separate narratives, the Parable of the Vineyard, the history of mankind, and the life of Christ, are depicted in parallel episodes set into and around medallions linked by spiraling foliate rinceaux. Elaborate 'IN' ('principio') compositions, often populated with symbolic or narrative subjects, are a particular feature of Mosan illumination, for example, the Bibles of St Hubert des Ardennes and St Mary de Parc.

The earliest monument of Mosan metalwork, remarkable for the technical brilliance of its workmanship and the effortless classicism of its style, is generally considered to be the monumental brass font (1107–18) attributed to *Rainer of Huy, now in the church of St Barthélémy, Liège. Its basin, resting on (originally twelve) oxen, evokes the 'sea of brass' in the courtyard of Solomon's temple (1 Kings 7:23–26). On its sides in high relief are depicted New Testament episodes relating to the theme of *baptism. This juxtaposition of an Old Testament prototype with its New Testament fulfilment was to become a hallmark of Mosan *iconography.

By the 1140s Mosan metalworkers had perfected the art of champlevé enamel on gilded copper. Several of the most important examples were created for the abbey of *Stavelot under its abbot *Wibald (r. 1130–58): for example, the Stavelot portable altar, the retable of St Remaclus (destroyed, but known from a drawing and surviving fragments), the head reliquary (1145) of the sainted pope Alexander I, and the Stavelot Triptych in the Morgan Library, New York (1156–8). Letters exchanged between Wibald and a certain 'G' (*Godefroid of Huy?) indicate that at least some of the artists in his employ were independent lay professionals.

Stylistic and iconographical features of the Liège font and the Stavelot metalwork objects also appear in a distinctive and important group of Mosan illuminated MSS (1150s–70s) that includes the Floreffe Bible, the Averbode Gospels, a fragmentary picture cycle, possibly from a Psalter (Berlin, Kupferstichkabinett, ms. 78 A 6), and the Louvain Gospels in *Brussels.

Mosan art is also known for elaborate typological iconography, in which individual figures, scenes, and symbolic personifications are combined in tightly structured compositions glossed with inscriptions. Examples from the mid 12th century include the frontispieces of the Floreffe Bible and the Guennol triptych reliquary of the True Cross. Perhaps the best-known example is the somewhat later ambo made by the goldsmith *Nicholas of Verdun for Klosterneuburg abbey in Austria (1181). Its three panels, each composed of three registers of champlevé enamel plaques, offer a typological reading of history. Each episode of Christ's life (the era of Grace, *sub gratia*) is paralleled with two Old Testament episodes, one from the period before the giving of the law to Moses (*ante legem*) and one after it (*sub lege*). These plaques, and the same artist's repoussé figures of prophets made for the Three Kings Shrine in *Cologne cathedral (1190–1200), signal the birth of the 'year 1200' or early Gothic figural style in sculpture and painting.

Mosan metalwork production continued well into the 13th century. In the 1230s Hugo, of the *Augustinian *priory of Oignies, demonstrated equal brilliance in a variety of metalwork techniques as well as in the quite different realm of calligraphy and illumination (Treasure of Oignies, convent of the Soeurs de Notre-Dame, Namur). From this date, the influence of northern French/Parisian Gothic began to supplant indigenous stylistic traditions, and Mosan art became increasingly assimilated to wider artistic currents.

See also ART AND ARCHITECTURE: GOTHIC/ROMANESQUE; TYPOLOGY. AMB

W. Cahn, *Romanesque Bible Illumination* (1982).
G. Chapman, *Mosan Art: An Annotated Bibliography* (1988).
S. Collon-Gevaert, J. Lejeune, and J. Stiennon, eds, *Art mosan aux XIe et XIIe siècles* (1961).
C. Dumortier, ed., *La salle aux trésors: chefs-d'oeuvre de l'art roman et mosan* (1999).
A. Legner, ed., *Rhein und Maas: Kunst und Kultur, 800–1400*, 3 vols (1972–3).

art and architecture: Mozarabic A Castilian word, *Mozarab*, derives from the Arabic *mustarib* (meaning Arabised). The label *Mozarabic* is generally used to describe the art and architecture of Christians living in the areas of the Iberian Peninsula ruled by Muslims after the Arab invasion in 711, or that art which was produced by Arabised Christians who had emigrated to re-conquered Christian territory (*see* RECONQUISTA) on the Iberian Peninsula. Mozarabic art and architecture is best characterized as a synthesis of *Visigothic, Romanesque, and Islamic decorative elements and motifs. Unfortunately, few Mozarab objects or buildings survive.

Among the best surviving examples of Mozarabic art belong to the so-called 'Beatus Apocalypses', a collection of MSS dating to the 10th and 11th centuries. The text and images of these Apocalypse MSS are based on the commentaries of *Beatus of Liébana, an 8th-century Spanish monk and mystic. Most of these MSS were produced in *monasteries and provide valuable information about *scribes and *artists as well as monastic *scriptoria. Flat backgrounds, figural abstraction, and vibrant colours are characteristic features of the illustrated pages of these MSS.

The churches of S. Miguel de Escalada near *León (913) and Santa Maria Melque in the province of *Toledo (*c.*8th century) are the principal surviving examples of the Mozarab style in architecture. Characteristic features of this architecture include stone construction, horseshoe arches, and ribbed domes. LT

J. F. Arenas, *Arquitectura mozárabe* (1972).
J. C. Aznar, 'Arquitectura española del siglo X: Mozárabe y de la repoblación', *Goya*, 52 (1963), 206–19.
—— 'El arte de la miniatura española en el siglo X', *Goya*, 64–5 (1964), 266–87.
J. D. Dodds, *Architecture and Ideology in Early Medieval Spain* (1990).
J. Fontaine, *L'art mozarabe* (1977).
M. Gómez-Moreno, *Iglesias Mozárabes* (1919).
J. Williams, *Early Spanish Manuscript Illumination* (1977).

art and architecture: Norman

1. Historical context
2. Architecture in France
3. Architecture in England
4. Normans in Sicily and southern Italy
5. MS illumination

1. *Historical context*

Norman is a contraction of 'Norsemen'. The Norse or *Vikings were quite successful, following the beginning of their attacks on western Europe in 795. They settled extensively in Britain and Ireland, and also in what had been a western section of the *Carolingian empire. This would become, over the course of the 10th century, the Duchy of *Normandy.

The Normans assimilated into western European culture, adopting the local language (French), religion (Christianity), architectural styles (Romanesque), social organization (land-based *feudalism), and so on. By the time of the *Norman Conquest of England in 1066, they called themselves *Franci*, and their Scandinavian origins were apparent only in their hairstyles and marriage customs.

2. *Architecture in France*

Many of the earliest and most important Norman structures in Normandy itself are now lost, but we have records and physical evidence that allow us to reconstruct the style of these works. *Rouen, the Norman administrative capital, was the first major city to be overhauled. The street layout was returned to its Roman grid plan, probably under Duke William Longsword (927–42). His successors, Richard I (942/3–96) and Richard II (996–1026), followed by constructing a new, two-storey ducal palace, with an attached *chapel.

Richard I sponsored a religious revival, including the restoration of many *monasteries. Since their new context was Carolingian, early works are generally Carolingian in style. The earliest surviving evidence of such works is the small church of St-Pierre, Jumièges. Probably from the 10th century, this structure follows Carolingian antecedents in that it lacks decorative mouldings or elaborations to divide the piers from the walls and *arches. Soon after, however, the style changed to incorporate more recent trends in both architecture and *monasticism. The new cathedral at Rouen, begun by Archbishop Robert (989–1037), son of Duke Richard I, was rather similar to *Fulbert's great *cathedral at Chartres. Likewise, monastic reformers were invited from *Lotharingia, Burgundy, and Italy, in the effort to 'modernize' Normandy. Indeed, twenty religious houses were founded by the Normans between 1035 and 1066, a trend of aggressive building that was only to intensify in England after the Conquest.

Early-11th-century works were characterized by simple plans, rectangular *naves with narrower choirs, flint construction with *ashlar limited to corners and around typically narrow windows, and minimal sculptural decoration, even at major sites. The techniques and materials used in Normandy in this period are found throughout the French region. Notre-Dame (Jumièges) demonstrates the pre-Conquest Norman Romanesque style. Built between 1050 and 1067, it has matching towers in the Ottonian fashion, but an innovative nave, with alternating compound piers and round columns, articulated nave shafts and *pilaster strips, all used to support a wooden roof that, in fact, required far less structural support. The focus from the exterior was on the verticality of the west façade, and on the interior, on the articulation of the wall surfaces. The focal points were to shift dramatically after the Conquest.

Perhaps the most prominent Norman work on the Continent, as opposed to the number of major Norman works in Britain, is *Mont-St-Michel, founded in 1023 (though most of the surviving fabric dates to after 1058). This work is noteworthy for its remarkable site. It sits on a tall, sharp rock, projecting 250 feet upward out of the English Channel, surrounded by a bed of quicksand. Until recently, the island was accessible only at low tide, when a path was revealed. This site provides a highly dramatic setting for a work of architecture.

The rock was originally a Celtic funeral site until 708, when St Aubert, bishop of *Avranches, saw St Michael appear at the top, commanding him to build a church there. He then obtained *relics to turn the location into a *pilgrimage site. It was maintained by a small number of monks in individual cells. In 966, a *Benedictine *monastery was founded on the mount by the duke, in order to regulate the flow of pilgrims. This function, combined with numerous setbacks and a military role in the conquest of England, inspired what was then an unusual, if not unique, form of architecture—the castellar monastery. This one conglomeration of buildings, perched atop the rock, served as monastery, *castle, sanctuary, and eventually as the seat of the Brotherhood of St-Michel-de-la-Mer, an order of *knights that occupied the site in the 13th century. Indeed, the Norman work actually served as a foundation for later works of the 12th and 13th centuries.

The original Norman portion, dating to the 10th century, consists of a seven-*bay church dedicated to Notre-Dame-sous-Terre, which in turn sits on a round *oratory constructed under the aegis of St Aubert, at the pinnacle of the rock. The Normans added the conventual buildings in a three-storey construction north of the church, including among other structures guest rooms on the lowest level, a two-aisled *promenoir*, as there was no room for a full *cloister, a library, and a *refectory on the middle level, and the dormitory at the top.

The great Norman church that was built at the very summit of the rock is a 12th-century structure, following the abbey's increased importance after the Norman Conquest. It was constructed under Abbot Robert de Torigni (1154–86), who was a close councillor of *Henry II of England.

3. Architecture in England

The Normans are, perhaps, more well known for the architecture they produced in England than that from Normandy. Here, architecture was used as a means to control and impress the local population. In these years, more monumental structures were built in England than anywhere else in the world, and many of these are powerful statements of AN engineering, finances, and artistry.

4. Normans in Sicily and southern Italy

The Normans established a kingdom in Sicily in 1130, under *Roger II, which endured in one state or another until passing on to *Charles I of Anjou in 1266. Many great churches were constructed in Calabria, just before the period of the monarchy, though the only one to survive in any significant fashion is Gerace. Following the Conquest, the new Norman churches in Sicily had notable similarities with those in England, such as the long nave at *Palermo and the western towers at Cefalù, as well as decorative motifs throughout. Use of local techniques suggests that local craftsmen were employed, though it does appear that some English craftsmen were likely involved as well.

5. MS illumination

Early Norman illumination differs considerably, not only from location to location and MS to MS. Highly varied *initials may be found even within a single MS. The initials are frequently either in the shape of plant and animal forms, or filled with them. As in their architecture, the Normans were first influenced by *Carolingian works. This was followed by a greater impact from AS sources, direct or indirect, before the production of a coherent, consistent style of their own. Following the Conquest, there were many overlaps in production techniques and styles, leading later toward an 'international' style.

Initials are the dominant decorative element, though frontispieces are also important. Norman work is frequently characterized by use of thick paints and dull colours, particularly purples, and by the use of rosy dots on the cheeks of figures. A combination of fully painted and outlined images are not uncommon, and do not necessarily indicate an unfinished work. The works fall into two groups, those from Mont-St-Michel and those from Lower Normandy. These—from the abbeys of *Bayeux, St-Évroult, Lyre, Préaulx, La-Croix-St-Leufroi, and *Bec—share a number of similar features, including a preference for initial letters with thickly painted foliage in reds and greens, often accompanied by animal, *dragon, and human figures. Such works would come to have a strong influence on AN MSS in England. *See also* ART, ANGLO-SAXON; ART AND ARCHITECTURE: ANGLO-NORMAN / OTTONIAN / ROMANESQUE. ASM

J. J. G. Alexander, *Norman Illumination at Mont St Michel, 966–1100* (1970).

M. Baylé, 'Norman Architecture around the Year 1000: Its Place in the Art of North-Western Europe', *Anglo-Norman Studies 22: Proceedings of the Battle Conference*, ed. C. Harper-Bill (1999), 1–28.

W. Braunfels, *Monasteries of Western Europe* (1972).

R. A. Brown, *The Normans* (1984).
R. F. Cassady, *The Norman Achievement* (1986).
D. C. Douglas, *The Norman Achievement, 1050–1100* (1969).
E. Fernie, *The Architecture of Norman England* (2000).
D. Matthew, *The Norman Kingdom of Sicily* (1992).
Musée des antiquités, Rouen, and Musée des beaux-arts, Caen, *Tresors des Abbayes Normandes* (1979).
T. Rowley, *The Normans* (2004).
E. Searle, *Predatory Kinship and the Creation of Norman Power, 840–1066: Model and Evidences* (1988).
H. Takayama, *The Administration of the Norman Kingdom of Sicily* (1993).
S. N. Vaughn, *The Abbey of Bec and the Anglo-Norman State, 1034–1136* (1981).
F. Wormald, *The Survival of Anglo-Saxon Illumination after the Norman Conquest* (1944).
H. Zettel, *Das Bild der Normannen und der Normanneneinfalle in westfrankischen, ostfrankischen und angelsachsischen Quellen des 8. bis 11. Jahrhunderts* (1977).

art and architecture: Ottonian As befits a term derived from the political sphere, Ottonian art and architecture refers to those buildings and works of art produced in the Germanic lands (and surrounding areas) that were under the hegemony of three successive Germanic kings named Otto, as well as the last Saxon ruler, *Henry II. As a stylistic definition, the term has been extended to include the period under the succeeding Salian rulers Conrad II, Henry III, and Henry IV, until the last quarter of the 11th century and the *Investiture Controversy.

1. Saxon royal and aristocratic patronage
2. Salian royal patronage
3. Ecclesiastical patronage
4. Women patrons

1. *Saxon royal and aristocratic patronage*

As self-styled successors to the *Carolingian dynasty, Ottonian rulers sought imperial *coronation in Rome and vied with the Byzantine empire. For the *cathedral of the newly founded see of *Magdeburg, Otto I imported porphyry columns, much as *Charlemagne had done in the palace *chapel at *Aachen. Otto, the first member of the dynasty to be crowned Roman emperor by the pope, also commissioned an imperial crown that, with some modifications, became one of the primary insignia of the German Empire (Vienna, Treasury).

An ivory likely made in *Italy represents Otto II and his wife, Theophano, being crowned by Christ (Cluny Museum, Paris). Marriage to Theophano, most likely a niece of the Byzantine emperor Nicephorus Phocas, provided the ruling Ottonian house with political legitimacy, and the Byzantine imperial garb in the ivory indicates how the Ottonians looked to *Byzantium for both ideological and artistic exemplars.

A *prayer book made for the young Otto III at the behest of his mother, Theophano, and Archbishop *Willigis of *Mainz reveals the three iconographic pillars of Ottonian art (Munich, Bayerische Staatsbibliothek). The first representation of the enthroned ruler is based on Late Antique models; the orant Otto beneath a *Deesis relies on contemporary Byzantine *iconography; the king prostrated before Christ is derived from Carolingian sources. Carolingian models provided the greatest impetus for Ottonian art, though the changes from those models are revealing. Among the most famous Ottonian ruler images is Otto III in a *gospel book made for Aachen (cathedral treasury) in which he appears raised above earth within a mandorla and flanked by evangelist symbols. The composition is based on Carolingian *Maiestas Domini* imagery and in the Aachen Gospels is situated where the picture of Christ in Majesty ought to appear; Otto is understood as a virtual substitute for Christ and the picture underscores the sacral nature of Ottonian *kingship. Such ruler *portraits in *liturgical books integrated the sovereign into the religious fabric of the realm.

Although itinerant, each Ottonian and Salian ruler favoured a particular location. Otto III's devotion to Aachen is evident in the jewel-encrusted *cross he gave to the cathedral. Evoking the celestial Jerusalem, the cross is notable for its central cameo of Augustus Caesar, which simultaneously communicated Otto's own status as Roman emperor and his protection under the cross. His successor, Henry II, enriched the foundations of his native *Bavaria. Book illumination and *metalwork flourished especially in *Regensburg, the source of luxurious *textiles that were produced for Henry and Queen Kunigunde and then given to the couple's newly founded see of *Bamberg.

Rulers were not the only figures to endow new ecclesiastical foundations. The *relics of St Cyriakus that Margrave Gero acquired from Rome were the focal point of the monastic church he commissioned *c.*960 at Gernrode in *Saxony. One of the best-preserved Ottonian churches, its imposing *westwork, substantial rectangular piers, and arcaded *gallery all add to the impression of monumentality and cubic clarity. Most remarkable is the 11th-century Easter Sepulchre in the southern aisle near the *altar. This enclosed limestone structure was used for *Easter drama, and the stucco *angel and Marys affixed to the walls are rare large-scale sculptures suggesting the interactive and performative functions of Ottonian art.

2. *Salian royal patronage*

Under the Salians, the focus of artistic production shifted to such centres as *Speyer, *Goslar, and *Echternach. The cathedral of Speyer was initiated in 1030 by Conrad II as a new dynastic centre and burial site; consecrated in 1061, the building echoed the form of such Roman structures as the audience hall in *Trier. Groin *vaults added during its rebuilding under Henry IV magnified the impressive scale of one of Europe's largest churches. Dynastic concerns are also evident in the sumptuous gospels painted in Echternach and given by Henry III to Speyer (Madrid, Escorial), which contain portraits not only of Henry and his wife, Agnes, but also of his parents, Conrad and Gisela; the piety of both couples is reflected in their painted proximity to Christ and Mary.

3. *Ecclesiastical patronage*

Although products of royal and imperial *patronage have received the greatest scholarly attention, men and women of the church were responsible for the creation of most Ottonian and Salian art and architecture. Two of the most energetic patrons were Archbishop *Egbert of Trier and Bishop *Bernward of *Hildesheim, both of whom used art and architecture to express their personal piety and to advance the standings of their sees. In the Codex Egberti of *c.*985 (Trier, Stadtbibliothek), Egbert is shown frontally enthroned between two monastic artists from *Reichenau. The New Testament cycle in this *lectionary is related iconographically to wall paintings in the church of Oberzell on Reichenau, testifying to the renewed importance of Christ's life in Ottonian theology and to the artistic networks within the Ottonian realm. Also notable is the book's stylistic and compositional reliance on Late Antique illustration (for example, the Vatican Vergil); the sensitive modelling and atmospheric backgrounds have been attributed to an exceptional artist dubbed the *Master of the Registrum Gregorii. Such luxurious metalwork objects as the foot reliquary of St Andrew were commissioned by Egbert in his campaign to increase the prestige of Trier.

According to his friend and biographer, Thangmar, Bernward actively participated in crafting the works produced in Hildesheim. In the monastic church of St Michael's founded by the bishop, a series of complex mathematical relationships can perhaps be attributed to Bernward himself. Exterior and interior reinforce the geometric and spatial clarity of the building, which is laid out in a symmetrical plan with a double choir, two crossing towers, and *apses at both ends. Two remarkable bronzes were likely commissioned for this church, though they are now found in the cathedral. One is a free-standing column, 3.79 m high, that evokes triumphal columns in Rome; here the images scrolling to the top recount the *miracles of Christ. Two doors, 4.72 m high (1.12 m wide) and each cast in a single piece, are a testament to the metalworking skills in Ottonian Hildesheim; their Old and New Testament reliefs are an early and clear instance of typological pairing. Similar juxtapositions are found in such other Ottonian works as a pair of ivories depicting Moses Receiving the Law and the Doubting Thomas, which visually articulate sophisticated notions of touch, vision, and belief. The importance of physicality is evident above all in the life-size wooden *crucifix commissioned by Archbishop Gero for *Cologne cathedral. Often admired for its subtle rendering of the dead Christ, the sculpture was meant to serve as a *reliquary; its power was increased through its representational verisimilitude and emotional impact.

4. *Women patrons*

The emotional expressiveness, dramatic gestures, and broad bands of cool colours that characterize most Ottonian *painting can be seen in the cycle of pictures in the Hitda Codex (Darmstadt, Universitäts- und Landesbibliothek). Made in the *scriptorium of Cologne, the gospels contain a representation of Hitda, abbess in nearby Meschede, and is representative of the important role played by such women in the patronage of Ottonian art. Female monastic institutions were established in large numbers throughout the Ottonian realms; they were sites of architectural activity, artistic production, and the accumulation of wealth in the form of art objects that often functioned as tangible witnesses to familial ties and memory. Abbess Mathilda of Essen appears on a luxurious processional cross together with her brother, Duke Otto of *Swabia (grandchildren of Otto I); Mathilda was also the likely patron of the freestanding gilt statue of the Virgin and Child still in the Essen cathedral treasury. A connection to the Virgin is also forged in the Uta Codex, a deluxe lectionary made in Regensburg for Abbess Uta; the complexity of the MS's iconographic programme indicates the high levels of *literacy among educated women in Ottonian society.

Despite its relatively short chronological span, the Ottonian and Salian period in central Europe was a period of artistic and architectural efflorescence, in which objects and buildings of great splendour and grandeur were produced to communicate the personal piety and politics of men and women of an intertwined church and state. *See also* AUREOLE; QUEDLINBURG; TYPOLOGY. ASC

G. Althoff, *Herrschaftsrepräsentation im ottonischen Sachsen* (1998).
K.-G. Beuckers, J. Cramer, and M. Imhof, *Die Ottonen* ([2]2006).
P. Bloch and H. Schnitzler, *Die ottonische Kölner Malerschule*, 2 vols (1967–70).
M. Brandt, ed., *Bernward von Hildesheim und das Zeitalter der Ottonen* (1993).
A. S. Cohen, *The Uta Codex: Art, Philosophy and Reform in Eleventh-Century Germany* (2000).
T. Head, 'Art and Artifice in Ottonian Trier', *Gesta*, 36 (1997), 65–82.
N. Hiscock, ed., *The White Mantle of Churches* (2003).
H. Hoffmann, *Buchkunst und Königtum im ottonischen und frühsalischen Reich* (1988).
P. Lasko, *Ars Sacra, 800–1200* ([2]1994).
H. Mayr-Harting, *Ottonian Book Illumination: An Historical Study*, 2 vols (1991).
P. E. Schramm, *Die deutschen Kaiser und Könige in Bildern ihrer Zeit, 751–1190*, ed. F. Mütherich ([2]1983).
L. C. Vegas, *L'arte ottoniana intorno al Mille* (2002).
A. Wieczorek and H.-M. Hinz, eds, *Europas Mitte um 1000* (2000).

art and architecture: Romanesque Term describing art produced in Europe between roughly 1000 and 1200.

1. Definition
2. Architecture
3. Monumental decoration
4. Portable arts
5. Secular and military works
6. Artists and aesthetics

1. *Definition*

'Romanesque' is a relatively recent label, coined in the early 1800s to identify the Roman heritage of round *arches and thick walls found in 11th- and 12th-century architecture. Implicit in the coining, however, was a pejorative acknowledgement of that heritage's transformation: like Romance languages, it represented the debasement of a classical standard.

The name has only ever had limited value: what is 'Roman' in this period's MS painting, metal casting, ivory carving, or even, when one searches beyond the arches, in this period's architecture? When, moreover, did the style begin? Earlier traditions such as AS, Ottonian, and Visigothic make it difficult to establish absolute thresholds for when Romanesque art, if understood as a distinct, international aesthetic, set itself apart. Romanesque's final phases are similarly murky. Scholars usually identify *St-Denis (1144) as the first *Gothic structure, whose thinner walls, *rib vaults, and delicate columns superseded Romanesque's heavy barrel *vaults and hefty piers, yet those latter traits continued even into the 13th century in many areas of Europe, particularly in the (Holy) *Roman Empire. Other means of defining the period's art—as a specific representational value, a set of iconographic issues, expressions of theological terms or social movements, modes of visuality or corporeality—may prove more searching, but they may also be just as fraught. For better or worse, 'Romanesque' lingers as a term of convenience.

2. *Architecture*

As one contemporary remarked, Europe cloaked itself in a 'white mantle of churches' shortly after the year 1000, rebuilding its *abbeys and *priories after shaking off decades of social instability. The 9th and 10th centuries produced a wealth of works, particularly liturgical objects and MSS, but a renewal of monumental production around 1000 was perceptible.

The new church constructions came in a variety of sizes and shapes. Vast abbeys and smaller priories supported the growth of *monasticism; modest parish churches assured a corps of priests to administer the *sacraments to townsfolk; private *chapels satisfied desires for intimate spaces; and *oratories marked the shrines of saintly souls. Most churches employed a Latin-cross plan, perpetuating a tradition inherited from the early Christian period, but builders also occasionally employed round and Greek-cross plans. *Naves could reach two or three stories high, some with spacious second-story galleries allowing light to flow in and others with no windows whatsoever. In smaller churches, *transepts were frequently omitted, but at *monasteries they were indispensable for liturgical use, offering monks space for additional *apses and *altars. Altars consecrated with saints' *relics attracted special devotion from monks and laity alike, with the most important relics of favoured martyrs drawing great crowds. This cult of saints and the *pilgrimage phenomenon it engendered significantly marked the artistic culture of the period, including the architecture. Some churches employed large *ambulatories around the choir to assist in pilgrims' circulation; some raised the floor of the choir higher than the level of the nave, creating space for a larger *crypt below to house the site's most important relics. At monasteries, the church plan also varied according to the type of religious order followed; *Cluniacs, *Cistercians, and *Carthusians, for example, all on the rise in this period, organized their churches and *cloisters to accommodate particular practices.

Chip-stone work inaugurated this building phase in the early 11th century, gradually giving way to evenly cut *ashlar. *Vaults were typically the rounded, or barrel, type, but before the end of the 11th century builders employed both pointed and groin vaults to channel better the lateral thrusts. Coordination between the walls and their vaults encouraged new forms of wall articulation, including variations in the type of supports (for example, piers, columns, engaged columns), wall arcading, and arches (for example, transverse) that reinforced the vault spans. Scholars generally consider the progressive exploitation of such features to have been crucial to the development of Romanesque architecture.

3. *Monumental decoration*

*Fresco and *sculpture were the two primary types of wall decoration in the new churches (although some regions, especially Italy, retained a taste for *mosaic and marble revetment). Numerous examples of painted apses survive, frequently depicting the Virgin enthroned or Christ in Majesty surrounded by saints. Last Judgement scenes were also frequent, particularly on west walls of the nave. Nave and transept walls typically provided sufficient expanses for extensive cycles drawn from the Life and Passion of Christ or the Old Testament. Geometric patterns also covered walls (many created to mimic hanging textiles) and polychromy survives on capitals and columns (for example, striated to reproduce the effect of marble).

Sculpture assumed an unprecedented importance in church decoration. As in earlier periods, capitals received foliage decoration, but Romanesque sculptors expanded both the decorative repertory and the range of sculpture's uses. Early in the 11th century, birds, lions, and mythical beasts began appearing on capitals as well as the human figure; by mid century, sculptors excelled at elaborate biblical and hagiographic scenes across capitals' multiple faces. Such 'historiated' capitals as those at *Moissac, *Toulouse, *Cluny, Gerona, and Monreale rank among the period's most celebrated works. Portals tended to receive the most concerted collections of sculpture, with friezes or large-scale reliefs lining porches, covering the arches of the doorway, decorating the *tympanum (where Christ in Majesty and the Last Judgement were favoured subjects), and covering even the doorposts themselves. At once sculptural and architectural, Romanesque carving played upon this tension, exploring the relation of the sculptural field to its architectural support and exploiting the expressions of form, particularly movement, in relation to architectural stasis.

Sculpture thrived in other contexts as well. Wood sculpture in the round, such as statues of the Madonna enthroned with the Christ Child, proliferated in all corners of Europe, as did large-scale sculptures of Christ crucified. Many of these works were also *reliquaries and featured a small hollow to receive a small cache of *relics. Marble altar tables and frontals received carved decoration, as did episcopal thrones, pulpits, and baptismal basins.

*Stained glass was another important form of monumental decoration, yet precious few examples survive (most post-mid 12th century). Glazing programmes featured figures isolated in bays, including standing or seated saints and biblical figures (*Augsburg, *Strasbourg, *Canterbury), the Virgin enthroned (Chartres), and ensembles recounting biblical stories (Chartres, *Troyes, St-Remi).

4. *Portable arts*

Bronze casting provided another medium for monumental decoration (for example, bronze doors), but refined *metal techniques also yielded an extraordinary output of *liturgical furnishings on a smaller scale. Modelled (*repoussé) sheets of copper, gold, or silver decorated large altar frontals and small coffrets. Chisel and filigree work also combined with firing techniques to produce colourful *enamel-filled panels (a technique made famous in Limoges-area workshops) that decorated reliquaries and book covers. Crosiers, liturgical combs, and vessels for honouring the *Eucharist were executed in ivory as well, the other favoured medium for sacred objects. The most famous centres of such production were either affiliated with great abbeys (*Stavelot, *Liège, *Magdeburg, *Bury St Edmunds) and/or with royal seats of power (*León, *Winchester).

MSS count among the most sumptuous works of the period, with painters continuing earlier traditions in the careful decoration of texts but also surpassing their predecessors. Books were the privilege of clerics and elite laymen and were in most cases produced by clerics, so the vast majority of decorated texts were liturgical in nature (for example, books for the sacraments, sacred readings). In Bibles, for example, the opening initials of each book may be decorated with a embellished ('decorated') letter; sometimes a 'historiated' letter contained within it figures drawn from the biblical book it introduced (for example, Job on his dung heap, Paul writing his epistles), painted in blues, reds, greens, ochre, and often with gold leaf highlights. Such 'illumination' (*illuminare*, to shine or make bright) could also cover a full page, displaying a single image, such as Christ in Majesty, or multiple scenes that condense the stories of an entire biblical book. Non-religious books receiving decoration include *encyclopedias, classical literary works, scientific and scholastic texts, as well as law and history MSS.

5. *Secular and military works*

A great deal of art produced in the period falls outside of ecclesiastic use. Military architecture flourished as never before, with donjons (dungeons), their surrounding walls, and entry gates all representing significant developments for monumental construction. The period saw a dramatic rise in the number and size of towns and cities, with accompanying changes in the structures of wood and stone houses, market halls, fountains, and other public monuments. Houses could even include carved capitals, reliefs, and decorative friezes. Apart from military equipment, the laity's personal effects survive only rarely. Nonetheless, game pieces, decorated mirror cases, and chiselled leather coffers all offer a glimpse of the care taken to decorate household items.

6. *Artists and aesthetics*

11th- and 12th-century descriptions of works of art can tend to have an arid tone, often offering little more than reportage of materials and dimensions. On the other hand, sufficient textual evidence also shows that craftsmen, their patrons, and the clerical public were sensitive to the quality of the raw materials, and they, moreover, appreciated the fine craftsmanship that transformed those materials into more brilliant and beautiful objects. The 12th-century treatise on art by the monk *Theophilus even gives guidelines and tips to assure high quality. As a sign of pride in authorship, *signatures frequently decorated MSS, and sculptors carved their names onto church façades, capitals, and altars. Patrons took pride as well, and accounts of abbots' and bishops' lives frequently list the building projects they had sponsored. Art in the period, whether destined for a religious function or the household, dazzled and amazed onlookers; in short, awakened aesthetic sensibilities. *See also* ART, ANGLO-SAXON; ART AND ARCHITECTURE: GOTHIC/OTTONIAN. RAM

Art of Medieval Spain, AD 500–1200, exhibition catalogue (1993).
F. Avril *et al.*, eds, *Le monde roman*, 2 vols (1982–3).

R. Budde, *Deutsche romanische Skulptur, 1050–1200* (1979).
W. Cahn, *Romanesque Bible Illumination* (1982).
K. J. Conant, *Carolingian and Romanesque Architecture, 800 to 1200* ([3]1979).
O. Demus, *Romanesque Mural Painting*, tr. M. Whitall (German original, 1968) (1970).
C. R. Dodwell, *Pictorial Arts of the West, 800–1200* (1993).
I. H. Forsyth, *The Throne of Wisdom: Wood Sculptures of the Madonna in Romanesque France* (1972).
M. F. Hearn, *Romanesque Sculpture: The Revival of Monumental Stone Sculpture in the Eleventh and Twelfth Centuries* (1981).
M. Gómez-Moreno, *El Arte románico español* (1934).
L. Grodecki, *Le vitrail roman* (1977).
H. E. Kubach, *Romanesque Architecture* (1975).
P. Lasko, *Ars Sacra, 800–1200* ([2]1994).
Lanfranco e Wiligelmo: Il Duomo di Modena, exhibition catalogue (1984).
A. Legner, *Ornamenta Ecclesiae: Kunst und Künstler der Romanik*, 3 vols, exhibition catalogue (1985).
P. de Palol, *Early Medieval Art in Spain*, tr. A. Jaffa (German original, 1965) (1967).
A. Petzold, *Romanesque Art* (1995).
M. Schapiro, *Romanesque Art: Selected Papers* (1977).
E. Vergnolle, *L'art roman en France* (1994).
M. Woelk, *Benedetto Antelami: die Werke in Parma und Fidenza* (1995).
G. Zarnecki *et al.*, eds, *English Romanesque Art, 1066–1200*, exhibition catalogue (1984).

art and architecture: Russian Receiving Christianity only in 988/9, the East Slavic Rus' expressly appropriated art and architecture based on Byzantine models and elaborated their own styles. *Kiev, *Novgorod, and *Vladimir (Suzdalia) define the major foci of Rus' accomplishments in the pre-Mongolian period, before the 1230s. Only after the battle at *Kulikovo (1380) did monumental arts revive. And only when Prince Ivan the Great (r. 1462–1505) commissioned architects Aristotele Fioravanti and Alevisio Novi to work in the *Kremlin did the Italian Renaissance significantly influence Russian architecture.

Though none earlier than the 17th century is preserved, the first Rus' churches must have been wooden. The tower-like masonry church of the Ascension (1530–32) at Kolomenskoe near *Moscow possibly derived from indigenous wooden tent-churches. It shows a typical Russian feature: superimposed decorative gables, the so-called *kokoshniki*.

Byzantine masters built the first acknowledged masonry church, that of the *Tithe of the Most Holy Mother of God* (989–96) in Kiev for Prince St *Vladimir (r. 980–1015). In emulation of *Constantinople, his son, *Iaroslav the Wise (r. 1019–54) enlarged and fortified Kiev, guarded by the 'Golden Gate' (1017–24), an elaborate city-gate structure. Besides churches of St Irene and St George, Prince Iaroslav built the *cathedral of *St Sophia (begun 1037) at the city centre as the metropolitan seat and his mausoleum. St Sophia displayed recognizable Rus' re-interpretations of conventional style: for example, the enlargement and elongation of a Byzantine cross-in-square church through progressive multiplication of its elements. St Sophia is a five-aisled, five-apsidal building, enveloped on three sides by two-tiered *galleries. Thirteen *domes crowned its pyramidal silhouette. Besides a marble *chancel screen and **opus sectile* pavement, the artisans from Constantinople created an exquisite *mosaic and *fresco programme, which included *portraits of Prince Iaroslav and his family. In the towers, secular themes represented his grandmother, Princess St *Olga (r. 945–63) and contemporary Byzantine emperors, documenting historical and cultural Byzantine-*Rus' ties. In response to his answered prayers to the Mother of God, Prince Iaroslav topped the Golden Gate with the church of the Annunciation, which held the image of *Our Lady of Kazan* until 1699. From Kiev these urban, architectural, and artistic models later spread north (for example, St Sophia in Novgorod, 1045–52; the Golden Gate of the city of Vladimir, 1164; or the Moscow Kremlin, 1470s).

The native East Slavs engaged in arts early, like Alimipii Pečerskii, who helped Constantinopolitan painters decorate the church of the Dormition (*c.*1073) in the *monastery of the Caves near Kiev. Renowned for their icons, first copied after Byzantine models, the East Slavic Rus' particularly venerated the Mother of God as a protector and *mediatrix*. When Prince Andrei Bogoliubskii (r. 1157–74) established Vladimir as his capital, the miraculous 12th-century Byzantine icon of *Our Lady of Vladimir* (Tretyakov gallery, Moscow) was tranferred and assumed the protection of the city (as it will, according to another legend, protect Moscow from the siege of *Tamerlane in 1395). A special feast of the '*Pokrov Bogoroditsy*' (the protection and the intercession of the Mother of God) was also introduced. The four-piered church of the *Pokrov* (1166) on the Nerl' exemplifies Vladimir architecture. Delicately proportioned, twice as tall as a typical Byzantine church of the same plan and size, unlike Byzantine churches it is made of stone. The origins of its *lukovitsa* (onion-shaped dome) and exterior sculpture, characteristic of Vladimir architecture, are still debated.

Never conquered by the *Tatars, Novgorod maintained broad international artistic links and had an uninterrupted tradition of building, icon, and polychrome *sculpture production for princely, aristocratic, and ecclesiastical patrons. The church of the Saviour on Nereditsa Hill (1198) illustrates a typical northern Rus' architectural feature, the *trefoil *zakomary* (arched gables). Its frescoes exemplify the Novgorod variant of Middle Byzantine *painting, with outlined linear drawing, oversized figures, anecdotal character, realistic touches, and inscriptions in the local dialect. The so-called 'Novgorod School' of icons also exhibits folk traditions and vibrant colour schemes.

By the 14th century numerous schools of painting existed —in *Pskov, *Iaroslavl', *Tver', and Moscow. 'Moscow

Example of Russian art and architecture: Korsun Doors of St Sophia cathedral, Novgorod.

School' paintings by *Theophanes the Greek influenced Andrei *Rublev and Daniil Chernyi to combine sophisticated theological concepts with Palaeologan art and Novgorod linearism, and to increase the size of their icons to fit Russian high iconostases (for example, *Old Testament Trinity* icon, 1410s, from the *Trinity-Sergii monastery, now in Tretyakov Gallery, Moscow). Embroidered as a summa of Orthodox faith and replica of the coeval Russian church, the so-called *Major Sakkos* of Metropolitan Photios (1408–31) (Kremlin Armoury, Moscow) is among the finest surviving medieval vestments. *See also* APSE; ART AND ARCHITECTURE: BYZANTINE; ICONOGRAPHY: ICONOSTASIS; LITURGICAL VESTMENTS. JBo

I. Grabar *et al.*, eds, *Istoriia russkogo iskusstva*, 13 vols ([2]1953–69).
G. H. Hamilton, *The Art and Architecture of Russia* ([3]1983).
A. Komeč, *Drevnerusskoe zodčestvo kontsa X–načala XII v* (1987).
Y. Petrova, ed., *Sacred Arts and City Life: The Glory of Medieval Novgorod* (2005).

art and architecture: Sasanian May be divided into three periods, the first beginning with the reign of Ardashir I (224–43), the second with the reign of Shapur II (309–79), and the third with the reign of Khusrau I (531–79) and ending with the Islamic conquest of *Iran. The primary function in all periods was the glorification of the king.

Early Sasanian architecture was marked by the introduction of the *dome on *squinches, which was combined with the traditional Parthian method of iwan (vaulted hall) construction in Ardashir's palaces (Qaleh-i Dukhtar, Firuzabad). Ardashir also revived the ancient tradition of carving rock reliefs, which displayed scenes of divine investiture and military triumph. Ardashir's son, Shapur I (243–73), won a series of victories over the Romans, and Roman captives produced much of the art of his city, Bishapur.

Shapur II imposed state controls on craftsmen and centralized the manufacture of silver plate, which began to bear scenes of the royal hunt. The 4th century also saw the development of monumental architectural stuccoes (Hajiabad, Kish), whose ornamental riches tempered the austerity of earlier Sasanian buildings.

After a 5th-century crisis, the Sasanian empire experienced a revival under Khusrau I and II. The great hall of Khusrau I at Ctesiphon, with its two massive iwans, is the most iconic of Sasanian buildings. Khusrau II (591–628) is best known for his rock-cut vaults within the *paradeisos* (a park for game) at Taq-i Bustan, carved with scenes of investiture and the hunt.

Sasanian art enjoyed a robust afterlife. Early Islamic silver borrowed liberally from Sasanian royal iconography, and Islamic literature imbued certain Sasanian monuments (Ctesiphon, Taq-i Bustan) with a network of legendary associations. In medieval Christendom, Sasanian art, particularly the 'throne of Khusrau', served as an ambivalent symbol for royal splendour and hubris. BWA

M. Azarnoush, *The Sasanian Manor House at Hajiabad, Iran* (1994).
L. Bier, *Sarvistan* (1986).
P. O. Harper, *Silver Vessels of the Sasanian Period* (1981).
G. Herrmann, *The Iranian Revival* (1977).
J. Kroger, *Sasanidischer Stuckdekor* (1982).
J. D. Movassat, *The Large Vault at Taq-i Bustan* (2005).
E. Yarshater, ed., *The Cambridge History of Iran* (1983), vol. 3/2.

art and architecture: Scandinavian Medieval art in *Scandinavia, *c.*775–1550, represents eight centuries of highly diverse crafts, techniques, functions, and aesthetics, and the development can be traced in a constantly changing pattern of indigenous traditions, local creativity, and interactions with western Europe.

1. Animal ornament, 400–775/800
2. Viking ornament, 775/800–1000
3. Late Viking, 1000–1100
4. Romanesque and Gothic architecture
5. Wooden (stave) churches
6. Pictorial arts and sculpture

1. *Animal ornament, 400–775/800*

The abstract art of animal ornament was created in the 5th–6th century, probably in Denmark. Bernhard Salin classified it in three chronological groups that later research has further subdivided. Style I was based ultimately on late Roman *metalwork and was disseminated in Scandinavia, on the continent, and in England. Style II was created around 600, by combining Style I-animals with ribbon *interlace, and it became popular in much of both ecclesiastical and secular ornament in 7th-century northwestern Europe, for example, the chieftains' graves at Vendel and Valsgärde (Sweden) and *Sutton Hoo (East Anglia). Style III, of the 8th and early 9th century, consists mainly of freely intertwining ribbon-shaped animals and is restricted to Scandinavia.

2. *Viking ornament, c.775/800–1000*

With the addition of semi-naturalistic animal motifs based on Frankish and AS models, Style III:E forms an important part of early *Viking ornament. The woodcarvings from a richly furnished woman's grave at *Oseberg (Norway), with a dendrochronological *ante quem* dating of 834, have given name to the Oseberg style which is generally dated to *c.*775/800–875. The Oseberg carvings display the manner in which highly competent craftsmen had integrated the Scandinavian and European elements, combining ribbon-shaped animals in loose and asymmetrical loop compositions of late Style III with semi-naturalistic animals and playful gripping-beasts of west-European origins. The Oseberg style was followed by the Borre style, *c.*875–950, which is characterized by close ribbon interlace, knots and ring-chains in equilateral compositions, continuing the by now traditional gripping-beast, and including plant motifs based on Frankish models. In the early 10th century the ribbon-shaped animal was reintroduced in the novel and more regular form, often S-shaped, of the so-called Jelling style. The combination of Borre and Jelling styles came to dominate ornament until *c.*950/75.

The Borre is the earliest style to have been used in the Scandinavian settlements in Iceland, the British Isles, and Russia. It is also the earliest Scandinavian ornament to have been used in a Christian context, namely on stone crosses in the Scandinavian settlements in the British Isles in the first half of the 10th century. Even in wood- and stone-carving, however, ornament of the early and middle Viking periods retains the carpet-pattern repetition of small, identical motifs that is characteristic of minor arts. It is also a paradox that animal ornament at the time of the fiercest raids on western Europe consisted mainly of the neutral ribbon-shaped animals and the playful gripping-beast. The change in size, format, and content came with Christianization. King Harald Gormson's *rune stone at Jelling, raised *c.*965 to commemorate his parents and himself, also proclaims his Christianization of the Danes. It shows the earliest surviving Scandinavian fight between lion and snake on one face and a large crucifixion scene in a scroll on the other. The motifs and their prominence on the surface are new, but their style is Scandinavian. This so-called Mammen style of the second half of the 10th century marks the start of late Viking ornament and the earliest phase of Christian art in Denmark.

3. *Late Viking, c.1000–1100*

The Ringerike style, *c.*1000–1050, is the earliest surviving Christian ornamental style in Norway, Sweden, and Iceland. It continued the motifs introduced with the Mammen style but with new details and composition schemes imported from Ottonian and AS ornament. The Urnes style, *c.*1025/50–1100/25, was a Scandinavian innovation built on the Ringerike and Mammen motifs and further developed the fight between animals. Characteristic of the Urnes style are the asymmetrical loop compositions, which were adaptable to any size and shape of object. Both the Ringerike and Urnes styles were used for Christian memorial rune stones and wooden church buildings as well as on jewellery, weapons, and everyday wooden utensils. Both styles

Urnes doorway, Norway.

Baptismal font by master mason Tove in Gumlösa church, Sweden, *c.*1190.

were used in all parts of Scandinavia and were also adopted in England and Ireland. Remnants of the Urnes-style loop compositions still occurred in otherwise Romanesque woodcarvings and metalwork of the 1130s. But mainly, the unified development of Scandinavian ornament came to an end around 1100, apparently quelled by the intense ecclesiastical building activity of the 12th century.

4. Romanesque and Gothic architecture

As in Europe, Scandinavian Romanesque cathedrals and parish churches in stone replaced the simpler church buildings of the 11th century, and architects, stone *masons, and stone carvers were brought in from abroad. The diversity of international contacts is highlighted by comparing some of the major cathedrals. *Lund, with altars consecrated between 1123 and 1146, is a close parallel to the *Kaiserdome* of *Speyer, *Worms, and *Bonn, and the architect(s) had presumably trained in a workshop connected with the Rhenish cathedrals. Ribe cathedral was begun *c.*1130. Its building stone was imported from the Eifel district, and the building itself is a unique paraphrase on continental models: an aisled nave, a transept that has the apse opening directly from the central bay, and the crossing surmounted by a dome. St Mary's church (*c.*1140–70) in *Bergen provides an outlying example of this general Rhenish/Romanesque type. AN models are, on the other hand, probable for the main *cathedrals on the Scandinavian peninsula. This influence survives in both a simple, undecorated version with a tower over the crossing, for example, in the cathedrals of Sigtuna and *Oslo, and with a more open plan and ornamented details in Stavanger and *Trondheim. In Denmark, the introduction of brick as building material on Sjælland in the 1170s, for example, *Roskilde cathedral, increased the emphasis on the structural elements and facilitated a seamless transition to a simple, unadorned Gothic architecture that is closely related to the North-German brick churches of the Baltic. In Sweden, Gothic architecture owed more to French prototypes, for example, *Uppsala cathedral, begun soon after 1273, final consecration 1435. In contrast, English models can be seen throughout the building of Trondheim cathedral, begun soon after 1152/3 and finished *c.*1300/1350.

5. Wooden (stave) churches

The earliest wooden churches, of the 10th century, with a construction set directly in the ground, belonged to a

Viklau church, Sweden.

pan-European building type that was brought in by the missionaries. In the 11th century ground sills on stone packing were introduced. By *c*.1130 the Romanesque stave church (*see* STAVKIRKE) had been created, with its distinctive composite of room units, and with dwarf galleries, cushion capitals, and doorways translated from Romanesque stone churches. The present stave church at Urnes, dendro-dated to the 1130s, is unique in having a richly decorated interior. Ornament on most other stave churches is concentrated to the exterior of doorway(s). With two exceptions, stave churches have survived only in Norway (26 original ones standing).

6. *Pictorial arts*

The pictorial arts of the Viking period can be glimpsed from haphazardly surviving monuments and *skaldic poems and must originally have been an important branch of the arts. Narrative representations dominate the approximately 35 picture stones of *c*.800 from *Gotland, the scenes on the cart and the tapestry from Oseberg, and a handful of skaldic **ekphraseis*. The tales refer to events of both Scandinavian myths and pan-European heroes, and pictures of riders, ships, and hunts suggest acquaintance with west-European secular iconography. Christian iconography of the 10th and 11th centuries survives in secular contexts: as pendant crucifixes (the earliest from a grave at *Birka, *c*.925–50), the large crucifixion in a vine-scroll on the Jelling stone, *c*.965, the Adoration of the Magi on the rune stone from Dynna (Norway) *c*.1025–50, and the frieze of standing saints, probably apostles in a Last Judgement, from what was arguably a private church at Flatatunga (Iceland), *c*.1050. Church furniture survives from the 12th century onwards and is wholly international in character. The eleven 'golden altars' in Denmark are important survivors of the *pala d'oro* tradition. They are made of hammered and gilt copper on a core of wood, in the European tradition, but their ornaments show indigenous stylistic details. The datings span the period *c*.1135–1235. All come from Jutland, with concentrations in the dioceses of Århus and Ribe. In Norway, approximately 30 painted wooden altar fronts survive, dated to *c*.1250–1350. Their motifs develop from devotional representations of the *Majestas Domini* and the Crucifixion to dramatic narratives including legends and apocrypha, again echoing the general development of European iconography.

The series of surviving figure sculpture in polychrome wood begins with imported crucifixes and Virgins in the 12th century, but import was soon superseded by local work. Both iconography and styles closely reflect their European models, for example, with the Virgin changing from *Sedes sapientiae* of the 12th to the heavenly queen and playful mother of the 13th–14th centuries, and the crucified from the crowned cosmic ruler to the tormented dead Man with the *crown of thorns. The iconography of saints, both in painting and sculpture, keeps closely to the European prototypes; even local saints like the Norwegian *Olaf and the Swedish *Birgitta are rendered according to internationally current schemata for respectively, male and female saints, being identifiable only by their attributes. Stylistically, English, German, and French influences are distinguishable. Wall painting that survives in Denmark and Sweden from shortly after 1100 onwards reflects mainly continental influences. After the *Black Death, artistic commissions declined, and in Norway the flourishing high Gothic workshops seem to have died completely. In Sweden and Denmark local traditions were taken up again around 1375/1400, and late medieval wall paintings demonstrate an interesting mixture of professional and folk art. The preferred *altar decoration in all three countries was now the modern, Netherlandish and North-German altarpieces with their scenes of three-dimensional, devotional or narrative, sculpture on the corpus and the inside of the doors, and paintings of scenes from the Bible or legends on the outside. The pattern of imported pieces is not identical in the three Scandinavian countries, but the importance of the Scandinavian

Mammen axehead. National Museum of Denmark.

market is indicated by the fact that two of Bernt Notke's major works were Scandinavian commissions: the altarpiece in Århus cathedral, dedicated 1479, and the stupendous sculpture group of St George and the dragon dedicated 1489 in Storkyrkan, Stockholm, commissioned by Sten Sture as a national monument to celebrate his victory over the Danes at Brunkaberg. *See also* ARCHITECTURE: ANGLO-SAXON; ART AND ARCHITECTURE: GOTHIC/ROMANESQUE. SHF

C. Ahrens, *Die frühen Holzkirchen Europas*, 2 vols (2001).
A. Andersson, *Medieval Wooden Sculpture in Sweden*, vols 2–3 (1966–80).
—— and P. Anker, *The Art of Scandinavia*, 2 vols (1970).
M. Blindheim, *Wooden Sculpture in Norway c.1100–1250* (1998).
—— *Gothic Painted Wooden Sculpture in Norway 1220–1350* (2004).
J. von Bonsdorff, *Kunstproduktion und Kunstverbreitung im Ostseeraum des Spätmittelalters* (1993).
S. H. Fuglesang, *Some Aspects of the Ringerike Style* (1980).
U. Haastrup and E. L. Lillie, eds, *Danske kalkmalerier*, 1–7 (1985–92).
E. B. Hohler, *Norwegian Stave Church Sculpture*, 2 vols (1999).
K. J. Krogh, 'The Royal Viking-age Monuments at Jelling in the Light of Recent Archaeological Excavations: A Preliminary Report', *Acta Archaeologica* 53 (1982), 183–216.
M. Malmanger *et al.*, eds, *Norwegian Medieval Altar Frontals and Related Material* (Acta ad archaeologiam et artium historiam pertinentia, 9) (1995).
M. Müller-Wille and L-O. Larsson, eds, *Tiere—Menschen—Götter: Wikingerzeitliche Kunststile und ihre neuzeitliche Rezeption* (2001).
P. Nørlund, *Gyldne altre* ([2]1968).
U. Plahter, E. B. Hohler, and N. Morgan. *Painted Altar Frontals of Norway 1250–1350*, 3 vols (2004).
E. Roesdahl and D. M. Wilson, *From Viking to Crusader* (1992).
Signums svenska konsthistoria, 1–3 (1990–91).
D. M. Wilson and O. Klindt-Jensen, *Viking Art* (1966; repr. 1980).

art and architecture: Seljuk Art and architecture produced during the Seljuk period is important in that it defined aesthetic and architectural expression in the central and eastern Islamic lands for the next several centuries. An abundant material record—*mosques, *tombs, tile work, *ceramics, *metalwork, *illuminated MSS—was left by Seljuk society before its collapse in the early 13th century. Part of the 10th-century tribal Oghuz migration from the steppes, the Seljuks had been Islamicized and recruited for military service in Transoxania on behalf of the Abbasid *caliphs. When they assumed control of Abbasid *Baghdad and what remained of their empire in 1055, the Seljuks and their military elite inaugurated a phase of *patronage whereby they sought to reinvent themselves from frontier *condottieri* to sophisticated, established legitimate rulers. This reinvention was strongest in their self-promotion as custodians of *Sunni orthodoxy, especially in light of the political and religious advances by the Egypt-based *Shiite Fatimids.

For this reason, we see considerable construction activity in religious edifices (*mosques, *madrasahs) from Iraq to Afghanistan, and therein a number of shifts in terms of aesthetics and functionality. With respect to mosque planning and structures, the Seljuks incorporated the pre-Islamic Persian conception of the domed chamber and the *ivan*. The domed chamber would house the *mihrab* (prayer niche) which would then be foregrounded by the *ivan*, a vaulted open hall standing at the end of a walled rectangular courtyard. Massive vaulted *arches such as these *ivans* had been the defining features of secular space in pre-Islamic Iran, as we see from the hall of enthronement (Taq-i Kisra) at the Sasanian capital of Ctesiphon. A fine example of this style of mosque construction and layout can be seen in the Jami Masjid in *Isfahan. The other distinctive feature of Seljuk mosque building were the *minarets, lofty cylindrical towers attached to either side of the *ivan*. Mosques from other periods and locations in the Islamic world tended to be square (for example the Great Mosque in *Kairouan) or spiral (for example the Great Mosque in Samarra). With extensive decorations in glazed and unglazed brick as well as complex tile mosaics, these 80–100-foot minarets were construed by the Seljuks as conspicuous proof of their legitimacy and piety. It was also this propagandistic principle which explains the wave of madrasa construction in the late 11th century. Formal centres of theological training, madrasas have been attributed to the administrative genius Nizam al-Mulk (d. 1092), who ordered the construction of these colleges in every principal Seljuk city. The generic form of a madrasah—assembly hall, inner sanctum, with rows of cells—has been linked in form and function to the small Buddhist temple-school complexes (*viharas*) which dotted the eastern Iranian landscape until the medieval period. Likewise, mausoleums and funerary structures produced during the Seljuk period have been connected with central Asian Turkic burial practices. There are two principal styles of Seljuk mausoleums: the tomb tower (cylindrical base with a coned roof) and the domed tomb (rectangular base with a domed roof). Religious architecture erected during the Seljuk period demonstrates the popularity of profiling sacred inscriptions, primarily Quranic Arabic, through inlaid tile work and stucco. Imperial palaces are well attested in contemporary chronicles for centres like Isfahan and Rayy, but these have long since been destroyed or dismantled.

The Seljuk period is also recognized for its glazed tile and ceramic wares production, and while physical evidence is scattered and inconsistent, there are sufficient grounds to believe that artisans were able to develop new methods of ceramic production. The most impressive luxury ceramic wares—complete with a rich palette of coloured glazes which profiled both scriptural and figural representation (*Quran, poetry, animals, humans, angels, and so forth)—was in Kashan (north of Isfahan). Seljuk *metalwork (ewers, lamps, jewellery) was noted for its impressive detail and use of inlaid work combining various metals. Illuminated double-paged frontispieces for Qurans were especially extravagant, and Seljuk-sponsored ateliers have been credited with introducing the 'East Persian' Kufic script to the repertoire of calligraphers and scribes. CPM

O. Grabar, 'The Visual Arts, 1050–1350', *Cambridge History of Iran*, vol. 5 (1968), 626–48.

R. Hillenbrand, *Islamic Architecture* (1994).

—— 'Saldjukids—VI. Art and Architecture', *EI*, vol. 8, 959–64.

art and architecture: Serbian From the 9th-century conversion to Christianity until the 11th century, the ecclesiastical art and architecture of the Serbs, both Orthodox and Roman Catholic, shared the concurrent accomplishments of the Croats, Latins, and Greeks. All of these groups cohabited the territories between the rivers Bojana and Cetina in Duklja (Zeta, Montenegro), Zahumlje (Herzegovina), and their littoral. Wall *paintings, donor *portraits, inscriptions in Greek and Latin, and architectural *sculpture on *windows, portals, capitals, *chancel screens, *ciboria, and baptismal fonts, reveal influences of pre-Romanesque, Romanesque, and Byzantine models. Instructive examples come from the 9th-century *rotunda of St Peter at Ras, in central *Serbia; the cross-in-square church of St Triphon at Kotor (809?), replaced by a Romanesque *cathedral in the mid 12th century; the 11th-century single-aisled church of St Michael in Ston; and the 11th-century *basilica of Archangel Michael in the fortified town Martinići, near Skadar Lake.

The best preserved, studied, and most comprehensive Serbian artistic achievements are related to churches and monasteries built from the period of the Nemanjić dynasty founded by *Joupan* Stefan Nemanja (r. 1169–96) until the Ottoman conquest in 1459. Byzantine, Romanesque and Gothic influences on Serbian arts were continuous and of various extent. Stefan Nemanja founded three churches built in three different building idioms. The Byzantines built the all-brick church of St Nicholas (1160s) at Kuršumlija, while local builders used stone for St George (or Djurdjevi Stupovi, 1170–71) near Novi Pazar. Stefan Nemanja's mausoleum, the church of the Mother of God (begun in 1183) at Studenica monastery, revetted in high-quality marble, blends Romanesque *corbel-tables and architectural sculpture with Byzantine spatial concepts and *domes into a new, 'Raška School', architectural style.

The use of Serbian language on *frescoes and distinctive local features such as the cult and image of Stefan Nemanja (St Symeon of Serbia) is first acknowledged at Studenica.

Comparable only to the *Hilandar *monastery on Mount Athos founded by Stefan Nemanja and his son Rastko (St *Sava of Serbia), Studenica remained of the greatest spiritual importance for the Serbs. Unique in its circular plan with the **katholikon* in the very centre, Studenica became the ultimate model for 13th-century monasteries at Ziča, Mileševa, Sopoćani, Morača, Gradac, Arilje, and their *katholika*. Their frescoes introduced classicizing elements of Late Byzantine art, exemplified by the paintings from the Holy Trinity church at Sopoćani (1273/4). Monumental and rhythmical compositions, harmonious colour-schemes, and oversized saints painted as antique heroes recurred during the Italian Renaissance period.

Under King Stefan Uroš II Milutin (r. 1282–1321) the churches of Bogorodica Ljeviška at Prizren, Kraljeva crkva at Studenica, St George at Staro Nagoričino, the Dormition of the Mother of God at Gračanica, and Hilandar *katholikon* reveal the major shift towards a 'Serbo-Byzantine' style in both monumental painting and architecture. Materialized by builders and painters, mostly trained in Thessalonian and Epirote idioms, these churches reach the best Late Byzantine achievements. Sculptural decoration and building technique of some other early-14th-century churches, like at Banjska and Dečani monasteries, show western influences.

Byzantine influences continued to prevail in 14th-century Serbian icons (for example, the icon of the *Presentation of the Virgin*, Hilandar monastery), *embroidery (for example, *King Milutin's epitaphios*, Museum of the Serbian Orthodox Church, Belgrade), *manuscripts (for example *Serbian Psalter*, Munich, Bayer. Staatsbibliothek, Cod. slav. 4), and wall painting. The largest extant painting programme in the Balkans, that from Dečani church, has more than 1,000 compositions, including the *Nemanjić Family Tree* (cf. 'Tree of Jesse'), and exemplifies the finest artistic accomplishments under Serbian patrons. The churches of the Holy Archangels near Prizren and of the Mother of God at Matejič built under Stefan Uroš IV Dušan (r. 1331–46; emperor 1346–55) and the churches of Archangel Michael at Lesnovo and St Demetrios in Markov Manastir, founded by the Serbian aristocracy, reflect the different tastes of their patrons and the presence of various builders and artists who drew their inspiration from *Constantinople, Thessaloniki, and the Adriatic coastal regions.

After the battle on the river Marica (1371) the Serbian state shrank in the north to the Morava valley, where an idiosyncratic national style, the so-called 'Morava School', emerged. The style is typified by a triconch church at Kalenić monastery (1407–17) and its rich stone and ceramo-plastic decoration. Its frescoes of the parables of Christ represent figures dressed in the costumes of contemporary Serbian *nobility. *See also* ART AND ARCHITECTURE: BYZANTINE/GOTHIC/ROMANESQUE; ICONOGRAPHY: ICONS. JBo

D. Bogdanović *et al.*, *Chilandar* (1978).
S. Ćurčić, *Gračanica* (1979).
V. Djurić, *Byzantinische Fresken in Jugoslawien* (Serbian original, 1974) (1976).
—— and G. Babić-Djordjević, *Srpska umetnost u srednjem veku*, 2 vols (1997).
G. Millet, *L'Ancien art serbe: Les Églises* (1919).
S. Popović, *Krst u krugu* (1994).
B. Todić, *Serbian Medieval Painting: The Age of Milutin* (1999).
—— and M. Čanak-Medić, *Manastir Dečani* (2005).

art and architecture: synagogue Although documentary evidence attests to the existence of early medieval synagogues, archaeological remains and buildings that allow an understanding of their appearance exist only from the high MA. In Europe, the political stabilization of the Rhineland that took place in the 9th and 10th centuries led to the re-establishment of Jewish communities in cities where Jews had lived during the *Roman Empire, as well as the founding of new communities.

1. Ashkenaz (Speyer, Worms, Prague, Regensburg, Buda)
2. North Africa
3. Iberia (Toledo, Córdoba, Portugal)

1. *Ashkenaz*

The oldest excavated synagogue in *Ashkenaz (the German lands) is the synagogue of *Speyer, built in 1104, whose basic features are repeated in later houses of worship. The entry to this masonry synagogue was on the north side; a niche for the Torah scrolls was situated in the east wall facing *Jerusalem, the direction of prayer; and the reader's desk was placed in the centre of the space to permit the entire congregation to hear the reading of the Torah. The extant arcaded *windows are bifurcated by columns with cushion capitals. In the 12th century, a vestibule was added and a **mikveh* or ritual bath with carved stone relief decorations was built nearby. In 1195, the synagogue was destroyed by fire (it had a wooden roof) and was rebuilt five years later. In the 13th century, it was again reconstructed. Enlarged Gothic windows were installed, and a women's prayer hall was added along the south side of the building. Windows cut into the south wall of the original men's synagogue allowed the women to follow the service.

Until 11 November, 1938 (*Kristallnacht*), the oldest extant medieval synagogue stood in nearby *Worms where it had been built on the site of an earlier house of worship dated 1034. The new synagogue was erected in 1174/5 as a double-*nave Romanesque building, a plan that was favoured by many Jewish congregations because it was used not for churches but for more secular purposes (although other plans having undivided spaces were also employed). The men's synagogue at Worms was subdivided by columns into two naves, each consisting of three groin-*vaulted bays. The ark for the Torah scrolls was built into the east wall, and the reader's desk was set between the two columns in the middle of the seating area. Vegetal and geometric motifs decorated the *tympanum over the main doorway.

The same ground plan, translated into Gothic style, was employed in the Altneuschul in *Prague erected in 1268, which is now the oldest existing medieval synagogue. In place of the figurative sculpture normally found on Gothic structures, the tympanum above the ark is filled with foliage and that over the main door bears a tree in relief, probably a rendering of the Tree of Life. Today, the floor level of the Altneuschul is below ground level, which may be a function of the deposit of debris over the centuries, or it may represent a deliberate effort on the part of the synagogue's patrons to achieve a sense of vertical monumentality despite medieval Christian restrictions on the height of Jewish houses of worship. The Altneu synagogue, like those in Speyer, Worms, and other German cities, originally had no space for women. Its *Frauenschul*, a space parallel to the men's synagogue but separated by a wall with small windows, dates to the 14th century. The reasons for the appearance in late medieval synagogues of new spaces for female worshippers are not yet clear.

*Regensburg had one of the most well-known Gothic synagogues, despite its demolition in 1519. In that year, the city council expelled the Jews from the city and decreed that the synagogue be demolished and a church erected on its site, a common practice in the later MA that expressed the victory of Christianity over Judaism. Prior to its destruction, the artist Albrecht Altdorfer (*c.*1482/5–1538), a member of the city council, recorded the synagogue's appearance in two

The interior of Worms synagogue before 1938.

*etchings. Excavations begun in 1995 confirmed many of the features of Altdorfer's depictions. A vestibule flanked the prayer hall, whose space was bisected by a row of columns between which the reader's desk was situated. *Rib vaults covered both the synagogue and the vestibule.

A twinned-nave synagogue was also erected in *Buda in 1461. Its interior space was subdivided by three large composite pillars of the same style as those in buildings dated 1458–90 that were erected for King *Matthias I Corvinus. After the Ottoman invasion of the city in 1541, Ottoman Jews also used the synagogue, adding painted amuletic decorations to its wall surfaces. The same two-nave plan

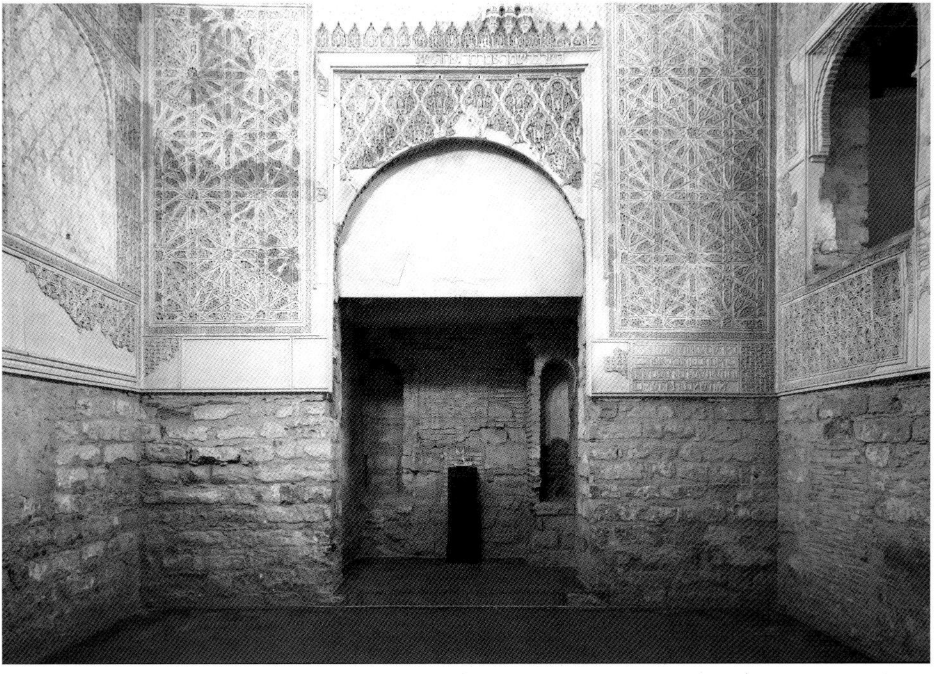

The interior of Córdoba synagogue.

appeared in the Old Synagogue of *Cracow built in the 15th century, perhaps brought eastward by Jews leaving German and Bohemian cities, but its form was soon superseded by other types of buildings under the influence of Italian architects and builders who were active in Poland from the 15th century onward.

2. *North Africa*

Most of the medieval Jewish population lived not in Europe, but in North Africa, Greater Syria, and Babylonia. We know little of their synagogues. In 1979, the structures below the 19th-century Ben Ezra synagogue of al-*Fustat (*Cairo) were examined by a team of archaeologists, and their findings were coordinated with textual documentation of the 11th to the 13th centuries found in the synagogue's *Geniza, a repository for old and worn writings in Hebrew script. An early synagogue was replaced in the years 1039–41 by a *basilica with columns separating the side aisles from the central nave. Above the aisles were galleries for female worshippers, entered from a separate staircase that rose on the exterior of the building. Short walls projecting from the centre of the east wall framed the niche for the Torah scrolls and the steps leading to it. Numerous dependencies surrounded the synagogue: a room for the rabbinical court; a *sukkah*, or temporary dwelling used during the Feast of Tabernacles; a well; and houses for various functionaries.

3. *Iberia*

The appearance of later North African synagogues may be reflected in two synagogues built in Mudéjar style (*see* ART, MUDÉJAR) in *Toledo, Spain. The earlier, now known as Santa Maria de la Blanca, was built in the 13th century, as a series of five parallel aisles separated by arcades of piers, a type of building commonly used for *mosques, like the 12th-century mosque in Tinmal, Morocco. The capitals of Santa Maria, the *spandrels, and the walls above are richly ornamented with stucco decoration. A similar synagogue existed in Segovia until the 19th century. This form of building may have arrived in Spain with the 12th-century *Almohad invasion.

A different plan was used by Isaac Mehab ben Ephraim, the patron of a synagogue built in *Córdoba in 1314/15. A small vestibule leads to the men's synagogue and houses stairs leading to the women's balcony. All of the walls are covered with rich stucco decoration, both vegetal motifs and inscriptions that include a dedicatory inscription. Between 1357–60, Samuel Abulafia, treasurer to *Pedro I of Castile, built a larger single-nave synagogue with a gallery for women along one side. Similar to the decoration of mosques, bands of biblical inscriptions, here Hebrew, fill a register at the top of the walls and surround the tripartite Torah shrine in the east wall. Floral stucco decorations cover the wall below, sometimes enclosing Arabic inscriptions referring to *Allah or God. Adjacent to the Torah niche is Abulafia's dedicatory inscription that enumerates the elements of a medieval synagogue:

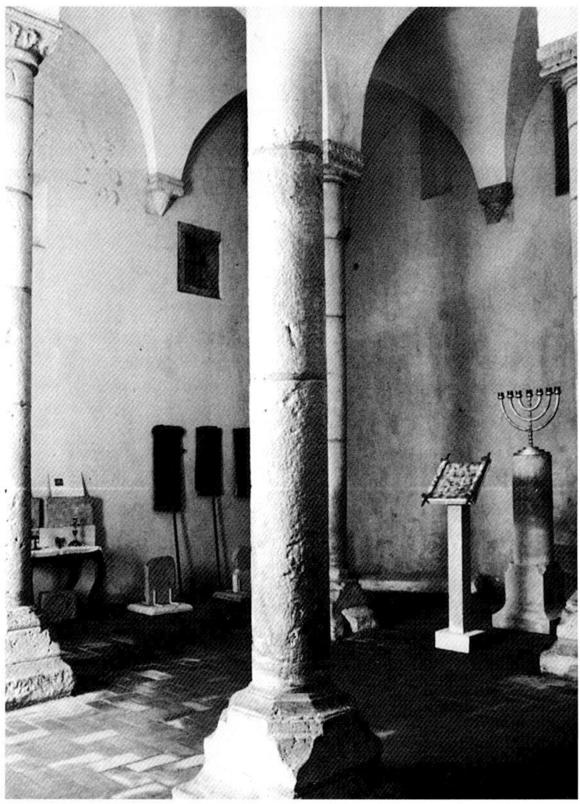
The interior of Tomar synagogue.

> the wooden tower [*almemor* or desk] for reading the law ... and its Torah scrolls and their crowns to God, and its lavers, and its lamps for illumination and its windows like the window of Ariel [Jerusalem], and its courts for those diligent in the perfect law and a residence for those who would sit in the shade of God....

Thus, the synagogue of the later MA was, like the 12th-century Ben Ezra in Cairo, not just a place of prayer, but also the seat of the rabbinical court and a hostel for those in need. Abulafia's mention of lamps and windows calls attention to the importance of light in a synagogue, where the entire congregation read the service.

In northern Portugal, the city of Tomar boasts a small synagogue which is a blend of Christian and Muslim elements. The plan, a central square surrounded by other square bays, was used for private mosques throughout the Dar-el-Islam, but the use of columns supporting the vaults points to Christian sources. It was on the Iberian Peninsula that the two worlds of medieval Jewry, those who lived in

Ashkenaz and those who lived under the rule of Islam, came together symbolically in the architecture of synagogues. VBM

Historisches Museum der Pfalz Speyer, *The Jews of Europe in the Middle Ages*, exhibition catalogue (2004).
R. Krautheimer, *Mittelälterliche Synagogen* (1927).
C. H. Krinsky, *Synagogues of Europe: Architecture, History, Meaning* (1985).
P. Lambert, ed., *Fortifications and the Synagogue: The Fortress of Babylon and the Ben Ezra Synagogue, Cairo* (1994).
R. Wischnitzer, *The Architecture of the European Synagogue* (1964).

artes poeticae The arts of poetry and prose are technical treatises or manuals that teach literary composition. As such, they give practical instruction on writing, not poetic theory. Although the art they promote had a long history, the major treatises were written between 1175 and 1280. They are *Matthew of Vendôme's *Ars versificatoria*; *Geoffrey of Vinsauf's *Poetria nova* and his *Documentum*; a longer, anonymous *Documentum* formerly attributed to Geoffrey; Gervase of Melkley's *Ars versificaria*; *John of Garland's *Parisiana Poetria*; and Eberhard the German's *Laborintus*. There are also numerous brief works on special topics such as description, *tropes and figures, and versification. There are also important commentaries on Geoffrey's *Poetria nova*.

The arts of poetry borrow from two major sources: rhetorical treatises, especially Cicero's *De inventione* and the pseudo-Ciceronian *Rhetorica ad Herennium*; and Horace's *Art of Poetry* was also a major influence. These works were read with the assistance of commentaries and *glosses. From them the treatises borrow new, medieval features of composition such as natural and artificial order, or arrangement of beginning, middle, and end in 'natural' chronological sequence or in 'artificial' order that follows a different sequence; material style, or conformity of descriptions to social order; and amplification and abbreviation, or the emphasis on specific tropes and figures to develop or shorten source material.

The scope of the treatises varies, suggesting gradual progression in scholastic study and practice of literary composition. Pupils begin with elementary exercises using tropes, figures of speech and thought, and versification. From there they pass to features of invention used in describing persons and things in intermediate works (Matthew of Vendôme). *Geoffrey of Vinsauf and *John of Garland treat the more advanced subjects of invention and disposition. Finally, students go on to study canonical masterpieces as models for imitation. The treatises recommend standard classical Latin authors, notably Vergil, Ovid, and Statius, as well as medieval works, especially those by *Bernard Silvestris, *Alan of Lille, and *Joseph of Exeter. Bernard's *Cosmographia* and Alan's *De planctu Naturae* are emphasized because they illustrate both verse and prose composition (*prosimetrum*). Imitation of models such as these developed compositional skills in the classroom by stressing features taught in the treatises; pupils imitated chosen passages or topics by writing set pieces (*praeexercitamina*). *John of Salisbury describes such activities in his *Metalogicon* with *Bernard of Chartres's teaching as illustration. *Gervase of Melkley refers to similar instruction imparted by *John of Hauville; this poet's *Architrenius* is a model text from which, Gervase asserts, one can learn all one needs to know about the art of poetry. FDK

A. Cizek, *Imitatio et tractatio: die literarische Grundlagen der Nachahmung in Antike und Mittelalter* (1994).
K. Friis-Jensen, 'Horace and the Early Writers of Arts of Poetry', *Sprachtheorien in Spätantike und Mittealter*, ed. S. Ebbesen (1995), 360–401.
D. Kelly, *The Arts of Poetry and Prose* (1991).
J. Y. Tilliette, *Des mots à la Parole: une lecture de la 'Poetria nova' de Geoffroy de Vinsauf* (2000).
J. O. Ward, *Ciceronian Rhetoric in Treatise, Scholion and Commentary* (1995).

Artevelde family Political family of *Ghent. **Jacob van Artevelde** (*c.*1290–1345), a broker and landowner, became chief captain of Ghent in 1338 at the time of an English wool embargo. He steered Ghent into an alliance with England and into domination over the rest of *Flanders through the *drie steden*, thus becoming *de facto* ruler of Flanders. The failure of English military ventures weakened van Artevelde. He survived a coup attempt in 1343 but was assassinated in 1345 when rumour spread that he intended to recognize the prince of Wales as count of Flanders. Between 1361 and 1370 his two older sons, **Jan** and **Jacob the younger**, took vengeance against those they considered responsible for their father's death. **Philip van Artevelde** (1340–82), Jacob's youngest son, was chief captain of Ghent January–November 1382. He was an even stronger English partisan than his father had been, but his hope of English help was disappointed. He used the first month of his captaincy to hunt down the eldest male descendants of all he considered implicated in his father's assassination but unpunished. He broke the blockade of Ghent with a sortie against *Bruges. He styled himself 'regent', and lived lavishly. He perished at the battle of West Rozebeke on 27 November 1382. DN

D. Nicholas, *The Van Arteveldes of Ghent: The Varieties of Vendetta and the Hero in History* (1988).
N. de Pauw, ed., *Cartulaire historique et généalogique des Artevelde* (1920).
H. van Werveke, *Jacques van Artevelde* (1942).

Arthur of Brittany (1187–*c.*1203) Grandson of *Henry II of England. He was named heir by his uncle, *Richard I, in 1190, and after the accession of King *John 'Lackland' (1199),

Artevelde family. The victory of the Ghents against Bruges, under the leadership of Philip van Artevelde.

his claim was supported by *Philip II Augustus of *France. Captured by John's forces in August 1202, he was probably murdered by John's orders soon thereafter. REM

J. Gillingham, *The Angevin Empire* ([2]2001).

Articella A collection of works used for medical education in Latin Europe. The term *Articella* (literally, The little Art) was given by the Renaissance press to a collection of works that from the 12th century became the basic canon of medical education in Latin Europe. Some MS traditions use this name while others prefer *Artesella*, *Ars medicinae*, or *Ars commentata*. The origin of the collection is still under discussion, but generally it is associated with the medical schools of Salerno. The earliest surviving MSS from the early 12th century already witness the establishment of a sequence of short works that began with the *Isagoge* of Johannitius (*Hunayn ibn Ishaq), were followed by the Hippocratic *Aphorisms* and *Prognostics*, and ended with two short treatises (attributed to Theophilus and Philaretus) that dealt with the two main diagnostic tools of Galenic medicine: the inspection of urines and the taking of the pulse. Later in the century *Galen's *Tegni* (*Microtegni*, *Ars parva*) was added to these, along with the commentary on it by Haly Ridwan.

The *Isagoge* is a Latin reworking of an Arabic introduction to Galenic medicine structured around those things that pertain to the body (the naturals); those that are external to it but pertain to the maintenance of health (the non-naturals); and those that pertain to the disease (things against nature). The *Tegni* is a compendium of the conceptual basis of the Galenic medical system. It is organized around three main themes: states of the body (healthy, neutral, and diseased), symptoms, and causes of disease. Less systematic than these two works are the Hippocratic *Aphorisms* with an aphoristic structure that allows it to deal with a wide number of topics; this was customarily followed by the *Prognostics*, which deals with theoretical and practical aspects of medical prognosis but in an all-encompassing sense that takes into account the past, present, and future of the disease. In the 13th century, a seventh work was added to the *Articella*, the Hippocratic *De regimine acutorum* (On the regimen in acute diseases); though it does not eschew theory, this work focuses on practical issues that are involved in the handling of therapeutic measures. The three Hippocratic texts were incorporated in the collection in their Latin versions from the Arabic or from the Greek and from the 13th century onwards were usually accompanied by commentaries by Galen. The presence of the commentaries altered the character of the collection since it determined how the collection was read and interpreted.

The *Articella* was a flexible teaching tool, open to local and temporary variation, as is reflected in the complex MS tradition. Nevertheless, the seven works named here formed the core of the collection printed in the Renaissance that enjoyed sixteen editions between 1476 and 1534. FS

P. O. Kristeller, 'Bartholomaeus, Musandinus and Maurus of Salerno and other Early Commentators on the *Articella*, with a Tentative List of Texts and Manuscripts', *IMU* 19 (1976), 57–87.

C. O'Boyle, *The Art of Medicine: Medical Teaching at the University of Paris, 1250–1400* (1998).

T. Pesenti, 'Le *Articelle* di Daniele di Marsilio Santasofia (†1410), professore di medicina', *Studi petrarcheschi* 7 (1990), 50–92.

artisans and craftwork From the early to the late MA in both western Europe and Islamic lands, artisans became increasingly specialized, producing both ordinary and *luxury goods for local consumption and as commodities in long-distance trade. Virtually all artisans learned their crafts through *apprenticeships, either informal within household or family workshop economies, or under formal apprenticeship contracts often under the aegis of craft *guilds. *Craft skill was often passed down through families, from fathers to sons and sometimes daughters, and from mothers to daughters.

The locales of craftwork varied with time and place. In the early MA women produced almost all cloth from *spinning to *weaving to finishing, sometimes in their own households. On the manor, women did this work in a designated workshop called a *gynaeceum*. In the later MA, the urban workshop was the usual site for artisanal production. As manufactures such as *textiles became commodities that fuelled long-distance *trade, weaving and finishing came to be controlled by male artisans in the *towns, while spinning was 'put out' to women working in their own homes in the countryside.

The length of apprenticeships depended on the initial age of the apprentice and the complexity of the craft. The average length was four or six years during which both skills and responsibilities gradually increased. Sometimes a masterpiece was required before the apprentice could become a *journeyman. These day labourers often travelled to find work (tramping), carrying techniques and innovations with them from one locale to another. Becoming a master was never automatic, because to do so required the acquisition of a workshop, often easier for the sons of masters than for other journeymen.

Great respect for craftwork is evident in the 12th-century treatise by *Theophilus Presbyter. In the late MA the status of some crafts rose sharply, particularly those involved in the *decorative arts and luxury trades such as *painting, *sculpture, and maiolica work. One result was the expansion of writings on particular crafts by artisans as well as others. *See also* ATELIER; CERAMICS; ESTATE MANAGEMENT AND ORGANIZATION; TEXTILES AND CLOTH-MAKING. POL

J. Amman and H. Sachs, *The Book of Trades (Ständebuch)*, ed. B. A. Rifkin (facsimile ed. of German original, 1568) (1973).

X. Barral i Altet, ed., *Artistes, artisans et production artistique au Moyen Age*, 3 vols ([3]1990).

S. A. Epstein, *Wage Labor and Guilds in Medieval Europe* (1991).

—— 'Craft Guilds, Apprenticeship, and Technological Change in Preindustrial Europe', *JEconH* 58 (1998), 684–713.

—— *Freedom and Growth: The Rise of States and Markets in Europe, 1300–1750* (2000).

J. R. Farr, *Artisans in Europe, 1300–1914* (2000).

D. Herlihy, *Opera Muliebria: Women and Work in Medieval Europe* (1990).

P. O. Long, *Openness, Secrecy, Authorship: Technical Arts and the Culture of Knowledge from Antiquity to the Renaissance* (2001).

G. Ovitt, Jr, *The Restoration of Perfection: Labor and Technology in Medieval Culture* (1986).

G. Rosser, 'Grafts, Guilds and the Negotiation of Work in the Medieval Town', *PaP* 154 (1997), 3–31.

M. Shatzmiller, *Labour in the Medieval Islamic World* (1994).

H. Swanson, *Medieval Artisans: An Urban Class in Late Medieval England* (1989).

Theophilus, *The Various Arts, On Diverse Arts*, ed. and tr. C. R. Dodwell (1961; repr. 1986).

artist In the MA the artist, or better *artifex* ('artificer'), was most frequently considered a practitioner of the *mechanical arts. Inextricably linked to his manual activities, he was viewed as a craftsman and was recruited from the *artisan class. However, a new attitude had emerged by the 14th century when the painter *Giotto, admired by *Dante, *Petrarch, and *Boccaccio, was presented as a creative intellectual. *See also* ART. FB

E. Castelnuovo, 'L'artista', *L'uomo medievale*, ed. J. Le Goff (1988), 235–69.

—— ed., *Artifex bonus: il mondo dell'artista medievale* (2004).

A. Martindale, *The Rise of the Artist in the Middle Ages and Early Renaissance* (1972).

Art of Dying (*Ars moriendi*) The *block-book of the *Ars moriendi*, reduced to eleven pictures, was one of the most popular and influential books circulating in Europe in the post-*plague era. Intended to prepare Christians for *death, the book portrays in vivid illustrations the various diabolical temptations awaiting them on their deathbed (despair, impatience, vainglory, avarice) with inspirations to help them stand firm. The final *woodcut depicts the moment of death as a triumph of self-will over temptation in which the devils are sent scrambling back into *hell.

SMB

P. Binski, *Medieval Death: Ritual and Representation* (1996).

Artois Strategically situated to facilitate trade among *England, *France, and the *Low Countries, Artois prospered during much of the MA. By the 5th century Franks ruled the region, and by the mid 9th century Odalric of Artois had established it as a county under *Carolingian dominion. In 863, *Charles II 'the Bald' gave Artois to his daughter Judith, at the time of her marriage to Baldwin 'Iron Arm', first count of *Flanders (d. 879). Artois lands remained part of the county of Flanders until 1180, when Isabelle of *Hainaut (1170–90), niece of Philip I of Flanders (1143–91), brought Artois as dowry in her marriage to the king of France, *Philip II Augustus. This king's grandson, *Louis IX, would in 1237 grant Artois as an *apanage to his brother, Robert (1216–50), who was followed by two long-lived successors, Robert II (1250–1302) and Mahaut (1268–1329). Although disputed by her cousin, Robert of Bethune (1287–1342), Mahaut retained possession and passed her lands to her own daughter, Jeanne of Burgundy (1291–1330), former queen of France. Upon Jeanne's death in 1330, Artois was united with the duchy of *Burgundy when her daughter, also named Jeanne (1308–49), married Eudes IV (1295–1350). Joan's nephew, Louis II of Flanders (1330–84), inherited Artois in 1361, but it reverted to Burgundian rule upon his death in 1384 due to the marriage of his daughter and heir, *Margaret, to Philip the Bold (1342–1404). Briefly part of France after 1482, it was ceded to the *Habsburgs in 1493.

TCH

P. Pierrard, *Histoire du Nord: Flandre, Artois, Hainaut, Picardie* (1978).

Arts, Faculty of the Provided the basic teaching for beginning students in medieval *universities. This propaedeutical teaching was a necessary requirement, in most places, for further study in one of the higher faculties (theology, *law, and *medicine). Not all students, however, proceeded to the higher faculties. Some left the university after their arts studies to engage in administrative careers or to teach in local schools in their region of origin; others continued to teach as *Master of Arts in their own faculty. The length of the study varied according to period and region: in 13th-century *Paris seven years was normal, but later on, for instance, in 14th-century German universities the course was much shorter.

From the beginning, the teaching programme at the Arts Faculty included not only the *'seven liberal arts', mainly *grammar and *logic but also the disciplines of the quadrivium (geometry, *astronomy, arithmetic, and *music). Especially after the *baccalaureate, a degree obtained after several years of study, a number of other disciplines were taught based on the Latin translations of the treatises of Aristotle: physics (natural *philosophy), *metaphysics, *cosmology, psychology, and so forth. Thus the Arts Faculty could also be called the faculty of philosophy.

The teaching methods were mainly the *lectio* and the *disputatio*. The *lectio* consisted in reading and commenting on the basic texts: the Master of Arts read aloud a portion of the text corresponding to the discipline he was to teach (for example, a passage of the *Physics* of Aristotle) and explained not only the literal meaning, but also the general sense and the intention of the author. He also raised and answered questions about the text (*quaestio*) concerning its difficulties and possible inconsistencies. He could, of course, use the *glosses or commentaries of earlier masters, but he was not allowed to simply read an already existing commentary and had to comment on the text independently. Many commentaries of Arts masters have survived.

The other main teaching method, the *disputatio*, was the organized and systematic discussion of questions arising from the reading of the texts or of independent questions. The students were supposed to participate in the disputations as opponents or respondents. There were several kinds of disputations: the discussions conducted by the master with his own students, the exercises for the students, the disputations during examinations, and the solemn disputation in which all the masters and students of the faculty participated. These teaching methods were the same in the higher faculties. Thus the students of the Arts Faculty, apart from learning the contents of the several disciplines, also learned the methods of analysing and reasoning they would need in their later studies. *See also* EDUCATION; MATHEMATICS.

OW

J. M. Fletcher, 'The Faculty of Arts', *The History of the University of Oxford, I: The Early Oxford Schools*, ed. J. I. Catto (1984), 369–99.

O. Weijers, *Le maniement du savoir: Pratiques intellectuelles à l'époque des premières universités (XIIIe–XIVe siècles)* (1996).

—— and L. Holtz, eds, *L'enseignement des disciplines à la Faculté des arts (Paris et Oxford, XIIIe–XVe siècles)* (1997).

Arundel, earls of Until the mid 13th century, these earls were also frequently known as earls of *Sussex, until this title fell into disuse. The Arundel title is the oldest extant earldom in the *peerage of *England. **Roger de Montgomery** was created earl of Arundel (or Sussex) about 1067. His title was forfeited by his eldest son in 1102. **William d'Aubigny** (or 'de Albini') was the next earl *c.*1139. There were five d'Aubigny earls until 1243, when Arundel itself was inherited by a coheir, **John FitzAlan**, whose grandson **Richard** was created earl of Arundel in 1289. He was the first of thirteen FitzAlan earls in direct descent down to

1580, when it passed to Philip *Howard, ancestor of the dukes of Norfolk, the current earls. *See also* ARUNDEL, THOMAS. MAH

G. E. Cokayne, *The Complete Peerage*, ed. V. Gibbs (1910), vol. 1.

Arundel, Thomas, archbishop of Canterbury (1353–1414) Younger son of the earl of *Arundel, he was bishop of *Ely at an extraordinarily young age (1373–88), archbishop of *York (1388–96), and then *Canterbury (1396–1414). Five times he held the post of Chancellor. WJD

M. Aston, *Thomas Arundel, A Study of Church Life in the Reign of Richard II* (1967).
J. Hughes, *Pastors and Visionaries* (1988).

Arundel's Constitutions (drafted 1407, published 1409). Provincial constitutions published by Archbishop *Arundel of *Canterbury. The thirteen articles cover preaching without licence, the production of vernacular books and scriptural translations, and the content of preaching and teaching; they also provide for a monthly examination of the religious beliefs of members of *Oxford University. They have been interpreted both as anti-*Lollard and as anti-Oxford in intention. SJa

Concilia Magnae Britanniae et Hiberniae, ed. D. Wilkins, vol. 3 (1737).
A. Hudson, *The Premature Reformation* (1988).
S. James, 'Debating Heresy: 15th-Century Vernacular Theology and Arundel's Constitutions', Ph.D. thesis (Cambridge, 2004).

Arzneibücher Medieval German compilations of medical knowledge, normally prepared in *monasteries, based on Graeco-Roman *medicine rather than on the Germanic medical tradition. These texts represent some of the earliest medical writing in German. Notable *Arzneibücher* include a German version of the *Macer Floridus, *De viribus herbarum* (composed *c.*1200), and the late-12th-century *Bartholomäus*. *See also* HERBALS. MPie

M. W. Adamson, 'Technical Literature (*Fachliteratur*)', *A Companion to Middle High German Literature to the 14th Century*, ed. F. G. Gentry (2002), 319–43.
W. Crossgrove, *Die deutsche Sachliteratur des Mittelalters* (1994).

Asaph the Physician Asaph Judaeus or 'Asaph ben Berachyahu', pseudonym attached to the 'Book of Remedies' (*Sepher Refuoth*), considered the oldest Hebrew medical work, variously dated from the 6th to the 10th century. Its place of origin, whether the Middle East or southern *Italy, is also debated. The work draws from *Galen, *Hippocrates, *Soranus, and Rufus of Ephesus, and treats *physiology, pathology, dietetics, prognosis, embryology, and pharmacology (*see* PHARMACY) relying on *Dioscorides. JS

A. Melzer, 'Asaph the Physician—The Man and his Book: A Historical-Philological Study of the Medical Treatise, *The Book of Drugs*', Ph.D. thesis (Wisconsin, 1972).
S. Muntner, *Mavo le-Sefer Asaf ha-Rofe* (1967).
D. E. Rhumer and A. G. Zupko, *Some Contributions by Jews to Pharmacy* (1960), 7–10.
J. Shatzmiller, 'In Search of the "Book of Remedies": Medicine and Astrology in Montpellier at the Turn of the Fourteenth Century', *AJS Review*, 7–8 (1982–3), 383–407.
L. Venetianer, *Asaf Judaeus: Der Älteste Medizinische Schriftsteller in Hebräischer Sprache* (1915).

Ascanians *See* BRANDENBURG, MARGRAVATE OF.

Ascension, Feast of *See* LITURGICAL YEAR; LITURGY.

asceticism Derived from *askesis* (a Greek word meaning 'training'), asceticism is the restriction or renunciation of bodily needs and pleasures in favour of spiritual attainment. Celibacy (the renunciation of sexual unions) and *fasting (the restriction of food consumption) are exemplary forms of asceticism. Christian asceticism developed from Graeco-Roman traditions. It was closely, but far from exclusively, associated with *monasticism. TFH

P. Brown, *The Body and Society: Men, Women, and Sexual Renunciation in Early Christianity* (1988).
C. Bynum, *Holy Feast, Holy Fast: The Religious Significance of Food to Medieval Women* (1987).
V. Wimbush and R. Valantasis, eds, *Asceticism* (2002).

aseity [Latin, 'from itself'] Theological term used to describe that which is the Ultimate Being; an entity that was not created and thus always has and will continue to exist. Applied to God by Church Fathers, theologians including *Thomas Aquinas affirmed God's possession of aseity by proving the non-aseity of the natural universe. *See also* ANSELM, ST; COSMOLOGY; ETERNITY OF THE WORLD; ONTOLOGICAL ARGUMENT, THE; THEOLOGY, WESTERN. LMP

New Catholic Encyclopedia (²2003), vol. 1, 778–80.

Ashari, Abu l-Hasan Ali ibn Ismail al- (*c.*874–935/6) Muslim theologian, founder of the Asharite school of Islamic *theology. Educated in *Basra in Mutazilite theology, he broke with its rationalism and moved to *Baghdad, where he died. FG

C. E. Bosworth, 'Aš'arī', *EIran*, vol. 2, 702–3.
I. Goldziher, *Introduction to Islamic Theology and Law*, tr. A. and R. Hamori (1981), 94–115.
M. E. Marmura, *The Cambridge Companion to Arabic Philosophy*, ed. P. Adamson and R. C. Taylor (2005), 141–50.

Asharites *See* ASHARI, AL-.

Asher ben Yehiel (d. 1327) Student of *Meir ben Barukh of Rothenburg. Escaping persecution, Asher and his family reached *Toledo in 1305. He compiled *Tosafot* to a number of tractates (based on *Samson ben Abraham of Sens), and wrote a Talmudic commentary (following the *Hilkhot ha-Rif*) collecting teachings of leading rabbis in both *Ashkenaz and *Sefarad. The published collection of Asher's **responsa* contains only some of those he wrote. EK

Y. D. Galinsky, 'Ha-Rosh ha-Ashkenazi bi-Sefarad', *Tarbiz*, 74 (2005), 389–413.

I. Ta-Shma, 'R. Asher u-Beno R. Ya'aqov Ba'al ha-Turim', *Pe'amim*, 46 (1991), 75–91.

Ashingdon, battle of Victory for the Danish king *Cnut over an English force under *Edmund II (Ironside) in battle at *Assandun* (*Essex), 18 October 1016. Cnut was accepted as king north of the Thames hereafter, well placed to take the English throne on Edmund's death in November 1016. SRIF

K. Lawson, *Cnut: The Danes in England in the Early Eleventh Century* (1993).

Ashkenaz Hebrew term denoting the Jewish settlement area in northwest Europe, initially on the banks of the *Rhine and the upper *river Danube, later understood to refer to *Germany, German Jewry, and German Jews (Ashkenazim). The name derives from Genesis 10:3; by the 11th century the term was well established. The first Jews settled in Ashkenaz during the 9th century. By the end of the 10th century, 4,000 to 5,000 Jews lived in Ashkenaz, but the communities grew quickly during the 11th century, when an intellectual and economic blossoming laid the foundations for the Ashkenazic identity. Owing to close cultural relations with the Jewish communities in the Rhineland, northern *France and even *England (with its short Jewish history) are mostly included in the term Ashkenaz, although a different term (Ẓarfat) existed in the MA and was used for both geographic and cultural purposes.

Jewish scholars in Ashkenaz focused their studies on the Bible, the *Talmud, and specific questions in Jewish law. Known for exegesis and **responsa*, they did not compose systematic treatments of Jewish law. Traces of their interaction with the surrounding Christian society, both influences and polemics, can be found in many texts and customs. Social structures that characterize Ashkenazic Judaism are monogamous families and autonomy of the local communities. Ashkenaz also developed its own prayer rite that spread from northern France to *Poland. In the 14th century the term also included Jewish communities in the Slavic countries which continued the Ashkenazic cultural heritage, including the use of a Judaeo-German language (*Yiddish). Ashkenaz is often used in contrast to *Sefarad, the Jewish cultural entity that developed on the Iberian Peninsula. EHo

A. Grossman, *The Early Sages of Ashkenaz* [Hebrew] (1988).

A. Haverkamp, ed., *Geschichte der Juden im Mittelalter von der Nordsee bis zu den Südalpen* (2002).

M. Toch, 'The Formation of a Diaspora: The Settlement of Jews in the Medieval German "Reich" ', *Aschkenas*, 7 (1997), 55–78.

—— *Die Juden im mittelalterlichen Reich* (1998).

ashlar Quarried and dressed *stone cut into rectangular blocks producing regular vertical and horizontal joints. Ashlar was used for wall facing and was tooled (smoothed) on its external face. *See also* BUILDING AND CONSTRUCTION; QUARRYING AND STONEMASONRY. LTC

R. Mark, ed., *Architectural Technology up to the Scientific Revolution* (1993).

L. F. Salzman, *Building in England down to 1540* (1952; repr. 1992).

Ash Wednesday The first day of *Lent. It was understood by the 7th century as occurring 40 days (not counting Sundays) before *Easter. The high medieval *liturgy featured the marking of a *cross in ashes on the foreheads of the faithful as they were reminded of their eventual return to the dust of the earth (Genesis 3:19). ECT

Ash-Wednesday.org, 17 July 2007 www.ash-wednesday.org.

Asinarius (*c.*1200) Anonymous Latin elegiac verse narrative composed probably in south *Germany, featuring the animal-bridegroom motif, here a prince in donkey's guise. It is embedded in a courtly context, into which many ancient elements (mythology, Ovidian colouring) are mixed. GKG

S. Rizzardi, ed., *Asinarius, Commedie latine del XII e XIII secolo*, ed. F. Bertini, vol. 4 (1983), 137–251.

J. M. Ziolkowski, *Fairy Tales from Before Fairy Tales* (2007), 200–230.

Asmatikon *See* LITURGICAL BOOKS, GREEK.

asperges The rite of sprinkling the church, officiants, and people with holy water before the celebration of *Mass, as a symbol of cleansing and a memorial of *baptism. DJKe

C. Goeb, 'The Asperges', *Orate Fratres*, 2 (1927–28), 338–42.

J. A. Jungmann, *The Mass of the Roman* Rite, tr. F. A. Brunner (German original, 1950) (1951; rev. and abridged ed. 1959).

aspersion *See* BAPTISM.

assart, assarting *See* ESTATE MANAGEMENT AND ORGANIZATION.

Assassins (Hashishin), **sect of** The Assassin movement was inaugurated by al-Hasan ibn al-Sabbah (d. 1124), a Persian who claimed descent from the Himyarite kings of South Arabia. Hassan received instruction in the Batinite system in Rayy, and after spending a year and a half in *Egypt returned to his native land as a Fatimid missionary. Here in 1090 he gained possession of the strong mountain fortress of *Alamut, northwest of Qazwin. This 'eagle's nest', as the name means, gave al-Sabbah and his successors an important central stronghold. From *Alamut the grand master with his disciples made surprise raids to capture other fortresses. In pursuit of their ends they made free and treacherous use of the dagger, making 'assassination' an art. Their secret organization developed an agnosticism which aimed to emancipate the followers from the clutches of doctrine and the superfluity of prophets, to believe nothing and dare all. The *fidais*, given hashish, stood ready to execute whatever orders the grand master issued. They were taught that revealed religion was for the masses, that only the true *imam and his representative (Hassan), to whom they owed unquestioning obedience, possessed divine truth, and that as they gained his secret knowledge, so would they gain hidden powers. Marco *Polo gave an account of the 'Old Man of the Mountain' and his followers, describing the taking of hashish that would make the followers think they were in the Muslim paradise.

The assassination in 1092 of the Seljuk vizier Nizam al-Mulk by a *fidai* disguised as a Sufi was the first of a series of mysterious murders that terrified the Muslim world. When in the same year Sultan Malikshah sent a disciplinary force against the fortress, its garrison made a night sortie and repelled the besieging army. Other attempts by *caliphs and sultans proved equally futile until finally the Mongol Hulagu, who destroyed the *caliphate, in 1256 seized the fortress together with its subsidiary castles in Persia. After the capture of Masjad in 1260 by the Mongols, the Mamluk *Baybars in 1272 dealt the Syrian Assassins the final blow. Since then the Assassins were scattered through northern Syria, Persia, Oman, Zanzibar, and *India. They acknowledge as titular head the Aga Khan, who claims descent through the last grand master of Alamut from Isma'il, the seventh imam. MD

B. Lewis, *The Assassins* (1975).

assembly, royal Assemblies met annually in 7th- and 8th-century Frankish and *Lombard kingdoms, and had regular venues in *Visigothic Spain and AS kingdoms. Political relationships were negotiated through discussions, conflicts staged and defused through rituals; offices were conferred or removed, petitions heard, military targets and war taxation approved, and laws promulgated. Assemblies often met at church feasts. English assemblies from the 13th century included *knights and urban spokesmen, along with nobles and bishops. JLN

S. Airlie, 'Talking Heads: Assemblies in Early Medieval Germany', *Political Assemblies in the Earlier Middle Ages*, ed. P. Barnwell and M. Mostert (2003), 29–46.

T. Reuter, 'Assembly Politics', *The Medieval World*, ed. P. Linehan and J. L. Nelson (2001), 432–50.

Asser (d. 908/9) Bishop of Sherborne (*c*.895–909) and biographer of *Alfred the Great of England. Of Welsh origin, Asser joined the court of King Alfred around 885 and played an important role in the intellectual life of Alfred's court. Asser's biography of Alfred presents the king in highly idealized terms but is nonetheless our most significant source of information for Alfred's life and reign. Some scholars have questioned the authenticity of the biography, but most accept it as genuine. WHS

S. Keynes and M. Lapidge, eds and trs, *Alfred the Great: Asser's Life of King Alfred and Other Contemporary Sources* (1983).

Asses, Feast of Either of two parodic liturgies associated with the Feast of *Fools. One honoured Balaam's Ass; the other, celebrated 14 January, honoured the ass of the Flight into Egypt. It featured antiphonal braying and the laudatory 'Prose of the Ass'. *See also* BOY BISHOP; FOOLS, FEAST OF; LITURGICAL YEAR; LITURGY. RSS

I. S. Gilhus, 'Carnival in Religion: The Feast of Fools in France', *Numen*, 37/1 (1990), 24–52.

—— 'Eselmesser', *Tradisjon*, 23 (1993), 19–29.

Assisi Located in the Umbrian region of central *Italy, Assisi is a small town, known as Assisium in Roman times. The town's ancient foundations are evidenced by the temple of Minerva in the city centre. During the MA, Assisi was engaged in a bitter rivalry with its neighbour, *Perugia, which culminated in a battle in 1202 for control of several small towns. Perugia emerged victorious. Assisi is best known as the birthplace and burial site of two beloved saints, *Francis, founder of the *Franciscan order, and *Clare, founder of the Poor Clares. Two churches dedicated to Francis, one on top of the other, were begun in 1228, the year that he was *canonized. The Upper and Lower churches were decorated by artists including Pietro *Lorenzetti, Simone *Martini, *Cimabue, and *Giotto. A church dedicated to Clare was begun in 1257. *See also* RELIGIOUS ORDERS. JEB

Assisi al tempo di San Francesco (1978).

A. Fortini, *Francis of Assisi*, tr. H. Moak (1981).

B. Kleinschmidt, *Die Basilika San Francesco in Assisi*, 3 vols (1915–28).

A. Smart, *The Assisi Problem and the Art of Giotto* (1971).

J. Wood, *Women, Art, and Spirituality* (1996).

assize The word 'assize' has several distinct meanings. During and after the reign of *Henry II it refers to a royal enactment, made with assent of the great men of the realm, which could deal with one or multiple topics. The Assize of *Clarendon (1166) is concerned with crime and new procedures for trying criminal cases. The Assize of *Northampton, in part expanding Clarendon's provisions but also dealing with non-criminal matters, was made at a council there (1176). Other assizes, such as the 1181 Assize of Arms or the 13th-century Assizes of Bread and Ale, had narrower focus.

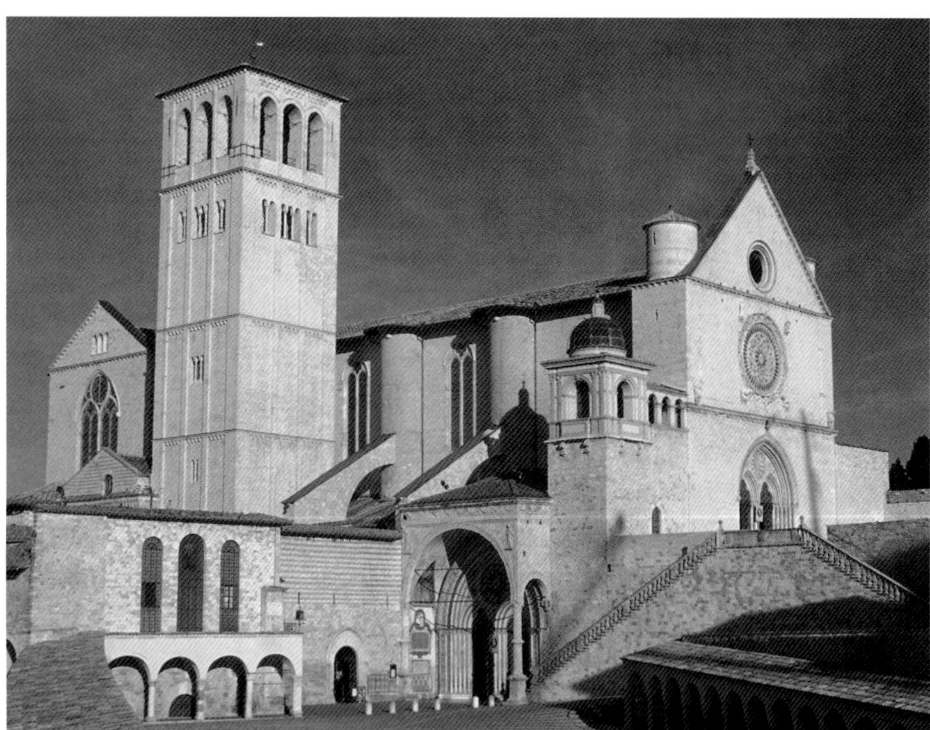

The cathedral in Assisi.

Assize also refers to a procedure for deciding specific controversies. The *Grand Assize (1179) provided a new means whereby a dispute concerning the right to land—brought to court by the writ of right—could be handled. Previously, the decision had been made by *battle; the Grand Assize gave a defendant/tenant the option to choose instead a *jurata* of twelve sworn knights who presented their conclusions on the matter in the king's court.

There were also four so-called petty assizes: Novel Disseisin, Mort d'Ancestor, Darrein Presentment, and Utrum. The first three are possessory; they did not determine ultimate right but protected a claimant against a defendant's alleged wrong. The Assize of Novel Disseisin probably dates from 1166, while provision for the Assize of Mort d'Ancestor is found in the Assize of Northampton. Both Novel Disseisin and Mort d'Ancestor determined which of two litigants should have the possession of land; a plaintiff in Mort d'Ancestor claimed to be the heir of a close ancestor who had been seised of the land when he died, and a plaintiff in Novel Disseisin claimed that he, while in seisin of the land, was wrongfully dispossessed. A plaintiff in Darrein Presentment (of uncertain date) claimed the right to name a parson to a church because he or the ancestor through whom he claimed had named the last parson in time of peace. The fourth petty assize, Utrum (1164), determined whether land was held as lay fee or in free alms (frankalmoign), important because ecclesiastical courts had jurisdiction over disputes concerning the latter. In each assize, the *sheriff assembled twelve free men called recognitors, who had knowledge of the situation and would inform the itinerant royal justices of the facts when the justices came into the county. The decision rested on the recognitors' finding; the gathered recognitors were themselves referred to as the assize. Use of the assizes eventually declined as new actions with fewer limitations came into being. The most often used, Novel Disseisin, began to be replaced in the 15th century, although it was not formally abolished (together with the other possessory assizes) until 1833.

In the 13th century, the system of *justices itinerant was further formalized. *Magna Carta *c*.12 provided that justices hearing assizes should visit each county twice a year, and later in the century the justices were allocated regular circuits. They were called justices of assize, and the periodic court sessions at which they presided were also called assizes. By statutes of 1299 and 1328, the justices were told also to try accused persons already in custody, at sessions of gaol delivery; later their jurisdiction was expanded to cover those not yet in gaol. Additionally, by the end of the 13th century the justices functioned as commissioners of *nisi prius*, hearing evidence and receiving jury verdicts in civil matters begun at Westminster and returning the verdicts there. However, all the sittings, held at the same time and place, came to be known as the assizes. The assize system endured with many modifications until 1971, when it was abolished.

In non-legal usage, the word 'assize' was also used in the later medieval and early modern centuries simply to mean 'size', particularly with reference to linear measurements, for example 'five foot of assize'. 'Assize' in that sense is found particularly in official records and in building contracts. JSL

P. Brand, 'Edward I and the Transformation of the English Judiciary', *The Making of the Common Law*, ed. idem (1992), 135–68.
F. W. Maitland, *The Forms of Action at Common Law*, ed. A. H. Chaytor and W. J. Whittaker (1909; repr. 1985).
C. A. F. Meekings, ed., Introduction to *Calendar of the General and Special Assize and General Gaol Delivery Commissions on the Dorses of the Patent Rolls: Richard II (1377–1399)* (1977).
D. W. Sutherland, *The Assize of Novel Disseisin* (1973).

Assizes of Romania Legal code enforced in the Frankish-occupied regions of the Byzantine Empire. The Assizes of Romania was a collection of 219 articles regulating feudal relations. It was introduced in 1204 after *Constantinople's capture by the Fourth Crusade, and was written down in the period 1333–46. IG

P. W. Topping, *Feudal Institutions as Revealed in the Assizes of Romania, the Law Code of Frankish Greece* (1949).

assonance *See* RHYME, LATIN.

Assumption, Feast of the *See* LITURGY.

astrolabe *See* ASTRONOMY.

astrological medicine refers to both a theoretical basis and the use of practical astrological calculation in medicine. In the Ptolemaic model of the cosmos, belief in celestial influences was all-pervasive. An extensive system of correspondences formed a coherent vision linking the celestial with the terrestrial. The planets, for example, were understood to exercise control over days of the week, hours of the day, parts of the body, *physiognomy, and healing plants. The sun and moon were especially important planets from a medical viewpoint, as the course and outcome of acute diseases could be predicted by motions of the moon, and those of chronic diseases, by the sun.

Another commonplace of medieval astrological medicine was the doctrine of the zodiac man (*homo signorum*), with man at the centre of the universe. Celestial influences from the macrocosm were reflected in the microcosm of the human body. Parts of the body were governed not only by the planets, but also—and more commonly—by signs of the *zodiac, with the head influenced by Aries and the feet by Pisces. Applications of this dominance varied, but a general rule was to forbid medical treatment to the part of the body at the time the zodiacal sign ruled. This doctrine was repeated in countless texts, both in Latin and the vernaculars, and illustrations of the so-called 'zodiac man' are ubiquitous in surviving MSS.

Arabic transmission of Greek medical learning that presumed celestial control of the body was introduced to western Europe in the 12th century. Astrological considerations were involved in *diagnosis, prognosis, and therapy and applied to concepts of the critical days of sickness and the best times to administer medicine or carry out *surgery. This knowledge initially appeared in Salerno, but wider application had to await the accessibility of accurate astronomical tables and instruments as well as the availability of texts on their use. Determining appropriate times for various actions, ascertained by 'nativities', 'interrogations', and 'elections', constituted a refined system that demanded technical knowledge and skills to calculate the most propitious moment.

Technical equipment in the form of tables and volvelles appeared increasingly in medical textbooks, calendars, and almanacs towards the end of the medieval period. Material evidence of the spread of medical applications of *astrology throughout society can be found in 15th-century portable almanacs suspended from a cord at the waist and consulted at the sickbed. In the learned medical astrology of the later MA, horoscopes were calculated for the onset of disease as well as for nativities and were used to determine critical days, as well as the duration and outcome of disease.

Astrology also merged with other aspects of medicine such as *uroscopy, and late medieval texts such as 'Urina non visa' appeared, which enabled the physician to determine uroscopic information regarding diagnosis, prognosis, or recommended therapy by astrological reckoning rather than by actual analysis of a patient's urine.

Instruction in astrology in medical faculties of *universities was controversial but took place in some Italian universities. In general, astrology was held in high esteem for its relevance to medicine, and astrological knowledge was widespread. University-trained physicians, the most prestigious of medical practitioners in the late MA, mastered the science of astrology, both its theoretical and practical implications, and many were renowned astrologers.

For less affluent people, less complicated procedures existed to determine celestial influence. For example, the days of the moon were considered relevant to illness and recovery, and medieval texts, often rhymed, which tell the significance of each day of the moon, survive.

Late medieval medical MSS reveal that astrological medicine extended from the highest levels of learning to practitioners with little or no professional training. Even laymen had access to knowledge of astrological principles. Texts on medical astrology became increasingly common in late medieval MSS. They range from lengthy, learned Latin treatises with complex tables to simple rhymes in vernacular languages for oral distribution. *See also* ARABIC MEDICINE IN THE LATIN WEST; MEDICAL ILLUSTRATION. IAJT

R. French, *Medicine Before Science: The Business of Medicine from the Middle Ages to the Enlightenment* (2003).

J. North, *Horoscopes and History* (1986).
C. Rawcliffe, *Medicine and Society in Later Medieval England* (1995).
N. Siraisi, *Medieval and Early Renaissance Medicine* (1990).
I. Taavitsainen, *Middle English Lunaries: A Study of the Genre* (1988).

astrology Astrology has been defined in many different ways, but in the MA, both in the Latin West and in Islam, most of its practitioners assumed that events on earth are determined by celestial events, although some took those to be only signs. Many feared the implications of determinism for *free will and responsibility for personal actions, insisting that the stars merely incline us to act in a certain way, but that they do not compel. The subject had its roots in early Babylonian divinatory practices, which were later blended with the remarkable mathematical *astronomy of their culture. Greek enthusiasm for the subject helps to explain why astrology became so highly valued by Rome, the Islamic nations, the Jews, and the Christian west. There were even echoes of traditions from further afield, for instance, chronological doctrines from *India and Mazdaism from *Persia. The Greeks handed on to the MA the belief that many of their astrological ideas had an origin in Egyptian hermeticism.

By the time the Greeks and Romans inherited those Near Eastern traditions of mathematized astrology, the subject had become subdivided. Some writings related the heavens at significant moments (such as the solstices or equinoxes, the time of a planetary conjunction, or the appearance of an *eclipse or comet) to the affairs of a people or nation or even to the whole world. Interrogatory astrology purported to answer questions about the future on the basis of the state of the heavens, and catarchic astrology (elections, the science of 'beginnings') claimed to be able to decide whether the time was ripe for the commencement of a given action. The best known branch of all was of course genethlialogical astrology, which related the state of the heavens at the moment of birth to an individual's character and future life-history. Medical astrology tended to combine all of these strands. Simpler doctrines associated *colours, *metals, *stones, plants, drugs, animals, weather patterns, days of the week, parts of the human body, diseases, facets of human psychology, and so forth with the planets and fixed stars. The notion of planetary or stellar divinity continued to flourish as a literary and artistic device, despite its irreligious cast.

In more formal astrology, Ptolemy's didactic treatise *Tetrabiblos* (2nd century AD, a work in four parts known in Latin as *Quadripartitum*) provided the basic structure for many subsequent compendia. Other influential classical writers included the Latin author Vettius Valens, Ptolemy's near contemporary, and the earlier Marcus Manilius, author of a didactic poem on astrology, from the first decades of the millennium. Increasingly, astrology was taught as a subject requiring astronomical expertise and indeed provided one of the strongest motivations for studying astronomy and *mathematics—without which such practices as the casting of horoscopes would have been impossible. There were other 'exact' methods used in genethlialogy, for example the complicated system of lots, namely points of the ecliptic (often therefore marked on the horoscopic figure) that were determined by the angular separation of the sun and moon or certain planets.

Islamic astrology grafted ideas from as far afield as India on Babylonian-Hellenistic astrology, but more significant was the amalgam of translations from Greek into Syriac, Arabic, and Hebrew. The result was a series of writings that were to become canonical in east and west. One very influential figure in the transmission was the Iraqi or Persian Jew *Masha'allah. The most significant Islamic writer of all was a close contemporary, *Abu Mashar, many of whose 40 treatises found their way to the west. He made popular the doctrine according to which political and religious fortunes of peoples rose and fell in phase with the so-called 'great conjunctions' of Saturn and Jupiter or Saturn and Mars. The idea was used to explain the timing of such historical events as the birth of Christ, the rise of Islam, and the rise and fall of sects generally. *Isidore of Seville, for example, could preach against 'superstitious astrology' while accepting great conjunctions and comets as prognosticators of revolution, war, and pestilence.

Under the Abbasid *caliphate in *Baghdad, astrology flourished side by side with astronomy. By the 12th century, 'scientific' astrological treatises were beginning to make their way from Near Eastern Islam into Europe via Muslim Spain. Between the 10th and 13th centuries, Jews were especially important in translating works by such as Masha'allah, Abu Mashar, and al-Qabisi from Arabic into the Romance languages of the region, from which Christian translators put them into Latin. The greatest translator of the 12th-century *Toledo group, *Gerard of Cremona, made or supervised translations of five astrological works—a small fraction, though, of the 87 translations with which he has been credited.

Under these influences astronomy and astrology began to outstrip in importance all other scientific subjects, with the possible exception of *medicine. From an astronomical point of view, the most valuable consequence of this activity was the stimulus it gave to the refinement of astronomical tables, especially the so-called 'Toledan tables' of the 11th century and later those done under the patronage of *Alfonso X of *Castile, in the 13th. Sicily was another important point of entry for astrology into the west. Thus, *Adelard of Bath travelled from *England to *France, *Italy, Sicily (where he learned Arabic), Syria, and possibly *Palestine and Spain. He translated Abu Mashar's *Lesser Introduction to Astrology* and an astrological work by *Thabit ibn Qurra, as well as astronomical tables. *Petrus Alfonsi,

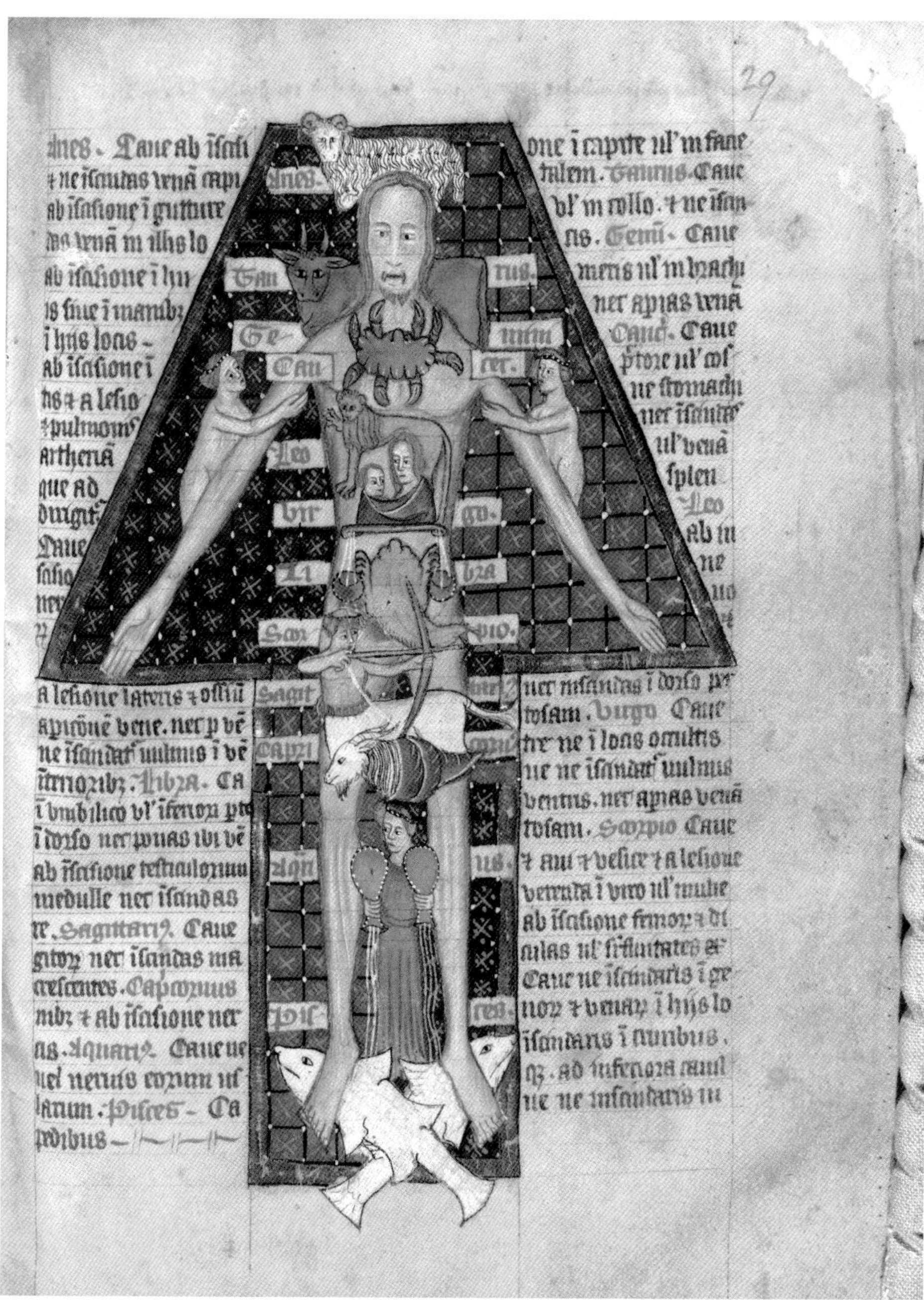

Zodiac man.

a Spanish Jew who converted to Christianity and who practised astrological methods in medicine, was like *Adelard for a time in the service of the English king *Henry I. Comparable patterns of influence can be traced in Italy, France, and *Germany, where, by the end of the 12th century, astrological *prognostication following Islamic authorities was commonplace. There was little inclination to advance or otherwise modify the science, as had been done in Islam. In both worlds it was common to keep astrology free from contamination by astral *magic and necromancy, not because these were disbelieved, but because of the attendant spiritual danger. Bishop Etienne Tempier's famous condemnations (1277) of Averroistic (Aristotelian) doctrines being currently taught in *Paris opposed the invocation of *demons, but not astrology as such. By the late MA, there were few popes and few bishops in whose entourage no scholar skilled in astrology was to be found. By the mid 12th century, astrology in various forms had become a recognized part of western intellectual life. By the 14th century, the place of astrology in the *university curriculum was

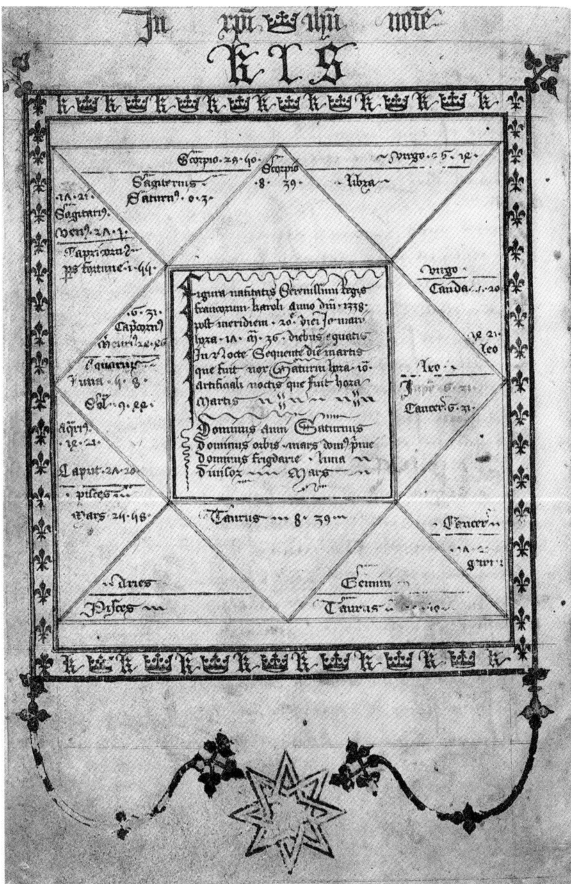

The horoscope of Charles V of France.

generally secure, making use of such texts as the commentary on John of Seville's translation of al-Qabisi (Alchabitius) by the Parisian John of Saxony (1331). After Paris, *Oxford was a leading European centre for such studies, as witnessed by John Ashenden's weighty *Summa iudicialis de accidentibus mundi* (1348).

The two greatest European poets of the 14th century, *Dante at the beginning and *Chaucer at the end, both wove much astrology into their writings, and it is a curious fact that their styles mirror those of the two poles of astrological practice, Dante writing in architectonic generalities and Chaucer silently performing precise calculations to pattern plot and imagery alike.

Very many astrologers, east and west, were connected in some way with royal courts. Birth horoscopes, the timing of a march to war or a coronation, or medical advice were all dispensed by astrologers. It became a habit in the late MA and afterwards for astrologers to collect together horoscopes of the famous. Only towards the end of the MA, and later helped by the introduction of *printing, did astrology begin to work its way down the social scale. The decline in astrology as a serious intellectual pursuit only came long after the ending of the MA. *See also* ASTROLOGICAL MEDICINE; COSMOLOGY; METEOROLOGY; PHARMACY.

JDN

Abu Mashar, *The Abbreviation of the Introduction to Astrology Together with the Medieval Latin Translation of Adelard of Bath*, ed. and tr. C. Burnett, K. Yamamoto, and M. Yano (1994).

J.-P. Boudet, *Lire dans le Ciel: La Bibliothèque de Simon de Phares, astrologue du XVe siècle* (1994).

Masha'allah, *The Astrological History*, tr. and ed. E. S. Kennedy and D. Pingree (1971).

J. D. North, *Horoscopes and History* (1986).

—— *Chaucer's Universe* (1988).

L. Thorndike, *A History of Magic and Experimental Science*, 8 vols (1923–58).

G. F. Vescovini and F. Barocelli, eds, *Filosofia, Scienza e Astrologia nel Trecento europeo: Biagio Pelacani Parmense* (1992).

astronomical tables *See* ASTRONOMY.

astronomy

astronomy Arguably the oldest of the sciences, astronomy had a long history before the dawn of the MA. By the 6th century, however, only the names and reputations of the great Greek astronomers remained in the Latin West. Any surviving astronomical knowledge was preserved in *encyclopedias and works on the *seven liberal arts. Neither the authors of these works nor the sources on which they relied had any direct experience of theoretical astronomy.

1. Astronomy in the quadrivium
2. *Computus*
3. Islam
4. Europe

1. *Astronomy in the quadrivium*

The astronomy of the quadrivium had been intended for the education of gentlemen, not of astronomers, and consequently, engaged very little in theoretical explanation of celestial motions. Just this sort of descriptive astronomy appears in *Macrobius' *Commentary on the Dream of Scipio* (end of the 4th century) and in *Martianus Capella's *Marriage of Mercury and Philology* (early 5th century), two works that attracted readers and commentators for centuries. Both works entertained their readers while educating them in basic facts of astronomy that remained unchallenged until *Copernicus. Each describes the spherical Earth stationary at the centre of a spherical cosmos, the outer sphere of which is adorned with fixed stars and turns around the Earth once a day. The seven planets share in this daily motion but also follow an eastward course against the background of a narrow band of stars called the ecliptic, each completing the circuit in different times. The ecliptic is inclined to the celestial equator, creating the equinoctial points where the two cross, and the solsticial points where they are farthest apart.

Martianus did not entirely avoid theory. He explained that the Sun takes more time to transit some equal arcs of the sky than it does others by proposing that the Earth is eccentric from the Sun's orbital centre. The fact that Mercury and Venus never stray very far from the Sun suggested that they orbit the Sun. Eleven hundred years later, Copernicus would praise Martianus for this intuition.

2. Computus

The astronomical portions of both the *Commentary* and the *Marriage* circulated independently, testifying to the topic's appeal. Yet there was little in these texts or others like them to aid in practical applications, such as finding the date of *Easter. The council of *Arles and the council of Nicaea (325) had stipulated that all Christendom should observe Easter on the same day—the Sunday following the first full moon after the vernal equinox (the paschal moon)—and that each community apply the same method to determine what that day would be. The effort to find that method involved debates between the ecclesial jurisdictions of Rome, Alexandria, and Ireland, which spawned a literature called *computus* (sometimes written as 'compotus'). One problem treated in computus was how to locate on the Julian calendar the date of the paschal moon. Authors of *computus* texts debated which arithmetical method best reconciled the incommensurable periods of lunar-solar cycles, the seven days of the week, and rates of various intercalations so as to allow the identification of Easter dates well before the paschal moon could actually be observed. The debate was resolved with the work of *Bede, who drew upon Roman and patristic authors as well as Irish *computus* texts to establish a computational method with ties to rudimentary astronomical theory.

Later *computus* texts were written by *Hrabanus Maurus, Helperic of Auxerre (late 10th century), and St *Abbo of Fleury, who also wrote *De ratione spere*, one of the few works on spherical astronomy before the rediscovery of Ptolemy.

3. Islam

Islamic scholars acquired the works of Ptolemy and Aristotle along with Persian and Indian texts in the 8th and beginning of the 9th centuries. Much as early Christians had done, Muslims debated the value of the newly acquired pagan learning. Its evident utility in the determination of time-dependent religious observances and of the *qibla*, the direction of Mecca, assured astronomy of acceptance in Islamic culture despite its close ties to *astrology. As the practice spread among *mosques of employing a timekeeper (*muwaqqit*), fewer astronomers needed to work as astrologers so that the notoriety attached to the latter for their challenge to God's exclusive knowledge of the future extended somewhat less to the former.

Medieval Arabic astrolabe used in astronomy.

The earliest tables, or *azyaj* (singular *zij*), such as those compiled by al-Fazari (d. 806) and al-*Khwarizmi, were derived from Sanskrit texts. Later tables, such as the ones produced by al-*Battani and Habash al-Hasib (*fl.* late 9th century), used new observations and Ptolemaic theory. The widely used *Toledan Tables* were compiled by al-*Zarqali, who recalculated the tables of al-Battani and al-Khwarizmi for the meridian of *Toledo. The emphasis on new observations resulted in improvements over Ptolemaic values for the obliquity of the ecliptic, the rate of precession of the equinoxes, and the discovery of the precession of the solar apogee, a motion not mentioned by Ptolemy.

Comparison of increasingly more precise observations with ancient records implied that the rate of precession was not constant. In his *De motu octave spere*, *Thabit ibn Qurra (826–901) proposed that the variable motion or trepidation was due to a long-term oscillatory motion superimposed on the uniform precessional motion of the stellar sphere. Astronomers until Tycho Brahe proposed theories to explain what was in fact an illusory departure from the uniform rate of precession.

Despite the success of Ptolemaic theory, Muslim astronomers saw it as cosmologically unsound. Ptolemy employed circles with centres displaced from the centre of the Earth, in violation of the geocentric requirement of Aristotelian *cosmology. He employed epicycles turning around a point on a rotating deferent, which violated the Aristotelian rule that a body can have only one proper motion. But Ptolemy's most egregious violation, in the eyes of medieval Aristotelians, was to tie the uniformity of a deferent's rotation to a point, called the 'equant', removed from the deferent's centre. In so doing, Ptolemy had abandoned the basic requirement that planetary motion be a compound of uniform circular motions. In one response, *Ibn Tufayl and al-*Bitruji postulated a single Earth-centred sphere for each planet and fit the mechanism for generating the planet's orbital path into the surface of its sphere.

Modification of Ptolemaic theory continued at the observatory of Meragha in the work of *Nasir al-Din al-Tusi, whose method of producing oscillatory motion from circular motion, later known as the 'Tusi couple', was adopted by many later astronomers. *Ibn al-Shatir employed it in his lunar theory, which bears a striking resemblance to that of Copernicus.

In addition to building large stationary observing instruments, Muslims also perfected the astrolabe. Described by *John Philoponus around 500, and constructed on principles of spherical projection known to Ptolemy, the astrolabe served as an observing tool and timekeeper. The standard astrolabe consists of a circular plate or *mater* bearing on one side a circular scale for measuring altitudes by means of a centrally pivoting viewer or 'alidade'. A recess on the other side accepts a disk called a *tympan that bears the projection of the celestial globe for a given latitude. Over the tympan is placed the *rete*, a map of the fixed stars and the zodiac. The *rete* can be rotated to place the stars in a portion of the sky indicated by the tympan. To use the astrolabe at a different latitude, it was only necessary to supply a tympan for that latitude. Instructions on how to build and use an astrolabe and its variants were written in Arabic from the 9th century on.

The ability of the astrolabe to represent three dimensions in two made it more portable, easier to use, and easier to manufacture than the three-dimensional arrangement of concentric rings known as the armilla or armillary sphere. Ptolemy had described the armillary sphere in the *Almagest* (5.1) and had used it as an observing tool. Although its use in that capacity declined after the improvement of the astrolabe and the invention of other instruments, it remained useful to astronomy teachers because it modelled the very circles—equator, ecliptic, horizon, and colure—that were the basic features of the medieval cosmos.

4. *Europe*

The presence of Islamic cultures in Sicily, southern *Italy, and southern Spain made possible the initial contact between the Latin West and the wealth of Arabic philosophy and science. The age of translation of Arabic works into Latin reached its peak in the 12th century, but as early as the 10th Europeans came in contact with Arabic astronomical knowledge. When Gerbert of Aurillac, the future *pope Silvester II, went to study in Spain, he may have seen and helped to circulate a treatise *De utilitate astrolabii*, one of the earliest Latin books on the subject.

By the 12th century, astronomers seeking access to Arabic learning were part of a larger effort to translate these works into Latin. The translations of *Adelard of Bath include a version of al-Khwarizmi's tables and Euclid's *Elements*. Adelard's original work *De opere astrolapus* also touches on Ptolemaic planetary theory. The *Almagest* and the *Toledan Tables* were translated from the Arabic by *Gerard of Cremona.

Along with works on astronomy, the translators of the 12th century also provided Europe with much of the Aristotelian corpus, which became the basis for the *arts faculty curriculum at European *universities from the 13th century on. But the homocentric system described in Aristotle's *De caelo* was of no use to astronomers, who instead drew upon Arabic works to compile an informal collection of teaching texts that came to be known as the *corpus astronomicum*. The most popular of the many introductory texts written in the 13th century with the title *De sphaera* was written around 1220 by *John of Sacrobosco.

Perceiving a need for new tables more firmly grounded in Ptolemaic theory than the *Toledan Tables*, *Alfonso X of *Castile assembled a group of astronomers who produced new tables in the late 13th century. In the 1320s a revised version of these Alfonsine Tables with new rules, or *canones*, was prepared by Jean de Lineres and John of Saxony. These became the authoritative tables for the remainder of the MA. The *canones* for these and other tables often circulated independently and were incorporated into the *corpus astronomicm*.

New works on the *computus* and on the *calendar continued to appear, including works by John of Sacrobosco and Robert *Grosseteste. Recommendations for calendar reform were made to *Pope Clement VI in 1345—in which year the vernal equinox arrived eight days early—and to the Council of *Constance, yet no action was taken until the establishment of the Gregorian calendar in 1582.

The tension between Ptolemaic planetary theory and Aristotelian cosmology experienced by Muslim astronomers remained a problem in the Latin West. *Henry of Langenstein may have voiced a popular belief in his *De reprobatione eccentricarum et epicyclorum* of 1304 that epicycles and eccentrics could not exist. In the absence of a physically tenable theory with equal success at predictions, the only option was to find a physical representation of Ptolemaic theory that surrendered none of its predictive ability. *Georg

Peurbach achieved this goal in 1454 in his *Theoricae novae planetarum*. Such was Ptolemy's unchallenged authority that Peurbach was then charged with producing a more easily accessible text of the *Almagest*, a project completed by *Regiomontanus and eventually printed in 1496.

Treatises on the astrolabe and other observing and calculating instruments continued to appear. *Richard of Wallingford designed several instruments, including a device equivalent in use to an armillary sphere but with straight instead of circular scales, making it easier to manufacture. Richard also designed mechanical *clocks, which were becoming the timekeepers of choice at *monasteries that could afford them, even though they required frequent correction based on old-fashioned celestial observation.

A puzzle and an irony attend the history of medieval astronomy. The puzzle is why astronomy in the west eventually made a discarded image of the Aristotelian cosmos, while astronomy in Islam did not. The irony is that this most demanding of academic disciplines could never have flourished without a sufficiently large population of competent practitioners. This population in turn could never have sustained itself without the remuneration available through the practice of astrology and *astrological medicine, the endeavours which made by far the widest use of astronomical prediction. But as the Aristotelian cosmos faded, and with it the rationale for astrology, astrologers and astronomers parted company, astrologers to the moribund realm of occult pursuits, astronomers to centuries of bold discoveries that astrologers could never have achieved. *See also* COUNCILS, ECCLESIASTICAL; SCIENCE, TRANSMISSION OF. PGSo

Bedae, *Opera de temporibus*, ed. C. W. Jones (1943).
O. Pederson, 'Astronomy', *Science in the Middle Ages*, ed. D. C. Lindberg (1978), 303–37.
G. Saliba, *A History of Arabic Astronomy* (1994).
W. H. Stahl, *Martianus Capella and the Seven Liberal Arts* (1971).

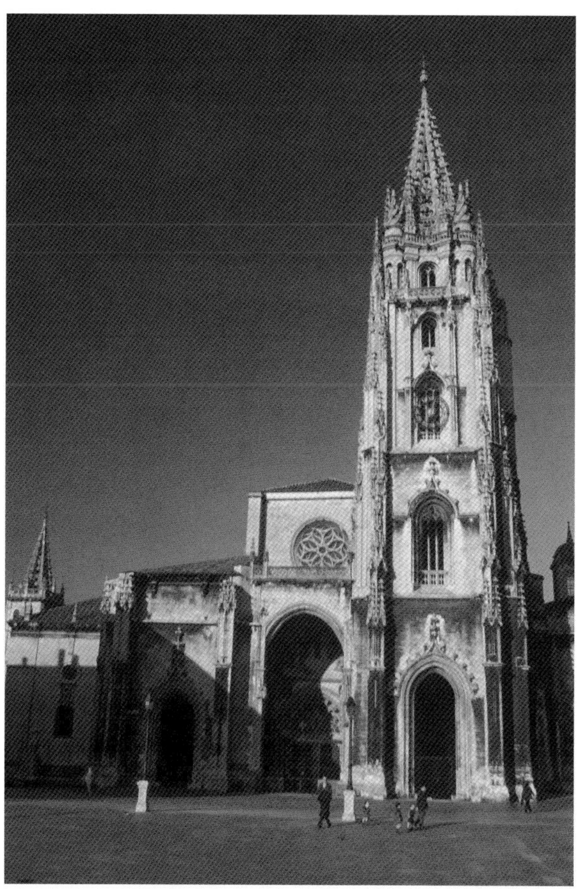

Cathedral de Oviedo in Asturias.

Asturias The Astures were one of the pre-Roman populations of Iberia who, like the Cantabrians and the Vascones or *Basques, put up a long resistance to Roman conquest. After the foundation of Astorga, however, the Asturian region experienced a more rapid penetration of Roman culture than did other northern regions. The region's *Visigothic history is barely known, but there are few signs of Asturian integration into the Gothic kingdom and an Asturian revolt is recorded under Sisebut (611/2–20).

The origins of the medieval kingdom of the Asturias are shrouded in legend. By the reign of Alfonso III (866–910), the kingdom had developed an interest in recording (or inventing) its own past, as witnessed by two major chronicles—the *Chronica Albeldense* and the *Chronicle of Alfonso III*. We are almost wholly reliant on these two sources, which seriously overstate the kingdom's early significance. In them, Asturian history begins with the victory of the nobleman Pelagius (Pelayo) over an Arab army at the battle of *Covadonga (718/22). Despite the mythic status of Pelayo and Covadonga—which grows with each medieval retelling—both are unknown to Arab sources and also to the Christian *Chronicle of 754*, written in that year under Arab rule in *Toledo.

The kingdom's real origins were rather more prosaic: the Asturias was captured in 714 in the first wave of Arab conquests, but a minor revolt *c*.720 convinced the region's new masters that the arduous and unproductive territory was simply not worth garrisoning. Although the chronicles record the history of Pelayo's successors, it is not till the reign of *Alfonso I that something like a genuine, if tiny, kingdom is discernable, sheltering behind the Asturian and Cantabrian mountains and initially centred on Cangas de Onis. Alfonso I is supposed to have withdrawn the Christian population from the *Duero valley in order to protect his kingdom from the Arabs, but this is probably a retrospective explanation of why the kingdom remained largely safe from Arab attack, despite opportunistic Asturian raids into *Galicia and the Meseta.

Another such invented tradition linked the new Asturian and the old Visigothic kingdom and is clearly attested by the reign of Alfonso II (791–842). Son of King Fruela I (757–68), Alfonso had been repeatedly passed over for the kingship in his childhood. That fact demonstrates the weakness of any hereditary principle in the Asturian monarchy, which had tangled dynastic connections with neighbouring Cantabria and Galicia, whose aristocracy was flattered by Asturian royal patronage of the emerging cult of Santiago. Alfonso II's long reign was troubled by civil war (in 801/2 he was briefly immured in a *monastery), but his decision to move his royal residence out of the mountains to Oviedo gave the Asturias its capital. His eventual successor, Ordoño I (850–66), began the real expansion of the Asturian kingdom, occupying several of the old Roman cities of the Meseta, most importantly *León and Astorga. After winning a victory over the *Basques in 859, Ordoño occupied the Basque region of Alava, a bone of future contention between *Castile-León and *Navarre.

Alfonso III (866–910), known as 'the Great', undertook the systematic incorporation of the northern Meseta and the Duero valley into his kingdom, something which was once envisaged as a literal repopulation and is now regarded as a process of political integration. He continued to build in the city of Oviedo and maintained Asturian patronage of *Santiago de Compostela, where he sponsored the construction of a church that lies beneath the extant *Romanesque cathedral. In 910, Alfonso was deposed by his own sons in obscure circumstances, though we do know that the count of *Galicia was heavily involved in the conspiracy. With the accessions of Alfonso's sons García (910–13/4) and Ordoño II (914–24), the centre of the Asturian kingdom was shifted again, from Oviedo to Zamora and then to León, which could more easily control the Asturian satellite principalities of Castille and Galicia. As a result, we normally cease to speak of a kingdom of the Asturias and begin to speak of the kingdom of León, though one is the direct successor of the other. MKu

J. Gil, J. L. Moralejo, and J. I. Ruiz de la Peña, *Crónicas asturianas* (1985).

A. B. Marroquín, *Orígines hispano-godos del reino de Asturias* (2000).

J. I. R. de la Peña, *La monarquía astur-leonesa: de Pelayo a Alfonso VI (718–1109)* (1995).

C. Sánchez-Albornoz, *Orígenes de la nación española: el Reino de Asturias*, 3 vols (1972–5).

asylum (sanctuary), **right of** Sanctuary afforded wrongdoers who fled to a church or other designated place protection from forcible removal and corporal punishment. While analogous protections were recognized in temples of the pre-Christian Mediterranean world, the medieval practice was linked with the penitential and intercessory practices of the church from the time of the late Roman Empire. In the MA, such protections extended to cemeteries, prayer *chapels, *hospitals, episcopal houses, and other edifices near or adjoining a church. Recognized and sanctioned by royal law, ecclesiastical law, and a host of local practices, sanctuary flourished in nearly all medieval legal traditions. In *England the administration of secular law incorporated sanctuary protection, and sanctuary claims were a routine feature of medieval English law. Papal restrictions and secular opposition significantly reduced the scope of sanctuary across Europe in the 16th and 17th centuries. The most recent edition of the code of canon *law omits all reference to sanctuary.

The word 'asylum' was rarely employed in medieval sources (even less in legal sources), but was reintroduced into juristic terminology by early modern civil jurists. KBS

J. C. Cox, *The Sanctuaries and Sanctuary Seekers of Medieval England* (1911).

A. Papadakis, 'Asylum', *ODB*, vol. 1, 217.

P. Timbal, *Le droit d'asile* (1939).

atelier Literally, 'workshop', a term with applications to several contexts: the physical space in which the artist/craftsman produced his work (for example, a house on the Rue Neuve Notre-Dame in *Paris); the relationship between a master craftsman (head of an 'atelier' or shop) and one or more assistants; and a work produced under a master's supervision, but not necessarily by his own hand (a *sculpture attributed to the 'atelier' of Nicola *Pisano). JHL

X. Barral i Altet, ed., *Artistes, artisans, et production artistique au Moyen Age*, 3 vols (1986–90).

Athanasian Creed *See* CREEDS: APOSTLES', ATHANASIAN, NICENE.

atomism The belief that extended magnitudes (for example, matter, time) are composed of atoms, be they minimal, extended particles (as in classical atomism) or unextended geometrical points. Swayed variously by Aristotle's strictures against the actual infinite and by geometrical arguments deriving from *Avicenna, most medieval thinkers rejected atomism. Important exceptions include the *Mutakallimun and Robert *Grosseteste. *See also* ARISTOTELIANISM; FORM AND MATTER; MATHEMATICS; MATTER THEORY; PHILOSOPHY, NATURAL. RCr

A. Pyle, *Atomism and its Critics: Problem Areas Associated with the Development of the Atomic Theory from Democritus to Newton* (1995).

atrium An internal courtyard in ancient Roman houses, the atrium denotes an open forecourt in ecclesiastical architecture, usually situated in front of the main entrance and surrounded by roofed porticoes. It serves as an area of transition and, if including a fountain or well, purification (the

Pope Leo I, 'the Great' (440–61), meeting with Attila the Hun. Painting by Raphael in the Vatican Museums.

*holy water *font is a remnant of this practice). It was especially frequent in early Christian times. SdB

J.-P. Caillet, 'Atrium, péristyle et cloître: des réalités si diverses?', *Der mittelalterliche Kreuzgang: Architektur, Funktion, und Programm* (2004), 57–65.
A. Frazer, 'Modes of European Courtyard Design before the Medieval Cloister', *Gesta*, 12 (1973), 1–12.

Attila (Etil, Etzel), ruler of the Huns (b. *c*.406; r. 434–53) Attila was first co-ruler with his brother Beda (d. *c*.445), then master of the Hunnic Empire that stretched from the western Eurasian steppe to Germany. His nomadic empire, with its centre in the *Carpathian Basin, included several Turkic and Germanic peoples. Having raided both the East Roman Balkans and the West Roman Gaul, the Huns were stopped in 451 by Aetius in the battle of Châlons (*Catalaunum*). After Attila's death, the empire fell apart and the Huns vanished from history. His memory is reflected in German and Norse sagas as well as in Hungarian chronicles. In the Germanic heroic tradition, he is portrayed either as powerful, helpful, and passive (German tradition) or as cruel and ruthless (Scandinavian tradition). *See also* DIETRICHEPIK; NIBELUNGENLIED; VǪLSUNGA SAGA; ÞIÐREKS SAGA AF BERN. JMB, CB

H. de Boor, *Das Attilabild in Geschichte, Legende und heroischer Dichtung* (1932; repr. 1963).
E. A. Thompson, *A History of Attila and the Huns* (1948; repr. 1999 as *The Huns*).
J. Williams, *Etzel der rîche* (1981).

Atto of Vercelli (d. 959×60), bishop; author of a commentary on the Pauline epistles, socio-political works (*De pressuris ecclesiasticis* and *Polypticum*), an episcopal capitulary, *sermons, and letters. RMe

J. Bauer, *Die Schrift 'De Pressuris Ecclesiasticis' des Bischofs Atto von Vercelli* (1975).
S. F. Wemple, *Atto of Vercelli: Church, State and Society in Tenth Century Italy* (1979).

Aubri (Alberic) **of Trois-Fontaines** (d. *c*.1251) Cistercian of Trois-Fontaines; author of an invaluable world chronicle (*c*.1232–41) annotated and continued by Giles of Orval and Maurice of Neufmoustier. JLB

Albrici monachi Trium Fontium Chronica, MGH.SS 23 (1874), 631–950.
M. Schmidt-Chazan, 'Aubri de Trois-Fontaines, un historien entre la France et l'Empire', *Annales de l'Est*, 36 (1984), 163–92.

Aucassin et Nicolette Unique example of *chantefable* (alternating spoken and sung narrative passages) in OFr. (*Picard, *c*.1200). A love-affair between a young French *noble and a Christian adoptee, who turns out to be daughter to the Saracen king of 'Cartage' (Cartagena), consistently foils what are presented as conventional expectations. The 'world-upside-down' Torelore episode and multiple upsetting of *gendered behaviour patterns are famous. The tone is consistently comic and often considered to be parodic, though there is much debate over the extent and mode of *parody. *See also* LANGUAGES: FRENCH; LITERATURES: FRENCH. JGi

P. Matarasso, tr., *Aucassin and Nicolette, and Other Tales* (1971).

Auch Archdiocese and capital of *Armagnac. An ecclesiastical and agricultural hub throughout the MA, the city attracted pilgrims to its *Benedictine priory of St-Orens in the

11th century, then flourished as a centre of *Cistercian agrarian expansion. LR

C. H. Berman, 'Medieval agriculture, the southern French countryside, and the early Cistercians: a study of forty-three monasteries', *TAPS* 76 (1986), 1–179.

A. Shaver-Crandell, P. Gerson, A. Stones, *The Pilgrim's Guide to Santiago de Compostela: A Gazetteer* (1995).

Audiëntie The court of appeal established in 1309 by Louis de Nevers, count of *Flanders, intending both to centralize comital power and challenge that of the county's leading cities. At first the court had a mixed financial and judicial character, overseeing the activities of comital bailiffs as well as investigating and ruling on appeals from lower courts and cases of disputed jurisdiction between smaller towns and feudal courts. Under Count Louis of Male (1346–84), however, the Audiëntie's role became exclusively judicial as its judges came to hold most of their sessions either in Male outside *Bruges or in *Ghent. JMMu

J. Buntinx, *De audientie van de graven van Vlaanderen, studie over het centraal grafelijk gerecht (c.1330–c.1409)* (1949).

Audradus Modicus (*fl.* 847–53) Frankish ecclesiastic and author. Previously at St-Martin, *Tours, Audradus became suffragan bishop of Sens (847). In 849 he presented *Pope Leo IV with a collection of his writings, including the poem *Liber de fonte vitae* and a book of apocalyptic visions concerning the *Carolingian empire. CDB

L. Traube, *'O Roma nobilis', Abhandlungen der Bayerischen Akademie der Wissenschaften* 19 (1891), 378–87.

Augsburg (city, bishopric) Attested since the 8th century on the site of Roman Augusta Vindelicorum. A document of 1156 confirms the bishop's lordship, conditioned by the citizens' community. An imperial city from 1316, later boasting prominent trading families (for example the *Fugger dynasty of merchant bankers) who promoted economic and cultural flowering. KS

W. Zorn, *Augsburg: Geschichte einer europäischen Stadt* ([4]2001).

augustalis, augustarius *See* MONEY AND COINAGE.

Augustine, Rule of Portions of certain documents attributed to St *Augustine of Hippo—Letter 211, Sermons 355 and 356, part of the rule directed to clerics or monks, the *Regula secunda*, and another entitled *De vita eremitica ad sororem liber*—were used by *Benedict, *Caesarius of Arles, and the *Codex Regularum* of *Benedict of Aniane. The 'Rule' or sections thereof were important in the development of the so-called Austin Canons, male and female, from the mid 11th century and beyond. Portions of the rules they used passed into later rules used by many congregations. RER

J. C. Dickinson, *The Origin of the Austin Canons and their Introduction into England* (1950).

R. E. Reynolds, 'An Early Rule for Canons Regular from Santa Maria de l'Estany (New York, Hispanic Society of America MS HC 380/819)', *Miscel·lània litúrgica catalana*, 10 (2001), 165–91.

Augustine, St, bishop of Hippo Regius (354–430) Born in Roman North Africa, Augustine died as the most influential mediator of Roman Christianity to the medieval and modern worlds. Young Augustine studied *grammar and *rhetoric and moved to Carthage where he began the pursuit of wisdom and worldly experience. His *Confessions* recall this period of experimentation and anxiety. In *Milan, the teacher of rhetoric encountered *Ambrose's sermons and experienced a conversion. Returning to North Africa, he was ordained priest and, soon after, bishop of Hippo (395/6).

As bishop, Augustine used his intellect, his insider's knowledge of pagan philosophy and theology, and his preaching charisma to combat belief systems that competed with the Christianity he espoused, composing many polemic works against the Manichees, the *Donatists, the *Arians, sceptics, Jews, and individuals. Fashioned in conflict and filtered through his education and experiences, his discussions of grace, *predestination, *free will, and the soul came to define Christian teaching for the west. He wrote on the arts and composed a handbook for educated Christians, the *De doctrina christiana*. His *City of God* defended Christianity against apologists for Roman *paganism and projected a vision of history situating humanity on a continuum between the cities of Man and of God.

The MA revered Augustine as a saint and accepted his writings as authoritative, though their full range, chronology, and context were imperfectly known. Medieval controversialists often enlisted Augustine on both sides of an argument. JJC

P. R. L. Brown, *Augustine of Hippo: A Biography* ([2]2000).

P. Courcelle, *Recherches sur les Confessions de S. Augustin* (1950).

E. D. English, ed., *Reading and Wisdom:* The De Doctrina Christiana *of Augustine in the Middle Ages* (1995).

R. A. Markus, *Saeculum: History and Society in the Theology of St Augustine* (1970).

J. J. O'Donnell, *Augustine: A New Biography* (2005).

Augustine of Canterbury, St (d. 604×9) First archbishop of *Canterbury. *Pope Gregory I the Great sent Augustine as Rome's first missionary to the *Anglo-Saxons in 597. King *Æthelbert of Kent welcomed Augustine and his small band of monks to Canterbury, where they established a religious centre. Æthelbert became the first AS king to convert to Christianity, and the pope designated Augustine the archbishop of England. MS

N. Brooks, *The Early History of the Church of Canterbury: Christ Church from 597–1066* (1984).

M. A. Green, *Saint Augustine of Canterbury* (1997).

H. Mayr-Harting, *The Coming of Christianity to Anglo-Saxon England* (1991).

Augustine of Ireland (Augustinus Hibernicus) (7th century) Irish author of *De mirabilibus sacrae scripture* (654/5), a rationalistic explanation for miracles in the Bible inspired by St *Augustine of Hippo, once thought to have been its author. AYH

De mirabilibus sacrae scripture, *PL* 35: 2149–200.

D. Bracken, 'Rationalism and the Bible in Seventh-Century Ireland', *Chronicon*, 2 (1998), 1–37.

Augustinian canons *See* RELIGIOUS ORDERS.

Augustinian friars *See* FRIARS; RELIGIOUS ORDERS.

Augustinianism St *Augustine of Hippo was indisputably the greatest authority after the Bible in the history of Christian thought in the western MA. Indeed, his influence was omnipresent in all areas of life. In psychology, Augustine bequeathed his own definition of the soul to the MA as the mainspring of intellectual and sensory knowledge. In spirituality, the inner self represented the ultimate possibility for perfection in the MA. Moreover, in noetics, as God is the source of intellectual knowledge, all knowledge is essentially dispensed in the form of illumination. Augustine also gave direction and meaning to history, which originated with Adam. After the original sin, humanity was a *massa perditionis* from which God saved some chosen people by his grace alone. The history of the world consisted of a sequence of six ages that began with the Fall and ended with final redemption.

Although following the Pelagian controversy Augustine's thought was universally lauded, it was never adopted in totality. First of all, his writings are extensive, prolific, and subtle and cannot be easily broken down. Furthermore, throughout the MA it was learned and understood in different ways. Augustine's work was mainly copied in the 9th and again in the 12th centuries before vernacular copying and *translation made him better known during the later centuries of the MA. Many *anthologies, among which the earliest and the best known was Eugippius' (*c*.455–*c*.535), aided in Augustine's thought being widely read.

An example of Augustinian mixed influence is the concept of 'political Augustinianism'. Augustine accepted that obedience was due to pagan emperors. But as the centuries passed, the idea that temporal power should be placed at the service of the church and be integrated within it gained supporters as well as critics.

The most important medieval thinkers were directly or indirectly influenced by Augustine's thought. Indeed, there were almost as many 'Augustinianisms' as there were readers of his works. Men as different as *Boethius and *John Scottus Eriugena integrated key Augustinian ideas into their own views. In the 12th century, despite his indisputable originality, *Anselm of Canterbury notably continued in the Augustinian tradition by considering faith as the very condition of knowledge. *Hugh of St-Victor was considered to be an *alter Augustinus* and restated many Augustinian ideas, such as God's union with the individual soul or the ideal of knowledge ending in wisdom. *Peter Lombard demonstrated Augustine's prestige in 12th-century schools by inserting more than a thousand of his quotations into **The Four Books of Sentences*, a theological textbook into the 16th century. These quotations would maintain Augustine's thought in the medieval mentality.

Theologians traditionally considered to be Augustinian include *Franciscans such as *Alexander of Hales, *Bonaventure, *John Peckham, and John *Duns Scotus, but also *Dominicans known to be Aristotelians such as *Thomas Aquinas. Similarly, the existence of an Augustinian school among the order of *canons cannot be underestimated. *Giles of Rome and *James of Viterbo are not easily classified, despite an indisputably Augustinian influence on their writings. This influence can also be found in works by Thomas *Bradwardine and Gregory of Rimini, who are generally looked on as 'neo-Augustinians'. In the 15th century, Augustine continued to nourish academic debates as well as new intellectual points of view. Jean *Gerson, Lorenzo *Valla, Marsilio *Ficino, and Pietro *Pomponazzi drew their inspiration on several accounts from Augustine. *See also* INVESTITURE CONTROVERSY; PAPAL STATES. CGi

H.-X. Arquillière, *L'augustinisme politique: essai sur la formation des théories politiques du Moyen Âge* (1934; repr. 1972).

P. Delhaye, 'Notes sur l'Augustinisme médiéval', *Mélanges de science religieuse*, 19 (1962), 100–109.

M. D. Jordan, 'Augustinianism', *The Routledge Encyclopedia of Philosophy*, ed. E. Craig (1998), 559–65.

H.-I. Marrou, *Saint Augustin et l'augustinisme* (1955; repr. 2003).

G. B. Matthews, ed., *The Augustinian Tradition* (1999).

M. Nicoletti, 'Augustinisme politique 2', *Saint Augustin, la Méditerranée et l'Europe IVe–XXIe siècle*, ed. A. D. Fitzgerald and M.-A. Vannier (English original, 1999) (2005), 114–19.

M. W. F. Stone, 'Augustine and Medieval Philosophy', *The Cambridge Companion to Augustine*, ed. E. Stump and N. Kretzmann (2001), 253–66.

Augustinian order Beginning in the 11th century a number of important *religious orders throughout western Europe, including the Augustinian canons, *Dominicans, Augustinian Hermits or Friars, Servites, Ursulines, Bridgettines, and Visitandines, adopted the rule of life traditionally known as the 'Rule of *Augustine'. Three major texts, long associated with St *Augustine of Hippo, together constitute the Rule that bears the bishop's name, namely: (1) the *Ordo monasterii*, which provides general regulations for *liturgy and life in a *monastery; (2) the *Praeceptum* or 'Rule', also for a male religious community; (3a) the *Obiurgatio*, in which Augustine reprimands disputing nuns (*Epistula* 211, sections 1–4); and (3b) the *Regularis informatio*, also known as the 'Rule for Nuns' (*Epistula* 211, sections 5–16). While many questions remain regarding these texts, their authorship, and their interrelationships, the work of Verheijen has shed considerable light on the textual, literary, and historical complexities of Augustine's Rule.

Although reformers in the *Carolingian period sought to re-establish the communal life of secular *clergy under a bishop that had been practised by Augustine but had since fallen out of favour, they did so not by having recourse to Augustine's Rule but rather by producing new ones such as the *Regula Canonicorum* of *Chrodegang of Metz and the *Institutio Canonicorum* of *Amalar of Metz. While these 8th-century *regulae* enjoyed wide use throughout Europe into the 11th century, *Gregorian reformers and their supporters found them lax and lacking in certain ways (for example, in allowing *canons private residences and personal property). New Gregorian collections of canon *law such as those of Anselm of Lucca (*Pope Alexander II), Deusdedit, and *Ivo of Chartres demonstrate how extensively the works of Augustine were being studied particularly among canons. In the late 11th and early 12th centuries these canons discovered and adopted Augustine's Rule for common life, which they understood as serving to correct the deficiencies of the Carolingian rules. Communities of canons living according to the Augustinian Rule quickly became known as 'canons regular' (*canonici regulares*) or Augustinian canons. The two most influential congregations of Augustinian canons were the Victorines, founded by *William of Champeaux in 1108 and established at the house of *St-Victor in *Paris, and the *Premonstratensians, founded by St *Norbert of Xanten at *Prémontré in 1120.

In the 13th century, several new mendicant orders including the Dominicans, Augustinian Hermits, and Servites also adopted the Rule of St Augustine after the Fourth Lateran *Council (1215) decreed that newly founded communities should take their rule and institutes from an already existing and approved religious order (Canon 13). In the 16th and 17th centuries the Augustinian Rule was adopted by the Ursuline and Visitation nuns, respectively. *See also* FRIARS; HERMITS; MONASTICISM; MONASTIC RULES AND CUSTOMARIES. FTH

J. Châtillon, *Le mouvement canonial au moyen âge: réforme de l'église, spiritualité et culture*, ed. P. Sicard (1992).

J. C. Dickinson, *The Origins of the Austin Canons and their Introduction into England* (1950).

L. Verheijen, *La Règle de saint Augustin*, 2 vols (1967).

Augustinus ('Triumphus') **of Ancona** (d. 1328) Italian *Augustinian; taught in *Padua and *Paris. In his *Summa de potestate ecclesiastica* Augustinus defended the absolute supremacy of papal power over both the temporal power and the council of the cardinals. He commented on several books of the Bible and on Aristotle. MTo

B. Ministeri, *De vita et operibus Augustini de Ancona* (1953).

Aulici Nobles of the royal court in 13th–14th-century (and later) *Hungary. *Iuvenes* (regardless of age) and *milites aulae regiae* performed various services for the king and were often promoted to aristocratic positions. They came to be increasingly distinct from the 'country nobility' and may be seen as representatives of a (limited) courtly culture in Hungary. JMB

Á. Kurcz, *Lovagi kultúra Magyarországon a 13.–14. században* (1988).

M. Rady, *Nobility, Land and Service in Medieval Hungary* (2000).

Aurelian of Réôme (*fl.* mid 9th century) Frankish clergyman and music theorist. His *Musica disciplina* provides the earliest theoretical descriptions of liturgical musical practice in the *Carolingian era and teaches the proper use of the eight church modes. REG

Aurelian of Réôme, *'Musica disciplina': A Revised Text, Translation, and Commentary*, tr. J. P. Ponte (1961).

aureole Variously shaped frame representing the light which envelops or radiates from a sacred figure. When the aureole encircles the head it is called a nimbus or *halo, and when the body a mandorla. JBo

A. N. Didron, *Christian Iconography*, tr. E. J. Millington (French original, 1851) ([2]1968), vol. 1, 107–65.

B. Fletcher, *A History of Architecture on the Comparative Method* ([13]1967), 1258.

Aureoli (Aureolus, Auriol)**, Petrus** (Peter) (*c.*1280–1322) French *Franciscan theologian and author of, among other things, an influential and extensive *commentary on *Peter Lombard's *Sentences*. He defended the *Immaculate Conception of the Virgin Mary and introduced theories on *predestination, divine foreknowledge, and the apparent existence (*esse apparens*) and human intellectual cognition of 'singulars'. *See also* NOMINALISM; WILLIAM OF OCKHAM; UNIVERSALS. VSy

C. Schabel, *Theology at Paris, 1316–1345* (2000).

K. H. Tachau, *Vision and Certitude in the Age of Ockham* (1988).

Aurillac (abbey) Established 894 by Count Géraud in the Haute-Auvergne, the well-endowed abbey enshrined its founder's *relics in an early *pilgrimage plan church and golden reliquary-bust. St-Géraud's prestige came also from its school, *scriptorium, and famous student, Gerbert (*Pope Silvester II), whose study of Arabic MSS enriched western science and *philosophy. LR

M. Durliat and P. Lebouteaux, 'L'Église Saint-Géraud d'Aurillac', *BAr* 8 (1975), 23–49.

P. Riché, *Gerbert d'Aurillac: Le pape de l'an mil* (1987).

Austrasia Eastern kingdom of the Rhineland ('Ripuarian') Franks, in what today is northeastern France, western Germany, Belgium, and Luxembourg. In the early 6th century the Merovingian king *Clovis I incorporated the Rhineland

Franks into his expanding kingdom, and thereafter Austrasia (the 'eastern realm') remained one of the three main kingdoms (alongside Neustria and *Burgundy) divided among Clovis's descendants. Austrasia was distinctive from Neustria and Burgundy in a number of ways: it was less Romanized, its Frankish inhabitants had their own law code (the *Lex Ripuaria*), and, while the Franks of Neustria were becoming Latin / Romance speakers, the Austrasian Franks remained predominantly Frankish (Germanic) speakers. Under the Merovingians the Franks of Austrasia usually demanded their own independent king, and during the 6th and 7th centuries the Austrasian and Neustrian nobles were often embroiled in bloody conflicts with each other. Austrasia had a number of important Roman and episcopal cities, including *Metz, *Trier, *Cologne, and *Mainz. It was from Austrasia that the Franks conquered and colonized eastward across the *Rhine into Main-Franconia, Alemannia, Thuringia, Bavaria, and eventually Saxony. The *Carolingian family that overthrew the Merovingian dynasty in 751 hailed from Austrasia, and it was in Austrasia that *Charlemagne built his new imperial capital of *Aachen. Austrasia gradually lost its geopolitical significance in the Carolingian empire, being replaced by the new realms of *Lotharingia and East Francia in the 9th and 10th centuries. EJG

E. James, *The Franks* (1988).
I. Wood, *The Merovingian Kingdoms, 450–751* (1994).

Austria *See* GERMANY.

authentic mode *See* MODES, MELODIC.

authors and authority Modern notions of professional writing were not present in the medieval mind. *Bonaventure typified the medieval view in describing the author (*auctor*) as one who writes one's own words along with those of others, while in so doing placing one's own words at the heart of the work's textual endeavour. Despite this understated consideration, it was generally held that the *auctor* drew his or her authority ultimately from God, and that the *auctor*'s works clearly respected and built upon received religious texts; these were not simply texts to be read for purely informative, or informal, purposes. When vernacular literature began to spread, it was not initially held to be authoritative but as serving to transmit stories or knowledge. It is with later medieval vernacular poets in particular, such as *Dante (for Italy) and *Chaucer (for England), where there emerges a more modern understanding of the authorial self, as ones who speak in readily identifiable and comparatively subjective voices. These same authors were able to advance socially and even politically through their acquired reputation as writers, and this fame further aided their works in being considered as authoritative literary models. GPF

J. A. Burrow, *Medieval Writers and their Work* ([2]2008).
A. J. Minnis, *Medieval Theory of Authorship: Scholastic Literary Attitudes in the Later Middle Ages* ([2]1988).
N. Watson, *Richard Rolle and the Invention of Authority* (1991).

autobiography of Charles IV of Luxembourg *See* CHARLES IV AUTOBIOGRAPHY.

auto da fé Portuguese term for the ritual of public *penance for condemned heretics conducted by the Spanish *Inquisition (Spanish, *auto de fé* 'test of faith'). The *auto da fé* evolved from a simple rite to a showy, expensive public spectacle in the mid 16th century. The ritual included a solemn public procession of the condemned, a *Mass, and the reading of sentences, which could include fines, banishment, imprisonment, flogging, the galleys, and the wearing of a *sanbenito* or penitential garment. Those condemned to death were normally led outside the city and burnt at a second ceremony following the principal one. Those who had fled or died were burnt in effigy. Nonetheless, artistic depictions focus on scenes of torture and burning. The first *auto da fé* took place in *Seville in 1481; others were also carried out in regions under Spanish rule including Portugal, *Italy, Brazil, Mexico, Peru, and Goa, *India. MMH

H. Kamen, *The Spanish Inquisition: A Historical Revision* (1997).
H. C. Lea, *A History of the Inquisition in Spain*, 4 vols (1906–7).
C. Maqueda Abreu, *El Auto de fé* (1992).
E. Peters, *Inquisition* (1988).

autopsy *See* DISSECTION AND AUTOPSY.

Autpert, Ambrose (d. 784) Born in *Provence, he became a monk at San Vincenzo on the Volturno near Benevento. His election as abbot in 777 led to internal disputes and he was forced to flee. His writings include a mystical *commentary on the Apocalypse, drawn on for the **Glossa ordinaria*. TNB

A. Autpert, *Opera*, ed. R. Weber, *CCCM* 27, 27A, 27B (1975).
C. Leonardi, 'Spiritualità di Ambrogio Autperto', *SMed* 9 (1968), 1–131.

Autun Founded by Augustus (hence Augustodunum), this fortified centre of Burgundian trade, church history, and rhetoric still has Roman remains. Its outstanding architectural monument is the 12th-century *Romanesque cathedral of St-Lazare, famous for the sculptural programme of *Gislebertus (*c.*1130). The Last Judgement *tympanum above the west door bears his signature—*Gislebertus hoc fecit* ('Gislebertus made this')—beneath the feet of Christ. Autun's Musée Rolin houses Gallo-Roman pieces, among

'Burning of the Heretics' (*auto da fé*) by Pedro Berruguete, *c.*1500. Prado Museum, Madrid.

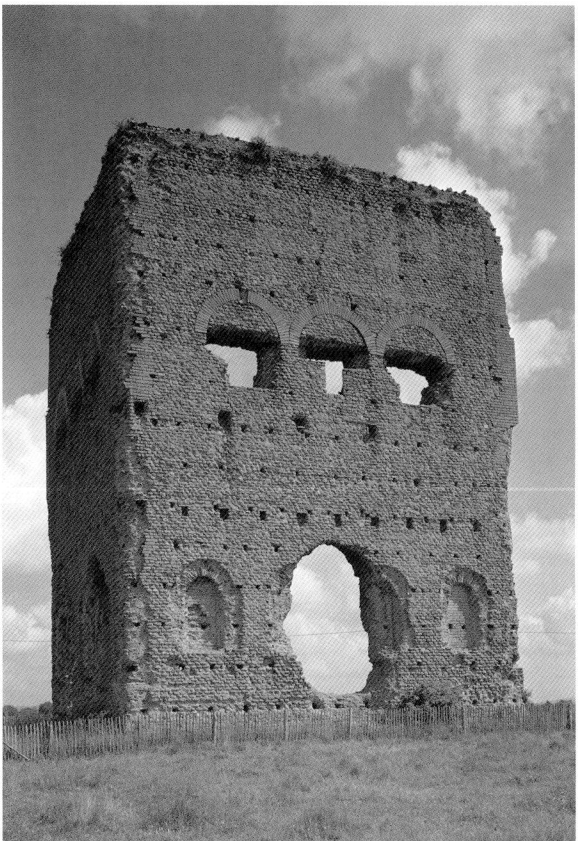

Janus temple in Autun.

them a representation of Eve, the first female nude of European medieval sculpture. RJC

D. Grivot, *Autun* (1967).
—— and G. Zarnecki, *Gislebertus: Sculptor of Autun* (1961).
R. Oursel, *Bourgogne romane* (⁷1979).

Auvergne Thinly settled territories in the uplands of the Massif Central with significant trade and pilgrimage traffic; county with ties to *Aquitaine beginning in the 8th century. Bishops of *Clermont played an important role, and the rich intellectual life and leading position of Christian institutions led to many well-known and influential men being trained in or originating from the Auvergne, such as Gerbert of Aurillac (*Pope Silvester II), *Peter the Venerable, *William of Auvergne, and *Durandus of St-Pourçain. *Philip II Augustus gained a foothold in the territory in the early 13th century. Much of the Auvergne became an apanage for *Louis IX's brother Alphonse (d. 1271). While divided amongst the county of Auvergne, royal holdings around Riom and Issoire, various local families, the counts of Forez, and the bishops of Clermont, Auvergne remained of interest to neighbouring lords as well as to the crown. It became a duchy with peerage status in 1360 when granted to John II's son John. The duchy was passed to the dukes of *Bourbon in the early 15th century. JFP

G. Bernage, A. Courtillé, and M. Mégemont, *La basse Auvergne médiévale: En hommage à Guillaume Revel et Gabriel Fournier* (2002).
G. Fournier, *Le peuplement rural en basse Auvergne durant le haut moyen âge* (1962).
C. Lauranson-Rosaz, *L'Auvergne et ses marges (Velay, Géraudan) du VIII*[e] *au XI*[e] *siècles: La fin du monde antique?* (1987).

Auxerre City on the Yonne river, *c.*195 km southeast of *Paris. It had become a bishopric by the mid 4th century and the seat of an important county by the 9th century. A *monastery dedicated to an ancient bishop, St *Germanus, flourished from the 9th century through the 12th, supporting a popular pilgrimage shrine for Germanus' *relics and a famous school, whose masters included *Haimo, *Heiric, and *Remigius. TFH

D. Iogna-Prat *et al.*, eds, *L'école carolingienne d'Auxerre* (1991).
T. Noble and T. Head, eds, *Soldiers of Christ* (1995).
Y. Sassier, *Recherches sur le pouvoir comtal en Auxerrois* (1980).

Auxilius (*fl.* 891–912) Neapolitan priest. After Pope Formosus (891–6) was posthumously condemned and all his acts and measures annulled, Auxilius wrote treatises, including *De ordinationibus a papa Formoso factis* and *Infensor et Defensor*, defending the validity of orders Formosus had conferred. HB

M. Bacchiega, *Papa Formoso: processo al cadavere* (1983).
E. Dümmler, *Auxilius und Vulgarius* (1866).
C. Gnocchi, 'Ausilio e Vulgario: L'eco della "questione formosiana" in area napoletana', *MEFRM* 107 (1995), 65–75.

Ava, Frau (d. 1127) The first female German writer known by name, Ava composed several works of religious literature, totaling around 2200 lines, which form a coherent whole as a song of praise for Christ and his redemption of mankind. MPie

J. A. Rushing, Jr, ed. and tr., *Ava's Old Testament Narratives: 'When the Old Law Passed Away'* (2003).

Avanzo, Jacopo (or Avanzi) (*fl.* 1363–84) Bolognese painter who signed a *panel of the *Crucifixion* (Rome, Colonna Gallery). The same powerful volumes, vigorous movements, and expressive characterization of the figures reappear in a *fresco of the *Massacre of the Idolaters* from the church at Mezzaratta (now Bologna, Pinacoteca Nazionale). FB

D. Benati, *Jacopo Avanzi nel rinnovamento della pittura padana del secondo Trecento* (1992).
G. L. Mellini, *Altichiero e Jacopo Avanzi* (1965).

Ave maris stella Anonymous office hymn in honour of the Virgin Mary, probably composed in the Carolingian period. In the 12th century the melody inspired the *sequence 'O Maria stella maris' and the *troubadour song 'Reis glorios'. The text was widely cited and commented upon. SB

AHMA 51 (1908), 140.
M. Fassler, *Gothic Song* (1993), 324–6.
H. Lausberg, *Der Hymnus 'Ave maris stella'* (1976).

Avencebrol *See* SOLOMON BEN JUDAH IBN GABIROL.

Ave regina caelorum *See* ANTIPHONS, MARIAN.

Averroës (Abu al-Walid Muhammad ibn Rushd) (1126–98) Andalusian philosopher, physician, and lawyer. Born in *Córdoba to a family of jurists, he was trained in Islamic law and also received instruction in *medicine, *mathematics, and *philosophy. Averroës was introduced to the *Almohad court in 1163 and was a court physician for the remainder of his life, except for a brief period of exile a few years before his death. Averroës was known also as 'the Commentator' owing to his extensive commentaries on the works of Aristotle and on Plato's *Republic*, which circulated widely in medieval academic environments. In addition to these massive works, Averroës also produced an original work of medicine, *Kitab al-Kulliyyat* ('Book of Generalities'), which became known as the *Colliget* and was often coupled with another work known as the *Liber Teisir* (*Kitab at-Taisir*, 'Book of Particularities') authored by his friend ibn Zuhr (in Latin, Avenzoar). His writings on Islamic law were also very extensive. The term 'Averroism' may be used to refer to various medieval and Renaissance interpretations of the philosopher's thought; this term can also be applied to other philosophical trends that emerged from the diffusion of his

Portrait of Averroës. Detail from *Triumph of St Thomas Aquinas*, *c.*1365.

commentaries, but did not necessarily reflect the original meaning of the philosopher's writings. Latin Averroism was particularly popular in the MA and the Renaissance at the universities of *Paris and *Bologna. The key tenets of Latin Averroism usually included the assertion that the world is eternal; the possibility that a problem may have multiple solutions, one religious and one logical or rational; the absence of a concept of providence; the uniqueness and immortality of the 'receptive intellect' for all men; and the mortality of the individual soul. From a Catholic religious perspective these theses were extremely controversial and were condemned in 1270 and again in 1277 by the archbishop of Paris, Etienne Tempier. This measure was part of Tempier's larger effort to eliminate secular and independent research regarding the origin of the world, thereby reducing the innovative appeal of philosophy as a discipline. Some historians argue that the effect of these prohibitions was exactly the reverse, and that they in fact promoted a clearer rationalist movement in *scholasticism, in which one could see the origins of modern secular and scientific thought. Among those targeted by Tempier's prohibitions were intellectuals such as *Siger of *Brabant, *Peter of Abano, Egidio Colonna, and *Thomas Aquinas. AMM

L. Bianchi, *Il vescovo e i filosofi: la condanna parigina del 1277 e l'evoluzione dell'aristotelismo scolastico* (1990).

Z. Kuksewicz, 'The Latin Averroism of the Late Thirteenth Century', *Averroismus im Mittelalter und in der Renaissance*, ed. F. Niewöhner and L. Sturlese (1994), 101–13.

A. de Libera and M. Hayoun, *Averroès et l'averroïsme* (1991).

—— 'Der lateinische Averroismus im Mittelalter und in der Früh-Renaissance', *Philosophy and Learning: Universities in the Middle Ages*, ed. M. Hoenen, J. Schneider, and G. Wieland (1995), 371–86.

J. M. Thijssen, '1277 Revisited: A New Interpretation of the Doctrinal Investigations of Thomas Aquinas and Giles of Rome', *Vivarium*, 35 (1997), 72–101.

Avesnes family Noble family of *Hainaut. Civil war erupted in *Flanders between the children of Countess *Margaret by her successive marriages to **Burchard of Avesnes** and **Guillaume of Dampierre**. *Louis IX of France arbitrated a compromise (1246) giving Flanders to the Dampierres and Hainaut to the Avesnes, but neither party accepted the verdict, and war lasted until 1257. **John of Avesnes** married **Aleid**, sister of Count William II of Holland, who as Emperor enfeoffed him with imperial Flanders. In 1299 Holland, Hainaut, and Zeeland were united under John of Avesnes, and the family ruled there until 1345. Arbitration in 1323 gave imperial Flanders to the Dampierres. DN

C. Duvivier, *Les influences françaises et germaniques en Belgique au XIIIe siècle: la querelle des Avesnes et des Dampierre jusqu'à la mort de Jean d'Avesnes (1257)* (1894).

Ave verum corpus Short eucharistic hymn by an anonymous composer of the 14th century. It could be sung after the preface or during the consecration at *Mass, or during the ceremony of Benediction. RER

Avicenna (Ibn Sina) (980–1037) Served under several Islamic princes in Bukhara, Gurganj, Rayy, Hamadan, Isfahan, as a philosopher, physician, vizier, and music theorist. He is said to have written more than 450 works, about half of which have survived. He re-cast Peripatetic *philosophy in several forms, of which the most famous, within and outside the Islamic world, was that of the *Shifa* ('The Cure') which, in four 'collections' (*jumal*), dealt with *logic, natural science, *mathematics, and metaphysics. His musical interests follow al-*Farabi: modes, genera, the Greater Perfect System, rhythm, principles of composition, and organology. As the representative of the philosopher, whose doctrines were suspect in the light of Islamic revelation, he was criticized by al-*Ghazali, but defended by *Averroës. Aside from 'western philosophy', in which the different views of authorities are compared, he developed an 'eastern philosophy' which gave only the 'true view' on each subject. Avicenna's systematic philosophy was an inspiration for the subsequent 'philosophy of Illumination' that dominated Iranian philosophy, but a more abiding influence was that of his logic, which replaced Aristotle's *Organon* as the basic teaching material throughout the Islamic world. Several parts of the *Shifa* were translated into Latin in the 12th and 13th centuries, including the sections on the soul, on animals, and on metaphysics. Avicenna was often quoted by scholastic philosophers as an alternative authority to Aristotle, and his theories of the five 'internal senses', the nature of vision, and the natural explanation of prophecy were influential. He is equally important, however, as a medical writer. His *Canon on Medicine*, in five parts, dealing respectively with general principles, simple medicines, illness (from head to toe), illnesses affecting the whole body, and compound medicines, was sufficient in itself as a *vade mecum* for doctors and, in its Latin translation made in the late 12th century by *Gerard of Cremona, became the basic textbook for the study of medicine in the west. It attracted numerous commentaries and was printed several times in the Renaissance. In the Islamic world after his death Avicenna was known as 'al-Shaikh al-Rais' ('the outstanding master'), which was interpreted by Gerard of Cremona as meaning 'elderly king' (*senex rex*), and led to an iconographical and literary tradition in which he was an actual king. CBu, JLY

D. Gutas, *Avicenna and the Aristotelian Tradition: Introduction to Reading Avicenna's Philosophical Works* (1988).

N. Siraisi, *Avicenna in Renaissance Italy: The Canon and Medical Teaching in Italian Universities after 1500* (1987).

O. Wright, 'Ibn Sina,' *NGD2* (2001), vol. 12, 46.

View of Avignon.

Avignon Situated on the banks of the Rhône in southern *France near its confluence with the Durance, in post-Roman times Avignon became part of the kingdom of *Arles and then the county of *Provence. When Provence was divided between the houses of *Toulouse and *Barcelona in 1125, Avignon, which lay near the frontier, was ruled jointly by both. In 1226 Louis VIII of France laid siege to the city because it sided with Raymond VI of Toulouse during the Albigensian Crusades, and it consequently lost its walls and many privileges. Although part of the Comtat Venaissin, which became a papal territory after the crusades, Avignon remained a possession of the counts of Provence.

In 1309 *Pope Clement V settled in Avignon because civil strife had made *Rome unsafe for him, and Avignon was on more neutral ground than could be found in France. In 1348 *Pope Clement VI purchased the city from Joanna of *Naples. Under papal patronage Avignon expanded into an important centre for late medieval art, learning, and culture as well as religious reform. The *papacy continued to reside in Avignon until 1378, and two *antipopes lived there from 1378 to 1418. After the resolution of the *schism, a papal legation was established in Avignon to govern the city in the pope's name. Avignon remained under papal sovereignty until the French Revolution. EFJ

S. Gagnière, *Histoire d'Avignon* (1979).
G. Mollat, *The Popes at Avignon, 1305–1378*, tr. Janet Love (1963).

Avignonese papacy *See* BABYLONIAN CAPTIVITY.

Avis, house of Founded along with the Avis dynasty by King João I of Portugal (1357–1433), Master of the Order of Avis and the illegitimate son of King *Pedro, when he seized the throne from his niece, Beatriz, daughter of his half-brother King Fernando (r. 1367–83). João's victory over the Castilians led by Juan I at the battle of *Aljubarrota in August 1385 cemented his claim to the Portuguese throne. Two years later, King João married Philippa, daughter of *John of Gaunt, duke of Lancaster. Much of Portugal's history in the 15th century revolves around the legitimate and illegitimate children of João I and their heirs. Duarte, the oldest legitimate son, succeeded to the throne in 1433. Pedro, the second oldest, served as regent during the minority of Alfonso V (r. 1438–81) and died at the battle of Alfarrobeira in 1449. Henry, the so-called 'Navigator' and Master of the Order of Christ, played an important role in Portugal's North African campaigns and later was involved in the exploration of the Atlantic islands and west Africa. João was Master of Santiago and Constable of Portugal. Fernando was Master of Avis and died as a hostage in North Africa in 1443. João's daughter Isabel married Philip, duke of *Burgundy, in 1429 and was the mother of Charles the Bold. João's illegitimate son, Afonso, became duke of *Braganza in 1442. Afonso and his two sons played important roles in the struggle between the powerful landed aristocracy and those who worked to promote greater centralization and royal power. The Avis dynasty's greatest claim to fame was that it presided over four decades of major overseas expansion during the reigns of two of João I's great-grandsons: João II (r. 1481–95) and Manuel I (r. 1495–1521). The Avis dynasty came to an end in 1580. FAD

A. H. de Oliveira Marques, *History of Portugal*, vol. 1 (1972).
P. E. Russell, *Prince Henry 'the Navigator': A Life* (2000).

aviticitas Entail in medieval *Hungary. The inalienable status of noble property, based on a tribal tradition that the

descensus estate should descend to brothers, collateral relatives, and kinsmen. It was extended to donations by King St *Stephen, and though King Andrew II's 1222 *Golden Bull introduced free alienation, was re-established by King *Louis the Great in 1351. APBá

A. Murarik, *Az ősiség alapintézményének eredete* (1938).

Avitus of Vienne *See* BIBLE EPIC.

Avranches Avranches is situated on a hill overlooking the Bay of Mont-St-Michel. Taken by the Franks in the early 6th century, it became a bishopric soon thereafter. Soon after the creation of the duchy of *Normandy, Avranches became a county seat. In 1203 agents of King *Philip II Augustus of *France took the town by force. Avranches changed hands often during the second half of the *Hundred Years War and in the subsequent conflict between the king of France and Charles the Bold. It was definitively restored to the French crown in 1468. EFJ

E. Pigeon, *Le diocèse d'Avranches* (repr. 1981).

Ayyubid dynasty Founded by *Saladin ibn Ayyub, ruler of *Egypt, Syria-Palestine, most of Mesopotamia, and Yemen. Saladin, a Kurd, succeeded his father as the governor of Takrit (Iraq), and in this capacity earned the gratitude of Nur ad-Din Zangi and acted as his chief commander in driving out the Turks. He was later detached to Egypt to assist in overpowering the Ismaili Fatimids. After years of struggle, he managed to take Egypt, but Shawar, the designated governor, died a few weeks thereafter, and as head of the troops Saladin was his natural successor. Egypt returned to being a Sunni province after two centuries. When Zangi died, Syria disintegrated and northern Syria was annexed to Egypt. Although Zangi's successors abolished the idea of fighting, Saladin used it to strengthen his position and by 1183 he became master of Egypt, Syria, and part of Hijaz. Stability was not achieved, and he then turned to the crusader states. He successfully drove the Franks out of *Palestine and Syria. Relying on his army inherited from Zangi and developed by himself, he had more than a hundred commanders in 1187 when he won the decisive battle of *Hattin. The Latins did manage to recover a major part of the Syro-Palestinan coast (thougn not *Jerusalem) before a treaty halted hostilities. Saladin died in 1193, and under his successors, al-Malik al-Adil and al-Malik al-Kamil, family rivalries for power ensued, as well as a clash with the *Seljuks. The Ayyubids could no longer depend on the *Almohads as allies; they thus pursued diplomacy and ceded most of the Frankish coastal towns. However, by the time of the Fifth Crusade, the Ayyubids were rivals in power with the Khwarizmians and ceded Jerusalem to the Christians on the condition of guaranteeing freedom of religion to all. The dynasty ended when al-Salih, al-Malik al-Kamil's son, could not face the Franks who had allied with al-Salih Ismail and Nasir Dawud of Karak. The Turkish army of al-Salih ushered in the Mamluk regime of Egypt in 1249. MD

W. C. Schultz, 'Ayyubids', *MedIsl* vol. 1, 84.

Azhar, al- (mosque, university) This imposing structure was erected by the Fatimid Muizz li-Din Allah in *Cairo in 970 to promote Shiite learning. Its reputation recovered under the Mamluks. It assumed central significance since *Egypt was prosperous, and was enlarged by the Ottomans. MD

A. Nanji, 'Azhar', *MedIsl* vol. 1, 84–5.

Azo (d. after 1229) Law professor at *Bologna for thirty years, ranked as the most influential law teacher of his time. Authoritative medieval commentaries on civil and canon law invariably treat his opinions with great respect. Azo's principal work was a *Summa* on Justinian's *Code* and *Institutes*. JABr

H. Lange, *Römisches Recht im Mittelalter* (1997).
J. A. C. Smith, *Medieval Law Teachers and Writers, Civilian and Canonist* (1975).

Azores The Azores archipelago is located in the central Atlantic and consists of nine islands. While Europeans, and particularly the Portuguese, may have been vaguely aware of its existence since the mid 14th century, its islands were explored and claimed for Portugal only between 1427 and 1451. Members of the royal family, particularly Prince *Henry the Navigator and his brother Prince Pedro, took an active interest in stimulating settlement and economic development, tasks handed over to their retainers and agents, both Portuguese and foreign (particularly from *Flanders and *England). While the population remained small in the 15th century, the islands quickly developed an export economy that included wheat, woad, and *urzela* (*Roccella tinctoria*). The Azores played an important role in the Portuguese overseas expansion and the Moroccan wars, both as a way station and a supplier of grain. IE

F. F. R. Fernández-Armesto, 'Medieval Atlantic Exploration: The Evidence of Maps', *Renaissance and Modern Studies*, 30 (1986), 12–34; repr. in *Portugal, the Pathfinder*, ed. G. D. Winius (1995), 41–70.
J. Marinho dos Santos, *Os Açores nos sécs. XV e XVI*, 2 vols (1989).
A. Vieira, *O comércio inter-insular nos sèculos XV e XVI. Madeira, Açores, e Canárias* (1987).
—— *Portugal y las isles del Atlántico* (1992).

azulejo *See* MOSAICS.

Minarets of al-Azhar mosque and university.

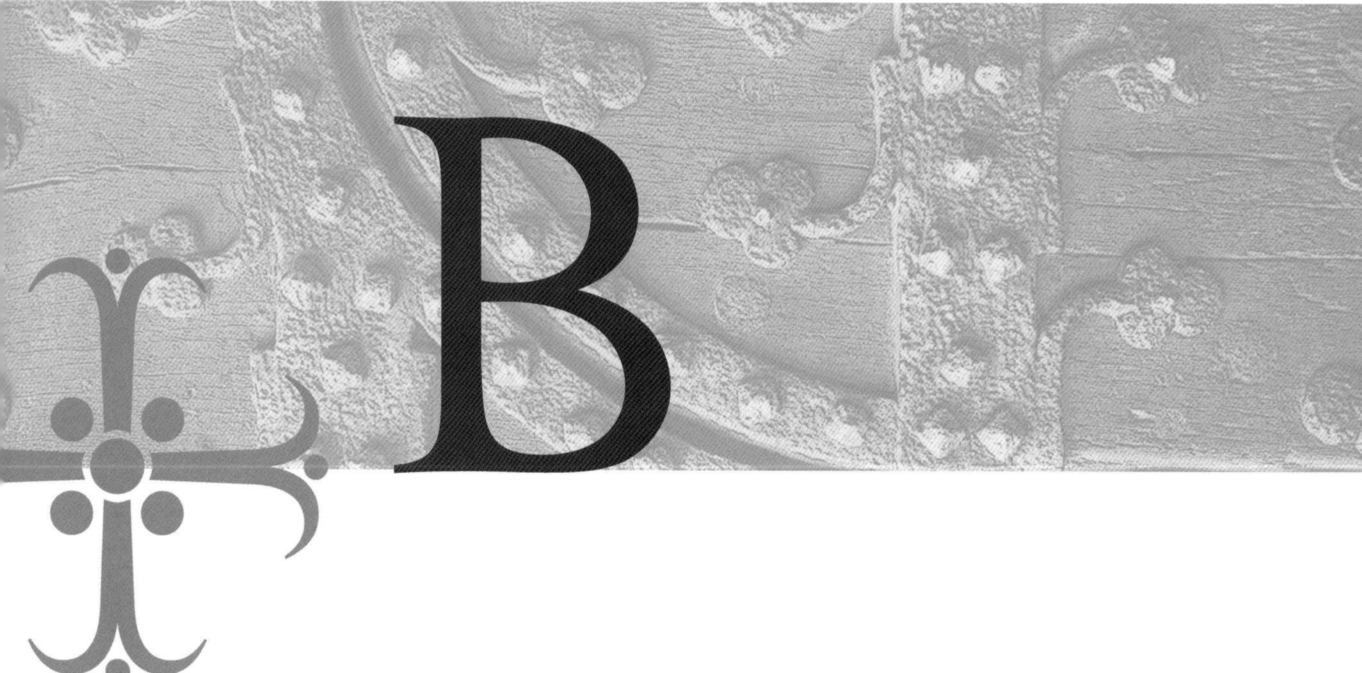

Babylonian captivity Babylon was synonymous in Christian tradition with immorality, and so the deportation of Judah to Babylon by Nebuchadnezzar in 597 and 586 BC, scene of the books of Daniel and Jeremiah, became for *Petrarch a metaphor for the residence of the *papal court in *Avignon. That sojourn began with the *election of *Pope John XXII in 1316, and ended either with the return of Gregory XI to Italy in 1376 or with the deposition of Benedict XIII of Avignon in 1417. *See also* ANTIPOPE; CONSTANCE, COUNCIL OF; SCHISM, GREAT WESTERN. DHW

P. Piur, ed., *Petrarcas Buch ohne Namen und die päpstliche Kurie* (1925).
B. Tuchman, 'The Papal Schism', in *A Distant Mirror* (1978).

baccalarius (*baccalaureus*, **bachelor**) In medieval *universities the bachelor (a term of vernacular origin) was a student in the second phase of his studies who had passed the examination of the baccalaureate, conducted a number of disputations, and obtained the right to teach. He taught courses of a different character to those of the *Master of Arts, treating the basic texts on a more superficial level (*cursorie*). He also assisted with the ordinary lectures of the master and participated in the magisterial disputations. *See also* ARTS, FACULTY OF THE. OW

M. Teeuwen, *The Vocabulary of Intellectual Life in the Middle Ages* (2003).
O. Weijers, *Terminologie des universités au XIIIe siècle* (1987).

Bacon, Roger (*c*.1214/20–*c*.1292) English scholar, educated at the *universities of *Oxford and *Paris, subsequently a *Franciscan *friar. By the end of the 16th century, Bacon had acquired a reputation as magician and sorcerer; by the end of the 19th century, he was widely judged a precursor of modern experimental science. Neither reputation is supported by the historical record. Bacon's genuine contribution was as a transitional figure in European intellectual history—one of the first Europeans to master and defend the whole (nearly) of the classical scientific tradition, newly available in Latin *translation.

An early lecturer on *Aristotle at the University of Paris, in mid career Bacon encountered the newer traditions of mathematical and *'experimental' science belonging to the classical tradition—a revelation and a turning point in his scholarly career. Bacon threw himself into the study of these portions of the classical tradition, producing a series of treatises designed to explain and defend their contents. Three of them (*Opus maius*, *Opus minus*, and *Opus tertium*), written in the 1260s at the request of *Pope Clement IV, contained a passionate appeal to the leaders of Christendom not to condemn this new learning, but to encourage its mastery and use. Bacon's argument, borrowed largely from *Augustine of Hippo, extolled the virtues of the classical tradition—especially *mathematics and 'experimental science' —and the benefits it offered Christendom, of which (he assured his readers) it would serve, if suitably disciplined, as faithful handmaiden.

The scientific discipline that Bacon most fully mastered was *optics or *perspectiva*, to which his *Opus maius*, *De multiplicatione specierum*, and *De speculis comburentibus* devoted more than 100,000 words. In these writings, Bacon synthesized the contents of the various ancient Greek and medieval Islamic optical traditions as developed over the preceding 1500 years, adjudicating differences, crafting compromises, and filling lacunae—thereby instructing his successors and shaping the science of optics for the next 350 years.

Bacon's reputation as a founder of modern experimental science is largely undeserved. He was a promoter of what he called 'scientia experimentalis', but this denoted a broad range of experiences, including reports of the experiences of others, the experience of divine illumination, and a body of lore allegedly gained by experiential means. Bacon did submit his theories to empirical tests and perform some experiments, but he was not original in so doing. DCL

R. Bacon, *Opus maius*, ed. J. H. Bridges, 3 vols (1900).
S. C. Easton, *Roger Bacon and his Search for a Universal Science* (1952).
J. M. G. Hackett, ed., *Roger Bacon and the Sciences: Commemorative Essays* (1997).
—— and T. S. Maloney, 'A Roger Bacon Bibliography (1957–85)', *NSchol*, 61 (1987), 184–207.
D. C. Lindberg, *Roger Bacon's Philosophy of Nature* (1983).
—— 'Science as Handmaiden: Roger Bacon and the Patristic Tradition', *Isis*, 78 (1987), 518–36.
—— *Roger Bacon and the Origin of Perspectiva in the Middle Ages* (1996).
A. G. Little, ed., *Roger Bacon Essays* (1914).
A. G. Molland, 'Roger Bacon and the Hermetic Tradition in Medieval Science', *Vivarium*, 31 (1993), 140–60.

Baden *Castle, dynasty of princes, and territory on the upper *Rhine (Baden-Württemberg, Germany). The castle of Baden-Baden is located on the western foothills of the *Black Forest on the banks of the Oos river, in the region of Karlsruhe. It was founded by Hermann II, son of Margrave Hermann of *Verona. As descendants of Duke Berthold of Carinthia the margraves benefited, like the *Zähringer, from the breakup of *Swabia, and they proved very successful in increasing the area of their holdings. The cities founded by the princes of Baden include Stuttgart (*c.*1220) and Karlsruhe (1715). Along with *Habsburg, *Wittelsbach, and *Württemberg, Baden ranked among the four leading principalities in southern Germany. The territory was fragmented between 1190 and 1503, dominated by the lines of Baden, Baden-Hachberg, and Baden-Sausenberg, later reunited by Bernard I (1364–1431) and Christoph I (1453–1527), and fragmented again in 1535, dominated by the lines of Baden-Baden (Protestant) and Baden-Durlach (Roman Catholic). AZ

'Baden', *LMA* vol. 1 (1980), 1337–8.
H. Schwarzmaier, 'Baden', in *Handbuch der baden-württembergischen Geschichte*, vol. 2 (1995), 164–246.

badge, Jewish Concern to segregate Christendom's Jewish minority intensified over the MA. The most demeaning technique was to require distinguishing external garb to identify Jews as 'different'. Such a demand was first made at the Fourth Lateran *Council (1215). The form varied, including coloured fabric patches worn on outer garments and specially shaped hats. While institution of this practice was slow, over time it became a feature of Jewish existence in Christian lands. *See also* ANTI-SEMITISM; JEWISH CLOTHING AND DISTINCTIVE DRESS. RC

R. Mellinkoff, *Outcasts* (1993).

Badius, Jodocus (d. 1535) Josse Bade was one of the most prolific printers in *Paris. Between 1503 and 1535 he published over 780 editions that reflected a broad cross-section of intellectual currents of the time, ranging from editions of classical authors, medieval *auctores*, and scholastic theology, *mysticism, and Christian devotional works. An avid grammarian, he published editions of *Alexander of Villa Dei's *Doctrinale* as well as humanist grammars, and wrote grammatical *commentaries on over 50 texts. *See also* GRAMMAR, LATIN; PRINTING AND PRINTED BOOK PRODUCTION. MLCr

P. Renouard, *Bibliographie des ouvrages édités, commentés ou imprimés par Josse Bade Ascensius, imprimeur et humaniste*, 3 vols (1908; repr. 1953).

Badon, Mount (Mons Badonicus, Mons Badonis) Yet to be identified securely as the site of a notable battle between Britons and Saxons *c.*500, it is said to have halted the advance of *Saxons into Romano-British territory. The Latin term *mons* ('hill') has suggested a hill fort. Associated with King Arthur in medieval tradition, Badon is first mentioned in *Gildas's *De excidio Britanniae* where it is only inferentially associated with the British war leader, Ambrosius Aurelianus. The early-9th-century *Historia Brittonum* treats Badon as the last of twelve battles fought by 'Arthur'. *See also* LITERATURES: ARTHURIAN LEGEND. SGw

B. Colgrave and R. A. B. Mynors, eds, *Bede's Ecclesiastical History of the English People* (1969).
E. Faral, ed., *La Légende Arthurienne* (1969), vol. 3 ('Historia Brittonum').
Gildas: The Ruin of Britain and Other Works, ed. M. Winterbottom (1978).

Baena, Juan Alfonso de (*c.*1375–*c.*1434) Court scribe, poet, and compiler of the eponymous *cancionero* (*c.*1430), whose roughly 500 poems are, for the most part, the unique testimony of the emergence of Castilian *court poetry. Baena's role as arbiter of taste is evident in his prefatory defence of poetry and critical rubrics. *See also* LITERATURES: CASTILIAN. JW

Cancionero de Juan Alfonso de Baena, ed. B. Dutton and J. González Cuenca (1993).

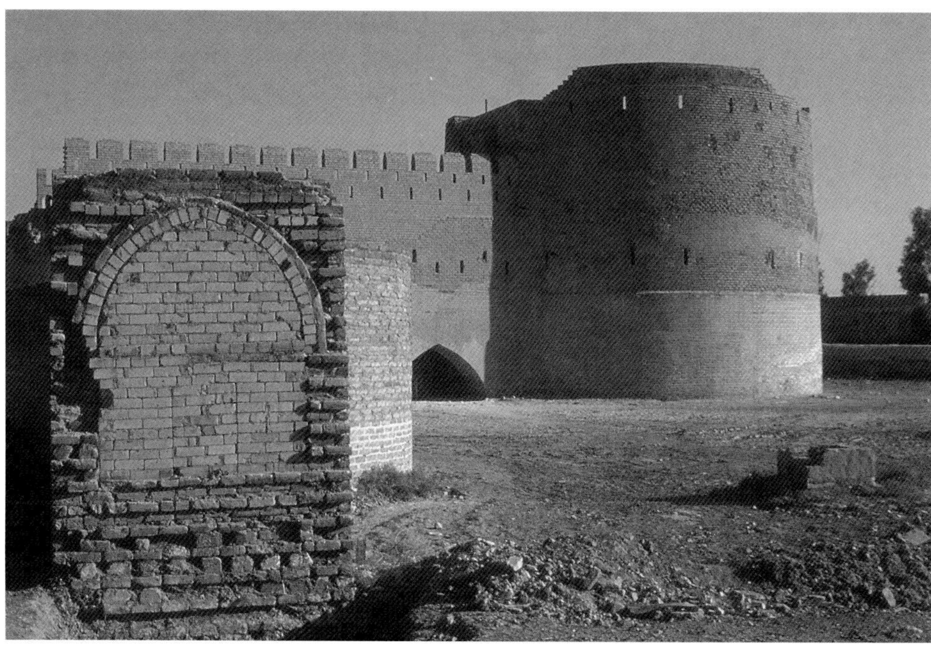

Bab el-Wastani, one of the town gates of Baghdad dating from the 11th century and rebuilt during the 13th century; remains of the town wall which was built around the Abbasid town 100 years before the Mongol attack; today a museum.

C. F. Fraker, *Studies on the 'Cancionero de Baena'* (1966).
J. Weiss, *The Poet's Art: Literary Theory in Castile, c.1400–60* (1990), 25–54.

Baerze, Jacques de (*c.*1384–99) Netherlands sculptor best remembered for the two carved altarpieces commissioned by Philip the Bold (duke of *Burgundy) in 1390. These were installed in the *Charterhouse of *Champmol in 1399 and were decorated by the painter Melchior Broederlam. Both works (now at *Dijon, Musée des Beaux-Arts) exhibit dense groupings of elegantly characterized figures set within richly embellished fields. FB

D. H. Hinkey, 'The Dijon Altarpiece by Melchior Broederlam and Jacques de Baerze: A Study of its Iconographic Integrity', Ph.D. thesis (UCLA, 1976).
C. Minott, 'The Meaning of the Baerze-Broederlam Altarpiece', in *A Tribute to Robert A. Koch: Studies in the Northern Renaissance* (1994), 131–46.

Baghdad Capital city founded in 762 by the Abbasid caliph al-*Mansur on the Tigris in southern Iraq; political, economic, and cultural centre of the Islamic world for several centuries thereafter. Iraq's agricultural wealth, *trade, and provincial taxes supported countless *translations of texts from Greek, Syriac, Persian, and Sanskrit into Arabic, as well as a boom in publishing and intellectual activity following the adoption of rag *paper technology from China. Baghdad's importance plummeted in 1258, when the Mongol Hulagu captured the city, executed the caliph, and established a new capital in Tabriz. *See also* CALIPHATE, ABBASID. DJSt

J. Lassner, *The Topography of Baghdad in the Early Middle Ages* (1970).

Baglar The opposition to King Sverrir Sigurðarson (1177–1202) in the Viken area established a 'flock' or political faction (ON *flokkr*) in 1196 called the *Baglar* ('croziers'). The leader of the group was Bishop Nikulás Árnason of *Oslo. Because of the conflicts between Sverrir and the church, the *Baglar* subsequently gained support from Archbishop Eiríkr Ívarsson (1189–1205). The reconciliation of Sverrir's son, King Hákon Sverrisson (1202–4), with the church created a new political atmosphere in the country, as the church from then on acted as a mediator between the flocks.

After Hákon's death, the battle between *Baglar* and **Birkibeinar* continued to 1208, and then, as a consequence of church intervention, a peace treaty was made at Kvitingsøy between the factions and the country divided between them. The Birkibeinar got control over northern and western Norway, while the eastern area came under the control of the *Baglar*. In 1217 the kings of both groups died, and *Hákon Hákonarson, King Sverrir Sigurðarson's grandson, became king, with support from leading magnates from both parties. JVS

K. Helle, *Norge blir en stat, 1130–1319* (1974).
—— *et al.*, eds, *The Cambridge History of Scandinavia*, vol. 1 (2003).

bagpipe *See* MUSICAL INSTRUMENTS.

bailiff (*bailli, bayle*) In England 'bailiff' applied generally to royal officials and, specifically, to royal representatives in the *'hundred' or to town administrators. On manorial *estates 'bailiffs' were superintendents. In France *bailli(e)* was originally a fiscal division; later, *bailli* referred to the king's local judicial and administrative representative. *See also* ADMINISTRATION, ROYAL. APK

J. Fesler, 'French Field Administration: The Beginnings', *Comparative Studies in Society and History*, 5 (1962), 76–111.

T. F. T. Plucknett, *The Medieval Bailiff* (1954).

bailiff (*baljuw*) **in the Low Countries** In *Flanders, *Philip of Alsace introduced the bailiff as chief officer in the 1170s. Salaried and without fixed term, he was a more reliable officer than the *castellan, from whom he took over most military and police functions and cases involving blood justice. He presided over *alderman courts in cities and castellanies, and was also collector of several comital revenues. The bailiff's income came from profits of justice; as wages were low, many were seduced into misconduct. In the 15th century the office was often farmed out. WP

D. Nicholas, *Medieval Flanders* (1992), 87–92, 237–42, 341–5.

baking *See* BREAD AND BAKING.

Balaton, Lake Located in western *Hungary; the largest freshwater lake in east central Europe. Its name comes from the Slavic *blatin'* ('muddy'). Before the late 19th century, the lake was surrounded by extensive wetlands. Once comprising a single, open water surface with the lake in the MA, western-northwestern bays developed into wetlands in the early modern period. Some of the extensively utilized islands of the same area shrank due to the late medieval–early modern rise of the water level.

Well-populated early medieval centres, such as Keszthely, the fortification of Fenékpuszta (Valcum), and Zalavár (*Mosapurg), located around the western shorelines, show a gradual transition towards the time of the late-9th-century Hungarian conquest. Newly founded *monasteries of the 11th century (for example, Tihany) received extensive landed properties by the lake, retaining them until the Turkish occupation of the mid 16th century. The high and late medieval Balaton area is characterized by a dense network of small and medium-sized settlements where *fishery and *wine production predominated, while the main continental route from *Buda towards the Adriatic Sea also led along the lake's shorelines. AKi

K. Bakay *et al.*, *Veszprém megye régészeti topográfiája: A keszthelyi és tapolcai járás* (1966).

J. Holub, *Zala megye középkori vízrajza* (1963).

K. Sági, 'A Balaton vízállás-tendenciái a történeti és kartográfiai adatok tükrében', *Veszprém Megyei Múzeumi Közlemények*, 7 (1968), 441–68.

B. M. Szőke, 'A korai középkor hagyatéka a Dunántúlon', *Ars Hungarica*, 2 (1999), 257–319.

Zs. Visy, *Hungarian Archaeology at the Turn of the Millennium* (2003).

baldachin (baldachinium, baldachinum) Originally a cloth ('baldacco', *silk from *Baghdad) canopy above a ritually important object, portable in a procession or fixed. It had an architectural counterpart in an *aedicula*, cupola, or tower over an *altar, shrine, throne, doorway, or statue, for example. A free-standing baldachin supported by columns over an altar is called a ciborium. *See also* EUCHARISTIC VENERATION AND VESSELS. SdB

A. Reinle, *Die Zeichensprache der Architektur* (1976), 337–44.

Baldr In Scandinavian mythology, the son of *Odin, killed by his brother Hǫðr, according to some texts, at *Loki's instigation, who will return after *Ragnarok. Baldr was long understood as a type of the Middle Eastern dying god, but the context of his story seems to be martial, and, taken as a whole, it involves not just Baldr's death and its permanence but also Odin's efforts to achieve vengeance. JLi

J. Lindow, *Norse Mythology: An Annotated Bibliography* (1988).

—— *Murder and Vengeance among the Gods: Baldr in Scandinavian Mythology* (1997).

—— *Norse Mythology: A Guide to the Gods, Heroes, Rituals, and Beliefs* (2001).

baldric *See* CLOTHING AND COSTUME.

Baldus de Ubaldis *See* BALDUS OF PERUGIA.

Baldus of Perugia (Baldus de Ubaldis) (1327–1400) The most influential jurist of the later 14th century. A native of *Perugia, he studied there under Federicus Petruccius and *Bartolo of Sassoferrato. He was awarded the doctorate in both types of *law (canon and civil or Roman) in 1347 and was appointed to a chair in Perugia, where, apart from sojourns at *Pisa, *Florence, and *Padua, he taught until 1390. Among his pupils were Francesco *Zabarella and Gregory XI. A prolific author, Baldus commented on the **Corpus iuris civilis*, the decretals or **Corpus iuris canonici*, the **Libri feudorum*, and the *Speculum judiciale* of Guillelmus *Durantis. He wrote numerous monographs on both laws and, as a consultant, produced over 2,500 **consilia*. Baldus was active in Perugian diplomacy, and intervened in the Great *Schism in support of Roman obedience. In 1390 Giangaleazzo *Visconti retained him as an adviser and professor at *Pavia, where he remained until his death. LDA

J. Canning, *The Political Thought of Baldus de Ubaldis* (1987).

V. Colli, 'Il cod. 351 della Biblioteca Capitolare "Feliniana" di Lucca: editori quattrocenteschi e "Libri consiliorum" di Baldo degli Ubaldi (1327–1400)', *Scritti di storia del diritto offerti dagli allievi a Domenico Maffei* (1991), 255–82.

K. Pennington, 'Baldus de Ubaldis', *Rivista internazionale di diritto commune*, 8 (1997), 35–61.

Baldwin I of Boulogne *See* JERUSALEM, KINGS OF.

Baldwin II of Le Bourcq *See* JERUSALEM, KINGS OF.

Baldwin III *See* JERUSALEM, KINGS OF.

Baldwin IV *See* JERUSALEM, KINGS OF.

Baldwin V *See* JERUSALEM, KINGS OF.

Baldwin family Counts of *Flanders. **Baldwin I** (r. *c.*863–79) held the *pagus Flandrensis* (the *Bruges district) and domains near *Ghent from *Charles II 'the Bald', after Baldwin's elopement with Charles's daughter Judith. **Baldwin II** (r. 879–918) defended Flanders against the *Scandinavians. He built *castle fortifications that served as centres of domain *administration and *militia. The term *Flandrae*, as distinct from *pagus Flandrensis*, was used for the count's entire territory in his time.

Baldwin III (d. 962) shared the rule with his father, *Arnulf 'the Great', as count of Flanders, but predeceased him. **Baldwin IV** (r. 988–1035) began the *castellany organization in Flanders and extended his administration into the newly conquered south. He had himself recognized as chief advocate of all churches in Flanders. After the 990s, Baldwin's relations with the French crown were peaceful. He campaigned east of the Scheldt, leading Henry II to invade Flanders in 1020.

Baldwin V (r. 1035–67) consolidated his predecessors' gains. In 1028 he married Adela, daughter of King Robert II of *Orléans ('the Pious'). His father's preoccupation with the eastern frontier had eased relations with the *Normans, and Baldwin V's daughter, *Matilda of Flanders, married *William I of England (or 'the Bastard' of Normandy). He continued to foster the churches. His main foreign policy problem was with Henry III in 'imperial Flanders' east of the Scheldt. **Baldwin VI** (1067–70) of Flanders (Baldwin I of *Hainaut) had married Richilde, widow of Count Herman of Hainaut, in 1051 in an agreement excluding Herman's two sons from the succession. After Baldwin's son **Arnulf III** was killed in 1071, rule in Hainaut reverted to Richilde and her son.

The brief reign of **Baldwin VII** (r. 1111–19), son of Count *Robert II 'the Jerusalemite' and Clementia of *Burgundy, was marred by civil war with his mother when he refused to return her marriage portion, and saw the rise to power at the Flemish court of *Charles 'the Good', son of *Robert I the Frisian's daughter by Cnut of Denmark.

Baldwin VIII (1191–4) (Baldwin V of Hainaut) succeeded his brother-in-law *Philip of Alsace as count. His short reign was spent consolidating his position against the nobles and against his predecessor's widow, Matilda. The succession of 1191 lost *Artois as the *dowry of Isabella, Baldwin VIII's daughter and queen of *Philip II Augustus of France. Baldwin VIII sided with the English as a way to counter the growing French threat to Flanders. He lost Flanders when his wife died in 1194; and when he died the next year, Flanders and Hainaut were reunited in the person of Baldwin IX, their son.

Baldwin IX (r. 1194–1206) 'of Constantinople', also Baldwin VI of Hainaut, had to pay relief and render homage to the French crown for Flanders, but in 1197 he resumed his father's alliance with England. The war ended temporarily in 1200 in the Treaty of Péronne, which returned some territory to Flanders, but not most of Artois. Baldwin IX went on *crusade and in 1204 was crowned emperor at *Constantinople, but was captured and killed by the Bulgarians. DN

J. W. Baldwin, *The Government of Philip Augustus: Foundations of French Royal Power in the Middle Ages* (1996).
F. L. Ganshof, *La Flandre sous les premiers comtes* (1943).
T. de Hemptinne, 'Vlaanderen en Henegouwen onder de erfgenamen van de Boudewijns, 1070–1244', *AGN* vol. 2 (1981), 372–98.
D. Nicholas, *Medieval Flanders* (1992).

Baldwin of Canterbury (*c.*1125–90) Archbishop of *Canterbury from 1185 until his death at *Acre during the Third *Crusade. Wrote *sermons and treatises on faith and the *Eucharist that continued to be influential well into the 15th century. WMH

C. Holdsworth, 'Baldwin of Forde, Cistercian and Archbishop of Canterbury', *Annual Report* [Friends of Lambeth Palace Library] (1989), 13–31.
C. Tyerman, *England and the Crusades, 1095–1588* (1988).

Baldwin of Luxembourg, archbishop-elector of Trier (1307–54) An influential prelate and statesman, brother of (Holy) *Roman emperor Henry VII and great-uncle of Emperor Charles IV. He helped to *elect both (with an intervening period of support, ultimately withdrawn,

Baldwin of Luxembourg: the seven electors. Miniature from Codex Balduineus, first half of the 14th century.

Cannon built in 1449 in Belgium and located at Edinburgh castle.

for Emperor Louis of *Bavaria). *See also* ROMAN EMPIRE [HOHENSTAUFEN DYNASTY]. MBo

G. Barraclough, *The Origins of Modern Germany* ([2]1962).
J. Mötsch and F. J. Heyen, eds, *Balduin von Luxemburg, Erzbischof von Trier, Kurfürst des Reiches, 1285–1354* (1985).

Ball, John (d. 1381) One of the leaders of the *Peasants' Rebellion of July 1381. A renegade priest and radical itinerant preacher for at least twenty years before the revolt, Ball was *excommunicated and repeatedly imprisoned for his seditious *sermons promoting social equality. He is credited with being the author of several letters in which he skilfully defends the uprising and shows cognizance of late medieval complaint literature and William *Langland's *Piers Plowman*. RJU

R. F. Green, 'John Ball's Letters: Literary History and Historical Literature', in *Chaucer's England: Literature in Historical Context*, ed. B. Hanawalt (1992), 176–200.
S. Justice, *Writing and Rebellion: England in 1381* (1994).

ballade Late medieval French poetic form. Ballades normally comprised three stanzas ending in a refrain, often followed by a half-stanza or *envoi*. Within these parameters, versification varied greatly. Primarily amorous, content diversified increasingly after the late 14th century. *See also* FORMES FIXES; LITERATURES: FRENCH. AA

D. Poirion, *Le Poète et le prince: l'évolution du lyrisme courtois de Guillaume de Machaut à Charles d'Orléans* (1965), 361–97.

ballata *See* LAUDA; POLYPHONY: 1300–1400; SONGS, POLYPHONIC.

Balliol family In 1292, *Edward I of England named **John Balliol** king of Scotland. Balliol, nicknamed 'Toom Tabard' ('empty coat'), ruled as Edward's puppet until 1296, when he opposed the invading English. Defeated, he abdicated and was imprisoned. John's son Edward supported the English in the 1330s in a vain attempt to gain the Scottish throne. *See also* SCOTLAND, IRELAND, WALES: SCOTLAND AND WALES 1064–1536. AMBr

C. McNamee, *The Wars of the Bruces* (1997).
R. Scott, *Robert the Bruce: King of Scots* (1996).

ballistics, cannon, and gunnery By the beginning of the 14th century Europeans had developed tube-shaped weapons, made in bronze or wrought iron, which used *gunpowder to discharge missiles from them, bolts (initially) and then balls made of *stone or *metal (lead or *iron). They were called by many names, but eventually became known generically as 'cannons' (from the French *canons*) or 'guns' (from the English *gynnes*). Although an entirely different *military *technology—requiring new state economic priorities, new support and supply structures and logistics, the acquisition of new natural resources, and even new strategies and tactics—within 150 years gunpowder weapons had come to dominate *warfare everywhere.

The first and most frequent use of gunpowder artillery was in *sieges. By the end of the 14th century guns were being fired frequently into towers, gates, and walls; although they did not often destroy these fortifications, their mere presence could intimidate those within into surrender. *Henry V of England used such a strategy in his conquest of northern France in 1417–20. At other times, however, depending on the determination and tenacity of the garrison and citizenry, fortified sites held out against even the heaviest bombardments, such as at *Orléans in 1428–9, Neuss in 1473–4, and Rhodes in 1480.

Also by the end of the 14th century large gunpowder artillery began appearing in battles, although it was not until hand-held guns could be produced in larger numbers—by the mid 15th century—that they affected tactical manoeuvres. At the same time guns were mounted on board *ships. More standardized than siege or battlefield artillery in barrel length, calibre, and chamber size, and capable of being loaded with powder and ball from the rear, they could be fired against other vessels and coastal fortifications. Finally, by the end of the MA military engineering or *gunners' manuals began to focus on the technology and ballistics of gunpowder weapons. KDV

K. Chase, *Firearms: A Global History to 1700* (2003).
B. S. Hall, *Weapons and Warfare in Renaissance Europe: Gunpowder, Technology, and Tactics* (1997).
R. D. Smith and R. R. Brown, *Mons Meg and her Sisters* (1989).
—— and K. DeVries, *The Artillery of the Dukes of Burgundy, 1363–1477* (2005).

Balmung In the **Nibelungenlied*, the *sword given to *Siegfried by Schilbung and Nibelung, as payment for his (ultimately unsuccessful) dividing up of their treasure. Siegfried kills Schilbung and Nibelung and their giant allies with Balmung. *Hagen acquires the sword after murdering Siegfried. When Hagen is captured by Dietrich in the epic's concluding scenes, *Kriemhild uses Balmung to decapitate him. WM

H. de Boor, ed., *Das Nibelungenlied* ([22]1988).
B. Raffel, tr., *Das Nibelungenlied* (2006).

Baltic Sea A large body of water that protected *Scandinavia from the major *migrations while facilitating later military and mercantile contacts with the peoples to the east and south. Though closed by ice in winter, the southern Baltic was crossed by *Vikings and merchants to *Novgorod, *Pskov, and Polotsk, and ultimately to the great *markets of the *Islamic and *Byzantine worlds. *Trade items included *fish (herring), amber, *textiles (cloth), and *iron from the *Low Countries, *forest products from *Rus' and *Livonia, and *grain from *Poland. WU

D. Kirby and M.-L. Hinkkanen, *The Baltic and North Seas* (2000).

Bamberg (town, bishopric) Settled since the 8th century, Bamberg was designated a **castrum* (10th century), then a *civitas*. With the bishopric founded in 1007, Emperor Henry II made it both a spiritual and political stronghold and an intellectual centre richly endowed with *manuscript production facilities. He and his wife, Kundigunde, are buried in the *cathedral. Provided with papal privileges, in the 13th century Bamberg became free of the *Mainz metropolitan league. A citizens' *commune is attested from the late 13th century. However, the city remained in episcopal power. Its cathedral, begun in 1111 by St *Otto, is famous for its *sculptural decoration. *See also* ROMAN EMPIRE [CAROLINGIAN, OTTONIAN, SALIAN/FRANCONIAN DYNASTIES]. KS

E. von Guttenberg, *Die Regesten der Bischöfe von Bamberg* (1932–63).
—— and A. Wendehorst, *Das Bistum Bamberg*, 2 vols (1937; repr. 1966).
B. Schimmelpfennig, *Bamberg im Mittelalter* (1964).

banates The term *banate* or *banat* designated a frontier province governed by a *ban*, a Slavic word meaning 'lord' or 'governor'. Thus *banat* maybe translated loosely as 'province'. The term designated territories in the northern Balkans along the southern frontier of the kingdom of *Hungary, serving as buffers against *Byzantine and *Serbian, later Ottoman, advance.

The southern border of the *banates* was fluid, depending on the balance of power between the kingdom and its neighbours. The most important ones—some of which were temporarily held by powerful *barons, even members of the royal family—were (from east to west) the *banates* of Szörény (Severin), Macsó (Mačva), Só (Sol), Srebrenik, and Jajce. From the late 15th century they gradually fell under Ottoman control. JMB

L. Thallóczy *et al.*, *Codex diplomaticus partium regno Hungariae adnexarum*, 3 vols (1903–12).

banderia [Italian *bandiera*, 'banner, flag'] Private armies of the rulers, lords, and prelates in medieval *Hungary. The *noble levy was increasingly replaced or augmented (from the late 13th century) with troops supplied by great landowners, mostly heavy cavalry, consisting mainly of the **familiaritas* of the banderial lords. Regulations about their size and tasks are known from the age of Sigismund of *Luxembourg. The size of a *banderium* seems to have varied, but consisted usually of *c.*100–200 mounted men. Occasionally, the troops of the counties in the levy were also called *banderia*. JMB

DRMH (1989–2006), vol. 2, 141–53.
J. Held, 'Military Reform in Early 15th-Century Hungary', *East European Quarterly*, 11 (1977), 129–39.

bandits and outlawry The MA are filled with legends of bandits, notably the 12th-century *Robin Hood and his merry band at Sherwood (or Barnsdale) Forest, praised in ballads that circulated widely in the 14th century. Especially during the later MA, bandits were commonplace. Outlawed members of the Ubaldini magnates and their peasant *fideli* ruled mountain passes between *Florence and Bologna. On the eve of the *Black Death, Roman bandits killed pilgrims and pillaged merchants en route to the Holy City, giving rise to *Cola di Rienzo's popular government bent on cleansing the territory of these scourges of *trade, commerce, and local stability. Bands of *malandrini* led by Mazziotto terrorized large tracts of the kingdom of *Naples through the 1370s. Such outlaws hardly posed as protectors of those in *poverty.

But other bands may have mixed personal profit with revolutionary zeal, such as the Tuchins, who terrorized large parts of the Massif Central, the *Auvergne, and *Languedoc from 1364 to their suppression in 1384 by the duke of *Berry. According to chronicler Michel Pintoin, they ruthlessly roasted merchants and tortured *clergy, but they also rebelled against *Charles V's escalation of taxes that burdened the poor. From letters of remission, however, they appear as little more than disgruntled nobles and soldiers settling scores and robbing the countryside for what they could get. SKC

M. Boudet, *La Jacquerie des Tuchins, 1363–84* (1895).

A. Leguai, 'Les Révoltes rurales dans le royaume de France du milieu du XIVᵉ siècle à la fin du XVᵉ', *MA* 88 (1982), 49–76.

Bangor, Antiphoner of Modern name of 7th-century MS in Irish scripts, containing *hymns and *antiphons for the monastic *Divine Office. Discovered at Bobbio, it includes a hymn honouring the abbots of Bangor (Ireland), plus some *Ambrosian Rite antiphons. *See also* LITURGICAL BOOKS; PALAEOGRAPHY; PSALMODY. PJ

M. Curran, *The Antiphonary of Bangor and the Early Irish Monastic Liturgy* (1984).

K. Gamber, ed., *Codices Liturgici Latini Antiquiores (CLLA)*, 2 vols ([2]1968), no. 150.

F. E. Warren, *The Antiphonary of Bangor*, 2 vols (1893–5).

banking, finance, and taxation Medieval financial and fiscal institutions owed little to ancient precedents, but were produced by the distinctive social, political, and economic features of medieval Europe. Medieval business techniques such as double-entry bookkeeping (*see* ACCOUNTING AND BOOKKEEPING), giro banking, maritime insurance, and the *bill of exchange were of enduring significance; and the fiscal innovations of late medieval governments laid the foundations for the early modern fiscal state.

1. Banking and finance
2. Taxation and public finance

1. *Banking and finance*

Medieval banking may be divided into (i) merchant banking, (ii) money-changing and deposit banking, and (iii) *moneylending and pawnbroking, though the boundaries between these sectors were rarely firm.

The origins of medieval banking lay in money-changing; indeed, the words 'bank' and 'banker' derive from the Latin for money-changer (*bancherius*) and the cloth-covered table (*bancus*) at which he conducted his business in urban markets and at international *fairs. The money-changer's expertise lay in assessing the fineness and relative value of the enormous variety of *gold and silver coins employed in commerce, and money-changing was often a secondary function of merchants active in international or inter-regional markets. Money-changers also functioned as local deposit bankers. By the 13th century, Italian money-changers were accepting deposits that could be used to settle payments by assignment or giro (It. *girare* 'to rotate'): instructions were usually given orally and recorded in the banker's ledgers, but written cheques were in use in 14th-century Tuscany. Overdrafts based on a fractional reserve system were usually confined to local transactions, though there is evidence that they played a more significant role in the later MA.

The rise of merchant banking was closely connected with the international trade fairs of northwestern Europe, particularly the Champagne *fairs, which served not only as markets for bulk goods and luxury commodities but as financial clearing-houses and money markets. By the 13th century, Italian merchants routinely employed credit instruments such as 'exchange contracts' (*instrumenta ex causa cambii*) to raise capital repayable in the local currency at the fair and 'fair letters' (*lettres de foire*) to defer outstanding balances to subsequent fairs. With the eclipse of the Champagne fairs in the early 14th century, travelling merchants were supplanted by sedentary merchant bankers operating in family firms, the biggest of which were based in *Florence: the Bardi, Peruzzi, and *Acciaiuoli. The companies were partnerships: capital was supplied by family members and outside partners for an agreed period, at the end of which dividends were paid in proportion to investment, and the company re-formed, usually with the same partners. Employing international networks of representatives, double-entry accounting, and the bill of exchange—by which sums could be remitted without physically transporting coins and which, by exploiting variations in exchange rates, evaded the *usury prohibition—such firms engaged in activities as diverse as trading in *wool, *grain, luxuries and *textiles, tax farming, manufacturing, the collection of papal revenues, and the provision of credit to rulers. When a combination of bad loans and conjunctural factors resulted in the collapse of the leading Florentine banks in the 1340s, the sector reformed into more modestly capitalized and less centrally organized firms, such as the Alberti, *Datini, and *Medici banks. The exceptionally well-documented firm of Francesco *Datini of Prato (d. 1410) was a network of trading, manufacturing, and financial concerns throughout the western Mediterranean coordinated by Datini through independent partnerships. The Medici bank combined wool and silk manufacturing with papal finance and the supply of credit through bills drawn on branches from *London to *Naples. Poor management and failure to adapt to new conditions created by the emergence of the *Lyons fairs as the leading financial clearing-house led to the decline of the Medici bank. Moreover, by the mid 15th century, Italian hegemony was being successfully challenged by transalpine financiers such as Jacques Coeur of *Bourges and the *Fuggers of *Augsburg, who combined finance with investment in *mining and smelting.

Moneylenders and pawnbrokers provided loans on little or no security at rates ranging from 12 to 43 per cent a year, and were usually the sole source of credit for workers and *peasants. Although usury was forbidden by canon *law, usurers and pawnbrokers operated openly everywhere in medieval Europe under royal or municipal licence. Many Italian communes, for example, authorized Jewish pawnbroking at rates of 20 per cent on payment of an annual fine, but by the 14th century the sector was dominated in most European centres by Piedmontese from Asti and Chieri, known popularly as 'Lombards' or *'Cahorsins'. Regarded with disdain, public usurers were often subject to violence and expulsion, and sometimes to prosecution in the church courts for restitution of their gains.

2. *Taxation and public finance*

Because of significant variations over time and between regions, the tax and fiscal regimes of medieval Europe defy easy characterization. In general, however, the 12th to 14th centuries marked a shift from dependence on traditional 'regalian' or feudal revenues to systems exploiting a wider range of resources.

Early medieval rulers typically relied on wealth extracted from lands under their immediate control (demesnes) to finance their households and associated activities; additional resources might derive from plunder or from feudal 'aids', which were levied on certain customary occasions or in extraordinary circumstances, for example, to make war. Because rulers' aristocratic retainers themselves depended on revenue-generating land grants (*fiefs)—the incomes of which they jealously protected and rulers were reluctant to tax—conditions did not lend themselves to systems of generalized taxation.

From the 12th century onward, however, the growth of agricultural productivity, urbanization, and trade provided rulers with new sources of income: licence fees for fairs or the right to conduct business, trade duties, excise and sales taxes on goods and services, fees for exploiting natural resources, *poll taxes, and compulsory or voluntary loans from financiers. In 1275, for example, Parliament granted the English king the right to impose export duties on wool and cloth; by the mid 14th century this had been extended to 'tunnage' on imported wine and 'poundage' on a variety of exported goods. By contrast, the kings of France depended mainly on internal sales taxes, especially the royal salt monopoly, and, beginning in the 15th century, the *taille*, a wealth tax levied on the non-noble population. Governments in heavily urbanized *Flanders and northern Italy favoured consumption taxes, for example, on *wine or beer, and *gabelles* and fees on goods passing through the city gates. Such taxes were often farmed, but the loss to rulers in the form of smaller yields was offset by the advantages of predictable revenue streams. In general, medieval rulers were reluctant to tax wealth directly, especially that of aristocracies and urban patriciates. The result was that taxation was highly regressive, falling most heavily on peasants and workers, and it is notable that insurrections from the mid 13th century onward were often triggered by insupportable or unjust levies.

Since revenues rarely matched expenditures, especially those connected with the rising costs of the *mercenaries often employed in late medieval *warfare, rulers and governments increasingly resorted to loans. In Germany, loans were secured by liens on royal property, but elsewhere they were usually advanced by Italian merchant bankers in return for tax farms and trading privileges. Such loans were nevertheless highly risky, and medieval rulers often defaulted. North Italian city-states such as *Florence and *Venice depended heavily on compulsory loans from wealthy citizens, and by the 14th century most cities had consolidated outstanding debts into funds (*monti*) paying annual rates of 5–15 per cent. Shares in the *monti* were marketable, and prices fluctuated with the government's fiscal health. In Flanders, the Rhineland, *Catalonia, and *Valencia, the preferred mechanism for raising capital was the annuity (*census*, *rente*, *censal*) secured by anticipated tax revenues: for a lump sum, investors purchased a fixed return for life or for several generations.

The various techniques developed by late medieval rulers for mobilizing capital were not uniformly diffused, and many would not be fully exploited until after 1500, as government expenditures rose with the increasing costs of warfare and administration. LDA

R. Bonney, ed., *The Rise of the Fiscal State* (1999).

F. Braudel, *Civilization and Capitalism, 15th–18th Century*, vol. 2: *The Wheels of Commerce*, tr. S. Reynolds (French original, 1979) (1982).

R. de Roover, *The Rise and Decline of the Medici Bank, 1397–1494* (1963).

E. S. Hunt, *The Medieval Super-Companies: A Study of the Peruzzi Company of Florence* (1994).

—— and J. M. Murray, *A History of Business in Medieval Europe, 1200–1500* (1999).

A. Molho, *Florentine Public Finances in the Early Renaissance, 1400–1433* (1971).

R. C. Mueller, *The Venetian Money Market: Banks, Panics, and the Public Debt, 1200–1500* (1997).

J. M. Murray, *Bruges, Cradle of Capitalism, 1280–1390* (2005).

M. North, *Von Aktie bis Zoll: Ein historisches Lexikon des Geldes* (1995).

P. Spufford, *Money and its Use in Medieval Europe* (1988).
C. Tilly, *Coercion, Capital, and European States, AD 990–1992* (1992).
H. Van der Wee, 'Monetary, Credit and Banking Systems', *Cambridge Economic History of Europe*, vol. 5, *The Economic Organization of Early Modern Europe*, ed. E. E. Rich and C. Wilson (1977), pp. 315–22.

banneret *See* CHIVALRY AND KNIGHTHOOD.

Bannockburn, battle of (1314) Fought between the armies of *Edward II of England and *Robert I of Scotland on 23–4 June 1314, Bannockburn holds a central place in Scottish history. Edward II sought to recover lost ground in Scotland and relieve Stirling Castle. His advance was blocked by Bruce's smaller host and forced onto unsuitable ground, before being routed by a rapid advance at dawn. Bannockburn confirmed Robert as effective ruler of Scotland. *See also* ANGLO-SCOTTISH WARS (1296–1513). MBr

G. W. S. Barrow, *Robert Bruce and the Community of the Realm of Scotland* ([2]2005).
D. Cornell, *Bannockburn: The Triumph of Robert the Bruce* (2009).

banns of marriage *See* KINSHIP, FAMILY, MARRIAGE, DIVORCE: IN WESTERN EUROPE.

Banská Bystrica (Besztercebánya, Neusohl) *Copper *mining town in medieval northern *Hungary. Refounded by German (probably *Thuringian) settlers on the estate of Zvolen castle (Zólyom, Sohl), it received a *charter from King Béla IV in 1255 that delineated the town's territory, including rich deposits of copper. From the 15th century it was a leading member of the alliance of Lower Hungarian mining towns, under the chamber of Kremnica (Körmöcbánya). The rights of mining copper and mercury were exploited from 1494 by the *Fugger-Thurzó enterprise. *See also* METALS AND METALLURGY. KSz

V. Mencl, *Středověká města na Slovensku* (1938), 84–7.
O. Paulinyi, 'Tulajdon és társadalom a Garam-vidéki bányavárosokban', *TSz* 5 (1962), 173–88.

Banu Musa (9th century) Three brothers, Muhammad (d. 873), Ahmad, and al-Hasan, famous for their *engineering works in *Baghdad. They got books from the *Byzantine Empire for *translation into Arabic and wrote books on *mathematics and *astronomy and *mechanics. The influential *Book of Ingenious Devices*, largely the work of Ahmad, described about a hundred small machines, including many trick vessels and six fountains. The vessels operated by different combinations of siphons, valves, pulleys, gears, cranks, miniature waterwheels, floats, and balances. POL

D. R. Hill, 'Banū Mūsā', *DSB* vol. 1, 443–6.
——ed. and tr., *The Book of Ingenious Devices by the Banū (Sons of) Mūsā bin Shākir* (1979).

baptism [Greek *baptismos*, 'washing, immersion'] This first of the church's seven *sacraments remits the initiate's sins to that point (including original sin), joins the initiate with the church, and identifies the initiate as Christian. The sacrament originates from Jesus' description of baptism in John 3:5. The rite requires that the initiate be washed in some way, with water of any kind, while the officiant states that he or she baptizes the initiate in the name of the Father, the Son, and the Holy Spirit. The rite is generally performed by *clergy, though it may also be performed by the *laity (men or women), even *heretics or *pagans, so long as their intent is to carry out the wishes of the church. When performed within a church by an attendant priest, the rite took place in a *baptistery, a distinct building, chamber, or section of a church containing a baptismal *font, the receptacle holding baptismal water; the Latin term *baptisterium* can refer to either the dedicated architectural space or the font, or both. Baptismal water could be blessed to endow the water with purificatory and healing powers (though this blessing is not necessary for the rite), and could be applied to uses other than baptism, including distribution after baptisms to the laity to bless their land and property.

According to canon *law, baptism was usually administered 'as soon as possible' (*quam primum*) after birth, in order to secure salvation and mitigate the effects of original sin. The primitive connection of baptism with *Sundays and holy days and the gathering of the Christian assembly was therefore largely obscured. The rite of baptism in the *Sarum Manual has three sections: 'The order for the making of a catechumen', 'The blessing of the font' (undertaken periodically), which included the *Litany of the Saints, and 'Concerning baptism'. The threefold structure shows that the rite was adapted over a millennium, from a staged baptismal rite embracing those able to answer for themselves as well as infants, to a composite rite for infants, in which godparents answered for the candidates. Candidates were administered exorcised salt, the *sign of the Cross (which made them catechumens), a pre-baptismal anointing with the oil of *exorcism, a triple administration of the water of baptism, a post-baptismal anointing with *chrism, a chrismal robe, and a lit candle. *See also* HOLY WATER; HOLY WATER FONT; SACRAMENTS. KRV, DJKe

P. Cramer, *Baptism and Change in the Early Middle Ages, c.200–c.1150* (1993).
J. D. C. Fisher, *Christian Initiation: Baptism in the Medieval West* (1965).
M. E. Johnson, *The Rites of Christian Initiation: Their Evolution and Interpretation* (1999).

baptistery A structure or a space containing the water *font used for *baptism. The early Christian baptistery was a more or less separate edifice, which might be connected to the church building or not. Many early baptisteries had a centralized arrangement with a low water basin in the middle—a design that survived in Italian *cathedrals until the 13th century. The general trend, however, was towards the incorporation of the font in a corner or *chapel of the main church, as a consequence of the introduction of infant baptism and the disappearance of collective baptismal rites on solemn occasions. SdB

J. G. Davies, *The Architectural Setting of Baptism* (1962).
S. Ristow, *Frühchristliche Baptisterien* (1998).

Bar, duchy of In northeast France, Bar was ruled by counts and *dukes whose allegiance vacillated between *France and the *Roman Empire. In 1419 the duchy was left to *René of Anjou, through whose heirs it was united to *Lorraine. EARB

G. Poull, *La Maison ducale de Bar* (1977).
H. Thomas, *Zwischen Regnum und Imperium: die Fürstentümer Bar und Lothringen zur Zeit Kaiser Karls IV* (1973).

barbarians Drawn from Greek cultural traditions, the term has been used to describe various peoples who entered the Roman Empire during late antiquity. One of the earliest depictions is that of Tacitus (AD 56–*c*.120), who portrayed them as 'noble savages' whose martial skill, morality, and marital fidelity stood in contrast to the corruptions of Rome. Later portrayals were less complimentary, as they were described as dishonest, disloyal, irrational, drunkards, slaves, unable to live by the rule of law, and unworthy opponents. These accounts reveal the long-standing connections between Romans and barbarians. Contact was often violent; Marcus Aurelius fought them, and barbarians contributed to the chaos in the empire in the 3rd century. Constantine, however, enrolled large numbers of them as soldiers, beginning the 'barbarization of the army' or, alternatively, the 'Romanization' of the barbarians, who had respected Roman power, traded with the Romans, and been introduced to the imperial traditions in the generations they had resided along the Roman frontiers. In the 4th and 5th centuries they were perceived as enemies, coming in large numbers, seeking to destroy the empire, but in fact they arrived in relatively small numbers and sought refuge from their enemies and a better life. They eventually converted to Christianity, and established successor kingdoms to the empire that continued into the early MA. *See also* MIGRATION OF PEOPLES. MCF

P. Heather, *Empires and Barbarians* (2009).
H. Wolfram, *The Roman Empire and its Germanic Peoples*, tr. T. Dunlap (German original, 1990) (1997).

Barbaro, Ermolao (*c*.1454–93) Venetian humanist and diplomat. He gained fame as a classical scholar for his textual criticism of Pliny the Elder and for his Latin translations of Greek philosophical texts. A Venetian patrician and senator, he served the Republic on numerous missions but died in exile. *See also* HUMANISM, LEGAL; TRANSLATION; VENICE. JAK

V. Branca, 'Ermolao Barbaro and Late Quattrocento Venetian Humanism', in *Renaissance Venice*, ed. J. R. Hale (1973), 218–43.

Barbastro Crusade (1064) Robert Crispin of *Normandy, William duke of Aquitaine, and Count Ermengol III of Urgell led a combined Christian army of Burgundian, Norman, Aquitanian, Italian, Catalan, and Aragonese troops that captured the Spanish Muslim city of Barbastro, located 60 miles northeast of Saragossa, in August 1064. The Muslim king of Saragossa, al-Muqtadir, soon recaptured the city, which remained contested between Christians and Muslims until Pere I of *Aragon secured it in 1101.

Historians have debated if this campaign should be considered the First *Crusade because of the *bull *Eos qui in Ispaniam* that *Pope Alexander II issued to the *clergy of Voltorno, Italy, *c*.1063. This bull contains the earliest surviving text of a papal crusading *indulgence. Without referring specifically to the Barbastro campaign, the bull absolved from *penance all *knights who went to Spain to fight, and gave them remission from sins committed during the campaign. This was the first papal bull to link religious *warfare with the relief of punishment for sin. Other historians have challenged the crusade status of Barbastro and questioned Alexander's role in organizing the campaign, raising the army, and selecting the leader. Another aspect of this debate questions if Barbastro changed the nature of the reconquest (*Reconquista) by introducing the *Gregorian reform programme into what had been a local conflict between Christians and Muslims within the peninsula, leading to the objectification of the Muslims in Christian eyes and exacerbating the reconquest. *See also* CHURCH HISTORY. TMV

A. Ferreiro, 'The Siege of Barbastro 1064–65: A Reassessment', *JMH* 9 (1983), 129–44.
J. G. Gaztambide, *Historia de la bula de la cruzada en España* (1958).
J. F. O'Callaghan, *Reconquest and Crusade in Medieval Spain* (2003).

barber surgeons A term strictly speaking seldom used in the MA, if at all. However, it is a convenient way of describing barbers who also offered medical services, especially *bloodletting and minor surgical procedures. The barber's red and white striped pole, still seen outside many shops, goes back to the need to advertise these services. Barbers belonged to trade *guilds, not medical guilds set up in Italian cities like *Florence, and were subject to the regulations of their guild. Far more numerous than *physicians or master *surgeons, they were often seen by the latter as competitors, no better than mere *empirics who would offer to set bones or mend hernias. Despite this, many barbers are known by their wills or inscriptions to have possessed

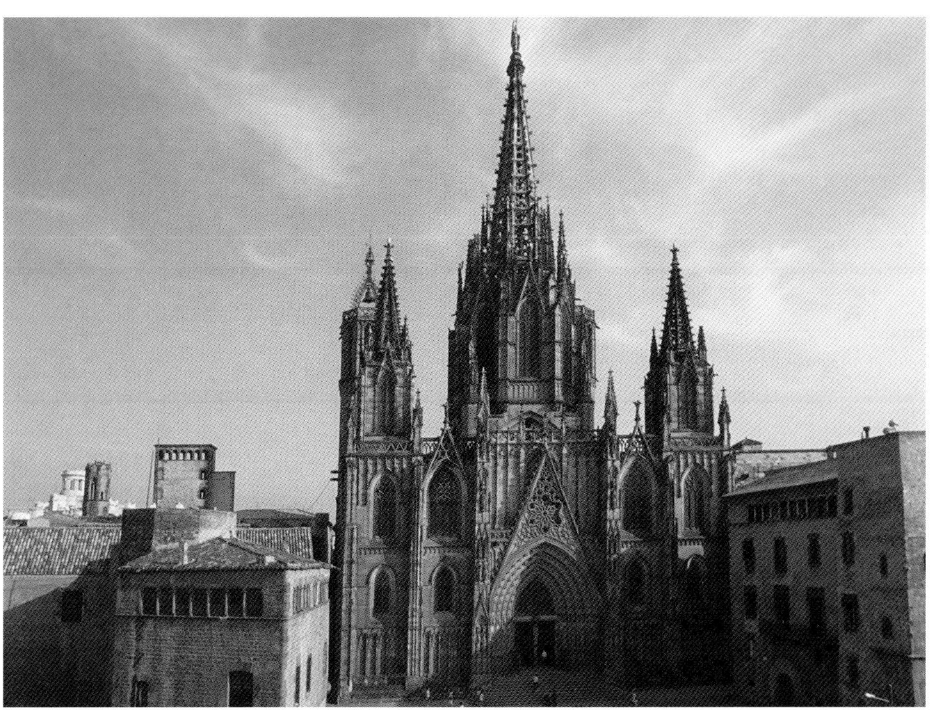

Cathedral of Barcelona.

or even commissioned medical books in the late MA, when medical books in the vernacular were written in large numbers. It is likely that the principal medical service offered by the barber was bloodletting. Since physicians were not expected to soil their hands with menial tasks, these were referred to barbers. *See also* MEDICAL TRAINING.

PMJ

T. Beck, *The Cutting Edge: Early History of the Surgeons of London* (1974).
K. Park, *Doctors and Medicine in Early Renaissance Florence* (1985).

barbotine *See* POTTERY, CERAMICS, AND TILE.

Barbour, John (1320×30–1395) Scottish author of oldest extant, large-scale vernacular literature. *The Bruce*, an epic composed in the 1370s in early *Scots, lent a patriotic boost after the struggles for independence. Appointed precentor (*cantor) of Dunkeld in 1355, and archdeacon of Aberdeen in 1357, Barbour enjoyed the *patronage of King *Robert II. Other works include the lost *The Stewartis Original* and *The Stewartis Genealogy*. *See also* SCOTLAND, IRELAND, WALES: SCOTLAND AND WALES 1064–1536.

MTA

J. Barbour, *The Bruce*, ed. A. A. M. Duncan (1997).

Barcelona A small Roman colony in Hispania Citerior, of less importance than Tarragona until superior defences enabled it to resist Germanic attacks in the late 3rd century. Evidence of Christian communities comes from this period, with Cugat martyred under Diocletian, then Bishop Pacian (360–90) becoming protector of the spiritual and cultural life of the city as imperial authority declined. Barcelona was capital to the *Visigoth king Athaulf (415), then the usurper Maximus (418–22), and the imperial pretender Sebastian (444). In 476 the city became an important centre of the Visigoth kingdom of *Toulouse. It would be capital to Teudis (531–48) before power shifted to central Spain. Provincial councils were held in Barcelona in 540 and 599. Under *Leovigild, the city had both Christian and *Arian bishops. It was captured by the Muslims (717–18), but its ecclesiastical and civil administration remained largely intact.

In 801, taken by forces under the overall command of *Louis the Pious, Barcelona became the major fortress on the southern frontier of the Frankish kingdom. Barcelona remained under the control of a count and a bishop, who was subject to *Narbonne. Ecclesiastical culture flourished, as did the Jewish community, and Mediterranean commerce increased. As *Carolingian power waned, closer ties were sought with Rome and *Córdoba, particularly under Count Borrell (947–92), but in 985 the city was subject to a devastating attack by al-*Mansur. The extent of the long-term damage remains a matter of great debate. In the two centuries that followed, the city expanded while the counts of Barcelona united the other Catalan counties around their town and joined *Catalonia with *Aragon from 1137. A major port, it was home to many merchants and traders, who greatly profited from its rise, as well as a flourishing Christian church (subject to Tarragona from 1154) and *religious orders and noted Jewish theologians, jurists, and poets.

In the 13th century, with the establishment of a Catalan navy, the city reached the height of its power. *Majorca was conquered (1230), and Barcelona provided many men and provisions for the Valencian conquest (1238). A number of businessmen, having gained great wealth through *trade and commerce, established themselves as the leading figures in the city. Representatives of the city's interests, backed by the support of the crown, could be found in all the major cities of the Mediterranean. The royal court spent increasing time in Barcelona and protected the position of the *artisans and the vibrant Jewish community, though attitudes towards the latter began to change. No less influential were the *Franciscans and the *Dominicans, whose number included Ramón de *Peñafort, the greatest lawyer of the age. Many of the walls of the city were built at this time, as well as palaces, dockyards, *hospitals, and churches. The representation of the citizens in government increased, though much power remained in the hands of a few councillors.

Prosperity continued well into the 14th century, but the 1333 famine, the *Black Death, and many subsequent *plagues took their toll. Conflicts between the crown, in a weakened financial state, and the town oligarchy increased. Massacres of the Jews in 1348 and 1391 bear witness to increased tensions and the decline in the city's fortunes, though courtly culture thrived, as did maritime commerce, into the first half of the 15th century. But with the impressive prosperity achieved by *Valencia, along with the establishment of the court in *Naples (1422), Barcelona's fortunes waned. As the city plunged into debt, it became divided into two political factions: the Biga, including landowners, stockholders, and some merchants, and the Busca, representing artisans, craftsmen, and other merchants and supported by the king. Neither the initial triumph of the Busca (1453) nor the subsequent struggle of the Biga and the *Generalitat against *Joan II over the question of the *remences* (a Catalan mode of *serfdom), ending in the surrender of Pedralbes (an area west of Barcelona, 1472), did anything to help Barcelona recover. After the end of the civil war there were, however, indications of renewed *demographic expansion and heightened trade. *See also* JEWS IN THE IBERIAN PENINSULA; RECONQUISTA. DJSm

S. Bensch, *Barcelona and its Rulers, 1096–1291* (1995).
A. Duran i Sanpere, *Barcelona i la seva història*, 3 vols (1973–5).
P. Freedman, *The Origins of Peasant Servitude in Medieval Catalonia* (1991).
Història de Barcelona: De la prehistòria al segle XVI, ed. A. Duran i Sanpere (1975).
R. Hughes, *Barcelona* (1992).
P. Orti Gost, *Renda i fiscalitat en un ciutat medieval: Barcelona (segles XII–XIV)* (2000).
C. Batlle, *La crisis social y económica de Barcelona a mediados del siglo XV*, 2 vols (1973).

Bardo of Mainz (d. 1051) Monk of *Fulda and abbot of Werden before becoming archbishop in 1031, Bardo was a familiar at the imperial court. In 1036 he consecrated the *cathedral of *Mainz, the completion of which he oversaw after a fire in 1009 damaged St *Willigis' great structure. *See also* ROMAN EMPIRE [CAROLINGIAN, OTTONIAN, SALIAN/FRANCONIAN DYNASTIES]. ASC

S. Coué, *Hagiographie im Kontext* (1996), 100–126.

bards *See* FILI.

bar form *See* FORMES FIXES.

Barlaam of Calabria (Seminara) (*c.*1290–1350) Italian humanist and Orthodox theologian, who advocated ecclesiastical union with Rome. He left Calabria for *Constantinople in 1330 and became abbot of the Soter (Saviour) *monastery until 1341. He attacked a form of mystical *asceticism, called *hesychasm, practised by the monks of Mount Athos, and when his position was successfully challenged by *Gregory Palamas, he was condemned. Barlaam returned to Italy, converted to Catholicism, and became the Roman Catholic bishop of Gerace. He wrote in Greek and Latin and left 21 anti-Latin treatises. Most of his works against Gregory Palamas have been destroyed. *See also* THEOLOGY, BYZANTINE. AES, MAG

Barlaam of Calabria, *PG*, vol. 151, 1255–82, 1301–64.
——*Opere contro i Latini: introduzione, storia dei testi, edizione critica, traduzione e indici*, ed. A. Fyrigos, 2 vols (1998).
A. Fyrigos, *Barlaam Calabro: L'uomo, l'opera, il pensiero* (2001).

Barlaam and Josaphat's saga A Christian adaptation of legends of the life of Buddha. The *hermit Barlaam converts Josaphat, the son of the king of *India, to Christianity with learned conversations and parables. The tale has been attributed to *John of Damascus (675–749), but it probably dates back to the 6th century. It was translated into Greek and from Greek into Latin in the 11th century. From Latin it was translated into most European vernaculars, and became very popular in the MA. MRin

Historia animae utilis de Barlaam et Ioasaph, ed. R. Volk (2009).

barn In medieval contexts, a structure for *grain storage. Successful grain storage was essential for survival in a world where meat, *fruits, and vegetables were luxuries, and local populations depended on usable grain stores during times of famine. Maintenance of a cool, dry environment was essential to avoid loss from mould and fire.

Medieval barns have been likened in design to both Gothic churches and Roman *basilicas. Generally, two rows of stone columns and arches encompassed a large central *'nave' bracketed by side-aisles under a single, massive, heavy-beamed gable.

*Tithe barns were built by religious institutions to store their allotted one-tenth share of the produce. Since tithes were a major source of wealth, the tithe barn was an important repository, constructed of quality materials and craftsmanship to reflect its high-status role in the medieval economy. *See also* BUILDING AND CONSTRUCTION; VERNACULAR BUILDINGS: CONSTRUCTION AND FORM. DJS

N. D. K. Brady, 'The Sacred Barn: Barn-Building in Southern England, 1100–1550: A Study of Grain Storage Technology and its Cultural Context', Ph.D. thesis (Cornell, 1996).

J. W. Griswold, *A Guide to Medieval English Tithe Barns* (1999).

M. Kirk, *Silent Spaces: The Last of the Great Aisled Barns* (1994).

Barna da Siena (*fl.* 1330–50) Undocumented Sienese painter. Recognized for his dramatic intensity, Barna legendarily died while painting the New Testament *frescoes in San Gimignano's collegiate *church. CGM

G. Freuler, 'Lippo Memmi's New Testament Cycle in the Collegiata in San Gimignano', *Arte Cristiana*, 713 (1985), 93–102.

F. Hofmann, *Der Freskenzyklus des Neuen Testaments in der Collegiata von San Gimignano* (1996).

Barnet, battle of On 14 April 1471, Easter Sunday morning, *Edward IV's army defeated the *Lancastrian forces of Richard *Neville, earl of Warwick, outside London. Heavy fog led to uncoordinated strategies and Warwick's death in battle. *See also* ROSES, WARS OF THE. LCA

J. Bruce, ed., *Historie of the Arrivall of Edward IV in England*, Camden Society (1838).

P. W. Hammond, *The Battles of Barnet and Tewkesbury* ([2]1993).

baron, baroness A specific title of *nobility, ranking below a viscount; also a member of the fifth and lowest rank of the English *peerage or a generic *feudal class that held land from a feudal superior. *William I, 'the Conqueror', introduced the title of baron to England. JCH

J. M. W. Bean, *From Lord to Patron: Lordship in Late Medieval England* (1989).

C. G. Wilson, *The English Nobility in the Late Middle Ages: The Fourteenth-Century Political Community* (1987).

baronial reform movement Named for the 1258–65 attempt by English *barons, led by Simon de *Montfort, to reassert their claims under *Magna Carta against King *Henry III. In 1258 the barons passed autonomous laws, and by 1260 Henry sought a counteracting papal endorsement. That year, open *warfare between king and barons resurfaced. The barons won at Lewes (1264), capturing Henry. At Evesham (1265) the barons were decisively defeated with many killed, including Simon, and rebel-owned lands were confiscated. JCH

C. Bémont, *Simon de Montfort*, tr. E. F. Jacob (French original, 1930) ([2]1974).

J. R. Maddicott, *Simon de Montfort* (1994).

R. F. Treharne, 'The Constitutional Problem in Thirteenth-Century England', in *Simon De Montfort and Baronial Reform: Thirteenth-Century Essays*, ed. E. B. Fryde (1986), 235–67.

Barons' War (1215–17) The struggles between rebellious *barons and King *John I continued after *Magna Carta (1215) was signed. The barons gained aid from *France, but after John's death (1216) and the subsequent *coronation of his 9-year-old son *Henry III, the French presence in England was seen as the greater threat. Magna Carta was reissued in Henry's name, so the barons changed sides against the French.

English civil war from 1264 to 1267 resumed issues at dispute during the first Barons' War. Rebellious barons under Simon de *Montfort sought to reassert Magna Carta and fought Henry III's army, led by his son *Edward (later I). Henry and Edward were defeated and captured. De Montfort then called the first English *parliament. Henry later escaped, resumed the conflict, and crushed de Montfort and the rebellious barons at Evesham (1265). JCH

P. Brand, *Kings, Barons, and Justices: The Making and Enforcement of Legislation in Thirteenth-Century England* (2003).

D. A. Carpenter, *The Reign of Henry III* (2003).

J. C. Holt, *Magna Carta* ([2]1992).

J. R. Maddicott, *Simon de Montfort* (1996).

R. F. Treharne, *Documents of the Baronial Movement of Reform and Rebellion, 1258–1267* (1973).

barrels Wooden containers made with staves of oak and beech and with hoops made of hazelnut or chestnut. Coopers fabricated barrels by bending the staves while heating them by a wood fire (which allowed them to bend) and sealing them with tar. The capacity of barrels and the units of *weights and measurement used ranged widely depending on the particular time, the location, and the contents —liquid or dry. Barrels were used to *transport many commodities, including oil, *wine, and fresh or salted *fish, such as anchovies, herring, and tuna (the latter from the *al-Andalus fisheries) all over Europe. *See also* OLIVES AND OLIVE OIL; WOOD AND WOODWORKING. RCór

J. G. Jenkins and R. A. Salaman, 'A Note on Coopering', in *A History of Technology*, ed. C. Singer *et al.*, vol. 3 (1957), 128–33.

H. Zug Tucci, 'Un aspetto trascurato del commercio medievale del vino', in *Studi memoria di Federigo Melis*, vol. 3 (1978), 311–48.

R. E. Zupko, *Italian Weights and Measures from the Middle Ages to the Nineteenth Century* (1981), 11–23.

——*A Dictionary of Weights and Measures for the British Isles: The Middle Ages to the Twentieth Century* (1985), 25–33.

Barsumas (Barsaumā), Nestorian bishop of Nisibis (d. 490×96) Student of Ibas at *Edessa; championed Nestorianism

Medieval barrel found at Paul Street, London.

in *Iran and Armenia. He left Edessa in 457 for Nisibis, becoming metropolitan in *c.*470 and establishing an academy to which he welcomed representatives of the School of Edessa on its closure in 489. Barsumas' *preaching won many Persian converts to the *church of the East, and the *patronage of King Firoz. He opposed both Miaphysitism and Zeno's Henotikon. Embroiled in disputes with Catholicos Babowai, he also opposed the celibacy requirement, marrying a former nun. Six of his *letters survive. *See also* THEOLOGY, BYZANTINE. SPC, AHR

A. H. Becker, *Fear of God and the Beginning of Wisdom: The School of Nisibis and Christian Scholastic Culture in Late Antique Mesopotamia* (2006).

S. Gero, *Barsauma of Nisibis and Persian Christianity in the Fifth Century* (1981).

A. Kazhdan, 'Barsauma', *ODB*, vol. 1, 258.

Barsumas (Barsaumas) **the Eutychian** (d. 458) A Monophysite archimandrite of a Syrian *monastery, Barsumas espoused and violently defended the doctrines of Eutyches: Christ's human nature was subsumed by the divine, or at least it was different from that of other humans. These were a reaction to Nestorianism. In 449, Barsumas was the first monk to be appointed as a judge at the *Council of Ephesus, where he represented the malcontent monastic party. Bringing with him a riotous band of 1,000 monks to the council, he coerced it into acquitting Eutyches. Barsumas spent the remainder of his life propagating the Eutychian doctrines in Syria. Jacobites (that is, the Syrian church) regard him as a saint and *miracle worker. His disciple, Samuel, spread Eutychianism to Armenia. *See also* CHURCH OF THE EAST; THEOLOGY, BYZANTINE. AHR

E. Honigmann, 'A Trial for Sorcery on August 22, AD 449', *Isis*, 35/4 (1944), 281–4.

E. Venable, 'Barsumas (the Eutychian)', in *A Dictionary of Christian Biography*, ed. W. Smith *et al.* (1877), vol. 1, 267.

Bartholomaeus Anglicanus *See* BARTHOLOMEW THE ENGLISHMAN.

Bartholomew of Bruges (*c.*1286–1356) Philosopher, physician, and commentator on Aristotelian and medical texts. *Master of Arts and doctor of *medicine (*Paris), he subsequently taught in the medical faculty at *Montpellier and served as physician to Count Guy I of *Blois. MTT

C. O'Boyle, 'The Founding of the French University Faculties of Medicine: The Life and Works of Bartholomew of Bruges (*c.*1286–1356)', Ph.D. thesis (Cambridge, 1987).

Bartholomew of Lucca *See* THOMISM.

Bartholomew of Messina (*fl.* 1258–66) Chief translator at the court of Manfred, king of Sicily. He translated works from Greek into Latin by Aristotle or pseudo-Aristotle (the *Magna moralia*, the *Physiognomia*, the *Problemata*, and the *Signa Aquarum*) and at least two medical texts by *Hippocrates (*On the Nature of the Child* and *On the Nature of Man*). His *translations are extremely literal, but the *Problemata*, dealing with a wide range of questions concerning nature (including sex), became very popular, especially as accompanied by the *commentary of *Peter of Abano. *See also* SCIENCE, TRANSMISSION OF. CBu

G. Marenghi, 'Un capitolo dell'Aristotele medievale: Bartolomeo da Messina traduttore dei *Problemata physica*', *Aevum*, 36 (1962), 268–83.

Bartholomew of Pisa (San Concordio) (*c.*1260–1347) *Dominican *canonist. He studied theology and law and later taught in Dominican schools in central Italy. In his own age he was renowned for the confession manual *Summa de casis conscientiae*, while today he is best remembered for his interests in the classical world. *See also* PENANCE; RENAISSANCE AND ANTIQUARIANISM. FB

Bartolomeo, *Ammaestramenti degli antichi*, ed. P. G. Colombi (1963).

C. Segre, ed., *Volgarizzamenti del Due e Trecento* (1953).

Bartholomew the Englishman (Bartholomaeus Anglicus) (*fl.* 1230) Author of one of the earliest medieval *encyclopedias, the *De rerum proprietatibus*. Bartholomew may have studied at *Oxford under Robert *Grosseteste in the early 13th century, and later taught at both *Paris and *Magdeburg. *De rerum proprietatibus* covers theology, *philosophy, and most of the 13th-century sciences. WHS

De proprietatibus rerum, tr. B. van den Abeele, 2 vols (2007).

Bartinoro (Bartinura), **Ovadia** (d. *c.*1509) Rabbi and *Mishnah commentator, who studied under Joseph Colon ben Solomon Trabotto (also known as Maharik). Along with his father, Ovadia was involved in *moneylending. In 1487 he left Italy for *Egypt and Israel, where he served a number of communities. PIAL

M. Hartum and A. David, 'Rabbi Ovadia Yare of Bartinoro and his Letters from the Land of Israel', in *Jews in Italy*, ed. H. Beinart (1988), 24–108.

Bartolo di Fredi (*fl.* 1353–1410) Painter from the Sienese School, who was influenced by Simone *Martini and Pietro *Lorenzetti. He ran a large and successful workshop in *Siena. His best known work is the *Adoration of the Magi* (1390s, Siena, Pinacoteca Nazionale). *See also* ATELIER. LHZ

F. Gaudenz, *Bartolo di Fredi Cini: ein Beitrag zur sienesischen Malerei des 14. Jahrhunderts* (1994).
P. Harpring, *The Sienese Trecento Painter Bartolo di Fredi* (1993).

Bartolo of Sassoferrato (Bartolus de Saxoferrato) (1313/14–1357) The most renowned civilian of the mid 14th century. An Umbrian, he studied in *Perugia under Cino of Pistoia and later in *Bologna, where he obtained a doctorate in 1334. He served as judge in several *communes before occupying the chair of civil law (or Roman *law) in *Pisa in 1339. From 1342 until his death Bartolo taught at Perugia. Active in public life, he was awarded citizenship and served as ambassador to *Charles IV in 1355. His commentaries on the entire **Corpus iuris civilis* exemplified scholastic jurisprudence at its most sophisticated, and enjoyed an authority second only to the **Glossa ordinaria*. In several influential treatises he dealt with topics as diverse as the government of *city-states, the assessment of witness testimony, riparian rights, *Franciscan *poverty, and *heraldry. A busy legal consultant, he left some 600 **consilia* (briefs) on specific points of law. LDA

S. Lepsius, 'Bartolus de Saxoferrato', *CALMA*, vol. 2, 101–56.
——*Der Richter und die Zeugin: Eine Studie zum 'Tractatus testimoniorum' des Bartolus von Sassoferrato mit Edition* (2003).
D. Quaglioni, *Politica e diritto nel trecento italiano: Il 'De tyranno' di Bartolo da Sassoferrato (1314–1357)* (1983).

Basel (Basilea, civitas Basiliensis) Basel, located on the elbow of the *Rhine, has been settled since 1200 BC. A mention of 'Basilia' appears in AD 374 as the earliest written record. From the early MA the *town served as the bishop's seat. The building of the Rhine Bridge (1220–30) strengthened Basel's position as a *trade/commercial centre and *transportation intersection. Since the 13th century there exists proof of fifteen *guilds, which were given seats on the Minor Council in 1382. In 1349 the Jewish community was murdered out of fear of the great *plague; in 1356 several *earthquakes and a conflagration destroyed large parts of the town. During 1431–48 a general ecclesiastical *council was held in Basel. During the 14th and 15th century it was emancipated from the bishop. In 1501 the city joined the *Swiss Confederation, and in 1521 it cut all ties to its episcopal city master. CSL

Historisches Lexikon der Schweiz (HLS), s.v. 'Basel (-Stadt)', 24 June 2008, www.hls-dhs-dss.ch.
G. Kreis and B. von Wartburg, eds, *Basel: Geschichte einer städtischen Gesellschaft* (2000).
R. Wackernagel, *Geschichte der Stadt Basel*, 4 vols (1907–24).

Basel (bishopric) Despite early Basel's Christianizing, a list of its bishops has existed only since AD 730; however, at *Charlemagne's court there was already proof of two bishops from *Basel holding leading positions. In the 11th century the *diocese's population boomed. During the *Investiture Controversy the diocese supported the emperor, and the bishops developed the city by building a new *cathedral, a new bridge, and defensive *castles and fortifications.

During the late MA the bishops had to pledge their seigneurial rights to the city council owing to economic distress, and the rise of the *guilds slowly displaced the power of the episcopal city masters. In the course of this change, the bishops retreated to Porrentruy. Nevertheless, only with the sanction of the bishops could the city council confirm the *election of the city mayor and headmaster of the guilds, who swore an *oath of obedience. In 1521 the city officially ended any episcopal affiliation, and in 1529 iconoclasm swept through Basel, introducing the new Protestant faith. CSL

V. Feller-Vest, s.v. 'Basel (Diözese)', *Historisches Lexikon der Schweiz (HLS)*, 28 July 2008, www.hls-dhs-dss.ch.
J.-C. Rebetez *et al.*, eds, *Pro Deo: Das Bistum Basel vom 4. bis ins 16. Jahrhundert* (2006) (French tr., *Pro Deo: L'ancien évêché de Bâle du IVe au XVIe siècle*, 2006).

Basel, Council of (1431–49) Last council of the *conciliar movement. It asserted its authority over the *papacy and achieved reunion with the *Hussites. *Pope Eugenius IV transferred the council to *Ferrara to accommodate Byzantine overtures for ecclesiastical reunion. Some at *Basel refused, deposed him, and elected another pope, thereby effecting another *schism, and thus discrediting conciliarism as a movement. *See also* COUNCILS, ECCLESIASTICAL. JRP

J. Helmrath, *Das Basler Konzil, 1431–1449: Forschungsstand und Probleme* (1978).
J. W. Stieber, *Pope Eugenius IV, the Council of Basel, and the Secular and Ecclesiastical Authorities in the Empire: The Conflict over Supreme Authority and Power in the Church* (1978).

Basil, Liturgy of St *See* BYZANTINE RITE; EUCHOLOGION.

Basil, Rule of St Composed by Basil the Great (329–79) about 356, it consists of 55 Greater Monastic Rules and 313 Lesser Rules, some of which may have been written by Basil's followers. Written in a catechetical format, its discussion of virtues and *vices is based on references to biblical passages. The Rule is followed by most eastern Orthodox and many Catholic *monasteries. PJS

A. Holmes, *A Life Pleasing to God: The Spirituality of the Rule of St Basil* (2000).

Basilian monks and nuns Those following the Rule of St Basil. Basilian life is cenobitic, with common meals, *prayers, and work, the last being an innovation on the earlier eremitical model. The most important Basilian of the MA was Theodore of Studium (759–836), an opponent of iconoclasm. Some Basilians are in communion with Rome. *See also* ICONOGRAPHY: ICONOCLASM; RELIGIOUS ORDERS. PJS

A. Gardner, *Theodore of Studium: His Life and Times* (2000).

basilica The term for an ancient Roman, oblong assembly hall became the common name for a building of Christian worship in late antiquity, regardless of its shape. In post-medieval architectural terminology, however, it designated, retrospectively, a specific building type, usually a church: oblong in shape, with a long central *nave flanked on each side by one or more aisles separated from each other by columns or pillars. In a strict sense, the central nave has a clerestory, that is, a wall zone above the aisle roofs, pierced by *windows. Sometimes there were *galleries above the aisles. The earliest Christian basilicas had colonnades with architraves, but the more flexible design of arcades soon became the norm.

The essential characteristics of the early Christian basilicas have been determinative for medieval and later church building: the pronounced longitudinal axis from the entrance to the *apse and the spatial hierarchy of central nave and aisles. The introduction of *vaults and their supports in the Byzantine world and in western Romanesque, however, stimulated the most profound changes of character compared to the original form of the late antique basilica. *See also* ART AND ARCHITECTURE: BYZANTINE/ROMANESQUE. SdB

F. W. Deichmann, *Einführung in die christliche Archäologie* (1983), 74–82.

D. Kinney, 'The Church Basilica', *Acta ad archaeologiam et artium historiam pertinentia*, 15 (2001), 115–35.

R. Krautheimer, 'The Constantinian Basilica', *DOP* 21 (1967), 117–40.

Basilica, The (*ta Basilika*) 'Imperial Laws', a series of Greek writings reorganizing and updating Justinian's 6th-century Latin **Corpus iuris civilis*. The project was begun under the Byzantine emperor Basil I and completed *c.*888 under Leo VI. The new work in its complete, revised form was contained in six volumes of 60 books, with the laws arranged by subject matter. The *corpus* was considered an official collection of actual laws, though it did preserve some obsolete prescriptions and terms. RSM

Basilicorum libri LX, ed. H. J. Scheltema and N. van der Wal, 8 vols (1953–88).

A. Schminck and A. Kazhdan, 'Basilika', *ODB*, vol. 1, 265–6.

Basin, Thomas (d. 1491) Bishop of Lisieux and archbishop of Caesarea. Having taken part in the *League of the Public Weal (1465), Basin fled France. Between 1471 and 1484, he wrote important chronicles of the reigns of *Charles VII and Louis XI, partly to explain and justify his actions. CDT

B. Guenée, *Between Church and State* (1991), 259–375.

bas instruments *See* MUSICAL INSTRUMENTS, CATEGORIZATION OF.

Basoche (Bazoche) Professional *guild of law clerks created in the 14th century, given the privilege of performing religious plays. They called themselves a 'parliament' and annually elected a 'king'. The guild influenced the development of comic *drama in the late MA through its didactic and festive practices. MBG

M. Bouhaïk-Gironès, 'La Basoche et le théâtre comique: identité sociale, pratiques et culture des clercs de justice (Paris, 1420–1550)', Ph.D. thesis (Paris, 2004).

Basques The Vascones or Basques are first recorded shortly before the turn of the Christian era, when they, along with the Astures and Cantabri, the last of the indigenous peoples of Iberia to be subdued, were finally conquered by the Romans. Basque itself is the only non-Indo-European language in western Europe, and the only Iberian language to have survived the Roman period. Both these facts suggest a very ancient origin for the Basque population in roughly its present-day home, but any further precision is impossible and highly politicized by modern developments.

The evidence for Basque integration into Roman provincial culture is unclear. Archaic forms of family organization seem to have survived in the Basque country while its neighbours were adopting Roman modes of social life. In late antiquity, 'Basque' remained a byword for the savage and uncivilized, though one need not believe in deliberate Basque resistance to Romanization. Unusually for the peninsular north, the Basques are better attested in the *Visigoth period than they are in the Roman, and are demonstrably hostile to the Visigoth monarchy. How Basque society was organized—even precisely what regions constituted

Vasconia in this period—is completely unknown, but there is no shortage of records of Gothic campaigns against the Basques. King *Leovigild won a victory over the Basques in the course of his conquest of the peninsula, even founding the city of Victoriacum—the modern site is disputed—to commemorate the event and provide a base from which the region could be secured. How little good that did is demonstrated by the repeated campaigns into the region that his successors found necessary. One of them, Roderic (710/11–711/12), had in fact been engaged in a Basque campaign when he was forced to march south to confront the Arab and *Berber invasion in which he lost his life—and in which the Visigothic kingdom was destroyed.

The Gothic monarchs were not the only ones to suffer from Basque depredations. It seems likely that Basque expansion out of the Pyrenees and into that part of southwestern Gaul that would become Gascony had begun in the course of the 7th century, exploiting periods of disorder in Frankish government. Certainly, the Frankish king *Dagobert I made a concerted effort to subdue the northern Pyrenees, forcing many Basque *seniores* to submit to him, though with little lasting effect: by the beginning of the 8th century, it is clear that a Gallic Vasconia existed in addition to the older Spanish one. We lack any real knowledge of the Spanish Basques in that century, though the Arab conquest of the Ebro valley may have confined Basque influence within the higher mountains. In Gaul, by contrast, we repeatedly see Basque warriors being recruited into the wars between the *Carolingians and the recalcitrant dukes of *Aquitaine. In this same period the Garonne river seems to have marked the boundary between Aquitaine proper and the new Gascony, though in later centuries the division fell further south, along the Adour. The most famous episode of 8th-century Basque history is the great victory over *Charlemagne's army at *Roncesvalles in 778, which effectively confined Frankish presence south of the Pyrenees to *Catalonia.

Though Frankish military campaigns centred on Pamplona and the valley of *Aragon continued into the 820s, around 824 Pamplona became independent under one Iñigo Arista. The history of his little kingdom during the rest of the 9th century is almost a total blank, though it seems that the Christian rulers of Pamplona maintained close ties to the Muslim overlords of Saragossa, the Banu Qasi. In the early 10th century, the new Jimeno dynasty is recorded in Pamplona. At the same time, the county of Viscaya is attested for the first time, while Guipúzcoa first appears a separate entity in the 11th century. By that time, the separate regions that make up the modern Vascongadas had all taken on something like their present territorial form, while the annexation to Pamplona of the territory around *Nájera created the base around which the kingdom of *Navarre would emerge in the 11th century. *See also* CHURCH HISTORY. MKu

R. Collins, *The Basques* (²1990).
J. M. Lacarra, *Historia política del reino de Navarro*, 3 vols (1972–3).
J. M. Novo Güisán, *Los pueblos vasco-cantábricos y galaicos en la Antigüedad Tardía, siglos III–IX* (1992).
M. Rouche, *L'Aquitaine des Wisigoths aux Arabes, 418–781* (1979).
C. Sánchez-Albornoz, *Vascos y Navarros en su primera historia* (²1976).

Basra (al-Basrah) City 420 km southeast of *Baghdad on the Shatt al-Arab, previously a *Persian settlement. Utbah ibn Ghazwan chose this location, on the orders of *Caliph *Umar ibn al-Khattab, to establish a military cantonment in 638 for control over the Persian Gulf route and as a base for further expeditions eastward. By the 9th century it had emerged as a leading commercial emporium for non-Arabs and the centre of a school of language study. It was, however, sacked in the *Mongol invasion. MD

S. C. Judd, 'Basra', *MedIsl*, vol. 1, 99.

basse danse A stately dance in 15th- and early-16th-century courts, with music improvised over a simple bass line. The term is mentioned *c.*1320 by *Toulouse poet Raimon de Cornet. The earliest documents to describe the steps are from 15th-century Italy. EAu

F. Crane, *Materials for the Study of the Fifteenth Century Basse Dance* (1968).
D. Heartz, 'The Basse Dance: Its Evolution circa 1450 to 1550', *Annales musicologiques*, 6 (1958–63), 287–340.

bastard feudalism A construct created by 19th-century historians to describe the transformation of feudal military obligations in the later MA. If *feudalism itself is a construct created by later historians to describe *land tenure, then bastard feudalism represents the degradation of this construct in England between the 11th and 15th centuries. In earlier, more ideal forms of feudalism, lords raised armies of *vassals, who performed *homage and provided military service in return for *fiefs. Over time, these personal relationships between lords and vassals deteriorated, forcing lords to hire armies composed of *mercenaries. Bastard feudalism coincided with the decline in royal power in England, marked by the crown's failure to exact feudal dues and obligations from its vassals which inhibited the monarch's ability to raise armies. At the same time, local and aristocratic power increased, enabling the *nobility to raise short-term armies of retainers. TMV

M. Hicks, *Bastard Feudalism* (1995).

bastides Planned villages and *towns founded in southwestern France *c.*1220–1370. Some were intended to attract *peasants to ameliorate agricultural production, others to control and defend an area or to fulfil administrative functions. Many were originally unfortified, then had walls built because of the *Hundred Years War. Founded by counts and kings, and sometimes by several lords who shared rights, bastides consisted of standardized allotments in a grid layout. Privileges attracted settlers. The *nobility, ecclesiastics, and *serfs were usually excluded, ensuring the legal equality of inhabitants. Lords taxed *trade and each allotment. *See also* LORDSHIP AND TOWN. NB

G. Bernard, *L'Aventure des bastides: villes nouvelles du Moyen Âge* (1998).

Bastille Fortress begun under *Charles V (1370), completed twelve years later, to guard the eastern approach to *Paris. Its two gates, one facing west toward Paris and the other east toward open country, were flanked by two donjons (dungeons) with four towers at each angle, all joined by a wall 3 m thick at the base and topped by a parapet walk. Manned by a captain and a force of around ten, it served as an *arsenal and *prison from the early 15th century until its destruction in 1789. RCl

C. Quétel, *La Bastille* (1989).

Bataille, Nicolas (*fl.* 1363–1399/1400) Parisian *tapestry merchant. Bataille mediated between *patrons and workshops, maintaining a stock of tapestries and cartoons, negotiating contracts, and advancing funds for materials. He arranged the production of the *Angers Apocalypse* (1373–80) for Louis of *Anjou. *See also* ANGERS; ATELIER. LJW

J. Guiffrey, 'Nicolas Bataille, tapissier parisien du XIVe siècle', *Mémoires de la Société de l'Histoire de Paris et de l'Île-de-France*, 10 (1884), 268–317.
J. Lestocquoy, *Deux siècles de l'histoire de la tapisserie (1300–1500)* (1978), 18–32.

Bate, Henry (1246–1310) Born in *Malines (Mechelen); died in Tongerloo. A philosopher, theologian, astronomer, astrologer, and musician, he was a pupil of *Thomas Aquinas. He was *cantor and *canon of the cathedral of St-Lambert (*Liège) and tutor to Guy de *Hainaut. He made astrolabes and dedicated *Magistralis compositio astrolabii* to his friend *William of Moerbeke. He also authored commentaries on the astrological works of Abraham *ibn Ezra and penned the *Speculum divinorum et quorundam naturalium*. *See also* ASTROLOGY; ASTRONOMY; PHILOSOPHY, WESTERN. LMP

T. Gregory, 'Platone e Aristotele nello *Speculum* di Enrico Bate di Malines', *Studi medievali*, 3/2 (1961), 302–19.
G. Guldentops, 'Henry Bate's Encyclopedism', in *Pre-Modern Encyclopedic Texts*, ed. P. Binkley (1997), 227–37.
G. Wallerand, 'Henri Bate de Malines et saint Thomas d'Aquin', *Revue Néoscolastique de Philosophie*, 36 (1934), 387–411.

Bath and Wells (see) *Edward 'the Elder' established a *diocese at Wells, *Somerset, within the *archdiocese of *Canterbury in 909 as a missionary outpost from *Glastonbury abbey. Bishop John of Villula moved the see to Bath *c.*1090, thus beginning the protracted antagonism concerning episcopal *elections; further animosity arose when Bishop Savaric (1192–1205) appropriated Glastonbury abbey, calling himself 'bishop of Glastonbury'. In 1219 *Pope Honorius III attempted to settle hostilities by authorizing the diocesan title 'Bath and Wells'. In 1245, *Pope Innocent IV ordained joint elections to be held alternately at Bath and Wells, with the conjoined title for the diocese. Secular *canons governed the *cathedral chapter. At the Dissolution (1538–40) Wells became the *cathedral church and Bath abbey a *parish church. LTC, WJD

C. M. Church, *Chapters in the Early History of the Church of Wells, AD 1136–1333* (1894).
W. Hunt, *Diocesan Histories: Bath and Wells* (1885).
E. A. Livingstone, 'Bath and Wells', in *Oxford Dictionary of the Christian Church* ([3]1997), 170.
Victoria County History: Somerset, vol. 2 (1911), 1–67.

baths Medicinal bathing in hot or mineral springs had been known since classical times. The baths at Pozzuoli near *Naples are only the most famous of these, commemorated in detailed illuminations for each separate spring. Wells were also associated with saints and were places to wash away disease with purifying *holy water. Bathing formed part of the *regimen of health prescribed by *physicians, enabling the evacuation of impurities from the body. The association of public bath houses with *prostitution, on the other hand, gave bathing a doubtful reputation, particularly where mixed bathing was allowed. *See also* CIVIC MEDICINE. PMJ

A. Karpozilos *et al.*, 'Baths', *ODB*, vol. 1, 271–2.
C. M. Kauffmann, *The Baths of Pozzuoli* (1959).
R. Porter, ed., *The Medical History of Waters and Spas* (1990).

Battani, Abu abd Allah Muhammad ibn Jabir al- (Albategnius, Albategni) (*c.*858–929) Arab astronomer, born in al-Raqqa (now north-central Syria). He authored several works on *astronomical and *astrological topics. His most successful work was known in Arabic as simply *Kitab al-zij* (Book of Astronomy), although it contained, in addition to tables and star catalogues, information on instrument-building and calculation. The son of an instrument maker, he improved upon existing astronomical *instruments (he was rumoured to have owned an astrolabe three cubits in diameter) and found new ways to use spherical trigonometry in his calculations. He acquired accurate values for the obliquity of the ecliptic and the length of the seasons and of the tropical year. The *Kitab al-zij* was translated into Latin in the mid 12th century and was printed in 1537 as *De motu stellarum* and in 1645 as *De scientia stellarum*. It was cited by *Copernicus, Riccioli, and Kepler. *See also* CALENDARS AND RECKONING OF TIME; COSMOLOGY; MATHEMATICS. PGSo

W. Hartner, 'Al-Battani', *DSB*, vol. 1, 507–16.
J. North, *The Norton History of Astronomy and Cosmology* (1994), 186–8.

Battle (abbey) *See* HASTINGS, BATTLE OF.

battle, trial by Widely practised, trial by battle (judicial combat) was a means of achieving a final decision between disputants. Not unlike the *ordeal, trial by battle relied on combatants' physical prowess to render a judgement in favour of the victorious party. Legal historians have distinguished between early medieval forms of trial by battle, thought to have been concerned with achieving a final decision, and later practices aimed at establishing legal proof of a fact. There is little evidence that trial by battle was known in England before the *Norman Conquest. Twelfth-century English legal writers already express hostility toward it, and it seems to have faded from English practice by the 14th century. KBS

R. Bartlett, *Trial by Fire and Water: The Medieval Judicial Ordeal* (1986).
G. E. Levi, ed., *Il duello giudizario: enciclopedia e bibliografia* (1932).
H. Nottarp, *Gottesurteilstudien* (1956).
P. Wormald, *The Making of English Law* (1999), 71–2.

battle axe *See* MILITARY ARTS.

Baude Cordier (d. 1397/8) Probably harpist and *organist at the court of Philip II 'the Bold', duke of *Burgundy (1380s–90s). He is attributed as the composer of nine *rondeaux, a *ballade, and a *Gloria, ranging from complex to simple in style. PML

G. Reaney, 'Cordier, Baude', *NGD2*, vol. 6, 255–6.
C. Wright, *Music at the Court of Burgundy, 1364–1419* (1979).

Baudri of Bourgueil (Baldricus) (*c*.1046–1130) Abbot of Bourgueil (*c*.1080), archbishop of Dol (1107). Baudri's collection of refined, witty Latin verse includes letters to male and female friends and *patrons, epitaphs, and occasional poetry. He also produced a history of the First *Crusade, *hagiographies, and *letters. *See also* EPIGRAM; LOIRE VALLEY POETS. BKB

Baudri of Bourgueil, *'Opera'*, *PL*, 162, 1043–58; 166, 1181–1280.
—— *Poèmes*, ed. J.-Y. Tilliette, 2 vols (1998, 2002).
G. Bond, *The Loving Subject: Desire, Eloquence, and Power in Romanesque France* (1995).

Baumstark, Anton Professor of *liturgy and eastern languages; taught in *Germany and the *Low Countries; founded and edited *Oriens Christianus* and *Jahrbuch für Liturgiewissenschaft*. His 654 works include *Liturgie comparée* (1940), in which he sought to trace the 'laws' of liturgical evolution. RER

T. Klauser, 'Anton Baumstark (1872–1948)', *Ephemerides Liturgicae*, 63 (1949), 185–207.

bautastein Large stone raised on end and secured in the ground. Without inscription, such stones served as memorials, fertility symbols, or grave markers, and were common in Norway, Sweden, and parts of Denmark and north Germany from the Iron Age and perhaps as early as the late Bronze Age. *See also* ARCHAEOLOGY: SCANDINAVIA AND ICELAND. REB

E. Skjelsvik, 'Bautastein', *KLNM* 1 (1956), 391–4.

Bautzen Capital of *Saxon Upper Lusatia (*Lausitz). Originally a Slavic settlement, Bautzen and its surroundings (Land Bautzen) were integrated into the Roman Empire by King Conrad II (1031). From 1081 to 1635 (with the exception of brief intervals), the Land Bautzen was granted by the empire to the *dukes—later kings—of *Bohemia. The city was the leading member of the Lusatian union of six cities founded in 1346. *See also* ROMAN EMPIRE [CAROLINGIAN, OTTONIAN, SALIAN/FRANCONIAN DYNASTIES]; SLAVS. GA

R. Reymann, ed., *Die Geschichte der Stadt Bautzen* (1902; repr. 1990).
Von Budissin nach Bautzen: Beiträge zur Geschichte der Stadt Bautzen (2002).

Bautzen, Treaty (Peace) **of** (1018) Throughout the MA almost all (Holy) *Roman emperors were forced to defend their northeastern borders. On 30 January 1018 a rare treaty was signed at Ortenberg *Castle in *Bautzen between Emperor Henry II and Duke Bolesław I of *Poland, ending fifteen years of *warfare. It allowed Henry to focus on other military concerns and Bolesław to extend his lands toward *Kiev and *Byzantium. *See also* ROMAN EMPIRE [CAROLINGIAN, OTTONIAN, SALIAN/FRANCONIAN DYNASTIES]. KDV

Von Budissin nach Bautzen: Beiträge zur Geschichte der Stadt Bautzen (2002).
H. Wolfram, *Conrad II, 990–1039: Emperor of the Three Kingdoms*, tr. D. A. Kaiser (2006).

Bavaria Emerging from Roman provinces, by the mid 6th century it was a Frankish-influenced barbarian *regnum* ruled by Garibald, the first Agilolfing *duke, whose family heartland lay in the east around *Regensburg and *Salzburg, where there may have been some Romanized survival. The western lands, nominally under ducal authority, often came under Frankish influence; nonetheless, the Agilolfingi enjoyed over two centuries of relative independence from the Franks. The Bavarians pursued diplomatic and marital ties with *Lombards, Franks, and their Slavic neighbours in the east while generally avoiding armed conflicts. The formal Christianization of Bavaria began in the late 7th and early 8th centuries under Duke Theodo I (*c*.680–725) and his sons, when three foreign missionaries were active in Bavaria: *Rupert at Salzburg, *Emmeram at Regensburg, and Corbinian at *Freising. Numerous religious communities were founded in the 8th and 9th centuries by the dukes and the newly Christianized elites. Under Tassilo III (748–88) the Bavarians incorporated Carinthia as a subject territory under its own duke (772).

The death of Duke Odilo (736–48) left his minor son Tassilo III under Pippin III's guardianship. Forced to submit as Pippin's *vassal, Tassilo surrendered Bavaria to his uncle and received it back as a benefice. Tassilo's attempts to maintain independence from the Franks ended in 788 when *Charlemagne annexed the duchy. Bavaria, however, retained its status as an intact sub-regnum within the greater Frankish polity, and continued to serve as the staging ground for forays against the (*Bohemia-)Moravians and other *Slavs. *Louis the German became Bavaria's ruler in 826; the duchy functioned as the heartland of his East Frankish kingdom until his death in 876. The last half of his reign, and those of his successors, were plagued by internal and frontier rebellions. The last *Carolingian, Louis the Child, died in 906; Bavaria then re-emerged as a tribal duchy under the *Luitpoldinger dynasty (906–47). Luitpoldinger resistance to subordination to the German kings manifested itself in their Hungarian policy, alternately one of conflict and cooperation.

In 947, Otto II granted the duchy to his younger brother Henry (948–55). His son, *Henry II (the Quarrelsome, 955–78, 983–95), rebelled against the emperor Otto II, then briefly served as Otto III's guardian before turning his attention to Bavarian constitutional reform. Another notable rebel was *Henry the Lion. Several Bavarian dukes ascended the imperial throne, notably Henry IV and Louis of Bavaria. In the 12th century Bavaria was a Welf (*Guelph) stronghold, and hence a centre of opposition to Hohenstaufen ambitions. Conflict and resistance had little effect on Bavaria's territorial integrity; its borders even today correspond reasonably well to those of the MA. *See also* ROMAN EMPIRE [CAROLINGIAN, OTTONIAN, SALIAN/FRANCONIAN/HOHENSTAUFEN DYNASTIES]. KLP

C. I. Hammer, *From Ducatus to Regnum: Ruling Bavaria under the Merovingians and Early Carolingians* (2007).

M. Spindler and A. Kraus, eds, *Handbuch der bayerischen Geschichte*, 2 vols ([3]1995).

Baybars (Baibars, Beibars, Bibars), **al-Bunduqdari** (*c.*1223–77) Fourth Bahri Mamluk sultan in *Egypt. He is said to have been a Turk purchased by the *Ayyubid sultan Salih and was called after his subsequent master. Militarily, he repulsed the *Mongols, suppressing rival princes. He also increased the efficiency of the postal system. By the end of his reign, he had led 38 campaigns in Syria alone. MD

R. Amitai, 'Baybars I', *MedIsl*, vol. 1, 101–3.

Bayeux A Gallic town, once the Roman *Civitas Baiocassium*, on the Aure river, near the English Channel. Its Roman street plan lasted into the 17th century. Conceded to the *Normans in 924, it became their organizing point in the west. It was governed, sometimes misgoverned, by wealthy, powerful 11th/12th-century bishops, including *William the Conqueror's half-brother *Odo (1049/50–1097). Later growth was less spectacular, but the result is the survival of an impressive *cathedral complex and 'Old Town'. *See also* BAYEUX EMBROIDERY. JMHo

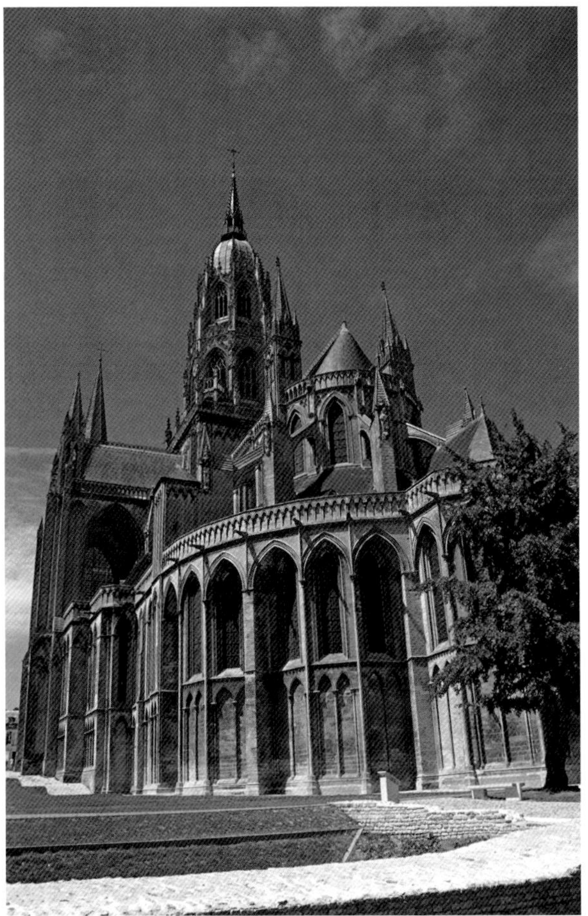

Bayeux: Notre-Dame cathedral.

D. Bates, *Normandy Before 1066* (1982), 128–32.

S. Gleason, *An Ecclesiastical Barony of the Middle Ages: The Bishopric of Bayeux, 1066–1204* (1936).

Bayeux Embroidery (Bayeux Tapestry) A 230ft-long by 1½ft-high wool-on-linen depiction of the *Norman Conquest. Though it is uncertain where, when, or by whom, the *textile was probably *embroidered under the *patronage of either *William the Conqueror's wife, *Matilda, or his brother *Odo of Bayeux, for exhibition in a palace or *cathedral. Its borders are decorated with flowers, exotic animals, and Aesopian fables.

Scenes from the Bayeux Embroidery (Tapestry).

Latin inscriptions accompany the main panels, which show *Harold II Godwinson in council with English king *Edward the Confessor, Harold's trip to *Normandy during which he is captured and taken to Duke William, and William and Harold's military expedition to *Brittany, at the end of which Harold swears an oath on *relics at *Bayeux, returns to England, and has himself crowned king upon Edward's death while Halley's comet appears. Thereupon, William has a fleet built, crosses the Channel, lands at Pevensey, and pillages. The battle of *Hastings is depicted in vivid detail, including William's feigned retreat, the arrow piercing Harold's eye, and the actual Anglo-Saxon retreat.

The right end may be missing 7–10ft. The textile also provides information about medieval land and sea *warfare and architecture. RHB

R. H. Bloch, *A Needle in the Right Hand of God: The Norman Conquest of 1066 and the Making and Meaning of the Bayeux Tapestry* (2006).
P. Bouet, B. Levy, and F. Neveux, eds, *The Bayeux Tapestry: Embroidering the Facts of History* (2004).
S. A. Brown, *The Bayeux Tapestry: History and Bibliography* (1988).
M. F. Foys *et al.*, eds, *The Bayeux Tapestry: New Interpretations* (2009).
L. Musset, *The Bayeux Tapestry* (2005).
D. Owen-Crocker, ed., *King Harold II and the Bayeux Tapestry* (2005).

bay system The division of a church's *nave and aisles into segments by means of projecting wall and, latterly, roof supports. *See also* ART AND ARCHITECTURE: GOTHIC; CHURCH TYPES; GOTHIC DESIGN AND CONSTRUCTION TECHNIQUES. DJR

J. Bony, *French Gothic Architecture in the 12th and 13th Centuries* (1983), 81–3.
W. Horn, 'On the Origins of the Mediaeval Bay System', *Journal of the Society of Architectural Historians*, 17 (1958), 2–23.

Béarn Region in the Pyrenees; first mentioned as a viscountcy in the Treaty of Verdun (843), opposite the county of Bigorre (both bishoprics). The first parliament (*Cour Major*) appeared in 1080. Part of the *duchy of *Aquitaine, it passed to the English crown when *Eleanor of Aquitaine married *Henry II (1152); it was subject to England until 1347. In 1290 it became part of the county of *Foix. Count Gaston III Fébus claimed it an independent *fiefdom (1347), and subsequently attacked Bigorre under the English occupation of Gascony. The city of Pau was fortified (11th century) and became the stronghold capital (1464).

Later, rule passed to the kingdom of *Navarre, rendering doubtful the kingdom of *France's claim to it (despite *Capetian dynastic descent). Even Henry III of Navarre, who in 1589 became Henry IV of France, kept personal estates separate from the crown. France demanded that the Navarrese king concede lands to France in 1607, yet Béarn and Lower Navarre (as independent counties) were not transferred. LMP

P. de Marca, *Histoire de Béarn* (1640; [2]1894).
P. Tucoo-Chala, *Petite Histoire de Béarn* (2000).

beast fable and epic The medieval tradition of the beast fable has its roots in classical antiquity, and since the time of Herodotus at least (*Histories* 2/134), it has been associated with the name of Aesop, although no fables written by him survive. Beast epic, in contrast, is a purely medieval creation, originating in the 11th–12th centuries.

The two *genres differ in form and mood. Whereas a beast fable is characteristically brief and simple in style, a beast epic is long and rhetorically elaborate; the fable is preceded or followed by a serious moral, based on the behaviour of the *animals in the narrative, while in the beast epic moral reflections are voiced by the animals themselves, and are the subject of comedy. Both genres can be given topical significance: fables were often used to make a point about a particular historical situation, while satire plays a large part in the medieval Latin beast *epic.

1. Beast fable
2. *Kalila and Dimna*
3. Beast epic
4. Sermons and later developments

1. *Beast fable*

The oldest surviving fable collection is by the Latin author Phaedrus (first half of the 1st century AD). The collection by the Greek author Babrius, which has some indirect links with the medieval tradition, is assigned to various dates but none earlier than the late 1st century. The collection of 42 Latin fables by Avianus (*c.*400), which largely derives from Babrius, was widely used as a school text throughout the MA. The difficult verse form used by Phaedrus (iambic senarii) was less suitable for Latin beginners than the elegiacs of Avianus; probably for this reason Phaedrus' fables were recast into prose, in a collection known as the *Romulus vulgaris*, supposedly translated from Aesop's Greek by one 'Romulus'. Its date is uncertain, but the oldest surviving MS is from the 9th century. The *didactic function of beast fables led to further revisions and adaptations, such as the fables of *Adhemar of Chabannes. Probably in the late 12th century, the Romulan fables were turned into elegiac verse, and this version outdid all others in popularity for the rest of the MA. The elegiac *Romulus* (ascribed by Hervieux, on quite inadequate grounds, to a certain 'Walter the Englishman') survives in nearly 200 MSS, and from the 13th to the 15th centuries this is what any educated person is most likely to have thought of as 'Aesop'.

At about the same time there appeared the earliest vernacular fable collection, written in Anglo-Norman, by *Marie de France. Its principal source is the *Romulus Nilantii*, but it also draws on the *Romulus vulgaris*, beast epic, eastern tales, and (perhaps) *folklore. Marie's collection was itself turned back into Latin (the so-called *Romulus* 'LBG'), and served as a source for the Hebrew *Fox Fables* by Berechiah ha-Nakdan. Other medieval French fable collections (*Isopets*) were based on the elegiac *Romulus*, the *Novus Aesopus* of *Alexander Neckam, or Avianus (*Avionnet*). The Romulan tradition also stimulated fable collections in German (for example, Gerhard von *Minden's 'Wolfenbüttel Aesop' and Ulrich *Boner's *Edelstein*, the 'Magdeburg Aesop') and in Italian.

2. Kalila and Dimna

One of the most unusual Latin fable collections is the *Novus Aesopus* written by an Italian named Baldo (*c.*1200). Despite its title, this is not an Aesopic collection, but a verse rendering of some of the moralizing animal stories found in the vast oriental tale collection that exists in many languages and is known variously as *Kalila and Dimna*, the *Panchatantra*, or *The Fables of Bidpai*. This work has a complex narrative structure, with stories embedded within other stories, and it also anthropomorphizes the animals more fully than Aesopic fables do; Baldo adapted the stories to the Aesopic model by splitting them into individual units and providing each with a separate moral. The Hebrew version of *Kalila and Dimna* was translated into Latin by John of Capua as the *Directorium humanae vitae* (*c.*1270); a later version (*c.*1313) by Raymond of *Béziers is a plagiarization of John's work.

3. *Beast epic*

The earliest representative of beast epic is the **Ecbasis captivi* (11th century), written in Latin hexameters. It is the story of a calf (representative of the monk-author), who runs away from home, falls into the hands of a wolf, and is eventually rescued by the rest of the herd, under the leadership of the fox. Inset into this narrative is the tale of the 'sick lion', which tells how the fox convinced the lion that he could be cured only by being wrapped in the skin of a newly flayed wolf. This story also forms the core of the **Ysengrimus* (1148–50), a full-scale epic of over 6,500 Latin elegiacs, which is the first work to name the wolf and fox 'Ysengrimus' and 'Reinardus', respectively, and to structure its narrative on the basis of their repeated attempts to outwit each other. The 'sick lion' story is found as an anonymous independent poem, datable to the *Carolingian period ('Aegrum fama fuit'), but its ultimate origins are obscure. Similarly, the cock-and-fox story (ultimately to become *Chaucer's 'Nun's Priest's Tale') does not appear in Phaedrus, but it has a precursor in *Alcuin's *De gallo*, and also appears as a long independent poem probably composed in the 11th century (*Gallus et vulpes*), before forming an episode of *Ysengrimus*. Other episodes of *Ysengrimus* are reworkings of Aesopic fable; the motif of the fox's 'sham death' is borrowed from the *bestiary. Another Latin beast epic, the *Speculum stultorum* (1180×90) of *Nigel Longchamp, breaks away from the fox-and-wolf model; it relates the adventures of the ass 'Burnellus' in search of a longer tail.

The *Ysengrimus* heralded an explosion of vernacular beast epics, beginning in the late 12th century with the earliest branches (II–Va) of the **Roman de Renart*, closely followed by the MHG *Reinhart Fuchs*. Over the next 300 years, Reynardian poems proliferated: in Flemish, *Van den Vos Reinaerde* and its later adaptation, *Reinaerts Historie*; in French, Jacquemart Gielée's *Renart le Nouvel*, the *Couronnement de Renart*, and *Renart le Contrefait*; in Franco-Italian, *Rainaldo e Lesengrino*; and, in Low German, *Reinke de Vos*.

4. *Sermons and later developments*

Meanwhile, the role of fables was extended through their use as *sermon *exempla. In the early 13th century, the English cleric Odo of Cheriton compiled a fable collection for use in *preaching (translated into French, and also into Spanish as the *Libro de los gatos*). Odo's collection included material from the bestiary and from the Reynardian tradition. The *Fables* of the 15th-century Scots writer Robert *Henryson similarly mixed Reynardian and Aesopic material.

With the age of *print, both beast fable and beast epic took on a new lease of life. In 1476/7 (Ulm edition) there appeared the huge collection of Latin fables (with German translations) assembled by Heinrich Steinhöwel, which included a *Life of Aesop*, the *Romulus vulgaris*, the elegiac *Romulus*, seventeen fables of uncertain source (the *extravagantes antiquae*), another seventeen translated from Greek, and selections of fables from Avianus, from the *Disciplina clericalis* of *Petrus Alfonsi, and from the *Facetiae* of Poggio *Bracciolini. Julien Macho's French translation of Steinhöwel's work was the source of

*Caxton's *Aesop*, printed in 1484. Already in 1481, Caxton had published *The History of Reynard the Fox*, his translation of the prose version of *Reinaerts Historie* printed by Gerard Leeu in 1479. JM

Der Novus Aesopus *des Baldo, Beiträge zur lateinischen Erzählungsliteratur des Mittelalters*, ed. A. Hilka (1928).
G. Dicke and K. Grubmüller, *Die Fabeln des Mittelalters und der frühen Neuzeit: Ein Katalog der deutschen versionen und ihrer lateinischen Entsprechungen* (1987).
Ecbasis Cuiusdam Captivi per Tropologiam, ed. K. Strecker, *MGH.SRG* (1935).
Les Fabulistes latins, ed. L. Hervieux, 5 vols ([2]1893–9).
Favolisti Latini Medievali, ed. F. Bertini, 8 vols (1984–).
C. Filosa, *La favola e la letteratura esopiana in Italia dal medio evo ai nostri giorni* (1952).
J. Flinn, *Le Roman de Renart dans la littérature française et dans les littératures étrangères au moyen âge* (1963).
'Gallus et Vulpes', ed. L. Herrmann, *Scriptorium*, 1 (1946–7), 260–66.
K. Grubmüller, *Meister Esopus: Untersuchungen zur Geschichte und Funktion der Fabel im Mittelalter* (1977).
H. R. Jauss, *Untersuchungen zur mittelalterlichen Tierdichtung* (1959).
B. M. Kaczynski and H. J. Westra, 'Aesop in the Middle Ages: The Transmission of the Sick Lion Fable and the Authorship of the St Gall Version', *Mittellateinisches Jahrbuch*, 17 (1982), 31–8.
F. P. Knapp, *Das lateinische Tierepos* (1979).
Marie de France: Fables, ed. and tr. H. Spiegel (1987).
Nigel de Longchamps, *Speculum Stultorum*, ed. J. H. Mozley and R. R. Raymo (1960).
J. Mann, *From Aesop to Reynard: Beast Literature in Medieval Britain* (2009).
M. Nøjgaard, *La Fable antique*, 2 vols (1964–7).
Recueil général des Isopets, ed. J. Bastin, 2 vols (1929–30).
Romulus, elegiac: The Fables of 'Walter of England', ed. A. E. Wright (1997).
Romulus vulgaris: Der lateinische Äsop des Romulus und die Prosa-Fassungen des Phädrus, ed. G. Thiele (1910).
E. Voigt, ed., *Kleinere lateinische Denkmäler der Thiersage aus dem zwölften bis vierzehnten Jahrhundert* (1878).
Ysengrimus: Text with Translation, Introduction, and Commentary, ed. J. Mann (1987).
J. M. Ziolkowski, *Talking Animals: Medieval Latin Beast Poetry, 750–1150* (1993).

beatific vision Immediate knowledge or direct perception of God, which *angels and the souls of the just enjoy in *heaven, considered the most intimate possible union with God and the final destiny of the redeemed. 'Beatific' indicates resultant happiness or blessedness. 'Vision' indicates direct apprehension of God 'as he is' (his essence) rather than a 'mediate' knowledge of God, something attainable by the human mind in this life. Controversies focusing on 'spiritual' versus bodily 'seeing', and Nature versus Grace, were partially resolved by *Pope Benedict XII's *Benedictus Deus* (1336). JCH

C. W. Bynum, *The Resurrection of the Body in Western Christianity, 200–1336* (1995).
M. Dykmans, *Pour et contre Jean XXII en 1333: deux traités avignonnais sur la vision béatifique* (1975).

Beatus manuscripts A group of MSS illustrating the *commentary on the Book of the Apocalypse, compiled *c.*776 from the patristic *exegetical literature by a Spanish monk, *Beatus of Liébana. *See also* LITERATURES: APOCALYPTIC. IDK

Actas del Simposio para el Estudio de los Códices del 'Comentario al Apocalipsis' de Beato de Liébana, 3 vols (1978–80).
J. Williams, *The Illustrated Beatus: A Corpus of the Illustrations of the Commentary on the Apocalypse*, 5 vols (1994–2003).

Beatus of Liébana (d. 798) A Spanish monk in Liébana (Cantabria), who in the 8th century authored a highly influential commentary on the Apocalypse. The significance of this commentary lay not so much in the text, which is a compilation of the ideas of previous authorities on the subject (especially Tyconius), as in the *manuscript illuminations that complement it in the many extant versions of the work.

Little is known about Beatus himself, except that he corresponded with *Alcuin and that he vigorously criticized *Adoptionism, preached by *Felix of Urgell and *Elipandus of *Toledo. The Adoptionist position, claiming that Christ was Son of God by adoption and not by essence, had been condemned as *heresy in 798 by Pope Leo III.

Beatus's *Commentary*, composed between 776 and 786, describes the Last Judgement and was extremely popular during the MA. Twenty-six MSS contain highly inventive, lavish illuminations. The biblical episodes depicted are meant to be interpreted allegorically rather than literally: the Vision of the Seventh Trumpet (Revelation 11:15, 12:17), the Four Horsemen (Rev. 6), the Heavenly Jerusalem (Rev. 21:9, 22:5), and others. In the first episode, for example, a woman and a child confront a red dragon with seven heads, and a war ensues in heaven. While some interpreted the woman as the Virgin *Mary and the child as Christ, others, including Beatus, saw them as personifications of the church and the Christian believer reborn through *baptism. This interpretation of Beatus's commentary was more prevalent than the eastern-derived Mariological one in the early western MA. *See also* LITERATURES: APOCALYPTIC. MPi

Adversus Elipandum libri duo, ed. B. Löfstedt, *CCCM* 59 (1984).
Sancti Beati a Liebana Commentarius in Apocalypsin, ed. E. Romero-Pose, 2 vols (1985).
J. Williams, 'Purpose and Imagery in the Apocalypse Commentary of Beatus of Liébana', in *The Apocalypse in the Middle Ages*, ed. R. K. Emmerson and B. McGinn (1992), 217–33.
—— *The Illustrated Beatus*, 5 vols (1994–2003).

Beaucaire A trading town on the main route from Italy to Spain at the Rhône, once in the kingdom of *Burgundy, then held by the counts of *Provence, then (1125) by the counts of *Toulouse. In the Albigensian *Crusade Beaucaire was taken by Simon de *Montfort but recovered by Raymond VI

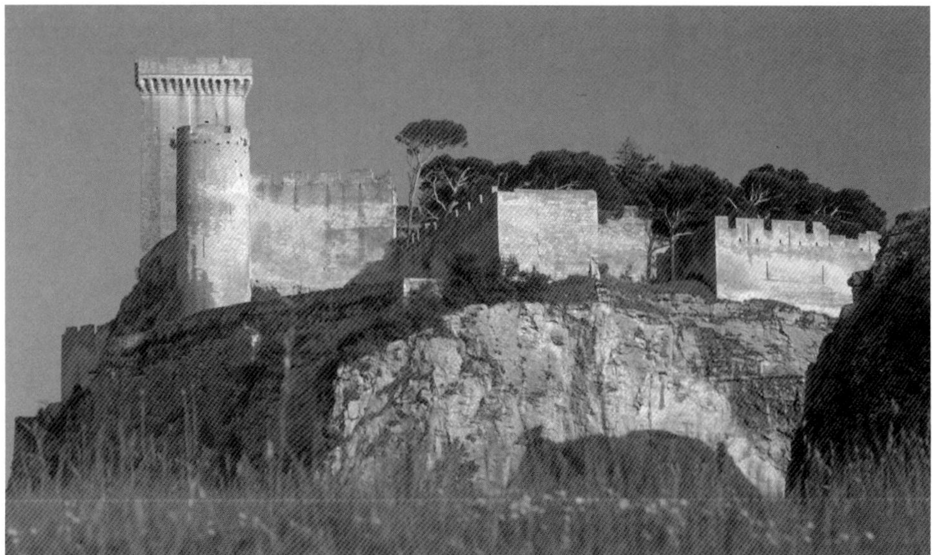
The castle at Beaucaire.

of Toulouse with the aid of the people, hence his grant of privileges (1217) to their Magdalen *Fair (22–27 July). *Louis IX made the town a free port and military headquarters of the seneschalcy (1229) of Beaucaire and Nîmes, confronting the *town of Tarascon across the river in imperial Provence. DHW

M. Contestin, *Beaucaire: Le Temps retrouvé* (1990).
O. Lombard, A. Michelozzi, M. Contestin, and J. Roche, *Beaucaire, notes historiques et archéologiques* (1974).

Beauchamp chapel (Warwick) Officially the Lady chapel of St Mary's collegiate church, this chantry and funerary *chapel was built in the 15th century by the Beauchamp family, earls of Warwick, and is a magnificent example of the Gothic style of architecture. *See also* ART AND ARCHITECTURE: GOTHIC; CHURCH, COLLEGIATE. SJER

N. Pevsner and A. Wedgwood, *Warwickshire* (1966).
A. F. J. Sinclair, *The Beauchamp Earls of Warwick in the Later Middle Ages* (1987).

Beaufort, Edmund *See* SOMERSET.

Beaufort, Henry *See* BEAUFORT FAMILY.

Beaufort, Lady Margaret *See* BEAUFORT FAMILY.

Beaufort family Named after a French *castle, John, Henry, Thomas, and Joan Beaufort were bastards of *John of Gaunt, *duke of *Lancaster (d. 1399) by his mistress, Katherine Swinford (née Roet, d. 1403), and half-siblings of *Henry IV of England. They were legitimated (except regarding the crown) when Katherine became Gaunt's third duchess. **Thomas** (d. 1426) became duke of *Exeter and guardian of *Henry VI. **Henry** (d. 1447) became Cardinal Beaufort and the principal statesman of Henry VI's minority. **Joan** (d. 1440) became countess of Westmorland and ancestress of the *Nevilles and most of the *peerage. **John**, earl of *Somerset (d. 1410), begat two dukes of Somerset, John (d. 1444), father of Lady Margaret Beaufort (d. 1509), who was the mother of *Henry VII, and, next, Edmund. Both dukes commanded in France, where Edmund lost *Normandy in 1450. A favourite of Henry VI, he was killed at *St Albans in 1455. Also committed *Lancastrians, his three sons were killed in the Wars of the *Roses: Duke Henry after *Hexham in 1464, dukes Edmund and John at *Tewkesbury in 1471. Charles Somerset, ancestor of the dukes of Beaufort, was Duke Henry's bastard. MAH

G. L. Harriss, *Cardinal Beaufort* (1988).
M. K. Jones and M. Underwood, *The King's Mother* (1992).

Beaujeu, house of The lords of Beaujeu were leading magnates of France whose estates in the Beaujolais passed in 1400 to the house of *Bourbon. *Anne of France, daughter of Louis XI, became lady of Beaujeu on marrying Pierre de Bourbon in 1471, and exercised significant power as regent during the minority of *Charles VIII. Louise of *Savoy, mother of Francis I, acquired Beaujolais, but the *lordship was restored to the Bourbon family in 1560. EARB

M. Méras, 'Le Dernier Seigneur de Beaujeu: Édouard II (1374–1400)', *BECh* 111 (1953), 107–23.
—— 'Beaujeu', *LMA*, vol. 1, 1754.

Beaumanoir, Philippe de (*c.*1250–96) Son of Philippe de Remy, whose verse compositions are sometimes ascribed to Beaumanoir, he was a royal *bailli* (*bailiff, administrator)

Beauchamp chapel, Warwick.

Bec abbey.

in *Poitou, *Vermandois, and *Senlis after an appointment by the count of *Clermont-en-Beauvaisis. He compiled Beauvais's laws of *custom *c.*1280–83. This celebrated compilation, edited three times and often hailed as the *chef-d'œuvre* of the genre, includes Beaumanoir's views of justice and records of a hundred cases, real or imaginary, that confirm rulings as customary law. FRPA

The Coutumes de Beauvaisis of Philippe de Beaumanoir, tr. F. R. P. Akehurst (1992).

Beauneveu, André (*c.*1335–1401/3) French sculptor and painter. In the 1360s he worked for *Charles V of France, executing four tombs in the abbey of *St-Denis. From 1386 he was employed by Jean, Duc de *Berry, for whom he created *sculptures, monumental *paintings, and *manuscript illuminations. *See also* SARCOPHAGUS AND TOMB. MCS

U. Heinrichs-Schreiber, *Vincennes und die höfische Skulptur* (1997).

F. Joubert, 'Illusionnisme monumental à la fin du XIVᵉ siècle', in F. Joubert and D. Sandron, *Pierre, lumière, couleur* (1999), 367–84.

Bec (abbey) Founded in central *Normandy in 1034 by the *knight Herluin, Bec, despite its initial obscurity, soon gained a reputation for piety and learning, producing two notable ecclesiastics: *Lanfranc and *Anselm, scholars and archbishops of *Canterbury. AJHi

S. N. Vaughn, *The Abbey of Bec and the Anglo-Norman State, 1034–1136* (1981).

Beccadelli, Antonio ('Il Panormita') (1394–1471) Sicilian poet, humanist, and diplomat. He spent his early years in northern and central *Italy, moving to *Naples in 1434, where he served *Alfonso V of *Aragon. He is best remembered for writing the *Hermaphroditus* (1425), a collection of bawdy Latin *epigrams. FB

D. Coppini, ed., *Antonii Panhormitae Hermaphroditus* (1990).

E. O'Connor, 'Panormita's Reply to his Critics: The *Hermaphroditus* and the Literary Defense', *Renaissance Quarterly*, 50 (1997), 985–1010.

Becket, St Thomas, archbishop of Canterbury (*c.*1120–70) English saint and *martyr. Becket, the son of a London merchant, was educated at *Merton priory and in *London and *Paris. After serving several years in the household of Theobald of *Bec, archbishop of Canterbury, Becket was named archdeacon of *Canterbury in 1154. In 1155, at Theobald's recommendation, *Henry II named Becket chancellor. They quickly developed a close friendship, so when Theobald died in 1161, Henry supported Becket's *election, believing Becket, as archbishop, would continue to serve the king's interests. Becket reluctantly accepted, was consecrated in 1162, and, to Henry's dismay, began wholeheartedly to defend the rights of the church.

The most troublesome issue between Henry and the church concerned whether *clergy accused of civil *crimes should be tried in civil or ecclesiastical courts. Henry asserted the crown's authority over the church through the Constitutions of *Clarendon, which he claimed upheld practices dating from the time of *Henry I. Becket refused to endorse these measures, intensifying their quarrel, so that by the end of 1164, Becket was living in exile in France.

*Pope Alexander III negotiated an uneasy peace between the two, and they were reconciled on 20 July 1170. However, during Becket's absence, Henry arranged for his son to be crowned by the archbishop of *York, infringing on Canterbury's right of *coronation, and despite their truce, Becket *excommunicated the bishops involved in the coronation. Henry, in a fit of temper, upbraided his men for allowing Becket to treat him thus. Four *knights of Henry's household, taking this as an order to assassinate Becket, travelled to Canterbury and, on 29 December 1170, murdered the archbishop in his *cathedral. *Miracles were attributed to Becket immediately after his death. He was *canonized in 1173. Henry did public *penance before Becket's tomb in 1174. Becket's shrine was a *pilgrimage site that drew people from all over Europe until its destruction by Henry VIII in 1538. MBKo

F. Barlow, *Thomas Becket* (1986).

A. Duggan, *Thomas Becket* (2004).

J. C. Robertson and J. B. Sheppard, eds, *Materials for the History of Thomas Becket, Archbishop of Canterbury*, 7 vols (1875–85).

Bede, St (The Venerable Bede) (*c*.673–735) AS *England's most learned, prolific, and influential Latin writer, the greatest scholar of the age, and, from shortly after his death, honoured as a *doctor of the church. Having entered the twin monastery of *Wearmouth and Jarrow as a child *oblate under the direction of abbots *Benedict Biscop and *Ceolfrith, he was the abbey's teacher and author in every discipline of the monastic curriculum. He appended his own brief autobiography, followed by the extensive list of his some 30 works, to the book for which he is now most renowned, *Historia ecclesiastica gentis Anglorum*.

This beautifully structured work traces the history of England from its earliest days to Bede's own, and sets the pattern for later medieval English historians. Among his accounts of many otherwise unrecorded events and personages, Bede tells of the first named Anglo-Saxon poet, *Cædmon, a stable boy in Abbess *Hilda's monastery at Whitby. The *History*'s positive record of the successful spread of the Gospel to England, originally by monastic missionaries from *Iona and especially from Rome under *Pope Gregory I as well as its more recent development, is counterbalanced by the long formal letter written to his disciple Archbishop *Egbert of York, with its negative rehearsal of contemporary evils in the *Northumbrian church.

As an *exegete Bede wrote numerous *commentaries on the *Bible, sometimes presenting a compilation of patristic authorities within his own organized treatment, sometimes writing on parts never before treated, such as *On the Tabernacle* and *On the Temple* for the Old Testament and on the *Seven Catholic Epistles* for the New. He wrote a number of *hagiographic works, most notably a poetic and prose version of the Life of St *Cuthbert, and he composed a number of *hymns, poems, and *epigrams. He left a warm account of his abbey and its abbots, and sent a number of formal letters on ecclesiastical polity and religious topics to prelates. To prepare students for biblical study and *monastic life he generated a number of educational treatises, and he wrote two manuals on the science of *computus*, the second of which, *De temporum ratione*, set the standard for calendrical reckoning for the entire MA. This ideal monk lived and died a scholarly saint. His life and career are now commemorated at *Bede's World* in Jarrow. *See also* CALENDARS AND RECKONING OF TIME; CONVERSION OF THE ENGLISH. GHB

Bede, *Ecclesiastical History of the English People*, ed. B. Colgrave and R. A. B. Mynors (1969).

Bede: On the Reckoning of Time, tr. F. Wallis, rev. edn. (2004).

Bede's World, 15 May 2008, www.bedesworld.co.uk/.

G. H. Brown, *Bede the Venerable* (1987).

P. Hunter Blair, *The World of Bede* ([2]1990).

M. Lapidge, ed., *Bede and his World: The Jarrow Lectures, 1959–1993* (1994).

Opera exegetica (Beda Venerabilis), tr. and ed. S. Connolly, A. G. Holder, D. Hurst, and W. T. Foley (1962–2001).

C. Plummer, *Baedae opera historica* (1896; repr. 1975), *CCSL* 118–23.

Bedouin Pastoral nomads of Arab descent, found today in the *Arabian Peninsula, parts of *Iran, Pakistan, Turkestan, North Africa, and the Sudan. Their mobile life exploits uncultivable land, practising herding and transhumancy. With a patrilineal and tribalistic family system, they prize *honour, preserving ancient values of hospitality, and depend on confederation of alliances. *See also* PASTORALISM AND TRANSHUMANCE. MD

I. Shahîd, *Byzantium and the Arabs in the Sixth Century*, 2 vols (2002).

beekeeping Honey was practically the only *sugar known during the MA. It frequently was used in *therapeutics, to sweeten drinks, and as a seasoning and preservative. In addition, beeswax was the basis of all medieval lighting. Medieval beekeeping practices did not evolve noticeably from those used in antiquity. They involved gathering the hive's material and harvesting the honey, which ideally happened twice a year, in late spring and autumn. *See also* FOOD, DRINK, AND DIET; HEATING AND LIGHTING; MEAD. GC

E. Crane, *The World History of Beekeeping and Honey Hunting* (1999).

P. Mane, 'Abeilles et apiculture dans l'iconographie médiévale', *Anthropozoologica*, 14–15 (1991), 25–48.

P. Marchenay, *L'Homme et l'abeille* (1979).

beer *See* ALE- AND BEER-MAKING.

beghards and beguines As early as the 12th century, women who wished to live an *apostolic life of manual labour, spiritual awakening, and voluntary *poverty without joining a formal *religious order banded together in informal communities without professing formal *vows, or even formally renouncing the possibility of *marriage. These groups often began in urban settings where the women supported themselves through handicrafts, especially *weaving and cloth-making. These groups became known as 'beguines', perhaps taking their name from *Lambert le Bèges (li Beges), a priest from *Liège, who advised women to live in community and to minister to the needy. Soon, many groups began taking short-term vows, including sworn chastity, and developing their own spiritual rituals, often with the aid of sympathetic monks or clerics, particularly the *Cistercians.

This was the height of the movement, with numerous theologians praising the beguine way of life and advocating their practices. An especially ardent supporter was *Jacques de Vitry, the bishop of *Acre and eventual *cardinal-legate. Under his guidance, the beguines gained quasi-official status, but also came under stricter regulations. Many were forced to accept conventual rules and spiritual advisers, curtailing their independence but also assuring freedom from persecution.

This immunity did not last, however, and by the late 13th century, beguines were persecuted as *heretics. In particular, they were often accused of being members of the *Free Spirit movement. Regulations became tighter, forbidding beguines to receive alms or to travel, and requiring them to submit to local spiritual authorities. Beguines also became subject to clerical abuses, and appealed to authorities themselves for relief from attempts at seduction. Eventually, beguines were episcopally organized into *parishes, brought directly under clerical supervision, especially from *Dominicans, and lost their autonomy. However, throughout their history, beguines remained laywomen.

Beguine spirituality was characterized by *mysticism and *asceticism, often practised in extreme measures. Members of the movement produced a number of influential treatises, including *Mechthild of Magdeburg's *Flowing Light of the Godhood*, *Hadewijch of Antwerp's *Visions*, and Beatrice of Nazareth's *Seven Manners of Loving*, as well as Marguerite *Porete's *Mirror of Simple Souls*, which was declared heretical and banned. Additionally, Jacques de Vitry produced a number of *vitae* of remarkable women such as Christina Mirabilis and Mary of Oignies.

A similar male vocation, the 'beghards', developed in the late 13th century. These communities lacked the popularity of beguinages, and reached prominence only in Belgium. Living communally and working together, also primarily in weaving, beghard groups resembled Lombard *Humiliati. Unlike beguines, beghards were often freed from taxes and dues, and were less subject to persecution. However, a number were caught up in the Free Spirit accusations. When they inadvertently came under papal sanctions, most beghards became *Franciscan tertiaries, resulting in very few changes in their lifestyle. *See also* COMMUNES AND COMMUNITY; LAITY. MMS

H. Geybels, *Vulgariter Beghinae: Eight Centuries of Beguine History in the Low Countries* (2004).

H. Grundmann, *Religious Movements in the Middle Ages*, tr. S. Rowan (1995).

W. Simons, *Cities of Ladies: Beguine Communities in the Medieval Low Countries, 1200–1565* (2001).

Behaim, Albert (*c*.1180–*c*.1260) German cleric, born and educated near Niederaltaich, *Bavaria; *canon in *Passau from 1212; went to Rome for the Fourth Lateran *Council in 1215, remaining there in a diplomatic post. He helped establish a political coalition against *Frederick II. In 1237 or 1238 he returned to Germany to settle a *dispute between the duke of Bavaria and the bishop of *Freising, but had to flee back to *Rome. Returning in 1240 to agitate against the emperor, he *excommunicated the bishop of *Salzburg, which led to his second expulsion (1241). He participated in the Council of *Lyons in 1245 and returned to Passau in 1247, before being forced to leave again. Finally, he settled in Passau (1250), where he died. He left a diary and memory book, the *Missivbuch*. *See also* LIBRI MEMORIALES. AC

Das Brief- und Memorialbuch des Albert Behaim, ed. T. Frenz and P. Herde, *MGH, Briefe des späten Mittelalters* (2000), vol. 1.

T. Frenz, 'Kaiser Friedrichs II. standhaftester Widersacher in Bayern: der Passauer Domdekan Albertus Bohemus', University of Passau, 15 May 2008, www.phil.uni-passau.de/histhw/diversa/Behaim_Wuerzburg.html.

Beheim, Michael (1416×18–1474×8) German poet. Originally a *weaver, then a soldier, then a wandering poet; murdered. He composed pessimistic satirical, autobiographical, political, and historical poems, fables, religious songs, and songs like the *Meistersingers', creating his own melodies. AC

A. Classen, *Die autobiographische Lyrik des europäischen Spätmittelalters* (1991).

W. C. McDonald, *'Whose Bread I Eat': The Song Poetry of Michel Beheim* (1981).

Behetrías Seigneurial lands of northern *Castile and part of *León, in which free landholders were able to move and to choose their lord. Also called *benefactoría*, this form of *commendation was originally distinct from that of other areas in northern Spain, where small landholders permanently gave up ownership of land to a lord in exchange for protection, a bond usually passed on through inheritance. Greater freedom and contractual advantage was available in the *behetrías* because these repopulation zones had fewer powerful landlords. Often small landholders acted collectively. The choice of lord could be completely open—*de mar a mar*—or, as increasingly occurred, restricted to a particular lineage—*behetrías de linaje.* Although the institution has been traced to as early as the 11th century, the greatest wealth of information about it derives from the *Libro becerro de behetrías* commissioned by *Pedro I in 1351 as a census of all landholding rights in a large area north of the *Duero river. *See also* LAND TENURE; LORDSHIP AND TOWN. APK

I. Alvarez Barge, 'Lordship and Landownership in the South of Old Castile in the Middle of the Fourteenth Century', *JMH* 23 (1997), 75–88.
Consejo Superior de Investigaciones Científicas, *Los señoríos de Behetría* (2003).
C. Estepa Díez, *Las behetrías castellanas* (2003).
G. Martínez Díez, *Libro becerro de las behetrías* (1981).

Beirut (Berytus) Ancient Phoenician city, a bishopric by the late 4th century, it also had a famous law school. Damaged by earthquake in 551, the city was captured by the Arabs in 635. Muawiya, *caliph of the Umayyad dynasty, brought in Persian *colonists, and commercial relations with *Damascus and *Egypt resumed, financing fortifications. In 1110 the *crusaders, after taking *Jerusalem, blockaded and took the city. Two years later the first Latin bishop, Baldwin of Boulogne, was consecrated. The reconquering Mamluks further fortified it before an 18th-century war destroyed the fortifications. *See also* CASTLES, FORTIFICATIONS, AND FORTRESSES; EDUCATION, SCHOOLS OF LAW. MD

N. Jidejian, *Beirut through the Ages* (1973).

Beleth, Jean (*fl.* 1162) Theologian; author of a *commentary on the entire *liturgy, *Summa de ecclesiasticis officiis*, drawing on *Amalar, *Honorius of *Autun, and *Gratian's **Decretum*, among others. Compiled in four recensions, it exists in over 180 MSS and influenced *Sicard of *Cremona and *Pope Innocent III. RER

H. Douteil, ed., *Summa de ecclesiasticis officiis*, *CCCM* 41/41A (1976).

Belgrade (Beograd) *Serbia's capital, Belgrade (Roman Singidunum) is situated at the confluence of the rivers Sava and Danube. Fortified by Justinian, then taken by the Avars, it appears under its *Slavic name in a papal letter dated 878. Since the Christianization of *Bulgaria (864), Belgrade was an episcopal see. Attested by its Bulgarian name in western sources, it survived Bulgarian rule and lasted through the *Byzantine period (1018–*c.*1190), when the border fortress was the target of Hungarian attacks. During the 12th-century Byzantine–Hungarian wars, Belgrade was a starting point for military operations in Hungarian territory. After the withdrawal of Byzantine forces at the end of the 12th century, until *c.*1232, Belgrade was, along with other fortresses on the Danube line, a point of contention between the Hungarian kingdom and the second Bulgarian Empire.

Later, Belgrade formed part of a dynastic territory bestowed on the female relatives of the king. In 1284 Belgrade and the region of Machva received the former king of Serbia, Stefan Dragutin (r. 1276–82, d. 1316), as son-in-law of the Hungarian king. Belgrade remained a Hungarian border fortress until 1404, when King Sigismund granted it to his *vassal, the Serbian *despot Stefan Lazarević (1389–1427), who made Belgrade his capital. After the despot's death in 1427, Belgrade was returned to *Hungary, resisting Ottoman sieges in 1440 and 1456. Surrounded by Ottoman territory, strongly garrisoned, Belgrade survived until 1521, when it came under Ottoman rule. SMĆ

A. Kazhdan, 'Singidunum', *ODB*, vol. 3, 1904.
J. Mijušković, *Beograd u srednjem veku* (1967).

bells *See* MUSICAL INSTRUMENTS.

bells, manufacture of Initially small bells were forged with the hammer from *iron, *copper, and bronze, or made with the lost wax process. With the advent of the church bell, probably in the 6th century, a variation of the wax process was developed specifically for bells. The process was described in detail by *Theophilus in the 12th century. Bell founders constructed a two-part mould made primarily of clay. The clay core formed the inside surface of the bell, over which a bell was modelled in wax or tallow; the whole was then covered with the outer part of the mould, called the mantle or cope, leaving holes for the wax to run out.

Typically, bell founders placed the mould in a pit and built a *furnace around it. They lit a *wood fire in the furnace, causing the clay to harden and the wax or tallow to escape. They repaired the escape holes with clay and then built up the furnace, leaving only a small aperture on top. They then lit another fire around the mould and kept it burning for 24 hours. In separate furnaces, they heated pots in which they melted the bronze. When the clay mould was red hot, they rapidly filled the pit with lightly compacted earth to support the mould and prevent it from breaking up under the molten alloy, which was then poured in. With the *metal solid but still hot, they removed the earth from around the mould, removed the mould from the pit, and extracted the clay core to prevent cracking as the bell cooled. When the mould was completely cold, they broke it away from the bell. They smoothed and polished the bell with appropriate tools and abrasives and tuned it by filing the metal away at the proper places. In the 15th century, bronze gun founding was developed directly from the methods of bell founding. POL

C. Blair and J. Blair, 'Copper Alloys', in *English Medieval Industries: Craftsmen, Techniques, and Products*, ed. J. Blair and N. Ramsay (1991), 81–105.

G. Elphick, *The Craft of the Bellfounder* (1988).
Theophilus, *The Various Arts: De Diversis Artibus*, tr. C. R. Dodwell (1986).
R. F. Tylecote, *The Early History of Metallurgy in Europe* (1987).

bell tower (campanile, steeple) A tower in which one or more *bells are hung, usually connected to churches, sometimes also to civic buildings. Towers had been chiefly part of fortifications in antiquity. Other tower-like structures were known as isolated funerary monuments. The integration of a bell tower into the architectural scheme of a religious building took place in the early MA, in part as a functional response to the acoustic requirements of bell ringing (the greater the height the further it could be heard) and initially sometimes for reasons of defence.

In all cases the towers acquired strong symbolical associations and were impressive monuments. The simple cubic towers of the early MA could develop into spectacular transparent structures in the Gothic period. Bell towers are usually integrated into the church complex close to the entrance. In some regions they are completely detached. Churches of special importance sometimes have a double tower façade or a tower group. A crossing tower that surmounts the church *transept is not always a bell tower in the strict sense: like a cupola, it is often designed as an inner space, meant to elevate and light a central area of the interior. SdB

O. Asendorf, *Mittelalterliche Türme im Deutschordensland Preußen: Untersuchungen zu ihrer Bedeutung und Funktion* (1998).
J. P. McAleer, 'The Tradition of Detached Bell Towers at Cathedral and Monastic Churches in Medieval England and Scotland (1066–1539)', *JBAA* 154 (2001), 54–83.
A. Priester, 'Bell Towers and Building Workshops in Medieval Rome', *Journal of the Society of Architectural Historians*, 52 (1993), 199–220.
'Tours et clochers à l'époque préromane et romane', *Journées Romanes de Cuxa*, 28 (1995–6).

bema The Greek term for a speaker's platform became the common designation for the *altar area in the *church of the East. The Byzantine *bema* usually includes the *apse and an enclosed zone in front of it, slightly raised above the *nave floor. The *bema* in synagogues is an elevated area, generally made of wood, for the reading of the scriptures. *See also* ART AND ARCHITECTURE: BYZANTINE/SYNAGOGUE. SdB

C. Peeters, *De liturgische dispositie van het vroegchristelijk kerkgebouw* (1969).

Benedicamus Domino ('Let us bless the Lord') *Versicle closing the hours of the *Divine Office (except *matins). It was sung by a soloist or group and answered by the choir with *Deo gratias* ('Thanks be to God'). Elaborations included borrowed melodies and *troping. DDH

A. W. Robertson, 'Benedicamus Domino', *NGD2*, vol. 3, 237–9.

Benedicite Canticle from the 'Song of the Three Children' in the biblical Book of Daniel (named from its first word, 'Bless [ye the Lord]'), sung on *Sundays and feasts in medieval Lauds in the *Divine Office. It was included in English translation in the 1549 English *Book of Common Prayer*. *See also* LITURGY. DJKe

R. F. Taft, *The Liturgy of the Hours in East and West* (1986).

Benedict, Rule of St *See* BENEDICT OF NURSIA, ST.

Benedict Biscop (d. 689) Briefly abbot of Sts Peter and Paul, *Canterbury, then founding abbot of *Wearmouth-Jarrow. In his five *pilgrimages to *Rome he acquired a great collection of books and art with which he endowed these twin monasteries. Their co-abbot, *Ceolfrith, succeeded him. GHB

Bede, *'Historia Abbatum'*, in *Baedae opera historica*, ed. C. Plummer (1896; repr. 1975), vol. 1, 364–77.
P. Wormald, 'Bede and Benedict Biscop', in *Famulus Christi*, ed. G. Bonner (1976), 141–69.

Benedictine order Refers generally, but anachronistically, to those monasteries of both men and women which use as their primary governing document the Rule of *Benedict of Nursia, written in the early 6th century. For several hundred years thereafter, Benedict's was but one of many rules used by *monasteries in western Christendom, although it was certainly one of the most influential. In the 9th century, under the authority of Emperor *Louis the Pious, *Benedict of Aniane made Benedict's Rule the standard constitution for monasteries throughout the *Carolingian Empire, and thence for much of western Europe. Most monastic communities of the following centuries were in a profound sense Benedictine, although many communities augmented the Rule by means of written *'customs' (*consuetudines*).

One of the central principles of the Rule was the self-governing independence of a monastic community. Individual Benedictine houses did, however, join together in loose affiliations, by such means as sharing 'customs'. These affiliations were one of the means by which monastic leaders of the late 10th and early 11th centuries tried to reform the monastic life, and most of the affiliations were centred on reformist foundations such as *Cluny and *Gorze.

In the later 11th and 12th centuries, new groups of monastic reformers undertook a more radical transformation of the monastic life, although in reference to Benedict's Rule. By a contemporary convention referring to the colours of their robes, the newer reform monks were called *White Monks, while more traditional Benedictines were called Black Monks. In the decades preceding the Fourth Lateran *Council (1215), the 'order' emerged as a new form of organizing religious communities. These organizations, such as the 'mendicant' orders, consisted of a group of communities subject to the rule of a single superior general, as opposed to the Benedictine model of individual communities subject to the rule of their abbot. Several groups of White Monks, such as the *Cistercian order, adopted this form of organization. Despite the influence of the mendicants and White Monks, traditional Benedictines continued to be an important part of the religious life of the western church through the late MA and Reformation to the present.

Benedictine monasteries began to organize into regional congregations, the earliest being that formed in England in 1204. These congregations retained a relatively loose structure. Such congregations continue today to be the organizational structure of Benedictine monasteries within the Roman Catholic church. Those congregations have banded together as a 'Benedictine Confederation', which is now the formal title of Benedictine *monasticism within the Catholic church. *See also* RELIGIOUS ORDERS. TFH

G. Constable, *Medieval Monasticism: A Select Bibliography* (1976).
D. Knowles, *The Monastic Order in England: A History of its Development from the Times of St Dunstan to the Fourth Lateran Council, 940–1216* ([2]1963).
—— *From Pachomius to Ignatius: A Study in the Constitutional History of the Religious Orders* (1966).
St John's University, 'The Order of St Benedict' (1995–2008), 15 May 2008, www.osb.org/.
P. Schmitz, *Histoire de l'Ordre de Saint-Benoît*, 7 vols ([2]1948–56).

Benedictional *See* LITURGICAL BOOKS, LATIN.

Benedict of Aniane, St (*c.*750–821) Professed in 774, he became a monastic reformer in *Carolingian Francia, seeking with imperial support to impose the Rule of St *Benedict and a uniform customary on all *monasteries of the empire. His ideals may have influenced those of *Cluny. MAC

P. Bonnerue, *Benedicti Anianensis Concordia regularum*, CCCM 168/168A (1999).
J. Semmler, 'Benedictus II: una regula—una consuetudo', in *Benedictine Culture, 750–1050*, ed. W. Lourdaux and D. Verhelst (1983), 1–49.

Benedict of Nursia, St (*c.*480–*c.*545) Author of what became the most important collection of monastic rules in western Christianity. Little is known about his life. His Rule is the only work to survive from his hand. Posthumously, *Pope Gregory I the Great included an account of Benedict's life in his *Dialogues*. According to Gregory, Benedict fled ordinary society to become a *hermit in the hilly district of Norcia, northeast of Rome. Eventually, he became an abbot of several *monasteries, a career which culminated in the abbacy of *Monte Cassino.

As abbot, he composed his Rule, which was intended, like contemporary works of this genre, to be a guide to the monastic life and a constitutional document for monastic communities. It is an original work of deep spiritual insight, which artfully combines, often verbatim, several extant traditions about the monastic life. Although influential for centuries after Benedict's death, it was not until the 9th century and the efforts of the monastic reformer *Benedict of Aniane that Benedict's Rule became the standard for monastic communities, first in the *Carolingian Empire and later in western Europe more generally. Over time, the monasteries of Monte Cassino and *Fleury both claimed to possess the *relics of Benedict, and thus be the centre of his posthumous cult. *See also* BENEDICTINE ORDER; CUSTOMARIES AND ORDINALS, MUSIC AND LITURGY IN; MONASTICISM. TFH

T. Fry *et al.*, eds, *RB 1980: The Rule of St Benedict in Latin and English with Notes* (1981).
Gregory the Great, *Dialogues*, tr. O. Zimmerman (1959).
La Règle de Saint Benoît, ed. A. de Vogüé and J. Neufville, 6 vols (1971–72).

Benedictus Section of the Roman *Mass following the first Hosanna of the *Sanctus. By the 16th century it was separately performed during the *Eucharistic veneration. In *polyphonic mass settings of the 15th and 16th centuries, the Benedictus was set as a separate movement. RF

J. A. Jungmann, *The Mass of the Roman Rite*, tr. F. A. Brunner (German original, 1948) (1961).

Benedictus qui venit *See* SANCTUS.

Benediktbeuern (abbey) Bavarian *monastery founded in 748. The community declined under Duke Arnulf of *Bavaria (907–37), then was destroyed by the Hungarians in 955. Bishop Ulrich of *Augsburg refounded it as a community of *canons; in 1032 *Tegernsee's abbot restored it as a *Benedictine house. The **Carmina Burana* MS was discovered in its *library. KLP

Chronicon Benedictoburanum, ed. G. H. Pertz, *MGH.SS* 11 (1851).
W. Störmer, 'Fernstraße und Kloster: Zur Verkehrs- und Herrschaftsstruktur des westlichen Altbayern im frühen Mittelalter', *Zeitschrift für bayerische Landesgeschichte*, 29 (1966), 299–343.

Benedikt Ried (*c.*1454–1534) *Architect and head of the *masons' *guild at Prague Castle. Before coming to *Prague in 1488/9, he built the fortifications of the *castle of Burghausen. In 1502 he finished the Vladislav Hall, using large-span *tracery *vaults. He built royal town churches in *Kutná Hora and Louny, as well as noble residences. The most important architect of Bohemian Late Gothic, he renewed Danubian architecture, and under *Jagiełłonian rule evolved a style in transition towards the Renaissance. *See also* ART, BOHEMIAN; ART AND ARCHITECTURE: GOTHIC. HLá

G. Fehr, *Benedikt Ried: Ein deutscher Baumeister zwischen Gotik und Renaissance in Böhmen* (1961).

benevolence Benevolences were *gifts to the king in his necessity (usually in wartime) that all English subjects were bound to make. *Edward IV systematically assessed his subjects on what they should give of their 'benevolence'. *Parliament abolished benevolences in 1484, but forced gifts and loans continued until 1628. MAH

G. L. Harriss, 'Aids, Loans, and Benevolences', *Historical Journal*, 6/1 (1963), 1–19.

Benjamin of Tudela (*fl.* 1160–75) Jewish rabbi and traveller whose diary constitutes an important source of information for medieval cities and Jewish communities. A native of Tudela (Spain), Benjamin set out *c.*1160 on an almost fifteen-year journey taking him to over 300 cities including *Rome, *Constantinople, *Jerusalem, and *Baghdad. Though he also claimed to have visited *India and China, scholars generally concur that he turned around upon reaching Baghdad. For each locale, Benjamin provided details regarding local customs, history, economic conditions, and *geography, as well as descriptions of the local Jewish population. Unusual for his epoch, Benjamin revealed his sources of information and is considered highly reliable. Scholars have attributed several objectives to his *travel and exploration, such as assessing the conditions of *Jewish quarters in the Mediterranean, private commercial pursuits, and *pilgrimage to holy Jewish sites. His *Itinerary* remains important for the study of medieval *urban life, geography, and Jewish communities. *See also* JEWS, MEDIEVAL. AHo

M. N. Adler, ed., *The Itinerary of Benjamin of Tudela: Critical Text, Translation, and Commentary* (1907).
H. Harboun, *Benjamin de Tudèle, 1165/66–1172/73* (1998).
V. B. Mann, J. D. Dodds, and T. F. Glick, eds, *Convivencia: Jews, Muslims, and Christians in Medieval Spain* (1992).
A. Muñiz-Huberman, *El mercader de Tudela* (1998).

Benno of Osnabrück (d. 1088) Bishop and royal adviser. Involved in church and state affairs, Benno supported Emperor Henry IV. Supervisor of royal public works, and perhaps himself an *architect, he was initially in charge of the reconstruction of *Speyer cathedral. *See also* ROMAN EMPIRE [CAROLINGIAN, OTTONIAN, SALIAN/FRANCONIAN DYNASTIES]. ASC

'Vita Bennonis II Episcopi Osnabrugensis', in *Lebensbeschreibungen einiger Bischöfe des 10.–12. Jahrhunderts*, ed. and tr. H. Kallfelz (1973).

Benoît de Ste-Maure (St-More) (12th century) Court poet and historian of *Henry II of England, succeeding *Wace, he authored the *Chronique des ducs de Normandie* and the massively influential *Roman de Troie* (*c.*1165) This vast poem expands to approximately 28,000 French octosyllabic lines the Latin prose narratives of the fall of Troy by *Dares and *Dictys, introducing several love stories between the Greeks and Trojans, notably that between Troilus and Cressida (Benoît calls her Briseide). *See also* LITERATURES: ANGLO-NORMAN; PLANTAGENET/ANGEVIN DYNASTY. SK

P. Eley, 'History and Romance in the *Chronique des ducs de Normandie*', *MÆ* 68 (1999), 81–95.
D. Rollo, *Historical Fabrication, Ethnic Fable, and French Romance in Twelfth-Century England* (1998).

Benvenutus Gapheus *See* MEDICINE.

Benzo of Alba *See* INVESTITURE CONTROVERSY.

Beowulf The premier example of early Germanic literature, *Beowulf* is an anonymous OE poem of 3,182 alliterative verses composed in AS England sometime between the late 7th and early 11th centuries, preserved in a single fire-damaged MS copy, BL Cotton Vitellius A.xv (*c.*1000). It recounts the career of Beowulf, last king of the Geats, a people once living in southern Sweden. As a young hero, Beowulf sails to the court of Hrothgar, king of the Danes, to fight Grendel, a cannibalistic being who has terrorized the kingdom for twelve years, occupying the great hall Heorot by night. This creature is a descendant of Cain, mankind's first murderer. The hero wrestles with Grendel, ripping off Grendel's arm as he flees. The next night, Grendel's mother takes revenge upon Hrothgar's most beloved retainer. Beowulf tracks her to a cave at the bottom of a mere and kills her. Then he returns home to Sweden and eventually becomes king of the Geats for 50 years, when a fire-breathing *dragon is aroused. Beowulf confronts the dragon alone, but a young kinsman comes to his aid and helps him to kill it. The old king dies of his injuries, after which treasure obtained from the dragon's hoard is reburied with him, as 'useless to men as it was before'. Three times the impending destruction of the Geats by their enemies is prophesied, the last by a 'Geatish woman' who laments by Beowulf's pyre. His companions say 'he was of kings in the world the mildest of men and most gracious, the kindest to his people and most eager for their esteem'. Though the poet was a Christian, he depicts the hero and other pre-Christian characters with much sympathy and respect. The agency of the Christian God is adduced in the victories of Beowulf, but ignored in his defeat. Beowulf himself invokes God's aid, but attributes the ultimate outcome of events to *wyrd*, a general principle of negative eventuality that brings all human efforts to failure. CRD

R. E. Bjork and J. D. Niles, eds, *A 'Beowulf' Handbook* (1997).
R. D. Fulk, R. E. Bjork, and J. D. Niles, eds, *Klaeber's 'Beowulf'* ([4]2008).
A. Orchard, *A Critical Companion to 'Beowulf'* (2003).

Berakhia ben Natronai Ha-Naqdan (*fl.* 1190) Fabulist and translator, who may be identical with 'Benedictus le Puncteur' of *Oxford. His *Mishlei Shualim* (Fox Fables), relying on the *Romulus* Latin translation of Aesop, may also have been taken from the *Ysopet* of *Marie de France (*c*.1170). *See also* BEAST FABLE AND EPIC. PIAL

W. Jackson, 'Introduction', in *Fables of a Jewish Aesop*, ed. M. Hadas (1967), ix–x.
C. Roth, *The Jews of Medieval Oxford* (1951).

Berbers North African ethnic group found today from *Egypt to the Atlantic and the Niger. Though they were partially converted to *Islam, they frequently revolted, sometimes in the name of *Shia and *Kharijism, and kept their own languages. They also established two strong but short-lived kingdoms in North Africa, the *Almoravids and the *Almohads, but never successfully united in a single polity. MD

V. Gonzalez, 'Berbers', *MedIsl*, vol. 1, 105–6.

Berceo, Gonzalo de (*c*.1196–*c*.1264) First named poet in Castilian. Born in La Rioja, Berceo was educated at the *Benedictine *monastery of San Millán de la Cogolla, and possibly the Estudio General de Palencia, before serving as a *notary to the monastery's abbot. Berceo's literary output is in *cuaderna vía* (quatrains of 14-syllable lines with a mid-line caesura and mono-rhyme), also favoured in the 13th-century *Poema de *Fernán González* and *Libro de *Alexandre*, and in the 14th century by Juan *Ruiz and *López de Ayala. Berceo's compositions comprise *hagiography (*Vida de Santo Domingo de Silos*, *Vida de San Millán de la Cogolla*, *Vida de Santa Oria*, *Martirio de San Lorenzo*), doctrinal works and hymns (*Sacrificio de la Misa*, *Signos del Juicio Final*, *Himnos*), and poems of Marian devotion (*Milagros de Nuestra Señora*, *Loores de Nuestra Señora*, *Duelo de la Virgen*). Some of these works, particularly the saints' lives and Marian poems, served as propaganda to promote the interests of the monastery of San Millán. *See also* ALFONSO X; LITERATURES: CASTILIAN. JG

G. de Berceo, *Obras completas*, ed. B. Dutton, 5 vols (1967–81).
G. Giménez Resano, *El mester poético de Gonzalo de Berceo* (1976).
J. E. Keller, *Gonzalo de Berceo* (1972).
J. Saugnieux, *Berceo y las culturas del siglo XIII* (1982).

Bercheure (Berchoire, Bersuire), **Pierre** (d. 1362) Prior of St-Éloy in *Paris, *encyclopedist, moralist, translator, and polemicist. He composed voluminous works of moral theology, including a *commentary on Ovid's *Metamorphoses*. He also translated portions of Livy's history of Rome for King Jean II. *See also* RENAISSANCE AND ANTIQUARIANISM. CDT

C. Samaran and J. Monfrin, 'Pierre Bersuire', *Histoire littéraire de France*, 39 (1962), 258–450.

Berengaria *See* RICHARD I.

Berengar of Tours (*c*.1010–88) Theologian involved in the 11th-century *Eucharistic controversy. Berengar appealed to reason instead of authority, leading him to question teachings concerning the Real Presence. He was condemned by *councils and refuted by *Lanfranc of Bec and others. MCF

G. Macy, *The Theologies of the Eucharist in the Early Scholastic Period* (1984).
J. de Montclos, *Lanfranc et Berengar: la controverse eucharistique du XIe siècle* (1971).

Bergamo Situated in the present-day Italian region of Lombardy, the city of Bergamo lies close to the Alpine foothills. During *Lombard rule (568/9–774), it was the site of an important *duchy that was transformed into a province after the Frankish conquest of the Lombard kingdom (774). Bergamo acquired a great deal of autonomy from the Italian king at the beginning of the 10th century, but set up a communal government only two centuries later. Even though the city often sided with the imperial party in opposition to *Milan, Bergamo was one of the founding members of the *Lombard League (1167), created against Emperor Frederick

The cathedral in Bergamo.

I. At the beginning of the 14th century, as a result of a long series of internal clashes, a *signorie* replaced the *commune. *See also* ROMAN EMPIRE [HOHENSTAUFEN DYNASTY]. LAB

G. Chittolini, ed., *Il Comune e la Signoria*, vol. 2 of *Storia economica e sociale di Bergamo* (1999).

J. Jarnut, *Bergamo 568–1098: Verfassungs-, Sozial- und Wirtschaftsgeschichte einer lombardischen Stadt in Mittelalter* (1979).

Berg dynasty The counts of Berg were related to the Ezzonen dynasty and appeared in the 11th century. In 1280 they moved to Düsseldorf. In 1348, the county of Berg merged with that of Jülich and the counts were elevated to *dukes. The line continued until 1609, when the last duke died without heirs. SMW

B. Gebhardt, *Handbuch der deutschen Geschichte* (1956), vol. 2.

Bergen Norwegian *town. Bergen probably became a bishop's seat and a legally confirmed urban community in the reign of King Olaf III Haraldsson (1067–93). The town grew into the all-important export channel for *fish and other west Nordic products. It became the first true political capital of Norway and the largest medieval town of *Scandinavia. German merchants increasingly took over the town's foreign *trade. In the mid 14th century, one of the most important *Hanseatic foreign trading stations (*Kontore*) was established there. KH

K. Helle, *Bergen bys historie* (1982), vol. 1.

K. Helle *et al.*, *Norsk byhistorie* (2006).

Berlin Founded as a merchant settlement on a Spree river crossing (late 12th century), Berlin was developed by the margraves of *Brandenburg, through *market, toll, and self-government privileges (mid 13th century). Town leaders created a council (1307), and joined the Hanseatic League. Margrave Frederick II abolished the council (1442), weakened ties to the *Hanse, and transformed Berlin (-Kölln) into a *Hohenzollern residence. FL

W. Ribbe, ed., *Geschichte Berlins* (1987), vol. 1.

berna A *tax collected from *Bohemian and Moravian cities by the rulers, originally as an extraordinary levy but later regularly. The ruler determined the amount to be collected. In contrast, the ordinary tax was collected only on specific occasions such as *coronations or royal weddings. At the beginning of the 14th century the *berna* came under the authority of the *noble diet of the land. RŠi

T. Borovský, 'Zvláštní berně v českém středověku', *Dějiny a současnost*, 24/2 (2002), 8–14.

Bernard, St, abbot of Clairvaux (1090–1153) Born in Fontaines-lès-Dijon, the son of Tescelin le Saur and Aleth de Montbard, both members of the Burgundian *nobility. Bernard entered the *Cistercian abbey of *Cîteaux in 1112, but left there in 1115 to establish the *monastery of *Clairvaux. He was *canonized in 1174, and made a *doctor of the church in 1830.

Bernard's influence in both religious and political spheres during his lifetime was immense, in spite of his monk's desire to be removed from worldly matters. His defence of Pope Innocent II during the papal schism of 1130–38 secured the support of the (Holy) *Roman emperor Lothair II. In 1146 Bernard was commissioned by *Pope Eugenius III to preach the doomed Second *Crusade, which he did most famously in a sermon given at *Vézelay, purportedly inspiring Louis VII of France to take up the Cross. His conservatism led him to oppose the intellectualism of scholastic theology. He fought publicly to secure the condemnation of one of its greatest proponents, Peter *Abelard.

Bernard's lasting influence can be measured in his impact on the religious life of the later MA. In his many theological and devotional writings, and especially in his *sermons in praise of the Virgin *Mary and his commentaries on the Song of Songs, Bernard formulated the basic tenets of contemplative and affective piety that would shape late medieval spirituality. LRa

Bernard of Clairvaux, *Works*, Cistercian Fathers series (1970–99).

G. R. Evans, *Bernard of Clairvaux* (2000).

Bernard de Gordon (*fl.* 1283–1309) Physician who spent his career at the University of *Montpellier. His well-organized writings covered the entire spectrum of *medical training and procedures, and his encyclopedic *Lilium medicinae* (1305) was authoritative for four centuries and was widely translated into the vernacular languages of Europe. Bernard believed that practice should be grounded in rational principles. His speculations, even at their most dialectical, aimed at health as the ultimate objective. *See also* MEDICINE; REGIMEN OF HEALTH. LED

L. Demaitre, 'Bernard de Gordon et son influence sur la pensée médicale aux XIVe et XVe siècles', in *Actes du Colloque international: 'L'Université de Montpellier et son rayonnement, XIIIe–XVe siècles' (17–19 mai 2001)*, ed. D. Le Blévec (2004), 103–31.

Bernard Gui (1261/2–1331) Dominican, historian, bishop, inquisitor. Born into Limousin *nobility, Bernard entered the Dominicans in 1279 (professed 1280), and studied *logic and theology. In 1290 he was appointed prior, serving at *Limoges, Albi, and *Carcassonne before becoming inquisitor of *Toulouse, where he led the struggle against heresy (1307–24). He served on papal diplomatic missions and was appointed bishop of Tuy in 1323. In 1324 he was transferred to Lodeve, where he served until his death.

Gui composed Latin theological works, saints' lives, and histories of the *papacy, Roman emperors, French kings, and the Dominicans. Many of his works were translated into French and Occitan and survive in numerous MSS.

His most important work was *Practica inquisitionis heretice pravitatis*, which outlines the proper means to conduct an *inquisition and includes detailed accounts of the beliefs of *Cathars, *Waldensians, and other heretics Gui encountered. *See also* LANGUAGES: OCCITAN. MCF

Bernard Gui, *Manuel de l'inquisiteur*, ed. and tr. G. Mollat, 2 vols (1926–27).
'Bernard Gui et son monde', *Cahiers de Fanjeaux*, 16 (1981).

Bernardino of Siena, St (1380–1444) One of the most influential preachers of 15th-century *Italy. Bernardino was born to the Albizzeschi family in Massa Marittima, but was orphaned very young. He joined the order of the *Franciscan Friars Minor in 1402, took his final *vows the next year, and was nominated Observant preacher in 1405. He delivered *sermons regularly from 1410 to 1426 in Tuscany, Lombardy, the Veneto, and Emilia-Romagna before being brought before *Pope Martin V in 1426 on charges of *heresy. Though his acquittal augmented his popularity, he later refused the bishoprics of *Siena, *Ferrara, and *Urbino, preferring instead to continue his *preaching throughout most of the Italian peninsula. Despite occasional subsequent accusations of heresy and no small amount of controversy, he was widely respected and enjoyed enormous popularity for his earthy, witty sermons, the depth of his secular learning, his passionate rhetorical skills, and his attempts on several occasions to bring peace to the turbulent region. He passed away in 1444 and was *canonized six years later. His numerous sermons are preserved in Latin and Italian, and his life was vividly portrayed by several contemporary *biographers. EMP

Atti del Convegno storico bernardiniano: in occasione del sesto centenario della nascita di S. Bernardino da Siena (1982).
F. D'Episcopo, ed., *S. Bernardino da Siena, predicatore e pellegrino* (1985).
Enciclopedia Bernardiniana, 2 vols (1980–84).
F. Mormando, *The Preacher's Demons* (1999).
I. Origo, *The World of San Bernardino* (1962).
C. Polecritti, *Preaching Peace in Renaissance Italy: Bernardino of Siena and his Audience* (2000).

Bernard of Auvergne (d. after 1307) *Dominican bachelor of theology in *Paris and bishop of *Clermont. Bernard is known for his work supporting *Thomas Aquinas's doctrines against a number of eminent Parisian theologians. In 1303 he took a position opposing *Pope Boniface VIII. *See also* BACCALARIUS. MTo

V. Heynk, 'Die Kontroverse zwischen Gottfried von Fontaines und Bernard von Auvergne O.P. um die Lehre des hl. Thomas von der *confessio informis*', *FrSt* 45 (1963), 1–40, 201–42.

Bernard of Chartres (d. *c.*1130) Breton philosopher. According to *John of Salisbury, Bernard was the most eminent *Neoplatonist of his time. He taught at the famous cathedral school of *Chartres, of which he served as chancellor until 1124. Bernard is the author of a *commentary on Calcidius' Latin version of the *Timaeus*, known as the *Glosae super Platonem*. SJM

Bernard of Chartres, *Glosae super Platonem*, ed. P. Dutton (1991).

Bernard of Cluny (Morlas, Morval, Morlaix) (*fl.* 12th century) Monk at *Cluny during the time of *Peter the Venerable. His *De contemptu mundi* provides a satire against the moral disruption of the time. From the late medieval period onward, he was often confused with another Bernard and monk of Cluny who wrote the *Consuetudines cluniacenses*. AJD

Bernard of Cluny, *De contemptu mundi by Bernard of Morval*, ed. H. C. Hoskier (1929).
G. J. Engelhardt, 'The *De contemptu mundi* of Bernardus Morvalensis: A Study in Commonplace', *MS* 22 (1960), 108–35.

Bernard of Morlaix *See* BERNARD OF CLUNY.

Bernard Silvestris (Silvester) (*fl.* 1130–50) Master at the *Tours cathedral school. His *Cosmographia*, a mythologized creation story in prose and verse, is an innovative manifestation of Chartrian *Neoplatonism. Bernard also wrote the poem *Mathematicus*, and *commentaries on several school authors are attributed to him. *See also* CHARTRES, SCHOOL OF. BKB

Bernard Silvestris, *Cosmographia*, tr. W. Wetherbee (1973), ed. P. Dronke (1978).
B. Stock, *Myth and Science in the Twelfth Century: A Study of Bernard Silvester* (1972).

Bernart de Ventadorn (*fl. c.*1145–80) The most renowned *troubadour, probably a younger son of the vice-comital Ventadorn family, despite his **vida* claiming he was the illegitimate son of a servant woman. He probably enjoyed *Plantagenet patronage for a time, as well as that of the count of Toulouse. The relatively large and widely disseminated surviving corpus (*c.*45) of quintessentially courtly lyrics largely defined the subsequent Occitan tradition and was widely imitated in Northern France and Germany. Though often formally complex, his exquisite lyrics seem effortless and beguilingly sincere. Of his some 40 extant songs, nineteen survive with music. SG

C. Appel, ed., *Bernart von Ventadorn: seine Lieder* (1915).
M. Lazar, *Bernard de Ventadour: chansons d'amour* (1966).
S. G. Nichols, Jr, *et al.*, *The Songs of Bernart de Ventadorn* (1962).

Bernicia The northernmost Anglian kingdom centred at Bamburgh and Yeavering. Ida, whose rule is traditionally dated to 547–59, founded the royal dynasty. During the late 6th and 7th centuries Bernicia expanded against the

Brittonic kingdoms of Gododdin to the north and *Rheged to the west, and finally won supremacy over *Deira, a rival Anglian kingdom to the south, with which it united to form the kingdom of *Northumbria in the mid 7th century. CRD

D. Dumville, 'The Origins of Northumbria', in *The Origins of Anglo-Saxon Kingdoms*, ed. S. Bassett (1989), 213–22.

B. Yorke, 'Northumbria', in *Kings and Kingdoms of Early Anglo-Saxon England* (1990), 72–99.

Berno, abbot of Cluny (d. 927) First abbot of the *monastery of *Cluny. Abbot of Baume, where he had implemented the reforms of *Benedict of *Aniane, Berno founded the monastery at Cluny in 910 at the behest of William, duke of *Aquitaine, and established its basic organization and internal structure. *See also* CLUNIAC ORDER. MCF

C. H. Lawrence, *Medieval Monasticism* (^{3}2000).

Bern(o) Augiensis, abbot of Reichenau (r. 1008–48) Music theorist and liturgist. His *Prologus in tonarium* (also called 'Musica Bernonis'), compiled between 1021 and 1036, was a popular textbook, widely distributed throughout the 11th and 12th centuries. The *Prologus* exhibits Berno's knowledge of earlier *music theory and contributes important information about *modal transposition. *Hermann the Lame ('Contractus') of Reichenau was one of his pupils. Berno also wrote *sermons, *letters, and liturgical offices (*historiae*), and gave the *vita* of *Ulrich of *Augsburg its third, definitive version. WB, REG

W. Berschin, *Eremus und Insula: St Gallen und die Reichenau im Mittelalter* (^{2}2005).

H. Oesch, *Berno und Hermann von Reichenau als Musiktheoretiker* (1961).

Bernold of Constance (d. 1100) Monk, polemicist, canonist, and historian. Perhaps the most learned figure of his time, Bernold belongs to a south German tradition of scholarship that also includes *Herman the Lame and *Berno (Augiensis) of *Reichenau. Bernold was a prolific author, and employed his massive erudition in the service of the reform programme of *Pope Gregory VII. His contribution to canon *law scholarship was particularly profound. PSH

Die Chroniken Bertholds von Reichenau und Bernolds von Konstanz, 1054–1100, ed. I. S. Robinson, *MGH.SRG.NS* 14 (2003).

I. S. Robinson, 'Zur Arbeitsweise Bernolds von Konstanz und seiner Kreises: Untersuchungen zum Schlettstäter Codex 13', *DAEM* 34 (1978), 51–122.

Berno of Reichenau *See* BERNO AUGIENSIS.

Bernward of Hildesheim, St (d. 1023) Bishop; teacher and adviser to Otto III. Bernward was a great artistic and architectural *patron, possibly personally involved in artistic production. The bronze doors and column for St Michael's *monastery, which Bernward founded, indicate the intellectual and technical sophistication of his projects. Bernward was *canonized in 1192. *See also* ROMAN EMPIRE [CAROLINGIAN, OTTONIAN, SALIAN/FRANCONIAN DYNASTIES]. ASC

M. Brandt and A. Eggebrecht, eds, *Bernward von Hildesheim und das Zeitalter der Ottonen*, 2 vols (1993).

F. Tschan, *Bernward of Hildesheim*, 3 vols (1942–52).

Béroul *See* TRISTAN AND YSEULT.

Berry, duchy of The province governed from *Bourges, now roughly the departments of Cher and Indre. A county controlled by the Frankish, then the French kings, Berry was part of the *dowry that *Eleanor of *Aquitaine brought to *Henry II of England (1152); Berry returned to the French crown in 1200. As a royal *apanage, Berry was made a duchy in 1360. The first duke was Jean de France (1340–1416). DHW

F. Lehoux, *Jean de France, duc de Berri, sa vie, son action politique (1340–1416)*, 4 vols (1966–8).

Berry, Jean de France, duc de (1340–1416) Son of King Jean II of France. Berry was an unsuccessful royal lieutenant and military commander, but did mediate between his brothers, the *dukes of *Orléans and *Burgundy, during the reign of *Charles VI. He was an important *patron of the arts, with a library of over three hundred illuminated MSS including the *Très Riches Heures*. *See also* LIMBOURG BROTHERS. CDT

F. Autrand, *Jean de Berry: L'art et le pouvoir* (2000).

F. Lehoux, *Jean de France, duc de Berri, sa vie, son action politique (1340–1416)*, 4 vols (1966–8).

Berserk [ON 'Bear-shirt'?] A fierce Scandinavian warrior clad in bear- or wolf-skin. Of Germanic cultic origin, he is best known from ON sagas, where he can have positive associations (for example, in *Egills saga*) but, far more often, negative ones moving toward the monstrous (for example, in *Ǫrvar-Odds saga*). *See also* ICELANDIC SAGAS. REB

D. Beard, 'The Berserkr in Icelandic Literature' in *Approaches to Oral Literature*, ed. R. Thelwall (1978), 99–114.

B. Blaney, 'Berserkr', *MedScan*, 37–8.

Berthold of Henneberg, archbishop of Mainz (1441–1504) Imperial reform advocate from the regional *nobility, with ties to the courts of Frederick III and Maximilian I. *See also* ROMAN EMPIRE [HABSBURG DYNASTY]. JFP

P.-J. Heinig, 'Ausblick auf einen neuen Präzeptor des Reiches: Erzbischof Berthold von Henneberg', in *Handbuch der Mainzer Kirchengeschichte*, ed. F. Jürgensmeier (2002), vol. 6.1/1–2, 550–54.

Berthold of Regensburg (d. 1272) German *Franciscan preacher; active in *Augsburg from 1240. Between 1254 and 1263 he toured the German-speaking lands. *Albertus Magnus asked him to *preach the *crusade against *heretics, but Berthold denounced *war. Three hundred and two MSS of his *sermons survive. AC

Berthold von Regensburg, *Vollständige Ausgabe seiner Predigten*, ed. F. Pfeiffer and J. Strobl, 2 vols (1862–80; repr. 1965).

—— *Sermones*, ed. and tr. C. Lecouteux and P. Marcque, 3 vols (1971).

C. Oechslin Weibel, *'ein übergülde aller der sælikeit . . .': Der Himmel und die anderen Eschata in den deutschen Predigten Bertholds von Regensburg* (2005).

Berthold of Zwiefalten (*c.*1089–*c.*1169) Born in *Württemberg; joined the *Benedictine house of Zwiefalten. He wrote the *Libellus de constructione Zwivildensis monasterii* as a continuation of Ortlieb of Zwiefalten's chronicle, and thrice was the abbot of his *monastery. AC

Die Zwiefalter Chronik Ortliebs und Bertholds, ed. and tr. E. König and K. O. Müller (1941).

L. Wallach, 'Studien zur Chronik Bertholds von Zwiefalten', *SMGB* 51 (1933), 83–110, 183–95.

Berthold von Holle (*fl.* 1251–70) MHG poet; composed three courtly verse romances, *Demantin*, *Crane*, and (the fragmentary) *Darifant*, in which the protagonists have to display ideal *knightly behaviour and amatory constancy despite challenges. The sources of all three works, written in a mix of MHG and Middle Low German, are unknown. *See also* COURTLY LOVE; LITERATURES: GERMANIC. AC

Demantin and *Crane*, ed. K. Bartsch (1875, 1858).

M. Wermke, *Elemente mündlicher Komposition in der ritterlichen Epik des späten 13. Jahrhunderts* (1988).

Bertran de Born (*fl. c.*1159–95, d. 1215) Noble *troubadour from the *Périgord. His 47 surviving lyrics are largely **sirventes*, combining a bellicose interpretation of **fin'amor* with robust *commentary on the political concerns of the day, particularly on the *feuding of his *Plantagenet overlords. His work was admired by *Dante, even though he placed him in the *Inferno* because of his love of strife and his bloodthirsty brutality. He probably entered holy orders at the end of his life (*c.*1196). One melody survives. SG

W. D. Paden, T. Sankowitch, and P. H. Stablein, eds, *The Poems of the Troubadour Bertran de Born* (1986).

Berwick-upon-Tweed Founded as a royal borough in the early 12th century and, until the late 13th, the wealthiest port and the most important urban centre in Scotland. Berwick fell to English assault in 1296 and thereafter began a slow but steady decline. It changed hands several times during the *Anglo-Scottish wars of the later medieval period, passing finally to the English in 1422. *See also* SCOTLAND, IRELAND, WALES: SCOTLAND AND WALES 1064–1536. CJN

R. Nicholson, *Scotland: The Later Middle Ages* (1978).

Besançon In the eastern French Franche-Comté region, Besançon is strategically located, surrounded on three sides by the river Doubs and on the fourth by a mountain. Passing from Roman to Alamannic to Frankish to *Carolingian rule, it was incorporated into the newly founded French *'palatine' county of *Burgundy in 986. In 1032 the county and city entered the domain of the empire and Besançon was elevated to an archbishopric, imperial *free city, and ecclesiastical seigneury. In 1290 the Bisontins obtained *communal rights, protected by the counts, then *dukes, of Burgundy. TCH

G. Maillet, 'Histoire du comté de Bourgogne ou Franche-Comté du IXe au XIVe siècle', 19 May 2008, gilles.maillet.free.fr/histoire/recit_bourgogne/recit_comte_bourgogne.htm.

besät, bisat *See* RUGS AND CARPETS.

Bescheidenheit *See* FREIDANK.

Bessarion, Cardinal John (1403/8–1472) Byzantine religious leader, philosopher, and scholar. The most influential of the Byzantine émigrés to Italy, he became a *cardinal of the Catholic church, wrote an important treatise arguing for the compatibility of *Neoplatonism and Christianity, and donated his large collection of Greek manuscripts to *Venice, where it formed the core of the Marciana Library. *See also* LIBRARIES, MEDIEVAL; PHILOSOPHY, BYZANTINE. JAK

J. Monfasani, *Byzantine Scholars in Renaissance Italy: Cardinal Bessarion and Others* (1995).

bestiary Genre of Latin or vernacular book, usually illustrated, that describes real and fabulous creatures and their Christian allegorical significance. True bestiaries descend from the Greek *Physiologus* (2nd-century?) and its Latin translations; they are classified according to the nature of their additions to it: the Bible, Solinus' Pliny epitome (2nd-century), *Isidore's *Etymologies*, *Ambrose's *Hexameron*, and *Hugh of Fouilloy's *Aviarium*, among other texts. Most bestiaries were produced in 12th- and 13th-century England, and have been linked to contemporary interest in exotic menageries and to the development of *heraldry.

Bestiaries are usually understood as monastic literature; recent scholarship speculates that Latin bestiaries were also used in elementary lay *education to teach both *literacy and the correct method of interpreting God's creation. They reflect the medieval view of the created world as a book in which divine truth could be symbolically read: the pelican, thought to revive its young with its own blood, is thus an image *in bono* of Christ sacrificing himself for mankind, while the ravenous wolf, interpreted *in malo*,

English bestiary, early 13th century (vellum).

represents the devil. Other creatures provide positive or negative ethical models.

Bestiaries do not invariably provide such moralizations of the animal behaviours they describe, and have sometimes also been regarded as attempts at *natural history. Thus, entries on the wolf accurately describe its brief breeding season, emphasize its danger to domestic flocks, and offer advice on how to fend it off, in addition to highlighting its diabolical associations.

Bestiaries declined in number after the 13th century, as more *encyclopedic works became popular. *See also* LITERATURES: ALLEGORICAL. RSS

R. Baxter, *Bestiaries and their Users in the Middle Ages* (1998).
W. B. Clark, *A Medieval Book of Beasts: The Second-Family Bestiary—Commentary, Art, Text, and Translation* (2006).
W. George and B. Yapp, *The Naming of the Beasts: Natural History in the Medieval Bestiary* (1991).
L. Houwen, ed., *The Deidis of Armorie: A Heraldic Treatise and Bestiary*, 2 vols (1994).
M. R. James, *The Bestiary* (1928).
F. McCulloch, *Medieval Latin and French Bestiaries* ([2]1962).
H. Wirtjes, ed., *The Middle English Physiologus* (1991).

Bethlehem City believed to be the birthplace of Jesus, site of a church begun by Constantine and enlarged and adorned by Justinian, Manuel I, and the *crusaders. Taken by the latter in 1099, it was a Latin bishopric for almost a century. *See also* PALESTINE. MD

J. Folda, *The Art of the Crusaders in the Holy Land* (1995).
L.-A. Hunt, 'The Mosaics of the Church of the Nativity in Bethlehem', *DOP* 45 (1991), 69–85.

betrothal rings, Jewish Part of the Jewish wedding ceremony is the groom's placing of a ring on the forefinger of the bride's right hand as a sign of her sanctification to him. Fourteenth-century *Ashkenazic rings have an architectural bezel, symbolizing the *Jerusalem temple and the couple's home, and are inscribed *mazal tov* ('good luck'). *See also* KETUBBOT; MARRIAGE RITES. VBM

Historisches Museum der Pfalz Speyer, *The Jews of Europe in the Middle Ages* (2004), 195, 199, 222.

Béziers Mediterranean city of *France, founded as a Roman legionary colony. One of seven bishoprics of the *Visigothic kingdom north of the Pyrenees, with a *cathedral founded in the 4th–6th centuries, it was conquered by Arabs *c.*719, then by Pepin the Short in 759 and integrated into the *Carolingian realm. By 900 dominion was shared by bishop and viscounts, ancestors of the *Trencavel family. Sacked in July 1209 by a *crusading army, its population was massacred. Later it became the seat of a royal vicariate. FLC

M. Bourin-Derruau, *Villages médiévaux en Bas-Languedoc: genèse d'une sociabilité* (1987).
J. Sagnes, ed., *Histoire de Béziers* (1986).

Bianchi e Neri ('Whites and Blacks') Tuscan *Guelph factions of the beginning of the 14th century. They were chiefly associated with *Florence and linked to the antagonism between the families of the Cerchi (Bianchi) and Donati (Neri). In 1301–2 the Neri, with the help of *Pope Boniface VIII and Charles of *Valois, expelled the Bianchi. The latter joined the Ghibellines, likewise exiled, but they failed to regain Florence. A large amnesty for the Bianchi was granted in 1311, but it excluded those, like *Dante, who supported the policy of Emperor Henry VII. *See also* LUXEMBOURG DYNASTY. GR

R. Davidsohn, *Forschungen zur älteren Geschichte von Florenz*, 4 vols (1896–1908).
V. Mazzoni, 'Dalla lotta di parte al governo delle fazioni: i guelfi e i ghibellini del territorio fiorentino nel Trecento', *Archivo Storico Italiano*, 160 (2002), 455–514.
J. M. Najemy, 'Dante and Florence', in *The Cambridge Companion to Dante*, ed. R. Jacoff (1993), 80–99.

Aerial view of the church of the Nativity in Bethlehem.

View of the river and castle at Béziers.

Bible, Hungarian-Hussite Three codices contain the earliest Hungarian translations of the Bible. Possibly translated by *Hussites, these are the Munich Codex (1466), containing the four gospels; the Vienna Codex (*c*.1450), containing Old Testament books; and the Apor Codex (*c*. late 15th–early 16th century), including a prose version of the Psalms. Written in Middle Hungarian, they are of great cultural and linguistic significance, serving to document literary and spoken language development and the rise of the vernacular. *See also* LANGUAGES: HUNGARIAN / MAGYAR; MANUSCRIPT STUDIES. AMD

J. von Farkas and G. Décsy, eds, *Der Münchener Kodex*, 2 vols (1958–66).
G. Mészöly, ed., *Bécsi Codex* (1916).
D. Szabó, ed., *Apor-Kódex: Bevezetéssel Ellátta és Hasonmásban Közzéteszi*, facs. edn. (1942).

Bible, illustration of the The illustration of the Bible, like its text, occupied a special place in the medieval world. The Bible's great length and varied content meant that biblical images were extraordinarily heterogeneous. The earliest surviving example of an illustrated (complete) Bible is the Codex Amiatinus (Florence, Bibl. Laur. MS Amiat. 1), which was made in *Northumbria (*Wearmouth and Jarrow) around 700 and exported to Rome in 716. It contains a full-page image of Christ in Majesty as a preface to the New Testament, and a number of pages of *diagrams and images at the start of the book. Their interpretation is controversial.

A perception that a Bible should be a huge volume with a few strategically placed full-page images carried on through the *Carolingian and Romanesque eras (Vivian Bible, S. Paolo Bible, Bury Bible, Winchester Bible), and occasionally in the Gothic period (Conradin Bible). A type of small-scale 'pocket' Bible, however, was developed in *Paris at the beginning of the 13th century, and this received a more or less standardized decoration, with very small images located in the opening initials to most of the biblical books. These 'Paris Bibles', with their minute script, were produced in large numbers.

From the early period onward, the vast majority of illuminated biblical MSS contained only a part of the biblical

Illustration of the Bible, Exodus 7, in Wenceslas Bible.

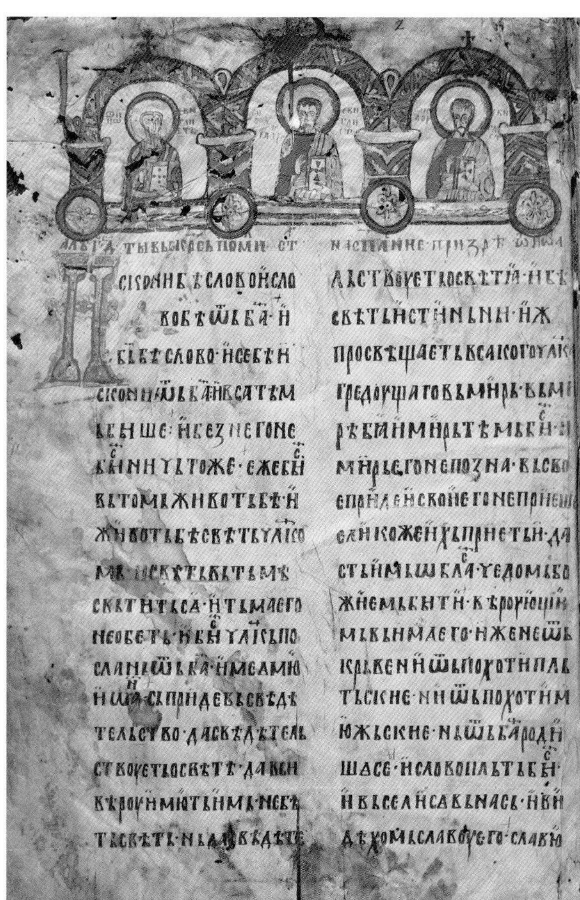

Illustration of the Bible in Miroslav Gospel Book, 12th century.

text: the Book of Psalms (in the *Psalter), the *gospels, or the Apocalypse, for example. Each of these books developed its own type or types of illumination, generally varying over time and by place of production. The Psalter often had images interspersed in the text at points that marked the division of the Psalms according to the *Divine Office of monastic usage (although such books were not made for monks). But much more conspicuous were the cycles of images that were often included as prefaces to the Psalms. Beginning in the 11th century, these cycles generally eschewed images of the life of David (author of the Psalms) in favour of a more or less lengthy sequence of biblical images, extending in some cases from Genesis to the Last Judgement (St Albans Psalter).

The gospels, by way of contrast, often contained images only of the four Evangelists, represented as medieval *scribes (rather than, for example, as inspired authors). Prefatory diagrams known as *canon tables, comprising columns of numbers, also received extraordinarily elaborate decoration. Because the story of Christ's life is recounted in parallel versions by the four Evangelists, it was practical to arrange images as a frontispiece cycle, following a single (visual) narrative. On occasions, rearranging the text to follow the demands of the *liturgy, as in the Gospel *Lectionary of Archbishop *Egbert of Trier (*c*.980), enabled the images to be integrated into the biblical text.

Different again was the arrangement of text and image in illustrated MSS of the Apocalypse (Revelation). In Iberia, the Apocalypse with the very lengthy commentary of *Beatus of Liébana was illuminated in the 9th–13th centuries. In northern Europe a different type of Apocalypse was produced, notably from the mid 13th century onwards (for example, Lambeth Apocalypse). In such Apocalypses the images closely represent the descriptive detail of the text. Some are picture books, in which every page has an image of similar format, and the amount of text varies. Although the biblical text is complete in some examples, it is heavily abbreviated or even absent in others.

Translating the Bible, or parts of it, into various vernaculars created new opportunities and possibilities for illumination. The Psalms were among the first biblical texts to be translated into French (*Eadwine Psalter, *c*.1150), and the Apocalypse was transcribed in a French version from *c*.1250. The massive *Bible historiale* (the Bible integrated with the *Historia Scholastica*) had great success as an illuminated book, especially from *c*.1350. Many more biblical images were supplied in MSS of the *Bible historiale* than in Latin Bibles. This total, however, was puny in comparison with the **Bible moralisée*, which was produced in only a few exemplars but had more than 5,000 images.

A separate category is formed by biblical images that lack a MS context: those executed in *enamel, sculpted on a *cathedral façade, painted on a wall, and so on. Only rarely were such images derived from MSS (Angers Apocalypse *tapestries). But they were potentially visible to a wide public, whereas miniatures in MSS were always for a limited clientele. *See also* BIBLE, TRANSLATIONS OF THE; BIBLIA PAUPERUM; LITERATURES: APOCALYPTIC; MANUSCRIPT ILLUMINATION. JHL

W. Cahn, *Romanesque Bible Illumination* (1982).
C. de Hamel, *The Book: A History of the Bible* (2001).
C. M. Kauffmann, *Biblical Imagery in Medieval England, 700–1550* (2003).
H. L. Kessler, *The Illustrated Bibles from Tours* (1977).
J. Lowden, *The Making of the Bibles moralisées*, 2 vols (2000).
N. G. Morgan, *The Lambeth Apocalypse* (1990).
MS Laurenziano Amiatino 1, facs. edn. (2002).
F. Muel, *La Tenture de l'Apocalypse d'Angers* ([2]1987).
St Albans Psalter, 12 October 2006, www.abdn.ac.uk/stalbanspsalter/index.shtml.
J. Williams, *The Illustrated Beatus*, 5 vols (1994–2003).

Bible, Latin The earliest Christians used a Greek Bible: the Jewish (Old Testament) Greek scriptures (the Septuagint), and the Christian texts canonized as the New Testament. By the 4th century the scripture *canon was basically closed; this is the Bible that was translated into Latin.

The Latin Old Testament included the books known today as 'Apocrypha' or deutero-canonical, books like Maccabees and others known in Greek but not Hebrew. In the Latin MA, some authors were more likely to quote Wisdom than Proverbs.

The medieval Latin Bible was more often found in parts than as a pandect, a complete collection copied together. Sometimes pandects were popular, usually because of Bible-copying programmes, part of revivals of scholarship. This is the case with the Alcuin Bibles of the 9th, the Display Bibles of the 12th, and the Paris Bibles of the 13th century. Most medieval Christians who could read the Bible in Latin and had biblical texts available (monastics and *schoolmen) had discrete sections of the Bible in separate books: the *gospels in an Evangeliary, a *Psalter, the Pauline epistles, and collections of wisdom texts. Christians had always preferred the codex to the scroll, so medieval Bible copies, pandects or part-books, were written on both sides of the page and bound together. Some of these were richly illustrated.

The earliest Latin translations of the Bible were anonymous; they are preserved by early fathers and in the *liturgy. In the late 4th century, *Jerome undertook a translation project resulting in a new Latin version known as the Vulgate. Jerome consulted the Hebrew for his Old Testament translations, and made one Psalms version directly from the Hebrew, but he also reproduced the Septuagint Old Testament. The authority of Jerome's version was mostly scholarly, and the Old Latin remained a liturgical text. Sometimes there were programmes to correct the Vulgate text; the Alcuin Bible and the Paris Bible are results of such efforts.

As the word 'Vulgate' implies, Jerome's translation was meant to be accessible to Christians in their own native tongue, Latin. As Christianity spread into western Europe, and vernacular *literacy gained importance, the Latin Bible became more remote from the centre of theological activity. This led to the early modern translations into German (Luther's Bible) and English (the Authorized or King James Bible) that spelled the eventual decline of the Latin Bible. *See also* MANUSCRIPT STUDIES. EAM

C. de Hamel, *The Book: A History of the Bible* (2001).
L. Light, 'French Bibles *c.*1200–30: A New Look at the Origin of the Paris Bible', in *The Early Medieval Bible*, ed. R. Gameson (1994), 155–76.
R. Loewe, 'The Medieval History of the Latin Vulgate', in *The Cambridge History of the Bible*, vol. 2, ed. G. W. H. Lampe (1969), 102–54.
B. Smalley, *The Study of the Bible in the Middle Ages* ([3]1983).
H. F. D. Sparks, 'Jerome as Biblical Scholar', in *The Cambridge History of the Bible*, vol. 1, ed. P. R. Ackroyd and C. E. Evans (1970), 510–41.

Bible, translations of the After the Greek Septuagint and the so-called Vetus Latina, *Jerome's Vulgate was gradually accepted in the west as standard. In the east, early translations were made into Coptic, Armenian, Ethiopic, and Syriac, this last important for the 5th-century Peshitta and for Tatian's 2nd-century *Diatessaron* or gospel harmony, subsequently translated into Latin and thence into 9th-century OHG.

The oldest Germanic vernacular translation of the Bible is attributed to the 4th-century *Visigothic bishop Wulfila (Latin, Ulfilas), written in an alphabet credited to him, but attested in codices of the 5th and 6th centuries. Of these, the most celebrated is the *Codex Argenteus*, written in silver and gold on reddish-purple parchment, containing 188 extant pages of the Gospel translations of Matthew, John, Luke, and Mark, that is, in 'western' sequence. The remaining five extant Wulfilian Bible codices are palimpsests, as are seven of the extant eight leaves of the Gothic 'Explication of the Gospel according to John' or *Skeireins*.

Other Continental vernacular translations of the Bible, parts and/or paraphrases thereof, abound from the 8th century onward in the Christianization of Germanic culture. Tatian's *Diatesseron* was anonymously translated into OHG prose from Latin at *Fulda *c.*830. Not a translation, but a poem based on the four gospels, the *Evangelienbuch* was composed *c.*870 by *Otfrid von Weissenburg, who is credited with introducing end-line rhyme into Germanic verse form. The third important text figure of the era is *Notker Teutonicus of *St Gall (*c.*1000). Less monumental are the prose translation of Matthew in the *Mondsee-Vienna Fragments (9th century), a prose Latin and German interlinear *Psalter (9th century), and, in Otfridian verse, 'Christ and the Samaritan Woman' (10th century) and Psalm 138 (10th century). William of Ebersberg's translation (11th century) of the Song of Songs was widely read.

The OS **Heliand*, an alliterative New Testament narrative poem depicting Christ as a Germanic lord, is the earliest epic of continental Germanic. Attested in five 9th–10th-century MSS, heterogeneous OS displays German and English interference. The OS *Genesis* is considered the source for its translation into the OE *Genesis B*.

Insular West Germanic, specifically OE, enjoyed a florescence of biblical translations and paraphrases, for example *Bede's reputed (but non-extant) Gospel of John (8th century); several OE glossed Psalters, foremost the Vespasian Psalter (8th/9th century); the *Cædmonian *Genesis*, *Exodus*, *Daniel* poems (*c.*1000); and the interlinear glossing of the *Lindisfarne Gospels (10th century) and the Rushworth Gospels (10th century).

Other continental Germanic biblical translations include the Old Low Franconian Wachtendonck Psalms (10th century), of which the Old Dutch Psalms 1–9 evince an underlying OHG translation. Biblical works continue in the later MA, for example the MHG *Genesis* and *Exodus*, verse epics extant in the Vienna and Millstatt codices (12th century); the Middle Dutch *Historijenbibel* (14th century); the Early New High German Augsburger Bibel (14th century) and Wenzel Bibel (14th century), culminating in the printing of Johann Mentelin's *Erste deutsche Bibel* (1466). *See also* BIBLE, HUNGARIAN-HUSSITE/ILLUSTRATION OF THE/LATIN; BIBLE EPIC; MANUSCRIPT STUDIES; TRANSLATIONS, BIBLE. IR

C. de Hamel, *The Book: A History of the Bible* (2001).
J. M. Jeep, ed., *Medieval Germany: An Encyclopedia* (2001).
J. Rogerson, *The Oxford Illustrated History of the Bible* (2001).
P. E. Szarmach, M. T. Tarovmina, and J. T. Rosenthal, eds, *Medieval England: An Encyclopedia* (1998).

bible epic The retelling of biblical narratives using the conventions of epic, Graeco-Roman or vernacular. The transposition of biblical texts into classical genres began before the Christian era, among Diaspora Jews. Christian biblical epic emerges early in the 4th century with Juvencus and Sedulius Caelius, in the context of the evangelization of the Roman upper classes. Most literary historians trace its origins to the attempt to provide an alternative to traditional epic, with its freight of *pagan cult and ideals, adopting the highest literary conventions to make scripture readable for the upper classes.

By the 5th century Nonnus of Panopolis had recast the Gospel of John as Homeric epic. The pedagogic tradition of transposition also must have played a role, yet any reasons for the emergence of biblical epic must be balanced against a poet's misgivings in adapting an inspired text, every word of which was filled with divine meaning. It is unlikely that Julian the Apostate's prohibition against Christians teaching pagan literature was a factor.

Inspired by Latin examples, vernacular biblical epics were written in OE and OS—including *Exodus*, *Genesis A* and *B*, and the **Heliand*, in double adaptations of Judaeo-Christian content and Graeco-Roman genre. The biblical epic allowed the writer to refashion the Bible narrative in light of contemporary theological problems and developments. In turn, works like Sedulius' *Carmen paschale* and Arator's versification of Acts found their way into the *exegetical tradition. *Bede notably used Arator as a source for his own *commentary. Although some later medieval works are classed as biblical epics, mere length does not define the genre. The production of biblical epic wanes with the rise of the *romance, which influences the writing of religious poetry in the later MA (for example, ME *Patience* and *Purity*), just as the classical epic did earlier. Religious *drama arguably usurps its evangelical role. Biblical narrative as epic is, however, reborn in the 16th century in texts stretching from *Croatia to England.

The biblical epic incorporated non-Christian poetics and vocabulary as well as many ideals carried over into the Christian *paideia*, first with Latin and Greek and later with the vernaculars. The appearance of the epic in the vernacular may represent an effort at evangelization, but is more likely to represent a conscious imitation of the intellectual life of the Christian empire and a confident assertion of vernacular talent and artistry taking its place within a scholarly, literary, and spiritual continuum reaching back to the original biblical authors. *See also* EDUCATION, JEWISH ELEMENTARY SCHOOLS; LANGUAGES: GERMANIC; LITERATURES: ENGLISH—ME PROSE AND POETRY/GERMANIC. HCOB

B. P. H. Green, *Latin Epics of the New Testament* (2006).
J. McClure, 'The Biblical Epic and its Audience in Late Antiquity', in *Papers of the Liverpool Latin Seminar*, 3 (1981), 305–21.
G. R. Murphy, *The Saxon Savior: The Germanic Transformation of the Gospel in the Ninth Century 'Heliand'* (1989).
P. G. Remley, *Old English Biblical Verse* (1996).
M. Roberts, *Biblical Epic and Rhetorical Paraphrase in Late Antiquity* (1985).
G. Shepherd, 'Scriptural Poetry', in *Continuations and Beginnings*, ed. E. G. Stanley (1966), 1–36.
C. P. E. Springer, *Gospel as Epic in Late Antiquity: The 'Carmen Paschale' of Sedulius* (1988).

Bible moralisée Biblical picture book with moralizing images and *commentary, made for queens and kings of *France *c.*1220–1400. Blanche of *Castile seems to have been the first *patron. Initially, texts were in French. The repetitive layout with eight images and texts per page is characteristic. The most complete examples have more than 5,000 images. *See also* BIBLE, ILLUSTRATION OF THE; BIBLIA PAUPERUM. JHL

R. Gonzálvez Ruiz, ed., *La Biblia de San Luis*, 5 vols (2001–4).
G. Guest, comm., *Bible moralisée* (1995).
J. Lowden, *The Making of the Bibles moralisées*, 2 vols (2000).

Biblia Pauperum ('Bible of the poor') A picture book with characteristic layout: a scene from the life of Christ flanked by two Old Testament typological parallels and four prophets holding relevant texts. Early examples have two such compositions per page. These books were probably devised in south Germany or Austria in the mid 13th century, and further popularized in German-speaking lands by *block book and printed versions from the 1460s onwards, mostly of 40 pages. *See also* BIBLE, ILLUSTRATION OF THE; BIBLE MORALISÉE; TYPOLOGY. JHL

G. Schmidt and A. Weckwerth, 'Biblia Pauperum', in *Lexikon der christliche Ikonographie* ([2]1994), vol. 1, 293–8.

Biel, Gabriel (d. 1495) Scholastic theologian. Probably the most representative figure of late medieval *nominalism, Biel professed to follow *William of Ockham. Influences of *Duns Scotus, *Thomas Aquinas, and *Bonaventure can be seen in his works. He joined the *Brethren of the Common Life in 1468. *See also* SCHOLASTICISM; THEOLOGY, WESTERN. AJD

W. M. Landen, 'Gabriel Biel and the Brethren of the Common Life in Germany', *CH* 20 (1951), 23–6.
H. A. Oberman, *The Harvest of Medieval Theology: Gabriel Biel and Late Medieval Nominalism* (1963).

Biernat of Lublin (*c.*1465–after 1529) First vernacular Polish author known by name. Plebeian by birth, he must have had some *education, since he became a priest serving as *chaplain at aristocratic courts. His versified *prayer book, *Raj duszny* (Soul's Paradise, 1513), was one of the first books printed in Poland. His chief work, *Żywot Ezopa* (The Life of Aesop, 1522), is a quasi-autobiographical tale narrated supposedly by the legendary *slave/sage himself and appended with over 200 'Aesop's fables'. *See also* BEAST FABLE AND EPIC. SBa

T. Witczak, *Literatura Sredniowiecza* (1990).
J. Woronczak, *Studia* (1993).
J. Ziomek, *Literatura Odrodzenia* (1987).

Bigod family It rose to status in post-Conquest *England within two generations. Through royal office and loyalty to King *Henry I, Roger Bigod (d. 1107) became extremely wealthy and powerful. His son Hugh (d. 1177) was made *earl of Norfolk. Hugh and later Bigod earls were often among the leaders in major rebellions, the second earl Roger (d. 1221) in 1215, the fourth earl Roger (d. 1270) in 1258, and the fifth earl Roger (d. 1306) in 1297. The fourth earl inherited the office of earl marshal of England. RCD

M. Morris, *The Bigod Earls of Norfolk in the Thirteenth Century* (2005).

bilingualism This could mean reading/writing/speaking Latin in addition to one's mother tongue, or denote competencies in multiple vernaculars. Multilingualism is documented throughout Europe, as in England, where elites *c.*1100–1300 enjoyed fluency in Latin, Anglo-Norman, and English. Bilingualism permeated *trade, *administration, law, scholarship, science, *medicine, *missions, and literature. Evidence exists in *macaronic literature, polyglot *grammars, *glosses and commentaries, scholastic colloquies, *letters, and *translations. The phenomenon of diglossia (register) identifies prestige domains (law, science, theology) emerging from language contact. The appearance of non-native lexemes and phrases in native writing highlights a similar exclusivity among bilinguals.

Borderlands remained bilingual. European elites spoke French as a status language from the 13th century onwards, while Provençal had cachet in France, Italy, and Spain. Mediterranean merchants communicated in Italian and Greek. Southern Italy, Spain, and Sicily nurtured contacts with Arabic speakers; scholars learned Hebrew from Jews. Bilingualism declined with the vernaculars' ascendancy. In England the language of science shifted to English between *c.*1375 and 1475; Latin–French–English miscellanies disappear by *c.*1350. The Latin diglossia distinguishing *Langland's *Piers Plowman* arose because English had gained prominence.

Bilingual competence varied. While accurate translations and grammars point to proficiency, some evidence manifests only rudimentary bilingualism. Walter of Bibbesworth composed his *Tretiz de Langage* *c.*1250 for English aristocratic women teaching their children elementary French: its limited scope shows that it was not written for adept bilinguals. Early German *dialogue manuals likewise demanded minimal competence. Popular academic 'bilingualism' may be represented by the 'Interpretation of Hebrew Names', a Latin dictionary of transliterated Hebrew names from scripture appended to most *Bibles from *c.*1200.

As for Latin–vernacular bilingualism, syntactic and lexical compatibility fostered the interpenetration of Latin and Romance tongues, but impeded it in Celtic- or Germanic-speaking regions. For example, French–Latin *glossaries preserve cognate *interpretamenta* proving a reliance on *etymological translation: French *communion* = Latin *communio*. Elsewhere in Europe, plausibly in *monastic classrooms, exploiting cognates was a strategy that enhanced bilingual learning. Since Latin affixes allowed meanings to be generalized from roots, knowledge of a small numbers of affixes and roots would yield a practical, if elementary, lexicon. 'Loan-translations' frequently accompany Germanic and Celtic glosses to Latin texts.

Translators with limited vocabulary could substitute hyponyms for more specific terms. The use of familiar synonyms for less common words represents the impulse to translate the same word identically irrespective of context. Approximation describes the translation of sense-units. All these strategies lead to changes in the meaning of acquired lexemes through the dominance of one's native tongue. 'Code-switching' could be used for conversational convenience, to negotiate identity, or to establish boundaries. *See also* LANGUAGES: ANGLO-NORMAN / CASTILIAN / SPANISH / FRENCH / GERMANIC / HEBREW / ITALIAN / LATIN, MEDIEVAL / OCCITAN. SGw

J. N. Adams, ed., *Bilingualism in Ancient Society* (2002).

B. Bischoff, 'The Study of Foreign Languages in the Middle Ages', *Speculum*, 36 (1961), 209–24.

T. W. Machan, 'Language Contact in *Piers Plowman*', *Speculum*, 69 (1994), 359–85.

H. Penzl, '"Gimer min ros": How German Was Taught in the Ninth and Eleventh Centuries', *German Quarterly*, 57 (1984), 392–401.

W. Rothwell, 'The Teaching of French in Medieval England', *Modern Language Review*, 63 (1968), 37–46.

J. Scahill, 'Trilingualism in Early Middle English Miscellanies: Languages and Literature', *Yearbook of English Studies*, 33 (2003), 18–32.

L. E. Voigts, 'What's the Word? Bilingualism in Late-Medieval England', *Speculum*, 71 (1996), 813–26.

bill of exchange Payment order executable in a different currency in a foreign market, requiring up to four parties dealing by sets between two places. Replacing the exchange contract in the middle of the 14th century, it becomes an essential instrument of credit and speculation through the practice of 'rechange'.

The 'deliverer' (lender) pays funds to a 'payee' (borrower) in another place by depositing domestic currency with a local 'taker' (payee's agent); in effect, the deliverer 'buys' a bill of exchange drawn on the payee's local account. When the bill arrives in the foreign place, the money is paid to the payee in his currency through the deliverer's agent there (the 'payer'). The bill can be repaid weeks or months later by reversing the process. The exchange and rechange practice provided the deliverer with a profit and obviated the need to transfer *bullion. *See also* COMMERCIAL REVOLUTION; MONEYLENDING, CREDIT, AND USURY. JHay

R. De Roover, *L'Évolution de la lettre de change, XIVe–XVIIIe siècles* (1953).

R. C. Mueller, *The Venetian Money Market: Banks, Panics, and the Public Debt, 1200–1500* (1997).

J. H. Munro, 'The Medieval Bill of Exchange', University of Toronto, 17 Apr. 2008, eh.net/coursesyllabi/syllabi/munro/BILLEXCH.htm.

Billung dynasty The Billung family of *nobles from *Saxony extended from the 9th until the 12th century. They emerged as rulers of Saxony in the Ottonian period. Otto I entrusted Hermann Billung with power, much to the chagrin of Hermann's brothers. A family *feud ensued as a result. The family ruled Saxony until 1106 when Magnus died without heirs. *See also* ROMAN EMPIRE [CAROLINGIAN, OTTONIAN, SALIAN / FRANCONIAN DYNASTIES]. SMW

B. Arnold, *Medieval Germany, 500–1300: A Political Interpretation* (1997).
K. Leyser, *Communication and Power in Medieval Europe: The Carolingian and Ottonian Centuries*, tr. T. Reuter (1994).
T. Reuter, *Germany in the Early Middle Ages, c.800–1056* (1991).

Binchois (de Bins), **Gilles** (*c*.1400–1460) Composer active at the court of *Burgundy, often paired with Guillaume *Du Fay. His music is prized for its melodic grace and clarity. RF

W. Rehm, ed., *Die Chansons von Gilles Binchois (1400–1460)* (1957).
C. Wright, *Music at the Court of Burgundy, 1354–1419* (1979).

biography, Latin 'Biography', the recording in writing of a life, is an expression retrojected from the 17th century, the standard Latin term being *vita*. (Other designations included *passio*, *gesta*, *legenda*, in some cases also *historia*, *translatio*, *miracula*, and even *epitaphium*.) Biography is neither a branch of historiography nor to be simply equated with hagiography as such—that is, saints' lives as defined by modern scholarship.

1. Origins and late antiquity
2. Early MA
3. Tenth and eleventh centuries
4. Twelfth and thirteenth centuries
5. Fourteenth century and after

1. *Origins and late antiquity*

Early biographies include the 3rd- and 4th-century Christian *martyr acts, such as the *Passio SS. Perpetuae et Felicitatis*. These may be compared with the writings associated with Cyprian of Carthage (d. 258): the *Acta (Passio) Cypriani*, written in plain style, and the rhetorical *Vita S. Cypriani* by Pontius of Carthage.

Following them, monks' lives became more popular. *Augustine was impressed by the 'Life of Antony' (d. 356), a classic of Christian biography that owed its appeal not only to Antony's example but also to the authority of its writer, Athanasius of Alexandria. The fame of the *Vita Antonii* prompted *Jerome to write three lives: the *Vita S. Pauli primi eremitae* (376), the *Vita S. Hilarionis*, and the *Vita Malchi monachi captivi* (both *c*.390). The 'Life of Malchus' showed that the hero of a Christian biography need not be a saint. Several of Jerome's *letters can also be considered mini-biographies.

St *Martin of Tours was the subject of a biography composed in his lifetime by *Sulpicius Severus which, with its sequels, became the most successful Latin biography of its time and much later.

Next, biographies of bishops began to flourish. A life of St *Ambrose of Milan was composed in 422 by his confidant, Paulinus. Augustine, who in his *Confessiones* (387) had furnished the prototype for autobiography, was himself the subject of a biography (*c*.435) by the North African bishop Possidius. His *Vita S. Augustini* describes Augustine's everyday habits, under the influence of Suetonius and Nepos.

Following Jerome's *De viris illustribus* (393), Gennadius of *Marseilles continued bishops' lives a century later (*c*.470–95). Around 530 there appeared in *Rome the serial biographies of popes that, with some interruptions, continued throughout the MA and were collected in the **Liber pontificalis*. A noteworthy feature of this work is the fact that saintliness is not a criterion for inclusion.

*Venantius Fortunatus composed many biographies of bishops and one of a woman, the *Vita S. Radegundis*, describing the life of *Radegunda, abbess of *Poitiers.

At the end of the 6th century *Gregory of Tours and *Pope Gregory I composed many short biographical notices. The *Dialogi* attributed to Gregory I (593/4) preserve the life of *Benedict and accounts of the lives of 49 other saints.

2. *Early MA*

The Merovingian era (482–751) produced a great number of bishops' *vitae*. Biography became the leading 7th-century literary genre. The most eminent *vita* of this epoch is that of a monk, the *Vita S. Columbani* of Jonas of Bobbio (*c*.642). In the first book Jonas describes the life of the Irishman *Columban (d. 615); in the second he recounts the lives of some of Columban's students, following New Testament models.

Italian biographical writing in the early MA followed Gregory I's *Dialogi*, with the exception of Rome, where until 870 papal *vitae* continued to be written on earlier patterns. The first pope whose *vita* incorporates elements of a saint's life was *Pope Paschal I. Somewhat later John the Deacon of Rome wrote (873–6) a biography of Gregory I, presented as a model pope.

An Italian speciality was the translation into Latin—first at Rome by *Anastasius Bibliothecarius and then at *Naples by a large number of translators active between 875 and 960—of Greek biographies and hagiographies.

Spain in the 7th century fostered biographical writing, producing among other works the *Vita S. Aemiliani* by *Braulio of Saragossa and the *Historia Wambae regis* by *Julian of Toledo. Though the Muslim conquest in 711 affected Latin culture in Spain, with Eulogius of *Córdoba, *Paulus Albarus of Córdoba, and the 'Mozarabic' or *'Córdoba martyrs' a Latin cultural island arose and continued.

Five biographies from Ireland—a land never part of the *Roman Empire but which used Latin—have survived: Cogitosus, *Vita (II) S. Brigidae*; Ultan (?), *Vita (I) S. Brigidae*; Muirchu, *Vita S. Patricii*; Tirechán, *Vita S. Patricii*; and *Adomnán, *Vita S. Columbae*, all written in the second half of the 7th century. The subsequent, most significant Hiberno-Latin biography was the **Navigatio Sancti Brendani*, a popular travel narrative.

The heirs to the *Irish church were the *Anglo-Saxons, who produced the following biographies during the first half of the 8th century: Anonymous of Whitby, *Liber beati et laudabilis viri Gregorii papae*; *Bede, *Vita S. Felicis*, *Vita S. Cuthberti metrica*, *Vita (II) S. Cuthberti*, *Historia abbatum*; *Eddius, *Vita S. Wilfridi*; Cuthbert of Jarrow, *De obitu Baedae*; and *Felix of Crowland, *Vita S. Guthlaci*. In the 10th century biographical writing again flourished in England, acquiring stylistic sophistication. For example, *Fridegodus of Canterbury's *Breviloquium vitae B. Wilfridi* (*c*.950) and the *Vita S. Dunstani* (*c*.1000) were written in a mannered style that did not long survive the *Norman Conquest.

Anglo-Latin biographical writing moved with English missionaries to the Continent around the middle of the 8th century. Willibald's *Liber S. Bonifatii* (*c*.760) and the nun *Hugeburc's biographies are stylistically more English than those of their Continental counterparts. In the areas of culture and *education the Anglo-Saxons played an important role during the first half-century of *Carolingian rule.

Carolingian classicism in biographical writing began in 800 with *Alcuin's preface to the *Vita (II) S. Richarii*, dedicated to *Charlemagne; it proposed a stylistic transformation of biography. Around 830 *Einhard wrote the *Vita Karoli*, modelled upon Suetonius. As others had made use of biblical formulas to portray their heroes' Christian virtues, so Einhard selected locutions from Suetonius to give Charlemagne a veneer of classical antiquity. Einhard had no successor; biographies of rulers developed along other lines. Thegan's *Vita Hludowici imperatoris* (*c*.837), written during the lifetime of *Louis the Pious, was composed *more annalium*, as *Walahfrid Strabo observed; and a second life of this emperor, composed immediately after his death by 'Astronomus', is best described as *gesta*.

Within the central Carolingian era (800–880), the 'official' biography deserves special mention. In *Fulda, founded by *Boniface in 744, each of the first five abbots received a *vita*: the most reflective and artful of all biographical products of Carolingian classicism, apart from Einhard's work, was the double biography, by *Paschasius Radbertus of *Corbie, of the abbots Adalhard (d. 826) and Wala of Corbie (d. 836).

Carolingian classicism was followed by a late mannerist phase when impressive works were produced. *Heiric of Auxerre composed *c*.875 the *Vita S. Germani*, the most significant metrical biography of the Carolingian era; *Notker Balbulus of *St Gall wrote (884–7) his *Gesta Karoli*, paraphrasing and varying Einhard's biography. The Carolingian impulse also spread abroad, stimulating *Asser's *De rebus gestis Aelfredi* in England (893).

3. Tenth and eleventh centuries

From 920 to 960 literary life languished, but then the new forces of *Cluny and the German *imperium* arose. Already St *Odo, second abbot of the reformed Cluny (910–1790), was a biographer, writing (before 942) the *Vita S. Geraldi*, with a noble layman as hero. Odo himself found a biographer in John of Salerno, whose *vita* begins the series of biographies of the abbots of Cluny. The most important subsequent ones are *Vita (I) S. Maioli* (954–94), by Syrus, *c*.1000; *Vita (I) S. Odilonis* (994–1049), by Jotsald, 1051–3; *Vita (I) S. Hugonis* (1049–1109), by Gilo, 1120–22; and *Vita (I) Petri Venerabilis* (1122–56), by Rudolf of Rudesheym, *c*.1160.

In central Europe *c*.960 a literary movement, in which biography played a strong role, resulted from the ascent of Otto I (936–73) and his successors. The most classical of these *vitae* are the *Gesta Ottonis* by *Hrotsvitha von Gandersheim and *Ruotger of Cologne's *Vita domni Brunonis*. Biography again set the pace for literature, enabling *Poland, Bohemia, and *Hungary to join the *orbis latinus*.

4. Twelfth and thirteenth centuries

During the *Investiture Controversy, central Europe's loss of power and influence extended also to literature. *Pope Gregory VII was treated by Wido of *Ferrara in the *De scismate Hildebrandi* (1086), a polemical treatise in biographical form; it was only later (*c*.1128) that Paul of Bernried, a German partisan of the pope, could describe him in a biography as a saint. We also have the highly rhetorical *Vita Heinrici IV imperatoris* (*c*.1107), a biography of Gregory's antagonist, in which the influence of Sallust is evident.

It was characteristic of the growth of biographical writing in the 12th century that at least five biographies appeared as a consequence of the *canonization of Abbot *Hugh of Cluny in 1120. Still more biographical efforts became associated with *Bernard of Clairvaux and Thomas *Becket of Canterbury. Bernard had a coterie of loyal biographers, who immediately recorded his every *miracle. Becket's murder prompted numerous authors, beginning with *John of Salisbury. There were soon Latin biographies everywhere, as the Latin-using world came to include Portugal, Denmark, Iceland, Sweden, Norway, Finland, and the Baltic lands. In Ireland once again a characteristic biographical literature appeared, the *Vitae sanctorum Hiberniae*. France in the high MA produced biographical works of particular interest: the *Vita Ludovici Grossi* by *Suger of *St-Denis and the autobiographies of *Guibert of Nogent (*De vita sua*) and *Abelard (*Historia calamitatum*). In Germany, biographical writing modelled on Jerome's *De viris illustribus* was revived by *Sigebert of Gembloux, *Honorius Augustodunensis, and *'Anonymous of Melk'.

The most important biographies of the 13th century were those of St *Francis, of which there are several versions, with Thomas of Celano (d. *c*.1260) introducing some of the saint's nonconformist character traits. These aspects were smoothed over in the official biography by *Bonaventure, who instead introduced a theological interpretation of Francis's life.

The 13th century was a critical period for Latin, which lost many fields of literature to vernaculars, including biography. Jean de *Joinville wrote his *Histoire de saint Louis* in OFr.; biographies of the German *mystics of the later MA were usually composed in MHG, and it was exceptional when *Gertrude of *Helfta wrote her spiritual autobiography in Latin.

5. *Fourteenth century and after*

In the 14th century a greater interest in classical antiquity arose, with decisive innovations originating in Italy. With *Petrarch an Italian movement once again stressed Latin. Petrarch composed his *De viris illustribus*, *vitae* of ancient Romans; *Boccaccio contrasted the *viri illustres* with a book *De claris mulieribus*.

For Petrarch the pre-eminent classical biographer was Suetonius. Soon after Petrarch's death, the *bioi paralleloi* of Plutarch began to appear in the west, though they did not enjoy immediate success. Only in 1440, with Giannozzo Manetti's *Vita Socratis et Senecae*, parallel Latin biographies fashioned after Plutarch, did Plutarch's *Lives* become the prime model for biography. *See also* LITERATURES: ANGLO-LATIN/HIBERNO-LATIN. WB

W. Berschin, 'Sueton und Plutarch im 14. Jahrhundert', in *Biographie und Autobiographie in der Renaissance*, ed. A. Buck (1983), 35–43.
—— *Biographie und Epochenstil im lateinischen Mittelalter*, 5 vols (1986–2004).
P. Cox, *Biography in Late Antiquity: A Quest for the Holy Man* (1983).
T. A. Dorey, ed., *Latin Biography* (1967).
A. Gransden, *Historical Writing in England*, 2 vols (1974–82).
H. Grundmann, *Geschichtsschreibung im Mittelalter* (1965).
G. Luck, 'Die Form der suetonischen Biographie und die frühen Heiligenviten', in *Mullus: Festschrift Theodor Klauser*, ed. A. Stuiber and A. Hermann (1964), 230–41.
G. Misch, *Geschichte der Autobiographie: Das Altertum* (1907), 2 vols (^{3}1949–50); tr. E. W. Dickes as *A History of Autobiography in Antiquity*, 2 vols (1950–51).
—— *Geschichte der Autobiographie: Das Mittelalter*, 3 vols (1955–67).
J. Romein, *Die Biographie* (1948).
D. A. Stauffer, *English Biography Before 1700* (1930; repr. 1964).

birchbark documents (East Slavic) East Slavic Cyrillic writings incised on birchbark strips, uncovered during excavations in *Novgorod and elsewhere. Isolated ones have been discovered in Ukraine, Belarus, and central Russia. By 2003 some 1,043 had been recorded (most from the 11th to mid 13th centuries); many more remain buried. They can be dated fairly accurately by dendrochronology, and provide a picture of linguistic, historical, and social development in northwestern *Rus' (11th–15th centuries).

They reveal elements of a vernacular not attested by the Church Slavonic language of high culture. Their contents concern business agreements, *trade inventories, *tax assessments, property ownership, *moneylending, military affairs, and everyday matters (*letters). What their existence says about the spread of *literacy in early Rus' among *boyars, tradesmen, *artisans, merchants, soldiers, and priests remains a matter of dispute. Some of the birchbarks contain alphabet exercises, readers, and even a child's drawings.

Linguistically, the birchbarks contain hitherto unrecorded lexical items and evidence of orthographic, phonological, and morphological developments in northwestern Rus' that often differ radically from those in the language typically reproduced on *parchment or in inscriptions in

Birchbark document from Novgorod, *c.*11th to mid 13th century.

the rest of East Slavic. Personal names have permitted the grouping of some texts and the identification of sites and objects with specific people, including artisans and their *patrons. *See also* ARCHAEOLOGY: RUSSIA, BELARUS, AND THE UKRAINE; LANGUAGES: SLAVIC; PROSOPOGRAPHY; SLAVS. MSF

S. Franklin, *Writing, Society and Culture in Early Rus* (2002).
V. L. Ianin, *Berestianye gramoty: 50 let otkrytiia i izucheniia* (2003).
M. W. Thompson, *Novgorod the Great: Excavations at the Medieval City Directed by A. V. Artsikovsky and B. A. Kolchin* (1967).
A. A. Zalizniak, *Drevnenovgorodskii dialekt* ([2]2004).

biretta *See* LITURGICAL VESTMENTS.

Birgitta (Bridget) **of Sweden, St** (*c*.1303–73) Mystic, founder of the Bridgettine order. She married Ulf Gudmarsson in 1316, with whom she had eight children, including St *Catherine of Sweden, the first abbess of Vadstena. After a *pilgrimage to *Santiago de Compostela in 1341–2, the couple retired to the *monastery of Alvastra, where Ulf died in 1344. Here Birgitta received some of her most important *visions and revelations, including the revelation of the Rule for a new monastic order. In 1349 she went to *Rome, accompanied by her two confessors and her daughter Catherine, and remained there for the rest of her life, except for travelling on pilgrimages. KW

B. Morris, *St Birgitta of Sweden* (1999).
T. Nyberg, ed., *Birgitta, hendes værk og hendes klostre i Norden* (1991).

Illumination of St Birgitta of Sweden from the Burnet Psalter, folio 28v.

Birinus, St (d. 649/50) First bishop of *Dorchester. Italian 'Apostle to the West Saxons', Birinus arrived in *Wessex in 634 and converted the king, Cynegils, who gave him Dorchester as his see. The little known of his work is contained in a conventional saint's life. REB

R. Love, ed. and tr., *Three Eleventh-Century Anglo-Latin Saints' Lives: 'Vita S. Birini', 'Vita et miracula S. Kenelmi' and 'Vita S. Rumwoldi'* (1996).

Birka An island-bound *Viking-age town, *c*.30 km west of Stockholm, with a wide hinterland. The site includes the Black Earth settlement area (*c*.7 ha), *c*.3,000 graves, and a defence system: a garrison area, ramparts, and a hill fort.

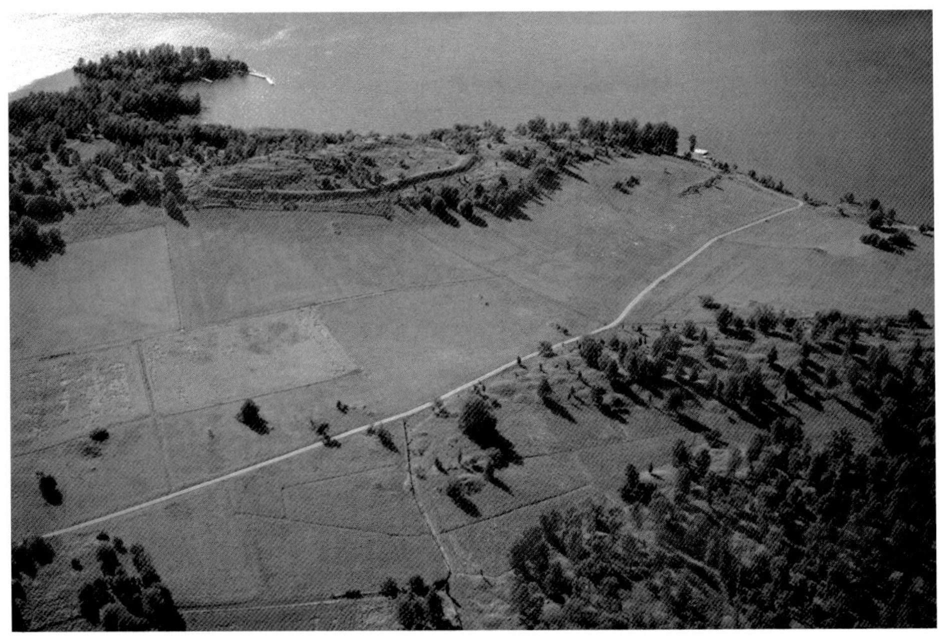

Aerial photo of Birka.

Extensive excavations in the 1870s and modern times date the site to *c*.750–970. Birka was part of a north European network, trading first with the *Carolingian empire and, after *c*.860, with the east. Birka is mentioned in the *Vita Ansgarii* and *Adam of *Bremen's *Gesta*. *See also* ANSGAR, ST; ARCHAEOLOGY: SCANDINAVIA AND ICELAND. BA

B. Ambrosiani and H. Clarke, eds, *Birka Studies* (1992–).
H. Arbman and G. Arwidsson, eds, *Birka*, 5 vols (1938–89).

Birkibeinar In the civil war period in Norway (*c*.1130–1217) many 'flocks' or political factions (ON *flokkar*) were established. In 1177 King Magnús Erlingsson (1161–84) defeated one of these, the so-called *Birkibeinar* ('Birchlegs'). After the defeat the group took as their king Sverrir Sigurðarson (1177–1202). He had been brought up in the Faroe Islands and claimed to be King Sigurðr Haraldsson's son. The *Birkibeinar* gained support from people in Trøndelag, Opplandene, and the more peripheral parts of Norway, whereas Magnús Erlingsson received aid from western Norway and the Viken.

Under Sverrir's great leadership and with skilful guerrilla *warfare, the *Birkibeinar* rose to power. They defeated Magnús Erlingsson in the battle of Fimreite in 1184. Magnús Erlingsson's supporters then established new factions under new leaders; one of these was the **Baglar*.

King Sverrir Sigurðarson died in 1202 and his son Hákon in 1204. Ingi Bárðarson then became the king of the *Birkibeinar*. He and the king of the *Baglar* died in 1217. *Hákon Hákonarson, King Sverrir Sigurðarson's grandson, then became king, with support from leading magnates of both parties. JVS

K. Helle, *Norge blir en stat 1130–1319* (1974).
—— *et al.*, eds, *The Cambridge History of Scandinavia* (2003), vol. 1.

Biruni, Abul-Rayhan Muhammad ibn Ahmad al- (973–1048) A Persian scholar from Khwarizm, al-Biruni wrote nearly 150 works that made powerful contributions to history, *medicine, *geography, *astronomy / *astrology, *mathematics, and mineralogy (*geology). His observational work caused him to travel widely, some of it reported in his highly original astronomical masterwork, the *Masudic Canon*. The *Maqalid ilm al-Haya* presents the recently reformulated spherical trigonometry and ascribes priority to his teacher, Abu Nasr Mansur. The *Exhaustive Treatise on Shadows* is a comprehensive study of gnomonics, foundational for sundials and for determining the times of Muslim prayer. Biruni's work on mathematical geography, the *Tahdid al-Amakin*, also takes inspiration from Muslim ritual by determining the *qibla* (the direction of *Mecca) and generalizing from it to many geodetic problems.

Other contributions include a comprehensive study of India's religion, philosophy, and culture; a catalogue of about 720 medicinal drugs; a chronology of ancient nations; and a scientific study of eighteen precious stones and metals. Although Biruni was not as well known in the west as some others, his scientific work was at the highest level of the medieval period. *See also* CLOCKS, SUNDIALS, AND TIMEKEEPING; PHARMACY. GVB

M.-T. Debarnot, *Al-Bīrūnī, Kitāb Maqālīd ʿilm al-Hay'a: la trigonométrie sphérique chez les Arabes de l'Est à la fin du Xᵉ siècle* (1985).
E. S. Kennedy, *A Commentary upon Bīrūnī's Kitāb Tahdīd al-Amākin* (1973).
—— *The Exhaustive Treatise on Shadows by Abu al-Rayhān Muhammad b. Ahmad al-Bīrūnī: Translation and Commentary*, 2 vols (1976).
E. C. Sachau, *Al-Beruni's India*, 2 vols (1910).

bishop's accoutrements Medieval episcopal dress could be extensive, and included *liturgical vestments common to other *clergy, such as the dalmatic and stole. But bishops wore special insignia and accoutrements called pontificals (*pontificalia*)—the mitre, crosier, ring, and gloves—on solemn and sacramental occasions as signs of dignity and rank in the ecclesiastical hierarchy. Other prelates such as mitred abbesses or protonotaries might display similar accoutrements, but they did so as papal privileges; bishops alone wore them by right.

The mitre, an ancient priestly headdress, appeared in the west in the 11th century and mainly on the heads of popes, but its use was shortly thereafter extended to the episcopacy at large. By the 11th century it had acquired its familiar form of two pointed halves (representing the testaments) with two vestigial ribbons (*infulae*) descending from the back. The crosier, a shepherd's staff as well as a sceptre, represents the bishop's pastoral and jurisdictional roles. Like other great lords, bishops might wear several rings, but the episcopal ring, a circlet set with a precious stone, was always worn on the third finger of the right hand. By the 8th century, gloves were added to the pontificals, apparently for aesthetic rather than practical purposes. A final accoutrement, the pallium, is a woven band worn around the shoulders of archbishops and given to them by the pope as a sign of their metropolitan status. *See also* LITURGY. WJD

J. Nainfa, *Costumes of Prelates of the Catholic Church* (1909).
C. Pocknee, *Liturgical Vesture: Its Origins and Development* (1960).

bishops' sagas Term used for historical accounts of Icelandic bishops from the 11th to the 14th centuries. They comprise *Hungrvaka* (an account of the first five bishops of Skálholt), the sagas of St Þorlákr Þorhallsson and Páll Jónsson, both of Skálholt, and the sagas of Jón Ǫgmundarson, *Guðmundr Arason, and Laurentius Kálfsson, all of Hólar. In addition, two tales (**þættir*) have been regarded as belonging to the bishops' sagas: the tales of Bishop Ísleifr and of Jón Halldórsson of Hólar. *See also* ICELANDIC SAGAS; THÓMAS SAGA ERKIBYSKUPS. KW

V. Ólason, ed., *Íslensk bókmenntasaga* (1992), vol. 1.
G. Turville-Petre, *Origins of Icelandic Literature* (1953).

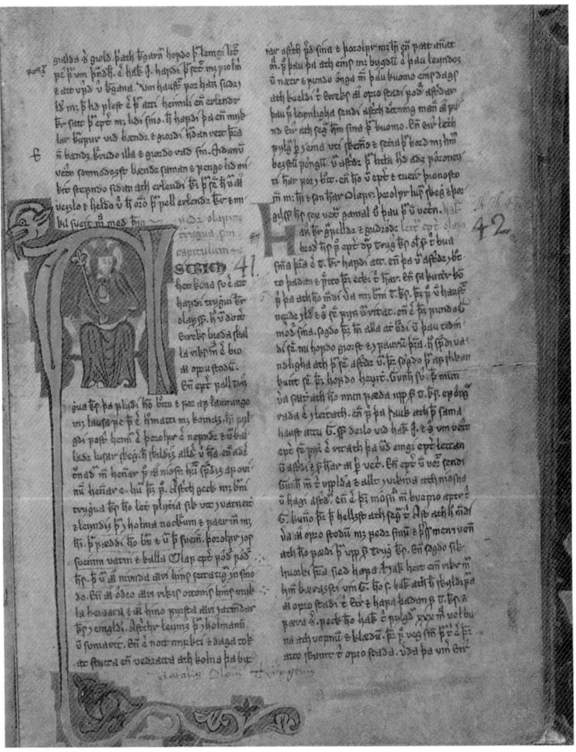

A page from the Bishop's Saga manuscript with a decorated initial.

Title page of the *Philostratus Chronicle*, one of Matthias Corvinus's MSS in his famous library. The flag of the Black Army was derived from the shield at the bottom of the page.

Bitruji, Nur al-Din al- (*fl.* 1200) Latinized as 'Alpetragius', he was an astronomer in Muslim Spain (*al-Andalus), who sought (with limited success) to reform Ptolemaic *astronomy to conform with Aristotle's physical principles. One of his goals was to eliminate both eccentrics and epicycles and to replace them with homocentric planetary models. In addition to the original Arabic of his work, medieval Hebrew and Latin versions had a certain diffusion. *See also* COSMOLOGY. BRG

B. R. Goldstein, *Al-Biṭrūjī: On the Principles of Astronomy* (1971).

J. Samsó, 'On al-Biṭrūjī and the *hay'a* Tradition in al-Andalus', *Islamic Astronomy and Medieval Spain*, 12 (1994).

M. H. Shank, 'Notes on al-Biṭrūjī Attributed to Regiomontanus', *Journal for the History of Astronomy*, 23 (1992), 15–30.

Bjarmaland Area of the Bjarmar, a Karelian tribe, east of Finnmark on the White Sea. Its mythical qualities as a heroic quest destination prompted the notion that there were two Bjarmalands (*Historia Norwegiae*; *Saxo Grammaticus). *See also* NORSE HEROIC LEGENDS. RFS

R. Simek, 'Elusive Elysia, or: Which Way to Glæsisvellir?', in *Sagnaskemmtun*, ed. R. Simek *et al.* (1986), 247–75.

'Black Army' of Matthias Corvinus The name the *mercenaries of King *Matthias I Corvinus of *Hungary took after the king's death. This army, originally recruited from soldiers of diverse central European countries, allowed the king to conquer extensive territories in Moravia, Silesia, and Austria. The size of the army is debated, but may have been as large as 15,000 men, probably the largest of its time in Europe. JMB

G. Rázsó, 'The Mercenary Army of King Mathias Corvinus', in B. K. Király and J. M. Bak, eds, *From Hunyadi to Rákóczi: War and Society in Late Medieval and Early Modern Hungary* (1982), 125–40.

Black Canons *See* RELIGIOUS ORDERS.

Black Death *See* PLAGUE AND EPIDEMICS.

Black Death, social and economic impact of the

The Black Death came from the east and raced through most of Europe in four years, 1347–51. Unlike the subtropical bubonic plague tied to rodents (*Y. pestis*), the Black Death spread almost as fast per diem as the later rodent disease spreads per annum. Their mortalities were also of different orders of magnitude. Even at its height in India, which accounted for over 95 per cent of deaths from *Y. pestis* in the 20th century, no city lost more than 3 per cent of its population to this disease. By comparison, tax records for *Florence suggest that as many as 80 per cent of the citizens died in four months alone in 1348. Finally, humans possess no natural immunity to *Y. pestis*, and as a result the age structure of its victims has not changed over the 20th century. By contrast, Europeans adapted rapidly to the Black Death killer; by its fourth wave in the 1380s, it had become mostly a children's disease, and according to the pope's doctor (Raymundus Chalmelli) far fewer now caught it and most of them survived. Such epidemiological differences are important for understanding the complexity of the psychological, social, and economic changes that ensued.

Historians have seen the Black Death as responsible for the *peasant revolts of the late 14th century, the end of *serfdom, the rise of vernacular languages, the Reformation, and even modernity itself. Whether the *plague alone can explain such broad and often distant changes is doubtful. The immediate and longer-term consequences of the Black Death often differed, could lead in opposite directions, and were not everywhere the same. For instance, immediately after the Black Death, places such as Florence vigorously recouped losses through quick rises in fertility and emigration from their hinterland. Curiously, this *demographic pattern changed in the 15th century. Fertility fell perhaps because the disease, although now less lethal, killed greater proportions of those who would replenish population—the young—and cities attracted fewer immigrants because the scarcity of rural *labour eventually meant improved conditions on the land.

The plague's consequences for social mobility and women also differed over time. Initially, the demographic catastrophes proved socially ameliorative for labourers. Shortages led to greater mobility; manual labourers could fill more skilled jobs, or move to other villages or *towns with more favourable conditions. Further, rising expectations led to new organizations of labourers, petitions, and revolts that extended their political rights and improved the conditions of their employment. Similarly, women filled jobs previously reserved for men. In Florence, a woman even became a recognized physician, and tax survey records show their control over property, north and south of the Alps, on the rise. These changes, however, were not to last through the 15th century. Soon male society reacted, imposing greater restrictions on *guild entry, and governments returned to more hierarchical, oligarchic rule than before the plague. *Artisans and labourers became increasingly marginalized with fewer political rights, and social mores reinvented aristocratic culture.

The economic and social consequences of the Black Death were not the same across Europe, as worsening conditions for rural labour in parts of eastern Europe attest. Nor were the Black Death or its successive strikes as 'universal' as contemporaries or historians today often assume. Plague may not have even touched places such as *Douai in *Flanders until 1400, and population losses in *Hainaut, *Holland, northern Germany, parts of *Poland, and Finland were notably lower than they were in many other cities and regions across Europe. Historians have yet to analyse these diverging demographic patterns, and their consequences for economic development and the transitions to early modern societies. *See also* WAGE LABOUR; WOMEN, ECONOMIC AND SOCIAL ROLES OF. SKC

The Brenner Debate: Agrarian Class Structure and Economic Development in Pre-industrial Europe, ed. T. H. Aston and C. H. E. Philpin (1985).

S. Cohn, 'Women and Work in the Renaissance', in *Gender and Society in Renaissance Italy*, ed. J. Brown and R. Davis (1997), 200–227.

—— *The Black Death Transformed: Disease and Culture in Early Renaissance Europe* (2002).

P. Goldberg, *Women, Work, and Life Cycle in a Medieval Economy: Women in York and Yorkshire, c.1300–1520* (1992).

J. Hatcher, *Plague, Population and the English Economy, 1348–1530* (1977).

D. Herlihy, *The Black Death and the Transformation of the West*, ed. S. Cohn (1997).

Black Forest Located in southwest Germany, it was the seat of power of the Alemanni in the early MA. Occupation of the region began in the 11th century. *Monasteries dedicated to St Blaise and to St Peter were established there at that time. SMW

The Black Forest.

H. O. Mühleisen *et al.*, eds, *Das Kloster St Peter auf dem Schwarzwald: Studien zu seiner Geschichte von der Gründung im 11. Jahrhundert bis zur frühen Neuzeit* (2001).

Black Friars *See* FRIARS; RELIGIOUS ORDERS.

Black Monks *See* RELIGIOUS ORDERS.

Black Sea (Mare Nigrum, Pontus Euxinus) The sea situated on the junction of the *trade routes from the east Mediterranean to further north and east. In the early MA most of its coastline belonged to *Byzantium. In the 13th–14th centuries Italian merchants colonized a considerable part of the northern Black Sea area. From the second half of the 15th century the Black Sea trade was taken over by Ottoman Turkey. MBK

A. Bryer and D. Winfield, *The Byzantine Monuments and Topography of the Pontos*, 2 vols (1985).

S. P. Karpov, *Trapesundskaya imperija i zapadnoevropejskie gosudarstva v XIII–XV vekakh* (1981).

bladder pipe *See* MUSICAL INSTRUMENTS.

Blasius of Parma (Biagio Pelacani) (d. 1416) Anti-Aristotelian Italian philosopher. Blasius defended mathematical measure and a materialistic, *atomistic, and deterministic philosophy, denying the immortality of the soul (for which he was condemned) and upholding the *eternity of the universe. *See also* ARISTOTELIANISM; ASTROLOGY; PHILOSOPHY, WESTERN. MTo

G. Federici Vescovini, *Astrologia e scienza: la crisi dell'aristotelismo sul cadere del Trecento e Biagio Pelacani da Parma* (1979).

——*Arti e filosofia nel secolo XIV: studi sulla tradizione aristotelica e i moderni* (1983).

Bligger von Steinach (*fl.* 1174–1209) MHG aristocratic poet, connected to the imperial court. He composed two *courtly love poems, lamenting his fruitless wooing, and a *didactic poem. *Gottfried von Strassburg and *Rudolf von Ems praised a narrative work, *Der Umbehanc* ('The Tapestry'), which has not survived. *See also* SPIELMANNSEPIK. AC

U. Meves, 'Urkundliche Bezeugungen der Minnesänger im 12. Jahrhundert', in *Literarische Interessenbildung im Mittelalter*, ed. J. Heinzle (1993), 75–105.

G. Schweikle, *Minnesang* (1989).

block book Made by *printing each page from a woodblock carved without using movable type; text was carved into the block. Chinese block books date from the 9th century; the most common European block books are the 15th-century *Biblia Pauperum and the *Ars moriendi* (**Art of Dying*). *See also* WOODCUT. EL

A. Hind, *An Introduction to the History of Woodcut* (1935), vol. 1, 207–64.

Blois Southeast of *Orléans, its *castle dominates the Loire. The town was important owing to river commerce and religious houses. The 10th century, when the Jewish community settled, saw the donjon (dungeon) built, but the town suffered during the *Hundred Years War. It was the seat of the Orléans dynasty from the mid 15th century and a royal property since Louis XII, who began reconstructing the castle, establishing the city as the cultural and *administrative centre of the realm. The legal reform decree 'Ordonnance de Blois' was issued there (1499). JFP

V. Aubourg *et al.*, *Blois, un château en l'an mil* (2000).

F. and P. Lesueur, *Le Château de Blois* (2005).

Blois, house of Powerful *duchy that grew from land given by *Louis the Pious in 835. It passed in the 10th century to Thibaut I, count of Blois, Chartres, *Tours, and *Provence, whose family ruled Blois until the 13th century. Holdings were expanded by marriage to include land in *Berry and *Champagne. With Champagne, Blois in the 11th and 12th centuries menaced the *Capetian kings. Among the descendants of Stephen of Blois and Adela, daughter of *William the Conqueror, was *Stephen of Blois, king of England. JKG

J. Dunbabin, *France in the Making, 843–1180* (1985).

E. Hallam, *Capetian France, 987–1328* (1980).

Blondel de Nesle (*fl.* 1175–1210) Early **trouvère*, who composed at least 23 songs on *courtly love. Technically competent if unoriginal, Blondel's lyrics are highly representative of the northern French lyric tradition. AA

Blondel de Nesle, *L'Œuvre lyrique: Textes*, ed. Y. Lepage (1994).

——*L'Œuvre lyrique de Blondel de Nesle: Mélodies*, ed. A. Bahat and G. le Vot (1996).

blood brother Fictive *kinship relationship apparently entered into by exchanging *oaths. Although the phenomenon is known cross-culturally, the most important medieval manifestations are from the North. The terms used in ON-Icelandic are *eiðbróðir* ('oath-brother'), *svarabróðir* ('sworn-brother'), and *fóstbróðir* ('foster-brother'), the latter two being most widely attested in the sagas.

The historical literary evidence situates blood brotherhood in the mechanisms of blood *feud, insofar as the oaths taken require the participants to avenge one another, just as actual brothers were so required by custom. On the obverse side, the Norwegian Gulaþing law has a provision allowing a man to take *wergeld* for a fallen 'oath-brother'. The provisions parallel those given to persons fostered into the family.

Two *Icelandic sagas, *Gísla saga* and *Fóstbrœðra saga*, describe rituals undertaken in connection with blood-brotherhood oaths in *pagan times, more than two centuries before the sagas were recorded. These involved passing under a strip of turf cut from the earth (a symbolic

Cityscape of Blois, including the river and bridge.

rebirth?) and, in *Gísla saga*, mingling blood in the soil. The more fantastic *fornaldarsǫgur* (sagas dealing with the ancient myths and hero legends of Germania, with the adventures of *Vikings, or with other exotic adventures in foreign lands) frequently invoke this motif. *See also* LAW, MEDIEVAL GERMAN. JLi

O. Bø, 'Fostbrorskap', *KLNM*, vol. 4 (1959), 540–41.

V. Guðmundsson, 'Fóstbrœðralag', in *Þrjár ritgjörðir sendar og tileinkaðar herra Páli Melsteð af Finni Jónssyni, Valtýr Guðmundssyni og Boga Th. Melsteð* (1891).

bloodletting Bloodletting was performed on healthy members of religious communities at regular intervals throughout the year. It is described in *monastic customaries and mentioned in *visitation records, account rolls, and *general chapter statutes. The practice originated in *Galeno-*Hippocratic prophylactic bloodletting, but came to differ from bleeding practices described in *medical texts. Dates derived from account rolls indicate that monastic bloodletting was scheduled in such a way as to avoid disruption to the monastic regimen, rather than according to medical calendars.

Its purpose was to preserve physical and spiritual health and to maintain communal discipline. After being bled, individuals would enjoy three days of rest and rich *food (usually including meat), and would reflect upon spiritual themes, presumably as set out in the 'seyney' or bloodletting books listed in the records of *Westminster Abbey. In the religious setting, where the body was often used as a model for the soul, bloodletting was the literal rendering of a powerful metaphor. *See also* PHLEBOTOMY AND HAEMATOSCOPY. MKKY

M. Cassidy-Welch, *Monastic Spaces and their Meanings* (2001), 133–65.

J. W. Clark, *The Observances in Use at the Augustinian Priory of S. Giles and S. Andrew at Barnwell, Cambridgeshire* (1897), lxi–lxxiii.

L. Gougaud, 'La Pratique de la phlébotomie dans les cloîtres', *RMab* 14 (1924), 1–13.

blood libel accusation By the end of the 12th century, the notion that Jews murdered Christians and the claim that they did so ritually, as a repetition of Jesus' crucifixion, had taken hold of many imaginations in western Christendom. The claim that Jews crucified Christian victims was associated with influential *Holy Week rituals. Since *Easter week and the Jewish observance of Passover often overlapped, it is not surprising that the allegations of Jewish involvement in ritual murder might elide into a sense of murder related to the Jewish holiday. Since the biblical narrative of the Israelites' deliverance from Egypt focuses on blood (Exodus 7:17–21, 12:7, 13, 22–23), it is perhaps not surprising that a new sense of Jewish *crime took hold during the middle decades of the 13th century, with the claim that Jews utilized Christian blood for Passover ritual observances.

As with many of the calumnies that emerged in western Christendom from the 12th century onward, church and state leaders investigated and repudiated the new blood libel. *Pope Innocent IV did so in 1247; more strikingly, Emperor *Frederick II convened a commission of experts, made up of former Jews considered both knowledgeable and unbiased in favour of Jews, to investigate the new claim. Based on the findings of this commission, the emperor denounced the claim and ordered that it not be recognized in his courts. Repeated repudiation notwithstanding, the blood libel accusation has proven the most durable of medieval calumnies, surfacing regularly down to the present. *See also* ANTI-SEMITISM. RC

A. Gross, 'The Blood Libel and the Blood of Circumcision: An Ashkenazic Custom that Disappeared in the Middle Ages', *JQR*, n.s. 86/1–2 (1995), 171–82.
N. Roth, 'Blood Libel', in *Medieval Jewish Civilization: An Encyclopedia* (2003), 119–21.

blood of Christ The blood struck from Christ's side by a lance (John 19:34) was central to patristic and medieval theologies of redemption. Conflated with the blood referred to by Christ in instituting the *Eucharist (Matthew 26:28), it was interpreted in the Epistle to the Hebrews as a substitution for Old Testament sacrifice. From the 11th century on, Christ's wounds and blood became important motifs in popular piety. A phrase attributed to *Bernard of Clairvaux, and used by *Pope Clement VI in the *bull *Unigenitus* (1343), asserted that one drop of Christ's blood was sufficient to redeem all humankind. *Visionaries such as *Peter Damian and *Catherine of Siena claimed to drink blood from Christ's side. In the central MA, a number of sites, such as Weingarten, claimed to possess *relics of Christ's blood. The 14th and 15th centuries saw many claims (for example, at Wilsnack in Germany and Daroca in Spain) that blood appeared miraculously on consecrated wafers. Some of these *miracles were supposedly the result of Jewish host desecrations, and were used to justify pogroms. *See also* ANTI-SEMITISM. CWB

C. Bynum, 'The Blood of Christ in the Later Middle Ages', *CH* 71 (2002), 685–715.
P. Dinzelbacher, 'Das Blut Christi in der Religiosität des Mittelalters', in *900 Jahre Heilig-Blut-Verehrung in Weingarten 1094–1994*, ed. N. Kruse and H. Rudolf (1994), vol. 1, 415–34.
J. H. Rohling, *The Blood of Christ in Christian Latin Literature Before the Year 1000* (1932).
M. Rubin, *Gentile Tales: The Narrative Assault on Late Medieval Jews* (1999).

Blore Heath, battle of On 23 September 1459, the earl of *Salisbury routed royal forces sent to hinder his support of *Richard, duke of York, and his challenge to *Henry VI's government. The skirmish hardened party lines, ultimately resulting in the *Yorkist capture of the throne by Richard's son *Edward IV. *See also* ROSES, WARS OF THE. LCA

R. A. Griffiths, *The Reign of King Henry VI* (1981).

Blume, Clemens (1862–1932) German hymnologist; a Jesuit from 1878, professor of liturgical studies at *Frankfurt from 1929. In 1897 he joined Guido Maria Dreves as one of the principal editors of *Analecta hymnica medii aevi* (from vol. 25). Blume published numerous articles and four volumes of *Hymnologische Beiträge* (1897–1900; repr. 1971). *See also* HYMNODY; LITURGICAL BOOKS. DDH

AHMA, 55 vols (1886–1922).

Boccaccio, Giovanni (1313–75) Founder of Italian prose literature and pre-eminent Latin humanist. Illegitimate son of Florentine merchant Boccaccino di Chellino and an unknown mother, Giovanni Boccaccio was born in the summer of 1313 in Tuscany, probably in *Florence. Details of Boccaccio's life are scarce and probably tainted by fictitious claims that Boccaccio himself makes in his literary works.

Accepted into the family of his father, Boccaccio passed his early youth in the intellectually rich ambience of Florence, at that time dominated *in absentia* by *Dante. As early as 1325 but certainly by 1327, young Giovanni moved to *Naples as an *apprentice in the powerful Bardi bank run by his father. Beyond his commercial *education, Boccaccio soaked up the cosmopolitan culture offered by Angevin Naples. Robert of *Anjou's court put Boccaccio into the orbit of intellectual luminaries outside his native Florentine sphere, including the historian Paolo Veneto, the early humanist Paolo da *Perugia, and the famed *astronomer Andalò da Negro. Boccaccio continued his particular Florentine education through contacts with Dante's old friend Cino da Pistoia. It is little wonder then that Boccaccio, much to his father's dismay, eschewed his study of *banking and of canon *law for the literary arts.

During Boccaccio's time in Naples he completed three works that reflect his unique literary education: *La Caccia di Diana* (1334?), *Filostrato* (1335?), and *Filocolo* (1336). Writing in the Florentine vernacular, Boccaccio remained faithful to Dante's stylistic agenda while incorporating the varied literary cultures of Naples into his text. As a result of his youthful erudition, these early works appear somewhat forced. Owing to a crisis in the Bardi bank, Boccaccio moved back to Florence in 1340 and began his most productive literary phase, writing *La Teseida* (1340–41), *Comedia delle Ninfe* or *Ameto* (1341–2), *Amorosa Visione* (1342–3), *Elegia di Madonna Fiammetta* (1343–4), and *Ninfale Fiesolano* (1346), as well as his collection of Latin poems *Bucolicum Carmen*. Although faithful to Dante's vernacular model, Boccaccio developed his own voice. His self-commentary on the *Teseida* suggests the erudition that made him a leading humanist. The unconventional complexity of the character of Fiammetta, his 'Beatrice' or poetic *senhal* (Provençal, 'code name' for dedicatee), belies Boccaccio's scepticism in Dante's *Dolce Stil Novo*.

After the death of his father in 1349, shortly after the calamitous *Black Death, Boccaccio assumed a more pronounced role in Florentine civic affairs while also undertaking more ambitious literary projects. The *plague and its social aftershocks provided the setting for Boccaccio's most famous work, the *Decameron* (1350–53). The model for Italian prose for centuries, this complex work illustrates Boccaccio's mastery of his structural, linguistic, and generic models. Beginning in the early 1350s, influenced by his friend and mentor Francesco Petrarca (*Petrarch), Boccaccio began cataloguing references to the classical deities in his broad humanistic reading. This exhaustive study resulted

Bloodletting man.

Vena cardiaca i. cordis uel conlis uaditur pro passionibus spiritualium membrorum

Vena cephalica i. capitis que pro passionibus capitis inciditur et cerebri

Vena media in fronte purgat emeroydas et frenesim et maniam

Vena in occipite media ualet contra querelam capitis et antiquam passionem

Vena in temporibus incisa si incidatur deinceps non fit effusio spermatis

Vena inter nares media purgat caput et auditum iuuat et confortat

Vena basilica i. epatica solet aperiri pro passionibus epatis et splenis

Vena in extremitate nasi media iuuat memoriam et purgat cerebrum

Vena purpurea aperitur pro passionibus internum

Vena in lingua media iuuat squinanciam et impedimentum loquele

Vena iliaca aperitur pro inferioribus passionibus membrorum

In collo duas uenas incidimus propter dolorem capitis et oculos reumatizantes

Vena pulsatiua media in cardiaca passione confert multum

Vena sub utraque ascella media facit ipsum quasi ridendo mori

Vena ad pollicem media contra liditatem corporis ualet multum

Vena in gibbo media purgat melancoliam et frenesim et maniam

Vena inter medium et auricularem media confert oculis et iuuat litargiam

Vena in poplitibus media facit ipsum cito incedere currentem

Vena media super uentrem ualet contra sciaticam passionem Sed alia media sub uentre ualet contra aliubum

Vena in utroque pede si aperiatur mensus et exterius humores purgat inferius

Vena ueniens ad pollicem pedis media ualet repletis uentositate et inflatis

Vena media super pollicem ualet contra inflationem et motus reumatis

Vena sub genu ab intra media sanguinem purgat de passione ne coaguletur

Vena sub genu ab extra media iuuat sciaticam et nefreticam et cruram in the *encyclopedic *Genealogia Deorum Gentilium* (1355–74). He also began another massive work dealing with classical *geography, *De Montibus, Silvis, Fontibus* (1355–74). The 1360s saw a continuation of Boccaccio's narrative development in Latin, notably with his historical works *De Casibus Virorum Illustrium* (1355–74) and *De Mulieribus Claris* (1361–75). Despite his shift to Latin, Boccaccio never ceased to champion the Tuscan vernacular. He composed three separate redactions of an almost *hagiographic life of Dante, *Trattatello in Laude di Dante* (1350, 1361, 1373). He wrote a vehemently misogynistic and most probably satirical *Corbaccio* (1355?). His final work is the unfinished *commentary on Dante's *Commedia, Esposizioni sopra la Comedia di Dante* (1373–5), commissioned by the city of Florence.

Of particular interest is Boccaccio's exchange of *letters with Petrarch, as well as his famous *Epistola Consolatoria a Pino de' Rossi* (1361–2). Boccaccio, with Petrarch, should be considered one of the first humanists. He discovered and assiduously copied classical texts such as Ovid's *Ibis* and Cicero's *Pro Cluentio*, and edited Dante's works in three autograph MSS. He was moderately successful in learning and reading Homer in classical Greek. Boccaccio's influence on the European narrative tradition stretches from *Chaucer to Borges. Boccaccio died in his family's provincial home in Certaldo in 1375, having merited the honour of forming, along with Dante and Petrarch, Italian literature's *tre corone*. *See also* LITERATURES: ITALIAN; PROSE STYLE, LATIN. JMH

G. Boccaccio, *Tutte le opere di Giovanni Boccaccio*, ed. V. Branca, 10 vols (1964–94).
V. Branca, *Boccaccio, the Man and his Works*, tr. R. Monges (1976).
R. Hollander, *Boccaccio's Two Venuses* (1977).
V. Kirkham, *Fabulous Vernacular: Boccaccio's Filocolo and the Art of Medieval Fiction* (2001).
G. Padoan, *Boccaccio, le muse, il Parnaso e l'Arno* (1978).
P. G. Ricci, *Studi sulla vita e le opere del Boccaccio* (1985).
V. Zaccaria, *Boccaccio narratore, storico, moralista e mitografo* (2001).

Bodel, Jean (*c*.1165–1209/10) *Arras-based author, the earliest important northern French urban writer. Bodel probably worked for the city's judiciary, and had connections with its leading families. In the early 13th century he contracted *leprosy, and died in a leper colony. His literary output is wide-ranging and original, and heavily influenced *Adam de la Halle and other later poets. Bodel's shorter works include nine *fabliaux, whose vivid, bawdy narratives contain elements of anticlerical satire; five **pastourelles*; and the *Congés*, a long and strikingly personal strophic poem composed after the onset of his leprosy, in which he takes his leave of Arras. In a substantial epic poem, the *Chanson des Saisnes*, Bodel recounts the war between *Charlemagne and the pagan *Saxon king Witikind: into this epic framework he weaves important motifs from other literary traditions, notably courtly *romance and urban realism. A similar fusion of *hagiographic, epic, and urban elements is apparent in the *Jeu de St Nicolas*, a play probably first performed in 1200. Captured in battle, a statue of St Nicholas is made to guard the victorious Saracen king's treasure, which is then stolen by three thieves distinctly from *Artois. The saint appears and orders the thieves to return the treasure, whereupon the Saracens convert. *See also* CHANSONS DE GESTE. AA

J. Bodel, *La Chanson des Saisnes*, ed. A. Brasseur (1989).
—— *Le Jeu de Saint Nicolas*, ed. J. Dufournet (2005).
C. Jacob-Hugon, *L'œuvre jongleresque de Jean Bodel: l'art de séduire un public* (1998).
P. Ruelle, ed., *Les Congés d'Arras* (1965).

body *See* ANATOMY AND PHYSIOLOGY; DEATH; GENDER; HUMOURS; NATURALS, NON-NATURALS, RES CONTRA NATURAM; PHYSIOGNOMY; REGIMEN OF HEALTH.

Boen (Boon), **Johannes** (d. 1367) Dutch music theorist, author of two treatises. His writings combine an interest in the mathematical traditions of *music theory with the practical concerns of the expanding use of chromaticism in music. CMB

W. Frobenius, *Johannes Boens 'Musica' und seine Konsonanzenlehre* (1971).
F. A. Gallo, ed., *Johannis Boen 'Ars (musica)'* (1972).

Boendale, Jan van (1279–1365) Author of *Brabantsche Yeesten*, *Boec van der Wraken*, and *Lekenspieghel*, an *encyclopedia of practical knowledge for the *laity. He also composed *dialogues, especially *Jans Testeye*, in which he praises the simplicity of *peasants and promotes the value of *education. DN

J. Van Gerven, 'Nationaal gevoel en stedelijke politieke visies in het 14de eeuwse Brabant: Het voorbeeld van Jan van Boendale', *Bijdragen tot de geschiedenis*, 59 (1976), 145–64.

Boethius, Anicius Manlius Severinus (*c*.480–*c*.524) Roman philosopher and statesman, often considered a Christian martyr in the MA. He spent most of his life as a cultivated aristocrat, pursuing a vast project of translating and introducing Greek *philosophy in Latin. He began by writing textbooks on arithmetic and music, based on Greek models, and gradually moved to translating all the works of Plato and *Aristotle and adding *commentaries. He almost completed the works on *logic, which included *translations and two commentaries each on Porphyry's *Isagoge*, the standard introduction to Aristotelian logic, and on Aristotle's *On Interpretation*, as well as one commentary on his *Categories*. Boethius draws heavily on the Greek commentary tradition, especially Porphyry, and his range includes problems of *metaphysics (*universals, modality) and semantics. He also wrote logical textbooks on topical (or semi-formal) reasoning and on different types of syllogism.

Boethius also became involved in the theological discussions between Latin and Greek Christians. The outcome was his five *opuscula sacra* ('Theological Tractates'). No. 4 is a simple presentation of Christian doctrine, and no. 3 is a purely philosophical discussion of God and goodness. Nos. 1 and 2 aim to establish doctrine about the *Trinity, and no. 5 discusses Christ's status as God and human, all by using Aristotelian physical and logical ideas to show the incoherence of heretical views.

In 522, Boethius accepted appointment as the highest official of *Theodoric, the Ostrogoth who ruled *Italy. Court intrigue and Boethius' wish to end corruption led to his rapid downfall. He was imprisoned and sentenced to death. Before being executed, he wrote his *Consolation of Philosophy*, a *dialogue with verse interludes, in which a personification of Philosophy appears to a despondent Boethius. By arguing with him rationally, Philosophy shows Boethius that he has lost nothing of real value through his fall from power and that, despite appearances, the human world is divinely ordered. Unlike worldly goods such as riches, power, and pleasure, the true good, which is what everyone really seeks, fulfils our desires. Evil-doers have only the semblance of power: in fact, they are weak and punish themselves through their wicked activities. In the last part of the dialogue, Philosophy answers Boethius' question about why God's foreknowledge does not mean that the future is fixed. In his eternity, she explains, God knows past, present, and future in the way we know the present, and we do not, for instance, determine the result of a chariot race by watching it.

Boethius's influence was vast. His logical translations were standard; his logical commentaries and textbooks formed the basis of the logic, including that of *Abelard, studied until *c.*1200. The *opuscula sacra* helped shape the analytical method of theology, and the *Consolation* was used by philosophers and theologians, including *Aquinas and *Albertus Magnus, and poets such as *Jean de Meun, *Dante, and *Chaucer alike. JMar

Boethius, *Tractates; The Consolation of Philosophy*, tr. H. F. Stewart, E. K. Rand, and S. J. Tester (1918; repr. 1973).
H. Chadwick, *Boethius: The Consolations of Music, Logic, Theology and Philosophy* (1981).
M. Gibson, ed., *Boethius: His Life, Thought, and Influence* (1981).
N. H. Kaylor, Jr, and P. E. Phillips, eds, *New Directions in Boethian Studies* (2007).
J. Marenbon, *Boethius* (2003).

Boethius, commentaries on (9th–12th centuries) Marginalia in MSS of *Boethius' *De institutione musica* often contain portions of an extensive *commentary called the *Glossa maior*. Topics include correspondences with other authorities, musical terminology, and *Neoplatonic philosophy. *See also* MUSIC THEORY. REG

Glossa maior in Institutionem musicam Boethii, ed. M. Bernhard and C. Bower, 4 vols (1993–6).

Boethius of Dacia (Boethius Dacus, Boethius the Dane) (d. *c.*1284) *Master of Arts at the University of *Paris and so-called 'radical Aristotelian' famous for defending heterodox opinions on human happiness and the *eternity of the world. Taught in the *arts faculty in Paris before 1277, when the Averroistic interpretation of his Aristotelian commentary was condemned. In *grammar he was an important exponent of the *modi significandi*. *See also* ARISTOTELIANISM; AVERROËS; GLOSS AND COMMENTARY. CJMc, PSE

Boethius of Dacia, *On the Supreme Good, On the Eternity of the World, On Dreams*, tr. J. Wippel (1987).
A. J. Celano, 'Boethius of Dacia: "On the Highest Good"', *Traditio*, 43 (1987), 199–214.
C. H. Lohr, 'Medieval Latin Aristotle Commentaries: Authors A–F', *Traditio*, 23 (1967), 313–413, esp. 385–8.
J. Pinborg, 'Die Entwicklung der Sprachtheorie im Mittelalter', *Beiträge zur Geschichte der Philosophie des Mittelalters*, 42/2 (1967), 77–86.

Bogomils *See* HERESY.

Bohemia (Moravia) The *duchy (later kingdom) of Bohemia and *margravate of Moravia occupied an important position in central Europe throughout the high and late MA. The Slavic Czechs (Češi) long formed the majority of this multi-ethnic society, whose history has been intertwined with that of western and eastern neighbours alike. Under some of the later *Přemyslid and especially the *Luxembourg rulers, Bohemia's status within the *Roman Empire increased; then the 15th-century *Hussite revolution transformed society while leading to the region's partial isolation.

1. Geography and early history
2. The Přemyslids
3. The Czech lands under the Luxembourgs
4. The Hussites

1. *Geography and early history*

Nearly surrounded by mountains, the central plain of Bohemia attracted humans since the Stone Ages. The Vltava (Moldau) river, originating in southern Bohemia, bisects the region before emptying into the *river Elbe. Bordering Bohemia to the southeast, Moravia takes its name from the Morava river that flows from the Sudeten Mountains south to the *river Danube. At their greatest extent, the crown lands of medieval Bohemia included not only Moravia but also neighbouring *Silesia and Lusatia (*Lausitz).

The name Bohemia derives from the Boii, the Celtic tribe inhabiting the region from the fourth century BC. Celtic dominance over Bohemia came to an end around the turn of the millennium as Germanic peoples, in some cases fleeing Roman military advances, moved in. *Slavs migrated westward across Moravia into Bohemia from the first half of the 6th century, where they began to assimilate local

Bohemia in Hussite times.

Germanic groups; archaeologists identify some of their earliest settlements by the presence of so-called 'Prague style' pottery. Conquered by the Turkic-speaking Avars in the 6th century, some Slavs in the region near the Frankish border revolted in 623, creating a short-lived political territory under the leadership of a Frankish merchant named Samo.

The first significant political and cultural unity to develop in this region centred on Moravia rather than Bohemia, where in the 9th century *Great Moravia extended its geographical power east and west after its foundation in the 830s. A close association with *Byzantium, in the persons of Sts *Cyril (Constantine) and Methodius, brought to Great Moravia from the 860s a Slavic-tongued Christianity that for a brief time looked to *Constantinople rather than *Rome; more lasting was the new script, *Old Church Slavonic.

2. *The Přemyslids*

In the 880s Great Moravia absorbed Bohemia, which earlier in the century had come under the periodic attack, and even loose control, of the Germanic rulers to the west. In 845, fourteen nobles (*duces*) from Bohemia had accepted Christianity from German bishops, though with limited effect. Under the patronage of Great Moravia, Bořivoj (d. *c.*890), the first documented leader of the Přemysl family, consolidated power in central Bohemia through controlling a series of forts. Bořivoj also accepted Christianity at the Moravian court. As Great Moravia collapsed, the Přemyslids gradually expanded their territory to include all of Bohemia by the end of the 10th century and Moravia in the early 11th. *Prague and its *castle area (Hradcin) increasingly dominated as the centre of the Czechs' political, economic, and religious life. A Jewish traveller from Spain in the 960s described Prague as a wealthy centre of long-distance *trade. It was also the burial place of St *Wenceslas, the Přemyslid martyr-duke, and from *c.*973 a bishopric.

In the 11th and 12th centuries, both the Czech lands and the *Přemysl dynasty flourished despite violently contested successions to the ducal throne. In these disputes, Moravia remained inextricably linked to Bohemia even as the dynasty treated it as a separate *apanage. Relations with the German emperors remained extremely important, while at the same time the dukes of Bohemia played an increasingly significant role in imperial politics. Christianization of the Czech lands neared completion as *Olomouc became Moravia's first bishopric in 1063. *Monastic communities increased in number and landed wealth once the *Premonstratensians and *Cistercians arrived in the mid

12th century; in the 13th century St *Agnes of Prague brought *Franciscans to Prague within a few years of that order's foundation.

Bohemia and its rulers—now kings—grew more wealthy in the 13th century: agricultural productivity increased with improved techniques and an orchestrated influx of predominantly Germanic settlers; new villages and new towns founded by *locatores* brought unprecedented income to kings and nobles alike, while silver *mines benefited the Přemyslid rulers in particular. This wealth and an imperial *interregnum helped Přemysl Otakar II (1253–78) extend his territory to the south and, as central Europe's most powerful ruler, vie for the imperial throne. The electors instead chose the weaker Rudolf IV of *Habsburg in 1273, and Přemysl Otakar, abandoned by many Bohemian nobles, died in the ensuing military struggles. A series of weak kings, hamstrung by ascendant *nobility, succeeded him until the last Přemyslid ruler was murdered in 1306.

3. *The Czech lands under the Luxembourgs*

Bohemian church leaders and the upper nobility worked to select a new king from competing external candidates. Finally, in 1310 an agreement with the German king Henry VII concluded several years of struggle: Henry's son, *John 'the Blind' of Luxembourg, would marry a Přemyslid princess and accept the Bohemian crown. King John managed to increase Bohemia's territory despite chronic struggles with Bohemia's powerful *barons. Yet he spent the majority of his reign as an absentee ruler, content to draw income from his kingdom while the barons wielded power.

Raised at the French court, John's son Charles invigorated Luxembourg rule in Bohemia when he returned there in 1333. Crowned king of Bohemia in 1346 and recognized as undisputed king of the Romans from 1347, *Charles IV was confirmed as emperor in 1355. Learned and ambitious, Charles significantly expanded the territory of the crown of Bohemia and the Luxembourg dynasty, primarily through well-chosen marriages and a liberal purse. Charles strengthened the status of Bohemia within the empire, most famously through the provisions of his *Golden Bull (1356). Culture flourished under his *patronage: Master Theodoric's *paintings for *Karlštejn Castle and *Peter Parler's *cathedral are among the best-known results.

Charles lavished attention on Prague, an archbishopric from 1344, overseeing the erection of the new cathedral and filling it with *relics from across Christendom, founding several religious houses, and dramatically expanding the city's scale with the establishment in 1348 of 'New Town'. He founded central Europe's first *university, *Charles University in Prague, while attempting to stimulate the long-distance trade routes passing through the city. Prague grew to become central Europe's largest city, with perhaps 40,000 inhabitants.

Charles's wide-ranging interests touched nearly every aspect of Bohemian society, though his initiatives did not invariably succeed. His *Maiestas Carolina*, for instance, proposed to reform the land law through which Bohemia's upper nobility exercised considerable power. When the barons baulked, the pragmatic emperor retracted his draft reforms. The nobles retained their influence through the *noble diets, from which even the urban elites of Prague were excluded.

At the death of Charles IV in 1378, Bohemia and the Luxembourg dynasty seemed likely to dominate central Europe for decades to come. One son, Wenceslas, had been elected king of the Romans; another, Sigismund, ruled *Brandenburg as margrave and had some claim to succeed the kings of *Poland and Hungary as well. Nevertheless, even apart from the weak reign of Wenceslas—he was embattled at home and deposed as German king in 1400—Bohemian society seems already to have been suffering. A general economic downturn in the later 14th century, in part due to the expensive diplomacy of Charles IV, combined with the first outbreaks of plague in Bohemia and Moravia, most seriously in 1380. Rising tensions between ethnically Czech and German inhabitants, particularly in the cities where Czechs had become more numerous, likewise seems to have set the stage for the crisis that enveloped the kingdom in the early 15th century.

4. *The Hussites*

The revolutionary Hussites drew their inspiration from John *Hus, the Prague University master executed for Wycliffite *heresy by the Council of *Constance in 1415. The movement began as an academic controversy between the predominantly German *nominalist masters and their Czech counterparts, who adopted some of *Wyclif's *realist positions but also drew inspiration from 14th-century Prague preachers like *Milíč of Kroměříž and Matthias of Janov. Long treated as late medieval heretics, the Hussites are now more commonly compared with the Protestant Reformers.

A spectrum of interests attracted a wide range of adherents to the movement, though from nearly the beginning it drew far more Czechs than Germans. The Four Articles of Prague (1420) expressed its central religious aims, including *communion in both kinds (*sub utraque specie*, hence their designation as *Utraquists) for the *laity. In the same year a more radical wing established a model evangelical community at *Tabor. Sigismund of Luxembourg, then king of the Romans and of Hungary, led unsuccessful *crusades against Bohemia to claim its crown. Other crusades followed, and were likewise repulsed by the *Hussite armies with their famous war wagons. In 1436 the Council of *Basel negotiated a compromise with the Utraquists, including the right for the laity to receive both bread and wine in communion. No pope ever confirmed this agreement (the *Compactata*), which accorded the Czech kingdom a unique status within Christendom; *George of Poděbrady, the so-called Hussite king, later held off yet another invading Catholic army. The military impasse and the interests of Bohemian nobles on both sides eventually stimulated the Peace of *Kutná Hora (1485), which reconciled Bohemian Catholics and Utraquists by allowing for broad mutual toleration.

This religious division continued to characterize Bohemian society under the *Jagiełłonian monarchs into the 16th century, while tacit acceptance of the principles of the Basel compromise helped maintain the peace. The nobles in particular had gained wealth and power at the expense of the church, but urban elites also emerged from the 15th century with a powerful voice within the Bohemian diet. *See also* ROMAN EMPIRE [HOHENSTAUFEN DYNASTY]; MIGRATION OF PEOPLES. DCM

P. M. Barford, *The Early Slavs: Culture and Society in Early Medieval Eastern Europe* (2001).
F. M. Bartoš, *Čechy v době husově 1378–1415* (1947).
M. Bláhová *et al.*, *Velké dějiny zemí Koruny české* (1999–2003), vols 1–5.
K. Bosl, ed., *Handbuch der Geschichte der Böhmischen Länder*, 2 vols (1967, 1974).
Z. V. David, *Finding the Middle Way: The Utraquists' Liberal Challenge to Rome and Luther* (2003).
F. Heymann, *John Žižka and the Hussite Revolution* (1955).
H. Kaminsky, *A History of the Hussite Revolution* (1967).
J. Klassen, *The Nobility and the Making of the Hussite Revolution* (1978).
F. Kutnar and J. Marek, *Přehledné dějiny českého a slovenského dějepisectví: Od počátků národní kultury až do sklonku třicátých let 20. století* (1997).
J. Nechutová, *Latinská literatura českého středověku do roku 1400* (2000).
O. Odložilík, *The Hussite King: Bohemia in European Affairs, 1440–1471* (1965).
F. Palacký, *Dějiny národa českého v Čechách a v Moravě*, 5 vols ([3]1876–78).
J. Purš and M. Kropilák, eds, *Přehled dějin Československa* (1980), vol. 1, 1.
F. Seibt, *Bohemia Sacra: Das Christentum in Böhmen, 973–1973* (1974).
—— *Karl IV.: Ein Kaiser in Europa, 1346 bis 1378* (1978).
F. Šmahel, *Husitská revoluce*, 4 vols (1993; German tr. 2002).
—— *Idea národa v husitských Čechach* (2000).
M. Teich, ed., *Bohemia in History* (1998).
V. V. Tomek, *Dějepis města Prahy*, 12 vols ([2]1892–1906).
D. Třeštík, *Počátky Přemyslovců: vstup Čechů do dějin (530–935)* (1997).
L. Wolverton, *Hastening Toward Prague: Power and Society in the Medieval Czech Lands* (2001).
J. Žemlička, *Čechy v době knížecí (1034–1198)* (1997).

Bohemian book illumination *Manuscript illuminations of the pre-Romanesque and Romanesque periods are scarce (the Gumboldt Legend, the Vyšehrad Gospels, Codex Gigas). In the first half of the 14th century, the *Passionale* of Abbess Cunigunde and the pictorial Velislav Bible follow the French linear style, whereas the *liturgical MSS of Queen Elisabeth Richenza are inspired by the Rhineland. Under *Charles IV, the court workshop (*atelier) produced a group known as the *Johannes von Neumarkt MSS, creating a Prague school influenced by Italy, resulting in such works as the *Liber Viaticus* of Johannes von Neumarkt (Jan ze Středy), the Missal of Provost Nicolas, and *Laus Mariae*. In the 1360s its style developed subtler decorative forms, shown in the *Orationale Arnesti*, the Missal of Johannes von Neumarkt, and the *Gospels of Johannes of Troppau. The school's activity peaked in the time of Wenceslas IV. Only a few MSS of its rich production are preserved: the six-volume Bible of Wenceslas IV, the romance *Willehalm* by *Wolfram von Eschenbach, *astrological MSS, and the *Golden Bull of Charles IV. With their ornate style and sophisticated content, they belong to the *International Style 1400; subsequently, painters continued working for the court (the Bible of Konrád of Vechta, the Gerona *Martyrology, the Hazmburg Missal, Emperor Sigismund's copy of *Peter Comestor, the *Bellifortis* of Konrád *Kyeser, *Mandeville's *Travels*). Large *graduals and hymnbooks of the 16th century represent Bohemian book illumination in the late Gothic and Renaissance periods. *See also* ART, BOHEMIAN. HJH, KHo

České iluminované rukopisy 13.–16. století, ed. J. Dvorský and J. Kropáček (1990).
J. Krása, *Die Handschriften König Wenzels IV.* (1971).

Bohemian Brethren Founded in 1457, a sect emerging from the *Hussite Wars. Teaching justification through faith and rejecting private property and episcopal authority, they were persecuted and fled to *Hungary and *Poland. Zinzendorf resurrected the movement in 1734. *See also* BOHEMIA. PJS

P. Brock, *The Political and Social Doctrines of the Unity of the Czech Brothers in the Fifteenth and Early Sixteenth Centuries* (1957).

Bohemond I of Taranto, prince of Antioch (d. 1111) Leading the *Normans in the First *Crusade, in 1098 he captured *Antioch, keeping the city and its hinterland himself. Spending 1100–1103 in Muslim captivity, in 1111 he became a *vassal of Alexius I. BAC

R. Hill, ed., *Gesta Francorum: The Deeds of the Franks* (1962).
J. Shepard, 'When Greek Meets Greek', *Byzantine and Modern Greek Studies*, 12 (1988), 185–277.

Böhm, Hans *See* NIKLASHAUSEN, DRUMMER OF.

Boileau, Étienne de (1210–70) Provost of *Paris in the 1260s. At the request of King *Louis IX, Boileau compiled a registry of the customs and regulations governing the Parisian guilds. The resulting *Livre des Métiers de Paris* of 1268 contains information on 101 *guilds. MFM

G. P. Depping, ed., *Réglemens sur les Arts et Métiers de Paris rédigés au XIIIe siècle, et connus sous le nom du Livre d'Étienne Boileau* (1837).

G. Fagniez, 'Études sur l'industrie et la classe industrielle à Paris au XIIIe et au XIVe siècle', *BEHE* 33 (1877).

Boinebroke, Jehan (d. *c.*1286) Patrician merchant of *Douai, whose will shows his involvement in his city's cloth industry. Some historians have argued that he embodies the early capitalist entrepreneur, whose vertical control of cloth production bears out *Pirenne's thesis that before 1302 the *textile industry in *Flanders was dominated by an elite of merchant drapers, who oppressed and exploited cloth workers. More recently, a revised interpretation argues that he functioned more as a financier, who bought *wool, sold it to *weavers, who organized production, and then in turn purchased and marketed the finished cloth. He came from a rich, politically powerful family, and served nine times as *alderman. At his death he possessed considerable real estate, as well as investments in *trade. *See also* BANKING, FINANCE, AND TAXATION. JMMu

G. Espinas, *Les Origines du capitalisme: Sire Jehan Boinebroke* (1933).

J.-L. Roch, 'De la nature du drapier médiéval', *RH* 202 (2000), 3–30.

Bois-Protat The oldest known extant woodblock fragment in Europe, the Bois-Protat is carved on the recto with an image of the Crucifixion and on the verso with an image of the Angel from an Annunciation. Found in Burgundy in 1898, it is thought to date from 1375–1400. *See also* WOODCUT. EL

A. Hind, *An Introduction to the History of Woodcut* (1935), vol. 1, 70–71.

Bollandists The Société des Bollandistes comprises Jesuits drawn primarily from Belgium. The purpose of the society is to study and publish the 'acts' of the saints (that is, all forms of *hagiography). Their scope includes saints who lived before the Reformation and works in the 'classical' languages of Christianity (Latin, Greek, and the so-called 'Oriental' languages, such as Syriac, Coptic, and Armenian). Their founder, John van Bolland (d. 1665), began the publication of the **Acta Sanctorum*, a collection of hagiography organized according to the *liturgical *calendar. The first two volumes, for January, were published in 1643. The last volume (1940) includes the saints of December.

Central to the Bollandist project has been the development of a rigorous methodology for the study of hagiography. Its application has resulted in the massive critical apparatus of the *Acta Sanctorum*, as well as the publication of numerous catalogues and research tools, including (since 1882) the journal *Analecta Bollandiana*. The Bollandists have effectively abandoned completion of the *Acta Sanctorum* in favour of these other projects, including electronic and internet resources. Their work constitutes one of the longest-lived cooperative ventures in the annals of scholarship, and remains essential to research in medieval hagiography. For current activities, consult their website. TFH

H. Delehaye, *The Work of the Bollandists through Three Centuries, 1615–1915* (1922) (French original, 1920) (²1959).

B. Joassart, *Hippolyte Delehaye: hagiographie critique et modernisme* (2000).

D. Knowles, *Great Historical Enterprises* (1963).

P. Peeters, *L'Oeuvre des Bollandistes* (²1961).

Société des Bollandistes, 'Christian Hagiography', 21 May 2008, www.kbr.be/~socboll/.

Bologna, University of The university developed out of the establishment in Bologna of law professionals and those who came to study under them in the late 11th century. *Irnerius taught at Bologna, where Justinian's **Corpus iuris civilis* was recovered in its entirety, and where *Gratian wrote his **Decretum* codifying canon *law.

International students, called *'nations', particularly lay students of civil law (that is, Roman *law), were unprotected by the statutes of the *commune of Bologna. To remedy this, Emperor Frederick I issued the decree *Habita* in 1158. The *papacy, too, took interest in the prestigious university and the jurists trained there.

Students provided teachers' fees and set their working conditions. They were an asset to the *town, which suffered economically from student flight in the early 13th century and in 1321 following clashes with Bolognese officials. From these migrations the University of *Padua and others were born.

Other disciplines eventually won independence from the all-important law faculties. Practitioners of medicine and their students were in Bologna from the early 13th century, but a faculty of *medicine emerged only by the 1260s. As for theology, Bologna had no faculty like those of *Oxford, *Paris, or *Cambridge until the mid 14th century. Before then, schools of theology run by mendicant orders assumed that role. RCE

Annali di storia delle università italiane (1997), vol. 1.

O. Capitani, ed., *L'università a Bologna: personaggi, momenti e luoghi dalle origini al XVI secolo* (1987).

H. de Ridder-Symoëns, ed., *A History of the University in Europe*, vol. 1, *Universities in the Middle Ages* (1992).

Bombolognus of Bologna (d. 1279×91) *Dominican, *lector principalis* in the **studium generale* of *Bologna, he wrote on *logic and completed a *commentary on the **Sentences*. He opposed *Thomas Aquinas, whose doctrine of theology as a science he considered incompatible with post-lapsarian human nature. LL

A. D'Amato, 'Bombolognus de Musolinis da Bologna', *Sapienza*, I (1948), 75–90, 232–52.
C. Piana, 'L'influsso di san Bonaventura nella cristologia di Bombologno di Bologna', *Antonianum*, 23 (1948), 475–500.

Bonanno Pisano (*fl.* 1179–86) Italian sculptor whose reputation rests on two surviving sets of bronze doors for *cathedrals in Monreale and *Pisa. Technically and artistically, these projects rank among the greatest achievements of Romanesque *sculpture. *See also* ART AND ARCHITECTURE: ROMANESQUE. FB

W. Melczer, *La porta di Bonanno a Monreale: teologia e poesia* (1987).
—— *La porta di Bonanno nel Duomo di Pisa: teologia ed immagine* (1988).

Bonaventure (1221–74) *Franciscan theologian, mystical writer; born John of Fidanza, in Bagnoregio, Italy. Educated at the local Franciscan house, then in *arts at *Paris, he entered the Franciscan order *c.*1245, studying theology under *Alexander of Hales. He was regent master from 1253 until 1257, when he was elected Franciscan minister general.

While regent master he wrote a *commentary on *Peter Lombard's **Sentences*, biblical commentaries, and theological treatises. His later writings comprised Franciscan history (*Apologia pauperum*), mystical works (*Itinerarium mentis in Deum*, The Soul's Journey into God), devotional treatises, and *sermons. His *Life of St Francis* (1263) was the only life the order approved. The *Collationes in Hexameron*, written as sermons, remained unfinished at his death at the Second Council of *Lyons. In theology Bonaventure was *Augustinian, rejecting much of the *Aristotelianism incorporated by his contemporary *Thomas Aquinas. Theology, *exegesis, and spirituality remained intertwined in his thought. GAZ

Bonaventure, *Opera omnia*, ed. PP. Collegii a S. Bonaventura, 11 vols in 28 (1882–1902).
—— *Works*, 5 vols (1960–70).
E. H. Cousins, *Bonaventure and the Coincidence of Opposites* (1978).
Z. Hayes, *The Hidden Center: Spirituality and Speculative Christology in St Bonaventure* (1981).
Lexique saint Bonaventure (1969).
S. Bonaventura, 1274–1974, 5 vols (1973–4).

Bondol (Bandol, Bandolf, Bruges)**, Jean de** (Jan Boudolf) (*fl.* 1368–81) South Netherlands painter and illuminator, active in France. He was court painter to *Charles V and was awarded a royal pension for life in 1380. *See also* BURGUNDIAN NETHERLANDS. LKE

F. Avril, *Manuscript Painting at the Court of France* (1978).
R. and M. Rouse, *Manuscripts and their Makers* (2000).

Boner (Bonerius)**, Ulrich** (*c.*1324–*c.*1349) Swiss *Dominican who wrote *Der Edelstein*, a popular collection of 100 moralizing fables on religious and political themes. Based on Latin sources, *Der Edelstein* was the first German work *printed with movable type and accompanied by *woodcuts (Bamberg, 1461). *See also* LITERATURES: GERMANIC. SKW

G. F. Benecke, ed., *Der Edelstein, getichtet von Bonerius* (1816).

Bonfini, Antonio (1427/34–1502) Born in Patrignone, from 1478 he taught Latin, Greek, *grammar, poetry, and *rhetoric in Recanati. He translated works by Hermogenes, Aphthonios, and Herodian into Latin, and wrote the history of Ascoli (lost). In 1486 he compiled the *genealogy of the Corvinus family (lost) and wrote a fictitious report on a *debate at the *Buda court. Having dedicated his works to *Matthias Corvinus, he entered his service, where he was charged with translating into Latin the works of Philostratus and *Filarete's architectural treatise.

In the spring of 1488 he settled permanently in *Hungary and began studying Hungarian history. He worked on this until the end of 1496, when he had a stroke; he died in Buda. His work *Rerum Hungaricarum decades* is the first humanist treatment of Hungarian history. He put the events of Hungarian history into a European context, showing them to be a continuous process, with recurrent movements of birth, death, and rebirth. He worked out a theory of the Hun–Avar–*Magyar identity, served the political goals of the *Hunyadi family, and created the image of Matthias accepted to this day. His work remained a standard until the 19th century and inspired several literary works. PKu

I. Fógel, B. Iványi, L. Juhász, M. Kulcsár, and P. Kulcsár, eds, *Rerum Hungaricarum decades*, 5 vols (1936–76).
L. Havas, 'La Tradition historiographique classique et la réception d'Antonio Bonfini dans l'historiographie latino-hongroise', in *Acta Conventus Neo-Latini Bonnensis*, ed. R. Schnur (2003), 361–70.
P. Kulcsár, *Bonfini magyar történetének forrásai és keletkezése* (1973).

Boniface, St, archbishop of Mainz (*c.*675–754) The 'Apostle of Germany', martyred at Dokkum. An *Anglo-Saxon by birth, named Wynfrith, he received the name Boniface from Pope Gregory II with his commission to *missionize the north. He felled the oak of the heathens at Geismar and founded seven *monasteries, notably *Fritzlar and *Fulda. Receiving the pallium from Pope Gregory II, he established episcopal sees at *Salzburg, *Eichstätt, *Regensburg, and *Passau. Early writings include a *grammar and a treatise on Latin metre, later ones his *Enigmata* and a large, influential correspondence. *See also* LETTERS; PAGANISM. GHB

Boniface, *Ars grammatica*, ed. G. Gebauer and B. Löfstedt, *CCSL* 133B (1980), 1–99.
—— *Enigmata Bonifatii*, ed. M. De Marco and F. Glorie, *CCSL* 133 (1968), 273–343.
T. Reuter, ed., *The Greatest Englishman: Essays on St Boniface and the Church at Crediton* (1980).
M. Tangl, ed., *Epistolae S. Bonifatii et Lullii*, *MGH.ES* (1916), vol. 1.

Bonizo (Bonitho) **of Sutri** (*c*.1045–*c*.1091) Bishop, historian, canonist, polemicist; author of works in defence of *Pope Gregory VII and the reform movement. *See also* INVESTITURE CONTROVERSY. DJH

W. Berschin, *Bonizo von Sutri: Leben und Werk* (1972).
Bonizo of Sutri, *Book to a Friend*, tr. I. S. Robinson, in *The Papal Reform of the Eleventh Century*, ed. idem (2004).

book binding The art of sewing *quires together within a cover into a single codex. The last step in *manuscript book production, binding protected codices and kept their contents in order. Most medieval books were bound in plain *parchment covers or wooden boards, tied or clasped at the open end. Titles were written in ink on the edges of the pages or on the spine. Wealthy *patrons commissioned luxurious decorative bindings for their books, while important sacred texts might be clad in ivory or valuable *metal and *gems, displaying the value of the material within. EL

M. L. Agati, *Il libro manoscritto* (2003).

Boppe (*fl.* 1280–90) German *gnomic poet-Meistersinger, thirty of whose songs survive, some noted. He discusses fundamental ethical and moral issues and reflects on the social and economic reality of his times. *See also* LITERATURES: GERMANIC. AC

H. Alex, *Der Spruchdichter Boppe* (1998).
J. Haustein, 'Beiläufiges zu sechs Boppe-Liedern', *ZDP* 119 (2000), 197–207.
J. Spicker, 'Geographische Kataloge bei Boppe', *ZDP* 119 (2000), 208–21.

Bordeaux City on the Garonne river in southwestern France; from Roman times, it was a *trading port actively connected to Spain and Britain. In 1154 the *duchy of Bordeaux, then controlled by the dukes of *Aquitaine, became an English possession. Under English rule, Bordeaux gained renown for its *wine production, and it became the chief exporter of wine to England. During the Gascon War (1294–1303) the French unsuccessfully besieged Bordeaux, but they ultimately regained the city in 1453. JHH

C. Higounet, *Bordeaux pendant le haut moyen âge* (1963).
Y. Renouard, *Bordeaux sous les rois d'Angleterre* (1965).

Boris and Gleb, Sts (d. 1015; f.d. 24 July) Princes of *Rostov and Murom, respectively, and saints. The sudden death of their father, Kievan prince St *Vladimir Sviatoslavich, in 1015 created a crisis in the succession. Sviatopolk, their elder half-brother, seized the throne, and then sent assassins to kill potential rivals. Boris declined the urging of Vladimir's retainers to oppose Sviatopolk. He was murdered without a struggle by Sviatopolk's men at his camp near the river Al'ta. Gleb, the younger of the two, was summoned to *Kiev by Sviatopolk, then killed en route on the *river Dnieper. A third brother, *Iaroslav the Wise, attacked Sviatopolk and drove him from the land.

By 1019, after Iaroslav had secured the Kievan throne, he ordered that the bodies of Boris and Gleb be honourably buried together in Vyshgorod, the royal compound north of Kiev. *Miracles were witnessed. *Archaeological evidence shows that they were initially revered as healers and dynastic patrons in Kiev. During the prelacy of Metropolitan John I (1019–35), they were recognized as local saints and *martyrs. By the mid 15th century, they were venerated as national saints of Muscovy and later, together with Vladimir, as holy ancestors of the Daniilovich princes. GL

G. D. Lenhoff, *The Martyred Princes Boris and Gleb* (1989).
L. Müller, 'Studien zur altrussischen Legende der Heiligen Boris und Gleb', *Zeitschrift für Slavische Philologie*, 23 (1954), 60–77; 25 (1956), 329–63; 27 (1959), 274–322; 30 (1962), 14–44.
A. Poppe, 'La Naissance du culte de Boris et Gleb', *CCM* 24 (1981), 29–53.

Borselen family, van Powerful aristocratic family from *Zeeland whose members served the counts of both *Flanders and *Holland. A Floris van Borselen was killed in 1323 defending the port of *Sluis against an attack of the *Bruges militia. A branch of the family acquired the *lordship of the town of Veere in Zeeland after 1250. JMMu

A. W. E. Dek, *Genealogie der Heren van Borselen* (1979).

Bosch, Hieronymus (Hieronymus van Aken) (d. 1516) Painter. Jheronimus (Jeroen) Bosch was born *c*.1450 in 's-Hertogenbosch, where he lived, worked, and was buried in the *cathedral by his brethren of the Lieve-Vrouwe-Broederschap. From a painters' family, he appears in the city archives from 1474 onwards. As one of the core members of the Broederschap, he was an important figure in the city, and his obituary calls him a 'famous painter'.

Bosch's paintings, often *triptychs, mainly cover religious themes, and are famous for their strange creatures and imaginative oddities. He worked for various Netherlands *patrons, but also for the *Burgundian court, so much of his work is in the Prado in Madrid. Because Bosch was already famous in his own age, his work was much copied, imitated, and falsified from the 16th century onwards. Consequently, the attribution of works to Bosch is still controversial. *See also* GUILDS [MERCHANT/CRAFT GUILDS]; PAINTING. AW

W. S. Gibson, *Hieronymus Bosch: An Annotated Bibliography* (1983).
L. Harris, *The Secret Heresy of Hieronymus Bosch* (1995).
J. Koldeweij *et al.*, *Hieronymus Bosch: New Insights into his Life and Work* (2001).
R. H. Marijnissen, *Hieronymus Bosch: The Complete Works* (1987).

Bosnia A territorial and political entity situated along the river of the same name between present-day Sarajevo and

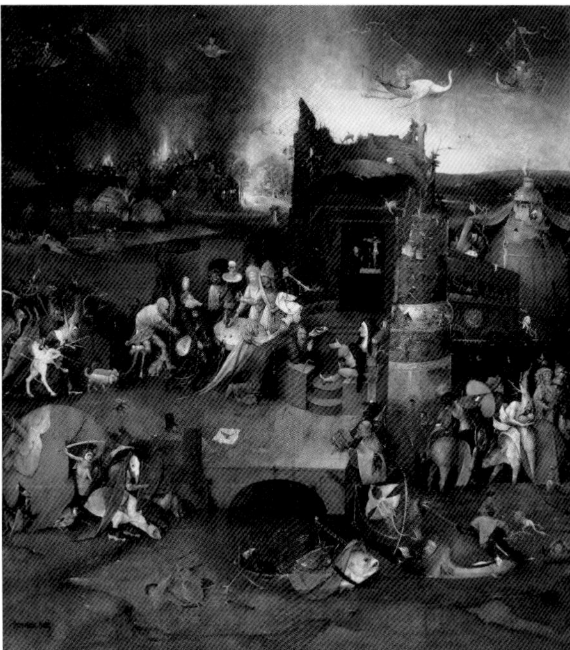

Detail of *Temptation of St Anthony* (oil on panel) by Hieronymus Bosch. National Museum of Ancient Art, Lisbon.

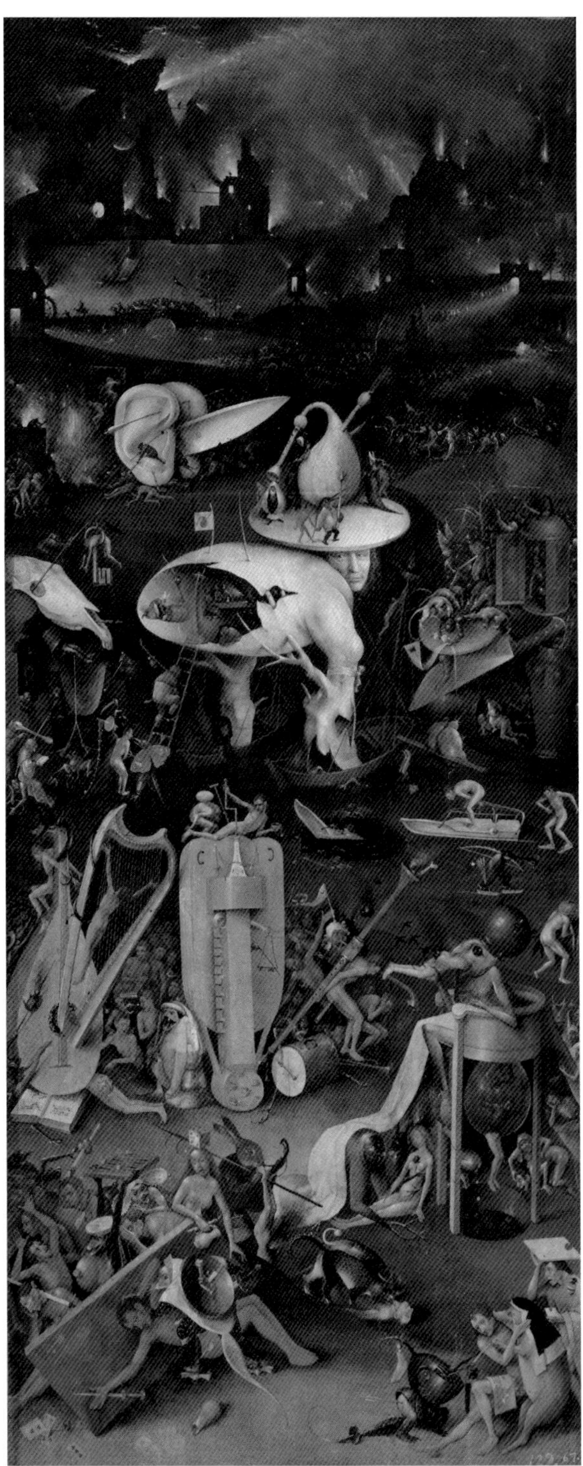

Detail of *Garden of Earthly Delights* (oil on panel) by Hieronymus Bosch. Prado, Madrid.

Zenica. Under this name it was first mentioned in Byzantine emperor Constantine Porphyrogenitus' mid-10th-century *De administrando imperio*. A process of ethno-polygenesis was begun by the *Slavs' 7th-century settlement in the area, which also included the autochthonous Illyrians and the Avars; they often settled in existing churches or forts. At least a century prior to the first mention of a Bosnian *ban* (prince) named Borić (1154–63), we have an image of Bosnia as an early *feudal state, which occasionally fell under the rule of *Serbian, *Croatian, or Byzantine rulers. With Ban Kulin (1180–1204), who was supported by *Pope Innocent III, Bosnia appears on the international political scene of east-central Europe, to remain there until its fall under Ottoman rule in 1463.

The opposing interests of *Byzantium and *Hungary clashed over Bosnia after *Constantinople fell in the Fourth *Crusade. The political position of Bosnian rulers was determined by the coordinated actions of *Rome and Hungary, which aimed to Latinize Bosnia's Slav bishopric. The result was the submission of the Bosnian bishopric to the metropolitan in Kalocsa in 1247 and, shortly afterwards (mid 1252 at the latest), the transfer of the Bosnian see to Đakovo. Thus Bosnia lost its bishopric, which opened up space for action by a separate Bosnian church and a specific shaping of the Bosnian religious environment.

Stjepan II (1322–53) and Tvrtko I Kotromanić (1353–91) advanced Bosnian borders to the Adriatic Sea and elevated Bosnia's international status by proclaiming a kingdom in

1377. From the late 14th century, the Ottomans began to step up military and political interference in Bosnian affairs. At the time, Bosnia found itself amidst the conflicting interests between Hungary, which impeded a hierarchical establishment of Roman Catholicism, and the Ottomans, who systematically destabilized the country politically and ruined it economically.

Images from its court culture—arts, *heraldry, official *seals, *literacy, architecture, *chivalry—represented Bosnia as a fruitful meeting point of Mediterranean and central European influences with *Venice, Dubrovnik, and Hungary as mediators. Bosnia's economy, based on the export of mineral ores (primarily silver, lead, and copper), was oriented to the Adriatic Sea, with Dubrovnik, *Split, and Venice as the most relevant *trade partners, achieving a high level. In the years before 1463, Bosnia was a prosperous participant in the east-central European region. *See also* BANATES; GOLD AND SILVER; METALWORK; MIGRATION OF PEOPLES; MINES AND MINING; TIN, PEWTER, AND LEAD. DLo

S. Ćirković, *Istorija srednjovekovne bosanske države* (1964).
—— 'Dvor i kultura u srednjovekovnoj bosanskoj državi', in *Bosna i Hercegovina u tokovima istorijskih i kulturnih kretanja u jugoistočnoj Evropi* (1987), 61–9.
F. Curta, *Southeastern Europe in the Middle Ages, 500–1250* (2006).
S. M. Džaja, 'Bosansko srednjovjekovlje kroz prizmu bosanske krune, grba i biskupije', *Jukić*, 15 (1985), 80–102.
J. V. A. Fine, Jr, *The Bosnian Church: A New Interpretation* (1975).
—— *The Early Medieval Balkans* (1983).
—— *The Late Medieval Balkans* (1987).
D. Lovrenović, *Na klizištu povijesti: Sveta kruna ugarska i Sveta kruna bosanska, 1387–1463* (2006).
M. Šunjić, *Bosna i Venecija: Odnosi u XIV i XV stoljeću* (1996).

Bosnian Christians (Krstjani) Earlier histories of the Bosnian church describe it as Bogomil (a dualistic *heresy), Orthodox, or syncretistic. More recently, it has been framed in a European context, as a custodian of order with its bishop (*djed*) having the power to crown Bosnian kings.

The first sign of a distinctly Bosnian church is based on unsuccessful attempts to Latinize the Bosnian bishopric away from its *Cyril-and-Methodius beginnings. Only later, through a combination of diplomacy and armed force by the *papacy and *Hungary, was the Bosnian see detached from Dubrovnik (1247) and placed under the metropolitanate of Kalocsa, with Đakovo as its centre. Thus Bosnia lost its bishop, but a different church emerged as an alternative to the Catholic see. As a result of the removal of direct jurisdictional dependence on Rome, the Bosnian church acquired its own followers and administrative structure. The nominally Catholic Bosnian *nobility adopted the new Christian confession, called 'the Bosnian religion' or 'our law' in historical documents, and medieval Bosnia became a scene of religious pluralism and political polycentrism. Still, some rulers and landed nobility vacillated among Catholic, Orthodox, and the Bosnian religion. Nevertheless, the 15th-century struggle between Rome and Hungary over the Bosnian bishopric had a crucial impact on the preservation of the Bosnian religion as a third Christian confession and a means of socialization.

Just as quickly as they emerged on the historical scene, however, the Bosnian Christians soon disappeared thanks to the penultimate Bosnian king Stjepan Tomaš (1443–61), who, accused by the west of handing over Smederevo to the Turks (1459), decided to eliminate the Bosnian church. Traces of the Bosnian Christians were preserved in the Ottoman public records (*defters*) after the fall of Bosnia in 1463, and give evidence that the name 'Christians' denoted not just monks but the lay followers of the Bosnian church as well.

Although there are no detailed, authentic descriptions of the hierarchy, *liturgy, and theology of the Bosnian church, historical sources do attest that its followers accepted the traditional *creeds (except for 'I believe in one holy Catholic and apostolic church'), venerated saints, practised *fasting, observed the normal Christian holidays, and held the entire Bible to be Holy Writ. This is why the Bosnian Christians might be termed, at worst, *schismatic rather than heretical, and certainly not 'Bogomils', a later (derogatory) term. DLo

S. Ćirković, 'Bosanska crkva u bosanskoj državi', in *Prilozi za istoriju BiH, 1: Društvo i privreda srednjovjekovne bosanske države* (1987), 195–254.
S. M. Džaja, 'Srednjovjekovna Crkva bosanska u procijepu suprotstavljenih kontekstualizacija', *Status*, 10 (2006), 250–55.
J. V. A. Fine, Jr, *The Bosnian Church: A New Interpretation* (1975).
D. Lovrenović, *Na klizištu povijesti: Sveta kruna ugarska i Sveta kruna bosanska, 1387–1463* (2006).
N. Malcolm, *Bosnia: A Short History* (1994).
L. Petrović, *Kršćani crkve bosanske* ([2]1999).

Bosworth Field, battle of Fought on 22 August 1485, between the *Yorkist king *Richard III and the *Lancastrian challenger, Henry Tudor, second earl of Richmond. Portions of Richard's forces defected, and he was defeated and killed, despite superior numbers. With the victory, Richmond became *Henry VII, initiating the *Tudor dynasty. The battle is traditionally regarded as the end of the Wars of the *Roses. *See also* YORK DYNASTY. MBKoz

M. Bennett, *The Battle of Bosworth* (1993).
P. Foss, *The Field of Redemore: The Battle of Bosworth, 1485* (1998).
D. T. Williams, *The Battle of Bosworth* (1996).

botany *See* NATURAL HISTORY.

Boucicaut, Jean II le Meingre, called (*c.*1366–1421) Marshal of France, governor of *Dauphiné and of *Genoa, *knight errant, and *crusader. He was captured at the battles of both *Nicopolis (1396) and *Agincourt (1415), and was the subject of a *chivalric *biography written in 1409. CDT

D. Lalande, ed., *Le Livre des faits du bon messire Jehan le Maingre, dit Bouciquaut* (1985).
——*Jean II le Meingre, dit Le Boucicault (1366–1421)* (1988).

Bourbon, duchy of Located in central France, its *castle became a *lordship centre in the 10th century. The lords moved their seat to Moulins (13th century) as they expanded their territories. Ties to the French crown were strengthened when Beatrix, the heiress, married *Louis IX's son Robert de *Clermont (1276). Their son Louis (I) was raised to the rank of *duke and peer in 1327–8. Louis II (d. 1410) built up the territory's *administration following the royal example. In recognition of their service to the crown, the dukes were granted properties and rights, extending their holdings in the 15th century to include Forez and parts of *Auvergne. The dynasty again joined the royal family with the marriage of Pierre II to Louis XI's eldest daughter, Anne (1473). JFP

A. Leguai, *Le Bourbonnais pendant la Guerre de Cent Ans* (1969).
Le Musée Anne-de-Beaujeu de Moulins, *Le Duché de Bourbon des origins au Connétable* (2001).

Bourbon, house of French noble dynasty that originated during the 10th century in the southern part of the county of *Bourges. From their ancestral *castle, Bourbon-L'Archambault, the scions of the Bourbon line became important aristocratic and military figures in the immediate vicinity and within the courts of the first *Capetian kings. The first male line of the family died out in 1198, to be continued by a cadet line founded by *Guy of Dampierre. This second house of Bourbon produced a number of successful lords who expanded their control over *Auvergne by war, and increased their influence outside of their own region by forging marriage ties to the houses of *Orléans and *Burgundy. The third Bourbon line began in 1268 when *Louis IX married his son, Robert of *Clermont, to the last surviving Bourbon heiress. From this propitious match the Bourbons advanced first to become *dukes in 1327 and then as important princes, officials, and military leaders during the *Valois dynasty. With the accession of Henry IV, the leader of the Huguenot party, in 1594, the Bourbons became French sovereigns and the architects of absolutism. *See also* KINGSHIP, QUEENSHIP, AND MONARCHY. DJK

D. Seward, *The Bourbon Kings of France* (1976).

Bourdichon, Jean (1457–1521) Prolific French illuminator and painter in *Tours, who was official painter to four successive kings, Louis XI to François I. His masterpiece is the *Grandes Heures* of *Anne of Brittany (Paris, BN, MS lat. 9474). *See also* HOURS, BOOKS OF; MANUSCRIPT ILLUMINATION. RSW

F. Avril and N. Reynaud, *Les Manuscrits à peintures en France, 1440–1520* (1993), 293–305.

bourgeois (burgher, borghese) Etymologically speaking, an inhabitant of a *burgus* (burgh), gradually equivalent to the judicial notion of *civis* (citizen, belonging to a city) as defined in urban privileges. Being or becoming a burgher (by birth, payment, following a chronologically defined residence, often followed by an *oath of allegiance) implied both rights and obligations—essentially the right of being judicially only subjected to the *aldermen of the city, and of freedom from a number of *feudal obligations (*Stadtluft macht frei*, 'the air of the town liberates'), and the obligation to participate in the defence and safeguarding of the *town by military service or more generally by paying *taxes.

Not all inhabitants of a city enjoyed the rights of burghers. Foreigners, *Jews, Arabs (non-Christians), and marginal people did not; women and *clergymen often had limited rights (regarding access to legal systems and political functions). The medieval burgher was socially speaking a man of the town: member of the *patriciate, member of a *guild, a merchant, or an intellectual. The burgher was clearly distinct from those living in the countryside; in some European urban landscapes, however (the *Low Countries, the *Rhineland, and the Swiss cantons), *buitenpoorters* or *Pfahlbürger* existed: they were essentially men from the country who had acquired burgher privileges (with judicial and fiscal responsibilities). *See also* TOWN AND COUNTRY; URBANISM. MGRB

M. Boone, 'Ceste frivole, dampnable et desraisonnable bourgeoisie': de vele gezichten van het laatmiddeleeuwse burgerbegrip in de Zuidelijke Nederlanden', in *Burger: Een geschiedenis van het begrip 'burger' in de Nederlanden*, ed. J. Kloek and K. Tilmans (2002), 33–53.
P. Boucheron, D. Menjot, and M. Boone, 'La ville médiévale', in *Histoire de L'Europe urbaine*, ed. J. L. Pinol (2003), vol. 1, 287–592.
'Neubürger im späten Mittelalter', *Zeitschrift für Historische Forschung*, Beiheft, 30 (2002).

Bourgeois de Paris The 'journal' of the 'bourgeois', an incomplete eyewitness account of what occurred in *Paris between 1405 and 1449. The author (possibly Jean Chuffart) was a doctor in theology, probably *canon of *Notre-Dame, and linked to the *hotel of Queen Isabella of Bavaria (1370–1435). Names of Parisian *aldermen and *clergy are given for each year. The journal describes how royalty, *university, and city functioned, and provides details of daily life. Regarding the civil war between *Armagnacs and Burgundians, the author supports the latter and criticizes the monarchy and *Joan of Arc. MGRB

C. Beaune, *Journal d'un bourgeois de Paris* (1990).

Bourges City located 230 km south of *Paris. Bourges was the capital of the Roman province of Aquitania Prima. In 250 it became a Christian bishopric and by 506 it was an

The cathedral at Bourges.

archbishopric. *Philip II established a royal *bailiff there, and *Capetian influence increased dramatically during the 13th century. In 1458 a council in Bourges established the *Pragmatic Sanction of the Gallican church. Bourges's *university was founded in 1463. TFH

G. Devailly, *Le Berry du Xe au milieu du XIIIe siècle* (1973).
F. Prevot and X. Barral i Altet, *Topographie chrétienne des cités de la Gaule, VI: Province ecclésiastique de Bourges* (1989).

Bourse Name given first to a town square, later to a building, where merchants met to transact business. It derived from a dynasty of *Bruges hostellers, the van der Buerse, whose establishment gave their name *Bourse* to the nearby square. By the 15th century, the city reserved the square for merchant business during set hours. *See also* GUILDS [MERCHANT/CRAFT GUILDS]; HOTELS, INNS, AND TAVERNS; TRADE AND COMMERCE. JMMu

'Ter Beurze Bruges', *BelgiumView*, 21 May 2008, www.belgiumview.com/belgiumview/tl3/view0001212.php4.

Bouvines, battle of (1214) *Philip II Augustus's French army faced combined imperial, English, Flemish, and Bolognese troops. In the centre the two armies fought to a standstill; on the wings the French routed their opponents. Emperor Otto IV escaped; *Ferrand of *Flanders and Reginald of Boulogne were imprisoned. Bouvines also led to English territorial losses in France. *See also* FRANCE [PHILIP II AUGUSTUS]. KDV

J. Bradbury, *Philip Augustus, King of France, 1180–1223* (1998).
G. Duby, *The Legend of Bouvines: War, Religion and Culture in the Middle Ages*, tr. C. Tihanyi (1990).

bow and arrow (crossbow, longbow) It is technology rather than length that distinguishes medieval bows. The regular bow, famed as the English longbow, was made of a single piece of *wood (yew for the longbow). Its strength came from the flexibility of the wood, strung in a D-shape with a *flax and *hemp string. The 'recurved' bow was of composite construction, with layers of wood, sinew, and horn glued together. Its two arms were strung forward, against the natural curve. Its construction did not require great length, as the recurved arms provided significant force. This shorter size also allowed it to be fired from horseback, a tactic favoured by the Huns, *Magyars, Turks, and *Mongols.

The crossbow consisted of a small bow attached to a long stock out of which protruded a trigger mechanism, usually a nut made of horn or some other hard surface out of the top and a lever from the bottom. Over the nut was placed the bowstring, which could be disengaged by squeezing the lever. In early crossbows the string was drawn by hand or by a claw attached to the *archer's belt; as he stood up, the string was drawn. Later bow-drawing aids included the 'goat's foot' lever, windlass, and cranequin. These became necessary as the bow, originally made of a composite construction like the recurved bow, began to be made of *metal in the later MA.

All medieval bows shot fletched arrows to which were attached sharpened *iron heads. *See also* ARMS AND ARMOUR; WARFARE. KDV

J. Bradbury, *The Medieval Archer* (1985).
D. Nicolle, *Crécy 1346: Triumph of the Longbow* (2000).
M. Strickland and R. Hardy, *The Great Warbow: From Hastings to the Mary Rose* (2005).

Bower, Walter (d. 1449) *Augustinian *canon, student at *St Andrews *University, and eventually abbot of Inchcolm. Author of the important chronicle entitled the *Scotichronicon*. Bower's training in canon *law and his regular attendance in *parliament and council lent a rare degree of accuracy to his account of Scottish history, especially in the period after 1424. *See also* SCOTLAND, IRELAND, WALES: SCOTLAND AND WALES 1064–1536. CJN

D. E. R. Watt, ed., *Scotichronicon by Walter Bower in Latin and English*, 9 vols (1987–98).

boyars Term documented for members of the ruling elite in Kievan *Rus', along with the roughly equivalent **druzhina*. By the 12th century 'boyar' became the usual term in almost all Rus' territories. In the *Moscow principality by the 14th century, the boyars were the primary *administrators and military commanders of the state, as well as advisers of the prince. In Moscow, the term came to signify not only members of the ruling elite in general but, in a more precise sense, those men from traditionally elite *clans whom the prince appointed to the rank of boyar. They were first in the court's service hierarchy and received all important court, administrative, and military offices. Though no clan had a prescriptive right to the rank, in practice the Moscow princes chose from only a few old Moscow boyar clans, gradually adding to this group some princely families from territories of Rus' and *Lithuania incorporated into the Moscow realm. By 1500, some 15 clans provided about 25 boyars. The number rose throughout the succeeding two centuries, especially by the late 17th century, when some 50–60 men held the rank. The boyars in Russia formed the core of the *duma*, the council of the grand prince, later tsar. Peter the Great ceased to make any new appointments to the rank after 1693, and it gradually disappeared. PB

N. S. Kollmann, *Kinship and Politics: The Making of the Muscovite Political System, 1345–1547* (1987).
A. E. Presniakov, *Kniazhoe pravo v drevnei Rusi* (1909).

boy bishop Choirboy elected mock bishop from the 11th century on. He performed non-sacramental episcopal duties from St Nicholas's Day (6 December) to the Feast of the Holy Innocents (28 December). *See also* FOOLS, FEAST OF; SACRAMENTS. RSS

M. Milway, 'Boy Bishops in Early Modern Europe: Ritual, Myth, and Reality', in *The Dramatic Tradition of the Middle Ages*, ed. C. Davidson (2005), 87–97.

Brabant Principality of the *Low Countries centring on *Brussels, *Antwerp, *Malines/Mechelen, and *Leuven,

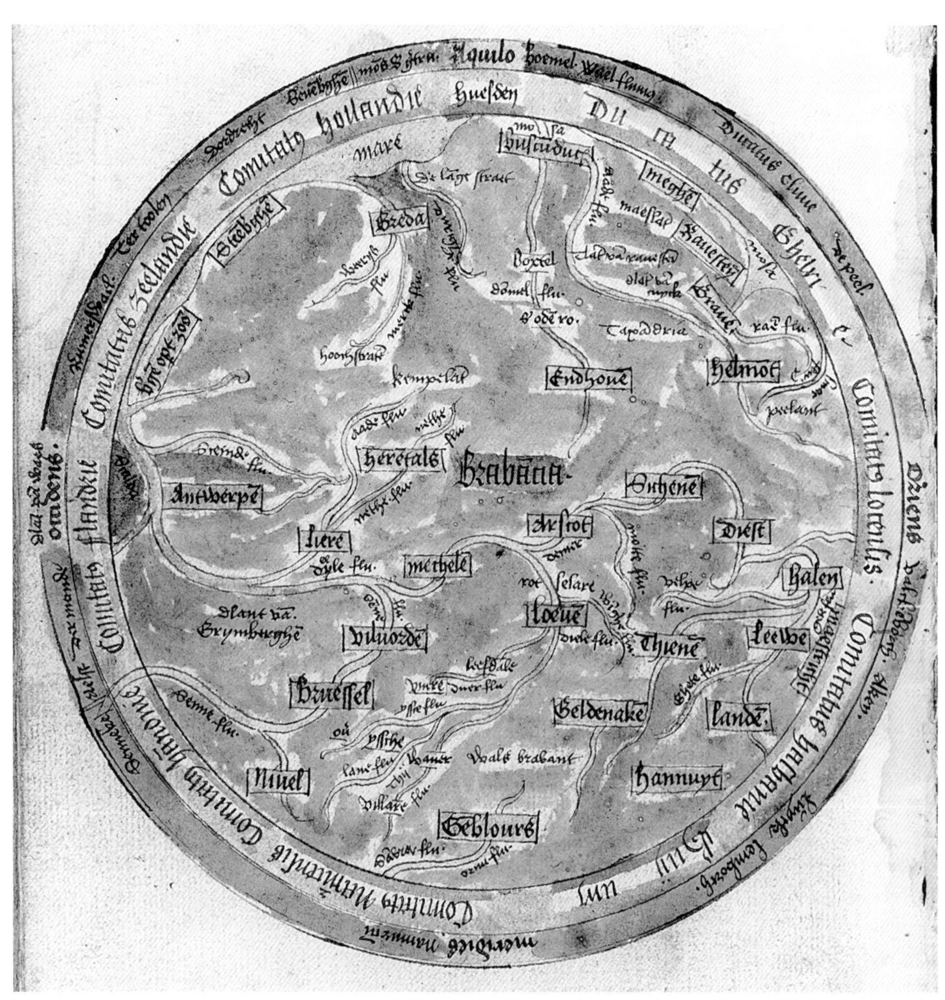

Map of Brabant, 16th century.

bordering the Scheldt and the Meuse, and *Hainaut, *Flanders, *Holland, and *Liège. Brabant controlled the major land route between the North Sea coast and the *Rhineland. It was primarily a Dutch-speaking area, although the nobles of south Brabant preferred French. Brabant had a large concentration of medium-size *towns controlling a considerable *textile industry and *trade.

1. Early territorial consolidation
2. Luxembourg era
3. Burgundian era
4. Trade and commerce

1. *Early territorial consolidation*

The nucleus of Brabant was the territory of the counts of Leuven, who by the early 11th century had expanded into the Brussels region. They were made dukes of Lower *Lorraine in 1106 and within a century had also accumulated other titles. The name Brabant was generally used from the early 13th century. A long war involving most of the Brabant *nobility ended with the reconciliation of the dukes with the Berthout family, and thereafter there was little danger from individual noble lineages.

Duke Henry I used the confusion in the empire, the *Angevin–*Capetian rivalry, and Flemish weakness after 1214 to his diplomatic advantage. Numerous princes recognized him as *feudal lord. However, most successions to Brabant between 1248 and 1430 involved either a minor or an heiress with a foreign husband. *John I was the first duke who favoured France. He annexed *Limburg in 1288 after a five-year war with *Guelders. Liège and Guelders remained antagonistic toward Brabant, whose territorial policy was to protect the route to *Cologne.

Even in the 13th century the dukes had to finance their territorial expansion by selling local governing and financial rights to the major cities. The 14th-century dukes were not strong figures, but a distinct consciousness that Brabant was a 'land' was emerging. John I made marriage alliances with Flanders and England. John II issued the Charter of *Kortenberg. John III had to face growing French influence. In 1329 *Philip VI tried to counter the growing power of Brabant with an alliance that included most other princes of the Low Countries, but it quickly deteriorated. Brabant joined England and Flanders but withdrew from the anti-French coalition in 1340.

2. *Luxembourg era*

John III's succession passed to his eldest daughter, Joan, wife of *Wenceslas of Luxembourg. Fearful that the duchy might be partitioned, the Brabanters extracted a new *charter of liberties in 1356. The invasion of *Louis of Male on behalf of his wife, Margaret, Joan's sister, forced Joan and Wenceslas to recognize Margaret as their successor in Brabant if they died childless. Unfortunately, they made the same promise to whoever happened to be the head of the house of *Luxembourg. These conflicting claims were still alive in 1430. Wenceslas and Joan were not popular in Brabant. When Wenceslas predeceased his wife in 1383, his nephew claimed Brabant, but Joan's right to rule was not contested seriously.

After 1383 Brabant was caught between rival power blocs. Joan favoured a *Burgundian succession, but this was opposed by the Estates of Brabant, which did permit the succession in 1406 of *Anthony, son of Philip of Burgundy and Joan's niece *Margaret of Flanders. Even before Brabant became Burgundian, there was some coordination of *administration with Flanders, ruled by Anthony's older brother John 'the Fearless', starting with a coinage union in 1384. Anthony died fighting for the French at *Agincourt in 1415 and was succeeded by his mentally incompetent son, *John IV. Brabant became entangled in the wars of Philip the Good (1419–67) of Burgundy to gain the inheritance. John IV died in 1427 and was succeeded by his brother, Philip, count of St-Pol, whose death in 1430 left Philip the Good sole heir to Brabant.

3. *Burgundian era*

Philip the Good spent more time in the Low Countries than in *Burgundy and preferred Brabant, less turbulent than Flanders. Brussels became his favourite residence. Duke Charles 'the Bold' (1467–77) established a central 'parliament' at Mechelen in 1473. In 1530 Brussels became the seat of government of the *Habsburg heirs of the Burgundian dukes. The acquisition of Brabant gave the Burgundians control of the ancient kingdom of Lower Lorraine, and thus Brabant became critical in the Burgundians' aspiration to have their domains promoted to a kingdom. Intermittent negotiations with the emperors from the 1430s ended in 1473 without a royal crown. Brabant participated in the struggles of the Low Countries after 1477 to eject the Habsburgs, but disorders were less serious than in Flanders.

4. *Trade and commerce*

Economically as well as politically, Brabant developed more slowly than Flanders. Brabant lacked a major river; the large towns were all on smaller streams that were deepened artificially. They developed in the late 12th century along the road from Bruges to the Rhineland. The 12th-century dukes gave privileges to Brussels, Leuven, Tienen, Zoutleeuw, Antwerp, Nivelles, and Gembloux. In the early 12th century Nivelles, Brussels, Antwerp, and Zoutleeuw built walls, and Brussels, Leuven, and Antwerp received *aldermen.

Brabant benefited from the Flemish commercial war with England (1270–74). The Brabant cities competed with the Flemish in the export of woollen cloth to the Mediterranean and the *Baltic, which involved links with England as the wool supplier. But Brabant was not well situated for the changed situation after 1363, when the English established their *wool *staple at *Calais. High English taxes on wool hurt everyone. Thus Brabantine cloth was not able to capitalize on the problems of Flemish luxury textiles. Worker–employer conflicts became more common from the 13th century. As early as 1249 the cities of Brabant agreed not to receive one another's rebellious *weavers and *fullers. Mechelen, however, was the only town where the *crafts took over the town government in the early 14th century. Brabant's internal political development was thus less chaotic than that of Flanders and more propitious to the development of internal *markets. DN

W. Nikolay, *Die Ausbildung der ständischen Verfassung in Geldern und Brabant während des 13. und 14. Jahrhunderts* (1985).
W. Prevenier and W. Blockmans, *The Promised Lands* (1999).
A. Uyttebrouck, *Le Gouvernement du duché de Brabant au bas moyen âge (1355–1430)* (1975).

Bracciolini, Poggio (1380–1459) Tuscan humanist and *manuscript copyist. Born near *Arezzo, he worked for the *papal court, later becoming chancellor of the Florentine republic. He rediscovered many lost works of classical literature and invented the humanist script. FB

P. Bracciolini, *Opera omnia*, ed. R. Fubini, 4 vols (1964–9).
—— *Lettere*, ed. H. Harth, 3 vols (1984–7).
R. Fubini and S. Caroti, eds, *Poggio Bracciolini nel VI centenario della nascita* (1980).

bracteate Term designating two distinct series of objects: Scandinavian gold pendants of the early MA, and the silver coins circulating in parts of central and northern Europe in the 12th and 13th centuries. Objects in both groups are round, thin pieces of metal, with a design struck on one side only.

Scandinavian gold bracteate pendants are classed into four types based on their iconography: a head derived from Roman coin *portraits; one or more standing male figures; a mounted warrior; or an ornamental animal. Many of the pieces bear inscriptions in *runic characters, which have led the images to be associated with religious figures, especially Woden (*Odin). They are found in hoards in *Scandinavia, often together with elaborate brooches, and in *burials in England, Germany, and Norway. Associated objects and skeletons link the bracteates to the feminine sphere, and date their period of manufacture and use from the mid 5th to the mid 6th century.

The bracteates of the central MA, produced in *Germany, Switzerland, *Bohemia, and Scandinavia, were silver coins of the penny denomination, and circulated together with two-sided pennies. To provide an ample surface for their complex imagery, the flans were hammered so thin that they could bear a die impression on only one side. Those of *Saxony of the 12th century, which bear images of rulers, saints, plants, *animals, and architecture, are regarded as among the most artistic of European coins. *See also* ARCHAEOLOGY: GERMANY/SCANDINAVIA; GEMS AND JEWELLERY; GOLD AND SILVER; MONEY AND COINAGE. AMSt

F. Berger, ed., *Die mittelalterlichen Brakteaten im Kestner-Museum Hannover* (1993).
Die Goldbrakteaten der Völkerwanderungszeit, 3 vols in 7 (1985–9).
P. Grierson, *The Coins of Medieval Europe* (1991).
K. Hauck, ed., *Der historische Horizont der Götterbild-Amulette aus der Übergangsepoche von der Spätantike zum Frühmittelalter* (1989).
L. Hedeager, 'Scandinavia', in *NCMH*, vol. 1: *c.500–c.700*, ed. P. Fouracre (2005), 496–523.

Bracton, Henry de (d. 1268) One must distinguish between the historical person Henry de Bracton and the work *De Legibus et Consuetudinibus Angliae* (*On the Laws and Customs of England*), commonly designated 'Bracton'. Bracton the man was clerk to William Ralegh, England's chief justice (1234–9), becoming a judge himself in 1245. The influential *De Legibus* was a collaborative effort involving Ralegh, Bracton, and other editors and redactors, containing passages from Roman and canon *law. Bracton both expounds the Roman law declaration 'what pleases the prince has the force of law' and asserts that the king must be subject to both God and the law. *See also* CUSTOM, LAW OF; LAW, ENGLISH COMMON. CJR

J. L. Barton, 'The Mystery of Bracton', *Journal of Legal History*, 14 (1993), 1–142.
S. Thorne, ed. and tr., *On the Laws and Customs of England*, 4 vols (1968–77).

Bradwardine, Thomas (*c.*1300–1349) *Augustinian theologian at *Oxford, and later archbishop of *Canterbury. Bradwardine opposed *atomism and applied the *Boethian theory of ratios to physics. He contested *Pelagianism and defended the non-distinction between past and future in God's knowledge. *See also* PHILOSOPHY, NATURAL. MTo

E. W. Dolnikowski, *Thomas Bradwardine: A View of Time and a Vision of Eternity in Fourteenth-Century Thought* (1995).
J.-F. Genest, *Prédétermination et liberté créée à Oxford au XIVe siècle: Buckingham contra Bradwardine* (1992).

Braga (archbishopric) Town and archbishopric in northern Portugal. Founded under Augustus, Braga (Bracara Augusta) became the capital of the province of Gallaecia created by Diocletian. It was an episcopal seat by the late 4th century, and its metropolitan status was established under Suevic rule. Three church councils (561, 572, and 675) convened there. *Martin of Bracara presided over the second and was probably responsible for the Suevic *Parochiale*, a list of churches and districts in thirteen *dioceses of the metropolitanate. The Arabs occupied Braga in the early 8th century.

Largest of the northern bracteates. Suspended from the neck as a magical amulet. A horse-like creature and a figure, probably Odin, are depicted.

Between the late 8th century and the 11th, several bishops of Lugo were titled bishops of Braga. Forgeries obscured their claims after King García of *Galicia restored Braga (1070), and the *papacy confirmed the metropolitanate (1099/1100). *Pope Innocent III resolved protracted litigation with *Santiago de Compostela in 1199. Although such rivalries had delayed Braga's restoration, ecclesiastical life flourished: a census, attributable to the late 11th century, tallies episcopal revenues from 573 parishes between the Lima and Ave rivers. Archbishop Gerald (1095/6–1108/9) was a monk of *Moissac, and *Aquitainian traits colour the *liturgy in the 12th-century *Missal of Mateus*.

War between Portugal and *Castile and the politics of the Great *Schism resulted in Braga's loss of Spanish suffragans to Compostela (1394), after *Lisbon, a new archbishopric, received Compostela's Portuguese suffragans. This conformity of ecclesiastical and political authority left Braga with three suffragans: Porto, Viseu, and Coimbra. Nonetheless, the see prospered under Archbishop Fernando da Guerra (1417–67), a member of the royal family, chancellor, and ecclesiastical reformer. JPD

IX Centenário da Dedicação da Sé de Braga, Congresso Internacional: Actas, 4 vols (1990).

J. O. Bragança, ed., *Missal de Mateus: manuscrito 1000 da Biblioteca Pública e Arquivo Distrital de Braga* (1975).

A. de J. da Costa, *O Bispo D. Pedro e a organização da diocese de Braga*, 2 vols (1959).

—— ed., *Liber Fidei Sanctae Bracarensis Ecclesiae*, 2 vols (1965).

P. David, *Études historiques sur la Galice et le Portugal du VIe au XIIe siècles* (1947).

J. Marques, *A Arquidiocese de Braga no século XV* (1988).

P. R. Rocha, *L'Office divin au Moyen Âge dans l'Église de Braga* (1980).

Braga, rite of Local form of the Roman rite practised in the *Braga *diocese (Portugal). The order of *Mass exhibits some *Gallican survivals also found in medieval French diocesan uses. PJ

J. O. Bragança, *Missal de Mateus* (1975).

A. L. Vaz, 'O Rito Bracarense', *Ora et Labora*, 18 (1972), 54–6, 143–53, 317–22, 387–95, 270–77; 19 (1973), 36–44, 135–52, 399–409; 20 (1974), 69–80, 158–69, 303–10.

Braganza (Bragança)**, house of** Begun by Afonso, count of Barcelos (*c*.1380–1461), the illegitimate son of João, Master of the Order of Avis and founder of the *Avis dynasty as King João I of Portugal (r. 1385–1433). The ducal house had its origins in 1401 at the marriage of Afonso with Beatriz, daughter of Nuno Álvarez Pereira, constable of Portugal, military hero of the war against *Castile (1383–5), and the wealthiest and most powerful *noble in the country. Nuno Álvarez Pereira gave lands and *castles to the couple, and King João I made Afonso count of Barcelos and gave him important properties.

In 1442 Afonso was given the title of *duke of Braganza by his half-brother, the regent Pedro. Afonso's oldest son, Afonso, count of Arraiolos and marquis of Valença, predeceased him, and the younger son, Fernando (1403–78), inherited the title of second duke of Braganza. The latter's son, also Fernando, third duke of Braganza, was executed for treason in 1483. The fourth duke, Jaime (1479–1532), returned to Portugal in 1496 after exile in Madrid and two years later was declared heir presumptive to the throne. In 1640, João, eighth duke of Braganza, was acclaimed king of Portugal, thus establishing the Braganza dynasty, which ruled Portugal until the overthrow of the monarchy in 1910. FAD

M. Soares de Cunha, *Linhagem, Parentesco e Poder: A Casa de Bragança, 1384–1483* (1990).

Brailes, William de (*fl. c*.1230–60) An English illuminator active in *Oxford. His name is recorded in several legal documents, and has been connected with the signature 'W. de Brailes' appearing in two MSS, in a book of *hours (BL, Add. MS 49999), and again in a *psalter (Cambridge, Fitzwilliam Museum, MS 330). *See also* MANUSCRIPT ILLUMINATION. LRa

C. Donovan, *The de Brailes Hours: Shaping the Book of Hours in Thirteenth-Century Oxford* (1991).

Bramham Moor Village in Yorkshire where, in 1408, Henry *Percy, earl of *Northumberland, fell in battle. Although Percy was instrumental in helping *Henry IV to secure the English throne in 1399, within a few years he had risen in revolt and allied himself with another rebel, Owain *Glyn Dŵr. CJN

R. R. Davies, *The Revolt of Owain Glyn Dŵr* (1997).

Brandenburg (town and bishopric) (founded 948, renewed 1161). Initially a *Slavic settlement, Brandenburg was conquered by Albrecht 'the Bear' in 1157. At that time Brandenburg consisted of several settlements that developed into independent municipalities: the old *town, the *cathedral town (on an island in the river Havel), and the new town (first attested 1196). From the 14th century until 1518, Brandenburg was a member of the *Hanse. GA

Germania Sacra, I: Die Bistümer der Kirchenprovinz Magdeburg, vol. 1 (1929; repr. 1963) and vol. 3 (1941; repr. 1963).
O. Tschirch, *Geschichte der Chur- und Hauptstadt Brandenburg an der Havel*, 2 vols (1928; [3]1941).

Brandenburg, margravate of Initially a settlement region of Germanic tribes, the heartland of the later Brandenburg marches was occupied by Slavic tribes in the 6th century. From the 8th century the region was the target of Frankish and then Saxon military expeditions. After the conquest of the Slavic Brennaburg (*Brandenburg) in winter 928/9 by Emperor Henry I, the North Marches were instituted (931), but lost during a rebellion of the *Slavs in 983.

The Ascanian period began with Albrecht 'the Bear', who was in possession of the German parts of the Old Marches from 1134 and inherited the Slavic dominions of the Brandenburg marches in 1150. The Ascanian dynasty successfully advanced the external and internal development of their patrimony by territorial acquisitions (New Marches, Land Lebus) as well as by founding new cities. However, from the beginning of the 14th century their political position was weakened by military conflicts. Already a participant in the election of the Roman king in the 12th century, the margrave of Brandenburg is mentioned in Eike of Repgow's **Sachsenspiegel* (around 1220/30) as 'kemerêre' (camerarius) of the Roman Empire and therefore one of the seven *electors. In the *Golden Bull of *Charles IV (1356) this office was formally acknowledged in imperial law.

When the Brandenburg branch of the Ascanian dynasty died out in 1319, the margravate, as a *fief of the Roman Empire, was seized by Louis the Bavarian (IV) and granted to his son Louis V. After long-lasting diplomatic efforts and military clashes, the Brandenburg marches were transferred to the *Luxembourg dynasty (1373). Sigismund, a younger son of Charles IV, became margrave of Brandenburg, but later—as king of *Hungary—pawned the margravate to Jobst of Moravia (1388). In 1415/17 the dominion was granted to burgrave Frederick VI of *Nuremberg, who was appointed margrave of Brandenburg. The intense efforts of the *Hohenzollern dynasty to consolidate the weakened territory prepared the ground for further expansion (Prussia). In 1473 Margrave Albert III Achilles formulated inheritance rules for the Hohenzollern dynasty. In the *dispositio Achillea* the Frankish dominions were parted from the Brandenburg marches and awarded to the younger son. *See also* ROMAN EMPIRE [CAROLINGIAN, OTTONIAN, SALIAN/FRANCONIAN/HOHENSTAUFEN DYNASTIES]. GA

H. Assing, *Brandenburg, Anhalt und Thüringen im Mittelalter: Askanier und Ludowinger beim Aufbau fürstlicher Territorialherrschaften*, ed. T. Köhn *et al.* (1997).
L. Dralle, *Slaven an Havel und Spree: Studien zur Geschichte des hevellisch-wilzischen Fürstentums (6. bis 10. Jahrhundert)* (1981).
H. Helbig, *Gesellschaft und Wirtschaft der Mark Brandenburg im Mittelalter* (1973).
H. Ludat, *An Elbe und Oder um das Jahr 1000: Skizzen zur Politik des Ottonenreiches und der slavischen Mächte in Mitteleuropa* (1971).
W. Neugebauer, *Die Hohenzollern* (1996), vol. 1.
E. Schmidt, *Die Mark Brandenburg unter den Askaniern (1134–1320)* (1973).
J. Schultze, *Die Mark Brandenburg* (1961–63; [3]2004), vols 1–3.

Braose (Briouze) **family** A *march of Wales family prominent in the political storms of King *John's reign. William III (d. 1211) fell afoul of John in 1207. William V was hanged by *Llywelyn ap Iorwerth in 1230. His *estates were divided between four co-heiresses. *See also* SCOTLAND, IRELAND, WALES: SCOTLAND AND WALES 1064–1536. PJAC

B. Holden, 'King John, the Braoses, and the Celtic Fringe, 1207–1216', *Albion*, 33 (2001), 1–23.
I. Rowlands, 'William de Braose and the Lordship of Brecon', *Bulletin of the Board of Celtic Studies*, 30 (1982–3), 123–33.

Braşov (**Brassó, Corona, Kronstadt**) Founded most probably in 1213 by the *Teutonic order in Burzenland, it became the largest town in *Transylvania in the 15th century. Strongly supported by the Hungarian kings in the 14th and 15th centuries, Braşov received trading privileges and the staple right (1369), which secured its position as a commercial centre in the international trade and with neighbouring *Wallachia and *Moldavia. MP

R. Manolescu, *Comerțul Țării Românești și Moldovei cu Brașovul, secolele XIV–XVI* (1965).
M. Philippi, *Die Bürger von Kronstadt im 14. und 15. Jahrhundert* (1986).
Quellen zur Geschichte der Stadt Kronstadt (Brassó), 9 vols (1886–1999).

brass *See* COPPER ALLOYS.

Bratislava (**Pozsony, Preßburg, Posonium**) Name (since 1919) of the capital of Slovakia, on the *river Danube. It was the border fortification and customs office of the *Hungarian kingdom. By the 13th century four churches were attested. After the Babenberg succession wars (1271–3), city walls were completed. *Town privilege, leading to *free royal city status, was granted in 1291, guaranteeing *Jews full rights. In 1466–85 Bratislava was the seat of the *Academia Istropolitana. *See also* THIRTIETH. RMa

R. Marsina, ed., *Bratislava-Preßburg, 1291–1991: Städte im Donauraum* (1993).
—— 'Preßburg/Bratislava: Hauptstadt der Slowakischen Republik', in *Hauptstädte zwischen Save, Bosporus und Dnjepr*, ed. H. Hepner (1998), 31–50.
T. Ortvay, *Geschichte der Stadt Preßburg*, 3 vols (1893–5).

Braulio of Saragossa (*c.*585–651) Bishop of Saragossa (631–51). The intellectual successor of *Isidore of Seville, Braulio is the author of the only significant collection of a single author's *letters to survive from *Visigothic Spain. Probably a native of La Rioja, he succeeded to the episcopate of Saragossa upon the death of the previous bishop, his elder brother John (619–31). Another brother, Fronimian, became abbot of the *monastery of St Aemilianus (San Millán de la Cogolla). Braulio's *vita* of Aemilianus, dedicated to his brother, is our sole historical source for Cantabria and La Rioja in the 6th century. Braulio's letter collection shows how extensive a role the most important bishops of the Visigothic kingdom could play in mid-7th-century politics, before the primacy of the see of *Toledo eclipsed the kingdom's other episcopal sees. Just as he had himself been influenced by Isidore, Braulio shaped the career of another important author, *Eugenius, later bishop of Toledo. MKu

Braulio, *Sancti Braulionis Caesaraugustani episcopi Vita Sancti Aemiliani*, ed. L. Vázquez de Parga (1943).
—— *Epistolario*, ed. L. Riesco Terrero (1975).
C. H. Lynch, *Saint Braulio, Bishop of Saragossa (631–651): His Life and Writings* (1938).

bread and baking Baking normally implied the use of a *stone or *brick oven throughout the MA, built in the kitchens of the very wealthy, but commoners reserved time at a communal oven or purchased baked goods from professional bakers. Alternatively, a householder could invest in a large *iron pot, with a tightly fitting lid; over a low fire and with hot coals on the lid, the pot (*thermospodium, testo, tegamo, trappe, trap*) functioned as a mini-oven and had the advantage of being portable. Of all the uses to which an oven was normally put in the MA, the baking of bread was primary.

Various *grains were ground into flour for bread, depending upon their cost and availability. Wheat, including spelt, along with rye, millet, and barley, were in common use. Those grains were frequently mixed; sometimes oats were added. The grain or grains determined the quality of the bread, varying in colour from white to dark, and in texture as well as in cost. On occasion peas, beans, lentils, rice, acorns, and chestnuts were ground for bread. Flour was mixed with water and a lump of fermented dough, reserved from a previous batch; the juxtaposition of bakery and brewery in *monastery plans suggests that fermenting barm was also used to raise bread dough.

Generally, no container was used in baking the dough. The standard 'loaf' of bread was a flat-bottomed mound. Its size tended not to be large so that it baked through without becoming too crusty. Fine table or *manchet* loaves were the size of a large bun. Sacramental bread was of the finest flour, the top of the risen dough occasionally inscribed with a religious symbol. Biscuits and wafers were made of looser, fine dough. The former was originally 'twice-baked'. The latter was baked in hot, flat-faced iron tongs that impressed a pattern on their surfaces.

Pastry dough was baked throughout the MA. Generally, the same cereal-grain flours for bread were used. A fine pastry dough of wheat flour could optionally include *olive oil, eggs (or egg yolks), *salt, *sugar, and rosewater (a distillate). The dough was rolled flat with a pin into a sheet for baked and deep-fried pies, tarts, and pasties. If a fluid filling was baked in an oven dish, the pastry shell could be of fine dough. If a pie was free-standing, coarser dough, rolled to an inch thick and optionally bound round with heavy greased paper and a cord, provided support for the filling. The fine pastry was considered edible, the coarse merely broken open and discarded. A solid chunk of meat, such as venison, might be wrapped in coarse dough. Turnovers of a fine dough were popular and could be baked or deep-fried. Batters, basically of flour and water, coated all sorts of foodstuffs, which generally were deep-fried. *See also* ALE- AND BEER-MAKING; FOOD, DRINK, AND DIET; FOODS, PREPARED. TPS

F. Desportes, *Le Pain au moyen âge* (1987).

breast feeding *See* GYNAECOLOGY AND OBSTETRICS.

Brehon Laws [from OIr. *brithem*, 'judge, jurist'] Irish legal texts often including pseudo-historical leading cases, composed *c*.7th–8th centuries, and preserved in 14th–16th-century MSS. *See also* EARLY IRISH SOCIETY. HCOB

D. A. Binchy, ed., *Corpus Iuris Hibernici*, 6 vols (1968).
F. Kelly, *A Guide to Early Irish Law* (1988).
K. McCone, *Pagan Past and Christian Present* (1990).
T. O'Loughlin, ed., *Adomnan at Birr AD 697: Essays in Commemoration of the Law of the Innocents* (2001).

Brembre, Nicholas (d. 1388) Grocer and mayor of *London in 1377 and 1383–5. As mayor, he supported the dominance of great merchants and traders in city politics. He was also an ally of *Richard II. When the Lords Appellant rose against the king, Brembre was executed. *See also* GUILDS [MERCHANT/CRAFT GUILDS]; MERCILESS PARLIAMENT; NORTHAMPTON, JOHN OF. JHH

R. Bird, *The Turbulent London of Richard II* (1949).

Bremen (suffragan) In 787 *Charlemagne founded the bishopric of Bremen in northern *Saxony as a missionary centre. In 848 it was united with the archbishopric of *Hamburg. EJG

Adam of Bremen, *History of the Archbishops of Hamburg-Bremen*, tr. F. J. Tschan, rev. edn. (2002).
I. Wood, *The Missionary Life: Saints and the Evangelisation of Europe, 400–1050* (2001).

Brendan (Brenainn)**, St**, abbot of Clonfert (484–577/83) Irish saint famous for his sea voyages and the subject of **Navigatio Sancti Brendani*. *See also* CELTIC CHURCH; TRAVEL AND MOBILITY. KR

W. R. J. Barron and G. S. Burgess, eds, *The Voyage of St Brendan: Representative Versions of the Legend in English Translation* (2002).
J. M. Wooding, ed., *The Otherworld Voyage in Early Irish Literature* (2000).

Brenner Pass The lowest (in altitude) and most developed *trade route over the *Alps was centred here. It grew in importance from the 14th century, since it was the only crossing able to handle wagons and, therefore, heavy goods

Bremen town hall.

A castle in Brescia.

(for example, *metal). Control of this pass was important to the *Habsburgs. *See also* ALPS AND ALPINE PASSES; INNSBRUCK; TRANSPORT, LAND; TYROL. JFP

H. Hassinger, 'Der Verkehr über Brenner und Reschen vom Ende des 13. bis in die zweite Hälfte des 18. Jahrhunderts', in *Festschrift Franz Huter* (1969), 137–94.
O. Wanka Edler von Rodlow, *Die Brennerstrasse im Alterthum und Mittelalter* (1900).

Brescia A Roman foundation, Brescia is located at the mouth of the Val Trompia midway between *Verona and *Bergamo. The seat of a bishop by the late 4th century, of a *duchy under the *Lombards, and of the Frankish Supponid counts in the 9th century, Brescia emerged as an important *trade centre in the 11th century. The earliest evidence of *communes dates from 1127, when the sources mention magistrates called *consuls, and in 1167 Brescia joined the *Lombard League. The city's internal politics reflected the party factionalism of *Milan, to which it was closely linked. Between 1227 and 1258 it was controlled by the Guelph *della Torre, but thereafter was dominated by a succession of *Guelph and Ghibelline **signorie*, a process intensified by the rise of the **popolo* in the later 13th century. In 1339, the *Visconti seized Brescia from the della *Scala of Verona, and thereafter it remained a Milanese possession until it was incorporated into the Venetian empire in 1426. LDA

L. Bethmann, ed., *Annales Brixienses*, *MGH.SS* 18 (1863; repr. 1990), 811–20.
Paul the Deacon, *Pauli Historia Langobardorum*, ed. G. Waitz, *MGH.SRG* 48 (1878; repr. 2005).
G. Treccani degli Alfieri, ed., *Storia di Brescia*, 5 vols (1963–4).

Breta sǫgur OIcel. translation (*c*.1200) of *Geoffrey of Monmouth's *Historia Regum Britanniae*. It is preserved only in a revised version in three 14th-century MSS. In these, the saga is written as a continuation of **Trójumanna saga*. The first six chapters of Geoffrey's text are substituted by a summary of Virgil's *Aeneid* as a transition from the Troy story to the history of the Brits. **Hauksbók* is the only MS containing a complete but somewhat abridged text of the saga. In the other MSS the saga has been reworked in the style of the courtly romances. Within *Hauksbók* the saga also contains the translation of the *Prophetiae Merlini* as one of the rare examples of an ON–Icel. translation into verse. *Merlínusspá* (Merlin's prophecies), as the poem is called, was probably translated by *Gunnlaugr Leifsson, who is well known for his sagas concerning the Norwegian kings Óláfr Tryggvason and St *Olaf. It is uncertain, however, whether he also translated the main text of Geoffrey's *Historia*. *See also* RENAISSANCE AND ANTIQUARIANISM; SCANDINAVIAN ROMANCES. SGr

Hauksbók, ed. F. and E. Jónsson (1892–6).

'Trójumanna saga ok Breta sögur', ed. J. Sigurðsson, *ANOH* (1848), 102–215; (1849), 3–145.
S. Würth, *Der 'Antikenroman' in der isländischen Literatur des Mittelalters* (1998).

Bretel, Jehan (*c.*1200–1272) *Bourgeois of *Arras; lay officer of St Vaast abbey; **trouvère*. Most of his seven *chansons* and about 90 **jeux-partis* survive with melodies. EAu

D. Di Croce, 'Jehan Bretel di Arras', *Atti dell'Istituto Veneto di Scienze, Lettere ed Arti*, 137 (1978–9), 203–20.
M. Gally, *Parler d'amour au puy d'Arras* (2004).

Brethren of the Common Life *See* DEVOTIO MODERNA.

Bretwalda Term used in the *Anglo-Saxon Chronicle* for a 'ruler of Britain'—a powerful king who dominated neighbouring kings. *Bede lists seven who held this position of *imperium*: *Ælle of *Sussex, *Ceawlin of *Wessex, *Æthelbert of *Kent, *Rædwald of *East Anglia, and *Edwin, *Oswald, and *Oswy of *Northumbria. The *Chronicle* later adds *Ecgberht of Wessex. *See also* ANNALS AND CHRONICLES: ENGLAND (1)—ANGLO-SAXON CHRONICLE. AMBr

J. Campbell, ed., *The Anglo-Saxons* (1982).
D. P. Kirby, *The Earliest English Kings* (2000).

breviary *See* LITURGICAL BOOKS, LATIN.

Breviary of Alaric (*Lex Romana Visigothorum*) Compilation of Roman *law promulgated in 506 by the Visigoth king Alaric II. Having a long relationship with Rome that stretched back to the 4th century, the *Visigoths had adopted many elements of Roman culture, language, and law when in the 5th century they established a great kingdom that stretched across France and Spain with *Toulouse as its capital. Though long retaining personal medieval Germanic *law as well as Arian Christianity, Visigoth kings slowly moved toward territorial law and Roman Catholicism.

This tension between a barbarian past and a Roman future was apparent in the great legal codifications Visigoth rulers sponsored down to the 7th century. In 476, Euric I issued a composite Roman-Germanic code that had a great influence on all later Iberian legislation. His son Alaric promulgated a great legal collection, the *Breviary*, which contained no Germanic elements and was fully Roman in its outlook and composition. Like the *Theodosian Code promulgated in 438, the *Breviary*, composed by unnamed legists serving in Alaric's court at Toulouse, attempted to upgrade and reorganize imperial law. This drastic change in national law only took place after Alaric had consulted with his *nobles and great *clergy and then brought the finished product before a Great Council for its approval. The code contained a selection of new laws or novels bracketing the reigns of Theodosius II and Severus, as well as long passages of judicial interpretation and theory from the imperial commentaries of Gaius, Papinian, and Paulus.

Though intended for use throughout Alaric's realm, the *Breviary* soon fell victim to geopolitical events that drastically altered the Visigoth world. When Alaric lost his life at the hands of his Frankish rival, *Clovis, at the battle of Vouillé in 507, the Visigoth kingdom was reduced to the Iberian Peninsula and its capital was now changed to *Toledo. This political catastrophe strongly affected the legislative direction taken by later Visigoth rulers, who followed the hybrid Germanic-Roman path pioneered by Euric's code down to the great territorial compilation issued under the 7th-century kings Chindaswinth and *Recceswinth, the 'Book of Judges' (*Liber Judiciorum*), which stands as the headwater of all subsequent Spanish and Portuguese law. Despite being rejected in its Iberian homeland, the *Breviary* had great influence on the formation of Justinian's *Code* issued in 534 and on all early medieval French law. DJK

A. d'Ors, 'La territorialidad del derecho en la época de los visigodos', *Estudios Visigóticos: Cuadernos del Instituto Jurídico Español*, 5 (1956), 91–124.
——*El Código de Eurico* (1960).
A. Garcí Gallo, 'Nacionalidad y territorialidad del derecho en la época visigoda', *Anuario de Historia del Derecho Español*, 13 (1936–41), 168–264.
——*Curso de historia del derecho español*, 2 vols (1971).
P. Meréa, *Estudios de direito visigótico* (1948).
C. Sánchez Albornoz, 'Pervivencia y crisis de la tradición jurídica romana en la España goda', *Settimane di studio del centro italiano di studi sull'alto medioevo*, 9 (1962), 128–99.
E. N. Van Kleffens, *Hispanic Law until the End of the Middle Ages* (1968).

Břevnov *Benedictine *monastery near *Prague, originally founded jointly by Duke Boleslav II (972–99) and Bishop Vojtěch/*Adalbert in 992/3, later settled by monks from Niederalteich who made it into a centre of ecclesiastical (*'Gregorian') reform. The *hermit St Vintíř (d. 1045) had close ties to Břevnov, where he was buried. A Romanesque *crypt, from before 1045, has survived at the site. Later building phases were in the mid 13th century and after 1306, when Abbot Paul II Bavor of Nečtiny (1290–1332) launched the construction of a Gothic church. The monastery was burned and destroyed by the *Taborites in 1420 and was not rebuilt until the 17th century.

Břevnov was a major cultural centre in *Bohemia, with a *scriptorium and a fine *library, and many of its scholars were in contact with other monastic communities. The philosopher Vojtěch Raňkův of Ježov (*c.*1320–88) was closely connected to Břevnov, and bequeathed his library to the community. The written records of the monastic economy (an inventory of the house and its dependent churches from

1390 and a register of its *estates) are unique examples of this type of source in Bohemia.

The monastery established several branch houses, such as Kostelec on the Vltava (*c.*1200) in south Bohemia and Police on the Metuje river (before 1260) in eastern Bohemia. Its priory in Broumov was raised to an abbey in 1296, and provided refuge for the Břevnov monks after 1420. RŠi

M. Bláhová and I. Hlaváček, eds, *Milénium břevnovského kláštera (993–1993)* (1993).

J. Hoffmann, ed., *Tausend Jahre Benediktiner in den Klöstern Břevnov: Braunau und Rohr* (1993).

Brian Boru (Borumha), high king of Ireland (r. 1002–14) Son of Cennedig, leader of the Dalcassians. The epithet *Borumha* signifies 'of the cattle tributes'. Having consolidated the Irish temporarily, Brian became celebrated as the enemy of the *Vikings. He died at the battle of *Clontarf, aged *c.*75. *See also* SCOTLAND, IRELAND, WALES: EARLY MEDIEVAL IRELAND TO 1166. DJS

F. D. Logan, *The Vikings in History* ([2]1991).

B. Ó Cuív, ed., *The Impact of the Scandinavian Invasions on the Celtic-speaking Peoples, c.800–1100* (1975).

brick making The production process of medieval bricks resembled the production of tiles. Loam (soil consisting of sand, clay, silt, and organic material) was dug in open-cast *mining with simple tools and left to weather for at least one winter. The weathering caused the organic components of the loam to decompose. Workers then watered the loam several times, and kneaded and mixed it. They stamped it with their feet and removed the coarse components. Loam with a high amount of clay was mixed with sand to prevent the bricks from cracking. It was then thrown into a wooden mould, and the surplus removed with hands or with wooden sticks. When forcefully thrown into the mould, the loam was squeezed into folds that remained and can be seen on the side surfaces of medieval bricks.

A characteristic of 12th- and 13th-century bricks is the hatching. Before the firing, workers beat, carved, or combed parallel lines onto the side surfaces of the brick. Hatching was not a technical necessity, but was ornamental. Hatched bricks were used for the most important parts of a building. After the unfired bricks were formed, they were tipped out of the mould onto the drying field and air-dried for several weeks. After an initial drying period, the bricks were set upright to dry the underside. To prevent damage caused by rain or other factors, the bricks were covered with straw mats.

The firing was accomplished in temporary kilns ('clamps') or solid kilns. It lasted about two weeks, during which the highest temperature of approximately 950° centigrade was maintained for about two days. The temperature varied inside the clamps as well as inside the kilns; only a few perfectly fired bricks resulted in addition to many over-fired or half-fired ('samel') bricks.

To make variously shaped bricks, workers either inserted additional wooden blocks into the mould or cut ordinary bricks into shape with the help of templates. They cut more elaborate pieces freehand out of lumps of loam.

*Glaze was used from the 12th century. Usually workers spread a lead mixture onto one side of the bricks (sometimes fired, sometimes not) and heated them again. The early black and green glazes were followed by yellow, red, brown, turquoise, and colourless glazes. *See also* POTTERY, CERAMICS, AND TILE. BCP

J. Campbell and W. Pryce, *Brick: A World History* (2003).

J. Cramer and D. Sack, eds, *Technik des Backsteinbaus im Europa des Mittelalters* (2004).

B. Perlich, *Mittelalterlicher Backsteinbau in Europa: Zur Frage nach der Herkunft der Backsteintechnik* (2006).

bridal quest epic Universal narrative type relating a young *nobleman's attempts to win a bride. They are especially popular in 12th- and 13th-century Germany (**Spielmannsepik*) and 13th- and 14th-century Scandinavia (*Saxo Grammaticus, **Þiðreks saga*, *Fornaldarsǫgur*). Early examples exist in Latin (*Fredegar, **Waltharius*) and also in Oriental, Byzantine, and Slavic literature and *folklore. CB

C. Bornholdt, *Engaging Moments: The Origins of Medieval Bridal-Quest Narrative* (2005).

M. Kalinke, *Bridal-Quest Romance in Medieval Iceland* (1990).

C. Schmid-Cadalbert, *Der 'Ortnit AW' als Brautwerbungsdichtung: Ein Beitrag zum Verständnis mittelhochdeutscher Schemaliteratur* (1985).

bridge-building brotherhoods (late 12th–mid 15th century) Three independent corporations in the Rhône valley whose members, primarily laymen, dedicated themselves to the construction, maintenance, and/or fiscal management of their respective bridges at *Avignon, *Lyons, and Pont-St-Esprit. By the early 14th century, the brotherhoods no longer controlled their respective bridges, and members turned their efforts from fundraising to serving in the *hospitals affiliated with each bridge. WAML

M. N. Boyer, 'The Bridge-Building Brotherhoods', *Speculum*, 39 (1964), 635–50.

P. Pansier, 'Histoire de l'ordre des frères du pont d'Avignon', *Annales d'Avignon et du Comtat Venaissin*, 7 (1920–21), 7–59.

bridges *See* ROADS AND BRIDGES.

Bridget, St *See* BIRGITTA OF SWEDEN, ST.

Bridget of Ireland, St (d. 524) Irish monastic founder associated with *Kildare; the third patron saint of Ireland and subject of two 7th-century *vitae* stressing her generosity and *miracles. *See also* BIOGRAPHY, LATIN; IRISH CHURCH, EARLY ORGANIZATION OF. HCOB

D. Ó hAodha, 'The Early Lives of St Brigit', *Kildare Archaeological Society Journal*, 15 (1971–6), 397–405.
R. Sharpe, 'Vitae S. Brigitae: The Oldest Texts', *Peritia*, 1 (1982), 81–106.

Bridgettine order *See* BIRGITTA OF SWEDEN, ST.

Brittany Culturally and politically distinct region occupying the *Armorica peninsula in northwestern France. Its status was that of a group of related *regna* (5th through 9th centuries), a kingdom (9th century), and an independent duchy (10th through 16th centuries). There are nine *broioù* or 'traditional regions': *León, Cornouaille, Trégor (the bishopric of Tréguier), *Vannes, St-Brieuc, Dol, *St-Malo (formerly the bishopric of Alet), *Rennes, and *Nantes.

During the 5th and 6th centuries, Brittonic Celts migrated from Britain to the Continent, where they absorbed remnants of Gallo-Roman ethnicity in what was then known as Ar(e)morica; later authors represented this *migration as a single vast movement. From 558 the Bretons fought the Franks; they were partially subjugated in the early 9th century and received the benefits of the Carolingian *Renaissance. Nominoë (841–51) and his descendants, Erispoë and Salomon, successfully fought the Carolingians, forcing them to recognize Brittany as an independent kingdom (863). Salomon's uncertain succession and *Viking incursions led to the kingdom's collapse (*c*.913–36). The Vikings were expelled by Alain Barbetorte, who established a *feudal duchy with its capital at Nantes.

The 10th and 11th centuries saw Brittany contested by the counts of Nantes and Cornouaille versus those of Rennes and pressured by the neighbouring principalities of *Anjou, *Blois, and *Normandy. Many Bretons participated in the *Norman Conquest of England. The *Plantagenets were overlords of Brittany from 1158 to 1203; after *Arthur of Brittany's murder, the Bretons aligned themselves with *Philip II of France, whose kinsman Pierre de *Dreux married Arthur's half-sister. There was relative peace until 1341, when the duke's death provoked a civil war in which France and England each backed a candidate. War concluded in 1366, when the English-backed candidate's son was made *duke. This and subsequent dukes made concerted attempts to create a sovereign principality within the larger kingdom of later medieval France. Military defeat by France (1487–91) and the marriage of the young duchess *Anne of Brittany to one French king after another led to the formal Edict of Union in 1532.

Brittany's distinctive character may partly be attributed (at least until the 12th century) to Celtic origins and ties with *Cornwall, Wales, and Ireland. The Breton language, which *c*.800 was scarcely distinguishable from Welsh and Cornish, would have been spoken throughout the 9th-century kingdom; in the eastern half it then gave way to French and Gallo, a Romance dialect. Brittany was a principal setting for Arthurian adventures, and is thought to have played a role in the oral transmission of the so-called **matière de Bretagne*, as suggested by the 'Breton lais' in OFr. and ME. No Breton-language literature survives from before the 15th century, but more recent *folklore is sometimes illuminating. *See also* LANGUAGES: FRENCH; LITERATURES: ARTHURIAN LEGEND. MBo

J. Balcou and Y. Le Gallo, eds, *Histoire littéraire et culturelle de la Bretagne* (1987).
A. Chédeville and H. Guillotel, *La Bretagne des saints et des rois, Ve–Xe siècle* (1984).
—— and N.-Y. Tonnerre, *La Bretagne féodale, XIe–XIIIe siècle* (1987).
J. A. Everhard, *Brittany and the Angevins* (2000).
L. Fleuriot, *Les Origines de la Bretagne* (1980).
P. Galliou and M. Jones, *The Bretons* (1991).
P.-R. Giot *et al.*, *Les Premiers Bretons d'Armorique* (2003).
M. Jones, *The Creation of Brittany* (1988).
—— *Between France and England* (2003).
J.-P. Leguay and H. Martin, *Fastes et malheurs de la Bretagne ducale* (1982).
B. Merdrignac, *Les Vies de saints Bretons durant le haut Moyen Âge (VIIe–XIIe siècle)* (1993).
J. Rio, *Mythes fondateurs de la Bretagne* (2000).

Brixen, Synod of (1080) The assembly of 30 Italian and German bishops who met in the presence of Henry IV, responding to his second deposition and *excommunication by *Pope Gregory VII. Not all of the accusations against the pope were scurrilous. The synod deposed Gregory and nominated Archbishop Wibert of *Ravenna in his place. URB

Briefe Heinrichs IV., ed. C. Erdmann (1937), appendix C.
J. Ziese, *Wibert von Ravenna* (1982).

Brixworth church This AS structure comprises a *nave, choir, rebuilt *apse, and beyond the apse, a ring *crypt. The nave was formerly flanked by a series of side chambers or *porticus*. It probably dates to the late 8th to mid 9th century. Brixworth has been identified, perhaps incorrectly, with Clofesho, the meeting place of church *councils. MFG

E. C. Fernie, *The Architecture of the Anglo-Saxons* (1983).

Brno (Brünn) Leading *administrative and *trading centre of *Great Moravia. It arose on the muddy (Old Slavic, *brn*) banks of the Svratka (Schwarzach) river by the mid 10th century. By the late 12th century settlement shifted several kilometres away to the Petrov hill, where a *Přemyslid castle and church of St Peter were built; the riverside settlement became known as Staré Brno (Old Brno). Brno grew rapidly during the first half of the 13th century, and achieved self-governance with its own laws (1243), *seal, town hall, and fortifications. In the 1250s *Otakar II built a new *castle here, Špilberk (Spielberg).

The religious houses of medieval Brno reflected the diversity of its inhabitants. German-speaking immigrants, who began arriving in the late 12th century, worshipped at the church of St James, while Czechs continued using the church of St Peter (today SS Peter and Paul *cathedral). The chapel of St Michael (demolished) served a small community of Italian or Walloon merchants. The synagogue and **mikveh* (ritual bath) of the Jewish community (1268 privilege) do not survive. Other institutions included the *Premonstratensian abbey of Zábrdovice (Obrowitz), outside the town wall; *Franciscan and *Dominican friaries (*c.*1230); a *beguine-like community known as the Herburg canonesses (1240s); and a *Cistercian nunnery at Staré Brno (founded 1323 by Eliška Rejčka, widow of Rudolf IV of Habsburg). SAH

Dějiny města Brna, ed. J. Dřímal (1969), vol. 1.

K. Kuča, *Města a městečka v Čechách, na Moravě a ve Slezku* (1996), vol. 1, 233–302.

F. Šujan, *Dějepis Brna*, Vlastivěda moravská ([2]1928).

Broederlam, Melchior *See* BAERZE, JACQUES DE.

bronze and brass *See* COPPER ALLOYS.

Bruce family (Bruis, Brix, Broase) (11th–14th centuries) Scottish dynasty of Norman-French descent, founded by Robert de Bruce III (d. 1189), though Robert de Bruce I (d. *c.*1094) came to England in 1066. Bruce influence peaked with two Scottish kings: Robert de Bruce VIII became *Robert I (1306), followed by *David II (1329–71). *See also* SCOTLAND, IRELAND, WALES: SCOTLAND AND WALES 1064–1536. MTA

G. W. S. Barrow, *Robert Bruce and the Community of the Realm of Scotland* (1996).

M. Brown, *The Wars of Scotland, 1214–1371* (2004).

Bruder Wernher MHG poet and musician, active *c.*1217–50. The description *Bruder* (brother) suggests that he was a religiously inclined layman (*see* LAITY) or eventually entered a *monastery. Seventy-six of his verses, focusing largely on politics and religion, survive. MPie

H. Brunner, 'Bruder Wernher', in *Verfasserlexikon* ([2]1999), vol. 10, 897–903.

Bruges From obscure Roman origins, through a period as a bastion of the counts of *Flanders, Bruges developed into the premier commercial city in northern Europe by the mid 14th century. Aided by the decline of the *fairs of Champagne and breakdown in internal security across continental Europe caused by war, Bruges came to combine the advantages of a highly developed port system, foreign merchant communities, and an unrivalled finance / payment system. Above all, it came to function as a node that brought together trading networks based in the great trading spheres of the North, *Baltic, and Mediterranean Seas.

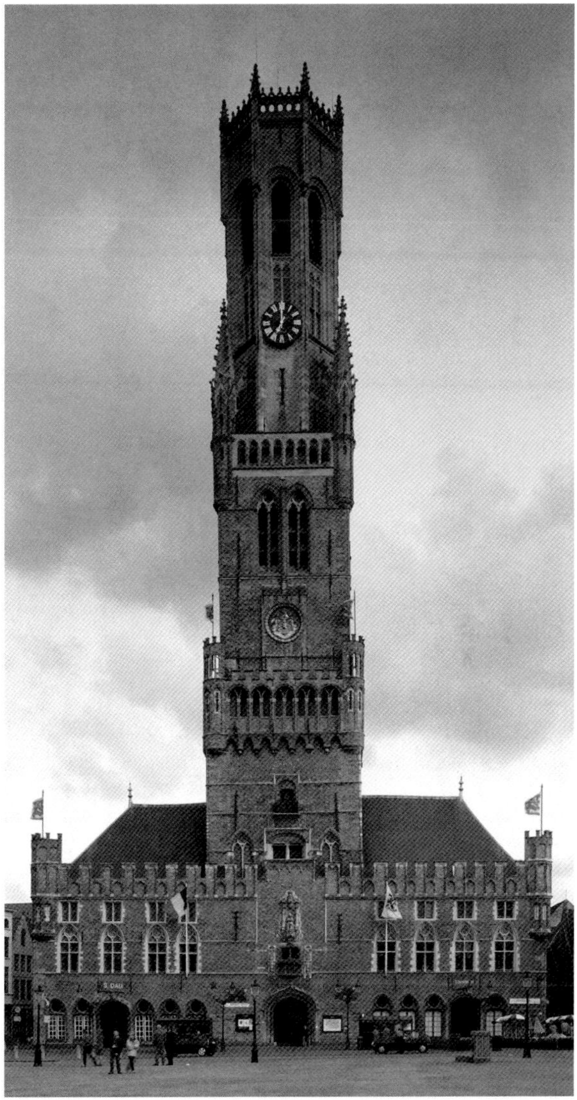

Belfry and market hall, Bruges.

Relatively little is known about the internal history of Bruges until the comital *notary and resident, *Galbert, wrote his history of the assassination of Count *Charles 'the Good' and the ensuing civil war. Though his intention was more *hagiographical than historical, Galbert's text provides a wealth of details about the social and political forces at work in the 12th-century town as it evolved from a regional *administrative centre and *marketplace to an international centre of manufacture and *trade. Although Bruges remained the seat of the *castellany of the Franc, and an ecclesiastical centre of importance, it was the cloth workers and merchants, who wrested a privilege of

Crane of Bruges, end of the 15th century.

self-government from the next would-be count in 1128, who made the city an economic wonder.

It was as a port and market in *wool and cloth that Bruges began to become prominent in the 13th century. Replacing nearby *Ypres as brokers of English and Flemish wool, Bruges merchants specialized in trade with England to such an extent that membership in the commercial *guild of England traders defined the city's political elite before 1300. Thereafter, the city was governed by commercial elites that included merchants, guildsmen, and old-line families who collectively strove to build a commercial city through investing in infrastructure, imposing social peace, and fashioning a hospitable environment for short- and long-term resident foreign merchants. By 1350, significant numbers of *Hanse, English, and Italian merchants met and traded in Bruges.

By the 14th century, many Bruges merchants had become experts in brokerage, hostelling, and partnering in import/export ventures with foreigners and countrymen alike. Arising from and abetting such businesses was a payment and credit system of great power and complexity, composed of Italian merchant banking companies, which could provide *bill of exchange transactions, thus enabling fund transfers over long distances, and local money-changers and hostellers, who together created a system of deposit *banking. The latter relied on an integrated system of book-keeping transfers, which was regional in scope, and so ubiquitous among merchants that money on deposit with Bruges changers or hostellers was routinely used in lieu of cash for commercial transactions all across northern Europe.

Changes in European trade and politics gradually eroded the commercial advantages Bruges offered, enabling *Antwerp to gradually gain the upper hand as a trading centre after 1500. Yet the shift was subtle if inexorable, and the city produced some of its greatest *artists, musicians, and *luxury products after 1430. *See also* ACCOUNTING AND BOOK-KEEPING; HOTELS, INNS, AND TAVERNS; MONEYLENDING, CREDIT, AND USURY; TEXTILES AND CLOTH-MAKING. JMMu

J. M. Murray, *Bruges, Cradle of Capitalism, 1280–1390* (2005).
J. B. Ross, *The Murder of Charles the Good* ([2]2005).

Brunanburh, battle of (937) Conflict between the English, led by King *Æthelstan and Eadmund, grandsons of *Alfred the Great, and combined Scottish, *Strathclyde Briton, and *Viking forces in which the English prevailed. The location of the battle is unknown, but it was probably the outcome of efforts by *Wessex to gain control of the whole of England. It is commemorated in a heroic, unusually nationalistic poem recorded in four MSS of the *Anglo-Saxon Chronicle*. *See also* MALDON, BATTLE OF. REB

J. Pope, ed., *Eight Old English Poems*, rev. R. D. Fulk ([3]2001), 58–61.
F. M. Stenton, *Anglo-Saxon England* ([3]1971), 342–3.

Brunelleschi, Filippo (1377–1446) Florentine architect and sculptor, who introduced a new classical style of *architecture based on the classical orders and his own system of proportions. He was famous for the *dome of the *cathedral in *Florence, completed in 1436. One of the largest masonry domes ever built, the space was too large for traditional *timber centring. Designing innovative lifting machines for the work, he distributed the weight on *ribs, laid the *brick in a herringbone pattern, and constructed the dome on a double-shell principle. *See also* RENAISSANCE AND ANTIQUARIANISM. POL

E. Battisti, *Filippo Brunelleschi* ([2]1983).
F. D. Prager and G. Scaglia, *Brunelleschi: Study of his Technology and Inventions* (1970).
H. Saalman, *Filippo Brunelleschi: The Cupola of Santa Maria del Fiore* (1980).

Brunhild (**Brunhilde, Brünhild, Brynhild**) Female protagonist in Germanic mythology and heroic tradition belonging to the Nibelung tradition; a *Valkyrie (shield-maiden) in the Scandinavian tradition (*eddic poetry,

**Vǫlsunga saga*, **Þiðreks saga*) and warrior queen in the **Nibelungenlied*. *See also* FOLKLORE AND MYTHOLOGY: GERMANIC/SCANDINAVIAN. CB

T. M. Andersson, *The Legend of Brunhild* (1980).

Bruni d'Arezzo (*c.*1370–1444) Tuscan humanist, historian, and orator. Bruni was apostolic secretary (1405–14) and chancellor of *Florence (1427–44), but is best remembered for his *History of the Florentine People* (1415–44), widely considered the first modern work of history. FB

Bruni d'Arezzo, *Historiarum Florentini populi libri XII*, ed. E. Santini (1926).

——*Opere letterarie e politiche*, ed. P. Viti (1996).

J. Hankins, ed., *Renaissance Civic Humanism: Reappraisals and Reflections* (2000).

Bruno, Giordano (1548–1600) Italian philosopher. After leaving the *Dominican order and fleeing Italy, he travelled in France, England, and Germany, developing an idiosyncratic and eclectic philosophical system that combined *Copernican heliocentrism, *Neoplatonic *metaphysics, Epicurean *atomism, and the art of memory (**memoria*). *Excommunicated by the Catholic, Lutheran, and Calvinist churches, he was tried by the *Inquisition and burned at the stake for *heresy. *See also* COSMOLOGY. JAK

I. Rowland, *Giordano Bruno*, (2008).

Bruno (Brun) **of Cologne, St** (*c.*925–65) Archbishop; duke of *Lorraine. Son of Henry I 'the Fowler' and brother of Otto I, Bruno was destined for an ecclesiastical life; he served as abbot of *Lorsch and *Corvey, chancellor of Germany (940), archbishop of *Cologne and duke of Lorraine (both 953). A scholar himself and *patron of a great cathedral school, Bruno was instrumental in forging the close ties between court and church that were a hallmark of Ottonian society. *See also* ROMAN EMPIRE [CAROLINGIAN, OTTONIAN, SALIAN/FRANCONIAN DYNASTIES]. ASC

J. Forse, 'Bruno of Cologne and the Networking of the Episcopate in Tenth-Century Germany', *German History*, 9 (1991), 263–79.

Bruno of Magdeburg and Merseburg (*fl.* 1082). German polemicist who served in the court of Archbishop Werner of *Magdeburg in the late 11th century. Bruno wrote his *Saxonicum Bellum* in 1082 as an apologia for the Saxon rebellion against King Henry IV of Germany (1056–1106). *See also* ROMAN EMPIRE [CAROLINGIAN, OTTONIAN, SALIAN/FRANCONIAN DYNASTIES]; SAXONY. PSH

H.-E. Lohmann, ed., *Brunos Buch vom Sachsenkrieg* (1937).

F.-J. Schmale, 'Zu Brunos Buch vom Sachsenkrieg', *DAEM* 18 (1962), 236–44.

Bruno of Querfurt, St (*c.*974–1009) Educated at *Magdeburg, Bruno was recruited to Otto III's court at Rome and became associated with the community to which *Adalbert of *Prague had belonged. Bruno followed Otto to *Ravenna, and in 1001 Otto sent Benedict of Benevento and a companion to *Poland to learn Slavonic and embark on a mission. In 1003 Bruno was sent to Magdeburg to be consecrated missionary bishop of the *Slavs; but Henry II was at war with the Polish ruler, so Bruno travelled to *Hungary, writing a draft of the *Life of Adalbert*. Later, he went on to *Rus', trying to work among the Petchenegs.

In 1007 he continued to Poland, where he found that Benedict and his companions had been murdered in 1003. Feeling responsible, Bruno composed a *Life of the Five Brothers*, lamenting his own failures. He also wrote a letter to Henry II, condemning his alliance with the *pagans against the Christian Poles, meanwhile giving an autobiographical account of his own missions. Finally, he set off to revive Adalbert's missionary work in the *Baltic, travelling to Prussia and then to *Lithuania, where he was martyred on 9 March 1009. An account of his *martyrdom was written by Wibert, who had been with him when he died. Both *Thietmar of *Merseburg and *Peter Damian provide some information on Bruno, but no full-scale *vita* was written. Bruno's own writings provide insight into his personality and his attitudes towards *missions. *See also* HAGIOGRAPHY; ROMAN EMPIRE [CAROLINGIAN, OTTONIAN, SALIAN/FRANCONIAN DYNASTIES]. IW

Bruno, *Epistola ad Henricum II Imperatorem*, ed. W. von Giesebrecht, in *Geschichte der deutschen Kaiserzeit* (^{4}1875), vol. 2, 689–92.

——*Passio sancti Adalberti episcopi et martyris*, ed. G. H. Pertz, *MGH.SS* 4 (1841).

——*Vita quinque fratrum Poloniae*, ed. R. Kade, *MGH.SS* 15/2 (1888).

R. Wenskus, *Studien zur historisch-politischen Gedankenwelt Bruns von Querfurt* (1956).

Wibert, *Hystoria de predicatione Episcopi Brunonis cum suis capellanis in Prussia et martyrio eorum*, ed. G. H. Pertz, *MGH.SS* 4 (1841).

I. N. Wood, *The Missionary Life: Saints and the Evangelisation of Europe, 400–1000* (2001).

Bruno of Segni, St (1045/9–1123) *Canon in *Siena, bishop of Segni (Latium), and abbot of *Monte Cassino. He collaborated with *Pope Gregory VII and his successors and authored biblical *commentaries and *sermons. *See also* EXEGESIS. PSto

R. Grégoire, *Bruno de Segni, exégète médiéval et théologien monastique* (1965).

B. Navarra, *San Bruno Astense, vescovo di Segni e abate di Montecassino* (1980).

Bruno the Carthusian, St (*c.*1032–1101) Founder of the *Carthusian order. Born in *Cologne, he attended school there and at *Rheims, eventually working in Rheims as a 'scholasticus'. In 1080 he abandoned teaching, building a hermitage in a remote forest. In 1084 he founded the Carthusians, establishing the first *monastery near *Grenoble, France. *See also* CHARTREUSE, LA GRANDE; HERMITS. GP

A. Ravier, *Saint Bruno, the Carthusian* (1995).

Brunschwig, Hieronymus (*c.*1450–1512/13) Surgeon from *Strasbourg, who prepared texts on medical subjects for the printer Johann Grüninger. His earliest book, a manual of *surgery in 1497, was followed by books on *distillation and the *plague in 1500, a revised version of his handbook on distillation in 1505, and a more comprehensive book on distillation in 1512. This last book incorporated sections on *herbal remedies, preparation of compound medicines, and a home *pharmacy for the poor. There were many reprints and numerous translations, especially into English, of these illustrated books in the 16th century. Brunschwig referred frequently to Latin authors, but he compiled his works from German translations. His audience was the increasingly literate German middle class, and ample use of *woodcuts in his works—which showed detailed and accurate processes and equipment, especially for *distillation—greatly increased their popular appeal. WCC

C. Probst, *Brunschwig und sein 'Buch der Cirurgia': Einführung in die Faksimileausgabe* (1967).

H. E. Sigerist, *Hieronymus Brunschwig and his Work* (1946).

Brunswick (Braunschweig) (duchy, town) The duchy of Brunswick-Lüneburg was the successor of the state of *Henry the Lion, duke of Saxony. His grandson Duke Otto received his Welf family's freehold lands (*see* ALLOD AND FREEHOLD) west of the *river Elbe in fief from Emperor Frederick II in 1235, and became an imperial prince. The family's holdings were subdivided frequently, with branches at Wolfenbüttel, Göttingen, and Grubenhagen. Brunswick-Lüneburg received a territorial constitution in 1392. It eventually became the electorate of Hanover.

The town of Brunswick existed in the 9th century, but its fortunes were transformed when Henry the Lion made its castle of Dankwarderode his favourite residence. Brunswick comprised five distinct settlements that were merged only in the late 13th century. Henry founded two of them: the Hagen, which became a weavers' quarter, and a commercial 'New City' between the Hagen and the Old City. Brunswick exported undressed cloth to *Flanders for finishing and was a major re-export depot for the metal products of Saxony. Much of Brunswick's prosperity came from its domination of its neighbour *Lüneburg and its lucrative *salt mines. Brunswick was the chief city of a Saxon League that was sometimes represented collectively in the Diet of the German *Hanse. It was governed by a merchant oligarchy; in 1374 a guild rebellion erupted that continued intermittently until 1386, when a regime was installed that represented the five districts of the city and the major crafts, but in practice the older lineages continued to dominate. Another revolutionary movement between 1487 and 1490 failed because the *guilds could not formulate a coherent programme. DN

H. Dürre, *Geschichte der Stadt Braunschweig im Mittelalter* (1861; repr. 1974).

Brussels The city developed around a market settlement on the Senne and a *castle of the dukes of *Brabant. The land route from *Bruges to the *Rhineland ran between them, and a wall linked the upper and lower towns in the 12th century. Brussels became the favourite residence of the dukes under Henry II (1235–48). In 1235 a *charter gave an annual magistracy of seven *schepenen*, chosen from ducal officials, and thirteen 'sworn' chosen from the burgesses. There were seven lineages, each of which furnished one *schepen*. While an effort to broaden the regime was defeated in 1306, the government was reformed in 1421 to include the *guilds in a subordinate role.

Brussels had a drapery guild by 1282 that set fullers' wages and hindered organizing by lower-status *textile workers. After 1306 *fullers and *weavers were forbidden to live within the walls. Wealthy Brusselers lived outside the walls, and after 1291 *peasants had to have their contracts concluded at Brussels to be sure of enforcement. By 1400 the villages around Brussels had been incorporated into the 'liberty' of the city. Brussels had a population of 40,000 by 1500 and was a favoured residence of the *Burgundian dukes. The Chamber of Accounts for Brabant, *Limburg, and *Luxembourg was fixed there, and in 1530 the centre of government of the *Habsburg governors-general of the *Low Countries was moved to Brussels. DN

F. Favresse, *L'Avènement du régime démocratique à Bruxelles pendant le Moyen Âge (1306–1423)* (1932).

M. Martens, ed., *Histoire de Bruxelles* (1976).

Bryennios, Manuel *See* MANUEL BRYENNIUS.

Bryennius, Nicephorus (Nikephoros Bryennios) (1062–*c.*1136) Byzantine general and historian who married Princess Anna Komnene and participated in the military campaigns of Alexius I Komnenos. In 1118 Anna Komnene tried to proclaim him emperor. Despite the failure of the plot, Bryennius became the general of Emperor John II Komnene and wrote *Hyle Historias* ('Historical Material'), covering the period 1070–79. *See also* BYZANTIUM. NVM

N. Bryennios, *Histoire*, ed. P. Gautier (1975).

A. Carile, 'La "Hyle Historias" del Cesare Niceforo Briennio', *Aevum*, 43 (1969), 56–87, 235–82.

Buch, captals of The title of 18 successive lords and three ladies (1274–1793) of La Teste de Buch, the *castle dominating the entrance of the Bassin d'Arcachon (Gironde). The most notable was Jean III de Grailly (1343–77), constable of *Aquitaine for *Edward, the 'Black Prince'. DHW

J. Delamare, *La Teste de Buch à travers les siècles* (1999).

ODNB, vol. 23, 257.

Buch, Jean III de Grailly, captal de (d. 1377) Gascon lord and founding member of the Order of the *Garter

(1348). He fought alongside *Edward of Woodstock, the 'Black Prince', at *Poitiers (1356) and *Nájera (1367), and took part in the suppression of the *Jacquerie. CDT

M. G. A. Vale, 'Grailly, Jean (III) de (d. 1377)', *ODNB*, vol. 23, 257–8.

Buckingham's rebellion (1483) It united disparate enemies of *Richard III, initially on behalf of *Edward V but later for Henry *Tudor (*Henry VII). Most were loyal, southern *Yorkists who escaped to France, but the rebellion is named after Richard's former ally Henry *Stafford, duke of Buckingham, who was the principal casualty. MAH

L. Gill, *Richard III and Buckingham's Rebellion* (1999).
M. A. Hicks, *Richard III* (2000).

bucolic *See* PASTORAL, MEDIEVAL LATIN; PATTERN POETRY.

Buda Founded in the 1240s by Germans from Pest who crossed the *river Danube to the greater safety of the Buda hill after the *Mongol-Tatar invasion of 1241. The new city took over the privileges, *seal, and even the German name (Ofen) of the earlier Pest settlement. Although the right of the citizens to elect their chief magistrate was confirmed in a royal privilege of 1244, the city's headman was, until the 1340s, appointed by the king. Buda stood at the hub of a network of *trade, mostly in *textiles, reaching to *Germany, *Poland, and *Transylvania. In the 15th century the city was home to representatives of some of central Europe's leading merchant firms. In the later 14th century the principal organs of royal *administration moved to Buda, and an extensive royal palace was constructed in the southern part of the city.

The population of Buda was sharply divided between merchants and *guildsmen and Germans and *Hungarians. Conflict between merchants and *artisans prompted an *urban revolt in 1402. In 1439 the largely Hungarian underclass rebelled against the city's German patrician elite. After 1439 the city's council was remodelled to give equal places to Hungarians and Germans. The overall population of Buda numbered 12,500–15,000 in the mid 15th century. Buda was sacked in 1526 by the Turks, who occupied the city from 1541 to 1686. MRa

L. Gerevich, *Budapest története* (1983), vols 1 and 2.
A. Kubinyi, *Die Anfänge Ofens* (1972).
M. Rady, *Medieval Buda* (1985).

Buda Stadtrecht Composed anonymously in German in the early 15th century. It describes the *custom law of *Buda, including the city's institutional organization, its main privileges, and commercial and fiscal regulations. MRa

L. Blazovich and J. Schmidt, *Buda város jogkönyve* (2001), vols 1 and 2.
K. Gönczi, *Ungarisches Stadtrecht aus europäischer Sicht* (1997).
K. Mollay, *Das Ofner Stadtrecht* (1959).

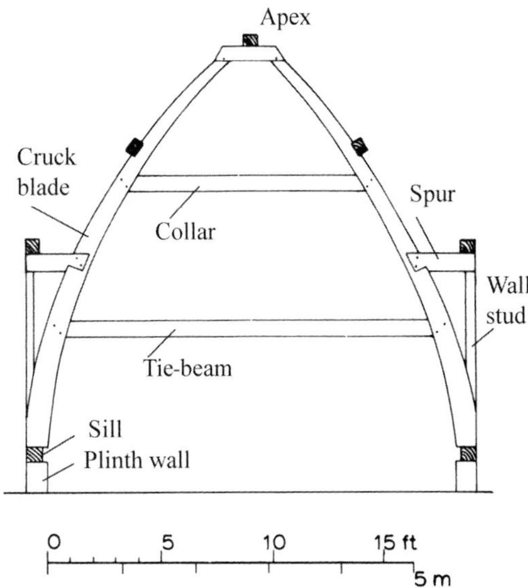

A typical cruck truss, based on an example in Warwickshire, England.

building and construction Architectural fabrication involving major exploitation of material resources and *technology.

1. General concepts
2. Labour (artisans)
3. Materials and transport
4. Northern Europe: revival and expansion
5. Masonry
6. Romanesque and Gothic
7. Timber
8. Metals
9. Tools and machinery

1. General concepts

Construction across medieval Europe from the 6th to the 16th century was largely determined by the availability of materials, accumulated technology, and *transport. Building in any material—*stone, *timber, reeds, clay, and *metals—required essential tools, craft expertise, and an understanding of the material's inherent physical properties, such as strength, durability, and workability, all of which imposed constraints on the builders. The varied medieval construction landscape, marked by *castles, *cathedrals, towers, walled towns, and gates, is characterized by material diversity as well as regional building types. While aisled buildings, masonry vaults, towers, and walled enclosures are ubiquitous, a marked contrast in materials, techniques, and structural forms delineates the differences between construction north of the *Alps and the Mediterranean region, the latter heavily influenced by Roman, Byzantine, and Islamic building traditions, such as in southern France, Spain, Italy, and the Balkans.

All major building enterprises were principally financed and technologically driven by ecclesiastical institutions and the social and military elites of medieval society. The spread of Christianity, *monasticism, and ties to Rome in the west militated against regionalism in ecclesiastical architecture; in particular, the church sponsored standardized plans for collegiate, monastic, and episcopal building complexes, such as the 9th-century idealized 'Plan of *St Gall'. Moreover, it fostered the creation of durable buildings, often based on Roman and Byzantine prototypes, as seen in the *Carolingian revival of large-scale masonry (for example, *Charlemagne's palace complex at *Aachen [795]). Usually, ecclesiastical and noble *patrons provided the economic means and ideological stimulus for the transmission of ideas, styles, materials, and technology, and selective elements of a 'high style' *architecture subsequently passed down the social scale to the *gentry, burghers (*bourgeois), eventually the *peasantry, and finally *vernacular buildings.

2. *Labour (artisans)*

Apart from the intermittent use of forced labour (diggers, hewers, carters, and so forth) conscripted for castle building and royal defences, the medieval workforce was made up of free men and dominated by a professional *artisan class whose trades underwent increased specialization; craftsmen experienced a general rise in social status during the high MA (1150–1350). The organization of the building trades that emerges in the records of the 12th century reveals a hierarchical structure, from masters, foremen, *journeymen, and so forth, down to the lowest common labourers; often, additional work was farmed out as task work. While it is difficult to generalize from varied accounts, most major building projects had a bureaucratic overseer, generally a cleric of the patron's household. Master *masons and carpenters combined the modern professions of civil *engineers, designers, and architects. They were trained in a craft tradition that included the practical arts of geometry and was identified by their characteristic *tools: the set square, dividers, compass, and measuring rod. Most importantly, the approach to building was experiential rather than theoretical. Medieval master builders were hands-on craftsmen, active at the construction site. Both masons and carpenters were often purveyors of materials, and owned *quarries or had privileged access to *forest and woodland resources.

3. *Materials and transport*

Building with local materials is traditionally one of the major criteria used to distinguish 'vernacular' from 'elite' architecture; the latter might require importing foreign expertise and high-quality materials. For certain materials, modes of transport had a profound influence on the organization of construction. The capacity of all conveyances, whether horse-drawn carts, boats, barges, or sailing *ships, determined the ultimate weight and size of structural components. For example, the prefabricated frame for Hugh *Herland's vast timber *roof for *Westminster Hall, London (*c.*1395–6), had no timber that exceeded 8.7 m in length and 1 m in breadth, but its transport required 2 carts drawn by 16 horses in 52 journeys, in addition to 263 separate cartloads of unspecified timber.

Given the physical limitations of pre-industrial conveyance, builders and their patrons supported extensive prefabrication linked to localized centres of manufacture (for example, lime kilns or ovens for *mortar, *brick, *ceramic tile, and *glass production). The primary structural materials, stone or timber, were routinely cut to size at the quarry or felling site before transport. While the economy of time and labour for this ancient practice is evident, the implications for the evolution of systematic construction are profound. For example, the large-scale extraction and cutting of stone, or the felling and converting of trees to specified dimensions, is predicated on a carefully worked-out design and a system for identifying the structural members. In addition to transport, the size and weight of individual components is correlated to the overall scale of the building and the master builder's understanding of the structural behaviour of a given material.

4. *Northern Europe: revival and expansion*

During the 12th and 13th centuries the building industry in northern Europe expanded the rate of production and especially the scale of construction. Technological advances in water and wind power, geared wheels, and steel-edged tools no doubt increased production, stimulated also by widespread economic growth. Tangible evidence of this architectural revival (and its legacy) is abundant. In any number of regions, the general scale, technical complexity, and aesthetic qualities of existing buildings dating from the 13th to the 16th century contrasts markedly with earlier (generally much smaller) rudimentary structures of wood, sod, and dry stone rubble, such as the *corbelled beehive huts at the 8th-century *monastery of Skellig Michael (or Sceilg Mhichil, an island off the coast of County Kerry, Ireland).

Timber-framed, aisled construction combined with masonry foundations proved to be *the* multi-purpose medieval building type. It enjoyed enormous longevity, extending from the earliest utilitarian structures and halls known from archaeology to the late medieval market halls of continental Europe. Within the long development of the residential hall and chamber block, the change from aisled to un-aisled interiors during the mid 13th century constitutes a major social and structural design change. The construction process is essentially that of the earlier aisled hall, but subsequent carpentry developments solved the technical challenge of wider internal spans.

5. *Masonry*

The most suitable material for the construction of load-bearing walls, foundations, and abutment was stone. Apart from the thin-walled High Gothic architecture of the Île-de-France, the salient feature of much medieval construction is thick-walled masonry designed to function in compression and to support stone vaults, towers, roofs, and *domes. From the widest geographical and chronological perspective, stone rubble was the most common material. Rubble was important in both mortared and dry-wall techniques. It was used in walls, foundations, wall cores, and as an aggregate with brick and *cement in *vault construction in *Ravenna, the Veneto, and the Balkans.

In northern Europe, from *Scandinavia to *Poland, elite buildings generally employed squared and dressed stone called *ashlar masonry, generally of limestone, sandstone, tufa, and where necessary basalt and granite. Limestone, such as the much favoured and widely exported *Caen stone of *Normandy, was used throughout Europe. It was also burnt for the production of lime for mortar as was gypsum for *plaster. In Italy and the eastern Mediterranean, marble was used for revetments or for load-bearing columns or piers (for example, Torcello cathedral *c.*1008, and St Mark's, *Venice, 1063–95).

In parts of England, Italy, northern Germany, the eastern Mediterranean, and the Balkans, fired brick construction developed at an early date. Ashlar, conglomerate, cement, baked brick, and tile were also combined, for both structural and decorative purposes, as in the famous land walls of *Constantinople, later imitated at *Caernarfon Castle (1296) in Wales; in alternating patterns at *St Albans Abbey, England (1077–88), where Roman brick was reused; and in the early-14th-century church of the Holy Virgin Hodegetria, in *Serbia. In northern Europe, medieval brickwork developed especially in urban architecture in the *Low Countries and the *Hanseatic towns of north Germany, such as *Lübeck.

6. *Romanesque and Gothic*

While Romanesque buildings are generally characterized by solid, load-bearing walls, a technical innovation that reduced the wall mass of stone without compromising stability appeared in the 11th century in northern France. This is the so-called double wall or 'thick-wall' construction, in which the inner and outer planes of the wall rise to full height and whose solidity is relieved by openings in the upper portions of the building (especially the conspicuous vaulted clerestory passages and fenestration). This voided wall was typical of AN building from the 11th to the 14th centuries.

The static problem of equilibrium became more critical with the advent of the taller and more skeletal, northern Gothic, 'thin-wall' construction which allowed a vast increase in fenestration. Since medieval walls and the stone vaults they carried were designed to function in compression, stability depended on the thickness of the wall, proper abutment, and structural geometry that distributed the forces appropriately within the central part of the wall. Medieval masons and carpenters approached wall, vault, and roof stability in several ways: masons used a rule-of-thumb ratio between wall height and thickness; they avoided eccentric (unbalanced) loading and inserted bonding courses between the inner and outer wall planes. Occasionally, they used *iron reinforcement, as in the chains embedded in the wall of the *Ste-Chapelle in Paris (1248) or the 13th-century iron ties at Westminster Abbey, London. In the thin-wall system developed in French High Gothic cathedrals, ashlar walls were strengthened by periodic abutments (wall buttresses and later flying buttresses). At the same time, roof carpenters devised better ways to seat their timberwork, using triangulated forms as well as exploiting the tensile properties of wood to contain the outward thrust atop high parapet walls. In Italy and southern Europe, however, building traditions had evolved that did not require these northern solutions, since the construction often incorporated tie beams, or roofs resting on stone diaphragm *arches, as widely found in *Catalonia (compare Guilermo *Abiell). Thus interior buttressing systems and trussed roofs remained a viable alternative to stone vaults.

7. *Timber*

In contrast to stone, which is strong in compression but has virtually no tensile (extension) strength, wood has roughly equal tensile and compressive capacities. Timber was the only widely available material with these attributes until the mass production of iron in the 18th century. As in roof structures, timber was essential to any masonry enterprise, for machinery, scaffolding, and *centring (form work).

Medieval timber construction has two primary forms: the skeletal, load-bearing frame that supports some form of infill, such as plaster, *wattle-and-daub, and so forth; and structures with load-bearing walls entirely of wood. Both forms coexisted from an early period and are geographically widely distributed. The skeletal type of construction, called 'timber framing', consists of an assembly of vertical posts, horizontal beams, and diagonal braces, creating a rectangular unit or box-frame. These box-frames correspond to the structural *bays that give linear articulation to the interior and exterior façades. This type of post-and-beam assembly dominated carpentry across Europe, and is distinguished from *cruck framing, whose heavy curved timbers form an A-frame. From the 13th to the 16th century these structures developed a number of regional variations and hybrids, whose evolution is complex and debated.

The second type of construction in wood has two variants: horizontal load-bearing walls ('log cabins'), found in

Scandinavia and eastern Europe, and vertical timbers, as in palisade walls. The most important manifestations of vertical walling are the Saxon church at Greensted, Essex, England (dendrochronological date: late 11th century) and the stave churches (*stavkirke) of Norway (mostly after 1200). In the stave churches, the larger corner and intermediate posts, along with interior arcade posts, act as a structural frame. Thus their builders, unlike those who used horizontal log construction, combined load-bearing frames with wooden palisade walls.

Along with masonry vaults, spires, and domes, timber roofs (with ceilings or open) constitute a major field of medieval engineering and experimentation. The purpose of the roof frame was to support the outer covering and to complete the building's external silhouette. Slate, lead, and stone or glazed tiles were common for elite architecture, in contrast to thatch, turf, stone, and wooden shingles for lower-status buildings.

Roofs fall into two distinct categories: open roofs that are meant to be seen and have an aesthetic role, and roofs above vaults, domes, and ceilings, where the structural carpentry remains unseen. For pitched roofs, the most important structural form is the triangulated truss, forming a rigid triangle with a tension tie that keeps the inclined rafters from spreading at their base.

8. *Metals*

Metals (chiefly iron, lead, and the low-carbon steel used for tools) were critical materials in medieval buildings made of wood, stone, or brick. The smith and plumber were skilled craftsmen, who contributed significantly (more than assumed) to fabricating *windows, door fittings, hinges, guttering, chimneys (*see* HEATING AND LIGHTING), and hearths. Metal clamps, tie-rods, chains, and iron bars called *dogges* were also used to reinforce masonry. Although wrought-iron ties were costly and difficult to produce, they were significant to reinforcement in pre-modern construction, especially in Italy and in tension members such as the tie-rods at Soissons cathedral (*c.*1170) or the 14th-century central hanger and trussing in the tower and spire of *Salisbury cathedral.

While iron was rarely used in timber assembly (jointing), iron nails and spikes, often of considerable size, figure conspicuously in building accounts such as those for *Henry III of England. In elite buildings, lead was used ubiquitously in northern Europe as a roofing material and to sheathe spires and belfries.

9. *Tools and machinery*

Tools for quarrying and working stone differed little from the ancient to the medieval period. Forged iron was the primary material used for spades, wedges, crowbars ('crowes'), hooks, chains, mallets, gavelocks (for splitting stone), and cutting saws. For dressing stone, a variety of bores (augers and gimlets), axes, hatchets, hammers, and chisels with iron blades or points (edged with steel) and handles of ash enabled masons to cut, plane, or strike the stone as required. Instruments such as rules, plumb bobs, squares, and dividers were used by several *crafts.

Construction machinery, or 'engines', consisted mainly of lifting devices: wooden cranes, pulleys, lewises, treadmills, and cogged wheels usually fashioned of oak, elm, or ash. Since medieval construction depended directly on human strength, machines had to be scaled to human proportions, as for example the simple *wheelbarrow, which appeared in the 13th century. Conveyances for materials, wheelbarrows, scaffolding, work platforms, ropes, and ladders appear in numerous contemporary *manuscript illuminations, as do the more complex operations of sawing or lifting heavy items using geared wheels to mechanically increase power through the difference in diameter between a larger (vertical) wheel (as in treadmills) and the smaller drum that winds a lifting rope. *See also* ART AND ARCHITECTURE: ANGLO-NORMAN / CAROLINGIAN / GOTHIC / ROMANESQUE; CHURCH, COLLEGIATE; HOUSING AND BUILDING TRADES. LTC

J. Blair and N. Ramsey, eds, *English Medieval Industries* (1991).
J. Bony, *French Gothic Architecture of the 12th and 13th Centuries* (1983).
H. M. Colvin, ed., *The History of the King's Works* (1963), vols 1 and 2.
S. Ćurčić, *Art and Architecture in the Balkans* (1984).
N. Davey, *A History of Building Materials* (1961).
A. Ferdiere, ed., *La Construction en pierre* (1999).
J. Fitchen, *The Construction of Gothic Cathedrals: A Study of Medieval Vault Erection* (1961).
F. Henry, 'Early Monasteries, Beehive Huts, and Dry-stone Houses in the Neighbourhood of Cahirciveen and Waterville (Co. Kerry)', *Proceedings of the Royal Irish Academy*, 58 (1957), 45–166.
R. J. Mainstone, *Developments in Structural Form* (1983).
R. Mark, ed., *Architectural Technology up to the Scientific Revolution* (1993).
K. Mijatev, *Die mittelalterliche Baukunst in Bulgarien*, tr. M. Matliev (1974).
R. Recht *et al.*, *Les Bâtisseurs des cathédrales gothiques* (1989).
L. F. Salzman, *Building in England down to 1540* (1952; repr. 1992).

Bukerel family *London family of merchants and moneyers, *c.*1100–*c.*1270. The name seems identical with the unexplained *Devon place name Buckerell. Members included six *sheriffs, four *aldermen, and a mayor, Andrew Bukerel (1231–7). Their principal city residence was called Bucklersbury, a name transferred to the adjacent street. *See also* MONEYLENDING, CREDIT, AND USURY. DKe

W. Page, *London: Its Origin and Early Development* (1923).
S. Reynolds, 'The Rulers of London in the Twelfth Century', *History*, 57 (1972), 337–57.

Bulgaria The first contacts of Danubian Bulgaria (founded *c.*681) with the European west date back to the first half of the 9th century. There was a stable alliance between Bulgaria and the Eastern Frankish kingdom, directed against *Great Moravia and *Byzantium. The conversion of the Bulgarians (*c.*864) contributed to the confrontation between the *papacy and Byzantium and helped reconfigure Europe. Though the ruler of Bulgaria, Boris-Michael I (852–89), opted for the Byzantine Orthodox form of Christianity, his successors maintained further contacts with the Holy See and the German Empire up to the Byzantine conquest in 1018.

The second Bulgarian state (1185–1396) continued its relations to the papacy and even concluded an ecclesiastical union with Rome (1204–35). It had to deal also with the Latin empire of *Constantinople (1204–61) and the growing power of Catholic *Hungary in the northwest Balkans. At the same time, Bulgaria established intensive commercial and political contacts with the maritime republics of Ragusa (Dubrovnik), *Venice, and *Genoa. The Ottoman conquest in the second half of the 14th century profoundly altered the situation in southeastern Europe, and almost interrupted Bulgarian contact with western Europe for about 400 years. ANN

R. Browning, 'Bulgaria', *ODB*, vol. 1, 332–4.
V. Gjuzelev, 'La Bulgarie, Venise et l'Empire Latin de Constantinople au milieu du XIIIe siècle', *Bulgarian Historical Review*, 3 (1975), 38–49.
S. Runciman, *A History of the First Bulgarian Empire* (1930).

bull, papal A solemn, open papal *letter, so called from the lead *seal (*bulla*), appended since the 6th century to such a letter by a cord of *hemp or *silk. The seal was stamped with the reigning pope's name and number on one side and the heads of Sts Peter and Paul on the other. DHW

NCE ([2]2003), vol. 2, 687.

bullion and bullion famine Gold and silver served as the basis of coinage while continuing to be used for utilitarian and decorative objects; silver was frequently alloyed with copper to produce low-value 'billon' coins. The relative value of the metals varied with their availability, but gold was usually worth 10 to 14 times as much as silver, silver about 100 times the same weight of copper.

In the early MA, bullion in Europe comprised mainly existing stocks from earlier periods, together with some silver sources such as that from *mines in Melle (*Poitou) in *Carolingian times. In the central MA, new sources of silver were exploited in the Harz Mountains of *Saxony (10th–11th centuries), *Freiberg, Friesach, and *Bohemia in central Europe, and Iglesias in *Sardinia (12th–13th centuries). Before the discovery (*c.*1325) of gold at Kremnica (Slovakia), within the kingdom of *Hungary, most European gold was derived from old stocks, from imported coins, or from gold dust brought from sub-Saharan Africa.

From *mint records and other sources it appears that in the later MA Europe suffered a shortage of gold and, especially, silver, which contributed to the decline of minting, the debasement of silver coinages, and the development of systems of credit and *banking. This situation was not fully alleviated until the arrival of new stocks of both metals from the New World, supplemented by further finds and exploitation of Bohemian silver deposits. *See also* GOLD AND SILVER; MONEY AND COINAGE. AMSt

P. Spufford, *Money and its Use in Medieval Europe* (1988).

Burchard of Ursberg (*c.*1177–*c.*1231) Ordained in 1202, in 1205 he joined the *Premonstratensians; in 1215 he became prior of Ursberg. Burchard was one of several authors who composed parts of a world chronicle (*Chronicon Urspergense*) between 1229 and 1230. While he copied from older chronicles, he relied on his own experiences for the years since 1190, being pro-Hohenstaufen and anti-papal. *See also* ROMAN EMPIRE [HOHENSTAUFEN DYNASTY]. AC

N. Backmund, *Die mittelalterlichen Geschichtsschreiber des Prämonstratenserordens* (1972), 8–33.
O. Holder-Egger and B. von Simson, eds, *Die Chronik des Propstes Burchard von Ursberg, MGH.SRG* ([2]1916).
W. Wulz, *Der spätstaufische Geschichtsschreiber Burchard von Ursberg* (1982).

Burchard of Worms (*c.*965–1025) Elected bishop of *Worms in 1000, Burchard compiled an influential, systematic canon *law collection addressing the issues of *penance, church discipline, and ecclesiology at the local *diocesan level. PSH

P. Fournier and G. le Bras, *Histoire des collections canoniques en occident depuis les Fausses Décrétales jusqu'au Décret de Gratien* (1931), vol. 1, 364–421.

burgage tenure The form of *land tenure in most English *towns or boroughs, notable for money rents (rather than services) and for its lack of restrictions on property transfers. Practice varied, but customs in major towns, especially *London, were often followed elsewhere. *See also* FIEF AND MONEY FIEF; NON-PRIVILEGE TOWNS. DKe

S. Reynolds, *Introduction to the History of English Medieval Towns* (1977).
J. Tait, *The English Medieval Borough* (1936).

Burggraf von Regensburg (d. *c.*1185) MHG *courtly love poet, associated with the counts of *Regensburg. He composed four stanzas (three in a woman's voice) using two different melodies; in one of the stanzas, contrary to courtly formulas, the woman serves the man. The male voice complains about courtly spies. *See also* MINNELIEDER. AC

J. Janota, 'Zum Burggrafen von Regensburg', in *Entstehung und Typen mittelalterlicher Lyrikhandschriften*, ed. A. Schwob (2001), 131–42.
O. Sayce, *The Medieval German Lyric, 1150–1300* (1982).

Burgh, Hubert de (d. 1243) A member of Prince John's *royal household, he became chamberlain in 1199 and served the king in various capacities. By 1215 he was justiciar, an office he continued to perform under *Henry III. In 1227 he was made *earl of *Kent and while in royal service accumulated great landholdings, but he fell from favour in 1232, was dismissed, and lost some of his lands. Subsequent specialization in royal *administration ended the kind of centralized authority de Burgh had held. RSO

C. Ellis, *Hubert de Burgh: A Study in Constancy* (1952).

Burghal Hidage A document (composed 884×914) cataloguing the defensive fortification network of *Wessex. It explicitly links land volume with defensive responsibility, demonstrating the growth of royal *administration. *See also* ALFRED THE GREAT; CASTLES, FORTIFICATIONS, AND FORTRESSES; WEIGHTS AND MEASURES. HCZ

D. Hill, 'The Burghal Hidage', *Medieval Archaeology*, 13 (1969), 84–92.

A. Rumble and D. Hill, eds, *The Defence of Wessex: The Burghal Hidage and Anglo-Saxon Fortifications* (1996).

Burgos Located on the banks of the Arlanzón river (*Castile), the city began as a military outpost in the 880s. Strategically placed, its *castle kept a watch for Muslim raids. By 1075, the translation of the bishopric of Oca to Burgos brought also a burgeoning ecclesiastical life. In 1080 the Council of Burgos led to the demise of the *Mozarabic *liturgy and its replacement by the Roman rite. By the 1150s, Burgos had grown into the leading Castilian economic centre. With the success of the *pilgrimage to *Santiago de Compostela, the city also became the most important stage along the pilgrimage road. Numerous foreign merchants settled there, a distribution hub for long-distance *trade.

By the 1250s, a mercantile and artisanal oligarchy dominated Burgos's civic and economic life. Under royal jurisdiction, Burgos played a major role as the site for the chancellery, as the first city to speak at the meetings of the *cortes*, and as a royal residence. Burgos's *militias also provided important support for the crown in its wars against the Muslims and against unruly *nobles. The kings rewarded the city and its ruling elite with numerous privileges, confirming Burgos's mercantile pre-eminence and the social and political standing of its *patriciate. So did the building of the *Cistercian monastery of Las Huelgas—which served as a royal residence and pantheon—and of a new Gothic *cathedral between 1170 and 1230.

With around 8,000 inhabitants *c.*1300 and a substantial Jewish (and a small *mudéjar*) population, Burgos began to wane in importance by the late 1300s. The conquest of *al-Andalus, above all that of *Seville, and the royal preference for Valladolid as the place for business meant a diminution of Burgos's role within the realm. In another blow, the 1391 pogroms led to the forced conversion or death of all of the city's Jews. Yet 15th-century Burgos still maintained an impressive mercantile connection with *Flanders, before its economic and demographic collapse in the 1550s. *See also* JEWS IN THE IBERIAN PENINSULA. TFR

C. Estepa *et al.*, *Burgos en la Edad Media* (1984).

T. Ruiz, *The City and the Realm: Burgos and Castile, 1080–1492* (1992).

Burgred of Mercia *See* MERCIA.

Burgundian Netherlands In 1369 *Louis of Male, count of *Flanders, married his only heir, *Margaret of Male, to Philip the Bold, duke of *Burgundy and son of John II, king of *France. In 1384 Philip the Bold succeeded as count of Flanders (1384–1404). Burgundy and Flanders were thus joined in a personal union. Philip soon developed supervision over the neighbouring territories in the Netherlands. In *Brabant he promoted his brother *Anthony as

Portrait of Charles the Bold, last duke of Burgundy (oil on panel), by Rogier van der Weyden. Gemäldegalerien of the Staatliche Museen, Berlin.

Burgos cathedral.

Portrait of John the Fearless (1371–1419), duke of Burgundy. Royal Museum of Fine Arts, Antwerp.

a potential heir from 1387, and in 1404 Anthony succeeded as duke. Philip realized several strategic matrimonial alliances. In 1385 his daughter Catherine married the son of the *Habsburg duke of Austria, and, in the double marriage of Cambrai, his eldest son John and his daughter Margaret both married within the *Wittelsbach dynasty of *Holland and *Hainaut. It remains difficult to tell if these alliances witnessed to a conscious intent by Philip to build a large new territorial complex, competing with the major European states; but later they may indeed be interpreted as first steps to the formation of a Burgundian state. Other symptoms of this ambition were the creation of central chambers of account and a central court, and the function of prime minister ('chancellor') with competence in all territories. Philip's military expedition against the Turks (1396) ended with a defeat in the battle of Nicopolis and the imprisonment of his son John. In the French–English conflict Philip needed diplomacy to maintain a delicate neutrality. Independently of the political position he concluded a commercial treaty with England (1396), crucial for Flemish industry and trade. Simultaneously he remained a loyal French prince, which allowed him to remain a member of the Regents' Council during the minority (1380–88) and illness (1392–1404) of the French king.

After Philip's death his widow, Margaret of Male, succeeded as countess of Flanders (1404–5), and his son John the Fearless as duke of Burgundy (1404–19) and in 1405 as count of Flanders. John's reign could not maintain the balance between loyalty to the crown of France and the priorities of the Burgundian dynasty. John ordered the murder of his main rival in the Regents' Council, Louis of Orléans (1407), which caused a civil war among the competing parties within France: the party of the French dauphin, the Burgundian faction ('Bourguignons'), the Cabochiens, and the Armagnac faction around the widow of Orléans and her son Charles. The conflict led to a total collapse of royal authority. This erasure of France's impact on the European scene opened perspectives for the international ambitions of the Burgundian duke. In France he dominated the political scene from 1408 to 1414. In the Netherlands John was confronted by fierce opposition from the cities in Flanders and *Liège. In 1407 he repressed the revolt of the citizens of *Bruges, but in 1410 he gave in and restored several privileges of the city. In 1408 he supported his nephew, John of Bavaria, prince-bishop of Liège, to end his conflict with the burghers of Liège in the battle of Othée. In 1414 a truce between *Armagnacs and Burgundians was concluded, but the conflict resumed. In 1418 John seized Paris in coalition with Queen Isabel, and took control of King *Charles VI and the royal treasury. In 1419 John the Fearless was murdered by an Armagnac commando on the bridge of Montereau, near Paris, where he intended to start negotiations with the dauphin.

Frustrated by the murder of his father, and encouraged by the Flemish cities, Philip the Good (1419–67) began his reign with the conclusion of the Treaty of *Troyes (1420), a significant move to an alliance with England and against France. In contrast with his predecessors, the disenchanted Philip seemed no longer interested in the traditional involvement in French domestic politics. More than his father and grandfather, he concentrated in the first years on state-building in his own territories, and increased central authority considerably. He consolidated his position as prime leader within the Low Countries, organizing political networks that furthered cohesion within the Burgundian state. In 1428–33 he prepared for the annexation of Holland, Zeeland, and Hainaut by progressively eliminating the power of Countess Jacqueline of Bavaria. In 1420–29 Philip purchased the strategically important county of *Namur. When John IV of Brabant, son and successor of the Burgundian duke Anthony, died in 1430, Philip diplomatically convinced the Estates of Brabant to accept him as their duke. The 1430s were decisive years, and showed the transition to nonaligned

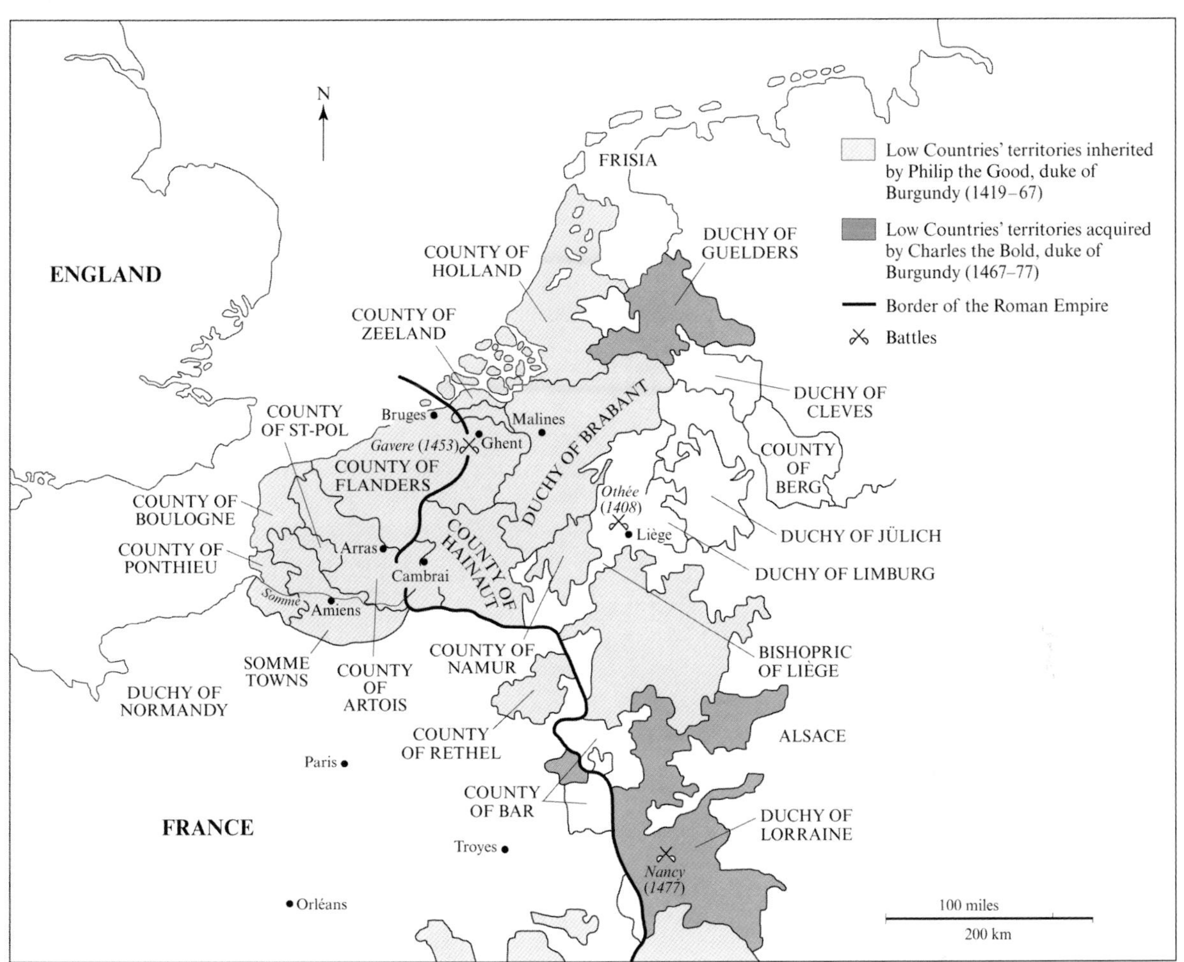

Burgundian Netherlands, 15th century.

international status and to Philip's increasing international prestige. A first sign, in 1430, was that he married not a French princess but the daughter of the king of Portugal, Isabella. The same year Philip founded the Order of the Golden Fleece, the perfect instrument to bind talented elites to the Burgundian dynasty. Philip's neutrality policy with respect to France and England reinforced the position of Burgundy as a great European power. This new status explains how Philip played a decisive role at the Council of *Basel (1431–4). In 1434 the German emperor Sigismund, aware of Burgundian territorial designs in Lorraine, formed an alliance with King *Charles VII of France, but Philip avoided this Franco-German encirclement by offering his own alliance to the king. This was a first step towards the exchange of the English–Burgundian coalition for a new pragmatic deal with France in the Treaty of *Arras (1435). The underlying economic argument for the shift was the growing import in Flanders of wool from Castile, making the Flemish textile industry less dependent on English raw materials. It was also an answer to what was considered aggressive dumping of English cloth on European markets. In the 1430s Philip the Good had to cope with serious domestic unrest, most strongly from Holland and Zeeland. In Flanders the urban uprisings (1430–38) had a clear social background, but were also directed against centralization. The last rebel, *Ghent, was defeated at the battle of Gavere (1453), followed by severe repression. Generally, however, Philip was convinced by his councillors that peace among the great European powers was the ultimate guarantee for economic growth in the Burgundian Netherlands, rightfully called 'Promised Lands' by contemporaries. The volume of trade doubled between 1400 and 1475.

Charles the Bold's (1467–77) third marriage with Margaret of York, sister of King *Edward IV, led to a new alliance with England. Charles demonstrated his independence towards France by creating a Burgundian High Court, the parlement of *Mechelen, replacing the royal parlement of *Paris. On the international scene Charles moved largely from the

Duke Philip the Good in session with his Great Council.

peace stance of his father to a war strategy, with a standing army and new taxation methods. Negotiations with the German emperor in 1473 for elevation to royal status did not reach a favourable conclusion. Though he realized the annexation of Guelders, his dream of the territorial cohesion of the northern and southern parts of the Burgundian state via a military conquest of Alsace and Lorraine failed. In this operation the duke died on the battlefield of Nancy in 1477.

Charles left as his only heir a politically inexperienced daughter aged 20, Mary of Burgundy. Threats to the dynasty came from without and within. The General Estates of the Burgundian Netherlands, though loyal to the duchess, used her weakness to restore several urban privileges, previously lost during the revolts against the dukes. Greater danger came from France, which took advantage of the situation by bringing the duchy of Burgundy back under the authority of the king (1477), and was suspected of more annexation plans. The answer was the marriage of Mary (1477) with Maximilian of Austria, the son of the German emperor. In 1482 Mary died in a hunting party, and her widower became regent for the entire minority of their son Philip. Maximilian could not prevent the loss of Franche-Comté and *Artois to France in 1482, in spite of numerous military expeditions against France that necessitated heavy taxes. This financial burden and the curtailment of urban autonomy caused endless domestic revolts, including a long imprisonment of Maximilian in Bruges (1488). Not before 1492 could his authority be restored.

Maximilian's son Philip the Fair (1494–1506) was better received, being accepted, unlike his father, as an indigenous ruler. His peaceful attitude towards France brought political goodwill amongst his subjects in the Low Countries. He also charmed them by favouring economic connections with England, crowned by the 'Intercursus magnus', a free-trade agreement, in 1496. At his death, in 1506, his young son *Charles V succeeded. In the following decades the Burgundian Netherlands moved in the power orbit of the Habsburg Empire. WP

W. Blockmans and W. Prevenier, *The Promised Lands: The Low Countries under Burgundian Rule, 1369–1530* (1999).

W. Prevenier and W. Blockmans, *The Burgundian Netherlands* (1986).

R. Vaughan, *Philip the Good* (1970).

—— *Charles the Bold* (1973).

—— *John the Fearless* (1979).

—— *Philip the Bold* (1979).

Burgundio of Pisa (*c.*1110–93) Emissary and judge whose influential translations of theology (*John of Damascus, John *Chrysostom), *medicine (*Galen), natural *philosophy (Aristotle), and law (Greek passages in Justinian's **Digest*) testify to the diplomatic and intellectual links between *Italy and *Byzantium. MR

P. Classen, *Burgundio von Pisa: Richter, Gesandter, Übersetzer* (1974).
G. Vuillemin-Diem and M. Rashad, 'Burgundio de Pise et ses manuscrits grecs d'Aristote: Laur. 87.7 et Laur. 81.18', *Recherches de théologie et philosophie médiévales*, 64 (1997), 136–98.

Burgundy (county) The county of Burgundy encompassed the area in eastern France known from the 12th century on as Franche-Comté, or 'free country'. Located between the kingdom of *France and the *Roman Empire and possessing thriving *salt mines, it was often fought over.

The county of Burgundy was not a separate entity until 986, being preceded by the 5th-century Alamanni, the 6th-century kingdoms of Burgundy and the Franks (part of the Merovingian and *Carolingian territories), and a refounded kingdom of *Burgundy in 888. Otto-William (962–1026) became its first count. His son Renaud I (986–1057) was named count palatine in 1037 by Conrad II (990–1039). The county remained a *fiefdom of the empire until 1127 when Count Renaud III (1093–1148) was victorious in battle and named the region *Franc Comte*.

Three decades later, Frederick I 'Barbarossa' again took control, first by military force and then by marriage to the count's daughter, Beatrice of Burgundy (r. 1148–84). Their son, Otto I (*c.*1167–1200), inherited the county, succeeded by his daughters, Jeanne (1191–1205) and Beatrice (1191–1231), and granddaughter, Adelaide of Burgundy (r. 1248–79). The next three generations of marriage, Otto IV (1248–1302) to Mahaut, countess of *Artois (1268–1329), Jeanne II (1291–1330) to Philip V of France (1293–1322), and Jeanne III (1308–49) to Eudes IV, *duke of Burgundy (1295–1350), saw the unification of the county first with France and then with the duchy, beginning the century and a half of Burgundian rule in Europe. *See also* PALATINATE. TCH

J. F. Benton, 'A.-A. Monteil et les comptes de Franche-Comté', *MA*, ser. 4, 74/3, 4 (1968), 495–506.
E. L. Cox, 'Burgundy, county of', *DMA*, vol. 2, 424–6.

Burgundy (duchy) The *Ducatus Burgundiae* is first mentioned in 1075, though the title *dux* was ascribed (918–20) to Richard 'the Justicer', count of *Autun (d. 921), and his sons Rudolph (d. 936) and Hugh the Black (d. 952). In the mid 10th century Hugh the Great (d. 956) seized the ducal title for the Robertiens. From Robert (d. 1076) to Philip I of Rouvres (d. 1361), the duchy of Burgundy was ruled by a junior branch of the *Capetians. It then reverted to King John II (d. 1364), who left the duchy to his fourth son, Philip 'the Bold' (d. 1404). Followed by John 'the Fearless' (d. 1419), Philip 'the Good' (d. 1467), and Charles I 'the Bold' (d. 1477), the *Valois princes ruled until the death of the last-named, when the duchy's states devolved to Louis XI of France.

The boundaries of the duchy of Burgundy shifted throughout the MA. The *Regnum Burgundiae* included *Mâcon, Chalon, Autun, Nevers, *Auxerre, *Sens, *Troyes, and *Langres, but the dukes' power over these territories was not stable. During the 12th century, the Capetian dukes consolidated their authority over *Dijon, Beaune, Autun, Avallon, Semur-en-Auxois, and Châtillon-sur-Seine. Their estates were further enlarged during the 13th and 14th centuries, mainly with Chalon (1237), the union with the county of Burgundy (1318), and alliance with the counts of *Flanders (1369). EMSC

M. Chaume, *Les Origines du duché de Bourgogne*, 4 vols (1925–37; repr. 1977).
J. Richard, *Les Ducs de Bourgogne et la formation du duché du XIe au XIVe siècle* (1954; repr. 1986).
R. Vaughan, *Valois Burgundy* (1975).

Burgundy (kingdom) Three different kingdoms of Burgundy were created and then absorbed by neighbouring kingdoms between late antiquity and the 11th century. All occupied portions of the region between present-day France and Germany, including the Jura Mountains and the *Alps, but did not completely overlap. Although the regional name was reused, there was essentially no political connection among the three.

The first kingdom of the Burgundians, centred between *Besançon and *Geneva, was one of several so-called 'barbarian' kingdoms established in Roman Gaul in the 5th century. This kingdom was conquered in the first half of the 6th century by the Merovingian kings of the Franks. In subsequent generations, Burgundy was one of the major divisions of Frankish lands (along with Neustria and *Austrasia). At its greatest extent, Merovingian Burgundy stretched from *Orléans to the Mediterranean.

When the *Carolingian dynasty replaced the Merovingians in the 8th century, Burgundy continued as a realm within the Frankish kingdom. Although much of Burgundy was culturally French, the region was divided along the Saône–Rhône basin by *Charlemagne's grandsons in the 9th century. The duchy of Burgundy, to the west, went to the French kingdom, while the kingdom of Burgundy, to the east, went to the *Roman Empire. In this period the kingdom was sometimes divided between Upper Burgundy, the northerly region that corresponded roughly to the 5th-century kingdom, and Lower Burgundy, stretching from *Lyons and *Vienne to *Arles.

An independent kingdom of Burgundy was revived in 879 under Boso, a counsellor and brother-in-law of *Charles II 'the Bald' of France. Boso sought to have himself *elected king of France after Charles's death and, although unsuccessful, he was elected king of Burgundy by the regional bishops. His kingdom—Lower Burgundy, also sometimes called *Provence or the kingdom of Arles—stretched from his capital at Vienne to the Mediterranean. Boso survived only eight years as king, but after his death, his son Louis managed to gain the support of the Carolingian king *Charles III 'the Fat' and take over his father's kingdom. But when Louis decided to conquer *Italy as well and to have himself crowned Roman emperor, his luck turned, and he was blinded by Berengar, king of Italy. He lived out his life in Burgundy / Provence in obscurity, and after his death his kingdom was absorbed into the empire.

Meanwhile, a separate kingdom of Burgundy (or Upper Burgundy) was created to the north of Boso's kingdom in 888, a year after his death. This kingdom was ruled by the Welf (*Guelph) dynasty for four generations. When the last king died in 1032, their kingdom was officially made part of the empire. In practice, however, it remained an independent county until Frederick I 'Barbarossa' took it over by marrying the heiress in the middle of the 12th century. *See also* THIERRY (THEUDERIC) III. CBB

C. B. Bouchard, *'Those of My Blood': Constructing Noble Families in Medieval Francia* (2001).

P. Fouracre, 'Francia in the Seventh Century', *NCMH*, vol. 1: *c.500–c.700*, ed. idem (2005), 371–96.

R. Poupardin, *Le Royaume de Bourgogne (888–1038): Étude sur les origines du royaume d'Arles* (1907).

R. Van Dam, 'Merovingian Gaul and the Frankish Conquests', *NCMH*, ed. P. Fouracre (2005), vol. 1, 193–231.

I. Wood, *The Merovingian Kingdoms, 450–751* (1994).

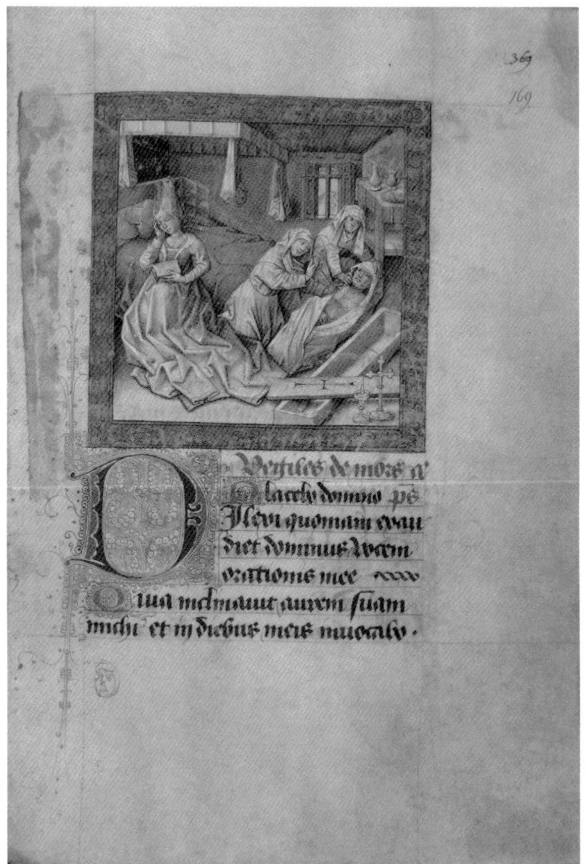

Body being prepared for burial.

burial customs and medieval cemeteries (500–1500)

The burial customs during the medieval period across Europe were, in broad terms, remarkably uniform, within and between the Christian, Muslim, and Jewish religions, although the details of practice varied widely. Christian burials followed no firm scriptural guidelines, and there is evidence that the early church was not concerned with burial rites until the 7th or 8th century. Jewish practice has, in many instances, kept to tradition and remained relatively unchanged. Early Islamic scholars produced codes of funerary law, dealing with far more than the handling of a Muslim corpse. The three major European and Middle Eastern religions—Christian, Muslim, and Jewish—have enough similarities to discuss them together. Pagan burial practices varied so widely that they are discussed separately at the end.

1. Burial customs
2. Cemeteries and graves
3. Pagan burials

1. *Burial customs*

In Muslim practice burial was expected on the same day as *death, and in Jewish practice a prompt burial was required. No particular time period was prescribed by Christianity, though local custom generally resulted in burial within three days. Each religion also had a defined funeral service for the body and soul of the deceased, the form of which developed over the centuries.

The preparation of the body for burial was reasonably consistent across religions with the body first being laid out, stripped, and washed. For Jews the deceased body was ritually unclean, and in Jewish cemeteries there was a building, a *beyt-tahara*, for the ritual preparation of corpses. In Muslim societies there was a room in the *mosque for washing bodies; strict rules determined who could perform this task (women could only wash a female body, men a man's body). In western European Christian tradition, the washing of the body was generally done by women, and the body could be prepared in any location, though usually in the home.

Throughout the MA there were two options for disposal: cremation or inhumation. The overwhelming majority of people across Europe and the Middle East were buried. All three religions allowed burial either directly into the earth or within a coffin, though Muslim coffin burials required some earth be put into it. Within Christian and Jewish practice there was one basic grave type—a rectangular hole in the ground. Christian graves were orientated east–west. Jewish graves were generally aligned the same way within an individual cemetery, though the alignment varied between cemeteries. There were two types of Muslim grave, the *lahd* and the *shaq*. The *lahd* grave was orientated north–south, with a crevice in the west side. The body was placed on its right-hand side facing *Mecca. Unburned bricks sealed the body, and the earth was back-filled. The *shaq* was a box-type grave with a plank placed on top, and the grave back-filled with earth. In Christian and Jewish burials the body is laid on its back, generally with the arms by the side or across the body. Cremation was banned by both Muslims and Jews, but Christian authorities used burning as a method of cleansing the souls of *heretics. The ashes might then be left or scattered.

2. *Cemeteries and graves*

The three religions had different attitudes to their cemeteries and the opening of old graves. The Christian cemetery normally surrounded a church or *chapel, and because of the theological belief that God will reconfigure the bodies at the Last Judgement, there was no spiritual problem when new graves replaced existing ones. Jewish cemeteries typically were walled *gardens away from settlements. Coffins were commonplace in Jewish cemeteries and were probably thought of as a way of containing the unclean body. The graves were kept distinctly separate, and no opening or disturbing them was permitted. If lack of space meant that graves had to be positioned on top of another, then the ground was built up to a depth of six hand-widths between graves. Disturbing graves was not permitted in Muslim cemeteries.

Grave goods in Christian, Muslim, or Jewish graves were rare. In all three religions the body was normally buried in a simple shroud or coffin. Occasionally, goods are found indicating the body was dressed for burial.

In all three religions the grave was marked, the most basic mark being the mound of the earth from digging the grave. In excavated medieval European Jewish cemeteries there are no indications of other grave markers, so presumably only the grave mound was used. In Christian and Muslim cemeteries graves could be marked with stones at the head of the grave, though on Muslim headstones writing was forbidden. Christian tradition also allowed above-ground tombs, which became more elaborate with time.

Medieval Jewish communities were actively encouraged to visit cemeteries, whereas Muslim texts are more circumspect. With Christian burials around and within churches, it was expected that people would visit and pray for the dead.

3. *Pagan burials*

In contrast to the major religions, *pagan burial practice was highly diverse. This variation has yet to be explained, but may be the result of an individual's devotion to a particular god or the practice of a wider social group.

In the early MA the pagan peoples who spread their belief systems across northern Europe were the *Anglo-Saxons from the *Baltic region, and then the *Vikings from *Scandinavia and Denmark. These peoples practised both inhumation and cremation. The northern areas of Europe were pagan for the greatest length of time, with the last great pagan state being the grand dukedom of *Lithuania, which was only converted to Christianity in the late 14th century. Pagan burial sites varied from small numbers of single mounds, called barrows, to mass cemeteries. One pagan burial practice of particular note was *ship burial, with the body being buried on dry land, or floated out to sea. Pagan graves could also range from containing simply a body to great treasure hoards, as discovered in 1939 at *Sutton Hoo in England. *See also* ABSOLUTIONS OF THE DEAD; ANOINTING OF THE DEAD; LIFE CYCLE, JEWISH RITES OF; OFFICE FOR THE DEAD; SARCOPHAGUS AND TOMB. CJD

S. Campbell and A. Green, eds, *The Archaeology of Death in the Ancient Near East* (1995).

M. Carver, *Sutton Hoo: The Burial Ground of Kings?* (1998).

C. Daniell, *Death and Burial in Medieval England, 1066–1550* (2001).

B. Effros, *Merovingian Mortuary Archaeology* (2003).

L. Halevi, *Muhammad's Grave: Death Rites and the Making of Islamic Society* (2007).

Buridan, John (Jean) (*c*.1295–1361) Career *arts *master and leading member of the *Picardy nation at the University of *Paris. Buridan was a brilliant logician and, thanks to his many students who spread his teachings and writings throughout *universities in Italy and central Europe, one of the most influential interpreters of Aristotle in the later MA. His logical masterwork, the *Summulae de Dialectica*, is a comprehensive textbook combining the traditional *logic of Aristotle with the newer, *nominalist methods focused on the semantics of terms and propositions. He brought the same innovative approach to the teaching of Aristotle, addressing various problems in Aristotle's *metaphysics and natural *philosophy through logical analysis. He popularized the theory of *impetus*, derived from *John Philoponus through the Arabic commentators—an account of projectile motion to replace the flawed Aristotelian theory of *antiperistasis*. His name is associated with 'Buridan's Ass', the parable of a donkey allegedly starving to death because it has no reason to choose between two equidistant and equally tempting piles of hay, though this illustration is not found in his writings. It is probably the work of later opponents, wishing to satirize Buridan's idea that freedom consists in the ability to defer choice. *See also* ARISTOTELIANISM; FREE WILL; MOTION. JAZ

J. Buridan, *Summulae de Dialectica*, tr. G. Klima (2001).
W. J. Courtenay, ed., 'John Buridan at the University of Paris', *Vivarium*, 42/1 (2004).
J. J. M. H. Thijssen and J. Zupko, eds, *The Metaphysics and Natural Philosophy of John Buridan* (2001).
J. Zupko, *John Buridan: Portrait of a 14th-Century Arts Master* (2003).

burin *See* ENGRAVING.

Burkhart von Hohenfels (*fl.* 1212–42) MHG poet. He composed eighteen songs, most of them *courtly love songs, as well as dance songs and *dialogues of young women (*Wechsel*), containing imagery of *hunting, *warfare, and nature. *See also* GOTTFRIED VON NEIFEN; MINNELIEDER; MINNESINGER. AC

T. Cramer, '"So sint doch gedanke fri"', in *Liebe als Literatur*, ed. R. Krohn (1983), 47–61.
H. Jaehrlink, *Die Gedichte Burkharts von Hohenfels* (1970).
M. Sydow, *Burkhart von Hohenfels und seine Lieder* (1901; repr. 1966).

Burley, Walter (*c*.1275–*c*.1345) English philosopher. He studied and taught logic at *Oxford, then theology at *Paris, engaging in debate with *William of Ockham. His commentaries on *Aristotle were widely admired well into the age of print. From 1327 on he was employed by *Edward III's government on diplomatic missions to the papal court at *Avignon. REB

Walter Burley, *On the Purity of the Art of Logic: The Shorter and Longer Treatises*, tr. and ed. P. V. Spade (2000).
J. Ottman and R. Wood, 'Walter Burley: His Life and Works', *Vivarium*, 37 (1999), 1–23.

burnt-clay castles *See* CASTLES, FORTIFICATIONS, AND FORTRESSES.

Bury St Edmunds (abbey) Founded in the early 7th century, the *monastery became in the 9th century the shrine of the king and saint *Edmund the Martyr. The abbey was a popular site of *pilgrimage and one of the most powerful monastic establishments in England. MS

A. Gransden, 'The Legends and Traditions Concerning the Origins of the Abbey of Bury St Edmunds', *EHR* 100 (1985), 1–24.

Busch, Jan (1399–1479/80) Born in Zwolle, died in *Hildesheim (the *Low Countries), the principal member of the *Brethren of the Common Life, and reformer of the Augustinian *canons whose home was established in *Windesheim near Zwolle. In his *Chronicon Windeshemense* he used for the first time the term **devotio moderna*. JK

F. W. Bautz, 'Busch, Johannes', *Biographisch-Bibliographisches Kirchenlexikon* (1990), vol. 1, 825–6.

buskins *See* LITURGICAL VESTMENTS.

Busnoys, Antoine (*c*.1430–92) French composer. Busnoys' *Mass setting based on the **homme armé* *cantus firmus was early and influential. His *chansons* and *motets show a mastery of abstract form and a keen sense of melodic energy and climax. RF

A. Busnoys, *Collected Works*, ed. R. Taruskin (1990).
P. Higgins, ed., *Antoine Busnoys: Method, Meaning, and Context in Late Medieval Music* (1999).

butter- and cheesemaking As *food, animal milk has two disadvantages: it spoils quickly and can easily be adulterated by an unscrupulous merchant. During the medieval period most milk was therefore used soon after being drawn from the cow, ewe, goat, or buffalo to make either cheese or, less commonly, butter. Because a significant portion of the liquid (buttermilk or whey), which contains bacteria, remained with the fat in the making of butter and cheese, spoilage in the long term was a hazard to both products. Adding *salt to the cheese curds or butter after churning was found to impede deterioration. When butter occasionally replaced pork fat and *olive oil as a frying medium by the 15th century, recipes direct that its excess salt be washed out first.

Butter was made in antiquity and throughout the MA. Essentially, it consists of the fat globules of milk, generally cow's milk because in it they are larger and can most easily be separated from the liquid. A slight warming of the milk in a pot, or simply letting it sit for a day or two, allowed the fat to rise and be skimmed off. Then it was beaten with a whisk in a bowl until butter formed; various wooden containers, cylindrical and square, were invented to churn larger quantities of butter. Only in the later MA was buttermaking anything but a domestic chore, assumed by women, for domestic consumption. In *Hildegard of Bingen and Anthimus (*De observatione ciborum*, 6th century) butter is mentioned solely as a medication.

Butter was most commonly known in northern Europe; between the 12th and 14th centuries Scandinavian countries traded butter and dried *fish for *wine. It was never much used in aristocratic kitchens—in part because animal grease and oil withstand higher frying temperatures. However, when variously coloured, sliced, or formed into small balls, larded with cloves, deep-fried until russet, and garnished with *sugar, butter was served on 14th- and 15th-century tables under some variant of the name *lait lardé* (see recipes in the *Viandier*, *Menagier de Paris*, and *Forme of Cury*).

Cheese afforded a more durable product from the milk fat of common domestic animals. In some form it had been known since pre-classical times. The initial step in making cheese was to warm whole milk slightly (to encourage bacteria to grow) and cause it to sour or curdle, generally by the admixture of rennet (the membrane of the stomach lining of a suckling calf), an acid (vinegar or citrus juice), or a vegetable extract (hyssop or cardoon). Then the clotted curds were squeezed in a cloth to remove as much whey as possible. The cheese was formed in a cloth or basket and set for whatever ageing was desired.

Cheeses were categorized as soft or hard, the former being fresh and probably without salt, the curd of the latter being salted, and ripened or aged, often with a protective covering of leaves or a coating of salt or oil in order to limit the penetration of unwanted bacteria. Given the risk of transporting milk any distance, cheeses were strictly local in their fabrication and qualities. As today, shapes, sizes, and added flavours further distinguished a large variety of regional cheeses.

In some places at some times Christian dietary restrictions occasionally forbade milk, butter, and cheese, particularly during *Lent. Their lean alternatives relied upon the oil of ground walnuts and especially ground almonds. Almond milk was in very common use in *cookery; a recipe for almond 'butter' appears in 1420. A pseudo-cheese could likewise be made from almond milk. *See also* ANIMAL HUSBANDRY; FRUITS AND NUTS; PHARMACY. TPS

I. Naso, *Formaggi nel medioevo: la 'Summa lacticiniorum' di Pantaleone da Confienza* (1990).

Buttington, battle of (893) Viewed as a key battle in AS history. After a long siege by Welsh and English forces led by *Alfred the Great, a *Viking (Danish) army broke out from their fortification, either at Buttington near Welshpool or (more probably) Buttington Tump near Chepstow. After fierce fighting, the surviving Vikings were forced to flee. *See also* ÆTHELWEARD; ENGLAND, ANGLO-SAXON. TE

A. Campbell, ed., *The Chronicle of Aethelweard* (1962).
M. Swanton, *The Anglo-Saxon Chronicle* (1996).

buttress *See* ARCHITECTS, ARCHITECTURE.

Buyids (Buwayhids) *Shia Muslim *emirs ruling Iraq and much of *Iran (945–1055). Three brothers founded the Buyid dynasty: Ali (Imad al-Dawla), in Fars; al-Hasan (Rukn al-Dawla), in Jibal; and Ahmad (Muizz al-Dawla), in Kirman and Khusistan. They came from Daylam, a northern Iranian region south of the Caspian known for powerful military men. In 945, Ahmad entered *Baghdad, overpowering the Abbasid *caliphate. Ahmad claimed to rule in the name of the caliph, continuing Abbasid traditions, but the emirate took over administrative functions and the Buyid military aristocracy allowed Shias to become a powerful force in the Islamic state.

Buyid emirs were ambitious builders, constructing palaces, *libraries, *hospitals, and other public buildings in cities such as Baghdad, *Shiraz, and *Isfahan. They also supported learning, including Arabic literature alongside a Persian literary revival. Though originally Zaydis (a moderate Shia group), the Buyids embraced 'twelver' Shiism (the largest Shia group, who believe in twelve divinely appointed *imams) and patronized its theologians.

By the early 11th century, the emirate was declining. This can be explained, in part, by an economic change: Indian Ocean commerce that had enriched Persian Gulf cities shifted to the Red Sea. By this time Buyid rulers had to contend with internal factionalism, the Fatimid *caliphate in *Egypt and Syria, and the *Ghaznavid dynasty in Afghanistan. The Buyid dynasty ended when the *Seljuks captured Baghdad in 1055. *See also* THEOLOGY, ISLAMIC. KL

C. Cahen, 'Buwayhids or Būyids', *EI* ([2]1960), vol. 1, 1350–57.
J. Donohue, *The Buwayhid Dynasty in Iraq* (2003).
J. Turner and R. Howes, 'Buyids', *MedIsl*, vol. 1, 124.

Byrhtferth of Ramsey (*c.*970–*c.*1020) Scholar, taught at *Ramsey by *Abbo of Fleury. Byrhtferth's scholarly output includes a *Computus*; a Latin and English *commentary thereon, entitled *Enchiridion*; a collection of materials to facilitate study of *Bede's scientific writings (*Glossae in Bedam*); Latin *biographies of Sts *Oswald of York and Ecgwine (Evesham's founder); and a historical compilation (based on Bede and *Asser) entitled *Historia regum*, treating the history of England from the 7th century until the death of *Alfred the Great. *See also* ENGLAND, ANGLO-SAXON. ML

Byrhtferth of Ramsey: Enchiridion, ed. P. S. Baker and M. Lapidge (1995).
Byrhtferth of Ramsey: The Lives of St Oswald and St Ecgwine, ed. M. Lapidge (2008).
M. Lapidge, *Anglo-Latin Literature, 900–1066* (1993), 293–417.

Byrhtnoth (d. 991) Thegn of *Æthelred II and hero and leader of the *AS forces in a battle against *Viking invaders at *Maldon. He was killed there and is commemorated in an OE poem named after the battle. REB

M. Locherbie-Cameron, 'Byrhtnoth and his Family', in *The Battle of Maldon, AD 911*, ed. D. Scragg (1991), 253–62.

Byzantine chant Liturgical music of the eastern Christian *Roman Empire. Liturgical languages included Greek, Syriac, *Coptic, *Old Church Slavonic, Armenian, and Georgian. The chants were composed through a process of 'centonization' (*see* PLAINSONG) and were usually notated monophonically, but not always performed as such because of the improvised *isokratema* (a continuous 'horizontal' tonal) accompaniment. The chants were stylized into practices: the *monastic and the *cathedral ('chanted') rites. The exceptional quantity of chants is diverse, and includes recitation tones, *psalms, *hymns (*troparion*, *kanon, **kontakion*), *prokeimena*, alleluia, *koinonika*, *cheroubika*, and *stichera*. *See also* LITURGY; MASS. DTM

D. E. Conomos, 'Chant', *ODB*, vol. 1, 409.

A. Lingas, *Introduction to Byzantine Chant* (forthcoming).

E. G. Wellesz, *A History of Byzantine Music and Hymnography* ([2]1961).

Byzantine dance Inherited from antiquity, with many types transmitted with rules for rhythm and *mele*, usually choreographed to the beats of poetic metres. A common thread can be traced through the tradition of circle dancing, called in literary and iconographical sources 'wrist holding'. Defended by Libanios as therapeutic to the spirit and body but condemned by the Church Fathers, dancing was not limited to any social class. The imperial palace had staged performances in ballets, pantomimes, and ceremonies. The *laity participated at *festivals, *carnivals, and taverns. Dancing also took place in sacred ceremonies: the 'Dance of Isaiah' at weddings, *Moirologia* (laments) at funerals, as well as the 'Taking of the Habit' and the 'Dance of Miriam'. *See also* DANCES AND DANCE MUSIC. DTM

D. Touliatos, 'The Evolution of Ancient Greek Music in Byzantium: Instruments, Women Musicians, Dance and Other Sundry Matters', in *Ancient Greek Music: Delphi* (1996), 77–88.

—— 'Byzantine Dancing in Secular and Sacred Spaces', *Technes and Archaiologia*, 91 (2004), 29–38.

Byzantine instruments Collectively called *organa*; adapted from ancient Greek models. The players of these instruments were called *paigniotai*. The imperial band had *salpinx* (trumpets), *boukina* (horns), *aulos* (reeds), *syrinx* (pipes), *crotala* (rattles), *tympana* (hand drums), and *cheirokymbala* (finger cymbals). There was also a court ensemble of bowed and plucked strings: *pandoura* (lute played with a plectrum), *kanonaki* (similar to the ancient 'magadis', a kind of dulcimer), psaltery (harp), *kithara* (lyre), four different sizes of *tamboura* (like the modern *bouzouki* or mandolin), *phandouros* (a three-stringed *tamboura*), Cappadocian *kemane* (a tall, slender, trapezoidal, bowed instrument), violas (bowed), and pneumatic organ (wind organ that replaced the *hydraulis* or water organ). The *semantron* (an elongated, cylindrical, bell-like instrument) and bells were used for *liturgies. For ceremonies at the imperial court, two golden organs were played simultaneously in a performance practice that was heterophonic or even polyphonic. *See also* MUSICAL INSTRUMENTS. DTM

W. Bachmann, 'Das byzantinische Musikinstrumentarium', in *Anfänge der slavischen Musik: Bratislava* (1964), 125–38.

Byzantine rite Known as the Constantinopolitan rite and followed by all Orthodox eastern churches.

1. Structure and uses
2. Liturgies
3. Feast day rites

1. *Structure and uses*

The structure of this rite was similar in organization to the western church's *liturgy (*Mass) and the *Divine Office: *Mesonyktikon* (midnight service); *Orthros* (equivalent to Matins and Lauds); *Hora prote* (Prime); *Hora trite* (Terce); *Hora hekte* (Sext); *Typika* (a short office between Sext and None); *Hora ennate* (None); *Apodeipnon* (Compline); and *Hesperinos* (Vespers). The Hours of the Office were known to be lengthy in content and can be found in the Horologion. In addition, the Byzantine rite was used for the following services: the sacraments (*baptism, *marriage, holy unction, and others), taking of the habit, *ordinations, inaugurations, funerals, *exorcisms, sanctifications, blessings on the 40th day for women having given birth, blessings of animals, and other rites for special feasts that are found in the *euchologion.

2. *Liturgies*

The Divine Liturgy is usually celebrated only on *Sundays, except at *monasteries, where it is celebrated daily, as are the Offices. The three standard Byzantine Divine Liturgies are St John *Chrysostom's, St Basil's, and the Liturgy of the *Presanctified Gifts. The St Basil Liturgy was first used in Caesarea, the metropolitan see of Basil, but was introduced to *Constantinople, and was the longest liturgy that was associated with solemn feast days. The St Chrysostom Liturgy was shorter than that of Basil and became the abbreviated common liturgy. The Liturgy of the Presanctified Gifts was usually celebrated during *Lent on Wednesdays and Fridays and on feast days when the holy gifts (bread and wine) were dedicated before their use on Sunday.

The Byzantine Divine Liturgy, in its three forms, had a rigid structure and retained many elements of the *Jewish liturgy of the synagogue, especially in congregational participation with a large number of responses after verses and the continual chanting of *Kyrie Eleison* for each call to *prayer. From its conception and development, *hymns were an important part of the liturgy: divine songs, known as *Prokeimena*, that were in the section of the catechumens between readings; *trisagion; Cherubic Hymn during the Great Entrance; and *Koinonikon* (*Eucharistic chant). Both the Liturgy and Offices contained components that were variable or fixed, similar to the Proper and Ordinary of the western rite.

The Byzantine rite also included a special archaic form referred to as the Cathedral Rite that was known to be practised in the Offices of Vespers and Orthros and Divine Liturgy in large *cathedrals, such as Hagia Sophia in Constantinople and Hagia Sophia in Thessalonica. This Cathedral Rite was known to have been used in *Byzantium as early as the 9th century, if not before, and remained in practice until 1430, when Thessalonica was captured by the Turks. In *Constantinople this rite fell into disuse in 1204 because of the occupation by the *crusaders that caused disruption and dislocation of chanters, resulting in a mixture of the cathedral and monastic Byzantine rite. Because this rite was known to have been chanted throughout, it was known as the chanted, choral, or '*asmatikos*' *akolouthia* (sung service) and pertained to Vespers, Orthros, and the Liturgy. Furthermore, this rite had an additional chanted office that was chanted between the Third (Terce) and Sixth (Sext) hours and was called the *Tritoekte*. The services of the chanted *akolouthia* were sung throughout by a large body of singers, specifically two choirs, the left and right choir directed by the *Domestikos* (Precentor), performed antiphonally. Even the prayers and supplications of the *clergy were intoned in a recitation style. This Cathedral Rite differed from the monastic rite, where the services were recited with a minimal amount of singing. Furthermore, this *akolouthia* was known to follow a special scheme of *psalms and antiphons from the Distributed *Psalter that indicated which psalms and accompanying antiphons, a selection of 68, were to be used for each day of the week within a two-week cycle.

3. Feast day rites

The Byzantine Rite for both movable and fixed feasts evolved from the earliest Christian liturgical practices of *Jerusalem and *Antioch. The *'Liturgy of Jerusalem', as documented in three sources (the pilgrimage of *Egeria, who described the liturgy for *Christmas and Epiphany *c.*383, an old Armenian *lectionary that narrated the services of *Holy Week in Jerusalem around the late 5th century, and a Georgian kanonarion of the 7th century), became the outline for the Offices. Furthermore, the liturgy of Antioch was the basis for the development of the Divine Liturgy of Constantinople. The earliest extant Greek source of the Byzantine rite is a Jerusalem *Typikon of the church of the Anastasis for Holy Week that dates from *c.*1122. By the end of the 11th and early 12th centuries the Byzantine rite had become codified, and its form has undergone few changes until the present day.

Unlike the west, the Byzantine rite is organized according to an eight-week cycle that corresponds to the eight modes of the *Oktoechos. For each week of the Byzantine calendar there is an assigned mode, and during *Easter week there is a different mode for each day. The Byzantine rite has fixed feasts, determined by the solar cycle, that follow the liturgical *calendar that begins 1 September (beginning of the indiction and the feast of St Symeon Stylites) and runs to 31 August (the Holy Girdle of the Theotokos). In another divergence from the western rite, the Propers of the Season (the fixed feasts) were celebrated only in the Office and not in the Eucharistic liturgy. This introduced an impressive augmentation of *stichera* hymns for the saints, martyrs, apostles, Theotokos, and the Lord. The movable feasts pertained to the cycle of Lent–Easter–Pentecost, and were governed by the lunar cycle. *See also* BYZANTINE CHANT; LITURGICAL BOOKS, GREEK; LITURGY OF ST JAMES. DTM

A. Baumstark, 'Denkmäler der Entstehungsgeschichte des byzantinischen Ritus', *Oriens christianus*, ser. 3, 2 (1927), 1–32.
R. F. Taft, 'Byzantine Rite', *ODB*, vol. 1, 343–4.
D. Touliatos, 'The "Chanted" Vespers Service', *Kleronomia*, 8 (1976), 107–28.
—— 'The Byzantine Orthros', *Byzantina*, 9 (1977), 325–83.

Byzantine secular music Patronized by the Byzantine court from the 4th century until the empire's fall (1453) in *dramas, pantomimes, ballets, banquets, pagan and political *festivals, Olympic games, and court ceremonies. Much information on this music was found in the writings of the Church Fathers, who denounced it as lascivious and referred to its performers as *prostitutes (*porni*). The 9th-century *Chronographia* of Theophanes the Confessor documents types of secular music and instruments.

Descriptions of secular court music are found in the *Book of Ceremonies* of Constantine VII Porphyrogennetus (905–59) and in the *De officiis* of Pseudo-Codinus (mid 14th century). Although *musical instruments were generally not allowed to be played in churches, much iconographical evidence is found in wall paintings and *liturgical books. There are few examples of secular music in extant Byzantine music MSS, and these are usually intermingled with liturgical music of the same period. The reason for this could be because much of the repertoire was improvised and disseminated through oral transmission.

Among the categories are Polychronia (acclamations or salutations sung for the imperial family, court ceremonies, anniversaries, and entertainments), Symposia / Sympotika (singing accompanied by instruments at banquets, a practice transmitted from ancient Greece), Teretismata or Kratemata (instrumental vocalizations using nonsense syllables with or without instrumental accompaniment), and Akritika (political or epic folk-songs). Composers of secular music are not documented until the late empire, and even then attributions are rare. Byzantine composers such as Joannes Koukouzeles, Xenos Korones, and Joannes Glykys contributed to the genre of Teretismata / Kratemata. Koukouzeles has even been given credit for dance music (National Library of Greece, MS 2604, fols 136v–37v). *See also* BYZANTINE DANCE; BYZANTINE INSTRUMENTS. DTM

D. Touliatos, 'Byzantine Secular Music', in *NGD2*, vol. 2, 756–7.
—— 'Nonsense Syllables in the Music of the Ancient Greek and Byzantine Traditions', *Journal of Musicology*, 7 (1989), 231–43.

Byzantium Conventional name for the state which evolved out of the eastern half of the later Roman Empire.

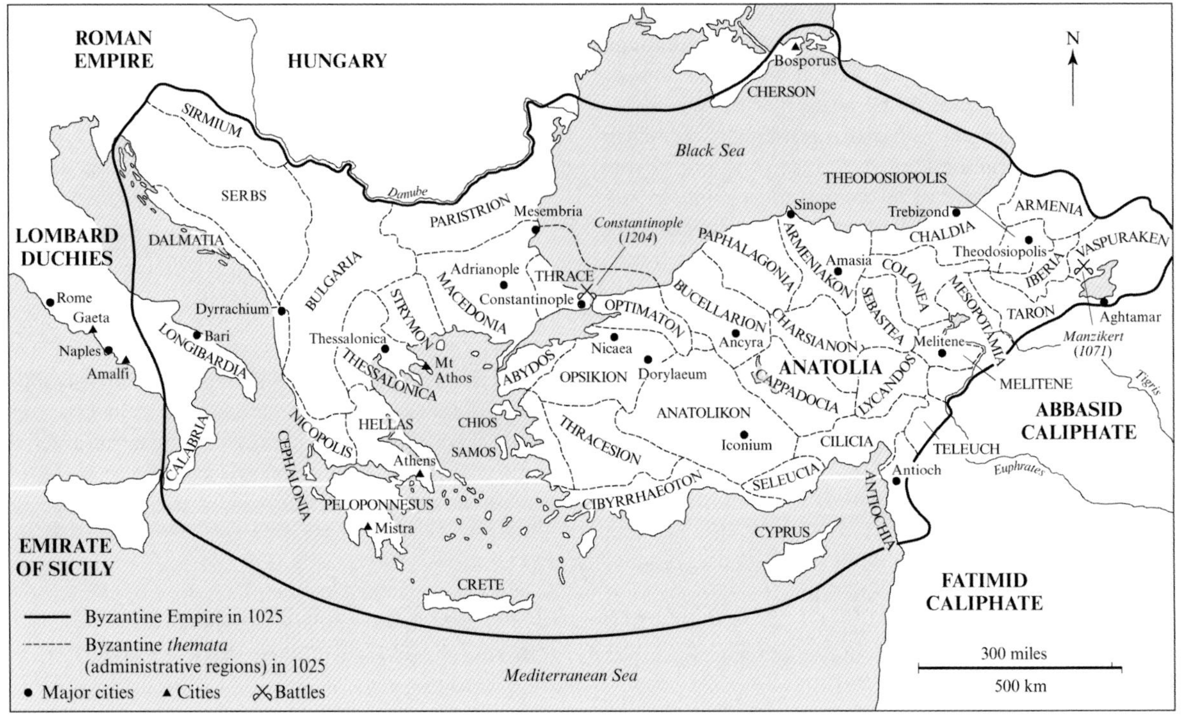

Byzantium in the 11th century.

1. Overview
2. Territory, demography, and language
3. Culture and economics
4. Religion
5. Relations to western Europe

1. *Overview*

Its beginnings are associated with the founding of *Constantinople as 'New Rome' by Constantine I (324) on the site of an ancient Greek colony on the Bosporus, Byzantion, whence 16th-century European scholars derived the name 'Byzantium'. Its long, turbulent history incubated Christianity's rise to hegemony in Europe, as well as the parting of ways between the eastern and western churches; it suffered the rise of *Islam, and both abetted and resisted the *crusades, until it succumbed to Ottoman domination after the fall of Constantinople in 1453. Byzantium's undeserved reputation as a den of intrigue and *mysticism has lent its name to the pejorative epithet 'Byzantine' largely as a result of Enlightenment prejudice against a perceived theocratic 'perversion' of ancient Rome's political virtues.

Often characterized as a combination of Hellenic culture, Roman political ideology, and Christian religion, Byzantium fashioned an evolving social, political, and cultural identity not reducible to its inherited ancient components. Chroniclers and historians wrote of their state and society as a unique, divinely sanctioned development. The Byzantines continued to refer to themselves as 'Romans' (*Rhomaioi*) and to their state as the 'empire of the Romans' (*basileia ton Rhomaion*). In day-to-day life, ecclesiastical ritual and economic activity shaped most people's self-image. Led by emperors who either inherited or seized authority, Byzantium relied on centralized policy in matters from foreign policy to faith.

2. *Territory, demography, and language*

The territory and demographic makeup of this empire fluctuated according to success or failure in keeping its frontiers. Gains around the Mediterranean under Justinian I (527–65) were followed by losses, as in the case of the Muslim conquests of *Egypt, *Palestine, and Syria in the 7th century, or the occasionally reversible erosion of Balkan or Italian territories by *Slavs (beginning in the 6th century) and *Normans (11th–12th centuries), respectively. In addition to the fortified capital, Constantinople, mainland Greece, some Aegean islands, the southern Balkans, and much of western Asia Minor formed the backbone of Byzantium until its further fragmentation under crusader potentates and Turkic warlords in the 13th and 14th centuries. By the time of its demise in the mid 15th century, Byzantium amounted to a city-state with pockets of territory in the Peloponnese, Thrace, and the Aegean.

Byzantium inherited a significant ethnic and linguistic diversity, and even some religious heterogeneity. Although predominantly Christian by the 7th century, at various times it ruled significant minorities of *pagans, *Jews, and Muslims. Greek, long the lingua franca of eastern Mediterranean cities, began to displace Latin as the language of imperial administration and law by the 6th century. Its pre-eminence in culture had never been challenged, and erudite use of Greek underpinned much of Byzantium's cultural self-confidence. Byzantium played a pivotal role in the transmission of classical knowledge to the Islamic world and to Renaissance Italy. Most of our surviving manuscripts of ancient Greek literature date from the 9th to the 14th centuries and were commissioned by Byzantine *patrons. Byzantine men of letters served as Greek tutors to the first Italian humanists around the time of Byzantium's impending collapse.

3. *Culture and economics*

The medieval character of Byzantine society is most apparent in the demise of late antique cities as junctions of commerce, culture, and politics in the 6th and 7th centuries. After the loss of Alexandria to the Muslims (*c*.641) and the decline of *Antioch following foreign invasions, Constantinople became the empire's only significant *urban centre, with Thessalonica, and later Corinth, distant seconds. Public and private *architecture diminished in size and quality. Opportunities for *education, *travel, and careers narrowed. The urbane culture of antiquity yielded to more uniform social regimes inspired by the popular authority of *monasticism and widening ecclesiastical jurisdiction. Civil and military organization remained centrally controlled. The extent of Byzantine *'feudalism' (*pronoia*) remains controversial. Systematic *taxation made Byzantium the richest state in Europe and the Near East, often attracting invaders. Its coinage was remarkably stable, and its agrarian economy was complemented by its pivotal location along important *trade routes. Constantinople's wealth was legendary in the MA. Economic activity was substantially regulated by the state: interest rates, profits, and prices were set by law and enforced through a system of *guilds and assessors. Over time the shrinking territories proved insufficient for financing the empire's defence, entrusted increasingly to *mercenaries.

4. *Religion*

A seamless continuum existed between sacred and secular life, as every sphere was thought to be within the purview of God. From the start, doctrinal differences over such things as the nature of Christ, marked by both sincerity and political expediency, undermined the internal stability of the empire. A large body of theological writing, along with church councils convened by emperors, including those of Nicaea (325) and Chalcedon (451), were much contested and helped shape the very nature of Christian belief, while alienating many dissenters (among them Arians, Miaphysites, and Paulicians) who would be labelled heretics. The Catholic/Orthodox split over doctrine and ecclesiastical primacy remains unresolved. Byzantine missionary work among Slavic peoples brought them into the Orthodox fold. The Byzantine religious sensibility also coloured Christianity in Ethiopia, Egypt, and Armenia.

5. *Relations to western Europe*

The importance of Byzantium for the study of the western MA has been largely overlooked in western curricula. It was central to the politics and economy of medieval Europe, as witnessed by wars and alliances with all the major kingdoms, French, Italian, Norman, and German. Its maritime trade pacts with *Venice and *Genoa helped catapult those cities to wealth and power. Its loss of and ostensible claim on the Holy Land served as cause and pretext for the crusades: their passage through Byzantine lands engendered mutual resentment as well as east–west cultural exchange.

ECB

H. Ahrweiler, *L'Idéologie politique de l'Empire byzantin* (1975).
A. M. Cameron, *The Byzantines* (2006).
G. Cavallo, ed., *The Byzantines*, tr. T. Dunlap *et al.* (1997).
J.-C. Cheynet, *Histoire de Byzance* (2005).
T. E. Gregory, *A History of Byzantium* (2005).
J. Herrin, *Byzantium* (2007).
A. Kazhdan and G. Constable, *People and Power in Byzantium* (1982).
A. E. Laiou, ed., *Economic History of Byzantium*, 3 vols (2002).
—— and Henry Maguire, eds, *Byzantium: A World Civilization* (1992).
W. L. MacDonald, 'Byzantium', in *Princeton Encyclopedia of Classical Sites*, ed. R. Stillwell *et al.* (1976), 177–9.
M. M. Mango, ed., *Byzantine Trade, 4th–12th Centuries* (2009).
M. Rautman, *Daily Life in the Byzantine Empire* (2006).
W. Treadgold, *A History of the Byzantine State and Society* (1997).

Cabala *See* MYSTICISM, JEWISH.

caballería, libros de ('chivalric romances') Sub-genre of the *romance. These lengthy episodic prose narratives recount the often marvellous adventures of knights errant and are frequently peopled with a myriad of characters such as damsels and sorcerers. Examples include the *Libro del caballero Zifar* (*c.*1300×1310) and **Amadís de Gaula*. The genre dates from the early 14th century onwards and was popular and influential both in the late MA and the Golden Age, inspiring Spanish explorers and chroniclers alike. Famously, the *libros de caballería* are satirized in Miguel de Cervantes's *Don Quixote* (1605 and 1615), in which the eponymous protagonist's obsession with chivalric romances drives him insane. *See also* CHANSONS DE GESTE. JG

E. B. C. Carbajal, L. P. Moro, and M. S. Pérez, eds, *Libros de caballerías (de 'Amadís' al 'Quijote'): poética, lectura, representación e identidad* (2002).

M. Harney, *Kinship and Marriage in Medieval Hispanic Chivalric Romance* (2001).

caballeros villanos A class of horsemen associated with towns in the Iberian Peninsula from the 11th through the 15th centuries. Their maintenance of a horse and its use in frontier combat enabled them to gain exemption from royal taxes and ultimately to claim a position at the lowest level in the aristocracy. They maintained resident status in their town, although often residing in the nearby countryside. They gave mobility to the urban militias both in defensive activity against Muslim raiders and as elements of the royal expeditionary armies. The *caballeros* were obligated to keep both their horses and their appropriate military gear ready for inspection as the combat season approached. They were most important in *Castile and gained in status as the monarchy allied with them as a counterweight to the higher aristocracy in the later MA. JFPo

L. G. de Valdeavellano, *Curso de historia de las instituciones españolas: De los orígenes al final de la Edad Media* (1968).

Cabasilas, Nicolas (1322/3–after 1391) Orthodox writer and theologian. He was a follower of *Gregory Palamas and was on the side of Emperor John VI Kantakouzenos after the civil war of 1341–7. Cabasilas was an author of wide-ranging interests, including theology, *rhetoric, *astronomy, and *law. *See also* THEOLOGY, BYZANTINE. NVM

Y. Spitzeris and C. Conticello, 'Nicolas Cabasilas Chamaetos', *La Théologie Byzantine et sa Tradition*, ed. C. G. Conticello and V. Conticello (2002), vol. 2, 315–410.

Cabochiens During the civil conflict between *Armagnacs and Burgundians, the butcher Simon Caboch led 'three thousand of the most miserable sort' in an attack against King *Charles VII's eldest son and imprisoned many noblemen sympathetic to the Armagnac side (*Chronique du religieux de St-Denys*). No doubt, the duke of *Burgundy lurked behind the scenes. But with assistance from the

University of *Paris, the Cabochiens imposed an ordinance of 258 articles on the king (26–27 May 1413), which severely restricted royal rights and prerogatives. The king signed them, but they never came into force. SKC

A. Coville, *Les premiers Valois et la Guerre de Cent Ans (1328–1422)* (1902).
R. Famiglietti, *Royal Intrigue: Crisis at the Court of Charles VI, 1392–1420* (1986).

caccia Italian poetic and musical genre of the 14th and early 15th centuries. The texts are strophic with a refrain (ritornello), and realistically depict *hunting and other outdoor scenes. Extant musical settings feature two texted, canonic upper voices above an instrumental part. BMW

G. Corsi, *Poesie musicali del Trecento* (1970).
K. von Fischer and G. d'Agostino, 'Caccia', *NGD2* (2001), vol. 4, 766–9.

Cadalus (**Cadelo, Honorius II**) (1009/10–1072) (antipope) Bishop of *Parma and *antipope (1061–64). Nominated by Agnes of Poitou, Cadalus became pope following the disputed election of *Pope Alexander II. His efforts to enter Rome failed, and a council in 1064 declared for Alexander. Lacking support, Cadalus nonetheless claimed to be the legitimate pope until his death. MCF

U.-R. Blumenthal, *The Investiture Controversy* (1988).

Cade, William (d. 1166) Cloth merchant and *moneylender of St-Omer, involved in the *London *money market. He lent money to persons of high and low standing, government officials, clerics, *Henry II, and possibly Thomas *Becket. Henry seized Cade's assets in *England in 1166. DN

H. Jenkinson, 'William Cade, a Financier of the Twelfth Century', *EHR* 28 (1913), 209–27.

Cade's Rebellion Popular rising in *Kent demanding reform. Jack Cade (d. 1450), possibly a Surrey yeoman who had fled abroad in 1448–9, was elected captain and formal demands were drawn up. The rebels briefly occupied *London in early July but were checked by the London militia, given a general pardon, and disbanded. Underlying issues included English defeats in *France, officials' corruption, and local grievances. The failure of *Henry VI's government to reform contributed to his deposition by *Edward IV a decade later. RSO

I. M. W. Harvey, *Jack Cade's Rebellion of 1450* (1991).

Cædmon Described as an illiterate layman in *Bede's *Historia ecclesiastica*, he was a herdsman at *Hild(a)'s *monastery of Whitby, *c.*670. Although his name suggests British descent, Bede records the tradition that a heavenly dream inspired Cædmon to paraphrase Christian subjects in the AS oral-formulaic verse style, an idiom suited to heroic themes. This innovation was widely emulated. One example of his oeuvre survives: the nine-line OE poem called 'Cædmon's Hymn'. SGw

B. Colgrave and R. A. B. Mynors, eds, *Bede's Ecclesiastical History of the English People* (1969).
D. P. O'Donnell, *Cædmon's Hymn: A Multimedia Study, Archive, and Edition* (2005).
J. Opland, *Anglo-Saxon Oral Poetry: A Study of the Traditions* (1980).

Cædwalla *See* WESSEX, KINGDOM AND EARLDOM OF.

Caen (Cadomum) Caen, in *Normandy on the Orne river, was the city of *William the Conqueror. William constructed two *monasteries (Abbaye-aux-Hommes and Abbaye-aux-Dames) and a *castle in the city during the 11th century, making it the capital of western Normandy. The name Caen is likely of Gaulish origin and may mean 'the field of combat'. The English captured the city in 1346 and again in 1417. GP

J. Strayer, 'Caen', *DMA*, vol. 3, 8.

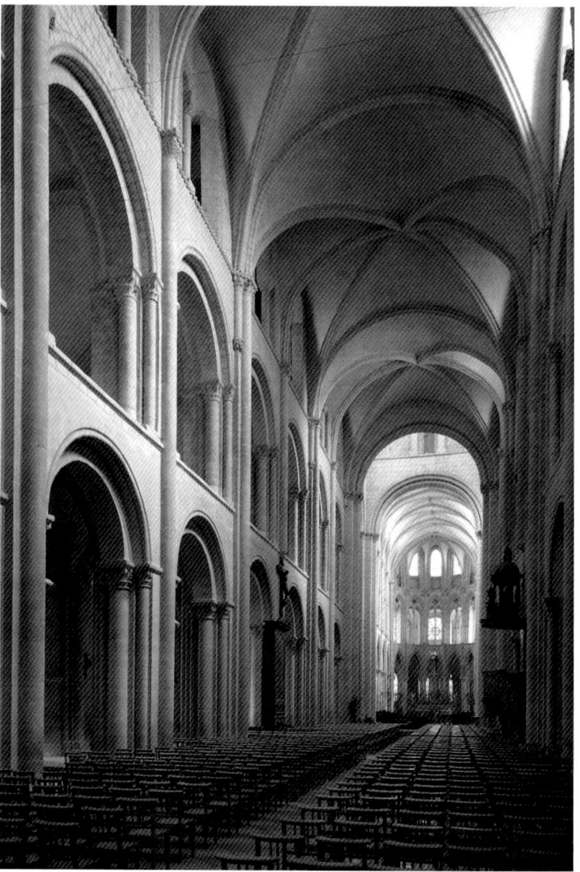

Interior of the church of St Étienne (Abbaye-aux-Hommes), Caen.

Caernarfon (Caernarvon) (castle) Situated at the southern end of the Menai Strait that flows between the mainland and the Isle of Anglesey, southwest of Bangor, in *Gwynedd, northwest Wales. King *Edward I of England's symbolic seat of power served as administrative and military capital and fortress-palace for the imperial prince of *Wales. The future *Edward II was reportedly born here on 25 April 1284, and a town charter granted 8 September 1284.

After the Welsh wars of 1282–3, Edward I planned the construction of four strategically conceived *castles to reinforce English domination: Beaumaris, Caernarvon, Conwy, and Harlech. Caernarvon was the most architecturally imposing and politically significant, the site being steeped in history and legend. The name is derived from the Welsh for the nearby Roman fort at Segontium, 'y gaer yn Arfon' (the stronghold in the land against Môn [Anglesey]), also known as Caer Segeint after the river Seiont near which it stood. *Gerald of Wales had reported a settlement at Kairarvon in 1188, probably inhabited by Welsh princes.

The first phase of construction (1283–92) was overseen by architect, master *mason, and military *engineer James of St George, a *Savoyard in Edward I's service since 1278 and at Caernarvon until 1287. His designs reflected the imperialism of Roman *Constantinople and capitalized on the Welsh legend of Macsen Wledig (Magnus Maximus, 340–88), exemplifying past greatness, present victory, and a new order. The site dictated an irregularly elongated plan: a Norman motte and bailey with an interior enclosure divided into upper / eastern and lower / western wards by a cross wall, flanked by thirteen spacious multi-angular towers, including two double-towered gatehouses—King's gate and Queen's gate—that opened into the upper ward. Eagle Tower, the largest, was twice the usual scale at 21 m diameter. Featuring substantial walls, protected entrances (portcullis and drawbridge), polychrome stonework, and ample provisions of food and weapons, the castle's shoreline access facilitated control of supplies to outposts and agricultural products from Anglesey to the rest of Wales.

The second building phase (1294–1330) was in response to a surprise Welsh revolt in 1294–5 led by Madog ap Llywelyn, a lord of Meirionydd. Repairs to the breached town walls and burned castle were supervised by master mason Walter of Hereford until 1301, when he was transferred to Scotland. After years of heavy expenditure, construction waned and ceased unfinished in 1330, though maintenance and garrisoning continued, withstanding sieges by Owain *Glyn Dŵr between 1401–04. Welsh exclusion eased with the accession of *Henry VII, a king of England with Welsh lineage, while Welsh adaptability to the English regime meant that by 1536 Caernarvon was largely controlled by Welsh *gentry. *See also* SCOTLAND, IRELAND, WALES: EARLY WALES TO 1064; LLYWELYN AP GRUFFUDD. MTA

A. H. Dodd, *A History of Caernarvonshire, 1284–1900* (1990).
M. Prestwich, 'Wales, Settlement and Rebellion', in *Edward I* (1988), 202–32.
A. J. Taylor, 'The Birth of Edward of Caernarvon and the Beginnings of Caernarvon Castle', *Hist(L)* 35 (1950), 256–61.
—— *Caernarfon Castle and Town Wall* (2001).
K. Williams-Jones, 'Caernarvon', in *Boroughs of Medieval Wales*, ed. R. A. Griffiths (1978), 73–101.

Caesarius, St, archbishop of Arles (*c.*470–542) Monk at *Lérins, bishop 502, granted the pallium and named vicar of Gaul by Pope Symmachus I (514). Caesarius presided over five church *councils (506–29) and helped eliminate semi-*Pelagianism. JJA

D. Bertrand *et al.*, *Césaire d'Arles et la christianisation de la Provence* (1994).
Clavis Patrum Latinorum, 1008–19.
W. E. Klingshirn, *Caesarius of Arles: The Making of a Christian Community in Late Antique Gaul* (1994).

Caesarius of Heisterbach (*c.*1180–1249) Born probably in *Cologne; joined the *Cistercians as a young man after he heard a story from the abbot of Heisterbach about how Mary and other female saints were seen wiping the faces of the monks of *Clairvaux while they harvested in the summer heat. Caesarius was fascinated with miracle narratives of this type. As novice master at Heisterbach, Caesarius collected eight hundred stories in his *Dialogus miraculorum* (1219–23). These exempla (*see* PROVERBS, RIDDLES, AND EXEMPLA) were meant to encourage novices to see their own dreams, hopes, and fears in terms of the experience of other monks and nuns. At the same time Caesarius included stories from the lives of lay persons. He enjoyed a good story for its own sake, and the dialogue form in many of the stories is often a mere formality.

Caesarius used to be said to have become prior of Heisterbach, but there is no medieval evidence for this. Presumably he continued as novice master and made new collections of stories, but none of them achieved the celebrity of the *Dialogue on Miracles*. BPM

Diálogo de milagros, ed. and tr. Z. Prieto Hernández (1998).
Dialogue on Miracles, tr. H. Scott and C. Bland (1929; repr. 1992).
Dialogus Miraculorum, ed. N. Nösges and H. Schneider, 4 vols (2008).

Cahors Market town, *pilgrimage centre, and seat of a bishopric in the Quercy region (southwest *France). An early-12th-century campaign refashioned the *nave of the *cathedral of St Stephen with two domed *bays following a contemporary regional practice, and by mid century had installed on the north doorway (west bay) a porch-portal structure with sculpture, similar to that at *Moissac. The Cahors doorway presents a massive compartmentalized *tympanum featuring the Ascension of Christ with

Caernarfon castle.

*angels, apostles, and vignettes illustrating Stephen's martyrdom. LR

M. Durliat, 'Cathédrale Saint-Etienne de Cahors: architecture et sculpture', *BM* 137 (1979), 285–340.
M. Vidal, *Quercy Roman* ([3]1978).

Cahorsin A native of *Cahors in southwestern *France, but by the mid 13th century a 'usurer' in popular usage (see, for example, *Dante, *Inferno* 11.50). Although Cahorsin merchants and bankers played a key role in 13th-century trade and finance, *usury rarely dominated their business. Nevertheless, 'Cahorsin', often paired with *'Lombard', came to denote any foreign *moneylender, particularly usurers from northern *Italy. For example, the 'Great Cahorsin', the publicly licensed pawnshop of *Bruges, was dominated by Piedmontese usurers. LDA

J. M. Murray, *Bruges, Cradle of Capitalism, 1280–1390* (2005).
Y. Renouard, 'Les Cahorsins, hommes d'affaires français du XIIIe siècle', *TRHS* 5th ser., 11 (1961), 43–67.

Cairo City strategically founded by the Fatimids in 969 at the foot of the Nile Delta near *Fustat. Under them and the Ayyubids and Mamluks it grew enormously in prosperity, with flourishing architecture and trade. MD

J. Abu-Lughod, *Cairo: One Thousand and One Years of the City Victorious* (1971).
S. Staffa, *Conquest and Fusion: The Social Evolution of Cairo 642–1850* (1977).

Cajetan, Thomas (Thomas de Vio) (1469–1534) Minister General of the *Dominican order (1508–18) and *cardinal from 1517. In 1518 Cajetan was sent as *legate of the *Holy See to the Imperial Diet of *Augsburg, and while there debated inconclusively with Martin Luther. He produced important *commentaries on works of *Thomas Aquinas, and in later life on much of the *Bible. RCr

J. Wicks, *Cajetan Responds: A Reader in Reformation Controversy* (1978).

Calais Seaport in northern *France, situated on an island at the narrowest point of the Channel 34 km (21 miles) from the coast of *England. Originally a fishing village without natural defences, it was fortified by the counts of Boulogne in the 13th century. In 1347, *Edward III of England captured Calais after an eleven-month siege. He subsequently expelled its townspeople, replacing them with English inhabitants. Calais remained English for two centuries, with strategic and economic importance to the kingdom. In 1363, it became the *staple port (designated export location) for England's wool trade, and it was also the base for English expeditions into France during the *Hundred Years War. The French re-took Calais in 1558. JHH

A. Derville and A. Vion, *Histoire de Calais* (1985).
H. Platelle and D. Clauzel, *Histoire des provinces françaises du Nord, II: Des principautés à l'empire de Charles-Quint* (1989).

First grand seal of Calais.

Calatrava, Order of Founded by Abbot Raymond of Fitero who, in 1158, received from Sancho III of *Castile the fortress of Calatrava on the Guadiana river. The monastic community assumed a military character to defend the position. In 1164, the foundation was affiliated to the *Cistercians and protected by *Pope Alexander III. In 1187, the abbot of Morimond was charged with visiting the order annually. The Calatravan knights guarded the Guadiana valley, thus protecting *Toledo. The order spread to *Aragon, *Galicia, and Portugal and the orders of *Alcántara, Avis, and Montesa became affiliates. After the Christian defeat at *Alarcos, the knights moved to Salvatierra which, after an heroic defence, fell to the *Almohads in 1211. After the Christian victory at Las *Navas, the knights established themselves at Calatrava la Nueva, playing an important part in the *Reconquista of the 13th century. Success brought them wealth but involved them in the machinations of Castilian politics, and their initial monastic vocation was lost. In 1489, Ferdinand II took over the order's administration. DJSm

C. A. Martínez, *Las Ordenes Militares Hispanicas en la Edad Media* (2003).
J. O'Callaghan, *The Spanish Military Order of Calatrava and its Affiliates* (1975).

calendar, ecclesiastical The *liturgy for every day of the year was governed by a cycle of seasons (*temporale*) and a cycle of saints (*sanctorale*). The *temporale* commemorated episodes in the life of Christ. Some (for example, *Christmas and Epiphany) fell on fixed dates, while others

(for example, *Easter and Pentecost) varied within limits. Most saints' days were fixed, and many saints, such as *Mary, Mother of Christ, and the Apostles, were universally commemorated. Other festivals were regional or merely local. *Calendars recorded the fixed anniversaries, often with notes on the solemnity of individual feasts. They also contained computistical information (for example, dominical letters) and astronomical data (for example, equinoxes and solstices). *See also* ASTRONOMY. JMM

B. Blackburn and L. Holford-Strevens, *The Oxford Companion to the Year* (1999).

A. Borst, 'Die karolingische Kalendarreform', *SMGH* 46 (1998).

J. Harper, *The Forms and Orders of Western Liturgy from the Tenth to the Eighteenth Century* (1991), 45–57.

calendar, liturgical *See* LITURGICAL YEAR.

calendars and reckoning of time Reckoning temporal units of a day or longer involves the calendar, *computus*, and chronology. A calendar orders days in a sequence culminating in the year. *Computus* calculates adjustments to calendar dates for a given year, particularly the date of *Easter. Chronology denotes a system for designating years. Medieval proposals to reform the calendar touched on all three methods.

1. Christian and non-Christian calendars
2. *Computus*
3. Chronology
4. Calendar reform

1. Christian and non-Christian calendars

By the mid 2nd century, the custom of commemorating the anniversaries of the martyrs tied Christian piety to the local civil calendar, which was, most often, the Julian calendar, our familiar solar calendar of 365 days (with a leap day every fourth year), commencing on 1 January and divided into twelve months of varying length, as inaugurated in Rome by Julius Caesar in 45 BC. The Christianization of the empire did not affect its structure apart from legislating the seven-day week with *Sunday as a public holy day. The content of the calendar, on the other hand, changed markedly as saints' days and fixed feasts replaced pagan celebrations. The Roman church's festal calendar came to dominate western Christendom through *missions, *Carolingian liturgical reforms, and the widening ecclesiastical authority of the *papacy. Nonetheless, important local variations persisted.

Visually, a medieval calendar is a generic Julian calendar with days arranged as a vertical list. Aligned with the dates on the right are feasts, saints' days, and astronomical notices. To the left of the dates are key letters used to customize this calendar for a particular year. The seven letters A–G ('Dominical' or Sunday letters) adjusted dates to weekdays (for years designated 'A', all A-days are Sundays, and so forth). Other key letters translated calendar dates into days of the lunar month or the position of the moon in the zodiac. The 'Golden Numbers', placed to the left of certain dates, indicated the year of the 19-year paschal lunar cycle (see below, section 2) when a new moon would fall on that date; the lunar phase on any calendar date could then be obtained by extrapolation.

Though the Roman manner of expressing dates was employed throughout the MA even in vernacular texts, forward counting from the first of the month, practised in *Byzantium from the 5th century onwards, gained popularity in the west from the 11th century. The notarial *consuetudo Bononiensis* (forward count to mid month, then reverse count to the end) can be found as far afield as *England from the mid 13th century. Leap Day continued to be inserted in the Roman fashion at 24 February, the *bissextus* or 'twice-sixth' kalends of March. Finally, texts of all kinds often designate the day by reference to the (nearest) saint's day, feast, or Sunday, often identified by the opening word(s) of the *introit of the *Mass for that day.

In western Europe, the ecclesiastical *calendar functioned as the civil calendar in most jurisdictions. However, the beginning of the civil year varied with locality (the church began the New Year at *Christmas); indeed these variations become more numerous with the passage of time (see Cordoliani for a useful table). *Iceland alone retained a distinctive secular public calendar.

By late antiquity, *Jews were using a calculated luni-solar calendar, with lunar months of 29 and 30 days, and periodic intercalations to bring the months into phase with the seasons. The rules for scheduling these intercalations were not solidified until the 11th century. The Jewish year varies between 353 and 385 days, depending on whether it is common or embolismic (with an intercalated month), 'deficient', ordinary, or 'abundant' (adjustments to avoid New Year falling on certain weekdays). The Muslim calendar, strictly lunar, begins each of its twelve months at the observed first visibility of the new moon.

2. Computus

Computus denotes the rules, formulae, tables, and expository texts used for constructing and adjusting a calendar. It also designates a treatise or volume devoted to this subject. Its main task, for Christian Europe, was to establish the date of Easter Sunday. Easter commemorates Christ's death and resurrection at the Jewish feast of Passover, celebrated at the full moon of the first lunar month (14 Nisan). Patristic writers assumed that Passover had to follow the vernal equinox. When the Julian calendar was inaugurated, the equinox fell on 25 March, and so it remained for many centuries. However, the calculated solar year of 365.25 days is longer than the astronomical tropical year (365.2422 days), so the equinox crept backwards in the calendar at the rate of one day in 128 years. This problem was noticed in antiquity,

Calendar on ivory showing saints' feast days, *c.*1500.

and the Alexandrian church adopted the corrected date of 21 March in the 4th century. No further correction was made, however, until Pope Gregory XIII mandated the reform of 1583 (see section 4 below).

Determining the date of Easter revolved around the following problems and questions:

(i) The stage of the moon on the vernal equinox and the date of the first full moon thereafter (the Easter terminus) must be established by calculation rather than by direct observation to accommodate pre-paschal observances such as Lent. A luni-solar cycle was therefore required, that is, a common denominator of solar and lunar years. Since the astronomical periods of the sun and moon are incommensurable, no luni-solar cycle is perfect, but several were tried out, of which the most accurate was the 19-year cycle ascribed to the ancient astronomer Meton of Athens.

(ii) Since Easter is celebrated on Sunday, it is essential to establish which calendar date the moon becomes full (Easter terminus) and what weekday that calendar date falls on, in order to find the next Sunday following, which will be Easter.

(iii) What is the permissible range of lunar dates on which Easter can fall? *Luna* 14–20, to underscore Christ's redemptive work as the true Paschal Lamb; or 16–22, to coincide at the earliest with the lunar anniversary of the Resurrection; or 15–21, to mirror the Jewish Feast of Unleavened Bread?

(iv) Given the conditions enumerated above, within what range of *calendar* dates in a Julian year could Easter fall?

The solution to all these problems was confounded by differences between the Alexandrian church and *Rome over the date of the equinox, the acceptable lunar and calendar dates, and what constituted a cycle. The achievement of

*Bede's *De temporum ratione* (725) was to provide the western church with a persuasive exposition of the Alexandrian *computus*, as set forth in the table of *Dionysius Exiguus (525). Dionysius' table had quietly replaced the very defective table of Victorius of Aquitaine (457) sometime between the mid 6th and mid 7th century. It adopted the 19-year Metonic luni-solar cycle, the 21 March equinox, Easter lunar limits of 15–21, and calendar limits of 22 March–25 April. *De temporum ratione* criticized not only Victorius but the British (and some Irish), who continued to use an 84-year paschal table. It also demonstrated how Dionysius' system produced a cycle of Easters over 532 years.

Bede's textbook was adopted by the Carolingian schools, and *computus* remained a staple of clerical training throughout the medieval period. However from the 12th century onwards, astronomical time-reckoning, or *computus naturalis*, emerged, stimulated by newly available translations, tables, and instruments. Late medieval calendars (for example, by John Somur and Nicholas of Lynn) are consequently equipped with tables of *eclipses and planetary positions and are, properly speaking, almanacs valid for specific spans of years.

3. *Chronology*

In the MA, both eponymous (for example, regnal year: 'the 12th year of Edward III') and absolute chronologies were employed. The *Byzantine Empire adopted regnal year dating for official documents in the reign of Justinian. In the west, regnal year dating was embraced only gradually: popes used it sporadically from 781, but the English chancery adopted it at the end of the 12th century. Regnal years were often adjusted to the civil year and could be reckoned from accession or coronation.

Absolute chronology designates years in a continuous numbered series or era, starting from an agreed epoch. Amongst Jews, the Creation era (eventually fixed from 3761 BC) gradually supplanted the Seleucid era (starting 312 BC) after the 9th century. Muslims dated from the *Hijra* (*Muhammad's migration to Medina on 13 September AD 622) after about AH 17, though in some jurisdictions they used the Roman era of the indictions (a 15-year cycle used by the bureaucracy of late imperial Rome and incorporated in some medieval contexts). But Christians were slow to develop a distinctive era, because the motives for chronology were diverse and seldom congruent.

One motive was *symbolic*: persuaded that the six days of Creation prefigured the course of history, that each day represented a thousand years, and that Christ arrived 'at the eleventh hour', Julius Africanus (2nd–3rd centuries) divided the 6,000 years of the world into twelve 'hours' of 500 years each, dating Christ's birth to *annus mundi* 5,500. Another motive was *computistical*: computists 'proved' the correctness of their cycles by showing how, when retrojected, they produced perfect data for the historic Passion and ultimately the Creation. A third impetus was *historical*: Eusebius of Caesarea's universal chronicle correlated the Incarnation to AM 5199; through its Latin translation by St *Jerome, it became the backbone of much early medieval historiography.

By the 5th century, a 'Christian era' counted from the Passion appears simultaneously in the histories of *Prosper of Aquitaine and the paschal tables of Victorius, though Alexandrian tables later preferred the 'era of the martyrs' (a euphemism for the era of Diocletian, commencing AD 284/5). Dionysius Exiguus calibrated his table to the year of Christ's incarnation (*annus Domini*), which he derived from the chronology in Eusebius/Jerome, but modified slightly for computistical convenience. The success of Dionysius' table encouraged acceptance of its era, particularly by annalists. Its adoption for official dating was slower in coming, but by the 11th century even the papal chancery used it. It did not always supplant other local chronologies (for example, the Spanish era, with epoch 1 January 38 BC, used in Iberia from *Visigothic times to the 14th or 15th centuries; in Spanish Moslem documents, this is the 'era of the Magi') or year counts (for example, indictions). The Byzantine Empire after the 9th century used an *annus mundi* era with epoch 5509 BC, and this was adopted by Russia.

4. *Calendar reform*

Annus domini was the first element of the Dionysian *computus* to attract criticism, notably by 11th-century computist-chronographers like *Abbo of Fleury, *Heriger of Lobbes, and Marianus Scottus. However, this debate was inconclusive and remained confined to scholarly circles. A more serious problem was posed by defects in the calculation of the lunar and solar periods on which the paschal *computus* rested. The drift of the equinox was very evident by the 12th century and could be calculated with precision by *computus naturalis*. Likewise, there was a glaring discrepancy between the computed and the visible moon, resulting from a miscalculation of the length of the synodic lunar month (one day accumulated in *c.*322 years). From the early 13th century to the *Gregorian Reform of 1583, scientists and prelates debated how to bring the calendar back into line with astronomical realities and keep it there. The first issue essentially entailed legislating the removal of the excess days from the Julian reckoning and setting the Golden Numbers back. The second problem, however, was scientific: the tropical solar year was plainly shorter than 365.25 days, but how much shorter? Put another way, how often would a Leap Year have to be omitted in order for the calendar to stay in step with the sun? Scholars like Robert *Grosseteste, *John of Sacrobosco, and Roger *Bacon advanced various estimates. A scientific commission mandated by *Pope Clement VI even proposed solving the lunar anomaly by scrapping the Metonic cycle in favour of planetary tables. No action, however, was taken either by the popes or by the great 15th-century *councils, despite the acute diagnosis of the astronomical issues by John of Gmunden and *Regiomontanus. *See also* ASTRONOMY; CLOCKS, SUNDIALS, AND TIME-KEEPING; LITURGICAL YEAR; LITURGY; MARTYROLOGY. FW

Bede, *De temporum ratione*, ed. C. W. Jones, *CCCM* 123b (1977).
—— *The Reckoning of Time*, tr. F. Wallis (1999).
A. Borst, *The Ordering of Time: From the Ancient Computus to the Modern Computer*, tr. A. Winnard (German original, 1990) (1999).
A. Capelli, *Cronologia, cronografia e calendario perpetuo dal principio dell'era cristiana ai giorni nostri: Tavole cronologico-sincrone e quadri sinottici per verificare le date storiche* ([2]1930).
C. R. Cheney, *Handbook of Dates for Students of English History* ([2]1995).
A. Cordoliani, 'Comput, chronologie, calendriers', in *L'Histoire et ses méthodes*, ed. C. Samaran (1961), 37–51.
C. V. Coyne, M. A. Hoskin, and O. Pedersen, eds, *The Gregorian Reform of the Calendar* (1983).
G. Declercq, *Anno Domini: The Origins of the Christian Era* (2000).
H. Grotefend, *Taschenbuch der Zeitrechnung des deutschen Mittelalters und der Neuzeit* ([10]1960).
C. W. Jones, *Bedae opera de temporibus* (1943).
—— *Bede, the Schools, and the Computus* (1994).
B. Krusch, *Studien zur christlich-mittelalterliche Chronologie: Der 84-jährige Osterzyklus* (1880).
—— *Studien zur christlich-mittelalterlichen Chronologie: Die Entstehung unserer heutigen Zeitrechnung* (1938).
D. McCarthy and A. Breen, *The Ante-Nicene Christian Pasch: 'De ratione paschali', the Paschal Tract of Anatolius, Bishop of Laodicea* (2003).
J. Moreton, 'John of Sacrobosco and the Calendar', *Viator*, 25 (1994), 229–44.
—— 'Robert Grosseteste and the Calendar', in *Robert Grosseteste: New Perspectives on his Thought and Scholarship*, ed. J. McEvoy (1997), 77–88.
D. Ó Cróinín, *Early Irish History and Chronology* (2003).
W. Stevens, *Cycles of Time and Scientific Learning in Medieval Europe* (1995).
A. Strobel, *Ursprung und Geschichte des frühchristlichen Osterkalendars* (1977).
R. D. Ware, 'Medieval Chronology: Theory and Practice', in *Medieval Studies: An Introduction*, ed. J. M. Powell ([2]1992), 252–77.

Calila e Dimna (*Kalila wa Dimna*) An extremely popular collection of animal stories tracing back to a 4th-century Sanskrit text, the *Panchatantra*. Translated into practically every language of the medieval Islamic and Christian worlds, this mirror for princes is centred around a pair of chatty, fable-spinning jackals—the scheming Dimna, who thirsts for recognition at the lion's court, and his more prudent brother Calila. The 6th-century Pehlevi translation by the Sassanian court physician Burzoe added more tales and an autobiographical preface. This version, now lost, was translated into Syriac, and most famously into Arabic by Abdullah Ibn al-Muqaffa, who added his own preface. This Arabic version gave rise to further translations into Persian, Turkish, and Greek and was versified in Arabic, Persian, and Turkish. In Europe, Ibn al-Muqaffa's Arabic text was translated twice into Hebrew and old Spanish. A Latin translation from the Hebrew, *Directorium vitae humanae* by John of Capua, became the source for subsequent translations into western European languages. Stories from the collection are found in many medieval works including *Petrus Alfonsi's *Disciplina Clericalis*, *Llull's *Llibre des Besties*, Lafontaine's *Fables*, and the *Roman de Renard*. *See also* ANIMALS, DOMESTIC, DRAFT, AND WILD; BEAST FABLE AND EPIC. LMA

J. M. C. Blecua and M. J. Lacarra, eds, *Calila e Dimna* (1985).

Calimala Outstanding *guild of medieval *Florence. Its members were merchants who engaged in foreign *trade and imported *wool cloth from *Flanders and northern *France for finishing. Among the seven *arti maggiori* of Florence, the Calimala played a vital role in the city's economic, political, and social life. It also maintained the *baptistery of S. Giovanni and the church of S. Miniato al Monte. FB

R. A. Goldthwaite *et al.*, *Due libri mastri degli Alberti: una grande compagnia di Calimala, 1348–1358*, 2 vols (1995).
J. M. Najemy, *Corporatism and Consensus in Florentine Politics, 1280–1400* (1982).
A. Sapori, *Una compagnia di Calimala ai primi del Trecento* (1932).

caliphate Office and jurisdiction of the caliph (*khalifa*), successor of *Muhammad. The first four *Medina-based caliphs (*Abu Bakr, *Umar, *Uthman, *Ali), the so-called 'rightly guided', were followed by dynastic caliphates, for example the Umayyads (661–750) and the Abbasids (750–1258). SMT

A. Asfaruddin, *Excellence and Precedence: Medieval Islamic Discourse on Legitimate Leadership* (2002).
P. Crone and M. Hinds, *God's Caliph: Religious Authority in the First Centuries of Islam* (1986).
H. Kennedy, *The Prophet and the Age of the Caliphates* ([2]2004).
W. Madelung, *The Succession to Muhammad: A Study of the Early Caliphate* (1997).

caliphate, Abbasid (749/50–1258) Founded by Abu al-Abbas al-Saffah; second *Sunni dynasty of the *Islamic empire, ruling for over five hundred years, with *Baghdad, founded by the second Abbasid caliph, al-*Mansur, as their seat of power.

The Abbasid caliphs claimed descent from Abbas ibn Abd al-Muttalib, *Muhammad's uncle, and fought the Umayyads believing themselves Muhammad's rightful heirs. The Abbasids based their claim to power on their religious righteousness as opposed to what they held to be the Umayyads' secularism and degeneration. Furthermore, unlike the desert-based Umayyads, the Abbasids envisioned a supranational order for the Muslim world. They gained the support of non-Arab Muslims (*mawali*), who under the Umayyads had remained outside the kinship-based society of Arab culture and were perceived as a lower class, and allied with the *Shiites who opposed the Umayyads.

The Abbasids' coming to power was seen by many as a revolution instituting new ways in place of the old, and in their campaign, launched from Persia, they called for an all-inclusive and egalitarian Islamic state. By shifting the seat of power from *Damascus to Baghdad the Abbasids stimulated a dynamic fusion of Arab and Persian cultures at all levels: political, administrative, literary, and artistic. This fusion was furthered by the inclusion of non-Arab Muslims in the Abbasids' court, though the strong presence of the Persian element alienated both the Khorasanian Arabs and the Shiites who had supported the Abbasids in their takeover. Once in power, the Abbasids embraced Sunni Islam and disavowed any support for Shiism. This led to conflicts and uprisings, resulting in the establishment of other Islamic dynasties such as that in *al-Andalus with its capital *Córdoba as a rival to Baghdad, the *Idrisid dynasty in the Maghreb, and the Fatimid dynasty in *Egypt.

Aside from these dynasties, the Abbasids faced challenges closer to home, especially after the fall of the Barmecides, a prominent Persian family of viziers. Late in his life Harun al-Rashid had his former vizier Jafar al-Barmaki executed (803). By the beginning of the 9th century, the caliphs' control was beginning to crumble; fighting broke out not only between Shiites and anti-Shiites but also between the two sons of Harun al-Rashid, al-Amin and al-Mamun, who fought for the throne. After a civil war al-Mamun became caliph and assigned to his brother al-Mutasim the task of creating an army of Circasso-Turkish slaves, known as the Mamluks, who would be loyal to him. Although the Mamluks provided the caliphate with a stable military force, they also created division between the caliphate and the peoples they ruled, especially as the Mamluks' power grew to dominate the caliphs who became figureheads. In February 1258 Baghdad was sacked by the Mongols, ending the Abbasid dynasty. ZSS

E. Hanne, 'Abbasids', *MedIsl*, vol. 1, 1–2.
H. Kennedy, *The Early Abbasid Caliphate* (1981).
—— *When Baghdad Ruled the Muslim World* (2005).
M. A. Shaban, *The Abbasid Revolution* (1970).

caliphate, Fatimid (909–1171) The Fatimids claimed to be descended from *Muhammad through his daughter *Fatima and her husband *Ali. They were an *Ismaili dynasty, direct descendants of the early *Shiites. Their empire extended from Palestine to Tunisia, where it was first established in 909. In 969 the Fatimids invaded *Egypt from Tunis and moved the seat of their caliphate to *Cairo as its new capital, building the al-*Azhar mosque as a training centre for missionaries. The Fatimid rulers called themselves caliphs, and rivalled the Sunni Abbasids in Baghdad whom they unsuccessfully tried to overthrow as leaders of the Muslim *Umma*. Nevertheless, by the beginning of the 11th century they claimed sovereignty over the whole North African coastal region, Sicily, southern Syria, the Hijaz, and Yemen.

Although the Fatimids espoused the official doctrine of Ismaili Shiism, promoting the belief that the Fatimid caliph was the only legitimate leader (therefore outlawing the practice of Sunni Islam), most of the Muslim population in their territories remained predominantly Sunni. With regard to other religions the Fatimids were known for their tolerance, except for one caliph, al-Hakim (r. 996–1021), who was known for his erratic behaviour; he ordered the destruction of the *Holy Sepulchre in *Jerusalem, and publicly proclaimed himself divine.

On the cultural level, Cairo, with al-Azhar, attracted Shiite scholars from all over the Muslim world, which gave rise to lively intellectual and religious debates as well as a corpus of Ismaili literature, theology, and *philosophy. In the social sphere the Fatimid dynasty played a major role in Arabizing most of North Africa. One famous move was the sending of Arab tribes to the *Berber regions of the Maghreb: *Ibn Khaldun commented on this event, highlighting the negative effects Arab nomads had on the sedentary Berbers.

The Fatimid dynasty was overthrown in 1171 by *Saladin, who founded the Ayyubid dynasty and restored Egypt to Sunni rule. ZSS

M. Brett, *The Rise of the Fatimids* (2001).
F. Daftary, 'Fatimids', *MedIsl*, vol. 1, 250–3.
H. Haji, *Founding the Fatimid State: The Rise of an Early Islamic Empire* (2006).
P. E. Walker, *Exploring an Islamic Empire: Fatimid History and its Sources* (2002).

caliphate, Umayyad (661–750) Islamic dynasty ruling from the death of *Ali ibn Abi Talib to that of Marwan II. The Umayyad caliphate was founded by Muawiya ibn Abi Sufyan of the Meccan clan of Umayya, and established itself in *Damascus, where Muawiya ruled as governor during the reign of *Uthman. The dynasty established Damascus as its capital, and instituted an administrative system that built on existing Byzantine structures and personnel. Arabic was declared the realm's official language, and an aniconic coinage with Arabophone inscriptions was issued. Umayyads built deluxe residences with Byzantine-style decoration, and imported artists to adorn the Damascus Great Mosque, transformed from a church.

This dynasty, the first Islamic state built on one family's claim to the right to rule, became reputed for running the state for its own profit, using harsh measures against its opponents. This resulted in the downfall of the Umayyads at the hands of the Abbasids. Opposition began soon after Muawiya's nomination of his son Yazid as his successor. This sparked many rebellions especially from among Ali's family, which ultimately divided Muslims into *Sunnis and *Shiites. After the Umayyads' defeat, the Abbasid armies hunted down all the Umayyads but one, Abd al-Rahman ibn Muawiya, who escaped to establish an Umayyad realm in *Córdoba. Under Umayyad rule in Spain (756–1031) *al-Andalus attained unprecedented prosperity, with art and architecture, philosophy, literature, and the sciences reaching high levels. While the Umayyads saw the expansion of the Islamic empire westward through North Africa as far as the Atlantic, across to Europe from the Iberian Peninsula, and eastward into central Asia and northwest India, it did not impose conversion to Islam which would have reduced the treasury's income from *jizya*, the *poll tax on non-Muslims. ZSS

S. S. Agha, *The Revolution that Toppled the Umayyads* (2003).
J. P. Berkey, *The Formation of Islam* (2003).
O. Grabar, 'Umayyad Palaces Reconsidered', *Ars Orientalis*, 23 (1992), 93–107.
G. R. Hawting, *The First Dynasty of Islam* (²2000).
—— 'Umayyads', *MedIsl*, vol. 2, 846–48.
R. Talgam, *The Stylistic Origins of Umayyad Sculpture*, 2 vols (2004).

calligraphy *See* WRITING AND WRITING MATERIALS.

Callimachus Experiens (Filippo Buonaccorsi) (1437–96) Italian humanist active in central Europe. After studying in Rome with Pomponio Leto, Buonaccorsi became involved in a conspiracy against Pope Paul II. He fled *Italy for *Poland in 1470, where he became tutor to the sons of King Casimir IV (1427–92). As Casimir's diplomat and chancellor, the renamed Callimachus tried to forge an alliance between the king and Frederick III against *Matthias Corvinus. After Casimir's death, Callimachus remained in the court of his son, King Albert. His major work, *Attila* (1489), while ostensibly about the 5th-century Hun, was actually a polemic against Matthias's expansionist policies. Callimachus wove criticism of Matthias into his treatment of Attila's Italian campaigns, knowing his readers would recognize the Hungarian king's policies under literary disguise. Yet there are signs that Callimachus grudgingly admired Matthias, not just in his epigrams, but also in his *Consilia* (1492). Anticipating Machiavelli, Callimachus describes the qualities an absolute ruler needs, in ways marked by Matthias's kingship. MDBi

Callimachi Experiensis Epistolae legationis responsa actiones res gestae Sigismundi, ed. A. T. Dzyatinski (1876).
—— *Attila: accedunt opuscula Quinti Aemiliani Cimbriaci ad Attilam pertinentia*, ed. T. Kardos (1932).
—— *Carmina*, ed. F. Sica (1981).
G. C. Garfagnini, ed., *Callimaco Esperiente, poeta e politico del 1400: Convegno internazionale di studi* (1987).
T. Kardos, *Callimachus: Tanulmány Mátyás király államrezonjáról* (1931).
G. Paparelli, *Callimaco Esperiente (Filippo Buonaccorsi)* (²1977).

Camaldolese, Order of *See* ROMUALD, ST.

Cambrai (Cambray) A politically valuable frontier town, Cambrai was near the French, Flemish, and German borders, with bishops dominant from the 10th century. Cambrai was a centre of cloth production in the later MA, and the cathedral's music school achieved international renown in the 15th and 16th centuries. JSO

W. Reinecke, *Geschichte der Stadt Cambrai bis zur Erteilung der Lex Godefridi (1227)* (1896).
L. Trenard, ed., *Histoire de Cambrai* (1982).

Cambrensis, Geraldus *See* GERALD OF WALES.

Cambridge (earldom) Held jointly with the earldom of Huntingdon by the Scottish royal family to 1237 (although it was unsuccessfully claimed separately twice in the 12th century). In 1340 *Edward III granted the earldom of Cambridge to his brother-in-law, then in 1362 to his fifth son, Edmund, later duke of *York. It then descended with the dukedom of York to *Edward IV, whose honours merged into the crown. RCD

G. E. Cokayne, ed., *The Complete Peerage of Britain*, 13 vols in 14 (1887), vol. 2, 492–77.

Cambridge, University of The town was a Norman outpost facing the Fens of *East Anglia on a commercially potent site where Roman roads crossed the river Granta (now Cam). The dues of the rich, annual Stourbridge *Fair were chartered to the *Augustinian Barnwell priory in 1211. Masters and scholars, most notably refugees from violence in *Oxford in 1209, came to teach in their own schools or to attend the schools of Barnwell and of the *Franciscans (from 1224). In 1231 *Henry III of England recognized the university under the judicial authority of the bishop of *Ely, and in 1233 *Pope Gregory IX granted it immunity from outside jurisdiction. To counterbalance the religious houses, Hugh de Balsham, bishop of Ely, founded the first college, Peterhouse (1284) on the model of *Merton College, Oxford. Other surviving medieval foundations are Clare (as University Hall, 1326), Pembroke (1347), Gonville and Caius (as Gonville Hall, 1348), Trinity Hall (1350), Corpus Christi (1352), Christ's (as Godshouse, 1439), King's (1441), Queens' (1448), St Catharine's (1473), Magdalene (as Buckingham, 1428), and Jesus (1496). St John's (1511) replaced the 13th-century Hospital of St John. Henry VIII folded King's Hall (1336) and Michaelhouse (1324) into his own Trinity College (1546). Canon and civil *law flourished in the 14th century with the energetic support of William Bateman, bishop of *Norwich (d. 1355), founder of Trinity Hall and re-founder of Gonville; orthodox theology dominated in the 15th. *See also* UNIVERSITIES. DHW

D. R. Leader, *The University to 1546* (1988), vol. 1 of *History of the University of Cambridge*.

Peterhouse, the earliest college of the University of Cambridge.

Cambridge Songs (Carmina cantabrigiensia) Latin anthology of some eighty secular and religious songs, both serious and comic, copied in Canterbury in the mid 11th century, now in *Cambridge. Many of the texts show German origins; some include *musical notation. They are distinct from the 'Later Cambridge Songs', a 12th-century collection. MJB

The Cambridge Songs (Carmina Cantabrigiensia), ed. and tr. J. Ziolkowski (1998).

Camelot *See* LITERATURES: ARTHURIAN LEGEND.

camera, apostolic Finance office of the *papal court (curia), directed by the chamberlain, a cardinal late in the 12th century. In the 14th century a cardinals' chamber separated, and the apostolic chamberlain, an archbishop, became principal minister of the papal government, head of a large bureau and scores of international collectors. DHW

Campanus of Novara (d. 1296) Italian astronomer and geometer, and editor of a widely used Latin text of Euclid's *Elements*. He authored works on the *calendar (*Computus major*), an introductory *astronomy text (*Tractatus de sphere*), and a more advanced treatise on Ptolemaic planetary theory later referred to as *Theorica planetarum*, which includes the earliest description in Latin of a planetary *equatorium, a device for calculating a planet's longitude. Also included are calculations of the distances and sizes of each of the planets. PGSo

F. S. Benjamin, Jr, and G. J. Toomer, *Campanus of Novara and Medieval Planetary Theory* (1971).

Campin, Robert (Master of Flémalle) (*fl. c.*1404–44) Netherlandish painter, dean of the Tournai guild (1426); probably taught Rogier van der *Weyden. No work signed by Campin is known, but all the panel paintings formerly attributed to a 'Master of Flémalle' (for example, the Merode Triptych) are now seen as his. AW

F. Thürlemann, *Robert Campin* (2002).

Camposanto (1278–1464) Cemetery in *Pisa. Constructed on the Campo dei Miracoli, its *frescoed *cloister encloses a 'sacred field' of earth transported from Golgotha during the Fourth *Crusade. *See also* BURIAL CUSTOMS AND MEDIEVAL CEMETERIES. CGM

C. Baracchini and E. Castelnuovo, eds, *Il Camposanto di Pisa* (1996).

M. Ronzani, *Un'idea trecentesca di cimitero: la construzione e l'uso del Camposanto nella Pisa del secolo XIV* (2005).

canals and locks *See* WATERWORKS.

Canary Islands Archipelago of volcanic islands located about 65 miles off the northwest shore of Africa on the Atlantic trade routes. The Canary Islands were Spain's first experience in claiming and exploiting already-occupied lands outside its peninsula. The islands, inhabited by the Guanches, were known in the classical period and were rediscovered by Castilian and Portuguese sailors. *Pope Clement VI claimed the right to dispose of the islands and awarded them in 1344 to Luis de la Cerda as a papal *fief. *Castile and Portugal both claimed the islands, sending expeditions to conquer and Christianize the native people.

French adventurers planned low-level economic exploitation and established plantations for *wine, *sugar, livestock, and wheat under the patronage of the kings of Castile. By the mid 15th century, conflict between Castile and Portugal had extended to the Canaries. As part of the Treaty of Alcaçovas in 1479, the Portuguese agreed to abandon their claims there in return for the islands of *Madeira and the *Azores. Under Queen Isabella I, Spain conquered the islands, settling Palma in 1490 and Tenerife in 1493. TMV

J. F. O'Callaghan, 'Castile, Portugal, and the Canary Islands: Claims and Counterclaims, 1344–1479', *Viator*, 24 (1993), 287–309.

J. H. Parry, *The Spanish Seaborne Empire* (1966).

Candlemas *See* VIRGIN MARY, LITURGICAL VENERATION OF.

candles *See* HEATING AND LIGHTING.

cannon *See* BALLISTICS, CANNON, AND GUNNERY; SIEGE MACHINES.

canon *See* CLERGY.

canoness A vowed religious woman who lived communally under a rule such as that of *Augustine and was governed by an abbess; canonesses were a parallel development to canons. The main work of canonesses was education in schools and the recitation of the *Divine Office. Canonesses lived under two vows, of obedience and chastity. Communities developed to be under one of two forms, secular (mainly noblewomen) and regular. AJD

Constitutions of the Regular Canonesses of the Order of St Augustine (1979).

I. Crusius, ed., *Studien zum Kanonissenstift* (2001).

D. Hamilton, *Chronicle of the English Augustinian Canonesses Regular* (1904).

canonical hours *See* DIVINE OFFICE.

canonists Teachers, writers, and practitioners specializing in canon *law. The term (ML *canonista*) was current from the beginning of the 13th century. Writers on *Gratian's **Decretum* may also be called decretists, while those who dealt with the *Decretals* of *Pope Gregory IX are frequently described as decretalists. JABr

K. Pennington and W. Hartmann, *Bio-Bibliographical Guide of Canonists*, faculty.cua.edu/pennington/biobibl.htm.

J. A. C. Smith, *Medieval Law Teachers and Writers, Civilian and Canonist* (1975).

canonization The first Christian saints, the early martyrs, were popularly acclaimed by the faithful, with no official process or oversight by the church hierarchy. When persecution of Christians ceased in the 4th century, prominent deceased bishops, nuns, monks, and civil rulers began to be proclaimed as saints. Saints' cults rapidly multiplied thereafter, along with *relics (some of dubious authenticity), *pilgrimages to saints' shrines, and accounts of *miracles. Bishops became increasingly involved in the selection and promotion of saints. Proclaiming a saint often involved a ritual exhumation and translation of the saint's remains to a new tomb, adding a feast day to the local liturgical *calendar, and the composition of a *vita* memorializing the saint's life, death, and miracles.

Papal interventions began in 993 when the bishop of *Augsburg asked Pope John XV and bishops assembled with him to recognize the sanctity of Bishop *Ulrich of Augsburg. The term 'canonization' was coined in the 11th century. In 1234, *Pope Gregory IX officially reserved the right of canonization to popes, but popular acclamation of saints continued to be widespread and accepted by *laity and *clergy. In the late MA, popes increased the legal procedures for verifying the sanctity of candidates for canonization, thus making the process more lengthy, costly, and difficult. Popes employed canonization as a vehicle for promoting specific models of sanctity. *See also* ACTA SANCTORUM; LITURGICAL YEAR; MARTYROLOGY. CMM

P. Delooz, *Sociologie et canonisations* (1969).

A. Vauchez, *Sainthood in the Later Middle Ages*, tr. Jean Birrell (French original, 1981) (1997).

D. Weinstein and R. M. Bell, *Saints and Society: The Two Worlds of Western Christendom, 1000–1700* (1982).

Canon of Scripture Texts included in the Bible as divinely inspired. Medieval Christianity accepted Esther 10:3f., Judith, Wisdom, Ecclesiasticus, Baruch, and Maccabees, later rejected by some. HCOB

R. T. Beckwith, *The Old Testament Canon of the New Testament Church and its Background in Early Judaism* (1985).

B. Metzger, *The Canon of the New Testament: Its Origin, Development, and Significance* (1987).

Canon of the Mass Eucharistic prayer (*canon*, 'rule') of the Roman rite, fixed from *c.*early 7th century. It includes a preface and series of petitions, traditionally designated by the opening Latin words of each section. *See also* MASS. DJKe

A. Hängi and I. Pahl, *Prex Eucharistica* ([2]1968).

J. A. Jungmann, *The Mass of the Roman Rite*, tr. F. A. Brunner (German original, 1950) (1951; rev. and abridged ed. 1959).

canons, regular and secular Clerics living in common under some approved rule or *canonicus*. Their origin lies in the early Christian presbyteral council of priests with whom the bishop shared his ministry and, often, his house. In response to the demands of evangelization beyond the mother church (*cathedra*), some of these priests ventured forth as missionaries and set up communities where they lived and prayed together. These clerical communities dotted the ecclesiastical landscape of early medieval Europe, especially in *cathedrals, but their way of life varied markedly. Some lived as monks espousing *poverty; others engaged in *pastoral care and kept personal property.

*Carolingian reformers attempted some clarification in making formal distinctions between *monasteries and canons' houses. The bishop of *Metz (St *Chrodegang) composed a simple rule for his cathedral clergy which became popular elsewhere in the empire. Other reform-minded bishops like Chrodegang drew up their own rules for *clergy living in common. Still, local colourations prevailed as did that chronic invitation to corruption, personal property. By the 11th century a more coherent provision was at hand in the so-called Rule of *Augustine. This rule of life, purportedly by the great bishop himself but probably written by an assistant, set out in brief how priests should live the common life in evangelical poverty. Those who adopted the Rule were called Regular or Augustinian (Austin) canons.

The rule's great popularity depended on the immense authority of its supposed author but also on the interpretability of its language. Some groups of canons emphasized the monastic features of the rule and formed independent communities dedicated to prayer and study in preference to traditional pastoral roles. These included the Victorines (Canons of *St-Victor) and the *Premonstratensian Canons (of Prémontré), both founded in the 12th century and under *Cistercian influence. Others emphasized the pastoral dimensions of the rule and set up almshouses in towns or hostels along travellers' routes such as the famous ones on St Bernard's Pass or along the pilgrims' route to *Santiago de Compostela.

Some bishops encouraged groups of clergy to live together under the guidance of local diocesan statutes rather than a rule which might, from a bishop's perspective, threaten divergent loyalties and arguments for canonical exemptions. Colleges of secular canons became associated with many cathedrals and the larger churches of a see. Like the regular canons, *education was a crucial component of these foundations, some of them later developing into *universities. But unlike the regular canons, seculars could own private property. They typically governed cathedrals and collegiate *churches through *chapters and elected leaders such as the provost or dean who ruled the chapter, the chancellor (*scholasticus*) who ran the cathedral school, the precentor (*cantor) who had charge of music, and the treasurer who managed the cathedral's funds. *See also* RELIGIOUS ORDERS. WJD

C. Deriene, 'Chanoines des origins au xiiii siècle', *DHGE*, vol. 12 (1951), 353–405.
K. Edwards, *The English Secular Cathedrals in the Middle Ages* (1967).
P. Frank, *Canonicorum regularium sodalitates et canonia* (1954).

canon table Concordance for the *gospels, created by Eusebius of Caesarea (4th century), providing a list of passages following the *liturgical year. Used by St *Jerome, they gained great popularity, especially for *manuscript books of the gospels. Canon tables are often illustrated by an architectural frame. ASM

M. P. Brown, *Understanding Illuminated Manuscripts* (1994).
R. G. Calkins, *Illuminated Books of the Middle Ages* (1983).
R. Nelson, 'Canon Tables' *ODB*, vol. 1, 374.

Canossa *Castle in Emilia, *Italy, 20 km southwest of Reggio Emilia; in 1077 site of the most famous incident of the *Investiture Controversy, a confrontation between the German King Henry IV and *Pope Gregory VII that undermined the authority of the emperors and bolstered that of the popes.

In January 1077, the recently excommunicated Henry made a desperate winter crossing of the *Alps. He was hoping to reconcile himself with Gregory before the pope could meet with German rebels determined to depose him. Henry found Gregory at the castle of Canossa, ancestral seat of the Margravine Matilda of Tuscany. Protected by Matilda's troops, the pope long refused to receive the penitent king. Henry was forced to stand humbly in the snow before Canossa's inner gate for three days, until Matilda and Abbot *Hugh of Cluny convinced Gregory to grant him *absolution.

The short-term victory was the king's. He had preserved his throne and by 1084 would be strong enough to force his way into Rome to receive the imperial crown. But the memory of his humiliation at Canossa seemed to validate Gregorian claims that the *papacy could judge and depose even the most powerful of secular rulers. The high medieval crisis of church and state had begun. DJH

Lampert of Hersfeld, *Annales*, ed. O. Holder-Egger, *MGH.SRG* 38 (1894), 283 ff.
K. F. Morrison, 'Canossa: A Revision', *Traditio*, 18 (1962), 121–48.
H. Zimmermann, *Der Canossagang von 1077: Wirkungen und Wirklichkeit* (1975).

Canossa, Meeting of (1077) In January 1077 a penitent Henry IV met *Pope Gregory VII at *Canossa to obtain absolution from the pope who had deposed and excommunicated him in February 1076. The king succeeded, thus preventing Gregory's journey to the *Augsburg assembly that was to decide the quarrel between Henry and the German princes. URB

I. S. Robinson, *Henry IV* (1999).

canso, canzone, chanson *Canso(n)* and *chanson* initially referred to the majority of texts sung by the *troubadours, and *canzone* is the name given to this lyrical form in the Italian vernacular. This *genre had its beginnings in the 12th

Henry IV and abbot of Cluny before Matilda asking her for intercession, on the way to Canossa.

century in the courts of southern France. It developed in France, northern Italy, and Cataluña, was imported by the *Sicilian School, and finally adopted as the most important poetic form by *Dante and canonized by *Petrarch.

According to the *vidas*, the troubadour *Giraut de Borneil first distinguished the term *canso* from the synonymous *vers*. *Canso* seems to be used critically for the first time by the anonymous Catalan author of the *Doctrina de compondre dictats*. It defined a composition of five to seven strophes (*coblas*, *stanze*) in rhymed verse. The *coblas* are organized in different patterns (some of which allow for mobility in the sequence of the stanzas, while others fix the order) both in order to preserve the text and as proof of the author's ability. The *canso* ends with a *tornada*, a shorter stanza containing the dedication to the addressee. In the *canzone*, each stanza consists of two parts (*fronte* and *sirma* or *coda*), which can in turn be divided into *piedi* and *volte*. The preferred verses of the *canzone* are hendecasyllables and septenaries, and the Italian counterpart of the *tornada* is the *commiato* or *congedo*.

In the *canso*, the first-person subject expresses his love for a lady, often unresponsive and distant. It is a celebration of **fin'amor*, and love is prescribed as its only subject. It depicts a relationship in which the *knight adopts a moral code in order to be worthy of the perfect lady. The song situates itself in the space of the desire between the knight and the lady, whose fulfilment is impossible, but it is not infrequently addressed to a male *patron, friend, or fellow poet. Among the most frequent *topoi* of the *canso* are the seasonal beginning, which allows a parallel between the mood of the poet and the season; the *senhal*, the pseudonym given to the lady, or sometimes patron; and the figure of the *gilos*, the opponent of the lovers. The expressions *trobar leu*, *trobar clus*, and *trobar ric/car* assessed the degree of obscurity and complexity of the poetry.

The Italian production of the 13th century differs from the forms developed in **langue d'oc* and *langue d'oïl* because the macrotext (*canzoniere* or *libro di poesia*, like Dante's *Vita nuova*) assumed primary importance over the single texts, in a growing tradition of self-commentary and self-interpretation. Furthermore, the divorce between poetry and music was almost immediate in the Italian tradition.

The first complete codification of the *canso/chanson/canzone* appeared in the *De Vulgari Eloquentia*, where Dante argued its superiority over all other genres (*DVE*, 2.3.1). With the poetry of Petrarch, the *canzone* received its consecration as the supreme genre of lyrical poetry. *See also* LITERATURES: OCCITAN. ESt

S. Gaunt and S. Kay, eds, *The Troubadours: An Introduction* (1999).

S. Huot, *From Song to Book: The Poetics of Writing in Old French Lyric and Lyrical Narrative Poetry* (1987).

M. Switten, *Music and Poetry in the Middle Ages: A Guide to Research on French and Occitan Song, 1100–1400* (1995).

W. Paden, *Medieval Lyric: Genres in Historical Context* (2000).

Canterbury (see) The primatial see of *England. The see was founded in 597 with the arrival of the mission to convert England, ordered by *Pope Gregory I and led by St *Augustine of Canterbury. While Gregory's plan called for the establishment of metropolitan sees at *London and *York, Augustine instead chose Canterbury as seat of the southern archbishop. By the end of the 12th century, Canterbury had jurisdiction over the majority of English sees, and had become a centre of intellectual activity. Canterbury's proximity to London and ecclesiastical authority often afforded its archbishops tremendous political power. Canterbury became an important *pilgrimage site after the martyrdom of Archbishop Thomas *Becket. *See also* CANTERBURY–YORK DISPUTE; DUNSTAN; LANFRANC; THEODORE OF TARSUS, ST. MBKo

Bede, *Bede's Ecclesiastical History of the English People*, ed. B. Colgrave and R. A. B. Mynors (1991).

E. Carpenter, *Cantuar: The Archbishops in their Office* ([3]1997).

I. J. Churchill, *Canterbury Administration*, 2 vols (1933).

Canterbury–York dispute A dispute centred on the archbishop of *Canterbury's contention that he was primate of all *England and the archbishop of *York's claim to a status equal to that of the archbishop of Canterbury. It took on special force in the generations following the *Norman Conquest. ECT

M. Gibson, 'Normans and Angevins', *A History of Canterbury Cathedral*, ed. P. Collinson, N. Ramsay, and M. Sparks ([2]2002), 38–68.

cantica nova *See* SEQUENCE.

cantiga 'Song' in Galician-Portuguese. Main genres are the male-voiced love song, usually with refrain; the female-voiced 'boyfriend song'; and the satirical invective song. The religious *Cantigas de Santa Maria*, from *Alfonso X's court, include *cantigas de miragre* ('miracle songs') with refrains. Music survives for six *cantigas de amigo* by *Martin Codax, seven *cantigas de amor* by *Dinis I of Portugal, and nearly all the Marian *cantigas*. MPF

M. Brea, ed., *Lírica profana galego-portuguesa*, 2 vols (1996).
B. M. de Castro, *As Cantigas de Santa Maria* (2005).
K. Kulp-Hill, tr., *Songs of Holy Mary of Alfonso X, the Wise* (2000).
G. Tavani, *La poesia lirica galego-portoghese* (1980–83).

cantigas de amigo *See* CANTIGA; LITERATURES: GALICIAN-PORTUGUESE.

cantigas de amor *See* CANTIGA; LITERATURES: GALICIAN-PORTUGUESE.

cantigas de Santa Maria *See* CANTIGA; LITERATURES: GALICIAN-PORTUGUESE.

Cantilupe, St Thomas de (St Thomas of Hereford) (*c*.1218–82) Bishop; canonized 1320. Studied canon *law at *Oxford and *Paris, and became chancellor of England (1265), but retired after Simon de *Montfort's defeat. As bishop he quarrelled with his former teacher, Archbishop Pecham, and died in *Rome appealing excommunication. RSO

M. Jancey, ed., *St Thomas Cantilupe, Bishop of Hereford* (1982).

Cantimpré, Thomas of (1201–72) *Dominican preacher, scholar and writer. Born in *Brabant, he joined the Augustinian *canons at Cantimpré, transferring after fifteen years to the Dominican order in *Leuven. Following studies in *Cologne and *Paris, he returned to Leuven to teach *philosophy and theology. His preaching was renowned throughout the *Low Countries, *France, and *Germany. The most influential of his compositions, *On the Nature of Things* (*Liber de natura rerum*), served over two centuries as a convenient guide to applying natural *philosophy to theology. SPM

R. S. Sweetman, 'Dominican Preaching in the Southern Low Countries, 1240–1260', Ph.D. diss. (Toronto, 1988).

cantio Latin term generally for 'song' (pre-14th century); thereafter applied to non-liturgical sacred song with strophic Latin texts. The latter was cultivated in monophonic and polyphonic textures, primarily by secular clergy and pedagogically by friars. BMW

J. Caldwell, 'Cantio', *NGD2*, vol. 5, 58–9.
D. Stevens, *Words and Music in the Middle Ages* (1986).

cantor (amarius, precentor) The cantor was one of the most important officers in medieval *monasteries and *cathedrals. From the *Carolingian period until the late 12th century (and in many places after that), he was in charge of the music and *liturgy, of the library, and of the *scriptorium. As he was the keeper of necrologies, he was also often responsible for the writing of chronicles and histories. MEF

M. E. Fassler, 'The Office of the Cantor in Early Western Monastic Rules and Customaries: A Preliminary Investigation', *EMH* 5 (1985), 29–51.
J. Grier, 'Roger de Chabannes (d. 1025), Cantor of St Martial, Limoges', *EMH* 14 (1995), 53–119.
—— *The Musical World of a Medieval Monk: Ademar de Chabannes in Eleventh-Century Aquitaine* (2006).

cantus coronatus Literally 'crowned song', although the exact meaning may lie anywhere from an awarded song to a mode of performance. Johannes de *Grocheio (*c*.1300) uses the expression, and a few **trouvère chansonniers* apply it to a dozen songs. JDH

H. van der Werf and W. Frobenius, 'Cantus coronatus', *Handwörterbuch der musikalischen Terminologie*, ed. H. H. Eggebrecht (1983).

cantus firmus (cantus prius factus) Borrowed melody, sacred or secular, set in *polyphony in slow note values in the tenor line. These pieces could be humble, elaborate (for example, *Busnoys's *Missa L'*homme armé*, based on a popular tune), or grandiose political *motets (for example, *Du Fay's *Nuper rosarum flores*). RF

E. Sparks, *Cantus Firmus in Mass and Motet* (1963).

canvas Made from *hemp, *flax, or combinations of these and/or *cotton. Coarse hempen canvas from rural looms was used for sacks and packing materials. Higher grade canvas, woven by urban artisans, was utilized for tents, pavilions, and sailcloth. In major port cities, sailcloth made from *linen or linen/cotton/hemp mixtures was woven and sewn by specialized workers according to meticulous prescriptions governing weight, density, and dimensions. In *Venice, the production of sailcloth was supervised by the *Arsenal. *See also* TEXTILES AND CLOTH-MAKING. MFM

M. F. Mazzaoui, *The Italian Cotton Industry in the Later Middle Ages, 1100–1600* (1981).

Capetians Royal dynasty whose members ruled *France in direct succession from the election of *Hugh Capet in 987 to the death of *Charles IV in 1328. The family came to power during the 10th century under the last *Carolingians. They were succeeded by a cadet branch, the *Valois. TFH

E. Hallam and J. Everard, *Capetian France, 987–1328* ([2]2001).
A. Lewis, *Royal Succession in Capetian France* (1981).

capitano del popolo Magistrate appointed to defend the **popolo* against elites in Italian *city-states. The office, first recorded in the mid 13th century, proliferated thereafter throughout northern Italy. The *capitano* was usually trained in law, recruited from afar, and appointed for six months to one year. *See also* CONSULATE; CONSULS. AHo

L. Martines, *Power and Imagination: City-states in Renaissance Italy* (1979).
A. Zorzi, 'The Popolo', in *Italy in the Age of the Renaissance: 1300–1550*, ed. J. M. Najemy (2004), 145–64.

Capitulare de villis vel curtis imperialis (812) An important regulatory document, or ordinance, for the administration of the imperial estates issued by *Charlemagne. A kind of blueprint for the entire *Carolingian imperial territory except *Italy and dependent on traditional Roman knowledge, the document offers detailed information about how to operate large estates, relying on a rotating field system. It includes such matters as how to raise animals, bees, and fish. Only a well-functioning system of estates could properly maintain an itinerant kingship and the Frankish army. AC

W. Elsner, *Zur Entstehung des Capitulare de villis* (1929).
F. L. Ganshof, *Frankish Institutions under Charlemagne* (1968).
A. E. Verhulst, *The Carolingian Economy* (2002).

capitulary A *Carolingian legal document recording administrative procedures or legislation enacted at the annual *assembly. *Charlemagne issued three types of capitularies: *capitula missorum*, administrative instruments that contained instructions for the *missi dominici* (a ruler's emissaries); the *capitula legibus addenda*, legislative acts that reformed existing laws; and *capitula per se scribenda*, such as *De villis* (770–800) or the Capitulary of *Frankfurt (794), that addressed subjects as varied as *estate management or *weights and measures. Most of Charlemagne's major capitularies addressed ecclesiastical reform, such as the Programmatic Capitulary (*Aachen, 802).

Charlemagne issued more capitularies after his imperial coronation in 800 than he did before, suggesting that the capitulary became an important tool to create and maintain imperial institutions in concord with ecclesiastic authorities. In all, some 200 Carolingian capitularies survive, partly because they were collected by the abbey of St Wandrille in 827. Despite these efforts, forged capitularies began appearing in the 9th century. Carloman issued the last capitulary in 884. TMV

J. R. Davis and M. M. Cormick, eds, *The Long Morning of Medieval Europe* (2008).
F. Ganshof, *Recherches sur les Capitulaires* (1958).
——*Frankish Institutions under Charlemagne*, tr. B. and M. Lyon (1968).
R. McKitterick, *The Carolingians and the Written Word* (1989).

Capréolus, John (Jean) (*c*.1380–1444) A *Dominican theologian whose major work was a defence of *Thomas Aquinas's theology against positions associated with *Duns Scotus, Petrus *Aureoli, and other 14th-century theologians. *See also* THOMISM. AVR

G. Bedouelle, R. Cessario, and K. White, eds, *Jean Capréolus en son temps (1380–1444)* (1997).
John Capréolus, *Thomistarum Principis Defensiones Theologiae Divi Thomae Aquinatis*, ed. C. Paban and T. Pègues, 7 vols (1900–1908; repr. 1967).

Caputiati (Capuciés) Lay *confraternity distinguished by their white hood with a lead badge of the Virgin and Child. Reacting against the brigandage in the *Auvergne *c*.1182, they swore to live decently, keeping the peace and fighting against lawbreakers. In arms with *Philip II Augustus in 1183, they helped massacre a brigand force, became politically significant, but soon were suppressed under charges of *heresy. DHW

DHGE vol. 11, 970–3.

Caput masses Three 15th-century polyphonic *Mass settings, one anonymous English, the others by Ockeghem and *Obrecht. Each is unified by a common *cantus firmus derived from the melisma on the word 'caput' in a *Maundy Thursday *antiphon. RF

M. Bukofzer, 'Caput: A Liturgico-Musical Study', *Studies in Medieval and Renaissance Music*, ed. idem (1950), 217–310.
A. Planchart, ed., *Missae Caput* (1964).

Carcassonne City dominating the Aude between *Narbonne and *Toulouse. A Roman colony later fortified by a 4th-century Visigothic fortress, then by Arabs (after 725). Bishopric established *c*.570. After Frankish conquest (late 8th century), seat of *Carolingian counts who came to rule *Béziers, Agde, *Foix, Comminges, and Bigorre. Principal city of the *Trencavel family from 1067, with a mint producing 'Ugonenc' pennies. Captured by crusaders (1209), it later became the seat of a royal seneschal. Its structures were restored in the 19th century. FLC

H. Débax, *La féodalité languedocienne* (2003).
G. Guilaine and D. Fabre, eds, *Histoire de Carcassonne* (2001).

Cardiff (Caerdydd) Borough in *Glamorgan, South Wales, near the confluence of the river Taff and Severn estuary. The medieval town was seeded by the foundation

Cardiff castle.

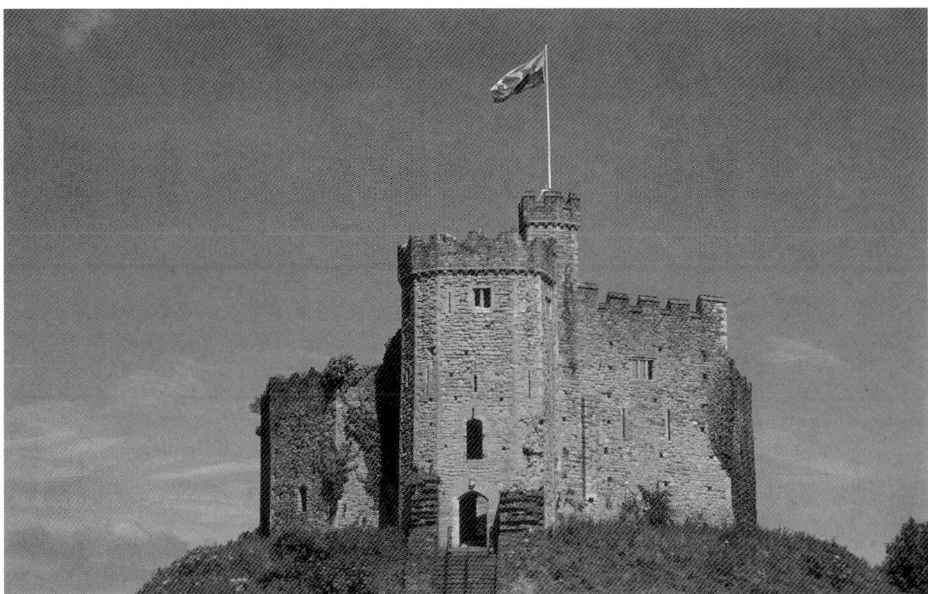

of the Norman motte and bailey castle in the late 11th century, built by Robert fitz Hamo on the site of Roman fortifications. Urbanization and expansion continued with the building of *parish churches, friaries, king's houses, tenements, and improvements to town defences. By the 1280s, Cardiff was the largest town in Wales, boasting 423 *burgages (urban plots). In 1451 Richard *Neville, earl of Warwick, issued a charter to the burgesses. The economic growth of the 13th century was followed by decline in the 14th century. A slow but steady recovery positioned Cardiff to become the national capital in 1955. *See also* SCOTLAND, IRELAND, WALES: EARLY WALES TO 1064. MTA

J. Davies, *A History of Wales* (1993).

—— *A Pocket Guide to Cardiff* (2002).

D. G. Walker, 'Cardiff', in *Boroughs of Medieval Wales*, ed. R. A. Griffiths (1978), 102–30.

cardinal A high church official, appointed by the pope. The cardinals (from Latin *cardo*, 'hinge') were defined as a 'sacred college' with clearly defined functions in the 11th century, when they became the electors of popes. There are three levels of cardinal: deacon, priest, and bishop. *See also* PAPACY. PGJ

G. D. Kittler, *The Papal Princes* (1960).

I. S. Robinson, *The Papacy, 1073–1198* (1990).

cardinal virtues *See* VICES AND VIRTUES.

carding and combing Two contrasting processes for preparing *wool for *spinning: combing aligned the fibres by means of a pair of long-toothed iron combs; carding evened the density of short-stapled wool with two leather-faced, wooden bats (cards) that included rows of wire hooks. FAP

D. Cardon, *La Draperie au Moyen Âge: Essor d'une Grande Industrie Européenne* (1999).

J. H. Munro, 'Combing, Carding and Bowing', in *The Cambridge History of Western Textiles*, vol. 1, ed. D. Jenkins (2003), 107–200.

Carlisle (see) Created by *Henry I in 1133 out of the archdiocese of *York and the earldom of Carlisle, it comprised northern Westmorland and most of Cumberland. The *Augustinian Canons' priory church was the *diocese's first *cathedral and the only English one governed by that *religious order. WJD

R. S. Ferguson, *Diocesan Histories: Carlisle* (1889).

Victoria County History: Cumberland, vol. 2 (1905), 1–210.

Carlos, prince of Viana (*c.*1421–61) Son of Juan II of *Aragon and Blanche of *Navarre, and author of a Chronicle of Navarre. Carlos (or Charles) was heir to the thrones of Navarre and Aragon-Catalonia. Upon the death of Blanche in 1441, Juan proclaimed himself king of Navarre and prevented the succession of Carlos, her heir. Instead, Juan named Carlos his lieutenant-general in Navarre. Carlos, supported by discontented nobles, fought Juan over his rights to Navarre and to Aragon between 1450 and 1460. Carlos had the support of his uncle, *Alfonso V the Magnanimous, who hoped to use Carlos as a lieutenant in the kingdoms of the Crown of *Aragon and may have thought to make him his heir. Juan, however, preferred Ferdinand (later Ferdinand el Catolico, king of Aragon), the son of his second marriage with Juana Enriques. Juan's refusal to reconcile with his oldest son led to his final break with Alfonso V in 1455–7. Carlos remained a focal point for discontent against Juan; later, upon Alfonso V's death, some Catalans plotted to crown Carlos king instead of Juan. Carlos predeceased his father. *See also* CATHOLIC MONARCHS. TMV

A. F. C. Ryder, *Alfonso the Magnanimous, King of Aragon, Naples, and Sicily, 1396–1458* (1990).

Carmel, Order of Mount *See* RELIGIOUS ORDERS.

Carmen de bello saxonico Composed in the winter of 1075/6, this verse *panegyric celebrated the victory of King Henry IV of Germany over the Saxon rebels in his kingdom. The anonymous author of the *Carmen* may perhaps be identical with the author of the near-contemporary *Vita Henrici IV imperatoris*. PSH

M. Schluck, *Die Vita Henrici IV Imperatoris: Ihre zeitgenössischen Quellen und ihr besonderes Verhältnis zum Carmen de bello Saxonico* (1979).

carmen figuratum *See* PATTERN POETRY.

Carmina Burana A compendium of over 200 Latin and German texts, largely in verse, assembled in *Germany in the early 13th century. The texts include satirical and goliardic pieces, love poems, and religious plays. MJB

Carmina Burana, ed. A. Hilka, O. Schumann, *et al.*, 2 vols in 4 (1930–71).

Carmina cantabrigiensia *See* CAMBRIDGE SONGS.

carnival A *festival rooted in ancient rituals of spring and fertility celebrated before *Lent when Christians engage in *penance, *fasting, and *prayer. Carnival afforded individuals the opportunity to act out fantasies and engage in behaviour normally inhibited during the rest of the year. LHZ

P. I. Barta, ed., *Carnivalizing Difference: Bakhtin and the Other* (2001).
C. Humphrey, *The Politics of Carnival: Festive Misrule in Medieval England* (2001).

carol (to 1400) A courtly or popular dance-song (12th–16th centuries); also an English form with Christmas-related texts, rooted in dance, featuring verse–refrain alternation, and with a popular flavour. PML

R. Greene, ed., *The Early English Carols* ([2]1977).
J. Stevens, ed., *Medieval Carols* ([2]1970).
—— *Words and Music in the Middle Ages: Song, Narrative, Dance and Drama, 1050–1350* (1986).

carol (1400–1500) English practice of joining popular and religious poetry in Latin and English with monophonic melodies and dance tunes, later elaborated in two and three voices. Many collections of polyphonic carols survive. RF

H. Keyte and A. Parrott, eds, *The New Oxford Book of Carols* (1992).
J. Stevens, *Music and Poetry in the Early Tudor Court* ([2]1979).

Carolingian dynasty Traditionally, the Carolingian family descended from a marriage alliance between two *Austrasian families, one headed by **Pippin I of Landen** (d. 639), *mayor of the palace (chief royal official), the other by *Arnulf, later bishop of *Metz. Arnulf's son married Pippin's daughter: their son **Pippin II of Herstal** won a victory at Tertry (687), established himself as mayor, and consolidated his family's position. When Pippin II died, his son by a second marriage, **Charles Martel**, struggled to secure the mayoral office and re-establish his family. By 737 he was ruling on his own, dividing his mayoral office between his sons **Pippin III** and **Carloman**. They faced provincial revolts and opposition from a half-brother; in 743 they restored a Merovingian to the throne. In 747 Carloman retired to a monastery, and Pippin began to gather support among the elite, who elected him king in 751. Pippin allied himself with the papacy, and Pope Stephen II, visiting Francia in 754, crowned and anointed Pippin, his wife, and their sons **Carloman** and **Charles**. Pippin held the royal office until his death, dividing the realm between his sons. When Carloman died in 771 Charles (*Charlemagne) secured the whole kingdom, and in 800 in Rome was crowned emperor by Pope Leo III. In 806 Charles divided his realm among his three legitimate sons, assigning the Frankish lands to **Charles**, and Italy and Aquitaine to **Pippin** and **Louis** respectively. Charles and Pippin died, so in 813 Charlemagne made Louis co-emperor and sole successor. In 817 Louis made his oldest son **Lothar** co-emperor and assigned his younger sons **Pippin** and **Louis** *Aquitaine and *Bavaria, in permanent subordination to Lothar. However, in 823 Louis had a fourth son, **Charles**, with his second wife. In trying to assign Charles a landed endowment Louis provoked a civil war (830–39). By 839 Pippin was dead and Louis had designated Lothar as heir to the empire, *Charles 'the Bald' as king of western Francia, and *Louis the German as king in Bavaria. On Louis's death (840) Charles and Louis allied against Lothar, and battle was joined until the Treaty of Verdun (843) whereby Charles received the western kingdom, Louis the lands east of the *Rhine, and Lothar the central lands from *Aachen to *Rome. Lothar (d. 855) divided his lands among his sons **Lothar II**, who received what came to be called *Lotharingia, **Charles**, who received *Provence, and *Louis II, who received Italy and the imperial title. **Louis the German** and **Charles the Bald** divided *Lotharingia in 870, and then Charles seized it on Louis's death and sought papal coronation as emperor. When two of Louis's sons died, and there were questions about the legitimacy of Charles 'the Bald's' surviving grandson, Louis the German's third son, *Charles III 'the Fat', briefly (885–8) reunited the empire. In 888 Charles's illegitimate son **Arnulf** succeeded as East Frankish king and became the last Carolingian emperor in 896. On his death in 900 his son **Louis IV 'the Child'**

After the Treaty of Verdun, 843.

succeeded in east Francia but died childless in 918. In the West Frankish kingdom Carolingians alternated with members of the *Robertian family. When **Louis V** (986–7) died the French nobles ignored his uncle and chose another Robertian, *Hugh Capet, whose family reigned in France until 1328. TFXN

W. Affeldt, 'Untersuchungen zur Königserhebung Pippins', *FMAS* 14 (1980), 95–187.
R. Gerberding, *The Rise of the Carolingians and the Liber Historiae Francorum* (1987).
I. Haselbach, *Aufstieg und Herrschaft der Karolinger in der Darstellung der sogenannten Annales Mettenses Priores* (1970).
E. Hlawitschka, 'Die Vorfahren Karls des Grossen', in *Karl der Grosse*, ed. W. Braunfels, vol. 1, *Persönlichkeit und Geschichte*, ed. H. Beumann (1965), 51–82.
S. Rösch, *Caroli Magni Progenies* (1977).
J. Semmler, 'Zur pippinid-karolingischen Sukzessionskrise 714–723', *DAEM* 33 (1977), 1–36.
K.-F. Werner, 'Die Nachkommen Karls des Grossen', in *Karl der Grosse*, ed. W. Braunfels, vol. 4, *Das Nachleben*, ed. Braunfels and P. E. Schramm (1965), 403–82.

Caron, Firminus *See* COMPOSERS, MINOR.

Carpathian mountains The highest sections of the Carpathians (*Montes Nivium*) formed boundaries between *Hungary and her neighbours: *Great Moravia, *Silesia, Greater *Poland, and Cumania, then the forming Romanian principalities in the late MA. Beyond groups (for example, *Székely*) in the high basins of the Carpathians for border protection, privileged populations of mainly German origin, specialized in trade and *mining, were settled in the northern (today in Slovakia) and the southern Carpathians (today in Romania) from the 12th century on. Germans and Hungarians, together with the Slavs in the north and the growing Romanian population in the southern and eastern Carpathians, resulted in a multilingual environment by the late MA. Connecting the *Hansa and the Levant, passes of the Carpathians played an important role in late medieval continental trade. Due to ore mining mainly in the northern Carpathians, Hungary became the first producer of gold, the second of silver, and a significant producer of copper in late medieval Europe. AKi

J. Kořan, *Přehledné dějiny československého hornictví* (1955).
A. Kubinyi, *Die mittelalterliche Städtebildung in südöstlichen Europa*, ed. H. Stoob (1977).
A. Maczak and H. Samsonowitz, *East Central Europe in Transition from the Fourteenth to the Seventeenth Century* (1985).
P. Z. Pach, *Levantine Trade in Hungary in the Middle Ages* (1975).
T. Răzvan, *Civilizatia românilor între medieval şi modern* (1987).
E. Westermann, ed., 'Bergbauvereine als Verbraucherzentren', *Vierteljahresschrift für Sozial- und Wirtschaftsgeschichte*, 130 (1996).

carpentry *See* WOOD AND WOODWORKING.

carpet page *See* MANUSCRIPT ILLUMINATION.

carrack A large sailing ship developed in the 14th century that carried a combination of square and *lateen sails, first on two and later on three masts. *See also* SHIPS, SEAFARING, AND NAVIGATION. RWU

Carrara family Italian comital family and lords of *Padua. In the 11th century the Carraresi held lands south of Padua and by the mid 12th century had acquired comital rights. Among the lesser feudal lineages of the region, the fortunes of the Carraresi rose in the late 13th century. Through judicious marriage alliances and the re-concentration of Carrara estates in the main line under **Giacomo da Carrara** (1264–1324), the family emerged as the most powerful in Padua by 1300. Threatened by Veronese expansionism, the *commune elected Giacomo as **signore* in 1318. The family's hegemony was consolidated by Giacomo's nephew **Marsilio, 'il Grande'** (1294–1338), and by **Francesco I, 'il Vecchio'** (1325–93), under whom power was concentrated in the Carrara household and exercised through signorial appointees. Francesco I and his son **Francesco Novello** (1359–1406) pursued an aggressive policy of territorial expansion at the expense of Padua's neighbours, provoking conflicts with the *Visconti of *Milan and with *Venice. In 1405 Venice conquered Padua, executed Francesco Novello, and exiled the Carrara family. The Carraresi are notable for their *patronage of several humanists, notably *Petrarch, who dedicated a treatise on government to Francesco I, and the educators Giovanni Conversini and Pier Paolo Vergerio. LDA

G. Conversini, *'De dilectione regnantium'*, in *Two Court Treatises*, ed. B. G. Kohl and J. Day (1987), 93–249.

B. G. Kohl, *Padua under the Carrara, 1318–1405* (1998).

F. Petrarca, *Rerum Senilium liber XIIII: Ad magnificum Franciscum de Carraria Padue dominum: Epistola I: Qualis esse debeat qui rem publicam regit*, ed. V. Ussani (1922).

carroccio Large ceremonial wagon symbolizing the honour and independence of an Italian city during the high MA. It carried the city's standard and an altar, and was often taken with the army to their military engagements. The earliest recorded *carroccio* was that of the Milanese at the defence of their city in 1038–9. KDV

E. Voltmer, *Il carroccio* (1994).

Cartagena, Alonso de (1385/6–1456) Son of Pablo de Santa María, chief rabbi then bishop of *Burgos following his conversion in 1390. Following an illustrious diplomatic career, Alonso inherited the bishopric on Pablo's death in 1435. A leading exponent of Castilian vernacular *humanism, he translated *Boccaccio, Seneca, Cicero, and Aristotle, debated *translation theory with Leonardo Bruni, and wrote treatises on lay piety, noble *education, *historiography, and the unity of the Christian faith (including an eloquent defence of converted *Jews). *See also* CARTAGENA, TERESA DE; CONVERSOS; LITERATURES: CASTILIAN. JW

O. T. Impey, 'Alfonso de Cartagena, traductor de Séneca y precursor del humanismo español', *Prohemio*, 3 (1972), 473–94.

J. N. H. Lawrance, *Un tratado de Alonso de Cartagena sobre la educación y los estudios literarios* (1979).

B. Rosenstock, *New Men: Conversos, Christian Theology, and Society in Fifteenth-Century Castile* (2002).

Cartagena, Teresa de (b. *c.*1420) Niece of Alonso de *Cartagena, a *Franciscan nun who wrote two spiritual treatises: the *Arboleda de los enfermos* (*c.*1450), a consolatory work inspired by her deafness, and the *Admiraçión operum Dey*, which includes an eloquent defence of female *literacy. Her learning and rhetorical strategies initiate a long line of literate Hispanic nuns. *See also* WOMEN, RELIGIOUS. JW

Arboleda de los enfermos y Admiraçión operum Dey, ed. L. J. Hutton (1967).

The Writings of Teresa de Cartagena, tr. D. Seidenspinner-Núñez (1998).

Carthusians, Order of An order combining elements of solitary and communal *monasticism, the Carthusians originated in 1084, when St *Bruno founded the Grande *Chartreuse in the *Dauphiné *Alps north of *Grenoble. The customs of the order were first redacted in 1127 by *Guigo I, fifth prior of the Grande Chartreuse, and approved by Pope Innocent II in 1133. Augmented customaries were adopted in 1271 and 1368. The first *general chapter of the order, of which the Grande Chartreuse was the mother-house, was held in 1140. Carthusian life was austere: gathering twice daily for the *liturgy, and for common meals only on Sundays and feast-days, the monks mainly engaged in solitary work and devotional exercises in hermitages grouped around a central cloister. Nuns adhering to Carthusian customs are attested from the mid 12th century and were formally approved in 1271. The order grew slowly, numbering just under 200 houses in the 15th century, most of them concentrated in the Dauphiné, Burgundy, and the Netherlands. The Grande Chartreuse has been destroyed several times, but the largest of medieval *charterhouses survives at Villeneuve-lès-Avignon in *Provence. *See also* HERMITS. LDA

B. Bligny, *Recueil des plus anciens actes de la Grande Chartreuse (1086–1196)* (1958).

P. De Leo, ed., *L'Ordine certosino e il papato dalla fondazione allo scisma d'Occidente* (2003).

P. Gröning, dir., *Die grosse Stille* (film) (2005).

Guigues I, 'Coutumes de Chartreuse', *Sources chrétiennes*, 313 (1984).

C. Le Couteulx, *Annales Ordinis Cartusiensis*, 8 vols (1887–91).

G. Schlegel and J. Hogg, eds, *Monasticon Cartusiense*, 4 vols (2004–).

carucate (Latin, *caruca* 'plough'). Term in *Domesday Book denoting both a unit of assessment and a *peasant landholding unit in the *Danelaw counties. Like the hide, the carucate amounted to a nominal 120 acres. SRIF

C. Hart, *The Danelaw* (1992).

R. Faith, *The English Peasantry and the Growth of Lordship* (1997).

F. W. Maitland, *Domesday Book and Beyond* (1897).

Cashel The Rock of Cashel in Munster was one of Ireland's greatest religious centres. A royal fort, the site was presented to the church in 1101 and became an episcopal see in Ireland's 12th-century reforms. King-bishop Cormac MacCarthy had a major Romanesque church built at Cashel, consecrated in 1134. PGJ

S. L. Hunt, *Cashel and its Abbeys: A Historical Guide* (1952).

D. G. Marnane, *Cashel: History and Guide* (2007).

Cashel, Synod of (1172) A church council, presided over by a papal *legate, which accepted *Henry II of England as lord of Ireland. According to Giraldus, the Irish bishops agreed that in matters such as *marriage law, *baptism of children, payment of tithes, and probate, they would in future follow English norms. JBG

M. T. Flanagan, 'Henry II, the Council of Cashel and the Irish Bishops', *Peritia*, 10 (1996), 184–211.

Casimir, St (1458–84) Prince of *Poland; second son of King Casimir IV and Queen Elizabeth. Offered the

Portrait of a Carthusian (1446) by Petrus Christus. The Metropolitan Museum of Art, New York.

Hungarian throne while a teenager, Casimir failed to defeat the Turks and returned to Poland. He served as king of Poland during his father's five-year absence and proved a capable administrator. He refused all offers of marriage, citing a vow of chastity. His feast day is 4 March. MMS

R. Brady, *Saint Casimir, 1458–1484* (1965).
S. Uminski, *The Royal Prince: The Story of Saint Casimir* (1971).

Caspe, Compromise of In 1412 the Compromise of Caspe ended a two-year interregnum in the Crown of *Aragon by granting the throne to Fernando de Antequera (Fernando I, 1412–16), a Castilian from the *Trastámara ruling family. Fernando's reign ended three centuries of Catalan political dominance of the Crown of *Aragon, a prosperous and strategically important Mediterranean kingdom. When King Martí the Humane died in 1410 without legitimate heir, the resultant four-way contest pitted Fernando against Federico de Luna, Jaume de Urgell, and Louis of *Anjou, duke of Calabria. The **cortes*, the *antipope Benedict XIII, and nine electors (three each from *Aragon, Catalunya, and *Valencia) excluded Luna because of his youth, leaving Urgell, grandson of King Alfonso IV (1327–36) and son-in-law of King Pedro IV (1336–87), with the strongest claim. The murder of the archbishop of Saragossa ended the hopes of both Urgell, who was implicated in his death, and Anjou, who was supported by the archbishop. TME

M. Dualde Serrano and C. M. Jos, *El compromiso de Caspe* ([2]1976).
S. Sobreques i Vidal, *El compromis de Casp i le noblesa catalana* (1973).

Cassel Small town in southwestern *Flanders. On 23 August 1328 the French army of *Philip VI defeated an army of Flemish rebels led by Niklaas *Zannekin. The so-called peasants' revolt—though many of the insurgents belonged to both the urban and rural middle classes—began in 1323 against the rule of Louis of Nevers, but turned out to be a more radical revolt against aristocratic rule in maritime Flanders. Repression was severe, and the cities and the rural districts of coastal Flanders temporarily lost some of their political autonomy. PSt

D. Nicholas, *Medieval Flanders* (1992).

Cassel, battle of (1328) After five years of Flemish rebellion, *Philip VI determined to end it militarily. Targeting a rebel army on the crest of Cassel hill, the French tried to lure the Flemings to fight on more even terrain below. But the Flemish surprise attack reached even the king's tents before being defeated by a quickly ordered cavalry charge. KDV

K. DeVries, *Infantry Warfare in the Early Fourteenth Century: Discipline, Tactics, and Technology* (1996).

Cassian, John (*c*.355–*c*.440) Monk and ascetic writer from southern Gaul, Cassian travelled in the east, especially *Egypt, and introduced rules of eastern *monasticism into the west. His most important works, *De Institutis* and *Collationes*, concern monastic life and sin. He was regarded in the MA as the originator of Semi-*Pelagianism. BEM

S. D. Driver, *John Cassian and the Reading of Egyptian Monastic Culture* (2002).
C. Stewart, *Cassian the Monk* (1998).

Cassiodorus, Flavius Magnus Aurelius (d. *c*.580) Ecclesiastical writer and statesman. His life comprised a secular and a sacred phase. Born *c*.485 into a distinguished senatorial family from Scyllaceum (Squillace) in southern *Italy, Cassiodorus initially opted for a political career, serving first as *consiliarius* (503–6), and then as *quaestor* (507–11), *consul ordinarius* (514), and *magister officiorum* (523–7). From there he moved on to the same distinguished rank held previously by his father, Praetorian Prefect of Italy (533–7). Around 538 he retired from public service and founded a monastery on his family estate, called Vivarium, intended to serve as a centre of Christian studies rivalling the secular tradition of the Roman rhetorical schools still flourishing in 6th-century Italy. Cassiodorus' surviving writings follow the lines of his secular and sacred vocations. They include the *Institutes* for Vivarium, the letters from his administrative correspondence which he entitled *Variae*, and his commentary on the Psalms. SDD

M. Cappuyns, 'Cassiodore', *DHGE* 11, 1349–1408.
S. Leanza, ed., *Cassiodoro: Dalla corte di Ravenna al Vivarium di Squillace* (1993).
J. O'Donnell, *Cassiodorus* (1979).
A. van de Vyver, 'Cassiodore et son oeuvre', *Speculum*, 6 (1931), 244–92.

cassock *See* LITURGICAL VESTMENTS.

castellan Polish official, who, until *c*.1300, exercised military and judicial authority in a specified area, based in a fortified site given by a ducal or royal authority. Thereafter much of his responsibilities were transferred to a newly established officer, the *starosta* (*capitaneus*). The castellan retained titular dignity, though separate from a *castle or territory, assuring him of a place in the diet and eventually in its upper house, the Senate. PWK

'Kasztelan', in *Słownik historii Polski*, ed. T. Łepkowski (1969), 131.
S. Kutrzeba, 'Starostowie, ich początki i rozwój do końca XIV wieku', *Rozprawy Akademii Umiejętności: wydział historyczno-filozoficzny*, 45 (1903), 231–348.

castellany The basic comital territorial structure of *Flanders from 993/4 on. The original military function broadened later into economic and judicial administration. Its court handled civil and criminal actions. In the 12th century several of its judicial functions moved to the *bailiffs. Most castellans' offices became honorific after 1400. WP

D. Nicholas, *Medieval Flanders* (1992), 82–9, 332–7, 363–6.

Castile Kingdom, originally a frontier county, definitively united with the kingdom of *León in 1230 and became the dominant realm of Iberia by the end of the MA.

1. Frontier county, to 1035
2. Rise of Castile, 1035–1157
3. Society and economy
4. Conquest and crisis, 1157–1284
5. A contested kingdom, 1284–1479

1. Frontier county, to 1035

Castile emerged in the early 9th century as a frontier county of the kingdom of *Asturias-León, strengthened by the creation of fortified sites such as *Burgos (884). Its border gradually reached the river *Duero by 912. The Duero region was resettled partly by *Mozarabs fleeing from *al-Andalus and through *presura* (appropriation) by migrants from Asturias and the *Basque country. There were significant numbers of free peasant smallholders, inhabiting an extensive network of *aldeas* (villages) and subject to a distinctive array of local laws and customs increasingly articulated from the 10th century in *fueros* (charters) granted by counts or other landowners. Recent Spanish historians, however, have rejected a traditional notion that Castile was not properly *feudalized.

The county became more autonomous in the 10th century, as the authority of the kingdom of Asturias-León waned. Count Fernán González (ruled 931–70) established marital ties with the rising royal house of *Navarre, and, assuming the title *gratia Dei comes*, established *de facto* patrimonial control over Castile; exploiting factional divisions, he led a movement to depose the newly crowned Sancho I 'the Fat' of León (958). Castile was ravaged by Muslim incursions later in the century, culminating in the raids of al-*Mansur, but benefited from the decline and fragmentation of the *caliphate. The counts collaborated with *Berber troops to defeat Mohammed II in 1009 and plundered the city of *Córdoba. The county fell under the aegis of *Sancho III 'el Mayor' of Navarre, who took possession of Castile in his sister's name and designated his son Fernando as the new count.

2. Rise of Castile, 1035–1157

To his inherited county of Castile, Fernando added the kingdom of León by defeating his brother-in-law Vermudo III (1037); he was recognized as king of Castile as well as León. Over the next century, military expansion—facilitated by heavy cavalry—brought sudden wealth to Castile. Fernando advanced against Muslim territories in the north of modern Portugal and elsewhere, acquiring the relics of *Isidore of Seville and transporting them to León, and enforced *paria* tributes in gold from the **taifa* kingdoms of *Seville, *Toledo, Badajoz, and Saragossa. Prosperity stimulated ties with France, particularly with the Burgundian reform monastery of *Cluny. Increasing French influence in Castile during the late 11th century was reflected in the appointment of French bishops to Palencia and Toledo, in the propagation of the Rule of St *Benedict, and in the new Roman liturgy, replacing its Visigothic-Mozarabic equivalent.

On his death in 1065, Fernando divided his realm among three sons, leaving *Galicia and Portugal to García (1065–72), León to *Alfonso VI, and Castile to Sancho II (1065–72). Sancho, frustrated by the partition, exiled García to Seville (1071), overthrew Alfonso, and was crowned king of León in 1072, but was assassinated—possibly with Alfonso's connivance—later that year. Alfonso VI now took possession of León, Galicia, and Castile (1072–1109), emerging as the most powerful of the peninsular kings and settling the frontier regions between the Duero and Tajo rivers. Castilian expansionism, however, provoked the intervention of the *Almoravids, bringing heavy defeats at Sagrajas (1086) and Uclés (1108) and interrupting the flow of *paria* tributes. Such problems were compounded by internal instability under *Urraca, leading to incursions by her estranged husband *Alfonso I el Batallador of Aragon.

These setbacks were reversed in the reign of *Alfonso VII, which witnessed imperial pretensions to dominion over other Christian kingdoms. Long before his death, Castile had moved into line with the crusading ethos forged at the papal curia. The move away from an earlier spirit of pragmatic coexistence can be traced from the beginning of the 12th century. Nonetheless, new scholarship has emphasized the permeability of the medieval frontier between Castile and al-Andalus. The romanticized figure of Rodrigo *Díaz de Vivar, *El Cid*, had been one mercenary among thousands who crossed the frontier to serve Muslim masters.

3. Society and economy

The nobility was a particularly dominant force in Castile. Its militaristic values permeated Castilian culture, and there were extremely close ties between the nobility and the monasteries. Military campaigning reinforced the development of this open elite, and especially before the mid 13th century the spoils of *Reconquista, which arguably retarded commercial enterprise in Castile, strengthened a symbiotic relationship between monarchy and nobility. The power of Castilian families like the Laras, Haros, and Castros derived in large part from their presence at the royal court and the temporary delegation of royal authority in the form of local *tenencias*. Landed estates were not yet comparable in size to the *mayorazgos* (entailed estates) of the late MA. Nonetheless, agrarian rents were an important form of

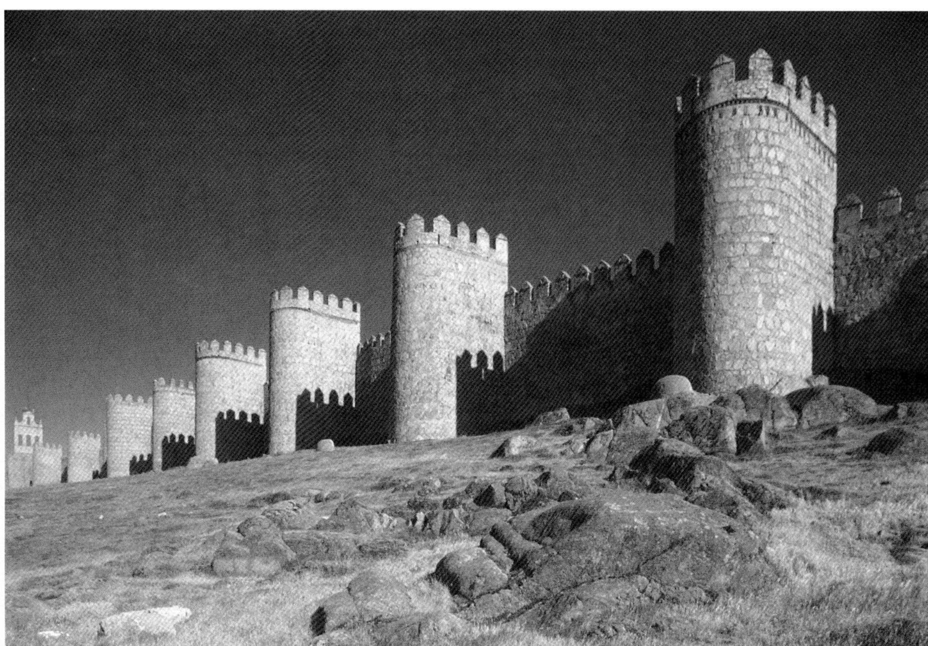

The fortress of Ávila, Castile.

income, and a rise in land values after the 11th century encouraged the growth of seigneurial lordships (*señoríos*) at the expense of peasant freeholders. Noblemen often oversaw repopulation, and many peasants became tenants on lands owned by lay lords (*solariegos*). By the 12th century, the jurisdictional relationship between lord and peasant was closely associated with the land itself. In *behetrías*, tenants had some room for choice in choosing a lord; the *Libro Becerro de Behetrías* (1352) provides an exceptional survey of landholding in northern Castile. In many parts of northern Castile, because of difficult soil conditions, extremes of climate, and under-population, pastoral transhumance was widespread.

The new vitality of the pilgrimage route to *Santiago de Compostela from the late 11th century provided an important stimulus for towns such as Nájera and Burgos. During the 12th and 13th centuries, some northern ecclesiastical towns tripled in size, while Castilian-Leónese armies conquered a number of thriving urban centres (including Cuenca and Toledo). Meanwhile, new fortified frontier towns including Ávila (1087), Segovia (*c.*1088), and *Salamanca (*c.*1100) enjoyed special royal *fueros* (charters) and played a particularly important role in resettlement because of difficulties posed by under-population; they were also integral to a process of feudal reorganization. The economy of such towns rested on livestock and raids into Muslim territory. Regional *fairs were established in Valladolid (1152) and Cáceres (1229); in the late MA, the most active fair was in Medina del Campo. Castilian merchants and craftsmen formed *cofradías* (*confraternities) to protect their economic interests. As military expansion declined after 1250, the production of merino wool became central to the economy. The perennial problem of under-population, later aggravated by the effects of the *Black Death, necessitated the rapid development of sheep raising—as well as cattle ranching—in the southern *meseta*, and the creation of the *Mesta. Zamora, Ávila, Segovia, and Soria developed important textile trades. Cantabrian and Basque ports, trading in iron, wine, textiles, and Castilian *wool, formed the Hermandad de las Marismas (1296). In the 14th century, the Castilian fleet promoted the commercial interests of Castilian merchant communities in *Bruges, *Rouen, and elsewhere, collaborating with the French in attacking English forces off La Rochelle (1372) and burning the English coastline in the 1370s. Domestically, the towns of Castile emerged as a significant political force, especially during royal minorities.

4. *Conquest and crisis, 1157–1284*

Alfonso VIII (1158–1214) led a new phase of Castilian expansion into Cuenca (1177) and toward the Guadiana river. He faced a dangerous counterattack by the *Almohads and was defeated heavily at Alarcos (1195), but emerged victorious at the pivotal battle of Las *Navas de Tolosa. By the time *Ferdinand III of Castile inherited the throne of León in 1230, the Almohad empire had disintegrated into new *taifa* kingdoms.

However, these developments were a mixed blessing for Castile. Ethnic tensions between Christian elite and Muslim subjects exploded in a *mudéjar* rebellion of 1264, backed by

Ibn al-Ahmar, king of *Granada; the subsequent expulsion of Muslims from Andalusia and Murcia aggravated underpopulation. The new territories were difficult to resettle; the conquests drastically diminished tribute payments; and an influx of precious metals catalysed spiralling inflation throughout Castile, threatening revenues. These economic problems accentuated social and political tensions under *Alfonso X, especially between the increasingly assertive crown and a conservative nobility, resulting in an aristocratic rising in 1272 and contributing to the rebellion of the *infante* Sancho (later Sancho IV, 1284–95) in 1282–4. The *caballeros villanos* of the royal Castilian towns took on greater political weight during this period. The **cortes*, a consultative outgrowth of the royal curia that had met infrequently between 1188 and 1250 in León and Castile, were now summoned more often to raise taxation (although their role declined in the later MA). Meanwhile, Alfonso faced hostility from the Castilian church, which had been taxed heavily to finance campaigns in Andalusia and had been poorly compensated in the newly conquered south. Clergymen accused him of reducing the church to servitude under the influence of his Jewish advisers. Alfonso's remarkable cultural achievements were therefore accompanied, and perhaps stimulated, by endemic political instability.

5. A contested kingdom, 1284–1479

The Marinids of Morocco posed a severe threat for three generations after 1275, when an army under Abu Yusuf crushed Alfonso X's forces near Écija. Sancho IV was able to recapture Tarifa, but the decisive moments occurred under Alfonso XI (1312–50), who defeated the Marinids at the battle of *Salado, thus ending North African intervention in Iberia, before taking Algeciras in 1344. Internal tensions within the governing elite proved more enduring. *Pedro I was deposed, and the civil war that led to this dynastic revolution was magnified by the *Hundred Years War.

The *Trastámara dynasty was secure by the reign of Enrique III (1390–1406). However, its authority rested upon aristocratic consensus, and therefore upon lavish grants of land and jurisdiction to the high nobility. Newly powerful noble lineages rose to great prominence, and by the mid 15th century the aristocracy enjoyed virtual economic hegemony. Its patrimonial and jurisdictional power provoked rising agrarian unrest (for example in Galicia, 1467), compounding growing social and ethnic malaise. Nor did the *mercedes* (royal grants) prevent endemic tensions between crown and nobility, although some families favoured co-operation with a strong monarchy through a system of royal favourites (*privanza*). Others, including the phenomenally wealthy Juan Pacheco, marquis of Villena, favoured limited monarchy and a powerful Royal Council composed of leading noblemen. This ideology was crystallized by opposition to the royal favourite Álvaro de *Luna. The nobility remained politically disunited, but the practical power of the crown was always limited in the face of noble privileges as well as urban *fueros*.

Despite civil strife, Castile was the dominant power on the peninsula: nearly four times the size of the mainland territories of Aragon and containing four-fifths of the population of peninsular Spain. Unlike the Crown of *Aragon, it was unified by a single language, coinage, administration, and fiscal structure and had enjoyed a period of unusual tranquillity in the first decade of *Enrique IV's reign. *See also* ALCÁNTARA, ORDER OF; CALATRAVA, ORDER OF; CATHOLIC MONARCHS; CONVIVENCIA; JEWS IN THE IBERIAN PENINSULA; JUAN II; NÁJERA, BATTLE OF; SANTIAGO, ORDER OF. SRD

S. Barton, *The Aristocracy in Twelfth-Century León and Castile* (1997).

I. Á. Borge, *Monarquía feudal y organización territorial: Alfoces y merindades en Castilla, siglos X–XIV* (1993).

R. Collins, *Early Medieval Spain: Unity in Diversity* (1995).

S. Doubleday, *The Lara Family: Crown and Nobility in Medieval Spain* (2001).

R. Fletcher, *The Quest for El Cid* (1989).

T. F. Glick, *From Muslim Fortress to Christian Castle: Social and Cultural Change in Medieval Spain* (1995).

H. Grassotti, *Las instituciones feudo-vassalláticas en León y Castilla*, 2 vols (1969).

R. Highfield, ed., *Spain in the Fifteenth Century* (1972).

J. N. Hillgarth, *The Spanish Kingdoms, 1250–1516*, 2 vols (1976–8).

H. Kamen, *Spain, 1469–1714: A Society of Conflict* (1983).

M. T. S.-Q. de León, *Linajes nobiliarios en León y Castilla, siglos IX–XIII* (1999).

P. Linehan, *Spanish Church and Society, 1150–1300* (1983).

—— *History and the Historians of Medieval Spain* (1993).

A. R. López, *La consolidación territorial de la monarquía feudal castellana: Expansión y fronteras durante el reinado de Fernando III* (1994).

A. McKay, *Spain in the Middle Ages: From Frontier to Empire* (1977).

J. F. O'Callaghan, *A History of Medieval Spain* (1975).

E. Procter, *Curia and Cortes in León and Castile, 1072–1295* (1980).

M. Á. L. Quesada, *Los señores de Andalucía: investigaciones sobre nobles y señoríos en los siglos XIII a XV* (1998).

B. F. Reilly, *The Contest of Christian and Muslim Spain* (1992).

—— *The Medieval Spains* (1993).

A. Rucqoi, ed., *Realidad e imágenes del poder: España a fines de la Edad Media* (1988).

castles, fortifications, and fortresses The castle—a combination of palace, which is unfortified, and fortress, which implies a purely military function—emerged on the European landscape from the 11th to 15th centuries and is perhaps the most universally recognized symbol of the MA. It served as fortress, residence, governmental centre, economic centre of an agricultural estate, and even stage for the enactment of the drama of courtly life and was the

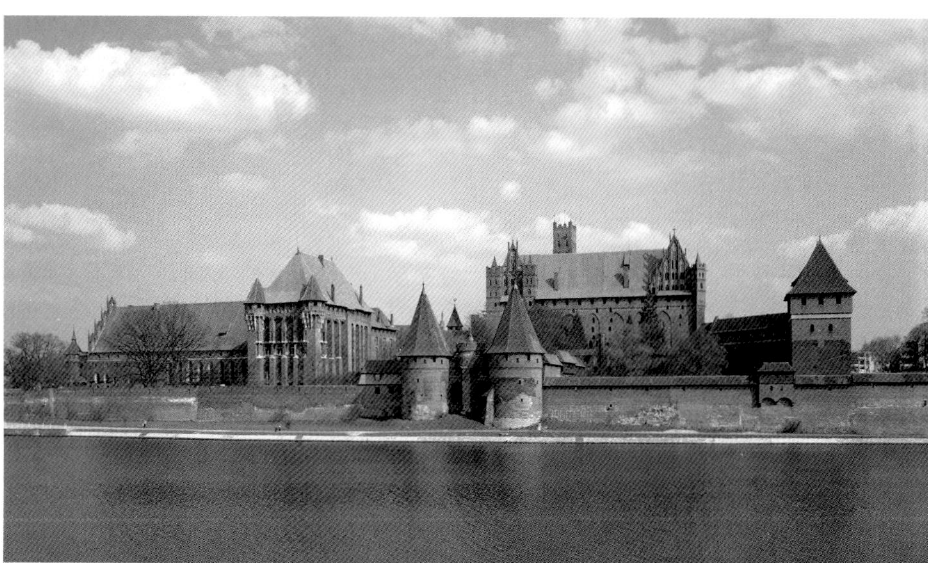

Malbork castle, Poland.

visible symbol of its owner's authority. Its name comes from the Latin *castrum and *castellum* (a walled enclosure or stronghold; any inhabited place in the early MA) and entered the vernacular languages of Europe as castle, *castillo*, *castello*, or *château*, although *burh*, *burg*, *borg*, *berg*, or *burgh* remained the preferred form in Germanic languages.

1. Early structures
2. Stonemasonry walls of the past
3. Castles of wood
4. First stone castles
5. The castle's role
6. Decline of the great tower
7. Centre of government

1. *Early structures*

Since the earliest times people built walls to define space, control livestock, and defend themselves. Two building traditions underlie castle construction in Europe: *stonemasonry learned from the Romans and characteristic of the Mediterranean world, and the *timber and earth structures characteristic of people living outside the Roman Empire. Celtic and Germanic people built timber and turf houses, surrounded by ditches and embankments (made from the earth removed for the ditches), and topped with wattle (woven branches) fences. In time they improved their defences with palisades, timber towers, and complex earthworks. These early buildings usually had circular plans, since a circular wall encloses the most territory within the shortest length.

In the 9th century, with the breakup of the *Carolingian empire and the onset of *Viking and *Magyar attacks, the need for building fortifications became paramount. Vikings were master carpenters, as witnessed by their *ships, and built circular (or ring) forts and staging area base camps (Trelleborg in Denmark), and trading centres that developed into true cities. When they settled in northern France (*Normandy), they continued the turf and timber tradition and developed what came to be known as the motte and bailey castle, a form popular with the Germanic peoples all over Europe, but today usually associated with Normans in France and England.

2. *Stonemasonry walls of the past*

The Romans introduced stone and mortar buildings to the rest of Europe. Wherever Roman armies marched, they built camps and towns with rectangular grid plans having major crossing streets with regularly disposed houses, barracks, or other buildings. Hadrian's Wall across northern Britain is typical. It consists of a single masonry wall of concrete with stone facing, varying between seven and nine feet thick and about fifteen feet tall, with regularly spaced towers, at one-mile intervals. The builders took advantage of the lay of the land, and the wall follows the crest of hills. The wall marked the boundary and functioned as a lookout post and a defence. The wall was crenellated, that is, raised portions (merlons) acted as shields for defenders and lower sections (crenels) permitted the defenders to shoot out over the wall. This wall is typical of the single-wall defensive system.

A more sophisticated defence in depth—double walls and a moat—was developed by Byzantine builders in the 5th century to defend *Constantinople. The walls were built of stone and concrete and bonded with brick, creating a banded effect that was not only effective but decorative and came to symbolize the imperial construction. The main wall was fifteen feet thick and defended by 96 towers, each of which

Wawel castle, Poland.

could become an independent fortress. The military engineers then constructed a second lower wall in front of the first, creating a killing field between them. Men on the high wall could see and shoot over the heads of those in the first line of defence. A moat (a water-filled ditch) protected the outer wall from tunnelling or battering rams. An attacking army faced a triple line of defence: they had to bridge the moat, break through a wall over six feet thick, and cross an open space before arriving at the main wall and towers, all the while fending off the *archers and rock-throwing machines on the walls. The land walls of Constantinople stood for 1000 years, serving as a model for military engineers and protecting the city. They were finally breached by the Turks using cannons in 1453.

3. Castles of wood

Timber and turf castles could be built rapidly and were especially useful when conquered territory had to be secured behind a rapidly moving army. *William the Conqueror built timber forts across England and may have brought prefabricated structures with him. These castles were essentially towers and stockades, which could be built rapidly and cheaply and required no specialized workmen.

Eighth- and ninth-century buildings were small, and some were designed to safeguard a small number of people and intended as a refuge during time of trouble. The tower could be built on a natural hill or on an artificial hill (a motte), created when a ditch was dug and a mound created. While the tower could provide living space, usually it was a last refuge, and a hall and other buildings stood near the tower. A wall and ditch surrounded the buildings, forming a yard known as a bailey. The motte and bailey castle is simply a man-made hill supporting a tower and a walled yard. Mottes varied in size, but Thetford, the largest motte in England, has a diameter at the base of 360 feet and a height of about 80 feet. As soon as possible, a tower was built on the motte to serve as the home for the lord or his constable (governor of the castle). This tower was called the 'great tower'. The words 'dungeon' and 'keep' were not used until the 14th century. The bailey in England is known as a 'ward'. Inside the bailey, timber and turf buildings housed people, animals, and supplies. By the 12th century at the height of castle building, the number of buildings inside the walls increased and included the public buildings: chapel and great hall, a residential chamber block and other sleeping quarters, kitchen, barns, stables, and storeroom. A well or some provision for water was necessary as well as a smithy, mill, and oven since the castle had to be self-sufficient.

Wooden castles, obviously, were vulnerable to fire. As soon as possible walls were converted to stone. The artificial mound of earth that formed the motte could not support the weight of stone walls, so natural hills were sought out. The cliff beside a river that formed a natural water barrier was especially prized.

4. First stone castles

Stone towers appeared in the Loire river valley as early as the 10th century (Langeais has been dated to 992). Loches, recently dated between 1012 and 1035, is the earliest surviving

Hradschin castle, Czech Republic.

Visegrád palace, Hungary.

great tower to combine the hall, lord's chamber, and chapel. In England William the Conqueror replaced the motte and bailey castles as soon as possible: the White Tower (so called because of plastered and whitewashed walls) of the *Tower of London is the most famous, but the early 12th-century keep at *Rochester is the largest surviving example—115 feet tall with additional ten-foot corner turrets and a plan about 70 feet on a side. These early stone keeps were square or rectangular in plan, with massive towers reinforcing the corners. Rochester had four stories: ground-floor storage, a principal floor divided into two double-height halls, and private rooms on the upper floors. Fireplaces, latrines, and small chambers were built in the thickness of the wall. Stairs in a separate fore-building provided access to the hall by way of a drawbridge. A *chapel was also located in the fore-building. A central opening allowed supplies to be raised from floor to floor by means of a windlass on the roof. The roof formed a firing platform for the garrison. At the top of the wall crenellations protected soldiers on the wall-walk (licences to crenellate, issued by the king as official permission to fortify a place, indicated a family's social status), and the garrison could build wooden platforms and walls (hoardings) out from the top of the wall to give extra protected space. Water and *sanitation were important considerations, and keeps were built over a spring or well whenever possible, and the buildings were provided with toilets, although with a direct drop into the ditch or moat. People bathed in portable tubs. Braziers, open fires, or wall fireplaces created smoke-filled rooms (chimneys came later), but because of the danger of fire, kitchens and bake ovens were usually placed in separate buildings in the courtyard. The chapel could be an independent building or, as at Rochester, a part of the fore-building. Castles had to be kept up to date; for example, in 1190 *Richard I (Lionheart) spent enormous

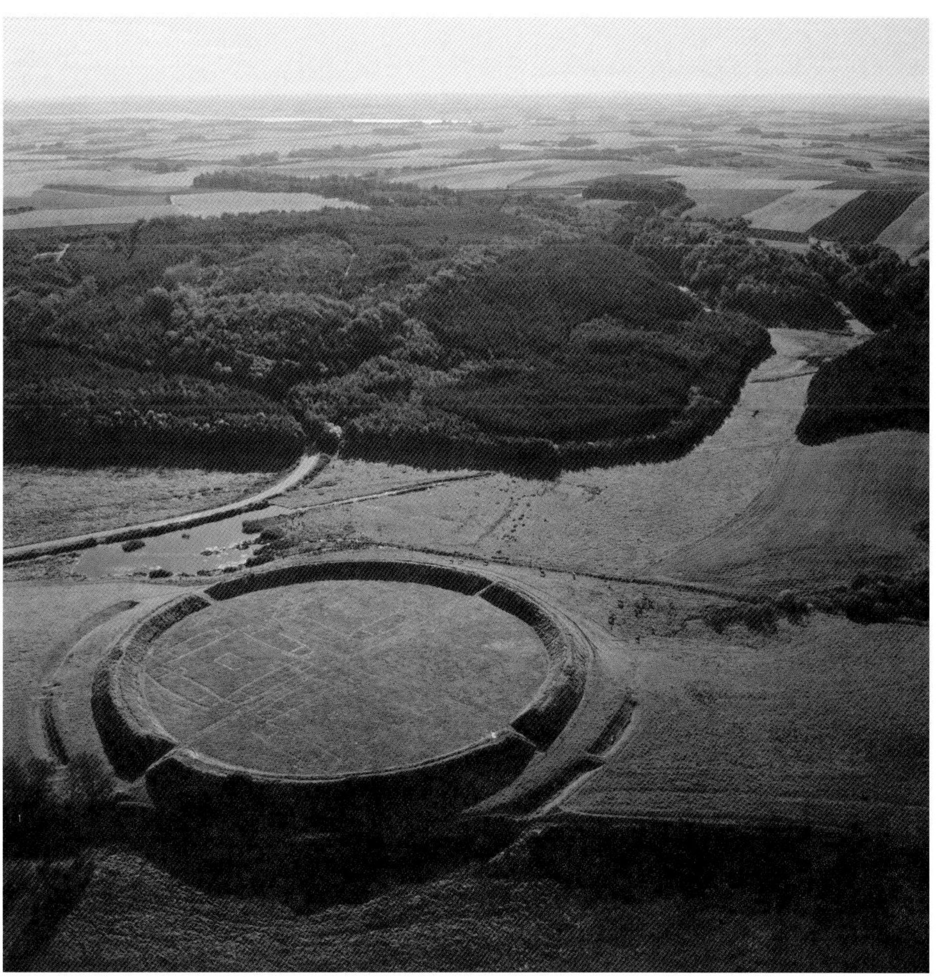
Ring fort reconstruction at Fyrkat, Denmark.

sums on a new ditch, bank, and curtain wall for the Tower of London.

5. *The castle's role*

A castle provided a secure residence and military headquarters for a ruler or lord of a territory. It enabled the resident commander to control the territory including borders and key transportation hubs. The lord or his constable oversaw his manors and fulfilled his feudal obligation to administer justice. The castle included a great hall and a prison. When the men were away at war or at court their wives often were left in charge, and many grand ladies led spirited defences of their lands and homes.

Although castles were symbols of authority and the social status of the families who owned them, they were built primarily to defend against siege *warfare, techniques developed centuries earlier. Medieval warfare consisted of long sieges and relatively short battles in the field, and rarely involved a large army. A well-built castle could be taken only through prolonged siege, that is, starvation, or by treachery. Advantage lay with the castle since it could be well provisioned while the attackers had to live off the land, and armies were dependent on feudal levies. Men were likely to be more interested in returning home to defend their own property than in maintaining a siege. An assault on a castle—only when negotiation, treachery, or starvation failed to prevail—meant that the attackers had to go over, under, or through the walls and then engage in hand-to-hand combat. To go over the wall required the construction of timber towers or the use of scaling ladders. Slower but more effective was tunnelling under the wall, causing it to collapse. To breach the walls the attackers could use battering rams and stone-throwing machines (very large catapults, the most powerful of which was the *trebuchet, a giant sling). To attempt to storm the castle gate was deadly. Gatehouses had sliding metal grilles (portcullis), drawbridges, changes of direction that defeated rams, and murder holes in the vaults. Nevertheless, for all their imposing defences and appearance, most castles stood for only a few years. From the 11th to the 13th centuries, castles stood as great military machines, but beginning in the 14th century and surely by the 15th and 16th centuries, they became symbolic buildings, their role in military strategy replaced by fortresses built to withstand artillery. The introduction of *gunpowder in wars irrevocably changed the nature of battles and affected the design of castles. The high walls of the castle made excellent targets for cannons; the new buildings needed distance rather than height.

6. *Decline of the great tower*

The great towers looked imposing, but they proved to be impractical for either fighting or living. Stacked rooms and spiral staircases made movement difficult. And these staircases weakened the corner turrets just at the tower's most vulnerable spot. Windows were needed for light and air but further weakened the walls. During a siege, the garrison had little flexibility, isolated as they were in a single tower. Straight walls proved difficult to defend because of blind spots. Windows reduced to arrow slits did not permit the archers to see the ground, although by the end of the 12th century sloping embrasures permitted archers to shoot downward and at angles. The best defence proved to be a very wide moat, river, or swamp, too wide and deep to jump, wade, fill, or bridge. The last of the great towers may well have been Richard I's *Château-Gaillard north of Paris. But even this magnificent keep with double walls around the court and independent fore-building could not withstand a prolonged siege, and the castle fell to the French in 1204.

7. *Centre of government*

In magnificent halls, the local ruler could hear petitions and administer justice. Towers could also serve as strongrooms to protect treasure and important documents. Increasing reliance on a money economy and on a rule of law required archives and treasuries. *Scribes worked in *chancery halls. The king and his great lords needed imposing, even intimidating, headquarters.

The great tower was replaced by a walled enclosure, which permitted more effective use of troops and better living conditions. The castle was designed with a curtain wall, that is, a wall seemingly hung like a curtain between towers, each of which functioned like a keep. The builders of the walls of Constantinople had seen the virtues of wall towers and curtain walls, and western crusaders learned from them. The curtain wall and tower design was known as the 'enceinte' or 'enclosure castle'. Two plans emerged—a series of courtyards that had to be taken one after another, or a concentric defence in which a second wall entirely surrounded the inner wall. Every section of the wall could be seen and defended from the mural towers, which were rounded rather than cubical, using cylindrical or D shapes, so that no flat surface faced a battering ram and every surface was visible. Stone machicolations replaced wooden hoardings. *See also* CAERNARFON; KARLŠTEJN CASTLE AND CHAPEL; KRAK DES CHEVALIERS; MONTSÉGUR; PRAGUE CASTLE; TRIM CASTLE; WINDSOR CASTLE AND CHAPEL. MStok

F. B. Andrews, *The Medieval Builder and his Methods* (1993).
T. S. R. Boase, *Castles and Churches of the Crusading Kingdom* (1967).
H. Colvin, A. J. Taylor, and R. A. Brown, *A History of the King's Works* (1963–82).
C. L. Coulson, *Castles in Medieval Society: Fortresses in England, France, and Ireland in the Central Middle Ages* (2003).
R. Higham and P. Barker, *Timber Castles* (1992).
M. Johnson, *Behind the Castle Gate: From Medieval to Renaissance* (2002).
H. Kennedy, *Crusader Castles* (1994).
J. Mesqui, *Châteaux et Enceintes de la France Médiévale* (1991–3).
N. J. G. Pounds, *The Medieval Castle in England and Wales: A Social and Political History* (1990).
M. Stokstad, *Medieval Castles* (2005).
A. H. Thompson, *Military Architecture in England During the Middle Ages* (1912).
S. Toy, *A History of Fortification from 3000 BC to AD 1700* (1955).
A. Tuulse, *Castles of the Western World*, tr. R. P. Girdwood (German original, 1958) (1958).

castrum Latin for 'fortification'; remained in use throughout the MA; however, unlike its Roman use, it almost always denoted a permanent fortified structure, not also a fortified camp. It was borrowed into Arabic (through Greek *kastron*) as *qasr*. By the later MA vernacular terms for castle—*château, schloss, castello, castellum*, and so forth—began to appear more frequently in Latin sources. KDV

J. F. Verbruggen, 'Note sur le sens des mots castrum, castellum, et quelques autres expressions qui désignent des fortifications', *Revue Belge de philologie et d'histoire*, 28 (1950), 147–55.

catacomb An underground passageway, notably that used as a cemetery with recesses for burials in walls and floors. Catacombs were developed in the later Roman Empire as a space-saving solution to the growing quantities of people who desired to be buried instead of cremated, Jews and Christians in particular. Several were renowned for martyrs' graves; some are decorated with wall paintings. Those in Rome soon turned into important places of collective Christian memory. After the translation of the *relics to churches inside the city, most catacombs fell into oblivion until the Counter-Reformation. *See also* BURIAL CUSTOMS AND MEDIEVAL CEMETERIES; MARTYROLOGY; SARCOPHAGUS AND TOMB. SdB

V. F. Nicolai, F. Bisconti, and D. Mazzoleni, *Le catacombe cristiane di Roma: origini, sviluppo, apparati decorativi, documentazione epigrafica* (1998).
J. Osborne, 'The Roman Catacombs in the Middle Ages', *Papers of the British School at Rome*, 53 (1985), 278–328.

Catalan Grand Company An organization of Catalonian, Aragonese, and other mercenaries, founded by Roger de Flor, a disgraced *Knight Templar. They fought in Sicily's Aragonese–Angevin wars, until the Peace of Caltabellota (1302) made them unwelcome. In 1303 they contracted with Byzantine emperor Andronicus II to fight Turkish advances in Asia Minor. Catalan operations there (1304), though successful, were marred by discord and local frictions. Rewarded anew, the Catalans were transferred to European Thrace. But the treacherous murder of Flor (April 1305) dissolved all loyalties. The Catalans established themselves independently around Gallipoli, plundering widely (1305–8), then moving into Thessaly (1309). After serving the Latin duke of Athens, they overthrew him (1311) and seized his territory. Under titular lordship of the Sicilian king and his descendants, then of other absentee patrons, the Catalans maintained their ranks and their control of Attica until finally driven out of Athens by Nero Acciajuoli (1388). *See also* CRUSADES; MERCENARY COMPANIES. JWB

A. E. Laiou, *Constantinople and the Latins: The Foreign Policy of Andronicus II, 1282–1328* (1972).
A. Rubió i Lluch, *Diplomatari de l'Orient Català* (1947; repr. 2001).
P. Lock, *The Franks in the Aegean, 1204–1500* (1995).
A. Lowe, *The Catalan Vengeance* (1972).
W. Miller, *The Latins in the Levant: A History of Frankish Greece (1204–1566)* (1908).
K. M. Setton, *Catalan Domination of Athens, 1311–1388* ([2]1975).

Catalonia Located in northeast Spain on the Mediterranean, Catalonia was a major maritime power as part of the Crown of *Aragon. The region was shaped by the counts of *Barcelona from the 9th century on.

1. Before the MA
2. The 6th through 7th centuries
3. The 8th through 10th centuries
4. The 11th through 12th centuries
5. The 13th through 15th centuries

1. *Before the MA*

The Greeks established colonies at Empúries and Roses; the Carthaginians and Romans disputed the territories in the second Punic War. The lands were permanently subjugated by the elder Cato. Sertorius used the region as his base against Sulla; Caesar fought the important Ilerdan campaign against Pompey. Latin, Roman *law, and coinage were introduced to lasting effect, Tarragona being the capital of Hispania Citerior, then of the Tarraconensis. Christianity arrived early, spread rapidly, suffered martyrdoms (Cugat, *Fructuosus), and maintained order when imperial authority waned. With the Germanic invasions from the 3rd century, the fortified city of Barcelona overtook Tarragona in importance, particularly in the early days of *Visigothic dominance.

2. *The 6th through 7th centuries*

The Ostrogothic Teudis (531–48) made Tarragona his capital, before power shifted to central Spain. The eastern Iberian peninsula then became a semi-autonomous zone, ruled by dukes and counts, while judges executed the law. Roses and Tarragona, at Byzantine instigation, rebelled against King *Leovigild but were defeated in 578. At Tarragona, Hermenegild was killed for refusing to renounce Catholicism (585). But it was the church, imbued with monastic spirituality, that provided the lasting influence while the Gothic element was absorbed into the Romanized world. The eastern Iberian peninsula revolted against Wamba under Duke Paul, but he was defeated in 673.

3. *The 8th through 10th centuries*

There were further revolts against Rodrigo in 710 and 711, aided by Byzantines and Arabs, the latter then devastating much of the region and then *Narbonne and *Toulouse (714–21), before being defeated at *Poitiers by Charles Martel (732). While the region of Tortosa, Tarragona, and Lleida became a part of the Muslim world for the next 400 years, the Moorish influence in the northern region of Catalonia was never strong and, while garrisons were stationed there, the civil and ecclesiastical administration in Girona and Barcelona and to the north remained largely intact. Taking advantage of internal dissension among Muslim rulers, the Franks under *Charlemagne and Louis absorbed Girona, Urgell, and Barcelona (785–801) but attempts to recapture Tortosa (808–9) failed. The fourteen counties of the eastern Pyrenean region thus came under the control of *Carolingian administration, subject to the rule of counts, of whom the count of Barcelona became pre-eminent. Roman liturgy and Reformed *Benedictine *monasticism arrived, while doctrinal dissent, provided by Bishop *Felix of Urgell's support of *Adoptionism, was eliminated. As Carolingian rule disintegrated, the counts, many of them sons and grandsons of Count Guifré of Barcelona (870–97), administered the counties almost independently, notably Sunyer (911–47) at Barcelona, Girona, and Osona; Miró II (897–927) at Cerdanya, Conflent, Berguedà, and Besalú; and Sunifred II (897–950) at Urgell. Cerdanya and Conflent looked to Rome for support (950–51), and a number of monasteries received papal exemption. Count Borrell II of Barcelona and Urgell (947–92) allied with *Córdoba, an alliance that served him ill when al-*Mansur broke with him, defeated him in battle, and sacked Barcelona (985).

4. *The 11th through 12th centuries*

In the lands under Muslim rule, irrigation was developed for farming, *mosques were constructed, and there were impressive *castles at Tortosa, Lleida, and Siurana. But the *caliphate of Córdoba collapsed in 1031, and a group of petty states, the **taifas*, took its place, notably at Lleida, Tortosa, and *Valencia, and these now formed the principal

Roman fortified bridge in Besalú, Catalonia.

opposition to the Christians, for whom the early 11th century would be an age of learning and letters under Oliba (971–1046), abbot of *Ripoll and bishop of Vic. This was coupled with a remarkable economic expansion that attracted people from the mountains to the plains. Again it would be for the church, inaugurating the *Peace and Truce of God, to maintain social order as comtal authority collapsed. Castellans ravaged the lands, and peasants were maltreated, a situation that did not improve when Ramon Berenguer I (1035–76) of Barcelona in trying to re-establish his hold on authority created a new aristocracy of enfeoffed knights and castellans, that is, *castlàns*, whence Catalonia. Through the imposition of the Peace and Truce, shrewd marriage alliances, dominance of the *taifa* rulers, entrance into the Mediterranean trading world, and encouragement of the papal reform movement in their lands, the counts consolidated their position, though the rise of the *Almoravids checked their ambitions to the South. Under Ramon Berenguer III (1097–1131), the county of *Provence was gained through marriage (1112), Cerdanya was annexed (1117), and Tarragona restored (1129) through the efforts of St Oleguer and Robert Burdet. By this time a Catalan identity existed, strengthened by a distinctive Catalan language. Under *Ramon Berenguer IV, Catalonia was united to the kingdom of *Aragon when the count was married to Petronilla (1137), daughter of Ramiro II. Thereafter, neither can Catalonia be understood without Aragon nor Aragon without Catalonia. Ramon Berenguer conquered Tortosa, Lleida, and Fraga (1148–9) and extended comtal power in *Languedoc. His advisers produced the *Usatges of Barcelona*, which stressed his regnal authority. A uniform fiscal administration for the counties was developed. *Cistercians arrived, most notably at Poblet (1150–53), while the ecclesiastical province of Tarragona was restored (1154). The *Almohad rise caused Alfonso II (1162–96) and Peter II (1196–1213) of Aragon to concentrate on the consolidation of power in their realms, particularly by securing control of castles, and to look beyond the Pyrenees, first opposing, then in alliance with, Toulouse.

5. The 13th through 15th centuries

But victory at Las *Navas de Tolosa opened up the south, while defeat at *Muret, confirmed by the Treaty of *Corbeil, closed the path north, though the crown long maintained possessions in Provence. After a period of economic and political crisis, the Catalans rallied to the cause of James I of Aragon (1213–76), playing the lead role in the conquests of *Majorca (1229), Valencia (1238), and Murcia (1266) and in their repopulation. Catalan trade, favoured by royal protection, expanded rapidly throughout the Mediterranean, and the centre of government shifted from Lleida (definitively part of Catalonia from 1244) to Barcelona. The Jewish community flourished there, the *Dominicans and *Franciscans throughout Catalonia. The barons fought (often successfully) to maintain their customs against the influx of Roman and canon *law, which tended to favour the crown. The reign of *Peter III saw the subjugation of the northern barons (1281), and Catalan expansion into Sicily (1282), resulting in a *crusade against the crown and the French invasion of Catalonia, which ended in Catalan victory following the defeat of the French fleet by Ruggerio di Loria (1285). Majorca (reconquered 1287) and Sicily now dominated

Catalan affairs, James II (1291–1327) attempting to exchange the latter for *Sardinia and Corsica with the approval of *Pope Boniface VIII. But the Sicilians defiantly elected James's brother Frederick (1291–1337) as their king; many Catalans settled there, and strong commercial ties were established. The duchy of Athens was founded (1311) and Sardinia conquered (1324). At home, the first *university was established at Lleida (1300), the developing *cortes* expressed the united powers of king, magnates, townsmen, and clerics, and royal administration became increasingly professionalized. Catalan, used by the missionary Ramon *Llull, the physician *Arnau de Villanova, and the chroniclers *Desclot and *Muntaner, established itself as a language of learning. Though Peter IV (1336–87) won victory over the Genoese in Sardinia (1354), and improved relations with Sicily, war (1357–75) with *Castile proved disastrous for Catalonia, facing crippling depopulation exacerbated by serious famines, the *Black Death, and various subsequent plagues. The attacks on Jews in 1391 at Barcelona, Lleida, Girona, Tarragona, and *Perpignan are indicative of increased social tension. Martin I (1395–1410) sought to diminish the dissensions between the various sections of society, as well as to foster learning. During the Great *Schism, Benedict XIII took up residence first at Perpignan, then in Barcelona (1409). Under *Trastámaran rule, Catalonia suffered a severe economic crisis, worsened by earthquakes (1427–8), while problems in the administration of justice and with the *remença* *peasants escalated. Economic hardship led to the creation of two opposed groups in Barcelona: the *Biga*, mainly representing landowners and honoured citizens, and the *Busca*, representing artisans, craftsmen, and merchants. They were, however, united in opposition to *Joan II when he arrested his own son Charles of Viana in 1460, and in 1462 following the revolt of the *remença* peasants, a civil war broke out in Catalonia, lasting until 1472, the background of which lay chiefly with the unresolved tensions between the various sections of Catalan society. The main beneficiary of the war was the French crown, which extended its interests into the north of Catalonia. In the reign of Ferdinand II (1479–1516), Catalonia's situation stabilized and there were indications of an economic upturn at the end of the 15th century. *See also* PEÑAFORT, RAMÓN DE; TRADE AND COMMERCE: MEDITERRANEAN EUROPEAN; VISIGOTHS IN SPAIN. DJSm

R. d'Abadal, *Els primers comtes catalans* (1961).
D. Abulafia, *The Western Mediterranean Kingdoms* (1997).
C. Batlle, *L'expansió baixmedieval [segles XIII–XV]* (1988).
T. Bisson, *The Medieval Crown of Aragon* (1986).
J. N. Farreras and P. Wolff, eds, *Histoire de la Catalogne* (1982).
P. Freedman, *The Origins of Peasant Servitude in Medieval Catalonia* (1991).
J. Hillgarth, *The Problem of a Catalan Mediterranean Empire 1229–1327* (1975).
J. Salrach, *El procés de feudalització [segles III–XII]* (1987).

catapults *See* SIEGE MACHINES.

catechumen *See* BAPTISM.

Categories In the *Categories*, Aristotle distinguishes between substances and nine types of accident, which, together, constitute the ten categories or ten highest *genera*. Substances are particulars of natural kinds, although Aristotle also recognizes secondary substances (*universals) of natural kinds. Hence, 'Socrates' is a particular or primary substance, while 'man' is a universal or secondary substance. The accidents are quantity, quality, relation, place, time, position, state, action, and affection (passivity or being acted upon), which further define a substance (for example, 'position' describes an object as a result of an action: Socrates 'sitting'). Although the *Categories* can be read as being about language, it can also be taken as setting out a basic *metaphysics.

Early medieval Latin readers were especially attracted to this text, because *Augustine boasts in the **Confessions* about his proficiency in understanding it, and he argues that God fits properly into only one category, that of substance. A Latin paraphrase of the *Categories* was wrongly attributed to Augustine, and it provided the main means of studying this work in the 9th and 10th centuries. The *Categories* gave a setting where an interest in theology (how can God be described in human language? and how do Trinitarian relations fit the category of relation?) could unite with an enthusiasm for *logic. In the 12th century, the work provided a metaphysical grid. In its opening section, it distinguishes between particular and universal substances and particular and universal accidents. Realists accepted the existence of all four; 12th-century nominalists, like *Abelard, usually accepted the existence of particular substances *and* accidents, but not of universals of any sort.

The *Categories* became less central once Aristotle's metaphysics became known in the 13th century, although the text was important for *William of Ockham, who argued that only substances and some qualities (and, for theological purposes, some quantities) are real items in the world. *See also* ARISTOTELIANISM; NOMINALISM; REALISM; SCHOLASTICISM; TRINITY. JMar

J. Biard and I. Rosier-Catach, eds, *La tradition médiévale des Catégories, XIIe–XVe* (2003).
O. Bruun and L. Corti, eds, *Les Catégories et leur histoire* (2005).

Cathars and Catharism The name given to the heretics and *heresy of southern *France and *Italy of the 12th and 13th centuries. Catharism taught a dualist religious doctrine and organizational structure that presented the greatest challenge to the medieval church. From the Greek *katharos* (pure), the Cathars were also known as Albigensians, Bulgari, and, in the vernacular, as 'heretics' or 'sodomites', but called themselves 'Christians' or 'Good Men' and 'Good Women'. Harassed by *inquisition and *crusades, Catharism experienced revivals in the late 13th and 14th centuries before disappearing in the 14th century.

1. Origins
2. Growth and suppression
3. Practice
4. Doctrine

1. *Origins*

Although sometimes traced to the early 11th century, the origins of Catharism are usually located in the mid 12th century with the arrival of Bogomil missionaries at *Cologne in 1143 and the re-emergence of dualist heretics there in 1163 and the debate between dualist heretics and churchmen at Lombers in 1165. In 1167, Nicetas, a representative of the absolute dualist Bogomil church of Dragovista (or Drugunthia), preached in southern France and Italy and converted many to his version of the faith. With representatives of various Cathar churches of France, he attended the council of St Félix-de-Caraman (between *Carcassonne and *Toulouse), where episcopal boundaries were established. Although the veracity of the account of this council, which comes from the 17th century, has been questioned, most accept it as evidence of the influence of Bogomil teachings on western heresy. Indeed, the combination of western dissidence and Bogomil dualism led to the emergence of Catharism.

2. *Growth and suppression*

Catharism grew during the later 12th century as many Christians were drawn to the heresy by the holy lives of Cathar preachers, the *perfecti*. The apparent growth of the heresy concerned the church hierarchy, and efforts were made to convert the Cathars back to the faith. Preaching missions were undertaken by *Cistercian monks and by St *Dominic. Despite the holiness of these missionaries, Catharism flourished in southern France, in part because of the support it received from the local nobility, including the counts of Toulouse, and others who were critical of clerical corruption and worldliness. The success of Catharism drew the attention of *Pope Innocent III, who sent a papal *legate to bring the count and region back to obedience to Rome. The legate's murder led to the Albigensian Crusade, which forced the submission of the count, who agreed to suppress heresy. The count was assisted by the inquisition in 1233–4, which increased the pressure on the Cathars, many of whom fled to northern Italy. In 1244, the stronghold of *Montségur was taken and some 200 Cathars were captured and burned, and Italian authorities increased persecution of the Cathars, burning 178 in *Verona. Despite persecution, Catharism underwent a revival from 1290 to 1309/10 in southern France, and *Montaillou emerged as the last Cathar centre in the early 14th century. The loss of the support of the nobility and persecution, however, led to the eradication of Catharism, which disappears from the records after the capture of the last Cathar bishop in 1329.

3. *Practice*

The Cathars developed a highly organized hierarchy that rivalled that of the church of Rome. At the top of the order were the bishops, who administered the *consolamentum*, the ritual that elevated the ordinary believer, man or woman, to the rank of *perfectus* (perfect). The 'perfects' adopted a life of *poverty, *celibacy (avoiding physical contact with the opposite sex), and regular prayer, and travelled about preaching the faith and confessing the *laity. They also performed the *apparellamentum*, a confession that served to purify them of minor infractions, and performed the ritual of blessing of the bread at meals. Their message and criticism of the *clergy and Catholic sacraments and their personal piety attracted many to the heresy, including those who supported the heresy without fully joining it. The Cathar laity was not expected to live as strictly as the perfects but supported the perfects with food, lodging, and protection and attended their sermons. They honoured the perfects with the *melioramentum*, which was a form of confession and request that the perfects pray for them.

4. *Doctrine*

Cathar churches taught either an absolute or moderate dualism, which associated creation with the evil god or Satan, who was identified with the God of the Old Testament. Cathar absolute dualism maintained that the good God and Satan were both eternal and without end, whereas the moderate dualism of other Cathars held that Satan was subject to God and that evil would be consumed at the end of time. According to the absolute dualist Cathars, the evil god invaded heaven and captured and imprisoned the angels in created bodies. Moderate dualist Cathars taught that Satan was a fallen angel who created the world and made human bodies out of clay into which he imprisoned the fallen angels. Because they saw the material world as evil and the creation of the evil god of the Old Testament, the Cathars rejected the Hebrew Scriptures and material creation. Cathar perfects were celibate and believed children were the work of the devil. They ate no meat because it was thought to contain the soul of a fallen angel; the Cathars believed in transmigration of the soul and held that only life as a perfected Cathar would lead to release of imprisoned souls. Milk, eggs, and cheese were eliminated from the diet because they were seen as the product of coition. Cathar dualism also contributed to a docetist Christology in which Christ did not assume human flesh but only appeared to do so and only seemed to suffer crucifixion. He was born of Mary, according to one myth, by entering into her ear.

See also DOCETISM. MCF

A. Borst, *Die Katharer* (1953).
A. Brenon, *Les Femmes Cathares* (1992).
J. Duvernoy, *Le Catharisme*, 2 vols (1976–9).
M. Lambert, *The Cathars* ([3]1998).
C. Lansing, *Power and Purity: Cathar Heresy in Medieval Italy* (1998).
E. Le Roy Ladurie, *Montaillou: village Occitan de 1294 à 1324* (1975).
M. Pegg, *The Corruption of Angels: The Great Inquisition of 1245–1246* (2001).
R. Weiss, *The Yellow Cross: The Story of the Last Cathars' Rebellion Against the Inquisition* (2000).

cathedral The church designated to be the official seat of a diocesan bishop and containing the *cathedra* or bishop's chair. In the late Roman Empire, a bishop would select one of the churches built in an existing *civitas* as his seat. Normally, this would be a relatively conspicuous building inside the city walls, but exceptions existed. The bishop's chair was placed in the centre of the *apse; later on one side of the high *altar.

In the MA, the cathedral became the symbol of ecclesiastical power and civic identity, in various degrees of importance in relation to each other. As a rule, the best available architects and artists were recruited to work on the cathedral, which was expected to display particular splendour. (In some regions, the city council was the real authority in building matters.) In the course of the MA, the liturgical duties of the bishop were only rarely carried out in the cathedral. Administration and daily worship were delegated to the *cathedral chapter of *canons or to a community of monks (such as in England). *See also* BISHOP'S ACCOUTREMENTS; CLERGY; DIOCESE; HOLY SEE. SdB

M. Imhof, *Deutschlands Kathedralen: Geschichte und Baugeschichte aller Bischofskirchen von der Spätantike bis heute* (2006).
S. E. Lehmberg, *The Reformation of Cathedrals: Cathedrals in English Society 1485–1603* (1988).
N. Pevsner and P. Metcalf, *The Cathedrals of England* (1985).
A. Prache, *Cathédrales d'Europe* (1999).
W. Schlink, 'Existait-il un programme d'ensemble pour les cathédrales au Moyen Age?', in *Le monde des cathédrales*, ed. R. Recht (2003), 13–40.
W. Vroom, *De financiering van de kathedraalbouw in de middeleeuwen* (1981).

cathedral chapter The college of *clergy, usually *canons, responsible for the spiritual and temporal administration of the *cathedral. This includes the daily rounds of *liturgy and chanting the *Divine Office. Among the *chapter leaders are the Dean or Provost, Precentor, Treasurer, and Chancellor. *See also* CANTOR. WJD

K. Edwards, *English Secular Cathedrals in the Middle Ages* (1949).
A. H. Thompson, *The Cathedral Churches of England* (1925).

Catherine of Genoa, St (1447–1510) Caterina Fieschi Adorno was an aristocratic married laywoman, hospital director, spiritual reformer, and *mystic. Her *Life* and teachings—the *Spiritual Dialogue* and *Treatise on Purgatory*—were published in 1551. *See also* PURGATORY. MBo

Catherine of Genoa, *Purgation and Purgatory; The Spiritual Dialogue*, tr. S. Hughes (1979).
U. B. da Genova, *S. Caterina Fieschi Adorno*, 2 vols (1960–62).
F. von Hügel, *The Mystical Element of Religion* (1908).

Catherine of Siena, St (*c*.1347–80) *Dominican penitent, religious reformer, and author; a key figure in the late medieval culture of affective spirituality and female sanctity. Catherine's writings—including more than 380 extant letters and a visionary book (the *Dialogo della divina provvidenza*)—constitute one of the great achievements of

Portrait of St Catherine of Siena from a fresco by Andrea Vanni in the chapel of the vaults, church of S. Domenico, Siena.

Italian vernacular religious literature. Born into a family prominent in the cloth trade in *Siena, around the age of twenty Catherine joined a local group of female penitents and soon afterwards began an unusually public career in causes like the settlement of the contest between the *papacy and *Florence known as the 'War of the Eight Saints'; renewal of the *crusade movement; ecclesiastical reform; and the return of the *papacy to *Rome from *Avignon. After the disputed papal election of 1378 until her death in April 1380, Catherine outspokenly supported the Roman obedience and *Pope Urban VI. She was canonized in 1461. FTL

Catherine of Siena, *Dialogue*, tr. S. Noffke (1980).
—— *Opera omnia*, ed. F. Sbaffoni, CD-ROM (2002).
—— *Letters of Catherine of Siena*, tr. S. Noffke, 4 vols (2000–2008).
F. T. Luongo, *The Saintly Politics of Catherine of Siena* (2006).
Raymond of Capua, *Legenda Sancti Catherine Senensis*, *AASS* 3, 862–967.
K. Scott, '*Io Caterina*: Oral Culture and Ecclesiastical Politics in the Letters of Catherine of Siena', in *Dear Sister: Medieval Women and the Epistolary Genre*, ed. K. Cherewatuk and U. Wiethaus (1993), 87–121.
E. D. Theseider, 'Caterina di Siena, santa', *DBI*, vol. 22, 361–79.

Catherine of Sweden, St (1331–81) Daughter of St *Birgitta of Sweden; abbess of Vadstena convent; married (chastely) to Eggart von Kürnen; widowed *c*.1350. Catherine spent almost 25 years in *Rome with her mother, until Birgitta died. Then she returned to Sweden, directing her efforts towards obtaining her mother's *canonization, and securing official papal approval for the Bridgettine order (1376). *See also* RELIGIOUS ORDERS. MMS

Bridget of Sweden, *Life and Selected Revelations*, ed. M. Harris and K. Ryle (1990).
B. Morris, *St Birgitta of Sweden* (1999).

Catherine of Valois (1401–37) Queen to *Henry V of *England, youngest daughter of the mad king *Charles VI of *France, Catherine was married as part of the treaty of *Troyes (1420) to Henry. She bore him *Henry VI. Her subsequent liaison/marriage to Owen *Tudor produced four Tudor children. MAH

M. Jones, 'Catherine [Catherine of Valois], 1401–37', *ODNB* vol. 10, 545–7.

Catholic Monarchs (Ferdinand and Isabella) Isabella (1451–1504) was the daughter of King John II of *Castile and his second wife, Isabella of Portugal. John died when his daughter was three years old, and Isabella was raised by her Portuguese mother and grandmother in Arévalo until her half-brother King Henry IV brought her to court in 1464. A pawn in Castilian politics, Isabella in 1469 married, without royal permission, Ferdinand (1452–1516), heir to the Crown of *Aragon and already king of Sicily.

Upon the death of Henry IV in 1474, with the support of *Aragon and part of the Castilian nobility, Isabella claimed the Castilian crown in a contest with Henry's daughter Juana, whose paternity was challenged, supported by Portugal and the remainder of the Castilian nobility. Isabella's forces won the civil war and assumed full control in Castile by 1479, when Ferdinand succeeded his father as king of Aragon.

Although their kingdoms remained legally separate, Ferdinand and Isabella together settled political unrest in Castile and Aragon, conducted an anti-French foreign policy, launched successful campaigns in Italy, took control of the *Canary Islands, sponsored the trans-Atlantic voyages of Christopher *Columbus, and laid the foundations of Spain's American empire. They installed the *Inquisition in Castile and Aragon and in 1492 forced Spain's Jews to choose between conversion to Christianity or expulsion. In the same year, they conquered *Granada, the last Muslim stronghold in western Europe.

After Isabella's death, Ferdinand became regent in Castile for their daughter Juana, widow of Philip the Handsome and deemed mentally unstable. Ferdinand later married Germaine de Foix and intervened in Spanish *Navarre to bring it under Castilian control. Upon Ferdinand's death in 1516, the grandson of the Catholic Monarchs, Charles, assumed the crowns of Castile and Aragon and later became German emperor. WDP

T. de Azcona, *Isabel la Católica: Estudio crítico de su vida y reinado* (1993).
D. A. Boruchoff, ed., *Isabel la Católica, Queen of Castile* (2003).
J. Edwards, *Ferdinand and Isabella* (2004).
P. K. Liss, *Isabel the Queen* (1992).
B. F. Weissberger, *Isabel Rules: Constructing Queenship, Wielding Power* (2004).

Cauchon, Pierre, bishop of Beauvais (*c*.1371–1442) Cauchon was a partisan of Burgundian and English interests during their occupation of northern *France. He is best known for his role as the principal judge in the trial of *Joan of Arc in 1431, following her capture within his diocese. CDT

F. Neveux, *L'évêque Pierre Cauchon* (1987).

cauda Literally 'tail': a melismatic passage on a *conductus's penultimate text syllable or that of a strophe within one; usually notated in a clear modal rhythm, unlike the syllabically texted sections that precede it. RAB

M. Everist, 'Reception and Recomposition in the Polyphonic *Conductus cum caudis*: The Metz Fragment', *Journal of the Royal Musicological Association*, 125 (2000), 135–63.

Caulites, Order of (val des Choux) *See* RELIGIOUS ORDERS.

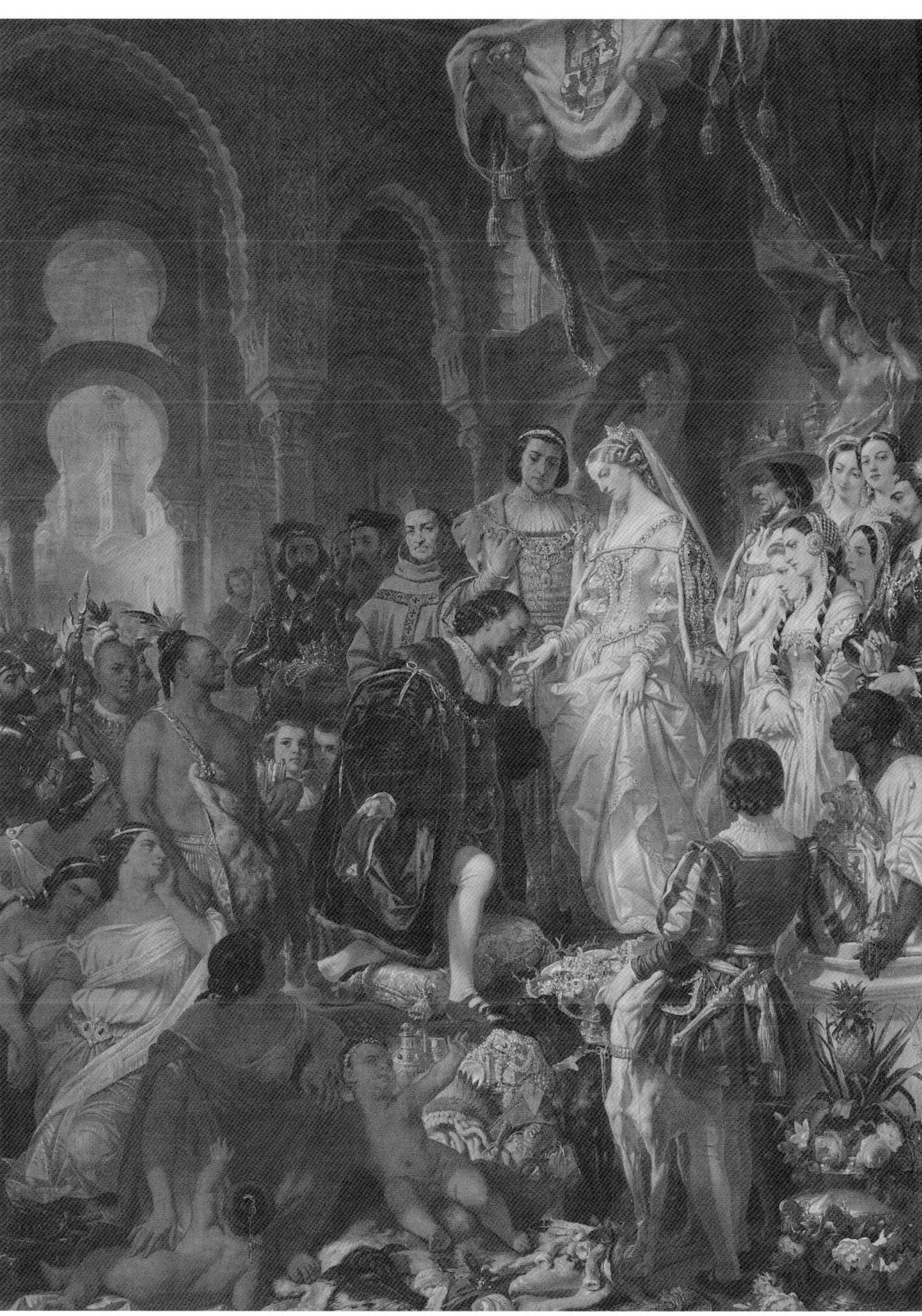

Christopher Columbus before the Catholic Monarchs Ferdinand and Isabella.

causation *See* PHILOSOPHY, NATURAL.

cautery A significant part of *surgery in the western MA. Actual cautery involved the placing of heated irons on the body to sear a particular area, whereas potential cautery used caustic medicines instead of heated irons. Cautery was used not only to removed diseased tissue and seal wounds but also to eliminate superfluous cold and moist *humours of the body and prevent the spread of corrupt humours to different parts of the body. Cautery diagrams showed the appropriate points at which cauteries should be applied to treat particular ailments. *See also* INSTRUMENTS, MEDICAL AND SURGICAL. PMJ

P. M. Jones, *Medieval Medicine in Illuminated Manuscripts* (1998).

M. S. Spink and G. L. Lewis, trs, *Albucasis on Surgery and Instruments* (1973).

B. Ventura and A. Raspadori, 'Il cauterio e la sua evoluzione', *Rivista di storia della medicina*, 10 (2000), 523–43.

Painting of Pierre Cauchon at the burning of Joan of Arc.

Cavallini, Pietro (*c*.1240–*c*.1310) Roman painter and mosaicist. *Apse *mosaics of the Life of the Virgin in Santa Maria in Trastevere (*c*.1291) and *frescoes of the Last Judgement and the nave cycles (largely destroyed) in the *nave of Santa Cecilia in Trastevere (*c*.1293) are authoritative, as is the Old Testament cycle (mostly destroyed). At *Naples (1308) the frescoes in the Duomo of Santa Maria Donnaregina and San Domenico Maggiore are attributed to him. SR

P. Hetherington, *Pietro Cavallini* (1979).
G. Matthiae, *Pietro Cavallini* (1972).
A. Tomei, *Pietro Cavallini* (2000).

Caxton, William (1422?–91) The first English printer. Born in *Kent and receiving a good education, he was apprenticed in the cloth trade. Travelling as an *apprentice, he saw his first printing press in *Cologne in 1471, possibly taking a part in its operation. In that same year he had completed a *translation from French of the *Recuyell of the Histories of Troy*. It proved popular, and in 1475, in *Bruges, he produced a printed edition to meet the demand for copies, the first book printed in English. Other publications followed, and in 1476 at *Westminster he set up the first press in England. The following year Caxton published *Dictes and Sayings of the Philosophers*, the first dated book printed in England. In 1483 he published an edition of *Chaucer's *Canterbury Tales*, which he characterized as a corrected version of one published about six years earlier. Among numerous publications, some 96 in all, often of Caxton's own translations from various sources, other notable productions include *Malory's *Morte d'Arthur*, printed in 1484; the *Golden Legend*, the translation of which

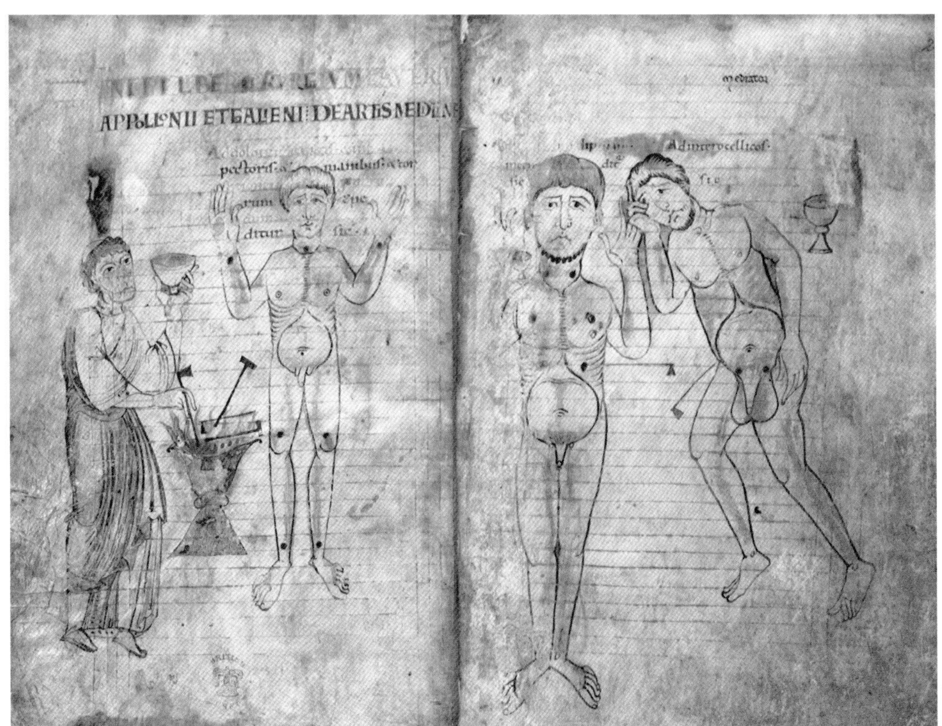

Surgeon heating cautery irons.

was completed in 1483, although the date of its printing is uncertain; and the *Eneydos*, translated and printed around 1490. The preface to the last contains an important discussion of the English language. Caxton did extensive work as a translator, and roughly a third of the productions of his press were his own translations. His continuation of Ranulf *Higden's *Polychronicon*, the addition of an eighth book, is the most substantial example surviving of Caxton's original prose. He had completed a translation of St *Jerome's *Lives of the Fathers* just before his death, and it was published by his apprentice and successor, Wynkyn de Worde, in 1495. *See also* JACOB OF VORAGINE; PRINTING AND PRINTED BOOK PRODUCTION; TEXTILES AND CLOTH-MAKING. MS

N. F. Blake, ed., *Caxton's Own Prose* (1973).
W. J. B. Crotch, *The Prologues and Epilogues of William Caxton* (1928; repr. 1971).
L. Hellinga, *Caxton in Focus: The Beginning of Printing in England* (1982).
—— 'Printing', in *The Cambridge History of the Book in Britain*, ed. eadem and J. B. Trapp (1998), vol. 3, 65–108.
G. D. Painter, *William Caxton: A Biography* (1976).

Ceawlin, king of Wessex (d. 593) Early English ruler (*c*.560–91) during whose reign the *Anglo-Saxons established control over southern Britain. Though little is known of his life, the *Anglo-Saxon Chronicle* records him winning a series of battles against the native Britons before succumbing to internecine conflict. *See also* BRETWALDA; ENGLAND, ANGLO-SAXON. ASR

F. Stenton, *Anglo-Saxon England* ([3]1971).
M. Swanton, tr., *The Anglo-Saxon Chronicle* (1998).

Cedrenus, George (Georgios Kedrenos) (*fl.* 11th century) Historian; wrote a chronicle (*synopsis historion*) from the creation of the world to 1057 (the beginning of the reign of Isaakios Komnenos), using and compiling various historiographers (*Theophanes, Georgios Monachos, and especially John Scylitzes). MAG

I. Bekker, *Georgius Cedrenus*, 2 vols (1838–9).
A. Kazhdan, 'Kedrenos, George', *ODB*, vol. 2, 1118.
R. Maisano, 'Sulla tradizione manoscritta di Giorgio Cedreno', *RSBN* 14–16 (1977–9), 179–201.

celestial movers *See* MOTION.

celestial spheres *See* ASTRONOMY; COSMOLOGY.

Celestina Late-15th-century work in dialogue by Fernando de Rojas. There is still debate among critics about whether it should be classified as a novel or drama.

The *Celestina* tells the tale of how the passion of a young nobleman, Calisto, for Melibea ends in disaster, with not only the death of the two lovers, but also that of several of their servants and of Celestina, the go-between and witch employed by Calisto to seduce the object of his desire. The final act consists of the lament of Pleberio, Melibea's father, for his deceased daughter and the cruelty of the world.

The first extant edition of the work appeared in *Burgos in 1499 under the title *Comedia de Calisto y Melibea* and was divided into sixteen acts. By 1502 an expanded version had appeared, with five new acts and interpolations in many of the existing acts. The title of this version was *Tragicomedia de Calisto y Melibea*, although it is better known as *La Celestina*, reflecting the crucial role of the eponymous go-between in the text.

Rojas, a law student at the University of *Salamanca and a *converso (Jewish convert to Christianity), claims not to have penned the text's first act. Rather he says he discovered it and decided to continue the tale of Calisto and Melibea in his own style, influenced by *Petrarch, the late medieval humanistic comedy in Latin, and sentimental *romances. Rojas's work proved immensely popular, achieving success not only in its original Spanish in the form of multiple editions and sequels by other authors, but also in numerous translations including Italian, French, English, German, and Dutch. *See also* LITERATURES: CASTILIAN. JG

C. F. Fraker, *'Celestina': Genre and Rhetoric* (1990).
S. Gilman, *The Art of 'La Celestina'* (1956).
—— *The Spain of Fernando de Rojas* (1972).
S. López-Ríos, ed., *Estudios sobre la 'Celestina'* (2001).
M. R. L. de Malkiel, *La originalidad artística de 'La Celestina'* (1962).
I. Michael and D. G. Pattison, eds, *Context, Meaning and Reception of 'Celestina': A Fifth Centenary Symposium*, special issue of *Bulletin of Hispanic Studies*, 78 (2001).
D. S. Severin, *Memory in 'La Celestina'* (1970).

Celestines, Order of *See* RELIGIOUS ORDERS.

celibacy of the clergy Christian views on this subject have varied considerably between regions and over time. During the first three centuries AD, each of the largely independent Christian communities developed its own rules for the sexual behaviour of its ministers. When *councils and synods began to legislate for groups of churches, from the 4th century on, rather different positions on clerical celibacy emerged in the western and eastern halves of the disintegrating Roman Empire. It became the rule in the west that deacons, priests, and bishops were not to marry, and if they had already been married before *ordination, they were to abstain from having sex with their wives. In fact, they were forbidden to live with or have as housekeeper any woman who was not 'above suspicion' by reason of kinship or advanced age. In the east, it was generally only bishops who were required to abstain from marital relations: when they were elected, their wives were expected to retire to a convent. On the other hand, priests and deacons who were married before ordination were allowed to live with their wives and to have 'lawful intercourse' with them. Tensions between the eastern and western churches on this subject were already evident by the 7th century, and became more pronounced during the so-called *Schism of 1054.

Yet in practice the sexual behaviour of the *clergy in the two regions was not so very different. While clerical celibacy was theoretically the rule in most parts of the west by the 6th century, enforcement was sporadic and often ineffective. As late as the 11th century, many clerics continued to marry and generate children, even after ordination; some writers openly defended this behaviour. It took the concerted efforts of a series of reformers over the course of the 11th and early 12th centuries to silence the defenders of clerical marriage and reassert the 'law of continence' for those in major orders. And, even then, enforcement remained a problem. While few clerics were openly married after the 12th century, a very substantial minority continued to live with women, or frequent prostitutes (*see* ADULTERY AND CONCUBINAGE), throughout the later MA.

In the 16th century, Protestant thinkers rejected medieval teachings on clerical celibacy, and asserted the benefits of marriage for the clergy as well as the *laity. *See also* GREGORIAN REFORM. MM

M. Boelens, *Die Klerikerehe in der Gesetzgebung der Kirche unter besonderer Berücksichtigung der Strafe* (1968).
P. Brown, *The Body and Society: Men, Women, and Sexual Renunciation in Early Christianity* (1988).
M. Frassetto, ed., *Medieval Purity and Piety: Essays on Medieval Clerical Celibacy and Religious Reform* (1998).
E. Frauenknecht, *Der Verteidigung der Priesterehe in der Reformzeit* (1997).
A. Vauchez, 'La question du célibat ecclésiastique dans l'Occident médiéval: un état de la recherche', in *Medieval Spirituality in Scandinavia and Europe: A Collection of Essays in Honour of Tore Nyberg*, ed. L. Bisgaard, C. S. Jensen, K. V. Jensen, and J. Lind (2001), 21–32.

Celtic church The Celtic church is a popular, but imprecise, expression referring to the churches of the Celtic-speaking peoples in the early MA.

1. The origins of the Celtic church as an idea
2. The problem of the Celtic church as a concept
3. Common roots and contribution

1. *The origins of the Celtic church as an idea*

The idea of a Celtic church has its roots in the Reformation. For Protestants, the early Celtic saints embodied evangelical purity and a church wholly independent of Rome; the Reformation represented a return to the values of the indigenous British Christianity of a golden age. This interpretation came to dominate historical perceptions in the succeeding centuries, and from it was born, in the 19th century, the concept of the 'Celtic church'.

2. *The problem of the Celtic church as a concept*

The concept of the Celtic church can no longer easily be defended: it implies a single institutional body that covered the Celtic lands, and the parts of northern *England influenced by *Iona. This demonstrably was not the case. A misconception has also grown up that the 'Celtic church' was peculiarly monastic in character. This 'Celtic' *monasticism has been understood as something different from the Christianity that entered England from Rome with St *Augustine of Canterbury, the latter dominated by bishops and papal authority. 'Celtic' monasticism, scholars supposed, was peculiarly inspired by the writings of the Egyptian Desert Fathers, channelled to the British Isles via *Lérins and monks from Gaul. But the evidence that once supported this view was discredited in the 1960s. The only churchman in early medieval Britain who certainly visited Lérins and the leading monasteries of Gaul was St Augustine, himself a monk. Two further predispositions led historians to think that the 'Celtic church' differed from the Gallo-Roman mainstream. First, monastic terminology in the Irish church of the 8th to 11th centuries was misunderstood, and led to a theory of a peculiarly structured church characterized by monastic organization. In fact, the same terminology applied in Gaul and AS England, being the usual language of the church before *Carolingian (and later) reforms emphasized the different roles of secular and monastic churches. The second predisposition was that the 'Celtic church' had to be different from the Continental and English churches, and characterized more by personal devotion than by episcopal jurisdiction. But little of what was once thought distinctive about the nature of the church in Celtic lands is any longer accepted. It can no longer be doubted that Ireland, Wales, and Scotland were subject to territorial episcopal jurisdiction; all that is unclear is its effectiveness. Any weakness in episcopal governance, moreover, argues directly against the coherence of a Celtic church. Christianity in the Gaelic world, in particular, lacked a governing structure that could hold together a single church against the power of particularistic secular rulers and the separatist tendencies of ideologically various monastic groups. In these circumstances it was hard to find any uniformity of thought or practice after the 6th century.

3. *Common roots and contribution*

All this being said, we may nevertheless notice a number of striking common features among the churches of the Celtic peoples: an intensely local pastoral structure, an obsession with a plethora of local saints (often preserved in place names), and an unusually close relationship between the ministry of the church and the religious life. These similarities may have had their roots in a monastic movement centred in western Britain during the 6th century, the legacy of the British monk *Gildas. In the 6th century we see an exchange of ideas, influences, and influential personnel between Britain, *Brittany, and Ireland. The oldest *penitential texts are those of Gildas and his approximate contemporaries, Uinniau and *Columban; compilations of these texts were made in Britain and Ireland, and included in MSS that transmitted the canon-material of these islands, through Brittany, to the principal libraries of Europe, where it is still preserved. This penitential writing, and the collection of ancient authorities that came with it, are perhaps the most notable contribution of the Celtic churches to the ecclesiastical practice of Europe. Richard Sharpe, in arguing this case, has suggested that if it were ever possible to use the term 'Celtic church', it would be at this time of close contact and intellectual exchange, in the second half of the 6th century. When Columbanus wrote to *Pope Gregory I the Great, he distinguished the churches of Britain and Ireland from 'those of Gaul', using the phrase *ecclesiae occidentis*, 'the churches of the west'. Perhaps this is the closest we can come to recognizing the existence of a Celtic church. *See also* COLUMBA, ST. JRD

M. W. Barley and R. P. C. Hanson, eds, *Christianity in Britain, 300–700* (1968).
J. Blair and R. Sharpe, eds, *Pastoral Care before the Parish* (1992).
N. K. Chadwick, *The Age of the Saints in the Early Celtic Church* (1961).
W. Davies, 'The Myth of the Celtic Church', in *The Early Church in Wales and the West*, ed. N. Edwards and A. Lane (1992), 12–21.
D. N. Dumville, 'The Origins and Early History of Insular Monasticism', *Bulletin of the Institute of Oriental and Occidental Studies, Kansai University*, 30 (1997), 85–108.
C. Etchingham, *Church Organisation in Ireland, AD 650–1000* (1999).
L. Gougaud, *Christianity in Celtic Lands: A History of the Churches of the Celts* (1932).
K. Hughes, 'The Celtic Church: Is This a Valid Concept?', *Cambridge Medieval Celtic Studies*, 1 (1981), 1–20.
D. E. Meek, *The Quest for Celtic Christianity* (2000).
R. Sharpe, 'Gildas as a Father of the Church', in *Gildas: New Approaches*, ed. M. Lapidge and D. N. Dumville (1984), 193–205.
A. T. Thacker and R. Sharpe, eds, *Local Saints and Local Churches in the Early Medieval West* (2002).
F. E. Warren, *The Liturgy and Ritual of the Celtic Church*, ed. J. Stevenson ([2]1987).
H. Zimmer, *The Celtic Church in Great Britain and Ireland* (1902).

cement A strong *mortar containing clay, used as a binding material in masonry construction. Cement often had hydraulic properties and was exploited in underwater structures. The medieval composition varied, but it frequently contained wax, pitch, resin, and/or ceramic tile dust. LTC

N. Davey, *A History of Building Materials* (1961).
L. F. Salzman, *Building in England down to 1540* (1952; repr. 1992).

Cennini, Cennino (*c*.1370–*c*.1440) Italian painter in the tradition of *Giotto, who wrote a *manual on *painting. *Il libro dell'arte* is an important source of information for medieval techniques of painting and related *crafts. In addition to numerous technical instructions, Cennini discusses the importance of *drawing, the training of painters, and the use of poetry by painters. *See also* PAINTING, TECHNIQUES OF. POL

C. Cennini, *Il libro dell'arte*, ed. F. Brunello (1971).
——*Il libro dell'arte*, ed. M. Serchi (1991).
C. D'Andrea Cennini, *The Craftsman's Handbook: The Italian 'Il Libro Dell'Arte'*, tr. D. V. Thompson, Jr (1933; repr. 1954).

censer *See* LITURGICAL FURNISHINGS.

centena, centenarius Following the fall of the western Roman Empire, some administrative divisions and titles persisted. One of those remaining in Gaul and Hispania was the *centena* or *centuria*. It corresponded approximately to the Roman Imperial *pagus*, although the original had been based on the ancient governance of 'one hundred families'. The head of the *centena* was the *centenarius*, who acted as a lower or village judge. *See also* HUNDRED. KDV

A. C. Murray, '"*Pax et disciplina*": Roman Public Law and the Merovingian State', in *From Roman Provinces to Medieval Kingdoms*, ed. T. F. X. Noble (2006), 376–85.

Cent Nouvelles Nouvelles A collection of 100 short tales purportedly told by the Philip the Good, duke of *Burgundy (ruled 1419–56), and various of his courtiers, and seemingly recording the atmosphere and exchanges at his court. However, a dedicatory preface and the attribution of some of the tales to an 'author' suggest the work is a carefully confected adaptation of *Boccaccio's **Decameron*, known in French as the *Cent Nouvelles*; suggestions as to this author's identity include Antoine de *la Sale. Most of the tales are comic and licentious, some exhibiting aristocratic libertinage, others resembling *fabliaux; but whereas fabliaux allow cleverness to succeed against power, the *Cent Nouvelles Nouvelles* mainly rejoice in aristocratic control of the lower orders, in men's control of women, and in the inability of women and the lower orders to control themselves. SK

F. P. Sweetser, ed., *Les Cent Nouvelles Nouvelles* ([2]1996).

cento A work composed by rearranging lines from earlier texts. The form thrives in a setting that fosters intensive study of standard texts, permitting passages to be recognized easily even out of context. The classical period, with its fairly standard curriculum, saw the rise of the cento, which most often employed the works of poets such as Virgil and Horace. Medieval authors also constructed centos from the classical poets, but the Bible became an important additional mine for quotations.

The earliest surviving Latin cento, the *Medea* of Hosidius Geta, was formed from lines of Virgil, and dates from the late 3rd century. Its fame was later eclipsed by the 4th-century

Cento of Faltonia Proba, a retelling of the Bible composed entirely of passages from Virgil. *Jerome disapproved of the work, but it was lauded by later writers such as *Boccaccio and *Christine de Pizan. Post-classical texts could also be exploited for centos: such is the case with the 15th-century *Trivita studentium* of Goswin Kempgyn, which was constructed of lines from a 12th-century grammatical treatise, the *Doctrinale* of *Alexander of Villa Dei.

The cento served an important liturgical function in the construction of plainchant, where passages from different parts of the Bible were juxtaposed in ways that emphasized their typological similarities. Other centos satirized ecclesiastical wrongdoing. The *Garcineida* or *Tractatus Garsiae* (*c.*1099), assembled from texts ranging from the Bible to Terence, mocked the venality of a historical archbishop. The most widely circulating humorous cento was the *Evangelium secundum marcas argenti*, which rearranged passages from the Bible to form a similar satire on ecclesiastical greed. Lines from the Bible were also used to form nonsense narratives, exploiting to the fullest the potential of the cento to make nonsense of the original text. MJB

M. Bayless, *Parody in the Middle Ages* (1996).
M. Bažil, '*Centones Christiani*' (2008).
M. Bernhard, *Goswin Kempgyn de Nussia, Trivita Studentium* (1976).
E. A. Clark and D. F. Hatch, *The Golden Bough, The Oaken Cross: The Vergilian Cento of Faltonia Betitia Proba* (1981).
S. McGill, *Virgil Recomposed* (2005).
R. Thomson, *Tractatus Garsiae* (1973).

centonization *See* PLAINSONG.

centring Temporary formwork erected to support the dead load of a stone *arch, *vault, or *dome during construction. While earth was used as formwork, the majority of medieval centring was *timber. The most critical operation in vault construction was removing the formwork at which point the masonry had to support its own weight. *See also* BUILDING AND CONSTRUCTION. LTC

J. Fitchen, *The Construction of Gothic Cathedrals* (1961).

Ceolfrith (abbot) (*c.*642–716) Disciple of Bishop *Wilfrid at Ripon and of Abbot *Benedict Biscop, Ceolfrith became prior of *Wearmouth monastery in 674, and abbot in 681 of its sister foundation Jarrow, where *Bede spent his life. In 688 Ceolfrith became abbot of both houses, among the most celebrated centres of learning in Europe. Ceolfrith followed Roman rather than Irish customs and travelled widely, both in England and on the continent during multiple pilgrimages to Rome. He commissioned three Bible pandects, one of which survives as the Codex Amiatinus, the oldest complete MS of the Latin Bible. SGw

S. Coates, 'Ceolfrid: History, Hagiography, and Memory in Seventh- and Eighth-Century Wearmouth-Jarrow', *JMH* 25 (1999), 69–86.
B. Colgrave and R. A. B. Mynors, eds, *Bede's Ecclesiastical History of the English People* (1969).
C. Plummer, ed., *Venerabilis Baedae Opera Historica* (1896), vol. 1 ('Historia Abbatum').

Ceolwulf of Mercia *See* MERCIA.

Ceolwulf of Northumbria *See* NORTHUMBRIA.

ceramics Perhaps the most frequently studied archaeological artefact is *pottery, or ceramics, because of their durability and stylistic differences. Ceramic comes from the Greek word *κέραμος* meaning potter's earth, potter's clay, or earthen vessel. Today, the term ceramic generally means any vessel or item made from clay fired at high temperatures. Pottery, which has been around since prehistoric times, is wet clay that is shaped into desired forms (bowl, jug, pitcher, and so forth) and then baked at high temperature. This produces an extremely hard substance that can hold liquids without leaking and lasts for many years, but has the disadvantage of breaking easily. To an archaeologist or historian, ceramics can serve as historical evidence in four ways. First, they are used for dating purposes, such as determining when a place, building, or town was inhabited. Second, they provide evidence for distribution and contact between different peoples and regions. Third, they can serve as an indication of a person's or group's status or function. Finally, they can help determine a building or room's function or use.

Ceramics are typically broken down into large, general categories based on usage. Fine ware is the pottery typically used for the consumption of food and drink at the table, sometimes referred to as tableware. It is usually of higher quality than other pottery classes, with distinctive decoration and forms, and was traded widely. *Cooking ware, usually produced locally, was used for the preparation and short-term storage of food in the kitchen. Coarse wares are undecorated vessels, typically used for storage. The most common coarse wares were the transport and storage vessels known as amphorae. They were the predominant container used in seaborne trade and are the most common item uncovered by archaeologists in shipwrecks.

Medieval ceramics from countries in western Europe were typically of a lower quality than those imported from places in the east, such as the Byzantine or *Islamic empires. Early medieval pottery in western Europe was often handmade by a potter using a technique called coil-building. These vessels were typically coarse, constructed from clay that contained numerous impurities, and undecorated. It was only in the later medieval period that western Europe began to use *glazes and create highly decorative pieces similar to what was being produced in the east. RSM

P. Davey and R. Hodges, *Ceramics and Trade: The Production and Distribution of Later Medieval Pottery in North-west Europe* (1983).
V. Everson, H. Hodges, and J. G. Hunt, eds, *Medieval Pottery from Excavations* (1974).
M. McCarthy and C. Brooks, *Medieval Pottery in Britain AD 900–1600* (1988).
S. Moorhouse, 'The Medieval Pottery Industry and its Markets', in *Medieval Industry*, ed. D. W. Crossley (1981), 96–125.
C. Orton, *The Pottery from Medieval Novgorod and its Regions* (2006).
—— P. Tyers, and A. Vince, *Pottery in Archaeology* (1993).
P. Rice, *Pottery Analysis: A Sourcebook* (1987).

Cerdic, king of Wessex (d. 534) Ruler of the Gewisse of the upper Thames and founder of a dynasty from which the West Saxon kings claimed descent. His name is derived from the Brittonic name *Caraticos*. *See also* WESSEX. CRD

R. Coates, 'On Some Controversy surrounding *Gewissae/Gewissei*, *Cerdic* and *Ceawlin*', *Nomina*, 13 (1989–90), 1–11.
B. Yorke, *Wessex in the Early Middle Ages* (1995).

Cerverí de Girona (*fl.* 1259–85) The Catalan *troubadour Guillem de Cervera composed 114 lyrical pieces, and five in narrative verse, under the pseudonym Cerverí de Girona, while he used his real name for a verse book of *proverbs. During his twenty-year service to *Peter III 'el Gran', he developed a distinctive style, marked by verbal wit and technical craftsmanship. His production covers a variety of genres and topics, including the contemporary fashion for moral topics, dance forms, and metrical experimentation, the politics that concerned his patron, and lively portraits of the court and the poet. His works bridge the gap between the troubadour tradition and later Catalan poets, among whom he was considered an authority. *See also* LITERATURES: CATALAN. MC

M. Cabré, *Cerverí de Girona and his Poetic Traditions* (1999).
Cerverí de Girona, Grup SGR de Cultura i Literatura a la Baixa Edat Mitjana, 13 April 2007, www.narpan.net.
M. de Riquer, *Obras completas del trovador Cerverí de Girona* (1947).

chace (chase) Formerly royal forest granted to a subject. Grant of a chace included exemption from *forest law and some royal forest rights. These included the power to imprison hunters, trespassers, and those seeking to cut the lord's timber. RSO

G. J. Turner, *Select Pleas of the Forest*, Selden Society, vol. 13 (1901 [1899]).

Chad (Ceadda), **St**, bishop of Lichfield (*c.*620–72) Brother of St Cedd and St Cynibild; missionary monk to Ireland; abbot of Lastingham. Appointed bishop of *York in *Wilfrid's absence, Chad was deposed upon his return, but subsequently was named bishop of *Lichfield. He built numerous churches and *monasteries, many with miraculous *pilgrim wells. MMS

J. Austerberry, *Chad: Bishop and Saint* (1984).
I. Macdonald, *Saints of Northumbria* (1997).

Chalcondyles (Chalcocondylas), **Demetrius** (1424–1511) Greek scholar based in Italy. Born in Athens, Chalcondyles moved to Italy in 1447 where he spent his life as a teacher of Greek and philosophy at *Padua, *Florence, and *Milan. He published the first printed editions of Homer, Isocrates, and the Suda lexicon, as well as a Greek *grammar. *See also* ENCYCLOPEDIAS; PHILOSOPHY, BYZANTINE. IG

D. J. Geanakoplos, 'The Discourse of Demetrius Chalcondyles on the Inauguration of Greek Studies at the University of Padua in 1463', *Studies in the Renaissance*, 21 (1974), 118–44.

Chalcondyles (Chalcocondylas), **Laonicus** (*c.*1423–after 1461) Historian; only a few details of his life are known. In 1447 he was a pupil of Georgius Gemistus *Pletho at Mistra. He wrote a history about the rise of the Turks in ten books covering the period from 1298 to 1463. *See also* SELJUK TURKS. MAG

E. Darkó, *Laonici Chalcocendylae historiarum demonstrationes, I–II* (1922–7).
H. Wurm and E. Gamillscheg, 'Bemerkungen zu Laonikos Chalkokondyles', *JÖB* 42 (1992), 213–9.

chalice *See* EUCHARISTIC VENERATION AND VESSELS.

chamber, king's *See* ROYAL HOUSEHOLD.

chamberlain *See* ROYAL HOUSEHOLD.

Chambre des Comptes Central financial institution of the French monarchy, imitated in French principalities, 'imported' in the *Burgundian Netherlands by the *Valois dukes of *Burgundy (1386: Chambre des Comptes in *Lille). King *Philip II Augustus's reign witnessed (*c.*1200) the activity of a branch of the **curia regis* specialized in the financial control of royal officers and of urban finances. Under *Louis IX, their action was formalized (ordinance of 1256). During the reign of *Philip IV the Fair the '*camera compotorum*' appears (1292); its meetings took place in the Temple, from 1303 onwards in the new royal palace in the 'Cité'. Its masters had extensive judicial powers and kept the archives and thus the memory of the State. MGRB

E. Aerts, *Geschiedenis en archief van de Rekenkamers* (1996).
P. Contamine and O. Mattéoni, eds, *La France des principautés: Les Chambres des comptes XIVᵉ–XVᵉ siècles* (1996).

Champagne Province of *France. During the MA, the influential counts of Champagne were virtually independent of their nominal suzerain, the king of France, until the conquest of Champagne by Philip III the Bold in 1273. Under the *patronage of the Countess Marie (1145–98), daughter of *Eleanor of Aquitaine, and her husband Henri, the court of Champagne became an influential literary centre, yielding authors such as *Chrétien de Troyes and *Andreas Capellanus. Champagne was also famous for the *fairs that achieved their height in the 13th century, with goods converging from the *Low Countries, *Italy, Spain, and *Germany. SJM

M. Crubelliere *et al.*, *Histoire de la Champagne* (1975).

Champmol *Carthusian monastery outside *Dijon founded by Philip III the Bold (1383) as a dynastic burial site for the Burgundian dukes; almost completely destroyed during the French Revolution. Surviving fragments include remarkable sculpture by Claus *Sluter and his nephew Claus de *Werve, including the famous 'Well of Moses'. SAH

R. Prochno, *Die Kartause von Champmol* (2002).

chancel The chancel is the part of the church, traditionally on the eastern end, that contains the *altar and is normally reserved for clerical use. The term is often used interchangeably with choir. ARS

E. Lucie-Smith, 'Chancel', in *The Thames and Hudson Dictionary of Art Terms* ([2]2004).

R. Toman, ed., *Romanesque: Architecture, Sculpture, Painting* (1997).

chancel screen A divider between the church sanctuary where *clergy or monks worshipped and the *nave where lay people attended services. In the early MA it stood shoulder height and was made of rectangular panels of wood or stone. In the 13th century enlarged screens included *altars, *chapels, and rich sculptural or painted decoration. They often had upper galleries for choirs or *pulpits and supported *crucifixes. CAB

N. Bock, P. Kurmann, S. Romano, and J.-M. Spieser, eds, *Art, Cérémonial et Liturgie au Moyen Âge* (2002).

chancery Royal or episcopal office that issued official documents and preserved records; modern scholarship also uses the word to describe public notaries producing documents on behalf of communes or municipalities. The *cancellarius*, a minor court official in the late Roman Empire and early Ostrogothic kingdom, probably was the intermediary between the court and the public. With the decline of the Roman imperial system in the west, the emerging successor states retained both the office and title. The papal chancery provided an institutional continuum between the west and the imperial chancery in *Constantinople. The papal chancery also established procedures to ensure the authenticity of legal documents and identify forgeries produced to substantiate false claims.

Under the *Carolingians, the *cancellarius* was the same as a notary, and could be either a layman or a cleric. The secretariat prepared letters and documents, while the chancery ensured their legal authenticity and preservation. The chancery was entrusted with matters of policy, preservation of royal privileges, taxation, and settling disputes over rights and property. Already in the 9th century the chancellor was an important government official; *Hincmar of Rheims wrote in *Ad procures regni pro institutione Carolomanni regis* that Carolingian chancellors needed discretion, fidelity, and the ability to keep secrets. In *England, the chancery also operated as a court, with the chancellor as judge. As the office became an important part of maintaining sovereign power, descriptions of the qualifications and duties of the chancellor (of which discretion and faithfulness were still paramount) were incorporated into statute law. As the status of the chancellor's office rose, it seems that he had less to do with the actual workings of the chancery and more to do with matters of state. The chancellor became a chief officer of the realm, in attendance upon the king. This meant that the actual work of the chancery was performed by subordinates. The substitution of *paper for *parchment (first in the Crown of *Aragon, after James I conquered Jativa and its paper *mills in 1248) increased the amount of government paperwork. By the 15th century, the chancery focused on the distribution and management of routine legal instruments, while another secretariat evolved to handle more confidential manners.

Lay and clerical chancery practices overlapped. Some rulers, local administrators, and even ecclesiastical institutions relied upon public *notaries to produce documents. Other monarchs appointed bishops as chancellors, who became members of the royal council. Lay chanceries also adopted numerous papal innovations, included sealing letters, maintaining registers of charters and letters, and the adoption of a particular chancery hand. In the late 11th century the papal chancery developed a rhythmic system of stressed and unstressed syllables at the end of clauses and sentences, called the *cursus*, which helped prevent forgery. *Pope Innocent III, in *De crimine falsi* (1198), set standards for determining the authenticity of papal documents, which included scrutiny of the subject matter, the writing, the style, the seals, and the signatures. Other chanceries embellished formats (such as elongating the letters along the top lines or the layout of the signatures), used variations in the material or attachment of seals (lead or wax, hanging, attached, or impressed), or incorporated drawn *signa*, all in the effort to identify unauthorized copies or forgeries. Notaries also, by law, maintained registers of the charters they drew up and followed authorized formats to produce authentic legal documents.

Diplomatics is the study of chancery practices, and it provides invaluable information about literacy, record-keeping, law, and administrative structures. The evolving format of record-keeping helps document the evolution of government. Despite reliance upon papal models, chancery practices differed throughout the west, and understanding

the history of the medieval chancery depends upon close scrutiny of surviving original charters. Chanceries and notarial records are also a good source for tracking *literacy and incidents of *bilingualism. TMV

G. Barraclough, *Public Notaries and the Papal Curia* (1934).
A. de Boüard, *Manuel de diplomatique, française et pontificale*, 2 vols (1929–51).
R. I. Burns, *Diplomatarium of the Crusader Kingdom of Valencia*, vol. 1 (1985).
D. A. Carpenter, 'The English Chancery in the Thirteenth Century', in *Écrit et pouvoir dans les chancelleries médiévales*, ed. K. Fianu and D. Guth (1997), 25–53.
M. T. Clanchy, *From Memory to Written Record: England 1066–1307* (1993).
O. Guyotjeannin *et al.*, *Diplomatique médiévale* (1993).
R. L. Poole, *Lectures on the History of the Papal Chancery down to the Time of Innocent III* (1915).

Chancery, Court of An English court of equity—a court where judgments were based on a notion of fairness rather than strict interpretation of statutory and case law—that developed in the late 14th century and gained official recognition in the 15th century.

The Court derived its status from the position and authority of the Chancellor, the king's primary administrator and the head of the royal secretariat. At times, he was also the king's confessor and thus was considered the king's 'conscience'. Indeed, petitioners to the Chancellor and the Court often made direct appeal to the 'justice' and 'conscience' of the king. Owing to his status, the Chancellor was delegated by the king to receive subjects' petitions for royal redress of their grievances. By the 15th century, the Chancellor and judges under him, forming the Court of Chancery, became the official source for the administration of justice that allegedly could not be dispensed fairly in the courts of common law. Petitioners to the Court often referred to the bias of juries or local officials toward the opposing party, the intimidation of the other party, or simply the inelasticity of existing law. DET

M. E. Avery, 'The History of Equitable Jurisdiction of Chancery before 1460', *BIHR* 42 (1969), 129–44.
W. P. Baildon, ed., *Select Cases in Chancery* (1896).
A. Harding, *The Law Courts of Medieval England* (1973).
T. F. T. Plucknett, *A Concise History of Common Law* ([5]1956).

change, theories of *See* PHILOSOPHY, NATURAL.

Channel Islands Archipelago off the coast of northwest *France, comprising the islands of Jersey, Guernsey, Alderney, Brechou, Great Sark, Little Sark, Herm, Jethou, and Lihou. Formerly part of *Normandy, the islands remained under the direct control of the English crown after the loss of Normandy in 1204, with a warden appointed to the defence of the islands, collection of ducal revenues, and administration of the lay courts. The islands remained under French ecclesiastical control (diocese of Coutances) until taken into the jurisdiction of *Winchester in 1568. JCF

J. Le Patourel, *The Medieval Administration of the Channel Islands, 1199–1399* (1937; repr. 2004).

chanson *See* POLYPHONIC CHANSON; SONGS, POLYPHONIC.

Chanson de Roland One of the earliest surviving and best-known of the **chansons de geste*, relating the death of *Charlemagne's nephew Roland in an ambush while retreating from Spain, followed by Charlemagne's revenge on the Saracens and prosecution of the traitor *Ganelon. The celebrated assonanced *Roland* (*c.*1098) is uncharacteristic of *chansons de geste* by its unity, intensity, and concision. It survives in full in only one MS (Bodleian Digby 23, the 'Oxford *Roland*'); better attested and more typical is the rhymed *Roland* (*c.*1180), which simplifies the moral landscape while diffusing the narrative focus, notably expanding the roles of Ganelon and Aude, Roland's betrothed.

Scholarship has traditionally focused on the Oxford text, especially on Roland's refusal to summon Charlemagne's help and later volte-face (the famous 'horn scenes'). Some critics consider the hero tragically flawed by *démesure*, others seek a contemporary rationale for his actions. However, the criticisms lodged by Roland's companion Olivier demonstrate that the hero does not represent a consensual warrior ethos, while comparison with the saintly Roland of the rhymed texts highlights the distance between Oxford's Roland and Christian models.

Recent investigations of the poem's construction of French *nationhood have focused on *feudal versus monarchist ideologies or on the treatment of Saracens. Conclusions must take into account the fact that most surviving redactions are not strictly 'French', but AN, Franco-Venetian, or originating from Imperial territory. *See also* CHIVALRY AND KNIGHTHOOD; KINGSHIP, QUEENSHIP, AND MONARCHY; LITERATURES: FRENCH; ROLANDSLIED; WARFARE. JGi

G. S. Burgess, tr., *The Song of Roland* (1990).
P. Haidu, *The Subject of Violence: The 'Song of Roland' and the Birth of the State* (1993).
S. Kinoshita, *Medieval Boundaries: Rethinking Difference in Old French Literature* (2006).

chansons de geste Also known, not uncontroversially, as OFr. epic. They appear as narrative poems, extant from *c.*1100, throughout the medieval period (including late prose reworkings) and in all the French-language dialects within and beyond *France, though particularly prevalent in Franco-Italian. They are characteristically written in *laisses*: groups of a varying number of lines united in some early cases by final assonance, otherwise by rhyme. Decasyllabic and dodecasyllabic (*alexandrine) lines predominate. They were

celebrated by 19th-century scholars for their supposed nationalism, moral heroism, and piety. Much the most famous is the *Chanson de Roland.

Chansons de geste were traditionally contrasted to courtly *romance as constituting an exclusively masculine, martial domain of feudal *warfare, warrior values, and male bonding. Only the few pre-1150 works were taken into account in this view. Romances were thought to have rapidly supplanted and pushed them into decadence. However, the majority of the 100-plus surviving poems are contemporary with romances. New, inclusive views of the *genre have therefore developed. Critics have argued against ascribing the fantastical settings, baroque adventures, and love stories included in later examples to an extraneous 'romance influence' denaturing the epic. *Chansons de geste* and romance represent alternative responses to the same baronial, courtly world. One influential viewpoint (Kay) analyses the genres as each other's 'political unconscious', presenting complementary analyses of the tensions experienced by elite groups in late *feudal society. This interpretation may be advanced at more micro levels: even the most unified *chansons* have an episodic structure in which sections of narrative offer divergent perspectives.

A similarly dynamic relation holds between poems in the different *gestes* or songs about the deeds of various families (*geste* can mean all of these). Three were famously defined by Bertrand de Bar-sur-Aube in his **Girart de Vienne* (*c.*1180) as centring (i) on *Charlemagne, king and emperor of the Franks, in his struggles against the Saracens; (ii) on the *barons related to Garin de Monglane (*see* GUILLAUME D'ORANGE CYCLE) and loyal to the king; and (iii) on the rebellious, treacherous clan of *Doon de Mayence. Although neither exhaustive nor adequate to the surviving texts, this classification does identify how key themes are diversely treated.

Chansons de geste differ from romances by their broad political canvas and their emphasis on the public dimensions of phenomena that romances address in the private realm. Thus conflicts between *knights or between lords and *vassals as well as marital and erotic affections and tensions are played out as allegiance, enmity, or betrayal on battlefields involving vast social groups. Violence is a constant concern and regarded quite variously, its constructive and destructive aspects explored. Solutions to internecine conflict include a strong central authority, king, or emperor, and solidarity against a joint enemy—often religious. The greater historicity and realism of *chansons de geste* in contrast to romance depend in part on the former's orientation towards the public, political and large-scale, which are important components in modern definitions of the historical and the real. Their engagement with contemporary politics—with the high MA of their writing rather than the often Carolingian past of their setting—is considered transparent relative to that of romance. Charlemagne rather than Arthur was claimed as a model by the *Capetian and *Valois kings of *France.

Chansons de geste were once deemed 'popular' in the sense of being addressed to the common people. Although this view is now untenable, modern popular fiction provides productive conceptual models. The vexed question opposing traditionalists, who held that *chansons de geste* were collective oral compositions only incidentally written down, to individualists (Bédieristes) regarding them as poetically crafted and authored texts, was illuminated by Rychner's comparisons with *oral story-telling in the modern Balkans, leading to the currently dominant, neo-traditionalist position. Similarly, film sequels, prequels, and remakes make interesting analogies to the grouping in *gestes*, and especially to the 13th-century tendency to group certain *chansons* in cyclical MSS, rewriting existing texts and composing new ones to follow the fortunes of a charismatic hero or villain (the most developed is that of Guillaume d'Orange). Modern exploitation of violence in popular cinema, while clearly not a key to medieval uses, raises new perspectives on *chansons de geste* aesthetics. *Feud in *chansons de geste* is at once a stimulus to fear and excitement and a means of generating further narrative. *See also* LITERATURES: ARTHURIAN LEGEND. JGi

J. Bédier, *Les Légendes épiques: Recherches sur la formation des chansons de geste*, 4 vols (1908–13).
S. Kay, *The 'Chansons de geste' in the Age of Romance: Political Fictions* (1995).
J. Rychner, *La Chanson de geste: Essai sur l'art épique des jongleurs* (1955).
F. Suard, *La Chanson de geste* (1993).

Chantilly The road northeast from *Paris to *Senlis was dominated by this 12th-century castle of the family Le Bouteiller, hereditary royal butlers, on the southern edge of the forest of Chantilly. The old donjon was obliterated by the magnificent château built by the constable Anne de *Montmorency (1493–1567). Here the Institut de France maintains the Musée Condé with its choice collection of medieval MSS, hundreds of them illustrated. DHW

G. Macon, *Chantilly: The Castle, the Park, the Stables*, tr. M. Veigneau (French original, 1927) (1929).

Chantilly codex *See* POLYPHONIC MUSIC, SOURCES: 1300–1400.

chantry chapels *See* CHAPEL.

chapel An enclosed or semi-enclosed space with an *altar; free-standing or one of many similar smaller-scaled spaces around or behind an *apse or along *transept or *nave.

Chapels originated with the cult of *relics and also served as liturgical spaces. The commonest examples, royal and

Aerial view of Château de Chantilly.

episcopal chapels, can be large, for example, *Vincennes, *Ste-Chapelle, or the palatine chapels in Aix (*Aachen) or *Palermo, and even two-storied (Laon and *Rheims).

In the 13th century, chapels were built by private patrons in veneration of a saint or for commemorative prayer; these were usually controlled by *clergy. CAB

C. Du Cange, *Glossarium mediae et infimae latinitatis* (1678; 1954), vol. 2, 115–18.

chapel royal *See* CHAPEL.

chaplain A large class of priest with pastoral responsibilities shaped according to the institution they served. Most medieval chaplains were hired priests (*stipendarii*) who assisted the parish *rector or vicar. Other chaplains were attached to *hospitals, almshouses, chantries, royal *chapels, and *oratories. *See also* CLERGY. WJD

J. Godfrey, *The English Parish, 600–1300* (1969).
J. Moorman, *Church Life in England in the Thirteenth Century* (1946).

chapter (capitulum) *Capitulum* originally referred to the portion of the Rule of *Benedict read at daily meetings in *monasteries. It came to denote the meeting itself, and the meeting space was called the *chapter house. *Capitulum* also designated *canons serving *cathedrals and collegiate *churches. *See also* MONASTICISM. GP

C. H. Lawrence, *Medieval Monasticism: Forms of Religious Life in Western Europe in the Middle Ages* ([2]1989).

chapter house Many monastic and *cathedral complexes included rooms used for meetings of their governing bodies. While continental chapter houses were usually buildings of little architectural distinction, highly decorated polygonal structures became typical of English foundations during the 13th and 14th centuries. *See also* CHAPTER; MONASTERY. ARS

R. Stalley, *Early Medieval Architecture* (1999).
E. Toman, ed., *The Art of Gothic: Architecture, Sculpture, Painting* (1998).

chapter of faults A meeting in *monasteries presided over by the abbot for the public acknowledgment of faults. When called upon, a monk confessed his guilt or failure in observance of the monastic discipline. The daily *chapter meeting often included a period for the admission of faults. *See also* MONASTICISM. GP

M. Wolter, *The Principles of Monasticism*, tr. B. A. Sause (Latin original, 1880) (1962).

charcoal Partially burned wood of various plant species, usually obtained in the medieval period by burning wood slowly over many days in a pit covered by earth (smothered burning). Often made from any fallen branches and shrubs, charcoal was also prepared from specific woods that produced a higher quality product, such as beech, ilex, pine, and, in the Mediterranean region, heather, the latter used in

the *furnaces of blacksmiths and coppersmiths. Charcoal production was carried out in *forests where the producers collected wood from places designated by public powers who enforced rotation to prevent depletion. The charcoal burners would *transport the charcoal to the cities on the backs of animals. It was sold in *markets or in specific locations in the *towns, which sometimes came to be represented in urban toponymy (for example, the Door of Charcoal—*Puerta del Carbon*—in *Granada).

Unlike wood, charcoal is light and burns without producing excessive ash or smoke. Medieval people used charcoal as a domestic *fuel for *heating and *cooking, for drying hops, as an ingredient and fuel in *glass-making, in the manufacture of medicines (*see* PHARMACY) and *soap, as a *pigment, and in metallurgical processes, especially *iron smelting. From the early 14th century it was used to make *gunpowder. RCór, POL

R. Bechmann, *Trees and Man: The Forest in the Middle Ages*, tr. K. Dunham (French original, 1984) (1990).

Charlemagne (Charles the Great) (*c.*742–814) Elder son of the Frankish magnate Pippin who displaced the last Merovingian king and assumed the title of king of the Franks in 751. In 754, Pope Stephen II came to Francia and consecrated Charles and his brother Carloman (b. 752) kings along with their father. The brothers learned Frankish leadership strategies: taking booty to secure aristocratic support, simultaneously protecting and exploiting churches, and marrying noble Frankish wives. This preliminary dynastic consolidation was strained when Pippin divided the Frankish realm equally between his sons (768).

Carloman's death (5 December 771) was good news for Charles, but his widow and two sons fled to the *Lombard king Desiderius who tried to persuade *Pope Hadrian I to consecrate the boys kings of the Franks. Meanwhile Charles attacked the Saxons, invaded Lombardy, captured the nephews and Desiderius, and took over the Lombard kingdom (June 774). Charles rejoiced in the Saxons' acceptance of Christianity (778), then campaigned against the *Basques in northeast Spain. As the Franks returned home, the booty-laden rearguard was slaughtered at *Roncesvalles (kernel of the **Chanson de Roland*). Defeat and harvest-failure stimulated a new agenda of legal and judicial reform, *famine relief, and *fasting and *penance (sketched at Herstal in 779).

In Rome in 781, Charles had Pope Hadrian consecrate his two youngest sons to kingdoms in *Italy and *Aquitaine, and sealed an alliance with the Byzantine regent Irene by betrothing his daughter Rotrud to Constantine VI. In 787 Irene and Constantine, with papal approval, summoned a council at Nicaea to restore icon-veneration, unilaterally broke off the betrothal arrangement, and sent a fleet to support Charles's enemies, the Beneventans. Charles pressured the pope into line and forced the Beneventan duke to switch sides, then deposed another enemy, the Bavarian duke

The coronation of Emperor Charlemagne by Pope Leo III on Christmas Eve AD 800, from *Chroniques des empereurs* by David Aubert (1462).

Tassilo, and took over *Bavaria (788). Charles's second son and namesake was established as his heir in Francia (790).

In the 790s, Charles unrolled an enlarged ideological campaign: a large palace begun at *Aachen and an attempt to dig a canal between the *river Danube and the *Rhine; the production of historical writing about the Franks and their king; and religious reform. Charles's eldest son attacked him, as did the Beneventans, the Saxons, and the Avars, but the son was crushed, the Avars were defeated, the Beneventans were contained by Charles's son Pippin, and the Saxons gradually accepted Frankish rule, even as Charles's other son, Louis, built a kingdom in Aquitaine. In *Byzantium, Irene's blinding of her own son and assumption of imperial power weakened Roman authority in west and east. In 799, Pope Leo III fled to *Paderborn, and Charles, with court and army, returned to Rome, where an assembly declared a Roman imperial vacancy. On Christmas Day 800 Charles was crowned emperor by the pope.

Thereafter, Charlemagne was based mostly at his Aachen court where embassies came from the caliph in *Baghdad. Administrative records, letters, and poems show a burst of governmental activity, with repeated oath-swearings, extended religious reform, and a remaking of the elites and the army. The empire Charlemagne bequeathed (814) to his sole surviving son, *Louis the Pious, was a going concern. JLN

B. Bastert, *Karl der Grosse in den europäischen Literaturen des Mittelalters* (2004).
—— *Karl der Grosse und Europa* (2004).
R. Morrissey, *Charlemagne and France*, tr. C. Tihanyi (French original, 1997) (2003).
J. Story, ed., *Charlemagne: Empire and Society* (2005).
L. Thorpe, tr., *Two Lives of Charlemagne* (1969).

Charles, duke of Orléans (1394–1465) French poet, son of Louis, duke of Orléans. Captured at *Agincourt, Charles spent 25 years in captivity in *England; after returning to *France, he built up a literary circle in *Blois. Charles composed poetry throughout his adult life, concentrating primarily upon allegorical *ballades and *rondeaux on amatory themes. He gradually developed a distinctive allegorical style, in which ambiguity plays a major part. AA

M.-J. Arn, ed., *Charles d'Orléans in England, 1415–1440* (2000).
Charles d'Orléans, *Poésies*, ed. P. Champion, 2 vols (1923–7).
A. Planche, *Charles d'Orléans ou la recherche d'un langage* (1975).

Charles ('the Good'), count of Flanders (1081–1127) Related to *Flanders' ruling house through his mother, he was raised in his mother's homeland. He succeeded his cousin, Baldwin VII, and distinguished himself as a defender of the church, champion of the poor, and enemy of lawlessness. Charles's investigation of the servile origins of a prominent family unleashed a wave of violence that took his life by assassination and plunged Flanders into a struggle involving the towns, *France, and *England. *Galbert of Bruges's hagiographical account of his life has become a classic. JMMu

J. B. Ross, *The Murder of Charles the Good* ([2]1982).

Charles I of Anjou, king of Naples (1226/7–1285) Count of *Provence by marriage, he was named count of *Anjou and Maine by his brother, *Louis IX, in 1246. Urban IV enticed him to make an expedition to *Italy in order to counterbalance the power of the Hohenstaufens. By 1265, Charles had aligned ample support from his allies to be crowned king of Sicily and to organize an assault on Manfred, whom he defeated the following year at the battle of Benevento. In 1268, Charles routed the forces of Conradin, the last Hohenstaufen claimant, and definitively established his position as king of the Regno. Though he pursued interests in Greece as well, Michael Palaeologus, his allies, and, eventually, Pope Gregory X effectively stopped the *Angevin spread eastward. Upon the succession of the French pope, Martin IV, the tides changed, and Charles began preparations for a siege on *Constantinople. The plans were curtailed, however, by a rebellion in 1282, known as the Sicilian Vespers, in which he lost Sicily to *Peter III of *Aragon. Onerous levels of *taxation are typically cited as factors leading to unrest in Sicily, although this theory has recently been challenged. EMP

J. Dunbabin, *Charles I of Anjou: Power, Kingship and State-Making in Thirteenth-Century Europe* (1998).
M. Fuiano, *Carlo I d'Angiò in Italia* (1974).
P. Herde, *Karl I von Anjou* (1979).
E. Jordan, *Les origines de la domination angevine en Italie*, 2 vols (1960).
É. Léonard, *Les Angevins de Naples* (1954).
S. Runciman, *The Sicilian Vespers* (1958).

Charles I of Navarre *See* CHARLES IV ('THE FAIR'); NAVARRE, KINGS AND QUEENS OF.

Charles II ('the Bad') (b. 1332) Count of Évreux (1343–87) and king of *Navarre (1349–87). In 1350, Charles executed the constable of *France, Raoul de Brienne, and was implicated in the assassination of his successor, Charles of Spain, four years later. Following a brief imprisonment, Charles became the leader of the opposition to his father-in-law, King Jean II. Though he was one of the nobles involved in the repression of the *Jacquerie, his brief flirtation with the Parisians and the English undermined his support in France. In 1364, he was driven from his Norman lands by Bertrand *Du Guesclin. The sobriquet 'El Malo' was given to him in the 16th century by Navarrese historians. CDT

D. M. Bessen, 'Charles II of Navarre and John the Good', Ph.D. thesis (Toronto, 1983).
R. Cazelles, *Société politique, noblesse et couronne sous Jean le Bon et Charles V* (1982).

Charles II ('the Bald'), emperor and king of France (823–77) Charles was the son of *Louis the Pious and his second wife Judith; his birth upset the succession plan of 817 and caused rebellions by Charles's half-brothers. During the civil wars following Louis's death, Charles joined with his brother *Louis the German against Lothar and Pepin I of Aquitaine. The Treaty of Verdun (843) granted Charles the western kingdom, which he ruled effectively despite revolts by Pepin and invasions by Louis the German. Good relations with his kingdom's bishops, especially *Hincmar of Rheims, were critical to his success against invasion and to establishing his royal position. By 860 he sought to expand his authority. On Christmas day 875 he was crowned emperor, ruling the middle kingdom as well. After Louis the German's death Charles seized *Aachen but failed to control Louis's kingdom. He promoted cultural and artistic life and presided over a great flowering of the Carolingian *Renaissance. MCF

M. Gibson and J. L. Nelson, eds, *Charles the Bald: Court and Kingdom* (1981).
J. L. Nelson, *Charles the Bald* (1992).

Charles III ('the Fat') (839–88) (emperor) Son of *Louis the German, Charles became king of Alemannia on his father's death in 876. In 879 he assumed the crown of *Italy, and in 881 Pope John VIII crowned him emperor. In 885 he became king of West Francia, thus bringing the entire empire under his authority. *Viking raids, illness, and rebellion led him to abdicate (887). He also commissioned *Notker Balbulus to write a life of *Charlemagne. MCF

S. McLean, *Kingship and Politics in the Late Ninth Century: Charles the Fat and the End of the Carolingian Empire* (2003).

Charles III ('the Simple'), king of France (r. 898–923) Called 'the Simple' from Latin *simplex*, better understood as 'straightforward', Charles, a *Carolingian, was respected by *France's *clergy and by *Germany's Henry I. In 911 he defeated the Northmen and granted them *Normandy provided they convert to Christianity, and was recognized by the nobles of *Lotharingia as king. Charles's attention to Lotharingia alienated the nobles of France, who rebelled in the 920s. Captured by Count Herbert of *Vermandois in 923, Charles remained imprisoned until his death. MCF

P. Riché, *The Carolingians: A Family Who Forged Europe*, tr. M. I. Allen (French original, 1983) (1993).

Charles IV (1316–78) King of *Bohemia and German emperor. The eldest son of John of Luxembourg and Elisabeth Přemyslovna, he made Bohemia a major centre of European culture. During his reign *Prague was raised to the status of an archbishopric (1344), endowed with a *university (1348), and embellished with many fine buildings in the Gothic style. He wrote a *hagiography of St *Wenceslas

The coronation of Charles II ('the Bald'), with the archbishops of Rheims and Treves, from the *Sacrementaire de Metz*.

and his own autobiography in Latin (*Vita Caroli*; *see* CHARLES IV AUTOBIOGRAPHY). AT

F. Seibt, *Kaiser Karl IV.: Staatsmann und Mäzen* ([2]1978).
——*Karl IV.: Ein Kaiser in Europa, 1346 bis 1378* (1994).

Charles IV ('the Fair'), king of France (r. 1322–8) Last monarch of the *Capetian line. A son of *Philip IV and Jeanne of Navarre, Charles followed his brother, Philip V, as king of France and Navarre in 1322. Attempting to dominate his aristocracy and *clergy, Charles proved an inept fiscal manager whose policies could have led to a full-blown financial crisis had his reign been longer. Despite three marriages between 1307 and 1328, Charles had no sons and his death precipitated a succession crisis which led inexorably to the *Hundred Years War. *See also* NAVARRE, KINGS AND QUEENS OF. DJK

P. S. Lewis, *Late Medieval France* (1968).

Charles IV Autobiography (*Vita Caroli*) The Autobiography, though probably not entirely from Charles's own hand, is a rare example of a personal memoir by a medieval ruler. The narrative covers the events of Charles's

Head of Charles IV from St Vitus cathedral.

youth from his birth and childhood, spent mainly in the court of the kings of France, his role in his father John of Luxembourg's Italian campaigns, and his activities in Bohemia and in the Silesian conflicts, up to his election as king of the Romans in 1346. Out of the twenty chapters, five include his thoughts on the perfect ruler and some sermon-like excurses and gospel commentaries. Two early Czech translations survive, preserved in 15th-century MSS, as well as a 15th-century German translation. BN

E. Hillenbrand, *Vita Caroli Quarti/Die Autobiographie Karls IV.* (1979).

B. Nagy and F. Schaer, *Karoli IV Imperatoris Romanorum vita ab eo ipso conscripta et hystoria nova de Sancto Wenceslao martyre—The Autobiography of Emperor Charles IV and his Legend of St Wenceslas* (2001).

K. Pfisterer and W. Bulst, *Karoli IV Imp. Rom. Vita ab eo ipso conscripta* (1950).

Charles IV of Luxembourg *See* ROMAN EMPIRE [HOHENSTAUFEN DYNASTY].

Charles V ('the Wise'), king of France (b. 1338; r. 1364–80) Charles was the first heir to the French throne to be styled dauphin of Viennois. While his father, Jean II, was a prisoner in *England following the battle of *Poitiers (1356), Charles served as royal lieutenant and regent during the time of the *Jacquerie riots in *Paris, the machinations of Charles of *Navarre, and an English invasion in 1359. After he inherited the throne in 1364, the situation rapidly improved. A new tax system financed the army with which *Du Guesclin defeated the Navarrese in 1364. Charles's brother Philip the Good married the heiress to *Flanders and *Artois, preventing the English from controlling these strategic lands. *Du Guesclin secured the Castilian throne for an ally of France who provided a fleet that defeated the English off La Rochelle (1372). Following the revival of the *Hundred Years War in 1369, French forces quickly recovered the majority of lands held by the English.

Charles V had the *Louvre restored and created the first royal library in France, including many books written or translated for him by a remarkable intellectual circle. In a biography written in 1404, *Christine de Pizan praised the king for his wisdom and cemented the contentious view that he was personally responsible for the French recovery. CDT

R. Cazelles, *Société politique, noblesse et couronne sous Jean le Bon et Charles V* (1982).

R. Delachenal, *Histoire de Charles V*, 5 vols (1909–31).

Charles VI ('the Mad'), king of France (1380–1422) Afflicted with paranoid schizophrenia since age 23, Charles illustrated the dangers inherent in the French concept of kingship: he ruled with full power and was kept from governing only when incapacitated; contemporaries could not always accurately assess his condition. Intermittent war with *England and periods of factional civil war (the *Armagnacs and Burgundians) did make treachery a reality. The military successes of *Henry V of England after *Agincourt and the treasonous behaviour of Charles's heir (*Charles VII) caused Charles VI to disinherit his heir, arrange for his daughter Catherine to marry Henry V, and accept the Treaty of *Troyes (1420), which stipulated that Henry would rule *France concurrently with Charles and then succeed him as king. RCF

R. C. Famiglietti, *Royal Intrigue: Crisis at the Court of Charles VI 1392–1420* (1986).

B. Guenée, *La folie du roi Charles VI* (2004).

Charles VII ('the Well-Served'), king of France (b. 1403; r. 1422–61) The eldest surviving son of *Charles VI and Isabeau of *Bavaria, Charles (VII) was disinherited in favour of *Henry V of England in the treaty of *Troyes (1420). When Henry and Charles VI died in quick succession in 1422, *France was split between the supporters of the infant *Henry VI north of the Loire, and the regime of Charles VII in the south. Aided by *Joan of Arc, Charles's forces secured dramatic victories in 1429, but the real turning point occurred in 1435 when *Burgundy abandoned the English and supported Charles. In 1445, the king and his advisors, particularly Arthur de *Richemont and Pierre de Brézé, implemented substantial military reforms which underpinned the reconquest of Normandy and *Aquitaine from the English between 1449 and 1453. Despite these successes, for which he was given the sobriquet 'the Victorious', Charles continued to face noble opposition to his attempts to consolidate royal power, most notably in the *Praguerie (1440). CDT

G. du F. de Beaucourt, *Histoire de Charles VII*, 6 vols (1881–91).
M. G. A. Vale, *Charles VII* (1974).

Charles VIII, king of France, Jerusalem, and Sicily (1470–98) Son of Louis XI and Charlotte of *Savoy, betrothed to Marguerite of Austria in 1482, king in 1483, Charles assumed power in 1488 after the regency of his sister Anne. Having subdued *Brittany, he married the duchess Anne in 1491. Aiming to gain Sicily and launch a crusade against the Turks, he invaded *Italy in 1494 and conquered *Naples, only to lose it in 1496 after the battle of Fornova in 1495. After his accidental death without heirs at 27, the crown passed to his cousin Louis XII. EARB

Y. Labande-Mailfert, *Charles VIII et son milieu (1470–1498): la jeunesse au pouvoir* (1975).
—— *Charles VIII: Le vouloir et la destinée* (1986).
R. W. Scheller, 'Imperial Themes in Art and Literature of the Early French Renaissance: The Period of Charles VIII', *Simiolus*, 12 (1981–2), 5–69.

Charles University Towards the end of the 13th century, an attempt by King Wenceslas II to institute a university in *Prague was thwarted by the Bohemian nobility. However, the efforts were successfully pursued by the Czech and Roman king (emperor since 1355), *Charles IV, right from the outset of his rule. Having gained consent from Pope Clement VI, who, on 26 January 1347, granted his *bull to a four-faculty university, he used his power as Bohemian king to issue a foundation charter, on 7 April 1348, which, in theoretical reference to older teachings in *Bologna and *Paris, aspired to unite the irreconcilable. The new university was put under the charge of the Prague archbishop, to act as chancellor.

While fully fledged tuition took a while to develop, the chairs of medicine, law, and theology staged readings immediately, inviting scholars from abroad, Italy in particular, and drawing upon some of the local regular studies. Although materially provided for by the Bohemian kingdom, the university won a general confirmation through the so-called Eisenach Diploma, from 14 January 1349, granted by Charles by virtue of being Roman king.

The university soon became consolidated, especially when the Charles and All Saints colleges, the two oldest, were set up in 1366. It was divided into four university nations (Bohemian, Bavarian, Saxon, and Polish) and, in 1372, the independent University of Law was constituted within the **studium generale*. The second half of the 14th century saw more universities founded in central Europe under the influence of Prague which, however, remained attractive even for students from remote countries (Scandinavia). Eminent foreign theologists worked there. With the leadership of John *Hus, himself influenced by John *Wyclif, Czech masters with their realism gained more importance. The *Kutná Hora decree, issued by Wenceslas IV on 18 January 1409, substantially enhanced the Czech element among the university nations. This resulted in secession of foreign students, reducing the university to an institution of regional standing which became the main authority of the Czech conservative right wing of the Hussite movement, progressively offering studies no higher than the Faculty of Arts. Although the Hussite revolution brought it to a halt over several years, its activities were later restored and, in the years 1447–8, the university opened itself to Catholic influences. Nonetheless, it remained a *Utraquist regional institution, with major influence on education in the country. IH

F. Kavka and J. Petráň, eds, *Dějiny Univerzity Karlovy*, vol. 1: *1347/48–1622* (1995).
Monumenta historica Universitatis Carolo-Ferdinandeae, 1–3 (1830–48).
P. Moraw, 'Die Universität Prag im Mittelalter', in *Die Universität zu Prag* (1986), 9–134.
H. de Ridder-Symoens, ed., *A History of the University in Europe*, vol. 1 (1992).
F. Šmahel, 'Die Anfänge der Prager Universität. Kritische Reflexionen zum Jubiläum, eines "nationalen Monumenst"', *Historica*, n.s., vols 3–4 (1996–7), 7–50.
V. V. Tomek, *Děje university pražské*, vol. 1: *1348–1437* (1849).
J. Tříška, *Životopisný slovník předhusitské pražské univerzity (1348–1409)* (1981).

charms, incantations, and amulets were shaped by ancient traditions of beneficent, and sometimes maleficent, magic inherited from late antiquity. Medieval amulets and magic bowls of eastern Mediterranean Jewish and Islamic origins display motifs, structures, and purposes that parallel European texts. Similarly, late antique materials in the Greek magical papyri commingle Egyptian, Graeco-Roman, Jewish, and Coptic Christian elements that bear resemblances to European charms.

The word charm (French *charme*, German *Zauber*, Italian *incanto*) comes from the Latin word *carmen*, a hymn or secular song. In the late 4th century, *Marcellus of *Bordeaux used *carmen* to indicate a short text to be performed by recitation or in writing for healing purposes. Instructions for performance are typically included in medieval charms, which often entail medical, magical, and religious rituals. Charms survive formally inscribed in texts, casually jotted in margins, and written upon artifacts, such as *parchment rolls, that were meant to be used as amulets. Within Christian communities, authorities who condemned the use of 'incantations' (*incantationes*), which are magical texts derived from outside the Christian tradition and potentially demonic, as magical practice did not always condemn charms, which were widely used. Charms were employed for many reasons such as to relieve fevers, staunch bleeding, prevent toothache, aid in conception and in childbirth, cure impotence, and cure and prevent falling sickness as well as attacks of elves and 'wicked spirits'. Medieval charms relied heavily on Christian motifs, both biblical and apocryphal, early Christian commentaries, saints' lives, and *liturgical materials. Some curative charms in the MSS consist entirely of prayers invoking saints or the power of the wounds of Christ.

Amulets are objects believed to have special powers. They were to be hung around the neck, attached to limbs, hidden in clothing, or kept within the house. Natural materials, such as precious stones, *herbs, nuts, and animal parts were valued for their healing and apotropaic powers. The Middleham Jewel in the York Museum is a fine example of medieval amuletic jewellery with its combination of engraved images, inscription, and border of saints; its case slides open to reveal a hidden container suitable for a relic. Tiny reliquaries to be worn on the body, and other devotional objects such as *pilgrim badges or small *ampullae containing water with a tincture of a saint's blood or bits of the cross, were worn or hung in homes for protection. Some amulets consisted primarily of words and signs inscribed on a thin sheet of metal (*lamina*) or piece of parchment (*breve*). *See also* MAGIC AND WITCHCRAFT; MEDICINE; RELICS; RELIGIOUS HEALING. LTO

E. Bozoky, *Charmes et Prières Apotropaïques* (2003).
L. Hansmann and L. Kriss-Rettenbeck, *Amulett und Talisman: Erscheinungsform und Geschichte* ([2]1977).
K. L. Jolly, *Popular Religion in Late Saxon England* (1996).
P. M. Jones and L. T. Olsan, 'Middleham Jewel: Ritual, Power, and Devotion', *Viator*, 31 (2000), 249–90.
M. W. Meyer and R. Smith, *Ancient Christian Magic* (1999).
L. T. Olsan, 'Charms in Medieval Memory', in *Charms and Charming in Europe*, ed. J. Roper (2004), 59–88.
E. Savage-Smith, 'Magic and Islam', in *Science, Tools, and Magic, Part One: Body and Spirit, Mapping the Universe*, ed. T. Maddison and idem (1997), 59–148.
L. H. Schiffman and M. Swartz, *Hebrew and Aramaic Incantation Texts from the Cairo Genizah* (1992).
D. C. Skemer, 'Written Amulets and the Medieval Book', *Scrittura e civiltà*, 23 (1999), 263–305.

charnel house From the Latin *carnarium*, a building or chamber in which bones were placed after being disinterred by the digging of new graves. LKE

P. Binski, *Medieval Death* (1996).
N. Orme, 'The Charnel Chapel of Exeter Cathedral', in *Medieval Art and Architecture at Exeter Cathedral*, ed. K. Francis (1991), 162–71.

Charny, Geoffroi de (*c*.1300–1356) French *knight who carried the royal banner at the battle of *Poitiers (1356). Charny also wrote the *Livre de chevalerie*, a treatise on the training and qualities expected of a young man-at-arms. CDT

G. de Charny, *The Book of Chivalry of Geoffroi de Charny*, ed. R. W. Kaeuper and E. Kennedy (1996).

Charolais County in southern Burgundy around city of Charolles with ties to *Autun, *Cluny. First countess (1272) was Béatrix, wife of Robert de *Clermont (sixth son of French king *Louis IX). Changed hands often between French royal claimants and dukes of *Burgundy during *Hundred Years War and later in 15th century. Nobility declared for Mary of Burgundy at death of Duke Charles the Bold in 1477. Became Habsburg territory with her marriage to Archduke Maximilian. (Claims recognized by King *Charles VIII of France in Treaty of *Senlis, 1493.) JFP

H. Elie, *Le Charolais dans l'histoire européenne* (1955).
M. Denizeau, *Histoire de Charelles* (1900; repr. 1992).

Charroux (monastery) Founded in the late 8th century on the Charente river, south of *Poitiers. In 989 the first council of the *Peace of God occurred there. TFH

T. Head, 'The Development of the Peace of God in Aquitaine (970–1005)', *Speculum*, 74 (1999), 656–86.
P. de Monsabert, ed., *Chartes et documents pour servir à l'histoire de l'abbaye de Charroux* (1910).

charter, private Designation (now thought anachronistic, but still used) for documents issued by people other than rulers or popes to record legal transactions. WCB

H. Fichtenau, *Das Urkundenwesen in Österreich vom 8. bis zum frühen 13. Jahrhundert* (1971).
O. Guyotjeannin, J. Pycke, and B.-M. Tock, *Diplomatique médiévale* (1993).
R. Sharpe, 'The Use of Writs in the Eleventh Century', *ASE* 32 (2003), 247–91.

charterhouse English name of *Carthusian monasteries. *Bruno the Carthusian founded the first *maison chartreuse* in the 1080s in the French alpine region of Dauphine near *Grenoble. King *Henry II founded the first charterhouse in *England at Witham in 1178. *See also* CHARTREUSE, LA GRANDE; MONASTERY. GP

J. Burton, *Monastic and Religious Orders in Britain, 1000–1300* (1994).

Charter of 1356 *See* 'JOYOUS ENTRY'.

charters of franchise and liberties A charter is a document addressed to a generality of people, usually containing a notification of a grant. A liberty or franchise (OFr. 'freedom') is an exemption from an aspect of a ruler's jurisdiction, of varying extent, usually within territorial bounds. Franchises were in effect a delegation of royal justice. In AN charters, the grant of such rights is usually found in a clause whereby land is to be held 'with' certain rights. In contrast, where property (or those living on it) was exempted from (for example) tolls, then that property is usually said to be held 'free and quit' of such charges. The one does not imply the other. Despite *Bracton's opinion to the contrary, the right to hold a liberty did not depend on the existence of a charter demonstrating that right. The statute **quo warranto* (1290) established that if a lord could demonstrate that they had held a liberty from the reign of *Richard I, they could continue to enjoy it; and they would also be given 'a title' to evidence that right. MH

H. M. Cam, 'The Evolution of the Mediaeval English Franchise', *Speculum*, 32 (1957), 427–42.
N. D. Hurnard, 'The Anglo-Norman Franchises', *EHR* 64 (1949), 290–327, 434–60.
R. Sharpe, 'The Use of Writs in the Eleventh Century', *ASE* 32 (2003), 247–91, at 249.
—— 'Address and Delivery in Anglo-Norman Royal Charters', in *Charters and Charter Scholarship in Britain and Ireland*, ed. M. T. Flanagan and J. A. Green (2005), 32–52, at 46–52.

Chartier, Alain (1385×95–1430) French author. A diplomat employed by the royal household, Chartier composed didactic, satirical, and amatory works in French and Latin. His ethical concerns and use of allegory heavily influenced the *Rhétoriqueurs; particularly important are *La Belle Dame sans merci* (1424), an amatory dialogue in verse, and the *Quadrilogue invectif* (1422), an allegorical debate in prose on the sorry condition of *France. *See also* LITERATURES: ALLEGORICAL. AA

J. C. Laidlaw, ed., *The Poetical Works of Alain Chartier* (1974).
F. Rouy, *L'Esthétique du traité moral d'après les œuvres d'Alain Chartier* (1980).

Chartres, school of The cathedral school became famous under the teacher and bishop *Fulcher of Chartres (d. 1028). The school's emphases included the harmony of faith and reason, and the harmony of biblical revelation and Platonic *cosmology. The *humanism of the school was founded upon study of the classical authors and Plato as well as *Macrobius and *Boethius. Famous scholars who were educated at the school included *Berengar of Tours, *William of Conches, *Bernard Silvestris, and *Clarembald of Arras. Famous chancellors of the school included *Bernard of Chartres, *Gilbert de la Porrée, and *Thierry of Chartres. *See also* NEOPLATONISM. AJD

P. Ellard, *The Sacred Cosmos* (2007).
E. Jeauneau, *'Lectio Philosophorum': Recherches dus l'École de Chartres* (1973).
R. W. Southern, 'The Schools of Paris and the School of Chartres', in *Renaissance and Renewal in the 12th Century*, ed. R. L. Benson and G. Constable (1982), 113–37.

Chartreuse, La Grande A *monastery in the French *Alps near *Grenoble, founded in 1084 by the reformer St *Bruno of *Cologne. Chartreuse gave birth to the

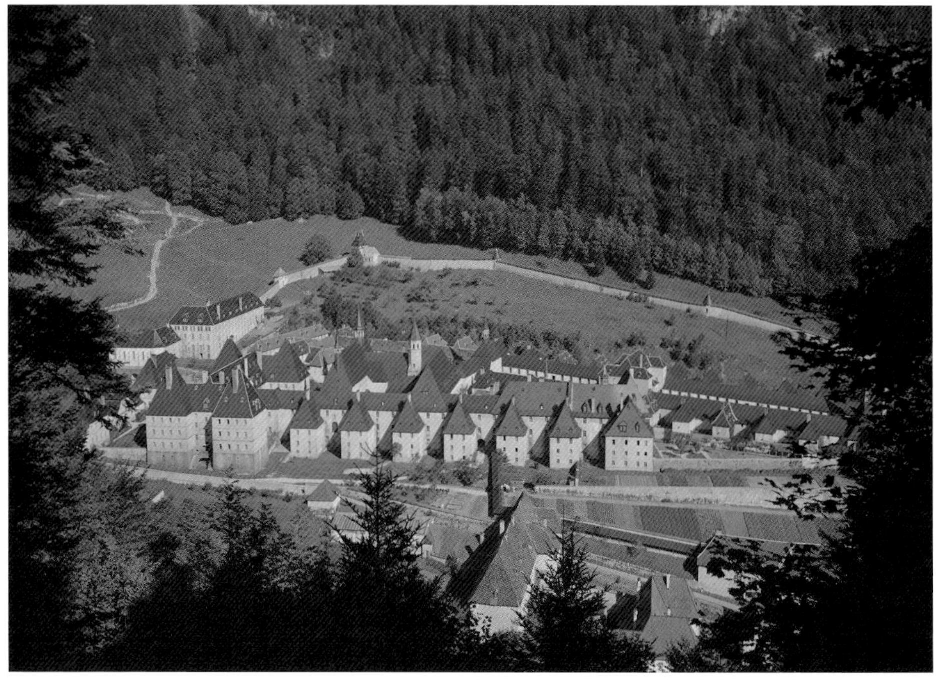

Aerial view of La Grande Chartreuse.

Remains of Château-Galliard.

*Carthusian order, dedicated to eremitical silence and seclusion within a monastic community. The monastery, briefly closed in the early 20th century, is still in operation today. PGJ

H. Leyser, *Hermits and the New Monasticism* (1984).

Chartreuse of Lövöld (Városlőd) The most important and richest of the Hungarian *Carthusian *monasteries, founded by Louis the Great in 1346. The church, modified in the late 15th century and rebuilt in 1747–61, has a single *nave and a polygonal sanctuary. A dozen MSS and incunabula, some of them in bindings typical of the place, are known from its library, for example a collection of *sermons (*Érdy codex*, Budapest, Országos Széchényi Könyvtár, MNy 9) written in Hungarian in 1526–7 by the 'Anonymous Carthusian'. BZS

P. Csengel and L. Gere, 'Előzetes beszámoló a városlődi karthauzi kolostor kutatásáról', *Műemlékvédelmi Szemle*, 6/1 (1996), 53–84.

Chastellain, Georges (*c.*1414–75) After studies at *Leuven, he entered the Burgundian court service in 1446, becoming official historiographer of Philip the Good in 1455 and ducal counsellor in 1457. Only fragments of his *Chronique* (1419–74) are preserved. He also composed poems and moralizing literature. WP

G. Small, *Chastellain and the Shaping of Valois Burgundy* (1997).

chasuble *See* LITURGICAL VESTMENTS.

Château-Gaillard The 'Lively Castle' built by *Richard I (Lionheart) between 1196 and 1198. Set on high bluffs overlooking the Seine, this fortress was constructed to block an easy French advance into *Normandy. Costing over £12,000 to complete, the unusual structure incorporated many elements of castle architecture Richard had seen on the Third *Crusade. Containing three wards, high curtain walls, and many towers, the *castle was linked by bridge to fortresses in the Seine. Despite its seemingly impregnable nature, the fortress fell to *Philip II Augustus in 1204 after a short siege. DJK

P. Warner, *Sieges of the Middle Ages* (1994).

Châtelain de Coucy (*fl.* 1186–1203) A prominent *trouvère* whose family owned the castle of Coucy (Picardy); he may have been Guy de Thourotte. He was the subject of the legend of the eaten heart in the *Roman du Castelain de Coucy* *c.*1300. JDH

J.-B. de Laborde, *Essai sur la musique ancienne et moderne* (1780), vol. 2.

A. Lerond, *Chansons attribuées au Chastelain de Coucy* (1963).

A. A. Perry, 'La symbolique du cœur dans quelques chansons du Châtelain de Coucy', *RlangR* 83 (1979), 237–43.

Châtelet Parisian fortress built in the early 12th century by Louis VI on the right bank of the Seine. It was the seat and the *prison of the royal provost of Paris, who oversaw administrative, policy, judicial, and fiscal tasks in the *Prévôté* and viscountcy of *Paris. MBG

C. Desmaze, *Le Châtelet de Paris, son organisation, ses privilèges (1060–1862)* (1863).
F. Lot and R. Fawtier, 'Le Châtelet', *Histoire des institutions françaises au Moyen Âge*, vol. 2: *Institutions royales* (1958), 372–85.
F. Olivier-Martin, *Histoire de la coutume de la prévôté et vicomté de Paris*, 2 vols (1922–30).

Chaucer, Geoffrey (*c*.1342–1400) The leading ME poet, arguably *England's greatest non-dramatic poet was born to a *London vintner family and is buried in *Westminster Abbey, where his tomb, erected in 1556, became the focus of Poets' Corner.

1. Life
2. Works
3. Influence

1. *Life*

First recorded in 1357 in the service of Elizabeth, countess of Ulster, Chaucer soon moved into the service of *Edward III, and later *Richard II. There is no information as to his education, though he was exceptionally widely read for a layman, in French, Latin, and, unusually for an Englishman of this period, in Italian. He was employed on royal service abroad in *France, in Spain in 1366, and in *Italy in 1372–3 and 1378. He held a number of demanding administrative posts, including the controllership of the London wool customs (1374–85) and the clerkship of the king's works (1389–91). He was a justice of the peace for *Kent and represented the county in the 1386 parliament.

There are numerous records of payments to Chaucer by Edward III, Richard II, and *Henry IV, and to both himself and his wife Philippa by *John of Gaunt (whose second wife she served), but none is identifiable as *patronage for his poetry. His primary audience probably consisted of men of his own rank, including the poet John *Gower, but aristocratic or royal readership is suggested by *The Book of the Duchess* (John of Gaunt), the original version of *The Legend of Good Women* (Anne of Bohemia), and the short advice poem *Lack of Steadfastness*.

Chaucer largely avoids direct political comment. He mentions the *Peasants' Rebellion of 1381 in a humorous

Portrait of Geoffrey Chaucer from Ellesmere manuscript of the *Canterbury Tales*.

context: the apparently orthodox Parson of the *Canterbury Tales* is accused by the Host of *Lollardy, and the Wife of Bath uses Lollard terminology as well as making a determined female attempt at biblical *exegesis, but his own views remain a matter of conjecture.

2. Works

The dominant spoken and written language at the royal court in Chaucer's early years was Anglo- or continental French. It was his achievement to make English the first choice of poetic language for the most sophisticated audiences. Probably his earliest work in English was a translation of the **Roman de la rose*, though of the three extant ME fragments only the first is likely to be his. His first original work to survive, *The Book of the Duchess* (a dream vision on the death of Blanche, first wife of John of Gaunt, d. 1368), is in effect written in dialogue with the *Roman* and the love narratives of Guillaume de *Machaut. He became acquainted with the great literature of the Italian Trecento through his visits to Italy. *Boccaccio's works provided the source narratives for the 'Knight's Tale' and *Troilus and Criseyde* and influenced the *Canterbury Tales*, and he made the first translation of one of *Petrarch's sonnets into English. His borrowings from and allusions to *Dante range from the wholly serious (such as the end of *Troilus*) to the sceptical, but he was clearly deeply impressed by him as a vernacular poet. He shows a familiarity too with classical poetry, especially Ovid and Virgil, though he offers as much resistance as homage; and he was strongly influenced by the *Consolation of Philosophy* of *Boethius, which he translated as the prose *Boece* c.1380.

Chaucer's works show a mixture of all these influences turned to highly original purposes. *The Parliament of Fowls*, a bird debate in dream form on the varieties of love, may possibly reflect on Richard II's marriage negotiations. *The House of Fame* is a dream meditation on the nature of literary authority, customarily dated before the *Parliament* on grounds of metre (tetrametre as against his innovative seven-line rhyme royal stanza), and is increasingly read as a theoretical link between *Troilus and Criseyde*, his great poem of love and betrayal completed in the mid 1380s, and the *Canterbury Tales*, which occupied him for the later years of his life. Two of the *Tales*, the 'Knight's' and 'Second Nun's', are mentioned in his *Legend of Good Women* (? late 1380s, revised after 1394) as the story of Palamon and Arcite and the life of St Cecilia, and were probably initially written as independent poems. The *Tales*, told by a group of pilgrims on the road to the shrine of St Thomas *Becket at *Canterbury, show to the full Chaucer's range from irony to high seriousness, his ear for individual voices, revolutionary vocabulary, and spacious syntax. The work remained uncompleted at his death, with only 24 tales written.

3. Influence

Chaucer was immediately recognized as a giant of English literature. He is the first English poet whose followers, starting with Thomas *Hoccleve and John *Lydgate, identify themselves by reference to him. The *Tales* was one of the first works to be printed in England, and he is the only ME poet to have been continuously read from his own time to the present. The first complete *Works* (an unprecedented English equivalent of the authoritative Latin *Opera*) was published in 1532 and expanded in various editions down to 1598; scholarly editing began with Thomas Tyrwhitt in 1775–8. Attempts to align him to both sides of the Reformation, especially the Protestant, were made during the 16th century. Major poets who imitated, adapted, or translated him include the Scottish Robert *Henryson, Spenser, Shakespeare, Milton, Dryden, Pope, and Wordsworth. His works continue a vibrant life in the modern world through media as various as opera, film, television, and animation.

HC

G. Chaucer, *The Riverside Chaucer*, gen. ed. L. G. Benson (1987).
S. Ellis, ed., *Chaucer: An Oxford Guide* (2005).

Oxford Guides to Chaucer
H. Cooper, *The Canterbury Tales* ([2]1996);
A. Minnis, *The Shorter Poems* (1995);
B. Windeatt, *Troilus and Criseyde* (1992).
D. Pearsall, *The Life of Geoffrey Chaucer* (1992).
P. Strohm, *Social Chaucer* (1989).

Cheb (Eger) City on the border between *Bohemia, *Bavaria, and *Saxony, first documented as *Egire* in 1061. Even though an important place on the trade routes to the west, it was regarded as marginal by the *Přemyslids and thus settled mainly by Germans. The Hohenstaufen rulers acquired it in 1146, replaced the Slavic fort with an imperial palace (*Pfalz*), and organized a system of *ministeriales* as guards against the Czechs. In 1167, Frederick I was keen to strengthen the region as important imperial property; in 1203 Cheb was first named a city, becoming a mint in 1235. John of Luxembourg acquired the property for the Bohemian crown and *Charles IV granted it extensive privileges. Cheb remained Catholic during the *Hussite wars, but facilitated transaction between the imperial and the Hussite side. In 1432, the delegates of the Council of *Basel met here with Hussite theologians. Cheb remained important into early modern times. MPo

'Eger', in *Handbuch der historischen Stätten Böhmen und Mähren* (1998), 119–26.
W. Schlesinger, *Egerland, Vogtland, Plassenland* (1937).
K. Siegl, *Eger und das Egerland im Wandel der Zeiten* (1931).

cheese and cheesemaking *See* BUTTER- AND CHEESEMAKING.

cheironomy Conducting music with the hands. Byzantine art often depicts musicians signalling with finger gestures, but their meanings are lost. Western evidence for such a practice is rare, but exists. An important issue is whether medieval neumatic notations originated as iconic transcriptions of hand gestures: this seems most plausible for some Byzantine neumes. PJ

E. Cardine, *Gregorian Semiology*, tr. R. M. Fowels (1982).

H. Hucke, 'Die Cheironomie und die Entstehung der Neumenschrift', *Musikforschung*, 32 (1979), 1–16.

M. Huglo, 'La chironomie médiévale', *Revue de musicologie*, 49 (1963), 155–71.

N. K. Moran, *Singers in Late Byzantine and Slavonic Painting* (1986).

chekker [French *eschiquier*; German *Schachtbrett*] Earliest designation for a stringed keyboard instrument, first used 1360. It may have referred to the clavichord, also documented mid 14th century. The name may derive from the instrument's resemblance to a medieval counting-board ('exchequer'). KAM

N. Meeùs, 'The "Chekker"', *Organ Yearbook*, 16 (1985), 5–25.

C. Page, 'The Myth of the Chekker', *Early Music*, 7 (1979), 482–9.

Chelčický, Peter (*c.*1390–1460) Bohemian reformer. He spent his entire life in his native south *Bohemia except for a brief stay in *Prague in 1419–20, where he met and disputed with *Hus's successor, *Jakoubek of Stříbro, on the principle of the morally justified war. Chelčický rejected St *Augustine's and *Wyclif's claim that war was sometimes justifiable, a radical form of pacifism he expounded in *On Spiritual Warfare*. In this and subsequent works (in Czech) he attacked the *Taborite abandonment of the communal ideals of the primitive church. In *On the Triple Division of Society*, Chelčický denounces the tripartite division of medieval society defended by his contemporaries as a betrayal of Christ's gospel of love and equality. His belief that all territorial authority is a form of violence and that the corruption of society began with the official acceptance of Christianity by the Roman imperial establishment is explored in *The Net of Faith* (*c.*1440). Chelčický's ideas were put into practice by his followers, who founded the *Unitas Fratrum* in 1467. *See also* HUSSITE WARS AND LEADERS. AT

P. Brock, *The Political and Social Doctrines of the Unity of Czech Brethren* (1957).

M. L. Wagner, *Peter Chelčický: A Radical Separatist from Hussite Bohemia* (1983).

Cherbourg Port in the Contentin Peninsula, northwest *France; the first territory conquered by *Vikings. L'Abbaye du Voeu, built in *Plantagenet times, fell victim to 13th-century English raids. A key strategic location during the *Hundred Years War; sovereignty changed six times. Rule remained French Catholic despite many Protestant efforts during the Wars of Religion (1563, 1574). LMP

G. Duby, ed., *Histoire de la France urbaine* (1980).

Chernigov (**Chernihiv**) Chernigov, on the *river Dnieper, first appeared in the *Primary Chronicle* under the year 907. In the 11th–13th centuries it was the capital of a powerful, expansionist principality, whose princes often occupied the throne of *Kiev. Chernigov was destroyed by the Mongols in 1239. In the mid 13th century it was incorporated into the principality of Briansk and a century later into *Lithuania. JPH

M. Dimnik, *Mikhail, Prince of Chernigov and Grand Prince of Kiev 1224–1246* (1981).

—— *The Dynasty of Chernigov 1054–1146* (1994).

V. I. Mezentsev, 'The Masonry Churches of Medieval Chernihiv', *Harvard Ukrainian Studies*, 11 (1987), 365–83.

Cherson (Chersones) A town in the *Crimea. In 711 Justinian II sent a punitive expedition to Cherson, which later turned into a rebellion against him. *Cyril (Constantine) studied Hebrew grammar in Cherson *c.*860. The Kievan prince *Vladimir Monomakh was baptized in Cherson in 988 after laying successful siege to the town. Cherson did not recover after the *Tatar devastation and ceased to exist by the mid 15th century. MBK

V. G. Chentsova, 'Materialy k istorii Chersona v srednie veka', *Materialy po Arkheologii, Istorii i Etnografii Tavriki*, 5 (1996), 171–84.

A. I. Romanchuk, *Chersones 12–14 vekov* (1986).

A. L. Yakobson, *Srednevekovyj Krym* (1964).

chess *See* SPORTS, GAMES, AND PASTIMES.

Chester-le-Street (bishopric) Established by the episcopal community of St *Cuthbert in 883 after seven years' wandering following their flight from *Viking attacks on *Lindisfarne. Honoured by the West Saxon royal house, the congregation moved to *Durham in 995 under Aldwin. SRIF

G. Bonner, D. Rollason, and C. Stancliffe, eds, *St Cuthbert, his Cult and his Community to AD 1200* (1989).

Chevalier, Ulysse (1841–1923) French bibliographer and historian. His *Bibliothèque liturgique* includes a *Repertorium hymnologicum* (1892–1912) with bibliographical entries on over 42,000 mainly liturgical Latin texts. The *Repertoire des sources historiques du moyen âge* consists of a *Bio-bibliographie* (1875–86) on historical personages from AD 1–1500 and a *Topo-bibliographie* (1894–1903) for places and other topics. DDH

chevauchée [French, 'to ride'] A practice common during the *Hundred Years War, the chevauchée was an armed raid into enemy territory. With the aim of destruction, pillage, and demoralization, chevauchées were generally conducted against civilian populations. *See also* MILITARY ARTS. MS

A. Curry and M. Hughes, eds, *Arms, Armies, and Fortifications in the Hundred Years War* (1994).

chevet The combination of *apse and radiating *chapels at the sanctuary end of a church. Probably originally designed to facilitate veneration of *relics in *pilgrimage churches of 10th–11th-century *France and Spain. DJR

K. J. Conant, *Carolingian and Romanesque Architecture, 800–1200* (1978), 139–41.
E. Shortell, 'Dismembering Saint Quentin: Gothic Architecture and the Display of Relics', *Gesta*, 36 (1997), 32–47.

childbirth *See* GYNAECOLOGY AND OBSTETRICS.

children in central and eastern Europe The source evidence about children and their role in the medieval society of central and eastern Europe is as sparse as it often is elsewhere. Ecclesiastical and secular legal sources deal with childbirth and with determining age for majority and marriage. The Slavic Orthodox churches' view of childbirth was ambivalent. The birth of a child was thought good, but sexual intercourse was seen as bad. This could lead to clerical opinion that these acts were not related: a woman conceived not so much through intercourse as because of God's will. Illegitimate births, however, were proof of sexual misconduct. Orthodox concepts about the 'impurity' of the new mother and of childbirth generally went far beyond western notions. Anyone attending the birth of a child, and even the building where the birth took place, became impure and had to be ritually purified. The theology of the Bogomil heretics of the Balkans went even further by declaring procreation evil and seeing children as small demons. Contrary to this, and also different from Catholic opinions, *Hussite theologians saw children in a new and positive light, citing Matthew 18:3 and other gospel texts. Children were incorporated into society by *baptism, and participated from an early age in Hussite church life as well as in social struggles. Holy *Communion was administered under both kinds even to babies. Children were also among the first Hussite martyrs.

In the Orthodox church naming the newborn on the eighth day after birth meant its entry into the community, while baptism was generally performed on the fortieth day after birth and marked full membership in the community. If there was danger that the child would die before that day, the priest was supposed to baptize it immediately. Slavic Orthodox church laws regularly dealt with infanticide, which was seen not as murder but as a sexual offence (*see* ABORTION, CONTRACEPTION, AND INFANTICIDE). Compared to western Europe, Orthodox society seems to have been much more intolerant of illegitimacy. This implies that the victims of infanticide were frequently illegitimate children. The Orthodox Christian canons set conditions of age for the establishment of a valid marriage, prohibiting the marriage of girls under twelve and of boys under fifteen. On average, girls married at thirteen or fourteen. Among the aristocracy, marriage for some girls was arranged at the age of eight or even five. Although the parents generally made the marriage arrangements, their children's wishes were not completely overlooked. Church canons made parents who gave their children in marriage against their will subject to a fine.

Based on older customary law, the Hungarian **Tripartitum* of Werbőczy (1517) refers to full age (*perfecta aetas*), meaning full legal capacity, at 24 for men and 16 for women. Concerning *imperfecta aetas* it distinguishes between non-lawful age (*illegitima aetas*) and lawful age (*legitima aetas*), the latter reached by boys at 14 and girls at 12, and allowing a person to act as a plaintiff or defendant in court, to appoint attorneys, or to make a testament. In *Poland, the 1423 statutes of Warta fixed the lawful age at 15 (12 for the whole state). The Hungarian *Tripartitum* regarded children born to a noble father and a non-noble mother as true nobles, but not vice versa. When a nobleman adopted a person of ignoble or servile status as his son, then this person and his offspring were also considered true nobles.

For some regions, for example in *Pomerania, *Lithuania, *Moldavia, and *Wallachia, late medieval sources attest to the selling of children of low social status. The value of a child was similar to that of a domestic animal, such as a cow or horse. As in the west, hagiographic sources and miracle stories regularly mention accidents and illnesses of children and refer to the corresponding problems of society. There is only a little information about children's games in the written sources of this area. Archaeology, however, offers evidence of children's toys made of stone, brick, wood, metal, or clay. Concerning children's *education, of the nobility in particular, the influence of western European ideas can be recognized. In *Hungary, the beginning of the medieval school system was connected with the foundation of the *Benedictine house of *Pannonhalma in 996. In the following centuries a number of cathedral chapter schools and parish schools were established. The 14th and 15th centuries were the main period for the foundation and further formation of parish schools and secular schools in urban spaces. A similar development can be recognized in other regions of central Europe. GJ

J. Bardach, 'L'enfant dans l'ancien droit polonaise et lituanien jusqu'à la fin du XVIIIe siècle', *L'enfant*, vol. 2: *Europe médiévale et moderne*, *RSJB* 36 (1976), 601–33.

A. Csizmadia, 'L'enfant dans le droit hongrois depuis le Moyen Age jusqu'au milieu du XIXe siècle', *L'enfant*, vol. 2: *Europe médiévale et moderne*, *RSJB* 36 (1976), 517–41.

M. Delimata, 'Wypadki losowe z udziałem dzieci w świetle średniowiecznych polskich katalogów cudów świętych', *Kwartalnik historii kultury materialnej*, 51 (2003), 327–35.

A. Herlea, 'Aspects de l'histoire du statut juridique de l'enfant en Roumanie', *L'enfant*, vol. 2: *Europe médiévale et moderne*, *RSJB* 36 (1976), 543–600.

E. Levin, 'Infanticide in Pre-Petrine Russia', *JGO* 34 (1986), 215–24.

——'Childbirth in Pre-Petrine Russia: Canon Law and Popular Traditions', in *Russia's Women: Accommodation, Resistance, Transformation*, ed. B. E. Clements *et al.* (1991), 44–59.

S. Petényi, *Games and Toys in Medieval and Early Modern Hungary* (1994).

N. Rejchrtová, 'Hussitism and Children', *Communio viatorum*, 22 (1979), 201–4.

M. Szeftel, 'Le statut juridique de l'enfant en Russie avant Pierre le Grand', *L'enfant*, vol. 2: *Europe médiévale et moderne*, *RSJB* 36 (1976), 635–56.

K. Szende and P. Szábo, eds, *A magyar iskola első évszázadai/Die ersten Jahrhunderte des Schulwesens in Ungarn (996–1526)* (1996).

children in England Medieval people inherited ideas about human life from the classical world. Life was seen as a sequence of stages—'the ages of man'. Infancy up to the age of seven was viewed as a time of growth, childhood from seven to fourteen as one of play, and adolescence from fourteen onwards as one of physical, intellectual, and sexual development.

1. Overview
2. Upbringing
3. Culture
4. Education
5. Adolescence

1. *Overview*

Children under the age of fourteen formed a large part of the population of medieval *England, perhaps as much as a third. The death rate among children was high by modern standards. It has been suggested that 25 per cent of children may have died in their first year, half as many (12.5 per cent) between one and four, and a quarter as many (6 per cent) between five and nine. There is no evidence that this mortality lessened parental affection and care for children, and the interest of adults in children can be traced throughout the MA.

Little survives about adult attitudes to children during the AS period (500–1066), although *burials show that children were often buried with grave-goods, like adults, and that children with deformities were cared for and enabled to grow up. Opinions about childhood become clearer in the 12th century, due to lawmaking by the church and in lay society. Lawmakers tended to place the boundary between childhood and adulthood at puberty, which was understood to happen at twelve for girls and fourteen for boys. The church came to regard children as too immature to commit sins or to understand adult concepts and duties. On these grounds they were forbidden to marry, excused from confessing to a priest, and excluded from sharing in the sacrament of the *Eucharist. Secular justice took a similar path, developing a concept of the age of legal responsibility at about puberty, although there are rare references to children receiving adult punishments.

By about 1250 scholars based in *France, such as Bartholomew Glanville, *Giles of Rome, and *Vincent of Beauvais, were discussing childhood and children's *education in learned writings. By about 1400 children were portrayed in art—especially in scenes of everyday life in *manuscript illuminations. Children seldom feature in literature from England before 1400, although some romances describe how their heroes and heroines were born and brought up. After that date, however, children's literature begins to survive on a significant scale in the English language. It includes works of wise instruction, technical treatises, and a few stories. There are also records of adolescent children reading adult fiction, such as romances, the works of *Chaucer, and ballads of *Robin Hood.

2. *Upbringing*

Birth took place in a private chamber from which men were excluded, and was followed by *baptism. The early Christian practice of centring baptism on the two great festivals of *Easter and Pentecost (Whitsuntide) gradually gave way to baptizing children on the day they were born, which was the dominant custom by the 12th century. At baptism a child was made a member of the church, given a forename, and provided with godparents to assist the parents in its upbringing. Forenames were sometimes chosen by parents, reflecting family traditions, but it was common for the senior godparent of the child's own gender to give it his or her own forename.

Babies were breast-fed until they were two or more, usually by their mothers except in noble families where wet nurses were employed. Gradually, they were weaned on soft foods. Parents provided care and training, and records of fatal accidents to small children suggest that boys and girls soon became aware of their *gender and followed their gender parent in daily tasks. Such accidents were taken seriously by the authorities and involved a *coroner's *inquest as they did for adults. Corporal punishment was familiar throughout society and was probably used in homes, although social commentators criticized parents for indulgence towards children rather than harsh discipline. Children were given tasks in keeping with their ages. As they grew older these might include lighter domestic or agricultural duties, but they were not capable of doing serious work until about the age of puberty when they began to acquire strength of an adult kind.

Growing up involved acquaintance with religion, but there was little structured education of children in this respect until the Reformation. Parents and godparents were expected to teach them basic *prayers in Latin (the Lord's Prayer, Apostles' *Creed, and later Hail Mary) and how to behave in church. Church law after the 12th century asked little of children in terms of duties. Only on reaching puberty did they acquire the adult obligations of confessing to a priest at least once a year, receiving the Eucharist at Easter, attending church, and paying church dues.

3. *Culture*

Medieval children possessed their own culture, encompassing material possessions, toys, games, speech, rhymes, and songs. Childhood required special clothes, from infant wrappings to miniature versions of adult dress, and cradles and walking frames were in use. A toy-making industry existed by about 1300, and archaeological finds from *London include miniature *knights on horseback and tiny utensils such as cups, plates, jugs, and skillets, all formed from moulds. Dolls existed, but have not survived since they were made of cloth or wood. Children are mentioned making their own toys: boats from pieces of bread, spears from sticks, and small houses from stones. Many games and *sports were played, from games of skill with cherry stones and tops to activities such as archery, football, and dancing. The oral culture of children is not recorded until the 14th and 15th centuries, when scraps of verse and songs are noted in books, especially school notebooks. These point to the existence of nursery rhymes similar to (but not identical with) those of later times, as well as to children knowing and sharing in the songs and phrases of adults.

4. *Education*

The education of children in England can be traced from the 7th century. Initially, it centred on the training of boys as monks, girls as nuns, and other boys as 'secular clergy'—those *clergy who lived in the everyday world and eventually ministered in parish churches. This education was based on the learning of Latin and was usually provided in *monasteries and nunneries. Education spread to some of the *laity as early as the 7th century, and by the end of the 9th century it often took the form of learning to read and write in English rather than Latin. Schools of a modern kind, free-standing and open to the public, first appear in records in the 1070s, and became numerous thereafter, although monasteries, friaries, and nunneries continued to do some educational work. Boys tended to be taught in schools and girls at home. Education began with the Latin alphabet, and many boys and girls proceeded no further in Latin, using the skill chiefly to read in their own language, either English or, between the 12th and the 15th centuries, French. Only a minority of boys went on to learn Latin *grammar and to become proficient in the language. Their studies also gave them a knowledge of *linguistics, the ability to write, and an acquaintance with Latin literature including some classical Latin poetry up to the 13th century but chiefly medieval Christian poetry between 1300 and 1500. Women (even nuns) rarely learnt Latin grammar after 1200, and their abilities in the language were chiefly restricted to being able to pronounce texts from Latin prayer books in a devout manner, without a full understanding of the meaning.

5. *Adolescence*

Most children began to do serious work once they reached puberty. Sometimes this took place at home, involving agricultural labour or a craft, but it was common to send adolescents away from home to be servants to other people. Places as servants varied widely, from working on farms or in domestic service to *apprenticeships in which one learnt a skilled *craft or *trade. Apprenticeship tended to exclude the very poor. Boys of the wealthier classes often continued their schooling during their adolescence, especially if they were envisaged as having careers in the church, law, or administration. Other boys were employed in churches as choristers or clerks. The wealthiest children of all—those of the *nobility and more important *gentry—often entered the households of other nobility or leading churchmen, where they acted as pages or retainers, learnt aristocratic manners, and in some cases underwent training in *military arts.

Although some aristocracy married in the teens, the population as a whole did not do so until their mid twenties. Entry to church careers also tended to be late, ranging from the mid teens in some religious houses up to 24, the age of *ordination as a priest. It followed that children passed a long period from puberty until the mid twenties in which they were partly, yet not fully, independent, away from home but not in households of their own. Like modern adolescents they bonded with others of their own gender, sometimes (in the case of youths) engaging in violence, and gradually making links with the opposite sex.

There was no clear end to childhood. The age of majority varied in different social groups and depended on whether fathers were alive or not, so that it ranged from the early teens until the age of twenty-one. In this respect, as so many others, medieval childhood comprised a wide range of experiences. Its history was as rich and complex as the history of society as a whole. *See also* CHILDREN IN [VARIOUS GEOGRAPHICAL REGIONS]; EDUCATION; GYNAECOLOGY AND OBSTETRICS; KINSHIP, FAMILY, MARRIAGE, DIVORCE: IN WESTERN EUROPE; LITERACY AND WRITING. NO

P. Ariès, *Centuries of Childhood* (1960).
S. Crawford, *Childhood in Anglo-Saxon England* (1999).
D. Gardiner, *English Girlhood at School* (1929).

B. Hanawalt, *The Ties that Bound: Peasant Families in Medieval England* (1986).
N. Orme, *From Childhood to Chivalry: The Education of the English Kings and Aristocracy, 1066–1530* (1984).
——*Medieval Children* (2001).
——*Medieval Schools* (2006).

children in France The medieval child was initially studied by the French '*Annales* school'. In 1960 Philippe Ariès claimed that medieval people had no awareness of childhood, which sparked a vigorous debate. Although they appear infrequently in textual sources, it is possible to reconstruct the lives of medieval children in both aristocratic and popular settings from visual representations and from excavated children's objects. Documentation increases from the 12th century onwards.

1. Childhood
2. The child at home
3. The child outside
4. The child at school
5. The child at work
6. The child in the castle

1. *Childhood*
Childhood was defined as the first two phases of life: *infantia*, to the age of four or seven, and *pueritia*, until twelve or fourteen, when a child was considered grown up. Children were named when baptized, shortly after birth. Infant mortality was high; children's bodies often received special burial. Generally children were free till the 'age of reason' at seven. In the country, children remained with their parents until marriage. In other situations, it was customary for boys especially to leave their family while still children, to learn elsewhere. All of French society was involved in children's lives as caregivers and educators.

2. *The child at home*
Small children stayed in the house, where they were raised by their mother and older siblings. Children of high birth and orphans in orphanages were fed by a wet nurse. Children's clothing was generally simple, except for the elite, and consisted of various layers over an undershirt. A household contained an extended family, with five children on average. Within the family a child had its own role. Parents could choose to give a child to a *monastery to give it a better start or because of its behaviour or family position. For these *oblates, orders created pedagogical programmes, including exceptions to the strict rules (for example in diet). Child-monks had special tasks within the community.

3. *The child outside*
Books of miracle stories often mention accidents that happened to children at home, on the streets, at work, and at school, giving the overall impression that they had considerable freedom to go about. Legal sources confirm the picture that falling or drowning were dangers for children. To youngsters out in the streets semi-official duties were assigned, such as accompanying funerals and taking part in processions. Childhood delinquency existed as well, as did kidnapping and child prostitution; beggars displayed children to attract pity. It was widely believed that prayers by children were the most effective. Children's games varied with the seasons and were often playful imitations of adult life.

4. *The child at school*
Historians have tended to underestimate the amount of schooling received by children, especially by girls. In *France, most children had access to the basics: reading, writing, and counting. The founding of schools, already promoted by *Charlemagne, was encouraged by the Lateran *councils of 1179 and 1215. From the 12th century onwards, there were parish schools for children in every neighbourhood, and grammar schools in the towns, plus a dense network of rural schools. The school year began after the autumn vintage and lasted about forty-four weeks, with vacations at Easter and Christmas; St Nicholas' feast was the holiday of schoolchildren. School started at dawn, and pupils had long days, with breaks for meals, recreation, and Mass; schoolchildren made up the choirs. In winter, many schools chose a *'boy bishop' who performed in church but also led his fellow pupils in festivities. School pupils had their own material culture: schoolbags held wax tablets, styluses, counting tokens, and spinning tops. Schoolchildren were the responsibility of their master, even outside school hours; beatings with rod or paddle were a regular punishment.

5. *The child at work*
Children were put to work gradually, in the family business, or as *apprentices. Peasants' children mostly helped in the fields; watching herds was a child's task. Placing a child with a master usually included a contract regulating both parties' duties and rights. Work hours were from dawn to dusk (though there must have been breaks). Most contracts concern children of twelve years or older, except for orphans or abandoned children. When children were paid, it was always less than adults. As a rule, children were not exploited before adolescence, except for the very poor and in a few jobs that required children because of their small size (for example, mining, cleaning wells). The labour of young girls fell mostly outside the realm of the paid and regulated.

6. *The child in the castle*
Owing to the nature of our sources, the children of French nobility are best known. Most *castles had a special area for women and children, where young nobles were taught by a private tutor. Boys went away at age seven to the castles of family friends. Pages came to the castle to receive a knightly education; they also served the noblewomen. Manuals (for

example, *'mirrors of princes') show what was expected of the sons and daughters of the nobility: to be polite, modest, and good-humoured. Archaeological finds from castles show that boys played with little *knight figures, girls with dolls and miniature kitchenware. Both sexes ran around in the gardens and kept *animal pets, while indoors they played nine men's morris, backgammon, and chess (the noble game). The higher one was in the social scale, the more exceptional one's childhood could be: the luxury enjoyed by the young Jean de *Berry is well documented. AW

D. Alexandre-Bidon and D. Lett, *Children in the Middle Ages*, tr. J. Gladding (French original, 1997) (1999).
P. Ariès, *Centuries of Childhood* (1960).
M. de Jong, *In Samuel's Image* (1996).
J.-M. Mehl, *Les jeux en Royaume de France: du XIIIe au début du XVe siècle* (1990).
L.-H. Parias and M. Rouche, *Histoire générale de l'enseignement et de l'éducation en France*, vol. 1, *Des origines à la Renaissance* (1981).
P. Riché and D. Alexandre-Bidon, *L'Enfance au Moyen Âge* (1994).
S. Shahar, *Childhood in the Middle Ages* (1990).

children in Germany and Austria Since the publication of Philippe Ariès's ground-breaking study of the history of childhood, medieval children in *Germany and Austria as well as in *France have become one of the liveliest areas of historians' research and publication. These small persons' experience—as infants and little boys and girls as well as maturing youth of all social classes—is elusive, less represented in documentary and literary sources than the lives of other medieval groups, especially of elite adult males. Yet recent decades have seen scholars' attempted reconstruction of both the experience of medieval childhood and contemporary adults' understanding of childhood from a variety of documentary, literary, theological, and artistic sources.

1. The European context
2. Children in visual sources
3. Children in literary sources

1. The European context

Scholarly interpretation affirms that children in Germany and Austria shared the material and emotional circumstances of other young Europeans. The harsh conditions of material life led to high infant and child mortality, but medieval adults' frequent bereavement did not prevent their cherishing high hopes for their own offspring and for youngsters in general; moderns' frequent assumption that childhood has been understood and valued as a distinctive developmental stage and that only modern children have been embraced by their families of origin in a high level of concern and affect has now been conclusively demonstrated to be ill-founded. Medieval people loved their children. Both lay and monastic authors portrayed children as pure, quasi-saintly in their innocence. In practical terms, medieval parents invested heavily in the protection and education of their communities' youngest members.

2. Children in visual sources

Among sources for the realities of medieval childhood and adult perspectives on children's nature and development, visual materials hold special value. Jesus himself is the most frequently represented child in medieval art in general, and images of him reveal details of children's attire and other material maintenance. Further, depictions of the young Christ are suggestive of the ways in which the cult of the child Jesus, important to Europeans' piety from the 12th century forward, at once reflected and transformed notions of appropriate parental behaviour and feelings. German plastic arts offer plentiful representations of the child Jesus in the Holy Family, that is, the triad of Mary, Joseph, and the Child, as well as in the Holy Kinship, that is, Jesus' matrilineage, with his grandmother Anne and his many cousins and uncles.

German artists favoured the Holy Family in the high MA, later developing interest in the horizontally extended family of the Virgin. Sculptors emphasized first the highly affective nature of the relationship between Mary and her son, then the importance of both maternal and grandmotherly roles in forging family unity and providing for young children. Images such as the striking *Holy Kinship* from *c.*1510 in the Thüringer Museum, Eisenach, with its ten adult males, five women, and ten infants and toddlers, suggest the importance of women in medieval private life and of the familial framework as a context for child-rearing. Images from the late medieval cult of *Joseph, again abundantly represented, document the importance of adult male support and affection for children. In concert, these visual memorials to family life emphasize the child as the focus of parental affection and investment.

3. Children in literary sources

Medieval German literature likewise represents the conditions and valuation of children in central Europe. James Schulz has argued compellingly that MHG literature evinces appreciation of childhood as a developmental stage marked by purity and possibility. MHG works such as *Wolfram von Eschenbach's *Willehalm* nonetheless represent children, especially boys, as less attached to their parents and more independent of their families of origin than studies in family history such as David Herlihy's *Medieval Households* have asserted were characteristic of wider medieval culture. MHG texts likewise generally fail to acknowledge that childhood ends in adolescence, such as moderns generally recognize and as family historians such as Michael Goodich recognize in medieval hagiographical sources. In medieval German *romances youthful maturity seems immediately to succeed childhood and extend up to the fourth decade of males' lives, while marriage and childbearing quickly transform little girls, like the Enite of Hartmann's *Erec*, into fully adult women.

MHG texts clearly speak to the assumptions of a noble readership about children and youth in elite culture, but may bear little direct relationship to the realities of most youngsters' lives. Their evidence must therefore be conflated carefully with other literary and documentary sources affirming that medieval people recognized both childhood and adolescence as distinct stages, and treated infants, children, and youth accordingly. German texts thus challenge historians' response to a pan-European literature and documentation on childhood, merging scepticism about human nature with awareness of developmental change and expressing appreciation of children as familial and community responsibilities and resources. The German MA shared a high valuation of children with recent times, but its adults understood and articulated the youngest persons' experience in categories that remind scholars of historical boys' and girls' distance from the modern experience of childhood. CLN

P. Ariès, *Centuries of Childhood: A Social History of Family Life*, tr. R. Baldick (French original 1960) (1962).
M. Goodich, 'Sexuality, Family, and the Supernatural in the Fourteenth Century', *Journal of the History of Sexuality*, 4 (1995), 280–95.
D. Herlihy, *Medieval Households* (1985).
N. Orme, *Medieval Children* (2001).
J. A. Schultz, *The Knowledge of Childhood in the German Middle Ages, 1100–1350* (1995).
——'No Girls, No Boys, No Families: On the Construction of Childhood in Texts of the German Middle Ages', *JEGP* 94 (1995), 59–81.
S. Shahar, *Childhood in the Middle Ages* (1990).
P. Sheingorn, 'Appropriating the Holy Kinship: Gender and Family History', in *Interpreting Cultural Symbols: St Anne in Late Medieval Society*, ed. K. Ashley and eadem (1990), 169–86.

children in Islam In pre-Islamic Arabia, as in many ancient societies, unwanted female children could be buried alive, as described in the *Quran: 'And they assign daughters for God!—Glory to Him!—And for themselves (sons, the issue) they desire! When news is brought to one of them of (the birth of) a female (child), his face darkens, and he is filled with inward grief! With shame does he hide himself from people, because of the bad news he has had! Shall he retain it on (sufferance and) contempt, or bury it in the dust? Ah, what an evil (choice) they decide on!' (*Al-Nahl*: 57, 58, 59). The advent of Islam placed greater value on childhood. An inalienable right of children according to Islam is the right to life: thus it forbids infanticide and *abortion, and asserts the rights of children regardless of gender.

Islamic belief holds that children are born into the world possessing a primordial conformity with truth (*al-fitra*). It is then their parents' job to turn them into Muslims, Jews, or Christians. The child's clear heart and soul are able to absorb whatever they are exposed to, which makes it the parents' responsibility to turn their offspring into good Muslims by teaching them proper values and manners, and by being role models themselves.

The Quran clearly explains children's claims on their parents: while it is the mother's duty to suckle her child up to the age of two, it is the father's duty to provide for the lactating mother: 'The mothers shall give suck to their offspring for two whole years, if the father desires to complete the term. But he shall bear the cost of their food and clothing on equitable terms. No soul shall have a burden laid on it greater than it can bear' (*Al-Baqara*: 233). On the other hand, parents may agree to wean their child at a suitable time, and may agree to appoint a wet nurse to suckle their children, provided that they pay her for her services, a practice that existed in pre-Islamic Arabia (*Muhammad is said to have been entrusted to a wet nurse). Furthermore, while pre-Islamic Arabian mothers were rebuked for giving birth to female children, the Quran warns that 'No mother shall be treated unfairly on account of her child, nor father on account of his child; an heir shall be chargeable in the same way' (*Al-Baqara*: 233).

Prophetic tradition also contributed to the institution of children's rights in Islam. Muhammad's conduct with children is related to have been exemplary, and his affection for his own children and grandchildren and for others' children serves as guidance. On showing affection to children, Al-Bukhari reports that Abu Hurayra related the following: 'Allah's messenger (peace and blessing of Allah be upon him) kissed Hasan ben Ali while al-Aqra ben Habis was sitting with him. Al-Aqra said: "I have ten children and I have never kissed any of them." The messenger of Allah (peace and blessing of Allah be upon him) looked at him and said: "To a person who shows no affection [to others] no mercy will be shown" '(Hamid, 24).

Kindness to children was required of a good Muslim parent. Abu Hurayra related that a man came to Muhammad with a child whom he hugged frequently. Muhammad asked him whether he loved the child, and when the man replied in the affirmative, Muhammad said, 'Allah is more compassionate to you than you are to your child, as he is the Most Merciful of the merciful' (Hamid, 53). Muhammad also advised people to treat their children equally and never favour one child over another. In a **hadith* reported by Al-Bukhari (Hamid, 25), Muhammad is reported to have told a man who wanted him to witness his giving of a particular present to one of his children whom he dearly loved that he should not favour him over his other children and should give equally to all his children. Muhammad is reported also to have spoken about equality between girls and boys in a society previously known for female infanticide. He reminded Muslims that God reserves great reward for those who bring up girls and treat them with kindness (Hamid, 23).

As for orphans, Islam instituted their rights: in the absence or death of their parents, children are to be taken in by their relatives. A guardian to look after their well-being and property is appointed until they reach puberty. Muhammad told his followers that a kind guardian of orphans has great rewards from God, saying: ' "I and the guardian of the orphan will be like this in paradise", crossing his index and middle fingers' (Hamid, 29).

On child-rearing Muslims often refer to prophetic traditions and the Quran. An illustrative example is the *Sura of Luqman*. Luqman the wise tells his son about righteousness and the ways of God, which consist of modesty, moderation, and the worship of the one and only God (*Luqman*: 13, 16, 17, 18, 19). For their part, children have duties towards their parents and society as a whole. The first duty is to be good to their parents, to obey and respect them (*Luqman*: 14, 15) as they ought, respect elders, care for the weak and aged, and observe their religious duties. ZSS

H. Abd al-Ati, *The Family Structure in Islam* (1977).
A. Giladi, *Children of Islam* (1992).
A. A. Hamid, *Moral Teachings of Islam: Prophetic Traditions* (2003).
Y. Yildirim, 'Children and Childhood', *MedIsl*, vol. 1, 150.

children in Jewish society Children were the expected and desired outcome of every marriage. As such they were a central component of medieval Jewish society. Despite this, medieval Jewish texts do not devote many discussions to the place of children in society. Rather they focus on a variety of everyday and legal issues in which children are involved, such as procreation, rituals of childhood, education, and care.

1. Procreation
2. Infant care
3. Religious education
4. Conceptions of childhood

1. Procreation

In medieval Jewish society, procreation was considered an important and positive commandment, one which both increased the population and glorified God's name. If a couple was married for more than ten years and did not produce offspring, some traditions sanctioned forced divorce. In *Germany and northern *France such divorces were significantly reduced. In other places, such as Spain and *Egypt, in many such cases men were allowed to take a second wife or to divorce their first wives. Procreation was considered a male and not a female obligation, but women could state that they desired children so they would have someone to lean on in old age.

Medieval Jewish sources describe the efforts families went to in order to ensure the birth of offspring. Women were attended to by *midwives from the time of their marriage and throughout their married lives. Jewish medical theories were in line with general medieval *medicine, following Aristotle. Infant mortality was much like that in surrounding societies. Boys were much preferred, as in all pre-modern societies, although many sources show that girls, like boys, were loved and cared for. Scholars have estimated that the average urban Jewish family had three to four children.

2. Infant care

The primary caregivers for infants and young children were female: mothers, servants, and wet nurses. The number of caretakers depended on the financial abilities of any given family, but the sources indicate that many families had servants and wet nurses who helped with childcare. Sources that describe infancy and childhood focus mainly on feeding infants and on infant mortality and protection from death. According to Jewish law, mothers were obligated as part of their marriage contract to nurse their children until the age of 24 months. Widowed and divorced women could not remarry until their children were weaned.

Children were their parents' responsibility. According to the *Mishnah, a father was obligated to circumcise his son, redeem him (redemption of the firstborn), teach him Torah and a profession, see him married, and, according to some versions, teach him to swim.

These obligations pertained to all male children; ancient sources are unclear as to obligations towards daughters. In any case, in medieval sources, the formal obligation of parents toward their children seems to be that of supporting them until age six. However, in reality most parents supported their children until they were married and sometimes continued to support them during the first years of their marriages. In cases in which the family did not or could not support their children, they were appointed guardians, and in some cases the local Jewish court would take responsibility for the child's well-being.

3. Religious education

Both boys and girls received religious *education. The boys often studied at a school situated in the local synagogue with teachers chosen by their parents or appointed by the community. Their studies were often also supported by donations made by community members who obtained books and paper for them. Every Jewish boy learned how to read Hebrew and follow the prayers and the Bible. More affluent families tutored their children at home. The more talented students continued to study for many years, travelling to different cities, whereas the others joined their families' trades or learned a new trade after two or three years of schooling.

Girls were educated in the home, often by male tutors. While there is little evidence of Jewish women's ability to read Hebrew, we know they were taught the basic laws pertaining to keeping a kosher household, observing the holidays, and ritual purity. Medieval sources also attest to women praying in Hebrew and in the vernacular and being regular participants in synagogue life, with which they were familiar. In addition to religious education, girls were taught sewing, embroidery, and housework by their mothers and other women in their surroundings.

The age of religious obligation was the traditional age of thirteen for boys and twelve for girls, an age also associated with sexual maturity. However, during the high MA, there is no evidence of a rite of passage connected with this transition. In Germany and northern France a rite of passage was celebrated when male children first began their schooling; we have no rite of passage connected with age thirteen in any Jewish community. The bar mitzvah was first celebrated only during the early modern period. Sources also reveal that many obligations later considered to be those of adults were observed by children during the high MA, as soon as their parents and teachers thought they could accept them.

4. Conceptions of childhood

Few medieval texts present Jewish conceptions of childhood; the very word 'childhood' (based on the Psalms) is mentioned only rarely in Hebrew texts. However, the few texts we do have reveal a variety of concepts. Some see children as easily moulded and influenced, and recommend good mentors; others see children as pure and God-fearing. Many texts discuss the importance of a spiritual and not just a physical education. EMB

J. Cohen, *'Be Fertile and Increase, Fill the Earth and Master It': The Ancient and Medieval Career of a Biblical Text* (1989).

S. Goldin, 'Die Beziehung der jüdischen Familie im Mittelalter zu Kind und Kindheit', *Jahrbuch der Kindheit*, 6 (1989), 211–56.

E. Kanarfogel, *Jewish Education and Society in the High Middle Ages* (1992).

I. Marcus, *Rituals of Childhood: Jewish Acculturation in Medieval Europe* (1996).

I. Ta-Shma, 'Children in Medieval Germanic Jewry: A Perspective on Ariès from Jewish Sources', *Studies in Medieval and Renaissance History*, 12 (1991), 263–80.

children in the Low Countries Affection between parents and children did certainly exist in the MA. Parents did not press children to leave the family at a young age to engage in economic activity. Medieval visual art and literature, as well as texts from legal theory and practice, suggest the widespread existence of love and of professional and pedagogic care of parents for their offspring.

In a strongly urbanized area like the late medieval Netherlands, with its sophisticated industrial and commercial network, general and professional *education was a necessity. As early as the 12th century *Ghent organized lay schools in which merchants' children learned the skills they would need in business. *Douai had seven schoolmasters in 1204, Valenciennes 49 (some of them women) in 1388. All men and a quarter of women received schooling. In elementary schools boys and girls between seven and twelve were educated in arithmetic, reading, writing, hymn-singing, and catechism. Girls were considered to be worth the investment of even a secondary education, the 'Latin school'. Wills and deeds of gift show that many women, owners of books, must have been literate, able to help with bookkeeping in their husbands' businesses, and in a position to take over in widowhood. Non-discrimination was dictated by perception of the importance of a professional career.

From the age of twelve (in some cases fourteen) the paths of the sexes diverged. Boys started to specialize in a craft and so became apprenticed to a master. Afterwards they became paid *journeymen, and after persisting for years they could become masters. Only a few girls entered a craft. Most women went straight into paid work, mostly domestic service and hospital care, some as saleswomen. Education was also a process of socializing and an introduction to the rules of the game of the social group to which they belonged by birth. Young people learned not only a trade, but also ideas about the value of work and social status. Another part of psychological and moral education took place within the family, fathers being more occupied with their sons, mothers with their daughters.

Under the pressure of urbanization and economic efficiency the model of the nuclear, or conjugal, family, without grandparents and without adult children, had already emerged in the Low Countries around 1300. Indeed most children left their parents' home to go and live separately, as soon as they got a job. Between ages eighteen and twenty-one children were regarded as adults and ready for marriage, though this theory did not work in practice. In the cities boys married on average at 27; girls, less tied to strict *apprenticeships, at twenty-one. In the countryside, where schooling and apprenticeship were less strict, marriage started earlier.

Medieval parents had an all-embracing judicial authority over their underage children. This could be brought to an end in three ways: emancipation, the death of the parents, or the marriage of the children. In *Flanders, but not in the other territories of the Netherlands, from 1546 on, parental authority ceased at majority, and emancipating majority was then set at the age of 25. Before 1546 this automatic process did not exist, so that emancipation could then only be realized by marriage or by explicit emancipation. In the third option, the death of the parents, guardianship and arrangements for maintenance ('houdenisse'), involving members of the extended family, came into effect. On the death of a mother the father continued to exercise all these rights; on the death of a father the mother exercised full guardianship.

Because children's labour before marriage and before emancipation was a source of income for the nuclear family, parents often tried to postpone the marriage. Parents also constantly developed strategies to influence the partners' choice. These actions, however, varied fundamentally given the social status of the family. In the wealthy classes marriage was a component of the family strategy for expanding the total family resources and forming connections with desirable families. Family patrimony also included social prestige and connections. As parental consent was not required for the ceremony in church, negotiations between the two families were always busy but never easy. In Flanders girls did not have to be provided with a dowry, because they had a formal right to the family patrimony and their part of the inheritance.

In less wealthy families the struggle for life was quite different, with a clear stress on affinity, and on care and protection of the offspring. In the crafts nepotism was never absent. Not only did sons of guild members enjoy priority over outsiders, sons of masters were exempt to amass the working capital needed to become a master, an insidious obligation for outsiders. A second area of affection appears in the care for illegitimate children, a logical concern after all, as they are often the result of an affectionate relationship between unmarried or adulterous partners. Three-generation families may have been exceptional in the Low Countries; there is plenty of evidence of the affection of children for their aged parents.

Care for orphans is certainly proof of the existence of affection between generations. Their interests were guaranteed by their parents' will, by a detailed inventory of the parents' property, and (if lacking) by the general succession legislation. Explicit legislation summarized the obligations and the resources available for maintenance by guardians. Urban *aldermen supervised the appointment of guardians, in a well-established priority: the closest family came first, followed by more distant relatives in descending order. Orphans of first-generation immigrants often had no identifiable relatives in town: they went to strangers. Indigent orphans went straight to an orphanage. Before the age of 14 guardians were to care for all elementary needs; after this age orphans could get jobs and become a source of income for their guardian family. Orphan status ended with marriage, entering a convent, or being 'breaded out' (explicit emancipation). WP

M. Danneel, *Weduwen en wezen in het laat-middeleeuwse Gent* (1995).

children in Scandinavia Known by the thousands from archaeological excavations and osteological analyses of *burial grounds and churchyards. The most informative documentary sources are the *hagiographic miracle collections.

1. Grave ritual
2. Death rate
3. Standard of living
4. Living children

1. *Grave ritual*

During the Iron Age (AD 500–1000), children were cremated as were adults and buried in individual graves or in double graves with an adult. Artefacts associated with children are few, typically non-existent. Inhumation graves occur in southernmost Scandinavia and in urban sites such as *Birka. These graves may be much more informative with boys buried like merchants or warriors, and girls buried in display dresses.

In the Christian churchyards from the 10th century on, children's graves regularly lack artefacts. *Sámi children's graves in central and north Scandinavia from around AD 900–1100, however, were sometimes richly furnished.

Before Christianization, many children were sometimes buried in the same cairn or in special parts of the burial grounds. Within the churchyards, there were sometimes special areas or mass graves for children.

2. *Death rate*

In the cremation burial grounds, rarely more than five to ten per cent of the buried are children. In contemporary southern Scandinavian inhumation burial grounds, there may be as many as 50–70 per cent.

Urban churchyards typically contain 10–25 per cent children's graves. The churchyard at Hamar cathedral in southeast Norway contains 26 per cent. Rural churchyards may contain considerably higher percentages, for example, 58 per cent at the Västerhus church in central Sweden.

Though problematic, the evidence suggests that 40–60 per cent of all individuals died before the age of twelve to fifteen. At thoroughly analysed sites, it has been demonstrated that 50–70 per cent of the individuals who died before the age of twelve months died during their first few days or weeks of life. Most children were not buried in a way as to make archaeological excavation and recording possible.

3. *Standard of living*

Children's skeletons at a few medieval churchyards (AD 1000–1500) make it possible to discuss their standard of living. At rural Västerhus, they were weaned at about two years. That period and the following three to four years were characterized by stress. Enamel hypoplasia is found in 43 per cent of individuals aged ten to sixteen and in 59 per cent of those aged 20 to 40 at death. For the individuals over 40, the percentage is lower, suggesting that childhood stress caused early death. In urban *Lund in southern Sweden, 23 per cent of individuals aged twelve to fifteen show enamel hypoplasia.

In urban Sigtuna, the occurrence of enamel hypoplasia is fourteen per cent for all individuals. At the Sigtuna churchyards, it has also been noted that about fifteen per cent of the children suffered from anaemia or disc hernia, indicating that they were poorly nourished or had ailing backs from some kind of stress or trauma. Osteological analysis suggests that children lived in harsh conditions and that their health became at risk as urban life developed. Girls suffered more from stress than boys did.

A few cases of women who died during pregnancy or childbirth are known. They have been buried together with the foetus or the newborn infant who did not survive.

4. *Living children*

Less is known about living children than dead. Toys and children's furniture are hard to recognize in archaeological excavations, although there are finds of dolls, ocarinas, marbles, and bark boats. Children are sometimes seen in church paintings and illuminated MSS.

The collections of stories of miracles by future saints are informative. Not surprisingly, they tell a lot about children's misfortunes and diseases.

Stories about boys injured in different ways are more common (73 per cent) than those about girls (27 per cent). Boys lived more hazardous lives than girls, especially around the age of ten to twelve, when the children started to take part in daily tasks together with the adults. The boys accompanying their fathers fishing, wood-cutting, and handling horses were in danger as were girls helping their mothers handle the fireplace and cauldrons with boiling water.

Otherwise, misfortunes most often happened to children one to four years old, when they started to walk and were curious about the world. They fell from roofs, got lost, mishandled knives, drowned, and so on. Girls drowned as often as boys, but in other ways boys seem to have been more adventurous. Infants up to about one were carried by their mothers during work in and out of doors, while toddlers one to four years were often left on their own because of their parents' hard working day.

Stories of disease are recorded in equal numbers for girls and boys. Of 99 stories, twelve concern infants less than one year old. After that, there are about five to six stories per year in the one-to-eight-year age group, and after that, the number decreases to one per year until the children were thirteen years old. These numbers correspond to the osteologically recorded child mortality during the first year of life.

The stories tell of parents who loved their children, girls as much as boys. They made great efforts to save their children from harm, search together with dozens of neighbours for them when they were lost, and donate generously to the church and saints when they were injured or ill. SW

C. Arcini, *Health and Disease in Early Lund: Osteo-Pathologic Studies of 3,305 Individuals Buried in the First Cemetery Area of Lund 990–1536* (1999).

E. Iregren and L. Redin, 'Assemblages of Children's Bones in a Medieval Churchyard in Sweden—Results of Epidemics, Warfare, Infanticide or Simply Disturbed Graves?' in *Investigaciones en Biodiversidad Humana*, ed. T. A. Varela (2000), 259–69.

A. Kjellström, *The Urban Farmer: Osteological Analysis of Skeletons from Medieval Sigtuna Interpreted in a Socioeconomic Perspective* (2005).

C. Krötzl, 'Parent–Child Relations in Medieval Scandinavia According to Scandinavian Miracle Collections', *Scandinavian Journal of History*, 14 (1989), 21–37.

T. Swärdstedt, *Odontological Aspects of a Medieval Population in the Province of Jämtland/Mid-Sweden* (1966).

S. Welinder, 'The Cultural Construction of Childhood in Scandinavia, 3500 BC–1350 AD', *Current Swedish Archaeology*, 6 (1998), 185–204.

children in Scotland, Ireland, and Wales Information on children is known largely from medieval Irish and Welsh legal and literary sources, but is somewhat more sparse for medieval Scotland.

1. Pregnancy
2. Paternity and affiliation
3. Age markers
4. Fostering and education
5. Play

1. *Pregnancy*

Pregnancy is afforded a degree of protection within the legal texts. The termination of a pregnancy was deemed homicide in the eyes of the medieval Irish and Welsh legal scribes with compensation necessary upon the destruction of a foetus. The gender of the foetus was presumed to be male. Where the health and welfare of a pregnant woman were concerned, her food cravings were to be satiated, within reason, in order to prevent a possible lack of sustenance which might in turn endanger the pregnancy. Similarly, a man in the midst of a court case whose wife went into labour was permitted to postpone the court case in order that he might seek a *midwife to ensure the best conditions for delivery.

2. *Paternity and affiliation*

Both medieval Irish and Welsh legal texts focus on the issues of paternity and how a child is affiliated to a kin-group. Recognition of paternity was vital in determining the status and life-path of a child in medieval Celtic society, with the male and female child's honour-price calculated as a fraction of his/her father's worth. Inheritance of land was partible among all recognized or affiliated sons, irrespective of the nature of the marital or sexual relationship which led to conception. Consequently, the official recognition of the child was of vital importance in Celtic society, and it is not surprising that this was a contentious area within the legal domain. A woman could bring a case of paternity when within her church, upon her deathbed, or if she was in a position to support her claim upon the child coming of age. The man could refute the claim or recognize the child resulting in the acceptance into the kin-group.

3. Age markers
The medieval Irish legal *scribes bestow the honour-price of a cleric on a child up to the age of seven, at which point the child's worth becomes a fraction of his/her father's. The Welsh legal tradition also reflects a shift in a child's capabilities and responsibilities within society occurring at this age: a child was held to have obtained better reason at this point in the life cycle. Three age divisions are mentioned within the medieval Irish context for a male child: up to seven years of age; from seven to twelve years; and from twelve to fourteen or seventeen years. Seven and fourteen years of age are noted as the pivotal times within the medieval Welsh tradition. For a female child, the age of seven saw a greater degree of responsibility being bestowed on the child, along with twelve noted in both traditions as a time when marriage may have been a consideration.

4. Fostering and education
The practice of fosterage was particularly prevalent in medieval Ireland. A medieval Irish legal text, *Cáin Íarraith* ('The Law of Fosterage Fee'), details aspects of child-rearing and fosterage in particular. In this system, a child was reared and educated in another household. This could commence at any time in a child's life, from the wet-nursing stage to when a child comes of age. Fosterage was an arrangement by mutual consent between families. There were two types of fosterage: one for payment and one out of affection. The primary difference between them was that with the former, the foster-parents bore no responsibility or financial liability for the crimes committed on or by the child. The fostering fee (in cattle or goods) was graded according to the child's status, along with items needed by the child.

The *education of the child lay at the heart of this regulated institution; a penalty of two-thirds of the fosterage-fee was incurred should the education be considered defective. The nature of the education was determined by the status and needs of the child. There was a strong pastoral flavour to the education of the children of the free-man grade—the herding of and tending to animals, kiln-drying, wood-cutting. More noble pursuits of playing board games, horse riding, and swimming were taught to children of higher grades. In a hierarchical society, gradations permeated all aspects of life of the child. Indeed, the legal texts specified different colour, texture, and ornament for the *clothing of the children of different social grades, and also their diet and what condiments were permitted for each grade.

The methods of discipline noted are verbal chastisement, fasting, and physical punishment, which could not leave a mark or blemish. The age of the child, the nature of the crime committed, and the number of previous offences were all taken into consideration when the appropriate punishment was determined. The age groupings noted for disciplinary purposes were up to the age of seven, seven to twelve years, and twelve to seventeen years, illustrating a medieval understanding of child development and behaviour.

Normally, the period of fosterage came to an end upon coming of age: fourteen for a girl, 'the age of choice', that is, possible marriage, and seventeen for a boy. Two specific infringements noted in this fostering process were the returning or taking of the child prematurely, and therefore the completion of fosterage was strictly regulated. The period of fosterage could be terminated if there was neglect or abuse.

Fosterage was an important political and social mechanism through which a child bound families together. All those involved in the process were legally connected for their lifetime. A foster-child had a responsibility to help care for his foster-parents in old age or in times of destitution. Foster-siblings were entitled to payment in the form of compensation were a foster-sibling to be murdered at any point in the life cycle. Vital lifelong bonds and social ties were formed through this child-rearing process.

Fosterage finds only brief mention within the medieval Welsh legal tradition, with children on the whole being presented as remaining at their 'father's dish', that is, at his table, for their childhood. The father had the right to discipline his child until the male child had come of age at fourteen years. At this time, he was presented to his lord, who in turn assumed responsibility for the youth. For a daughter, it was at twelve years of age that she might continue to remain with her father's permission in the homestead or, alternatively, enter into a marriage. It was, however, recommended that she refrain from pregnancy until her fourteenth year.

5. Play
The practical education of the child takes precedence in the legal sources. However, we also read of 'early playthings' in the medieval Irish legal texts, and of items in a child's possession—a scabbard, a hitting bat, balls, hoops—with dogs, cats, and herons as pets. Episodes of children at play can be found in both poetic and narrative sources. One extant fragmentary legal tract specifically deals with injuries inflicted on and by children during play activities, thus reflecting the possible dangers involved while at play. There have been a range of toys discovered in the layers of *Viking *Dublin—a boat, sword, a wooden horse—all of which indicate the material culture of the child. BNíC

T. Charles-Edwards, *Early Irish and Welsh Kinship* (1993).
F. Kelly, *A Guide to Early Irish Law* (1988), 86–90.

children in Spain and Portugal Religious practice and political and legal authority all influenced children's lives in medieval Spain and Portugal. The subject remains thinly studied compared to other European regions.

1. Perceptions of childhood
2. Abandonment
3. Infancy, to age two
4. Children aged two to seven
5. Children aged seven to fourteen
6. Adolescents

1. *Perceptions of childhood*

*Isidore of Seville and other authors divided childhood into stages, typically *infantia* (birth to age seven), *pueritia* (from seven to twelve or fourteen), and *adulescentia* (from twelve or fourteen to adulthood). Seventh-century Visigothic *laws assigned *wergeld* based on age: a boy under the age of one had a price of 30 solidi, increasing each year until a twenty-year-old male reached the maximum of 300 solidi. The blood prices for girls under age fifteen were half that of boys. Both Muslim and Christian authors viewed children ambivalently. While children were often perceived as innocent, Isidore, among other Christian authors, emphasized original sin and the infant's essential depravity. Similarly, some Muslim authors, including al-*Ghazali, emphasize the child's ignorance and lack of willpower.

2. *Abandonment*

Some families abandoned illegitimate children or those they could not easily support. In Iberia, such children seem to have been regularly enslaved, although, in the early MA, abandoned children were often adopted by childless couples.

Between 1000 and 1200, economic growth and changing inheritance customs made child abandonment less common, but abandonment seems to have increased after 1200. Shelters for abandoned children appeared in the 14th century in *Castile and in the early 15th in *Aragon. In the absence of orphanages, hospitals took in abandoned children, who were first entrusted to a series of wet nurses, and frequently died young. Foundling boys were apprenticed as early as age five, while girls usually became domestic servants.

At times, the loss or abandonment of young children fuelled accusations that Jews stole Christian children. Two such accusations were made in Spain in 1294, and the *Barcelona Jewish community forestalled similar charges by quickly burying a dead baby found in the Jewish meat market in 1301.

3. *Infancy, to age two*

Most infants were nursed by their mothers, but wealthy parents often resorted to wet nurses, who were usually poorer, lower-status women, often servants of a different religion from the parents. Most infants were also swaddled until they were old enough to walk, which made it easier to carry them.

Newborn Christians were usually baptized within the first week of life. Jewish and Muslim boys were ritually circumcised, usually between seven and fourteen days old. Muslim newborns of both sexes might experience other religious rituals such as reciting the call to prayer into a child's ear.

4. *Children aged two to seven*

Mothers cared for and taught these children, imparting religious education and, in more elite households, basic *literacy. In large families, older siblings helped care for younger, while wealthy mothers were assisted by servants or slaves. Children of peasants or craftsmen accompanied their parents about their daily tasks, tending livestock and other chores as they grew older. Children also had time for play; surviving evidence indicates the existence of dolls, balls, games, and puppets. Before the practice waned in the 12th century, Christian children were sometimes given to *monasteries as *oblates. Hispanic canon *law of the 7th century decreed that oblates must keep their vows as adults, though this rule was later relaxed.

5. *Children aged seven to fourteen*

In peasant families, older children had increased responsibility for tending to livestock, younger siblings, and other household chores, usually differentiated by gender. In towns, sons of artisans often began *apprenticeships. Sons of the nobility were frequently sent to other households for their training. In both social groups, girls stayed at home or in convents.

Among Christians, boys who intended to become merchants or clergy were most likely to have formal schooling, with increasing opportunities after *c.*1100. The Catalan author Ramon *Llull viewed apprenticeship in a trade as the most useful education for boys. Among Jewish families, boys studied Hebrew, Torah, and *Talmud. Under the Umayyads, schooling in Arabic and Islamic law was common for boys. In later centuries, Christians often suppressed Islamic schools. The Muslim population became concentrated in the lower classes, limiting Muslim children's access to formal education. Christian, Jewish, or Muslim girls rarely attended schools, though they might study at home with parents or tutors.

6. *Adolescents*

By some standards, adolescents over age twelve (for girls) or fourteen (for boys) were not children at all. Christians could legally marry, and many Iberian law codes declared orphans independent at this age. In practice, marriage and financial resources determined adult status. Jewish boys attained adulthood at age thirteen, when they were ceremonially admitted to the Torah. For most girls of all three faiths, marriage signalled the end of adolescence; for boys, economic independence was a more important marker. While most adolescents were still financially and legally dependent, they were increasingly active participants in the adult worlds of work, politics, religion, and community life.

MMH

D. Alexandre-Bidon and D. Lett, *Children in the Middle Ages: Fifth–Fifteenth Centuries*, tr. J. Gladding (French original, 1997) (1999).

J. Boswell, *The Kindness of Strangers: The Abandonment of Children in Western Europe from Late Antiquity to the Renaissance* (1988).

J. W. Brodman, *Charity and Welfare: Hospitals and the Poor in Medieval Catalonia* (1998).

A. Giladi, *Children of Islam: Concepts of Childhood in Medieval Muslim Society* (1992).

D. Herlihy, 'Medieval Children', in *Women, Family and Society in Medieval Europe*, ed. A. Molho (1995), 215–46.

M. M. McLaughlin, 'Survivors and Surrogates: Children and Parents from the Ninth to the Thirteenth Centuries', in *The History of Childhood*, ed. L. deMause (1974), 101–81.

D. Nicholas, 'Childhood in Medieval Europe', in *Children in Historical and Comparative Perspective: An International Handbook and Research Guide*, ed J. M. Hawes and N. R. Hiner (1991), 31–52.

S. Shahar, *Childhood in the Middle Ages*, tr. Chaya Galai (Hebrew original, 1990) (1992).

chimes *See* MUSICAL INSTRUMENTS.

chimneys and heating *See* HEATING AND LIGHTING.

Chinon In Touraine; renowned for its *castle and, as the residence of *Charles VII in 1428–9, the location of the convening of the Estates General by the king and of *Joan of Arc's petition to join the king's forces. JKG

H. Brocourt, *Chinon: Petite ville de grand renom* (1973).

J. Mesqui, *Chateaux-forts et fortifications en France* (1997).

chivalry and knighthood The profession of a *knight was inextricably linked to concepts of chivalry. Chivalry was initially associated with *warfare and with those who bore arms; later, the term carried ethical and even religious overtones and the ideal of chivalry functioned as a code of conduct for knights. Knights and those aspiring to the chivalric life were expected to excel in feats of arms, exhibit courtly behaviour, and devote themselves to the service of God.

1. Chivalry and chivalric virtues
2. Courtesy books
3. Courtly love
4. Christian chivalry
5. Tournaments
6. Knights and knighthood

1. *Chivalry and chivalric virtues*

The term 'chivalry' derives from Old French *chevalerie* and from the medieval Latin *caballarius*, meaning 'horseback rider'. A consistent definition of chivalry is elusive due to the subtle shifts in meaning and to variations in usage, both medieval and modern. In some circumstances, chivalry refers to a company of knights or horsemen equipped for battle. The term also refers to the status of a knight, emphasizing both his membership in a distinct social group and his occupation as a military retainer. Throughout the medieval period, chivalry was associated with a knight's martial activities; in the 12th century and onwards, chivalry also carried ethical or religious overtones and was best understood as a code of knightly conduct that governed moral, religious, and social behaviour. In literary texts, particularly the **chansons de geste* and courtly *romances, the chivalric knight is one who exhibits knightly virtues, such as largesse, courtesy, courage, honour, and service, and who displays military prowess, excelling in feats of arms both on the battlefield and in tournaments. Above all, knights were expected to be without fear and beyond reproach.

2. *Courtesy books*

References to chivalry are found not only in vernacular literature but also in *courtesy books. Courtesy books were manuals directed to a particular group of people that outlined proper codes of conduct; these books were prevalent during the MA and some were written for knights. Books on chivalry provided instruction in the proper appearance of and appropriate behaviour for a knight, and outlined his responsibilities. Examples of courtesy books intended for those interested in chivalric life and customs include Geoffroi de *Charny's *Livre de chevalerie* (14th century) and Ramon *Llull's *Libre del orde de cavayleria* (*c.*1276), translated into English by William *Caxton. Knights as noble gentlemen were expected to exhibit suitable virtues, such as honour, courtesy, loyalty, piety, governance, and moderation.

3. *Courtly love*

Lyrical poems performed in the 12th and 13th centuries by *troubadours in *France and by *minnesingers in *Germany praised the ideal of *courtly love, which informs conceptions of chivalry. Courtly love refers to the obedience, loyalty, and service owed to the knight's beloved. It is the knight's devotion to his lady and to the ideal of courtly love that ennobles him, inspiring him to perform great deeds in order to prove himself worthy of his lady's love or win her favour. The courtly relationship between the knight and his lady was modelled on the feudal relationship between the knight and his liege lord, to whom the knight pledged allegiance and military service. The ideals of courtly love are best exemplified by Sir *Lancelot and his adoration of, and loyalty to, Lady *Guinevere in the poems of *Chrétien de Troyes. The relationship between Sir Lancelot and Guinevere illustrates the sometimes conflicting nature of chivalry. Lancelot swears an oath of loyalty to his liege lord King Arthur but, in pledging his love to Guinevere, Arthur's wife and queen, the knight violates his feudal obligations for the sake of the courtly love ideal. However, the ideals of chivalry—courtesy, bravery, piety, and devotion to one's beloved and brothers-in-arms—could not ameliorate the brutalities of knightly violence; indeed, there was a growing disparity between the ideals of knighthood and the social reality of knighthood.

4. *Christian chivalry*

Chivalric virtues were influenced by Christianity and by the church's desire to control the destructive potential of knights and to legitimate the use of knightly force in defence of the church and religious causes. The heedless violence of knights and their disruption of the social order prompted the church to try and regulate the martial activities of knighthood. Synodal legislation in France, such as the *Peace of God (*Pax Dei*) in the 10th century and the Truce of God (*Treuga Dei*) in the 11th century, was designed to maintain peace and order by prohibiting violence during a specified period; by ensuring the protection of church property, members of the *clergy, and other non-combatants; and by circumscribing warfare between knights. Although the church attempted to control knightly violence, it was tolerant of the legitimate use of force by knights who were needed to defend the church and the Christian faith, to maintain peace and order, and to protect the weak.

The ideal knight was thus a pious knight devoted to serving God and to fighting the enemies of the church. During the 11th century in Europe, Christian knights were characterized as the righteous armed force of Christendom, becoming knights of Christ (*Militia Christi). During the 12th century, military orders of knights were formed to protect Christian *pilgrims in the Holy Land. These orders of chivalry, such as the *Knights Templar and *Knights Hospitaller, were brotherhoods of religious knights who took vows of *poverty, chastity, and obedience, and who upheld the chivalric virtues of knighthood. The ideal of Christian knighthood illustrates the tension between the devotion of God in the service of peace and the realities of warfare.

5. *Tournaments*

An acceptable means of channelling knightly aggression in the absence of war was the tournament. Tournaments were known as 'schools of prowess', offering knights the opportunity to demonstrate their martial skill and to train for war. Knights competed in tournaments in accordance with codified rules, ensuring that combat occurred in a designated area between fellow combatants. Gradually, the tournament became a great *sport and, as Kaeuper observes, 'the great social event of chivalry', a ritualized event that emphasized chivalric ideals and pageantry (164). Tournaments were a feature of chivalric life both for actual knights and for knights portrayed in literature.

6. *Knights and knighthood*

Throughout western Europe, knights (*milites*) emerged as a separate class of military retainers in the 10th century, and remained a social group distinct from the *nobility (*nobiles*) until the 13th century. The term *miles* initially had the connotation of subservience and referred to knights of low social status and power. However, knighthood became associated with the nobility, united by a common vocation and ideology. In Germany, for example, a class of unfree knights (*ministeriales*) blended into the free nobility during the 13th century, whereas knighthood fused with the nobility during the course of the 12th century in regions of France, suggesting that this process was not uniform. The ethos of chivalry, with its emphasis on *courtliness, consolidated the social dominance of knights and confirmed their innate nobility as members of the social elite who deserved their positions of power.

Knights thus were members of the landholding class, who rendered *homage and military service to a lord in return for a *fief. As a mounted warrior, the knight required a warhorse in addition to such necessary equipment as his hauberk, helmet, shield, *lance, and *sword. Aspirants to knighthood were called squires; they served as attendants to knights, caring for their masters' horses and carrying their equipment. While in his master's service, a squire might be trained in the art of combat with the expectation of becoming a knight. Beneath the rank of squire was that of a page; pages typically served as attendants and were also aspirants to knighthood, although the term page could also refer to a common soldier. Entry into knighthood was marked with the ceremony of investiture with arms, occurring once mastery of martial skill had been established. However, the cost of chivalric life rose during the later MA, and, as a result, the number of dubbed knights who were active diminished in England and in France. Nevertheless, chivalry remained a source of inspiration for those seeking the chivalric life and wishing to emulate its virtues. *See also* FEUDALISM. JLS

R. W. Barber, *Tournaments: Jousts, Chivalry, and Pageants in the Middle Ages* (1989).

C. B. Bouchard, *'Strong of Body, Brave and Noble': Chivalry and Society in Medieval France* (1998).

J. Bumke, *The Concept of Knighthood in the Middle Ages*, tr. W. T. and E. Jackson (German original, 1964) (1982).

D. Burnley, *Courtliness and Literature in Medieval England* (1997).

J. R. Goodman, *Chivalry and Exploration, 1298–1630* (1998).

C. S. Jaeger, *The Origins of Courtliness: Civilizing Trends and the Formation of Courtly Ideals, 939–1210* (1985).

R. W. Kaeuper, *Chivalry and Violence in Medieval Europe* (1999).

M. H. Keen, *Chivalry* (1984).

M. Strickland, *War and Chivalry: The Conduct and Perception of War in England and Normandy, 1066–1217* (1996).

Chobham (Chabham)**, Thomas** (*c.*1160–*c.*1236) *Paris-educated theologian and student of *Peter the Chanter, later Dean of *Salisbury. He wrote the immensely influential *Summa de Penitentia*, a lucid summary of scholastic theology accessible to *parish priests. *See also* CLERGY. WJD

T. Chobham, *Summa confessorum*, ed. F. Broomfield (1968).
G. Evans, 'Thomas of Chobham on Preaching and Exegesis', *Recherches de théologie ancienne et médiévale*, 52 (1985), 159–70.

Chrétien (Crestien) **de Troyes** (*c.*1135–83) The most refined and self-consciously creative northern French poet of the 12th century, Chrétien is primarily known for five verse romances whose dates cannot be precisely fixed but which were probably composed in this order from *c.*1170: *Erec et Enide* (a version of the story of 'The Fair Unknown'), *Cligès* (a witty riposte to the *Tristan story), *Yvain* or *Le Chevalier au lion* (which revisits the themes of *Erec*), *Lancelot* or *Le Chevalier de la Charrette* (the oldest narrative of Lancelot's love for Guenevere), and *Perceval* or *Le Conte du *graal* (the earliest surviving story involving the Holy Grail). Evidently in contact with *troubadours from southern *France, Chrétien also composed lyrics, of which two survive. We know, from his prologue to *Cligès*, that he wrote other, probably Ovidian, tales; these are lost except perhaps for the *Philomela*, if the narrative incorporated into the *Ovide moralisé* is his. Scholars have proposed a number of additional attributions, the most widely accepted being *Guillaume d'Angleterre*, the tale of a family divided and reunited and the mighty saved by humility whose narrator names himself 'Crestien'. Probably from Troyes in *Champagne, Chrétien dedicates the *Lancelot* to Marie, countess of Champagne; the *Perceval* is dedicated to Philip of Alsace who died in 1191. Although speculations abound, nothing else is known of Chrétien's life. Both these latter works are unfinished, perhaps because of the tedium of writing for commission. The conclusion to the *Lancelot* is claimed by Godefroy de Lagny, while the *Perceval* attracted several different continuations.

In the five canonical *romances, the court of Arthur provides a backdrop to the career of an individual *knight. The increasing inertia of the king contrasts with the knight's activity in chivalric adventure. In *Erec*, this enables the hero successfully to integrate *chivalry, marriage, and kingship, but subsequent romances are disconcertingly permeated by irony that undermines the hero's achievements. In *Cligès*, the protagonist is united with his beloved thanks only to the ingenuity of their servants, hers contributing magical potions in imitation of the Tristan legend while his constructs an ingenious hideaway. Cligès is eventually crowned emperor, but only following the apoplectic demise of his uncle who had usurped the throne. Although Yvain, like Erec, is a king's son, he never assumes a throne and his attempts to combine marriage and chivalry lead to a marital breakdown that is reversed only via a rather unconvincingly choreographed reconciliation. The narrative of the *Lancelot* stagnates while the hero is in prison; his *adultery with the queen is incapable of narrative resolution. The *Perceval* boasts the most bathetic of all Chrétien's heroes, a naive lad always asking questions but never the right ones; the romance tails off with him wandering adrift in the forest. This downward spiral of attainment of male characters is matched by declining prominence in the female ones. Enide plays an almost equal role with Erec, but later female leads are increasingly sidelined by the plot (like Blanchefleur in the *Perceval*), or become (like Guenevere in the *Lancelot*) almost caricatural.

Diminution of his characters makes Chrétien's art stand out more confidently, a divergence sometimes characterized as one between 'clergie' (the order of clerks like Chrétien, and their learning) and 'chevalerie' (knights and their achievements). Chrétien is a superlative poet. Elaborate rhyme, extended metaphors, and patterns of repetition adorn his narrative as much as his lyrical works. In his earliest romances, as in the lyrics, his 'clergie' leads him to foreground relations between his own and other well-known texts, most notably *Tristan* and **Roman d'Eneas*. In his later works, literary performance is more bound up with enigma. The lion that accompanies Yvain on his adventures must be meaningful, but of what? Lancelot's ride on the cart marks him out, but how? The grail is the enigmatic object *par excellence* that no question from Perceval elucidates.

Chrétien's prestige was important in transmitting Arthurian material to other European literatures and to the *prose romances of the following century, but his true heirs are probably the virtuoso authors of non-Arthurian verse romance like Jean *Renart and *Jean de Meun. *See also* LITERATURES: ARTHURIAN LEGEND. SK

N. J. Lacy and J. T. Grimbert, eds, *A Companion to Chrétien de Troyes* (2005).
S. Kay, 'Who was Chrétien de Troyes?', *Arthurian Literature*, 15 (1997), 1–35.
D. Kelly, ed., *The Romances of Chrétien de Troyes: A Symposium* (1985).
D. D. R. Owen, tr., *Chrétien de Troyes: The Arthurian Romances* (1987).

chrism [Greek, *chrisma*; Latin, *chrisma*, *unctio*] Scented oil used by the eastern and western churches in the *sacraments of *baptism, confirmation, holy orders, and extreme unction, and in the consecration of churches and sacred objects. The origin of the term is Greek, meaning 'oil' or 'unguent' as well as 'the process of anointing' with them. Its main ingredient, *olive oil, is mixed with balsam and sometimes additional aromatic substances that enhance its fragrance. In order to fulfil its role in the administration of sacraments, the charismatic oil is blessed in a special ceremony during Holy (or *Maundy) Thursday. In the western tradition this holy oil is blessed by the bishop, while in the eastern tradition that role falls to the *patriarch and other chief hierarchs of the autocephalous churches. The use of chrism in the Latin *coronation ritual of monarchs is recorded as early as the 7th century, while *Byzantium adopted it later (after 1204). The unction with sanctified oil symbolically conferred the gift of the Holy Spirit upon the anointed and gave them the power to carry on their spiritual roles of Christian converts, members of the *clergy, or divinely ordained rulers. TPN

M. Dudley and G. Rowell, eds, *The Oil of Gladness: Anointing in the Christian Tradition* (1993).
E. Eichmann, *Die Kaiserkrönung im Abendland*, 2 vols (1942).
P. Hofmeister, *Die heiligen Öle in der morgen- und abendländischen Kirche* (1948).
L. L. Mitchell, *Baptismal Anointing* (1966).
D. M. Nicol, '*Kaisersalbung*: The Unction of Emperors in Late Byzantine Coronation Ritual', *BMGS* 2 (1976), 37–52.

Christian I von Buch, archbishop of Mainz (1163–83) Imperial archchancellor (1167–83) who, as imperial legate and lieutenant (*Statthalter*) in *Italy, supported Frederick I and popes of the imperial party through administrative, diplomatic, and military service. FL

W. Georgi, *Friedrich Barbarossa und die auswärtigen Mächte: Studien zur Aussenpolitik 1159–1180* (1990).

Christian King, Most (Most Christian Majesty) By the 14th century, this diplomatic formula used by the *papacy in correspondence with kings had become an exclusive privilege of the French crown, embodying the doctrine that these kings were uniquely chosen by, and loyal to, God. CDT

J. Krynen, '*Rex christianissimus*: A Medieval Theme at the Roots of French Absolutism', *History and Anthropology*, 4 (1989), 79–96.

Christian of Prussia (d. 1245) First bishop of Prussia, 1215–45. Christian, a *Cistercian monk, led missionary enterprises in Prussia against heavy obstacles that included six years of imprisonment by the Prussians. He founded the Knights of Dobrin and encouraged the *Teutonic order's role in the region. PGJ

E. Christiansen, *The Northern Crusades* ([2]1997).
W. L. Urban, *The Teutonic Knights* (2003).

Christian of Stavelot (9th century) Probably from Burgundy, Christian spent his monastic life and teaching career at *Stavelot. His commentary on Matthew emphasized literal, historical interpretations. JLN

In Matthaeum, In Lucam, In Joannem, PL, vol. 106, 1261–1520.
M. Ponesse, 'The Instruction of Monks in Christian of Stavelot's Commentary on the Gospel of Matthew', *Journal of Medieval Latin*, 18 (2008), 24–35.

Christian poetry in Iceland Prose texts from the time of the conversion of Iceland (*Landnámabók*, *Kristni saga*, *Óláfs saga Tryggvasonar en mesta*) quote fragments of Christian verse, and the 11th-century skalds Hallfreðr Óttarsson, Skapti Þóroddsson, and Sighvatr Þórðarson all composed poems on Christian themes. Sighvatr's *Erfidrápa* and the *Glælognskviða* of Þórarinn loftunga, memorial lays on St Óláfr, are the earliest fully developed Christian poems. The poetry of the 12th century shows an increased interest in theology and rhetoric. Einarr Skúlason's *Geisli* and the anonymous *Plácítus drápa* are significant as the earliest surviving skaldic *drápur* and bear witness to the learning of their authors. AM MS 757a 4to is an anthology of Christian *drápur* from the 12th and 13th centuries: *Harmsól*, *Leiðarvísan*, *Líknarbraut*, *Heilags anda vísur*, *Máríudrápa*, and *Gyðingsvísur*. The non-skaldic *Sólarljóð* is difficult to date: there are no medieval MSS. Composed in the eddic ljóðaháttr, it is a vision of the otherworld and shows the influence of traditional Nordic religion. The 14th-century *Lilja*, still popular in Iceland, is a majestic *drápa* of 100 stanzas in *hrynhent* metre. The cause for the canonization of Bishop Guðmundr Arason led to the composition of hagiographic poems in his honour by Arngrímr Brandsson, Einarr Gilsson, and Árni Jónsson in the mid 14th century. The relatively large corpus of Christian poetry of the late 14th and 15th centuries has received too little scholarly attention. Its non-native devotional themes and imagery reflect the conventional Christian piety of the time, but its metrical experimentation is noteworthy. MLC

K. Attwood, ed., 'The Poems of MS AM 757a 4to', Ph.D. thesis (Leeds, 1996).
M. Chase, ed., *Einarr Skúlason's Geisli* (2005).
J. Helgason, ed., *Íslenzk miðaldakvæði* (1936–8).
F. Jónsson, ed., *Den norsk-islandske skjaldedigtning* (1912–15).
W. Lange, *Studien zur christlichen Dichtung der Nordgermanen* (1958).
J. Louis-Jensen, ed., '*Plácítus drápa*', in *Plácidus saga*, ed. J. Tucker (1998), 87–124.
G. Nordal, *Tools of Literacy* (2000).
——S. Tómasson, and V. Ólason, eds, *Íslensk bókmenntasaga*, vols 1–2 (1992–3).
H. Schottmann, *Die isländische Mariendichtung* (1973).
G. Tate, 'Líknarbraut', Ph.D. thesis (Cornell, 1974).
K. Wrightson, ed., *Fourteenth-Century Icelandic Verse on the Virgin Mary* (2001).

Christina of Markyate (*c*.1097–1161) As a young woman, Christina made a private *vow of virginity that was challenged by a lustful bishop and by her forced marriage. In resistance, Christina fled dressed in men's clothes. She studied in hiding with the *anchoress Alfwen, then later with the *hermit Roger. Eventually, her marriage was annulled, and she continued her reclusive life. Her reputation grew, and with the assistance of Abbot Geoffrey of *St

Albans, she made a formal profession and founded a convent for her many followers. MMS

S. Fanous and H. Leyser, eds, *Christina of Markyate: A Twelfth-Century Holy Woman* (2005).
C. H. Talbot, ed., *The Life of Christina of Markyate* (1959).

Christine de Pizan (Pisan) (1364–1430) Formerly disregarded and even reviled as a bluestocking, she is now the most widely studied medieval French author, partly for her contribution to the prehistory of feminism, and as a thinker and public intellectual. Born in *Italy, Christine was the daughter of Thomas de Pizan, astronomer and physician at the court of *Charles V of *France. Her happy marriage to Estienne du Castel ended tragically with his premature death; financially embarrassed, she began writing *c.*1393 in order to support her three children and widowed mother. Her oeuvre is permeated by a sense that it needs to compensate for immense personal loss, and the growing confidence that it does.

Her early writings are mainly addressed to the mainstream of courtly literature in her own day, whether in her *ballades (especially the *Cent ballades d'amant et de dame*), her contributions to the *querelle* (dispute) over the **Roman de la rose*, which began with the *Epistre au dieu d'amours* of 1399 and continued through 1401–2, or her beautifully ironic *dit amoureux Le duc des vrais amants* (1403–5). In such works Christine challenges the prevailing male-centred view of love on the grounds that men's satisfactions are directly detrimental to women's honour and thus their happiness.

Increasingly assured and ambitious as her career advances, she deliberately emulates canonical male authors: *Dante and *Boethius in *Le Chemin de Long estude* (1402), Ovid in *La Mutacion de Fortune* (1402), *Augustine and *Boccaccio in *La Cité des dames* (1405). She never let her *gender stand in the way of pronouncing authoritatively on history, government, or the art of war, contributing incisively on all these topics. Her high-impact literary production was matched by astute management in the compilation and dedication of her books; Queen Isabeau of *Bavaria was a major patron.

A talented versifier rather than a great poet, her post-1405 works are all in prose, though she terms it 'poetrie' because it requires intellectual interpretation. Her best known work is the *Cité des dames* in which lives of exemplary women are arranged in a defensive structure to protect and restore women's reputations. Her last work is the *Ditie Jeanne d'Arc* (1429). *See also* WOMEN IN FRANCE. SK

R. Brown-Grant, *Christine de Pizan and the Moral Defence of Women: Reading beyond Gender* (1999).
Christine de Pizan, *Cent ballades d'amant et de dame*, ed. J. Cerquiglini (1982).
——*Le Chemin de longue étude*, ed. A. Tarnowski (2000).
——*La Città delle dame*, ed. E. J. Richards, tr. P. Caraffi (1997).
——*Le Livre de la mutacion de fortune*, ed. S. Solente (1959).
——*Le Livre du duc des vrais amans*, ed. T. S. Fenster (1995).
M. Desmond, ed., *Christine de Pizan and the Categories of Difference* (1998).
——and P. Sheingorn, *Myth, Montage, and Visuality in Late Medieval Manuscript Culture: Christine de Pizan's Epistre Othea* (2003).

Christmas Annual Christian holy day celebrating the birth of Jesus, son of God. The calendar of Philocalus (354) records the earliest official 25 December observance. A seemingly Christian appropriation of extant pagan festivities associated with Mithra and the sun's birthday, liturgical developments in the MA gave rise to the Twelve Days of Christmas in which 25 December, 1 January, and 6 January were particularly marked by ecclesiastical *masses and customary feasting and foolery. *See also* HOLY FOLLY; LITURGY. MTA

T. Gulevich, *Encyclopaedia of Christmas* (2000).
R. Hutton, *The Stations of the Sun: A History of the Ritual Year in Britain* (1996).
F. X. Weiser, *Handbook of Christian Feasts and Customs* (1958).

Chrodegang, St, bishop of Metz (d. 766) Born to a Frankish aristocratic family *c.*700; became bishop of *Metz sometime in the 740s. His *Regula canonicorum*, written for the cathedral *canons, was adopted as the standard rule for secular religious across the Frankish empire in 817. MAC

J. Bertram, *The Chrodegang Rules: The Rules for the Common Life of the Secular Clergy from the Eighth and Ninth Centuries* (2005).
M. A. Claussen, *The Reform of the Frankish Church: Chrodegang of Metz and the Regula canonicorum in the Eighth Century* (2005).

Chrysostom, Liturgy of St John One of the three Byzantine liturgies, in dominant use since the 13th century. It is divided into two sections: Mass of the Catechumens (opening antiphons and hymns with the Little Entrance, troparia, acclamations, *trisagion, Prokeimenon, pre-gospel chants, invocation) and Mass of the Faithful (Cheroubikon sung at the Great Entrance, Niceno-Constantinopolitan Creed, chants with anaphora and Sanctus—trisagion, *Axion estin*, Communion, post-communion hymns, benediction, and apolytikion, Proper **kontakion* with dismissal hymns). DTM

R. F. Taft, *A History of the Liturgy of St John Chrysostom*, 5 vols (1975–2000).

Chur (town, bishopric) Bishopric (late 4th century?) first mentioned 614. The bishopric, formerly under *Milan, was assigned in 843 to the *Mainz archbishops, who increased their power over the town in the 10th century. The city had its own seal from 1282, but achieved autonomy as the centre of the *Gotteshausbund* (founded 1367) in the 15th century. The bishop's court remained independent. GSi

U. Jecklin, *Churer Stadtgeschichte*, vol. 1 (1993).

church, collegiate A church served and administered by a college of *canons or other *clergy living together and engaged in a common ecclesiastical endeavour. These clerics collectively came to be termed a *chapter (*capitulum*), with a dean as its head. Collegiate churches were similar to *cathedrals in organization but were not the seat of a bishopric. GP

J. Burton, *Monastic and Religious Orders in Britain, 1000–1300* (1994).

church history The central institution of medieval society, the church underwent important changes during the MA, and its evolution had a profound effect on the general history of the period. The main structures of the church included the *papacy, the episcopal hierarchy, and monastic foundations, each of which experienced significant growth and transformation during the MA.

1. Origins
2. Institutions and Carolingian reform
3. Decadence and Gregorian Reform
4. Monastic reform and new achievements
5. Decline and new challenges

1. Origins

The medieval church traces its origins to the earliest followers of Jesus and the communities they established. Although subject to sometimes intense persecution, the primitive church survived to become the official religion of the Roman Empire. The conversion of the emperor Constantine (d. 337) and, to a lesser extent, Theodosius' (d. 395) declaration of Catholic Christianity as the official religion of the empire helped lay the foundation for the medieval church. The actions of these emperors brought about the conversion of their subjects, and missionaries began to preach the faith among the Germanic tribes.

2. Institutions and Carolingian reform

During the early MA, the church endured despite the disappearance of Roman political structures and strove to convert the new Germanic rulers of the western empire and their followers from paganism or Arian Christianity to Catholic Christianity. In this period the central institutions of the medieval church took shape. In the 6th century, *Benedict of Nursia composed a rule that would become the standard *monastic rule of Latin Europe. The success of the rule was due to its humanity and to the support given it and its author by *Pope Gregory I. Gregory also elevated the status of the papacy throughout the west. His pastoral rule provided a model for the proper life of the bishops, and his sermons and other writings shaped medieval spirituality. He strengthened ties with rulers in *Italy and Gaul and sent missionaries to England in 595. In the 7th and 8th centuries English missionaries would spread the faith on the continent and reform the church. Reform would receive greater impetus from the *Carolingian dynasty. Carolingian rulers supported monastic life, oversaw the restructuring of the hierarchy, and forged close relations with the papacy. *Charlemagne and other members of his line promoted missionary activity and spread the faith as a result of their military conquests. Carolingian legislation sought to improve religious life and reformed the *Mass and canon *law throughout the empire. The first great doctrinal controversies of the MA occurred under the Carolingians, including debates over predestination and the Eucharist, and important exegetical and theological works were produced by Carolingian ecclesiastics.

3. Decadence and Gregorian Reform

During the 10th century, the vigour of the Carolingian reforms diminished, and, as is traditionally held, the church, especially the papacy, experienced a period of corruption and decline that lasted into the 11th century. Although long held, this view of the decadence of the church prior to the age of *Gregorian Reform has given way to a more nuanced view that recognizes reform involved a rejection of very real abuses in the church and a changing understanding of the relationship of the church and the world. The movement associated with the monastery of *Cluny was one of the first expressions of reform and was a centre of renewed religious life and independence from earthly authority. Cluniac monks were seen as living the holiest of lives, and a large network of houses was established thanks to a series of great abbots, including *Odo, *Mayeul, *Odilo, and *Hugh. These abbots came to exercise great influence on the wider world, and their actions are often identified as contributing to the reform of the papacy.

Perhaps the most dramatic and important development of the medieval church, the Gregorian Reform reshaped church belief and practice, altered relations with the state, and laid the foundation for the papal monarchy. Initiated by *Pope Leo IX in 1049, Gregorian Reform focused on the twin evils of *simony (the buying and selling of church offices) and *Nicolaitism (clerical marriage), both of which underwent a process of increased attention and redefinition during this period. Leo also asserted the sovereignty of the pope over all Christians and exercised his authority outside of Italy. With the support of like-minded churchmen, including *Peter Damian and *Humbert of Silva Candida, Leo and his successors sought to reform the church, remove lay authority over the church, and assert the primacy of the papacy. These goals were strenuously pursued by *Pope Gregory VII, who is perhaps best known for his role in the *Investiture Controversy, the bitter struggle with Henry IV of Germany. Although forced from Rome by Henry and replaced by an *antipope, Gregory triumphed because his vision of the church and papacy prevailed and shaped developments well into the next century.

4. Monastic reform and new achievements
The 12th century was a time of dramatic growth for the church when new forms of religious life emerged and institutional and intellectual development took place. A new understanding of the person of Jesus Christ emerged that emphasized the human Jesus rather than the divine Christ. This change was reflected in the growing devotion to the *apostolic life (*vita apostolica*) that was manifest in the lives of *Robert of Arbrissel, who founded a new order of *canons and was embraced by the church, and heretics such as *Henri of Lausanne whose vehement denunciations of the *clergy and life of *poverty attracted the opposition of the church. Along with new orders of canons, a new monastic reform movement appeared that introduced a more austere reading of the Rule of St *Benedict and sought to restore the balance of work and prayer. Established at Cîteaux by St *Robert of Molesme, the *Cistercian order enjoyed dramatic growth as a result of the charisma of its greatest member, *Bernard of Clairvaux. Changes in spiritual and monastic life were paralleled by the growth of the papal monarchy as the popes exercised increasing authority over religious and temporal matters despite occasional conflicts with kings and emperors. The greatest of them, *Pope Innocent III, extended papal power, intervened in political affairs, proclaimed *crusades, approved new religious orders, and convoked the Fourth Lateran *Council.

In the 13th century the medieval church reached its apex. The *Franciscans and the *Dominicans grew rapidly and provided an important bulwark against heresy, which had grown significantly in the late 12th century. The great heresies, the *Waldensians and the *Cathars, were suppressed by crusade and the establishment of the *inquisition in the 1230s. The *art and architecture of the Gothic style manifested the growth and increasing sophistication of the medieval church, and was paralleled in this by the theological achievements of St *Thomas Aquinas and other university masters. And the papacy emerged triumphant in its long struggle with the empire with the defeat and demise of the Hohenstaufen line.

5. Decline and new challenges
The late medieval church saw the unravelling of its great achievements. The theological work of Aquinas was undermined by the writings of John *Duns Scotus and *William of Ockham. Despite its victory over the emperors, the papacy faced a greater challenge from *Philip IV of *France, whose humiliation of *Pope Boniface VIII led to the rise of the Avignon papacy (the so-called *'Babylonian captivity') and, ultimately, the Great *Schism of 1378–1415. Although effective administrators, the Avignon popes often failed to provide spiritual leadership and were perceived as servants of the French king. Institutional authority broke down further in the face of absentee clerics who held multiple church offices and provided inadequate religious guidance. The popularity of *pilgrimages and the cult of the saints were revived, and mystics like *Catherine of Siena and Meister *Eckhart became influential. The *laity found alternate means of spiritual consolation, joining lay brotherhoods or the Beguines, a semi-monastic woman's movement (*see* BEGHARDS AND BEGUINES). Despite these difficulties, the church remained one of the central institutions in medieval society and, in many ways, Martin Luther attacked the successes and strengths of the medieval church as well as its failures and weaknesses. *See also* LAY BROTHER; MONASTICISM. MCF

U.-R. Blumenthal, *The Investiture Controversy* (1988).
P. Brown, *The Cult of the Saints: Its Rise and Function in Latin Christianity* (1981).
—— *The Rise of Western Christendom: Triumph and Diversity, 200–1000 AD* ([2]2003).
M. D. Chenu, *Nature, Man, and Society in the Twelfth Century*, tr. J. Taylor and L. K. Little (French original, 1966) (1968).
M. Lambert, *Medieval Heresy: Popular Movements from the Gregorian Reform to the Reformation* ([3]2002).
C. H. Lawrence, *The Friars: The Impact of the Early Mendicant Movement on Western Society* (1994).
—— *Medieval Monasticism: Forms of Religious Life in Western Europe in the Middle Ages* ([3]2000).
P. Llewellyn, *Rome in the Dark Ages* (1971).
J. Lynch, *The Medieval Church: A Brief History* (1992).
J. Pelikan, *The Growth of Medieval Theology (600–1300)* (1978).
I. S. Robinson, *The Papacy 1073–1198* (1990).
W. Ullman, *The Growth of Papal Government in the Middle Ages* ([3]1970).
A. Vauchez, *Sainthood in the Later Middle Ages*, tr. J. Birrell (French original, 1988) (1997).
J. M. Wallace-Hadrill, *The Frankish Church* (1984).

church modes *See* MODES, MELODIC.

church of the East (Assyrian church of the East) Known as the East Syrian, Chaldean, Assyrian, Malabar, Nestorian, or Persian Rite that followed the Antiochene Rite. The church, existing from as early as the 2nd century and using the Syriac language, was located mostly in Persian territory after the 5th century. It largely followed the Byzantine / Constantinopolitan liturgical forms. DTM

C. Baumer, *The Church of the East* (2006).

church types Since the early centuries of Christianity there has been a predilection for longitudinal spaces for the performance of the *liturgy. In the Constantinian period this basic building type was dramatically expanded by the adoption of the *basilica plan, which consists of a longitudinal *nave flanked by aisles on either side (a total of four aisles), and which culminates in an *apse containing the main *altar. The origins of the early Christian basilica can be found in the secular basilicas (meeting halls) of antiquity.

Iona
Lindisfarne
Armagh
Jarrow
Kells
Ripon
Whitby
Durrow
York
St Asaph
Abingdon
Glastonbury
Canterbury
Utrecht
Hamburg
Bremen
Paderborn
Magdeburg
Ghent
St Omar
Cologne
Corvey
Liège
Fulda
Rouen
Corbie
Echternach
Mainz
Würzburg
Prague
Atlantic Ocean
Jumièges
Rheims
Trier
St Emmeram (Regensburg)
Dol
Paris
Remiremont
Freising
Passau
Luxueil
Reichenau
Tegernsee
Mondsee
Tours
Fleury
Citeaux
Konstanz
Salzburg
Bourges
Besançon
Basle
St Gall
Cluny
Chur
Aquileia
Lyons
Tarentaise
Brescia
Milan
Verona
Bordeaux
Vienne
Lugo
CATHARS
Bobbio
Ravenna
Auch
Arles
Aix
WALDENSIANS
Narbonne
Florence
Assisi
CATHARS
Rome
San Vicenzo
Monte Cassino
Thessalonica
Capua
Mediterranean Sea
Mediterrane Sea
200 miles
400 km
N

Church (early).

- ■ Patriarchal seats
- ● Archbishoprics
- ▲ Important bishoprics
- □ Monasteries founded before 800
- ○ Monasteries founded after 800
- — Approximate boundary line between Catholic (Roman) and Orthodox (Byzantine) spheres of influence, *c*.1000
- Approximate extent of Christianity
- Area conquered by Arab Muslim invaders, 622–*c*.750

Constantinian buildings were, however, remarkably varied in type depending on site and function. At shrines of great importance, as at St Peter's, the church of the Nativity in *Bethlehem, or the *Holy Sepulchre in *Jerusalem, the basilica was combined with transverse or centralized spaces and sometimes with courtyards. The *transept at St Peter's was the first introduction of a transverse axis across a longitudinal plan and is associated with the veneration of the apostle in this part of the building. At Bethlehem and in Jerusalem, however, the Constantinian basilicas adjoined rounded spaces to commemorate a holy place: in Bethlehem an octagon was constructed over the site of the grotto of the nativity of Christ, and in Jerusalem there was a courtyard and martyrium (circular structure) over the site of Christ's crucifixion.

The central plan was associated from an early date with the veneration of holy persons or holy places. Buildings on a central plan were also often used as monuments to the dead and for burial, as can be seen, for example, at S. Costanza in *Rome. It is probably for this reason that it was adopted at an early date for baptisteries in the early Christian period: a notable example is the octagonal Lateran *baptistery in Rome. The central plan type, however, is not well adapted to the western liturgy and was therefore rarely used for churches with regular services.

The basilica form remained at the core of later church architecture. However, the basilica in the Romanesque period expands dramatically by an extension of the transept and by an increase of space around the apse and main altar with *ambulatory and radiating *chapels; by the Gothic period this had become a standard feature. The development of the east end of a church reflected the importance of the cult of *relics and the growing numbers of *clergy, especially the *cathedral chapters of *canons, which could include as many as a hundred or more members.

In the east, a type of church plan developed that can be seen as a fusion of the centralized and longitudinal plan: the Greek cross, or double-shell plan, typical of Byzantine architecture. Here the main focus area is covered by a *dome, and this central square is contained in a larger square. A series of smaller square or rectangular units served as aisles and often contained the lay public, making the transition from the outer shell to the inner core. *See also* ART AND ARCHITECTURE: BYZANTINE/GOTHIC/ROMANESQUE. CAB

G. Dehio, *Die Kirchliche Baukunst des Abendlandes: Historisch und systematisch dargestellt* (1969).

R. Krautheimer, *Early Christian and Byzantine Architecture* (1986).

ciborium *See* EUCHARISTIC VENERATION AND VESSELS.

Ciconia, Johannes (*c*.1370–1412) Native of *Liège; composer and theorist at *Padua. Ciconia wrote both sacred and secular music (ceremonial and political Latin motets, ornate French songs, and Italian ballatas, including some settings of texts by Francesco Giustiniani) and the speculative music theory treatise *Nova musica*, one book of which was later revised as the *De proportionibus*. OBE, RF

J. Ciconia, *Nova musica* and *De proportionibus*, ed. O. Ellsworth (1993).

—— *The Works of Johannes Ciconia*, ed. M. Bent and A. Hallmark (1985).

A. Hallmark, '*Protector, imo verus pater*: Francesco Zabarella's Patronage of Johannes Ciconia', *Music in Renaissance Cities and Courts: Studies in Honor of Lewis Lockwood*, ed. J. A. Owens and A. M. Cummings (1997), 153–68.

Cid, Cantar de Mio (*Poema de Mio Cid*) An anonymous Spanish epic from the mid-to-late 12th or early 13th century. The *Cantar* recounts the adventures of Rodrigo *Díaz de Vivar, known as the Cid, from the Arabic for lord. Born *c*.1043, the Cid was a *knight during the reigns of Fernando I (1035–65), Sancho II (1065–72), and *Alfonso VI. The Cid's relationship with his third feudal lord was often strained, and resulted in the Cid's exile on two occasions (1081–7, 1089–92).

The *Cantar* is found in one MS, the first folio of which is missing, and begins *in media res* at the point of the Cid's imminent departure from his homeland following his exile. Like the later Cidian epic **Mocedades de Rodrigo*, the *Cantar* was composed in traditional epic verse-form (irregular assonanced lines averaging fourteen to sixteen syllables). Various theories have been advanced regarding the origins of the *Cantar*, some placing its roots in popular tradition, others identifying composition by a learned author.

Although the work is divided into three sections (*cantares*), the thematic structure of the *Cantar* is bipartite, centring on the double loss and restoration of the hero's honour. The first half deals with the Cid's exile, and consequent loss of public honour, which he re-establishes by conquering Muslim-held territory, and lavishing gifts on Alfonso VI. In the second half, it is the eponymous hero's private honour which is tarnished by his sons-in-law, the Infantes de Carrión, through their violence against the Cid's daughters. Of course the Cid restores his honour once more, but this time he does so with recourse to the law. It is through these tribulations that the Cid demonstrates the traditional qualities of an epic hero: *fortitudo* and *sapientia*.

JG

A. D. Deyermond, ed., *'Mio Cid' Studies* (1977).

J. J. Duggan, *The 'Cantar de mio Cid': Poetic Creation in its Economic and Social Contexts* (1989).

M. Harney, *Kinship and Polity in the 'Poema de Mio Cid'* (1993).

M. E. Lacarra, *'Poema de Mio Cid', realidad histórica e ideología* (1980).

C. Smith, *The Making of the 'Poema de mio Cid'* (1983).

Cimabue, Giovanni (*c*.1240–*c*.1302) Born as Cenni di Pepe in *Florence, he was a painter and mosaicist, influenced by Byzantine and ancient art. A document of 1272 attests to him as being in *Rome. He worked on the *mosaics of the *baptistery in Florence and the murals in the choir and *transept in the Upper church of St *Francis at *Assisi around 1280. He also painted the Maestà of the Virgin for Santa Trinità at Florence (now Uffizi) and for St Francesco, *Pisa (now Paris, Louvre). Two painted wooden *crucifixes, one in *Arezzo (St Dominic), the other in Florence (Santa Croce), were badly damaged by flood (1966). *Dante Alighieri wrote in the *Divina Commedia* (*Purgatory*, 11.94) that his reputation was superseded by that of *Giotto. *See also* ART AND ARCHITECTURE: BYZANTINE. SR

E. Battisti, *Cimabue* (1963).
L. Bellosi, *Cimabue* (1998).
J. White, *The Birth and Rebirth of Pictorial Space* (1957).

cincture *See* LITURGICAL VESTMENTS.

Cinque Ports Confederacy of southeast English ports, named after the five 'head' ports of Hastings, (New) Romney, Hythe, Dover, and Sandwich. *Edward I granted them privileges in return for providing ships for royal service, and their rights were formalized under royal charter in 1278. There were eventually 32 ancillary ports or 'limbs'. *See also* CHARTERS OF FRANCHISE AND LIBERTIES. JCF

K. M. Murray, *The Constitutional History of the Cinque Ports* (1935).

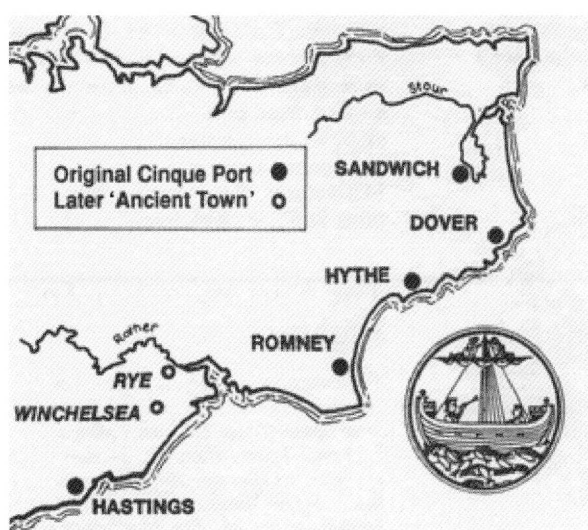

Map and herald of Cinque Ports.

Ciompi, Revolt of the (1378) Three major uprisings occurred in *Florence during the summer of 1378. In mid June, Salvestro de' *Medici staged a constitutional revolt against the magnate-dominated *Guelph Party, which had used its prerogatives to debar individuals from holding office. A month later, disenfranchised workers mostly of the *wool industry (the *popolo minuto*) stormed the Palazzo Signoria, established a government dominated by wool workers (the emergency council of thirty-two), and created three new *guilds that represented nearly all working men in Florence. At the end of August, wool workers (the *Otto di S. Maria Novella*) tried to push the revolution further but failed. The new government of guildsmen endured until January 1382, when a counter-revolution restored the oligarchy. SKC

G. Brucker, 'The Ciompi Revolution', in *Florentine Studies: Politics and Society in Renaissance Florence*, ed. N. Rubinstein (1968), 314–56.
S. Cohn, *The Laboring Classes in Renaissance Florence* (1980).
A. Stella, *La révolte des Ciompi: les hommes, les lieux, le travail* (1993).

Circumcision, Feast of the *See* LITURGICAL YEAR; LITURGY.

Circumspecte Agatis Though previous kings, both before and after the conquest of *England, had issued *writs confirming the freedoms of the church, and in particular the jurisdiction of the church, this English writ of 1285 issued by King *Edward I defined the extent of the jurisdiction of church courts more fully than before. *See also* ANGLO-SAXON CHURCH; CLARENDON, CONSTITUTIONS OF. FGP

E. B. Graves, '"Circumspecte Agatis"', *EHR* 43.169 (1928), 1–20.
D. Millon, 'Circumspecte Agatis Revisited', *Law & History Review*, 2.1 (1983), 105–27.

Cistercian chant The founders believed that liturgical innovation upset the traditional monastic balance amongst ceremony, labour, and study. Excising what were regarded as non-authentic hymns, they replaced inherited chant with the purportedly ancient *hymnody of *Metz. Mid-12th-century reformers, especially *Bernard of Clairvaux, reworked this material and made modest additions but resisted the introduction of *tropes and *sequences into the *liturgy. BRN

C. Maître, *La réforme cistercienne du plain-chant* (1995).
C. Waddell, 'The Origin and Early Evolution of the Cistercian Antiphonary', in *The Cistercian Spirit: A Symposium*, ed. M. B. Pennington (1970), 190–223.

Cistercian entrepreneurs The economies of *Cistercian *monasteries during the central MA varied considerably. Geographical circumstance and differing levels of ambition determined development. The paradigmatic Cistercian agricultural strategy was to take donations of property and fuse them with land acquired through purchase or exchange into unified production entities called granges. Work was done by members of the community vowed to consecrated labour (*lay brothers) with the assistance of secular farmhands.

Among the most remunerative products of Cistercian granges in western continental Europe was *wine. The Cistercians were also major players in the *wool trade, particularly in England, providing raw materials for a growing international market. The *White Monks had potentially profitable *mills, ovens, *mines, forges, and *salt works as well. In the 12th century the main outlets for monastic products were local *markets and regional *fairs. From the 1130s the Cistercians established warehouses in major commercial centres to store and sell their surplus. By 1170 they owned properties even in smaller towns, housing not only monastic products but also the managers of the order's economic interests and community members passing through on business.

The 12th- and early-13th-century Cistercians were also bankers. Some houses received deposits from noblemen seeking security for their treasures. Other monasteries were in the *moneylending and mortgage business, supplying cash loans in exchange for collateral that was returned when the principal was paid. Although Cistercian legislators were keen to ensure that *usury be avoided in such transactions, mortgaging was still lucrative. Borrowers received only one-half to two-thirds of what the pawn was worth, and if they died or were unable to pay the debt in time, the monks assumed ownership at below market value.

While wealthier Cistercian abbeys were prospering in the nascent commercial economy of the late 12th century, the less well-to-do were flagging. Some were in the red as a result of wine purchases. Others suffered from a surfeit of personnel, the burdens of hospitality, and overspending on building projects or real estate. Additional houses, resource-poor or hemmed in by other monasteries, simply never got off the ground. The 13th century brought additional economic challenges. The patrimony of prosperous abbeys could no longer be adequately managed by traditional methods. Already in 1208 the *general chapter approved the leasing of distant or 'less useful' properties. The difficulty of property management became more acute when the number of lay brothers entering the order began to decline. The trickle of leasing became a torrent, so that by the 14th century most Cistercians were no longer entrepreneurs but made their living as rentiers. *See also* ESTATE MANAGEMENT AND ORGANIZATION; FURNACES AND FORGES. BRN

C. Berman, *Medieval Agriculture, the Southern French Countryside, and the Early Cistercians* (1986).

C. B. Bouchard, *Holy Entrepreneurs* (1991).

R. A. Donkin, *The Cistercians: Studies in the Geography of Medieval England and Wales* (1978).

Économie cistercienne: géographie–mutations (1983).

J. E. Madden, 'Business Monks, Banker Monks, Bankrupt Monks', *CHR* 49 (1963), 341–64.

M. Toepfer, *Die Konversen der Zisterzienser* (1983).

D. H. Williams, *The Cistercians in the Early Middle Ages* (1998).

Cistercian liturgy *Cîteaux inherited its liturgy from Molesme, the home of its founders. The Cistercians attempted a return to primitive *Benedictine observance *c.*1108. A second reform was instituted before 1147 to correct musical errors and respond to contemporary religiosity. Guided by authority and/or reason, 12th-century Cistercian reformers bequeathed to posterity, especially in the chant, a liturgy of austerity and brevity. BRN

B. K. Lackner, 'The Liturgy of Early Cîteaux', in *Studies in Medieval Cistercian History* (1971), 1–34.

C. Maître, 'Authority and Reason in the Cistercian Theory of Music', *CiSt* 29 (1994), 197–208.

Cistercian order Order of monks and nuns originating as an 11th-century reform of the *Benedictines. St *Robert of Molesme attempted reforms at his own *monastery and others before gathering a group of hermits into a Benedictine community in Molesme. The community soon founded the New Monastery at *Cîteaux (1098) where twenty-one of the Molesme brothers joined Robert. The reforms were continued by *Alberic and Stephen *Harding after Robert was sent back to Molesme by papal request.

The ideals of this new order included a return to the principles of the 'primitive' observance of the Rule of *Benedict in which manual labour was emphasized. Unlike Benedictine houses, which often sought naturally defensible sites on mountains or on prominences, the Cistercians sought sites alongside rivers in valleys far away from civilization. Cistercian art and architecture favoured ascetical ideals and employed minimal decoration. These customs stood over and against the *Cluniac developments in high liturgy, in which manual labour was de-emphasized, and which involved elaborate decorations in church statuary, stained glass, and vestments.

Cîteaux formed a central hub in the fledgling Cistercian order, although the monasteries were organized as autonomous communities. In the 13th century, autonomy would become officially regulated among the men of the order by an annual chapter meeting of the college of abbots and a system of annual visitations to smaller houses. The early history of the order is told through the *Exordium Cistercii* and the *Exordium parvum*. The early organization was outlined by the early constitution of the order, the *Carta Caritatis*.

Within a generation of the order's foundation, the Cistercians had produced well-known and influential mystics, preachers, abbots, and spiritual writers. Foremost among them was *Bernard of Clairvaux, as well as his friend William of St-Thierry, a spiritual writer, the Yorkshire abbot *Aelred of Rievaulx, and the abbot *Isaac of Stella. Bernard of Clairvaux also helped preach the Second *Crusade.

Monks of the Cistercian order often served as spiritual directors to women, and from early on the order attracted numerous women who sought to join the order or turned existing convents into Cistercian houses; some of the earliest Cistercian women's foundations include Jully and La Tart in *France, Las Huelgas in Spain, and Sinningthwaite in *England. However, from the 13th century the order claimed not to have women's houses and officially organized the system of general chapters to include men's houses only. AJD

C. Berman, *The Cistercian Evolution* (1999).
L. Bouyer, *The Cistercian Heritage* (1958).
E. R. Elder, ed., *New Monastery: Texts and Studies on the Early Cistercians* (1998).
J. Leclercq, *Bernard of Clairvaux and the Cistercian Spirit* (1976).
L. Lekai, *The Cistercians: Ideals and Reality* (1977).
B. P. McGuire, *Friendship and Faith: Cistercian Men, Women, and their Stories, 1100–1200* (2002).
M. B. Pennington, *The Cistercians* (1992).
E. Scholl, ed., *In the School of Love: An Anthology of Early Cistercian Texts* (2000).

Cîteaux (Notre-Dame de Cîteaux) (abbey) The *Cistercian order's motherhouse near *Dijon, founded by St *Robert of Molesme in 1098. Cîteaux seeded over five hundred daughter houses by 1300 and was known for scribal production, agricultural innovation, and employment of laypersons. EMW

B. K. Lackner, *The Eleventh-Century Background of Cîteaux* (1972).
L. J. Lekai, *Nicholas Cotheret's Annals of Cîteaux* (1982).

City of God (*De Civitate Dei*) A reaction to pagan criticisms following Alaric's sack of *Rome in 410, St *Augustine of Hippo's 'great and arduous work', written 413–27, uses extensive classical learning to argue against both *paganism and Christian triumphalism. AKG

R. A. Markus, *Saeculum: History and Society in the Theology of Saint Augustine* (1970).
G. O'Daly, *Augustine's City of God: A Reader's Guide* (1999).

city-state The city-state—a recent concept—was a medieval city that, after conquering a territorial state, did not modify its municipal institutions to govern the new entity. The original city exerted sole sovereignty, while the conquered territories were its 'subjects'. (Another term is 'merchant republic'.) This institution developed outside of the feudal framework, and independently of royal or comital power which retained its dynastic character. The title of duke (doge) or prince, held by the chief of executive power, was bestowed after election by a council; the election would be ratified by the freemen gathered in the forum. This power was not hereditary.

The real power was in the collective possession of prominent men—the richest merchants, bankers, shipowners—who owned a patrimony of town estates and rural lands, and who succeeded in reducing the influence of the free assemblies, before transforming themselves, at the end of the 13th century, into an aristocracy, so as to monopolize power and council seats, and to elect magistrates, who were also noble. The former magistrates, stripped of their authority, would often form a senate—a limited council that managed power and delegated to a 'college of elders' the responsibility for finances, war, seafaring, and town planning.

These cities succeeded in conquering territories and in enlarging their dominion over other cities. They confiscated the goods of local potentates, which they sold to their own nobility, and set about reducing the influence of the old institutions of those towns and their urban aristocracies, instead sending magistrates (rectors) to administer them. The taxes taken from these subject-territories enriched the city-state, which redistributed them partly for the defence of its new borders.

Which cities fit this definition? *Genoa and *Venice; *Pisa at the time of its independence. Ancona attempted to give itself this status, and Ragusa (Dubrovnik) succeeded in doing so. *Bruges and *Ghent, however, despite their power, remained subjects first of the count of *Flanders, and then of the duke of *Burgundy. Certain Swiss towns—*Zürich, Berne, *Geneva—might claim this status, given the extent of their autonomy from the empire. For the chief towns of the Germanic *Hanse—*Lübeck, *Hamburg, and Danzig—the concept of the 'free city' would be more appropriate, as these ports did not subjugate neighbouring towns. The city-state model seems to have been best realized at *Novgorod, a new town created during the period of commercial relations established by the *Varangians with *Byzantium along the Russian rivers. Novgorod dominated an immense territory; within the city sovereign power was exercised by an assembly, which everyone of free status could attend provided they listen for the bell convoking it. This assembly elected a prince, but the town itself was its own prince, 'Lord Novgorod the Great', that declared war and signed commercial treaties. As in the Italian cities, Novgorod's society was divided between the aristocrats, who monopolized power, and the citizens. JCHo

J.-C. Hocquet, 'City State and Market Economy', in *The Origins of the Modern State in Europe: Economic Systems and State Finance*, ed. R. Bonney (1995), 81–100.
—— *Venise au Moyen Âge* ([2]2005).

civic medicine The policy of hiring medical practitioners occurred among a number of civic governments in Europe throughout the MA. *Physicians and *surgeons received a salary in exchange for their service in treating the population (often with special attention to the destitute), as well as for providing expert opinions in murder cases and during health crises such as epidemics. The earliest cases of medieval civic doctors can be found in *Byzantium, with the founding of the imperial hospital adjacent to the Pantocrator monastery, established and regulated by Emperor John II Komnenos in 1136. The hospital served all the citizens of *Constantinople, including the sick poor who could not afford a doctor's fee; compared to western European *hospitals where physicians and surgeons started to appear only after the *Black Death, the Pantocrator hospital was peculiar for the constant presence of physicians of both sexes, who alternated their civic employment with private practice. Earlier examples of civic practitioners in Byzantium, albeit less well documented, date back to the time of Justinian, who in 532 reorganized state doctors by affiliating them with Christian hospitals.

Affiliation with royal hospitals was also indirectly related to one of the earliest and largest royal hospitals for the sick poor in Great Britain, St Peter's hospital at *York, founded in 936 by King *Æthelstan. The number, remuneration, and availability of practitioners varied in each city that hired them for public service. Documented cases in northern *Italy, *France, and the Crown of *Aragon rarely present a large number of doctors on a city's payroll in the 13th–14th centuries. The most notable exception is *Venice, where since 1324 the government had an average of 21 salaried doctors (nine physicians and twelve surgeons); after 1348 and until the late 14th century, the city employed an average of eighteen practitioners. In the Crown of *Aragon, on the other hand, the mere presence of municipal doctors for consultation seemed to be the government's primary preoccupation, and in Florence, at least in the decades immediately following the *Black Death, the ranks of municipal practitioners (all surgeons) swelled to five. In *Florence and the Crown of Aragon, contrary to what happened in Venice and Constantinople, there is no evidence of governmental control over the fees a municipal doctor would receive from his patients. In cities such as *Parma, *Urbino, and *Milan, tax exemption for the physicians practising in the city was the reward for treating the sick poor. In Venice, the treatment of the destitute without charge, in addition to being included in contracts for civic practitioners, was also a means for physicians and surgeons to build a reputation and obtain municipal employment. When the demand for doctors was not influenced by epidemics and wars, remuneration of physicians and surgeons often depended on their reputation within the city, as well as abroad.

A university degree was not always a prerequisite for a physician's hire, as, for example, in the Crown of Aragon, in Florence, or in Venice. Reputation and necessity frequently trumped the authority of a degree in the hiring of municipal doctors. Age and length of service for the government were also factors considered in all cities for the calculation of a practitioner's salary. Assisting the army in war, a service common especially to surgeons in Europe, was also highly regarded by municipal and state governments in their hiring procedures. A routine duty of surgeons specifically, and of all civic practitioners in general, was testifying in criminal cases to provide a medical assessment of the cause of death or the nature of wounds. In this respect, Venice also obligated its salaried doctors, as early as 1368, to attend an annual *dissection for didactic purposes. AMM

D. Jacquart, *Le milieu médical en France du XIIe au XVe siécle* (1981).
E. J. Kealey, *Medieval Medicus* (1981).
M. R. McVaugh, *Medicine Before the Plague* (1993).
T. S. Miller, *The Birth of the Hospital in the Byzantine Empire* (1997).
V. Nutton, 'Continuity or Rediscovery? The City Physician in Classical Antiquity and Mediaeval Italy', in *The Town and State Physician in Europe from the Middle Ages to the Enlightenment*, ed. A. W. Russell (1981), 9–46.
K. Park, *Doctors and Medicine in Early Renaissance Florence* (1985).
—— 'Healing the Poor', in *Medicine and Charity before the Welfare State*, ed. J. Barry and C. Jones (1991), 26–45.
M. Rubin, 'Imagining Medieval Hospitals', in *Medicine and Charity before the Welfare State*, 14–25.

civil law *See* LAW, ROMAN.

Clairvaux (town, abbey) Town in the *Champagne region of *France, *c.*124 km from Dijon. On 25 June 1115, *Bernard of Clairvaux and his companions established a *Cistercian *monastery in the valley of the Aube. Records indicate that the monastery had as many as 700 monks at its height and possessed an impressive library. GP

T. N. Kinder, *Cistercian Europe: Architecture of Contemplation* (2002).

clan and kindred [Latin *genus*, *generatio*; Polish *plęme*, *ród*; Hungarian *nemzetség*; Old Croatian *pleme*] Predominant type of kinship structure among Polish, Hungarian, and Croatian nobility in the high MA; a group of agnatic kinsmen, with membership defined by descent from a real or fictitious ancestor. Whether such kindred groups had some formal leadership and common policy is unclear, but kinship connections were used for providing supportive manpower. In principle, each kindred group had a particular place of origin and residence, and shared landed property, common symbols, and a cultic centre, although these elements were not equally valued in different cases (in *Poland the role of *heraldry and common devices or battle cries were particularly important for the 'heraldic clans' [*herb*]). It was based on the rule of partible inheritance among male kinsmen with no pronounced restrictions on members' right to marry, while women had only the right of usufruct of landed property (upon marriage they were usually paid in money, jewellery, or other movable goods). The female side might even be discriminated against by the introduction of special legal institutes (the *quarta puellarum*). Such principles were usually expressed in customary law codes (the **Tripartitum*, the Poljica *law code, and so forth), but whether they were strictly upheld in practice is debated. Kindred groups existed on almost all levels of nobility: among aristocracy, and middling and lesser nobility (such as castle warriors and **servientes regis*), as well as among urban nobility in Dalmatian cities (the patriciate). There were also 'artificial' kindred groups, bound together by a voluntary union, usually in cases of immigrant knights (cases recorded in both Poland and *Hungary), as well as cases of the adoption of newcomers into the existing clans (the most famous being the agreement of Horodło in 1413, incorporating the Lithuanian nobles into Polish clans). The number of members in a particular group varied, from small clans of only a few families to the great ones comprising several thousand members (especially in Poland). Such clans apparently developed from broader cognatic kinship groupings characteristic of the nobility in the whole of Europe in the early MA, but from the 11th century that system started to be gradually replaced. This change seems to have begun in the south sometime after 1000, to be completed in the next two centuries. The weakening of solidarity among kinsmen leading to the decline of the clans as a major organizational type started in different areas at different rates as early as the 14th century, and was usually influenced by both the rise of territorial organization of the nobility and the growth of centralist governments. *See also* KINSHIP, FAMILY, MARRIAGE, DIVORCE: IN [VARIOUS]. DKa

E. Fügedi, *The Elefánthy: The Hungarian Nobleman and his Kindred* (1998).
A. Gąsiorowski, ed., *The Polish Nobility in the Middle Ages: Anthologies* (1984), 7–20, 123–76.
D. Karbić, 'The Šubići of Bribir: A Case Study of a Croatian Medieval Kindred', Ph.D. thesis (Central European University, Budapest, 2000).
M. Rady, *Nobility, Land and Service in Medieval Hungary* (2000), 96–109.

Clanvowe, Sir John (*c.*1341–91) English courtier and diplomat under the reigns of *Edward III and *Richard II. Author of *The Two Ways*, a religious prose treatise reflecting on the human choice between good and evil, and *The Book of Cupid* (sometimes called *The Cuckoo and the Nightingale*), a St Valentine's Day dream vision emulating Geoffrey *Chaucer's dream poetry. RJU

V. J. Scattergood, ed., *The Works of Sir John Clanvowe* (1975).

Clanvowe, Sir Thomas (*fl. c.*1400) A prominent English courtier during the reigns of *Richard II and *Henry IV, erroneously held to be the author of the late medieval poem *The Book of Cupid* (also known as *The Cuckoo and the Nightingale*). *See also* CLANVOWE, SIR JOHN. RJU

V. J. Scattergood, 'The Authorship of *The Boke of Cupide*', *Anglia*, 82 (1964), 37–49.

Clare family Prominent in *England from the *Norman Conquest to the 14th century, the Clares gained substantial holdings in Ireland and Wales as well as in England. The family's male line ended in 1314, but the three daughters of **Gilbert de Clare** carried on the tradition: one married Piers *Gaveston, another Hugh *Despenser, and the eldest, holder of the title of **Lady of Clare**, endowed Clare College, *Cambridge University. MS

M. Altschul, *A Baronial Family in Medieval England: The Clares, 1217–1314* (1965).
J. C. Ward, 'Royal Service and Reward: the Clare Family and the Crown, 1066–1154', *Anglo-Norman Studies*, 11 (1989), 261–78.

Clarembald (Clarenbaud) **of Arras** Taught at *Laon in the 1150s; wrote a Genesis commentary attempting to reconcile biblical teaching with the cosmogony of Plato's *Timaeus*, and a commentary on two of *Boethius' *opuscula sacra*, based on the teaching of *Thierry of Chartres and *Hugh of St-Victor. JMar

The Boethian Commentaries of Clarembald of Arras, tr. D. B. George and J. R. Fortin (2002).
The Life and Works of Clarembald of Arras, ed. N. M. Häring (1965).

Clarence, dukes of Title first created in 1362 for the third son of *Edward III, Lionel of *Antwerp, reflecting the rights and estates of his wife the **De Clare** heiress. After an active career in Ireland, Lionel died without sons in 1368, but his daughter's marriage to the *Mortimer earl of March linked him to later *Yorkist kings. The title was revived in 1412 for the second son of *Henry IV, *Thomas of *Lancaster, killed at the battle of Baugé (1421) without heirs. It was conferred in 1461 by *Edward IV upon his younger brother George (*Plantagenet), to bolster the legitimacy of the new Yorkist line with links to Edward III through the Mortimer family. George's disloyal actions led to his execution for treason in 1478 and forfeiture of all honours. The title was not conferred again until 1789. LCA

G. E. Cokayne, ed., *The Complete Peerage*, 12 vols (²1910–59), vol. 3, 257–61.
M. A. Hicks, *False, Fleeting, Perjur'd Clarence* (²1992).

Clarendon, Assize of (early 1166) Dealing with criminal justice administration by the *justices itinerant sent out that year, it gave the crown exclusive jurisdiction over robbery, murder, and theft, also providing for the *jury of presentment (ancestor of the grand jury). Those presented were tried by *compurgation or *ordeal and, even if acquitted, were forced, if of ill repute, to *abjure the realm. It was extended and amended by the Assize of *Northampton (1176). JSL

W. Stubbs, ed., *Select Charters and Other Illustrations of English Constitutional History to the Reign of Edward I* (1870; rev. H. W. C. Davis, ⁹1913).

Clarendon, Constitutions of (1164) Reflecting the long struggle between *Rome and European rulers, the Constitutions of Clarendon sprang from *Henry II's attempt to roll back recent civil advances of the English church. Most of the Clarendon articles, especially those dealing with clerical landholding and civil status as well as the king's role in abbatial elections, were well-established practices. Innovations mandating that 'criminous clerks' be judged and punished largely in royal courts and forbidding English clergy to appeal to Rome without royal consent caused great clerical opposition and presaged Thomas *Becket's murder in 1170. DJK

F. Barlow, *Thomas Becket* (1986).

Clare (Clara) **of Assisi, St** (1193/94–1253) Clare was born into an aristocratic family but came under the influence of *Francis of Assisi and his message of radical *poverty when she heard him preach in 1210. The following year she rejected an arranged marriage and, with her sister Agnes, joined Francis' disciples. They formed the core of a group of cloistered women following Francis' teachings who in time became the Order of Poor Clares (also known as the Clarissas). Towards the end of her life, Clare composed a *Rule* for her order in which she reasserted Francis' call for near absolute poverty, admonishing her sisters 'not to receive or hold onto any possessions or property acquired through an intermediary or even anything that might reasonably be called property'. This *Rule* only received official approval by *Pope Innocent IV two days before her death. She was canonized in 1255 by *Pope Alexander IV. TFH

Clare of Assisi, *Ecrits*, ed. M.-F. Becker, J.-F. Godet, and T. Matura (1985).
——*Early Documents*, tr. R. Armstrong (1993).
I. Peterson, *Clare of Assisi: A Biographical Study* (1993).

***clas* churches** Major Welsh churches with an associated community of *claswyr* (men of the *clas*) or *canons. The *clas* is referred to in the Welsh Laws, and was headed by an abbot, the *claswyr* having hereditary rights in the church. The *clas* was partly or wholly laicized by the 12th or 13th century. *See also* HYWEL DDA, LAWS OF. JRD

H. Pryce, *Native Law and the Church in Medieval Wales* (1993).

classical tradition: art and architecture *See* RENAISSANCE AND ANTIQUARIANISM.

Claudianus Mamertus (*c*.425–*c*.474) Gallic theologian and monk. In his *De statu animae* Claudianus demonstrated the incorporeal nature of the soul, using Greek philosophical literature. He was a precursor of *scholasticism. *See also* PHILOSOPHY, WESTERN. IDK

C. Brittain, 'No Place for a Platonist Soul in Fifth-Century Gaul?', in *Society and Culture in Late Antique Gaul*, ed. R. W. Mathisen and D. Shanzer (2001), 237–60.
M. Di Marco, *La polemica sull'anima tra 'Fausto di Riez' e Claudiano Mamerto* (1995).

Claudius of Turin (d. *c*.828/40) *Carolingian biblical exegete. Appointed bishop in 816, he preached against the decoration of the church of Turin, fearing 'idolatry' and sparking a backlash against his thought. JJC

P. Boulhol, *Claude de Turin: Un évêque iconoclaste dans l'Occident carolingien* (2002).
J. Cavadini, 'Claudius of Turin and the Augustinian Tradition', *Proceedings of the PMR Conference*, 11 (1986), 43–50.
M. Gorman, 'The Commentary on Genesis of Claudius of Turin and Biblical Studies under Louis the Pious', *Speculum*, 72 (1997), 279–329.

clausula In *Notre-Dame **organum*, a *discant section, with primarily note-against-note *polyphony proceeding in *modal rhythms in consonant, mostly contrary, motion; usually occurring where a melisma appears in the chant *tenor. RAB

R. A. Baltzer, 'Notation, Rhythm, and Style in the Two-Voice Notre Dame Clausula', Ph.D. thesis (Boston, 1974).
R. Flotzinger, *Der Discantussatz im Magnus liber und seiner Nachfolge* (1969).

Clauwaerts Political faction in *Flanders supporting the count of Flanders in his conflict with the king of *France *c*.1300; named 'claws' after the lion on the comital coat of arms. Most members were workers and artisans; some were patricians. WP

D. Nicholas, *Medieval Flanders* (1992), 190.
W. Prevenier, 'La Bourgeoisie en Flandre au XIIIe siècle', *Revue de l'université de Bruxelles* (1978), 407–28.

clavichord *See* MUSICAL INSTRUMENTS.

Clement VII (1378–94) (antipope) Son of the count of *Geneva, bishop of Thérouanne, then *Cambrai, created cardinal by Gregory XI (1371). *Legate in the war against *Florence, he permitted the massacre of Cesena (1377). He voted for *Pope Urban VI (8 April 1378) but joined the cardinals in rejecting him and was himself elected at Fondi (20 September) as Clement VII, beginning the Great *Schism. *See also* BABYLONIAN CAPTIVITY. DHW

Clement of Llanthony Augustinian *canon and prior of Llanthony priory (Gwent, Wales) in the 1160s. His writings include *Unum ex quatuor*, a widely circulated *gospel harmony with extensive *commentary, later translated into ME as *Oon of Foure*. *See also* RELIGIOUS ORDERS. TNB

G. R. Evans, 'Llanthony, Clement of (d. after 1169)', *ODNB*, vol. 34, 91.

J. R. Harris, 'The Gospel Harmony of Clement of Llanthony', *Journal of Biblical Literature*, 43 (1924), 349–62.

clergy The clerical order set apart from the *laity for service in the church. In apostolic times, clergy was a far broader concept and included a wide variety of ministries in service to the Christian community. But the clergy soon came to be more narrowly defined in relationship to the ministry of the *altar and according to a stricter hierarchical model.

1. Bishop and major orders
2. Minor orders
3. Secular, regular, parish, and chapel clergy
4. Education and discipline

1. *Bishop and major orders*

The bishop was the first priest of the community and ruled over it as pastor, teacher, and judge. He shared most of his pastoral responsibilities with the community elders—the presbyterate or college of priests—and both, in turn, were assisted by the deacons. As these ministries expanded to meet the needs of a larger church, subdeacons were instituted to assist deacons in caring for the poor and in service of the altar. By association and in anticipation of the higher orders, younger men were admitted to the clerical state as apprentices in various ministries.

In the wake of the 11th-century reform movement and 12th-century development in theology and canon *law, these earlier and looser distinctions were expanded into a complex clerical system. This included defined ranks within the clergy and associated jurisdictions in which their order was expressed. There were seven clerical ranks excluding the bishop who, having the fullness of priesthood, possessed all lesser ranks of order. The major orders were priest, deacon, and subdeacon. Priests shared in the bishop's original ministry of the *Eucharist by celebrating daily *Mass. They also carried out the basic *pastoral care of *parish communities in the celebration of the other *sacraments (though ordination and confirmation were reserved to the bishop). The principal duties of deacons were to read the Gospel of the day and lead the congregation in song. Subdeacons assisted in the preparation of the altar for the Eucharist. Their graduation from minor orders was not insignificant as it entailed a promise of *celibacy, at least in the west.

2. *Minor orders*

The *minor orders included porter, lector, exorcist, and acolyte. Porters had charge of the church doors, lectors read the epistle at Mass, exorcists assisted at *baptism and, by their association with *holy water, the blessings of things and people, and acolytes, approaching this great divide between minor and major orders, were allowed to approach the altar and carry the *Eucharistic vessels. These seven ranks were also degrees of clerical status and pastoral service that should be passed through decorously before advancing to the next. Thus receiving more than one order at the same time was prohibited. While it was not considered an order as such, First Tonsure, which could be received as early as seven years, marked the intention of a youth for service in the church and gave him clerical status. Thereafter, *tonsure was meant to be one defining sign of a person's clerical status from acolyte to archbishop.

3. *Secular, regular, parish, and chapel clergy*

A further distinction among clerics was in kind as well as rank: secular clerics laboured in the world of parishes and *chapels and were subject to their local bishop. Regular clerics were admitted to holy orders for service within their religious houses and were usually ordained as their communities needed them.

Many parishes in the MA supported clerics of varying ranks. The *rector, a cleric who need not necessarily be a priest, was in possession of the parish as an ecclesiastical benefice. His responsibilities included funding other necessary clerical positions for the pastoral needs of the parish community. Those were held by the curate who had the 'cure of souls'. He might also be a vicar, if the rector was non-residential. Parishes that had need or could afford them hired assisting *chaplains. Chantry priests had the service of a particular altar or chapel in the church and sang masses daily for the founders of the chantry. Numerous clerics were in the employ of great lords, secular and lay, as private chaplains, *scribes, secretaries, councillors, and teachers.

4. *Education and discipline*

Clerical *education was as varied a prospect as the men who needed pastoral training. Most clerics in the MA learned their pastoral craft as *apprentices to the local parish curate, and hence learned for good or ill. Some were supported by family or church for an education in a parish or cathedral school. Even fewer were able to seek advanced study at a *university, but provision for this was possible. All candidates for orders had to be examined at *ordination for basic learning, perhaps even the confident promise of it, appropriate to the order sought. They also needed to show proof of age, legitimacy of birth, and sponsorship (from some reputable personage or community) of their moral worthiness.

Long past ordination, clerics were supposed to be scrutinized on how they continued to live according to the requirements of their canonical order. Documents from diocesan visitations indicate concerns about clerics frequenting taverns, managing secular business enterprises, not keeping their tonsures, wearing colourful or expensive

Chanting clergy in procession, Brussels.

clothing, or bearing arms. Of gravest concern was that they lived chastely.

Clerics who offended the law were tried according to their status in Christian society. Precisely how this 'benefit of clergy' operated within the courts varied from one country to the next, but in theory clergy were to be tried for alleged crimes in the church's courts and, if found guilty, punished accordingly. Punishment for felonies could entail languishing in an ecclesiastical prison but more often resulted in deposition from clerical rank and nullification of that judicial benefit once enjoyed. Proof of clerical status in a criminal context was rarely easy: tonsure was an unreliable brand of safety, though sometimes demonstrated learning, at least on the first offence, was acceptable proof. WJD

G. Franzen, 'Tradition in Medieval Canon Law', in *The Sacrament of Holy Orders* (1962), 202–18.

G. Le Bras, *Institutions ecclésiastiques de la Chrétienté medievale* (1964).

W. J. Sheils and D. Wood, eds, *The Ministry: Clerical and Lay* (1989).

J. Shinners and W. Dohar, *Pastors and the Care of Souls in Medieval England* (1998).

Clericis Laicos A papal *bull issued by *Pope Boniface VIII in 1296 forbidding prelates or ecclesiastical superiors from paying any part of their income or revenue from the church to secular lords, and similarly forbidding secular lords from receiving income from clergymen. Those who did were declared ipso facto *excommunicate. The purpose of this bull was to prevent secular states from taxing *clergy, especially in *France and *England. The pope's inability to enforce the bull revealed the weakness of the papal monarchy. SMB

C. T. Wood, *Philip the Fair and Boniface VIII: State vs. Papacy* (1967).

clerk *See* CLERGY.

Clermont One of the oldest cities in *France. With a population of *c.*15,000 to 30,000 in the 2nd century, it was also one of the largest cities of Roman Gaul. Originally known as *Nemessos* (Gaulish for 'sacred forest'), it was renamed after the castle 'Clarus Mons' in 848. Clermont's fame as an episcopal city, beginning with the tenure of *Sidonius Apollinaris in the 5th century, grew during the MA, and *Pope Urban II preached the First Crusade at the Council of Clermont (a mixed synod of ecclesiastics and laymen) in November 1095. SJM